SPECIAL INDIAN EDITION

PRINCIPLES OF CORPORATE FINANCE

EIGHTH EDITION

RICHARD A. BREALEY
Professor of Finance
London Business School

STEWART C. MYERS
Gordon Y Billard Professor of Finance
Sloan School of Management
Massachusetts Institute of Technology

FRANKLIN ALLEN
Nippon Life Professor of Finance
The Wharton School

PITABAS MOHANTY
Professor of Finance
Xavier Labour Relations Institute (XLRI)
Jamshedpur

Tata McGraw Hill Education Private Limited
NEW DELHI

McGraw-Hill Offices
New Delhi New York St Louis San Francisco Auckland Bogotá Caracas
Kuala Lumpur Lisbon London Madrid Mexico City Milan Montreal
San Juan Santiago Singapore Sydney Tokyo Toronto

Tata McGraw-Hill

Principles of Corporate Finance, 8/e

Indian Adaptation done by arrangement with The McGraw-Hill Companies, Inc., New York

Sales territories: India, Pakistan, Nepal, Bangladesh, Sri Lanka and Bhutan

Sixth reprint 2009
RYCQCRQFDRAXB

Tata McGraw-Hill Edition 2007

ISBN-13: 978-0-07-063580-7
ISBN-10: 0-07-063580-3

Published by Tata McGraw Hill Education Private Limited,
7 West Patel Nagar, New Delhi 110 008, and Typeset at
Script Makers, 19, A 1-B, DDA Market, Paschim Vihar,
New Delhi 110 063 and printed at Sai Printo Pack Pvt. Ltd.,
A-102/4 Phase II, Okhla Industrial Area, New Delhi - 110 020

Cover Printer: SDR

The McGraw·Hill Companies

To Our Parents

ABOUT THE AUTHORS

RICHARD A. BREALEY

Professor of Finance at the London Business School. He is the former president of the European Finance Association and a former director of the American Finance Association. He is a fellow of the British Academy and has served as a special advisor to the Governor of the Bank of England and director of a number of financial institutions. Other books written by Professor Brealey include *Introduction to Risk and Return from Common Stocks.*

STEWART C. MYERS

Gordon Y Billard Professor of Finance at MIT's Sloan School of Management. He is past president of the American Finance Association and a research associate of the National Bureau of Economic Research. His research has focused on financing decisions, valuation methods, the cost of capital, and financial aspects of government regulation of business. Dr. Myers is a director of The Brattle Group, Inc., and is active as a financial consultant.

FRANKLIN ALLEN

Nippon Life Professor of Finance at the Wharton School of the University of Pennsylvania. He is past president of the American Finance Association, Western Finance Association and Society for Financial Studies. His research has focused on financial innovation, asset price bubbles, comparing financial systems, and financial crises. He is a scientific adviser at the Sveriges Riksbank (Sweden's central bank).

PITABAS MOHANTY

Professor of Finance, Xavier Labour Relations Institute (XLRI), Jamshedpur, India. He is a Fellow of the Indian Institute of Management Bangalore. A gold medalist in MA (Applied Economics) he is also a chartered financial analyst and a cost accountant. He has got more than ten years of teaching experience in investments and Corporate Finance. He has co-authored the Special Indian Edition of the book on ***Investments*** published by **McGraw-Hill**. He won the Best Young Teacher Award from AIMS in 2002, the first prize in two consecutive years in the Capital Markets Conference organized by the UTI Institute of Capital Markets, the prestigious Citibank Research Excellence Award in IIM Bangalore and the Best Research Paper Award from AIMS in 1999.

PREFACE

This book describes the theory and practice of corporate finance with particular emphasis on financial environment. We hardly need to explain why financial managers need to master the practical aspects of their job, but we should spell out why down-to-earth managers need to bother with theory.

Managers learn from experience how to cope with routine problems. But the best managers are also able to respond to change. To do so you need more than time-honored rules of thumb; you must understand *why* companies and financial markets behave the way they do. In other words, you need a *theory* of finance.

Does that sound intimidating? It shouldn't. Good theory helps you to grasp what is going on in the world around you. It helps you to ask the right questions when times change and new problems need to be analyzed. It also tells you which things you do *not* need to worry about. Throughout this book we show how managers use financial theory to solve practical problems.

Of course, the theory presented in this book is not perfect and complete—no theory is. There are some famous controversies where financial economists cannot agree. We have not glossed over these disagreements. We set out the arguments for each side and tell you where we stand.

Much of this book is concerned with understanding what financial managers do and why. But we also say what financial managers *should* do to increase company value. Where theory suggests that financial managers are making mistakes, we say so, while admitting that there may be hidden reasons for their actions. In brief, we have tried to be fair but to pull no punches.

CHANGES IN THIS EDITION

Principles is written for students of financial management. For many readers it is their first look at the world of finance. Therefore, in each edition we try to make the book simpler, clearer, and more fun to read. But the book is also used extensively as a reference and guide for practicing managers around the world. Therefore we also strive to make each edition more comprehensive and authoritative. We believe that this edition is better for both the student and the practicing manager. Here are some of the major changes.

The most important change that we have brought out in this edition is its focus on Indian financial environment. In almost all the chapters, you will find discussion on Indian companies, reference to Indian research results, India-specific chapter-end questions, and Indian examples. And this has not come at the cost of having lower exposure to international examples and research.

Indian corporate finance managers do not operate in a vacuum and awareness of international research results and laws are as relevant to them as to any manager operating from the US, or Russia. In this book, we maintain a judicious balance between having an India-centric view of corporate finance and having an international outlook on the subject at the same time.

Recent financial scandals have highlighted the importance of good systems of corporate governance. In Chapter 34, we compare financial markets, institutions, and corporate governance around the world. We explain why these different systems have developed and we discuss their relative strengths and weaknesses.

Chapter 34 is not the only place where we have increased coverage of the agency problems of motivating and controlling managers. For example, Chapter 2 contains an expanded section on corporate goals and corporate governance and Chapter 12 includes a deeper discussion of executive compensation structures and the measurement of managers' performance.

We have also expanded coverage of behavioral finance. The first natural place to introduce behavioral issues is in the discussion of market efficiency in Chapter 13, but we also circle back to the topic in later chapters. For example, we ask whether an understanding of behavioral psychology can help us to understand new issue pricing, dividend policy, and mergers.

Chapters 16 and 19 have also been rewritten. Chapter 16 now speaks more broadly about payout policy, not just about cash dividends. This responds to the growth in stock repurchases as a way to return cash to stockholders. Chapter 19 now shows how to use the weighted average cost of capital to value companies or divisions of companies. By covering valuation after we have discussed capital structure, we are able to introduce and work through more complex and realistic valuation problems.

Financial managers work in an international environment. Therefore in this edition we have continued to add international material. International issues are the subject matter of Chapter 28 (Managing International Risks) and Chapter 34 (Governance and Corporate Control around the World). But you will also find many international examples throughout the rest of the book.

The eighth edition is more web-friendly than the seventh. There are more web references in the text and we have included an updated and expanded list of useful websites at the beginning of each part. We have also included a list of useful Indian websites towards the end of the book. We have also added web exercises that give the reader the opportunity to gain experience with useful financial websites.

As every first-grader knows, it is easier to add than subtract, so to make way for these new topics we have needed to do some judicious pruning. Readers familiar with earlier editions will notice two places where we have consolidated. First, we have combined the two chapters on cash management and credit management. We believe that as a result the main tasks of working capital management come through with less clutter. Second, we no longer have a separate chapter on convertible debt and warrants. Instead, we describe them in Chapter 25, which reviews the many different kinds of debt that companies issue.

MAKING LEARNING EASIER

Each chapter of the book includes an introductory preview, a summary, and an annotated list of suggestions for further reading. There is a quick and easy quiz, practice questions on both numerical and conceptual topics, and a few challenge questions. Many questions use financial data on actual companies, which the reader can download from the websites mentioned in the book itself. Answers to the quiz questions may be found at the end of the book, along with a glossary and tables for calculating present values and pricing options. We have also provided for each chapter concept review questions and have keyed these to the page in the book where the topic is discussed. Sample questions are shown at the end of each chapter. The full set of Concept Review Questions is available on the CD that comes with the book and on the book's website **www.mhhe.com/bmam8e**.

The mini-cases at the end of each chapter have been revised and include specific questions to guide the case analyses. Answers to the mini-cases are available to instructors on this book's website.

A new feature of this edition is that a number of tables are now shown in the text as Excel spreadsheets. In these cases an equivalent "live" spreadsheet is contained on the book's CD and on the website. Readers can use these live spreadsheets to understand better the calculations behind the table and to see the effect of changing the underlying data. A number of end-of-chapter questions ask the student to use the spreadsheets to check that they understand the effect of changing inputs.

The 35 chapters in this book are divided into 11 parts. Each part includes a short introduction that explains the sequence of topics. Parts 1 to 3 of the book cover valuation and capital investment decisions, and Parts 4 to 8 discuss long-term financing. Part 9 focuses on financial planning and short-term financial decisions. Part 10 looks at mergers and corporate control. Part 11 concludes. We realize that instructors will wish to select from these topics and many will prefer a different sequence. Therefore, we have ensured that the text is modular, so that topics can be introduced in several logical orders. For example, there should be no difficulty in reading the material on financial statement analysis and short-term financial decisions before the chapters on valuation and capital investment.

SUPPLEMENTS

In this edition, we have gone to great lengths to ensure that our supplements are equal in quality and authority to the text itself.

For the Student

Student CD-ROM

Packaged with each new text is a CD-ROM for students that contains many features designed to enhance the classroom experience. Eleven learning modules from the Finance Tutor Series are included. Some of the featured modules are: Time Value of Money, Stock and Bond Valuation, and Capital Budgeting. In each module, students answer questions and solve problems that not only assess their general understanding of the subject, but also their ability to apply that understanding in real-world business contexts. In "Practice Mode," students learn as they go by receiving in depth feedback on each response before proceeding to the next question. Students who want to assess their current knowledge may select "Test Mode," where they read an extensive evaluation report after they have completed the test.

Also included are the PowerPoint presentation slides, Excel spreadsheet templates, Interactive Quizzes, Concept Review Questions,

Interactive FinSims, video clips, and many useful web links.

Online Learning Center
www.mhhe.com/bmam8e
Find a wealth of information online! This site contains information about the book and the authors as well as teaching and learning materials for the instructor and the student, including:

- **Interactive FinSims** This newly developed asset consists of multiple simulations of key financial topics. Ideal for students to use in order to reinforce their knowledge and gain additional practice in strengthening their skills.
- **Online Quizzes** These multiple choice questions are provided as an additional testing and reinforcement tool for students. Each quiz is organized by chapter to test the specific concepts presented in that particular chapter. Immediate scoring of the quiz will occur upon submission and the correct answers will be provided.
- **Standard & Poor's Educational Version of Market Insight** McGraw-Hill is proud to partner with Standard & Poor's by offering students access to the educational version of Market Insight.

ACKNOWLEDGMENTS

We have a long list of people to thank for their helpful criticism of earlier editions and for assistance in preparing this one. They include Aleijda de Cazenove Balsan, Kedran Garrison, Adam Kolasinski, Robert Pindyck, and Gretchen Slemmons at MIT; Stefania Uccheddu at London Business School; Lynda Borucki, Marjorie Fischer, Larry Kolbe, Michael Vilbert, and Bente Villadsen at The Brattle Group, Inc.; John Stonier at Airbus Industries; Alex Triantis at the University of Maryland; Julie Wulf and Jinghua Yan at the University of Pennsylvania, and Simon Gervais at Duke University. We would also like to thank all those at McGraw-Hill/Irwin who worked on the book, including Steve Patterson, Publisher; Rhonda Seelinger, Executive Marketing Manager; Christina Kouvelis, Developmental Editor; Lori Koetters, Senior Project Manager; Keith McPherson, Design Director; Joyce Chappetto, Media Project Manager, Carol Loreth, Senior Supplement Producer; and Rose Hepburn, Senior Production Supervisor.

We want to express our appreciation to those instructors whose insightful comments and suggestions were invaluable to us during this revision:

Noyan Arsen *Koc University*
Jan Bartholdy *ASB, Denmark*
Penny Belk *Loughborough University*
Eric Benrud *University of Baltimore*
Peter Berman *University of New Haven*
Jean Canil *University of Adelaide*
John Cooney *Texas Tech University*
William Dimovski *Deakin University, Melbourne*
Robert Duvic *University of Texas at Austin*
Robert Everett *Johns Hopkins University*
Christopher Geczy *University of Pennsylvania*
Stuart Gillan *University of Delaware*
Ning Gong *Melbourne Business School*
Mark Griffiths *Thunderbird, American School of International Management*
Winfried Hallerbach *Erasmus University, Rotterdam*
Milton Harris *University of Chicago*
Glenn Henderson *University of Cincinnati*
Ronald Hoffmeister *Arizona State University*
Ravi Jagannathan *Northwestern University*
Jarl Kallberg *NYU, Stern School of Business*
Steve Kaplan *University of Chicago*

Arif Khurshed *Manchester Business School*
Ken Kim *University of Wisconsin—Milwaukee*
C. R. Krishnaswamy *Western Michigan University*
George Kutner *Marquette University*
David Lovatt *University of East Anglia*
Debbie Lucas *Northwestern University*
Brian Lucey *Trinity College, Dublin*
George McCabe *University of Nebraska*
Joe Messina *San Francisco State University*
Dag Michalson *Bl, Oslo*
Peter Moles *University of Edinburgh*
Claus Parum *Copenhagen Business School*
Dilip Patro *Rutgers University*
John Percival *University of Pennsylvania*
Latha Ramchand *University of Houston*
Narendar V. Rao *Northeastern University*
Raghavendra Rau *Purdue University*
Tom Rietz *University of Iowa*
Robert Ritchey *Texas Tech University*
Mo Rodriguez *Texas Christian University*
John Rozycki *Drake University*
Brad Scott *Webster University*
Richard Simonds *Michigan State University*
Bernell Stone *Brigham Young University*
Shrinivasan Sundaram *Ball State University*
Avanidhar Subrahmanyam *UCLA*
Stephen Todd *Loyola University—Chicago*
Ilias Tsiakas *University of Warwick*
David Vang *St. Thomas University*
John Wald *Rutgers University*
Kelly Welch *University of Kansas*
Jill Wetmore *Saginaw Valley State University*
Matt Will *University of Indianapolis*
Art Wilson *George Washington University*

This list is surely incomplete. We know how much we owe to our colleagues at the London Business School, MIT's Sloan School of Management, and the University of Pennsylvania's Wharton School and XLRI, Jamshedpur. In many cases, the ideas that appear in this book are as much their ideas as ours. Finally, we record the continuing thanks due to our wives, Diana, Maureen, and Sally, and Leepi who were unaware when they married us that they were also marrying the ***Principles of Corporate Finance.***

Richard A. Brealey

Stewart C. Myers

Franklin Allen

Pitabas Mohanty

CONCEPT REVIEW QUESTIONS

These questions review the concepts illustrated within each chapter and are new to this edition. The first three questions are featured in the text, and additional questions are found on the book Web site at www.mhhe.com/bmam8e and on the Student CD-ROM packaged with the text, denoted by an instructional banner.

CONCEPT REVIEW QUESTIONS

1. What is the difference between a discount rate and a discount factor? (page 16)
2. How can risk be incorporated into PVs and NPVs? (page 17)
3. Write down the formulas for an investment's NPV and rate of return. Prove that NPV is positive *only* if the rate of return exceeds the opportunity cost of capital. (page 18)

For additional Concept Review Questions, please visit us at www.mhhe.com/bmam8e or refer to your Student C

NEW AND ENHANCED PEDAGOGY

In this edition of *Principles of Corporate Finance,* we've included several more features to help students succeed in learning the fundamental concepts of financial management.

WEB EXERCISES

Now included among the end-of-chapter material in selected chapters are Web Exercises that give students the opportunity to gain real-world experience with useful financial Web sites.

WEB EXERCISES

There are dozens of Web sites that provide calculators to help with personal financial decisions. Two good examples are **www.quicken.com** and **www.smartmoney.com.** (Note that both calculators assume simple interest to convert the monthly interest rate to an annual rate. In other words, the annual interest rate is quoted as 12 times the monthly rate.)

1. Suppose that you have Rs. 5,000 in the bank and plan to save Rs. 500 a month. If you earn a return of 12 percent a year (1 percent a month), how much will you have accumulated by the time that you retire in 30 years? Now log in to the Quicken site and click on *Bills and Banking* to find a nice savings calculator. Use this to check your answer.
2. Suppose that you take out a 30-year mortgage loan of Rs. 200,000 at an interest rate of 10 percent. What is your total monthly payment? How much of the first month's payment goes to reduce the size of the loan? How much ... after two years ...

		Year					
		1	2	3	4	5	6
1.	Cash flow	100	200	250	298	298	298
2.	Book value at start of year, straight-line depreciation	1,000	833	667	500	333	167
3.	Book value at end of year, straight-line depreciation	833	667	500	333	167	0
4.	Book depreciation	167	167	167	167	167	167
5.	Book income (1 - 4)	-67	+33	+83	+131	+131	+131
6.	Book ROI	-.067	+.04	+.124	+.262	0.393	+.787
7.	EVA	-167	-50	+17	+81	+96	+115

TABLE 12.3 Forecasted book income, ROI, and EVA for the proposed Jamshedpur store. Book ROI and EVA are underestimated for the first two years and overestimated thereafter.

Please visit us at www.mhhe.com/bmam8e or refer to your Student CD

11. In the International Mulch and Compost example (Section 6.2), we assumed that losses on the project could be used to offset taxable profits elswhere in the corporation. Suppose that the losses had to be carried forward and offset against future taxable profits from the project. How would the project NPV change? What is the value of the company's ability to use the tax deductions immediately?

12. Table 6.8 shows investment and projected income in euros for Flanel's new perfume factory. Note that the format of Table 6.8 matches Table 6.1. Go to the live Excel spreadsheet versions of Table 6.8 on this book's CD or at **www.mhhe.com/bmam8e.** ...recast cash flows and calculate NPV. ... nominal co... 11 perc...

Please visit us at www.mhhe.com/bmam8e or refer to your St...

EXCEL INTEGRATION

New to this edition, selected exhibits have been set as Excel spreadsheets and new end-of-chapter Excel questions have also been included. The templates are available on the book Web site at **www.mhhe.com/bmam8e** and on the Student CD-ROM packaged with the text, denoted by an icon.

Please visit us at
www.mhhe.com/bmam8e
or refer to your
Student CD .

FINANCE IN THE NEWS BOXES

Relevant news articles from financial publications appear in various chapters throughout the text. Aimed at bringing real life into the classroom, these boxes provide insight into the business world today.

FINANCE IN THE NEWS

THE HAZARDS OF SECURED BANK LENDING

The National Safety Council of Australia's Victoria Division had been a sleepy outfit until John Friedrich took over. Under its new management, NSC members trained like commandos and were prepared to go anywhere and do anything. They saved people from drowning, they fought fires, found lost bushwalkers and went down mines. Their lavish equipment included 22 helicopters, 8 aircraft and a mini-submarine. Soon the NSC began selling its services internationally.

Unfortunately the NSC's paramilitary outfit ... of dollars to ... more than it ... gap ...

check that their loans were safe. Sometimes a suspicious banker would ask to inspect a particular container. Friedrich would then explain that it was away on exercise, fly the banker across the country in a light plane and point to a container well out in the bush. The container would of course be empty, but the banker had no way to know that.

Six years after Friedrich was appointed CEO, his massive fraud was uncovered. But a few days before a warrant could be issued, Friedrich disappeared. Although he was eventually caught ... arrested, he shot ...

a. Draw a graph similar to Figure 8.7 showing how the expected return varies with beta.

STANDARD &POOR'S

b. What is the risk premium on the market?

c. What is the required return on an investment with a beta of 1.5?

d. If an investment with a beta of .8 offers an expected return of 9.8 percent, does it have a positive NPV?

e. If the market expects a return of 11.2 percent from stock X, what is its beta?

9. You can get the data for most of the companies in Table 8.2 from www.in.finance.yahoo.com. For those that are covered, use the Excel SLOPE function to recalculate betas from the monthly returns. Use as many monthly returns as available, up to a maximum of 60 months. Recalculate expected rates of return from the CAPM formula, using a current risk-free rate and a market risk premium of 11 percent. How have the expected returns changed from the figures reported in Table ...

STANDARD &POOR'S

STANDARD & POOR'S INTEGRATION

Among the end-of-chapter material in selected chapters are newly expanded problems directly incorporating the Educational Version of Market Insight, a service based on S&P's renowned Compustat database. These problems provide you with an easy method of including current real-world data into your course.

PART INTRODUCTIONS

New introductions have been added to each part explaining links between different concepts. They include real-world examples that provide motivation for the chapters that follow.

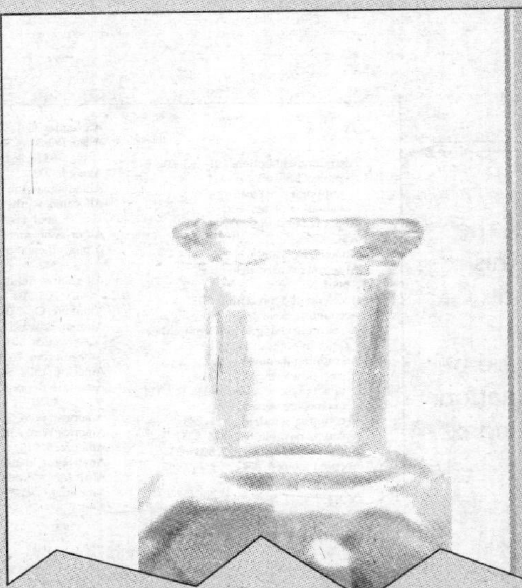

PART [1]

VALUE

IN 2003 TOYOTA announced plans to build a new $800 million automobile plant in San Antonio, Texas. Meanwhile, in Girardeau, Missouri, Procter & Gamble had started installation of a new machine to produce annually 80,000 tons of paper towel and tissues.

What was special about these developments? Nothing! We cite them because they are typical of the investments in new products and equipment that are being made each day in the United States and the rest of the world.

Presumably, Toyota and Procter & Gamble decided to undertake the investments bec...

MINI-CASES

To enhance the concepts discussed within a chapter, mini-cases are included in selected chapters and have been updated so students can apply their knowledge to typical real-world scenarios.

82 PART I Value

MINI-CASE
Reeby Sports

Ten years ago, in 1995, George Reeby founded a small mail-order company selling high-quality sports equipment. Since those early days Reeby Sports has grown steadily and been consistently profitable. The company has issued 2 million shares, all of which are owned by George Reeby and his five children.

For some months George has been wondering whether the time has come to take the company public. This would allow him to cash in on part of his investment and would make it easier for the firm to raise capital should it wish to expand in the future.

But how much are the shares worth? George's first instinct is to look at the firm's balance sheet, which shows that the book value of the equity is $ 26.34 million, or $ 13.17 per share. A share price of $ 13.17 would put the stock on a P/E ratio of 6.6. That is quite a bit lower than the 13.1 P/E ratio of Reeby's larger rival, Molly Sports.

George suspects that book value is not necessarily a good guide to a share's market value. He thinks of his daughter Jenny, who works in an investment bank. She would undoubtedly know what the shares are worth. He decides to phone her after she finishes work that evening at 9 o'clock or before she starts the next day at 6.00 ...

... some basic data on the ... that is hi...

PART FIVE RELATED WEB SITES

Dividend policy and leverage decisions may be influenced by tax rates. Here are some sites with information on tax rates:

www.taxsites.com (includes links to sites providing tax rates for a variety of countries)

finance.yahoo.com (information on personal tax rates)

www.quicken.com (information on personal tax rates)

You can get information on recent dividend announcements on:

www.fulldisclosure.com

aol.ccbn.com

www.ex-dividend.com

For information on the capital structure of individual firms as well as industries:

finance.yahoo.com

ValuePro provides software and data for estimating WACCs:

www.valuepro.net

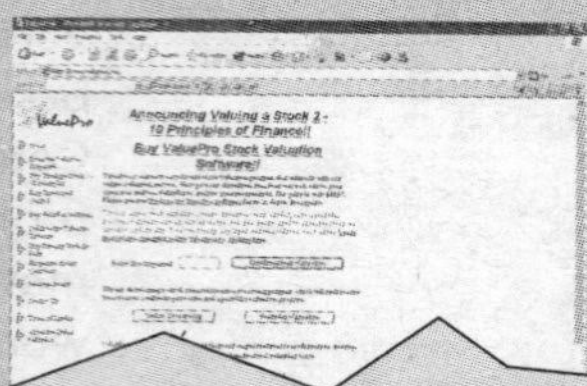

WEB SITE LISTINGS

In today's world the Internet provides students and instructors with a useful and powerful tool. An updated and expanded list of relevant Web sites is provided at the beginning of each part for ease in referencing the best sites for financial data and information.

INDEX

Because many concepts in financial management are relevant around the world, the international coverage in this text has been updated and enhanced—Latin and Asian influence in particular can be noted. To make this information easier to access, a global index has been created.

BRIEF CONTENTS

CONTENTS

Part One

VALUE 3

Chapter 1

Chapter 2

Chapter 3

CONTENTS

CONTENTS

CONTENTS

CONTENTS

Part Four
FINANCING DECISIONS AND MARKET EFFICIENCY

Chapter 13

Chapter 14

Chapter 15

Part Five
PAYOUT POLICY AND CAPITAL STRUCTURE

Chapter 16

CONTENTS

CONTENTS

PRINCIPLES OF CORPORATE FINANCE

PART ONE RELATED WEB SITES

Chapter 1 describes the role of the financial manager. More information on careers and salaries in finance can be found at:

www.careers-in-finance.com

www.careers.wsj.com

www.wageweb.com

Material on corporate governance is available on:

www.corpgov.net

www.thecorporatelibrary.com

Chapters 2 and 3 show how to value future cash flows. Many Web sites that are concerned with personal finance provide discussions of the time value of money and calculators. For example, try:

www.bankrate.com

www.money.cnn.com

www.quicken.com

www.smartmoney.com

Chapter 4 explains how bonds and stocks are valued. Helpful material and data on bond markets are available on

www.finpipe.com (good explanations of bond markets from a Canadian site perspective)

www.investinginbonds.com (Bond Market Association, contains useful bond data and links)

www.investorguide.com (good explanations of bond and equity markets)

bonds.yahoo.com

money.cnn.com/markets/bondcenter (market commentary)

www.federalreserve.gov (the research section contains historical data on interest rates)

www.stls.frb.org (Federal Reserve Bank of St Louis)

www.ustreas.gov (U.S. Treasury, includes current bond prices and yields)

Most major stock exchanges have good Web sites. See, for example:

www.nyse.com (New York Stock Exchange)

www.nasdaq.com (Nasdaq)

www.londonstockexchange.com (London Stock Exchange)

www.tse.or.jp (Tokyo Stock Exchange)

www.123world.com/stockexchanges (links to national exchanges)

www.rba.co.uk (links to national exchanges)

www.fibv.com (World Federation of Stock Exchanges, very useful comparative statistics)

Data on stock market indexes can be found on:

www.djindexes.com (Dow Jones indexes)

www.spglobal.com (Standard & Poor's indexes)

www.wilshire.com (return data for Wilshire set of indexes)

www.msci.com (return data for MSCI set of indexes)

www.barra.com (market indexes with information on dividend yields, P/Es, etc.)

Here is a selection of sites with market commentary and data on individual firms and stocks:

finance.yahoo.com (particularly useful)

www.bloomberg.com

hoovers.com

www.investor.reuters.com

www.cbs.marketwatch.com

money.cnn.com

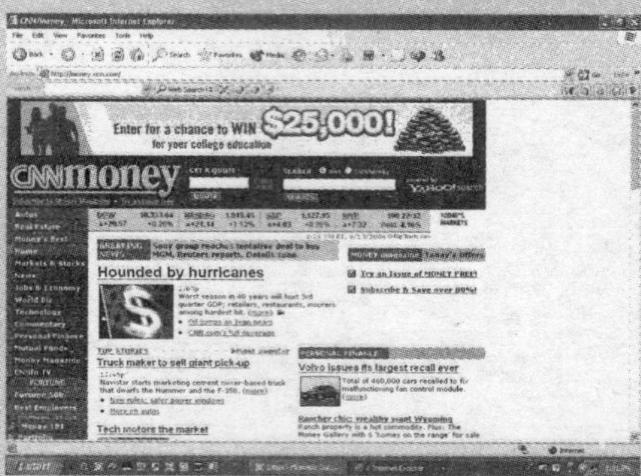

moneycentral.msn.com (links to msn sites for several overseas markets)

www.euroland.com (useful source of quotes for European markets)

www.zacks.com (includes consensus earnings forecasts)

www.valueline.com (includes free sample analyses and long-term earnings forecasts for Dow Jones stocks)

Two useful sites for estimating stock values with the dividend discount model are:

www.dividenddiscountmodel.com

www.valuepro.net

PART [1]

VALUE

IN 2003 TOYOTA announced plans to build a new $800 million automobile plant in San Antonio, Texas. Meanwhile, in Girardeau, Missouri, Procter & Gamble had started installation of a new machine to produce annually 80,000 tons of paper towel and tissues.

What was special about these developments? Nothing! We cite them because they are typical of the investments in new products and equipment that are being made each day in the United States and the rest of the world.

Presumably, Toyota and Procter & Gamble decided to undertake the investments because they thought that the new plant was worth more than it cost. But that raises an obvious question: How can firms calculate what an investment is worth when its returns may stretch 10, 20, or more years into the future?

This is the topic of Part 1. To set the scene, Chapter 1 shows how businesses are organized and describes the role that the financial manager plays in evaluating investments and finding the money to pay for them. Chapter 2 starts to build a theory of value. By the end of Chapter 6, you should be able to tackle a standard investment decision, such as those faced by Toyota and Procter & Gamble.

CHAPTER [1]

FINANCE AND THE FINANCIAL MANAGER

THIS BOOK IS about financial decisions made by corporations. We should start by saying what these decisions are and why they are important.

Corporations face two broad financial questions: What investments should the firm make? and How should it pay for those investments? The first question involves spending money; the second involves raising it.

The secret of success in financial management is to increase value. That is a simple statement, but not very helpful. It is like advising an investor in the stock market to "Buy low, sell high." The problem is how to do it.

There may be a few activities in which one can read a textbook and then do it, but financial management is not one of them. That is why finance is worth studying. Who wants to work in a field where there is no room for judgment, experience, creativity, and a pinch of luck? Although this book cannot supply any of these items, it does present the concepts and information on which good financial decisions are based, and it shows you how to use the tools of the trade of finance.

We start in this chapter by explaining what a corporation is and introducing you to the responsibilities of its financial managers. We will distinguish *real assets* from *financial assets* and *capital investment decisions* from *financing decisions*. We stress the importance of financial markets, both national and international, to the financial manager.

Finance is about money and markets, but it is also about people. The success of a corporation depends on how well it harnesses everyone to work to a common end. The financial manager must appreciate the conflicting objectives often encountered in financial management. Resolving conflicts is particularly difficult when people have different information. This is an important theme which runs through to the last chapter of this book. In this chapter we will start with some definitions and examples.

1.1 WHAT IS A CORPORATION?

Not all businesses are corporations. Small ventures can be owned and managed by a single individual. These are called *sole proprietorships*. In other cases several people may join to own and manage a *partnership*.[1] However, this book is about *corporate* finance. So we need to explain what a **corporation** is.

Almost all large and medium-sized businesses are organized as corporations. For example, Infosys, Tata Motors, Reliance Industries, and ITC are corporations. So are overseas businesses, such as British Petroleum, Unilever, Nestlé, Volkswagen, and Sony. In each case the firm is owned by stockholders who hold shares in the business.

When a corporation is first established, its shares may all be held by a small group of investors, perhaps the company's managers and a few backers. In this case the shares are not publicly traded and the company is *closely held*. Eventually, when the firm grows and new shares are issued to raise additional capital, its shares will be widely traded. Such corporations are known as *public companies*. Most well-known corporations in India are public companies.[2] In many other countries, it's common for large companies to remain in private hands.

By organizing as a corporation, a business can attract a wide variety of investors. Some may hold only a single share worth a few rupees, cast only a single vote, and receive a tiny proportion of profits and dividends. Shareholders may also include giant pension funds and insurance companies

[1]Many professional businesses, such as accounting and legal firms, are partnerships. Most large investment banks in the US started as partnerships, but eventually these companies and their financing needs grew too large for them to continue in this form. Goldman Sachs, the last of the leading investment-bank partnerships, issued shares and became a public corporation in 1998.

[2]In India, we find both public limited and private limited companies. A private limited company must have a minimum paid-up capital of Rs. 1 lakhs and at least two members (and maximum of 50 members). A public limited company must have a minimum paid-up capital of Rs. 5 lakhs and at least seven members.

whose investment may run to millions of shares and hundreds of millions of rupees, and who are entitled to a correspondingly large number of votes and proportion of profits and dividends.

Although the stockholders own the corporation, they do not manage it. Instead, they vote to elect a *board of directors*. Some of these directors may be drawn from top management, but others are non-executive directors, who are not employed by the firm. The board of directors represents the shareholders. It appoints top management and is supposed to ensure that managers act in the shareholders' best interests.

This *separation of ownership and management* gives corporations permanence.[3] Even if managers quit or are dismissed and replaced, the corporation can survive, and today's stockholders can sell all their shares to new investors without disrupting the operations of the business.

Unlike partnerships and sole proprietorships, corporations have **limited liability,** which means that stockholders cannot be held personally responsible for the firm's debts. When Enron and WorldCom went belly-up in 2002—two of the largest bankruptcies ever—no one demanded that their stockholders put up more money to cover the companies' debts. Stockholders can lose their entire investment, but no more.

Although a corporation is owned by its stockholders, it is legally distinct from them. It is based on memorandum of association and articles of association that set out the purpose of the business, how many shares can be issued, and so on. For many legal purposes, the corporation is considered as a resident of its state. As a legal "person," it can borrow or lend money, and it can sue or be sued. It pays its own taxes (but it cannot vote!).

Because the corporation is distinct from its shareholders, it can do things that partnerships and sole proprietorships cannot. For example, it can raise money by selling new shares to investors and it can buy those shares back. One corporation can make a takeover bid for another and then merge the two businesses.

There are also some *disadvantages* to organizing as a corporation. Managing a corporation's legal machinery and communicating with shareholders can be time-consuming and costly. Furthermore, in India, there is an important tax drawback. Because the corporation is a separate legal entity, it is taxed separately. So corporations pay tax on their profits, and in addition pay dividend distribution tax on any dividend they pay to the shareholders. In the United States, the corporations pay the taxes first on the profits, and, in addition, the shareholders pay tax on any dividends that they receive from the company.

1.2 THE ROLE OF THE FINANCIAL MANAGER

To carry on business, corporations need an almost endless variety of **real assets.** Many of these assets are tangible, such as machinery, factories, and offices; others are intangible, such as technical expertise, trademarks, and patents. All of them need to be paid for. To obtain the necessary money, the corporation sells claims on its real assets and on the cash those assets will generate. These claims are called **financial assets** or **securities.** For example, if the company borrows money from the bank, the bank gets a written promise that the money will be repaid with interest. Thus the bank trades cash for

[3]Corporations can be immortal, but as per the Indian Partnership Act, 1932, a partnership firm can be dissolved by the Court, by agreement, by operation of law, on the happening of some contingency, or by notice of any partner (if the partnership is by will). A sole proprietorship also will have an end because the proprietor is mortal.

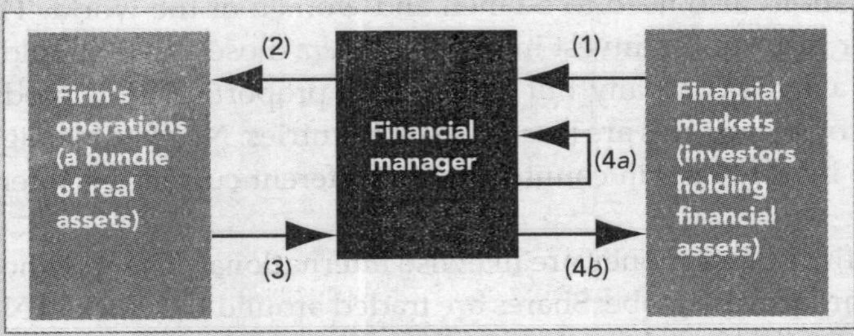

FIGURE 1.1

Flow of cash between financial markets and the firm's operations. Key: (1) Cash raised by selling financial assets to investors; (2) cash invested in the firm's operations and used to purchase real assets; (3) cash generated by the firm's operations; (4a) cash reinvested; (4b) cash returned to investors.

a financial asset. Financial assets include not only bank loans but also shares of stock, bonds, and a dizzying variety of specialized securities.[4]

The financial manager stands between the firm's operations and the **financial** (or **capital) markets,** where investors hold the financial assets issued by the firm.[5] The financial manager's role is illustrated in Figure 1.1, which traces the flow of cash from investors to the firm and back to investors again. The flow starts when the firm sells securities to raise cash (arrow 1 in the figure). The cash is used to purchase real assets used in the firm's operations (arrow 2). Later, if the firm does well, the real assets generate cash inflows which more than repay the initial investment (arrow 3). Finally, the cash is either reinvested (arrow 4*a*) or returned to the investors who bought the securities (arrow 4*b*). Of course, the choice between arrows 4*a* and 4*b* is not completely free. For example, if a bank lends money at stage 1, the bank has to be repaid the money plus interest at stage 4*b*.

Our diagram takes us back to the financial manager's two basic questions. First, what real assets should the firm invest in? Second, how should the cash for the investment be raised? The answer to the first question is the firm's **investment,** or **capital budgeting, decision.** The answer to the second is the firm's **financing decision.**

Investment and financing decisions are typically *separated,* that is, analyzed independently. When an investment opportunity or "project" is identified, the financial manager first asks whether the project is worth more than the capital required to undertake it. If the answer is yes, he or she then considers how the project should be financed.

But the separation of investment and financing decisions does *not* mean that the financial manager can forget about investors and financial markets when analyzing capital investment projects. As we will see in the next chapter, the fundamental financial objective of the firm is to maximize the value of the cash invested in the firm by its stockholders. Look again at Figure 1.1. Stockholders are happy to contribute cash at arrow 1 only if the decisions made at arrow 2 generate at least adequate returns at arrow 3. "Adequate" means returns at least equal to the returns that stockholders could earn by investing in financial markets. If your firm's projects consistently generate *in*adequate returns, your shareholders will want their money back.

[4]We review these securities in Chapters 14 and 25.

[5]You will hear financial managers use the terms *financial markets* and *capital markets* almost synonymously. But *capital markets* are, strictly speaking, the source of long-term financing only. Short-term financing comes from the *money market*. "Short-term" means less than one year. We use the term *financial markets* to refer to all sources of financing.

Financial managers of large corporations also need to be men and women of the world. They must decide not only *which* assets their firm should invest in but also *where* those assets should be located. Take Nestlé, for example. It is a Swiss company, but only a small proportion of its production takes place in Switzerland. Its 520 or so factories are located in 82 countries. Nestlé's managers must therefore know how to evaluate investments in countries with different currencies, interest rates, inflation rates, and tax systems.

The financial markets in which the firm raises money are likewise international. The stockholders of large corporations are scattered around the globe. Shares are traded around the clock in New York, London, Tokyo, Mumbai and other financial centers. Bonds and bank loans move easily across national borders. A corporation that needs to raise cash doesn't have to borrow from its hometown bank. Day-to-day cash management also becomes a complex task for firms that produce or sell in different countries. For example, think of the problems that Nestlé's financial managers face in keeping track of the cash receipts and payments in 82 countries.

We admit that Nestlé is unusual, but few financial managers can close their eyes to international financial issues. So throughout the book we will pay attention to differences in financial systems and examine the problems of investing and raising money internationally.

The financial manager does not work in a vacuum. A wide range of financial institutions has grown up to supply the firm with capital and to offer a variety of other financial services. For example, the firm may go to a bank to raise short-term debt or to an insurance company for a longer-term loan. It may raise cash by selling additional shares to mutual funds, pension funds, and other investors. It may engage a merchant banker to advise on a new issue of shares or to assist in merger negotiations. And so on. The firm's financial manager needs a good understanding of how requests will be viewed by these financial institutions. Likewise, to understand the firm's needs and how best to satisfy them, the managers of the financial institutions must also have a good grasp of the principles of corporate finance.

1.3 WHO IS THE FINANCIAL MANAGER?

In this book we will use the term *financial manager* to refer to anyone responsible for a significant investment or financing decision. But only in the smallest firms is a single person responsible for all the decisions discussed in this book. In most cases, responsibility is dispersed. Top management is of course continuously involved in financial decisions. But the engineer who designs a new production facility is also involved: The design determines the kind of real assets the firm will hold. The marketing manager who commits to a major advertising campaign is also making an important investment decision. The campaign is an investment in an intangible asset that is expected to pay off in future sales and earnings.

Nevertheless there are some managers who specialize in finance. Their roles are summarized in Figure 1.2. The **treasurer** is responsible for looking after the firm's cash, raising new capital, and maintaining relationships with banks, stockholders, and other investors who hold the firm's securities.

For small firms, the treasurer is likely to be the only financial executive. Larger corporations also have a **controller,** who prepares the financial statements, manages the firm's internal accounting, and looks after its tax obligations. You can see that the treasurer and controller have different

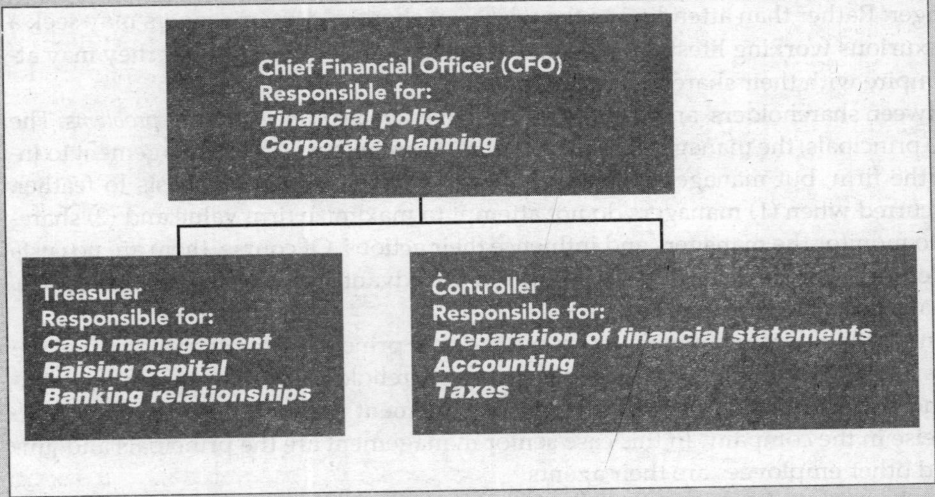

FIGURE 1.2

Senior financial managers in large corporations.

functions: The treasurer's main responsibility is to obtain and manage the firm's capital, whereas the controller ensures that the money is used efficiently.

Still larger firms usually appoint a **chief financial officer (CFO)** to oversee both the treasurer's and the controller's work. The CFO is deeply involved in financial policy and corporate planning. Often he or she will have general managerial responsibilities beyond strictly financial issues and may also be a member of the board of directors.

The controller or CFO is responsible for organizing and supervising the capital budgeting process. However, major capital investment projects are so closely tied to plans for product development, production, and marketing that managers from these areas are inevitably drawn into planning and analyzing the projects. If the firm has staff members specializing in corporate planning, they too are naturally involved in capital budgeting.

Because of the importance of many financial issues, ultimate decisions often rest by law or by custom with the board of directors. For example, only the board has the legal power to declare a dividend or to sanction a public issue of securities. Boards usually delegate decisions for small or medium-sized investment outlays, but the authority to approve large investments is almost never delegated.

1.4 SEPARATION OF OWNERSHIP AND MANAGEMENT

In large businesses separation of ownership and management is a practical necessity. Major corporations may have hundreds of thousands of shareholders. There is no way for all of them to be actively involved in management: It would be like running Mumbai City through a series of town meetings for all its citizens. Authority has to be delegated to managers.

The separation of ownership and management has clear advantages. It allows share ownership to change without interfering with the operation of the business. It allows the firm to hire professional managers. But it also brings problems if the managers' and owners' objectives differ. You can see the danger: Rather than attending to the wishes of shareholders, managers may seek a more leisurely or luxurious working lifestyle; they may shun unpopular decisions, or they may attempt to build an empire with their shareholders' money.

Such conflicts between shareholders' and managers' objectives create *principal–agent problems*. The shareholders are the principals; the managers are their agents. Shareholders want management to increase the value of the firm, but managers may have their own axes to grind or nests to feather. **Agency costs** are incurred when (1) managers do not attempt to maximize firm value and (2) shareholders incur costs to monitor the managers and influence their actions. Of course, there are no costs when the shareholders are also the managers. That is one of the advantages of a sole proprietorship. Owner–managers have no conflicts of interest.

Conflicts between shareholders and managers are not the only principal–agent problems that the financial manager is likely to encounter. For example, just as shareholders need to encourage managers to work for the shareholders' interests, so senior management needs to think about how to motivate everyone else in the company. In this case senior management are the principals and junior management and other employees are their agents.

Agency costs can also arise in financing. In normal times, the banks and bondholders who lend the company money are united with the shareholders in wanting the company to prosper, but when the firm gets into trouble, this unity of purpose can break down. At such times decisive action may be necessary to rescue the firm, but lenders are concerned to get their money back and are reluctant to see the firm making risky changes that could imperil the safety of their loans. Squabbles may even break out between different lenders as they see the company heading for possible bankruptcy and jostle for a better place in the queue of creditors.

Think of the company's overall value as a pie that is divided among a number of claimants. These include the management and the shareholders, as well as the company's workforce and the banks and investors who have bought the company's debt. The government is a claimant too, since it gets to tax corporate profits.

All these claimants are bound together in a complex web of contracts and understandings. For example, when banks lend money to the firm, they insist on a formal contract stating the rate of interest and repayment dates, perhaps placing restrictions on dividends or additional borrowing. But you can't devise written rules to cover every possible future event. So written contracts are incomplete and need to be supplemented by understandings and by arrangements that help to align the interests of the various parties.

Principal–agent problems would be easier to resolve if everyone had the same information. That is rarely the case in finance. Managers, shareholders, and lenders may all have different information about the value of a real or financial asset, and it may be many years before all the information is revealed. Financial managers need to recognize these *information asymmetries* and find ways to reassure investors that there are no nasty surprises on the way.

Here is one example. Suppose you are the financial manager of a company that has been newly formed to develop and bring to market a drug to cure toetitis. At a meeting with potential investors you present the results of clinical trials, show upbeat reports by an independent market research company, and forecast profits amply sufficient to justify further investment. But the potential investors are still worried that you may know more than they do. What can you do to convince them that you are telling the truth? Just saying "Trust me" won't do the trick. Perhaps you need to *signal* your integrity by putting your money where your mouth is. For example, investors are likely to

Differences in information	Different objectives
Stock prices and returns (13)	Managers vs. stockholders (2, 12, 32, 33, 34)
Issues of shares and other securities (15, 18, 25)	Top management vs. operating management (12)
Dividends (16)	Stockholders vs. banks and other lenders (18)
Financing (18)	

FIGURE 1.3

Differences in objectives and information can complicate financial decisions. We address these issues at several points in this book (chapter numbers in parentheses).

have more confidence in your plans if they see that you and the other managers have large personal stakes in the new enterprise. Therefore your decision to invest your own money can provide information to investors about the true prospects of the firm.

In later chapters we will look more carefully at how corporations tackle the problems created by differences in objectives and information. Figure 1.3 summarizes the main issues and signposts the chapters where they receive most attention.

1.5 TOPICS COVERED IN THIS BOOK

We have mentioned how financial managers face two broad decisions—which real assets the firm should invest in and how to raise the cash to pay for them. Thus, the investment decision typically precedes the financial decision. That is how we have organized this book. Parts 1 to 3 are almost entirely devoted to different aspects of the investment decision. The first topic is how to value assets, the second is the link between risk and value, and the third is the management of the capital investment process. Our discussion of these topics occupies Chapters 2 through 12.

Parts 4 to 7 are concerned with financing decisions. Part 4 starts by discussing three general issues: Can the financial manager assume that the market will fairly value the firm's securities? What are the main sources of finance that firms use? and what are the procedures for making a new issue of securities? Part 5 continues the analysis of the financing decision by looking at how much the firm should pay out to its shareholders and how much it should borrow. We then move on to look at options and how they are valued. Options are often tacked on to an issue of corporate securities and they often lurk in the *real* assets that the company owns. Having mastered options, we proceed in Part 7 to look at how debt is valued and the many different types of debt financing.

An important part of the financial manager's job is to judge which risks the firm should take on and which can be eliminated. Part 8 looks at risk management, both domestically and internationally.

Part 9 covers financial planning and short-term financial management. We address a variety of practical topics, including short- and longer-term forecasting, channels for short-term borrowing or investment, management of cash and marketable securities, and management of accounts receivable (money lent by the firm to its customers).

Part 10 looks at mergers and acquisitions and, more generally, at the control and governance of the firm. We also discuss how companies in different countries are structured to provide the right incentives for management and the right degree of control by outside investors.

Part 11 is our conclusion. It also discusses some of the things that we *don't* know about finance. If you can be the first to solve any of these puzzles, you will be justifiably famous.

SUMMARY

In Chapter 2 we will begin with the most basic concepts of asset valuation. However, we should first sum up the principal points made in this introductory chapter.

Large businesses are usually organized as corporations. Corporations have three important features. First, they are legally distinct from their owners and pay their own taxes. Second, corporations provide limited liability, which means that the stockholders who own the corporation cannot be held responsible for the firm's debts. Third, the owners of a corporation are not usually the managers.

The overall task of the financial manager can be broken down into (1) the investment, or capital budgeting, decision and (2) the financing decision. In other words, the firm has to decide (1) what real assets to buy and (2) how to raise the necessary cash.

In small companies there is often only one financial executive, the treasurer. However, most companies have both a treasurer and a controller. The treasurer's job is to obtain and manage the company's financing, while the controller's job is to confirm that the money is used correctly. In large firms there is also a chief financial officer or CFO.

Shareholders want managers to increase the value of the company's stock. Managers may have different objectives. This potential conflict of interest is termed a principal–agent problem. Any loss of value that results from such conflicts is termed an agency cost. Of course there may be other conflicts of interest. For example, the interests of the shareholders may sometimes conflict with those of the firm's banks and bondholders. These and other agency problems become more complicated when agents have more or better information than the principals.

The financial manager plays on an international stage and must understand how international financial markets operate and how to evaluate overseas investments. We discuss international corporate finance at many different points in the chapters that follow.

FURTHER READING

In India, finance managers read *The Economic Times, The Business Standard, The Financial Express, The Business Line* (or all of these) daily. You should too. You should also read the Asian edition of *The Wall Street Journal. The Times of India*, and a few other all-India newspapers have good business and financial sections, but they are no substitute for the above business dailies mentioned. The business and financial sections of most of the other Indian dailies are, except for local news, worthless for the finance manager.

The Business Today, The Business India, The Business World, etc. contain useful financial sections, and there are several magazines (like the *Financial Analyst*) that specialize in finance. Some of the good international publications include *Euromoney, Corporate Finance, Journal of Applied Corporate Finance, Risk*, and *CFO Magazine*. This list does not include research journals as the *Journal of Finance, Journal of Financial Economics, Review of Financial Studies*, and *Financial Management*. In the following chapters we give specific references to pertinent research.

CONCEPT REVIEW QUESTIONS

1. What is meant by limited liability? Do corporations have limited liability? What about sole proprietorships? (page 6)
2. There is an important tax drawback in the United States to organizing as a corporation. What is it? (page 6)
3. Firms invest in real assets and finance them by selling financial assets. Give some examples of each. (page 6)

For additional Concept Review Questions, please visit us at www.mhhe.com/bmam8e or refer to your Student CD.

QUIZ

1. Read the following passage: "Companies usually buy (*a*) assets. These include both tangible assets such as (*b*) and intangible assets such as (*c*). In order to pay for these assets, they sell (*d*) assets such as (*e*). The decision about which assets to buy is usually termed the (*f*) or (*g*) decision. The decision about how to raise the money is usually termed the (*h*) decision." Now fit each of the following terms into the most appropriate space: *financing, real, bonds, investment, executive airplanes, financial, capital budgeting, brand names.*
2. Vocabulary test. Explain the differences between:
   a. Real and financial assets.
   b. Capital budgeting and financing decisions.
   c. Closely held and public corporations.
   d. Limited and unlimited liability.
   e. Corporation and partnership.
3. Which of the following are real assets, and which are financial?
   a. A share of stock.
   b. A personal IOU.
   c. A trademark.
   d. A factory.
   e. Undeveloped land.
   f. The balance in the firm's checking account.
   g. An experienced and hardworking sales force.
   h. A corporate bond.
4. What are the main *disadvantages* of the corporate form of organization?
5. Which of the following statements more accurately describe the treasurer than the controller?
   a. Likely to be the only financial executive in small firms.
   b. Monitors capital expenditures to make sure that they are not misappropriated.
   c. Responsible for investing the firm's spare cash.
   d. Responsible for arranging any issue of common stock.
   e. Responsible for the company's tax affairs.
6. Which of the following statements always apply to corporations?
   a. Unlimited liability.
   b. Limited life.
   c. Ownership can be transferred without affecting operations.
   d. Managers can be fired with no effect on ownership.
   e. Shares must be widely traded.
7. In most large corporations, ownership and management are separated. What are the main implications of this separation?

CHAPTER [2]

PRESENT VALUES, THE OBJECTIVES OF THE FIRM, AND CORPORATE GOVERNANCE

COMPANIES INVEST in a variety of real assets. These include tangible assets such as plant and machinery and intangible assets such as management contracts and patents. The object of the investment, or capital budgeting, decision is to find real assets that are worth more than they cost. In this chapter we will take the first, most basic steps toward understanding how assets are valued.

There are a few cases in which it is not that difficult to estimate asset values. In real estate, for example, you can hire a professional appraiser to do it for you. Suppose you own a warehouse. The odds are that your appraiser's estimate of its value will be within a few percent of what the building would actually sell for.[1] After all, there is continuous activity in the real estate market, and the appraiser's stock-in-trade is knowledge of the prices at which similar properties have recently changed hands. Thus the problem of valuing real estate is simplified by the existence of an active market in which all kinds of properties are bought and sold. For many purposes no formal theory of value is needed. We can take the market's word for it.

But we need to go deeper than that. First, it is important to know how asset values are reached in an active market. Even if you can take the appraiser's word for it, it is important to understand *why* that warehouse is worth, say, Rs. 250,000 and not a higher or lower figure. Second, the market for most corporate assets is pretty thin. Look in the classified advertisements in *The Economic Times:* It is not often that you see a blast furnace for sale.

Companies are always searching for assets that are worth more to them than to others. That warehouse is worth more to you if you can manage it better than others can. But in that case, looking at the price of similar buildings will not tell you what the warehouse is worth under your management. You need to know how asset values are determined. In other words, you need a theory of value.

This chapter starts to develop that theory. We lead off with a simple numerical example: Should you invest in a new office building in the hope of selling it at a profit next year? We shall explain that you should do so if net present value is positive, that is, if the new building's value today exceeds the investment that is required. A positive net present value implies that the rate of return on your investment is higher than the opportunity cost of capital.

This chapter's first task is to define and explain net present value, rate of return, and opportunity cost of capital. The second task is to explain *why* financial managers need to search for investments with positive net present values. Here we will come to the fundamental objective of corporate finance: maximizing the current value of the firm's shares. We will explain why all shareholders should support this objective and why it makes more sense than other corporate goals, such as "maximizing profits."

Finally, we turn to the *managers'* objectives and discuss some of the mechanisms that help to align the managers' and stockholders' interests. We ask whether attempts to increase shareholder value need be at the expense of workers, customers, or the community at large.

In this chapter we will stick to the simplest problems to make basic ideas clear. Readers with a taste for complication will find plenty to satisfy them in later chapters.

[1] Needless to say, there are some properties that appraisers find nearly impossible to value—for example, nobody knows the potential selling price of the Taj Mahal, the Parthenon, or Windsor Castle.

2.1 INTRODUCTION TO PRESENT VALUE

If you find an investment opportunity, how do you decide whether it is worthwhile? Suppose you come across a vacant lot that you can buy for Rs. 50,000. Your real estate adviser thinks there will be a shortage of office space a year from now and that an office building will fetch Rs. 420,000. For simplicity, we will assume that this Rs. 420,000 is a sure thing. The total cost of buying the land and constructing the building would be Rs. 370,000. Thus you would be investing Rs. 370,000 now to generate Rs. 420,000 a year hence. You should go ahead if the **present value (PV)** of the Rs. 420,000 payoff is greater than the investment of Rs. 370,000. Therefore, you need to ask, What is the value today of Rs. 420,000 to be received one year from now, and is that present value greater than Rs. 370,000?

Calculating Future Value and Present Value

The first basic principle of finance is that *a rupee today is worth more than a rupee tomorrow,* because the rupee today can be invested to start earning interest immediately. Financial managers refer to this as the *time value of money.* Suppose that the rate of interest on Indian Government securities is 5 percent per year. If you invest Rs. 400,000 at 5 percent interest, you will have Rs. 400,000 × 1.05 = Rs. 420,000 a year from now. The **future value** of Rs. 400,000 today is 1.05 × Rs. 400,000 = Rs. 420,000 a year from now.

In our example, we know the *future* value (the office building that will be worth Rs. 420,000), but we need to find the *present* value of that future payoff. Think again of the time value of money. Since Re. 1 in hand today is worth more than Re. 1 next year, Re. 1 next year must be worth *less* than Re. 1 today. Therefore Rs. 420,000 next year must be worth less than Rs. 420,000 today—but how much less? The answer is Rs. 400,000, because investors can put up Rs. 400,000 today, earn 5 percent interest, and get Rs. 420,000 next year.

The arithmetic of present value is simple. Just run our future value calculation in reverse. If the interest rate is 5 percent, then the present value of Rs. 420,000 one year from now is Rs. 420,000/1.05 = Rs. 400,000. To find the present value, we divide the future cash flow by 1.05, or multiply it by 1/1.05. This multiplier (1/1.05 in our example) is called the **discount factor.** In general, if C_1 denotes the expected payoff at date 1 (one year hence), then

$$\text{Present value (PV)} = \text{discount factor} \times C_1$$

This discount factor is the value today of Re. 1 received in the future. It is expressed as the reciprocal of 1 plus a rate of return:

$$\text{Discount factor} = \frac{1}{1+r}$$

The rate of return r is the reward that investors demand for accepting delayed payment.

To calculate present value, we discount expected payoffs by the rate of return offered by equivalent investment alternatives in the capital market. This rate of return is the **discount rate, hurdle rate,** or **opportunity cost of capital.** It is called the opportunity cost because it is the return foregone by investing in the project rather than investing in securities. In our example the opportunity cost was 5 percent. Present value was obtained by dividing Rs. 420,000 by 1.05:

$$\text{PV} = \text{discount factor} \times C_1 = \frac{1}{1+r} \times C_1 = \frac{420{,}000}{1.05} = \text{Rs. } 400{,}000$$

Let us assume that as soon as you have bought the land and begun construction, you decide to sell your project. How much could you sell it for? That is an easy question. Since the property will be worth Rs. 420,000 in a year, investors would be willing to pay Rs. 400,000 for it today. That is what it would cost them to get a Rs. 420,000 payoff from investing in government securities. Of course, you could always sell your property for less, but why sell for less than the market will bear? The Rs. 400,000 present value is the only feasible price that satisfies both buyer and seller. Therefore, the present value of the property is also its market price.

Net Present Value

The office building is worth Rs. 400,000, but this does not mean you are Rs. 400,000 better off. You committed Rs. 370,000 and therefore the **net present value (NPV)** is Rs. 30,000. Net present value is found by subtracting the required investment:

$$\text{NPV} = \text{PV} - \text{required investment} = 400{,}000 - 370{,}000 = \text{Rs. } 30{,}000$$

In other words, your office development is worth more than it costs—it makes a *net* contribution to value and increases your wealth. The formula for calculating NPV can be written as

$$\text{NPV} = C_0 + \frac{C_1}{1+r}$$

remembering that C_0, the cash flow at time 0 (that is, today), will usually be a negative number. In other words, C_0 is an investment and therefore a cash outflow. In our example, $C_0 = -\text{Rs. } 370{,}000$.

Risk and Present Value

We made one unrealistic assumption in our discussion of the office development: Your real estate adviser cannot be certain about future values of office buildings. The Rs. 420,000 represents the best forecast, but it is not a sure thing.

If the future value of the building is risky, our calculation of NPV is wrong. Investors could achieve Rs. 420,000 with certainty by buying Rs. 400,000 worth of Indian Government securities, so they would not buy your building for that amount. You would have to cut your asking price to attract investors' interest.

Here we can invoke a second basic financial principle: *A safe rupee is worth more than a risky one.* Most investors avoid risk when they can do so without sacrificing return. However, the concepts of present value and the opportunity cost of capital still make sense for risky investments. It is still proper to discount the payoff by the rate of return offered by an equivalent investment. But we have to think of *expected* payoffs and the *expected* rates of return on other investments.[2]

Not all investments are equally risky. The office development is more risky than a government security but less risky than a start-up biotech venture. Suppose you believe the project is as risky as investment in the stock market and that stocks are forecasted to return 12 percent. Then 12 percent becomes the opportunity cost of capital. That is what you are giving up by not investing in equally risky securities. Now recompute NPV:

$$\text{PV} = \frac{420{,}000}{1.12} = \text{Rs. } 375{,}000$$

$$\text{NPV} = \text{PV} - 370{,}000 = \text{Rs. } 5{,}000$$

The office building still makes a net contribution to value, but the increase in your wealth is smaller than in our first calculation, which assumed that the future value of the office building was risk-free.

[2] We define "expected" more carefully in Chapter 9. For now think of expected payoff as a realistic forecast, neither optimistic nor pessimistic. Forecasts of expected payoffs are correct on average.

The value of the office building depends, therefore, on the timing of the cash flows and their uncertainty. The Rs. 420,000 payoff would be exactly that if it could be realized instantaneously. If the office building is as risk-free as government securities, the one-year delay *reduces value* by Rs. 20,000 to Rs. 400,000. If the building is as risky as investment in the stock market, then uncertainty further reduces value by Rs. 25,000 to Rs. 375,000.

If other investors agree with your forecast of a Rs. 420,000 payoff and your assessment of its risk, then your property ought to be worth Rs. 375,000 once construction is underway. If you tried to sell it for more, there would be no takers, because the property would then offer an expected rate of return lower than the 12 percent available in the stock market. Thus the office building's present value is also its market value.

Unfortunately, adjusting asset values for both time and uncertainty is often more complicated than our example suggests. Therefore, we will take the two effects separately. For the most part, we will dodge the problem of risk in Chapters 2 through 6, either by treating all cash flows as if they were known with certainty or by talking about expected cash flows and expected rates of return without worrying how risk is defined or measured. Then in Chapter 7 we will turn to the problem of understanding how financial markets cope with risk.

Present Values and Rates of Return

We have decided that construction of the office building is a smart thing to do, since it is worth more than it costs—it has a positive net present value and creates wealth for you. To calculate how much it is worth, we worked out how much you would need to pay to achieve the same payoff by investing directly in securities. The project's present value is equal to its future income discounted at the rate of return offered by these securities.

We can state our decision rule in another way: Our real estate venture is worth undertaking because its rate of return exceeds the cost of capital. The rate of return on the investment in the office building is simply the profit as a proportion of the initial outlay:

$$\text{Return} = \frac{\text{profit}}{\text{investment}} = \frac{420{,}000 - 370{,}000}{370{,}000} = .135, \text{ or } 13.5\%$$

The cost of capital is once again the return foregone by *not* investing in securities. If the office building is as risky as investing in the stock market, the return foregone is 12 percent. Since the 13.5 percent return on the office building exceeds the 12 percent opportunity cost, you should go ahead with the project.

Here, then, we have two equivalent decision rules for capital investment:[3]

- *Net present value rule.* Accept investments that have positive net present values.
- *Rate of return rule.* Accept investments that offer rates of return in excess of their opportunity costs of capital.[4]

[3] You might check for yourself that these are equivalent rules. In other words, if the return of Rs. 50,000/Rs. 370,000 is greater than r, then the net present value −Rs. 370,000 + [Rs. 420,000/$(1 + r)$] *must* be greater than 0.

[4] The two rules can conflict when there are cash flows at more than two dates. We address this problem in Chapter 5.

The Opportunity Cost of Capital

The opportunity cost of capital is such an important concept that we will give one more example. You are offered the following opportunity: Invest Rs. 100,000 today and, depending on the state of the economy at the end of the year, you will receive one of these equally probable payoffs:

Slump	Normal	Boom
Rs. 80,000	Rs. 110,000	Rs.140,000

Since the three scenarios all have probability 1/3, the expected payoff is

$$C_1 = \left(\frac{1}{3}\right)(80{,}000 + 110{,}000 + 140{,}000) = \text{Rs } 110{,}000$$

This represents an expected return of 10 percent on the investment of Rs. 100,000. But what's the right discount rate?

You search for a common stock with the same risk as the investment. Stock X turns out to be a perfect match. X's price next year, given a normal economy, is forecasted at Rs. 110. The stock price will be lower in a slump and higher in a boom, but to the same degrees as your investment (Rs. 80 in a slump and Rs. 140 in a boom). You conclude that the risks of stock X and your investment are identical.

Stock X's current price is Rs. 95.65. It offers an expected rate of return of 15 percent:

$$\text{Expected return} = \frac{\text{expected profit}}{\text{investment}} = \frac{110 - 95.65}{95.65} = .15, \text{ or } 15\%$$

This is the expected return that you are giving up by investing in the project rather than the stock market. In other words, it is the project's opportunity cost of capital.

To value the project, discount the expected cash flow by the opportunity cost of capital:

$$PV = \frac{110{,}000}{1.15} = \text{Rs. } 95{,}650$$

This is the amount it would cost investors in the stock market to buy an expected cash flow of Rs. 110,000. (They could do this by buying 1,000 shares of stock X.) It is therefore also the sum that investors would be prepared to pay for your project.

To calculate net present value, deduct the initial investment:

$$NPV = 95{,}650 - 100{,}000 = -\text{Rs. } 4{,}350$$

The project is worth Rs. 4,350 less than it costs. It is *not* worth undertaking. Instead of creating wealth, it would destroy wealth and make you worse off, compared with investing in the stock market.

Notice that you come to the same conclusion if you compare the expected project return with the cost of capital:

$$\text{Expected return on project} = \frac{\text{expected profit}}{\text{investment}} = \frac{110{,}000 - 100{,}000}{100{,}000} = .10, \text{ or } 10\%$$

The 10 percent expected return on the project is less than the 15 percent return investors could expect to earn by investing in stock X, so the project is not worthwhile.

Of course in real life it's impossible to restrict the future states of the economy to just "slump," "normal," and "boom." We have also simplified by assuming a perfect match between the payoffs of 1,000 shares of stock X and the payoffs to the investment project. The main point of the example does carry through to real life, however. Remember this: The opportunity cost of capital for an investment project is the expected rate of return demanded by investors in common stocks or other securities subject to the same risks as the project. When you discount the project's expected cash flow at its opportunity cost of capital, the resulting present value is the amount investors would be willing to pay for the project. Any time you find and launch a positive-NPV project (a project with present value exceeding its outlay) you have created wealth and are better off.

A Source of Confusion

Here is a possible source of confusion. Suppose a banker approaches. "Your company is a fine and safe business with few debts," she says. "My bank will lend you the Rs. 100,000 that you need for the project at 8 percent." Does that mean that the cost of capital for the project is 8 percent? If so, the project would be worth doing. At an 8 percent cost of capital, PV would be 110,000/1.08 = Rs. 101,852 and NPV = 101,852 − 100,000 = +Rs. 1,852.

But that can't be right. First, the interest rate on the loan has nothing to do with the risk of the project: It reflects the good health of your existing business. Second, whether you take the loan or not, you still face the choice between the project, which offers an expected return of 10 percent, or the equally risky stock which gives an expected return of 15 percent. A financial manager who borrows at 8 percent and invests at 10 percent is not smart, but stupid, if the company or its shareholders can borrow at 8 percent and buy an equally risky investment offering 15 percent. That is why the 15 percent expected return on the stock is the opportunity cost of capital for the project.

2.2 FOUNDATIONS OF THE NET PRESENT VALUE RULE

The net present value rule seems sensible enough. It worked for you when you decided to buy that vacant lot and constructed an office building on it. But will the rule work for everybody? Your investment objective—to earn a high return next year—may not be shared by others. Let us introduce this next question with the following scenario.

Your first day on the job You have just been hired by the stockholder relations department at Tata Steel. The annual shareholders' meeting is scheduled for your first day of work, and you are asked to attend. The meeting itself seems routine, but you note how carefully the CEO explains Tata Steel's plans of future acquisitions. Tata Steel has just completed the Rs. 1313 crores acquisition of the Singapore-based NatSteel. The extra explanation makes sense, you realize, because the acquisition involves expenditures exceeding hundreds of crores of rupees.

After the formal meeting you mingle at the shareholders' coffee hour. You can't help overhearing a rather heated exchange between an elderly woman, evidently retired, and an earnest young man:

Retired woman: The company's spending a fortune on new acquisitions. Why did they buy 100% stake in that Singapore based firm? It cost the company Rs. 1313 crores, and it may not pay off for decades. Let someone else look for steel in Singapore. The company could better use the money to pay higher dividends. I could use a bigger dividend.

Earnest young man: Would you like to see some pictures of my new daughter Puja? Of course you would—don't worry, I've only got a dozen. I bought the Tata Steel shares for her. She needs diapers, not dividends. Our company should invest for the long run. That Steel from Singapore will pay for her college education.

You are tempted to intervene, but hesitate. What should you say? They are only two of many thousand Tata Steel shareholders, and even they can't agree. Could the acquisition of a steel company be good news for little Puja and bad news for the retired lady? What about other stockholders? Some may combine long-run objectives with high risk aversion. Some may be happy to take chances that Tata Steel shares will go up and generate a short-run profit. Could a risk-averse, long-term investor and a risk-tolerant, short-term investor agree with Puja's dad on the wisdom of Tata Steel's investment in a steel company in Singapore?

The answer to these questions is yes: all of Tata Steel's stockholders should be able to agree on its investment plans, provided that the investments all have positive NPVs and that all stockholders have equal access to capital markets. We now demonstrate that theorem.

How Capital Markets Reconcile Preferences for Current vs. Future Consumption

You can look forward to a stream of income from your future employment. Unless you have some way of storing or anticipating the income, you will be compelled to consume it as it arrives. If the bulk of your income comes late in life, the result could be hunger now and gluttony later. The capital market solves this problem by allowing you to trade between rupees today and rupees in the future and vice versa. You can therefore consume moderately both now and in the future no matter when your income comes.

Suppose you have a nest egg of exactly Rs. 370,000 in cash. You could spend all of it today. You could invest it all at 5 percent interest and consume 1.05 × Rs. 370,000 = Rs. 388,500 a year from now. Or you could split the difference, consuming Rs. 185,000 now and putting the remaining Rs. 185,000 to work at 5 percent, so you can consume 1.05 × Rs. 185,000 = Rs. 194,250 next year. Or you could arrange many other blends of present and future consumption. The entire range of possibilities is shown by the blue line in Figure 2.1. The slope of this line is determined by the 5 percent interest rate.

Now suppose you also have the opportunity to invest your nest egg of Rs. 370,000 in the office-building development described earlier. This will produce a surefire Rs. 420,000 next year. But that does not mean you can't consume anything today. You can borrow against your future income. With an interest rate of 5 percent, you can borrow and spend up to Rs. 420,000/1.05 = Rs. 400,000. By varying the amount you borrow you can obtain any mixture of consumption this year and next. These possibie mixtures are shown by the green line in Figure 2.1. No matter what your preferences are, you are clearly better off investing in the office building. Investing in the building adds value. It increases your wealth. It moves you up from the blue to the green line in Figure 2.1. That is why

FIGURE 2.1

Effects of investing Rs 370,000 in the office-building project. Consumption opportunities are enlarged by the project's Rs 30,000 positive NPV. With the project, you can pick a time pattern of consumption along the outer green line, which starts at the project's present value of Rs 400,000. No matter what *your* preferred consumption plan, you are better off with the project.

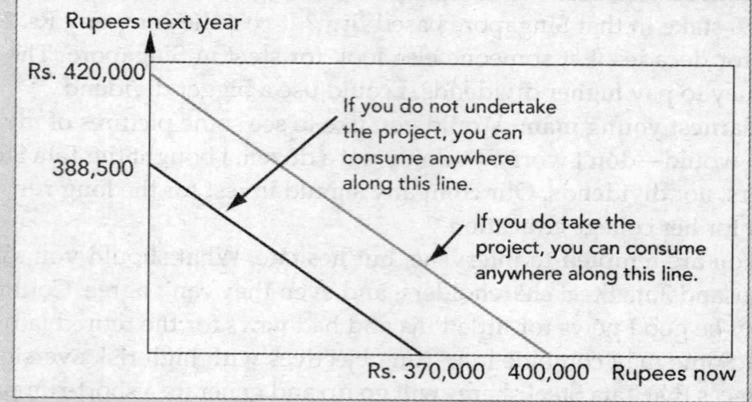

the NPV rule makes sense. Whenever you accept a positive-NPV investment project, you have extra wealth that can be spent now or in the future.[5]

We can now see how the existence of a well-functioning capital market allows investors with different time patterns of desired consumption to agree on whether investment projects should be undertaken. Suppose that there are two investors with entirely different preferences. Think of A as an ant, who wishes to save for the future, and of G as a grasshopper, who would prefer to spend all his wealth on some ephemeral frolic, taking no heed of tomorrow. Each has been offered the opportunity to invest Rs. 185,000 in a 50 percent share in the office building.

You can see from Figure 2.2 that A would clearly be happy to invest in the building. If she invests in the building, she will have 0.5 × Rs. 420,000 = Rs. 210,000 to spend at the end of the year. If she invested her Rs. 185,000 in the capital market, she would have only 1.05 × Rs. 185,000 = Rs. 194,250 to spend.[6]

But what about G, who wants money now, not in one year's time? He too is happy to invest, because he can borrow against the future payoff of the investment project. As you can see from Figure 2.2, investing gives him Rs. 15,000 more to spend today (210,000/1.05 = Rs. 200,000).

[5] The exact balance between present and future consumption that each individual will choose depends on personal preferences. Readers who are familiar with economic theory will recognize that the choice can be represented by adding indifference curves for each individual to Figure 2.1. The preferred combination of present and future consumption is the point of tangency between the interest-rate line and the individual's indifference curve. In other words, each individual will borrow or lend until 1 plus the interest rate equals the marginal rate of time preference (i.e., the slope of the indifference curve). A more formal graphical analysis of investment and the choice between present and future consumption is on the Brealey-Myers-Allen Web site at **www.mhhe.com/bmam8e.**

[6] If A did not have Rs 185,000 to invest, it would pay for her to borrow it. At the end of the year she could repay the loan out of the proceeds from her share in the office building. That would leave her with an additional 210,000 − 194,250 = Rs 15,750 to spend. Similarly, it would pay for G to borrow at 5 percent to invest in a building offering a return of 13.5 percent.

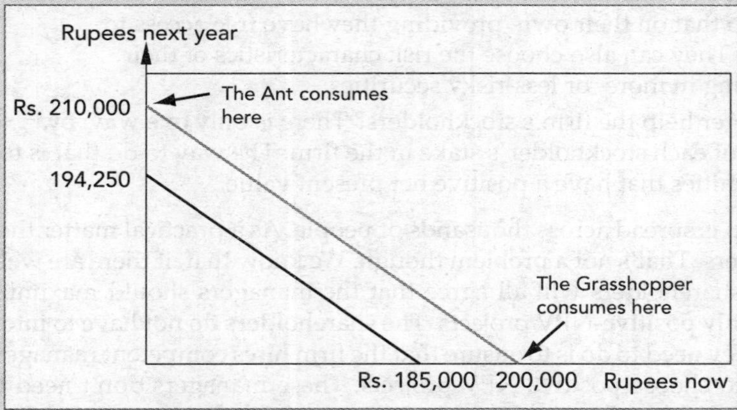

FIGURE 2.2

In this case both the Ant and the Grasshopper have a half-share in the building project. Both are Rs 15,000 richer by undertaking the project. The grasshopper chooses to spend this money now, while the ant prefers to postpone doing so until next year.

The key condition that allows A and G to agree on building the new office is that both have access to a well-functioning, competitive capital market, in which they can borrow and lend at the same rate. Whenever firms discount cash flows at capital market rates, they are implicitly assuming that their shareholders have equal access to competitive capital markets.

It is easy to see how our net present value rule would be damaged if we did not have such a well-functioning capital market. For example, suppose that G could not easily borrow against future income. In that case he might well prefer to spend his cash today rather than invest it in an office building. If A and G were shareholders in the same enterprise, there would be no simple way to reconcile their different objectives.

No one believes unreservedly that capital markets function perfectly. Later in this book we will discuss several cases in which differences in taxation, transaction costs, and other imperfections must be taken into account in financial decision making. However, we will also discuss research that indicates that, in general, capital markets function fairly well. That is one good reason for relying on net present value as a corporate objective. Another good reason is that net present value makes common sense; we will see that it gives obviously silly answers less frequently than its major competitors. But for now, having glimpsed the problems of imperfect markets, we shall, like an economist in a shipwreck, simply *assume* our life jacket and swim safely to shore.

A Fundamental Result

Our justification of the net present value rule was restricted to two periods and to certain cash flows. However, the rule also makes sense for uncertain cash flows that extend far into the future. The argument goes like this:

1. A financial manager should act in the interests of the firm's owners, its stockholders. Each stockholder wants three things:
   a. To be as rich as possible, that is, to maximize current wealth.
   b. To transform that wealth into whatever time pattern of consumption he or she desires.
   c. To choose the risk characteristics of that consumption plan.

2. But stockholders do not need the financial manager's help to achieve the best time pattern of consumption. They can do that on their own, providing they have free access to competitive capital markets. They can also choose the risk characteristics of their consumption plan by investing in more- or less-risky securities.
3. How can the financial manager help the firm's stockholders? There is only one way: by increasing the market value of each stockholder's stake in the firm. The way to do that is to seize all investment opportunities that have a positive net present value.

In large corporations ownership is spread across thousands of people. As a practical matter they need to delegate control to managers. That's not a problem though. We know that, if there are well-functioning capital markets, the shareholders will all agree that the managers should maximize shareholder wealth by choosing only positive-NPV projects. The shareholders do not have to interfere in day-to-day decisions. All they need to do is to ensure that the firm hires competent managers who have the correct incentives to choose positive-NPV projects. These managers don't need to know the preferences of each shareholder. They just need to follow one simple instruction: Maximize NPV.

In some countries capital markets do not function so well, and shareholders with different time preferences and risk tolerances may disagree about what firms should invest in. This could reduce the demand for shares of widely owned corporations. Such countries generally have more family-owned and state-owned firms and a greater concentration of control and wealth. For example, in Indonesia, the Philippines, and Thailand the largest 10 families control half of corporate assets.[7] In India, capital markets function reasonably well. The top 10 business groups in India control 13.5% of the total corporate assets in India.[8]

Other Corporate Goals

Sometimes you hear managers speak as if the corporation has other financial goals. For example, they may say that their job is to maximize profits. That sounds reasonable. After all, don't shareholders prefer to own a profitable company rather than an unprofitable one? But taken literally, profit maximization doesn't make sense as a corporate objective. Here are three reasons:

1. Maximizing profits? Which year's profits? Shareholders might not want a manager to increase next year's profits at the expense of profits in later years.
2. A company may be able to increase future profits by cutting its dividend and investing the cash. That is not in the shareholders' interest if the company earns only a low return on the investment.
3. Different accountants may calculate profits in different ways. So you may find that a decision that improves profits in one accountant's eyes will reduce them in another's.

[7] See S. Claessens, S. Djankov, and L.H.P. Lang, "The Separation of Ownership and Control in East Asian Corporations," *Journal of Financial Economics* 58 (2000), pp. 81–112, and R. La Porta, F. Lopez-de-Silanes, and A. Shleifer, "Corporate Ownership Around the World," *Journal of Finance* 59 (April 1999), pp. 30–45. For a theoretical analysis of family ownership see M. Burkart, F. Panunzi, and A. Shleifer, "Family Firms," *Journal of Finance* 58 (October 2003), pp. 2167–2201.

[8] Source: Power database. Data based on 9734 companies as on 30th March, 2006.

In contrast to maximizing profits, the net present value rule recognizes the time value of money and the difference between project rates of return and opportunity costs of capital. It also focuses on cash flow, and thus is immune to disagreements about accounting profits.

2.3 CORPORATE GOALS AND CORPORATE GOVERNANCE

We have explained that managers can best serve the interests of shareholders by investing in projects with a positive net present value. But this takes us back to the principal–agent problem highlighted in Chapter 1. How can the shareholders (the principals) ensure that management (their agents) don't simply look after their own interests? Shareholders can't spend their lives watching managers to check that they are pursuing the shareholders' interests rather than the management's own interests. However, good systems of *corporate governance* can help to ensure that the shareholders' pockets are close to the managers' hearts.[9]

A company's board of directors is elected by the shareholders and is supposed to represent them. Board of directors are sometimes portrayed as passive stooges who always champion the incumbent management. But when company performance starts to slide and managers do not offer a credible recovery plan, boards do act. In recent years the chief executives of Boeing, Eastman Kodak, Ford Motor, Hollinger International, and Lands End were all forced to step aside when their companies' profitability deteriorated and the need for new strategies became clear.

If shareholders believe that the corporation is underperforming and that the board of directors is not sufficiently aggressive in holding managers to task, they can try to replace the board in the next election. If they succeed, the new board will appoint a new management team. But these attempts to vote in a new board are expensive and rarely successful.[10] Thus dissidents do not usually stand and fight but sell their shares instead.

Selling, however, can send a powerful message. If enough shareholders bail out, the stock price tumbles. This damages top management's reputation and compensation. Part of the top managers' paychecks comes from bonuses tied to the company's earnings or from stock options, which pay off if the stock price rises but are worthless if the price falls below a stated threshold. This motivates managers to increase earnings and the stock price.[11]

If managers and directors do not maximize value, there is always the threat of a takeover. The further a company's stock price falls, due to lax management or wrong-headed policies, the easier it is for another company or group of investors to buy up a majority of the shares. The old manage-

[9] Prof. J R Varma of IIM Ahmedabad has observed that the corporate governance problem in India is completely different from that of the Anglo-American system. In India, there is a conflict of interest between the promoter shareholders (who mostly control the management) and the public shareholders. So it would be foolish to expect the Board in India to discipline the shareholders from whom it derives all its powers. See Varma, J.R., 1997, "Corporate Governance in India: Disciplining the Dominant Shareholder," IIMB Management Review, December, pp. 5–18.

[10] These contests are called *proxy fights*. See Chapter 14.

[11] Some critics say that the incentives created by stock options are excessively powerful, because they tempt managers to try to pump up stock prices so that the options can be cashed in for short-run profits. There are certainly examples of such behavior. WorldCom, for example, inflated its reported profits by various tricks to support an inflated stock price. WorldCom has now emerged from bankruptcy, with new management, as MCI. Debacles like WorldCom's seem to be exceptions and not the rule, however.

ment team is then likely to find itself out on the street and its place taken by a fresh team prepared to make the changes needed to realize the company's value.

These arrangements ensure that few managers at the top of major U.S. corporations are lazy or inattentive to stockholders' interests. On the contrary—the pressure to perform can be intense.

Should Managers Look after the Interests of Their Shareholders?

We have described managers as the agents of shareholders. But perhaps this begs the question. Is it desirable for managers to act in the selfish interests of their shareholders? Does a focus on enriching the shareholders mean that managers must act as greedy mercenaries riding roughshod over the weak and helpless?

Most of this book is devoted to financial policies that increase a firm's value. None of these policies requires gallops over the weak and helpless. In most instances, there is little conflict between doing well (maximizing value) and doing good. Profitable firms are those with satisfied customers and loyal employees; firms with dissatisfied customers and a disgruntled workforce will probably end up with declining profits and a low stock price.

Of course, when we say that the objective of the firm is to maximize shareholder wealth, we do not mean that anything goes. The law deters managers from making blatantly dishonest decisions, but most managers are not simply concerned with observing the letter of the law or with keeping to written contracts. In business and finance, as in other day-to-day affairs, there are unwritten, implicit rules of behavior. To work efficiently together, we need to trust each other. Thus huge financial deals are regularly completed on a handshake, and each side knows that the other will not renege later if things turn sour.[12]

In many financial transactions, one party has more information than the other. It can be difficult to be sure of the quality of the asset or service that you are buying. This opens up plenty of opportunities for financial sharp practice and outright fraud. The response of honest firms is to distinguish themselves by building long-term relationships with their customers and establishing a name for fair dealing and financial integrity. Major banks and securities firms know that their most valuable asset is their reputation. When something happens to undermine that reputation, the costs can be enormous. Here is one example.

The Market-Timing Scandal In the latter half of 2003, the mutual fund industry confronted a market-timing scandal. Market timing exploits the fact that stock markets in different parts of the world close at different times. If there is a strong upward surge in the U.S. stock market, then it is likely that stock prices will rise when markets open in Asia and Europe the next day. Traders who can buy international funds at prices set *before* the surge in U.S. stock prices can often make substantial profits. Similar profits tempt traders who see a sharp fall in the U.S. market and can sell international funds at stale prices. U.S. fund-management companies were not supposed to allow such trading, but some did. When the scandal came to light these companies suffered huge withdrawals, which severely damaged prospects for future revenues and profits. For example, after it

[12] In U.S. law, a contract can be valid even if it is not written down. Of course documentation is prudent, but contracts are enforced if it can be shown that the parties reached a clear understanding and agreement. For example, in 1984, the top management of Getty Oil gave a verbal agreement to merge with Pennzoil. Then Texaco arrived with a higher bid and won the prize. Pennzoil sued—and won—arguing that Texaco had broken up a valid contract.

was disclosed that managers at Putnam Investments had allowed market-timing trades, the company's funds suffered outflows of $ 30 billion in two months. Putnam was also fined $ 100 million and obliged to pay $ 10 million in compensation.

Should Firms Be Managed for Shareholders or All Stakeholders?

It is often suggested that firms should be managed on behalf of all stakeholders, not just stockholders. Other stakeholders include employees, customers, suppliers, and the communities where the firm's plants and offices are located.

Different countries take very different views on what the corporation's aims should be. In the United States, the United Kingdom, and other "Anglo-Saxon" economies, the idea of maximizing shareholder value is widely accepted as the chief financial goal of the firm.[13] In other countries, workers' interests are put forward much more strongly. In Germany, for example, workers in large companies have the right to elect up to half the directors to the companies' supervisory boards. As a result they have a significant role in the governance of the firm and less attention is paid to the shareholders.[14] In Japan managers usually view the interests of shareholders to be on a par with or even subordinate to the interests of employees and customers. For example, Toyota's business philosophy is "to realize stable, long-term growth by working hard to strike a balance between the requirements of people and society, the global environment and the world economy. . . . to grow with all of our stakeholders, including our customers, shareholders, employees, and business partners."[15]

Figures 2.3 and 2.4 summarize the results of interviews with executives from large companies in five countries. Japanese, German, and French executives think that their firms should be run for all stakeholders, while U.S. and U.K. executives say that shareholders come first. When asked about the trade-off between job security and dividends, almost all Japanese executives and the majority of German and French executives believe that job security should come first. By contrast, most U.S. and U.K. executives believe dividends should come first.

As capital markets have become more global, there has been greater pressure for companies in all countries to adopt wealth creation for shareholders as a primary goal. A number of German companies, including DaimlerChrysler and Deutsche Bank, have listed on the New York Stock Exchange and announced their primary goal as wealth creation for shareholders. In Japan there has been less movement in this direction. For example, the chairman of Toyota has suggested that it would be irresponsible to pursue shareholders' interests. On the other hand, the aggregate market value of Toyota's shares is significantly greater than the market values of GM's and Ford's, even though GM and Ford each make more vehicles than Toyota. So perhaps there is not too much conflict between these goals in practice.

[13] In India, the corporate objective in the private sector is largely biased towards shareholders' wealth maximization philosophy. The Kumar Managalam Birla Committee on Corporate Governance in India, in its draft report observed that "The fundamental objective of corporate governance is the enhancement of the long-term shareholder value while at the same time protecting the interests of other stakeholders". See www.ecgi.org/codes/documents/draft report.pdf.

[14] The following quote from the German banker Carl Fürstenberg (1850–1933) offers an extreme version of how shareholders were once regarded by German managers: "Shareholders are stupid and impertinent—stupid because they give their money to somebody else without any effective control over what the person is doing with it and impertinent because they ask for a dividend as a reward for their stupidity." Quoted by M. Hellwig, "On the Economics and Politics of Corporate Finance and Corporate Control," X. Vives, ed., *Corporate Governance* (Cambridge, UK: Cambridge University Press, 2000), p. 109.

[15] Toyota *Annual Report*, 2003, p. 10.

FIGURE 2.3

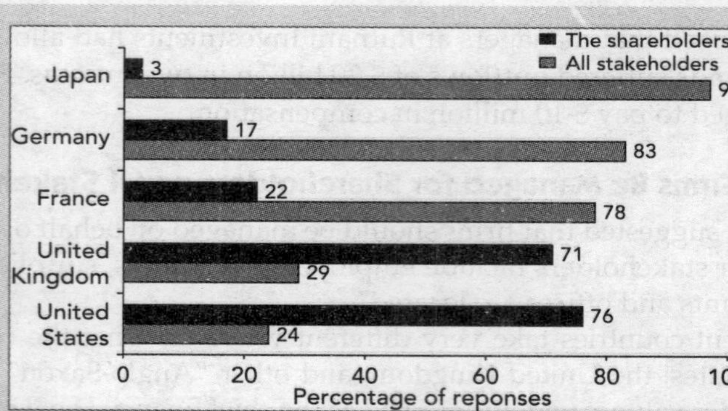

Whose Company Is It? The views of 378 managers from five countries.

Source: M. Yoshimori, "Whose Company Is It? The Concept of the Corporation in Japan and the West," *Long Range Planning*, Vol. 28 (August 1995), pp. 33–44. Copyright 1995 with permission from Elsevier Science

FIGURE 2.4

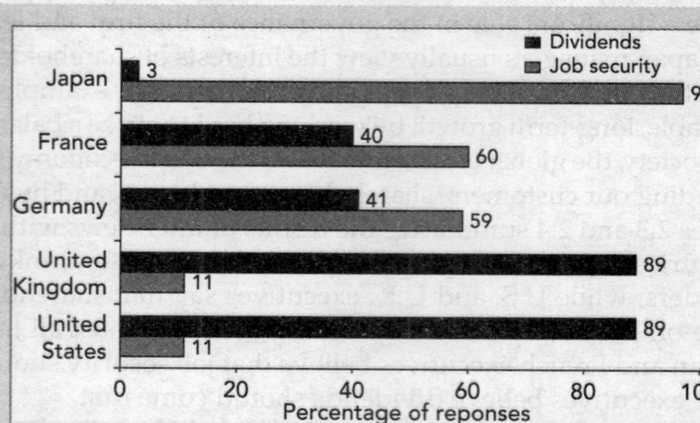

Which is more important—job security for employees or shareholder dividends? The views of 399 managers from five countries.

Source: M. Yoshimori, "Whose Company Is It? The Concept of the Corporation in Japan and the West," *Long Range Planning*, Vol. 28 (August 1995), pp. 33–44. Copyright 1995 with permission from Elsevier Science

SUMMARY

This chapter focuses on the financial objectives of the corporation. We saw that firms can best help their shareholders by accepting all projects with positive net present values and rejecting projects with negative net present values. The net present value of a project measures the wealth created by the project.

To find net present value we first calculate present value. Just discount future cash flow by an appropriate rate r, usually called the discount rate, hurdle rate, or *opportunity cost of capital:*

$$\text{Present value (PV)} = \frac{C_1}{1+r}$$

Net present value is present value plus any immediate cash flow:

$$\text{Net present value (NPV)} = C_0 + \frac{C_1}{1+r}$$

Remember that C_0 is negative if the immediate cash flow is an investment, that is, if it is a cash outflow.

The discount rate is determined by rates of return prevailing in capital markets. If the future cash flow is absolutely safe, then the discount rate is the interest rate on safe securities such as U.S. government debt. If the future cash flow is uncertain, then the expected cash flow should be discounted at the expected rate of return offered by equivalent-risk securities. We will talk more about risk and the cost of capital in Chapters 7 to 9.

Cash flows are discounted for two simple reasons: (1) because a rupee today is worth more than a rupee tomorrow, and (2) because a safe rupees is worth more than a risky one. Formulas for PV and NPV are numerical expressions of these ideas. The capital market is the market where safe and risky future cash flows are traded. That is why we look to rates of return prevailing in the capital markets to determine how much to discount for time and risk. By calculating the present value of an asset, we are estimating how much people will pay for it if they have the alternative of investing in the capital markets.

The net present value rule allows efficient separation of ownership and management. A manager who invests only in assets with positive net present values serves the best interests of each one of the firm's shareholders, regardless of differences in their wealth, risk aversion, or preferences for short- or long-term returns. The capital market makes this separation possible. Each shareholder can use the capital market to construct a personal investment plan tailored to his or her own requirements. For example, there is no need for the firm to arrange its investment policy to obtain a sequence of cash flows that matches its shareholders' preferred time patterns of consumption. The shareholders can shift funds forward or back over time perfectly well on their own, provided they have free access to well-functioning, competitive capital markets. In fact, their plan for consumption over time is limited by only two things: their personal wealth (or lack of it) and the interest rate at which they can borrow or lend. The financial manager cannot affect the interest rate but can increase shareholders' wealth. The way to do so is to invest in assets having positive net present values.

There are several institutional arrangements that help to ensure that managers pay close attention to the value of the firm:

- Managers are spurred on by incentive schemes, such as stock options, which pay off big if shareholders gain but are valueless if they do not.
- Managers' actions are subject to the scrutiny of the board of directors.
- Shirkers are likely to find that they are ousted by more energetic managers. This competition may arise within the firm, but poorly performing companies are also more likely to be taken over. The takeover typically brings in a fresh management team.

Recent events in the mutual fund industry underline the importance of ethical behavior. Managers should play fair by employees, suppliers, and customers, partly because they know it is for the common good, but partly because they know that their firm's most valuable asset is its reputation. Of course ethical issues do arise in financial management, and whenever unscrupulous managers abuse their positions, they harm the economy and society as a whole, because we all trust each other a little less.

In countries such as France, Germany, and Japan, managers give more weight to the interests of all stakeholders, rather than just to shareholders. However, globalization of capital markets has put increasing pressure on companies to pursue shareholders' interests.

The financial manager is asked to pursue financial goals. The firm may trade off financial goals against the goals of other stakeholders, but it cannot make trade-offs rationally unless it knows what the financial goals are. In this book we take maximization of shareholder value as the chief *financial* goal for the firm.

FURTHER READING

The pioneering works on the net present value rule are:

I. Fisher: *The Theory of Interest*, Augustus M. Kelley, Publishers. New York, 1965. Reprinted from the 1930 edition.

J. Hirshleifer: "On the Theory of Optimal Investment Decision," *Journal of Political Economy*, 66 (August 1958), pp. 329–352.

If you would like to dig deeper into the question of how managers can be motivated to maximize shareholder wealth, we suggest:

J. E. Core, W. R. Guay, and D. F. Larcker, "Executive Equity Compensation and Incentives: A Survey," *Federal Reserve Bank of New York Economic Policy Review*, 9 (April 2003), pp. 27–50. **www.ny.frb.org/research/epr/03v09n1/0304core.pdf.**

Two useful readings on ethical issues in finance:

C. W. Smith, Jr., "Economics and Ethics: The Case of Salomon Brothers," *Journal of Applied Corporate Finance* 5 (Summer 1992), pp. 23–28.

J. Brickley, C. W. Smith, Jr., and J. Zimmerman, "Ethics, Incentives, and Organizational Design," *Journal of Applied Corporate Finance* 7 (Summer 1994), pp. 8–19.

CONCEPT REVIEW QUESTIONS

1. What is the difference between a discount rate and a discount factor? (page 16)
2. How can risk be incorporated into PVs and NPVs? (page 17)
3. Write down the formulas for an investment's NPV and rate of return. Prove that NPV is positive *only* if the rate of return exceeds the opportunity cost of capital. (page 18)

For additional Concept Review Questions, please visit us at www.mhhe.com/bmam8e or refer to your Student CD.

QUIZ

1. C_0 is the initial cash flow on an investment, and C_1 is the cash flow at the end of one year. The symbol r is the discount rate.
   a. Is C_0 usually positive or negative?
   b. What is the formula for the present value of the investment?
   c. What is the formula for the net present value?
   d. The symbol r is often termed the *opportunity cost of capital.* Why?
   e. If the investment is risk-free, what is the appropriate measure of r?
2. If the present value of Rs. 150 paid at the end of one year is Rs. 130, what is the one-year discount factor? What is the discount rate?
3. Calculate the one-year discount factor DF_1 for discount rates of (a) 10 percent, (b) 20 percent, and (c) 30 percent.
4. A merchant pays Rs. 100,000 for a load of grain and is certain that it can be resold at the end of one year for Rs. 132,000.
   a. What is the return on this investment?
   b. If this return is *lower* than the rate of interest, does the investment have a positive or a negative NPV?
   c. If the rate of interest is 10 percent, what is the PV of the investment?
   d. What is the NPV?
5. Define the opportunity cost of capital. How in principle would you find the opportunity cost of capital for a risk-free asset? For a risky asset?
6. Look back to the numerical example graphed in Figure 2.1. Suppose the interest rate is 20 percent. What would the ant (*A*) and grasshopper (*G*) do if they both start with Rs. 185,000? Would they invest in the office building? Would they borrow or lend? How much and when would each consume?

7. We can imagine the financial manager doing several things on behalf of the firm's stockholders. For example, the manager might:
   a. Make shareholders as wealthy as possible by investing in real assets with positive NPVs.
   b. Modify the firm's investment plan to help shareholders achieve a particular time pattern of consumption.
   c. Choose high- or low-risk assets to match shareholders' risk preferences.
   d. Help balance shareholders' checkbooks.

   But in well-functioning capital markets, shareholders will vote for *only one* of these goals. Which one? Why?
8. Why would one expect managers to act in shareholders' interests? Give some reasons.
9. If a financial institution is caught up in a financial scandal, would you expect its value to fall by more or less than the amount of any fines and settlement payments? Explain.

PRACTICE QUESTIONS

1. What is the net present value of a *firm's* investment in an Indian T bill security yielding 5 percent and maturing in one year? *Hint:* What is the opportunity cost of capital? Ignore taxes.
2. A parcel of land costs Rs. 500,000. For an additional Rs. 800,000 you can build a motel on the property. The land and motel should be worth Rs. 1,500,000 next year. Suppose that common stocks with the same risk as this investment offer a 10 percent expected return. Would you construct the motel? Why or why not?
3. Calculate the NPV and rate of return for each of the following investments. The opportunity cost of capital is 20 percent for all four investments.

Investment	Initial Cash Flow, C_0	Cash Flow in Year 1, C_1
1	−10,000	+18,000
2	−5,000	+9,000
3	−5,000	+5,700
4	−2,000	+4,000

   a. Which investment is most valuable?
   b. Suppose each investment would require use of the same parcel of land. Therefore you can take only one. Which one? *Hint:* What is the firm's objective: to earn a high rate of return or to increase firm value?
4. In Section 2.1, we analyzed the possible construction of an office building on a plot of land appraised at Rs. 50,000. We concluded that this investment had a positive NPV of Rs. 5,000 at a discount rate of 12 percent.

   Suppose E. Coli Associates, a firm of genetic engineers, offers to purchase the land for Rs. 58,000, Rs. 20,000 paid immediately and Rs. 38,000 after one year. Indian government securities maturing in one year yield 5 percent.
   a. Assume E. Coli is sure to pay the second Rs. 38,000 installment. Should you take its offer or start on the office building? Explain.
   b. Suppose you are *not* sure E. Coli will pay. You observe that other investors demand a 10 percent return on their loans to E. Coli. Assume that the other investors have correctly assessed the risks that E. Coli will not be able to pay. Should you accept E. Coli's offer?
5. Norman Gerrymander has just received a $ 2 million bequest. How should he invest it? There are four immediate alternatives.
   a. Investment in one-year U.S. government securities yielding 5 percent.
   b. A loan to Norman's nephew Gerald, who has for years aspired to open a big Cajun restaurant in Duluth. Gerald had arranged a one-year bank loan for $ 900,000, at 10 percent, but asks for a loan from Norman at 7 percent.

c. Investment in the stock market. The expected rate of return is 12 percent.
d. Investment in local real estate, which Norman judges is about as risky as the stock market. The opportunity at hand would cost $ 1 million and is forecasted to be worth $ 1.1 million after one year.

Which of these investments have positive NPVs? Which would you advise Norman to take?

6. Show that your answers to Practice Question 5 are consistent with the rate of return rule for investment decisions.
7. Take another look at investment opportunity (d) in Practice Question 5. Suppose a bank offers Norman a $ 600,000 personal loan at 8 percent. (Norman is a long-time customer of the bank and has an excellent credit history.) Suppose Norman borrows the money, invests $ 1 million in real estate opportunity (d) and puts the rest of his money in opportunity (c), the stock market. Is this a smart move? Explain.
8. Ms. Espinoza is retired and depends on her investments for her income. Mr. Liu is a young executive who wants to save for the future. Both are stockholders in Scaled Composites, LLC, which is building SpaceShipOne to take commercial passengers into space. This investment's payoff is many years away. Assume it has a positive NPV for Mr. Liu. Explain why its investment also makes sense for Ms. Espinoza.
9. Answer this question by drawing graphs like Figure 2.1. Casper Milktoast has Rs. 200,000 available to support consumption in periods 0 (now) and 1 (next year). He wants to consume *exactly* the same amount in each period. The interest rate is 8 percent. There is no risk.
   a. How much should he invest, and how much can he consume in each period?
   b. Suppose Casper is given an opportunity to invest up to Rs. 200,000 at 10 percent risk-free. The interest rate stays at 8 percent. What should he do, and how much can he consume in each period?
   c. What is the NPV of the opportunity in (b)?

CHALLENGE QUESTIONS

1. For an outlay of Rs. 8 million you can purchase a tanker load of bucolic acid delivered in Rotterdam one year hence. Unfortunately the net cash flow from selling the tanker load will be very sensitive to the growth rate of the world economy:

Slump	Normal	Boom
Rs 8 million	Rs 12 million	Rs16 million

   a. What is the expected cash flow? Assume the three outcomes for the economy are equally likely.
   b. What is the expected rate of return on the investment in the project?
   c. One share of stock Z is selling for Rs. 10. The stock has the following payoffs after one year:

Slump	Normal	Boom
Rs 8	Rs 12	Rs 16

   Calculate the expected rate of return offered by stock Z. Explain why this is the opportunity cost of capital for your bucolic acid project.
   d. Calculate the project's NPV. Is the project a good investment? Explain why.

2. In real life the future health of the economy cannot be reduced to three equally probable states like slump, normal, and boom. But we'll keep that simplification for one more example.

Your company has identified two more projects, B and C. Each will require a Rs. 5 million outlay immediately. The possible payoffs at year 1, are in millions:

	Slump	Normal	Boom
B	4	6	8
C	5	5.5	6

You have identified the possible payoffs to investors in three stocks, X, Y, and Z:

		Payoff at Year 1		
	Current Price per Share	Slump	Normal	Boom
X	95.65	80	110	140
Y	40	40	44	48
Z	10	8	12	16

a. What are the expected cash inflows of projects B and C?
b. What are the expected rates of return offered by stocks, X, Y, and Z?
c. What are the opportunity costs of capital for projects B and C? *Hint:* Calculate the percentage differences, slump versus normal and boom versus normal, for stocks X, Y, and Z. Match up to the percentage differences in B's and C's payoffs.
d. What are the NPVs of projects B and C?
e. Suppose B and C are launched and Rs. 5 million are invested in each. How much will they add to the total market value of your company's shares?

CHAPTER [3]

HOW TO CALCULATE PRESENT VALUES

IN CHAPTER 2 we learned how to work out the value of an asset that produces cash exactly one year from now. But we did not explain how to value assets that produce cash two years from now or in several future years. That is the first task for this chapter. We will then have a look at some shortcut methods for calculating present values and at some specialized present value formulas. In particular we will show how to value an investment that makes a steady stream of payments forever (a *perpetuity*) and one that produces a steady stream for a limited period (an *annuity*). We will also look at investments that produce growing streams of payments.

The term *interest rate* sounds straightforward enough, but we will see that it can be defined in various ways. We will first explain the distinction between *compound interest* and *simple interest*. Then we will discuss the difference between the nominal interest rate and the real interest rate. This difference arises because the purchasing power of interest income is reduced by inflation.

By then you will deserve some payoff for the mental investment you have made in learning how to calculate present values. Therefore we will try out these new tools on bonds and stocks in the next chapter. After that we will tackle the firm's capital investment decisions at a practical level of detail.

For simplicity, every problem in this chapter is set out in rupees, but the concepts and calculations are identical in euros, yen, or any other currency.

3.1 VALUING LONG-LIVED ASSETS

Do you remember how to calculate the present value (PV) of an asset that produces a cash flow (C_1) one year from now?

$$PV = DF_1 \times C_1 = \frac{C_1}{1 + r_1}$$

The discount factor for the year-1 cash flow is DF_1, and r_1 is the opportunity cost of investing your money for one year. Suppose you will receive a certain cash inflow of Rs. 100 next year ($C_1 = 100$) and the rate of interest on one-year Indian. Treasury notes is 7 percent ($r_1 = .07$). Then present value equals

$$PV = \frac{C_1}{1 + r_1} = \frac{100}{1.07} = \text{Rs. } 93.46$$

The present value of a cash flow two years hence can be written in a similar way as

$$PV = DF_2 \times C_2 = \frac{C_2}{(1 + r_2)^2}$$

C_2 is the year-2 cash flow, DF_2 is the discount factor for the year-2 cash flow, and r_2 is the annual rate of interest on money invested for two years. Suppose you get a cash flow of Rs. 200 in year 2 ($C_2 =$ 200). The rate of interest on two-year Treasury notes is 7.7 percent per year ($r_2 = .077$); this means that a rupee invested in two-year notes will grow to $1.077^2 =$ Rs. 1.16 by the end of two years. The present value of your year-2 cash flow equals

$$PV = \frac{C_2}{(1 + r_2)^2} = \frac{200}{(1.077)^2} = \text{Rs. } 172.42$$

FIGURE 3.1

Present value of an investment providing cash flows of Rs 100 in year 1 and Rs 200 in year 2.

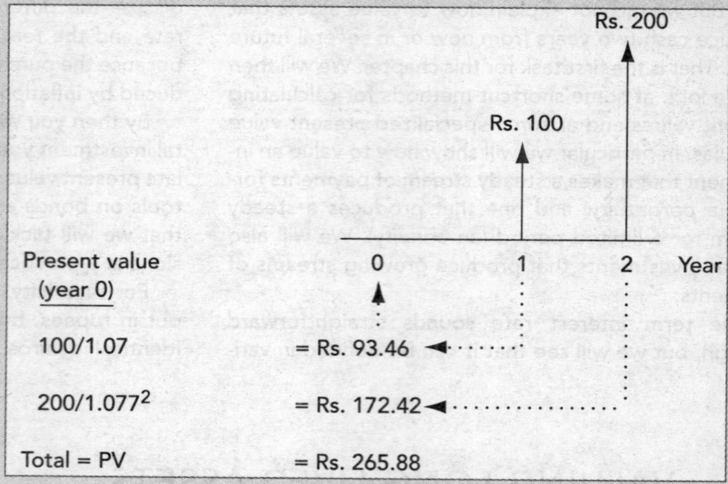

Valuing Cash Flows in Several Periods

One of the nice things about present values is that they are all expressed in current rupees—so you can add them up. In other words, the present value of cash flow A + B is equal to the present value of cash flow A plus the present value of cash flow B. For example, suppose you are now offered an investment that produces a cash flow of Rs. 100 in year 1 and a further cash flow of Rs. 200 in year 2. The one-year interest rate is 7 percent and the two-year rate is 7.7 percent. Figure 3.1 shows that the value today of the first year's flow is $C_1/(1 + r_1) = 100/1.07 =$ Rs. 93.46 and that the value of the second year's flow is $C_2/(1 + r_2)^2 = 200/1.077^2 =$ Rs. 172.42. Our rule for adding present values tells us that the *total* present value of the investment is

$$\text{PV} = \frac{C_1}{1+r_1} + \frac{C_2}{(1+r_2)^2} = \frac{100}{1.07} + \frac{200}{1.077^2} = \text{Rs. } 265.88$$

We can continue to apply the additivity rule to find the present value of an extended stream of cash flows:

$$\text{PV} = \frac{C_1}{1+r_1} + \frac{C_2}{(1+r_2)^2} + \frac{C_3}{(1+r_3)^3} + \cdots$$

This is called the **discounted cash flow (or DCF)** formula. A shorthand way to write it is

$$\text{PV} = \sum \frac{C_t}{(1+r_t)^t}$$

where Σ refers to the sum of the series. To find the *net* present value (NPV) we add the (usually negative) initial cash flow, just as in Chapter 2:

$$\text{NPV} = C_0 + \text{PV} = C_0 + \sum \frac{C_t}{(1+r_t)^t}$$

Why the Discount Factor Declines as Futurity Increases— And a Digression on Money Machines

If a rupee tomorrow is worth less than a rupee today, one might suspect that a rupee the day after tomorrow should be worth even less. In other words, the discount factor DF_2 should be less than the discount factor DF_1. But is this *necessarily* so, when there is a different interest rate r_t for each period?

Suppose r_1 is 20 percent and r_2 is 7 percent. Then

$$DF_1 = \frac{1}{1.20} = .83$$

$$DF_2 = \frac{1}{(1.07)^2} = .87$$

Apparently the rupee received the day after tomorrow is *not* necessarily worth less than the rupee received tomorrow.

But there is something wrong with this example. Anyone who could borrow and lend at these interest rates could become a millionaire overnight. Let us see how such a "money machine" would work. Suppose the first person to spot the opportunity is Sowmya Kapoor. Ms. Kapoor first lends Rs. 1,000 for one year at 20 percent. That is an attractive enough return, but she notices that there is a way to earn an *immediate* surefire profit on her investment. She reasons as follows. Next year she will have Rs. 1,200 which can be reinvested for a further year. Although she does not know what interest rates will be at that time, she does know that she can always put the money in a checking account and be certain of having Rs. 1,200 at the end of year 2. Her next step, therefore, is to go to her bank and borrow the present value of this Rs. 1,200. At 7 percent interest this present value is

$$PV = \frac{1200}{(1.07)^2} = \text{Rs. } 1{,}048$$

So Ms. Kapoor borrows Rs. 1,048, invests Rs. 1,000, and walks away with a profit of Rs. 48. If that does not sound like very much, notice that by borrowing more and investing more she can make much larger profits. For example, if she borrows Rs. 21,778,584 and invests Rs. 20,778,584, she would become a millionaire.

Of course this story is completely fanciful. Such an opportunity would not last long in capital markets like ours. Any bank that allowed you to lend for one year at 20 percent and borrow for two years at 7 percent would soon be wiped out by a rush of small investors hoping to become millionaires and a rush of millionaires hoping to become billionaires. There are, however, two lessons to our story. The first is that a rupee tomorrow *cannot* be worth less than a rupee the day after tomorrow. In other words, the value of a rupee received at the end of one year (DF_1) must be greater than the value of a rupee received at the end of two years (DF_2). There must be some extra gain from lending for two periods rather than one: $(1 + r_2)^2$ must be greater than $1 + r_1$.[1]

Our second lesson is a more general one and can be summed up by the precept "There is no such thing as a money machine." In well-functioning capital markets, any potential money machine will

[1] The extra return for lending two years rather than one is often referred to as a *forward rate of return*. Our rule implies that the forward rate cannot be negative.

be eliminated almost instantaneously by investors who try to take advantage of it. Therefore, beware of self-styled experts who offer you a chance to participate in a sure thing. The technical term for money machine is *arbitrage*. In well-functioning capital markets there are no opportunities for arbitrage.

Later in the book we will invoke the *absence* of arbitrage opportunities to prove several useful properties about security prices. That is, we will make statements like "The prices of securities X and Y must be in the following relationship—otherwise there would be potential arbitrage profits and capital markets would not be in equilibrium."

Ruling out arbitrage profits does not require that interest rates be the same for each future period. This relationship between the interest rate and the maturity of the cash flow is called the **term structure of interest rates.** We are going to look at term structure in Chapter 23, but for now we will finesse the issue by assuming that the term structure is "flat"—in other words, the interest rate is the same regardless of the date of the cash flow. This means that we can replace the series of interest rates $r_1, r_2, \ldots, r_t$, etc., with a single rate r and that we can write the present value formula as

$$PV = \frac{C_1}{1+r} + \frac{C_2}{(1+r)^2} + \cdots$$

Calculating PVs and NPVs

You have some bad news about your office building venture (the one described at the start of Chapter 2). The contractor says that construction will take two years instead of one and requests payment on the following schedule:

1. A Rs. 120,000 down payment now. (Note that the land, worth Rs. 50,000, must also be committed now.)
2. A Rs. 100,000 progress payment after one year.
3. A final payment of Rs. 100,000 when the building is ready for occupancy at the end of the second year.

Your real estate adviser maintains that despite the delay the building will be worth Rs. 420,000 when completed.

All this yields a new set of cash-flow forecasts:

Period	t = 0	t = 1	t = 2
Land	−50,000		
Construction	−120,000	−100,000	−100,000
Payoff			+420,000
Total	$C_0 = -170{,}000$	$C_1 = -100{,}000$	$C_2 = +320{,}000$

If the interest rate is 5 percent, then NPV is

$$NPV = C_0 + \frac{C_1}{1+r} + \frac{C_2}{(1+r)^2}$$

$$= -170{,}000 - \frac{100{,}000}{1.05} + \frac{320{,}000}{(1.05)^2}$$

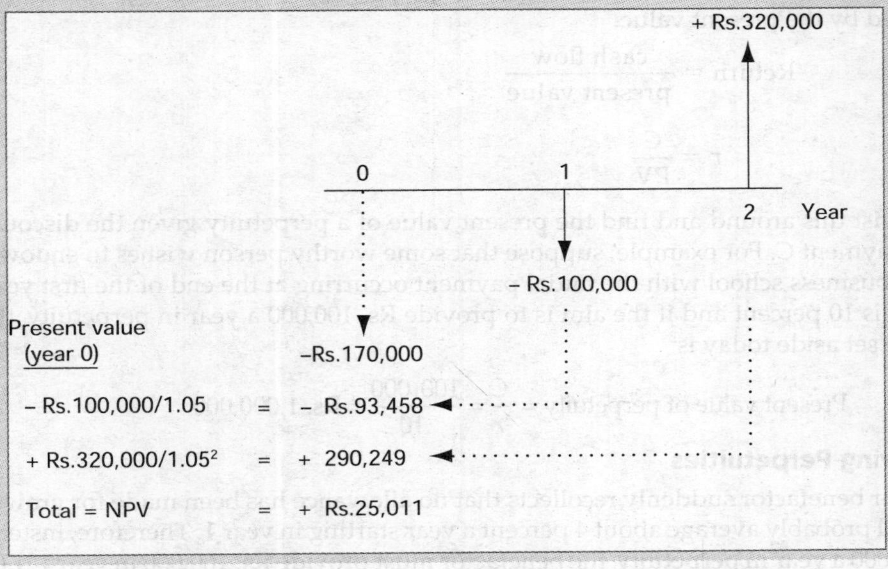

FIGURE 3.2

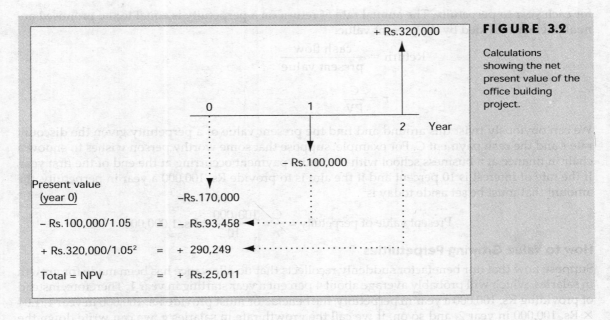

Calculations showing the net present value of the office building project.

Fortunately the news about your office venture is not all bad. The contractor is willing to accept a delayed payment, which means that the present value of the contractor's fee is less than before. This partly offsets the delay in the payoff. As Figure 3.2 shows, the net present value is Rs. 25,011—not a substantial decrease from the Rs. 30,000 calculated in Chapter 2. Since the net present value is positive, you should still go ahead.[2]

The calculations in Figure 3.2 required just a few keystrokes on a calculator. Real problems can be much more complicated, however, so financial managers usually turn to financial calculators especially programmed for present value calculations or to spreadsheet programs on personal computers. The Web site for this book contains two Web appendices that should get you started in using financial calculators and Excel spreadsheets to solve problems like those in this chapter. In case you should find yourself without a calculator or computer, we have included tables at the end of the book that can be used to solve a variety of present value problems.

3.2 LOOKING FOR SHORTCUTS—PERPETUITIES AND ANNUITIES

Sometimes there are shortcuts that make it easy to calculate present values. Let us look at some examples.

Among the securities that have been issued by the British government are so-called **perpetuities.** These are bonds that the government is under no obligation to repay but that offer a fixed income

[2]We assume the cash flows are safe. If they are risky forecasts, the opportunity cost of capital could be higher, say 12 percent. NPV at 12 percent is negative.

for each year to perpetuity. The annual rate of return on a perpetuity is equal to the promised annual payment divided by the present value:

$$\text{Return} = \frac{\text{cash flow}}{\text{present value}}$$

$$r = \frac{C}{\text{PV}}$$

We can obviously twist this around and find the present value of a perpetuity given the discount rate r and the cash payment C. For example, suppose that some worthy person wishes to endow a chair in finance at a business school with the initial payment occurring at the end of the first year. If the rate of interest is 10 percent and if the aim is to provide Rs. 100,000 a year in perpetuity, the amount that must be set aside today is[3]

$$\text{Present value of perpetuity} = \frac{C}{r} = \frac{100{,}000}{.10} = \text{Rs. } 1{,}000{,}000$$

How to Value Growing Perpetuities

Suppose now that our benefactor suddenly recollects that no allowance has been made for growth in salaries, which will probably average about 4 percent a year starting in year 1. Therefore, instead of providing Rs. 100,000 a year in perpetuity, the benefactor must provide Rs. 100,000 in year 1, 1.04 × Rs. 100,000 in year 2, and so on. If we call the growth rate in salaries g, we can write down the present value of this stream of cash flows as follows:

$$\text{PV} = \frac{C_1}{1+r} + \frac{C_2}{(1+r)^2} + \frac{C_3}{(1+r)^3} + \cdots$$
$$= \frac{C_1}{1+r} + \frac{C_1(1+g)}{(1+r)^2} + \frac{C_1(1+g)^2}{(1+r)^3} + \cdots$$

Fortunately, there is a simple formula for the sum of this geometric series.[4] If we assume that r is greater than g, our clumsy-looking calculation simplifies to

[3]You can check this by writing down the present value formula

$$\text{PV} = \frac{C}{1+r} + \frac{C}{(1+r)^2} + \frac{C}{(1+r)^3} + \cdots$$

Now let $C/(1+r) = a$ and $1/(1+r) = x$. Then we have (1) $\text{PV} = a(1 + x + x^2 + \ldots)$.
Multiplying both sides by x, we have (2) $\text{PV}x = a(x + x^2 + \ldots)$.
Subtracting (2) from (1) gives us $\text{PV}(1 - x) = a$. Therefore, substituting for a and x,

$$\text{PV}\left(1 - \frac{1}{1+r}\right) = \frac{C}{1+r}$$

Multiplying both sides by $(1 + r)$ and rearranging gives

$$\text{PV} = \frac{C}{r}$$

[4]We need to calculate the sum of an infinite geometric series $\text{PV} = a(1 + x + x^2 + \ldots)$ where $a = C_1/(1+r)$ and $x = (1+g)/(1+r)$. In footnote 3 we showed that the sum of such a series is $a/(1 - x)$. Substituting for a and x in this formula,

$$\text{PV} = \frac{C_1}{r - g}$$

$$\text{Present value of growing perpetuity} = \frac{C_1}{r-g}$$

Therefore, if our benefactor wants to provide perpetually an annual sum that keeps pace with the growth rate in salaries, the amount that must be set aside today is

$$PV = \frac{C_1}{r-g} = \frac{100{,}000}{.10-.04} = \text{Rs. } 1{,}666{,}667$$

How to Value Annuities

An **annuity** is an asset that pays a fixed sum each year for a specified number of years. The equal-payment house mortgage or installment credit agreement are common examples of annuities.

Figure 3.3 illustrates a simple trick for valuing annuities. The first row represents a perpetuity that produces a cash flow of C in each year beginning in year 1. It has a present value of

$$PV = \frac{C}{r}$$

The second row represents a second perpetuity that produces a cash flow of C in each year *beginning in year* $t+1$. It will have a present value of C/r in year t and it therefore has a present value today of

$$PV = \frac{C}{r(1+r)^t}$$

Both perpetuities provide a cash flow from year $t+1$ onward. The only difference between the two perpetuities is that the first one *also* provides a cash flow in each of the years 1 through t. In other words, the difference between the two perpetuities is an annuity of C for t years. The present value of this annuity is, therefore, the difference between the values of the two perpetuities:[5]

$$\text{Present value of annuity} = C\left[\frac{1}{r} - \frac{1}{r(1+r)^t}\right]$$

[5]Again we can work this out from first principles. We need to calculate the sum of the finite geometric series (1) $PV = a(1 + x + x^2 + \ldots + x^{t-1})$.
where $a = C/(1+r)$ and $x = 1/(1+r)$.
Multiplying both sides by x, we have (2) $PVx = a(x + x^2 + \ldots + x^t)$.
Subtracting (2) from (1) gives us $PV(1-x) = a(1-x^t)$.
Therefore, substituting for a and x,

$$PV\left(1 - \frac{1}{1+r}\right) = C\left[\frac{1}{1+r} - \frac{1}{(1+r)^{t+1}}\right]$$

Multiplying both sides by $(1+r)$ and rearranging gives

$$PV = C\left[\frac{1}{r} - \frac{1}{r(1+r)^t}\right]$$

FIGURE 3.3

An annuity that makes payments in each of years 1 to t is equal to the difference between two perpetuities.

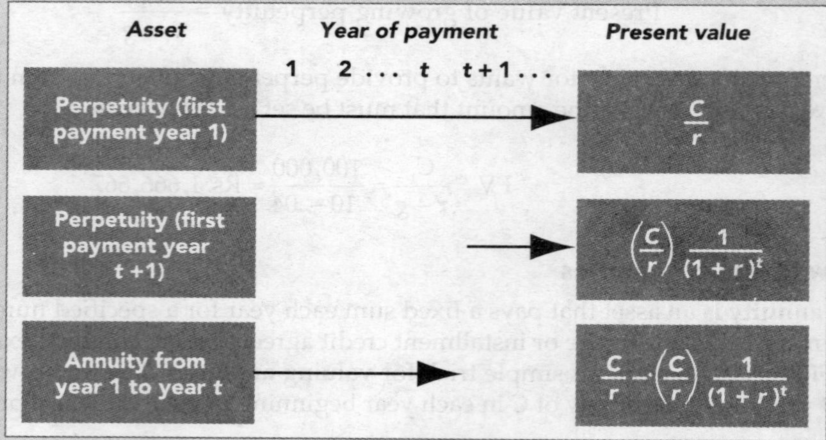

The expression in brackets is the *annuity factor,* which is the present value at discount rate r of an annuity of Re. 1 paid at the end of each of t periods.[6]

Suppose, for example, that our benefactor begins to vacillate and wonders what it would cost to endow a chair providing Rs. 100,000 a year for only 20 years. The answer calculated from our formula is

$$PV = 100{,}000\left[\frac{1}{.10} - \frac{1}{.10(1.10)^{20}}\right] = 100{,}000 \times 8.514 = \text{Rs. } 851{,}400$$

Appendix Table 3 at the end of the book is a table of annuity factors. You can look there to find the factor 8.514 if you don't have a calculator or computer handy.

Remember that the annuity formula assumes that the first payment occurs one period hence. If the first cash payment occurs immediately, we would need to discount each cash flow by one less year. So the present value would be increased by the multiple $(1 + r)$. For example, if our benefactor were prepared to make 20 annual payments *starting immediately,* the value would be Rs. 851,400 × 1.10 = Rs. 936,540. An annuity offering an immediate payment is known as an *annuity due.*

---

[6]Sometimes you may need to value a stream of payments that start in year 1, grow at the rate g until year t, and then stop. The formula for this *growing annuity* is

$$PV = C_1\left[\frac{1}{(r-g)} - \frac{1}{(r-g)} \times \frac{(1+g)^t}{(1+r)^t}\right]$$

Suppose that our benefactor wants to provide for a 4 percent annual raise, starting from year 1 and ending with the final payment in year 20. The growing annuity is Rs. 100,000 at date $t = 1$, Rs. 104,000 at date $t = 2$, etc. Then the PV is

$$PV = 100{,}000\left[\frac{1}{(.10-.04)} - \frac{1}{(.10-.04)} \times \frac{(1.04)^{20}}{(1.10)^{20}}\right] = \text{Rs. } 1{,}123{,}839.$$

The formula accounts for t years of growth in the term $(1 + g)^t$. You can see why by sketching a version of Figure 3.3 for *growing* annuities. You will end up showing the difference between a growing perpetuity that starts at date $t = 1$ and a second growing perpetuity that begins at $t + 1$ (year 21 in our numerical example). Thus, even though we start with cash flow at $t = 1$, not date $t = 0$, we have to account for t periods of growth.

You should always be on the lookout for ways in which you can use these formulas to make life easier. For example, we sometimes need to calculate how much a series of annual payments earning a fixed annual interest rate would amass to by the end of t periods. In this case it is easiest to calculate the *present* value, and then multiply it by $(1 + r)^t$ to find the future value.[7] Thus, suppose our benefactor wished to know how much wealth Rs. 100,000 would produce if it were invested each year instead of being given to those no-good academics. The answer would be

$$\text{Future value} = \text{PV} \times 1.10^{20} = \text{Rs. } 851{,}400 \times 6.727 = \text{Rs. } 5.73 \text{ million}$$

Annuity problems can be confusing on first acquaintance, but you will find that with practice they are generally straightforward. Here are two examples where you need to use the annuity formula to find the annuity payment *given* the present value.

Example 1: Choosing the Rental Payment Three years have passed; you have completed that office building and are about to sell it for Rs. 420,000. Now someone comes along and offers to rent it for 8 years for a fixed annual rental of Rs. 8,000. At the end of this period you would be able to sell the building. Your real estate adviser estimates that prices of office buildings will increase by 3 percent a year. The discount rate is 5 percent.

You should accept the offer only if its NPV is positive, that is, only if PV (rent in years 1 through 8) + PV(sale proceeds in year 8) *exceeds* sale proceeds today. At the end of eight years the office building can be sold for $420{,}000 \times 1.03^8$ = Rs. 532,043. The present value of this sum is $532{,}043/1.05^8$ = Rs. 360,108. Since you could sell the office building today for Rs. 420,000, the delay in selling the building costs you 420,000 − 360,108 = Rs. 59,892. Therefore the present value of the eight annual rental payments that you receive must be at least equal to this cost. In other words,

$$\text{Minimum acceptable rent} \times [1/.05 - 1/(.05 \times 1.05^8)] = \text{Rs. } 59{,}892$$
$$\text{Minimum Acceptable Rent} \times 6.463 = \text{Rs. } 59{,}892$$
$$\text{Minimum Acceptable Rent} = 59{,}892/6.463 = \text{Rs. } 9{,}267$$

You would do better to sell your office building today rather than rent it out at Rs. 8,000 for each of the next eight years.

Example 2: Home Mortgages Suppose that you take out a Rs. 250,000 house mortgage from your local savings bank. The bank requires you to repay the mortgage in equal monthly installments over the next 30 years. It must therefore set the monthly payments so that they have a present value of Rs. 250,000. Thus

$$\text{PV} = \text{mortgage payment} \times \text{360-month annuity factor} = \text{Rs. } 250{,}000$$
$$\text{Mortgage payment} = \text{Rs. } 250{,}000/\text{360-month annuity factor}$$

---

[7]For example, suppose you receive a cash flow of C in year 6. If you invest this cash flow at an interest rate of r, you will have by year 10 an investment worth $C(1 + r)^4$. You can get the same answer by calculating the *present value* of the cash flow PV $= C/(1 + r)^6$ and then working out how much you would have by year 10 if you invested this sum today:

$$\text{Future value} = \text{PV}(1 + r)^{10} = \frac{C}{(1 + r)^6} \times (1 + r)^{10} = C(1 + r)^4$$

Year	Beginning-of-Year Balance	Year-end Interest on Balance	Total Year-end Payment	Amortization of Loan	End-of-Year Balance
1	Rs. 1,000.00	Rs. 100.00	Rs. 315.47	Rs. 215.47	Rs. 784.53
2	784.53	78.45	315.47	237.02	547.51
3	547.51	54.75	315.47	260.72	286.79
4	286.79	28.68	315.47	286.79	0

TABLE 3.1

An example of an amortizing loan. If you borrow Rs. 1,000 at an interest rate of 10 percent, you would need to make an annual payment of Rs. 315.47 over 4 years to repay that loan with interest.

Suppose that the interest rate is 1 percent a month. Then

$$\text{360-month annuity factor} = \left[\frac{1}{.01} - \frac{1}{.01(1.01)^{360}}\right] = 97.218$$

and

$$\text{Mortgage payment} = 250{,}000/97.218 = \text{Rs. } 2{,}572$$

The mortgage loan is an example of an *amortizing loan.* "Amortizing" means that part of the monthly payment is used to pay interest on the loan and part is used to reduce the amount of the loan.

Table 3.1 illustrates another amortizing loan. This time it is a four-year loan of Rs. 1,000 with an interest rate of 10 percent and annual payments. The annual payment needed to repay the loan is Rs. 315.47. In other words, Rs. 1,000 divided by the four-year annuity factor is Rs. 315.47. At the end of the first year, the interest charge is 10 percent of Rs. 1,000, or Rs. 100. So Rs. 100 of the first payment is absorbed by interest, and the remaining Rs. 215.47 is used to reduce (or "amortize") the loan balance to Rs. 784.53.

Next year, the outstanding balance is lower, so the interest charge is only Rs. 78.45. Therefore Rs. 315.47 − 78.45 = Rs. 237.02 can be applied to amortization. Because the loan is progressively paid off, the fraction of each payment devoted to interest steadily falls over time, while the fraction used to reduce the loan increases. By the end of year 4 the amortization is just enough to reduce the balance of the loan to zero.

3.3 COMPOUND INTEREST AND PRESENT VALUES

There is an important distinction between **compound interest** and **simple interest.** When money is invested at compound interest, each interest payment is reinvested to earn more interest in subsequent periods. In contrast, the opportunity to earn interest on interest is not provided by an investment that pays only simple interest.

Table 3.2 compares the growth of Rs. 100 invested at compound versus simple interest. Notice that in the simple interest case, *the interest is paid only on the initial investment of Rs. 100*. Your wealth therefore increases by just Rs. 10 a year. In the compound interest case, you earn 10 percent on your initial investment in the first year, which gives you a balance at the end of the year of 100×1.10 = Rs. 110. Then in the second year you earn 10 percent on this Rs. 110, which gives you a balance at the end of the second year of 100×1.10^2 = Rs. 121.

	Simple Interest						Compound Interest				
Year	Starting Balance	+	Interest	=	Ending Balance	Starting Balance	+	Ending Interest	=	Balance
1	Rs. 100	+	10	=	Rs. 110	Rs. 100	+	10	=	Rs. 110
2	110	+	10	=	120	110	+	11	=	121
3	120	+	10	=	130	121	+	12.1	=	133.1
4	130	+	10	=	140	133.1	+	13.3	=	146.4
10	190	+	10	=	200	236	+	24	=	259
100	1,090	+	10	=	1,100	1,252,783	+	125,278	=	1,378,061
200	2,090	+	10	=	2,100	17,264,116,042	+	1,726,411,604	=	18,990,527,646
229	2,380	+	10	=	2,390	273,862,277,847	+	27,386,227,785	=	301,248,505,631

TABLE 3.2

Value of Rs. 100 invested at 10 percent simple and compound interest.

Table 3.2 shows that the difference between simple and compound interest is nil for a one-period investment, trivial for a two-period investment, but overwhelming for an investment of 10 years or more. A sum of \$ 100 invested during the American Revolution and earning compound interest of 10 percent a year would now be worth over \$ 300 billion. If only your ancestors could have put away a few paise.

The two top lines in Figure 3.4 compare the results of investing Rs. 100 at 10 percent simple interest and at 10 percent compound interest. It looks as if the rate of growth is constant under simple interest and accelerates under compound interest. However, this is an optical illusion. We know that under compound interest our wealth grows at a *constant* rate of 10 percent. Figure 3.5 is in fact a more useful presentation. Here the numbers are plotted on a semilogarithmic scale and the constant compound growth rates show up as straight lines.

Problems in finance almost always involve compound interest rather than simple interest, and therefore financial people always assume that you are talking about compound interest unless you specify otherwise. Discounting is a process of compound interest. Some people find it intuitively helpful to replace the question, What is the present value of Rs. 100 to be received 10 years from now, if the opportunity cost of capital is 10 percent? With the question, How much would I have to invest now in order to receive Rs. 100 after 10 years, given an interest rate of 10 percent? The answer to the first question is

$$PV = \frac{100}{(1.10)^{10}} = \text{Rs. } 38.55$$

And the answer to the second question is

$$\text{Investment} \times (1.10)^{10} = \text{Rs. } 100$$

$$\text{Investment} = \frac{100}{(1.10)^{10}} = \text{Rs. } 38.55$$

The bottom lines in Figures 3.4 and 3.5 show the growth path of an initial investment of Rs. 38.55 to its terminal value of Rs. 100. One can think of discounting as traveling *back* along the bottom line, from future value to present value.

FIGURE 3.4

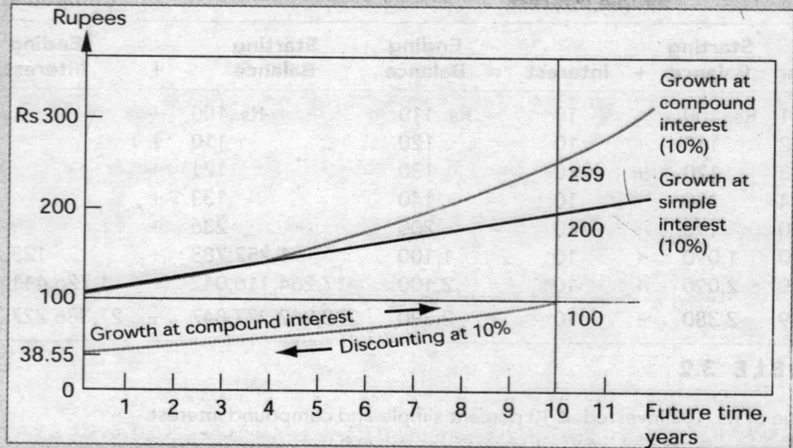

Compound interest versus simple interest. The top two ascending lines show the growth of Rs. 100 invested at simple and compound interest. The longer the funds are invested, the greater the advantage with compound interest. The bottom line shows that Rs. 38.55 must be invested now to obtain Rs. 100 after 10 periods. Conversely, the present value of Rs 100 to be received after 10 years is Rs. 38.55.

FIGURE 3.5

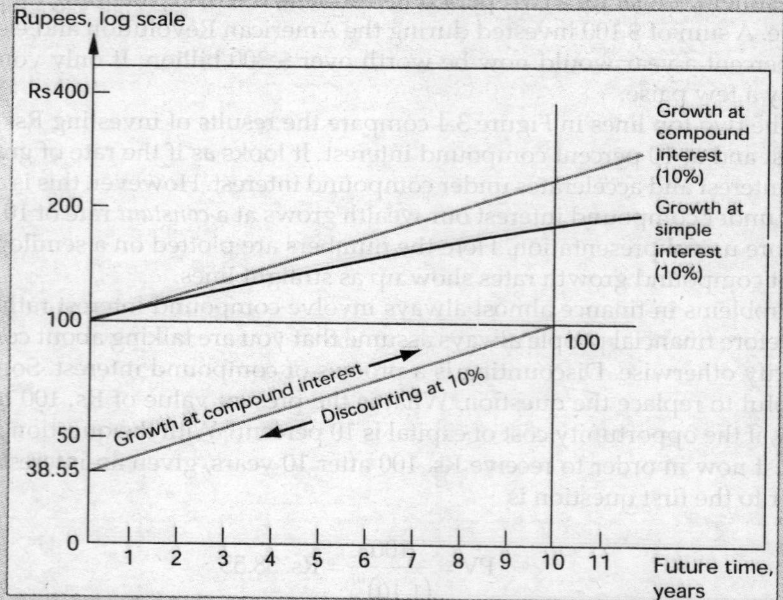

The same story as Figure 3.4, except that the vertical scale is logarithmic. A constant compound rate of growth means a straight ascending line. This graph makes clear that the growth rate of funds invested at simple interest actually *declines* as time passes.

A Note on Compounding Intervals

So far we have implicitly assumed that each cash flow occurs at the end of the year. This is sometimes the case. For example, in France and Germany most corporations pay interest on their bonds annually. However, in India and the United States most pay interest semiannually. In these countries, the investor can earn an additional six months' interest on the first payment, so that an investment of Rs. 100 in a bond that paid interest of 10 percent per annum compounded semiannually would amount to Rs. 105 after the first six months, and by the end of the year it would amount to

$1.05^2 \times 100 =$ Rs. 110.25. In other words, 10 percent compounded semiannually is equivalent to 10.25 percent compounded annually.

Let's take another example. Suppose a bank offers you an automobile loan with a 6 percent interest rate. If you are required to pay interest monthly, you will need to pay each month one-twelfth of the annual rate, that is, $6/12 = .5$ percent a month. Because the monthly return is compounded, the true annual interest rate on your loan is not 6 percent, but $1.005^{12} - 1 = .0617$, or 6.17 percent.

In general, an investment of Re. 1 at a rate of r per annum compounded m times a year amounts by the end of the year to $[1 + (r/m)]^m$, and the equivalent annually compounded rate of interest is $[1 + (r/m)]^m - 1$.

Continuous Compounding

In the case of our automobile loan example m was 12 and the interest rate was 6 percent. The annually compounded rate was therefore $[1 + (r/m)]^m - 1 = [1 + .06/12]^{12} - 1 = .0617$, or 6.17 percent. Instead of compounding interest monthly, the rate could be compounded weekly ($m = 52$) or daily ($m = 365$). In fact there is no limit to how frequent payments could be or how short the compounding interval. One can imagine a situation where the payments are spread evenly and continuously throughout the year, and the interest rate is continuously compounded.[8] In this case m is infinite.

It turns out that there are many occasions in finance when continuous compounding is useful. As we will see shortly, one application is in capital budgeting. Another important application is in option pricing models, such as the Black–Scholes model that we will introduce in Chapter 21. These are continuous time models. So you will find that most computer programs for calculating option values will ask for the continuously compounded interest rate.

It may seem that a lot of calculations would be needed to find a continuously compounded interest rate. However, think back to your high school algebra. You may recall that as m approaches infinity $[1 + (r/m)]^m$ approaches $(2.718)^r$. The figure 2.718—or e, as it is called—is the base for natural logarithms. Therefore, Re. 1 invested at a continuously compounded rate of r will grow to $e^r = (2.718)^r$ by the end of the first year. By the end of t years it will grow to $e^{rt} = (2.718)^{rt}$.

Example 1 Suppose you invest Re. 1 at a continuously compounded rate of 11 percent ($r = .11$) for one year ($t = 1$). The end-year value is $e^{.11}$, or Rs. 1.116. In other words, investing at 11 percent a year *continuously* compounded is exactly the same as investing at 11.6 percent a year *annually* compounded.

Example 2 Suppose you invest Re. 1 at a continuously compounded rate of 11 percent ($r = .11$) for two years ($t = 2$). The final value of the investment is $e^{rt} = e^{.22}$, or Rs. 1.246.

Sometimes it may be more reasonable to assume that the cash flows from a project are spread evenly over the year rather than occurring at the year's end. It is easy to adapt our previous formulas to handle this. For example, suppose that we wish to compute the present value of a perpetuity

[8] When we talk about *continuous* payments, we are pretending that money can be dispensed in a continuous stream like water out of a faucet. One can never quite do this. For example, instead of paying out Rs. 100,000 every year, our benefactor could pay out Rs. 100 every 8¾ hours or Re. 1 every 5¼ minutes or 1 paisa every 3⅙ seconds but could not pay it out *continuously*. Financial managers *pretend* that payments are continuous rather than hourly, daily, or weekly because (1) it simplifies the calculations, and (2) it gives a *very* close approximation to the NPV of frequent payments.

of C rupees a year. We already know that if the payment is made at the end of the year, we divide the payment by the *annually* compounded rate of *r:*

$$PV = \frac{C}{r}$$

If the same total payment is made in an even stream throughout the year, we use the same formula but substitute the *continuously* compounded rate.

Example 3 Suppose the annually compounded rate is 18.5 percent. The present value of a Rs. 100 perpetuity, with each cash flow received at the end of the year, is 100/.185 = Rs. 540.54. If the cash flow is received continuously, we must divide Rs. 100 by 17 percent, because 17 percent continuously compounded is equivalent to 18.5 percent annually compounded ($e^{.17} = 1.185$). The present value of the continuous cash flow stream is 100/.17 = Rs. 588.24. Investors are prepared to pay more for the continuous cash payments because the cash starts to flow in immediately.

For any other continuous payments, we can always use our formula for valuing annuities. For instance, suppose that our philanthropist has thought more seriously and decided to found a home for elderly donkeys, which will cost Rs. 100,000 a year, starting immediately, and spread evenly over 20 years. Previously, we used the annually compounded rate of 10 percent; now we must use the continuously compounded rate of $r = 9.53$ percent ($e^{.0953} = 1.10$). To cover such an expenditure, then, our philanthropist needs to set aside the following sum:[9]

$$PV = C\left(\frac{1}{r} - \frac{1}{r} \times \frac{1}{e^{rt}}\right)$$

$$= 100{,}000\left(\frac{1}{.0953} - \frac{1}{.0953} \times \frac{1}{6.727}\right) = 100{,}000 \times 8.932 = \text{Rs. } 893{,}200$$

If you look back at our earlier discussion of annuities, you will notice that the present value of Rs. 100,000 paid at the *end* of each of the 20 years was Rs. 851,400. Therefore, it costs the philanthropist Rs. 41,800—or 5 percent—more to provide a continuous payment stream.

Often in finance we need only a ballpark estimate of present value. An error of 5 percent in a present value calculation may be perfectly acceptable. In such cases it doesn't usually matter whether we assume that cash flows occur at the end of the year or in a continuous stream. At other times precision matters, and we do need to worry about the exact frequency of the cash flows.

[9]Remember that an annuity is simply the difference between a perpetuity received today and a perpetuity received in year *t*. A continuous stream of *C* rupees a year in perpetuity is worth *C*/*r*, where *r* is the continuously compounded rate. Our annuity, then, is worth

$$PV = \frac{C}{r} - \text{present value of } \frac{C}{r} \text{ received in year } t$$

Since *r* is the continuously compounded rate, *C*/*r* received in year *t* is worth $(C/r) \times (1/e^{rt})$ today. Our annuity formula is therefore

$$PV = \frac{C}{r} - \frac{C}{r} \times \frac{1}{e^{rt}}$$

sometimes written as

$$\frac{C}{r}(1 - e^{-rt})$$

3.4 NOMINAL AND REAL RATES OF INTEREST

If you invest Rs. 1,000 in a bank deposit offering an interest rate of 10 percent, the bank promises to pay you Rs. 1,100 at the end of the year. But it makes no promises about what the Rs. 1,100 will buy. That will depend on the rate of inflation over the year. If the prices of goods and services increase by more than 10 percent, you have lost ground in terms of the goods that you can buy.

Several indexes are used to track the general level of prices. Both the Consumer Price Index (CPI) and the Wholesale Price Index (WPI) are quite popular in India. CPI measures the number of rupees it takes to pay for a typical family's purchases. The WPI reflects the change in the wholesale prices during a year over a pre-defined base year. In India, we use 1993-94 as the base year for WPI calculations. Prior to 1993, the base period was 1981-82. We can estimate the inflation rate by studying the change in WPI from one year to the next year. Figure 3.6 shows the rate of inflation in India from 1948-49 till 2005-06. Inflation touched a peak of 26% in 1973-74, both due to a crop failure and the skyrocketing oil prices. This figure, however, pales into insignificance compared with inflation of Germany in 1923, which was more than 20 billion percent a year (nearly 5 percent per day). Of course, prices do not always rise. For example, in recent years, Japan, Argentina, and Hong Kong have all faced a problem of deflation. India experienced deflation in the year 1951-52, and again in the year 1954-55.

Economists sometimes talk about current, or nominal, rupees versus constant, or real, rupees. For example, the *nominal* cash flow from your one-year bank deposit is Rs. 1,100. But suppose prices of goods rise over the year by 6 percent; then each rupee will buy you 6 percent fewer goods next year than it does today. So at the end of the year Rs. 1,100 will buy the same quantity of goods as 1,100/1.06 = Rs. 1,037.74 today. The nominal payoff on the deposit is Rs. 1,100, but the *real* payoff is only Rs. 1,037.74.

The general formula for converting nominal cash flows at a future period t to real cash flows is

$$\text{Real cash flow} = \frac{\text{nominal cash flow}}{(1 + \text{inflation rate})^t}$$

For example, if you were to invest that Rs. 1,000 for 20 years at 10 percent, your future nominal payoff would be $1{,}000 \times 1.1^{20}$ = Rs. 6,727.50, but with an inflation rate of 6 percent a year, the real value of that payoff would be $6{,}727.50/1.06^{20}$ = Rs. 2,097.67. In other words, you will have roughly six times as many rupees as you have today, but you will be able to buy only twice as many goods.

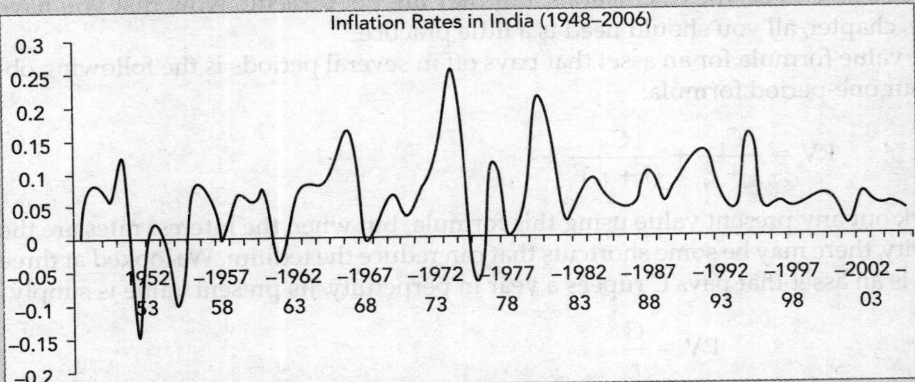

FIGURE 3.6

Annual rates of inflation in India from 1948-49—2005-06.

Source: Data compiled from www.rbi.org.in.

When the bank quotes you a 10 percent interest rate, it is quoting a nominal interest rate. The rate tells you how rapidly your money will grow:

Invest Current Rupees		Receive Period-1 Rupees	Result
1,000	→	1,100	10% *nominal* rate of return

However, with an inflation rate of 6 percent you are only 3.774 percent better off at the end of the year than at the start:

Invest Current Rupees		Expected Real Value of Period-1 Receipts	Result
1,000	→	1,037.74	3.774% expected *real* rate of return

Thus, we could say, "The bank account offers a 10 percent nominal rate of return," or "It offers a 3.774 percent expected real rate of return." Note that the nominal rate is certain but the real rate is only expected. The actual real rate cannot be calculated until the end of the year arrives and the inflation rate is known.

The 10 percent nominal rate of return, with 6 percent inflation, translates into a 3.774 percent real rate of return. The formula for calculating the real rate of return is

$$\begin{aligned} 1 + r_{\text{nominal}} &= (1 + r_{\text{real}})(1 + \text{inflation rate}) \\ &= 1 + r_{\text{real}} + \text{inflation rate} + (r_{\text{real}})(\text{inflation rate}) \end{aligned}$$

In our example,

$$1.10 = 1.03774 \times 1.06$$

SUMMARY

The difficult thing in any present value exercise is to set up the problem correctly. Once you have done that, you must be able to do the calculations, but they are not difficult. Now that you have worked through this chapter, all you should need is a little practice.

The basic present value formula for an asset that pays off in several periods is the following obvious extension of our one-period formula:

$$PV = \frac{C_1}{1 + r_1} + \frac{C_2}{(1 + r_2)^2} + \cdots$$

You can always work out any present value using this formula, but when the interest rates are the same for each maturity, there may be some shortcuts that can reduce the tedium. We looked at three such cases. The first is an asset that pays C rupees a year in perpetuity. Its present value is simply

$$PV = \frac{C}{r}$$

The second is an asset whose payments increase at a steady rate g in perpetuity. Its present value is

$$PV = \frac{C_1}{r - g}$$

The third is an annuity that pays C rupees a year for t years. To find its present value we take the difference between the values of two perpetuities:

$$PV = C\left[\frac{1}{r} - \frac{1}{r(1+r)^t}\right]$$

Remember that these shortcut formulas assume that the first cash flow occurs at the end of one year.

Our next step was to show that discounting is a process of compound interest. Present value is the amount that we would have to invest now at compound interest r in order to produce the cash flows C_1, C_2, etc. When someone offers to lend us a rupee at an annual rate of r, we should always check how frequently the interest is to be compounded. If the compounding interval is annual, we will have to repay $(1 + r)^t$ rupees; on the other hand, if the compounding period is continuous, we will have to repay 2.718^{rt} (or, as it is usually expressed, e^{rt}) rupees. In capital budgeting we often assume that the cash flows occur at the end of each year, and therefore we discount them at an annually compounded rate of interest. Sometimes, however, it may be better to assume that they are spread evenly over the year; in this case we must make use of continuous compounding.

It is important to distinguish between *nominal* cash flows (the actual number of rupees that you will pay or receive) and *real* cash flows, which are adjusted for inflation. Similarly, an investment may promise a high *nominal* interest rate, but, if inflation is also high, the *real* interest rate may be low or even negative.

We introduced in this chapter two very important ideas which we will come across several times again. The first is that you can add present values: If your formula for the present value of A + B is not the same as your formula for the present value of A plus the present value of B, you have made a mistake. The second idea is that arbitrage opportunities or money machines are rare and soon vanish. If you think you have found one, go back and check your calculations.

WEB EXERCISES

There are dozens of Web sites that provide calculators to help with personal financial decisions. Two good examples are **www.quicken.com** and **www.smartmoney.com.** (Note that both calculators assume simple interest to convert the monthly interest rate to an annual rate. In other words, the annual interest rate is quoted as 12 times the monthly rate.)

1. Suppose that you have Rs. 5,000 in the bank and plan to save Rs. 500 a month. If you earn a return of 12 percent a year (1 percent a month), how much will you have accumulated by the time that you retire in 30 years? Now log in to the Quicken site and click on *Bills and Banking* to find a nice savings calculator. Use this to check your answer.
2. Suppose that you take out a 30-year mortgage loan of Rs. 200,000 at an interest rate of 10 percent. What is your total monthly payment? How much of the first month's payment goes to reduce the size of the loan? How much of the payment after two years goes to reduce the amount of the loan? You can check your answers by logging in to the personal finance page of **www.smartmoney.com** and using the mortgage calculator.

CONCEPT REVIEW QUESTIONS

1. Write down the formula for the present value of an investment that produces cash flows of C_1, C_2 and C_3. (page 36)
2. What is the formula for the two-year discount factor, DF_2? (page 37)
3. Can the two-period discount rate (r_2) ever be smaller than the one-period rate (r_1)? (page 37)

For additional Concept Review Questions, please visit us at www.mhhe.com/bmam8e or refer to your Student CD.

QUIZ

1. At an interest rate of 12 percent, the six-year discount factor is .507. How many rupees is Re. .507 worth in six years if invested at 12 percent?
2. If the PV of Rs. 139 is Rs. 125, what is the discount factor?
3. If the cost of capital is 9 percent, what is the PV of Rs. 374 paid in year 9?
4. A project produces a cash flow of Rs. 432 in year 1, Rs. 137 in year 2, and Rs. 797 in year 3. If the cost of capital is 15 percent, what is the project's PV?
5. If you invest Rs. 100 at an interest rate of 15 percent, how much will you have at the end of eight years?
6. An investment costs Rs. 1,548 and pays Rs. 138 in perpetuity. If the interest rate is 9 percent, what is the NPV?
7. A common stock will pay a cash dividend of Rs. 4 next year. After that, the dividends are expected to increase indefinitely at 4 percent per year. If the discount rate is 14 percent, what is the PV of the stream of dividend payments?
8. In May 1998 a retired couple plunked down $1 to buy a Powerball lottery ticket and won a record $194 million. However, this sum was to be paid in 25 equal annual installments. If the first installment was received immediately and the interest rate was 9 percent, how much was the prize worth?
9. The interest rate is 10 percent.
   a. What is the PV of an asset that pays Re. 1 a year in perpetuity?
   b. The value of an asset that appreciates at 10 percent per annum approximately doubles in seven years. What is the approximate PV of an asset that pays Re. 1 a year in perpetuity beginning in year 8?
   c. What is the approximate PV of an asset that pays Re. 1 a year for each of the next seven years?
   d. A piece of land produces an income that grows by 5 percent per annum. If the first year's income is Rs. 10,000, what is the value of the land?
10. **a.** The cost of a new automobile is Rs. 10,000. If the interest rate is 5 percent, how much would you have to set aside now to provide this sum in five years?
    b. You have to pay Rs. 12,000 a year in school fees at the end of each of the next six years. If the interest rate is 8 percent, how much do you need to set aside today to cover these bills?
    c. You have invested Rs. 60,476 at 8 percent. After paying the above school fees, how much would remain at the end of the six years?
11. You have the opportunity to invest in the Belgravian Republic at 25 percent interest. The inflation rate is 21 percent. What is the real rate of interest?
12. The continuously compounded interest rate is 12 percent.
    a. You invest Rs. 1,000 at this rate. What is the investment worth after five years?
    b. What is the PV of Rs. 5 million to be received in eight years?
    c. What is the PV of a continuous stream of cash flows, amounting to Rs. 2,000 per year, starting immediately and continuing for 15 years?
13. You are quoted an interest rate of 6 percent on an investment of Rs. 10 million. What is the value of your investment after four years if the interest rate is compounded:
    a. Annually, **b.** monthly, or **c.** continuously?

PRACTICE QUESTIONS

1. What is the PV of Rs. 100 received in:
   a. Year 10 (at a discount rate of 1 percent).
   b. Year 10 (at a discount rate of 13 percent).
   c. Year 15 (at a discount rate of 25 percent).
   d. Each of years 1 through 3 (at a discount rate of 12 percent).
2. a. If the one-year discount factor is .905, what is the one-year interest rate?
   b. If the two-year interest rate is 10.5 percent, what is the two-year discount factor?
   c. Given these one- and two-year discount factors, calculate the two-year annuity factor.
   d. If the PV of Rs. 10 a year for three years is Rs. 24.65, what is the three-year annuity factor?
   e. From your answers to (c) and (d), calculate the three-year discount factor.
3. A factory costs Rs. 800,000. You reckon that it will produce an inflow after operating costs of Rs. 170,000 a year for 10 years. If the opportunity cost of capital is 14 percent, what is the net present value of the factory? What will the factory be worth at the end of five years?
4. A machine costs Rs. 380,000 and is expected to produce the following cash flows:

Year	1	2	3	4	5	6	7	8	9	10
Cash flow (Rs. 000s)	50	57	75	80	85	92	92	80	68	50

   If the cost of capital is 12 percent, what is the machine's NPV?
5. Mike Polanski is 30 years of age and his salary next year will be $40,000. Mike forecasts that his salary will increase at a steady rate of 5 percent per annum until his retirement at age 60.
   a. If the discount rate is 8 percent, what is the PV of these future salary payments?
   b. If Mike saves 5 percent of his salary each year and invests these savings at an interest rate of 8 percent, how much will he have saved by age 60?
   c. If Mike plans to spend these savings in even amounts over the subsequent 20 years, how much can he spend each year?

excel

Please visit us at www.mhhe.com/bmam8e or refer to your Student CD.

6. A factory costs Rs. 400,000. It will produce an inflow after operating costs of Rs. 100,000 in year 1, Rs. 200,000 in year 2, and Rs. 300,000 in year 3. The opportunity cost of capital is 12 percent. Calculate the NPV.
7. Halcyon Lines is considering the purchase of a new bulk carrier for $8 million. The forecasted revenues are $5 million a year and operating costs are $4 million. A major refit costing $2 million will be required after both the fifth and tenth years. After 15 years, the ship is expected to be sold for scrap at $1.5 million. If the discount rate is 8 percent, what is the ship's NPV?
8. As winner of a breakfast cereal competition, you can choose one of the following prizes:
   a. $100,000 now.
   b. $180,000 at the end of five years.
   c. $11,400 a year forever.
   d. $19,000 for each of 10 years.
   e. $6,500 next year and increasing thereafter by 5 percent a year forever.

   If the interest rate is 12 percent, which is the most valuable prize?
9. Siegfried Basset is 65 years of age and has a life expectancy of 12 more years. He wishes to invest $20,000 in an annuity that will make a level payment at the end of each year until his death. If the interest rate is 8 percent, what income can Mr. Basset expect to receive each year?
10. David and Helen Zhang are saving to buy a boat at the end of five years. If the boat costs $20,000 and they can earn 10 percent a year on their savings, how much do they need to put aside at the end of years 1 through 5?
11. Kangaroo Autos is offering free credit on a new Rs. 10,000 car. You pay Rs. 1,000 down and then Rs. 300 a month for the next 30 months. Turtle Motors next door does not offer free credit but will give you Rs. 1,000 off the list price. If the rate of interest is 10 percent a year, (about .83 percent a month) which company is offering the better deal?

12. Recalculate the NPV of the office building venture in Section 3.1 at interest rates of 5, 10, and 15 percent. Plot the points on a graph with NPV on the vertical axis and the discount rates on the horizontal axis. At what discount rate (approximately) would the project have zero NPV? Check your answer.

13. If the interest rate is 7 percent, what is the value of the following three investments?
    a. An investment that offers you Rs. 100 a year in perpetuity with the payment at the *end* of each year.
    b. A similar investment with the payment at the *beginning* of each year.
    c. A similar investment with the payment spread evenly over each year.

14. Refer back to Section 3.2. If the rate of interest is 8 percent rather than 10 percent, how much would our benefactor need to set aside to provide each of the following?
    a. Rs. 100,000 at the end of each year in perpetuity.
    b. A perpetuity that pays Rs. 100,000 at the end of the first year and that grows at 4 percent a year.
    c. Rs. 100,000 at the end of each year for 20 years.
    d. Rs. 100,000 a year spread evenly over 20 years.

15. How much will you have at the end of 20 years if you invest Rs. 100 today at 15 percent *annually* compounded? How much will you have if you invest at 15 percent *continuously* compounded?

16. You have just read an advertisement stating, "Pay us Rs. 100 a year for 10 years and we will pay you Rs. 100 a year thereafter in perpetuity." If this is a fair deal, what is the rate of interest?

17. Which would you prefer?
    a. An investment paying interest of 12 percent compounded annually.
    b. An investment paying interest of 11.7 percent compounded semiannually.
    c. An investment paying 11.5 percent compounded continuously.

    Work out the value of each of these investments after 1, 5, and 20 years.

18. Fill in the blanks in the following table:

Nominal Interest Rate (%)	Inflation Rate (%)	Real Interest Rate (%)
6	1	
—	10	12
9	—	3

19. In 1880 five aboriginal trackers were each promised the equivalent of 100 Australian dollars for helping to capture the notorious outlaw Ned Kelley. In 1993 the granddaughters of two of the trackers claimed that this reward had not been paid. The prime minister of Victoria stated that, if this was true, the government would be happy to pay the $100. However, the granddaughters also claimed that they were entitled to compound interest. How much was each entitled to if the interest rate was 5 percent? What if it was 10 percent?

20. A leasing contract calls for an immediate payment of Rs. 100,000 and nine subsequent Rs. 100,000 semiannual payments at six-month intervals. What is the PV of these payments if the *annual* discount rate is 8 percent?

Please visit us at www.mhhe.com/bmam8e or refer to your Student CD.

21. In August 1994 *The Wall Street Journal* reported that the winner of the Massachusetts State Lottery prize had the misfortune to be both bankrupt and in prison for fraud. The prize was $9,420,713, to be paid in 19 equal annual installments. (There were 20 installments, but the winner had already received the first payment.) The bankruptcy court judge ruled that the prize should be sold off to the highest bidder and the proceeds used to pay off the creditors.

a. If the interest rate was 8 percent, how much would you have been prepared to bid for the prize?

b. Enhance Reinsurance Company was reported to have offered $4.2 million. Use Excel to find the return that the company was looking for.

excel

Please visit us at www.mhhe.com/bmam8e or refer to your Student CD .

22. A mortgage requires you to pay Rs. 70,000 at the end of each of the next eight years. The interest rate is 8 percent.
   a. What is the present value of these payments?
   b. Calculate for each year the loan balance that remains outstanding, the interest payment on the loan, and the reduction in the loan balance.

23. You estimate that by the time you retire in 35 years, you will have accumulated savings of Rs. 2 million. If the interest rate is 8 percent and you live 15 years after retirement, what annual level of expenditure will those savings support?

   Unfortunately, inflation will eat into the value of your retirement income. Assume a 4 percent inflation rate and work out a spending program for your retirement that will allow you to maintain a level *real* expenditure during retirement.

24. You are considering the purchase of an apartment complex that currently generates a net cash flow of Rs. 400,000 per year. You normally demand a 10 percent rate of return on such investments. Future cash flows are expected to grow with inflation at 4 percent per year from today's level. How much would you be willing to pay for the complex if it:
   a. Will produce cash flows forever?
   b. Will have to be torn down in 20 years? Assume that the site will be worth Rs. 5 million at that time net of demolition costs. (The Rs. 5 million includes 20 years' inflation.)

   Now calculate the real discount rate corresponding to the 10 percent nominal rate. Redo the calculations for parts (a) and (b) using real cash flows. (Your answers should not change.)

25. Vernal Pool, a self-employed herpetologist, wants to put aside a fixed fraction of her annual income as savings for retirement. Ms. Pool is now 40 years old and makes $40,000 a year. She expects her income to increase by 2 percentage points over inflation (e.g., 4 percent inflation means a 6 percent increase in income). She wants to accumulate $500,000 in real terms to retire at age 70. What fraction of her income does she need to set aside? Assume her retirement funds are conservatively invested at an expected real rate of return of 5 percent a year. Ignore taxes.

CHALLENGE QUESTIONS

1. Here are two useful rules of thumb. The "Rule of 72" says that with discrete compounding the time it takes for an investment to double in value is roughly 72/interest rate (in percent). The "Rule of 69" says that with continuous compounding the time that it takes to double is *exactly* 69.3/interest rate (in percent).
   a. If the annually compounded interest rate is 12 percent, use the Rule of 72 to calculate roughly how long it takes before your money doubles. Now work it out exactly.
   b. Can you prove the Rule of 69?

2. Use Excel to construct your own set of annuity tables.

3. You own an oil pipeline which will generate a Rs. 2 million cash return over the coming year. The pipeline's operating costs are negligible, and it is expected to last for a very long time. Unfortunately, the volume of oil shipped is declining, and cash flows are expected to decline by 4 percent per year. The discount rate is 10 percent.
   a. What is the PV of the pipeline's cash flows if its cash flows are assumed to last forever?
   b. What is the PV of the cash flows if the pipeline is scrapped after 20 years?

CHAPTER [4]

THE VALUE OF BONDS AND COMMON STOCKS

WE SHOULD WARN you that being a financial expert has its occupational hazards. One is being cornered at cocktail parties by people who are eager to explain their system for making creamy profits by investing in common stocks. Fortunately, these bores go into temporary hibernation whenever the market goes down.

We may exaggerate the perils of the trade. The point is that there is no easy way to ensure superior investment performance. Later in the book we will show that in well-functioning capital markets changes in security prices are fundamentally unpredictable. Therefore, in this chapter, when we propose to use the concept of present value to price common stocks, we are not promising you a key to investment success; we simply believe that the idea can help you to understand why some investments are priced higher than others.

Why should you care? If you want to know the value of a firm's stock, why can't you look up the stock price in the newspaper? Unfortunately, that is not always possible. For example, you may be the founder of a successful business. You currently own all the shares but are thinking of going public by selling off shares to other investors. You and your advisers need to estimate the price at which those shares can be sold.

There is also another, deeper reason why managers need to understand how shares are valued. We have stated that, if a firm acts in its shareholders' interest, it should accept those investments that increase the value of their stake in the firm. But in order to do this, it is necessary to understand what determines the shares' value.

We begin with a brief review of how bonds are valued. It is brief because we shall be considering some of the refinements of bond valuation in Chapter 23. We then turn to common stocks. We look at how stocks are traded and explain the basic principles of share valuation and the use of discounted-cash-flow models to estimate expected rates of return.

These principles lead us to the fundamental difference between growth and income stocks. (It is not simply a question of whether the company is able to increase profits but whether it can also earn a superior return on its new investments.) Once you understand the essential ingredients for a growth stock, you will be well-equipped to interpret earnings–price ratios properly. You will find that these ratios are not reliable measures of expected returns or the firm's cost of capital.

A word of caution before we proceed. Everybody knows that common stocks are risky and that some are more risky than others. Therefore, investors will not commit funds to stocks unless the expected rates of return are commensurate with the risks. But we say next to nothing in this chapter about the linkages between risk and expected return. A more careful treatment of risk starts in Chapter 7.

4.1 USING PRESENT VALUE FORMULAS TO VALUE BONDS

When governments or companies borrow money, they often do so by issuing bonds. A bond is simply a long-term debt. If you own a bond, you receive a fixed set of cash payoffs: Each year until the bond matures, you collect an interest payment; then at maturity, you also get back the face value of the bond. The face value of the bond is known as the *principal*. Therefore, when the bond matures, the issuer pays you principal and interest.

A Short Trip to Germany to Value a Government Bond

We will start our discussion of bond values with a visit to Germany, where the government issues long-term bonds known as "bunds" (short for *Bundesanleihen*). These bonds pay interest and principal in euros (€s). For example, suppose that in January 2004 you decided to buy €100 face value of the 5.375 percent bund maturing in January 2010. Each year until 2010 you receive an interest payment of $.05375 \times 100 =$ €5.375. This amount is the bond's *coupon*.[1] When the bond matures in 2010 the government pays you the final €5.375 interest, plus the €100 face value. So the cash flows from owning the bond are as follows:

Cash Flows (€)					
2005	**2006**	**2007**	**2008**	**2009**	**2010**
€5.375	€5.375	€5.375	€5.375	€5.375	€105.375

What is the present value of these payoffs? To determine that, you need to look at the return provided by similar securities. In January 2004 other medium-term German government bonds offered a return of about 3.8 percent. That is what you were giving up when you bought the 5.375 percent bonds. Therefore, to value the 5.375 percent bonds you need to discount the cash flows at 3.8 percent:

$$PV = \frac{5.375}{1.038} + \frac{5.375}{(1.038)^2} + \frac{5.375}{(1.038)^3} + \frac{5.375}{(1.038)^4} + \frac{5.375}{(1.038)^5} + \frac{105.375}{(1.038)^6} = 108.31$$

Bond prices are usually expressed as a percentage of face value. Thus we can say that your 5.375 percent bund is worth 108.31 percent.

You may have noticed a shortcut way to value this bond. Your purchase is like a package of two investments. The first investment pays off the six annual coupon payments of €5.375 each, and the second investment pays off the €100 face value at maturity. Therefore, you can use the annuity formula to value the coupon payments and add on the present value of the final payment:

$$\begin{aligned} PV(\text{bond}) &= PV(\text{coupon payments}) + PV(\text{final payment}) \\ &= (\text{coupon} \times \text{6-year annuity factor}) + (\text{final payment} \times \text{discount factor}) \\ &= 5.375\left[\frac{1}{.038} - \frac{1}{.038(1.038)^6}\right] + \frac{100}{(1.038)^6} = 28.36 + 79.95 = 108.31 \end{aligned}$$

Any bond can be valued as a package of an annuity (the coupon payments) and a single payment (the repayment of the face value).

Rather than asking the value of the bond, we could have phrased our question the other way around: If the price of the bond is 108.31, what return do investors expect? In that case, we need to find the value of r that solves the following equation:

$$108.31 = \frac{5.375}{1+r} + \frac{5.375}{(1+r)^2} + \frac{5.375}{(1+r)^3} + \frac{5.375}{(1+r)^4} + \frac{5.375}{(1+r)^5} + \frac{105.375}{(1+r)^6}$$

This rate r is called the bond's **yield to maturity.** In our case r is 3.8 percent. If you discount the cash flows at 3.8 percent, you arrive at the bond's price of 108.31. The only *general* procedure for calcu-

[1]Bonds used to come with coupons attached, which had to be clipped off and presented to the issuer to obtain the interest payments. This is still the case with *bearer bonds,* where the only evidence of indebtedness is the bond itself. In many parts of the world bearer bonds are still issued and are popular with investors who would rather remain anonymous. The alternative is for the borrower to issue *registered bonds,* in which case the identity of the bond's owner is recorded and coupon payments are sent automatically. Bunds are registered bonds.

lating the yield to maturity is trial and error, but spreadsheet programs or specially programmed electronic calculators will usually do the trick.

The formula that we used for calculating the present value of the government bond was slightly different from the general present value formula that we developed in § 3.1, where we allowed r_1, the rate of return offered by the capital market on one-year investments, to differ from r_2, the rate of return on two-year investments. Then we finessed this problem by assuming that investors use the same rate to discount cash flows occurring in different years. In valuing our German government bond, we again assumed that investors use the same rate to discount cash flows occurring in different years. That does not matter as long as the term structure is flat, with short-term rates approximately the same as long-term rates. But when the term structure is not flat, professional bond investors discount each cash flow at a different rate. There will be more about that in Chapter 23.

What Happens When Interest Rates Change?

Interest rates fluctuate. For example, during the past 30 years yields on six-year German government bonds have been as low as 3.2 percent and as high as 11.2 percent. In periods of severe economic crisis, interest rates can sometimes rise to several hundred percent.

How do such changes in interest rates affect bond prices? Suppose, for example, that German bond yields fall to 2 percent. Then the price of our six-year bund would rise to

$$PV = \frac{5.375}{1.02} + \frac{5.375}{(1.02)^2} + \frac{5.375}{(1.02)^3} + \frac{5.375}{(1.02)^4} + \frac{5.375}{(1.02)^5} + \frac{105.375}{(1.02)^6} = 118.90$$

If yields jumped to 10 percent, then price would fall to

$$PV = \frac{5.375}{1.10} + \frac{5.375}{(1.10)^2} + \frac{5.375}{(1.10)^3} + \frac{5.375}{(1.10)^4} + \frac{5.375}{(1.10)^5} + \frac{105.375}{(1.10)^6} = 79.86$$

Not surprisingly, the higher the interest rate that investors demand, the less that they will be prepared to pay for the bond.

Some bonds are more affected than others by a change in the interest rate. The effect is greatest when the cash flows on the bond last for many years. The effect is trivial if the bond matures tomorrow.

Back to India: Semiannual Coupons and Bond Prices

We now need to hop back to India and look at a typical Indian G-Sec (short form of Government Securities), the 8.66% bond of 2016. This is similar to our German bund except that, like most bonds in India, this Government security makes coupon payments *semiannually*, so that instead of receiving 8.66% interest once a year, bondholders receive 4.33% interest every *half*-year. The face value of the bond is Rs. 100, so the six-monthly payment on each bond is 0.0433 × Rs. 100 = Rs. 4.33.

Because interest is semiannual, yields on Indian G-Secs are usually quoted as semiannually compounded yields. In March 2006, you could buy the 8.66% bond on a yield of 7.94 percent. Since this was a semiannually compounded yield, the yield over six months was 7.94/2 = 3.97%. Now we can calculate the value of the G-Sec recognizing that the coupons are received semiannually and that the quoted yield is a semiannually compounded rate:

$$PV = \frac{4.33}{1.0397} + \frac{4.33}{(1.0397)^2} + \frac{4.33}{(1.0397)^3} + \ldots + \frac{4.33}{(1.0397)^{19}} + \frac{104.33}{(1.0397)^{20}}$$
$$= \text{Rs. } 104.91$$

Each G-Sec is worth Rs. 104.91 or 104.91 percent of the face value.

By April 2006 the interest rate had increased to 8% per year, or 8/2 = 4% semiannually. So the bond's value decreased to Rs. 104.48:

$$PV = \frac{4.33}{1.04} + \frac{4.33}{(1.04)^2} + \frac{4.33}{(1.04)^3} + \ldots + \frac{4.33}{(1.04)^{19}} + \frac{104.33}{(1.04)^{20}}$$
$$= \text{Rs. } 104.48$$

or 104.48% of face value.

We need to move on and look at how common stocks are traded and valued.

4.2 HOW COMMON STOCKS ARE TRADED

There are 275.5 million shares of Infosys, and as on 31st March, 2006, these shares were owned by about 196 thousand shareholders[2]. They included the promoters, large foreign institutional investors (FIIs), mutual funds, corporate bodies that each won several million shares, as well as individuals who own a handful of shares. If you owned one share of Infosys, you would own 0.0000000003 percent of the company and have a claim on the same tiny fraction of Infosys's profits. Of course, the more shares you own, the larger your "share" of the company.

If Infosys wishes to raise additional capital, it may do so either by borrowing or by selling new shares to investors. Sales of new shares to raise new capital are said to occur in the *primary market*. But most trades in Infosys shares take place in existing shares, which investors buy from each other. These trades do not raise new capital for the firm. This market for secondhand shares is known as the secondary market. The principal secondary markets for Infosys shares are the Mumbai Stock Exchange and the National Stock Exchange[3].

Suppose that you are the head trader of a mutual fund that wishes to buy 100,000 shares of Infosys. You contact your broker, who then places the order directly in the National Stock Exchange Limited. The NSE uses a nation-wide fully-automated screen-based trading system (SBTS) where a member of NSE can enter the price and the number of shares he wants to buy (or sell) and the transaction gets executed as soon as the system finds a matching sale (or buy) order. The order placed by your broker will get executed as soon as the system finds a matching order. If no one is prepared to sell at your price, the order will enter into the limit order book maintained by the exchange for each stock. The NSE trading system is known as the *National Exchange for Automated Trading*, or NEAT.

The National Stock Exchange is not the only exchange in India. Since the shares of Infosys are listed in the Mumbai Stock Exchange and the Bangalore Stock Exchange, your broker could have placed the order with either of these exchanges. Both Mumbai Stock Exchange and Bangalore Stock

[2]Source: http://www.infosys.com/investor/investor_frm.asp

[3]Infosys shares are also listed at Bangalore Stock Exchange.

Exchange follow similar automated trading systems, known as BSE On Line Trading or BOLT and Bangalore Electronic Securities Trading (BEST) respectively.

The prices at which stocks are traded are summarized in the daily press. If you search for Infosys in the stock listing pages of any business daily, you should find something similar to the following[4]:

52 Weeks			Div		Vol		Net
High	Low	Stock (SYM)	Yld	PE	(100s)	Close	Change
3449	1876.9	Infosys (INFOSYSTECH)[5]	.0.2%	39.52	1539	3177.9	1.4%

You can see that on 29th April, 2006, investors traded a total of 1539 × 100 = 153900 shares of Infosys stock in the NSE. By the close of the day, the stock traded at Rs. 3177.9 a share, up by 1.4% from the day before. Since there were about 275.5 million shares of Infosys outstanding, investors were placing a total value on the stock of Rs. 875.5 billion.

Buying stocks is a risky occupation. Over the previous year, Infosys stock traded as high as Rs. 3449, but at one point dropped to Rs. 1876.4. An unfortunate investor who bought at the 52-week high and sold at the 52-week low would have lost nearly 46% of his or her investment. Of course, you do not come across such people at cocktail parties; they either keep quite or aren't invited.

Most business dailies also provide certain additional facts about Infosys's stock. The dividend yield on Infosys stock is 0.2 percent, and the ratio of the stock price to earnings (P/E ratio) is 39.52. We will explain shortly why investors pay attention to these figures.

4.3 HOW COMMON STOCKS ARE VALUED

Think back to the last chapter, where we described how to value future cash flows. The discounted-cash-flow (DCF) formula for the present value of a stock is just the same as it is for the present value of any other asset. We just discount the cash flows by the return that can be earned in the capital market on securities of comparable risk. Shareholders receive cash from the company in the form of a stream of dividends. So

$$\text{PV(stock)} = \text{PV(expected future dividends)}$$

At first sight this statement may seem surprising. When investors buy stocks, they usually expect to receive a dividend, but they also hope to make a capital gain. Why does our formula for present value say nothing about capital gains? As we now explain, there is no inconsistency.

[4]Figures are as on 29th April, 2006. The stock prices are the NSE quoted prices.

[5]Here, INFOSYSTECH' refers to the symbol NSE has assigned to Infosys's stock. The BSE symbol for Infosys is 500209.

Today's Price

The cash payoff to owners of common stocks comes in two forms: (1) cash dividends and (2) capital gains or losses. Suppose that the current price of a share is P_0, that the expected price at the end of a year is P_1, and that the expected dividend per share is DIV_1. The rate of return that investors expect from this share over the next year is defined as the expected dividend per share DIV_1 plus the expected price appreciation per share $P_1 - P_0$, all divided by the price at the start of the year P_0:

$$\text{Expected return} = r = \frac{DIV_1 + P_1 - P_0}{P_0}$$

This expected return is often called the **market capitalization rate.**

Suppose Fledgling Electronics stock is selling for Rs. 100 a share ($P_0 = 100$). Investors expect a Rs. 5 cash dividend over the next year ($DIV_1 = 5$). They also expect the stock to sell for Rs. 110 a year hence ($P_1 = 110$). Then the expected return to the stockholders is 15 percent:

$$r = \frac{5 + 110 - 100}{100} = .15, \text{ or } 15\%$$

On the other hand, if you are given investors' forecasts of dividend and price and the expected return offered by other equally risky stocks, you can predict today's price:

$$\text{Price} = P_0 = \frac{DIV_1 + P_1}{1 + r}$$

For Fledgling Electronics $DIV_1 = 5$ and $P_1 = 110$. If r, the expected return on securities in the same risk class as Fledgling, is 15 percent, then today's price should be Rs. 100:

$$P_0 = \frac{5 + 110}{1.15} = \text{Rs. } 100$$

How do we know that Rs. 100 is the right price? Because no other price could survive in competitive capital markets. What if P_0 were above Rs. 100? Then Fledgling stock would offer an expected rate of return that was *lower* than other securities of equivalent risk. Investors would shift their capital to the other securities and in the process would force down the price of Fledgling stock. If P_0 were less than Rs. 100, the process would reverse. Fledgling's stock would offer a higher rate of return than comparable securities. In that case, investors would rush to buy, forcing the price up to Rs. 100.

The general conclusion is that at each point in time *all securities in an equivalent risk class are priced to offer the same expected return.* This is a condition for equilibrium in well-functioning capital markets. It is also common sense.

But What Determines Next Year's Price?

We have managed to explain today's stock price P_0 in terms of the dividend DIV_1 and the expected price next year P_1. Future stock prices are not easy things to forecast directly. But think about what determines next year's price. If our price formula holds now, it ought to hold then as well:

$$P_1 = \frac{DIV_2 + P_2}{1 + r}$$

That is, a year from now investors will be looking out at dividends in year 2 and price at the end of year 2. Thus we can forecast P_1 by forecasting DIV_2 and P_2, and we can express P_0 in terms of DIV_1, DIV_2, and P_2:

$$P_0 = \frac{1}{1+r}(DIV_1 + P_1) = \frac{1}{1+r}\left(DIV_1 + \frac{DIV_2 + P_2}{1+r}\right) = \frac{DIV_1}{1+r} + \frac{DIV_2 + P_2}{(1+r)^2}$$

Take Fledgling Electronics. A plausible explanation why investors expect its stock price to rise by the end of the first year is that they expect higher dividends and still more capital gains in the second. For example, suppose that they are looking today for dividends of Rs. 5.50 in year 2 and a subsequent price of Rs. 121. That would imply a price at the end of year 1 of

$$P_1 = \frac{5.50 + 121}{1.15} = \text{Rs. } 110$$

Today's price can then be computed either from our original formula

$$P_0 = \frac{DIV_1 + P_1}{1+r} = \frac{5.00 + 110}{1.15} = \text{Rs. } 100$$

or from our expanded formula

$$P_0 = \frac{DIV_1}{1+r} + \frac{DIV_2 + P_2}{(1+r)^2} = \frac{5.00}{1.15} + \frac{5.50 + 121}{(1.15)^2} = \text{Rs. } 100$$

We have succeeded in relating today's price to the forecasted dividends for two years (DIV_1 and DIV_2) plus the forecasted price at the end of the *second* year (P_2). You will probably not be surprised to learn that we could go on to replace P_2 by $(DIV_3 + P_3)/(1 + r)$ and relate today's price to the forecasted dividends for three years (DIV_1, DIV_2, and DIV_3) plus the forecasted price at the end of the *third* year (P_3). In fact we can look as far out into the future as we like, removing *P*s as we go. Let us call this final period *H*. This gives us a general stock price formula:

$$P_0 = \frac{DIV_1}{1+r} + \frac{DIV_2}{(1+r)^2} + \cdots + \frac{DIV_H + P_H}{(1+r)^H}$$

$$= \sum_{t=1}^{H} \frac{DIV_t}{(1+r)^t} + \frac{P_H}{(1+r)^H}$$

The expression $\sum_{t=1}^{H}$ simply means the sum of the discounted dividends from year 1 to year *H*.

Table 4.1 continues the Fledgling Electronics example for various time horizons, assuming that the dividends are expected to increase at a steady 10 percent compound rate. The expected price P_t increases at the same rate each year. Each line in the table represents an application of our general formula for a different value of *H*. Figure 4.1 provides a graphical representation of the table. Each column shows the present value of the dividends up to the time horizon and the present value of the price at the horizon. As the horizon recedes, the dividend stream accounts for an increasing proportion of present value, but the *total* present value of dividends plus terminal price always equals Rs. 100.

TABLE 4.1

Applying the stock valuation formula to Fledgling Electronics.

Assumptions:
1. Dividends increase at 10 percent per year, compounded.
2. Capitalization rate is 15 percent.

	Expected Future Values		Present Values		
Horizon Period (H)	**Dividend (DIV_t)**	**Price (P_t)**	**Cumulative Dividends**	**Future Price**	**Total**
0	—	100	—	—	100
1	5.00	110	4.35	95.65	100
2	5.50	121	8.51	91.49	100
3	6.05	133.10	12.48	87.52	100
4	6.66	146.41	16.29	83.71	100
10	11.79	259.37	35.89	64.11	100
20	30.58	672.75	58.89	41.11	100
50	533.59	11,739.09	89.17	10.83	100
100	62,639.15	1,378,061.23	98.83	1.17	100

FIGURE 4.1

As your horizon recedes, the present value of the future price (shaded area) declines but the present value of the stream of dividends (unshaded area) increases. The total present value (future price and dividends) remains the same.

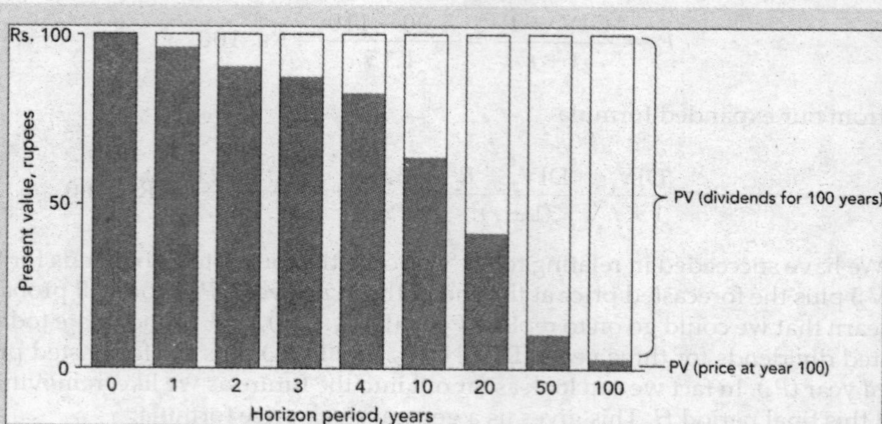

How far out could we look? In principle the horizon period H could be infinitely distant. Common stocks do not expire of old age. Barring such corporate hazards as bankruptcy or acquisition, they are immortal. (For example, one of the earliest corporations, the Hudson's Bay Company, was incorporated in 1670 and is still going strong as a major Canadian retailer.) As H approaches infinity, the present value of the terminal price ought to approach zero, as it does in the final column of Figure 4.1. We can, therefore, forget about the terminal price entirely and express today's price as the present value of a perpetual stream of cash dividends. This is usually written as

$$P_0 = \sum_{t=1}^{\infty} \frac{DIV_t}{(1+r)^t}$$

where ∞ indicates infinity.

This discounted-cash-flow (DCF) formula for the present value of a stock is just the same as it is for the present value of any other asset. We just discount the cash flows—in this case the dividend stream—by the return that can be earned in the capital market on securities of comparable risk. Some find the DCF formula implausible because it seems to ignore capital gains. But we know that the formula was *derived* from the assumption that price in any period is determined by expected dividends *and* capital gains over the next period.

Notice that it is *not* correct to say that the value of a share is equal to the sum of the discounted stream of earnings per share. Earnings are generally larger than dividends because part of those earnings is reinvested in new plant, equipment, and working capital. Discounting earnings would recognize the rewards of that investment (a higher *future* dividend) but not the sacrifice (a lower dividend *today*). The correct formulation states that share value is equal to the discounted stream of dividends per share.

4.4 ESTIMATING THE COST OF EQUITY CAPITAL

In Chapter 3 we encountered some simplified versions of the basic present value formula. Let us see whether they offer any insights into stock values. Suppose, for example, that we forecast a constant growth rate for a company's dividends. This does not preclude year-to-year deviations from the trend: It means only that *expected* dividends grow at a constant rate. Such an investment would be just another example of the growing perpetuity that we helped our fickle philanthropist to evaluate in the last chapter. To find its present value we must divide the first year's cash payment by the difference between the discount rate and the growth rate:

$$P_0 = \frac{\text{DIV}_1}{r - g}$$

Remember that we can use this formula only when g, the anticipated growth rate, is less than r, the discount rate. As g approaches r, the stock price becomes infinite. Obviously r must be greater than g if growth really is perpetual.

Our growing perpetuity formula explains P_0 in terms of next year's expected dividend DIV_1, the projected growth trend g, and the expected rate of return on other securities of comparable risk r. Alternatively, the formula can be used to obtain an estimate of r from DIV_1, P_0, and g:

$$r = \frac{\text{DIV}_1}{P_0} + g$$

The market capitalization rate equals the **dividend yield** (DIV_1/P_0) plus the expected rate of growth in dividends (g).

These two formulas are much easier to work with than the general statement that "price equals the present value of expected future dividends."[6] Here is a practical example.

[6]These formulas were first developed in 1938 by Williams and were rediscovered by Gordon and Shapiro. See J. B. Williams, *The Theory of Investment Value* (Cambridge, MA: Harvard University Press, 1938); and M. J. Gordon and E. Shapiro, "Capital Equipment Analysis: The Required Rate of Profit," *Management Science* 3 (October 1956), pp. 102–110.

Using the DCF Model to Set Gas and Electricity Prices

The prices charged by local electric and gas utilities in the US are regulated by state commissions. The regulators try to keep consumer prices down but are supposed to allow the utilities to earn a fair rate of return. But what is fair? It is usually interpreted as r, the market capitalization rate for the firm's common stock. That is, the fair rate of return on equity for a public utility ought to be the rate offered by securities that have the same risk as the utility's common stock.[7]

Small variations in estimates of this return can have a substantial effect on the prices charged to the customers and on the firm's profits. So both utilities and regulators devote considerable resources to estimating r. They call r the **cost of equity capital.** Utilities are mature, stable companies which ought to offer tailor-made cases for application of the constant-growth DCF formula.[8]

Suppose you wished to estimate the cost of equity for Cascade Natural Gas, a local natural gas distribution company. Its stock was selling for \$ 22.35 per share at the start of 2004. Dividend payments for the next year were expected to be \$ 1.03 a share. Thus it was a simple matter to calculate the first half of the DCF formula:

$$\text{Dividend yield} = \frac{\text{DIV}_1}{P_0} = \frac{1.03}{22.35} = .046, \text{ or } 4.6\%$$

The hard part is estimating g, the expected rate of dividend growth. One option is to consult the views of security analysts who study the prospects for each company. Analysts are rarely prepared to stick their necks out by forecasting dividends to kingdom come, but they often forecast growth rates over the next five years, and these estimates may provide an indication of the expected long-run growth path. In the case of Cascade, analysts in 2004 were forecasting an annual growth of 5.7 percent.[9] This, together with the dividend yield, gave an estimate of the cost of equity capital:

$$r = \frac{\text{DIV}_1}{P_0} + g = .046 + .057 = .103, \text{ or } 10.3\%$$

An alternative approach to estimating long-run growth starts with the **payout ratio**, the ratio of dividends to earnings per share (EPS). For Cascade, this was forecasted at 66 percent. In other words, each year the company was plowing back into the business about 44 percent of earnings per share:

$$\text{Plowback ratio} = 1 - \text{payout ratio} = 1 - \frac{\text{DIV}}{\text{EPS}} = 1 - .66 = .44$$

[7]This is the accepted interpretation of the U.S. Supreme Court's directive in 1944 that "the returns to the equity owner [of a regulated business] should be commensurate with returns on investments in other enterprises having corresponding risks." *Federal Power Commission v. Hope Natural Gas Company*, 302 U.S. 591 at 603.

[8]There are many exceptions to this statement. For example, Pacific Gas & Electric (PG&E), which serves northern California, used to be a mature, stable company until the California energy crisis of 2000 sent wholesale electric prices sky-high. PG&E was not allowed to pass these price increases on to retail customers. The company lost more than \$3.5 billion in 2000 and was forced to declare bankruptcy in 2001. PG&E emerged from bankruptcy in 2004, but we may have to wait a while before it is again a suitable subject for the constant-growth DCF formula.

[9]In this calculation we're assuming that earnings and dividends are forecasted to grow forever at the same rate g. We'll show how to relax this assumption later in this chapter. The growth rate was based on the average earnings growth forecasted by Value Line and IBES. IBES compiles and averages forecasts made by security analysts. Value Line publishes its own analysts' forecasts.

Also, Cascade's ratio of earnings per share to book equity per share was about 12 percent. This is its **return on equity,** or **ROE:**

$$\text{Return on equity} = \text{ROE} = \frac{\text{EPS}}{\text{book equity per share}} = .12$$

If Cascade earns 12 percent of book equity and reinvests 44 percent of income, then book equity will increase by $.44 \times .12 = .053$ or 5.3 percent. Earnings and dividends per share will also increase by 5.3 percent:

$$\text{Dividend growth rate} = g = \text{plowback ratio} \times \text{ROE} = .44 \times .12 = .053$$

That gives a second estimate of the market capitalization rate:

$$r = \frac{\text{DIV}_1}{P_0} + g = .046 + .053 = .099, \text{ or } 9.9\%$$

Although this estimate of the market capitalization rate for Cascade stock seems reasonable enough, there are obvious dangers in analyzing any single firm's stock with the constant-growth DCF formula. First, the underlying assumption of regular future growth is at best an approximation. Second, even if it is an acceptable approximation, errors inevitably creep into the estimate of g. Our two methods for calculating the cost of equity gave similar answers. That was a lucky chance; different methods can sometimes give very different answers.

Remember, Cascade's cost of equity is not its personal property. In well-functioning capital markets investors capitalize the dividends of all securities in Cascade's risk class at exactly the same rate. But any estimate of r for a single common stock is "noisy" and subject to error. Good practice does not put too much weight on single-company cost-of-equity estimates. It collects samples of similar companies, estimates r for each, and takes an average. The average gives a more reliable benchmark for decision making.

Table 4.2 shows DCF cost-of-equity estimates for Cascade and seven other gas distribution companies. These are all stable, mature companies for which the constant-growth DCF formula *ought* to work. Notice the variation in the cost-of-equity estimates. Some of the variation may reflect differences in the risk, but some is just noise. The average estimate is 10.2 percent.

Table 4.3 gives another example of DCF cost-of-equity estimates, this time for U.S. railroads in 2002.

Of course, you are not restricted to analyzing expected returns for particular industries; you can also use the DCF formula to estimate the expected return for the entire stock market. For example, Figure 4.2 shows the results of an exercise by Marston and Harris, which used analysts' forecasts of five-year earnings growth to produce DCF estimates of the average cost of equity for companies in the Standard & Poor's Index. You can see that as interest rates fell between 1982 and 1998, the estimated cost of equity fell from nearly 20 percent to just under 15 percent. The margin between the cost of equity and the rate of interest was much more stable and averaged 9.3 percent over the 17-year period.

Estimates of this kind are only as good as the long-term forecasts on which they are based. For example, several studies have observed that security analysts are subject to behavioral biases and their forecasts tend to be over-optimistic.[10] If so, such DCF estimates of the cost of equity should be regarded as upper estimates of the true figure.

[10]See, for example, A. Dugar and S. Nathan, "The Effect of Investment Banking Relationships on Financial Analysts' Earnings Investment Recommendations," *Contemporary Accounting Research* 12 (1995), pp. 131–160.

	Stock Price	Dividend Annual Rate[a]	Dividend Yield	Long-term Growth Rate	DCF Cost of Equity	Multistage DCF Cost of Equity[b]
Atmos Energy	$25.14	$1.31	5.2%	6.0%	11.2%	10.4%
Cascade Natural Gas	22.35	1.03	4.6	5.7	10.3	11.3
Keyspan	36.39	1.93	5.3	6.1	11.4	10.4
Laclede Group	29.37	1.41	4.8	3.6	8.4	9.5
Peoples' Energy	42.30	2.33	5.5	5.9	11.4	10.5
South Jersey Industries	44.14	1.85	4.2	5.3	9.5	9.4
Southwest Gas	23.42	.87	3.7	6.9	10.6	9.5
WGL Holdings	27.81	1.36	4.9	4.2	9.1	9.2
				Average	10.2	10.0

TABLE 4.2

Cost-of-equity estimates for local gas distribution companies at the start of 2004. The long-term growth rate is based on security analysts' forecasts. In the multistage DCF model, growth after 2007 is assumed to adjust gradually to the estimated long-term growth rate of Gross Domestic Product (GDP).

[a]Projected dividends, based on current dividend and one year's growth.
[b]Long-term GDP growth forecasted at 3.6%.
Source: The Brattle Group, Inc.

	Average Dividend Yield[a]	Forecasted Growth Rate[b]	Cost of Equity
Burlington Northern Santa Fe	1.85%	9.12%	10.97%
CSX	1.29	11.37	12.66
Norfolk Southern	1.27	11.79	13.06
Union Pacific	1.44	12.05	13.49
Weighted average[c]	1.48	11.13	12.61

TABLE 4.3

DCF cost-of-equity estimates for U.S. railroads, 2002.

[a]Average of monthly dividend yields during 2002.
[b]Based on I/B/E/S averages of security analysts' growth forecasts.
[c]Weights based on total market values of the railroads' common stock.
Source: U.S. Surface Transportation Board, "Railroad Cost of Capital—2002," June 19, 2003.

Some Warnings about Constant-Growth Formulas

The simple constant-growth DCF formula is an extremely useful rule of thumb, but no more than that. Naive trust in the formula has led many financial analysts to silly conclusions.

We have stressed the difficulty of estimating r by analysis of one stock only. Try to use a large sample of equivalent-risk securities. Even that may not work, but at least it gives the analyst a fighting chance, because the inevitable errors in estimating r for a single security tend to balance out across a broad sample.

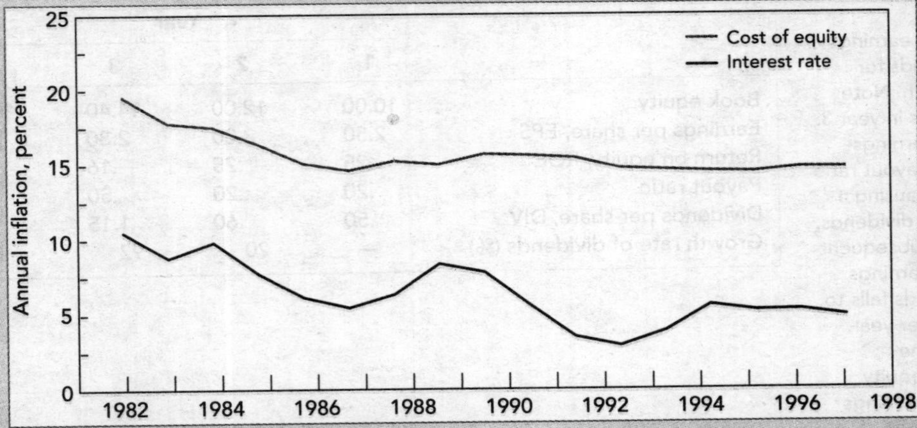

FIGURE 4.2

DCF estimates of the average cost-of-equity capital for companies in Standard & Poor's Composite Index, 1982–1998. The dividend growth rate *g*, is taken from analysts' forecasts of five-year earnings growth.

Source: R. S. Harris and F. C. Marston, "The Market Risk Premium: Expectational Estimates Using Analysts' Forecasts," *Journal of Applied Finance* 11 (2001), pp. 6–16. Reprinted with permission from the Financial Management Association International.

In addition, resist the temptation to apply the formula to firms having high current rates of growth. Such growth can rarely be sustained indefinitely, but the constant-growth DCF formula assumes it can. This erroneous assumption leads to an overestimate of *r*.[11]

Consider Growth-Tech, Inc., a firm with DIV_1 = Rs. 0.50 and P_0 = Rs. 50. The firm has plowed back 80 percent of earnings and has had a return on equity (ROE) of 25 percent. This means that *in the past*

$$\text{Dividend growth rate} = \text{plowback ratio} \times \text{ROE} = .80 \times .25 = .20$$

The temptation is to assume that the future long-term growth rate *g* also equals .20. This would imply

$$r = \frac{.50}{50.00} + .20 = .21$$

But this is silly. No firm can continue growing at 20 percent per year forever, except possibly under extreme inflationary conditions. Eventually, profitability will fall and the firm will respond by investing less.

In real life the return on equity will decline gradually over time, but for simplicity let's assume it suddenly drops to 16 percent at year 3 and the firm responds by plowing back only 50 percent of earnings. Then *g* drops to .50(.16) = .08.

[11]Table 4.3 may be an example of such an overestimate. One wonders whether the large railroads listed there can really sustain the 11 percent forecasted growth rate.

TABLE 4.4

Forecasted earnings and dividends for Growth-Tech. Note the changes in year 3: ROE and earnings drop, but payout ratio increases, causing a big jump in dividends. However, subsequent growth in earnings and dividends falls to 8 percent per year. Note that the increase in equity equals the earnings not paid out as dividends.

	Year			
	1	2	3	4
Book equity	10.00	12.00	14.40	15.55
Earnings per share, EPS	2.50	3.00	2.30	2.49
Return on equity, ROE	.25	.25	.16	.16
Payout ratio	.20	.20	.50	.50
Dividends per share, DIV	.50	.60	1.15	1.24
Growth rate of dividends (%)	—	20	92	8

Table 4.4 shows what's going on. Growth-Tech starts year 1 with book equity of Rs. 10.00 per share. It earns Rs. 2.50, pays out 50 paise as dividends, and plows back Rs. 2. Thus it starts year 2 with book equity of Rs. 10 + 2 = Rs. 12. After another year at the same ROE and payout, it starts year 3 with equity of Rs. 14.40. However, ROE drops to .16, and the firm earns only Rs. 2.30. Dividends go up to Rs. 1.15, because the payout ratio increases, but the firm has only Rs. 1.15 to plow back. Therefore subsequent growth in earnings and dividends drops to 8 percent.

Now we can use our general DCF formula:

$$P_0 = \frac{DIV_1}{1+r} + \frac{DIV_2}{(1+r)^2} + \frac{DIV_3 + P_3}{(1+r)^3}$$

Investors in year 3 will view Growth-Tech as offering 8 percent per year dividend growth. So we can use the constant-growth formula to calculate P_3:

$$P_3 = \frac{DIV_4}{r - .08}$$

$$P_0 = \frac{DIV_1}{1+r} + \frac{DIV_2}{(1+r)^2} + \frac{DIV_3}{(1+r)^3} + \frac{1}{(1+r)^3}\frac{DIV_4}{r-.08}$$

$$= \frac{.50}{1+r} + \frac{.60}{(1+r)^2} + \frac{1.15}{(1+r)^3} + \frac{1}{(1+r)^3}\frac{1.24}{r-.08}$$

We have to use trial and error to find the value of r that makes P_0 equal Rs. 50. It turns out that the r implicit in these more realistic forecasts is approximately .099, quite a difference from our "constant-growth" estimate of .21.

DCF Valuation with Varying Growth Rates

Our present value calculations for Growth-Tech used a *two-stage* DCF valuation model. In the first stage (years 1 and 2), Growth-Tech is highly profitable (ROE = 25 percent), and it plows back 80 percent of earnings. Book equity, earnings, and dividends increase by 20 percent per year. In the second stage, starting in year 3, profitability and plowback decline, and earnings settle into long-term growth at 8 percent. Dividends jump up to Rs. 1.15 in year 3, and then also grow at 8 percent.

	Year			
	1	2	3	4
Book equity at start of year	10.00	10.40	10.82	11.25
Earnings per share, EPS	.40	.73	1.08	1.12
Return on equity, ROE	.04	.07	.10	.10
Dividends per share, DIV	0	.31	.65	.67
Growth rate of dividends (%)	—	—	110	4

TABLE 4.5

Forecasted earnings and dividends for Phoenix.com. The company can initiate and increase dividends as profitability (ROE) recovers. Note that the increase in book equity equals the earnings not paid out as dividends.

Growth rates can vary for many reasons. Sometimes growth is high in the short run not because the firm is unusually profitable, but because it is recovering from an episode of *low* profitability. Table 4.5 displays projected earnings and dividends for Phoenix.com, which is gradually regaining financial health after a near meltdown. The company's equity is growing at a moderate 4 percent. ROE in year 1 is only 4 percent, however, so Phoenix has to reinvest all its earnings, leaving no cash for dividends. As profitability increases in years 2 and 3, an increasing dividend can be paid. Finally, starting in year 4, Phoenix settles into steady-state growth, with equity, earnings, and dividends all increasing at 4 percent per year.

Assume the cost of equity is 10 percent. Then Phoenix shares should be worth \$ 9.13 per share:

$$P_0 = \underbrace{\frac{0}{1.1} + \frac{.31}{(1.1)^2} + \frac{.65}{(1.1)^3}}_{\text{PV (first-stage dividends)}} + \underbrace{\frac{1}{(1.1)^3}\frac{.67}{(.10 - .04)}}_{\text{PV (second-stage dividends)}} = \$\ 9.13$$

You could go on to valuation models with three or more stages. For example, the far-right column of Table 4.2 presents multistage DCF estimates of the cost of equity for our old friend Cascade and seven other local gas distribution companies. In this case the long-term growth rates reported in the table do not continue forever. After 2007, each company's growth rate gradually adjusts to an estimated long-term growth rate for Gross Domestic Product (GDP). From 2013 on, all firms' dividends are forecasted to grow with GDP at 5.3 percent. The resulting cost-of-equity estimates average out to about 10 percent, just slightly lower than the estimates from the simple, perpetual-growth model. The dispersion of the cost-of-equity estimates is reduced, however.

We must leave you with two warnings about DCF formulas for valuing common stocks or estimating the cost of equity. First, it's almost always worthwhile to lay out a simple spreadsheet, like Table 4.4 or 4.5, to ensure that your dividend projections are consistent with the company's earnings and the investments that are required. Second, be careful about using DCF valuation formulas to test whether the market is correct in its assessment of a stock's value. If your estimate of the value is different from that of the market, it is probably because you have used poor dividend forecasts. Remember what we said at the beginning of this chapter about simple ways of making money on the stock market: There aren't any.

4.5 THE LINK BETWEEN STOCK PRICE AND EARNINGS PER SHARE

Investors often use the terms *growth stocks* and *income stocks*. They buy growth stocks primarily for the expectation of capital gains, and they are interested in the future growth of earnings rather than in next year's dividends. On the other hand, they buy income stocks primarily for the cash dividends. Let us see whether these distinctions make sense.

Imagine first the case of a company that does not grow at all. It does not plow back any earnings and simply produces a constant stream of dividends. Its stock would resemble the perpetual bond described in the last chapter. Remember that the return on a perpetuity is equal to the yearly cash flow divided by the present value. The expected return on our share would thus be equal to the yearly dividend divided by the share price (i.e., the dividend yield). Since all the earnings are paid out as dividends, the expected return is also equal to the earnings per share divided by the share price (i.e., the earnings–price ratio). For example, if the dividend is Rs. 10 a share and the stock price is Rs. 100, we have

$$\begin{aligned}\text{Expected return} &= \text{dividend yield} = \text{earnings–price ratio}\\ &= \frac{\text{DIV}_1}{P_0} = \frac{\text{EPS}_1}{P_0}\\ &= \frac{10.00}{100} = .10\end{aligned}$$

The price equals

$$P_0 = \frac{\text{DIV}_1}{r} = \frac{\text{EPS}_1}{r} = \frac{10.00}{.10} = 100$$

The expected return for *growing* firms can *also* equal the earnings–price ratio. The key is whether earnings are reinvested to provide a return equal to the market capitalization rate. For example, suppose our monotonous company suddenly hears of an opportunity to invest Rs. 10 a share next year. This would mean no dividend at $t = 1$. However, the company expects that in each subsequent year the project would earn Re. 1 per share, so that the dividend could be increased to Rs. 11 a share.

Let us assume that this investment opportunity has about the same risk as the existing business. Then we can discount its cash flow at the 10 percent rate to find its net present value at year 1:

$$\text{Net present value per share at year 1} = -10 + \frac{1}{.10} = 0$$

Thus the investment opportunity will make no contribution to the company's value. Its prospective return is equal to the opportunity cost of capital.

What effect will the decision to undertake the project have on the company's share price? Clearly none. The reduction in value caused by the nil dividend in year 1 is exactly offset by the increase in value caused by the extra dividends in later years. Therefore, once again the market capitalization rate equals the earnings–price ratio:

$$r = \frac{\text{EPS}_1}{P_0} = \frac{10}{100} = .10$$

Project Rate of Return	Incremental Cash Flow, C	Project NPV in Year 1[a]	Project's Impact on Share Price in Year 0[b]	Share Price in Year 0, P_0	$\frac{EPS_1}{P_0}$	r
.05	Re. .50	− Rs. 5.00	− Rs. 4.55	Rs. 95.45	.105	.10
.10	1.00	0	0	100.00	.10	.10
.15	1.50	+ 5.00	+ 4.55	104.55	.096	.10
.20	2.00	+ 10.00	+ 9.09	109.09	.092	.10

TABLE 4.6

Effect on stock price of investing an additional Rs. 10 in year 1 at different rates of return. Notice that the earnings–price ratio overestimates *r* when the project has negative NPV and underestimates it when the project has positive NPV.

[a]Project costs Rs. 10.00 (EPS_1). NPV = −10 + *C*/*r*, where *r* = .10.
[b]NPV is calculated at year 1. To find the impact on P_0, discount for one year at *r* = .10.

Table 4.6 repeats our example for different assumptions about the cash flow generated by the new project. Note that the earnings–price ratio, measured in terms of EPS_1, next year's expected earnings, equals the market capitalization rate (*r*) *only* when the new project's NPV = 0. This is an extremely important point—managers frequently make poor financial decisions because they confuse earnings–price ratios with the market capitalization rate.

In general, we can think of stock price as the capitalized value of average earnings under a no-growth policy, plus **PVGO**, the **net present value of growth opportunities:**

$$P_0 = \frac{EPS_1}{r} + PVGO$$

The earnings–price ratio, therefore, equals

$$\frac{EPS}{P_0} = r\left(1 - \frac{PVGO}{P_0}\right)$$

It will underestimate *r* if PVGO is positive and overestimate it if PVGO is negative. The latter case is less likely, since firms are rarely *forced* to take projects with negative net present values.

Calculating the Present Value of Growth Opportunities for Fledgling Electronics

In our last example both dividends and earnings were expected to grow, but this growth made no net contribution to the stock price. The stock was in this sense an "income stock." Be careful not to equate firm performance with the growth in earnings per share. A company that reinvests earnings at below the market capitalization rate *r* may increase earnings but will certainly reduce the share value.

Now let us turn to that well-known *growth stock*, Fledgling Electronics. You may remember that Fledgling's market capitalization rate, *r*, is 15 percent. The company is expected to pay a dividend of Rs. 5 in the first year, and thereafter the dividend is predicted to increase indefinitely by 10 percent a year. We can, therefore, use the simplified constant-growth formula to work out Fledgling's price:

$$P_0 = \frac{DIV_1}{r - g} = \frac{5}{.15 - .10} = \text{Rs. } 100$$

Suppose that Fledgling has earnings per share of Rs. 8.33. Its payout ratio is then

$$\text{Payout ratio} = \frac{DIV_1}{EPS_1} = \frac{5.00}{8.33} = .6$$

In other words, the company is plowing back 1 − .6, or 40 percent of earnings. Suppose also that Fledgling's ratio of earnings to book equity is ROE = .25. This explains the growth rate of 10 percent:

$$\text{Growth rate} = g = \text{plowback ratio} \times \text{ROE} = .4 \times .25 = .10$$

The capitalized value of Fledgling's earnings per share if it had a no-growth policy would be

$$\frac{EPS_1}{r} = \frac{8.33}{.15} = \text{Rs. } 55.56$$

But we know that the value of Fledgling stock is Rs. 100. The difference of Rs. 44.44 must be the amount that investors are paying for growth opportunities. Let's see if we can explain that figure.

Each year Fledgling plows back 40 percent of its earnings into new assets. In the first year Fledgling invests Rs. 3.33 at a permanent 25 percent return on equity. Thus the cash generated by this investment is .25 × 3.33 = Rs. .83 per year starting at $t = 2$. The net present value of the investment as of $t = 1$ is

$$NPV_1 = -3.33 + \frac{.83}{.15} = \text{Rs. } 2.22$$

Everything is the same in year 2 except that Fledgling will invest Rs. 3.67, 10 percent more than in year 1 (remember $g = .10$). Therefore at $t = 2$ an investment is made with a net present value of

$$NPV_2 = -3.67 + \frac{.83 \times 1.10}{.15} = \text{Rs. } 2.44$$

Thus the payoff to the owners of Fledgling Electronics stock can be represented as the sum of (1) a level stream of earnings, which could be paid out as cash dividends if the firm did not grow, and (2) a set of tickets, one for each future year, representing the opportunity to make investments having positive NPVs. We know that the first component of the value of the share is

$$\text{Present value of level stream of earnings} = \frac{EPS_1}{r} = \frac{8.33}{.15} = \text{Rs. } 55.56$$

The first ticket is worth Rs. 2.22 in $t = 1$, the second is worth Rs. 2.22 × 1.10 = Rs. 2.44 in $t = 2$, the third is worth Rs. 2.44 × 1.10 = Rs. 2.69 in $t = 3$. These are the forecasted cash values of the tickets. We know how to value a stream of future cash values that grows at 10 percent per year: Use the constant-growth DCF formula, replacing the forecasted dividends with forecasted ticket values:

$$\text{Present value of growth opportunities} = PVGO = \frac{NPV_1}{r - g} = \frac{2.22}{.15 - .10} = \text{Rs. } 44.44$$

Stock	Stock Price, P_0 (April 2006)	EPS[a]	Cost of Equity, r[b]	PVGO	PVGO, Percent of Stock Price
Income stocks:					
Thermax	311.4	84.65	14.00%	−293.24	−0.94
GE Shipping	261.3	29.07	11.50%	8.52	0.03
Steel Authority of India	83.3	12.54	15.90%	4.43	0.05
Tata Steel Limited	536.4	63.05	14.50%	101.57	0.19
Growth stocks:					
Zee Telefilms	238.45	7.85	21.20%	201.42	0.84
Wipro	558.55	18.85	22.90%	476.24	0.85
Ranbaxy Laboratories	431.6	18.11	11.90%	279.42	0.65
Siemens	5682.7	207.45	11.90%	3939.42	0.69
Bharti Tele Ventures	412.85	17.67	13.50%	281.96	0.68

TABLE 4.7

Estimated PVGOs

[a]EPS is the forecasted earnings for the year ended 31 March, 2007. We obtain the consensus forecast figures from the website of icicdirect.com

[b]The cost of equity was estimated by using the capital asset pricing model. We describe this model and how to use it in § 8.2 and § 9.2. For this example, we used a market risk premium of 9.87% and a risk-free rate of 5 percent.

Now everything checks:

$$\begin{aligned}\text{Share price} &= \text{present value of level stream of earnings} \\ &\quad + \text{present value of growth opportunities} \\ &= \frac{\text{EPS}_1}{r} + \text{PVGO} \\ &= \text{Rs. } 55.56 + \text{Rs. } 44.44 \\ &= \text{Rs. } 100\end{aligned}$$

Why is Fledgling Electronics a growth stock? Not because it is expanding at 10 percent per year. It is a growth stock because the net present value of its future investments accounts for a significant fraction (about 44 percent) of the stock's price.

Stock prices today reflect investors' expectations of future operating *and investment* performance. Growth stocks sell at high price–earnings ratios because investors are willing to pay now for expected superior returns on investments that have not yet been made.

Some Examples of Growth Opportunities

Stocks such as Wipro and Bharti Televentures are often described as growth stocks, while those of mature firms like Tata Steel and GE Shipping are regarded as income stocks. Let's check it out. The first column of Table 4.7 shows the stock price for each of these stocks in the beginning of April, 2006. The remaining columns estimate PVGO as a proportion of the stock price.

Remember, if there are no growth opportunities, present value equals the average future earnings from existing assets discounted at the market capitalization rate. We used an average of current and forecasted earnings as a measure of the earning power of existing assets. You can see that most of the value of the growth stocks comes from PVGO, that is, from investors' expectations that the company will be able to earn more than the cost of capital on its future investments. By contrast, most of the value of our sample of income stocks derives from the earning power of the existing assets.

What about Thermax? Its estimated PVGO is *negative*. What was the stock market telling us? There are two possible messages. One is that investors expected Thermax to invest in *negative*-NPV projects that would reduce its value. The second possibility is that we have overestimated the earning power of Thermax's existing assets and attributed too much value to these assets and too little to PVGO. We suspect that the second message is the correct one: It is not easy to divine investors' true expectations of future earnings.

Some companies have such extensive growth opportunities that they prefer to pay no dividends for long periods of time. For example, up to the time that we wrote this chapter, "glamour stocks" such as Amazon and Dell Computer had never paid a dividend, because any cash paid out to investors would have meant either slower growth or raising capital by some other means. Investors were happy to forgo immediate cash dividends in exchange for increasing earnings and the expectation of high dividends some time in the future.

SUMMARY

In this chapter we have used our newfound knowledge of present values to examine the market price of common stocks. The value of a stock is equal to the stream of cash payments discounted at the rate of return that investors expect to receive on other securities with equivalent risks.

Common stocks do not have a fixed maturity; their cash payments consist of an indefinite stream of dividends. Therefore, the present value of a common stock is

$$\text{PV} = \sum_{t=1}^{\infty} \frac{\text{DIV}_t}{(1+r)^t}$$

However, we did not just *assume* that investors purchase common stocks solely for dividends. In fact, we began with the assumption that investors have relatively short horizons and invest for both dividends and capital gains. Our fundamental valuation formula is, therefore,

$$P_0 = \frac{\text{DIV}_1 + P_1}{1+r}$$

This is a condition of market equilibrium. If it did not hold, the share would be overpriced or underpriced, and investors would rush to sell or buy it. The flood of sellers or buyers would force the price to adjust so that the fundamental valuation formula holds.

This formula will hold in each future period as well as the present. That allowed us to express next year's forecasted price in terms of the subsequent stream of dividends $\text{DIV}_2, \text{DIV}_3, \ldots$

We also made use of the formula for a growing perpetuity presented in Chapter 3. If dividends are expected to grow forever at a constant rate of g, then

$$P_0 = \frac{\text{DIV}_1}{r-g}$$

It is often helpful to twist this formula around and use it to estimate the market capitalization rate r, given P_0 and estimates of DIV_1 and g:

$$r = \frac{DIV_1}{P_0} + g$$

Remember, however, that this formula rests on a *very* strict assumption: constant dividend growth in perpetuity. This may be an acceptable assumption for mature, low-risk firms, but for many firms, near-term growth is unsustainably high. In that case, you may wish to use a *two-stage* DCF formula, where near-term dividends are forecasted and valued, and the constant-growth DCF formula is used to forecast the value of the shares at the start of the long run. The near-term dividends and the future share value are then discounted to present value.

The general DCF formula can be transformed into a statement about earnings and growth opportunities:

$$P_0 = \frac{EPS_1}{r} + PVGO$$

The ratio EPS_1/r is the capitalized value of the earnings per share that the firm would generate under a no-growth policy. PVGO is the net present value of the investments that the firm will make in order to grow. A growth stock is one for which PVGO is large relative to the capitalized value of EPS. Most growth stocks are stocks of rapidly expanding firms, but expansion alone does not create a high PVGO. What matters is the profitability of the new investments.

In earlier chapters you should have acquired—we hope painlessly—a knowledge of the basic principles of valuing assets and a facility with the mechanics of discounting. Now you know something of how common stocks are valued and market capitalization rates estimated. In Chapter 5 we can begin to apply all this knowledge in a more specific analysis of capital budgeting decisions.

FURTHER READING

There are a number of discussions of the valuation of common stocks in investment texts. We suggest:

Z. Bodie, A. Kane, and A. J. Marcus: *Investments*, 6th ed., Irwin/McGraw-Hill, 2005.

W. F. Sharpe, G. J. Alexander, and J. V. Bailey: *Investments*, 6th ed., Prentice-Hall, Inc., Englewood Cliffs, NJ, 1999.

J. B. Williams's original work remains very readable. See particularly Chapter V of:

J. B. Williams: *The Theory of Investment Value*, Harvard University Press, Cambridge, MA, 1938.

Leibowitz and Kogelman call PVGO the "franchise factor." They analyze it in detail in:

M. L. Leibowitz and S. Kogelman: "Inside the P/E Ratio: The Franchise Factor," *Financial Analysts Journal*, 46 (November–December 1990), pp. 17–35.

Myers and Borucki cover the practical problems encountered in estimating DCF costs of equity for regulated companies; Harris and Marston report DCF estimates of rates of return for the stock market as a whole:

S. C. Myers and L. S. Borucki: "Discounted Cash Flow Estimates of the Cost of Equity Capital—A Case Study," *Financial Markets, Institutions and Instruments*, 3 (August 1994), pp. 9–45.

R. S. Harris and F. C. Marston: "The Market Risk Premium: Expectational Estimates Using Analysts' Forecasts," *Journal of Applied Finance*, 11:6–16 (2001).

CONCEPT REVIEW QUESTIONS

1. Fill in the blanks: The market value of a bond is the present value of its _______ and _______ payments. (page 58)
2. What is meant by a bond's yield to maturity and how is it calculated? (page 58)
3. If interest rates rise, do bond prices rise or fall? (page 59)

For additional Concept Review Questions, please visit us at www.mhhe.com/bmam8e or refer to your Student CD.

QUIZ

1. A 10-year Treasury bond is issued with a face value of Rs. 1,000, paying interest of Rs. 60 a year. If market yields increase shortly after the T-bond is issued, what happens to the bond's:
   a. coupon rate?
   b. price?
   c. yield to maturity?
2. A bond with a coupon rate of 8 percent is selling at a price of 97 percent. Is the bond's yield to maturity more or less than 8 percent?
3. True or false?
   a. All stocks in an equivalent-risk class are priced to offer the same expected rate of return.
   b. The value of a share equals the PV of future dividends per share.
4. Respond briefly to the following statement:
   "You say stock price equals the present value of future dividends? That's crazy! All the investors I know are looking for capital gains."
5. Company X is expected to pay an end-of-year dividend of Rs. 10 a share. After the dividend its stock is expected to sell at Rs. 110. If the market capitalization rate is 10 percent, what is the current stock price?
6. Company Y does not plow back any earnings and is expected to produce a level dividend stream of Rs. 5 a share. If the current stock price is Rs. 40, what is the market capitalization rate?
7. Company Z's earnings and dividends per share are expected to grow indefinitely by 5 percent a year. If next year's dividend is Rs. 10 and the market capitalization rate is 8 percent, what is the current stock price?
8. Company Z-prime is like Z in all respects save one: Its growth will stop after year 4. In year 5 and afterward, it will pay out all earnings as dividends. What is Z-prime's stock price? Assume next year's EPS is Rs. 15.
9. If company Z (see question 7) were to distribute all its earnings, it could maintain a level dividend stream of Rs. 15 a share. How much is the market actually paying per share for growth opportunities?
10. Consider three investors:
    a. Mr. Single invests for one year.
    b. Ms. Double invests for two years.
    c. Mrs. Triple invests for three years.

    Assume each invests in company Z (see question 7). Show that each expects to earn a rate of return of 8 percent per year.
11. True or false? Explain.
    a. The value of a share equals the discounted stream of future earnings per share.
    b. The value of a share equals the PV of earnings per share assuming the firm does not grow, plus the NPV of future growth opportunities.
12. Under what conditions does r, a stock's market capitalization rate, equal its earnings–price ratio EPS_1/P_0?

PRACTICE QUESTIONS

1. Suppose that 5-year government bonds are selling on a yield of 4 percent. Value a 5-year bond with a 6 percent coupon. Start by assuming that the bond is issued by a continental European government and makes annual coupon payments. Then renew your work assuming that the bond is issued by the RBI, so that the bond pays semi-annual coupons and the yield refers to a semi-annually compounded rate.
2. Refer again to Practice Question 1. How would the bond value in each case change if interest rates fall to 3 percent?
3. A 6-year government bond makes annual coupon payments of 5 percent and offers a yield of 3 percent annually compounded. Suppose that one year later the bond still yields 3 percent. What return has the bondholder earned over the 12-month period? Now suppose instead that the bond yield is 2 percent at the end of the year. What return would the bondholder earn in this case?
4. Look in a recent issue of the *Business Line* at Stock Market Listings.
   a. What is the latest price of HLL stock?
   b. What are the annual dividend payment and the dividend yield on HLL stock?
   c. What would the yield be if HLL changed its yearly dividend to Rs. 4.00?
   d. What is the P/E on HLL stock?
   e. Use the P/E to calculate HLL's earnings per share.
   f. Is HLL's P/E higher or lower than that of Grasim Industries?
   g. What are the possible reasons for the difference in P/E?

eXcel

Please visit us at www.mhhe.com/bmam8e or refer to your Student CD.

5. Rework Table 4.1 under the assumption that the dividend on Fledgling Electronics is Rs. 10 next year and that it is expected to grow by 5 percent a year. The capitalization rate is 15 percent.
6. In March 2004, Fly Paper's stock sold for about Rs. 73. Security analysts were forecasting a long-term earnings growth rate of 8.5 percent. The company is expected to pay a dividend of Rs. 1.68 per share.
   a. Assume dividends are expected to grow along with earnings at $g = 8.5$ percent per year in perpetuity. What rate of return r were investors expecting?
   b. Fly Paper was expected to earn about 12 percent on book equity and to pay out about 50 percent of earnings as dividends. What do these forecasts imply for g? For r? Use the perpetual-growth DCF formula.
7. Consider the following three stocks:
   a. Stock A is expected to provide a dividend of Rs. 10 a share forever.
   b. Stock B is expected to pay a dividend of Rs. 5 next year. Thereafter, dividend growth is expected to be 4 percent a year forever.
   c. Stock C is expected to pay a dividend of Rs. 5 next year. Thereafter, dividend growth is expected to be 20 percent a year for 5 years (i.e., until year 6) and zero thereafter.

   If the market capitalization rate for each stock is 10 percent, which stock is the most valuable? What if the capitalization rate is 7 percent?
8. Pigeon Express currently plows back 40 percent of its earnings and earns a return of 20 percent on this investment. The dividend yield on the stock is 4 percent.
   a. Assuming that Pigeon can continue to plow back this proportion of earnings and earn a 20 percent return on the investment, how rapidly will earnings and dividends grow? What is the expected return on Pigeon stock?
   b. Suppose that management suddenly announces that future investment opportunities have dried up. Now Pigeon intends to pay out all its earnings. How will the stock price change?
   c. Suppose that management simply announces that the expected return on new investment will in the future be the same as the market capitalization rate. Now what is Pigeon stock price?

STANDARD & POOR'S

9. Look up General Mills, Inc., and Kellogg Co. on the Standard & Poor's Market Insight website (**www.mhhe.com/edumarketinsight**). The companies' ticker symbols are GIS and K.

a. What are the current dividend yield and price–earnings ratio (P/E) for each company? How do the yields and P/Es compare to the average for the food industry and for the stock market as a whole? (The stock market is represented by the S & P 500 index.)

b. What are the growth rates of earnings per share (EPS) and dividends for each company over the last five years? Do these growth rates appear to reflect a steady trend that could be projected for the long-run future?

c. Would you be confident in applying the constant-growth DCF valuation model to these companies' stocks? Why or why not?

STANDARD & POOR'S

10. Look up the following companies on the Standard & Poor's Market Insight website (**www.mhhe.com/edumarketinsight**): Citigroup (C), Dell Computer (DELL), Dow Chemical (DOW), Harley Davidson (HDI), and Pfizer, Inc. (PFE). Look at "Financial Highlights" and "Company Profile" for each company. You will note wide differences in these companies' price–earnings ratios. What are the possible explanations for these differences? Which would you classify as growth (high-PVGO) stocks and which as income stocks?

11. Vega Motor Corporation has pulled off a miraculous recovery. Four years ago, it was near bankruptcy. Now its charismatic leader, a corporate folk hero, may run for president.

Vega has just announced a Re. 1 per share dividend, the first since the crisis hit. Analysts expect an increase to a "normal" Rs. 3 as the company completes its recovery over the next three years. After that, dividend growth is expected to settle down to a moderate long-term growth rate of 6 percent.

Vega stock is selling at Rs. 50 per share. What is the expected long-run rate of return from buying the stock at this price? Assume dividends of Re. 1, Rs. 2, and Rs. 3 for years 1, 2, 3. A little trial and error will be necessary to find r.

12. Each of the following formulas for determining shareholders' required rate of return can be right or wrong depending on the circumstances:

a. $r = \dfrac{DIV_1}{P_0} + g$

b. $r = \dfrac{EPS_1}{P_0}$

For each formula construct a *simple* numerical example showing that the formula can give wrong answers and explain why the error occurs. Then construct another simple numerical example for which the formula gives the right answer.

13. Alpha Corp's earnings and dividends are growing at 15 percent per year. Beta Corp's earnings and dividends are growing at 8 percent per year. The companies' assets, earnings, and dividends per share are now (at date 0) exactly the same. Yet PVGO accounts for a greater fraction of Beta Corp's stock price. How is this possible? *Hint:* There is more than one possible explanation.

14. Look again at the financial forecasts for Growth-Tech given in Table 4.4. This time assume you *know* that the opportunity cost of capital is $r = .12$ (discard the .099 figure calculated in the text). Assume you do *not* know Growth-Tech's stock value. Otherwise follow the assumptions given in the text.

a. Calculate the value of Growth-Tech stock.

b. What part of that value reflects the discounted value of P_3, the price forecasted for year 3?

c. What part of P_3 reflects the present value of growth opportunities (PVGO) after year 3?

d. Suppose that competition will catch up with Growth-Tech by year 4, so that it can earn only its cost of capital on any investments made in year 4 or subsequently. What is Growth-Tech stock worth now under this assumption? (Make additional assumptions if necessary.)

STANDARD &POOR'S

15. Visit the website of **www.icicidirect.com/research**/ and select company snapshot. The website contains information for all the companies in Table 4.7 except for Infosys. Update the calculations of PVGO as a percentage of stock price. For simplicity assume that the cost of equity of Infosys is 16%. You can find the consensus EMP forecasts from the website itself.

16. Compost Science, Inc. (CSI), is in the business of converting Boston's sewage sludge into fertilizer. The business is not in itself very profitable. However, to induce CSI to remain in business, the Metropolitan District Commission (MDC) has agreed to pay whatever amount is necessary to yield CSI a 10 percent book return on equity. At the end of the year CSI is expected to pay a $ 4 dividend. It has been reinvesting 40 percent of earnings and growing at 4 percent a year.

a. Suppose CSI continues on this growth trend. What is the expected long-run rate of return from purchasing the stock at $ 100? What part of the $ 100 price is attributable to the present value of growth opportunities?

b. Now the MDC announces a plan for CSI to treat Cambridge sewage. CSI's plant will, therefore, be expanded gradually over 5 years. This means that CSI will have to reinvest 80 percent of its earnings for 5 years. Starting in year 6, however, it will again be able to pay out 60 percent of earnings. What will be CSI's stock price once this announcement is made and its consequences for CSI are known?

17. Look one more time at Table 4.1, which applies the DCF stock valuation formula to Fledgling Electronics. The CEO, having just learned that stock value is the present value of future dividends, proposes that Fledgling pay a bumper dividend of Rs. 15 a share in period 1. The extra cash would have to be raised by an issue of new shares. Recalculate Table 4.1 assuming that profits and payout ratios in all subsequent years are unchanged. You should find that the total present value of dividends *per existing share* is unchanged at Rs. 100. Why?

CHALLENGE QUESTIONS

1. Write a spreadsheet program to construct a series of bond tables that show the present value of a bond given the coupon rate, maturity, and yield to maturity. Assume that coupon payments are semiannual and yields are compounded semiannually.

2. The constant-growth DCF formula

$$P_0 = \frac{\text{DIV}_1}{r-g}$$

is sometimes written as

$$P_0 = \frac{\text{ROE}(1-b)\text{BVPS}}{r-b\text{ROE}}$$

where BVPS is book equity value per share, b is the plowback ratio, and ROE is the ratio of earnings per share to BVPS. Use this equation to show how the price-to-book ratio varies as ROE changes. What is price-to-book when ROE $= r$?

3. Portfolio managers are frequently paid a proportion of the funds under management. Suppose you manage a Rs. 100 million equity portfolio offering a dividend yield (DIV_1/P_0) of 5 percent. Dividends and portfolio value are expected to grow at a constant rate. Your annual fee for managing this portfolio is .5 percent of portfolio value and is calculated at the end of each year. Assuming that you will continue to manage the portfolio from now to eternity, what is the present value of the management contract? How would the contract value change if you invested in stocks with a 4 percent yield?

MINI-CASE
Reeby Sports

Ten years ago, in 1995, George Reeby founded a small mail-order company selling high-quality sports equipment. Since those early days Reeby Sports has grown steadily and been consistently profitable. The company has issued 2 million shares, all of which are owned by George Reeby and his five children.

For some months George has been wondering whether the time has come to take the company public. This would allow him to cash in on part of his investment and would make it easier for the firm to raise capital should it wish to expand in the future.

But how much are the shares worth? George's first instinct is to look at the firm's balance sheet, which shows that the book value of the equity is \$ 26.34 million, or \$ 13.17 per share. A share price of \$ 13.17 would put the stock on a P/E ratio of 6.6. That is quite a bit lower than the 13.1 P/E ratio of Reeby's larger rival, Molly Sports.

George suspects that book value is not necessarily a good guide to a share's market value. He thinks of his daughter Jenny, who works in an investment bank. She would undoubtedly know what the shares are worth. He decides to phone her after she finishes work that evening at 9 o'clock or before she starts the next day at 6.00 A.M.

Before phoning, George jots down some basic data on the company's profitability. After recovering from its early losses, the company has earned a return that is higher than its estimated 10 percent cost of capital. George is fairly confident that the company could continue to grow fairly steadily for the next 6 to 8 years. In fact he feels that the company's growth has been somewhat held back in the last few years by the demands from two of the children for the company to make large dividend payments. Perhaps, if the company went public, it could hold back on dividends and plow more money back into the business.

There are some clouds on the horizon. Competition is increasing and only that morning Molly Sports announced plans to form a mail-order division. George is worried that beyond the next six or so years it might become difficult to find worthwhile investment opportunities.

George realizes that Jenny will need to know much more about the prospects for the business before she can put a final figure on the value of Reeby Sports, but he hopes that the information is sufficient for her to give a preliminary indication of the value of the shares.

	1996	1997	1998	1999	2000	2001	2002	2003	2004	2005E
Earnings per share, \$	−2.10	−0.70	0.23	0.81	1.10	1.30	1.52	1.64	2.00	2.03
Dividend, \$	0.00	0.00	0.00	0.20	0.20	0.30	0.30	0.60	0.60	0.80
Book value per share, \$	9.80	7.70	7.00	7.61	8.51	9.51	10.73	11.77	13.17	14.40
ROE, %	−27.0	−7.1	3.0	11.6	14.5	15.3	16.0	15.3	17.0	15.4

QUESTIONS

1. Help Jenny to forecast dividend payments for Reeby Sports and to estimate the value of the stock. You do not need to provide a single figure. For example, you may wish to calculate two figures, one on the assumption that the opportunity for further profitable investment is reduced in year 6 and another on the assumption that it is reduced in year 8.
2. How much of your estimate of the value of Reeby's stock comes from the present value of growth opportunities?

CHAPTER [5]

WHY NET PRESENT VALUE LEADS TO BETTER INVESTMENT DECISIONS THAN OTHER CRITERIA

A COMPANY'S SHAREHOLDERS prefer to be rich rather than poor. Therefore, they want the firm to invest in every project that is worth more than it costs. The difference between a project's value and its cost is its *net present value (NPV)*. Companies can best help their shareholders by investing in all projects with a positive NPV and rejecting those with a negative NPV.

We start this chapter with a review of the net present value rule. We then turn to some other measures that companies may look at when making investment decisions. The first two of these measures, the project's payback period and its book rate of return, are little better than rules of thumb, easy to calculate and easy to communicate. Although there is a place for rules of thumb in this world, an engineer needs something more accurate when designing a 100-story building, and a financial manager needs more than a rule of thumb when making a substantial capital investment decision.

Instead of calculating a project's NPV, companies often compare the expected rate of return from investing in the project with the return that shareholders could earn on equivalent-risk investments in the capital market. The company accepts those projects that provide a higher return than shareholders could earn for themselves. If used correctly, this rate of return rule should always identify projects that increase firm value. However, we shall see that the rule sets several traps for the unwary.

We conclude the chapter by showing how to cope with situations when the firm has only limited capital. This raises two problems. One is computational. In simple cases we just choose those projects that give the highest NPV per dollar invested, but more elaborate techniques are sometimes needed to sort through the possible alternatives. The other problem is to decide whether capital rationing really exists and whether it invalidates the net present value rule. Guess what? NPV, properly interpreted, wins out in the end.

5.1 A REVIEW OF THE BASICS

Vegetron's chief financial officer (CFO) is wondering how to analyze a proposed $ 1 million investment in a new venture called project X. He asks what you think.

Your response should be as follows: "First, forecast the cash flows generated by project X over its economic life. Second, determine the appropriate opportunity cost of capital. This should reflect both the time value of money and the risk involved in project X. Third, use this opportunity cost of capital to discount the future cash flows of project X. The sum of the discounted cash flows is called present value (PV). Fourth, calculate *net* present value (NPV) by subtracting the $ 1 million investment from PV. Invest in project X if its NPV is greater than zero."

However, Vegetron's CFO is unmoved by your sagacity. He asks why NPV is so important.

Your reply: "Let us look at what is best for Vegetron stockholders. They want you to make their Vegetron shares as valuable as possible."

"Right now Vegetron's total market value (price per share times the number of shares outstanding) is $ 10 million. That includes $ 1 million cash we can invest in project X. The value of Vegetron's other assets and opportunities must therefore be $ 9 million. We have to decide whether it is better to keep the $ 1 million cash and reject project X or to spend the cash and accept project X. Let us call the value of the new project PV. Then the choice is as follows:

	Market Value ($ millions)	
Asset	Reject Project X	Accept Project X
Cash	1	0
Other assets	9	9
Project X	0	PV
	10	9 + PV

"Clearly project X is worthwhile if its present value, PV, is greater than $ 1 million, that is, if net present value is positive."

CFO: "How do I know that the PV of project X will actually show up in Vegetron's market value?"

Your reply: "Suppose we set up a new, independent firm X, whose only asset is project X. What would be the market value of firm X?

"Investors would forecast the dividends firm X would pay and discount those dividends by the expected rate of return of securities having similar risks. We know that stock prices are equal to the present value of forecasted dividends.

"Since project X is the only asset, the dividend payments we would expect firm X to pay are exactly the cash flows we have forecasted for project X. Moreover, the rate investors would use to discount firm X's dividends is exactly the rate we should use to discount project X's cash flows.

"I agree that firm X is entirely hypothetical. But if project X is accepted, investors holding Vegetron stock will really hold a portfolio of project X and the firm's other assets. We know the other assets are worth $ 9 million considered as a separate venture. Since asset values add up, we can easily figure out the portfolio value once we calculate the value of project X as a separate venture.

"By calculating the present value of project X, we are replicating the process by which the common stock of firm X would be valued in capital markets."

CFO: "The one thing I don't understand is where the discount rate comes from."

Your reply: "I agree that the discount rate is difficult to measure precisely. But it is easy to see what we are *trying* to measure. The discount rate is the opportunity cost of investing in the project rather than in the capital market. In other words, instead of accepting a project, the firm can always give the cash to the shareholders and let them invest it in financial assets.

"You can see the trade-off (Figure 5.1). The opportunity cost of taking the project is the return shareholders could have earned had they invested the funds on their own. When we discount the project's cash flows by the expected rate of return on financial assets, we are measuring how much investors would be prepared to pay for your project."

"But which financial assets?" Vegetron's CFO queries. "The fact that investors expect only 12 percent on IBM stock does not mean that we should purchase Fly-by-Night Electronics if it offers 13 percent."

Your reply: "The opportunity-cost concept makes sense only if assets of equivalent risk are compared. In general, you should identify financial assets with risks equivalent to the project under consideration, estimate the expected rate of return on these assets, and use this rate as the opportunity cost."

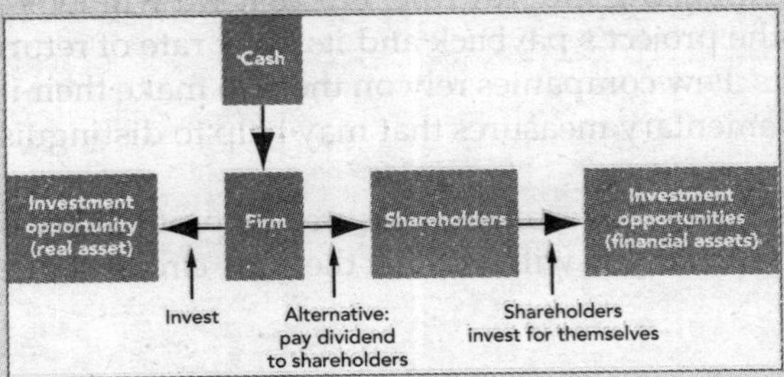

FIGURE 5.1

The firm can either keep and reinvest cash or return it to investors. (Arrows represent possible cash flows or transfers.) If cash is reinvested, the opportunity cost is the expected rate of return that shareholders could have obtained by investing in financial assets.

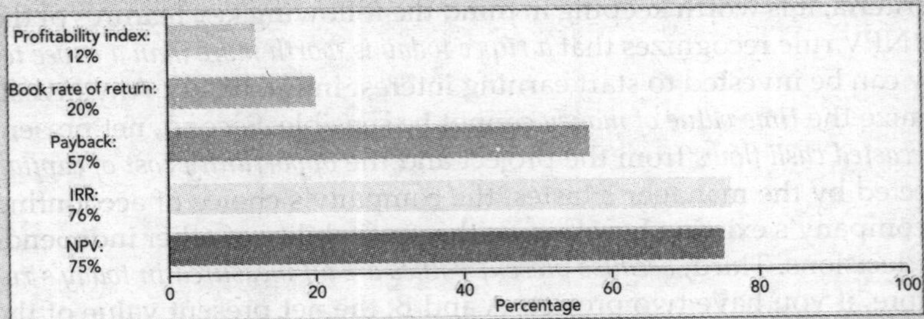

FIGURE 5.2a

Survey evidence on the percentage of CFOs who always, or almost always, use a particular technique for evaluating investment projects.

Source: Reprinted from J. R. Graham and C. R. Harvey, "The Theory and Practice of Finance: Evidence from the Field," *Journal of Financial Economics* 61 (2001), pp. 187–243, © 2001 with permission from Elsevier Science.

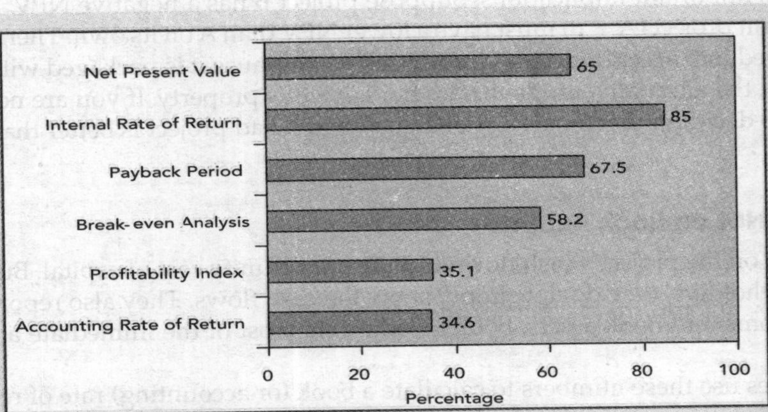

FIGURE 5.2b

Survey evidence on the percentage of Indian CFOs who use a particular technique for evaluating investment projects.

Source: Anand, M., 2002, "Corporate Finance Practices in India: A Survey," *Vikalpa*, October-December, Vol. 27, No. 4, pp.29-56. Reprinted with permission.

Net Present Value's Competitors

When you advised the CFO to calculate the project's NPV, you were in good company. These days, 75% of the firms (65% of firms in india) calculate net present value when deciding on investment projects. However, as you can see from Figure 5.2a and Figure 5.2b, NPV is not the only investment criterion that companies use, and firms often look at more than one measure of a project's attractiveness.

About 85 percent of the firms calculate the project's internal rate of return (or IRR) in India while doing project appraisal. The IRR rule is a close relative of NPV and, used properly, it will give the same answer. You therefore need to understand the IRR rule and how to take care when using it.

A large part of this chapter is concerned with explaining the IRR rule, but first we will look at two other measures of a project's attractiveness—the project's payback and its book rate of return. As we will see, both measures have obvious defects. Few companies rely on them to make their investment decisions, but they do use them as supplementary measures that may help to distinguish the marginal project from the no-brainer.

Later in the chapter we will also come across one further investment measure, the profitability index. As you can see from Figure 5.2, it is not often used, but you will find that there are circumstances in which this measure has some special advantages.

Three Points to Remember about NPV

As we look at these alternative criteria, it is worth keeping in mind the following key features of the net present value rule. First, the NPV rule recognizes that *a rupee today is worth more than a rupee tomorrow,* because the rupee today can be invested to start earning interest immediately. Any investment rule which does not recognize the *time value of money* cannot be sensible. Second, net present value depends solely on the *forecasted cash flows* from the project and the *opportunity cost of capital.* Any investment rule that is affected by the manager's tastes, the company's choice of accounting method, the profitability of the company's existing business, or the profitability of other independent projects will lead to inferior decisions. Third, *because present values are all measured in today's rupees, you can add them up.* Therefore, if you have two projects A and B, the net present value of the combined investment is

$$\text{NPV}(A + B) = \text{NPV}(A) + \text{NPV}(B)$$

This adding-up property has important implications. Suppose project B has a negative NPV. If you tack it onto project A, the joint project (A + B) must have a lower NPV than A on its own. Therefore, you are unlikely to be misled into accepting a poor project (B) just because it is packaged with a good one (A). As we shall see, the alternative measures do not have this property. If you are not careful, you may be tricked into deciding that a package of a good and a bad project is better than the good project on its own.

NPV Depends on Cash Flow, Not on Book Returns

Net present value depends only on the project's cash flows and the opportunity cost of capital. But when companies report to shareholders, they do not simply show the cash flows. They also report book—that is, accounting—income and book assets; book income gets most of the immediate attention.

Financial managers sometimes use these numbers to calculate a book (or accounting) rate of return on a proposed investment. In other words, they look at the prospective book income as a proportion of the book value of the assets that the firm is proposing to acquire:

$$\text{Book rate of return} = \frac{\text{book income}}{\text{book assets}}$$

Cash flows and book income are often very different. For example, the accountant labels some cash outflows as *capital investments* and others as *operating expenses.* The operating expenses are, of course, deducted immediately from each year's income. The capital expenditures are put on the firm's balance sheet and then depreciated. The annual depreciation charge is deducted from each year's income. Thus the book rate of return depends on which items the accountant chooses to treat as capital investments and how rapidly they are depreciated.[1]

Now the merits of an investment project do not depend on how accountants classify the cash flows[2] and few companies these days make investment decisions just on the basis of the book rate of return. But managers know that the company's shareholders pay considerable attention to book measures of profitability and naturally they think (and worry) about how major projects would affect the company's book return. Those projects that will reduce the company's book return may be scrutinized more carefully by senior management.

You can see the dangers here. The company's book rate of return may not be a good measure of true profitability. It is also an *average* across all of the firm's activities. The average profitability of past investments is not usually the right hurdle for new investments. Think of a firm that has been exceptionally lucky and successful. Say its average book return is 24 percent, double shareholders' 12 percent opportunity cost of capital. Should it demand that all *new* investments offer 24 percent or better? Clearly not: That would mean passing up many positive-NPV opportunities with rates of return between 12 and 24 percent.

We will come back to the book rate of return in Chapter 12, when we look more closely at accounting measures of financial performance.

5.2 PAYBACK

Some companies require that the initial outlay on any project should be recoverable within a specified period. The **payback period** of a project is found by counting the number of years it takes before the cumulative forecasted cash flow equals the initial investment.

Consider the following three projects:

	Cash Flows (Rs.)				Payback	
Project	C_0	C_1	C_2	C_3	**Period (years)**	**NPV at 10%**
A	−2,000	500	500	5,000	3	+2,624
B	−2,000	500	1,800	0	2	−58
C	−2,000	1,800	500	0	2	+50

Project A involves an initial investment of Rs. 2,000 ($C_0 = -2{,}000$) followed by cash inflows during the next three years. Suppose the opportunity cost of capital is 10 percent. Then project A has an NPV of +Rs. 2,624:

$$\text{NPV(A)} = -2{,}000 + \frac{500}{1.10} + \frac{500}{1.10^2} + \frac{5{,}000}{1.10^3} = +\text{Rs. } 2{,}624$$

[1]This chapter's mini-case contains simple illustrations of how book rates of return are calculated and of the difference between accounting income and project cash flow. Read the case if you wish to refresh your understanding of these topics. Better still, do the case calculations.

[2]Of course, the depreciation method used for tax purposes does have cash consequences which should be taken into account in calculating NPV. We cover depreciation and taxes in the next chapter.

Project B also requires an initial investment of Rs. 2,000 but produces a cash inflow of Rs. 500 in year 1 and Rs. 1,800 in year 2. At a 10 percent opportunity cost of capital project B has an NPV of −Rs. 58:

$$\text{NPV(B)} = -2{,}000 + \frac{500}{1.10} + \frac{1{,}800}{1.10^2} = -\text{Rs. } 58$$

The third project, C, involves the same initial outlay as the other two projects but its first-period cash flow is larger. It has an NPV of +Rs. 50.

$$\text{NPV(C)} = -2{,}000 + \frac{1{,}800}{1.10} + \frac{500}{1.10^2} = +\text{Rs. } 50$$

The net present value rule tells us to accept projects A and C but to reject project B.

The Payback Rule

Now look at how rapidly each project pays back its initial investment. With project A you take three years to recover the Rs. 2,000 investment; with projects B and C you take only two years. If the firm used the *payback rule* with a cutoff period of two years, it would accept only projects B and C; if it used the payback rule with a cutoff period of three or more years, it would accept all three projects. Therefore, regardless of the choice of cutoff period, the payback rule gives answers different from the net present value rule.

You can see why payback can give misleading answers:

1. *The payback rule ignores all cash flows after the cutoff date.* If the cutoff date is two years, the payback rule rejects project A regardless of the size of the cash inflow in year 3.
2. *The payback rule gives equal weight to all cash flows before the cutoff date.* The payback rule says that projects B and C are equally attractive, but because C's cash inflows occur earlier, C has the higher net present value at any discount rate.

In order to use the payback rule, a firm has to decide on an appropriate cutoff date. If it uses the same cutoff regardless of project life, it will tend to accept many poor short-lived projects and reject many good long-lived ones.

Some companies discount the cash flows before they compute the payback period. The *discounted-payback rule* asks, How many periods does the project have to last in order to make sense in terms of net present value? This modification to the payback rule surmounts the objection that equal weight is given to all flows before the cutoff date. However, the discounted-payback rule still takes no account of any cash flows after the cutoff date.

The simplicity of payback makes it an easy device for *describing* investment projects. Managers talk casually about quick-payback projects in the same way that investors talk about high-P/E common stocks, but the payback period of a project does not usually govern their decisions. Some managers *do* use payback in judging investment proposals. We don't know why. Maybe these managers don't believe the more distant cash-flow forecasts and in frustration decide to discard entirely all forecasts beyond the payback period.

5.3 INTERNAL (OR DISCOUNTED-CASH-FLOW) RATE OF RETURN

Whereas payback and return on book are ad hoc measures, internal rate of return has a much more respectable ancestry and is recommended in many finance texts. If, therefore, we dwell more on its deficiencies, it is not because they are more numerous but because they are less obvious.

In Chapter 2 we noted that the net present value rule could also be expressed in terms of rate of return, which would lead to the following rule: "Accept investment opportunities offering rates of return in excess of their opportunity costs of capital." That statement, properly interpreted, is absolutely correct. However, interpretation is not always easy for long-lived investment projects.

There is no ambiguity in defining the true rate of return of an investment that generates a single payoff after one period:

$$\text{Rate of return} = \frac{\text{payoff}}{\text{investment}} - 1$$

Alternatively, we could write down the NPV of the investment and find that discount rate which makes NPV = 0.

$$\text{NPV} = C_0 + \frac{C_1}{1 + \text{discount rate}} = 0$$

implies

$$\text{Discount rate} = \frac{C_1}{-C_0} - 1$$

Of course C_1 is the payoff and $-C_0$ is the required investment, and so our two equations say exactly the same thing. *The discount rate that makes NPV = 0 is also the rate of return.*

Unfortunately, there is no wholly satisfactory way of defining the true rate of return of a long-lived asset. The best available concept is the so-called **discounted-cash-flow (DCF) rate of return** or **internal rate of return (IRR).** The internal rate of return is used frequently in finance. It can be a handy measure, but, as we shall see, it can also be a misleading measure. You should, therefore, know how to calculate it and how to use it properly.

Calculating the IRR

The internal rate of return is defined as the rate of discount which makes NPV = 0. This means that to find the IRR for an investment project lasting *T* years, we must solve for IRR in the following expression:

$$\text{NPV} = C_0 + \frac{C_1}{1 + \text{IRR}} + \frac{C_2}{(1 + \text{IRR})^2} + \cdots + \frac{C_T}{(1 + \text{IRR})^T} = 0$$

FIGURE 5.3

This project costs Rs. 4,000 and then produces cash inflows of Rs. 2,000 in year 1 and Rs. 4,000 in year 2. Its internal rate of return (IRR) is 28 percent, the rate of discount at which NPV is zero.

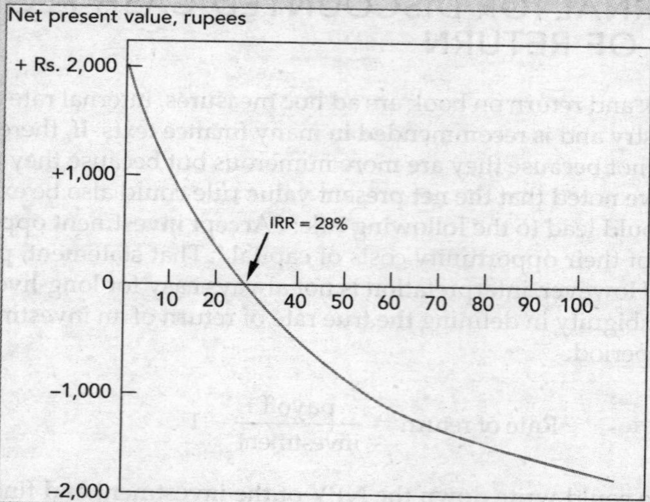

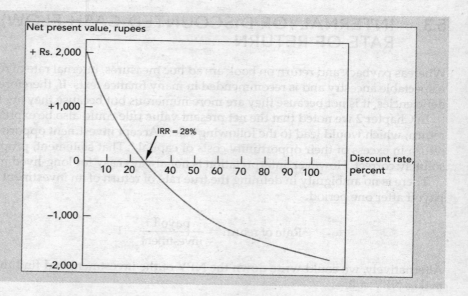

Actual calculation of IRR usually involves trial and error. For example, consider a project that produces the following flows:

Cash Flows (Rs.)		
C_0	C_1	C_2
−4,000	+2,000	+4,000

The internal rate of return is IRR in the equation

$$NPV = -4{,}000 + \frac{2{,}000}{1 + IRR} + \frac{4{,}000}{(1 + IRR)^2} = 0$$

Let us arbitrarily try a zero discount rate. In this case NPV is not zero but +Rs. 2,000:

$$NPV = -4{,}000 + \frac{2{,}000}{1.0} + \frac{4{,}000}{(1.0)^2} = +\text{Rs. } 2{,}000$$

The NPV is positive; therefore, the IRR must be greater than zero. The next step might be to try a discount rate of 50 percent. In this case net present value is −Rs. 889:

$$NPV = -4{,}000 + \frac{2{,}000}{1.50} + \frac{4{,}000}{(1.50)^2} = -\text{Rs. } 889$$

The NPV is negative; therefore, the IRR must be less than 50 percent. In Figure 5.3 we have plotted the net present values implied by a range of discount rates. From this we can see that a discount rate of 28 percent gives the desired net present value of zero. Therefore IRR is 28 percent.

The easiest way to calculate IRR, if you have to do it by hand, is to plot three or four combinations of NPV and discount rate on a graph like Figure 5.3, connect the points with a smooth line, and read off the discount rate at which NPV = 0. It is of course quicker and more accurate to use a computer or a specially programmed calculator, and this is what most financial managers do.

Some people confuse the internal rate of return and the opportunity cost of capital because both appear as discount rates in the NPV formula. The internal rate of return is a *profitability measure* that depends solely on the amount and timing of the project cash flows. The opportunity cost of capital is a *standard of profitability* which we use to calculate how much the project is worth. The opportunity cost of capital is established in capital markets. It is the expected rate of return offered by other assets with the same risk as the project being evaluated.

The IRR Rule

The internal rate of return rule is to accept an investment project if the opportunity cost of capital is less than the internal rate of return. You can see the reasoning behind this idea if you look again at Figure 5.3. If the opportunity cost of capital is less than the 28 percent IRR, then the project has a *positive* NPV when discounted at the opportunity cost of capital. If it is equal to the IRR, the project has a *zero* NPV. And if it is greater than the IRR, the project has a *negative* NPV. Therefore, when we compare the opportunity cost of capital with the IRR on our project, we are effectively asking whether our project has a positive NPV. This is true not only for our example. The rule will give the same answer as the net present value rule *whenever the NPV of a project is a smoothly declining function of the discount rate.*

Many firms use internal rate of return as a criterion in preference to net present value. We think that this is a pity. Although, properly stated, the two criteria are formally equivalent, the internal rate of return rule contains several pitfalls.

Pitfall 1—Lending or Borrowing?

Not all cash-flow streams have NPVs that decline as the discount rate increases. Consider the following projects A and B:

	Cash Flows (Rs.)			
Project	C_0	C_1	IRR	NPV at 10%
A	−1,000	+1,500	+50%	+364
B	+1,000	−1,500	+50%	−364

Each project has an IRR of 50 percent. (In other words, −1,000 + 1,500/1.50 = 0 *and* + 1,000 − 1,500/1.50 = 0.)

Does this mean that they are equally attractive? Clearly not, for in the case of A, where we are initially paying out Rs. 1,000, we are *lending* money at 50 percent; in the case of B, where we are initially receiving Rs. 1,000, we are *borrowing* money at 50 percent. When we lend money, we want a *high* rate of return; when we borrow money, we want a *low* rate of return.

If you plot a graph like Figure 5.3 for project B, you will find that NPV increases as the discount rate increases. Obviously the internal rate of return rule, as we stated it above, won't work in this case; we have to look for an IRR *less* than the opportunity cost of capital.

Pitfall 2—Multiple Rates of Return

Helmsley Iron is proposing to develop a new strip mine in Western Australia. The mine involves an initial investment of $A 60 million and is expected to produce a cash inflow of $A 12 million a year for the next nine years. At the end of that time the company will incur $A 15 million of cleanup costs. Thus the cash flows from the project are:

Cash flows (millions of Australian dollars)				
C_0	C_1	. . .	C_9	C_{10}
−60	12		12	−15

Helmsley calculates the project's IRR and its NPV as follows:

IRR (%)	NPV at 10%
−44.0 *and* 11.6	$A 3.3 million

Note that there are *two* discount rates that make NPV = 0. That is, *each* of the following statements holds:

$$\text{NPV} = -60 + \frac{12}{.56} + \frac{12}{.56^2} + \cdots + \frac{12}{.56^9} - \frac{15}{.56^{10}} = 0$$

$$\text{NPV} = -60 + \frac{12}{1.116} + \frac{12}{1.116^2} + \cdots + \frac{12}{1.116^9} - \frac{15}{1.116^{10}} = 0$$

In other words, the investment has an IRR of both −44.0 *and* 11.6 percent. Figure 5.4 shows how this comes about. As the discount rate increases, NPV initially rises and then declines. The reason for this is the double change in the sign of the cash-flow stream. There can be as many internal rates of return for a project as there are changes in the sign of the cash flows.[3]

Decommissioning costs are an obvious reason that cash flows can go from positive to negative, but you can probably think of a number of other cases where the company needs to plan for later expenditures. Ships periodically need to go into dry dock for a refit, hotels may receive a major face-lift, machine parts may need replacement, and so on.

Whenever the cash-flow stream is expected to change sign more than once, the company typically sees more than one IRR.

As if this is not difficult enough, there are also cases in which *no* internal rate of return exists. For example, project C has a positive net present value at all discount rates:

	Cash Flows ($)				
Project	C_0	C_1	C_2	IRR (%)	NPV at 10%
C	+1,000	−3,000	+2,500	None	+339

[3]By Descartes's "rule of signs" there can be as many different solutions to a polynomial as there are changes of sign. For a discussion of the problem of multiple rates of return, see J. H. Lorie and L. J. Savage, "Three Problems in Rationing Capital," *Journal of Business* 28 (October 1955), pp. 229–239; and E. Solomon, "The Arithmetic of Capital Budgeting," *Journal of Business* 29 (April 1956), pp. 124–129.

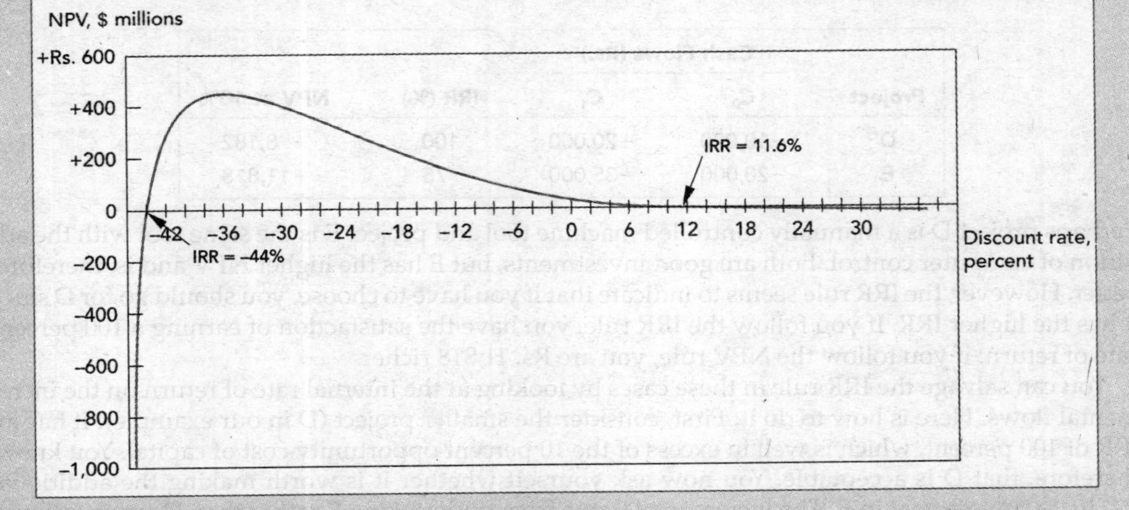

FIGURE 5.4

Helmsley Iron's mine has two internal rates of return. NPV = 0 when the discount rate is −44 percent *and* when it is +11.6 percent.

A number of adaptations of the IRR rule have been devised for such cases. Not only are they inadequate, but they also are unnecessary, for the simple solution is to use net present value.[4]

Pitfall 3—Mutually Exclusive Projects

Firms often have to choose from among several alternative ways of doing the same job or using the same facility. In other words, they need to choose from among **mutually exclusive projects.** Here too the IRR rule can be misleading.

---

[4]Companies sometimes get around the problem of multiple rates of return by discounting the later cash flows back at the cost of capital until there remains only one change in the sign of the cash flows. A *modified internal rate of return* can then be calculated on this revised series. In our example, the modified IRR is calculated as follows:

1. Calculate the present value of the year 9 and 10 cash flows in year 8:

$$\text{PV in year 9} = +12/1.1 - 15/1.1^2 = -1.49$$

2. Add to the year 8 cash flow the present value of subsequent cash flows:

$$C_8 + \text{PV (subsequent cash flows)} = +12 - 1.49 = 10.51$$

3. Since there is now only one change in the sign of the cash flows, the revised series has a unique rate of return, which is 11.5 percent:

$$\text{NPV} = -60 + \frac{12}{1.115} + \frac{12}{1.115^2} + \cdots + \frac{12}{1.115^7} + \frac{10.51}{1.115^8} = 0$$

Since the modified IRR of 11.5 percent is greater than the cost of capital (and the initial cash flow is negative), the project has a positive NPV when valued at the cost of capital.

Of course, it would be much easier in such cases to abandon the IRR rule and just calculate project NPV.

Consider projects D and E:

	Cash Flows (Rs.)			
Project	C_0	C_1	IRR (%)	NPV at 10%
D	−10,000	+20,000	100	+ 8,182
E	−20,000	+35,000	75	+11,818

Perhaps project D is a manually controlled machine tool and project E is the same tool with the addition of computer control. Both are good investments, but E has the higher NPV and is, therefore, better. However, the IRR rule seems to indicate that if you have to choose, you should go for D since it has the higher IRR. If you follow the IRR rule, you have the satisfaction of earning a 100 percent rate of return; if you follow the NPV rule, you are Rs. 11,818 richer.

You can salvage the IRR rule in these cases by looking at the internal rate of return on the incremental flows. Here is how to do it: First, consider the smaller project (D in our example). It has an IRR of 100 percent, which is well in excess of the 10 percent opportunity cost of capital. You know, therefore, that D is acceptable. You now ask yourself whether it is worth making the additional Rs. 10,000 investment in E. The incremental flows from undertaking E rather than D are as follows:

	Cash Flows (Rs.)			
Project	C_0	C_1	IRR (%)	NPV at 10%
E − D	−10,000	+15,000	50	+3,636

The IRR on the incremental investment is 50 percent, which is also well in excess of the 10 percent opportunity cost of capital. So you should prefer project E to project D.[5]

Unless you look at the incremental expenditure, IRR is unreliable in ranking projects of different scale. It is also unreliable in ranking projects which offer different patterns of cash flow over time. For example, suppose the firm can take project F *or* project G but not both (ignore H for the moment):

	Cash Flows (Rs.)								
Project	C_0	C_1	C_2	C_3	C_4	C_5	Etc.	IRR (%)	NPV at 10%
F	−9,000	+6,000	+5,000	+4,000	0	0	. . .	33	3,592
G	−9,000	+1,800	+1,800	+1,800	+1,800	+1,800	. . .	20	9,000
H		−6,000	+1,200	+1,200	+1,200	+1,200	. . .	20	6,000

Project F has a higher IRR, but project G has the higher NPV. Figure 5.5 shows why the two rules give different answers. The blue line gives the net present value of project F at different rates of discount. Since a discount rate of 33 percent produces a net present value of zero, this is the internal rate of return for project F. Similarly, the green line shows the net present value of project G at different discount rates. The IRR of project G is 20 percent. (We assume project G's cash flows continue

[5]You may, however, find that you have jumped out of the frying pan into the fire. The series of incremental cash flows may involve several changes in sign. In this case there are likely to be multiple IRRs and you will be forced to use the NPV rule after all.

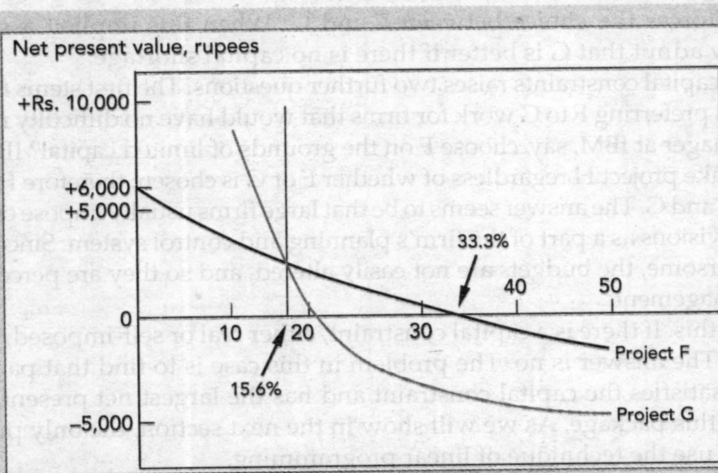

FIGURE 5.5

The IRR of project F exceeds that of project G, but the NPV of project F is higher *only* if the discount rate is greater than 15.6 percent.

indefinitely.) Note that project G has a higher NPV so long as the opportunity cost of capital is less than 15.6 percent.

The reason that IRR is misleading is that the total cash inflow of project G is larger but tends to occur later. Therefore, when the discount rate is low, G has the higher NPV; when the discount rate is high, F has the higher NPV. (You can see from Figure 5.5 that the two projects have the *same* NPV when the discount rate is 15.6 percent.) The internal rates of return on the two projects tell us that at a discount rate of 20 percent G has a zero NPV (IRR = 20 percent) and F has a positive NPV. Thus if the opportunity cost of capital were 20 percent, investors would place a higher value on the shorter-lived project F. But in our example the opportunity cost of capital is not 20 percent but 10 percent. Investors are prepared to pay relatively high prices for longer-lived securities, and so they will pay a relatively high price for the longer-lived project. At a 10 percent cost of capital, an investment in G has an NPV of Rs. 9,000 and an investment in F has an NPV of only Rs. 3,592.[6]

This is a favorite example of ours. We have gotten many businesspeople's reactions to it. When asked to choose between F and G, many choose F. The reason seems to be the rapid payback generated by project F. In other words, they believe that if they take F, they will also be able to take a later project like H (note that H can be financed using the cash flows from F), whereas if they take G, they won't have money enough for H. In other words they implicitly assume that it is a

[6]It is often suggested that the choice between the net present value rule and the internal rate of return rule should depend on the probable reinvestment rate. This is wrong. The prospective return on another *independent* investment should *never* be allowed to influence the investment decision. For a discussion of the reinvestment assumption see A. A. Alchian, "The Rate of Interest, Fisher's Rate of Return over Cost and Keynes' Internal Rate of Return," *American Economic Review* 45 (December 1955), pp. 938–942.

shortage of capital which forces the choice between F and G. When this implicit assumption is brought out, they usually admit that G is better if there is no capital shortage.

But the introduction of capital constraints raises two further questions. The first stems from the fact that most of the executives preferring F to G work for firms that would have no difficulty raising more capital. Why would a manager at IBM, say, choose F on the grounds of limited capital? IBM can raise plenty of capital and can take project H regardless of whether F or G is chosen; therefore H should not affect the choice between F and G. The answer seems to be that large firms usually impose capital budgets on divisions and subdivisions as a part of the firm's planning and control system. Since the system is complicated and cumbersome, the budgets are not easily altered, and so they are perceived as real constraints by middle management.

The second question is this. If there is a capital constraint, either real or self-imposed, should IRR be used to rank projects? The answer is no. The problem in this case is to find that package of investment projects which satisfies the capital constraint and has the largest net present value. The IRR rule will not identify this package. As we will show in the next section, the only practical and general way to do so is to use the technique of linear programming.

When we have to choose between projects F and G, it is easiest to compare the net present values. But if your heart is set on the IRR rule, you can use it as long as you look at the internal rate of return on the incremental flows. The procedure is exactly the same as we showed above. First, you check that project F has a satisfactory IRR. Then you look at the return on the additional investment in G.

	Cash Flows (Rs.)								
Project	C_0	C_1	C_2	C_3	C_4	C_5	Etc.	IRR (%)	NPV at 10%
G − F	0	−4,200	−3,200	−2,200	+1,800	+1,800	. . .	15.6	+5,408

The IRR on the incremental investment in G is 15.6 percent. Since this is greater than the opportunity cost of capital, you should undertake G rather than F.

Pitfall 4—What Happens When We Can't Finesse the Term Structure of Interest Rates?

We have simplified our discussion of capital budgeting by assuming that the opportunity cost of capital is the same for all the cash flows, C_1, C_2, C_3, etc. Remember our most general formula for calculating net present value:

$$\text{NPV} = C_0 + \frac{C_1}{1 + r_1} + \frac{C_2}{(1 + r_2)^2} + \frac{C_3}{(1 + r_3)^3} + \cdots$$

In other words, we discount C_1 at the opportunity cost of capital for one year, C_2 at the opportunity cost of capital for two years, and so on. The IRR rule tells us to accept a project if the IRR is greater than the opportunity cost of capital. But what do we do when we have several opportunity costs? Do we compare IRR with $r_1, r_2, r_3, \ldots$? Actually we would have to compute a complex weighted average of these rates to obtain a number comparable to IRR.

What does this mean for capital budgeting? It means trouble for the IRR rule whenever the term structure of interest rates becomes important. In a situation where it is important, we have to compare the project IRR with the expected IRR (yield to maturity) offered by a traded security that (1) is equivalent in risk to the project and (2) offers the same time pattern of cash flows as the project. Such a comparison is easier said than done.

Many firms use the IRR, thereby implicitly assuming that there is no difference between short-term and long-term rates of interest. They do this for the same reason that we have so far finessed the term structure: simplicity.[7]

The Verdict on IRR

We have given four examples of things that can go wrong with IRR. We spent much less space on payback or return on book. Does this mean that IRR is worse than the other two measures? Quite the contrary. There is little point in dwelling on the deficiencies of payback or return on book. They are clearly ad hoc measures which often lead to silly conclusions. The IRR rule has a much more respectable ancestry. It is less easy to use than NPV, but, used properly, it gives the same answer.

Nowadays few large corporations use the return on book (accounting rate of return) as their primary measure of project attractiveness[8]. Most use discounted cash flow or "DCF," and for many companies DCF means IRR, not NPV. For "normal" investment projects with an initial cash outflow followed by a series of cash inflows, there is no difficulty in using the internal rate of return to make a simple accept/reject decision. However, we think that financial managers need to worry more about Pitfall 3. Financial managers never see all possible projects. Most projects are proposed by operating managers. A company that instructs nonfinancial managers to look first at project IRRs prompts a search for those projects with the highest IRRs rather than the highest NPVs. It also encourages managers to *modify* projects so that their IRRs are higher. Where do you typically find the highest IRRs? In short-lived projects requiring little up-front investment. Such projects may not add much to the value of the firm.

We don't know why so many companies pay such close attention to the internal rate of return, but we suspect that it may reflect the fact that management does not trust the forecasts it receives. Suppose that two plant managers approach you with proposals for two new investments. Both have a positive NPV of Rs. 1,400 at the company's 8 percent cost of capital, but you nevertheless decide to accept project A and reject B. Are you being irrational?

The cash flows for the two projects and their NPVs are set out in the table below. You can see that, although both proposals have the same NPV, project A involves an investment of Rs. 9,000, while B requires an investment of Rs. 9 million. Investing Rs. 9,000 to make Rs. 1,400 is clearly an attractive proposition, and this shows up in A's IRR of nearly 16 percent. Investing Rs. 9 million to make Rs. 1,400 might also be worth doing if you could be *sure* of the plant manager's forecasts, but there is almost no room for error in project B. You could spend time and money checking the cash-flow forecasts, but is it really worth the effort? Most managers would look at the IRR and decide that, if the cost of capital is 8 percent, a project that offers a return of 8.01 percent is not worth the worrying time.

	Cash Flows (Rs. thousands)					
Project	C_0	C_1	C_2	C_3	NPV at 8%	IRR (%)
A	−9.0	2.9	4.0	5.4	1.4	15.58
B	−9,000	2,560	3,540	4,530	1.4	8.01

[7]In Chapter 9 we will look at some other cases in which it would be misleading to use the same discount rate for both short-term and long-term cash flows.

[8]In figure 5.2 if you compare the Indian survey findings with the U.S. survey findings,you will notice one major difference. NPV rule is more popular than the payback rule in the U.S. Not so in India. In India, both the measures seem to be equally popular with the CFOs.

5.4 CHOOSING CAPITAL INVESTMENTS WHEN RESOURCES ARE LIMITED

Our entire discussion of methods of capital budgeting has rested on the proposition that the wealth of a firm's shareholders is highest if the firm accepts *every* project that has a positive net present value. Suppose, however, that there are limitations on the investment program that prevent the company from undertaking all such projects. Economists call this *capital rationing*. When capital is rationed, we need a method of selecting the package of projects that is within the company's resources yet gives the highest possible net present value.

An Easy Problem in Capital Rationing

Let us start with a simple example. The opportunity cost of capital is 10 percent, and our company has the following opportunities:

	Cash Flows (Rs. millions)			
Project	C_0	C_1	C_2	**NPV at 10%**
A	−10	+30	+5	21
B	−5	+5	+20	16
C	−5	+5	+15	12

All three projects are attractive, but suppose that the firm is limited to spending Rs. 10 million. In that case, it can invest *either* in project A *or* in projects B and C, but it cannot invest in all three. Although individually B and C have lower net present values than project A, when taken together they have the higher net present value. Here we cannot choose between projects solely on the basis of net present values. When funds are limited, we need to concentrate on getting the biggest bang for our buck. In other words, we must pick the projects that offer the highest net present value per rupee of initial outlay. This ratio is known as the **profitability index:**[9]

$$\text{Profitability index} = \frac{\text{net present value}}{\text{investment}}$$

For our three projects the profitability index is calculated as follows:[10]

Project	Investment (Rs. millions)	NPV (Rs. millions)	Profitability Index
A	10	21	2.1
B	5	16	3.2
C	5	12	2.4

[9]If a project requires outlays in two or more periods, the denominator should be the present value of the outlays. A few companies do not discount the benefits or costs before calculating the profitability index. The less said about these companies the better.

[10]Sometimes the profitability index is defined as the ratio of the present value to initial outlay, that is, as PV/investment. This measure is also known as the *benefit–cost ratio*. To calculate the benefit–cost ratio, simply add 1.0 to each profitability index. Project rankings are unchanged.

Project B has the highest profitability index and C has the next highest. Therefore, if our budget limit is Rs. 10 million, we should accept these two projects.[11]

Unfortunately, there are some limitations to this simple ranking method. One of the most serious is that it breaks down whenever more than one resource is rationed.[12] For example, suppose that the firm can raise only Rs. 10 million for investment in *each* of years 0 and 1 and that the menu of possible projects is expanded to include an investment next year in project D:

	Cash Flows (Rs. millions)				
Project	C_0	C_1	C_2	NPV at 10%	Profitability Index
A	−10	+30	+5	21	2.1
B	−5	+5	+20	16	3.2
C	−5	+5	+15	12	2.4
D	0	−40	+60	13	0.4

One strategy is to accept projects B and C; however, if we do this, we cannot also accept D, which costs more than our budget limit for period 1. An alternative is to accept project A in period 0. Although this has a lower net present value than the combination of B and C, it provides a Rs. 30 million positive cash flow in period 1. When this is added to the Rs. 10 million budget, we can also afford to undertake D next year. A and D have *lower* profitability indexes than B and C, but they have a *higher* total net present value.

The reason that ranking on the profitability index fails in this example is that resources are constrained in each of two periods. In fact, this ranking method is inadequate whenever there is *any* other constraint on the choice of projects. This means that it cannot cope with cases in which two projects are mutually exclusive or in which one project is dependent on another.

For example, suppose that you have a long menu of possible projects starting this year and next. There is a limit on how much you can invest in each year. Perhaps also you can't undertake both projects alpha and beta (they both require the same piece of land), and you can't invest in project gamma unless you invest in delta (gamma is simply an add-on to delta). You need to find the package of projects that satisfies all these constraints and gives the highest NPV.

One way to tackle such a problem is to work through all possible combinations of projects. For each combination you first check whether the projects satisfy the constraints and then calculate the net present value. But it is smarter to recognize that linear programming (LP) techniques are specially designed to search through such possible combinations and that you can hand the problem to a computer that is equipped to solve LPs.[13]

[11]If a project has a positive profitability index, it must also have a positive NPV. Therefore, firms sometimes use the profitability index to select projects when capital is *not* limited. However, like the IRR, the profitability index can be misleading when used to choose between mutually exclusive projects. For example, suppose you were forced to choose between (1) investing Rs. 100 in a project whose payoffs have a present value of Rs. 200 or (2) investing Rs. 1 million in a project whose payoffs have a present value of Rs.1.5 million. The first investment has the higher profitability index; the second makes you richer.

[12]It may also break down if it causes some money to be left over. It might be better to spend all the available funds even if this involves accepting a project with a slightly lower NPV.

[13]On our Web site at **www.mhhe.com/bmam8e** we show how linear programming can be used to select from the four projects in our earlier example. For more detail on the application of linear programming to capital budgeting problems, see H. M. Weingartner, *Mathematical Programming and the Analysis of Capital Budgeting Problems* (Englewood Cliffs, NJ: Prentice-Hall, Inc., 1963).

Uses of Capital Rationing Models

Linear programming models seem tailor-made for solving capital budgeting problems when resources are limited. Why then are they not universally accepted either in theory or in practice? One reason is that these models can turn out to be very complex. Second, as with any sophisticated long-range planning tool, there is the general problem of getting good data. It is just not worth applying costly, sophisticated methods to poor data. Furthermore, these models are based on the assumption that all future investment opportunities are known. In reality, the discovery of investment ideas is an unfolding process.

Our most serious misgivings center on the basic assumption that capital is limited. When we come to discuss company financing, we shall see that most large corporations do not face capital rationing and can raise large sums of money on fair terms. Why then do many company presidents tell their subordinates that capital is limited? If they are right, the capital market is seriously imperfect. What then are they doing maximizing NPV?[14] We might be tempted to suppose that if capital is not rationed, they do not *need* to use linear programming and, if it is rationed, then surely they *ought* not to use it. But that would be too quick a judgment. Let us look at this problem more deliberately.

Soft Rationing Many firms' capital constraints are "soft." They reflect no imperfections in capital markets. Instead they are provisional limits adopted by management as an aid to financial control.

Some ambitious divisional managers habitually overstate their investment opportunities. Rather than trying to distinguish which projects really are worthwhile, headquarters may find it simpler to impose an upper limit on divisional expenditures and thereby force the divisions to set their own priorities. In such instances budget limits are a rough but effective way of dealing with biased cash-flow forecasts. In other cases management may believe that very rapid corporate growth could impose intolerable strains on management and the organization. Since it is difficult to quantify such constraints explicitly, the budget limit may be used as a proxy.

Because such budget limits have nothing to do with any inefficiency in the capital market, there is no contradiction in using an LP model in the division to maximize net present value subject to the budget constraint. On the other hand, there is not much point in elaborate selection procedures if the cash-flow forecasts of the division are seriously biased.

Even if capital is not rationed, other resources may be. The availability of management time, skilled labor, or even other capital equipment often constitutes an important constraint on a company's growth.

Hard Rationing Soft rationing should never cost the firm anything. If capital constraints become tight enough to hurt—in the sense that projects with significant positive NPVs are passed up—then the firm raises more money and loosens the constraint. But what if it *can't* raise more money—what if it faces *hard* rationing?

Hard rationing implies market imperfections, but that does not necessarily mean we have to throw away net present value as a criterion for capital budgeting. It depends on the nature of the imperfection.

Arizona Aquaculture, Inc. (AAI), borrows as much as the banks will lend it, yet it still has good investment opportunities. This is not hard rationing so long as AAI can issue stock. But perhaps it

[14] Don't forget that in Chapter 2 we had to assume perfect capital markets to derive the NPV rule.

can't. Perhaps the founder and majority shareholder vetoes the idea from fear of losing control of the firm. Perhaps a stock issue would bring costly red tape or legal complications.[15]

This does not invalidate the NPV rule. AAI's *shareholders* can borrow or lend, sell their shares, or buy more. They have free access to security markets. The type of portfolio they hold is independent of AAI's financing or investment decisions. The only way AAI can help its shareholders is to make them richer. Thus AAI should invest its available cash in the package of projects having the largest aggregate net present value.

A barrier between the firm and capital markets does not undermine net present value so long as the barrier is the *only* market imperfection. The important thing is that the firm's *shareholders* have free access to well-functioning capital markets.

The net present value rule *is* undermined when imperfections restrict shareholders' portfolio choice. Suppose that Nevada Aquaculture, Inc. (NAI), is solely owned by its founder, Alexander Turbot. Mr. Turbot has no cash or credit remaining, but he is convinced that expansion of his operation is a high-NPV investment. He has tried to sell stock but has found that prospective investors, skeptical of prospects for fish farming in the desert, offer him much less than he thinks his firm is worth. For Mr. Turbot capital markets hardly exist. It makes little sense for him to discount prospective cash flows at a market opportunity cost of capital.

[15] A majority owner who is "locked in" and has much personal wealth tied up in AAI may be effectively cut off from capital markets. The NPV rule may not make sense to such an owner, though it will to the other shareholders.

SUMMARY

If you are going to persuade your company to use the net present value rule, you must be prepared to explain why other rules may *not* lead to correct decisions. That is why we have examined three alternative investment criteria in this chapter.

Some firms look at the book rate of return on the project. In this case the company decides which cash payments are capital expenditures and picks the appropriate rate to depreciate these expenditures. It then calculates the ratio of book income to the book value of the investment. Few companies nowadays base their investment decision simply on the book rate of return, but shareholders pay attention to book measures of firm profitability and some managers therefore look with a jaundiced eye on projects that would damage the company's book rate of return.

Some companies use the payback method to make investment decisions. In other words, they accept only those projects that recover their initial investment within some specified period. Payback is an ad hoc rule. It ignores the timing of cash flows within the payback period, and it ignores subsequent cash flows entirely. It therefore takes no account of the opportunity cost of capital.

The internal rate of return (IRR) is defined as the rate of discount at which a project would have zero NPV. It is a handy measure and widely used in finance; you should therefore know how to calculate it. The IRR rule states that companies should accept any investment offering an IRR in excess of the opportunity cost of capital. The IRR rule is, like net present value, a technique based on discounted cash flows. It will therefore give the correct answer if properly used. The problem is that it is easily misapplied. There are four things to look out for:

1. *Lending or borrowing*? If a project offers positive cash flows followed by negative flows, NPV can *rise* as the discount rate is increased. You should accept such projects if their IRR is *less* than the opportunity cost of capital.
2. *Multiple rates of return*. If there is more than one change in the sign of the cash flows, the project may have several IRRs or no IRR at all.
3. *Mutually exclusive projects*. The IRR rule may give the wrong ranking of mutually exclusive projects that differ in economic life or in scale of required investment. If you insist on using IRR to rank mutually exclusive projects, you must examine the IRR on each incremental investment.
4. *The cost of capital for near-term cash flows may be different from the cost for distant cash flows*. The IRR rule requires you to compare the project's IRR with the opportunity cost of capital. But sometimes there is an opportunity cost of capital for one-year cash flows, a different cost of capital for two-year cash flows, and so on. In these cases there is no simple yardstick for evaluating the IRR of a project.

If you are going to the expense of collecting cash-flow forecasts, you might as well use them properly. Ad hoc criteria should therefore have no role in the firm's decisions, and the net present value rule should be employed in preference to other techniques. Having said that, we must be careful not to exaggerate the payoff of proper technique. Technique is important, but it is by no means the only determinant of the success of a capital expenditure program. If the forecasts of cash flows are poor, even the most careful application of the net present value rule will fail.

In developing the NPV rule, we assumed that the company can maximize shareholder wealth by accepting every project that is worth more than it costs. But, if capital is strictly limited, then it may not be possible to take every project with a positive NPV. If capital is rationed in only one period, then the firm should follow a simple rule: Calculate each project's profitability index, which is the project's net present value per rupee of investment. Then pick the projects with the highest profitability indexes until you run out of capital. Unfortunately, this procedure fails when capital is rationed in more than one period or when there are other constraints on project choice. The only general solution is linear programming.

Hard capital rationing always reflects a market imperfection—a barrier between the firm and capital markets. If that barrier also implies that the firm's shareholders lack free access to a well-functioning capital market, the very foundations of net present value crumble. Fortunately, hard rationing is rare for corporations in the United States. Many firms do use soft capital rationing, however. That is, they set up self-imposed limits as a means of financial planning and control.

FURTHER READING

For a *survey of capital budgeting procedures*, see:

J. Graham and C. Harvey, "How CFOs Make Capital Budgeting and Capital Structure Decisions," *Journal of Applied Corporate Finance*, 15 (Spring 2002), pp. 8–23.

CONCEPT REVIEW QUESTIONS

1. "Most firms use only one measure of a project's attractiveness." True or false? (page 87)
2. "Payback gives too much weight to cash flows that occur after the cutoff date." True or false? (page 90)
3. Your CEO insists that all projects should have a payback period of four years or less. As a result, attractive long-lived projects are being turned down. The CEO is willing to switch to a discounted payback with the same four-year cutoff period. Would this be an improvement? (page 90)

For additional Concept Review Questions, please visit us at www.mhhe.com/bmam8e or refer to your Student CD.

QUIZ

1. a. What is the payback period on each of the following projects?

	Cash Flows (Rs.)				
Project	C_0	C_1	C_2	C_3	C_4
A	−5,000	+1,000	+1,000	+3,000	0
B	−1,000	0	+1,000	+2,000	+3,000
C	−5,000	+1,000	+1,000	+3,000	+5,000

b. *Given* that you wish to use the payback rule with a cutoff period of two years, which projects would you accept?
c. If you use a cutoff period of three years, which projects would you accept?
d. If the opportunity cost of capital is 10 percent, which projects have positive NPVs?
e. "If a firm uses a single cutoff period for all projects, it is likely to accept too many short-lived projects." True or false?
f. If the firm uses the discounted-payback rule, will it accept any negative-NPV projects? Will it turn down positive-NPV projects? Explain.

2. Write down the equation defining a project's internal rate of return (IRR). In practice how is IRR calculated?
3. a. Calculate the net present value of the following project for discount rates of 0, 50, and 100 percent:

Cash Flows (Rs.)		
C_0	C_1	C_2
−6,750	+4,500	+18,000

b. What is the IRR of the project?

4. You have the chance to participate in a project that produces the following cash flows:

Cash Flows (Rs.)		
C_0	C_1	C_2
+5,000	+4,000	−11,000

The internal rate of return is 13 percent. If the opportunity cost of capital is 10 percent, would you accept the offer?

5. Consider a project with the following cash flows:

C_0	C_1	C_2
−100	+200	−75

a. How many internal rates of return does this project have?
b. Which of the following numbers is the project IRR:
(i) −50%; (ii) −12%; (iii) +5%; (iv) +50%?
c. The opportunity cost of capital is 20 percent. Is this an attractive project? Briefly explain.

6. Consider projects Alpha and Beta:

	Cash Flows (Rs.)			
Project	C_0	C_1	C_2	IRR (%)
Alpha	−400,000	+241,000	+293,000	21
Beta	−200,000	+131,000	+172,000	31

The opportunity cost of capital is 8 percent.

Suppose you can undertake Alpha or Beta, but not both. Use the IRR rule to make the choice. *Hint:* What's the incremental investment in Alpha?

7. Suppose you have the following investment opportunities, but only Rs. 90,000 available for investment. Which projects should you take?

Project	NPV	Investment
1	5,000	10,000
2	5,000	5,000
3	10,000	90,000
4	15,000	60,000
5	15,000	75,000
6	3,000	15,000

PRACTICE QUESTIONS

1. Consider the following projects:

	Cash Flows (Rs.)					
Project	C_0	C_1	C_2	C_3	C_4	C_5
A	−1,000	+1,000	0	0	0	0
B	−2,000	+1,000	+1,000	+4,000	+1,000	+1,000
C	−3,000	+1,000	+1,000	0	+1,000	+1,000

a. If the opportunity cost of capital is 10 percent, which projects have a positive NPV?
b. Calculate the payback period for each project.
c. Which project(s) would a firm using the payback rule accept if the cutoff period is three years?

2. Respond to the following comments:
   a. "I like the IRR rule. I can use it to rank projects without having to specify a discount rate."
   b. "I like the payback rule. As long as the minimum payback period is short, the rule makes sure that the company takes no borderline projects. That reduces risk."
3. Calculate the IRR (or IRRs) for the following project:

C_0	C_1	C_2	C_3
−3,000	+3,500	+4,000	−4,000

   For what range of discount rates does the project have positive NPV?
4. Consider the following two mutually exclusive projects:

	Cash Flows (Rs.)			
Project	C_0	C_1	C_2	C_3
A	−100	+60	+60	0
B	−110	0	0	+140

   a. Calculate the NPV of each project for discount rates of 0, 10, and 20 percent. Plot these on a graph with NPV on the vertical axis and discount rate on the horizontal axis.
   b. What is the approximate IRR for each project?
   c. In what circumstances should the company accept project A?
   d. Calculate the NPV of the incremental investment (B − A) for discount rates of 0, 10, and 20 percent. Plot these on your graph. Show that the circumstances in which you would accept A are also those in which the IRR on the incremental investment is less than the opportunity cost of capital.
5. Mr. Cyrus Clops, the president of Giant Enterprises, has to make a choice between two possible investments:

	Cash Flows (Rs. thousands)			
Project	C_0	C_1	C_2	**IRR (%)**
A	−400	+250	+300	23
B	−200	+140	+179	36

   The opportunity cost of capital is 9 percent. Mr. Clops is tempted to take B, which has the higher IRR.
   a. Explain to Mr. Clops why this is not the correct procedure.
   b. Show him how to adapt the IRR rule to choose the best project.
   c. Show him that this project also has the higher NPV.
6. The Titanic Shipbuilding Company has a noncancelable contract to build a small cargo vessel. Construction involves a cash outlay of Rs. 250,000 at the end of each of the next two years. At the end of the third year the company will receive payment of Rs. 650,000. The company can speed up construction by working an extra shift. In this case there will be a cash outlay of Rs. 550,000 at the end of the first year followed by a cash payment of Rs. 650,000 at the end of the second year. Use the IRR rule to show the (approximate) range of opportunity costs of capital at which the company should work the extra shift.

7. Look again at projects D and E in Section 5.3. Assume that the projects are mutually exclusive and that the opportunity cost of capital is 10 percent.
   a. Calculate the profitability index for each project.
   b. Show how the profitability-index rule can be used to select the superior project.
8. Borghia Pharmaceuticals has Rs. 1 million allocated for capital expenditures. Which of the following projects should the company accept to stay within the Rs. 1 million budget? How much does the budget limit cost the company in terms of its market value? The opportunity cost of capital for each project is 11 percent.

Project	Investment (Rs. thousands)	NPV (Rs. thousands)	IRR (%)
1	300	66	17.2
2	200	–4	10.7
3	250	43	16.6
4	100	14	12.1
5	100	7	11.8
6	350	63	18.0
7	400	48	13.5

CHALLENGE QUESTIONS

1. Some people believe firmly, even passionately, that ranking projects on IRR is OK if each project's cash flows can be reinvested at the project's IRR. They also say that the NPV rule "assumes that cash flows are reinvested at the opportunity cost of capital." Think carefully about these statements. Are they true? Are they helpful?
2. Look again at the project cash flows in Practice Question 3. Calculate the modified IRR as defined in footnote 4 in Section 5.3. Assume the cost of capital is 12 percent.

   Now try the following variation on the modified IRR concept. Figure out the fraction x such that x times C_1 and C_2 has the same present value as (minus) C_3.

$$xC_1 + \frac{xC_2}{1.12} = -\frac{C_3}{1.12^2}$$

   Define the modified project IRR as the solution of

$$C_0 + \frac{(1-x)C_1}{1+\text{IRR}} + \frac{(1-x)C_2}{(1+\text{IRR})^2} = 0$$

   Now you have two modified IRRs. Which is more meaningful? If you can't decide, what do you conclude about the usefulness of modified IRRs?
3. Consider the following capital rationing problem:

Project	C_0	C_1	C_2	NPV
W	–10,000	–10,000	0	+6,700
X	0	–20,000	+5,000	+9,000
Y	–10,000	+5,000	+5,000	+0
Z	–15,000	+5,000	+4,000	–1,500
Financing available	20,000	20,000	20,000	

   Set up this problem as a linear program and solve it.

   You can allow partial investments, that is, $0 \le x \le 1$. Calculate and interpret the shadow prices[16] on the capital constraints.

[16] A shadow price is the marginal change in the objective for a marginal change in the constraint.

MINI-CASE

Vegetron's CFO Calls Again

(The first episode of this story was presented in Section 5.1.)

Later that afternoon, Vegetron's CFO bursts into your office in a state of anxious confusion. The problem, he explains, is a last-minute proposal for a change in the design of the fermentation tanks that Vegetron will build to extract hydrated zirconium from a stockpile of powdered ore. The CFO has brought a printout (Table 5.1) of the forecasted revenues, costs, income, and book rates of return for the standard, low-temperature design. Vegetron's engineers have just proposed an alternative high-temperature design that will extract most of the hydrated zirconium over a shorter period, five instead of seven years. The forecasts for the high-temperature method are given in Table 5.2.[17]

CFO: Why do these engineers always have a bright idea at the last minute? But you've got to admit the high-temperature process looks good. We'll get a faster payback, and the rate of return beats Vegetron's 9 percent cost of capital in every year except the first. Let's see, income is $ 30,000 per year. Average investment is half the $ 400,000 capital outlay, or $ 200,000, so the average rate of return is 30,000/200,000, or 15 percent—a lot better than the 9 percent hurdle rate. The average rate of return for the low-temperature process is not that good, only 28,000/200,000, or 14 percent. Of course we might get a higher

TABLE 5.1

Income statement and book rates of return for high-temperature extraction of hydrated zirconium ($ thousands).

*Straight-line depreciation over five years is 400/5 = 80, or $ 80,000 per year.

†Capital investment is $ 400,000 in year 0.

	Year				
	1	2	3	4	5
1. Revenue	180	180	180	180	180
2. Operating costs	70	70	70	70	70
3. Depreciation*	80	80	80	80	80
4. Net income	30	30	30	30	30
5. Start-of-year book value†	400	320	240	160	80
6. Book rate of return (4 ÷ 5)	7.5%	9.4%	12.5%	18.75%	37.5%

TABLE 5.2

Income statement and book rates of return for low-temperature extraction of hydrated zirconium ($ thousands).

*Rounded. Straight-line depreciation over seven years is 400/7 = 57.14, or $57,140 per year.

†Capital investment is $ 400,000 in year 0.

	Year						
	1	2	3	4	5	6	7
1. Revenue	140	140	140	140	140	140	140
2. Operating costs	55	55	55	55	55	55	55
3. Depreciation*	57	57	57	57	57	57	57
4. Net income	28	28	28	28	28	28	28
5. Start-of-year book value†	400	343	286	229	171	114	57
6. Book rate of return (4 ÷ 5)	7%	8.2%	9.8%	12.2%	16.4%	24.6%	49.1%

[17]For simplicity we have ignored taxes. There will be plenty about taxes in Chapter 6.

rate of return for the low-temperature proposal if we depreciated the investment faster—do you think we should try that?

You: Let's not fixate on book accounting numbers. Book income is not the same as cash flow to Vegetron or its investors. Book rates of return don't measure the true rate of return.

CFO: But people use accounting numbers all the time. We have to publish them in our annual report to investors.

You: Accounting numbers have many valid uses, but they're not a sound basis for capital investment decisions. Accounting changes can have big effects on book income or rate of return, even when cash flows are unchanged.

Here's an example. Suppose the accountant depreciates the capital investment for the low-temperature process over six years rather than seven. Then income for years 1 to 6 goes down, because depreciation is higher. Income for year 7 goes up because the depreciation for that year becomes zero. But there is no effect on year-to-year cash flows, because depreciation is not a cash outlay. It is simply the accountant's device for spreading out the "recovery" of the up-front capital outlay over the life of the project.

CFO: So how do we get cash flows?

You: In these cases it's easy. Depreciation is the only noncash entry in your spreadsheets (Tables 5.1 and 5.2), so we can just leave it out of the calculation. Cash flow equals revenue minus operating costs. For the high-temperature process, annual cash flow is:

$$\text{Cash flow} = \text{revenue} - \text{operating cost} = 180 - 70 = 110, \text{ or } \$\,110{,}000.$$

CFO: In effect you're adding back depreciation, because depreciation is a noncash accounting expense.

You: Right. You could also do it that way:

$$\text{Cash flow} = \text{net income} + \text{depreciation} = 30 + 80 = 110, \text{ or } \$\,110{,}000.$$

CFO: Of course. I remember all this now, but book returns seem important when someone shoves them in front of your nose.

You: It's not clear which project is better. The high-temperature process appears to be less efficient. It has higher operating costs and generates less total revenue over the life of the project, but of course it generates more cash flow in years 1 to 5.

CFO: Maybe the processes are equally good from a financial point of view. If so we'll stick with the low-temperature process rather than switching at the last minute.

You: We'll have to lay out the cash flows and calculate NPV for each process.

CFO: OK, do that. I'll be back in a half hour—and I also want to see each project's true, DCF rate of return.

QUESTIONS

1. Are the book rates of return reported in Table 5.1 useful inputs for the capital investment decision?
2. Calculate NPV and IRR for each process. What is your recommendation? Be ready to explain to the CFO.

CHAPTER [6]

MAKING INVESTMENT DECISIONS WITH THE NET PRESENT VALUE RULE

WE HOPE THAT by now you are convinced that wise investment decisions are based on the net present value rule. In this chapter we can think about how to apply the rule to practical capital investment decisions. Our task is threefold. First, what should be discounted? We know the answer in principle: Discount cash flows. But useful forecasts of cash flows do not arrive on a silver platter. Often the financial manager has to make do with raw data supplied by specialists in product design, production, marketing, and so on.

This information has to be checked for completeness, consistency, and accuracy. The financial manager has to ferret out hidden cash flows and take care to reject accounting entries that look like cash flows but truly are not.

Second, how does the financial manager pull everything together into a forecast of overall, "bottom-line" cash flows? This requires careful tracking of taxes, changes in working capital, inflation and the end-of-project "salvage values" of plant, property, and equipment. We will work through a realistic example.

Third, how should a financial manager apply the net present value rule when choosing between investments in plant or equipment with different economic lives? For example, suppose you must decide between machine Y, with a 5-year useful life, and machine Z, with a 10-year useful life. The present value of Y's lifetime investment and operating costs is naturally less than Z's, because Z will last twice as long. Does that necessarily make Y the better choice? Of course not.

We will show you how to transform the present value of an asset's investment and operating costs into an *equivalent annual cost*, that is, the total cost per year of buying and operating the asset. We will also show how to use equivalent annual costs to decide when to replace aging plant or equipment.

Choices between short- and long-lived production facilities, or between new and existing facilities, almost always involve project *interactions*, because a decision about one project cannot be separated from a decision about another, or from future decisions. We close this chapter with further examples of project interactions, for example, the choice between investing now and waiting to invest later.

6.1 WHAT TO DISCOUNT

Up to this point we have been concerned mainly with the mechanics of discounting and with the net present value rule for project appraisal. We have glossed over the problem of deciding *what* to discount. When you are faced with this problem, you should always stick to three general rules:

1. Only cash flow is relevant.
2. Always estimate cash flows on an incremental basis.
3. Be consistent in your treatment of inflation.

We will discuss each of these rules in turn.

Only Cash Flow is Relevant

The first and most important point: Net present value depends on future cash flows. Cash flow is the simplest possible concept; it is just the difference between rupees received and rupees paid out. Many people nevertheless confuse cash flow with accounting profits.

Accountants *start* with "rupees in" and "rupees out," but to obtain accounting income they adjust these inputs in two important ways. First, they try to show profit as it is *earned* rather than when the company and the customer get around to paying their bills. Second, they sort cash outflows into two categories: current expenses and capital expenses. They deduct current expenses when calculating profit but do *not* deduct capital expenses. Instead they depreciate capital expenses over a number of years and deduct the annual depreciation charge from profits. As a result of these procedures, profits include some cash flows and exclude others, and they are reduced by depreciation charges, which are not cash flows at all.

It is not always easy to translate the customary accounting data back into actual rupees—rupees you can buy beer with. If you are in doubt about what is a cash flow, simply count the rupees coming in and take away the rupees going out. Don't assume without checking that you can find cash flow by routine manipulations of accounting data.

Always estimate cash flows on an after-tax basis. Some firms do not deduct tax payments. They try to offset this mistake by discounting the cash flows before taxes at a rate higher than the opportunity cost of capital. Unfortunately, there is no reliable formula for making such adjustments to the discount rate.

You should also make sure that cash flows are recorded *only when they occur* and not when work is undertaken or a liability is incurred. For example, taxes should be discounted from their actual payment date, not from the time when the tax liability is recorded in the firm's books.

Estimate Cash Flows on an Incremental Basis

The value of a project depends on *all* the additional cash flows that follow from project acceptance. Here are some things to watch for when you are deciding which cash flows should be included:

Do Not Confuse Average with Incremental Payoffs Most managers naturally hesitate to throw good money after bad. For example, they are reluctant to invest more money in a losing division. But occasionally you will encounter turnaround opportunities in which the *incremental* NPV on investment in a loser is strongly positive.

Conversely, it does not always make sense to throw good money after good. A division with an outstanding past profitability record may have run out of good opportunities. You would not pay a large sum for a 20-year-old horse, sentiment aside, regardless of how many races that horse had won or how many champions it had sired.

Here is another example illustrating the difference between average and incremental returns: Suppose that a railroad bridge is in urgent need of repair. With the bridge the railroad can continue to operate; without the bridge it can't. In this case the payoff from the repair work consists of all the benefits of operating the railroad. The incremental NPV of such an investment may be enormous. Of course, these benefits should be net of all other costs and all subsequent repairs; otherwise the company may be misled into rebuilding an unprofitable railroad piece by piece.

Include All Incidental Effects It is important to include all incidental effects on the remainder of the business. For example, a branch line for a railroad may have a negative NPV when considered in isolation, but still be a worthwhile investment when one allows for the additional traffic that it brings to the main line.

These incidental effects can extend into the far future. When GE, Pratt & Whitney, or Rolls Royce commits to the design and production of a new jet engine, cash inflows are not limited to revenues from engine sales. Once sold, an engine may be in service for 20 years or more, and during that time there is a steady demand for replacement parts. Some engine manufacturers also run profitable service and overhaul facilities. Finally, once an engine is proven in service, there are opportunities to offer modified or improved versions for other uses. All these "downstream" activities generate significant incremental cash inflows.

Do Not Forget Working Capital Requirements Net working capital (often referred to simply as *working capital*) is the difference between a company's short-term assets and liabilities. The principal short-term assets are accounts receivable (customers' unpaid bills) and inventories of raw materials and finished goods. The principal short-term liabilities are accounts payable (bills that *you* have not paid). Most projects entail an additional investment in working capital. This investment should, therefore, be recognized in your cash-flow forecasts. By the same token, when the project comes to an end, you can usually recover some of the investment. This is treated as a cash inflow. We will supply a numerical example of working-capital investment later in this chapter.

Include Opportunity Costs The cost of a resource may be relevant to the investment decision even when no cash changes hands. For example, suppose a new manufacturing operation uses land which could otherwise be sold for Rs. 100,000. This resource is not free: It has an opportunity cost, which is the cash it could generate for the company if the project were rejected and the resource were sold or put to some other productive use.

This example prompts us to warn you against judging projects on the basis of "before versus after." The proper comparison is "with or without." A manager comparing before versus after might not assign any value to the land because the firm owns it both before and after:

Before	Take Project	After	Cash Flow, Before versus After
Firm owns land	→	Firm still owns land	0

The proper comparison, with or without, is as follows:

With	Take Project	After	Cash Flow, with Project
Firm owns land	→	Firm still owns land	0

Without	Do Not Take Project	After	Cash Flow, without Project
	→	Firm sells land for Rs. 100,000	Rs. 100,000

Comparing the two possible "afters," we see that the firm gives up Rs. 100,000 by undertaking the project. This reasoning still holds if the land will not be sold but is worth Rs. 100,000 to the firm in some other use.

Sometimes opportunity costs may be very difficult to estimate; however, where the resource can be freely traded, its opportunity cost is simply equal to the market price. Why? It cannot be otherwise. If the value of a parcel of land to the firm is less than its market price, the firm will sell it. On the other hand, the opportunity cost of using land in a particular project cannot exceed the cost of buying an equivalent parcel to replace it.

Forget Sunk Costs Sunk costs are like spilled milk: They are past and irreversible outflows. Because sunk costs are bygones, they cannot be affected by the decision to accept or reject the project, and so they should be ignored.

For an elderly, but classic, example we jump back to 1971, when Lockheed sought a federal guarantee for a bank loan to continue development of the TriStar airplane. Lockheed and its supporters argued it would be foolish to abandon a project on which nearly $ 1 billion had already been spent. Some of Lockheed's critics countered that it would be equally foolish to continue with a project that offered no prospect of a satisfactory return on that $ 1 billion. Both groups were guilty of the *sunk-cost fallacy;* the $ 1 billion was irrecoverable and, therefore, irrelevant.[1]

Beware of Allocated Overhead Costs We have already mentioned that the accountant's objective is not always the same as the investment analyst's. A case in point is the allocation of overhead costs. Overheads include such items as supervisory salaries, rent, heat, and light. These overheads may not be related to any particular project, but they have to be paid for somehow. Therefore, when the accountant assigns costs to the firm's projects, a charge for overhead is usually made. Now our principle of incremental cash flows says that in investment appraisal we should include only the *extra* expenses that would result from the project. A project may generate extra overhead expenses; then again, it may not. We should be cautious about assuming that the accountant's allocation of overheads represents the true extra expenses that would be incurred.

Treat Inflation Consistently

As we pointed out in Chapter 3, interest rates are usually quoted in *nominal* rather than *real* terms. For example, if you buy a one-year 8 percent Treasury bond, the government promises to pay you Rs. 1,080 at the end of the year, but it does not promise what that Rs. 1,080 will buy. Investors take inflation into account when they decide what is a fair rate of interest.

Suppose that the yield on the Treasury bond is 8 percent and that next year's inflation is expected to be 6 percent. If you buy the bond, you get back Rs. 1,080 in year-1 rupees, which are worth 6 percent less than current rupees. The nominal payoff is Rs. 1,080, but the expected *real* value of your payoff is 1,080/1.06 = Rs. 1,019. Thus we could say, "The *nominal* rate of interest on the bond is 8 percent," *or* "The expected *real* rate of interest is 1.9 percent." Remember that the formula linking the nominal interest rate and the real rate is

$$1 + r_{\text{nominal}} = (1 + r_{\text{real}})(1 + \text{inflation rate})$$

If the discount rate is stated in nominal terms, then consistency requires that cash flows be estimated in nominal terms, taking account of trends in selling price, labor and materials cost, etc. This calls for more than simply applying a single assumed inflation rate to all components of cash flow. Labor cost per hour of work, for example, normally increases at a faster rate than the consumer price index because of improvements in productivity and increasing real wages throughout the

[1]See U. E. Reinhardt, "Break-Even Analysis for Lockheed's TriStar: An Application of Financial Theory," *Journal of Finance*, 28 (September 1973), pp. 821–838.

economy. Tax savings from depreciation do *not* increase with inflation; they are constant in nominal terms because tax law in India allows only the original cost of assets to be depreciated.

Of course, there is nothing wrong with discounting real cash flows at a real discount rate. In fact, this is standard procedure in countries with high and volatile inflation. Here is a simple example showing that real and nominal discounting, properly applied, always give the same present value.

Suppose your firm usually forecasts cash flows in nominal terms and discounts at a 15 percent nominal rate. In this particular case, however, you are given project cash flows estimated in real terms, that is, current rupees:

Real Cash Flows (Rs. thousands)			
C_0	C_1	C_2	C_3
−100	+35	+50	+30

It would be inconsistent to discount these real cash flows at 15 percent. You have two alternatives: Either restate the cash flows in nominal terms and discount at 15 percent, or restate the discount rate in real terms and use it to discount the real cash flows.

Assume that inflation is projected at 10 percent a year. Then the cash flow for year 1, which is Rs. 35,000 in current rupees, will be 35,000 × 1.10 = Rs. 38,500 in year-1 rupees. Similarly the cash flow for year 2 will be 50,000 × $(1.10)^2$ = Rs. 60,500 in year-2 rupees, and so on. If we discount these nominal cash flows at the 15 percent nominal discount rate, we have

$$\text{NPV} = -100 + \frac{38.5}{1.15} + \frac{60.5}{(1.15)^2} + \frac{39.9}{(1.15)^3} = 5.5, \text{ or Rs. } 5{,}500$$

Instead of converting the cash-flow forecasts into nominal terms, we could convert the discount rate into real terms by using the following relationship:

$$\text{Real discount rate} = \frac{1 + \text{nominal discount rate}}{1 + \text{inflation rate}} - 1$$

In our example this gives

$$\text{Real discount rate} = \frac{1.15}{1.10} - 1 = .045, \text{ or } 4.5\%$$

If we now discount the real cash flows by the real discount rate, we have an NPV of Rs. 5,500, just as before:

$$\text{NPV} = -100 + \frac{35}{1.045} + \frac{50}{(1.045)^2} + \frac{30}{(1.045)^3} = 5.5, \text{ or Rs. } 5{,}500$$

Note that the real discount rate is approximately equal to the *difference* between the nominal discount rate of 15 percent and the inflation rate of 10 percent. Discounting at 15 − 10 = 5 percent would give NPV = Rs. 4,600—not exactly right, but close.

The message of all this is quite simple. Discount nominal cash flows at a nominal discount rate. Discount real cash flows at a real rate. *Never* mix real cash flows with nominal discount rates or nominal flows with real rates.

6.2 EXAMPLE—IM&C'S FERTILIZER PROJECT

As the newly appointed financial manager of International Mulch and Compost Company (IM&C), you are about to analyze a proposal for marketing guano as a garden fertilizer. (IM&C's planned advertising campaign features a rustic gentleman who steps out of a vegetable patch singing, "All my troubles have guano way.")[2]

You are given the forecasts shown in Table 6.1.[3] The project requires an investment of Rs. 10 million in plant and machinery (line 1). This machinery can be dismantled and sold for net proceeds estimated at Rs. 4 million in year 7 (line 1, column 7). This amount is your forecast of the plant's *salvage value.*

Whoever prepared Table 6.1 depreciated the capital investment over six years using 15%[4] as the depreciation rate. The estimated salvage value of the plant and machinery (Rs. 3.771 million) is lower than your forecasted salvage value of Rs. 4 million. Since the Income Tax Act in India prescribes written down value (WDV) method to depreciate assets, we have used WDV method here.[5] Under this method annual depreciation equals a constant proportion of the written down value of the asset at the beginning of the year. The WDV depreciation in year t is

Depreciation in year t = Beginning of the Year 't' (same as close of year 't-1') Book Value of the Asset × Depreciation Rate

Thus for example, in year 2, the depreciation is 15% of beginning of year 2 book value (Rs. 8.5 million), that is, Rs. 1.275 million.

Lines 6 through 12 in Table 6.1 show a simplified income statement for the guano project.[6] This will be our starting point for estimating cash flow. In preparing this table IM&C's managers recognized the effect of inflation on prices and costs. Not all cash flows are equally affected by inflation. For example, wages generally rise faster than the inflation rate. So labor costs per ton of guano will rise in real terms unless technological advances allow more efficient use of labor. On the other hand, inflation has no effect on the tax savings provided by the depreciation deduction, since the Income Tax Act allows you to depreciate only the original cost of the equipment, regardless of what happens to prices after the investment is made.

Table 6.2 derives cash-flow forecasts from the investment and income data given in Table 6.1. Cash flow from operations is defined as sales less cost of goods sold, other costs, and taxes. The remaining cash flows include the changes in working capital, the initial capital investment, and the recovery of your estimated salvage value. If, as you expect, the salvage value turns out higher than the depreciated value of the machinery, you will have to pay tax on the difference. So you must also include this figure in your cash-flow forecast.

---

[2]Sorry.

[3]"Live" Excel versions of Tables 6.1, 6.2, 6.4, 6.5, 6.6, and 6.8 are available on the book's web site, **www.mhhe.com/bma8e.** However, in this book, we have re-estimated the depreciation figures by using WDV (rather than SLM, as has been assumed in the US edition of the book) and hence you will find some difference between the figures given in the book and the ones given in the website.

[4]The depreciation rate on plant and machinery in India has been reduced to 15% (from 25%) after the 2005 Budget.

[5]From the assessment year 1998-99, a business unit engaged in generation and distribution of power has the option of claiming depreciation using straight line method for any asset acquired after March 31, 1997.

[6]We have departed from the usual profit and loss account format by separating depreciation from costs of goods sold.

		Period							
		0	1	2	3	4	5	6	7
1	Capital Investment	10,000.0							(4000)[a]
2	Accumulated Depreciation		1500	2775	3858.75	4779.938	5562.947	6228.505	0.0
3	Year-end book value	10,000.0	8,500	7,225	6,141	5,220	4,437	3,771	0.0
4	Working Capital		550	1289	3261	4890	3583	2002	0.0
5	Total book value (3 + 4)		9050	8514	9402.25	10110.06	8020.053	5773.495	0.0
6	Sales		523	12887	32610	48901	35834	19717	
7	Cost of Goods Sold[b]		837	7729	19552	29345	21492	11830	
8	Other costs[c]	4,000.0	2200	1210	1331	1464	1611	1772	
9	Depreciation		1500	1275	1083.75	921.1875	783.0094	665.558	0.0
10	Pre-tax Profit (6 - 7 - 8 - 9)	(4,000.0)	(4,014.0)	2673	10643.25	17170.81	11947.99	5449.442	229.4[d]
11	Tax at 33.66%[f]	(1364)[e]	(1,351.1)	899.7318	3582.518	5779.695	4021.694	1834.282	76.9
12	Profit after tax (10 - 11)	(2,653.0)	(2,662.9)	1773.268	7060.732	11391.12	7926.297	3615.16	152.5

TABLE 6.1

IM&C's guano project—projections (Rs. thousands) reflecting inflation.

[a]Salvage value.
[b]We have departed from the usual profit and loss account format by *not* including depriciation in cost of goods sold. Instead, we break out depreciation separately (see line 9).
[c]Start-up costs in years 0, 1, and general administrative costs in years 1 to 6.
[d]Here, we assume the difference between the salvage value and the ending book value of 3771.5 to be taxable profit. In India a company is unlikely to pay any tax on this. We explain it later.
[e]Here, we assume that IM&C is an otherwise profitable company and that its profits in the first two years are much higher than the loss from this project.
[f]This assumes 30% normal tax rate, 10% surcharge and 2% education cess.

Please visit us at www.mhhe.com/bmam8e or refer to your Student CD.

		Period							
		0	1	2	3	4	5	6	7
1	Sales		523	12,887	32,610	48,901	35,834	19,717	
2	Cost of Goods Sold		837	7,729	19,552	29,345	21,492	11,830	
3	Other Costs	4,000	2,200	1,210	1,331	1,464	1,611	1,772	
4	Tax on Operations	(1,346)	(1,351)	900	3,583	5,780	4,022	1,834	
5	Cash flow from operations (1 - 2 - 3 - 4)	(2,654)	(1,163)	3,048	8,144	12,312	8,709	4,281	
6	Change in working capital		(550)	(739)	(1,972)	(1,629)	1,307	1,581	2,002
7	Capital investment and disposal	(10,000)							3923[a]
8	Net cash flow (5 + 6 + 7)	(12,654)	(1,713)	2,309	6,172	10,683	10,016	5,862	5,925
9	Present value at 20%	(12,654)	(1,427)	1,604	3,572	5,152	4,025	1,963	1,654
	Net present value	3,889							

TABLE 6.2

IM&C's guano project—cash-flow analysis (Rs. thousands).

[a]Salvage value of Rs. 4,000 less tax of Rs. 77 on the difference between salvage value and ending book value.

Please visit us at www.mhhe.com/bmam8e or refer to your Student CD.

IM&C estimates the nominal opportunity cost of capital for projects of this type as 20 percent. When all cash flows are added up and discounted, the guano project is seen to offer a net present value of about Rs. 3.9 million:

$$\text{NPV} = -12{,}654 - \frac{1713}{1.2} + \frac{2309}{(1.2)^2} + \frac{6172}{(1.2)^3} + \frac{10683}{(1.2)^4} + \frac{10016}{(1.2)^5}$$
$$+ \frac{5862}{(1.2)^6} + \frac{5925}{(1.2)^7} = +3889, \text{ or Rs. } 3{,}889{,}000$$

Separating Investment and Financing Decisions

Our analysis of the guano project takes no notice of how that project is financed. It may be that IM&C will decide to finance partly by debt, but if it does we will not subtract the debt proceeds from the required investment, nor will we recognize interest and principal payments as cash outflows. We analyze the project as if it were all equity-financed, treating all cash outflows as coming from stockholders and all cash inflows as going to them.

We approach the problem in this way so that we can separate the analysis of the investment decision from the financing decision. Then, when we have calculated NPV, we can undertake a separate analysis of financing. Financing decisions and their possible interactions with investment decisions are covered later in the book.

Investments in Working Capital

Now here is an important point. You can see from line 6 of Table 6.2 that working capital increases in the early and middle years of the project. What is working capital? you may ask, and why does it increase?

Working capital summarizes the net investment in short-term assets associated with a firm, business, or project. Its most important components are *inventory, accounts receivable,* and *accounts payable.* The guano project's requirements for working capital in year 2 might be as follows:

$$\begin{array}{ccccccc} \text{Working capital} & = & \text{inventory} & + & \text{accounts receivable} & - & \text{accounts payable} \\ \text{Rs. } 1{,}289 & = & 635 & + & 1{,}030 & - & 376 \end{array}$$

Why does working capital increase? There are several possibilities:

1. Sales recorded on the income statement overstate actual cash receipts from guano shipments because sales are increasing and customers are slow to pay their bills. Therefore, accounts receivable increase.
2. It takes several months for processed guano to age properly. Thus, as projected sales increase, larger inventories have to be held in the aging sheds.
3. An offsetting effect occurs if payments for materials and services used in guano production are delayed. In this case accounts payable will increase.

The additional investment in working capital from year 2 to 3 might be

$$\begin{array}{ccccccc} \text{Additional investment working capital} & = & \text{increase in inventory} & + & \text{increase in accounts receivable} & - & \text{increase in accounts payable} \\ \text{Rs. } 1{,}972 & = & 972 & + & 1{,}500 & - & 500 \end{array}$$

A more detailed cash-flow forecast for year 3 would look like Table 6.3.

Cash Flows		Data from Forecasted Income Statement		Working-Capital Changes
Cash inflow	=	Sales	−	Increase in accounts receivable
Rs. 31,110	=	32,610	−	1,500
Cash outflow	=	Cost of goods sold, other costs, and taxes	+	Increase in inventory net of increase in accounts payable
Rs. 24,9378	=	(19,552 + 1,331 + 3,583)	+	(972 − 500)
		Net cash flow = cash inflow − cash outflow		
		Rs. 6,172 = 31,110 − 24,938		

TABLE 6.3

Details of cash-flow forecast for IM&C's guano project in year 3 (Rs. thousands).

Instead of worrying about changes in working capital, you could estimate cash flow directly by counting the rupees coming in from customers and deducting the rupees going out to suppliers. You would also deduct all cash spent on production, including cash spent for goods held in inventory. In other words,

1. If you replace each year's sales with that year's cash payments received from customers, you don't have to worry about accounts receivable.
2. If you replace cost of goods sold with cash payments for labor, materials, and other costs of production, you don't have to keep track of inventory or accounts payable.

However, you would still have to construct a projected income statement to estimate taxes.

We discuss the links between cash flow and working capital in much greater detail in Chapter 31.

A Further Note on Depreciation

Depreciation is a noncash expense; it is important only because it reduces taxable income. It provides an annual tax shield equal to the product of depreciation and the marginal tax rate. Thus for example, in our case, the tax shield in year 1 is given by:

$$\text{Tax shield} = \text{depreciation} \times \text{tax rate}$$
$$= 1{,}500 \times 0.3366 = 504.9, \text{ or Rs. } 504{,}900$$

The present value of the tax shields (for all the six years put together) is Rs. 1,260,370 at a 20% discount rate.[7]

Now if IM&C could just get those tax shields sooner, they would be worth more, right? If a company is allowed to use a higher depreciation rate in the initial part of the life of the asset, it will get the tax shields sooner. In the US, tax laws allow accelerated depreciation, whereby a company can compute depreciation at a higher rate in the initial part of the life of the asset.

In India, a company can (on top of normal depreciation) claim additional depreciation under certain situations. The Finance Act 2005 amended Section 32 of the Income Tax Act in India to increase the rate of additional depreciation to 20 percent (from 15%) on new plant and machinery (other than ships and aircraft), acquired and installed after 31st March, 2005. Prior to this amendment, only new

[7]By discounting the depreciation tax shields at 20 percent, we assume that they are as risky as the other cash flows. Since they depend only on tax rates, depreciation method, and IM&C's ability to generate taxable income, they are probably less risky. In some contexts (the analysis of financial leases, for example) depreciation tax shields are treated as safe, nominal cash flows and are discounted at an after-tax borrowing or lending rate. See Chapter 26.

undertakings were granted the additional depreciation. The Finance Act, 2005, however, reduced the normal depreciation rate on plant and machinery to 15% (from 25%).[8]

Let's assume that the guano project started after 31st March 2005 and hence qualifies for the additional depreciation of 20%. IM&C can claim this additional depreciation in the first year. Therefore IM&C can write-off 35% of the depriciable investment in year 1, as soon as the assets are placed in service, then 15% of the written down value from year 2 till year 6. Here are the tax shields for the guano project.

	Year					
	1	2	3	4	5	6
Normal Depreciation	1500.0	975.0	828.8	704.4	598.8	509.0
Additional depreciation	2000.0	0.0	0.0	0.0	0.0	0.0
Total tax depreciation	3500.0	975.0	828.8	704.4	598.8	509.0
Tax shield (tax depreciation x tax rate, t = 0.3366)	1155.0	321.0	273.5	232.5	197.6	168.0

TABLE 6.4

Estimation of depreciation tax shield (Rs. thousands) when additional depreciation is allowed.

The present value of the tax shields is Rs. 1,592,000, about Rs. 331,600 higher than the earlier estimate we get by ignoring additional depreciation.

Table 6.5 recalculates the guano project's impact on IM&C's future tax bills, and Table 6.6 shows revised after-tax cash flows and present value. This time, we have incorporated realistic assumptions about taxes. We, of course, arrive at a higher NPV than in Table 6.2, because that table ignored the additional present value of additional depreciation.

There is one possible additional problem lurking in the woodwork behind Table 6.5: it is the *minimum alternative tax (MAT)*[9], which can limit or defer the tax shields of additional depreciation or other tax preference items. As per Section 115JB of the Income Tax Act in India, if tax payable by a company (ignoring the provisions of Section 115JB of the Income Tax Act) is lower than 11.22% of the book profit, then the effective tax liability of the company will be 11.22% of the *book profit*. For the purpose of MAT, *book profit* is estimated from the *net profit* (as reported to the shareholders) after making certain adjustments. One of the adjustments requires adding back the excess depreciation to the net profit of the company. In a few cases, this can partially neutralize the benefits of having additional depreciation. We will discuss about MAT in Chapter 26, rather than here. So make a mental note not to sign off on a capital budgeting analysis without checking whether your company is subject to the minimum alternative tax.

A Final Comment on Taxes

In India, depreciation is normally computed on the written down value of the block of assets. Here a 'block of assets' refers to a group of similar assets (belonging to the same class) and having the same rate of depreciation. Thus for example, as per the Income Tax Act in India, all the furniture and fittings (including electrical fittings) form one block of assets with a WDV depreciation rate of 10 percent. Similarly certain types of plant and equipment will form another block of assets with WDV depreciation rate of 15%, and so on.

---

[8]See http://incometaxindia.gov.in/Notifications/IncomeTaxAct/2005/Notification672005.pdf for the depreciation rates for the different types of assets in India.

[9]Refer to Section 115JB of the Income Tax Act of India, 1961.

		Period							
		0	1	2	3	4	5	6	7
1	Capital Investment	10,000.0							(4000)[a]
2	Accumulated Depreciation		3500	4475	5303.75	6008.188	6606.959	7115.915	0.0
3	Year-end book value	10,000.0	6,500	5,525	4,696	3,992	3,393	2,884	0.0
4	Working Capital		550	1289	3261	4890	3583	2002	0.0
5	Total book value (3 + 4)		7050	6814	7957.25	8881.813	6976.041	4886.085	0.0
6	Sales		523	12887	32610	48901	35834	19717	
7	Cost of Goods Sold[b]		837	7729	19552	29345	21492	11830	
8	Other costs[c]	4,000.0	2200	1210	1331	1464	1611	1772	
9	Depreciation		3500	975	828.75	704.4375	598.7719	508.9561	0.0
10	Pre-tax Profit (6 - 7 - 8 - 9)	(4,000.0)	(6,014.0)	2973	10898.25	17387.56	12132.23	5606.044	1116[d]
11	Tax at 33.66%[f]	(1346.4)[e]	(2,024.3)	1000.712	3668.351	5852.654	4083.708	1886.994	375.6
12	Profit after tax (10 - 11)	(2,653.6)	(3,989.7)	1972.288	7229.899	11534.91	8048.52	3719.05	740.3

TABLE 6.5

IM&C's guano project - projections (Rs. thousands) reflecting inflation.

[a]Salvage Value
[b]We have departed from the usual profit and loss account format by *not* including depreciation in cost of goods sold. Instead, we break out depreciation separately (see line 9).
[c]Start-up costs in years 0, 1, and general administrative costs in years 1 to 6.
[d]Here, we assume the difference between the salvage value and the ending book value of 2884 to be a taxable profit.
[e]Here, we assume that IM&C is an otherwise profitable company and that its profit in the first two years are much higher than the loss from this project.
[f]This assume 30% normal tax rate, 10% surcharge, and 2% education cess.

		Period							
		0	1	2	3	4	5	6	7
1	Sales		523	12,887	32,610	48,901	35,834	19,717	
2	Cost of Goods Sold		837	7,729	19,552	29,345	21,492	11,830	
3	Other Costs	4,000	2,200	1,210	1,331	1,464	1,611	1,772	
4	Tax on Operations	(1,346)	(1,985)	981	3,596	5,738	4,004	1,850	
5	Cash flow from operations (1 - 2 - 3 - 4)	(2,654)	(529)	2,967	8,131	12,354	8,727	4,265	
6	Change in working capital		(550)	(739)	(1,972)	(1,629)	1,307	1,581	2,002
7	Capital investment and disposal	(10,000)							3625[a]
8	Net cash flow (5 + 6 + 7)	(12,654)	(1,079)	2,228	6,159	10,725	10,034	5,846	5,626
9	Present value at 20%	(12,654)	(899)	1,547	3,564	5,172	4,033	1,958	1,570
	Net present value	4,169							

TABLE 6.6

IM&C's guano project - cash flow analysis (Rs. thousands).

[a]Salvage value of Rs. 4000 less tax of Rs. 375 on the difference between salvage value and ending book value.

In the guano example, we assumed that when IM&C sells the asset at a gain, it has to pay tax on the difference between the sale proceeds and the written down value of the asset. In India, tax authorities follow a different system however. Section 50 of the Income Tax Act, 1961 prescribes the following procedure to determine the tax implications of sale of assets.[10]

Step 1: Determine the net consideration (sale proceeds) by deducting any expense incurred while selling (or transferring) the asset from the actual consideration received while selling the asset. Thus for example, in the guano project, we assumed that IM&C will receive Rs. 4 million by selling the asset after the sixth year. If we further assume that IM&C will incur an additional cost of Rs. 1 lakh to sell the asset, then the net consideration will be Rs. 3.9 million.

[10]Source: http://incometaxindia.gov.in/publications/4_Compute_Your_Capital_Gains/Chapter4.asp.

Step 2: Determine the short term capital gain by deducting the written down value of the block of assets from the net consideration. Here, it is important to understand that we subtract the written down value of the block of assets (and ***not*** the asset sold) from the net consideration to derive the short term capital gains.

To illustrate, in the guano example, the written down value of the asset at the end of year 6 was Rs. 2.88 million (Table 6.5). Suppose, this asset is part of a block, whose written down value at the time was more than Rs. 4 million, then the difference between Rs. 4 million (or Rs. 3.9 million, if one considers the cost incurred while selling the asset) and Rs. 2.88 million will not be treated as capital gains. Therefore the cash flow in year 7 (in both Table 6.1, and Table 6.5) will be higher by the tax that IM&C does not have to pay. The NPV of the project will accordingly be higher by the present value of the excess tax computed.

All large Indian corporations keep two separate sets of books, one for stockholders and one for the Income Tax Department. It is common to use straight-line depreciation (using the rates provided in the Schedule XIV of the Companies Act) on the stockholder books and written down value rates on the tax books. The Income Tax Department does not object to this as it is perfectly legal to do so, and it makes the firm's reported earnings higher than if written down value method were used everywhere.[11] There are many other differences between tax books and shareholder books.[12]

Project Analysis

Let us review. Several pages ago, you embarked on an analysis of IM&C's guano project. You started with a simplified statement of assets and income for the project that you used to develop a series of cash-flow forecasts. Then you remembered accelerated depreciation and had to recalculate cash flows and NPV.

You were lucky to get away with just two NPV calculations. In real situations, it often takes several tries to purge all inconsistencies and mistakes. Then there are "what if" questions. For example: What if inflation rages at 15 percent per year, rather than 5? What if technical problems delay start-up to year 2? What if gardeners prefer chemical fertilizers to your natural product?

You won't truly understand the guano project until all relevant what-if questions are answered. *Project analysis* is more than one or two NPV calculations, as we will see in Chapter 10.

Calculating NPV in Other Countries and Currencies

Before you become too deeply immersed in guano, we should take a quick look at another company that is facing a capital investment decision. This time it is the French firm, Flanel s.a., which is contemplating investment in a facility to produce a new range of fragrances. The basic principles are the same: Flanel needs to determine whether the present value of the future cash flows exceeds the initial investment. But there are a few differences that arise from the change in project location:

1. Flanel must produce a set of cash-flow forecasts like those that we developed for the guano project, but in this case the project cash flows are stated in euros, the European currency.
2. In developing these cash-flow forecasts, the company needs to recognize that prices and costs will be influenced by the French inflation rate.
3. When they calculate taxable income, French companies cannot use accelerated depreciation. (Remember that companies in India can use additional depreciation of 20% of the written down value of any plant and machinery acquired and installed after 31st March, 2005.)

[11]Thus for example, Schedule XIV of the Companies Act recommends a straight line rate of 4.75% (single shift) for plant and machinery against the WDV rate of 15% prescribed by the Income Tax Act.

[12]This separation of tax accounts from shareholder accounts is not found worldwide. In Japan, for example, taxes reported to shareholders must equal taxes paid to the government; ditto for France and many other European countries.

4. Profits from Flanel's project are liable to the French rate of corporate tax. This is currently 35.4 percent, a trifle higher than the rate in the United States.
5. Just as IM&C calculated the net present value of its investment in India by discounting the expected rupee cash flows at the rupee cost of capital, so Flanel can evaluate an investment in France by discounting the expected euro cash flows at the euro cost of capital. To calculate the opportunity cost of capital for the fragrances project, Flanel needs to ask what return its shareholders are giving up by investing their euros in the project rather than investing them in the capital market. If the project were risk-free, the opportunity cost of investing in the project would be the interest rate on safe euro investments, for example, euro bonds issued by the French government. As we write this the 10-year euro interest rate slightly below 3.5%, about 3% lower than the rate on Indian 10-year rupee rate. But since the project is not risk-free, Flanel needs to ask how much risk it is asking its shareholders to bear and what extra return they demand for taking on this risk. A similar company in India might come up with a different answer to this question. We will discuss risk and the cost of capital in Chapters 7 through 9.

You can see from this example that the principles of valuation of capital investments are the same worldwide. A spreadsheet table for Flanel's project could have exactly the same format as Table 6.6.[13] But inputs and assumptions have to conform to local conditions.

6.3 EQUIVALENT ANNUAL COSTS

When you calculate NPV, you transform future, year-by-year cash flows into a lump-sum value expressed in today's rupees (dollars or euros, or other relevant currency). But sometimes it's helpful to reverse the calculation, transforming an investment today into an equivalent stream of future cash flows. Consider the following example.

Investing to Produce Reformulated Gasoline at California Refineries

In the early 1990s, the California Air Resources Board (CARB) started planning its "Phase 2" requirements for reformulated gasoline (RFG). RFG is gasoline blended to tight specifications designed to reduce pollution from motor vehicles. CARB consulted with refiners, environmentalists, and other interested parties to design these specifications.

As the outline for the Phase 2 requirements emerged, refiners realized that substantial capital investments would be required to upgrade California refineries. What might these investments mean for the retail price of gasoline? A refiner might ask: "Suppose my company invests $ 400 million to upgrade our refinery to meet Phase 2. How much extra revenue would we need every year to recover that cost?" Let's see if we can help the refiner out.

[13] You can tackle Flanel's project in Practice Question 12.

Assume $ 400 million of capital investment and a real (inflation-adjusted) cost of capital of 7 percent. The new equipment lasts for 25 years, and does not change raw-material and operating costs. How much additional revenue does it take to cover the $ 400 million investment? The answer is simple: Just find the 25-year annuity with a present value equal to $ 400 million.

$$\text{PV of annuity} = \text{annuity payment} \times \text{25-year annuity factor}$$

At a 7 percent cost of capital, the 25-year annuity factor is 11.65.

$$\$\,400 \text{ million} = \text{annuity payment} \times 11.65$$
$$\text{Annuity payment} = \$\,34.3 \text{ million per year}^{14}$$

This annuity is called an **equivalent annual cost.** Equivalent annual cost is the annual cash flow sufficient to recover a capital investment, including the cost of capital for that investment, over the investment's economic life.

Equivalent annual costs are handy—and sometimes essential—tools of finance. Here is a further example.

Choosing between Long- and Short-Lived Equipment

Suppose the firm is forced to choose between two machines, A and B. The two machines are designed differently but have identical capacity and do exactly the same job. Machine A costs Rs. 15,000 and will last three years. It costs Rs. 5,000 per year to run. Machine B is an economy model costing only Rs. 10,000, but it will last only two years and costs Rs. 6,000 per year to run. These are real cash flows: The costs are forecasted in rupees of constant purchasing power.

Because the two machines produce exactly the same product, the only way to choose between them is on the basis of cost. Suppose we compute the present value of cost:

	Costs (Rs. thousands)				
Machine	C_0	C_1	C_2	C_3	PV at 6% (Rs. thousands)
A	+15	+5	+5	+5	28.37
B	+10	+6	+6		21.00

Should we take machine B, the one with the lower present value of costs? Not necessarily, because B will have to be replaced a year earlier than A. In other words, the timing of a future investment decision is contingent on today's choice of A or B.

[14]For simplicity we have ignored taxes. Taxes would enter this calculation in two ways. First, the $ 400 million investment would generate depreciation tax shields. The easiest way to handle these tax shields is to calculate their PV and subtract it from the initial outlay. For example, if the PV of depreciation tax shields is $ 83 million, equivalent annual cost would be calculated on an after-tax investment base of $ 400 − 83 = $ 317 million. Second, our annuity payment is after-tax. To actually achieve after-tax revenues of, say, $ 34.3 million, the refiner would have to achieve pretax revenue sufficient to pay tax and have $ 34.3 million left over. If the tax rate is 35 percent, the required pretax revenue is 34.3/(1 − .35) = $ 52.8 million. Note how the after-tax figure is "grossed up" by dividing by one minus the tax rate.

So, a machine with total PV(costs) of Rs. 21,000 spread over three years (0, 1, and 2) is not necessarily better than a competing machine with PV(costs) of Rs. 28,370 spread over four years (0 through 3). We have to convert total PV(costs) to a cost per year, that is, to an equivalent annual cost. For machine A, the annual cost turns out to be 10.61, or Rs. 10,610 per year:

	Costs (Rs. thousands)				
Machine	C_0	C_1	C_2	C_3	**PV at 6% (Rs. thousands)**
Machine A	+15	+5	+5	+5	28.37
Equivalent annual cost		+10.61	+10.61	+10.61	28.37

We calculated the equivalent annual cost by finding the three-year annuity with the same present value as A's lifetime costs.

$$\text{PV of annuity} = \text{PV of A's costs} = 28.37$$
$$= \text{annuity payment} \times \text{three-year annuity factor}$$

The annuity factor is 2.673 for three years and a 6 percent real cost of capital, so

$$\text{Annuity payment} = \frac{28.37}{2.673} = 10.61$$

A similar calculation for machine B gives:

	Costs (Rs. thousands)			
	C_0	C_1	C_2	**PV at 6% (Rs. thousands)**
Machine B	+10	+6	+6	21.00
Equivalent annual cost		+11.45	+11.45	21.00

Machine A is better, because its equivalent annual cost is less (Rs. 10,610 versus Rs. 11,450 for machine B).

You can think of the equivalent annual cost of machine A or B as an annual rental charge. Suppose the financial manager is asked to *rent* machine A to the plant manager actually in charge of production. There will be three equal rental payments starting in year 1. The three payments must recover both the original cost of machine A in year 0 and the cost of running it in years 1 to 3. Therefore the financial manager has to make sure that the rental payments are worth Rs. 28,370, the total PV(costs) of machine A. You can see that the financial manager would calculate a fair rental payment equal to machine A's equivalent annual cost.

Our rule for choosing between plant and equipment with different economic lines is, therefore, to select the asset with the lowest fair rental charge, that is, the lowest equivalent annual cost.

Equivalent Annual Cost and Inflation The equivalent annual costs we just calculated are *real* annuities based on forecasted *real* costs and a 6 percent *real* discount rate. We could, of course, restate the annuities in nominal terms. Suppose the expected inflation rate is 5 percent; we multiply the first cash flow of the annuity by 1.05, the second by $(1.05)^2 = 1.105$, and so on.

		C_0	C_1	C_2	C_3
A	Real annuity		10.61	10.61	10.61
	Nominal cash flow		11.14	11.70	12.28
B	Real annuity		11.45	11.45	
	Nominal cash flow		12.02	12.62	

Note that B is still inferior to A. Of course the present values of the nominal and real cash flows are identical. Just remember to discount the real annuity at the real rate and the equivalent nominal cash flows at the consistent nominal rate.[15]

When you use equivalent annual costs simply for comparison of costs per period, as we did for machines A and B, we strongly recommend doing the calculations in real terms.[16] But if you actually rent out the machine to the plant manager, or anyone else, be careful to specify that the rental payments be "indexed" to inflation. If inflation runs on at 5 percent per year and rental payments do not increase proportionally, then the real value of the rental payments must decline and will not cover the full cost of buying and operating the machine.

Equivalent Annual Cost and Technological Change So far we have the following simple rule: Two or more streams of cash outflows with different lengths or time patterns can be compared by converting their present values to equivalent annual costs. Just remember to do the calculations in real terms.

Now any rule this simple cannot be completely general. For example, when we evaluated machine A versus machine B, we implicitly assumed that their fair rental charges would *continue* at Rs. 10,610 versus Rs. 11,450. This will be so only if the *real* costs of buying and operating the machines stay the same.

Suppose that this is not the case. Suppose that thanks to technological improvements new machines each year cost 20 percent less in real terms to buy and operate. In this case future owners of brand-new, lower-cost machines will be able to cut their rental cost by 20 percent, and owners of old machines will be forced to match this reduction. Thus, we now need to ask: If the real level of rents declines by 20 percent a year, how much will it cost to rent each machine?

If the rent for year 1 is rent_1, rent for year 2 is $\text{rent}_2 = .8 \times \text{rent}_1$. Rent_3 is $.8 \times \text{rent}_2$, or $.64 \times \text{rent}_1$. The owner of each machine must set the rents sufficiently high to recover the present value of the costs. In the case of machine A,

$$\text{PV of renting machine A} = \frac{\text{rent}_1}{1.06} + \frac{\text{rent}_2}{(1.06)^2} + \frac{\text{rent}_3}{(1.06)^3} = 28.37$$

$$= \frac{\text{rent}_1}{1.06} + \frac{.8(\text{rent}_1)}{(1.06)^2} + \frac{.64(\text{rent}_1)}{(1.06)^3} = 28.37$$

$$\text{rent}_1 = 12.94, \text{ or Rs. } 12{,}940$$

[15]The nominal discount rate is

$$r_{\text{nominal}} = (1 + r_{\text{real}})(1 + \text{inflation rate}) - 1$$
$$= (1.06)(1.05) - 1 = .113, \text{ or } 11.3\%$$

Discounting the nominal annuities at this rate gives the same present values as discounting the real annuities at 6 percent.

[16]Do *not* calculate equivalent annual costs as level *nominal* annuities. This procedure can give incorrect rankings of true equivalent annual costs at high inflation rates. See Challenge Question 2 at the end of this chapter for an example.

For machine B,

$$\text{PV of renting machine B} = \frac{\text{rent}_1}{1.06} + \frac{.8(\text{rent}_1)}{(1.06)^2} = 21.00$$

$$\text{rent}_1 = 12.69, \text{ or Rs. } 12{,}690$$

The merits of the two machines are now reversed. Once we recognize that technology is expected to reduce the real costs of new machines, then it pays to buy the shorter-lived machine B rather than become locked into an aging technology with machine A in year 3.

You can imagine other complications. Perhaps machine C will arrive in year 1 with an even lower equivalent annual cost. You would then need to consider scrapping or selling machine B at year 1 (more on this decision below). The financial manager could not choose between machines A and B in year 0 without taking a detailed look at what each machine could be replaced with.

Comparing equivalent annual costs should never be a mechanical exercise; always think about the assumptions that are implicit in the comparison. Finally, remember why equivalent annual costs are necessary in the first place. The reason is that A and B will be replaced at different future dates. The choice between them therefore affects future investment decisions. If subsequent decisions are not affected by the initial choice (for example, because neither machine will be replaced) then we do *not need to take future decisions into account.*[17]

Equivalent Annual Cost and Taxes We have not mentioned taxes. But you surely realized that machine A and B's lifetime costs should be calculated after-tax, recognizing that operating costs are tax-deductible and that capital investment generates depreciation tax shields.

Deciding When to Replace an Existing Machine

The previous example took the life of each machine as fixed. In practice the point at which equipment is replaced reflects economic considerations rather than total physical collapse. *We* must decide when to replace. The machine will rarely decide for us.

Here is a common problem. You are operating an elderly machine that is expected to produce a net cash *inflow* of Rs. 4,000 in the coming year and Rs. 4,000 next year. After that it will give up the ghost. You can replace it now with a new machine, which costs Rs. 15,000 but is much more efficient and will provide a cash inflow of Rs. 8,000 a year for three years. You want to know whether you should replace your equipment now or wait a year.

We can calculate the NPV of the new machine and also its *equivalent annual cash flow,* that is, the three-year annuity that has the same net present value:

	Cash Flows (Rs. thousands)				
	C_0	C_1	C_2	C_3	NPV at 6% (Rs. thousands)
New machine	−15	+8	+8	+8	6.38
Equivalent annual cash flow		+2.387	+2.387	+2.387	6.38

[17]However, if neither machine will be replaced, then we have to consider the extra revenue generated by machine A in its third year, when it will be operating but B will not.

In other words, the cash flows of the new machine are equivalent to an annuity of Rs. 2,387 per year. So we can equally well ask at what point we would want to replace our old machine with a new one producing Rs. 2,387 a year. When the question is put this way, the answer is obvious. As long as your old machine can generate a cash flow of Rs. 4,000 a year, who wants to put in its place a new one that generates only Rs. 2,387 a year?

It is a simple matter to incorporate salvage values into this calculation. Suppose that the current salvage value is Rs. 8,000 and next year's value is Rs. 7,000. Let us see where you come out next year if you wait and then sell. On one hand, you gain Rs. 7,000, but you lose today's salvage value *plus* a year's return on that money. That is, $8{,}000 \times 1.06 =$ Rs. 8,480. Your net loss is $8{,}480 - 7{,}000 =$ Rs. 1,480, which only partly offsets the operating gain. You should not replace yet.

Remember that the logic of such comparisons requires that the new machine be the best of the available alternatives and that it in turn be replaced at the optimal point.

Cost of Excess Capacity

Any firm with a centralized information system (computer servers, storage, software, and telecommunication links) encounters many proposals for using it. Recently installed systems tend to have excess capacity, and since the immediate marginal costs of using them seem to be negligible, management often encourages new uses. Sooner or later, however, the load on a system increases to the point at which management must either terminate the uses it originally encouraged or invest in another system several years earlier than it had planned. Such problems can be avoided if a proper charge is made for the use of spare capacity.

Suppose we have a new investment project that requires heavy use of an existing information system. The effect of adopting the project is to bring the purchase date of a new, more capable system forward from year 4 to year 3. This new system has a life of five years, and at a discount rate of 6 percent the present value of the cost of buying and operating it is Rs. 500,000.

We begin by converting the Rs. 500,000 present value of cost of the new system to an equivalent annual cost of Rs. 118,700 for each of five years.[18] Of course, when the new system in turn wears out, we will replace it with another. So we face the prospect of future information-system expenses of Rs. 118,700 a year. If we undertake the new project, the series of expenses begins in year 4; if we do not undertake it, the series begins in year 5. The new project, therefore, results in an *additional* cost of Rs. 118,700 in year 4. This has a present value of $118{,}700/(1.06)^4$, or about Rs. 94,000. This cost is properly charged against the new project. When we recognize it, the NPV of the project may prove to be negative. If so, we still need to check whether it is worthwhile undertaking the project now and abandoning it later, when the excess capacity of the present system disappears.

6.4 PROJECT INTERACTIONS

Almost all decisions about capital expenditure involve either–or choices. The firm can build either a 90,000-square-foot warehouse in northern South Dakota or a 100,000-square-foot warehouse in southern North Dakota. It can heat it either by oil or natural gas, and so on. These mutually exclusive options are simple examples of *project interactions*.

[18]The present value of Rs. 118,700 for five years discounted at 6 percent is Rs. 500,000.

All of the examples in the last section involved project interactions. Think back to the first example, the choice between machine A, with a three-year life, and machine B, with a two-year life. A and B interact because they are mutually exclusive, and also because the choice of A or B ripples forward to affect future machine purchases.

Project interactions can arise in countless ways. The literature of industrial engineering sometimes addresses cases of extreme complexity and difficulty. We will be content with two more simple but important examples.

Case 1: Optimal Timing of Investment

The fact that a project has a positive NPV does not mean that it is best undertaken now. It might be even more valuable if undertaken in the future. Similarly, a project with a currently negative NPV might become a valuable opportunity if we wait a bit. Thus *any* project has two mutually exclusive alternatives: Do it now, or wait and invest later.

The question of optimal timing of investment is not difficult under conditions of certainty. We first examine alternative dates *(t)* for making the investment and calculate its net *future* value as of each date. Then, in order to find which of the alternatives would add most to the firm's *current* value, we must work out

$$\frac{\text{Net future value as of date } t}{(1+r)^t}$$

For example, suppose you own a large tract of inaccessible timber. In order to harvest it, you have to invest a substantial amount in access roads and other facilities. The longer you wait, the higher the investment required. On the other hand, lumber prices will rise as you wait, and the trees will keep growing, although at a gradually decreasing rate.

Let us suppose that the net present value of the harvest at different *future* dates is as follows:

	Year of Harvest					
	0	**1**	**2**	**3**	**4**	**5**
Net *future* value (Rs. thousands)	50	64.4	77.5	89.4	100	109.4
Change in value from previous year (%)		+28.8	+20.3	+15.4	+11.9	+9.4

As you can see, the longer you defer cutting the timber, the more money you will make. However, your concern is with the date that maximizes the net *present* value of your investment, that is, its contribution to the value of your firm *today.* You therefore need to discount the net future value of the harvest back to the present. Suppose the appropriate discount rate is 10 percent. Then if you harvest the timber in year 1, it has a net *present* value of Rs. 58,500:

$$\text{NPV if harvested in year 1} = \frac{64.4}{1.10} = 58.5\text{, or Rs. } 58{,}500$$

The net present value (at $t = 0$) for other harvest dates is as follows:

	Year of Harvest					
	0	1	2	3	4	5
Net present value (Rs. thousands)	50	58.5	64.0	67.2	68.3	67.9

The optimal point to harvest the timber is year 4 because this is the point that maximizes NPV.

Notice that before year 4 the net future value of the timber increases by more than 10 percent a year: The gain in value is greater than the cost of the capital that is tied up in the project. After year 4 the gain in value is still positive but less than the cost of capital. You maximize the net present value of your investment if you harvest your timber as soon as the rate of increase in value drops below the cost of capital.[19]

The problem of optimal timing of investment under uncertainty is, of course, much more complicated. An opportunity not taken at $t = 0$ might be either more or less attractive at $t = 1$; there is rarely any way of knowing for sure. Perhaps it is better to strike while the iron is hot even if there is a chance it will become hotter. On the other hand, if you wait a bit you might obtain more information and avoid a bad mistake.[20]

Case 2: Fluctuating Load Factors

Although a Rs. 10 million warehouse may have a positive net present value, it should be built only if it has a higher NPV than a Rs. 9 million alternative. In other words, the NPV of the Rs. 1 million *marginal* investment required to buy the more expensive warehouse must be positive.

One case in which this is easily forgotten is when equipment is needed to meet fluctuating demand. Consider the following problem: A widget manufacturer operates two machines, each of which has a capacity of 1,000 units a year. They have an indefinite life and no salvage value, and so the only costs are the operating expenses of Rs. 2 per widget. Widget manufacture, as everyone knows, is a seasonal business, and widgets are perishable. During the fall and winter, when demand is high, each machine produces at capacity. During the spring and summer, each machine works at 50 percent of capacity. If the discount rate is 10 percent and the machines are kept indefinitely, the present value of the costs is Rs. 30,000:

[19]Our timber-cutting example conveys the right idea about investment timing, but it misses an important practical point: The sooner you cut the first crop of trees, the sooner the second crop can start growing. Thus, the value of the second crop depends on when you cut the first. This more complex and realistic problem might be solved in one of two ways:

1. Find the cutting dates that maximize the present value of a series of harvests, taking account of the different growth rates of young and old trees.
2. Repeat our calculations, counting the future market value of cut-over land as part of the payoff to the first harvest. The value of cut-over land includes the present value of all subsequent harvests.

The second solution is far simpler if you can figure out what cut-over land will be worth.

[20]We return to optimal investment timing under uncertainty in Chapters 10 and 22.

	Two Old Machines
Annual output per machine	750 units
Operating cost per machine	2 × 750 = Rs. 1,500
PV operating cost per machine	1,500/.10 = Rs. 15,000
PV operating cost of two machines	2 × 15,000 = Rs. 30,000

The company is considering whether to replace these machines with newer equipment. The new machines have a similar capacity, and so two would still be needed to meet peak demand. Each new machine costs Rs. 6,000 and lasts indefinitely. Operating expenses are only Re. 1 per unit. On this basis the company calculates that the present value of the costs of two new machines would be Rs. 27,000:

	Two New Machines
Annual output per machine	750 units
Capital cost per machine	Rs. 6,000
Operating cost per machine	1 × 750 = Rs. 750
PV total cost per machine	6,000 + 750/.10 = Rs. 13,500
PV total cost of two machines	2 × 13,500 = Rs. 27,000

Therefore, it scraps both old machines and buys two new ones.

The company was quite right in thinking that two new machines are better than two old ones, but unfortunately it forgot to investigate a third alternative: to replace just one of the old machines. Since the new machine has low operating costs, it would pay to operate it at capacity all year. The remaining old machine could then be kept simply to meet peak demand. The present value of the costs under this strategy is Rs. 26,000:

	One Old Machine	One New Machine
Annual output per machine	500 units	1,000 units
Capital cost per machine	0	Rs. 6,000
Operating cost per machine	2 × 500 = Rs. 1,000	1 × 1,000 = Rs. 1,000
PV total cost per machine	1,000/.10 = Rs. 10,000	6,000 + 1,000/.10 = Rs. 16,000
PV total cost of both machines	Rs. 26,000	

Replacing one machine saves Rs. 4,000; replacing two machines saves only Rs. 3,000. The net present value of the *marginal* investment in the second machine is −Rs. 1,000.

SUMMARY

By now present value calculations should be a matter of routine. However, forecasting cash flows will never be routine. It will always be a skilled, hazardous occupation. Mistakes can be minimized by following three rules:

1. Concentrate on cash flows after taxes. Be wary of accounting data masquerading as cash-flow data.
2. Always judge investments on an incremental basis. Tirelessly track down all cash-flow consequences of your decision. Include opportunity costs. Ignore sunk costs.
3. Treat inflation consistently. Discount nominal cash-flow forecasts at nominal rates and real forecasts at real rates.

We worked through a detailed numerical example (IM&C's guano project), showing the basic steps in calculating project NPV. Remember to track changes in working capital, and stay alert for differences between tax depreciation and the depreciation used in reports to shareholders.

The principles of valuing capital investment projects are the same worldwide, but inputs and assumptions vary by country and currency. For example, cash flows from a project undertaken in France would be in euros, not rupees, and would be forecasted after French taxes.

We might add still another rule: Recognize project interactions. Decisions involving only a choice of accepting or rejecting a project rarely exist, since capital projects can rarely be isolated from other projects or alternatives. The simplest decision normally encountered is to accept or reject or delay. A project having a positive NPV if undertaken today may have a still higher NPV if undertaken tomorrow.

Projects also interact because they are mutually exclusive. You can install machine A or B, for example, but not both. When mutually exclusive choices involve different lengths or time patterns of cash outflows, comparison is difficult unless you convert present values to equivalent annual costs. Think of the equivalent annual cost as the period-by-period rental payment necessary to cover all the cash outflows. Choose A over B, other things equal, if A has the lower equivalent annual cost. Remember, though, to calculate equivalent annual costs in real terms and adjust for technological change if necessary.

This chapter is concerned with the mechanics of applying the net present value rule in practical situations. All our analysis boils down to two simple themes. First, be careful about the definition of alternative projects. Make sure you are comparing like with like. Second, make sure that your calculations include all incremental cash flows.

CONCEPT REVIEW QUESTIONS

1. Why should the financial manager *include* opportunity costs but *ignore* sunk costs when evaluating a proposed capital investment? Give an example of each case. (pages 115–116)
2. Suppose a forgetful manager makes the mistake of discounting nominal project cash flows at a real discount rate. Inflation is projected at 4 percent per year. Does the manager overestimate or underestimate NPV? Assume that the project's NPV is positive with proper discounting. (pages 116–118)
3. What does it mean to "separate investment and financing decisions"? Are interest payments treated as an expense in a standard NPV analysis? (pages 120)

For additional Concept Review Questions, please visit us at www.mhhe.com/bmam8e or refer to your Student CD.

QUIZ

1. Which of the following should be treated as incremental cash flows when deciding whether to invest in a new manufacturing plant? The site is already owned by the company, but existing buildings would need to be demolished.
   a. The market value of the site and existing buildings.
   b. Demolition costs and site clearance.
   c. The cost of a new access road put in last year.
   d. Lost earnings on other products due to executive time spent on the new facility.
   e. A proportion of the cost of leasing the president's jet airplane.

f. Future depreciation of the new plant.
g. The reduction in the corporation's tax bill resulting from tax depreciation of the new plant.
h. The initial investment in inventories of raw materials.
i. Money already spent on engineering design of the new plant.

2. Mr. Art Deco will be paid Rs. 100,000 one year hence. This is a nominal flow, which he discounts at an 8 percent nominal discount rate:

$$PV = \frac{100,000}{1.08} = \text{Rs. } 92,593$$

The inflation rate is 4 percent.

Calculate the PV of Mr. Deco's payment using the equivalent *real* cash flow and *real* discount rate. (You should get exactly the same answer as he did.)

3. True or false?
   a. A project's depreciation tax shields depend on the actual future rate of inflation.
   b. Project cash flows should take account of interest paid on any borrowing undertaken to finance the project.
   c. In the U.S., income reported to the tax authorities must equal income reported to shareholders.
   d. Accelerated depreciation reduces near-term project cash flows and therefore reduces project NPV.

4. How does the PV of depreciation tax shields vary if (i) the additional depreciation is allowed throughout the life of the asset rather than only in the first year of its operation, if (ii) the normal depreciation rate is 25% and there is no additional depreciation?

5. The following table tracks the main components of working capital over the life of a four-year project.

	2004	2005	2006	2007	2008
Accounts receivable	0	150,000	225,000	190,000	0
Inventory	75,000	130,000	130,000	95,000	0
Accounts payable	25,000	50,000	50,000	35,000	0

Calculate net working capital and the cash inflows and outflows due to investment in working capital.

6. When appraising mutually exclusive investments in plant and equipment, financial managers calculate the investments' equivalent annual costs and rank the investments on this basis. Why is this necessary? Why not just compare the investments' NPVs? Explain briefly.

7. Air conditioning for a college dormitory will cost Rs. 1.5 million to install and Rs. 200,000 per year to operate. The system should last 25 years. The real cost of capital is 5 percent, and the college pays no taxes. What is the equivalent annual cost?

8. Machines A and B are mutually exclusive and are expected to produce the following real cash flows:

	Cash Flows (Rs. thousands)			
Machine	C_0	C_1	C_2	C_3
A	−100	+110	+121	
B	−120	+110	+121	+133

The real opportunity cost of capital is 10 percent.
   a. Calculate the NPV of each machine.
   b. Calculate the equivalent annual cash flow from each machine.
   c. Which machine should you buy?

9. Machine C was purchased five years ago for Rs. 200,000 and produces an annual cash flow of Rs. 80,000. It has no salvage value but is expected to last another five years. The company can replace machine C with machine B (see question 8) *either* now *or* at the end of five years. Which should it do?

PRACTICE QUESTIONS

1. Restate the net cash flows in Table 6.6 in real terms. Discount the restated cash flows at a real discount rate. Assume a 20 percent *nominal* rate and 10 percent expected inflation. NPV should be unchanged at +3,802, or Rs. 3,802,000.

2. In 1898 Simon North announced plans to construct a funeral home on land he owned and rented out as a storage area for railway carts. (A local newspaper commended Mr. North for not putting the cart before the hearse.) Rental income from the site barely covered real estate taxes, but the site was valued at $ 45,000. However, Mr. North had refused several offers for the land and planned to continue renting it out if for some reason the funeral home was not built. Therefore he did not include the value of the land as an outlay in his NPV analysis of the funeral home. Was this the correct procedure? Explain.

3. Each of the following statements is true. Explain why they are consistent.

a. When a company introduces a new product, or expands production of an existing product, investment in net working capital is usually an important cash outflow.

b. Forecasting changes in net working capital is not necessary if the timing of *all* cash inflows and outflows is carefully specified.

4. Mrs. Malhotra, the treasurer of Ideal Pune, has a problem. The company has just ordered a new kiln for Rs. 40 lakhs. Of this sum, Rs. 5 lakhs is described by the supplier as an installation cost. Mrs. Malhotra does not know whether the Income Tax Department will permit the company to treat this as a tax-deductible current expense, or as a capital investment. In the latter case, the company could depreciate Rs. 5 lakhs by using 15% as the WDV depreciation rate over a period of 5 years. In this case, she can also charge the written down value of the kiln at the end of the fifth year as depreciation in the sixth year. How will the IT Department's decision affect the after-tax cost of the kiln? The tax rate is 33.66% and the opportunity cost of capital is 15%.

excel

Please visit us at www.mhhe.com/bmam8e or refer to your Student CD .

5. A project requires an initial investment of Rs. 10 lakhs, and is expected to produce a cash inflow before tax of Rs. 2.6 lakhs for five years. Company A has substantial accumulated tax losses and is unlikely to pay taxes in the foreseeable future. Company B pays corporate taxes at a rate of 33.66% and can depreciate the investment for tax purposes using a WDV depreciation rate of 15% in the first four years. Company B can charge the entire written down value of the project as depreciation in the fifth year. Suppose, the opportunity cost of capital is 8 percent. Ignore inflation.

a. Calculate project NPV for each company.

b. What is the IRR of the after-tax cash flows for each company? What does comparison of the IRRs suggest is the effective corporate tax rate?

excel

Please visit us at www.mhhe.com/bmam8e or refer to your Student CD .

6. Go back to the guano project again.

a. How does the guano project's NPV change if IM&C is forced to depriciate the asset by using 10% as the depreciation rate?

b. New engineering estimates raise the possibility that capital investment will be more than Rs. 10 million, perhaps as much as Rs. 15 million. On the other hand, you believe that the 20 percent cost of capital is unrealistically high and that the true cost of capital is about 11 percent. Is the project still attractive under these alternative assumptions?

c. Continue with the assumed Rs. 15 million capital investment and the 11 percent cost of capital. What if sales, cost of goods sold, and net working capital are each 10 percent higher in every year? Recalculate NPV. *Note:* Enter the revised sales, cost, and working-capital forecasts in the spreadsheet for Table 6.1.

d. Assume that IM&C does not have to pay any tax in year 7, following Section 50 of the Income Tax Act in India. Re-estimate the NPV of the project.

excel

Please visit us at www.mhhe.com/bmam8e or refer to your Student CD .

7. A widget manufacturer currently produces 200,000 units a year. It buys widget lids from an outside supplier at a price of Rs. 2 a lid. The plant manager believes that it would be cheaper to make these lids rather than buy them. Direct production costs are estimated to be only Rs. 1.50 a lid. The necessary machinery would cost Rs. 150,000 and would last 10 years. This investment could be written off for tax purposes using the seven-year tax depreciation schedule. The plant manager estimates that the operation would require additional working capital of Rs. 30,000 but argues that this sum can be ignored since it is recoverable at the end of the 10 years. If the company pays tax at a rate of 35 percent and the opportunity cost of capital is 15 percent, would you support the plant manager's proposal? State clearly any additional assumptions that you need to make.

eXcel

Please visit us at www.mhhe.com/bmam8e or refer to your Student CD.

8. Reliable Electric is considering a proposal to manufacture a new type of industrial electric motor which would replace most of its existing product line. A research break-through has given Reliable a two-year lead on its competitors. The project proposal is summarized in Table 6.7.
   a. Read the notes to the table carefully. Which entries make sense? Which do not? Why or why not?
   b. What additional information would you need to construct a version of Table 6.7 that makes sense?
   c. Construct such a table and recalculate NPV. Make additional assumptions as necessary.

	2003	2004	2005	2006–2013
1. Capital expenditure	−10,400			
2. Research and development	−2,000			
3. Working capital	−4,000			
4. Revenue		8,000	16,000	40,000
5. Operating costs		−4,000	−8,000	−20,000
6. Overhead		−800	−1,600	−4,000
7. Depreciation		−1,040	−1,040	−1,040
8. Interest		−2,160	−2,160	−2,160
9. Income	−2,000	0	3,200	12,800
10. Tax	0	0	420	4,480
11. Net cash flow	−16,400	0	2,780	8,320
12. Net present value = +13,932				

TABLE 6.7

Cash flows and present value of Reliable Electric's proposed investment (Rs. thousands). See Practice Question 8.

Notes:

1. *Capital expenditure:* Rs. 8 million for new machinery and Rs. 2.4 million for a warehouse extension. The full cost of the extension has been charged to this project, although only about half of the space is currently needed. Since the new machinery will be housed in an existing factory building, no charge has been made for land and building.
2. *Research and development:* Rs. 1.82 million spent in 2002. This figure was corrected for 10 percent inflation from the time of expenditure to date. Thus 1.82 × 1.1 = Rs. 2 million.
3. *Working capital:* Initial investment in inventories.
4. *Revenue:* These figures assume sales of 2,000 motors in 2004, 4,000 in 2005, and 10,000 per year from 2006 through 2013. The initial unit price of Rs. 4,000 is forecasted to remain constant in real terms.
5. *Operating costs:* These include all direct and indirect costs. Indirect costs (heat, light, power, fringe benefits, etc.) are assumed to be 200 percent of direct labor costs. Operating costs per unit are forecasted to remain constant in real terms at Rs. 2,000.
6. *Overhead:* Marketing and administrative costs, assumed equal to 10 percent of revenue.
7. *Depreciation:* Straight-line for 10 years.
8. *Interest:* Charged on capital expenditure and working capital at Reliable's current borrowing rate of 15 percent.
9. *Income:* Revenue less the sum of research and development, operating costs, overhead, depreciation, and interest.
10. *Tax:* 35 percent of income. However, income is negative in 2003. This loss is carried forward and deducted from taxable income in 2005.
11. *Net cash flow:* Assumed equal to income less tax.
12. *Net present value:* NPV of net cash flow at a 15 percent discount rate.

9. Marsha Jones has bought a used Mercedes horse transporter for her Connecticut estate. It cost $ 35,000. The object is to save on horse transporter rentals.

Marsha had been renting a transporter every other week for $ 200 per day plus $ 1.00 per mile. Most of the trips are 80 or 100 miles in total. Marsha usually gives the driver a $ 40 tip. With the new transporter she will only have to pay for diesel fuel and maintenance, at about $ .45 per mile. Insurance costs for Marsha's transporter are $ 1,200 per year.

The transporter will probably be worth $ 15,000 (in real terms) after eight years, when Marsha's horse Nike will be ready to retire.

Is the transporter a positive-NPV investment? Assume a nominal discount rate of 9 percent and a 3 percent forecasted inflation rate. Marsha's transporter is a personal outlay, not a business or financial investment, so taxes can be ignored.

excel

Please visit us at www.mhhe.com/bmam8e or refer to your Student CD.

10. United Pigpen is considering a proposal to manufacture high-protein hog feed. The project would make use of an existing warehouse, which is currently rented out to a neighboring firm. The next year's rental charge on the warehouse is Rs. 100,000, and thereafter the rent is expected to grow in line with inflation at 4 percent a year. In addition to using the warehouse, the proposal envisages an investment in plant and equipment of Rs. 1.2 million. This could be depreciated for tax purposes straight-line over 10 years. However, Pigpen expects to terminate the project at the end of eight years and to resell the plant and equipment in year 8 for Rs. 400,000. Finally, the project requires an initial investment in working capital of Rs. 350,000. Thereafter, working capital is forecasted to be 10 percent of sales in each of years 1 through 7.

Year 1 sales of hog feed are expected to be Rs. 4.2 million, and thereafter sales are forecast to grow by 5 percent a year, slightly faster than the inflation rate. Manufacturing costs are expected to be 90 percent of sales, and profits are subject to tax at 35 percent. The cost of capital is 12 percent.

What is the NPV of Pigpen's project?

11. In the International Mulch and Compost example (Section 6.2), we assumed that losses on the project could be used to offset taxable profits elswhere in the corporation. Suppose that the losses had to be carried forward and offset against future taxable profits from the project. How would the project NPV change? What is the value of the company's ability to use the tax deductions immediately?

excel

Please visit us at www.mhhe.com/bmam8e or refer to your Student CD.

12. Table 6.8 shows investment and projected income in euros for Flanel's new perfume factory. Note that the format of Table 6.8 matches Table 6.1. Go to the live Excel spreadsheet versions of Table 6.8 on this book's CD or at **www.mhhe.com/bmam8e**. Forecast cash flows and calculate NPV. The nominal cost of capital in euros is 11 percent.

13. As a result of improvements in product engineering, United Automation is able to sell one of its two milling machines. Both machines perform the same function but differ in age. The newer machine could be sold today for $ 50,000. Its operating costs are $ 20,000 a year, but in five years the machine will require a $ 20,000 overhaul. Thereafter operating costs will be $ 30,000 until the machine is finally sold in year 10 for $ 5,000.

The older machine could be sold today for $ 25,000. If it is kept, it will need an immediate $ 20,000 overhaul. Thereafter operating costs will be $ 30,000 a year until the machine is finally sold in year 5 for $ 5,000.

Both machines are fully depreciated for tax purposes. The company pays tax at 35 percent. Cash flows have been forecasted in real terms. The real cost of capital is 12 percent.

Which machine should United Automation sell? Explain the assumptions underlying your answer.

excel

Please visit us at www.mhhe.com/bmam8e or refer to your Student CD.

14. Hayden Inc. has a number of copiers that were bought four years ago for Rs. 20,000. Currently maintenance costs Rs. 2,000 a year, but the maintenance agreement expires at the end of two years and thereafter the annual maintenance charge will rise to Rs. 8,000. The machines have a current resale value of Rs. 8,000, but at the end of year 2 their value will have fallen to Rs. 3,500. By the end of year 6 the machines will be valueless and would be scrapped.

		Period								
		0	1	2	3	4	5	6	7	8
1.	Capital investment	83.5								-12.0
2.	Accumulated depreciation		11.9	23.9	35.8	47.7	59.6	71.6	83.5	
3.	Year-end book value	83.5	71.6	59.6	47.7	35.8	23.9	11.9	0.0	
4.	Working capital	2.3	4.4	7.6	6.9	5.3	3.2	2.5	0.0	
5.	Total book value (3 + 4)	85.8	76.0	67.2	54.6	41.1	27.1	14.4	0.0	
6.	Sales		27.0	51.3	89.1	81.0	62.1	37.8	29.7	
7.	Cost of goods sold		9.2	17.4	30.3	27.5	21.1	12.9	10.1	
8.	Other costs		15.5	15.5	5.2	5.2	5.2	5.2	5.2	
9.	Depreciation		11.9	11.9	11.9	11.9	11.9	11.9	11.9	
10.	Pretax profit (6 - 7 - 8 - 9)		-9.6	6.5	41.7	36.4	23.9	7.8	2.5	
11.	Tax at 34.4%		-3.4	2.3	14.8	12.9	8.5	2.8	0.9	-4.2
12.	Profit after tax (10 - 11)		-6.2	4.2	26.9	23.5	15.4	5.0	1.6	-7.8

TABLE 6.8

Projected investment and income for Flanel's new perfume factory. Figures in millions of euros.

Note: The format of this table matches Table 6.1. Cost of goods sold excludes depreciation.

excel

Please visit us at www.mhhe.com/bmam8e or refer to your Student CD

Hayden is considering replacing the copiers with new machines that would do essentially the same job. These machines cost Rs. 25,000, and the company can take out an eight-year maintenance contract for Rs. 1,000 a year. The machines will have no value by the end of the eight years and will be scrapped.

Both machines are depreciated by using 15% WDV depreciation rate, and the tax rate is 35 percent. Assume for simplicity that the inflation rate is zero. The real cost of capital is 7 percent.

When should Hayden replace its copiers?

15. Return to the start of Section 6.3, where we calculated the equivalent annual cost of producing reformulated gasoline in California. Capital investment was $ 400 million. Suppose this amount can be depreciated for tax purposes on the 10-year MACRS schedule from Table 6.4. The marginal tax rate, including California taxes, is 39 percent, the cost of capital is 7 percent, and there is no inflation. The refinery improvements have an economic life of 25 years.

a. Calculate the after-tax equivalent annual cost. *Hint:* It's easiest to use the PV of depreciation tax shields as an offset to the initial investment.

b. How much extra would retail gasoline customers have to pay to cover this equivalent annual cost? *Note:* Extra income from higher retail prices would be taxed.

16. You own 500 acres of timberland, with young timber worth Rs. 40,000 if logged now. This represents 1,000 cords of wood worth Rs. 40 per cord net of costs of cutting and hauling. A paper company has offered to purchase your tract for Rs. 140,000. Should you accept the offer? You have the following information:

Years	Yearly Growth Rate of Cords per Acre
1–4	16%
5–8	11
9–13	4
14 and subsequent years	1

- You expect price per cord to increase at 4 percent per year indefinitely.
- The cost of capital is 9 percent. Ignore taxes.
- The market value of your land would be Rs. 100 per acre if you cut and removed the timber this year. The value of cut-over land is also expected to grow at 4 percent per year indefinitely.

17. The Borstal Company has to choose between two machines that do the same job but have different lives. The two machines have the following costs:

Year	Machine A	Machine B
0	\$ 40,000	\$ 50,000
1	10,000	8,000
2	10,000	8,000
3	10,000 + replace	8,000
4		8,000 + replace

These costs are expressed in real terms.

a. Suppose you are Borstal's financial manager. If you had to buy one or the other machine and rent it to the production manager for that machine's economic life, what annual rental payment would you have to charge? Assume a 6 percent real discount rate and ignore taxes.

b. Which machine should Borstal buy?

c. Usually the rental payments you derived in part (a) are just hypothetical—a way of calculating and interpreting equivalent annual cost. Suppose you actually do buy one of the machines and rent it to the production manager. How much would you actually have to charge in each future year if there is steady 8 percent per year inflation? *Note:* The rental payments calculated in part (a) are real cash flows. You would have to mark up those payments to cover inflation.

18. Look again at your calculations for question 17 above. Suppose that technological change is expected to reduce costs by 10 percent per year. There will be new machines in year 1 that cost 10 percent less to buy and operate than A and B. In year 2 there will be a second crop of new machines incorporating a further 10 percent reduction, and so on. How does this change the equivalent annual costs of machines A and B?

19. The president's executive jet is not fully utilized. You judge that its use by other officers would increase direct operating costs by only \$ 20,000 a year and would save \$ 100,000 a year in airline bills. On the other hand, you believe that with the increased use the company will need to replace the jet at the end of three years rather than four. A new jet costs \$ 1.1 million and (at its current low rate of use) has a life of six years. Assume that the company does not pay taxes. All cash flows are forecasted in real terms. The real opportunity cost of capital is 8 percent. Should you try to persuade the president to allow other officers to use the plane?

CHALLENGE QUESTIONS

1. One measure of the effective tax rate is the difference between the IRRs of pretax and after-tax cash flows, divided by the pretax IRR. Consider, for example, an investment I generating a perpetual stream of pretax cash flows C. The pretax IRR is C/I, and the after-tax IRR is $C(1-T_C)/I$, where T_C is the statutory tax rate. The effective rate, call it T_E, is

$$T_E = \frac{C/I - C(1-T_c)/I}{C/I} = T_c$$

In this case the effective rate equals the statutory rate.

a. Calculate T_E for the guano project in Section 6.2.

b. How does the effective rate depend on the tax depreciation schedule? On the inflation rate?

c. Consider a project where all of the up-front investment is treated as an expense for tax purposes. What is the effective tax rate for such a project?

2. We warned that equivalent annual costs should be calculated in real terms. We did not fully explain why. This problem will show you.

Look back to the cash flows for machines A and B (in "Choosing between Long- and Short-Lived Equipment"). The present values of purchase and operating costs are 28.37 (over three years for A) and 21.00 (over two years for B). The real discount rate is 6 percent, and the inflation rate is 5 percent.

a. Calculate the three- and two-year *level nominal* annuities which have present values of 28.37 and 21.00. Explain why these annuities are *not* realistic estimates of equivalent annual costs. (*Hint:* In real life machinery rentals increase with inflation.)

b. Suppose the inflation rate increases to 25 percent. The real interest rate stays at 6 percent. Recalculate the level nominal annuities. Note that the *ranking* of machines A and B appears to change. Why?

MINI-CASE

New Economy Transport (A)

The New Economy Transport Company (NETCO) was formed in 1952 to carry cargo and passengers between ports in the Pacific Northwest and Alaska. By 2005 its fleet had grown to four vessels, including a small dry-cargo vessel, the *Vital Spark*.

The *Vital Spark* is 25 years old and badly in need of an overhaul. Peter Handy, the finance director, has just been presented with a proposal that would require the following expenditures:

Overhaul engine and generators	$ 340,000
Replace radar and other electronic equipment	75,000
Repairs to hull and superstructure	310,000
Painting and other repairs	95,000
	$ 820,000

Mr. Handy believes that all these outlays could be depreciated for tax purposes in the seven-year MACRS class.

NETCO's chief engineer, McPhail, estimates the post-overhaul operating costs as follows:

Fuel	$ 450,000
Labor and benefits	480,000
Maintenance	141,000
Other	110,000
	$ 1,181,000

These costs generally increase with inflation, which is forecasted at 2.5 percent a year.

The *Vital Spark* is carried on NETCO's books at a net depreciated value of only $ 100,000, but could probably be sold "as is," along with an extensive inventory of spare parts, for $ 200,000. The book value of the spare parts inventory is $ 40,000. Sale of the *Vital Spark* would generate an immediate tax liability on the difference between sale price and book value.

The chief engineer also suggests installation of a brand-new engine and control system, which would cost an extra $ 600,000.[20] This additional equipment would not substantially improve the *Vital Spark*'s performance, but would result in the following reduced annual fuel, labor, and maintenance costs:

Fuel	$ 400,000
Labor and benefits	405,000
Maintenance	105,000
Other	110,000
	$ 1,020,000

Overhaul of the *Vital Spark* would take it out of service for several months. The overhauled vessel would resume commercial service next year. Based on past experience, Mr. Handy believes that it would generate revenues of about $ 1.4 million next year, increasing with inflation thereafter.

But the *Vital Spark* cannot continue forever. Even if overhauled, its useful life is probably no more than 10 years, 12 years at the most. Its salvage value when finally taken out of service will be trivial.

NETCO is a conservatively financed firm in a mature business. It normally evaluates capital investments using an 11 percent cost of capital. This is a nominal, not a real, rate. NETCO's tax rate is 35 percent.

QUESTION

1. Calculate the NPV of the proposed overhaul of the *Vital Spark*, with and without the new engine and control system. To do the calculation, you will have to prepare a spreadsheet table showing all costs after taxes over the vessel's remaining economic life. Take special care with your assumptions about depreciation tax shields and inflation.

New Economy Transport (B)

There is no question that the *Vital Spark* needs an overhaul soon. However, Mr. Handy feels it unwise to proceed without also considering the purchase of a new vessel. Cohn and Doyle, Inc., a Wisconsin shipyard, has approached NETCO with a design incorporating a Kort nozzle, extensively automated navigation and power control systems, and much more comfortable accommodations for the crew. Estimated annual operating costs of the new vessel are:

Fuel	$ 380,000
Labor and benefits	330,000
Maintenance	70,000
Other	105,000
	$ 885,000

The crew would require additional training to handle the new vessel's more complex and sophisticated equipment. Training would probably cost $ 50,000 next year.

The estimated operating costs for the new vessel assume that it would be operated in the same way as the *Vital Spark*. However, the new vessel should be able to handle a larger load on some routes, which could generate additional revenues, net of additional out-of-pocket costs, of as much as $ 100,000 per year. Moreover, a new vessel would have useful service life of 20 years or more.

Cohn and Doyle offered the new vessel for a fixed price of $ 3,000,000, payable half immediately and half on delivery next year.

[20]This additional outlay would also qualify for tax depreciation in the seven-year MACRS class.

Mr. Handy stepped out on the foredeck of the *Vital Spark* as she chugged down the Cook Inlet. "A rusty old tub," he muttered, "but she's never let us down. I'll bet we could keep her going until next year while Cohn and Doyle are building her replacement. We could use up the spare parts to keep her going. We might even be able to sell or scrap her for book value when her replacement arrives.

"But how do I compare the NPV of a new ship with the old *Vital Spark*? Sure, I could run a 20-year NPV spreadsheet, but I don't have a clue how the replacement will be used in 2020 or 2025. Maybe I could compare the overall *cost* of overhauling and operating the *Vital Spark* to the cost of buying and operating the proposed replacement."

QUESTIONS

1. Calculate and compare the equivalent annual costs of (a) overhauling and operating the *Vital Spark* for 12 more years, and (b) buying and operating the proposed replacement vessel for 20 years. What should Mr. Handy do if the replacement's annual costs are the same or lower?
2. Suppose the replacement's equivalent annual costs are higher than the *Vital Spark*'s. What additional information should Mr. Handy seek in this case?

PART TWO RELATED WEB SITES

Chapter 7 provides an overview of long-term returns on stocks and bonds. You can find long-term securities' price data on:

www.globalfindata.com

www.econ.yale.edu/~shiller (Robert Shiller's home page)

In Chapter 8 we explain why risk can be measured by "beta." Equity betas for individual stocks can be found on Yahoo! (or you can download the stock prices from Yahoo! and calculate your own measures):

finance.yahoo.com

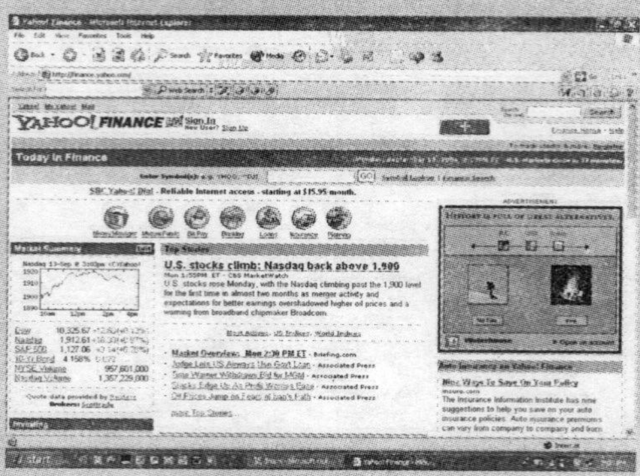

Chapter 9 looks at portfolio construction. Campbell Harvey's home page includes software to calculate efficient frontiers for portfolios of two or three assets:

www.duke.edu/~charvey

Data on the Fama–French factors are published on Ken French's Web site:

mba.tuck.dartmouth.edu/pages/faculty/ken.french

PART [2]

RISK

AMAZON.COM STOCK STARTED trading in May 1997 at a price of $ 1.73. By December 1999, the stock price had risen by over 6,000 percent. Within little more than a year it had slumped by 90 percent. These gyrations in Amazon's stock price were unusually large, but they remind us how risky investment in common stocks can be.

Most investors are not adrenaline junkies; they don't enjoy taking risks. Therefore they require a higher expected return from risky investments. Companies recognize this in their capital budgeting decisions. An investment in a risky new project adds value only if the expected return is higher than investors could expect from an equally risky investment in the capital market.

But that raises two questions. How should risk be measured? And what is the relationship between risk and expected return? We tackle these two questions in Part 2.

CHAPTER [7]

INTRODUCTION TO RISK, RETURN, AND THE OPPORTUNITY COST OF CAPITAL

WE HAVE MANAGED to go through six chapters without directly addressing the problem of risk, but now the jig is up. We can no longer be satisfied with vague statements like "The opportunity cost of capital depends on the risk of the project." We need to know how risk is defined, what the links are between risk and the opportunity cost of capital, and how the financial manager can cope with risk in practical situations.

In this chapter we concentrate on the first of these issues and leave the other two to Chapters 8 and 9. We start by summarizing more than 100 years of evidence on rates of return in capital markets. Then we take a first look at investment risks and show how they can be reduced by portfolio diversification. We introduce you to beta, the standard risk measure for individual securities.

The themes of this chapter, then, are portfolio risk, security risk, and diversification. For the most part, we take the view of the individual investor. But at the end of the chapter we turn the problem around and ask whether diversification makes sense as a corporate objective.

7.1 OVER A CENTURY OF CAPITAL MARKET HISTORY (IN US) IN ONE EASY LESSON

Financial analysts are blessed with an enormous quantity of data. There are comprehensive databases of the prices of U.S. stocks, bonds, options, commodities, as well as huge amounts of data for securities in other countries. We will focus on a study by Dimson, Marsh, and Staunton that measures the historical performance of three portfolios of U.S. securities:[1]

1. A portfolio of Treasury bills, that is, U.S. government debt securities maturing in less than one year.[2]
2. A portfolio of U.S. government bonds.
3. A portfolio of U.S. common stocks.

These investments offer different degrees of risk. Treasury bills are about as safe an investment as you can make. There is no risk of default, and their short maturity means that the prices of Treasury bills are relatively stable. In fact, an investor who wishes to lend money for, say, three months can achieve a perfectly certain payoff by purchasing a Treasury bill maturing in three months. However, the investor cannot lock in a **real** rate of return: There is still some uncertainty about inflation.

By switching to long-term government bonds, the investor acquires an asset whose price fluctuates as interest rates vary. (Bond prices fall when interest rates rise and rise when interest rates fall.) An investor who shifts from bonds to common stocks shares in all the ups and downs of the issuing companies.

Figure 7.1 shows how your money would have grown if you had invested $ 1 at the start of 1900 and reinvested all dividend or interest income in each of the three portfolios.[3] Figure 7.2 is identical except that it depicts the growth in the **real** value of the portfolio. We will focus here on nominal values.

[1]See E. Dimson, P. R. Marsh, and M. Staunton, *Triumph of the Optimists: 101 Years of Investment Returns* (Princeton, NJ: Princeton University Press, 2002).

[2] Treasury bills were not issued before 1919. Before that date the interest rate used is the commercial paper rate.

[3]Portfolio values are plotted on a log scale. If they were not, the ending values for the common stock portfolio would run off the top of the page.

FIGURE 7.1

How an investment of $ 1 at the start of 1900 would have grown, assuming reinvestment of all dividend and interest payments.

Source: E. Dimson, P. R. Marsh, and M. Staunton, *Triumph of the Optimists: 101 Years of Investment Returns* (Princeton, NJ: Princeton University Press, 2002), with updates provided by the authors.

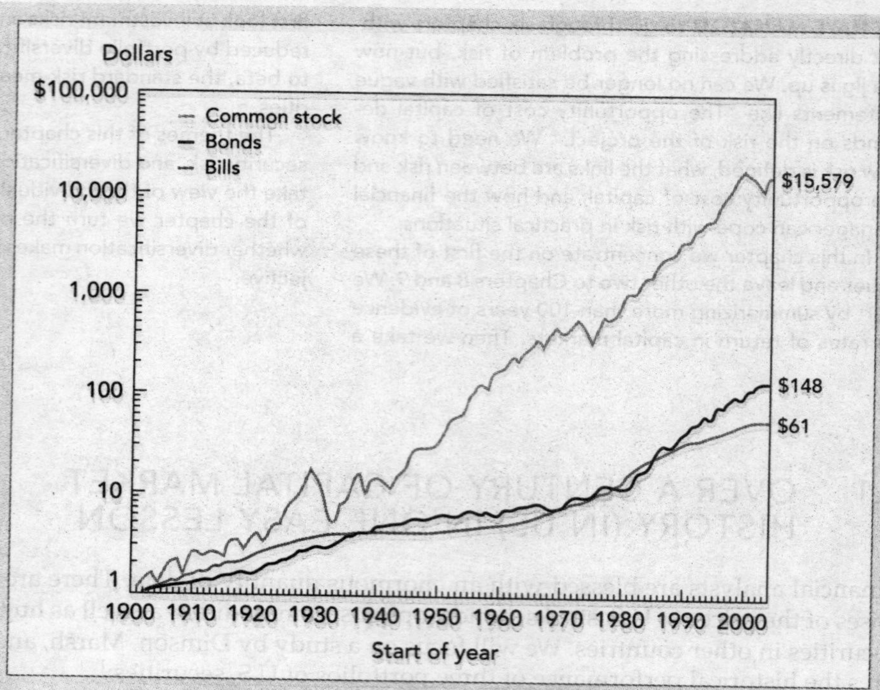

FIGURE 7.1A

How an investment of Rs. 100 in India at the start of 1978–79 would have grown assuming reinvestment of all the dividend and interest income..

Source: Data compiled from www.rbi.org.in.

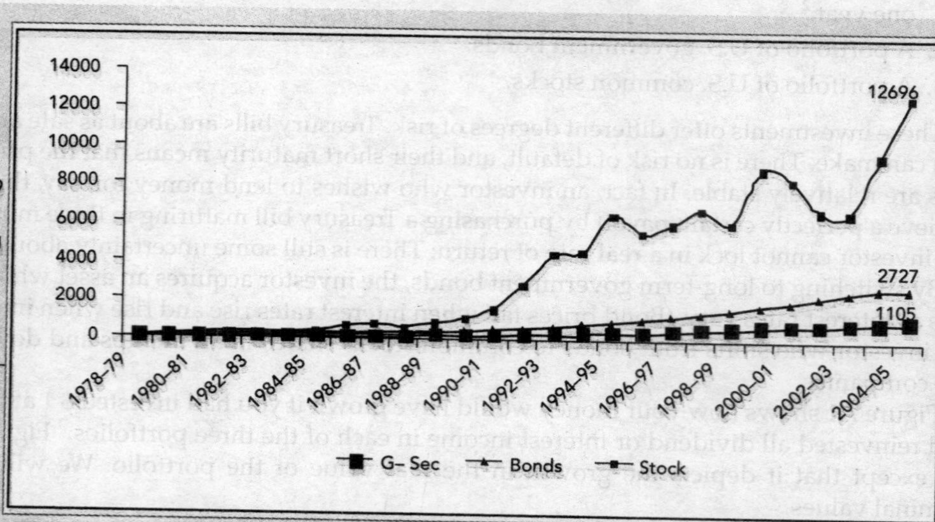

	Average Annual Rate of Return		Average Risk Premium (Extra Return versus Treasury Bills)
	Nominal	Real	
Treasury bills	4.1	1.1	0
Government bonds	5.2	2.3	1.2
Common stocks	11.7	8.5	7.6

TABLE 7.1

Average rates of return on U.S. Treasury bills, government bonds, and common stocks, 1900–2003 (figures in percent per year)

Source: E. Dimson, P. R. Marsh, and M. Staunton, *Triumph of the Optimists: 101 Years of Investment Returns*, (Princeton, NJ: Princeton University Press, 2002), with updates provided by the authors.

Investment performance coincides with our intuitive risk ranking. A dollar invested in the safest investment, Treasury bills, would have grown to \$ 61 by the end of 2003, barely enough to keep up with inflation. An investment in long-term Treasury bonds would have produced \$ 148. Common stocks were in a class by themselves. An investor who placed a dollar in the stocks of large U.S. firms would have received \$ 15,579.

We can also calculate the rate of return from these portfolios for each year from 1900 to 2003. This rate of return reflects both cash receipts—dividends or interest—and the capital gains or losses realized during the year. Averages of the 104 annual rates of return for each portfolio are shown in Table 7.1.

Since 1900 Treasury bills have provided the lowest average return—4.1 percent per year in *nominal* terms and 1.1 percent in *real* terms. In other words, the average rate of inflation over this period was about 3 percent per year. Common stocks were again the winners. Stocks of major corporations provided an average nominal return of 11.7 percent. By taking on the risk of common stocks, investors earned a risk premium of $11.7 - 4.1 = 7.6$ percent over the return on Treasury bills.

You may ask why we look back over such a long period to measure average rates of return. The reason is that annual rates of return for common stocks fluctuate so much that averages taken over short periods are meaningless. Our only hope of gaining insights from historical rates of return is to look at a very long period.[4]

[4]We cannot be sure that this period is truly representative and that the average is not distorted by a few unusually high or low returns. The reliability of an estimate of the average is usually measured by its *standard error.* For example, the standard error of our estimate of the average risk premium on common stocks is 2.0 percent. There is a 95 percent chance that the *true* average is within plus or minus 2 standard errors of the 7.6 percent estimate. In other words, if you said that the true average was between 3.6 and 11.6 percent, you would have a 95 percent chance of being right. *Technical note:* The standard error of the average is equal to the standard deviation divided by the square root of the number of observations. In our case the standard deviation is 20.1 percent, and therefore the standard error is $20.1 / \sqrt{104} = 2.0$.

FIGURE 7.2

How an investment of $ 1 at the start of 1900 would have grown in real terms, assuming reinvestment of all dividend and interest payments. Compare this plot with Figure 7.1, and note how inflation has eroded the purchasing power of returns to investors.

Source: E. Dimson, P. R. Marsh, and M. Staunton, *Triumph of the Optimists: 101 Years of Investment Returns* (Princeton, NJ: Princeton University Press, 2002), with updates provided by the authors.

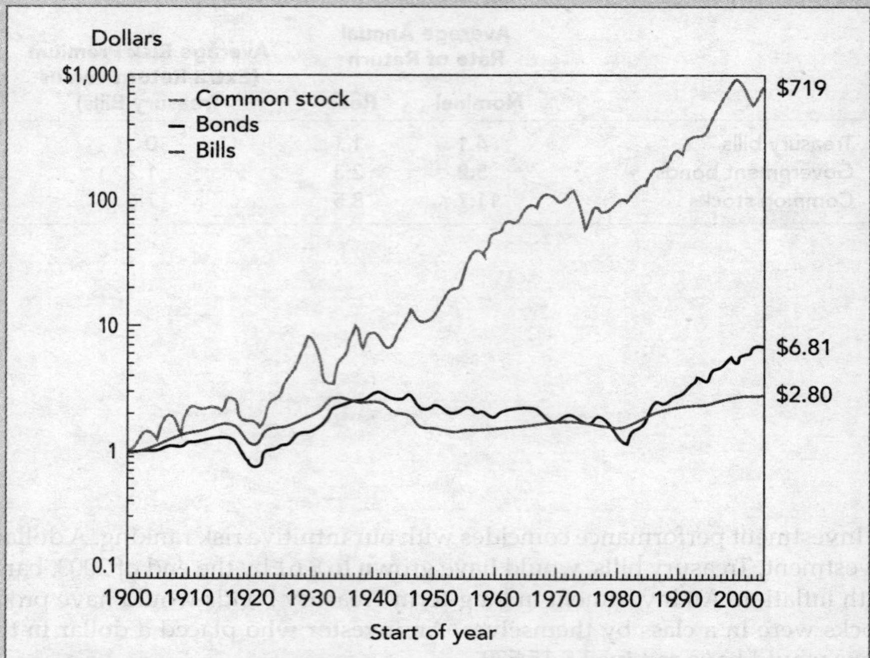

FIGURE 7.2A

How an investment of Rs. 100 in India at the start of 1978–79 would have grown in real terms, assuming reinvestment of all interest payments. Compare this plot with Figure 7.1.A, and note how inflation has eroded the purchasing power of returns to investors.

Source: Data compiled from www.rbi.org.in

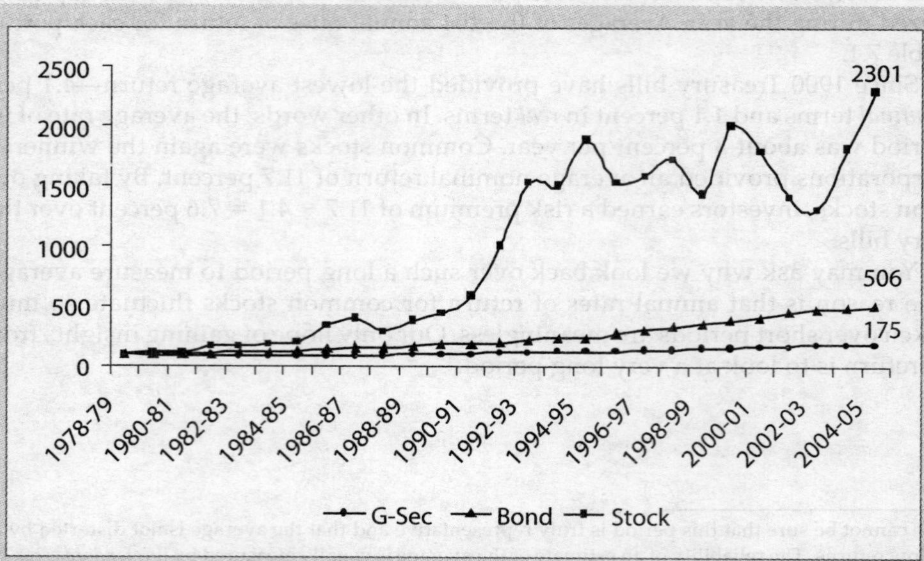

What about evidence from India? Though the Mumbai Stock Exchange started functioning from as early as 1875, it started compiling the BSE sensitivity index (Sensex) only from 1986. The base-year of Sensex is 1978–79 and the base value is 100. The website of the Reserve Bank of India contains the monthly data on Sensex from 1978–79[5]. We estimate the yearly returns on Sensex from 1978-79 by using the data from this website. We also obtain estimates of yields on 1-year Government Securities, popularly known as G-Secs (a proxy for risk free rate of return) and the prime lending rate (a proxy for AAA rated corporate bond rate) from the website of RBI.

In Figure 7.1.A, we show how your money would have grown if you had invested Rs. 100 at the start of 1978–79 and reinvested the dividend and interest income in these portfolios[6]. Figure 7.2.A is identical except that it depicts the growth in the real value of the portfolio.

We can see from Figures 7.1 and 7.1A that the investment performance of the three portfolios coincides with our intuitive risk ranking in India also. In Table 7.1.A, we report the rate of return from these portfolios. This rate of return reflects both cash receipts – dividends and interest – and the capital gains or losses realized (only for the stock portfolio) during the year.

	Average Annual Rate of Return		Average Risk Premium (Extra Return versus 1-year G-Sec Yields)
	Nominal	Real	
1-Year G-Sec Yield	9.74	2.34	0
AAA-Rated Corporate Bonds	14.16	6.55	4.42
Common stocks	23.04	15.78	13.30

TABLE 7.1A

Average rates of return on 5-year bank deposits, AAA-rated corporate bonds and common stocks, 1978–2005 in India (Figures in percent per year)

Source: Compiled from www.rbi.org.in

Since 1979–80, the 1-year Government Securities in India have provided the lowest average return, 9.74 percent per year, in nominal terms and 2.34 percent in real terms. In other words, the average rate of inflation over this period was about 7.4 percent per year. Common stocks were clearly the winners. Stocks of the Sensex 30 corporations provided an average nominal return of 23 percent. By taking on the risk of common stocks, investors earned a risk premium of 13.3 percent over the return on 1-year G-Secs[7].

Arithmetic Averages and Compound Annual Returns

Notice that the average returns shown in Tables 7.1 and 7.1 A are arithmetic averages. Thus for example, in Table 7.1 A, we simply added twenty-six annual returns and divided by 26. The arithmetic average is higher than the compound annual return over the period. The 104-year compound annual return for the S&P index was 9.7 percent.[8] The 26-year compound annual return for the Sensex was 20.48 percent.

[5]See http://www.rbi.org.in/scripts/Statistics.aspx

[6] While computing Sensex, BSE adjusts for rights issue, bonus issue, mergers, spin-offs, conversion of debentures, buyback of shares and other corporate restructurings. It however, makes no adjustment for dividend. We assume that the dividend yield on Sensex is a constant 3.1 percent during 1979–2005. This has been the average dividend yield on Sensex during 1979–2005.

[7]If we consider only the 1990–2005 period, then the risk premium on Sensex comes to a mere 9 percent

[8] This was calculated from $(1 + r)^{104} = 15{,}579$, which implies $r = .097$. *Technical note:* For lognormally distributed returns the annual compound return is equal to the arithmetic average return minus half the variance. For example, the annual standard deviation of returns on the U.S. market was about .20, or 20 percent. Variance was therefore $.20^2$, or .04. The compound annual return is $.04/2 = .02$, or 2 percentage points less than the arithmetic average.

The proper uses of arithmetic and compound rates of return from past investments are often misunderstood. Therefore, we call a brief time-out for a clarifying example.

Suppose that the price of Big Oil's common stock is Rs. 100. There is an equal chance that at the end of the year the stock will be worth Rs. 90, Rs. 110, or Rs. 130. Therefore, the return could be −10 percent, +10 percent, or +30 percent (we assume that Big Oil does not pay a dividend). The *expected* return is ⅓(−10 + 10 + 30) = +10 percent.

If we run the process in reverse and discount the expected cash flow by the expected rate of return, we obtain the value of Big Oil's stock:

$$PV = \frac{110}{1.10} = \text{Rs. } 100$$

The expected return of 10 percent is therefore the correct rate at which to discount the expected cash flow from Big Oil's stock. It is also the opportunity cost of capital for investments that have the same degree of risk as Big Oil.

Now suppose that we observe the returns on Big Oil stock over a large number of years. If the odds are unchanged, the return will be −10 percent in a third of the years, +10 percent in a further third, and +30 percent in the remaining years. The arithmetic average of these yearly returns is

$$\frac{-10 + 10 + 30}{3} = +10\%$$

Thus the arithmetic average of the returns correctly measures the opportunity cost of capital for investments of similar risk to Big Oil stock.[9]

The average compound annual return[10] on Big Oil stock would be

$$(.9 \times 1.1 \times 1.3)^{1/3} - 1 = .088, \text{ or } 8.8\%,$$

which is *less* than the opportunity cost of capital. Investors would not be willing to invest in a project that offered an 8.8 percent expected return if they could get an expected return of 10 percent in the capital markets. The net present value of such a project would be

$$NPV = -100 + \frac{108.8}{1.1} = -1.1$$

Moral: If the cost of capital is estimated from historical returns or risk premiums, use arithmetic averages, not compound annual rates of return.[11]

---

[9]You sometimes hear that the arithmetic average correctly measures the opportunity cost of capital for one-year cash flows, but not for more distant ones. Let us check. Suppose that you expect to receive a cash flow of Rs. 121 in year 2. We know that one-year hence investors will value that cash flow by discounting at 10 percent (the arithmetic average of possible returns). In other words, at the end of the year they will be willing to pay $PV_1 = 121/1.10$ = Rs. 110 for the expected cash flow. But we already know how to value an asset that pays off Rs. 110 in year 1—just discount at the 10 percent opportunity cost of capital. Thus $PV_0 = PV_1/1.10 = 110/1.1$ = Rs. 100. Our example demonstrates that the arithmetic average (10 percent in our example) provides a correct measure of the opportunity cost of capital regardless of the timing of the cash flow.

[10]The compound annual return is often referred to as the *geometric average* return.

[11]Our discussion above assumed that we *knew* that the returns of −10, +10, and +30 percent were equally likely. For an analysis of the effect of uncertainty about the expected return see I. A. Cooper, "Arithmetic Versus Geometric Mean Estimators: Setting Discount Rates for Capital Budgeting," *European Financial Management* 2 (July 1996), pp. 157–167.

Using Historical Evidence to Evaluate Today's Cost of Capital

Suppose there is an investment project which you *know*—don't ask how—has the same risk as Sensex. We will say that it has the same degree of risk as the *market portfolio*, although this is speaking somewhat loosely, because the index does not include all risky securities. What rate should you use to discount this project's forecasted cash flows?

Clearly you should use the currently expected rate of return on the market portfolio; that is the return investors would forgo by investing in the proposed project. Let us call this market return r_m. One way to estimate r_m is to assume that the future will be like the past and that today's investors expect to receive the same "normal" rates of return revealed by the averages shown in Table 7.1.A. In this case, you would set r_m at 20 percent, the average of past market returns.

Unfortunately, this is *not* the way to do it; r_m is not likely to be stable over time. Remember that it is the sum of the risk-free interest rate r_f and a premium for risk. We know that r_f varies. For example, in 1991–92 the yield on 1-year G-Sec was 17.3 percent. May be in that year, the investors were not content to hold common stocks offering an expected return of only 20 percent.

If you need to estimate the return that investors expect to receive, a more sensible procedure is to take the 1-year G-Sec yield and add 13.3 percent, the average risk premium shown in Table 7.1.A For example as we write this in early 2006 the 1-year G-Sec yield is about 6.22%. Adding on the average risk premium, therefore, gives

$$r_m(2006) = r_f(2006) + \text{normal risk premium}$$
$$= 0.0622 + 0.133 = 0.1952, \text{ or about } 19.52\%$$

The crucial assumption here is that there is a normal, stable risk premium on the market portfolio, so that the expected *future* risk premium can be measured by the average past risk premium.

Even with 26 years of data, we can't estimate the market risk premium exactly[12]; nor can we be sure that investors today are demanding the same reward for risk that they were 10 or 20 years ago. All this leaves plenty of room for argument about what the risk premium really is.[13]

Many financial managers and economists believe that long-run historical returns are the best measure available. Others have a gut instinct that investors don't need such a large risk premium to persuade them to hold common stocks.[14] For example, two recent surveys of financial economists revealed that they expected a risk premium of between 5.5 percent and 7 percent,[15] while surveys of chief financial officers have suggested an average risk premium of 5.6 percent.[16]

---

[12]Even with more than 100 years of data for the US, we cannot estimate the expected market risk premium in the US exactly.

[13]Some of the disagreements simply reflect the fact that the risk premium is sometimes defined in different ways. Some measure the average difference between stock returns and the returns (or yields) on long-term bonds. Others measure the difference between the compound rate of growth on stocks and the interest rate. As we explained above, this is not an appropriate measure of the cost of capital.

[14]There is some theory behind this instinct. The high risk premium earned in the market seems to imply that investors are extremely risk-averse. If that is true, investors ought to cut back their consumption when stock prices fall and wealth decreases. But the evidence suggests that when stock prices fall, investors spend at nearly the same rate. This is difficult to reconcile with high risk aversion and a high market risk premium. See R. Mehra and E. Prescott, "The Equity Premium: A Puzzle," *Journal of Monetary Economics* 15 (1985), pp. 145–161.

[15]The 7 percent figure comes from a survey conducted in 1998 and is reported in Ivo Welch, "Views of Financial Economists on the Equity Premium and on Professional Controversies," *Journal of Business* 73 (2000), pp. 501–537. The 5.5 percent figure comes from a follow-up survey in 2001, reported in Ivo Welch, "The Equity Premium Consensus Forecast Revisited," Cowles Foundation Discussion Paper No. 1325, Yale School of Management, September 2001.

[16]These surveys were conducted between 2000 and 2003 and are reported in J. R. Graham and C. R. Harvey, "Expectations of Equity Risk Premia, Volatility and Asymmetry from a Corporate Finance Perspective" working paper, Duke University, Fuqua School of Business, July 2003. The CFOs forecasted a risk premium of 3.8 percent over 10-year Treasury bond yields, which is equivalent to 5.6 percent over the yield on 3-month Treasury bills.

If you believe that the expected market risk premium is less than the historical average, you probably also believe that history has been unexpectedly kind to investors in the United States and that their good luck is unlikely to be repeated. Here are two reasons that history *may* overstate the risk premium that investors demand today.

Reason 1 Since 1900 the United States has been among the world's most prosperous countries. Other economies have languished or been wracked by war or civil unrest. By focusing on equity returns in the United States, we may obtain a biased view of what investors expected. Perhaps the historical averages miss the possibility that the United States could have turned out to be one of these less-fortunate countries.[17]

Figure 7.3 sheds some light on this issue. It is taken from a comprehensive study by Dimson, Marsh, and Staunton of market returns in 16 countries and shows the average risk premium in each country between 1900 and 2003.[18] Although U.S. investors are far from top of the form in terms of risk premium that they have earned, they do appear to have been slightly luckier than the average investor in the 16 countries.

In Figure 7.3 Danish stocks come bottom of the league; the average risk premium in Denmark was only 4.3 percent. The clear winner was Italy with a premium of 10.7 percent. Some of these differences between countries may reflect differences in risk. For example, Italian stocks have been particularly variable and investors may have required a higher return to compensate. But remember how difficult it is to make precise estimates of what investors expected. You probably would not be too far out if you concluded that the *expected* risk premium was the same in each country.

Reason 2 Stock prices in the United States have for some years outpaced the growth in company dividends or earnings. For example, between 1950 and 2000 dividend yields in the United States fell from 7.2 percent to 1.2 percent. It seems unlikely that investors *expected* such a sharp decline in yields, in which case some part of the actual return during this period was *unexpected*.

Some believe that the low dividend yields at the end of the twentieth century reflected optimism that the new economy would lead to a golden age of prosperity and surging profits, but others attribute the low yields to a reduction in the market risk premium. Perhaps the growth in mutual funds has made it easier for individuals to diversify away part of their risk, or perhaps pension funds and other financial institutions have found that they also could reduce their risk by investing part of their funds overseas. If these investors can eliminate more of their risk than in the past, they may become content with a lower return.

To see how a rise in stock prices can stem from a fall in the risk premium, suppose that a stock is expected to pay a dividend next year of \$ 12 ($DIV_1 = 12$). The stock yields 3 percent and the dividend is expected to grow indefinitely by 7 percent a year ($g = .07$). Therefore the total return that

---

[17]This possibility was suggested in P. Jorion and W. N. Goetzmann, "Global Stock Markets in the Twentieth Century," *Journal of Finance* 54 (June 1999), pp. 953–980.

[18]See E. Dimson, P. R. Marsh, and M. Staunton, *Triumph of the Optimists: 101 Years of Investment Returns* (Princeton, NJ: Princeton University Press, 2002).

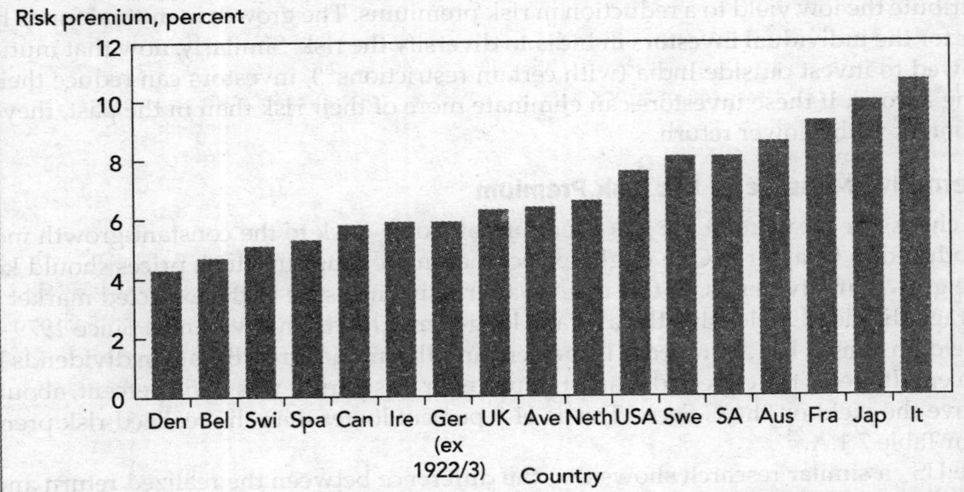

FIGURE 7.3

Average market risk premia (nominal return on stocks minus nominal return on bills), 1900–2003.

Source: E. Dimson, P. R. Marsh, and M. Staunton, *Triumph of the Optimists: 101 Years of Investment Returns* (Princeton, NJ: Princeton University Press, 2002), with updates provided by the authors.

investors expect is $r = 3 + 7 = 10$ percent. We can find the stock's value by plugging these numbers into the constant-growth formula that we introduced in Chapter 3:

$$PV = DIV_1/(r - g) = 12/(.10 - .07) = \$\,400$$

Imagine that investors now revise downward their required return to $r = 9$ percent. The dividend yield falls to 2 percent and the value of the stock rises to

$$PV = DIV_1/(r - g) = 12/(.09 - .07) = \$\,600$$

Thus a fall from 10 percent to 9 percent in the required return leads to a 50 percent rise in the stock price. If we include this price rise in our measures of past returns, we will be doubly wrong in our estimate of the risk premium. First, we will overestimate the return that investors required in the past. Second, we will fail to recognize that the return investors require in the future is lower than they needed in the past.

What about the market risk premium in India? Sensex has registered an excess return of 13.3 percent over the yield on 1-year G-Sec (our proxy for risk-free rate in India) over the last 26 years. Given the high volatility observed in the stock market, we certainly need much more than 26 years of data to estimate the equity risk premium with some confidence.

The dividend yield on the Sensex 30 companies has fallen from 8.38%[19] (in 1979–80) to 1.29% in 2005–06. If we assume that investors never expected such a sharp decline in dividend yield, then it

[19]This has happened despite the fact that some of the low dividend-paying companies like SAIL, Arvind Mills, Hindustan Motors, and Premier Auto have been replaced with high dividend-paying stocks like Infosys, Hero Honda, and Wipro in Sensex.

is obvious that part of the return they earned in the latter part of the study was unexpected. One may attribute the low yield to a reduction in risk premiums. The growth in mutual funds has made it easier for the individual investors in India to diversify the risk. Similarly, now that mutual funds are allowed to invest outside India (with certain restrictions[20]), investors can reduce their risk by investing abroad. If these investors can eliminate more of their risk than in the past, they may become content with a lower return.

An Alternative Measure of the Risk Premium

We can check our measure of the risk premium by going back to the constant-growth model that we introduced in Chapter 4. One might expect that in the long run stock prices should keep pace with the growth in dividends. In this case an alternative measure of the expected market return is the average dividend yield plus the average long-term growth in dividends. Since 1979–80, dividend yield on Sensex has averaged 3.1[21] percent and the annual growth rate in dividends has been 8.43 percent. It seems the expected market return over this period was 11.53 percent, about 1.8 percent above the yield on the G-Secs. This is 11.5 percent lower than the realized risk premium reported in Table 7.1.A.[22]

In the US , a similar research shows that the difference between the realized return and the actual return after 1900 is 5.3 percent. Fama and French have pointed out that much of this difference is due to the second half of the twentieth century, when dividend yields fell sharply.[23] Since 1950 dividend yields have averaged under 3.9 percent and the annual growth in dividends has been 5.4 percent.

This suggests that the expected market return during this period was $3.9 + 5.4 = 9.3$ percent, or 4 percent above the average risk-free interest rate since 1950.

Out of this debate only one firm conclusion emerges: Do not trust anyone who claims to *know* what returns investors expect. History contains some clues, but ultimately we have to judge whether investors on average have received what they expected. Many financial economists rely on the evidence of history and therefore work with a risk premium of about 7.5% in the US and 13% in India. The remainder generally uses a somewhat lower figure. If we consider the post-1991 period, then the risk premium is about 4 percent lower than the historical average of 13.3 percent. Many analysts would be happy to ignore the pre-1991 period because liberalization in the capital market in India started after 1991. We have no official position on the issue, but we believe that a range of 9 to 13 percent is reasonable for the risk premium in India.

Period of Study	Sensex Return	Average G-Sec Yield	Equity Risk Premium
1978–2005	23.04	9.74	13.30
1991–2005	19.86	10.82	9.05

[20]See http://www.indiainbusiness.nic.in/invest-abroad/inv-guidelines.htm for details of the restrictions that apply.

[21]If we exclude the pre-1991 period, the average dividend yield on Sensex 1.58 percent and the growth rate in dividends is 12.33 percent.

[22]Note, however, that depending on your forecasts of dividend growth, the constant-growth model can come up with estimates of the expected risk premium that are either higher or lower than the realized premium. In Chapter 4 we described a study by Marston and Harris, which used the constant-growth model to estimate the market risk premium. The study, which employed analysts' forecasts of long-term earnings growth, estimated that the expected risk-premium was 9.3 percent. However, we also noted in Chapter 4 that analysts tend to be unduly optimistic in their earnings forecasts.

[23]See E. F. Fama and K. R. French, "The Equity Premium," *Journal of Finance* 57 (April 2002), pp. 637–659. Fama and French quote even lower estimates of the risk premium. The difference largely reflects the fact that they define the risk premium as the difference between market returns and the commercial paper rate. Except for the years 1900–1918, the interest rates used in Table 7.1 are the rates on U.S. Treasury bills.

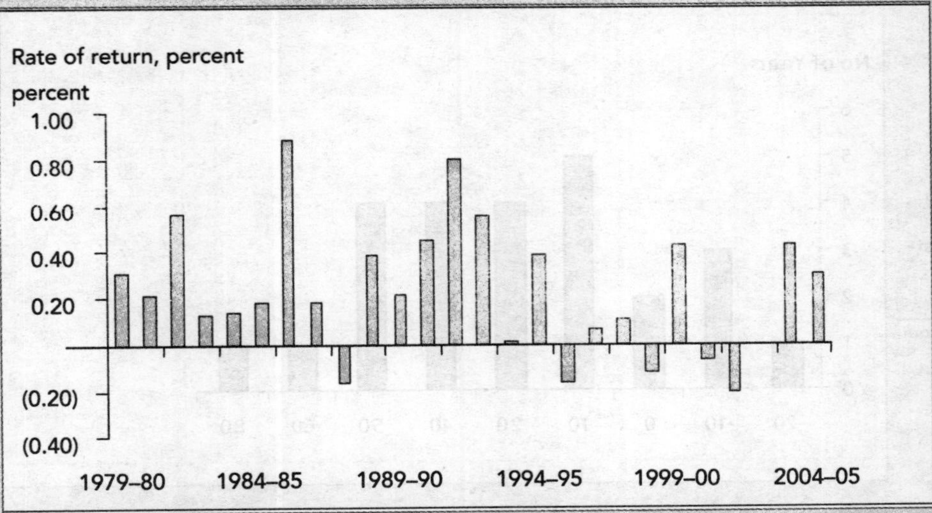

FIGURE 7.4

The stock market has been a profitable but extremely variable investment.

Source: Compiled from www.rbi.org.in

7.2 MEASURING PORTFOLIO RISK

You now have a couple of benchmarks. You know the discount rate for safe projects, and you have an estimate of the rate for average-risk projects. But you *don't* know yet how to estimate discount rates for assets that do not fit these simple cases. To do that, you have to learn (1) how to measure risk and (2) the relationship between risks borne and risk premiums demanded.

Figure 7.4 shows the 26 years of return of Indian common stocks (we use Sensex as a proxy for this). The fluctuations in year-to-year returns are remarkably wide. The highest annual return was 88% in 1985–86. In four of the last 26 years, the returns on Sensex exceeded 50 percent. However, there were negative returns in six of the last 25 years, the worst being–20 percent in 2001–02.

Another way of presenting these data is by a histogram or frequency distribution. This is done in Figure 7.5, where the variability of year-to-year returns shows up in the wide "spread" of outcomes.

Variance and Standard Deviation

The standard statistical measures of spread are **variance** and **standard deviation.** The variance of the market return is the expected squared deviation from the expected return. In other words,

$$\text{Variance } (\tilde{r}_m) = \text{the expected value of } (\tilde{r}_m - r_m)^2$$

FIGURE 7.5

Histogram of the annual rates of return from the stock market in India, 1979–80 to 2004–05, showing wide spread of returns from investment in common stocks.

Source: Compiled from www.rbi.org.in

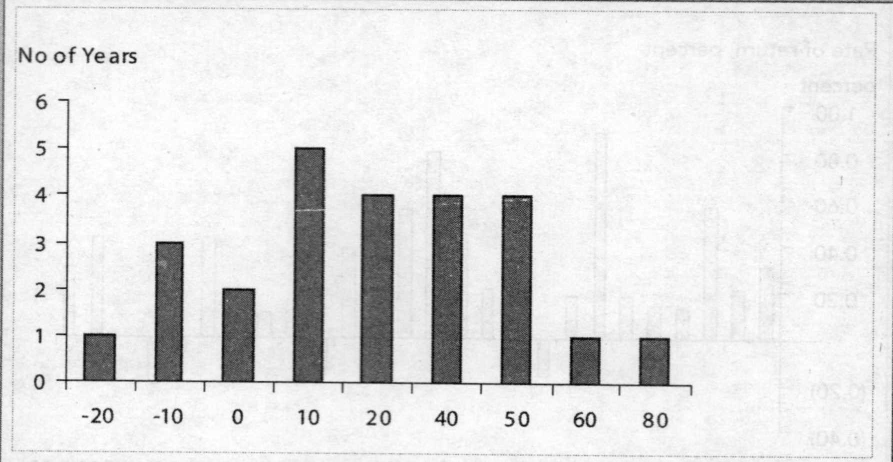

where $\tilde{r}_m$ is the actual return and r_m is the expected return.[24] The standard deviation is simply the square root of the variance:

$$\text{Standard deviation of } \tilde{r}_m = \sqrt{\text{variance } (\tilde{r}_m)}$$

Standard deviation is often denoted by σ and variance by σ^2.

Here is a very simple example showing how variance and standard deviation are calculated. Suppose that you are offered the chance to play the following game. You start by investing Rs. 100. Then two coins are flipped. For each head that comes up you get back your starting balance *plus* 30 percent, and for each tail that comes up you get back your starting balance *less* 10 percent. Clearly there are four possible outcomes:

- Head + head: You gain 60 percent.
- Head + tail: You gain 20 percent.
- Tail + head: You gain 20 percent.
- Tail + tail: You lose 20 percent.

There is a chance of 1 in 4, or 0.25, that you will make 60 percent; a chance of 2 in 4, or 0.5, that you will make 20 percent, and a chance if 1 in 4, or 0.25, that you will lose 20 percent. The game's expected return is, therefore, a weighted average of the possible outcomes:

[24]One more technical point: When variance is estimated from a sample of *observed* returns, we add the squared deviations and divide by $N - 1$, where N is the number of observations. We divide by $N - 1$ rather than N to correct for what is called *the loss of a degree of freedom*. The formula is

$$\text{Variance } (\tilde{r}_m) = \frac{1}{N-1} \sum_{t=1}^{N} (\tilde{r}_{mt} - r_m)^2$$

where $\tilde{r}_{mt}$ is the market return in period t and r_m is the mean of the values of $\tilde{r}_{mt}$.

TABLE 7.2
The coin-tossing game: Calculating variance and standard deviation

(1) Percent Rate of Return ($\tilde{r}$)	(2) Deviation from Expected Return ($\tilde{r} - r$)	(3) Squared Deviation $(\tilde{r} - r)^2$	(4) Probability	(5) Probability × Squared Deviation
+60	+40	1600	0.25	400
+20	0	0	0.5	0
−20	−40	1600	0.25	400
			Variance = Expected value of $(\tilde{r} - r)^2$ =	800
			Standard deviation = $\sqrt{\text{variance}} = \sqrt{800}$ =	28.28

$$\text{Expected return} = (0.25 \times 60) + (0.5 \times 20) + (0.25 \times -20) = +20\%$$

Table 7.2 shows the variance of the percentage return is 800. Standard deviation is the square root of 800, or 28 percent.

One way of defining uncertainty is to say that more things can happen than will happen. The risk of an asset can be completely expressed, as we did for the coin-tossing game, by writing all possible outcomes and the probability of each. In practice this is cumbersome and often impossible. Therefore we use variance or standard deviation to summarize the spread of possible outcomes.[25]

These measures are natural indexes of risk.[26] If the outcome of the coin-tossing game had been certain, the standard deviation would have been zero. The actual standard deviation is positive because we *don't* know what will happen.

Or think of a second game, the same as the first except that each head means a 50 percent gain and each tail means a 30 percent loss. Again, there are four equally likely outcomes:

- Head + head: You gain 100 percent.
- Head + tail: You gain 20 percent.
- Tail + head: You gain 20 percent.
- Tail + tail: You lose 60 percent.

For this game, the expected return is 20 percent, the same as that of the first game. But its standard deviation is double that of the first game, 56 percent versus 28 percent. By this measure, the second game is twice as risky as the first.

Measuring Variability

In principle, you could estimate the variability of any portfolio of stocks or bonds by the procedure just described. You would identify the possible outcomes, assign a probability to each outcome, and grind through the calculations. But where do the probabilities come from? You can't look them up in the newspaper; newspapers seem to go out of their way to avoid definite statements about

[25]Which of the two we use is solely a matter of convenience. Since standard deviation is in the same units as the rate of return, it is generally more convenient to use standard deviation. However, when we are talking about the *proportion* of risk that is due to some factor, it is less confusing to work in terms of the variance.

[26]As we explain in Chapter 8, standard deviation and variance are the correct measures of risk if the returns are normally distributed.

prospects for securities. We once saw an article headlined "Bond Prices Possibly Set to Move Sharply Either Way." Stockbrokers are much the same. Yours may respond to your query about possible market outcomes with a statement like this:

> The market currently appears to be undergoing a period of consolidation. For the intermediate term, we would take a constructive view, provided economic recovery continues. The market could be up 20 percent a year from now, perhaps more if inflation continues low. On the other hand, . . .

The Delphic oracle gave advice, but no probabilities.

Most financial analysts start by observing past variability. Of course, there is no risk in hindsight, but it is reasonable to assume that portfolios with histories of high variability also have the least predictable future performance.

The annual standard deviations and variances observed for our three portfolios over the period 1979–2005 were:[27]

Portfolio	Standard Deviation (σ)	Variance (σ^2)
1-Year G-Sec Yields	3.57	12.74
AAA-Rated Corporate Bonds	2.43	5.90
Common stocks	28.37	804.86

As expected, 1-year G-Secs were the least variable security, and common stocks were the most variable. AAA-rated corporate bonds hold the middle ground.

You may find it interesting to compare the coin-tossing game and the stock markets alternative investments. The stock market generated an average annual return of 23 percent with a standard deviation of 28.37 percent. The game offers 20 and 28.28 percent, respectively. Your gambling friends may have come up with a crude representation of the stock market.

Figure 7.6 compares the standard deviation of stock market returns in 16 countries over the same 104-year period. Canada occupies low field with a standard deviation of 16.8 percent, but most of the other countries cluster together with percentage standard deviations in the low 20s. It is interesting to note that the Indian stock market is as volatile as the Japanese stock market.

Of course, there is no reason to suppose that the market's variability should stay the same over more than a century. For example, Germany, Italy, and Japan now have much more stable economies and markets than they did in the years leading up to and including the Second World War. As you can see from the following table, variability in India has remained quite stable in the last 20 years (excepting for the 1990–94 period).[28]

---

[27]In discussing the riskiness of *bonds*, be careful to specify the time period and whether you are speaking in real or nominal terms. The *nominal* return on a long-term government bond is absolutely certain to an investor who holds on until maturity; in other words, it is risk-free if you forget about inflation. After all, the government can always print money to pay off its debts. However, the real return on Treasury securities is uncertain because no one knows how much each future dollar will buy.

The bond returns were measured annually. The returns reflect year-to-year changes in bond prices as well as interest received. The *one-year* returns on long-term bonds are risky in *both* real and nominal terms.

[28]These standard deviations are calculated from daily data. Annual observations are insufficient for estimating volatility over five-year periods. The daily variance is converted into an annual variance by multiplying by 240 (approximate number of trading days in a year). That is, the variance of the daily return is 1/240th of the annual variance. The longer you hold a security or portfolio, the more risk you have to bear. This conversion assumes that successive daily returns are statistically independent. This is, in fact, a good assumption, as we will show in Chapter 13.

Period	Market Standard Deviation (σ_m)
1984–89	24.91%
1990–94	35.92
1995–99	25.11
2000–04	25.47

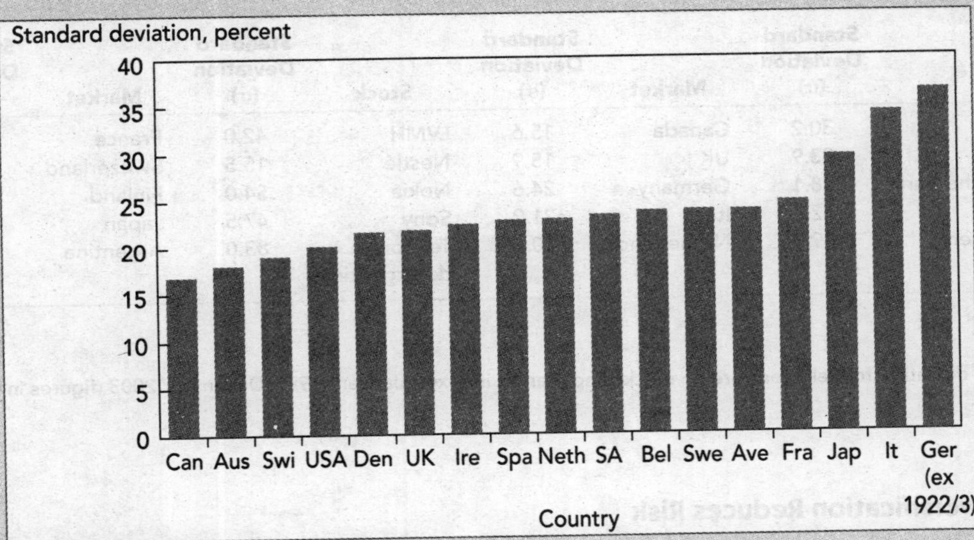

FIGURE 7.6

The risk (standard deviation of annual returns) of markets around the world, 1900–2003.

Source: E. Dimson, P. R. Marsh, and M. Staunton, *Triumph of the Optimists: 101 Years of Global Investment Returns* (Princeton, NJ: Princeton University Press, 2002), with updates provided by the authors.

These figures do not support the widespread impression of especially volatile stock prices in recent years. However, there were brief periods of extremely high volatility. Sensex fell by more than 16.5 percent during two trading days (14th and 17th of May[29]) after the 2004 Parliament election results were announced. The standard deviation of the market for the week surrounding these two days was equivalent to 117 percent per year. Fortunately, volatility dropped to 30 percent in the next week itself.

[29] 15th and 16th of May were holidays.

TABLE 7.3

Standard deviations for selected Indian stocks, April 2001–March 2006 (figures in percent per year)

Stock	Standard Deviation (σ)	Stock	Standard Deviation (σ)
L & T	56.87%	BHEL	38.67%
ICICI Bank	45.05	Ranbaxy Laboratories	33.05
Tata Steel	42.77	HLL	29.53
Satyam Computer Services	41.89	Reliance Industries	29.28
ONGC	40.12	HDFC Bank	24.92

Stock	Standard Deviation (σ)	Market	Standard Deviation (σ)	Stock	Standard Deviation (σ)	Market	Standard Deviation (σ)
Alcan	30.2	Canada	15.6	LVMH	42.0	France	21.4
BP	23.9	UK	15.9	Nestlé	15.5	Switzerland	15.6
Deutsche Bank	38.1	Germany	24.6	Nokia	54.0	Finland	40.3
Fiat	32.7	Italy	21.2	Sony	47.5	Japan	17.9
Heineken	19.9	Netherlands	20.4	Telefonica de Argentina	83.0	Argentina	42.5

TABLE 7.4

Standard deviation for selected foreign stocks and market indexes, January 1999–December 2003 (figures in percent per year).

How Diversification Reduces Risk

We can calculate our measures of variability equally well for individual securities and portfolios of securities. Of course, the level of variability over 100 years is less interesting for specific companies than for the market portfolio—it is a rare company that faces the same business risks today as it did a century ago.

Table 7.3 presents estimated standard deviations for 10 well-known common stocks of India for a recent five-year period[30]. Do these standard deviations look high to you? They should. Remember that the market portfolio's standard deviation was about 22.8 percent during the same five-year period. Of our individual stocks, only HDFC Bank came close to this figure. L&T was two-and-half times more volatile than the market portfolio.

Take a look also at Table 7.4, which shows the standard deviations of some well-known stocks from different countries and of the markets in which they trade. Some of these stocks are much more variable than others, but you can see that once again the individual stocks are for the most part more variable than the market indexes.

[30] These standard deviations are calculated from monthly data.

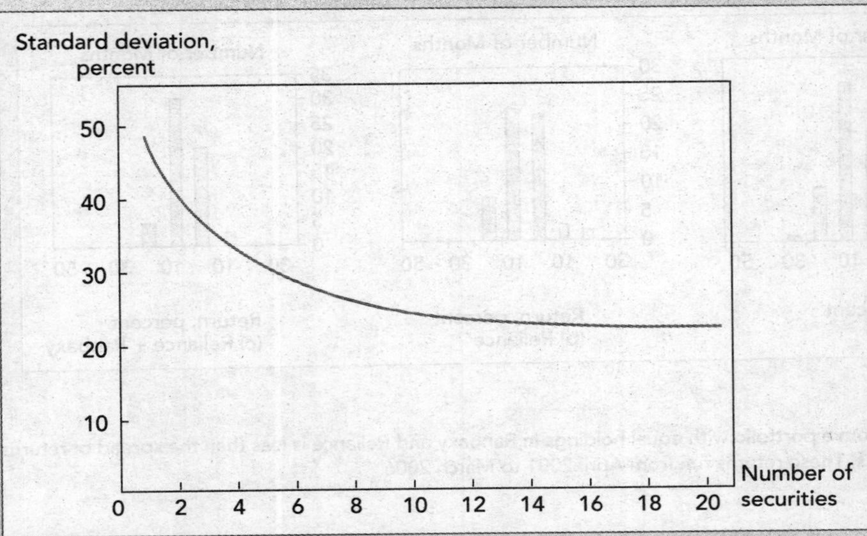

FIGURE 7.7

The risk (standard deviation) of randomly selected portfolios containing different numbers of New York Stock Exchange stocks. Notice that diversification reduces risk rapidly at first, then more slowly.

Source: M. Statman, "How Many Stocks Make a Diversified Portfolio?" *Journal of Financial and Quantitative Analysis* 22 (September 1987), pp. 353–363.

This raises an important question: The market portfolio is made up of individual stocks, so why doesn't its variability reflect the average variability of its components? The answer is that *diversification reduces variability.*

Even a little diversification can provide a substantial reduction in variability. Suppose you calculate and compare the standard deviations of randomly chosen one-stock portfolios, two-stock portfolios, five-stock portfolios, etc. A high proportion of the investments would be in the stocks of small companies and individually very risky. However, you can see from Figure 7.7 that diversification can cut the variability of US returns about in half. Notice also that you can get most of this benefit with relatively few stocks: The improvement is slight when the number of securities is increased beyond, say, 20 or 30.[31] Obaidullah (1994)[32] also reports similar findings from India. The author finds that almost half of the risk of an individual security is non-systematic risk and is eliminated by diversification.

Diversification works because prices of different stocks do not move exactly together. Statisticians make the same point when they say that stock price changes are less than perfectly correlated. Look, for example, at Figure 7.8. The first two panels show histograms of the monthly returns for Ranbaxy Laboratories and Reliance Industries stocks over the 60-month period beginning in April 2001. As we showed in table 7.3, during this period neither stock was particularly risky, and the (annualized) standard deviation of their monthly returns was about 30 percent. Nevertheless, if you had invested all your cash in Ranbaxy, there would have been four occasions that you would have lost at least 10 percent of your investment. If you had put all your money in Reliance Industries

[31] There is some evidence that in recent years stocks have become individually more risky but have moved less closely together. Consequently, you need to hold more stocks to get the bulk of the gains from diversification. See J. Y. Campbell, M. Lettau, B. G. Malkiel, and Y. Xu, "Have Individual Stocks Become More Volatile? An Empirical Exploration of Idiosyncratic Risk," *Journal of Finance* 56 (February 2001), pp. 1–43.

[32] M Obaidullah, 1994, Indian Stock Market: Theories and Evidence, ICFAI Publication, Hyderabad, India. The sample period for this study was 1986–90

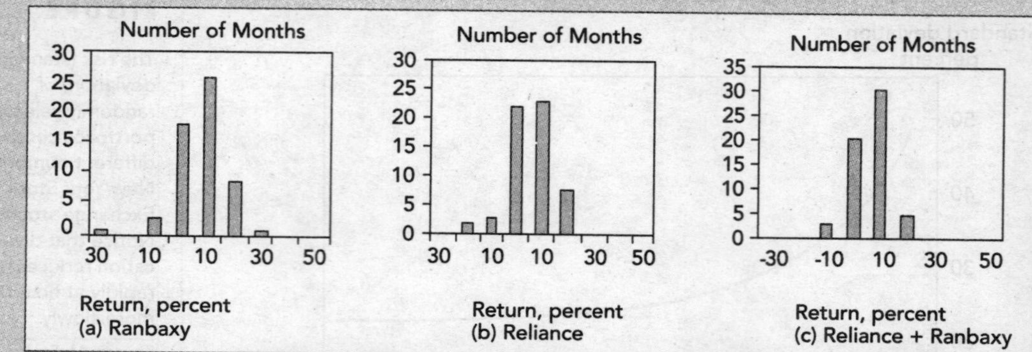

FIGURE 7.8

The spread of returns from a portfolio with equal holdings in Ranbaxy and Reliance is less than the spread of returns from the individual stocks. These returns run from April 2001 to March 2006.

stock, you would have lost at least 10 percent of your investment on five occasions. Now look at the third histogram in Figure 7.8, which shows the distribution of monthly returns on a portfolio that was evenly distributed between Ranbaxy and Reliance. On many occasions a decline in the value of one stock was offset by a rise in the price of the other[33], so that even this limited diversification would have evened out many of the peaks and the troughs. For example, there would have been only three months that you would have lost more than 10 percent of your money and you would never have experienced a loss greater than 19 percent. The maximum loss for Reliance in any single month was 33 percent and it was 22 percent for Ranbaxy.[34]

The risk that potentially can be eliminated by diversification is called **unique risk.**[35] Unique risk stems from the fact that many of the perils that surround an individual company are peculiar to that company and perhaps its immediate competitors. But there is also some risk that you can't avoid, regardless of how much you diversify. This risk is generally known as **market risk.**[36] Market risk stems from the fact that there are other economywide perils that threaten all businesses. That is why stocks have a tendency to move together. And that is why investors are exposed to market uncertainties, no matter how many stocks they hold.

In Figure 7.9 we have divided risk into its two parts—unique risk and market risk. If you have only a single stock, unique risk is very important; but once you have a portfolio of 20 or more stocks, diversification has done the bulk of its work. For a reasonably well-diversified portfolio, only market risk matters. Therefore, the predominant source of uncertainty for a diversified investor is that the market will rise or plummet, carrying the investor's portfolio with it.

[33]Over this period, the correlation between the returns on the two stocks was 0.238.

[34]The standard deviations of Reliance and Ranbaxy were 29 and 33 percent, respectively. The standard deviation of a portfolio with half invested in each was 23 percent.

[35]Unique risk may be called *unsystematic risk, residual risk, specific risk,* or *diversifiable risk.*

[36]Market risk may be called *systematic risk* or *undiversifiable risk.*

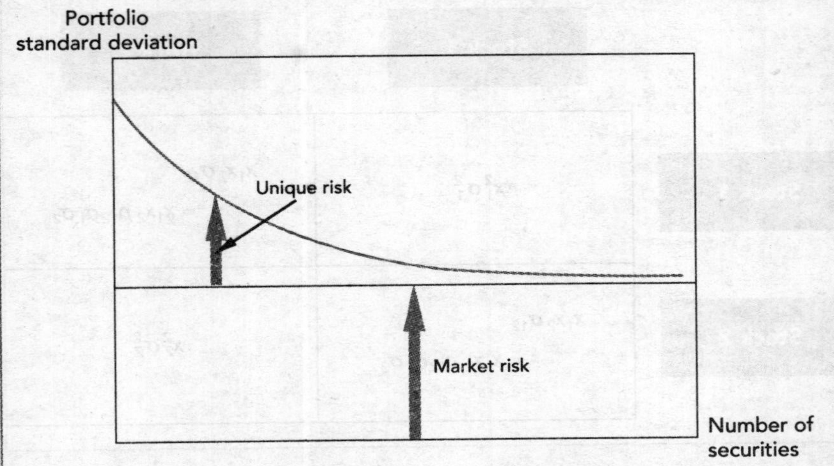

FIGURE 7.9

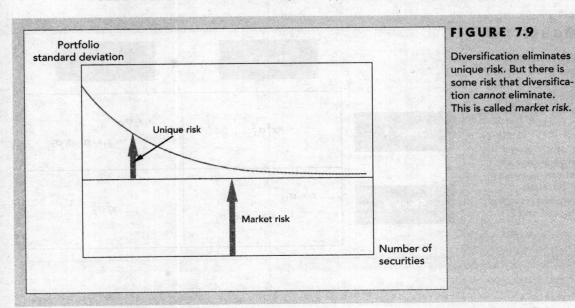

Diversification eliminates unique risk. But there is some risk that diversification *cannot* eliminate. This is called *market risk.*

7.3 CALCULATING PORTFOLIO RISK

We have given you an intuitive idea of how diversification reduces risk, but to understand fully the effect of diversification, you need to know how the risk of a portfolio depends on the risk of the individual shares.

Suppose that 47 percent of your portfolio is invested in Reliance Energy and the remainder is invested in Grasim Industries. You expect that over the coming year Reliance Energy will give a return of 17 percent and Grasim, 14 percent. The expected return on your portfolio is simply a weighted average of the expected returns on the individual stocks:[37]

$$\text{Expected portfolio return} = (0.47 \times 17) + (0.53 \times 14) = 15.41\%$$

Calculating the expected portfolio return is easy. The hard part is to work out the risk of your portfolio. In the past the standard deviation of returns was 37 percent for Reliance Energy and 33 percent for Grasim. You believe that these figures are a good representation of the spread of possible future outcomes. At first you may be inclined to assume that the standard deviation of the portfolio is a weighted average of the standard deviation of the two stocks, that is (0.47 × 37) + (0.53 × 33) = 34.88 percent. That would be correct *only* if the prices of the two stocks moved in perfect lockstep. In any other case, diversification reduces the risk below this figure.

The exact procedure for calculating the risk of a two-stock portfolio is given in Figure 7.10. You need to fill in four boxes. To complete the top-left box, you weight the variance of the returns on

[37] Let's check this. Suppose you invest Rs. 47 in Reliance Energy and Rs. 53 in Grasim. The expected rupee return on your Reliance Energy holding is 0.17 × 47 = Rs. 7.99, and on Grasim it is 0.14 × 53 = Rs. 7.42. The expected rupee return on your portfolio is Rs. 7.99 + Rs. 7.42 = Rs. 15.41. The portfolio *rate* of return is Rs. 15.41/100 = 15.41, or 15.41 percent.

FIGURE 7.10

The variance of a two-stock portfolio is the sum of these four boxes. x_1, x_2 = proportions invested in stocks 1 and 2; σ_1^2, σ_2^2, = variances of stock returns; σ_{12} = covariance of returns ($\rho_{12}\sigma_1\sigma_2$); ρ_{12} = correlation between returns on stocks 1 and 2.

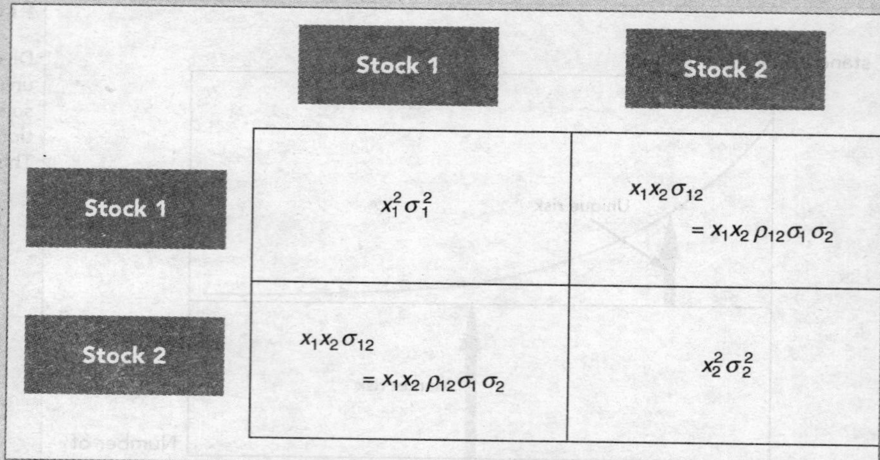

stock 1 (σ_1^2) by the *square* of the proportion invested in it (x_1^2). Similarly, to complete the bottom-right box, you weight the variance of the returns on stock 2 (σ_2^2) by the *square* of the proportion invested in stock 2 (x_2^2).

The entries in these diagonal boxes depend on the variances of stocks 1 and 2; the entries in the other two boxes depend on their **covariance.** As you might guess, the covariance is a measure of the degree to which the two stocks "covary." The covariance can be expressed as the product of the correlation coefficient ρ_{12} and the two standard deviations:[38]

$$\text{Covariance between stocks 1 and 2} = \sigma_{12} = \rho_{12}\sigma_1\sigma_2$$

For the most part stocks tend to move together. In this case the correlation coefficient ρ_{12} is positive, and therefore the covariance σ_{12} is also positive. If the prospects of the stocks were wholly unrelated, both the correlation coefficient and the covariance would be zero; and if the stocks tended to move in opposite directions, the correlation coefficient and the covariance would be negative. Just as you weighted the variances by the square of the proportion invested, so you must weight the covariance by the *product* of the two proportionate holdings x_1 and x_2.

Once you have completed these four boxes, you simply add the entries to obtain the portfolio variance:

$$\text{Portfolio variance} = x_1^2\sigma_1^2 + x_2^2\sigma_2^2 + 2(x_1x_2\rho_{12}\sigma_1\sigma_2)$$

The portfolio standard deviation is, of course, the square root of the variance.

[38] Another way to define the covariance is as follows:

$$\text{Covariance between stocks 1 and 2} = \sigma_{12} = \text{expected value of } (\tilde{r}_1 - r_1) \times (\tilde{r}_2 - r_2)$$

Note that any security's covariance with itself is just its variance:

$$\sigma_{11} = \text{expected value of } (\tilde{r}_1 - r_1) \times (\tilde{r}_1 - r_1)$$
$$= \text{expected value of } (\tilde{r}_1 - r_1)^2 = \text{variance of stock } 1 = \sigma_1^2.$$

Now you can try putting in some figures for Reliance and Ranbaxy. We said earlier that if the two stocks were perfectly correlated, the standard deviation of the portfolio would lie 47 percent of the way between the standard deviations of the two stocks. Let us check this by filling in the boxes with $\rho_{12} = +1$.

	Reliance Energy	Grasim
Reliance Energy	$x_1^2\sigma_1^2 = (0.47)^2 \times (37)^2$	$x_1x_2\rho_{12}\sigma_1\sigma_2 = (0.47) \times (0.53) \times 1 \times (37) \times (33)$
Grasim	$x_1x_2\rho_{12}\sigma_1\sigma_2 = (0.47) \times (0.53) \times 1 \times (37) \times (33)$	$x_2^2\sigma_2^2 = (0.53)^2 \times (33)^2$

The variance of your portfolio is the sum of these entries:

$$\text{Portfolio variance} = [(0.47)^2 \times (37)^2] + [(0.53)^2 \times (33)^2] + 2(0.47 \times 0.53 \times 1 \times 33 \times 37)$$
$$= 1216.61$$

The standard deviation is $\sqrt{1216.61} = 34.88$ percent, or 40 percent of the way between 33 and 37.

Reliance Energy and Grasim do not move in perfect lockstep. If past experience is any guide, the correlation between the two stocks is about 0.52. If we go through the same exercise again with $\rho_{12} = 0.52$, we find

$$\text{Portfolio variance} = [(0.47)^2 \times (37)^2] + [(0.53)^2 \times (33)^2] + 2(0.47 \times 0.53 \times 0.52 \times 33 \times 37)$$
$$= 924.63$$

The standard deviation is $\sqrt{924.63} = 30.41$ percent. The risk is now less than 47 percent of the way between 33 and 37 percent. In fact, it is less than the risk of investing in either Reliance Energy or Grasim alone.

The greatest payoff to diversification comes when the two stocks are negatively correlated. Unfortunately, this almost never occurs, but just for illustration, let's assume it for Reliance Energy and Grasim. And as long as we are being unrealistic, we might as well go whole hog and assume perfect negative correlation ($\rho_{12} = -1$). In this case,

$$\text{Portfolio variance} = [(0.47)^2 \times (37)^2] + [(0.53)^2 \times (33)^2] + 2(0.47 \times 0.53 \times (-1) \times 37 \times 33) = 0$$

When there is perfect negative correlation, there is always a portfolio strategy (represented by a particular set of portfolio weights) which will completely eliminate risk[39]. It is too bad perfect negative correlation doesn't really occur between common stocks.

General Formula for Computing Portfolio Risk

The method for calculating portfolio risk can easily be extended to portfolios of three or more securities. We just have to fill in a larger number of boxes. Each of those down the diagonal—the shaded boxes in Figure 7.11—contains the variance weighted by the square of the proportion invested. Each

[39]Since the standard deviation of Reliance is (37/33) times that of Grasim, you need to invest (37/33) times more in Grasim to eliminate risk in this two-stock portfolio.

FIGURE 7.11

To find the variance of an N-stock portfolio, we must add the entries in a matrix like this. The diagonal cells contain variance terms ($x_i^2\sigma^2_i$), and the off-diagonal cells contain covariance terms ($x_i x_j \sigma_{ij}$).

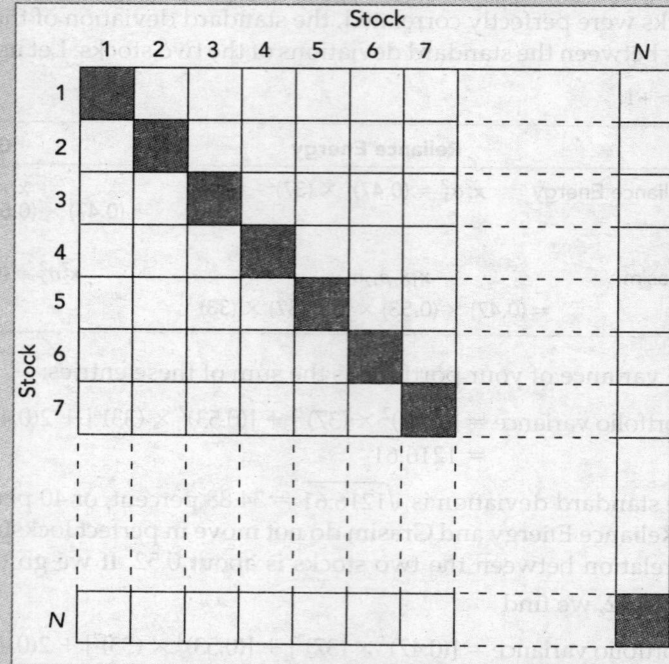

of the other boxes contains the covariance between that pair of securities, weighted by the product of the proportions invested.[40]

Limits to Diversification

Did you notice in Figure 7.11 how much more important the covariances become as we add more securities to the portfolio? When there are just two securities, there are equal numbers of variance boxes and of covariance boxes. When there are many securities, the number of covariances is much larger than the number of variances. Thus the variability of a well-diversified portfolio reflects mainly the covariances.

Suppose we are dealing with portfolios in which equal investments are made in each of N stocks. The proportion invested in each stock is, therefore, $1/N$. So in each variance box we have $(1/N)^2$ times the variance, and in each covariance box we have $(1/N)^2$ times the covariance. There are N variance boxes and $N^2 - N$ covariance boxes. Therefore,

[40] The formal equivalent to "add up all the boxes" is

$$\text{Portfolio variance} = \sum_{i=1}^{N}\sum_{j=1}^{N} x_i x_j \sigma_{ij}$$

Notice that when $i = j$, σ_{ij} is just the variance of stock i.

$$\text{Portfolio variance} = N\left(\frac{1}{N}\right)^2 \times \text{average variance}$$
$$+ (N^2 - N)\left(\frac{1}{N}\right)^2 \times \text{average covariance}$$
$$= \frac{1}{N} \times \text{average variance} + \left(1 - \frac{1}{N}\right) \times \text{average covariance}$$

Notice that as N increases, the portfolio variance steadily approaches the average covariance. If the average covariance were zero, it would be possible to eliminate *all* risk by holding a sufficient number of securities. Unfortunately common stocks move together, not independently. Thus most of the stocks that the investor can actually buy are tied together in a web of positive covariances which set the limit to the benefits of diversification. Now we can understand the precise meaning of the market risk portrayed in Figure 7.9. It is the average covariance which constitutes the bedrock of risk remaining after diversification has done its work.

7.4 HOW INDIVIDUAL SECURITIES AFFECT PORTFOLIO RISK

We presented earlier some data on the variability of 10 individual Indian stocks. L&T had the highest standard deviation and HDFC Bank had the lowest. If you had held L&T on its own, the spread of possible returns would have been two-and-half times greater than if you had held HDFC Bank on its own. But that is not a very interesting fact. Wise investors do not put all their eggs into just one basket: they reduce their risk by diversification. They are therefore interested in the effect that each stock will have on the risk of their portfolio.

This brings us to one of the principal themes of this chapter. *The risk of a well-diversified portfolio depends on the market risk of the securities included in the portfolio.* Tattoo that statement on your forehead if you can't remember it any other way. It is one of the most important ideas in this book.

Market Risk is Measured by Beta

If you want to know the contribution of an individual security to the risk of a well-diversified portfolio, it is no good thinking about how risky that security is if held in isolation—you need to measure its *market risk,* and that boils down to measuring how sensitive it is to market movements. This sensitivity is called **beta** (β).

Stocks with betas greater than 1.0 tend to amplify the overall movements of the market. Stocks with betas between 0 and 1.0 tend to move in the same direction as the market, but not as far. Of course, the market is the portfolio of all stocks, so the "average" stock has a beta of 1.0. Table 7.5 reports betas for the 10 well-known common stocks we referred to earlier.

Over the five years from April 2001 to March 2006, Tata Steel had a beta of 1.47. If the future resembles the past, it means that on average, when the market rises an extra 1 percent, Tata Steel's stock price will rise by an extra 1.47 percent. When the market falls by 2 percent, Tata Steel's stock prices will fall an extra $2 \times 1.47 = 2.94$ percent. Thus a line fitted to a plot of Tata Steel's returns versus market returns has a slope of 1.47. See Figure 7.12.

TABLE 7.5

Betas for selected Indian stocks, April 2001–March 2006.

Stock	Beta (β)	Stock	Beta (β)
L & T	1.54	ONGC	0.99
Tata Steel	1.47	Reliance Industries	0.98
ICICI Bank	1.44	HLL	0.87
Satyam Computer Services	1.35	Ranbaxy Laboratories	0.73
BHEL	1.25	HDFC Bank	0.63

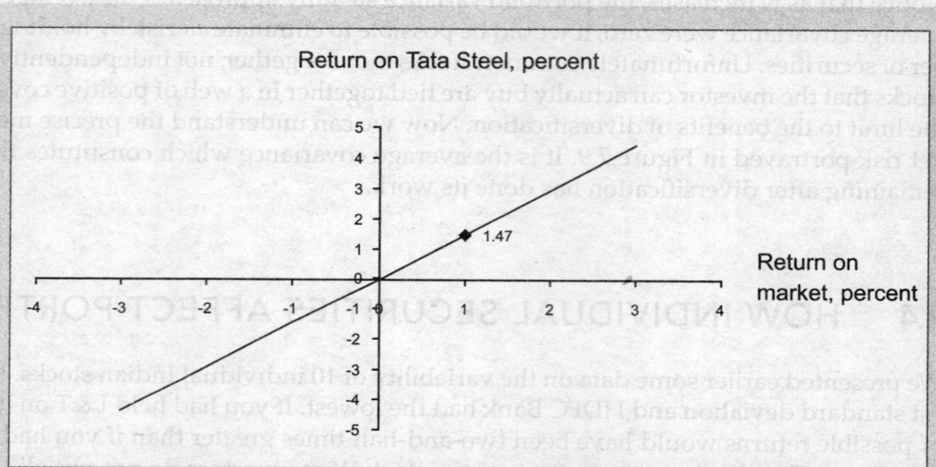

FIGURE 7.12

The return on Tata Steel stock changes on average by 1.47 percent for each additional 1 percent change in the market return. Beta is therefore 1.47.

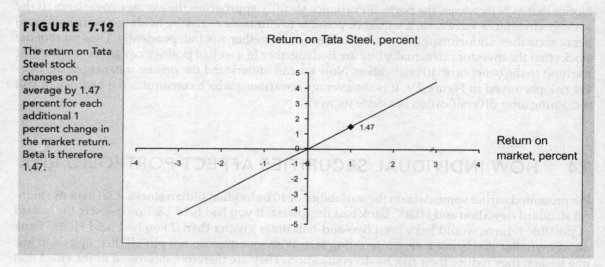

Of course, Tata Steel's stock returns are not perfectly correlated with market returns. The company is also subject to unique risk, so the actual returns will be scattered about the line in Figure 7.12. Sometimes, Tata Steel will head south while the market goes north and vice versa.

Of the ten stocks in Table 7.5, L&T has the highest beta. HDFC Bank is at the other extreme. A line fitted to a plot of HDFC Bank's returns versus market returns would be less steep: its slope would be only 0.63. Notice that many of the stocks that have high standard deviations also have high betas. But that is always not so. For example, ONGC, which has a relatively high standard deviation, has joined the low-beta stocks in the right-hand column of Table 7.5. It seems that while ONGC is a risky investment on its own, it makes a relatively low contribution to the risk of a diversified portfolio.

Just as we can measure how the returns of an Indian stock are affected by fluctuations in the Indian market, so we can measure how stocks in other countries are affected by movements in *their* markets. Table 7.6 shows the betas for the sample of foreign stocks.

Stock	Beta	Stock	Beta
Alcan	.85	LVMH	1.53
BP	.86	Nestlé	.42
Deutsche Bank	1.18	Nokia	1.31
Fiat	.82	Sony	1.62
Heineken	.17	Telefonica de Argentina	1.42

TABLE 7.6

Betas for foreign stocks, January 1999–December 2003 (beta is measured relative to the stock's home market).

Why Security Betas Determine Portfolio Risk

Let us review the two crucial points about security risk and portfolio risk:

- Market risk accounts for most of the risk of a well-diversified portfolio.
- The beta of an individual security measures its sensitivity to market movements.

It is easy to see where we are headed: In a portfolio context, a security's risk is measured by beta. Perhaps we could just jump to that conclusion, but we would rather explain it. In fact, we will offer two explanations.

Explanation 1: Where's Bedrock? Look back to Figure 7.9, which shows how the standard deviation of portfolio return depends on the number of securities in the portfolio. With more securities, and therefore better diversification, portfolio risk declines until all unique risk is eliminated and only the bedrock of market risk remains.

Where's bedrock? It depends on the average beta of the securities selected.

Suppose we constructed a portfolio containing a large number of stocks—500, say—drawn randomly from the whole market. What would we get? The market itself, or a portfolio *very* close to it. The portfolio beta would be 1.0, and the correlation with the market would be 1.0. If the standard deviation of the market were 20 percent (roughly its average for 1900–2003), then the portfolio standard deviation would also be 20 percent. This is shown by the middle line in Figure 7.13.

But suppose we constructed the portfolio from a large group of stocks with an average beta of 1.5. Again we would end up with a 500-stock portfolio with virtually no unique risk—a portfolio that moves almost in lockstep with the market. However, *this* portfolio's standard deviation would be 30 percent, 1.5 times that of the market.[41] A well-diversified portfolio with a beta of 1.5 will amplify every market move by 50 percent and end up with 150 percent of the market's risk. The upper line in Figure 7.13 shows this case.

Of course, we could repeat the same experiment with stocks with a beta of .5 and end up with a well-diversified portfolio half as risky as the market. You can see this also in Figure 7.13.

[41] A 500-stock portfolio with $\beta = 1.5$ would still have some unique risk because it would be unduly concentrated in high-beta industries. Its actual standard deviation would be a bit higher than 30 percent. If that worries you, relax; we will show you in Chapter 8 how you can construct a fully diversified portfolio with a beta of 1.5 by borrowing and investing in the market portfolio.

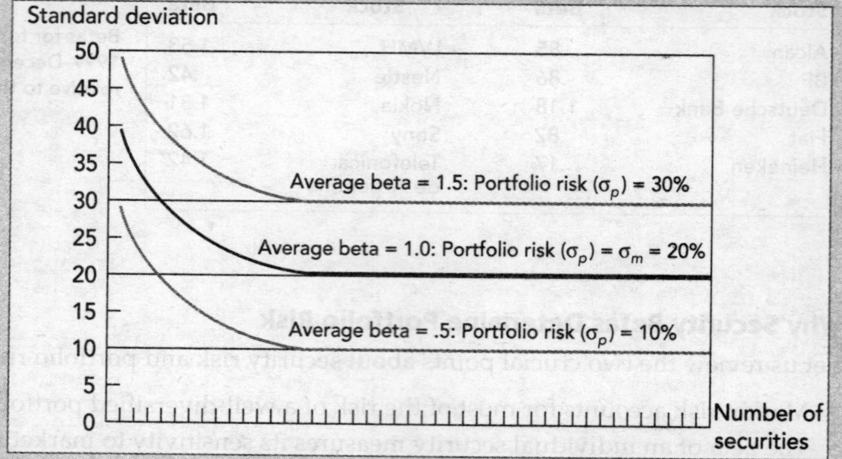

FIGURE 7.13

The middle line shows that a well-diversified portfolio of randomly selected stocks ends up with $\beta = 1$ and a standard deviation equal to the market's—in this case 20 percent. The upper line shows that a well-diversified portfolio with $\beta = 1.5$ has a standard deviation of about 30 percent—1.5 times that of the market. The lower line shows that a well-diversified portfolio with $\beta = .5$ has a standard deviation of about 10 percent—half that of the market.

The general point is this: the risk of a well-diversified portfolio is proportional to the portfolio beta, which equals the average beta of the securities included in the portfolio. This shows you how portfolio risk is driven by security betas.

Explanation 2: Betas and Covariances. A statistician would define the beta of stock *i* as

$$\beta_i = \frac{\sigma_{im}}{\sigma_m^2}$$

where σ_{im} is the covariance between stock *i*'s return and the market return, and σ_m^2 is the variance of the market return.

It turns out that this ratio of covariance to variance measures a stock's contribution to portfolio risk. You can see this by looking back at our calculations for the risk of the portfolio of Reliance Energy and Grasim.

Remember that the risk of this portfolio was the sum of the following cells:

	Reliance Energy	Grasim
Reliance Energy	$(0.47)^2 \times (37)^2$	$(0.47) \times (0.53) \times 0.52 \times (37) \times (33)$
Grasim	$(0.47) \times (0.53) \times 0.52 \times (37) \times (33)$	$(0.53)^2 \times (33)^2$

If we add each *row* of cells, we can see how much of the portfolio's risk comes from Reliance Energy and how much comes from Grasim:

Stock	Contribution to Risk
Reliance Energy	$0.47 \times \{[0.47 \times 37^2] + [0.53 \times 0.52 \times 37 \times 33]\} = 0.47 \times 979.94$
Grasim	$0.53 \times \{[0.53 \times 33^2] + [0.47 \times 0.52 \times 37 \times 33]\} = 0.53 \times 875.58$
	Total portfolio variance 924.63

Reliance Energy's contribution to portfolio risk depends on its relative importance in the portfolio (0.47) and its average covariance with the stocks in the portfolio (979.94). (Notice that the average covariance of Reliance Energy with the portfolio includes its covariance with itself, i.e., its variance.) The *proportion* of the risk that comes from the Reliance Energy holding is

$$\text{Relative market value} \times \frac{\text{average covariance}}{\text{portfolio variance}} = 0.47 \times \frac{979.94}{924.63} = 0.47 \times 1.06 = 0.5$$

Similarly, Grasim's contribution to portfolio risk depends on its relative importance in the portfolio (0.53) and its average covariance with the stocks in the portfolio (875.58). The proportion of the risk that comes from the Grasim holding is also 0.5:

$$0.53 \times \frac{875.58}{924.63} = 0.53 \times 0.946 = 0.5$$

In each case the proportion depends on two numbers: the relative size of the holding (0.47 or 0.53) and a measure of the effect of that holding on portfolio risk (1.06 or 0.946). The latter values are the betas of Reliance Energy and Grasim *relative to that portfolio*. On average, an extra 1 percent change in the value of the portfolio would be associated with an extra 1.06 percent change in the value of Reliance Energy and a 0.946 percent change in the value of Grasim.

To calculate Reliance Energy's beta relative to the portfolio, we simply take the covariance of Reliance Energy with the portfolio and divide by the portfolio variance. The idea is exactly the same if we wish to calculate the beta of Reliance Energy *relative to the market portfolio*. We just calculate its covariance with the market portfolio and divide by the variance of the market:

$$\begin{array}{c}\text{Beta relative to market portfolio} \\ \text{(or, more simply, beta)}\end{array} = \frac{\text{covariance with market}}{\text{variance of market}} = \frac{\sigma_{im}}{\sigma_m^2}$$

7.5 DIVERSIFICATION AND VALUE ADDITIVITY

We have seen that diversification reduces risk and, therefore, makes sense for investors. But does it also make sense for the firm? Is a diversified firm more attractive to investors than an undiversified one? If it is, we have an *extremely* disturbing result. If diversification is an appropriate corporate objective, each project has to be analyzed as a potential addition to the firm's portfolio of assets. The value of the diversified package would be greater than the sum of the parts. So present values would no longer add.

Diversification is undoubtedly a good thing, but that does not mean that firms should practice it. If investors were *not* able to hold a large number of securities, then they might want firms to diversify for them. But investors *can* diversify.[42] In many ways they can do so more easily than firms. Individuals can invest in the steel industry this week and pull out next week. A firm cannot do that.

[42]One of the simplest ways for an individual to diversify is to buy shares in a mutual fund that holds a diversified portfolio.

To be sure, the individual would have to pay brokerage fees on the purchase and sale of steel company shares, but think of the time and expense for a firm to acquire a steel company or to start up a new steel-making operation.

You can probably see where we are heading. If investors can diversify on their own account, they will not pay any *extra* for firms that diversify. And if they have a sufficiently wide choice of securities, they will not pay any *less* because they are unable to invest separately in each factory. Therefore, in countries like the United States, which have large and competitive capital markets, diversification does not add to a firm's value or subtract from it. The total value is the sum of its parts.

This conclusion is important for corporate finance, because it justifies adding present values. The concept of *value additivity* is so important that we will give a formal definition of it. If the capital market establishes a value PV(A) for asset A and PV(B) for B, the market value of a firm that holds only these two assets is

$$\text{PV(AB)} = \text{PV(A)} + \text{PV(B)}$$

A three-asset firm combining assets A, B, and C would be worth PV(ABC) = PV(A) + PV(B) + PV(C), and so on for any number of assets.

We have relied on intuitive arguments for value additivity. But the concept is a general one that can be proved formally by several different routes.[43] The concept seems to be widely accepted, for thousands of managers add thousands of present values daily, usually without thinking about it.

[43]You may wish to refer to the Appendix to Chapter 32, which discusses diversification and value additivity in the context of mergers.

SUMMARY

Our review of capital market history showed that the returns to investors have varied according to the risks they have borne. At one extreme, very safe securities like U.S. Treasury bills have provided an average return over 104 years of only 4.1 percent a year. The riskiest securities that we looked at were common stocks. The stock market provided an average return of 11.7 percent, a premium of 7.6 percent over the safe rate of interest.

This gives us two benchmarks for the opportunity cost of capital. If we are evaluating a safe project, we discount at the current risk-free rate of interest. If we are evaluating a project of average risk, we discount at the expected return on the average common stock. Historical evidence suggests that this return is 7.6 percent above the risk-free rate, but many financial managers and economists opt for a lower figure. That still leaves us with a lot of assets that don't fit these simple cases. Before we can deal with them, we need to learn how to measure risk.

Risk is best judged in a portfolio context. Most investors do not put all their eggs into one basket: They diversify. Thus the effective risk of any security cannot be judged by an examination of that security alone. Part of the uncertainty about the security's return is diversified away when the security is grouped with others in a portfolio.

Risk in investment means that future returns are unpredictable. This spread of possible outcomes is usually measured by standard deviation. The standard deviation of the *market portfolio*, generally represented by the Standard and Poor's Composite Index, is around 15 to 20 percent a year.

Most individual stocks have higher standard deviations than this, but much of their variability represents *unique* risk that can be eliminated by diversification. Diversification cannot eliminate *market* risk. Diversified portfolios are exposed to variation in the general level of the market.

A security's contribution to the risk of a well-diversified portfolio depends on how the security is liable to be affected by a general market decline. This sensitivity to market movements is known as *beta* (β). Beta measures the amount that investors expect the stock price to change for each additional 1 percent change in the market. The average beta of all stocks is 1.0. A stock with a beta greater than 1 is unusually sensitive to market movements; a stock with a beta below 1 is unusually insensitive to market movements. The standard deviation of a well-diversified portfolio is proportional to its beta. Thus a diversified portfolio invested in stocks with a beta of 2.0 will have twice the risk of a diversified portfolio with a beta of 1.0.

One theme of this chapter is that diversification is a good thing *for the investor*. This does not imply that *firms* should diversify. Corporate diversification is redundant if investors can diversify on their own account. Since diversification does not affect the firm value, present values add even when risk is explicitly considered. Thanks to *value additivity*, the net present value rule for capital budgeting works even under uncertainty. In this chapter we have introduced you to a number of formulas. They are reproduced in the endpapers to the book. You should take a look and check that you understand them.

FURTHER READING

A very valuable record of the performance of United States securities since 1926 is:

Ibbotson Associates, Inc.: *Stocks, Bonds, Bills, and Inflation, 2004 Yearbook*, Wiley, New York, 2004.

Dimson, Marsh, and Staunton compare market returns in 16 countries over the years 1900–2001 in:

E. Dimson, P. R. Marsh, and M. Staunton: *Triumph of the Optimists: 101 Years of Global Equity Returns*, Princeton University Press, 2002.

For a somewhat technical survey of the literature on the market risk premium, see:

M. J. Brennan, "Corporate Investment Policy," in G. M. Constantinides, M. Harris, and R. M. Stulz (eds.), *Handbook of the Economics of Finance*, Elsevier Science, 2003.

Books on the risk premium include:

B. Cornell, *The Equity Risk Premium: The Long-Run Future of the Stock Market*, Wiley, New York, 1999.

R. Ibbotson, W. Goetzmann, and B. Kogut, *The Equity Risk Premium: Research and Practice*, Oxford University Press, 2004.

There have been several studies of the way that standard deviation is reduced by diversification, including:

M. Statman: "How Many Stocks Make a Diversified Portfolio?" *Journal of Financial and Quantitative Analysis*, 22 (September 1987), pp. 353–364.

CONCEPT REVIEW QUESTIONS

1. Explain the difference between the arithmetic average and the compound annual return. Which one is higher? (page 150)
2. If stock prices rise faster than dividends, one possible explanation is that the cost of capital has fallen. Explain why. Would an average of past returns over- or underestimate the cost of capital? (pages 154-155)
3. What are the formulas for the variance and standard deviation of returns? (pages 157–158)

For additional Concept Review Questions, please visit us at www.mhhe.com/bmam8e or refer to your Student CD.

QUIZ

1. A game of chance offers the following odds and payoffs. Each play of the game costs Rs. 100, so the net profit per play is the payoff less Rs. 100.

Probability	Payoff	Net Profit
.10	Rs. 500	Rs. 400
.50	100	0
.40	0	−100

What are the expected cash payoff and expected rate of return? Calculate the variance and standard deviation of this rate of return.

2. The following table shows the nominal returns on the Indian stocks and the rate of inflation.
   a. What was the standard deviation of the market returns?
   b. Calculate the average real return.

Year	Nominal Stock Return on Sensex	Inflation (%)
1995–96	−0.157	0.043
1996–97	0.070	0.053
1997–98	0.112	0.044
1998–99	−0.120	0.051
1999–00	0.423	0.063
2000–01	−0.066	0.054

3. Mr. Rakesh Sabharwal, ace mutual fund manager, produced the following percentage rates of return from 1999 to 2003. Rates of return on Sensex are given for comparison.

	1998–99	1999–00	2000–01	2001–02	2002–03
Mr. Rajesh Sabharwal	−6.20%	48.07%	−1.50%	−6.91%	−1.10%
Sensex	−12.0%	42.3%	−6.6%	−19.9%	−0.3%

Calculate the average return and standard deviation of Mr. Sabharwal's mutual fund. Did he do better or worse than Sensex by these measures?

4. True or false?
   a. Investors prefer diversified companies because they are less risky.
   b. If stocks were perfectly positively correlated, diversification would not reduce risk.
   c. The contribution of a stock to the risk of a well-diversified portfolio depends on its market risk.
   d. A well-diversified portfolio with a beta of 2.0 is twice as risky as the market portfolio.
   e. An undiversified portfolio with a beta of 2.0 is less than twice as risky as the market portfolio.

5. In which of the following situations would you get the largest reduction in risk by spreading your investment across two stocks?
   a. The two shares are perfectly correlated.
   b. There is no correlation.
   c. There is modest negative correlation.
   d. There is perfect negative correlation.

6. To calculate the variance of a three-stock portfolio, you need to add nine boxes:

Use the same symbols that we used in this chapter; for example, x_1 = proportion invested in stock 1 and σ_{12} = covariance between stocks 1 and 2. Now complete the nine boxes.

TABLE 7.7

See Quiz Question 9.

Stock	Stock Return if Market Return Is:	
	−10%	+10%
A	0	+20
B	−20	+20
C	−30	0
D	+15	+15
E	+10	−10

7. Suppose the standard deviation of the market return is 20 percent.
   a. What is the standard deviation of returns on a well-diversified portfolio with a beta of 1.3?
   b. What is the standard deviation of returns on a well-diversified portfolio with a beta of 0?
   c. A well-diversified portfolio has a standard deviation of 15 percent. What is its beta?
   d. A poorly diversified portfolio has a standard deviation of 20 percent. What can you say about its beta?
8. A portfolio contains equal investments in 10 stocks. Five have a beta of 1.2; the remainder have a beta of 1.4. What is the portfolio beta?
   a. 1.3.
   b. Greater than 1.3 because the portfolio is not completely diversified.
   c. Less than 1.3 because diversification reduces beta.
9. What is the beta of each of the stocks shown in Table 7.7?

PRACTICE QUESTIONS

1. Here are the inflation rates and Indian stock market and Treasury Bill returns between 2001 and 2006:

Year	Sensex returns	Inflation	T-Bill rate
2000–01	−6.61%	5.35%	7.20%
2001–02	−19.93%	1.62%	6.10%
2002–03	−0.33%	6.29%	4.74%
2002–04	42.32%	4.54%	5.28%
2004–05	29.86%	4.98%	5.88%
2005–06	19.33%	7.40%	6.22%

(Source: www.rbi.orb.in, and www.fimmda.org)

Please visit us at www.mhhe.com/bmam8e or refer to your Student CD.

   a. What was the real return on the stock market each year?
   b. What was the average real return?
   c. What was the risk premium in each year?
   d. What was the average risk premium?
   e. What was the standard deviation of the risk premium?
2. You will find data on all of the companies in Table 7.3 in the website of National Stock Exchange of India (www.nseindia.com[44]). Pick at least three companies. For each company, download the daily prices

[44]If you have access to the Prowess database of CMIE, you can directly get the adjusted monthly returns of these stocks. The website of NSE gives only the unadjusted prices. You can also download monthly prices data for some of the stocks from www.in.finance.yahoo.com

in an Excel spreadsheet. Estimate the monthly returns from these data. Calculate each company's variance and standard deviation from the monthly returns given on the spreadsheet. The Excel functions are VAR and STDEV. Convert the standard deviations from monthly to annual units by multiplying by the square root of 12. How has the standard deviations of these stocks changed, compared with the figures reported in table 7.3?

3. Each of the following statements is dangerous or misleading. Explain why.
   a. A long-term Indian government bond is always absolutely safe.
   b. All investors should prefer stocks to bonds because stocks offer higher long-run rates of return.
   c. The best practical forecast of future rates of return on the stock market is a 5- or 10- year average of historical returns.

eXcel

Please visit us at www.mhhe.com/bmam8e or refer to your Student CD .

4. Hippique s.a., which owns a stable of racehorses, has just invested in a mysterious black stallion with great form but disputed bloodlines. Some experts in horseflesh predict the horse will win the coveted Prix de Bidet; others argue that it should be put out to grass. Is this a risky investment for Hippique shareholders? Explain.

5. Lonesome Gulch Mines has a standard deviation of 42 percent per year and a beta of +.10. Amalgamated Copper has a standard deviation of 31 percent a year and a beta of +.66. Explain why Lonesome Gulch is the safer investment for a diversified investor.

eXcel

Please visit us at www.mhhe.com/bmam8e or refer to your Student CD .

6. Lambeth Walk invests 60 percent of his funds in stock I and the balance in stock J. The standard deviation of returns on I is 10 percent, and on J it is 20 percent. Calculate the variance of portfolio returns, assuming
   a. The correlation between the returns is 1.0.
   b. The correlation is .5.
   c. The correlation is 0.

7. a. How many variance terms and how many covariance terms do you need to calculate the risk of a 100-share portfolio?
   b. Suppose all stocks had a standard deviation of 30 percent and a correlation with each other of .4. What is the standard deviation of the returns on a portfolio that has equal holdings in 50 stocks?
   c. What is the standard deviation of a fully diversified portfolio of such stocks?

STANDARD &POOR'S

8. Suppose that the standard deviation of returns from a typical share is about .40 (or 40 percent) a year. The correlation between the returns of each pair of shares is about .3.
   a. Calculate the variance and standard deviation of the returns on a portfolio that has equal investments in two shares, three shares, and so on, up to 10 shares.
   b. Use your estimates to draw a graph like Figure 7.9. How large is the underlying market risk that cannot be diversified away?
   c. Now repeat the problem, assuming that the correlation between each pair of stocks is zero.

eXcel

Please visit us at www.mhhe.com/bmam8e or refer to your Student CD .

9. Download the daily closing prices of HLL, Reliance and ITC from the website of the NSE (www.nseindia.com). Estimate the monthly returns from these data.
   a. Calculate the annual standard deviation of returns from each company, using the most recent three years of monthly returns. Use the Excel function STDEV. Multiply by the square root of 12 to convert to annual units.
   b. Use the Excel function CORREL to calculate the correlation coefficient between the monthly returns for each pair of stocks.
   c. Calculate the standard deviation of returns for a portfolio with equal investments in each of the three stocks.

eXcel

Please visit us at www.mhhe.com/bmam8e or refer to your Student CD .

STANDARD &POOR'S

10. Table 7.8 shows standard deviations and correlation coefficients for seven stocks from different countries. Calculate the variance of a portfolio with equal investments in each stock.

11. Download data on daily stock prices of any three companies given in Table 7.5 from the website of the NSE (www.nseindia.com). Similarly download the daily closing prices of Nifty. Estimate the monthly returns of these three stocks and Nifty. Beta is calculated by the Excel function SLOPE, where the "y" range

	Correlation Coefficients							
	Alcan	BP	Deutsche Bank	KLM	LVMH	Nestlé	Sony	Standard Deviation
Alcan	1.0	.39	.55	.54	.61	.26	.36	30.2%
BP		1.0	.23	.29	.22	.30	.14	23.9
Deutsche Bank			1.0	.36	.48	.16	.39	38.1
KLM				1.0	.49	.32	.19	54.5
LVMH					1.0	.02	.50	42.0
Nestlé						1.0	.10	15.5
Sony							1.0	47.5

TABLE 7.8

Standard deviations of returns and correlation coefficients for a sample of seven stocks.

Note: Correlations and standard deviations are calculated using returns in each country's own currency; in other words, they assume that the investor is protected against exchange risk.

refers to the company's return (the dependent variable) and the "x" range refers to the market returns (the independent variable). Calculate the betas. How have they changed from the betas reported in Table 7.5?

12. Your eccentric Aunt Claudia has left you $ 50,000 in Alcan shares plus $ 50,000 cash. Unfortunately her will requires that the Alcan stock not be sold for one year and the $ 50,000 cash must be entirely invested in one of the stocks shown in Table 7.8. What is the safest attainable portfolio under these restrictions?

13. There are few, if any, real companies with negative betas. But suppose you found one with $\beta = -.25$.
    a. How would you expect this stock's rate of return to change if the overall market rose by an extra 5 percent? What if the market fell by an extra 5 percent?
    b. You have Rs. 1 million invested in a well-diversified portfolio of stocks. Now you receive an additional Rs. 20,000 bequest. Which of the following actions will yield the safest overall portfolio return?
        i. Invest Rs. 20,000 in Treasury bills (which have $\beta = 0$).
        ii. Invest Rs. 20,000 in stocks with $\beta = 1$.
        iii. Invest Rs. 20,000 in the stock with $\beta = -.25$.

        Explain your answer.

14. Download the daily closing prices for Maruti Udyog Limited and Tata Chemicals from the website of the NSE (www.nseindia.org). Estimate the monthly returns from this.
    a. Calculate each company's beta, following the procedure described in Practise Question 11.
    b. Calculate the annual standard deviation of the market return from the monthly returns for Nifty. Use the Excel function STDEV, and multiply by the square root of 12 to convert to annual units. Also calculate the annual standard deviations of Maruti and Tata Chemicals.
    c. Let's assume that your answers to (a) and (b) are good forecasts. What would be the standard deviation of a well-diversified portfolio of stocks with betas equal to Maruti's beta? How about a well-diversified portfolio of stocks with Tata Chemicals' beta?
    d. How much of the total risk of Maruti was unique risk? How much of Tata Chemicals'?

STANDARD & POOR'S

15. In footnote 38 we gave the formula for the covariance. The following table shows a worked example of how to calculate the covariance and correlation coefficient between the returns on 2 stocks:

Month	Return on A ($\tilde{r}_A$)	Return on B ($\tilde{r}_B$)	$(\tilde{r}_A - r_A)^2$	$(\tilde{r}_B - r_B)^2$	$(\tilde{r}_A - r_A) \times (\tilde{r}_B - r_B)$
1	11	7	$(11 - 4)^2 = 49$	$(7 - 3)^2 = 16$	28
2	9	8	$(9 - 4)^2 = 25$	$(8 - 3)^2 = 25$	25
3	0	−5	$(0 - 4)^2 = 16$	$(-5 - 3)^2 = 64$	32
4	−4	2	$(-4 - 4)^2 = 64$	$(2 - 3)^2 = 1$	8
Sums	16	12	154	106	93
Averages	$r_A = 16/4 = 4$	$r_B = 12/4 = 3$			
Variances	$\sigma_A^2 = 154/4 = 38.5$	$\sigma_B^2 = 106/4 = 26.5$			
Standard deviations	$\sigma_A = \sqrt{38.5} = 6.20$	$\sigma_B = \sqrt{26.5} = 5.15$			
Covariance	$\sigma_{AB} = 93/4 = 23.25$				
Correlation	$\sigma_{AB}/(\sigma_A \times \sigma_B) = 23.25/(6.20 \times 5.15) = .73$				

Now use the monthly prices of Maruti and Tata Chemicals that you downloaded for Practise Question 14 and calculate the covariance and correlation coefficient between the two sets of returns.

CHALLENGE QUESTIONS

1. Here are some historical data on the risk characteristics of Wipro and Tata Motors:

	Wipro	Tata Motors
β (beta)	1.25	1.33
Yearly standard deviation of return (%)	41.88	40.57

The standard deviation of the return on the market (Sensex) was 22.8%.

a. The correlation coefficient between Wipro's returns versus Tata Motors' return is 0.72. What is the standard deviation of a portfolio invested half in Wipro and half in Tata Motors?

b. What is the standard deviation of a portfolio invested one-third in Wipro, one-third in Tata Motors and one-third in Treasury Bills?

c. What is the standard deviation if the portfolio is split evenly between Wipro and Tata Motors and is financed at 50 percent margin, i.e., the investor puts up only 50 percent of the total amount and borrows the balance from a broker?

d. What is the approximate standard deviation of a portfolio composed of 100 stocks with betas of 1.25 like Wipro? How about 100 stocks like Tata Motors? Hint: Part (d) should not require anything but the simplest arithmetic to answer.

2. Suppose that Treasury bills offer a return of about 6 percent and the expected market risk premium is 8.5 percent. The standard deviation of Treasury-bill returns is zero and the standard deviation of market returns is 20 percent. Use the formula for portfolio risk to calculate the standard deviation of portfolios with

different proportions in Treasury bills and the market. (Note that the covariance of two rates of return must be zero when the standard deviation of one return is zero.) Graph the expected returns and standard deviations.

3. Select two bank stocks and two oil stocks and then calculate the returns for 60 recent months. (Daily stock price and index data can be obtained from www.nseindia.com)
   a. Use the Excel STDEV and CORREL functions to calculate the standard deviation of monthly returns for each of these stocks and the correlation between each pair of stocks.
   b. Use your results to find the standard deviation of a portfolio that is evenly divided between different pairs of stocks. Do you reduce risk more by diversifying across stocks in the same industry or those in different industries?
4. Calculate the beta of each of the stocks in Table 7.8 relative to a portfolio with equal investments in each stock.

excel

Please visit us at www.mhhe.com/bmam8e or refer to your Student CD.

CHAPTER [8]

RISK AND RETURN

IN CHAPTER 7 we began to come to grips with the problem of measuring risk. Here is the story so far.

The stock market is risky because there is a spread of possible outcomes. The usual measure of this spread is the standard deviation or variance. The risk of any stock can be broken down into two parts. There is the *unique risk* that is peculiar to that stock, and there is the *market risk* that is associated with marketwide variations. Investors can eliminate unique risk by holding a well-diversified portfolio, but they cannot eliminate market risk. *All* the risk of a fully diversified portfolio is market risk.

A stock's contribution to the risk of a fully diversified portfolio depends on its sensitivity to market changes. This sensitivity is generally known as *beta*. A security with a beta of 1.0 has average market risk—a well-diversified portfolio of such securities has the same standard deviation as the market index. A security with a beta of .5 has below-average market risk—a well-diversified portfolio of these securities tends to move half as far as the market moves and has half the market's standard deviation.

In this chapter we build on this newfound knowledge. We present leading theories linking risk and return in a competitive economy, and we show how these theories can be used to estimate the returns required by investors in different stock market investments. We start with the most widely used theory, the capital asset pricing model, which builds directly on the ideas developed in the last chapter. We will also look at another class of models, known as arbitrage pricing or factor models. Then in Chapter 9 we show how these ideas can help the financial manager cope with risk in practical capital budgeting situations.

8.1 HARRY MARKOWITZ AND THE BIRTH OF PORTFOLIO THEORY

Most of the ideas in Chapter 7 date back to an article written in 1952 by Harry Markowitz.[1] Markowitz drew attention to the common practice of portfolio diversification and showed exactly how an investor can reduce the standard deviation of portfolio returns by choosing stocks that do not move exactly together. But Markowitz did not stop there; he went on to work out the basic principles of portfolio construction. These principles are the foundation for much of what has been written about the relationship between risk and return.

We begin with Figure 8.1, which shows a histogram of the daily returns on Grasim Industries from 1994 to 2006. On this histogram we have superimposed a bell-shaped normal distribution. The result is typical: when measured over some fairly short interval, the past rates of return on any stock conform closely to a normal distribution.[2]

Normal distributions can be completely defined by two numbers. One is the average or expected return; the other is the variance or standard deviation. Now you can see why in Chapter 7 we discussed the calculation of expected return and standard deviation. They are not just arbitrary measures: if returns are normally distributed, they are the *only* two measures that an investor need consider.

---

[1] H. M. Markowitz, "Portfolio Selection," *Journal of Finance* 7 (March 1952), pp. 77–91.

[2] If you were to measure returns over *long* intervals, the distribution would be skewed. For example, you would encounter returns greater than 100 percent but none less than −100 percent. The distribution of returns over periods of, say, one year would be better approximated by a *lognormal* distribution. The lognormal distribution, like the normal, is completely specified by its mean and standard deviation.

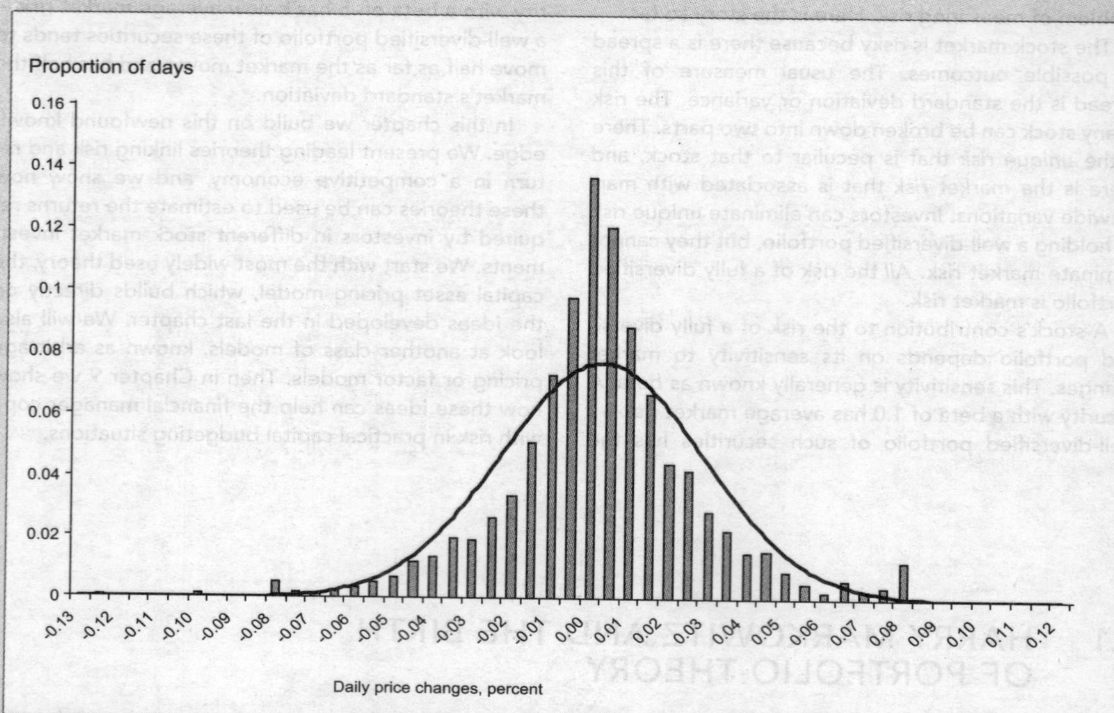

FIGURE 8.1

Daily price changes for Grasim Industries are approximately normally distributed. This plot spans November 1994 to March 2006.

Figure 8.2 pictures the distribution of possible returns from two investments. Both offer an expected return of 10 percent, but A has the much wider spread of possible outcomes. Its standard deviation is 15 percent; the standard deviation of B is 7.5 percent. Most investors dislike uncertainty and would therefore prefer B to A.

Figure 8.3 pictures the distribution of returns from two other investments. This time both have the *same* standard deviation, but the expected return is 20 percent from stock C and only 10 percent from stock D. Most investors like high expected return and would therefore prefer C to D.

Combining Stocks into Portfolios

Suppose that you are wondering whether to invest in shares of Grasim Industries or Reliance Energy. You decide that Grasim offers an expected return of 14 percent and Reliance Energy offers an expected return of 17 percent. After looking at the past variability of the two stocks, you also decide that the standard deviation of returns is 33 percent for Grasim and 37 percent for Reliance Energy. Reliance Energy offers the higher expected return, but is more risky.

Now there is no reason to restrict yourself to holding only one stock. For example, in Section 7.3 we analyzed what would happen if you invested 53% of your money in Grasim and 47% in Reliance Energy. The expected return on this portfolio is 15.41 percent, which is simply a weighted average of the expected returns on the two holdings. What about the risk of this portfolio? We know that, thanks to diversification, the portfolio risk is less than the average of the risks of the separate

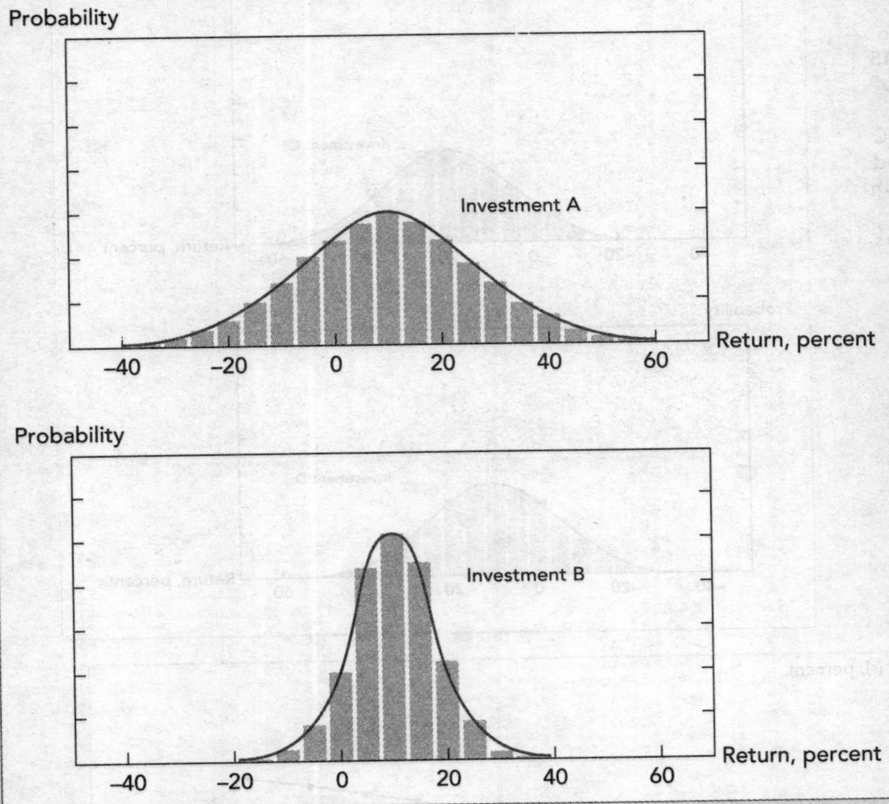

FIGURE 8.2

These two investments both have an *expected* return of 10 percent but because investment A has the greater spread of *possible* returns, it is more risky than B. We can measure this spread by the standard deviation. Investment A has a standard deviation of 15 percent; B, 7.5 percent. Most investors would prefer B to A.

stocks. In fact, on the basis of past experience the standard deviation of this portfolio is 30.41 percent[3].

In Figure 8.4 we have plotted the expected return and risk that you could achieve by different combinations of the two stocks. Which of these combinations is the best? That depends on your stomach. If you want to stake all on getting rich quickly, you will do best to put all your money in Reliance Energy. If you want a more peaceful life, you should invest most of your money in Grasim. To minimize risk you should keep a small investment in Reliance Energy[4].

In practice, you are not limited to investing in only two stocks. Our next task, therefore, is to find a way to identify the best portfolios of 10, 100, or 1,000 stocks.

---

[3]We pointed out in Section 7.3 that the correlation between the returns of Grasim and Reliance Energy is 0.52. The variance of a portfolio that is 53 percent invested in Grasim and 47 percent invested in Reliance Energy is

$$\begin{aligned}\text{Variance} &= x_1^2\sigma_1^2 + x_2^2\sigma_2^2 + 2x_1x_2\rho_{12}\sigma_1\sigma_2 \\ &= [(0.47)^2 \times (37)^2] + [(0.53)^2 \times (33)^2] + 2(0.47 \times 0.53 \times 1 \times 33 \times 37) \\ &= 1216.61\end{aligned}$$

The portfolio standard deviation is $\sqrt{1216.61} = 34.88$ percent.

[4]The portfolio with the minimum risk has 61.8 percent in Grasim. We assume in Figure 8.4 that you may not take negative positions in either stock, i.e., we rule out short sales.

FIGURE 8.3

The standard deviation of possible returns is 15 percent for both these investments, but the expected return from C is 20 percent compared with an expected return from D of only 10 percent. Most investors would prefer C to D.

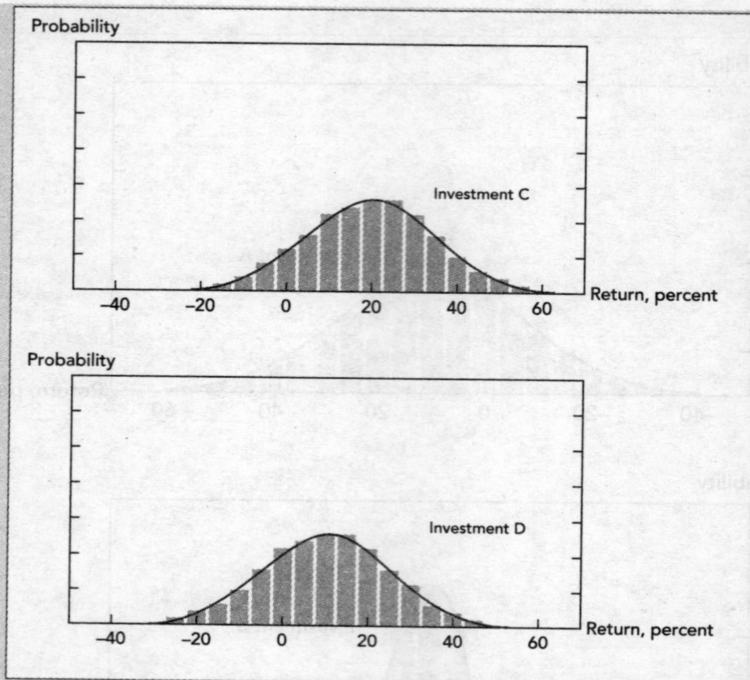

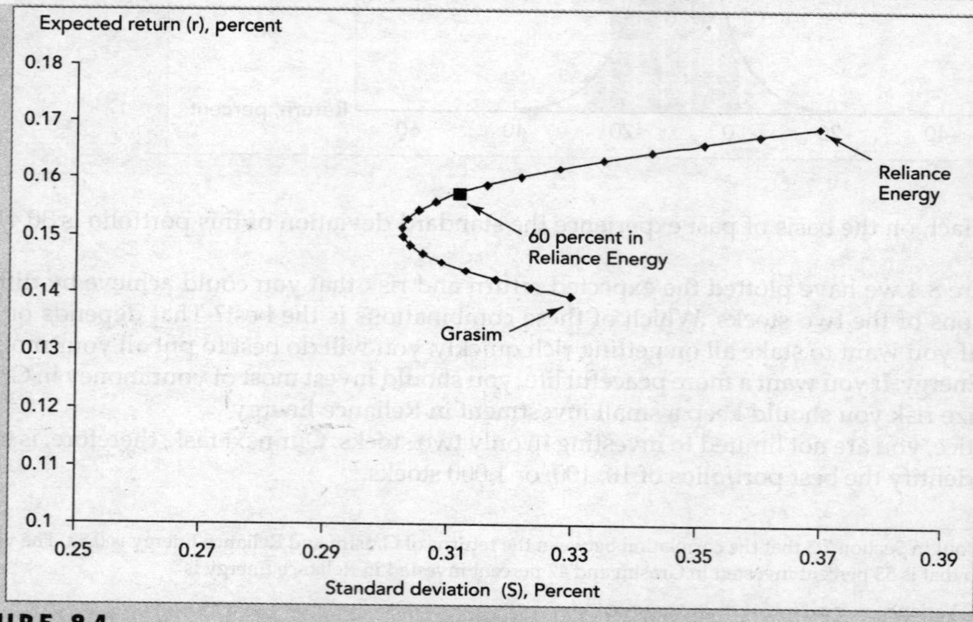

FIGURE 8.4

The curved line illustrates how expected return and standard deviation change as you hold different combinations of two stocks. For example, if you invest 40 percent of your money in Reliance Energy and the remaining in Grasim, your expected return is 15.8 percent, which is 40 percent of the way between the expected returns on the two stocks. The standard deviation is 31.17 percent, which is less than 40 percent of the way between the standard deviations between the two stocks. This is because diversification reduces risk.

Stocks	Expected Return	Standard Deviation	Efficient Portfolios—Percentages Allocated to Each Stock			
			A	B	C	D
Grasim_indistries	14%	33%				
Reliance_Energy_Ltd.	17%	37%			12%	14%
ACC	16%	31%		19%	7%	20%
BHEL	19%	39%			16%	7%
Gujarat_Ambuja_Cements_Ltd.	13%	29%				
Hero_Honda_Motors	15%	31%			9%	10%
HDFC	14%	26%			11%	34%
Infosys	19%	40%		27%	25%	15%
L_T	22%	57%	100%	23%	8%	
TELCO	20%	41%		31%	12%	
Expected portfolio return			22%	20%	18%	16%
Portfolio standard deviation			57%	34.10%	27.60%	23.15%

TABLE 8.1

Examples of efficient portfolios chosen from 10 stocks.

Note: Standard deviations and correlations between stock returns were estimated from monthly stock returns, November 94–March 2006. Efficient portfolios are calculated assuming that short sales are prohibited.

We'll start with 10. Suppose that you can choose a portfolio from any of the stocks listed in the first column of Table 8.1. After analyzing the prospects for each firm, you come up with the return forecasts shown in the second column of the table. You use data for the past five years to estimate the risk of each stock (column 3) and the correlation between the returns on each pair of stocks.[5]

Now turn to Figure 8.5. each dot (shaped as "•") marks the combination of risk and return offered by a different individual security. For example, L & T Limited (marked "A" in the figure) has the highest standard deviation; it also offers the highest expected return. It is represented by the "•" at the upper right of Figure 8.5.

By mixing investment in individual securities, you can obtain an even wider selection of risk and return: in fact, *anywhere* in the shaded area in Figure 8.5. But where in the shaded area is best? Well, what is your goal? Which direction do you want to go? The answer should be obvious: You want to go up (to increase expected return) and to the left (to reduce risk). Go as far as you can, and you will end up with one of the portfolios that lies along the heavy solid line. Markowitz called them **efficient portfolios.** These portfolios are clearly better than any in the interior of the shaded area.

We will not calculate this set of efficient portfolios here, but you may be interested in how to do it. Think back to the capital rationing problem in Section 5.4. There we wanted to deploy a limited amount of capital investment in a mixture of projects to give the highest total NPV. Here we want to deploy an investor's funds to give the highest expected return for a given standard deviation. In principle, both problems can be solved by hunting and pecking—but only in principle. To solve the

[5]There are 90 correlation coefficients, so we have not listed them in Table 8.1.

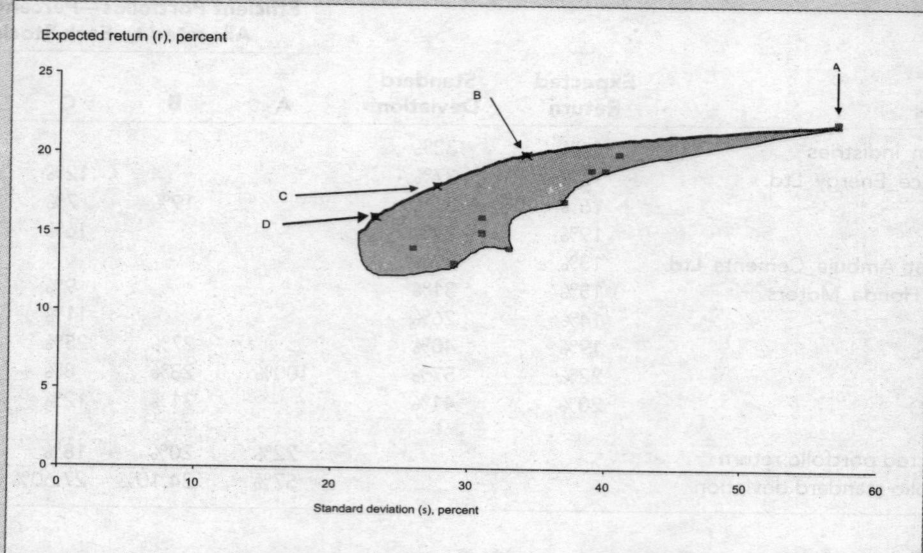

FIGURE 8.5

Each shaded box marked "▪" shows the expected return and the standard deviation of 1 of the 10 stocks in Table 8.1. The area between the dark and the thin line shows the possible combinations of expected return and standard deviation from investing in a mixture of these stocks. If you like high expected returns and dislike high standard deviations, you will prefer portfolios along the heavy line. These are efficient portfolios. We have marked the four efficient portfolios described in Table 8.1 (A, B, C, and D).

capital rationing problem, we can employ linear programming; to solve the portfolio problem, we would turn to a variant of linear programming known as *quadratic programming*. Given the expected return and standard deviation for each stock, as well as the correlation between each pair of stocks, we could give a computer a standard quadratic program and tell it to calculate the set of efficient portfolios.

Four of these efficient portfolios are marked in Figure 8.5. Their compositions are summarized in Table 8.1. Portfolio A offers the highest expected return; A is invested entirely in one stock, L&T Limited. Portfolio D offers much lower risk; you can see from table 8.1 that among others, it has 34 percent holding in HDFC, which had the lowest standard deviation. Notice that D also has 15 percent holding in Infosys, even though this stock is individually very risky. The reason? On past evidence the fortunes of Infosys are only weakly correlated with those of the other stocks in the portfolio and therefore Infosys provides additional diversification.

Table 8.1 also shows the compositions of two other efficient portfolios B and C with intermediate levels of risk and expected return.

We Introduce Borrowing and Lending

Of course, large investment funds can choose from thousands of stocks and thereby achieve a wider choice of risk and return. This choice is represented in Figure 8.6 by the shaded, broken-egg-shaped area. The set of efficient portfolios is again marked by the heavy curved line.

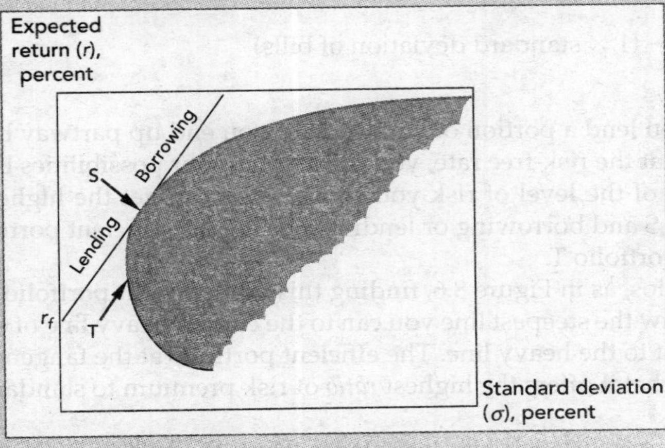

FIGURE 8.6

Lending and borrowing extend the range of investment possibilities. If you invest in portfolio S and lend or borrow at the risk-free interest rate, r_f, you can achieve any point along the straight line from r_f through S. This gives you a higher expected return for any level of risk than if you just invest in common stocks.

Now we introduce yet another possibility. Suppose that you can also lend or borrow money at some risk-free rate of interest r_f. If you invest some of your money in Treasury bills (i.e., lend money) and place the remainder in common stock portfolio S, you can obtain any combination of expected return and risk along the straight line joining r_f and S in Figure 8.6. Since borrowing is merely negative lending, you can extend the range of possibilities to the right of S by borrowing funds at an interest rate of r_f and investing them as well as your own money in portfolio S.

Let us put some numbers on this. Suppose that portfolio S has an expected return of 15 percent and a standard deviation of 16 percent. Treasury bills offer an interest rate (r_f) of 5 percent and are risk-free (i.e., their standard deviation is zero). If you invest half your money in portfolio S and lend the remainder at 5 percent, the expected return on your investment is halfway between the expected return on S and the interest rate on Treasury bills:

$$r = (\tfrac{1}{2} \times \text{expected return on S}) + (\tfrac{1}{2} \times \text{interest rate})$$
$$= 10\%$$

And the standard deviation is halfway between the standard deviation of S and the standard deviation of Treasury bills[6]:

$$\sigma = (\tfrac{1}{2} \times \text{standard deviation of S}) + (\tfrac{1}{2} \times \text{standard deviation of bills})$$
$$= 8\%$$

Or suppose that you decide to go for the big time: You borrow at the Treasury bill rate an amount equal to your initial wealth, and you invest everything in portfolio S. You have twice your own money invested in S, but you have to *pay* interest on the loan. Therefore your expected return is

$$r = (2 \times \text{expected return on S}) - (1 \times \text{interest rate})$$
$$= 25\%$$

[6]If you want to check this, write down the formula for the standard deviation of a two-stock portfolio:

$$\text{Standard deviation} = \sqrt{x_1^2\sigma_1^2 + x_2^2\sigma_2^2 + 2x_1x_2\rho_{12}\sigma_1\sigma_2}$$

Now see what happens when security 2 is riskless, i.e., when $\sigma_2 = 0$.

And the standard deviation of your investment is

$$\sigma = (2 \times \text{standard deviation of S}) - (1 \times \text{standard deviation of bills})$$
$$= 32\%$$

You can see from Figure 8.6 that when you lend a portion of your money, you end up partway between r_f and S; if you can borrow money at the risk-free rate, you can extend your possibilities beyond S. You can also see that regardless of the level of risk you choose, you can get the highest expected return by a mixture of portfolio S and borrowing or lending. S is the *best* efficient portfolio. There is no reason ever to hold, say, portfolio T.

If you have a graph of efficient portfolios, as in Figure 8.6, finding this best efficient portfolio is easy. Start on the vertical axis at r_f and draw the steepest line you can to the curved heavy line of efficient portfolios. That line will be tangent to the heavy line. The efficient portfolio at the tangency point is better than all the others. Notice that it offers the highest *ratio* of risk premium to standard deviation.

This means that we can separate the investor's job into two stages. First, the best portfolio of common stocks must be selected—S in our example. Second, this portfolio must be blended with borrowing or lending to obtain an exposure to risk that suits the particular investor's taste. Each investor, therefore, should put money into just two benchmark investments—a risky portfolio S and a risk-free loan (borrowing or lending).[7]

What does portfolio S look like? If you have better information than your rivals, you will want the portfolio to include relatively large investments in the stocks you think are undervalued. But in a competitive market you are unlikely to have a monopoly of good ideas. In that case there is no reason to hold a different portfolio of common stocks from anybody else. In other words, you might just as well hold the market portfolio. That is why many professional investors invest in a market-index portfolio and why most others hold well-diversified portfolios.

8.2 THE RELATIONSHIP BETWEEN RISK AND RETURN

In Chapter 7 we looked at the returns on selected investments. The least risky investment was the 1-year Government Security. Since the return in the G-Sec is fixed, it is unaffected by what happens to the market. In other words, the G-Secs have a beta of zero. We also considered a much riskier investment, the market portfolio of common stocks. This has the average market risk: Its beta is 1.0.

Wise investors do not take risks just for fun. They are playing with real money. Therefore they require a higher return from the market portfolio than from Government Securities or Treasury Bills. The difference between the return on the market and the interest rate is termed the *market risk premium*. Since 1978–79, the market risk premium ($r_m - r_f$) has averaged 13.3 percent a year in India.

In Figure 8.7 we have plotted the risk and expected return from Treasury bills and the market portfolio. You can see that Treasury bills have a beta of 0 and a risk premium of 0.[8] The market

---

[7]This *separation theorem* was first pointed out by J. Tobin in "Liquidity Preference as Behavior toward Risk," *Review of Economic Studies* 25 (February 1958), pp. 65–86.

[8]Remember that the risk premium is the difference between the investment's expected return and the risk-free rate. For Treasury bills, the difference is zero.

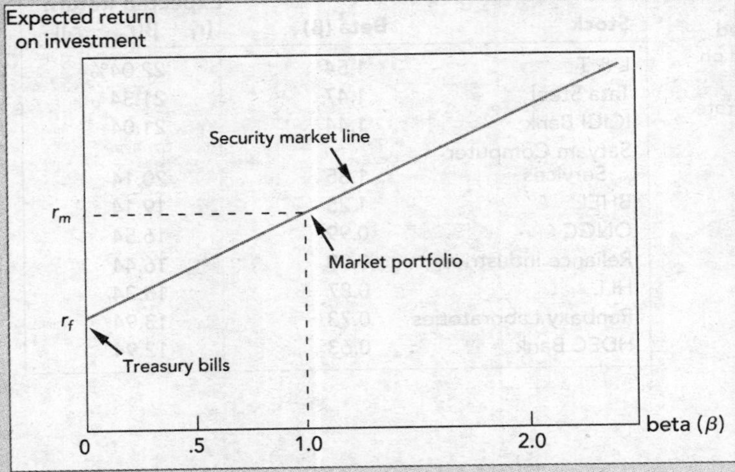

FIGURE 8.7

The capital asset pricing model states that the expected risk premium on each investment is proportional to its beta. This means that each investment should lie on the sloping security market line connecting Treasury bills and the market portfolio.

portfolio has a beta of 1.0 and a risk premium of $r_m - r_f$. This gives us two benchmarks for the expected risk premium. But what is the expected risk premium when beta is not 0 or 1?

In the mid-1960s three economists—William Sharpe, John Lintner, and Jack Treynor—produced an answer to this question.[9] Their answer is known as the **capital asset pricing model,** or **CAPM.** The model's message is both startling and simple. In a competitive market, the expected risk premium varies in direct proportion to beta. This means that in Figure 8.7 all investments must plot along the sloping line, known as the **security market line.** The expected risk premium on an investment with a beta of .5 is, therefore, *half* the expected risk premium on the market; the expected risk premium on an investment with a beta of 2.0 is *twice* the expected risk premium on the market. We can write this relationship as

Expected risk premium on stock = beta × expected risk premium on market

$$r - r_f = \beta(r_m - r_f)$$

Some Estimates of Expected Returns

Before we tell you where the formula comes from, let us use it to figure out what returns investors are looking for from particular stocks. To do this, we need three numbers: β, r_f, and $r_m - r_f$. We gave you estimates of the betas of 10 stocks in Table 7.5. In March 2006, the yield on 1-year G-Sec was about 6.64 percent.

How about the market risk premium? As we pointed out in the last chapter, we can't measure $r_m - r_f$ with precision. From past evidence it appears to be 13.3 percent, although many economists and financial managers would forecast a lower figure. Let's use 10 percent in this example.

[9] W. F. Sharpe, "Capital Asset Prices: A Theory of Market Equilibrium under Conditions of Risk," *Journal of Finance* 19 (September 1964), pp. 425–442 and J. Lintner, "The Valuation of Risk Assets and the Selection of Risky Investments in Stock Portfolios and Capital Budgets," *Review of Economics and Statistics* 47 (February 1965), pp. 13–37. Treynor's article has not been published.

TABLE 8.2

These estimates of the returns expected by investors in March 2006 were based on the capital asset pricing model. We assumed 6.64 percent for the risk free rate and 10 percent for the expected risk premium $r_m - r_f$.

Stock	Beta (β)	Expected Return $[r_f + \beta(r_m - r_f)]$
L & T	1.54	22.04%
Tata Steel	1.47	21.34
ICICI Bank	1.44	21.04
Satyam Computer Services	1.35	20.14
BHEL	1.25	19.14
ONGC	0.99	16.54
Reliance Industries	0.98	16.44
HLL	0.87	15.34
Ranbaxy Laboratories	0.73	13.94
HDFC Bank	0.63	12.94

Table 8.2 puts these numbers together to give an estimate of the expected return on each stock. The stock with the highest beta in our example is L&T. Our estimate of the expected return from L&T is 22 percent. The stock with the lowest beta is HDFC Bank. Our estimate of the expected return is 12.94 percent, 6.3 percent more than the yield on 1-year Government Securities.

You can also use the capital asset pricing model to find the discount rate for a new capital investment. For example, suppose that you are analyzing a proposal by ONGC to expand capacity. At what rate should you discount the forecast cash flows? According to Table 8.2, investors are looking for a return of 16.54 percent from businesses with the risk of ONGC. So the cost of capital for a further investment in the same business is 16.54 percent.[10]

In practice, choosing a discount rate is seldom so easy. (After all, you can't expect to be paid a fat salary just for plugging numbers into a formula.) For example, you must learn how to adjust for the extra risk caused by company borrowing. You will also need to consider the difference between short- and long-term interest rates. In 2006 the short-term rate was about 1.2 percent lower than the long-term rate. A cost of capital based on this rate would have been inappropriate for long-term capital investments. But these refinements can wait until later.[11]

Review of the Capital Asset Pricing Model

Let us review the basic principles of portfolio selection:

1. Investors like high expected return and low standard deviation. Common stock portfolios that offer the highest expected return for a given standard deviation are known as *efficient portfolios*.

[10]Remember that instead of investing in plant and machinery, the firm could return the money to the shareholders. The opportunity cost of investing is the return that shareholders could expect to earn by buying financial assets. This expected return depends on the market risk of the assets.

[11]Tax issues arise because a corporation must pay tax on income from an investment in Treasury bills or other interest-paying securities. It turns out that the correct discount rate for risk-free investments is the *after-tax* Treasury bill rate. We come back to this point in Chapter 19.

Various other points on the practical use of betas and the capital asset pricing model are covered in Chapter 9.

2. If the investor can lend or borrow at the risk-free rate of interest, one efficient portfolio is better than all the others: the portfolio that offers the highest ratio of risk premium to standard deviation (that is, portfolio S in Figure 8.6). A risk-averse investor will put part of his money in this efficient portfolio and part in the risk-free asset. A risk-tolerant investor may put all her money in this portfolio or she may borrow and put in even more.
3. The composition of this best efficient portfolio depends on the investor's assessments of expected returns, standard deviations, and correlations. But suppose everybody has the same information and the same assessments. If there is no superior information, each investor should hold the same portfolio as everybody else; in other words, everyone should hold the market portfolio.

Now let us go back to the risk of individual stocks:

4. Do not look at the risk of a stock in isolation but at its contribution to portfolio risk. This contribution depends on the stock's sensitivity to changes in the value of the portfolio.
5. A stock's sensitivity to changes in the value of the *market* portfolio is known as *beta*. Beta, therefore, measures the marginal contribution of a stock to the risk of the market portfolio.

Now if everyone holds the market portfolio, and if beta measures each security's contribution to the market portfolio risk, then it is no surprise that the risk premium demanded by investors is proportional to beta. That is what the CAPM says.

What If a Stock Did Not Lie on the Security Market Line?

Imagine that you encounter stock A in Figure 8.8. Would you buy it? We hope not[12]—if you want an investment with a beta of .5, you could get a higher expected return by investing half your money in Treasury bills and half in the market portfolio. If everybody shares your view of the stock's prospects, the price of A will have to fall until the expected return matches what you could get elsewhere.

What about stock B in Figure 8.8? Would you be tempted by its high return? You wouldn't if you were smart. You could get a higher expected return for the same beta by borrowing 50 paise for every rupee of your own money and investing in the market portfolio. Again, if everybody agrees with your assessment, the price of stock B cannot hold. It will have to fall until the expected return on B is equal to the expected return on the combination of borrowing and investment in the market portfolio.

We have made our point. An investor can always obtain an expected risk premium of $\beta(r_m - r_f)$ by holding a mixture of the market portfolio and a risk-free loan. So in well-functioning markets nobody will hold a stock that offers an expected risk premium of *less* than $\beta(r_m - r_f)$. But what about the other possibility? Are there stocks that offer a higher expected risk premium? In other words, are there any that lie above the security market line in Figure 8.8? If we take all stocks together, we have the market portfolio. Therefore, we know that stocks *on average* lie on the line. Since none lies

[12]Unless, of course, we were trying to sell it.

FIGURE 8.8

In equilibrium no stock can lie below the security market line. For example, instead of buying stock A, investors would prefer to lend part of their money and put the balance in the market portfolio. And instead of buying stock B, they would prefer to borrow and invest in the market portfolio.

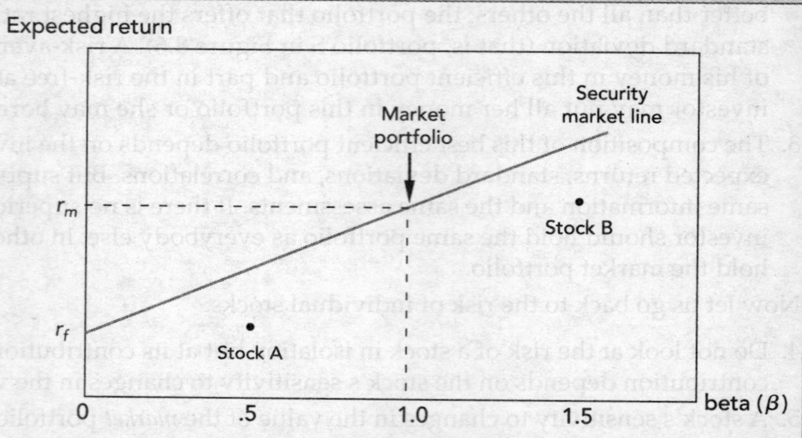

below the line, then there also can't be any that lie *above* the line. Thus each and every stock must lie on the security market line and offer an expected risk premium of

$$r - r_f = \beta(r_m - r_f)$$

8.3 VALIDITY AND ROLE OF THE CAPITAL ASSET PRICING MODEL

Any economic model is a simplified statement of reality. We need to simplify in order to interpret what is going on around us. But we also need to know how much faith we can place in our model.

Let us begin with some matters about which there is broad agreement. First, few people quarrel with the idea that investors require some extra return for taking on risk. That is why common stocks have given on average a higher return than the risk free assets in India. Who would want to invest in risky common stocks if they offered only the *same* expected return as bills? We would not, and we suspect you would not either.

Second, investors do appear to be concerned principally with those risks that they cannot eliminate by diversification. If this were not so, we should find that stock prices increase whenever two companies merge to spread their risks. And we should find that investment companies which invest in the shares of other firms are more highly valued than the shares they hold. But we do not observe either phenomenon. Mergers undertaken just to spread risk do not increase stock prices, and investment companies are no more highly valued than the stocks they hold.

The capital asset pricing model captures these ideas in a simple way. That is why financial managers find it a convenient tool for coming to grips with the slippery notion of risk and why nearly three-quarters of them use it to estimate the cost of capital.[13] It is also why economists often use the

[13]See J. R. Graham and C. R. Harvey, "The Theory and Practice of Corporate Finance: Evidence from the Field," *Journal of Financial Economics* 61 (2001), pp. 187–243. A number of the managers surveyed reported using more than one method to estimate the cost of capital. Seventy-three percent used the capital asset pricing model, while 39 percent stated they used the average historical stock return and 34 percent used the capital asset pricing model with some extra risk factors.

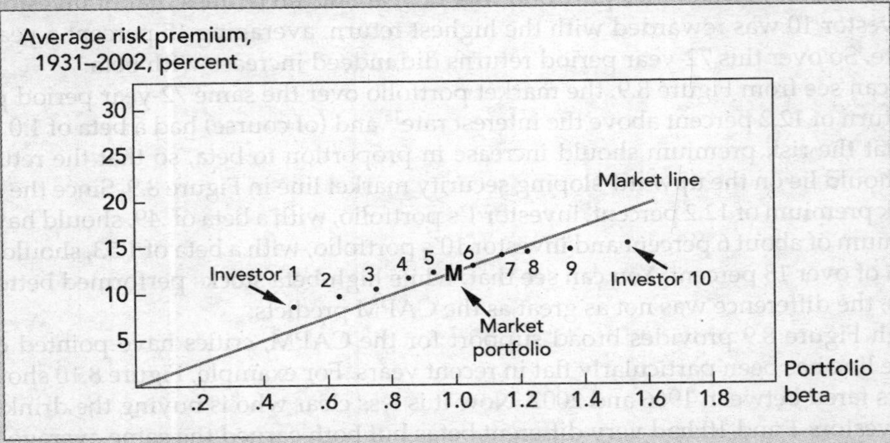

FIGURE 8.9

The capital asset pricing model states that the expected risk premium from any investment should lie on the security market line. The dots show the actual average risk premiums from portfolios with different betas. The high-beta portfolios generated higher average returns, just as predicted by the CAPM. But the high-beta portfolios plotted below the market line, and the low-beta portfolios plotted above. A line fitted to the 10 portfolio returns would be "flatter" than the market line.

Source: F. Black, "Beta and Return," *Journal of Portfolio Management* 20 (Fall 1993), pp. 8–18. We are grateful to Adam Kolasinski for updating the calculations.

capital asset pricing model to demonstrate important ideas in finance even when there are other ways to prove these ideas. But that does not mean that the capital asset pricing model is ultimate truth. We will see later that it has several unsatisfactory features, and we will look at some alternative theories. Nobody knows whether one of these alternative theories is eventually going to come out on top or whether there are other, better models of risk and return that have not yet seen the light of day.

Tests of the Capital Asset Pricing Model

Imagine that in 1931 ten investors gathered together in a Wall Street bar and agreed to establish investment trust funds for their children. Each investor decided to follow a different strategy. Investor 1 opted to buy the 10 percent of the New York Stock Exchange stocks with the lowest estimated betas; investor 2 chose the 10 percent with the next-lowest betas; and so on, up to investor 10, who proposed to buy the stocks with the highest betas. They also planned that at the end of each year they would reestimate the betas of all NYSE stocks and reconstitute their portfolios.[14] And so they parted with much cordiality and good wishes.

In time the 10 investors all passed away, but their children agreed to meet in early 2003 in the same bar to compare the performance of their portfolios. Figure 8.9 shows how they had fared. Investor 1's portfolio turned out to be much less risky than the market; its beta was only .49. However, investor 1 also realized the lowest return, 9 percent above the risk-free rate of interest. At the other

[14]Betas were estimated using returns over the previous 60 months.

extreme, the beta of investor 10's portfolio was 1.53, about three times that of investor 1's portfolio. But investor 10 was rewarded with the highest return, averaging 15 percent a year above the interest rate. So over this 72-year period returns did indeed increase with beta.

As you can see from Figure 8.9, the market portfolio over the same 72-year period provided an average return of 12.2 percent above the interest rate[15] and (of course) had a beta of 1.0. The CAPM predicts that the risk premium should increase in proportion to beta, so that the returns of each portfolio should lie on the upward-sloping security market line in Figure 8.9. Since the market provided a risk premium of 12.2 percent, investor 1's portfolio, with a beta of .49, should have provided a risk premium of about 6 percent and investor 10's portfolio, with a beta of 1.53, should have given a premium of over 18 percent. You can see that, while high-beta stocks performed better than low-beta stocks, the difference was not as great as the CAPM predicts.

Although Figure 8.9 provides broad support for the CAPM, critics have pointed out that the slope of the line has been particularly flat in recent years. For example, Figure 8.10 shows how our 10 investors fared between 1966 and 2002. Now it is less clear who is buying the drinks: The portfolios of investors 1 and 10 had very different betas but both earned the same average return over these 36 years. Of course, the line was correspondingly steeper before 1966. This is also shown in Figure 8.10

What is going on here? It is hard to say. Defenders of the capital asset pricing model emphasize that it is concerned with *expected* returns, whereas we can observe only *actual* returns. Actual stock returns reflect expectations, but they also embody lots of "noise"—the steady flow of surprises that conceal whether on average investors have received the returns they expected. This noise may make it impossible to judge whether the model holds better in one period than another.[16] Perhaps the best that we can do is to focus on the longest period for which there is reasonable data. This would take us back to Figure 8.9, which suggests that expected returns do indeed increase with beta, though less rapidly than the simple version of the CAPM predicts.[17]

The CAPM has also come under fire on a second front: Although return has not risen with beta in recent years, it has been related to other measures. For example, the green line in Figure 8.11 shows the cumulative difference between the returns on small-firm stocks and large-firm stocks. If you had bought the shares with the smallest market capitalizations and sold those with the largest capitalizations, this is how your wealth would have changed. You can see that small-cap stocks did not always do well, but over the long haul their owners have made substantially higher returns. Since the end of 1926 the average annual difference between the returns on the two groups of stocks has been 3.9 percent.

Now look at the blue line in Figure 8.11 which shows the cumulative difference between the returns on value stocks and growth stocks. Value stocks here are defined as those with high ratios of book value to market value. Growth stocks are those with low ratios of book to market. Notice that

[15]In Figure 8.9 the stocks in the "market portfolio" are weighted equally. Since the stocks of small firms have provided higher average returns than those of large firms, the risk premium on an equally weighted index is higher than on a value-weighted index. This is one reason for the difference between the 12.2 percent market risk premium in Figure 8.9 and the 7.6 percent premium reported in Table 7.1.

[16]A second problem with testing the model is that the market portfolio should contain all risky investments, including stocks, bonds, commodities, real estate—even human capital. Most market indexes contain only a sample of common stocks. See, for example, R. Roll, "A Critique of the Asset Pricing Theory's Tests; Part 1: On Past and Potential Testability of the Theory," *Journal of Financial Economics* 4 (March 1977), pp. 129–176.

[17]We say "simple version" because Fischer Black has shown that if there are borrowing restrictions, there should still exist a positive relationship between expected return and beta, but the security market line would be less steep as a result. See F. Black, "Capital Market Equilibrium with Restricted Borrowing," *Journal of Business* 45 (July 1972), pp. 444–455.

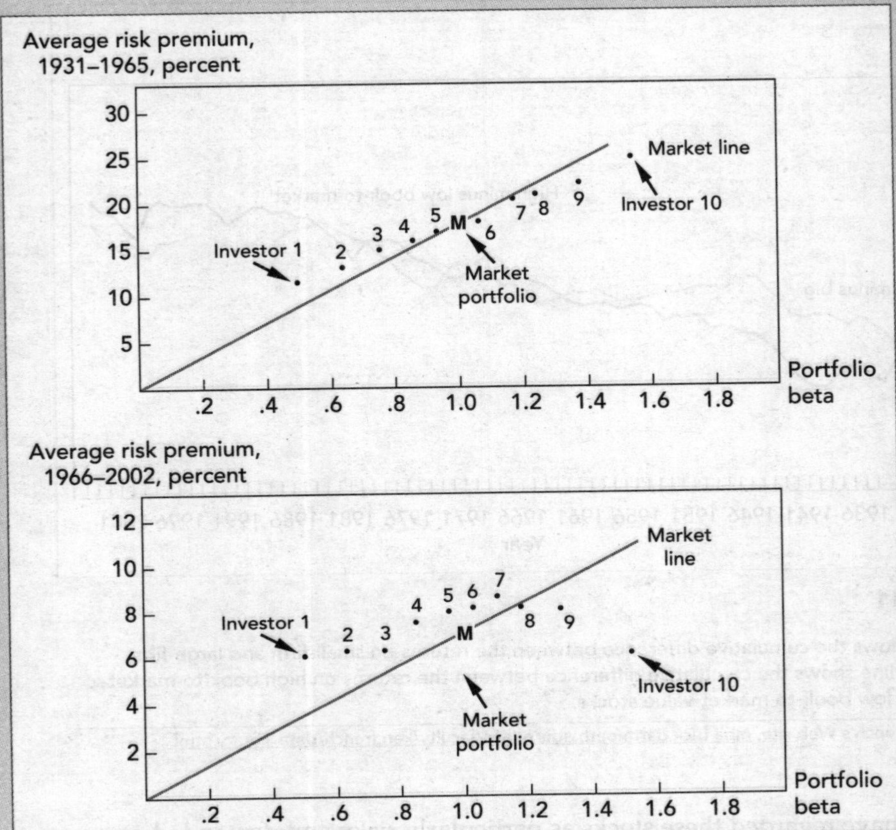

FIGURE 8.10

The relationship between beta and actual average return has been much weaker since the mid-1960s. In particular stocks with the highest betas have provided poor returns.

Source: F. Black, "Beta and Return," *Journal of Portfolio Management* 20 (Fall 1993), pp. 8–18. We are grateful to Adam Kolasinski for updating the calculations.

value stocks have provided a higher long-run return than growth stocks.[18] Since 1926 the average annual difference between the returns on value and growth stocks has been 4.4 percent.

Figure 8.11 does not fit well with the CAPM, which predicts that beta is the *only* reason that expected returns differ. It seems that investors saw risks in "small-cap" stocks and value stocks that were not captured by beta.[19] Take value stocks, for example. Many of these stocks may have sold below book value because the firms were in serious trouble; if the economy slowed unexpectedly, the firms might have collapsed altogether. Therefore, investors, whose jobs could also be on the line

[18]The small-firm effect was first documented by Rolf Banz in 1981. See R. Banz, "The Relationship between Return and Market Values of Common Stock," *Journal of Financial Economics* 9 (March 1981), pp. 3–18. Fama and French calculated the returns on portfolios designed to take advantage of the size effect and the book-to-market effect. See E. F. Fama and K. R. French, "The Cross-Section of Expected Stock Returns," *Journal of Financial Economics* 47 (June 1992), pp. 427–465. When calculating the returns on these portfolios, Fama and French control for differences in firm size when comparing stocks with low and high book-to-market ratios. Similarly, they control for differences in the book-to-market ratio when comparing small- and large-firm stocks. For details of the methodology and updated returns on the size and book-to-market factors see Kenneth French's Web site (**mba.tuck.dartmouth.edu/pages/faculty/ken.french/data_library.html**).

[19]The beta of the portfolio of small-company stocks has been on average nearly .20 higher than that of the large-company stocks, but the difference in beta is not nearly large enough to explain the difference in returns. There is no simple relationship between the return on the value- and growth-stock portfolios and beta.

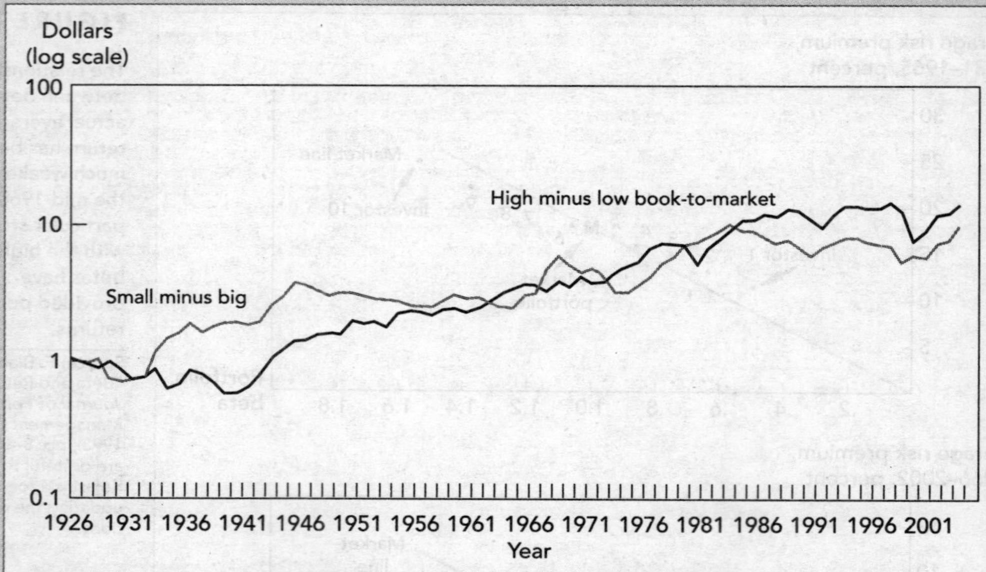

FIGURE 8.11

The green line shows the cumulative difference between the returns on small-firm and large-firm stocks. The blue line shows the cumulative difference between the returns on high book-to-market-value stocks and low book-to-market-value stocks.

Source: Kenneth French's Web site, mba.tuck.dartmouth.edu/pages/faculty/ken.french/data_library.html.

in a recession, may have regarded these stocks as particularly risky and demanded compensation in the form of higher expected returns. If that were the case, the simple version of the CAPM cannot be the whole truth.

In India, researchers have found very similar evidences, albeit by using data for a much smaller period. Obaidullah (1993), Ray (1994), and Mohanty (2002) find evidence against CAPM in the Indian capital market. Connor and Sehgal (2001) and Mohanty (2002) find evidence of Fama-French factors in the Indian context[20].

Again, it is hard to judge how seriously the CAPM is damaged by this finding. The relationship among stock returns and firm size and book-to-market ratio has been well documented. However, if you look long and hard at past returns, you are bound to find some strategy that just by chance would have worked in the past. This practice is known as "data-mining" or "data snooping." Maybe the size and book-to-market effects are simply chance results that stem from data snooping. If so, they should have vanished once they were discovered. There is some evidence that this is the

[20]See Obaidullah, M., "Does the CAPM Explain Actual Price behavior," Chartered Financial Analyst, November 1993, Ray, S., Capital Asset Pricing Model: The Indian Context, Unpublished Doctoral Dissertation, 1994, Indian Institute of Management, Bangalore. Connor, G., and S. Sehgal, Tests of Fama and French Model in India, May 2001, Paper can be downloaded from

www.1se.ac.uk/collections/accountingAndFinance/staff/connor/files/Fama%26FrenchIndia and Mohanty, P., Efficiency of the Market for Small Stock, NSE Research Initiative, April 2001.

case. If you look again at Figure 8.11, you will see that in the past 20 years small-firm stocks and value stocks have underperformed just about as often as they have overperformed.

There is no doubt that the evidence on the CAPM is less convincing than scholars once thought. But it will be hard to reject the CAPM beyond all reasonable doubt. Since data and statistics are unlikely to give final answers, the plausibility of the CAPM *theory* will have to be weighed along with the empirical "facts."

Assumptions behind the Capital Asset Pricing Model

The capital asset pricing model rests on several assumptions that we did not fully spell out. For example, we assumed that investment in U.S. Treasury bills is risk-free. It is true that there is little chance of default, but bills do not guarantee a *real* return. There is still some uncertainty about inflation. Another assumption was that investors can *borrow* money at the same rate of interest at which they can lend. Generally borrowing rates are higher than lending rates.

It turns out that many of these assumptions are not crucial, and with a little pushing and pulling it is possible to modify the capital asset pricing model to handle them. The really important idea is that investors are content to invest their money in a limited number of benchmark portfolios. (In the basic CAPM these benchmarks are Treasury bills and the market portfolio.)

In these modified CAPMs expected return still depends on market risk, but the definition of market risk depends on the nature of the benchmark portfolios.[21] In practice, none of these alternative capital asset pricing models is as widely used as the standard version.

8.4 SOME ALTERNATIVE THEORIES

Consumption Betas versus Market Betas

The capital asset pricing model pictures investors as solely concerned with the level and uncertainty of their future wealth. But this could be too simplistic. For example, investors may become accustomed to a particular standard of living, so that poverty tomorrow may be particularly difficult to bear if one were wealthy yesterday.[22] Behavioral psychologists have also observed that investors do not focus solely on the *current* value of their holdings, but look back at whether their investments are showing a profit. A gain, however small, may be an additional source of satisfaction. The capital asset pricing model does not allow for the possibility that investors may look back at the price at which they purchased stock and feel elated when their investment is in the black and depressed when it is in the red.[23]

[21]For example, see M. C. Jensen (ed.), *Studies in the Theory of Capital Markets*, Frederick A. Praeger, Inc., New York, 1972. In the introduction Jensen provides a very useful summary of some of these variations on the capital asset pricing model.

[22]See, for example, G. M. Constantinides, "Habit Formation: A Resolution of the Equity Premium Puzzle," *Journal of Political Economy* 98 (June 1990) pp. 519–543.

[23]We will discuss aversion to loss again in Chapter 13. The implications for asset pricing are explored in S. Benartzi and R. Thaler, "Myopic Loss Aversion and the Equity Premium Puzzle," *Quarterly Journal of Economics* 110 (1995), pp. 75–92; and in N. Barberis, M. Huang, and T. Santos, "Prospect Theory and Asset Prices," *Quarterly Journal of Economics* 116 (2001), pp. 1–53.

FIGURE 8.12

(a) The standard CAPM concentrates on how stocks contribute to the level and uncertainty of investor's wealth. Consumption is outside the model. (b) The consumption CAPM defines risk as a stock's contribution to uncertainty about consumption. Wealth (the intermediate step between stock returns and consumption) drops out of the model.

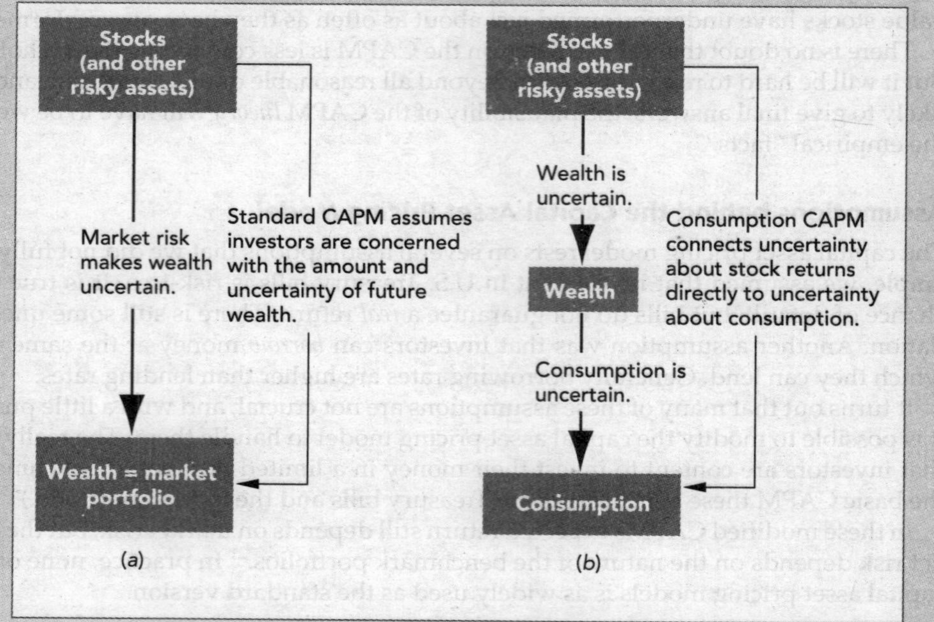

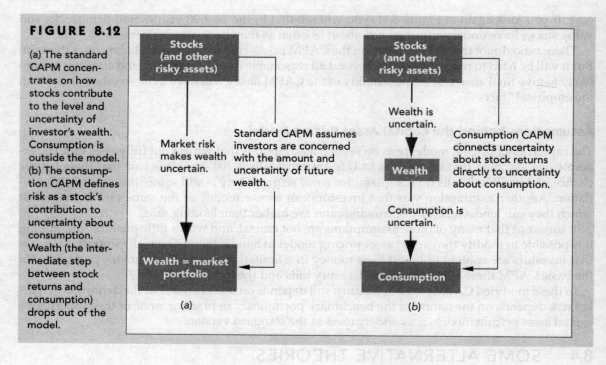

Of course, for most people wealth is not an end in itself. What good is wealth if you cannot spend it? People invest now to provide future consumption for themselves or for their families and heirs. The most important risks are those that might force a cutback of future consumption.

Douglas Breeden has developed a model in which a security's risk is measured by its sensitivity to changes in investors' consumption. If he is right, a stock's expected return should move in line with its *consumption beta* rather than its market beta. Figure 8.12 summarizes the chief differences between the standard and consumption CAPMs. In the standard model investors are concerned exclusively with the amount and uncertainty of their future wealth. Each investor's wealth ends up perfectly correlated with the return on the market portfolio; the demand for stocks and other risky assets is thus determined by their market risk. The deeper motive for investing—to provide for consumption—is outside the model.

In the consumption CAPM, uncertainty about stock returns is connected directly to uncertainty about consumption. Of course, consumption depends on wealth (portfolio value), but wealth does not appear explicitly in the model.

The consumption CAPM has several appealing features. For example, you do not have to identify the market or any other benchmark portfolio. You don't have to worry that Standard and Poor's Composite Index does not track returns on bonds, commodities, and real estate.

However, you do have to be able to measure consumption. *Quick:* How much did you consume last month? It is easy to count the hamburgers and movie tickets, but what about the depreciation on your car or washing machine or the daily cost of your homeowner's insurance policy? We suspect that your estimate of total consumption will rest on rough or arbitrary allocations and assumptions. And if it is hard for you to put a dollar value on your total consumption, think of the task facing a government statistician asked to estimate month-by-month consumption for all of us.

Compared to stock prices, estimated aggregate consumption changes smoothly and gradually over time. Changes in consumption often seem to be out of phase with the stock market. Individual stocks seem to have low or erratic consumption betas. Moreover, the volatility of consumption appears too low to explain the past average rates of return on common stocks unless one assumes unreasonably high investor risk aversion.[24] These problems may reflect our poor measures of consumption or perhaps poor models of how individuals distribute consumption over time. It seems too early for the consumption CAPM to see practical use.

Arbitrage Pricing Theory

The capital asset pricing theory begins with an analysis of how investors construct efficient portfolios. Stephen Ross's **arbitrage pricing theory,** or **APT,** comes from a different family entirely. It does not ask which portfolios are efficient. Instead, it starts by *assuming* that each stock's return depends partly on pervasive macroeconomic influences or "factors" and partly on "noise"—events that are unique to that company. Moreover, the return is assumed to obey the following simple relationship:

$$\text{Return} = a + b_1(r_{\text{factor 1}}) + b_2(r_{\text{factor 2}}) + b_3(r_{\text{factor 3}}) + \ldots + \text{noise}$$

The theory does not say what the factors are: There could be an oil price factor, an interest-rate factor, and so on. The return on the market portfolio *might* serve as one factor, but then again it might not.

Some stocks will be more sensitive to a particular factor than other stocks. ONGC would be more sensitive to an oil factor than, say, Titan. If factor 1 picks up unexpected changes in oil prices, b_1 will be higher for ONGC.

For any individual stock there are two sources of risk. First is the risk that stems from the pervasive macroeconomic factors which cannot be eliminated by diversification. Second is the risk arising from possible events that are unique to the company. Diversification eliminates unique risk, and diversified investors can therefore ignore it when deciding whether to buy or sell a stock. The expected risk premium on a stock is affected by factor or macroeconomic risk; it is *not* affected by unique risk.

Arbitrage pricing theory states that the expected risk premium on a stock should depend on the expected risk premium associated with each factor and the stock's sensitivity to each of the factors (b_1, b_2, b_3, etc.). Thus the formula is[25]

$$\begin{aligned}\text{Expected risk premium} &= r - r_f \\ &= b_1(r_{\text{factor 1}} - r_f) + b_2(r_{\text{factor 2}} - r_f) + \ldots\end{aligned}$$

Notice that this formula makes two statements:

1. If you plug in a value of zero for each of the b's in the formula, the expected risk premium is zero. A diversified portfolio that is constructed to have zero sensitivity to each macroeconomic factor is essentially risk-free and therefore must be priced to offer the risk-free rate of interest. If the portfolio offered a higher return, investors could make a risk-free

[24]See R. Mehra and E. C. Prescott, "The Equity Risk Premium: A Puzzle," *Journal of Monetary Economics* 15 (1985), pp. 145–161.

[25]There may be some macroeconomic factors that investors are simply not worried about. For example, some macroeconomists believe that money supply doesn't matter and therefore investors are not worried about inflation. Such factors would not command a risk premium. They would drop out of the APT formula for expected return.

(or "arbitrage") profit by borrowing to buy the portfolio. If it offered a lower return, you could make an arbitrage profit by running the strategy in reverse; in other words, you would *sell* the diversified zero-sensitivity portfolio and *invest* the proceeds in Indian Treasury bills.

2. A diversified portfolio that is constructed to have exposure to, say, factor 1, will offer a risk premium, which will vary in direct proportion to the portfolio's sensitivity to that factor. For example, imagine that you construct two portfolios, A and B, which are affected only by factor 1. If portfolio A is twice as sensitive to factor 1 as portfolio B, portfolio A must offer twice the risk premium. Therefore, if you divided your money equally between U.S. Treasury bills and portfolio A, your combined portfolio would have exactly the same sensitivity to factor 1 as portfolio B and would offer the same risk premium.

   Suppose that the arbitrage pricing formula did *not* hold. For example, suppose that the combination of Treasury bills and portfolio A offered a higher return. In that case investors could make an arbitrage profit by selling portfolio B and investing the proceeds in the mixture of bills and portfolio A.

The arbitrage that we have described applies to well-diversified portfolios, where the unique risk has been diversified away. But if the arbitrage pricing relationship holds for all diversified portfolios, it must generally hold for the individual stocks. Each stock must offer an expected return commensurate with its contribution to portfolio risk. In the APT, this contribution depends on the sensitivity of the stock's return to unexpected changes in the macroeconomic factors.

A Comparison of the Capital Asset Pricing Model and Arbitrage Pricing Theory

Like the capital asset pricing model, arbitrage pricing theory stresses that expected return depends on the risk stemming from economywide influences and is not affected by unique risk. You can think of the factors in arbitrage pricing as representing special portfolios of stocks that tend to be subject to a common influence. If the expected risk premium on each of these portfolios is proportional to the portfolio's market beta, then the arbitrage pricing theory and the capital asset pricing model will give the same answer. In any other case they will not.

How do the two theories stack up? Arbitrage pricing has some attractive features. For example, the market portfolio that plays such a central role in the capital asset pricing model does not feature in arbitrage pricing theory.[26] So we do not have to worry about the problem of measuring the market portfolio, and in principle we can test the arbitrage pricing theory even if we have data on only a sample of risky assets.

Unfortunately you win some and lose some. Arbitrage pricing theory does not tell us what the underlying factors are—unlike the capital asset pricing model, which collapses *all* macroeconomic risks into a well-defined *single* factor, the return on the market portfolio.

[26] Of course, the market portfolio *may* turn out to be one of the factors, but that is not a necessary implication of arbitrage pricing theory.

Factor	Estimated Risk Premium* ($r_{factor} - r_f$)
Yield spread	5.10%
Interest rate	−.61
Exchange rate	−.59
Real GNP	.49
Inflation	−.83
Market	6.36

TABLE 8.3

Estimated risk premiums for taking on factor risks, 1978–1990.

*The risk premiums have been scaled to represent the annual premiums for the average industrial stock in the Elton-Gruber-Mei sample.

Source: E. J. Elton, M. J. Gruber, and J. Mei, "Cost of Capital Using Arbitrage Pricing Theory: A Case Study of Nine New York Utilities," *Financial Markets, Institutions, and Instruments* 3 (August 1994), pp. 46–73.

APT Example

Arbitrage pricing theory will provide a good handle on expected returns only if we can (1) identify a reasonably short list of macroeconomic factors,[27] (2) measure the expected risk premium on each of these factors, and (3) measure the sensitivity of each stock to these factors. Let us look briefly at how Elton, Gruber, and Mei tackled each of these issues and estimated the cost of equity for a group of nine New York utilities.[28]

Step 1: Identify the Macroeconomic Factors Although APT does not tell us what the underlying economic factors are, Elton, Gruber, and Mei identified five principal factors that could affect either the cash flows themselves or the rate at which they are discounted. These factors are

Factor	Measured by
Yield spread	Return on long government bond *less* return on 30-day Treasury bills
Interest rate	Change in Treasury bill return
Exchange rate	Change in value of dollar relative to basket of currencies
Real GNP	Change in forecasts of real GNP
Inflation	Change in forecasts of inflation

To capture any remaining pervasive influences, Elton, Gruber, and Mei also included a sixth factor, the portion of the market return that could not be explained by the first five.

Step 2: Estimate the Risk Premium for Each Factor Some stocks are more exposed than others to a particular factor. So we can estimate the sensitivity of a sample of stocks to each factor and then measure how much extra return investors would have received in the past for taking on factor risk. The results are shown in Table 8.3.

---

[27]Some researchers have argued that there are four or five principal pervasive influences on stock prices, but others are not so sure. They point out that the more stocks you look at, the more factors you need to take into account. See, for example, P. J. Dhrymes, I. Friend, and N. B. Gultekin, "A Critical Re-examination of the Empirical Evidence on the Arbitrage Pricing Theory," *Journal of Finance* 39 (June 1984), pp. 323–346.

[28]See E. J. Elton, M. J. Gruber, and J. Mei, "Cost of Capital Using Arbitrage Pricing Theory: A Case Study of Nine New York Utilities," *Financial Markets, Institutions, and Instruments* 3 (August 1994), pp. 46–73. The study was prepared for the New York State Public Utility Commission.

TABLE 8.4

Using APT to estimate the expected risk premium for a portfolio of nine New York State utility stocks.

Source: E. J. Elton, M. J. Gruber, and J. Mei, "Cost of Capital Using Arbitrage Pricing Theory: A Case Study of Nine New York Utilities," *Financial Markets, Institutions, and Instruments* 3 (August 1994), tables 3 and 4. Reprinted by permission from Blackwell Publishers Journal Rights.

Factor	Factor Risk (b)	Expected Risk Premium ($r_{factor} - r_f$)	Factor Risk Premium $b(r_{factor} - r_f)$
Yield spread	1.04	5.10%	5.30%
Interest rate	−2.25	−.61	1.37
Exchange rate	.70	−.59	−.41
GNP	.17	.49	.08
Inflation	−.18	−.83	.15
Market	.32	6.36	2.04
Total			8.53%

For example, stocks with positive sensitivity to real GNP tended to have higher returns when real GNP increased. A stock with an average sensitivity gave investors an additional return of .49 percent a year compared with a stock that was completely unaffected by changes in real GNP. In other words, investors appeared to dislike "cyclical" stocks, whose returns were sensitive to economic activity, and demanded a higher return from these stocks.

By contrast, Table 8.3 shows that a stock with average exposure to *inflation* gave investors .83 percent a year *less* return than a stock with no exposure to inflation. Thus investors seemed to prefer stocks that protected them against inflation (stocks that did well when inflation accelerated), and they were willing to accept a lower expected return from such stocks.

Step 3: Estimate the Factor Sensitivities The estimates of the premiums for taking on factor risk can now be used to estimate the cost of equity for the group of New York State utilities. Remember, APT states that the risk premium for any asset depends on its sensitivities to factor risks (b) and the expected risk premium for each factor ($r_{factor} - r_f$). In this case there are six factors, so

$$r - r_f = b_1(r_{factor\ 1} - r_f) + b_2(r_{factor\ 2} - r_f) + \ldots + b_6(r_{factor\ 6} - r_f)$$

The first column of Table 8.4 shows the factor risks for the portfolio of utilities, and the second column shows the required risk premium for each factor (taken from Table 8.3). The third column is simply the product of these two numbers. It shows how much return investors demanded for taking on each factor risk. To find the expected risk premium, just add the figures in the final column:

$$\text{Expected risk premium} = r - r_f = 8.53\%$$

The one-year Treasury bill rate in December 1990, the end of the Elton–Gruber–Mei sample period, was about 7 percent, so the APT estimate of the expected return on New York State utility stocks was[29]

$$\begin{aligned}\text{Expected return} &= \text{risk-free interest rate} + \text{expected risk premium}\\ &= 7 + 8.53\\ &= 15.53, \text{ or about } 15.5\%\end{aligned}$$

[29]This estimate rests on risk premiums actually earned from 1978 to 1990, an unusually rewarding period for common stock investors. Estimates based on long-run market risk premiums would be lower. See E. J. Elton, M. J. Gruber, and J. Mei, "Cost of Capital Using Arbitrage Pricing Theory: A Case Study of Nine New York Utilities," *Financial Markets, Institutions, and Instruments* 3 (August 1994), pp. 46–73.

The Three-Factor Model

We noted earlier the research by Fama and French showing that stocks of small firms and those with a high book-to-market ratio have provided above-average returns. This could simply be a coincidence. But there is also evidence that these factors are related to company profitability and therefore may be picking up risk factors that are left out of the simple CAPM.[30]

If investors do demand an extra return for taking on exposure to these factors, then we have a measure of the expected return that looks very much like arbitrage pricing theory:

$$r - r_f = b_{\text{market}}\,(r_{\text{market factor}}) + b_{\text{size}}(r_{\text{size factor}}) + b_{\text{book-to-market}}\,(r_{\text{book-to-market factor}})$$

This is commonly known as the Fama–French three-factor model. Using it to estimate expected returns is exactly the same as applying the arbitrage pricing theory. Here is an example.[31]

Step 1: Identify the Factors Fama and French have already identified the three factors that appear to determine expected returns. The returns on each of these factors are

Factor	Measured by
Market factor	Return on market index *minus* risk-free interest rate
Size factor	Return on small-firm stocks *less* return on large-firm stocks
Book-to-market factor	Return on high book-to-market-ratio stocks *less* return on low book-to-market-ratio stocks

Step 2: Estimate the Risk Premium for Each Factor Here we need to rely on history. Fama and French find that between 1963 and 1994 the return on the market factor averaged about 5.2 percent per year, the difference between the return on small and large capitalization stocks was about 3.2 percent a year, while the difference between the annual return on stocks with high and low book-to-market ratios averaged 5.4 percent.[32]

Step 3: Estimate the Factor Sensitivities Some stocks are more sensitive than others to fluctuations in the returns on the three factors. Look, for example, at the first three columns of numbers in Table 8.5, which show some estimates by Fama and French of factor sensitivities for different industry groups. You can see, for example, that an increase of 1 percent in the return on the book-to-market factor *reduces* the return on computer stocks by .49 percent but *increases* the return on utility stocks by .38 percent.[33]

[30] E. F. Fama and K. R. French, "Size and Book-to-Market Factors in Earnings and Returns," *Journal of Finance* 50 (1995), pp. 131–155.

[31] The example is taken from E. F. Fama and K. R. French, "Industry Costs of Equity," *Journal of Financial Economics* 43 (1997), pp. 153–193. Fama and French emphasize the imprecision involved in using either the CAPM or an APT-style model to estimate the returns that investors expect.

[32] We saw earlier that over the longer period 1926-2002 the average annual difference between the returns on small and large capitalization stocks was 3.9 percent. The difference between the returns on stocks with high and low book-to-market ratios was 4.4 percent.

[33] A 1 percent return on the book-to-market factor means that stocks with a high book-to-market ratio provide a 1 percent higher return than those with a low ratio.

	Three-Factor Model				CAPM
	Factor Sensitivities				
	b_{market}	b_{size}	$b_{book\text{-}to\text{-}market}$	Expected Risk Premium*	Expected Risk Premium
Aircraft	1.15	.51	.00	7.54%	6.43%
Banks	1.13	.13	.35	8.08	5.55
Chemicals	1.13	−.03	.17	6.58	5.57
Computers	.90	.17	−.49	2.49	5.29
Construction	1.21	.21	−.09	6.42	6.52
Food	.88	−.07	−.03	4.09	4.44
Petroleum & gas	.96	−.35	.21	4.93	4.32
Pharmaceuticals	.84	−.25	−.63	.09	4.71
Tobacco	.86	−.04	.24	5.56	4.08
Utilities	.79	−.20	.38	5.41	3.39

TABLE 8.5

Estimates of industry risk premiums using the Fama-French three-factor model and the CAPM.

*The expected risk premium equals the factor sensitivities multiplied by the factor risk premiums, that is, $(b_{market} \times 5.2) + (b_{size} \times 3.2) + (b_{book\text{-}to\text{-}market} \times 5.4)$.

Source: Reprinted from *Journal of Financial Economics* 43 (1997). By E. F. Fama and K. R. French, "Industry Costs of Equity," pp. 153–193. Reprinted with permission of Elsevier Science.

Once you have an estimate of the factor sensitivities, it is a simple matter to multiply each of them by the expected factor return and add up the results. For example, the fourth column of numbers shows that the expected risk premium on computer stocks is $r - r_f = (.90 \times 5.2) + (.17 \times 3.2) - (.49 \times 5.4) = 2.49$ percent. Compare this figure with the risk premium estimated using the capital asset pricing model (the final column of Table 8.5). The three-factor model provides a substantially lower estimate of the risk premium for computer stocks than the CAPM. Why? Largely because computer stocks have a low exposure (−.49) to the book-to-market factor.

SUMMARY

The basic principles of portfolio selection boil down to a commonsense statement that investors try to increase the expected return on their portfolios and to reduce the standard deviation of that return. A portfolio that gives the highest expected return for a given standard deviation, or the lowest standard deviation for a given expected return, is known as an *efficient portfolio*. To work out which portfolios are efficient, an investor must be able to state the expected return and standard deviation of each stock and the degree of correlation between each pair of stocks.

Investors who are restricted to holding common stocks should choose efficient portfolios that suit their attitudes to risk. But investors who can also borrow and lend at the risk-free rate of interest should choose the *best* common stock portfolio *regardless* of their attitudes to risk. Having done that, they can then set the risk of their overall portfolio by deciding what proportion of their money they are willing to invest in stocks. The best efficient portfolio offers the highest ratio of forecasted risk premium to portfolio standard deviation.

For an investor who has only the same opportunities and information as everybody else, the best stock portfolio is the same as the best stock portfolio for other investors. In other words, he or she should invest in a mixture of the market portfolio and a risk-free loan (i.e., borrowing or lending).

A stock's marginal contribution to portfolio risk is measured by its sensitivity to changes in the value of the portfolio. The marginal contribution of a stock to the risk of the *market portfolio* is measured by *beta*. That is the fundamental idea behind the capital asset pricing model (CAPM), which concludes that each security's expected risk premium should increase in proportion to its beta:

$$\text{Expected risk premium} = \text{beta} \times \text{market risk premium}$$
$$r - r_f = \beta(r_m - r_f)$$

The capital asset pricing theory is the best-known model of risk and return. It is plausible and widely used but far from perfect. Actual returns are related to beta over the long run, but the relationship is not as strong as the CAPM predicts, and other factors seem to explain returns better since the mid-1960s. Stocks of small companies, and stocks with high book values relative to market prices, appear to have risks not captured by the CAPM.

The CAPM has also been criticized for its strong simplifying assumptions. A more recent theory called the *consumption* capital asset pricing model suggests that security risk reflects the sensitivity of returns to changes in investors' *consumption*. This theory calls for a consumption beta rather than a beta relative to the market portfolio.

The arbitrage pricing theory offers an alternative theory of risk and return. It states that the expected risk premium on a stock should depend on the stock's exposure to several pervasive macroeconomic factors that affect stock returns:

$$\text{Expected risk premium} = b_1(r_{\text{factor 1}} - r_f) + b_2(r_{\text{factor 2}} - r_f) + \ldots$$

Here b's represent the individual security's sensitivities to the factors, and $r_{\text{factor}} - r_f$ is the risk premium demanded by investors who are exposed to this factor.

Arbitrage pricing theory does not say what these factors are. It asks for economists to hunt for unknown game with their statistical tool kits. The hunters have returned with several possible factors that could affect the future dividends or the rate at which they are discounted.

Fama and French have suggested three different factors:

- The return on the market portfolio less the risk-free rate of interest.
- The difference between the return on small- and large-firm stocks.
- The difference between the return on stocks with high book-to-market ratios and stocks with low book-to-market ratios.

In the Fama–French three-factor model, the expected return on each stock depends on its exposure to these three factors.

Each of these different models of risk and return has its fan club. However, all financial economists agree on two basic ideas: (1) Investors require extra expected return for taking on risk, and (2) they appear to be concerned predominantly with the risk that they cannot eliminate by diversification.

FURTHER READING

The pioneering article on portfolio selection is:

H. M. Markowitz: "Portfolio Selection," *Journal of Finance*, 7 (March 1952), pp. 77–91.

There are a number of textbooks on portfolio selection which explain both Markowitz's original theory and some ingenious simplified versions. See, for example:

E. J. Elton, M. J. Gruber, S. J. Brown, and W. N. Goetzmann: *Modern Portfolio Theory and Investment Analysis*, 6th ed., John Wiley & Sons, New York, 2002.

Of the three pioneering articles on the capital asset pricing model, Jack Treynor's has never been published. The other two articles are:

W. F. Sharpe: "Capital Asset Prices: A Theory of Market Equilibrium under Conditions of Risk," *Journal of Finance*, 19 (September 1964), pp. 425–442.

J. Lintner: "The Valuation of Risk Assets and the Selection of Risky Investments in Stock Portfolios and Capital Budgets," *Review of Economics and Statistics*, 47 (February 1965), pp. 13–37.

The subsequent literature on the capital asset pricing model is enormous. Jensen's book provides a collection of some of the more important articles plus a very useful survey. Black's paper provides a test of the model, which we have updated in this chapter.

M. C. Jensen (ed.): *Studies in the Theory of Capital Markets*, Frederick A. Praeger, Inc., New York, 1972.

F. Black, "Beta and Return," *Journal of Portfolio Management*, 20 (Fall 1993) pp. 8–18.

Two useful, but difficult, review articles on important alternatives to the capital asset pricing model are:

W. E. Ferson, "Tests of Multi-Factor Pricing Models, Volatility, and Portfolio Performance," in G. M. Constantinides, M. Harris, and R. M. Stulz (eds.), *Handbook of the Economics of Finance*, Elsevier Science, 2003.

J. Y. Campbell, "Consumption-Based Asset Pricing," in G. M. Constantinides, M. Harris, and R. M. Stulz (eds.), *Handbook of the Economics of Finance*, Elsevier Science, 2003.

The most accessible implementation of APT is:

E. J. Elton, M. J. Gruber, and J. Mei, "Cost of Capital Using Arbitrage Pricing Theory: A Case Study of Nine New York Utilities," *Financial Markets, Institutions, and Instruments*, 3:46–73 (August 1994).

CONCEPT REVIEW QUESTIONS

1. If stock returns are normally distributed, the distribution can be completely defined by two numbers. What are they? (page 183)
2. What is meant by "the set of efficient portfolios"? (page 187)
3. If an investor can borrow and lend at the same rate of interest, should the choice of a common stock portfolio depend on the investor's willingness to bear risk? Why or why not? (page 189)

For additional Concept Review Questions, please visit us at www.mhhe.com/bmam8e or refer to your Student CD.

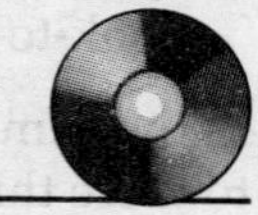

QUIZ

1. Here are returns and standard deviations for four investments.

	Return	Standard Deviation
Treasury bills	6%	0%
Stock P	10	14
Stock Q	14.5	28
Stock R	21.0	26

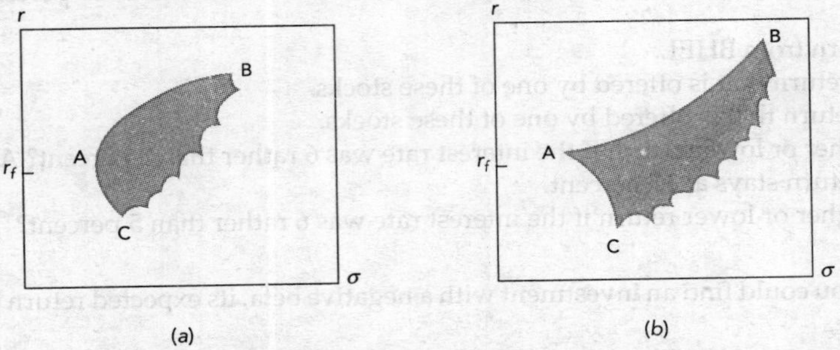

FIGURE 8.13

See Quiz Question 3.

Calculate the standard deviations of the following portfolios.

a. 50 percent in Treasury bills, 50 percent in stock P.

b. 50 percent each in Q and R, assuming the shares have

- perfect positive correlation
- perfect negative correlation
- no correlation

c. Plot a figure like Figure 8.4 for Q and R, assuming a correlation coefficient of .5.

d. Stock Q has a lower return than R but a higher standard deviation. Does that mean that Q's price is too high or that R's price is too low?

2. For each of the following pairs of investments, state which would always be preferred by a rational investor (assuming that these are the *only* investments available to the investor):

a. Portfolio A r = 18 percent σ = 20 percent
Portfolio B r = 14 percent σ = 20 percent

b. Portfolio C r = 15 percent σ = 18 percent
Portfolio D r = 13 percent σ = 8 percent

c. Portfolio E r = 14 percent σ = 16 percent
Portfolio F r = 14 percent σ = 10 percent

3. Figures 8.13*a* and 8.13*b* purport to show the range of attainable combinations of expected return and standard deviation.

a. Which diagram is incorrectly drawn and why?

b. Which is the efficient set of portfolios?

c. If r_f is the rate of interest, mark with an X the optimal stock portfolio.

4. a. Plot the following risky portfolios on a graph:

	Portfolio							
	A	B	C	D	E	F	G	H
Expected return (r), %	10	12.5	15	16	17	18	18	20
Standard deviation (σ), %	23	21	25	29	29	32	35	45

b. Five of these portfolios are efficient, and three are not. Which are *in*efficient ones?

c. Suppose you can also borrow and lend at an interest rate of 12 percent. Which of the above portfolios is best?

d. Suppose you are prepared to tolerate a standard deviation of 25 percent. What is the maximum expected return that you can achieve if you cannot borrow or lend?

e. What is your optimal strategy if you can borrow or lend at 12 percent and are prepared to tolerate a standard deviation of 25 percent? What is the maximum expected return that you can achieve with this risk?

5. Suppose that the Treasury Bill rate is 5 percent and the expected return on the market is 17 percent. Use the betas in Table 8.2 .
   a. Calculate the expected return from BHEL.
   b. Find the highest expected return that is offered by one of these stocks.
   c. Find the lowest expected return that is offered by one of these stocks.
   d. Would Ranbaxy offer a higher or lower return if the interest rate was 6 rather than 5 percent? Assume that the expected market return stays at 17 percent.
   e. Would Tata Steel offer a higher or lower return if the interest rate was 6 rather than 5 percent?
6. True or false?
   a. The CAPM implies that if you could find an investment with a negative beta, its expected return would be less than the interest rate.
   b. The expected return on an investment with a beta of 2.0 is twice as high as the expected return on the market.
   c. If a stock lies below the security market line, it is undervalued.
7. Consider a three-factor APT model. The factors and associated risk premiums are

Factor	Risk Premium
Change in GNP	5%
Change in energy prices	−1
Change in long-term interest rates	+2

   Calculate expected rates of return on the following stocks. The risk-free interest rate is 7 percent.
   a. A stock whose return is uncorrelated with all three factors.
   b. A stock with average exposure to each factor (i.e., with $b = 1$ for each).
   c. A pure-play energy stock with high exposure to the energy factor ($b = 2$) but zero exposure to the other two factors.
   d. An aluminum company stock with average sensitivity to changes in interest rates and GNP, but negative exposure of $b = -1.5$ to the energy factor. (The aluminum company is energy-intensive and suffers when energy prices rise.)

PRACTICE QUESTIONS

1. True or false? Explain or qualify as necessary.
   a. Investors demand higher expected rates of return on stocks with more variable rates of return.
   b. The CAPM predicts that a security with a beta of 0 will offer a zero expected return.
   c. An investor who puts Rs. 10,000 in Treasury bills and Rs. 20,000 in the market portfolio will have a beta of 2.0.
   d. Investors demand higher expected rates of return from stocks with returns that are highly exposed to macroeconomic risk.
   e. Investors demand higher expected rates of return from stocks with returns that are very sensitive to fluctuations in the stock market.
2. Look back at the calculation of Grasim and Reliance Energy in Section 8.1. Recalculate the expected portfolio return and standard deviation for different values of x_1 and x_2, assuming the correlation coefficient $\rho_{12} = 0$. Plot the range of possible combinations of expected return and standard deviation as in Figure 8.4. Repeat the problem for $\rho_{12} = +1$ and for $\rho_{12} = -1$.
3. Mark Harrywitz proposes to invest in two shares, X and Y. He expects a return of 12 percent from X and 8 percent from Y. The standard deviation of returns is 8 percent for X and 5 percent for Y. The correlation coefficient between the returns is .2.

a. Compute the expected return and standard deviation of the following portfolios:

Portfolio	Percentage in X	Percentage in Y
1	50	50
2	25	75
3	75	25

b. Sketch the set of portfolios composed of X and Y.

c. Suppose that Mr. Harrywitz can also borrow or lend at an interest rate of 5 percent. Show on your sketch how this alters his opportunities. Given that he can borrow or lend, what proportions of the common stock portfolio should be invested in X and Y?

4. Ebenezer Scrooge has invested 60 percent of his money in share A and the remainder in share B. He assesses their prospects as follows:

	A	B
Expected return (%)	15	20
Standard deviation (%)	20	22
Correlation between returns	.5	

a. What are the expected return and standard deviation of returns on his portfolio?

b. How would your answer change if the correlation coefficient was 0 or −.5?

c. Is Mr. Scrooge's portfolio better or worse than one invested entirely in share A, or is it not possible to say?

STANDARD &POOR'S

5. When we calculated the efficient portfolios in Table 8.1, we assumed that the investor could not hold short positions (that is, have negative holdings). The Student CD and the book Web site (www.mhhe.com/bmam8e) contain an Excel program for calculating the efficient frontier with short sales. (We are grateful to Simon Gervais for providing us with a copy of this program.)

excel

Please visit us at www.mhhe.com/bmam8e or refer to your Student CD.

a. Look at the efficient portfolios constructed from the 10 stocks in Table 8.1. How does the possibility of short sales improve the choices open to the investor?

b. Now download daily stock prices from www.nseindia.com and estimate monthly returns from that. Enter the past returns into the Excel program. (The program will take up to 10 years of returns.) Enter some plausible figures for the expected return on each stock and find the set of efficient portfolios.

STANDARD &POOR'S

6. Download daily stock prices for Tata Motors and Hindustan Levers from www.nseindia.com. Use the Excel function SLOPE to calculate beta for each company. (See practice question 7.11 for details)

a. Suppose the market index falls unexpectedly by 5 percent. By how much would you expect Tata Motors and HLL to fall?

b. Which is the riskier company for the well-diversified investor? How much riskier?

c. Suppose the Treasury bill rate is 5 percent and the expected return on Nifty is 16 percent. Use the CAPM to forecast the expected rate of return on each stock.

STANDARD &POOR'S

7. Download the monthly stock prices for Reliance Industries and Infosys from www.in.finance.yahoo.com.

a. Calculate the annual standard deviation for each company, using the most recent three years of monthly returns. Use the Excel function STDEV. Multiply by the square root of 12 to convert to annual basis.

b. Use the Excel function CORREL to calculate the correlation coeffiicient between the stocks' monthly returns.

c. Use the CAPM to estimate expected rates of return. Calculate betas, or download the beta estimates from www.nseindia.com. Use the current Treasury bill rate (download from www.fimmda.org) and a reasonable estimate of the market risk premium.

d. Construct a graph like Figure 8.4. What combination of Reliance and Infosys has the lowest portfolio risk? What is the expected return for this minimum-risk portfolio?

8. The Treasury bill rate is 4 percent, and the expected return on the market portfolio is 12 percent. Using the capital asset pricing model:

STANDARD &POOR'S

a. Draw a graph similar to Figure 8.7 showing how the expected return varies with beta.

b. What is the risk premium on the market?

c. What is the required return on an investment with a beta of 1.5?

d. If an investment with a beta of .8 offers an expected return of 9.8 percent, does it have a positive NPV?

e. If the market expects a return of 11.2 percent from stock X, what is its beta?

9. You can get the data for most of the companies in Table 8.2 from www.in.finance.yahoo.com. For those that are covered, use the Excel SLOPE function to recalculate betas from the monthly returns. Use as many monthly returns as available, up to a maximum of 60 months. Recalculate expected rates of return from the CAPM formula, using a current risk-free rate and a market risk premium of 11 percent. How have the expected returns changed from the figures reported in Table 8.2?

STANDARD &POOR'S

10. Go to the website of www.nseindia.com and find a low-risk income stock. Estimate the company's beta to confirm that it well below 1.0. Use monthly rates of return for the most recent three years. For the same period, estimate the annual standard deviation for the stock, the standard deviation of Nifty, and the correlation coefficient between returns on the stock and the Nifty. Forecast the expected rate of return for the stock, assuming the CAPM holds, with a market return of 17 percent and a risk-free rate of 6 percent.

a. Plot a graph like Figure 8.5 showing the combinations of risk and return from a portfolio invested in your low-risk stock and in the market. Vary the fraction invested in the stock from zero to 100 percent.

b. Suppose you can borrow or lend at 5 percent. Would you invest in some combination of your low-risk stock and the market? Or would you simply invest in the market? Explain.

c. Suppose you forecast a return on the stock that is 5 percentage points higher than the CAPM return used in part (a). Redo parts (a) and (b) with this higher forecasted return.

d. Find a high-beta stock and redo parts (a), (b), and (c).

11. Percival Hygiene has $10 million invested in long-term corporate bonds. This bond portfolio's expected annual rate of return is 9 percent, and the annual standard deviation is 10 percent.

Amanda Reckonwith, Percival's financial adviser, recommends that Percival consider investing in an index fund which closely tracks the Standard and Poor's 500 index. The index has an expected return of 14 percent, and its standard deviation is 16 percent.

a. Suppose Percival puts all his money in a combination of the index fund and Treasury bills. Can he thereby improve his expected rate of return without changing the risk of his portfolio? The Treasury bill yield is 6 percent.

b. Could Percival do even better by investing equal amounts in the corporate bond portfolio and the index fund? The correlation between the bond portfolio and the index fund is +.1.

12. Some true or false questions about the APT:

a. The APT factors cannot reflect diversifiable risks.

b. The market rate of return cannot be an APT factor.

c. There is no theory that specifically identifies the APT factors.

d. The APT model could be true but not very useful, for example, if the relevant factors change unpredictably.

13. Consider the following simplified APT model (compare Tables 8.3 and 8.4):

Factor	Expected Risk Premium
Market	6.4%
Interest rate	−.6
Yield spread	5.1

Calculate the expected return for the following stocks. Assume $r_f = 5$ percent.

	Factor Risk Exposures		
	Market	Interest Rate	Yield Spread
Stock	(b_1)	(b_2)	(b_3)
P	1.0	−2.0	−.2
P^2	1.2	0	.3
P^3	.3	.5	1.0

14. Look again at Practice Question 13. Consider a portfolio with equal investments in stocks P, P^2, and P^3.

a. What are the factor risk exposures for the portfolio?

b. What is the portfolio's expected return?

15. The following table shows the sensitivity of four stocks to the Fama-French factors in the nine years to 2000. Estimate the expected return on each stock assuming that the interest rate is 5 percent, the expected risk premium on the market is 10 percent, the expected risk premium on the size factor is 12 percent, and the expected risk premium on the book-to-market factor is 8 percent.

	Factor Sensitivities			
Factor	Bharat Forge Ltd.	Madras Petro Chem Ltd	Priyadarshini Cement Ltd.	Wimco Ltd.
Market	0.354	0.453	0.640	0.598
Size*	0.182	0.047	0.252	−0.075
Book-to-market†	0.363	− 0.007	−0.5595	−0.051

*Return on small-firm stocks less return on large-firm stocks.

†Return on high book-to-market-ratio stocks less return on low book-to-market-ratio stocks.

CHALLENGE QUESTIONS

1. In footnote 4 we noted that the minimum-risk portfolio contained an investment of 61.8 percent in Grasim and 38.2 per cent in Reliance Energy. Prove it. *Hint:* You need a little calculus to do so.
2. Look again at the set of efficient portfolios that we calculated in Section 8.1.
   a. If the interest rate is 10 percent, which of the four efficient portfolios should you hold?
   b. What is the beta of each holding relative to that portfolio? *Hint:* Remember that if a portfolio is efficient, the expected risk premium on each holding must be proportional to the beta of the stock *relative to that portfolio*.
   c. How would your answers to (a) and (b) change if the interest rate was 5 percent?
3. The following question illustrates the APT. Imagine that there are only two pervasive macroeconomic factors. Investments X, Y, and Z have the following sensitivities to these two factors:

Investment	b_1	b_2
X	1.75	.25
Y	−1.00	2.00
Z	2.00	1.00

We assume that the expected risk premium is 4 percent on factor 1 and 8 percent on factor 2. Treasury bills obviously offer zero risk premium.
   a. According to the APT, what is the risk premium on each of the three stocks?
   b. Suppose you buy Rs. 200 of X and Rs. 50 of Y and sell Rs. 150 of Z. What is the sensitivity of your portfolio to each of the two factors? What is the expected risk premium?
   c. Suppose you buy Rs. 80 of X and Rs. 60 of Y and sell Rs. 40 of Z. What is the sensitivity of your portfolio to each of the two factors? What is the expected risk premium?
   d. Finally, suppose you buy Rs. 160 of X and Rs. 20 of Y and sell Rs. 80 of Z. What is your portfolio's sensitivity now to each of the two factors? And what is the expected risk premium?
   e. Suggest two possible ways that you could construct a fund that has a sensitivity of .5 to factor 1 only. (Hint: One portfolio contains an investment in Treasury bills.) Now compare the risk premiums on each of these two investments.
   f. Suppose that the APT did *not* hold and that X offered a risk premium of 8 percent, Y offered a premium of 14 percent, and Z offered a premium of 16 percent. Devise an investment that has zero sensitivity to each factor and that has a positive risk premium.

CHAPTER [9]

CAPITAL BUDGETING AND RISK

LONG BEFORE THE development of modern theories linking risk and return, smart financial managers adjusted for risk in capital budgeting. They knew that risky projects are, other things equal, less valuable than safe ones—that is just common sense. Therefore they demanded higher rates of return from risky projects, or they based their decisions about risky projects on conservative forecasts of project cash flows.

Today most companies start with the *company cost of capital* as a benchmark risk-adjusted discount rate for new investments. The company cost of capital is the opportunity cost of capital for investment in the firm as a whole. It is usually calculated as a weighted average cost of capital, that is, the average rate of return demanded by investors in the company's debt and equity securities. Our first task in this chapter is to explain when the company cost of capital can, and cannot, be used to discount project cash flows. We shall see that it is the right discount rate for projects that have the same risk as the company's existing business. But if a project is riskier than the firm as it stands, the cost of capital *for the project* should be higher. Conversely, the project cost of capital for a safe project is lower.

The hardest part of estimating the company cost of capital is figuring out the expected rate of return to investors in the firm's stock. Many firms turn to the capital asset pricing model (CAPM) for an answer. The CAPM states that expected return equals the risk-free interest rate r_f plus a risk premium that depends on beta and the market risk premium $r_m - r_f$:

$$\text{Expected return} = r_f + \text{beta} \times (r_m - r_f)$$

We used this formula in the last chapter to estimate expected rates of return on a sample of common stocks, but we did not explain how to estimate beta. Unfortunately, you cannot look up beta in a newspaper or see it clearly by tracking a few day-by-day or month-by-month changes in stock price. But you can usually get an approximate measure by looking at how the stock price has responded on average to historical market fluctuations. Smart financial managers also look at average betas for portfolios of similar companies. Betas estimated for portfolios are more accurate than betas estimated for individual companies.

Sometimes you do not have a beta, or you get beta estimates that are just statistical garbage. In those cases, you can assess the project's operating leverage (its ratio of fixed to variable cost) and you can ask whether the project's future cash flows will be unusually sensitive to the business cycle. Cyclical projects with high operating leverage have high betas. But be careful not to confuse diversifiable risk with market risk. Diversifiable risk does not increase the cost of capital.

Betas vary from project to project. They can also vary over time. Some projects are riskier in youth than in old age, for example, and we may need a higher discount rate for the start-up stage of a project. But in most cases financial managers assume that project risk is the same in every future period and use a single risk-adjusted discount rate for all future cash flows. We will use *certainty equivalents* to illustrate how risk accumulates over time for ordinary projects.

We close the chapter with a brief look at risk and discount rates for international projects.

9.1 COMPANY AND PROJECT COSTS OF CAPITAL

The **company cost of capital** is defined as the expected return on a portfolio of all the company's existing securities. It is the opportunity cost of capital for investment in the firm's assets, and therefore the appropriate discount rate for the firm's average-risk projects.

FIGURE 9.1

A comparison between the company cost of capital rule and the required return under the capital asset pricing model. Satyam's company cost of capital is 20.14 percent. This is the correct discount rate only if the project beta is 1.35. In general, the correct discount rate increases as project beta increases. Satyam should accept projects with rates of return above the security market line relating required return to beta.

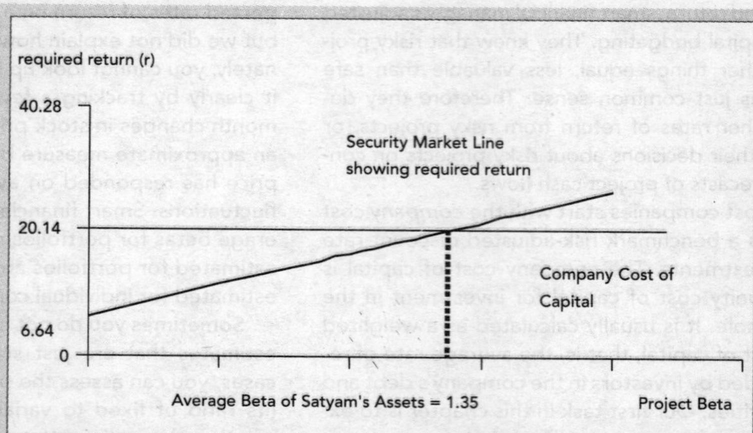

If the firm has no significant amount of debt outstanding, then the company's cost of capital is just the expected rate of return on the firm's stock. Many large, successful companies fit this special case, including Satyam Computer Services. In Table 8.2 we estimated that the investors require a return of 20.14 percent from Satyam common stock. If Satyam is contemplating an expansion of the firm's existing business, it would make sense to discount the forecasted cash flows at 20.14 percent.

The company cost of capital is *not* the correct discount rate if the new projects are more or less risky than the firm's existing business. Each project should in principle be evaluated at its *own* opportunity cost of capital. This is a clear implication of the value-additivity principle introduced in Chapter 7. For a firm composed of assets A and B, the firm value is

$$\text{Firm value} = \text{PV(AB)} = \text{PV(A)} + \text{PV(B)}$$
$$= \text{sum of separate asset values}$$

Here PV(A) and PV(B) are valued just as if they were mini-firms in which stockholders could invest directly. Investors would value A by discounting its forecasted cash flows at a rate reflecting the risk of A. They would value B by discounting at a rate reflecting the risk of B. The two discount rates will, in general, be different. If the present value of an asset depended on the identity of the company that bought it, present values would *not* add up, and we know they do add up. (Consider a portfolio of Rs. 1 million invested in Infosys and Rs. 1 millon invested in HLL. Would any reasonable investor say that the portfolio is worth anything more or less than Rs. 2 millon?)

If the firm considers investing in a third project C, it should also value C as if C were a mini-firm. That is, the firm should discount the cash flows of C at the expected rate of return that investors would demand to make a separate investment in C. *The true cost of capital depends on the use to which that capital is put.*

This means that Satyam Computer Services should accept any project that more than compensates for the project's beta. In other words, Satyam should accept any project lying above the upward-sloping security market line that links expected return to risk in Figure 9.1. If the project is high-risk, Satyam needs a higher prospective return than if the project is low-risk. Now contrast the company cost of capital rule, which accepts any project *regardless of its risk* as long as it offers a higher return than the *company's* cost of capital. In terms of Figure 9.1, the rule tells Satyam to accept any project above the horizontal cost of capital line, that is, any project offering a return more than 20.14 percent.

It is clearly silly to suggest that Satyam should demand the same rate of return from a very safe project as from a very risky one. If Satyam used the company cost of capital rule, it would reject many good low-risk projects and accept many poor high-risk projects. It is also silly to suggest that just because another company has a low company cost of capital, it is justified in accepting projects that Satyam would reject.

The notion that each company needs only one discount rate or cost of capital is widespread, but far from universal. Many firms require different returns from different categories of investment. For example, discount rates might be set as follows:

Category	Discount Rate
Speculative ventures	30%
New products	20
Expansion of existing business	15 (company cost of capital)
Cost improvement, known technology	10

Perfect Pitch and the Cost of Capital

The true cost of capital depends on project risk, not on the company undertaking the project. So why is so much time spent estimating the company cost of capital?

There are two reasons. First, many (maybe most) projects can be treated as average risk, that is, no more or less risky than the average of the company's other assets. For these projects the company cost of capital is the right discount rate. Second, the company cost of capital is a useful starting point for setting discount rates for unusually risky or safe projects. It is easier to add to, or subtract from, the company cost of capital than to estimate each project's cost of capital from scratch.

There is a good musical analogy here.[1] Most of us, lacking perfect pitch, need a well-defined reference point, like middle C, before we can sing on key. But anyone who can carry a tune gets *relative* pitches right. Businesspeople have good intuition about *relative* risks, at least in industries they are used to, but not about absolute risk or required rates of return. Therefore, they set a company-wide cost of capital as a benchmark. This is not the right hurdle rate for everything the company does, but adjustments can be made for more or less risky ventures.

That said, we have to admit that many large companies use the company cost of capital not just as a benchmark, but also as an all-purpose discount rate for every project proposal. Measuring differences in risk is difficult to do objectively, and financial managers shy away from intracorporate squabbles. ("My projects are safer than yours! I want a lower discount rate!" "No they're not! Your projects are riskier than a naked call option!"[2])

[1]The analogy is borrowed from S. C. Myers and L. S. Borucki, "Discounted Cash Flow Estimates of the Cost of Equity Capital—A Case Study," *Financial Markets, Institutions, and Investments* 3 (August 1994), p. 18.

[2]A "naked" call option is an option purchased with no offsetting (hedging) position in the underlying stock or in other options. We will get to options in Chapter 20.

When firms force use of a single company cost of capital, risk adjustment shifts from the discount rate to project cash flows. Top management may demand extra conservative cash-flow forecasts from extra-risky projects. They may refuse to sign off on an extra-risky project unless NPV, computed at the company cost of capital, is well above zero. Rough and ready risk adjustments are better than none at all.

Debt and the Company Cost of Capital

We defined the company cost of capital as "the expected return on a portfolio of all the company's existing securities." That portfolio usually includes debt as well as equity. Thus the cost of capital is estimated as a blend of the cost of debt (the interest rate) and the cost of equity (the expected rate of return demanded by investors in the firm's common stock).

If you owned a portfolio of all the firm's securities—100 percent of the debt and 100 percent of the equity—you would own the firm's assets lock, stock, and barrel. You would not share the cash flows with anyone; every rupee of cash the firm paid out would be paid to you. You can think of the company cost of capital as the expected return on this hypothetical portfolio. To calculate it, you just take a weighted average of the expected returns on the debt and the equity:

$$\text{Company cost of capital} = r_{\text{assets}} = r_{\text{portfolio}}$$

$$= \frac{\text{debt}}{\text{debt} + \text{equity}} r_{\text{debt}} + \frac{\text{equity}}{\text{debt} + \text{equity}} r_{\text{equity}}$$

For example, suppose that the firm's market-value balance sheet is:

Asset value	100	Debt value (*D*)	30
		Equity value (*E*)	70
Asset value	100	Firm value (*V*)	100

Note that the values of debt and equity add up to the firm value ($D + E = V$) and that the firm value equals the asset value. These figures are *market* values, not *book* (i.e., accounting) values: The market value of the firm's equity is often very different from its book value.

If investors expect a return of 7.5 percent on the debt and 15 percent on the equity, then the expected return on the assets must be:

$$r_{\text{assets}} = \frac{D}{V} r_{\text{debt}} + \frac{E}{V} r_{\text{equity}}$$

$$= \left(\frac{30}{100} \times 7.5\right) + \left(\frac{70}{100} \times 15\right) = 12.75\%$$

If the firm is contemplating investment in a project that has the same risk as the firm's existing business, the opportunity cost of capital for this project is the same as the firm's cost of capital; in other words, it is 12.75 percent.

Note that the company cost of capital is not the cost of debt, and not the cost of equity, but an average. Thus the blend is typically called the **weighted-average cost of capital** or "WACC." Estimating WACC can be just a trifle complicated, particularly when taxes are incorporated (interest is a tax-deductible expense) and changes in debt ratios must be considered. We defer these complications to Chapters 17 and 19. In this chapter we will concentrate on measuring the cost of equity. But please do not try to estimate and use the weighted-average cost of capital for any practical purpose until you have at least read Chapter 17.

9.2 MEASURING THE COST OF EQUITY

Suppose that you are considering an across-the-board expansion by your firm. Such an investment would have about the same degree of risk as the existing business. Therefore you should discount projected cash flows at a weighted-average cost of capital. To calculate the weighted-average cost of capital, you need an estimate of the cost of equity.

You decide to use the capital asset pricing model (CAPM). Here you are in good company: as we saw in the last chapter, most large U.S. companies do use the CAPM to estimate the cost of equity.[3] The CAPM says that

$$\text{Expected stock return} = r_f + \beta(r_m - r_f)$$

Now you have to estimate beta. Let us see how that is done in practice.

Estimating Beta

In principle we are interested in the future beta of the company's stock, but lacking a crystal ball, we turn first to historical evidence. For example, look at the scatter diagram at the top left of Figure 9.2. Each dot represents the return on HLL stock and the return on the market in a particular month. The plot starts in January 1998 and runs to December 2001, so there are 48 dots in all. The second diagram on the left shows a similar plot for the returns on Tata Steel stock, and the third shows a plot for Himachal Futuristics (HFCL) stock. In each case we have fitted a line through the points. The slope of the line[4] is an estimate of beta.[5] It tells us how much on average the stock price changed for each additional 1 percent change in the market index.

The right hand diagrams show similar plots for the same three stocks during the subsequent period ending in December 2005. Although slopes varied from the first to the second, there is little doubt that HLL's beta is much less than HFCL's or that Tata Steel's beta falls somewhere between the two. If you had used the past beta to predict its future beta, you would not have been too far off, for HLL and Tata Steel, although you missed on HFCL's beta, which decreased from 3.09 to 1.56 in the later period.

Only a small proportion of each stock's total risk comes from movements in the market. The rest is unique risk, which shows up in the scatter of points around the fitted lines in Figure 9.2. *R-squared* (R^2) measures the proportion of the total variation in the stock's returns that can be explained by market movements. For example, from 2002 to 2005, the R^2 of HLL was 0.49. In other words, only about one-half of HLL's risk was market risk and the remaining half was unique risk. The variance of returns on HLL stock was 888.86[6]. So we could say that the variance in stock returns that was due to the market was 0.49 × 888.86 = 435.5, and the variance of unique returns was 453.4.

[3]The CAPM is not the last word on risk and return, of course, but the principles and procedures covered in this chapter work just as well with other models such as arbitrage pricing theory (APT).

[4]We have used Excel to draw these scatter plots. Excel automatically scales the axes and hence you will not be able to guess the slope of the best-fit line by merely looking at the lines.

[5]Notice that you must regress the *returns* on the stock on the market *returns*. You would get a very similar estimate if you simply used the percentage *changes* in the stock price and the market index. But sometimes analysts make the mistake of regressing the stock price *level* on the *level* of the index and obtain nonsense results.

[6]This is an annual figure; we annualized the monthly variance by multiplying by 12. The standard deviation was $\sqrt{888.86}$ = 29.81 percent.

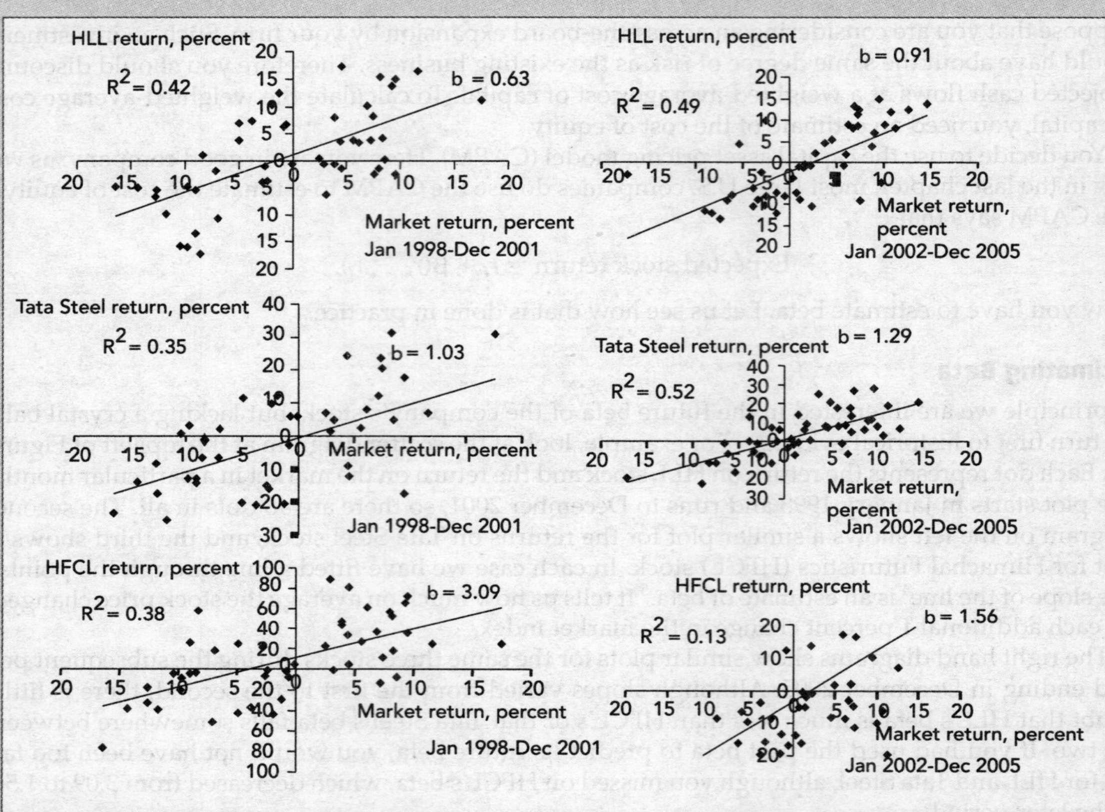

FIGURE 9.2

We have used past return to estimate the beats of three stocks for the periods January 1998 to December 2001 (left-hand diagrams) and January 2002 to December 2005 (right-hand diagrams). Beta is the slope of the fitted line. Notice that in both periods HLL had the lowest beta and HFCL the highest. We also report the proportion of total risk that is due to market movements (R^2).

	β_{equity}	Standard Error
Andhra Cements Ltd.	0.99	0.62
India Cements Ltd.	1.40	0.32
Madras Cements Ltd.	0.90	0.20
Shree Digvijay Cement Co. Ltd.	1.74	0.48
Cement Portfolio	1.26	0.29

TABLE 9.1

Estimated betas and standard errors for a sample of large cement manufacturing companies and for a portfolio of these companies, based on monthly returns from January 2001 to May 2006. The prcision of the portfolio beta is better than that of the betas of the individual companies note the lower standard error for the portfolio.

The estimates of beta shown in Figure 9.2 are just that. They are based on stock's returns in 48 particular months. The noise in returns can obscure the true beta. Therefore, statisticians calculate the *standard error* of the estimated beta to show the extent of possible mismeasurement. Then they set up a *confidence interval* of the estimated value plus or minus two standard errors. For example, the standard error of HFCL's estimated beta is 0.53 for the period 1998–2001. Thus the confidence interval for HFCL's beta is 3.09 plus or minus 1.96 × 0.53. If you state that the true beta for HFCL is between 2.05 and 4.13, you have a 95 percent chance of being right. Since the standard error of Tata Steel's beta is 0.21, we can be more confident of Tata Steel's beta and less confident of HFCL's.

Usually you will have more information (and thus more confidence) than this simple calculation suggests. For example, you know that HLL's estimated beta was way below 1 in the previous period, while HFCL's estimated beta was well above 1. Nevertheless, there is always a large margin of error when estimating the beta for individual stocks.

Fortunately, the estimated errors tend to cancel out when you estimate betas of *portfolios*.[7] That is why financial managers often turn to industry betas. For example. Table 9.1 shows estimates of beta and standard errors of these estimates for the common stocks of four cement companies in India. Two of the standard errors are above 0.4, large enough to preclude a precise estimate of any particular cement company's beta. However, the table also shows the estimated beta for a portfolio of all four cement stocks. Notice that the estimated industry beta is somewhat more reliable. This shows up in the lower standard error.

[7]If the observations are independent, the standard error of the estimated mean beta declines in proportion to the square root of the number of stocks in the portfolio.

The Expected Return on India Cement's Common Stock

Suppose that in the beginning of 2006 you have been asked to estimate the company cost of capital of India Cements Limited. Table 9.1 provides two clues about the true beta of India Cements' stock: the direct estimate of 1.4 and the average estimate for the industry of 1.26. We will use the industry average of 1.26.[8]

In early 2006, the risk-free interest was about 6.3 percent. Suppose you decide to use a market risk premium of 10 percent. The resulting estimate for India Cements' cost of equity is about 19 percent:

$$\text{Cost of equity} = \text{Expected return} = r_f + \beta(r_m - r_f)$$
$$= 6.3 + 1.29 \times 10 = 18.9\%$$

9.3 SETTING DISCOUNT RATES WHEN YOU DON'T HAVE A BETA

Stock or industry betas provide a rough guide to the risk encountered in various lines of business. But an asset beta for the cement business can take you only so far. Not all investments made in that industry are average-risk. And if you are the first to start a cement plant, you will not even have a useful industry beta to start with.

In some cases an asset is publicly traded. If so we can estimate risk from past prices. Suppose your company wants to assess the risk of investing in commercial real estate, for example, in a large office building for company headquarters. Here the company can turn to indexes of real estate prices and returns derived from sales and appraisals of commercial properties.[9]

What should a manager do if the asset has no such convenient price record? What if the proposed investment is not close enough to business as usual to justify using a company cost of capital?

These cases clearly call for judgment. For managers making that kind of judgment, we offer three pieces of advice.

1. *Avoid fudge factors.* Don't give in to the temptation to add fudge factors to the discount rate to offset things that could go wrong with the proposed investment. Adjust cash-flow forecasts first.

[8]Comparing the beta of India Cements with those of the other cement companies would be misleading if India Cement had a marginally higher or lower debt ratio.

[9]See Chapter 23 in D. Geltner and N. G. Miller, *Commercial Real Estate Analysis and Investment* (Englewood Cliffs, NJ: Prentice Hall, 2001).

2. *Think about the determinants of asset betas.* Often the characteristics of high- and low-beta assets can be observed when the beta itself cannot be.
3. *Don't be fooled by diversifiable risk.*

Let us expand on these points.

Avoid Fudge Factors in Discount Rates

We have defined risk, from the investor's viewpoint, as the standard deviation of portfolio return or the beta of a common stock or other security. But in everyday usage *risk* simply equals "bad outcome." People think of the risks of a project as a list of things that can go wrong. For example,

- A geologist looking for oil worries about the risk of a dry hole.
- A pharmaceutical manufacturer worries about the risk that a new drug that cures baldness may not be approved by the Food and Drug Administration.
- The owner of a resort hotel in a politically unstable part of the world worries about the risk of expropriation.

Managers often add fudge factors to discount rates to offset worries such as these.

This sort of adjustment makes us nervous. First, the bad outcomes we cited appear to reflect unique (i.e., diversifiable) risks that would not affect the expected rate of return demanded by investors. Second, the need for a discount rate adjustment usually arises because managers fail to give bad outcomes their due weight in cash-flow forecasts. The managers then try to offset that mistake by adding a fudge factor to the discount rate.

Example Project Z will produce just one cash flow, forecasted at Rs. 1 million at year 1. It is regarded as average risk, suitable for discounting at a 10 percent company cost of capital:

$$PV = \frac{C_1}{1+r} = \frac{1{,}000{,}000}{1.1} = \text{Rs. } 909{,}100$$

But now you discover that the company's engineers are behind schedule in developing the technology required for the project. They are confident it will work, but they admit to a small chance that it will not. You still see the *most likely* outcome as Rs. 1 million, but you also see some chance that project Z will generate *zero* cash flow next year.

Now the project's prospects are clouded by your new worry about technology. It must be worth less than the Rs. 909,100 you calculated before that worry arose. But how much less? There is *some* discount rate (10 percent plus a fudge factor) that will give the right value, but we do not know what that adjusted discount rate is.

We suggest you reconsider your original Rs. 1 million forecast for project Z's cash flow. Project cash flows are supposed to be *unbiased* forecasts, which give due weight to all possible outcomes, favorable and unfavorable. Managers making unbiased forecasts are correct on average. Sometimes their forecasts will turn out high, other times low, but their errors will average out over many projects.

If you forecast a cash flow of Rs. 1 million for projects like Z, you will overestimate the average cash flow, because every now and then you will hit a zero. Those zeros should be "averaged in" to your forecasts.

For many projects, the most likely cash flow is also the unbiased forecast. If there are three possible outcomes with the probabilities shown below, the unbiased forecast is Rs. 1 million. (The unbiased forecast is the sum of the probability-weighted cash flows.)

Possible Cash Flow	Probability	Probability-Weighted Cash Flow	Unbiased Forecast
1.2	.25	.3	
1.0	.50	.5	1.0, or Rs. 1 million
0.8	.25	.2	

This might describe the initial prospects of project Z. But if technological uncertainty introduces a 10 percent chance of a zero cash flow, the unbiased forecast could drop to Rs. 900,000:

Possible Cash Flow	Probability	Probability-Weighted Cash Flow	Unbiased Forecast
1.2	.225	.27	
1.0	.45	.45	.90, or Rs. 900,000
0.8	.225	.18	
0.0	.10	.0	

The present value is

$$PV = \frac{90}{1.1} = .818, \text{ or Rs. } 818{,}000$$

Now, of course, you can figure out the right fudge factor to add to the discount rate to apply to the original Rs. 1 million forecast to get the correct answer. But you have to think through possible cash flows to get that fudge factor; and once you have thought through the cash flows, you don't *need* the fudge factor.

Managers often work out a range of possible outcomes for major projects, sometimes with explicit probabilities attached. We give more elaborate examples and further discussion in Chapter 10. But even when a range of outcomes and probabilities is not explicitly written down, the manager can still consider the good and bad outcomes as well as the most likely one. When the bad outcomes outweigh the good, the cash-flow forecast should be reduced until balance is regained.

Step 1, then, is to do your best to make unbiased forecasts of a project's cash flows. Step 2 is to consider whether *investors* would regard the project as more or less risky than typical for a company or division. Here our advice is to search for characteristics of the asset that are associated with high or low betas. We wish we had a more fundamental scientific understanding of what these characteristics are. We see business risks surfacing in capital markets, but as yet there is no satisfactory theory describing how these risks are generated. Nevertheless, some things are known.

What Determines Asset Betas?

Cyclicality Many people intuitively associate risk with the variability of book, or accounting, earnings. But much of this variability reflects unique or diversifiable risk. Lone prospectors in search of gold look forward to extremely uncertain future earnings, but whether they strike it rich is not likely to depend on the performance of the market portfolio. Even if they do find gold, they do not bear much market risk. Therefore, an investment in gold has a high standard deviation but a relatively low beta.

What really counts is the strength of the relationship between the firm's earnings and the aggregate earnings on all real assets. We can measure this either by the *accounting beta* or by the *cash-flow beta*. These are just like a real beta except that changes in book earnings or cash flow are used in place of rates of return on securities. We would predict that firms with high accounting or cash-flow betas should also have high stock betas—and the prediction is correct.

This means that cyclical firms—firms whose revenues and earnings are strongly dependent on the state of the business cycle—tend to be high-beta firms. Thus you should demand a higher rate of return from investments whose performance is strongly tied to the performance of the economy.

Operating Leverage A production facility with high fixed costs, relative to variable costs, is said to have high *operating leverage*. High operating leverage means high risk. Let us see how this works.

The cash flows generated by any productive asset can be broken down into revenue, fixed costs, and variable costs:

$$\text{Cash flow} = \text{revenue} - \text{fixed cost} - \text{variable cost}$$

Costs are variable if they depend on the rate of output. Examples are raw materials, sales commissions, and some labor and maintenance costs. Fixed costs are cash outflows that occur regardless of whether the asset is active or idle, for example, property taxes or the wages of workers under contract.

We can break down the asset's present value in the same way:

$$\text{PV(asset)} = \text{PV(revenue)} - \text{PV(fixed cost)} - \text{PV(variable cost)}$$

Or equivalently

$$\text{PV(revenue)} = \text{PV(fixed cost)} + \text{PV(variable cost)} + \text{PV(asset)}$$

Those who *receive* the fixed costs are like debtholders in the project; they simply get a fixed payment. Those who receive the net cash flows from the asset are like holders of common stock; they get whatever is left after payment of the fixed costs.

We can now figure out how the asset's beta is related to the betas of the values of revenue and costs. The beta of PV(revenue) is a weighted average of the betas of its component parts:

$$\beta_{\text{revenue}} = \beta_{\text{fixed cost}} \frac{\text{PV(fixed cost)}}{\text{PV(revenue)}} + \beta_{\text{variable cost}} \frac{\text{PV(variable cost)}}{\text{PV(revenue)}} + \beta_{\text{assets}} \frac{\text{PV(asset)}}{\text{PV(revenue)}}$$

The fixed-cost beta should be about zero; whoever receives the fixed costs receives a fixed stream of cash flows.[10] The betas of the revenues and variable costs should be approximately the same, because they respond to the same underlying variable, the rate of output. Therefore, we can substitute $\beta_{\text{variable cost}}$ and solve for the asset beta. Remember that $\beta_{\text{fixed cost}} = 0$.

$$\beta_{\text{assets}} = \beta_{\text{revenue}} \frac{\text{PV(revenue)} - \text{PV(variable cost)}}{\text{PV(assets)}}$$

$$= \beta_{\text{revenue}} \left[1 + \frac{\text{PV(fixed cost)}}{\text{PV(assets)}} \right]$$

Thus, given the cyclicality of revenues (reflected in β_{revenue}), the asset beta is proportional to the ratio of the present value of fixed costs to the present value of the project.

Now you have a rule of thumb for judging the relative risks of alternative designs or technologies for producing the same project. Other things being equal, the alternative with the higher ratio of fixed costs to project value will have the higher project beta. Empirical tests confirm that companies with high operating leverage actually do have high betas.[11]

You cannot hope to estimate the relative risk of assets with any precision, but good managers examine any project from a variety of angles and look for clues as to its riskiness. They know that high market risk is a characteristic of cyclical ventures and of projects with high fixed costs. They think about the major uncertainties affecting the economy and consider how projects are affected by these uncertainties.[12]

Finally, do not confuse beta with diversifiable risk. A project may look extra-risky viewed at close range, but if the project's uncertainties are not correlated with the market or other macroeconomic risks, then the project is only average-risk to a diversified investor.

9.4 CERTAINTY EQUIVALENTS—ANOTHER WAY TO ADJUST FOR RISK

In practical capital budgeting, a single discount rate is usually applied to all future cash flows. For example, the financial manager might use the capital asset pricing model to estimate the cost of capital and then use this figure to discount each year's expected cash flow.

Among other things, the use of a constant discount rate assumes that project risk does not change over time, but remains constant year-in and year-out. We know that this cannot be strictly true, for the risks that companies are exposed to are constantly shifting. We are venturing here onto somewhat difficult ground, but there is a way to think about risk that can suggest a route through. It involves converting the expected cash flows to **certainty equivalents.** First we work through an

[10]The cash flows are not absolutely safe, of course. The firm may be able to shut down the plant and avoid the fixed costs entirely. We discuss this abandonment option in Chapters 10 and 22.

[11]See B. Lev, "On the Association between Operating Leverage and Risk," *Journal of Financial and Quantitative Analysis* 9 (September 1974), pp. 627–642; and G. N. Mandelker and S. G. Rhee, "The Impact of the Degrees of Operating and Financial Leverage on Systematic Risk of Common Stock," *Journal of Financial and Quantitative Analysis* 19 (March 1984), pp. 45–57.

[12]Sharpe's article on a "multibeta" interpretation of market risk offers a useful way of thinking about these uncertainties and tracing their impact on a firm's or project's risk. See W. F. Sharpe, "The Capital Asset Pricing Model: A 'Multi-Beta' Interpretation," in H. Levy and M. Sarnat (eds.), *Financial Decision Making under Uncertainty* (New York: Academic Press, 1977).

example showing what certainty equivalents are. Then, as a reward for your investment, we will use certainty equivalents to uncover what you are really assuming when you discount a series of future cash flows at a single risk-adjusted discount rate. We also value a project where risk changes over time and ordinary discounting fails.[13]

Valuation by Certainty Equivalents

Think back to the simple real estate investment that we used in Chapter 2 to introduce the concept of present value. You are considering construction of an office building that you plan to sell after one year for Rs. 420,000. Since that cash flow is uncertain, you discount at a risk-adjusted discount rate of 12 percent rather than the 5 percent risk-free rate of interest. This gives a present value of 420,000/1.12 = Rs. 375,000.

Suppose a real estate company now approaches and offers to fix the price at which it will buy the building from you at the end of the year. This guarantee would remove any uncertainty about the payoff on your investment. So you would accept a lower figure than the uncertain payoff of Rs. 420,000. But how much less? If the building has a present value of Rs. 375,000 and the interest rate is 5 percent, then

$$\text{PV} = \frac{\text{Certain cash flow}}{1.05} = 375{,}000$$

$$\text{Certain cash flow} = \text{Rs. } 393{,}750$$

In other words, a certain cash flow of Rs. 393,750 has exactly the same present value as an expected but uncertain cash flow of Rs. 420,000. The cash flow of Rs. 393,750 is therefore known as the *certainty-equivalent cash flow*. To compensate for both the delayed payoff and the uncertainty in real estate prices, you need a return of 420,000 − 375,000 = Rs. 45,000. One part of this difference compensates for the time value of money. The other part (Rs. 420,000 − 393,750 = Rs. 26,250) is a markdown or "haircut" to compensate for the risk attached to the forecasted cash flow of Rs. 420,000.

Our example illustrates two ways to value a risky cash flow C_1:

Method 1: Discount the risky cash flow at a *risk-adjusted discount rate* r that is greater than r_f.[14] The risk-adjusted discount rate adjusts for both time and risk. This is illustrated by the clockwise route in Figure 9.3.

Method 2: Find the certainty-equivalent cash flow and discount at the risk-free interest rate r_f. When you use this method, you need to ask, What is the smallest *certain* payoff for which I would exchange the risky cash flow C_1? This is called the *certainty equivalent* of C_1, denoted by CEQ_1.[15] Since CEQ_1 is the value equivalent of a safe cash flow, it is discounted at the risk-free

[13]Your investment will be rewarded further when we cover options in Chapters 20 and 21 and forward and futures pricing in Chapter 27. Option pricing formulas discount certainty equivalents. Forward and futures prices *are* certainty equivalents.

[14]The discount rate r can be less than r_f for assets with negative betas. But actual betas are almost always positive.

[15]CEQ_1 can be calculated directly from the capital asset pricing model. The certainty-equivalent form of the CAPM states that the certainty-equivalent value of the cash flow, C_1, is $C_1 - \lambda \text{ cov}(\tilde{C}_1, \tilde{r}_m)$. Cov $(\tilde{C}_1, \tilde{r}_m)$ is the covariance between the uncertain cash flow, $\tilde{C}_1$, and the return on the market, r_m. Lambda, λ, is a measure of the market price of risk. It is defined as $(r_m - r_f)/\sigma_m^2$. For example, if $r_m - r_f = .08$ and the standard deviation of market returns is $\sigma_m = .20$, then lambda $= .08/.20^2 = 2$. We show on our Web site **(www.mhhe.com/bmam8e)** how the CAPM formula can be twisted around into this certainty-equivalent form.

FIGURE 9.3

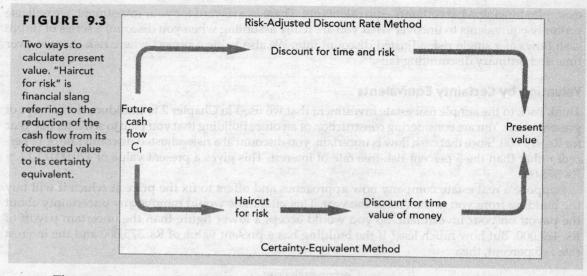

Two ways to calculate present value. "Haircut for risk" is financial slang referring to the reduction of the cash flow from its forecasted value to its certainty equivalent.

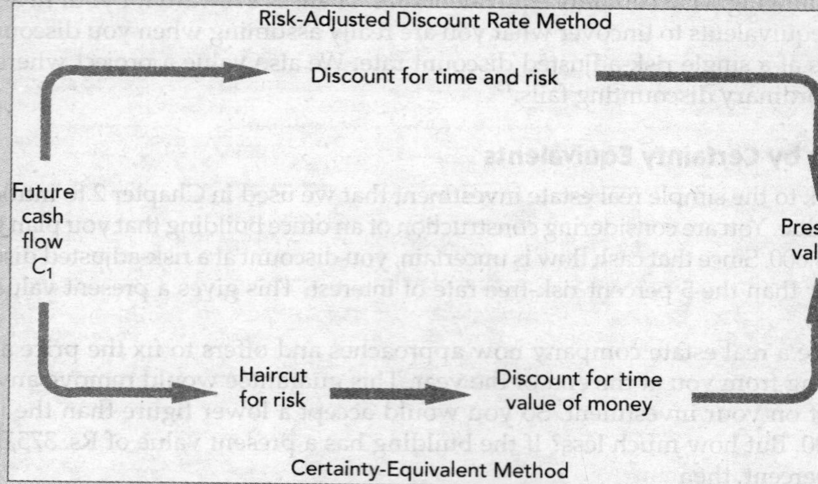

rate. The certainty-equivalent method makes *separate* adjustments for risk and time. This is illustrated by the counterclockwise route in Figure 9.3.

We now have two identical expressions for PV:

$$PV = \frac{C_1}{1+r} = \frac{CEQ_1}{1+r_f}$$

For cash flows two, three, or t years away,

$$PV = \frac{C_t}{(1+r)^t} = \frac{CEQ_t}{(1+r_f)^t}$$

When to Use a Single Risk-Adjusted Discount Rate for Long-Lived Assets

We are now in a position to examine what is implied when a constant risk-adjusted discount rate, r, is used to calculate a present value.

Consider two simple projects. Project A is expected to produce a cash flow of Rs. 100 million for each of three years. The risk-free interest rate is 6 percent, the market risk premium is 8 percent, and project A's beta is .75. You therefore calculate A's opportunity cost of capital as follows:

$$r = r_f + \beta(r_m - r_f)$$
$$= 6 + .75(8) = 12\%$$

Discounting at 12 percent gives the following present value for each cash flow:

Project A		
Year	**Cash Flow**	**PV at 12%**
1	100	89.3
2	100	79.7
3	100	71.2
	Total PV	240.2

Now compare these figures with the cash flows of project B. Notice that B's cash flows are lower than A's; but B's flows are safe, and therefore they are discounted at the risk-free interest rate. The *present value* of each year's cash flow is identical for the two projects.

Project B		
Year	Cash Flow	PV at 6%
1	94.6	89.3
2	89.6	79.7
3	84.8	71.2
	Total PV	240.2

In year 1 project A has a risky cash flow of 100. This has the same PV as the safe cash flow of 94.6 from project B. Therefore 94.6 is the certainty equivalent of 100. Since the two cash flows have the same PV, investors must be willing to give up 100 − 94.6 = 5.4 in expected year-1 income in order to get rid of the uncertainty.

In year 2 project A has a risky cash flow of 100, and B has a safe cash flow of 89.6. Again both flows have the same PV. Thus, to eliminate the uncertainty in year 2, investors are prepared to give up 100 − 89.6 = 10.4 of future income. To eliminate uncertainty in year 3, they are willing to give up 100 − 84.8 = 15.2 of future income.

To value project A, you discounted each cash flow at the same risk-adjusted discount rate of 12 percent. Now you can see what is implied when you did that. By using a constant rate, you effectively made a larger deduction for risk from the later cash flows:

Year	Forecasted Cash Flow for Project A	Certainty-Equivalent Cash Flow	Deduction for Risk
1	100	94.6	5.4
2	100	89.6	10.4
3	100	84.8	15.2

The second cash flow is riskier than the first because it is exposed to two years of market risk. The third cash flow is riskier still because it is exposed to three years of market risk. This increased risk is reflected in the steadily declining certainty equivalents.

Therefore, use of a constant risk-adjusted discount rate for a stream of cash flows assumes that risk accumulates at a constant rate as you look farther out into the future.

A Common Mistake

You sometimes hear people say that because distant cash flows are riskier, they should be discounted at a higher rate than earlier cash flows. That is quite wrong: We have just seen that using the same risk-adjusted discount rate for each year's cash flow implies a larger deduction for risk from the later cash flows. The reason is that the discount rate compensates for the risk borne *per period*. The more distant the cash flows, the greater the number of periods and the larger the *total* risk adjustment.

When You Cannot Use a Single Risk-Adjusted Discount Rate for Long-Lived Assets

Sometimes you will encounter problems where the use of a single risk-adjusted discount rate will get you into trouble. For example, later in the book we will look at how options are valued. Because an option's risk is continually changing, the certainty-equivalent method needs to be used.

Here is a disguised, simplified, and somewhat exaggerated version of an actual project proposal that one of the authors was asked to analyze. The scientists at Vegetron have come up with an electric mop, and the firm is ready to go ahead with pilot production and test marketing. The preliminary phase will take one year and cost Rs. 125,000. Management feels that there is only a 50 percent chance that pilot production and market tests will be successful. If they are, then Vegetron will build a Rs. 1 million plant that would generate an expected annual cash flow in perpetuity of Rs. 250,000 a year after taxes. If they are not successful, the project will have to be dropped.

The expected cash flows (in thousands of rupees) are

$$C_0 = -125$$

$$C_1 = 50\% \text{ chance of } -1{,}000 \text{ and } 50\% \text{ chance of } 0$$

$$= .5(-1{,}000) + .5(0) = -500$$

$$C_t \text{ for } t = 2, 3, \ldots = 50\% \text{ chance of } 250 \text{ and } 50\% \text{ chance of } 0$$

$$= .5(250) + .5(0) = 125$$

Management has little experience with consumer products and considers this a project of extremely high risk.[16] Therefore management discounts the cash flows at 25 percent, rather than at Vegetron's normal 10 percent standard:

$$\text{NPV} = -125 - \frac{500}{1.25} + \sum_{t=2}^{\infty} \frac{125}{(1.25)^t} = -125; \text{ or } -\text{Rs.}\,125{,}000$$

This seems to show that the project is not worthwhile.

Management's analysis is open to criticism if the first year's experiment resolves a high proportion of the risk. If the test phase is a failure, then there is no risk at all—the project is *certain* to be worthless. If it is a success, there could well be only normal risk from then on. That means there is a 50 percent chance that in one year Vegetron will have the opportunity to invest in a project of *normal* risk, for which the *normal* discount rate of 10 percent would be appropriate. Thus the firm has a 50 percent chance to invest Rs. 1 million in a project with a net present value of Rs. 1.5 million:

$$\text{Success} \rightarrow \text{NPV} = -1000 + \frac{250}{.10} = +1{,}500 \text{ (50\% chance)}$$

Pilot production and market tests

$$\text{Failure} \rightarrow \text{NPV} = 0 \text{ (50\% chance)}$$

[16] We will assume that they mean high *market risk* and that the difference between 25 and 10 percent is *not* a fudge factor introduced to offset optimistic cash-flow forecasts.

Thus we could view the project as offering an expected payoff of .5(1,500) + .5(0) = 750, or Rs. 750,000, at $t = 1$ on a Rs. 125,000 investment at $t = 0$. Of course, the certainty equivalent of the payoff is less than Rs. 750,000, but the difference would have to be very large to justify rejecting the project. For example, if the certainty equivalent is half the forecasted cash flow and the risk-free rate is 7 percent, the project is worth Rs. 225,500:

$$NPV = C_0 + \frac{CEQ_1}{1+r}$$

$$= 125 + \frac{.5(750)}{1.07} = 225.5, \text{ or Rs. } 225,500$$

This is not bad for a Rs. 125,000 investment—and quite a change from the negative-NPV that management got by discounting all future cash flows at 25 percent.

9.5 DISCOUNT RATES FOR INTERNATIONAL PROJECTS

We have shown how the CAPM can help to estimate the cost of capital for domestic investments by Indian companies. But can we extend the procedure to allow for investments in different countries? The answer is yes in principle, but naturally there are complications.

Foreign Investments Are Not Always Riskier

Pop Quiz: Which is riskier for an investor in the United States — the Standard and Poor's Composite Index or the stock market in India? If your answer is India, you are right. But probably you defined risk as the *total* volatility (standard deviation). But does investment in India have a high *beta*? How much does it add to the risk of a diversified portfolio held in the United States?

Table 9.2 shows estimated betas for the Indian market and for markets in seven other countries. The standard deviations in these markets were several times more than the US market, but only in India, Indonesia, and Thailand had a beta greater than 1. The reason is low correlation. For example, the standard deviation of the Brazilian market was 6.29 times that of the Standard and Poor's index, but the correlation coefficient was only 0.134. The beta was 6.29 × 0.134 = 0.84.

TABLE 9.2

	Ratio of Standard Deviations[a]	Correlation Coefficient	Beta[b]
Brazil	6.29	.134	.84
Egypt	5.67	.104	.59
India	6.10	.173	1.05
Indonesia	7.29	.176	1.28
Mexico	3.92	.131	.51
Poland	3.21	.264	.85
Thailand	6.32	.276	1.74
South Africa	4.04	.211	.85

Betas of eight country indexes versus the U.S. market, calculated from monthly returns, January 1999–December 2003. Despite high volatility, many of the betas are less than 1. The reason is the relatively low correlation with the U.S. market.

[a] Ratio of standard deviations of country index to Standard & Poor's Composite Index.

[b] Beta is the ratio of covariance to variance. Covariance can be written as $\sigma_{IM} = \rho_{IM}\,\sigma_I\,\sigma_M$; $\beta = \rho_{IM}\,\sigma_I\,\sigma_M/\sigma_M^2 = \rho\,(\sigma_I/\sigma_M)$, where I indicates the country index and M indicates the U.S. market.

Table 9.2 does not prove that investment abroad is always safer than at home. But it should remind you always to distinguish between diversifiable and market risk. The opportunity cost of capital should depend on market risk.

Foreign Investment in the United States

Suppose that Saravana Bhawan[17], the South Indian fast food joint, is considering opening a new restaurant in Jamshedpur. The financial manager forecasts rupee cash flows from the project and discounts these cash flows at the rupee cost of capital. She computes that cost of capital in the same way as her counterpart in a U.S. fast food joint. She estimates Saravana Bhawan's beta and the beta of a portfolio of Indian fast food joints. However, she calculates these betas relative to the *Indian* market index. Suppose that both measures point to a beta of 0.75 and that the expected return on the Indian market is 10 percent above the Indian interest rate. Then Saravana Bhawan needs to discount the rupee cash flows from the new restaurant at $0.75 \times 10 = 7.5$ percent above the Indian interest rate.

That is straightforward. But now suppose Saravana Bhawan considers opening several stores in the United States. Once again the financial manager measures beta relative to the Indian market index. But the fortunes of a U.S. restaurant will be less closely tied to the Indian market index. So the beta of the U.S. restaurant relative to the Indian index will be less than 1.1. But how much less? One useful guide is the beta of U.S. restaurant stocks relative to the Indian market. Let's assume that this beta is 0.5. Then Saravana Bhawan should discount the rupee cash flows from its U.S. project at $0.5 \times 10 = 5$ percent above the Indian interest rate.

Why does Saravana Bhawan's manager measure the beta of its investment relative to the Indian index, whereas her U.S. counterpart measures the beta relative to the U.S. index? The answer lies in Section 7.4, where we explained that risk cannot be considered in isolation; it depends on the other securities in the investor's portfolio. Beta measures risk *relative to the investor's portfolio*. If Indian investors already hold the Indian market, an additional rupee invested at home is just more of the same. But, if Indian investors hold the Indian market, an investment in the United States can reduce their risk. That explains why investment in a new restaurant in the United States is likely to have lower risk for Saravana Bhawan's shareholders than it would for McDonald's shareholders. It also explains why Saravana Bhawan's shareholders are willing to accept a lower return from such an investment as compared to the shareholders of McDonald[18].

When a company measures risk relative to its domestic market, its managers are implicitly assuming that shareholders simply hold domestic stocks. That is not a bad approximation, particularly in the case of India.[19] As of now, lots of restrictions apply when an Indian invests outside India[20].

Even U.S. investors generally invest only a small proportion of their money overseas even though they are legally allowed to reduce their risk by holding an internationally diversified port-

[17]In this example, we assume that Saravana Bhawan is owned by investors who have invested in diversified portfolios.

[18]When an investor holds an efficient portfolio, the expected reward for risk on each stock in the portfolio is proportional to its beta *relative to the portfolio*. So, If the Indian market index is an efficient portfolio for Indian investors, then these investors will want Saravana Bhawan to invest in a new restaurnt if the expected reward is proportional to its beta relative to the Indian market Index.

[19]But it can sometime be had approximation elsewhere. For small countries with open financial borders—Luxembourg, for example—a beta calculated relative to the local market has little value. Few investors in Luxembourg hold only local stocks.

[20]See http://www.indianbusiness.nic.in/invest-abroad/foreign-securities.htm for details.

folio. Why they do so is a puzzle.[21] It looks as if they are worried about the costs of investing overseas, but we do not understand what these costs include. Maybe it is more difficult to figure out which foreign shares to buy. Or perhaps investors are worried that a foreign government will expropriate their shares, restrict dividend payments, or catch them by a change in tax law[22].

Who knows? Perhaps in a few years investors will hold internationally diversified portfolios, and later editions of this book will recommend that firms calculate betas relative to the world market. If investors throughout the world held the world portfolio, then French and U.S. companies would both demand the same return from an investment in India, in the United States, in France, or in Egypt.

Do Some Countries Have a Lower Cost of Capital?

Some countries enjoy much lower rates of interest than others. For example, in April 2006, the 1-year t-bill yield is about 0.3 percent in Japan; it is 4.8 percent in the U.S., and 6.2 percent in India. People often conclude from this that Japanese companies enjoy lower cost of capital.

This view is one part confusion and one part probable truth. The confusion arises because the interest rate in Japan is measured in yen and the rate in the United States is measured in dollars. You would not say that a 10-inch-high rabbit was taller than a 9-foot elephant. You would be comparing their height in different units. In the same way it makes no sense to compare an interest rate in yen with a rate in dollars. The units are different.

But suppose that in each case you measure the interest rate in *real* terms. Then you are comparing like with like, and it does make sense to ask whether the costs of overseas investment can cause the *real* cost of capital to be lower in Japan. Japanese citizens have for a long time been big savers, but as they moved into a new century they were very worried about the future and were saving more than ever. That money could not be absorbed by Japanese industry and therefore had to be invested overseas. Japanese investors were not *compelled* to invest overseas: They needed to be enticed to do so. So the expected real returns on Japanese investments fell to the point that Japanese investors were willing to incur the costs of buying foreign securities. When a Japanese company wanted to finance a new project, it could tap into a pool of relatively low-cost funds.

[21]For an explanation of the cost of capital for international investments when there are costs to international diversification, see I. A. Cooper and E. Kaplanis, "Home Bias in Equity Portfolios and the Cost of Capital for Multinational Firms," *Journal of Applied Corporate Finance* 8 (Fall 1995), pp. 95–102.

[22]Part of this fear is not unfounded. The Sensex crashed by more than 800 points on June 18, 2006 after there were rumors that the Central Board of Direct Taxes (CBDT) was planning to increase the tax rate on short term capital gains on the foreign institutional investors in India. It is only after the Finance Minister clarified that the FIIs will not pay the higher tax that the market bounced back on June 19, 2006.

SUMMARY

In Chapter 8 we set out some basic principles for valuing risky assets. In this chapter we have shown you how to apply these principles to practical situations.

The problem is easiest when you believe that the project has the same market risk as the company's existing assets. In this case, the required return equals the required return on a portfolio of all the company's existing securities. This is called the *company cost of capital*.

The company cost of capital is the cost of capital for investment in the firm as a whole. It is usually calculated as a weighted-average cost of capital, that is, the average rate of return demanded by investors in the company's debt and equity securities. But in this chapter we focused mostly on the firm's cost of equity. We defined risk as beta, and we used the capital asset pricing model to estimate expected returns.

The most common way to estimate the beta of a stock is to figure out how the stock price has responded to market changes in the past. Of course, this will give you only an estimate of the stock's true beta. You may get a more reliable figure if you calculate an industry beta for a group of similar companies.

The company cost of capital is the correct discount rate for projects that have the same risk as the company's existing business. Many firms, however, use the company cost of capital to discount the forecasted cash flows on all new projects. This is a dangerous procedure. In principle, each project should be evaluated at its own opportunity cost of capital; the true cost of capital depends on the use to which the capital is put. If we wish to estimate the cost of capital for a particular project, it is *project risk* that counts. Of course the company cost of capital is fine as a discount rate for average-risk projects. It is also a useful starting point for estimating discount rates for safer or riskier projects.

Then we turned to the problem of assessing project risk. We provided several clues for managers seeking project betas. First, avoid adding fudge factors to discount rates to offset worries about bad project outcomes. Adjust cash-flow forecasts to give due weight to bad outcomes as well as good; *then* ask whether the chance of bad outcomes adds to the project's market risk. Second, you can often identify the characteristics of a high- or low-beta project even when the project beta cannot be calculated directly. For example, you can try to figure out how much the cash flows are affected by the overall performance of the economy: Cyclical investments are generally high-beta investments. You can also look at the project's operating leverage: Fixed production charges work like fixed debt charges; that is, they increase beta.Third, don't be fooled by diversifiable project risk. Don't increase the discount rate to offset risks that can be diversified away in stockholders' portfolios.

There is one more fence to jump. Most projects produce cash flows for several years. Firms generally use the same risk-adjusted rate to discount each of these cash flows. When they do this, they are implicitly assuming that cumulative risk increases at a constant rate as you look further into the future. That assumption is usually reasonable. It is precisely true when the project's future beta will be constant, that is, when risk *per period* is constant.

But exceptions sometimes prove the rule. Be on the alert for projects where risk clearly does not increase steadily. In these cases, you should break the project into segments within which the same discount rate can be reasonably used. Or you should use the certainty-equivalent version of the DCF model, which allows separate risk adjustments to each period's cash flow.

These basic principles apply internationally, but of course there are complications. The risk of a stock or real asset may depend on who's investing. For example, a Swiss investor would calculate a lower beta for Merck than an investor in the United States. Conversely, the U.S. investor would calculate a lower beta for a Swiss pharmaceutical company than a Swiss investor. Both investors see lower risk abroad because of the less-than-perfect correlation between the two countries' markets.

If all investors held the world market portfolio, none of this would matter. But there is a strong home-country bias. Perhaps some investors stay at home because they regard foreign investment as risky. We suspect they confuse total risk with market risk. For example, we showed examples of countries with extremely volatile stock markets. Most of these markets were nevertheless low-beta investments for an investor holding the U.S. market. Again, the reason was low correlation between markets.

FURTHER READING

There is a good review article by Rubinstein on the application of the capital asset pricing model to capital investment decisions:

M. E. Rubinstein: "A Mean-Variance Synthesis of Corporate Financial Theory," *Journal of Finance*, 28 (March 1973), pp. 167–182.

For some ideas on how one might break down the problem of estimating beta, see:

W. F. Sharpe: "The Capital Asset Pricing Model: A 'Multi-Beta' Interpretation," in H. Levy and M. Sarnat (eds.), *Financial Decision Making under Uncertainty*, Academic Press, New York, 1977.

Fama's article digs deeper into the implicit assumptions underlying ordinary DCF calculations. Cornell reconsiders the relative risks of near-term vs. distant cash flows.

E. F. Fama, "Discounting Under Uncertainty," *Journal of Business* 69 (October 1996), pp. 415–428.

B. Cornell, "Risk, Duration and Capital Budgeting: New Evidence on Some Old Questions," *Journal of Business* 72 (April 1999), pp. 183–200.

CONCEPT REVIEW QUESTIONS

1. Write out the formula for the company cost of capital, ignoring taxes. For what projects is this the correct discount rate? (page 218)
2. What are the advantages of an industry cost of capital rather than a cost of capital estimated for a single firm? (page 223)
3. Explain carefully how you would estimate beta for a publicly traded stock. (page 221)

For additional Concept Review Questions, please visit us at www.mhhe.com/bmam8e or refer to your Student CD.

QUIZ

1. Suppose a firm uses its company cost of capital to evaluate all projects. Will it underestimate or overestimate the value of high-risk projects?
2. Look back at the top right panel of Figure 9.2. What proportion of HLL's return was explained by market movements? What proportion was unique or diversifiable risk? How does the unique risk show up in the plot? Assume that the standard error is 0.12. What is the range of possible error in the beta estimate?

3. A company is financed 40 percent by risk-free debt. The interest rate is 10 percent, the expected market return is 18 percent, and the stock's beta is .5. What is the company cost of capital?
4. Gonzalez Farms is breeding a new, genetically engineered potato that should produce low-calorie French fries. Unfortunately the breeding program is not complete, and the new potato will have to be approved by the U.S. Food and Drug Administration. The overall probability of success in breeding and testing is only about 50 percent. The investment required is $15 million.

   Gonzalez Farms's ordinary cost of capital is 12 percent. How should the company forecast and discount future cash flows from the low-calorie potato? Should it use a discount rate greater than 12 percent? How about 24 percent, to account for the 50 percent chance of failure? Explain briefly.
5. True or false?
   a. Distant cash flows are riskier than near-term cash flows. Therefore long-term projects require higher risk-adjusted discount rates.
   b. Financial managers should always use the same risk-adjusted discount rate for short- and long-lived projects.
6. Which of these companies is likely to have the higher cost of capital?
   a. A's sales force is paid a fixed annual rate; B's is paid on a commission basis.
   b. C produces machine tools; D produces breakfast cereal.
7. True or false?
   a. The Indian stock market is much more volatile than the U.S. market.
   b. The betas of foreign stock markets (calculated relative to the U.S. market) are usually greater than 1.0.
   c. Investors concentrate their holdings in their home countries. This means that companies domiciled in different countries may calculate different discount rates for the same project.
8. A project has a forecasted cash flow of Rs. 110 in year 1 and Rs. 121 in year 2. The interest rate is 5 percent, the estimated risk premium on the market is 10 percent, and the project has a beta of .5. If you use a constant risk-adjusted discount rate, what is
   a. The PV of the project?
   b. The certainty-equivalent cash flow in year 1 and year 2?
   c. The ratio of the certainty-equivalent cash flows to the expected cash flows in years 1 and 2?

PRACTICE QUESTIONS

1. The total market value of the common stock of the Bangalore Real Estate Company is Rs. 6 million, and the total value of its debt is Rs. 4 million. The treasurer estimates that the beta of the stock is currently 1.5 and that the expected risk premium on the market is 6 percent. The Treasury bill rate is 4 percent. Assume for simplicity that Bangalore Real Estate debt is risk-free and the company does not pay tax.
   a. What is the required return on Bangalore Real Estate stock?
   b. Estimate the company cost of capital.
   c. What is the discount rate for an expansion of the company's present business?
   d. Suppose the company wants to diversify into the manufacture of rose-colored spectacles. The beta of unleveraged optical manufacturers is 1.2. Estimate the required return on Bangalore venture.

2. Nero Violins has the following capital structure:

Security	Beta	Total Market Value (Rs. millions)
Debt	0.0	Rs. 100
Preferred stock	0.20	40
Common stock	1.20	299

   a. What is the firm's asset beta? *Hint:* What is the beta of a portfolio of all the firm's securities?
   b. Assume that the CAPM is correct. What discount rate should Nero set for investments that expand the scale of its operations without changing its asset beta? Assume a risk-free interest rate of 5 percent and a market risk premium of 6 percent.

3. Look again at the companies listed in Table 8.2. Download the daily closing prices of the stocks for the last four years from www.nseindia.com. Download the daily closing level of Nifty from the website for the same four year. Estimate monthly returns from the data. From the respective companies' websites obtain data on dividend paid, bonus issue and stock split. Estimate the adjusted monthly returns from this. What percentage of the variance of each company's return is explained by the index? Use the excel function RSQ, which calculates R^2.

4. Pick any five of the companies identified in the previous question.
   a. Split the rates of return into any two consecutive two-year periods. Calculate betas for each period using Excel SLOPE function. How stable was each company's beta?
   b. Suppose you had used these betas to estimate expected rates of returns from the CAPM. Would your estimates have changed significantly from period to period?
   c. You may find it interesting to repeat your analysis using weekly returns.

5. The following table shows estimates of the risk of two well-known Canadian stocks:

	Standard Deviation %	R^2	Beta	Standard Error of Beta
Alcan	24	.15	.69	.21
Inco	29	.22	1.04	.26

   a. What proportion of each stock's risk was market risk, and what proportion was unique risk?
   b. What is the variance of Alcan? What is the unique variance?
   c. What is the confidence level on Inco's beta?
   d. If the CAPM is correct, what is the expected return on Alcan? Assume a risk-free interest rate of 5 percent and an expected market return of 12 percent.
   e. Suppose that next year the market provides a zero return. Knowing this, what return would you expect from Alcan?

6. Identify a sample of chemical companies listed in India. Obtain the daily closing prices data from www.nseindia.com.
   a. Estimate beta and R^2 for each company by using the monthly returns data. The Excel functions are SLOPE and RSQ.

b. Calculate an industry beta. Here is the best procedure: First calculate the monthly returns on an equally weighted portfolio of the stocks in your sample. Then calculate the industry beta using these portfolio returns. How does the R^2 of this portfolio compare to the average R^2 of the individual stocks?

c. Use the CAPM to calculate an average cost of equity (r_{equity}) for the chemicals industry. Use current interest rates (from www.fimmda.org) and a reasonable estimate of the market risk premium.

7. You are given the following information for Golden Fleece Financial.

Long-term debt outstanding:	Rs. 300,000
Current yield to maturity (r_{debt}):	8%
Number of shares of common stock:	10,000
Price per share:	Rs. 50
Book value per share:	Rs. 25
Expected rate of return on stock (r_{equity}):	15%

Calculate Golden Fleece's company cost of capital. Ignore taxes.

8. Look again at Table 9.1. This time we will concentrate on Andhra Cements.

a. Calculate Andhra Cements' cost of equity from the CAPM using its own beta estimate and the industry beta estimate. How different are your answers? Assume a risk-free rate of return of 6 percent and a market risk premium of 10 percent.

b. Can you be confident that Andhra Cements' true beta is *not* the industry beta?

c. Under what circumstances might you advise Andhra Cements to calculate its cost of equity based on its own beta estimate?

9. You run a perpetual encabulator machine, which generates revenues averaging Rs. 20 million per year. Raw material costs are 50 percent of revenues. These costs are variable—they are always proportional to revenues. There are no other operating costs. The cost of capital is 9 percent. Your firm's long-term borrowing rate is 6 percent.

Now you are approached by Studebaker Capital Corp., which proposes a fixed-price contract to supply raw materials at Rs. 10 million per year for 10 years.

a. What happens to the operating leverage and business risk of the encabulator machine if you agree to this fixed-price contract?

b. Calculate the present value of the encabulator machine with and without the fixed-price contract.

10. Mom and Pop Groceries has just dispatched a year's supply of groceries to the government of the Central Antarctic Republic. Payment of $ 250,000 will be made one year hence after the shipment arrives by snow train. Unfortunately there is a good chance of a coup d'état, in which case the new government will not pay. Mom and Pop's controller therefore decides to discount the payment at 40 percent, rather than at the company's 12 percent cost of capital.

a. What's wrong with using a 40 percent rate to offset political risk?

b. How much is the $ 250,000 payment really worth if the odds of a coup d'état are 25 percent?

11. An oil company is drilling a series of new wells on the perimeter of a producing oil field. About 20 percent of the new wells will be dry holes. Even if a new well strikes oil, there is still uncertainty about the amount of oil produced: 40 percent of new wells that strike oil produce only 1,000 barrels a day; 60 percent produce 5,000 barrels per day.

a. Forecast the annual cash revenues from a new perimeter well. Use a future oil price of $ 15 per barrel.

b. A geologist proposes to discount the cash flows of the new wells at 30 percent to offset the risk of dry holes. The oil company's normal cost of capital is 10 percent. Does this proposal make sense? Briefly explain why or why not.

12. Look back at project A in Section 9.4. Now assume that
  a. Expected cash flow is $ 150 per year for five years.
  b. The risk-free rate of interest is 5 percent.
  c. The market risk premium is 6 percent.
  d. The estimated beta is 1.2.

Recalculate the certainty-equivalent cash flows, and show that the ratio of these certainty-equivalent cash flows to the risky cash flows declines by a constant proportion each year.

13. A project has the following forecasted cash flows:

Cash Flows, $ Thousands			
C_0	C_1	C_2	C_3
−100	+40	+60	+50

The estimated project beta is 1.5. The market return r_m is 16 percent, and the risk-free rate r_f is 7 percent.
  a. Estimate the opportunity cost of capital and the project's PV (using the same rate to discount each cash flow).
  b. What are the certainty-equivalent cash flows in each year?
  c. What is the ratio of the certainty-equivalent cash flow to the expected cash flow in each year?
  d. Explain why this ratio declines.

14. Bharat Soaps Limited (BSL) is proposing to market a new brand of soap. The product will first be test-marketed for two years in Pune at an initial cost of Rs. 5,000,000. The test launch is not expected to produce any profits but should reveal consumer preferences. There is a 60 percent chance that demand will be satisfactory. In this case BSL will spend Rs. 50 million to launch the soap nationwide and will receive an expected annual profit of Rs. 7,000,000. If demand is not satisfactory, the soap will be withdrawn.

Once consumer preferences are known, the soap will be subject to an average degree of risk, and therefore, BSL requires a return of 12 percent on its investment. However, the initial test-market phase is viewed as much riskier, and BSL demands a return of 40 percent on its initial expenditure.

What is the NPV of this soap project?

15. Look at Table 9.2. What would the eight countries' betas be if the correlation coefficient for each was 0.5? Do the calculation and explain.

16. Consider the beta estimates for the country indexes shown in Table 9.2. Could this information be helpful to a U.S. company considering capital investment projects in these countries? Would a German company find this information useful? Explain.

CHALLENGE QUESTIONS

1. Suppose you are valuing a future stream of high-risk (high-beta) cash *outflows*. High risk means a high discount rate. But the higher the discount rate, the less the present value. This seems to say that the higher the risk of cash outflows, the less you should worry about them! Can that be right? Should the sign of the cash flow affect the appropriate discount rate? Explain.

2. An oil company executive is considering investing Rs. 10 million in one or both of two wells: Well 1 is expected to produce oil worth Rs. 3 million a year for 10 years; well 2 is expected to produce Rs. 2 million for 15 years. These are *real* (inflation-adjusted) cash flows.

The beta for *producing wells* is .9. The market risk premium is 8 percent, the nominal risk-free interest rate is 6 percent, and expected inflation is 4 percent.

The two wells are intended to develop a previously discovered oil field. Unfortunately there is still a 20 percent chance of a dry hole in each case. A dry hole means zero cash flows and a complete loss of the Rs. 10 million investment.

Ignore taxes and make further assumptions as necessary.

a. What is the correct real discount rate for cash flows from developed wells?

b. The oil company executive proposes to add 20 percentage points to the real discount rate to offset the risk of a dry hole. Calculate the NPV of each well with this adjusted discount rate.

c. What do *you* say the NPVs of the two wells are?

d. Is there any *single* fudge factor that could be added to the discount rate for developed wells that would yield the correct NPV for both wells? Explain.

3. If you have access to the "Data Analysis Tools[23]" in Excel, use the "regression" functions to investigate the reliability of the betas estimated in Practice Questions 4 and 6.

STANDARD &POOR'S

a. What are the standard errors of the betas from questions 4(a) and 4(c)? Given the standard errors, do you regard the different beta estimates obtained for each company as significantly different? (Perhaps the differences are just "noise.") What would you propose as the most reliable *forecast* of the beta of each company?

b. How reliable are the beta estimates from question 6(a)?

c. Compare the standard error of the industry beta from question 6(b) with the standard errors for individual-company betas. Given these standard errors, would you rely on the industry beta or betas for individual companies?

MINI-CASE

The Jones Family, Incorporated

The Scene: Early evening in an ordinary family room in Manhattan. Modern furniture, with old copies of *The Wall Street Journal* and the *Financial Times* scattered around. Autographed photos of Alan Greenspan and George Soros are prominently displayed. A picture window reveals a distant view of lights on the Hudson River. John Jones sits at a computer terminal, glumly sipping a glass of chardonnay and trading Japanese yen over the Internet. His wife Marsha enters.

Marsha: Hi, honey. Glad to be home. Lousy day on the trading floor, though. Dullsville. No volume. But I did manage to hedge next year's production from our copper mine. I couldn't get a good quote on the right package of futures contracts, so I arranged a commodity swap.

John doesn't reply.

Marsha: John, what's wrong? Have you been buying yen again? That's been a losing trade for weeks.

John: Well, yes. I shouldn't have gone to Goldman Sachs's foreign exchange brunch. But I've got to get out of the house somehow. I'm cooped up here all day calculating covariances and efficient risk-return trade-offs while you're out trading commodity futures. You get all the glamour and excitement.

Marsha: Don't worry dear, it will be over soon. We only recalculate our most efficient common stock portfolio once a quarter. Then you can go back to leveraged leases.

John: You trade, and I do all the worrying. Now there's a rumor that our leasing company is going to get a hostile takeover bid. I knew the debt ratio was too low, and you forgot to put on the poison pill. And now you've made a negative-NPV investment!

Marsha: What investment?

John: That wildcat oil well. Another well in that old Sourdough field. It's going to cost $ 5 million! Is there any oil down there?

Marsha: That Sourdough field has been good to us, John. Where do you think we got the capital for your yen trades? I bet we'll find oil. Our geologists say there's only a 30 percent chance of a dry hole.

[23] In case you do not have "Data Analysis Tools", you need to install the add-in your computer. Alternative, go to "Help" and select "Lotus 1-2-3 Help", Select 'Data' option there and you can also run regression by selecting 'regression'.

John: Even if we hit oil, I bet we'll only get 300 barrels of crude oil per day.

Marsha: That's 300 barrels day in, day out. There are 365 days in a year, Dear.

John and Marsha's teenage son Johnny bursts into the room.

Johnny: Hi, Dad! Hi, Mom! Guess what? I've made the junior varsity derivatives team! That means I can go on the field trip to the Chicago Board Options Exchange. (*Pauses.*) What's wrong?

John: Your mother has made another negative-NPV investment. A wildcat oil well, way up on the North Slope of Alaska.

Johnny: That's OK, Dad. Mom told me about it. I was going to do an NPV calculation yesterday, but I had to finish calculating the junk-bond default probabilities for my corporate finance homework. (*Grabs a financial calculator from his backpack.*) Let's see:
300 barrels a day times 365 days per year times \$ 25 per barrel when delivered in Los Angeles . . . that's \$ 2.7 million per year.

John: That's \$ 2.7 million *next* year, assuming that we find any oil at all. The chances can't be better than 90 percent. Then production will start declining by 5 percent every year. And we still have to pay \$10 per barrel in pipeline and tanker charges to ship the oil from the North Slope to Los Angeles. That's a fixed cost. We've got some serious operating leverage here.

Marsha: On the other hand, our energy consultants project increasing oil prices. If they increase with inflation, price per barrel should increase by roughly 2.5 percent per year. The wells ought to be able to keep pumping for at least 15 years.

Johnny: I'll calculate NPV after I finish with the default probabilities. The interest rate is 6 percent. Is it OK if I work with the beta of .8 and our usual figure of 7 percent for the market risk premium?

Marsha: I guess so, Johnny. But I am concerned about the fixed shipping costs.

John: (*Takes a deep breath and stands up.*) Anyway, how about a nice family dinner? I've reserved our usual table at the Four Seasons.

Everyone exits.

Announcer: Is the wildcat well really negative-NPV? Will John and Marsha have to fight a hostile takeover? Will Johnny's derivatives team use Black–Scholes or the binomial method? Find out in the next episode of The Jones Family, Incorporated.

You may not aspire to the Jones family's way of life, but you will learn about all their activities, from futures contracts to binomial option pricing, later in this book. Meanwhile, you may wish to replicate Johnny's NPV analysis.

QUESTIONS

1. Calculate the NPV of the wildcat oil well, taking account of the probability of a dry hole, the shipping costs, the decline in production, and the forecasted increase in oil prices. How long does production have to continue for the well to be a positive-NPV investment? Ignore taxes and other possible complications.
2. Now consider operating leverage. How should the fixed shipping costs be valued? Recalculate NPV. *Hint:* The Jones's oil company has an excellent credit rating. Its long-term borrowing rate is only 7 percent.

PART THREE RELATED WEB SITES

Software for project analysis (Chapter 10) is available on:

www.jaxworks.com (simple illustration of accounting breakeven analysis)

crystalball.com (demo of Crystal Ball™ simulation software)

home.uchicago.edu/~rmyerson (Roger Myerson's home page provides downloadable software for risk analysis and simulation)

The Corporate Library is a very useful source of information on executive compensation. BusinessWeek and Forbes produce regular reports on remuneration, and the Web site of Towers Perrin, the human resource consultancy, provides some extracts from its database:

www.thecorporatelibrary.com

www.towersperrin.com

www.forbes.com

www.businessweek.com

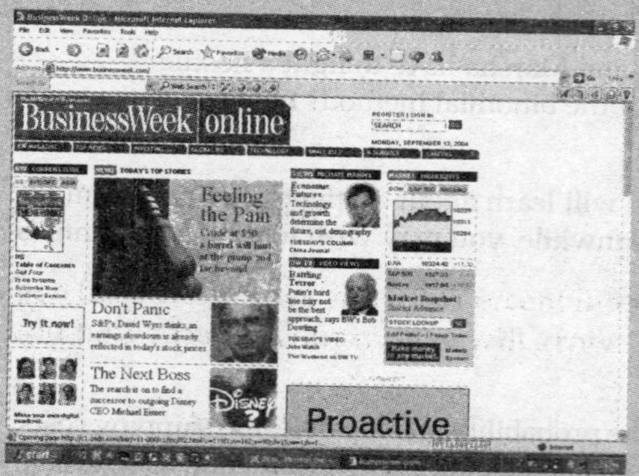

Chapter 12 describes how performance may be measured by EVA. Stern Stewart's site provides articles and data on EVA:

www.sternstewart.com

PART [3]

PRACTICAL PROBLEMS IN CAPITAL BUDGETING

EUROTUNNEL'S CONSTRUCTION OF a tunnel between England and France cost a record $15 billion. Before proceeding, the company developed cash-flow forecasts that indicated a satisfactory 14 percent return. Unfortunately, meticulous DCF calculations do not guarantee success. The tunnel proved more costly and took longer to build than anticipated. Also revenues were disappointing; 10 years after opening the tunnel, the company was still unable to earn enough to pay the interest on its debt. In exasperation a large group of shareholders rose up in revolt and sacked the entire board.

Of course, life is full of unpleasant surprises, but Part 3 shows how companies can take steps to minimize the chance that a project will turn out a loser. Chapter 10 describes how companies identify factors that could put a project below water. It also shows how firms build in the flexibility to expand if things go well, and cut back if disaster threatens.

Chapter 11 looks at how managers satisfy themselves that a project truly does have a positive NPV. They do not simply check the NPV calculations. They ask fundamental questions about the project. Does the firm have a strategic advantage or headstart over other firms? How will competitors react? Will their responses erode the project's profitability? For example, it seems likely that Eurotunnel's management underestimated just how sharply existing operators of channel ferries would cut their prices.

Finally, Chapter 12 shows how firms organize the investment process and provide managers and employees with the proper incentives to maximize firm value.

CHAPTER [10]

A PROJECT IS NOT A BLACK BOX

A back box is something that we accept and use but do not understand. For most of us a computer is a black box. We may know what it is supposed to do, but we do not understand how it works and, if something breaks, we cannot fix it.

We have been treating capital projects as black boxes. In other words, we have talked as if managers are handed unbiased cash-flow forecasts and their only task is to assess risk, choose the right discount rate, and crank out net present value. Actual financial managers will not rest until they understand what makes the project tick and what could go wrong with it. Remember Murphy's law, "If anything can go wrong, it will," and O'Reilly's corollary, "at the worst possible time."

Even if the project's risk is wholly diversifiable, you still need to understand why the venture could fail. Once you know that, you can decide whether it is worth trying to resolve the uncertainty. Maybe further expenditure on market research would clear up those doubts about acceptance by consumers, maybe another drill hole would give you a better idea of the size of the ore body, and maybe some further work on the test bed would confirm the durability of those welds. If the project really has a negative NPV, the sooner you can identify it, the better. And even if you decide that it is worth going ahead on the basis of present information, you do not want to be caught by surprise if things subsequently go wrong. You want to know the danger signals and the actions you might take.

We will show you how to use *sensitivity analysis, break-even analysis,* and *Monte Carlo simulation* to identify crucial assumptions and to explore what can go wrong. There is no magic in these techniques, just computer-assisted common sense. You do not need a license to use them.

Discounted-cash-flow analysis commonly assumes that companies hold assets passively, and it ignores the opportunities to expand the project if it is successful or to bail out if it is not. However, wise managers value these opportunities. They look for ways to capitalize on success and to reduce the costs of failure, and they are prepared to pay up for projects that give them this flexibility. Opportunities to modify projects as the future unfolds are known as *real options.* We describe several important real options, and we show how to use *decision trees* to set out these options' attributes and implications.

10.1 SENSITIVITY ANALYSIS

Uncertainty means that more things can happen than will happen. Whenever you are confronted with a cash-flow forecast, you should try to discover what else can happen.

Put yourself in the well-heeled shoes of the treasurer of the Otobai Company in Osaka, Japan. You are considering the introduction of an electrically powered motor scooter for city use. Your staff members have prepared the cash-flow forecasts shown in Table 10.1. Since NPV is positive at the 10 percent opportunity cost of capital, it appears to be worth going ahead.

$$\text{NPV} = -15 + \sum_{t=1}^{10} \frac{3}{(1.10)^t} = +\text{¥}3.43 \text{ billion}$$

TABLE 10.1

Preliminary cash-flow forecasts for Otobai's electric scooter project (figures in ¥ billions).

Assumptions:

1. Investment is depreciated over 10 years straight-line.
2. Income is taxed at a rate of 50 percent.

"Live" Excel versions of Tables 10.1 to 10.5 are available with this book's CD (included with the book at sale) and on the book's Web site, **www.mhhe.com/bmam8e.**

Please visit us at www.mhhe.com/bmam8e or refer to your Student CD .

		Year 0	Years 1-10
1.	Investment	15	
2.	Revenue		37.5
3.	Variable cost		30
4.	Fixed cost		3
5.	Depreciation		1.5
6.	Pretax Profit		3
7.	Tax		1.5
8.	Net profit		1.5
	Operating cash flow		3
	Net cash flow	-15	3

Before you decide, you want to delve into these forecasts and identify the key variables that determine whether the project succeeds or fails. It turns out that the marketing department has estimated revenue as follows:

$$\text{Unit sales} = \text{new product's share of market} \times \text{size of scooter market}$$
$$= .1 \times 1 \text{ million} = 100{,}000 \text{ scooters}$$

$$\text{Revenue} = \text{unit sales} \times \text{price per unit}$$
$$= 100{,}000 \times 375{,}000 = ¥37.5 \text{ billion}$$

The production department has estimated variable costs per unit as ¥300,000. Since projected volume is 100,000 scooters per year, total variable cost is ¥30 billion. Fixed costs are ¥3 billion per year. The initial investment can be depreciated on a straight-line basis over the 10-year period, and profits are taxed at a rate of 50 percent.

These seem to be the important things you need to know, but look out for unidentified variables. Perhaps there are patent problems, or perhaps you will need to invest in service stations that will recharge the scooter batteries. The greatest dangers often lie in these *unknown* unknowns, or "unk-unks," as scientists call them.

Having found no unk-unks (no doubt you will find them later), you conduct a **sensitivity analysis** with respect to market size, market share, and so on. To do this, the marketing and production staffs are asked to give optimistic and pessimistic estimates for the underlying variables. These are set out in the left-hand columns of Table 10.2. The right-hand side shows what happens to the project's net present value if the variables are set *one at a time* to their optimistic and pessimistic values. Your project appears to be by no means a sure thing. The most dangerous variables appear to be

	Range			NPV (billions of yen)		
Variable	Pessimistic	Expected	Optimistic	Pessimistic	Expected	Optimistic
Market size	.9 million	1 million	1.1 million	+1.1	+3.4	+5.7
Market share	.04	.1	.16	-10.4	+3.4	+17.3
Unit price	350,000 yen	375,000 yen	380,000 yen	-4.2	+3.4	+5.0
Unit variable cost	360,000 yen	300,000 yen	275,000 yen	-15.0	+3.4	+11.1
Fixed cost	4 billion yen	3 billion yen	2 billion yen	+.4	+3.4	+6.5

TABLE 10.2

To undertake a sensitivity analysis of the electric scooter project, we set each variable in turn at its most pessimistic or optimistic value and recalculate the NPV of the project.

excel

Please visit us at www.mhhe.com/bmam8e or refer to your Student CD

market share and unit variable cost. If market share is only .04 (and all other variables are as expected), then the project has an NPV of −¥10.4 billion. If unit variable cost is ¥360,000 (and all other variables are as expected), then the project has an NPV of −¥15 billion.

Value of Information

Now you can check whether you could resolve some of the uncertainty *before* your company parts with the ¥15 billion investment. Suppose that the pessimistic value for unit variable cost partly reflects the production department's worry that a particular machine will not work as designed and that the operation will have to be performed by other methods at an extra cost of ¥20,000 per unit. The chance that this will occur is only 1 in 10. But, if it does occur, the extra ¥20,000 unit cost will reduce after-tax cash flow by

$$\text{Unit sales} \times \text{additional unit cost} \times (1 - \text{tax rate})$$
$$= 100{,}000 \times 20{,}000 \times .50 = \text{¥}1 \text{ billion}$$

It would reduce the NPV of your project by

$$\sum_{t=1}^{10} \frac{1}{(1.10)^t} = \text{¥}6.14 \text{ billion},$$

putting the NPV of the scooter project underwater at +3.43 − 6.14 = −¥2.71 billion.

Suppose further that a ¥10 million pretest of the machine will reveal whether it will work and allow you to clear up the problem. It clearly pays to invest ¥10 million to avoid a 10 percent probability of a ¥6.14 billion fall in NPV. You are ahead by −10 + .10 × 6,140 = +¥604 million.

On the other hand, the value of additional information about market size is small. Because the project is acceptable even under pessimistic assumptions about market size, you are unlikely to be in trouble if you have misestimated that variable.

Limits to Sensitivity Analysis

Sensitivity analysis boils down to expressing cash flows in terms of key project variables and then calculating the consequences of misestimating the variables. It forces the manager to identify the underlying variables, indicates where additional information would be most useful, and helps to expose confused or inappropriate forecasts.

One drawback to sensitivity analysis is that it always gives somewhat ambiguous results. For example, what exactly does *optimistic* or *pessimistic* mean? The marketing department may be interpreting the terms in a different way from the production department. Ten years from now, after hundreds of projects, hindsight may show that the marketing department's pessimistic limit was exceeded twice as often as the production department's; but what you may discover 10 years hence is no help now. Of course, you could specify that, when you use the terms "pessimistic" and "optimistic," you mean that there is only a 10 percent chance that the actual value will prove to be worse than the pessimistic figure or better than the optimistic one. However, it is far from easy to extract a forecaster's notion of the true probabilities of possible outcomes.[1]

Another problem with sensitivity analysis is that the underlying variables are likely to be interrelated. What sense does it make to look at the effect in isolation of an increase in market size? If market size exceeds expectations, it is likely that demand will be stronger than you anticipated and unit prices will be higher. And why look in isolation at the effect of an increase in price? If inflation pushes prices to the upper end of your range, it is quite probable that costs will also be inflated.

Sometimes the analyst can get around these problems by defining underlying variables so that they are roughly independent. But you cannot push *one-at-a-time* sensitivity analysis too far. It is impossible to obtain expected, optimistic, and pessimistic values for total *project* cash flows from the information in Table 10.2.

Scenario Analysis

If the variables are interrelated, it may help to consider some alternative plausible scenarios. For example, perhaps the company economist is worried about the possibility of another sharp rise in world oil prices. The direct effect of this would be to encourage the use of electrically powered transportation. The popularity of compact cars after the oil price increases in 2004 leads you to estimate that an immediate 20 percent price rise in oil would enable you to capture an extra 3 percent of the scooter market. On the other hand, the economist also believes that higher oil prices would prompt a world recession and at the same time stimulate inflation. In that case, market size might be in the region of .8 million scooters and both prices and cost might be 15 percent higher than your initial estimates. Table 10.3 shows that this scenario of higher oil prices and recession would on balance help your new venture. Its NPV would increase to ¥6.5 billion.

Managers often find **scenario analysis** helpful. It allows them to look at different but *consistent* combinations of variables. Forecasters generally prefer to give an estimate of revenues or costs under a particular scenario than to give some absolute optimistic or pessimistic value.

---

[1] If you doubt this, try some simple experiments. Ask the person who repairs your television to state a numerical probability that your set will work for at least one more year. Or construct your own subjective probability distribution of the number of telephone calls you will receive next week. That ought to be easy. Try it.

		Cash Flows, Years 1-10, billions of yen	
		Base Case	High Oil Prices and Recession Case
1.	Revenue	37.5	44.9
2.	Variable cost	30.0	35.9
3.	Fixed cost	3.0	3.5
4.	Depreciation	1.5	1.5
5.	Pretax Profit (1 - 2 - 3 - 4)	3.0	4.0
6.	Tax	1.5	2.0
7.	Net profit (5 - 6)	1.5	2.0
8.	Net cash flow (4 + 7)	3.0	3.5
	PV of cash flows	+18.4	+21.5
	NPV	+3.4	+6.5
		Assumptions	
		Base Case	High Oil Prices and Recession Case
	Market size	1 million	.8 million
	Market share	.1	.13
	Unit price	375,000 yen	431,300 yen
	Unit variable cost	300,000 yen	345,000 yen
	Fixed cost	3 billion yen	3.5 billion yen

TABLE 10.3

How the NPV of the electric scooter project would be affected by higher oil prices and a world recession.

eXcel

Please visit us at www.mhhe.com/bmam8e or refer to your Student CD .

Break-Even Analysis

When we undertake a sensitivity analysis of a project or when we look at alternative scenarios, we are asking how serious it would be if sales or costs turned out to be worse than we forecasted. Managers sometimes prefer to rephrase this question and ask how bad sales can get before the project begins to lose money. This exercise is known as **break-even analysis.**[2]

In the left-hand portion of Table 10.4 we set out the revenues and costs of the electric scooter project under different assumptions about annual sales.[3] In the right-hand portion of the table we discount these revenues and costs to give the *present value* of the inflows and the *present value* of the outflows. Net present value is of course the difference between these numbers.

You can see that NPV is strongly negative if the company does not produce a single scooter. It is just positive if (as expected) the company sells 100,000 scooters and is strongly positive if it sells 200,000. Clearly the *zero*-NPV point occurs at a little under 100,000 scooters.

[2]For an excellent case study of break-even analysis see U. E. Reinhardt, "Break-Even Analysis for Lockheed's TriStar: An Application of Financial Theory," *Journal of Finance* 28 (September 1973), pp. 821–838.

[3]Notice that if the project makes a loss, this loss can be used to reduce the tax bill on the rest of the company's business. In this case the project produces a tax saving—the tax outflow is negative.

	Inflows	Outflows							
		Year 0	Years 1-10						
Unit Sales, Thousands	Revenues, Years 1-10	Investment	Variable Costs	Fixed Costs	Taxes	PV Inflows	PV Outflows	NPV
0	0	15	0	3	-2.25	0	19.6	-19.6
100	37.5	15	30	3	1.5	230.4	227.0	3.4
200	75.0	15	60	3	5.25	460.8	434.4	26.5

excel

Please visit us at www.mhhe.com/bmam8e or refer to your Student CD.

TABLE 10.4

NPV of electric scooter project under different assumptions about unit sales (figures in ¥ billions except as noted).

FIGURE 10.1

A break-even chart showing the present values of Otobai's cash inflows and outflows under different assumptions about unit sales. NPV is zero when sales are 85,000.

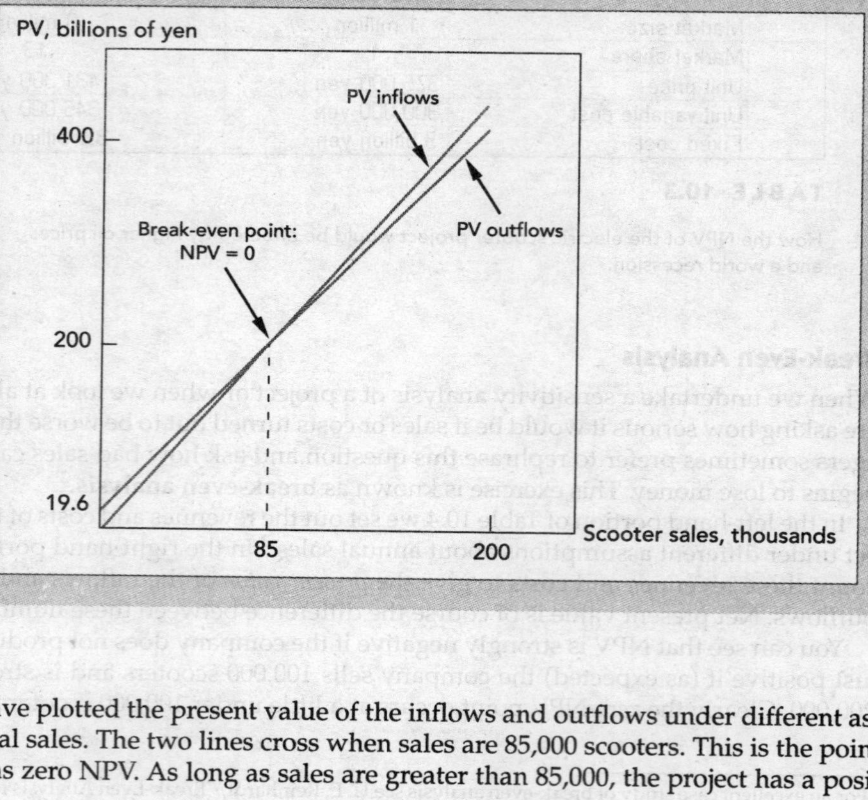

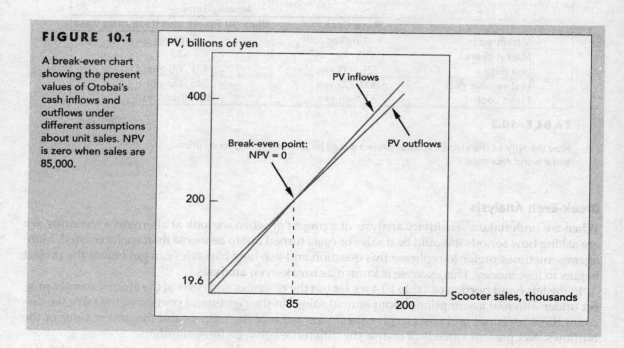

In Figure 10.1 we have plotted the present value of the inflows and outflows under different assumptions about annual sales. The two lines cross when sales are 85,000 scooters. This is the point at which the project has zero NPV. As long as sales are greater than 85,000, the project has a positive NPV.[4]

Managers frequently calculate break-even points in terms of accounting profits rather than present values. Table 10.5 shows Otobai's after-tax profits at three levels of scooter sales. Figure 10.2 once again plots revenues and costs against sales. But the story this time is different. Figure 10.2,

[4]We could also calculate break-even sales by plotting equivalent annual costs and revenues. Of course, the break-even point would be identical at 85,000 scooters.

Unit Sales, Thousands	Revenues	Variable Costs	Fixed Costs	Depreciation	Taxes	Total Costs	Profit after Tax
0	0	0	3	1.5	-2.25	2.25	-2.25
100	37.5	30	3	1.5	1.5	36.0	1.5
200	75.0	60	3	1.5	5.25	69.75	5.25

TABLE 10.5

The electric scooter project's accounting profit under different assumptions about unit sales (figures in ¥ billions except as noted).

excel

Please visit us at www.mhhe.com/bmam8e or refer to your Student CD.

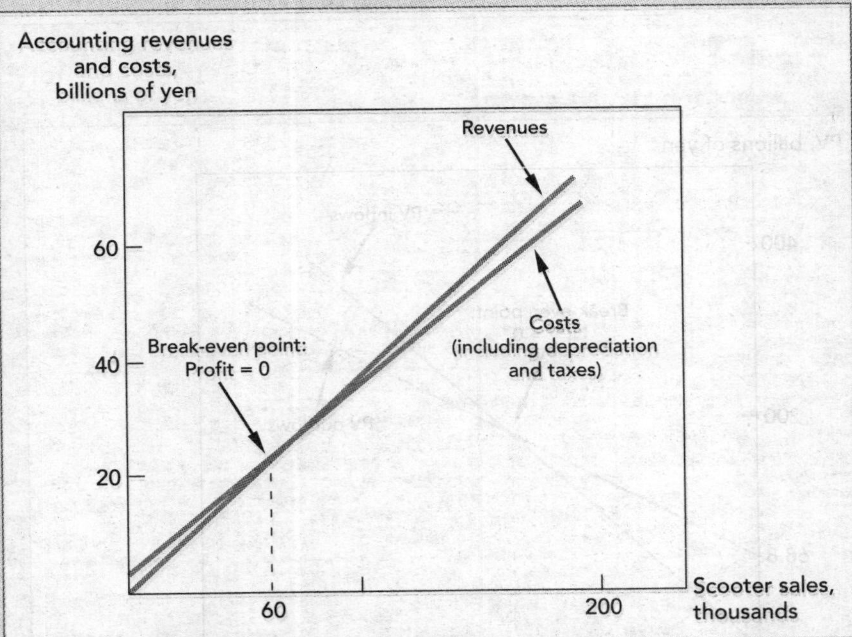

FIGURE 10.2

Sometimes break-even charts are constructed in terms of accounting numbers. After-tax profit is zero when sales are 60,000.

which is based on accounting profits, suggests a break-even of 60,000 scooters. Figure 10.1, which is based on present values, shows a break-even at 85,000 scooters. Why the difference?

When we work in terms of accounting profit, we deduct depreciation of ¥1.5 billion each year to cover the cost of the initial investment. If Otobai sells 60,000 scooters a year, revenues will be sufficient both to pay operating costs and to recover the initial outlay of ¥15 billion. But they will *not* be sufficient to repay the *opportunity cost of capital* on that ¥15 billion.

Operating Leverage and Break-Even Points

Break-even charts like Figure 10.1 help managers appreciate *operating leverage,* that is, project exposure to fixed costs. High operating leverage means high risk, other things equal, of course.

TABLE 10.6

Cash-flow forecasts and NPV for the electric scooter project, here assuming a production technology with high fixed costs but low total costs (figures in ¥ billions). Compare Table 10.1.

	Year 0	Years 1–10
Investment	15	
1. Revenue		37.5
2. Variable cost		12.0
3. Fixed cost		19.0
4. Depreciation		1.5
5. Pretax profit (1 − 2 − 3 − 4)		5.0
6. Tax		2.5
7. Net profit (5 − 6)		2.5
8. Operating cash flow (4 + 7)		4.0
Net cash flow	−15	+4.0

$$NPV = -15 + \sum_{t=1}^{10} \frac{4.0}{(1.1)^t} = +¥9.6 \text{ billion}$$

FIGURE 10.3

Break-even chart for an alternative production technology with higher fixed costs. Notice that break-even sales increase to 88,000. Compare Figure 10.1.

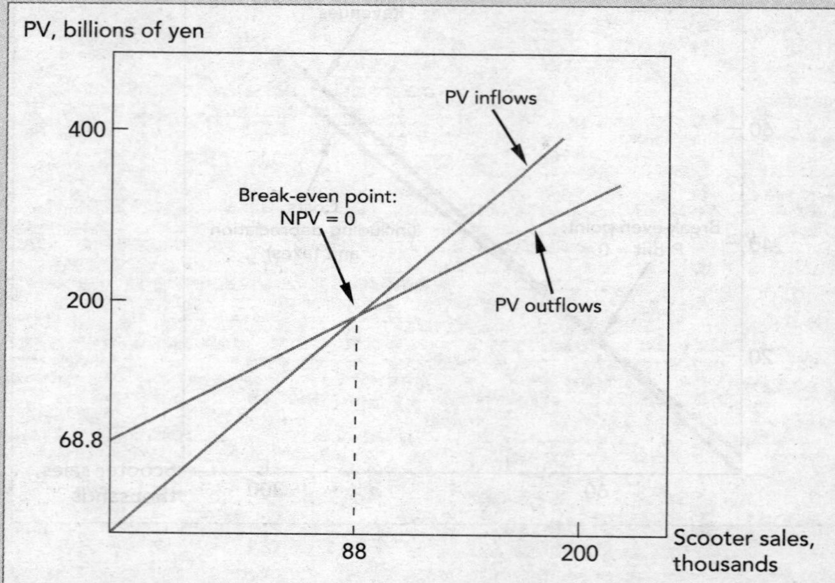

The electric scooter project had low fixed costs, only ¥3 billion against projected revenues of ¥37.5 billion. But suppose Otobai now considers a different production technology with lower variable costs of only ¥120,000 per unit (versus ¥300,000 per unit) but higher fixed costs of ¥19 billion. Total forecasted production costs are lower (12 + 19 = ¥31 billion versus ¥33 billion), so profitability improves—compare Table 10.6 to Table 10.1. Project NPV apparently increases to ¥9.6 billion.

Figure 10.3 is the new break-even chart. Break-even sales have *increased* to 88,000 (that's bad), even though total production costs have *fallen*. A new sensitivity analysis would show that project NPV is much more exposed to changes in market size, market share, or unit price. All of these differences can be traced to the higher fixed costs of the alternative production technology.

Is the alternative technology better than the original one? The financial manager would have to consider the alternative technology's higher business risk, and perhaps recompute NPV at a higher discount rate, before making a final decision.[5]

10.2 MONTE CARLO SIMULATION

Sensitivity analysis allows you to consider the effect of changing one variable at a time. By looking at the project under alternative scenarios, you can consider the effect of a *limited number* of plausible combinations of variables. **Monte Carlo simulation** is a tool for considering *all* possible combinations. It therefore enables you to inspect the entire distribution of project outcomes.

Imagine that you are a gambler at Monte Carlo. You know nothing about the laws of probability (few casual gamblers do), but a friend has suggested to you a complicated strategy for playing roulette. Your friend has not actually tested the strategy but is confident that it will *on the average* give you a 2½ percent return for every 50 spins of the wheel. Your friend's optimistic estimate for any series of 50 spins is a profit of 55 percent; your friend's pessimistic estimate is a loss of 50 percent. How can you find out whether these really are the odds? An easy but possibly expensive way is to start playing and record the outcome at the end of each series of 50 spins. After, say, 100 series of 50 spins each, plot a frequency distribution of the outcomes and calculate the average and upper and lower limits. If things look good, you can then get down to some serious gambling.

An alternative is to tell a computer to simulate the roulette wheel and the strategy. In other words, you could instruct the computer to draw numbers out of its hat to determine the outcome of each spin of the wheel and then to calculate how much you would make or lose from the particular gambling strategy.

That would be an example of Monte Carlo simulation. In capital budgeting we replace the gambling strategy with a model of the project, and the roulette wheel with a model of the world in which the project operates. Let us see how this might work with our project for an electrically powered scooter.

Simulating the Electric Scooter Project

Step 1: Modeling the Project The first step in any simulation is to give the computer a precise model of the project. For example, the sensitivity analysis of the scooter project was based on the following implicit model of cash flow:

$$\text{Cash flow} = (\text{revenues} - \text{costs} - \text{depreciation}) \times (1 - \text{tax rate}) + \text{depreciation}$$

$$\text{Revenues} = \text{market size} \times \text{market share} \times \text{unit price}$$

$$\text{Costs} = (\text{market size} \times \text{market share} \times \text{variable unit cost}) + \text{fixed cost}$$

This model of the project was all that you needed for the simpleminded sensitivity analysis that we described above. But if you wish to simulate the whole project, you need to think about how the variables are interrelated.

[5] He or she could use the procedures outlined in Section 9.3 to recalculate beta and come up with a new discount rate.

For example, consider the first variable—market size. The marketing department has estimated a market size of 1 million scooters in the first year of the project's life, but of course you do not know how things will work out. Actual market size will exceed or fall short of expectations by the amount of the department's forecast error:

$$\text{Market size, year 1} = \text{expected market size, year 1} \times (1 + \text{forecast error, year 1})$$

You *expect* the forecast error to be zero, but it could turn out to be positive or negative. Suppose, for example, that the actual market size turns out to be 1.1 million. That means a forecast error of 10 percent, or +.1:

$$\text{Market size, year 1} = 1 \times (1 + .1) = 1.1 \text{ million}$$

You can write the market size in the second year in exactly the same way:

$$\text{Market size, year 2} = \text{expected market size, year 2} \times (1 + \text{forecast error, year 2})$$

But at this point you must consider how the expected market size in year 2 is affected by what happens in year 1. If scooter sales are below expectations in year 1, it is likely that they will continue to be below in subsequent years. Suppose that a shortfall in sales in year 1 would lead you to revise down your forecast of sales in year 2 by a like amount. Then

$$\text{Expected market size, year 2} = \text{actual market size, year 1}$$

Now you can rewrite the market size in year 2 in terms of the actual market size in the previous year plus a forecast error:

$$\text{Market size, year 2} = \text{market size, year 1} \times (1 + \text{forecast error, year 2})$$

In the same way you can describe the expected market size in year 3 in terms of market size in year 2 and so on.

This set of equations illustrates how you can describe interdependence between different *periods*. But you also need to allow for interdependence between different *variables*. For example, the price of electrically powered scooters is likely to increase with market size. Suppose that this is the only uncertainty and that a 10 percent shortfall in market size would lead you to predict a 3 percent reduction in price. Then you could model the first year's price as follows:

$$\text{Price, year 1} = \text{expected price, year 1} \times (1 + .3 \times \text{error in market size forecast, year 1})$$

Then, if variations in market size exert a permanent effect on price, you can define the second year's price as

$$\begin{aligned}\text{Price, year 2} &= \text{expected price, year 2} \times (1 + .3 \times \text{error in market size forecast, year 2}) \\ &= \text{actual price, year 1} \times (1 + .3 \times \text{error in market size forecast, year 2})\end{aligned}$$

Notice how we have linked each period's selling price to the *actual* selling prices (including forecast error) in all previous periods. We used the same type of linkage for market size. These linkages mean that forecast errors accumulate; they do not cancel out over time. Thus, uncertainty *increases* with time: The farther out you look into the future, the more the actual price or market size may depart from your original forecast.

The complete model of your project would include a set of equations for each of the variables: market size, price, market share, unit variable cost, and fixed cost. Even if you allowed for only a few interdependencies between variables and across time, the result would be quite a complex list of equations.[6] Perhaps that is not a bad thing if it forces you to understand what the project is all about. Model building is like spinach: You may not like the taste, but it is good for you.

Step 2: Specifying Probabilities Remember the procedure for simulating the gambling strategy? The first step was to specify the strategy, the second was to specify the numbers on the roulette wheel, and the third was to tell the computer to select these numbers at random and calculate the results of the strategy:

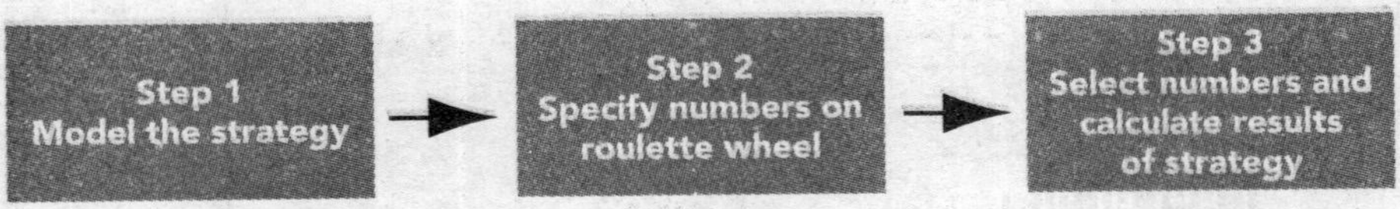

The steps are just the same for your scooter project:

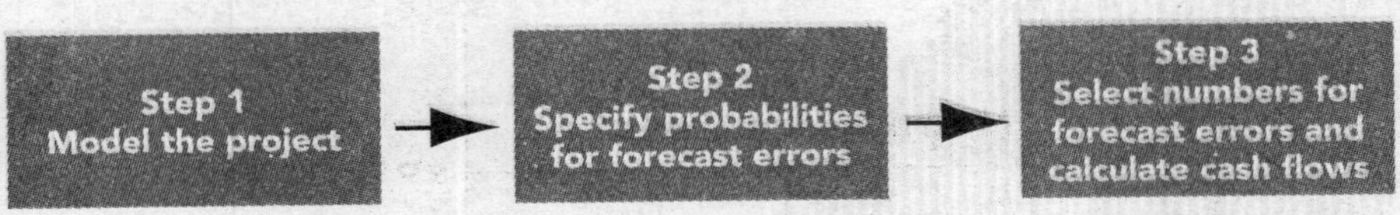

Think about how you might go about specifying your possible errors in forecasting market size. You *expect* market size to be 1 million scooters. You obviously don't think that you are underestimating or overestimating, so the expected forecast error is zero. On the other hand, the marketing department has given you a range of possible estimates. Market size could be as low as .85 million scooters or as high as 1.15 million scooters. Thus the forecast error has an expected value of 0 and a range of plus or minus 15 percent. If the marketing department has in fact given you the lowest and highest possible outcomes, actual market size should fall somewhere within this range with near certainty.[7]

That takes care of market size; now you need to draw up similar estimates of the possible forecast errors for each of the other variables that are in your model.

Step 3: Simulate the Cash Flows The computer now *samples* from the distribution of the forecast errors, calculates the resulting cash flows for each period, and records them. After many iterations you begin to get accurate estimates of the probability distributions of the project cash flows—accurate, that is, only to the extent that your model and the probability distributions of the forecast errors are accurate. Remember the GIGO principle: "Garbage in, garbage out."

Figure 10.4 shows part of the output from an actual simulation of the electric scooter project.[8] Note the positive skewness of the outcomes—very large outcomes are more likely than very small

[6]Specifying the interdependencies is the hardest and most important part of a simulation. If all components of project cash flows were unrelated, simulation would rarely be necessary.

[7]Suppose "near certainty" means "99 percent of the time." If forecast errors are normally distributed, this degree of certainty requires a range of plus or minus three standard deviations.

Other distributions could, of course, be used. For example, the marketing department may view any market size between .85 and 1.15 million scooters as *equally likely*. In that case the simulation would require a uniform (rectangular) distribution of forecast errors.

[8]These are actual outputs from Crystal Ball™ software. The simulation assumed annual forecast errors were normally distributed and ran through 10,000 trials. We thank Christopher Howe for running the simulation. An Excel program to simulate the Otobai project was kindly provided by Marek Jochec, and is available on the CD that accompanies the book and on the Web site, **www.mhhe.com/bmam8e.**

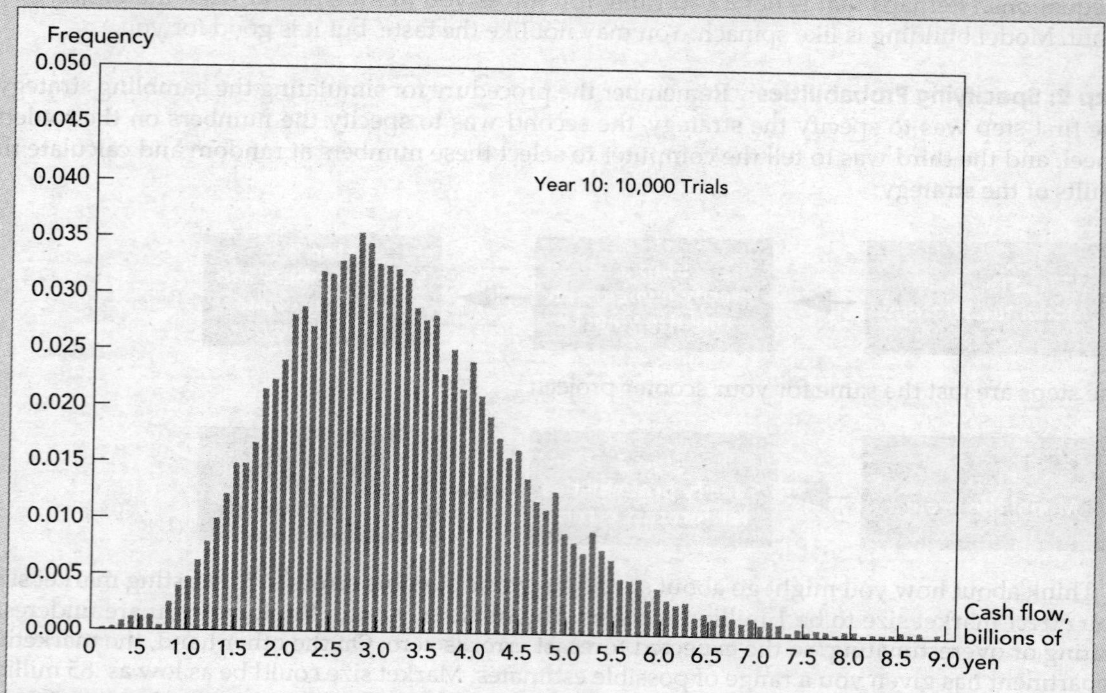

FIGURE 10.4

Simulation of cash flows for year 10 of the electric scooter project.

ones. This is common when forecast errors accumulate over time. Because of the skewness the average cash flow is somewhat higher than the most likely outcome; in other words, a bit to the right of the peak of the distribution.[9]

Step 4: Calculate Present Value The distributions of project cash flows should allow you to calculate the expected cash flows more accurately. In the final step you need to discount these expected cash flows to find present value.

Simulation of Pharmaceutical Research and Development

Simulation, though sometimes costly and complicated, has the obvious merit of compelling the forecaster to face up to uncertainty and to interdependencies. Once you have set up your simulation model, it is a simple matter to analyze the principal sources of uncertainty in the cash flows and to see how much you could reduce this uncertainty by improving the forecasts of sales or costs. You may also be able to explore the effect of possible modifications to the project.

[9]When you are working with cash-flow forecasts, bear in mind the distinction between the expected value and the most likely (or modal) value. Present values are based on *expected* cash flows—that is, the probability-weighted average of the possible future cash flows. If the distribution of possible outcomes is skewed to the right as in Figure 10.4, the expected cash flow will be greater than the most likely cash flow.

Several large pharmaceutical companies have used Monte Carlo simulation to analyze investments in research and development (R&D) of new drugs. Only a small fraction of drug candidates identified in basic research prove effective and achieve profitable production. At each phase of R&D, the company must decide whether to press on to the next phase or halt. The pharmaceutical companies face two kinds of uncertainty:

1. *Will the compound work?* Will it have harmful side effects? Will it ultimately gain FDA approval? (Most drugs do not: Of 10,000 promising compounds, only 1 or 2 may ever get to market. The 1 or 2 that are marketed have to generate enough cash flow to make up for the 9,999 or 9,998 that fail.)
2. *Market success.* FDA approval does not guarantee that a drug will sell. A competitor may be there first with a similar (or better) drug. The company may or may not be able to sell the drug worldwide. Selling prices and marketing costs are unknown.

Imagine that you are contemplating a research program that will investigate a promising class of compounds. Could you write down the expected cash inflows and outflows of the program up to 25 or 30 years in the future? We suggest that no mortal could do so without a model to help; simulation may provide the answer.[10]

Simulation may sound like a panacea for the world's ills, but, as usual, you pay for what you get. Sometimes you pay for more than you get. It is not just a matter of the time and money spent in building the model. It is extremely difficult to estimate interrelationships between variables and the underlying probability distributions, even when you are trying to be honest.[11] But in capital budgeting, forecasters are seldom completely impartial and the probability distributions on which simulations are based can be highly biased.

In practice, a simulation that attempts to be realistic will also be complex. Therefore the decision maker may delegate the task of constructing the model to management scientists or consultants. The danger here is that, even if the builders understand their creation, the decision maker cannot and therefore does not rely on it. This is a common but ironic experience: The model that was intended to open up black boxes ends up creating another one.

10.3 REAL OPTIONS AND DECISION TREES

If financial managers treat projects as black boxes, they may be tempted to think only of the first accept–reject decision and to ignore the subsequent investment decisions that may be tied to it. But if subsequent investment decisions depend on those made today, then today's decision may depend on what you plan to do tomorrow.

[10] N. A. Nichols, "Scientific Management at Merck: An Interview with CFO Judy Lewent," *Harvard Business Review* 72 (January–February 1994), p. 91.

[11] These difficulties are less severe for the pharmaceutical industry than for most other industries. Pharmaceutical companies have accumulated a great deal of information on the probabilities of scientific and clinical success and on the time and money required for clinical testing and FDA approval.

When you use discounted cash flow (DCF) to value a project, you implicitly assume that the firm will hold the assets passively. But managers are not paid to be dummies. After they have invested in a new project, they do not simply sit back and watch the future unfold. If things go well, the project may be expanded; if they go badly, the project may be cut back or abandoned altogether. Projects that can easily be modified in these ways are more valuable than those that do not provide such flexibility. The more uncertain the outlook, the more valuable this flexibility becomes.

That sounds obvious, but notice that sensitivity analysis and Monte Carlo simulation do not recognize the opportunity to modify projects.[12] For example, think back to the Otobai electric scooter project. In real life, if things go wrong with the project, Otobai would abandon to cut its losses. If so, the worst outcomes would not be as devastating as our sensitivity analysis and simulation suggested.

Options to modify projects are known as **real options.** Managers may not always use the term real option to describe these opportunities; for example, they may refer to "intangible advantages" of easy-to-modify projects. But when they review major investment proposals, these option intangibles are often the key to their decisions.

The Option to Expand

In 2000 FedEx placed an order for 10 Airbus A380 superjumbo transport planes for delivery in the years 2008–2011. Each flight of an A380 freighter will be capable of making a 200,000 pound dent in the massive volume of goods that FedEx carries each day, so the decision could have a huge impact on FedEx's worldwide business. If FedEx's long-haul airfreight business continues to expand and the superjumbo is efficient and reliable, the company will need more superjumbos. But it cannot be sure they will be needed.

Rather than placing further firm orders in 2000, FedEx secured a place in the Airbus production line by acquiring *options* to buy a "substantial number" of additional aircraft at a predetermined price. These options do not commit the company to expand but give it the flexibility to do so.

Figure 10.5 displays FedEx's expansion option as a simple **decision tree.** You can think of it as a game between FedEx and fate. Each square represents an action or decision by the company. Each circle represents an outcome revealed by fate. In this case there is only one outcome in 2007,[13] when fate reveals the airfreight demand and FedEx's capacity needs. FedEx then decides whether to exercise its options and buy additional A380s. Here the future decision is easy: Buy the airplanes only if demand is high and the company can operate them profitably. If demand is low, FedEx walks away and leaves Airbus with the problem of selling the planes that were reserved for FedEx to some other customer.

You can probably think of many other investments that take on added value because of the further options they provide. For example

- When launching a new product, companies often start with a pilot program to iron out possible design problems and to test the market. The company can evaluate the pilot and then decide whether to expand to full-scale production.

[12] Some simulation models *do* recognize the possibility of changing policy. For example, when a pharmaceutical company uses simulation to analyze its R&D decisions, it allows for the possibility that the company can abandon the development at each phase.

[13] We assume that FedEx can wait until 2007 to decide whether to acquire the additional planes.

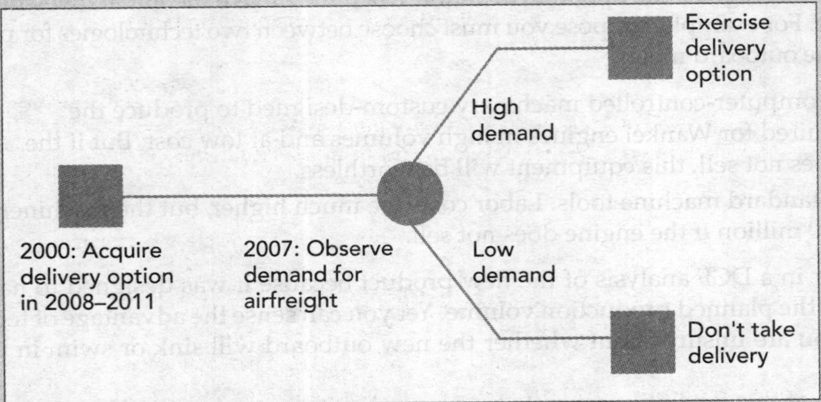

FIGURE 10.5

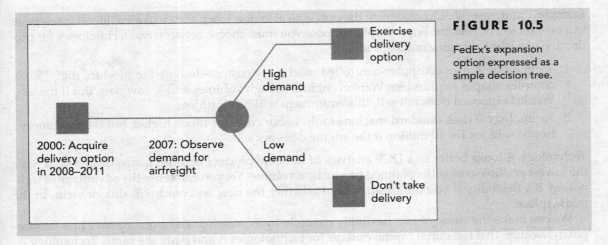

FedEx's expansion option expressed as a simple decision tree.

- When designing a factory, it can make sense to provide extra land or floor space to reduce the future cost of a second production line.
- When building a four-lane highway, it may pay to build six-lane bridges so that the road can be converted later to six lanes if traffic volumes turn out to be higher than expected.

Such options to expand do not show up in the assets that the company lists in its balance sheet, but investors are very aware of their existence. If a company has valuable real options that can allow it to invest in new profitable projects, its market value will be higher than the value of its physical assets now in place.

In Chapter 4 we showed how the present value of growth opportunities (PVGO) contributes to the value of a company's common stock. PVGO equals the forecasted total NPV of future investments. But it is better to think of PVGO as the value of the firm's *options* to invest and expand. The firm is not obliged to grow. It can invest more if the number of positive-NPV projects turns out high or slow down if that number turns out low. The flexibility to adapt investment to future opportunities is one of the factors that makes PVGO so valuable.

The Option to Abandon

If the option to expand has value, what about the decision to bail out? Projects do not just go on until assets expire of old age. The decision to terminate a project is usually taken by management, not by nature. Once the project is no longer profitable, the company will cut its losses and exercise its option to abandon the project.

Some assets are easier to bail out of than others. Tangible assets are usually easier to sell than intangible ones. It helps to have active secondhand markets, which really exist only for standardized items. Real estate, airplanes, trucks, and certain machine tools are likely to be relatively easy to sell. On the other hand, the knowledge accumulated by a software company's research and development program is a specialized intangible asset and probably would not have significant abandonment value. (Some assets, such as old mattresses, even have *negative* abandonment value; you have to pay to get rid of them. It is costly to decommission nuclear power plants or to reclaim land that has been strip-mined.)

Example Managers should recognize the option to abandon when they make the initial investment in a new project or venture. For example, suppose you must choose between two technologies for production of a Wankel-engine outboard motor.

1. Technology A uses computer-controlled machinery custom-designed to produce the complex shapes required for Wankel engines in high volumes and at low cost. But if the Wankel outboard does not sell, this equipment will be worthless.
2. Technology B uses standard machine tools. Labor costs are much higher, but the machinery can be sold for Rs. 10 million if the engine does not sell.

Technology A looks better in a DCF analysis of the new product because it was designed to have the lowest possible cost at the planned production volume. Yet you can sense the advantage of technology B's flexibility if you are unsure about whether the new outboard will sink or swim in the marketplace.

We can make the value of this flexibility concrete by expressing it as a real option. Just for simplicity, assume that the initial capital outlays for technologies A and B are the same. Technology A, with its low-cost customized machinery, will provide a payoff of Rs. 18.5 million if the outboard is popular with boat owners and Rs. 8.5 million if it is not. Think of these payoffs as the project's cash flow in its first year of production plus the present value of all subsequent cash flows. The corresponding payoffs to technology B are Rs. 18 million and Rs. 8 million.

	Payoffs from Producing Outboard (Rs. millions)	
	Technology A	**Technology B**
Buoyant demand	Rs. 18.5	Rs. 18
Sluggish demand	8.5	8

If you are obliged to continue in production regardless of how unprofitable the project turns out to be, then technology A is clearly the superior choice. But remember that at year-end you can bail out of technology B for Rs. 10 million. If the outboard is not a success in the market, you are better off selling the plant and equipment for Rs. 10 million than continuing with a project that has a present value of only Rs. 8 million.

Figure 10.6 summarizes this example as a decision tree. The abandonment option occurs at the right-hand boxes for Technology B. The decisions are obvious: continue if demand is buoyant, abandon otherwise. Thus the payoffs to Technology B are:

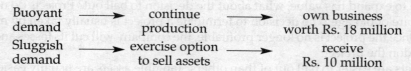

Buoyant demand	→	continue production	→	own business worth Rs. 18 million
Sluggish demand	→	exercise option to sell assets	→	receive Rs. 10 million

Technology B provides an insurance policy: If the outboard's sales are disappointing, you can abandon the project and recover Rs. 10 million. You can think of this abandonment option as an option to sell the assets for Rs. 10 million. The total value of the project using technology B is its DCF value, assuming that the company does not abandon, *plus* the value of the abandonment option. When you value this option, you are placing a value on flexibility.

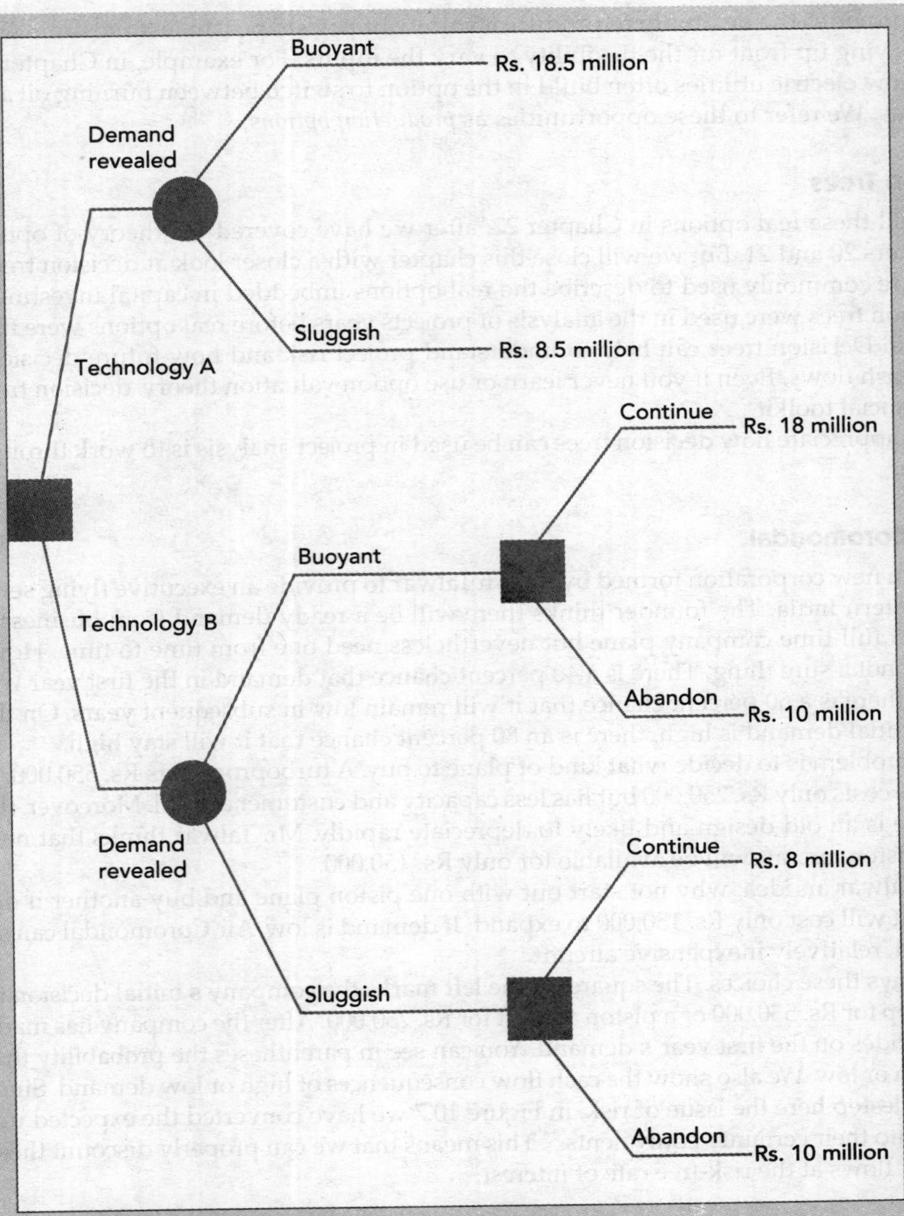

FIGURE 10.6

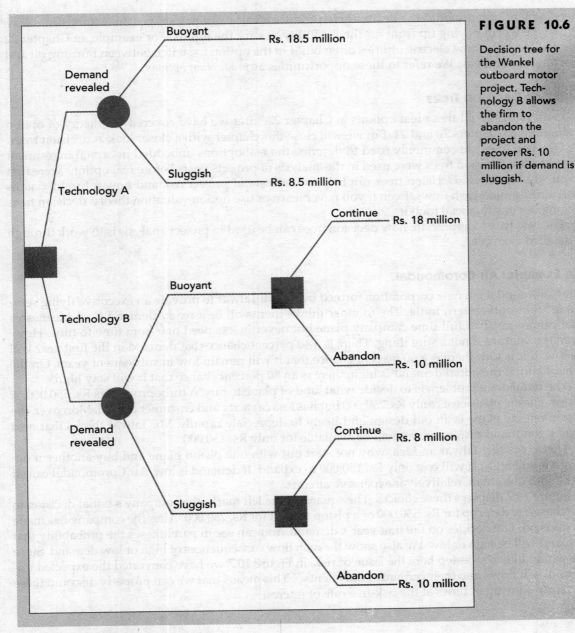

Decision tree for the Wankel outboard motor project. Technology B allows the firm to abandon the project and recover Rs. 10 million if demand is sluggish.

Two Other Real Options

These are not the only real options. For example, companies with positive-NPV projects are not obliged to undertake them right away. If the outlook is uncertain, you may be able to avoid a costly mistake by waiting a bit. Such options to postpone investment are called *timing options*.

When companies undertake new investments, they generally think about the possibility that at a later stage they may wish to modify the project. After all, today everybody may be demanding round pegs, but, who knows, tomorrow square ones could be all the rage. In that case you need a plant that provides the flexibility to produce a variety of peg shapes. In just the same way, it may be worth paying up front for the flexibility to vary the inputs. For example, in Chapter 22 we will describe how electric utilities often build in the option to switch between burning oil and burning natural gas. We refer to these opportunities as *production options*.

More on Decision Trees

We will return to all these real options in Chapter 22, after we have covered the theory of option valuation in Chapters 20 and 21. But we will close this chapter with a closer look at decision trees.

Decision trees are commonly used to describe the real options imbedded in capital investment projects. But decision trees were used in the analysis of projects years before real options were first explicitly identified. Decision trees can help to understand project risk and how future decisions will affect project cash flows. Even if you never learn or use option valuation theory, decision trees belong in your financial toolkit.

The best way to appreciate how decision trees can be used in project analysis is to work through a detailed example.

An Example: Air Coromondal

Air Coromondal is a new corporation formed by Rajesh Talwar to provide an executive flying service for the southeastern India. The founder thinks there will be a ready demand from businesses that cannot justify a full-time company plane but nevertheless need one from time to time. However, the venture is not a sure thing. There is a 40 percent chance that demand in the first year will be low. If it is low, there is a 60 percent chance that it will remain low in subsequent years. On the other hand, if the initial demand is high, there is an 80 percent chance that it will stay high.

The immediate problem is to decide what kind of plane to buy. A turboprop costs Rs. 550,000. A piston-engine plane costs only Rs. 250,000 but has less capacity and customer appeal. Moreover, the piston-engine plane is an old design and likely to depreciate rapidly. Mr. Talwar thinks that next year secondhand piston aircraft will be available for only Rs. 150,000.

That gives Mr. Talwar an idea: why not start out with one piston plane and buy another if demand is still high? It will cost only Rs. 150,000 to expand. If demand is low, Air Coromondal can sit tight with one small, relatively inexpensive aircraft.

Figure 10.7 displays these choices. The square on the left marks the company's initial decision to purchase a turboprop for Rs. 550,000 or a piston aircraft for Rs. 250,000. After the company has made its decision, fate decides on the first year's demand. You can see in parentheses the probability that demand will be high or low. We also show the cash flow consequences of high or low demand. Since we would like to sidestep here the issue of risk, in Figure 10.7 we have converted the expected uncertain cash flows into their certainty equivalents.[14] This means that we can properly discount these certainty-equivalent flows at the risk-free rate of interest.

[14]Certainty-equivalent cash flows are the sure-fire cash flows that would have the same present value as the actual uncertain flows. We described certainty-equivalent flows in Chapter 9 and showed how they can be used to calculate present values. We will use them in Chapters 21 and 22, when we show how to value options.

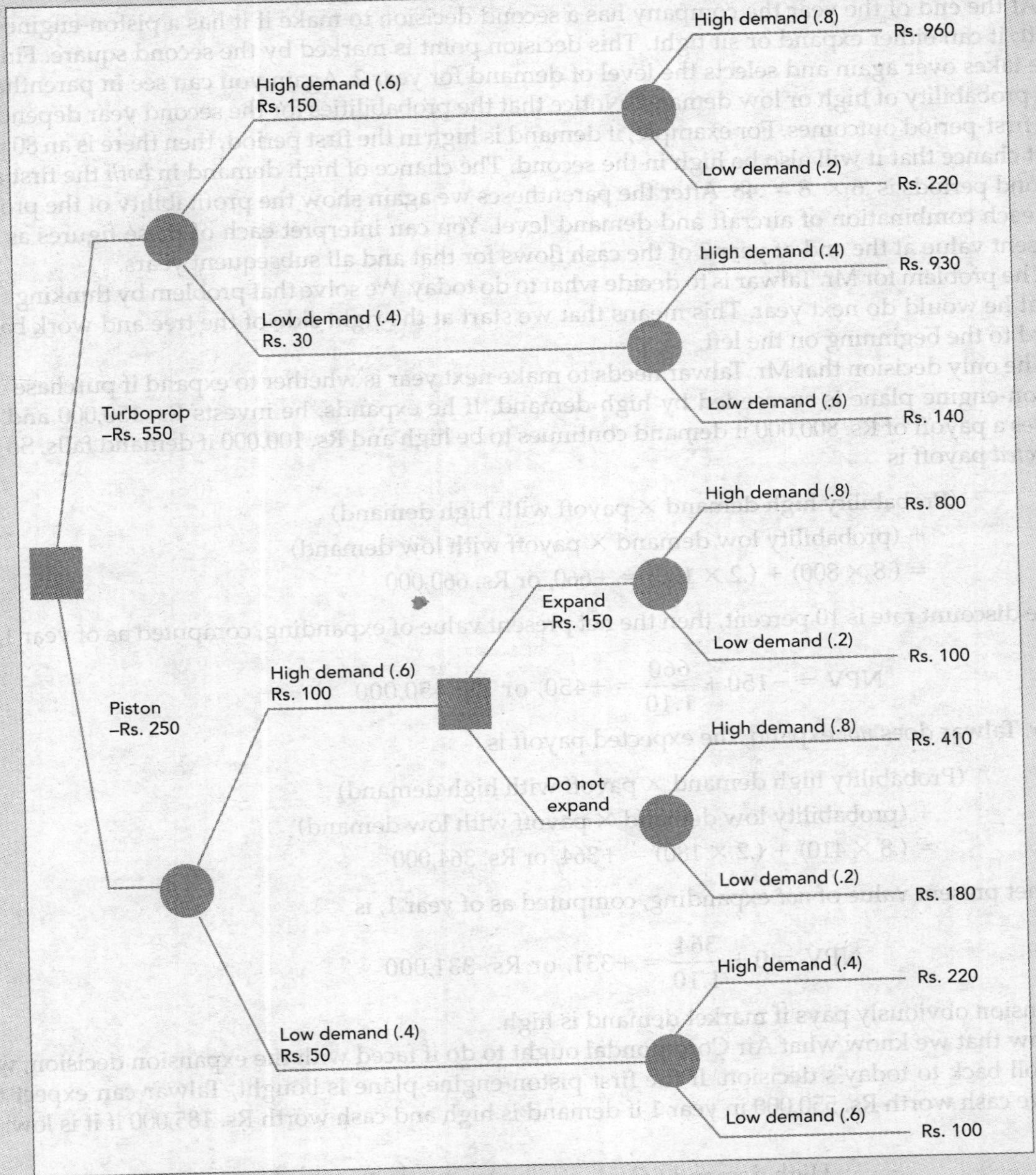

FIGURE 10.7

Decision tree for Air Coromondal. Should it buy a turboprop or a smaller piston-engine plane? A second piston plane can be purchased in year 1 if demand turns out to be high. (All figures are in thousands. Probabilities are in parentheses.)

At the end of the year the company has a second decision to make if it has a piston-engine aircraft: it can either expand or sit tight. This decision point is marked by the second square. Finally fate takes over again and selects the level of demand for year 2. Again you can see in parentheses the probability of high or low demand. Notice that the probabilities for the second year depend on the first-period outcomes. For example, if demand is high in the first period, then there is an 80 percent chance that it will also be high in the second. The chance of high demand in *both* the first and second periods is .6 × .8 = .48. After the parentheses we again show the profitability of the project for each combination of aircraft and demand level. You can interpret each of these figures as the present value at the end of year 2 of the cash flows for that and all subsequent years.

The problem for Mr. Talwar is to decide what to do today. We solve that problem by thinking first what he would do next year. This means that we start at the right side of the tree and work backward to the beginning on the left.

The only decision that Mr. Talwar needs to make next year is whether to expand if purchase of a piston-engine plane is succeeded by high demand. If he expands, he invests Rs. 150,000 and receives a payoff of Rs. 800,000 if demand continues to be high and Rs. 100,000 if demand falls. So his *expected* payoff is

(Probability high demand × payoff with high demand)
+ (probability low demand × payoff with low demand)
= (.8 × 800) + (.2 × 100) = +660, or Rs. 660,000

If the discount rate is 10 percent, then the net present value of expanding, computed as of year 1, is

$$\text{NPV} = -150 + \frac{660}{1.10} = +450, \text{ or Rs. } 450{,}000$$

If Mr. Talwar does *not* expand, the expected payoff is

(Probability high demand × payoff with high demand)
+ (probability low demand × payoff with low demand)
= (.8 × 410) + (.2 × 180) = +364, or Rs. 364,000

The net present value of *not* expanding, computed as of year 1, is

$$\text{NPV} = 0 + \frac{364}{1.10} = +331, \text{ or Rs. } 331{,}000$$

Expansion obviously pays if market demand is high.

Now that we know what Air Coromondal ought to do if faced with the expansion decision, we can roll back to today's decision. If the first piston-engine plane is bought, Talwar can expect to receive cash worth Rs. 550,000 in year 1 if demand is high and cash worth Rs. 185,000 if it is low:

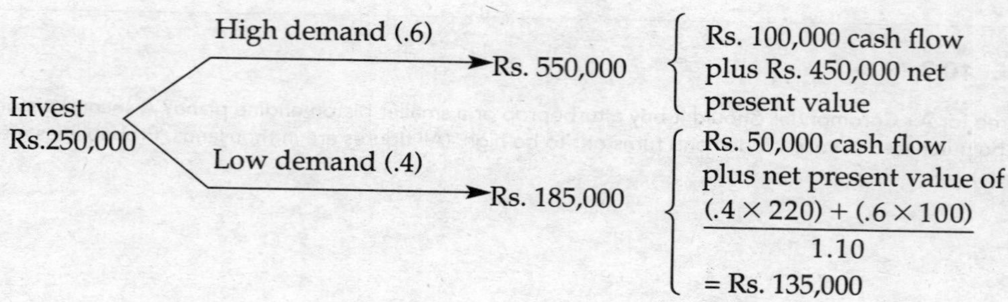

The net present value of the investment in the piston-engine plane is therefore Rs. 117,000:

$$NPV = -250 + \frac{.6(550) + .4(185)}{1.10} = +117, \text{ or Rs. } 117{,}000$$

If Air Coromondal buys the turboprop, there are no future decisions to analyze, and so there is no need to roll back. We just calculate expected cash flows and discount:

$$\begin{aligned} NPV &= -550 + \frac{.6(150) + .4(30)}{1.10} \\ &+ \frac{.6[.8(960) + .2(220)] + .4[.4(930) + .6(140)]}{(1.10)^2} \\ &= -550 + \frac{102}{1.10} + \frac{670}{(1.10)^2} = +96, \text{ or Rs. } 96{,}000 \end{aligned}$$

Thus the investment in the piston-engine plane has an NPV of Rs. 117,000; the investment in the turboprop has an NPV of Rs. 96,000. The piston-engine plane is the better bet. Note, however, that the choice would be different if we forgot to take account of the option to expand. In that case the NPV of the piston-engine plane would drop from Rs. 117,000 to Rs. 52,000:

$$\begin{aligned} NPV &= -250 + \frac{.6(100) + .4(50)}{1.10} \\ &+ \frac{.6[.8(410) + .2(180)] + .4[.4(220) + .6(100)]}{(1.10)^2} \\ &= +52, \text{ or Rs. } 52{,}000 \end{aligned}$$

The value of the option to expand is, therefore,

$$117 - 52 = +65, \text{ or Rs. } 65{,}000$$

The decision tree in Figure 10.7 recognizes that, if Mr. Talwar buys one piston-engine plane, he is not stuck with that decision. He has the option to expand by buying an additional plane if demand turns out to be unexpectedly high. But Figure 10.7 also assumes that, if Mr. Talwar goes for the big time by buying a turboprop, there is nothing that he can do if demand turns out to be unexpectedly *low*. That is unrealistic. If business in the first year is poor, it may pay for Mr. Talwar to sell the turboprop and abandon the venture entirely. In Figure 10.7 we could represent this option to bail out by adding an extra decision point (a further square) if the company buys the turboprop and first-year demand is low. If that happens, Mr. Talwar could decide either to sell the plane or to hold on and hope demand recovers. If the abandonment option is sufficiently valuable, it may make sense to take the turboprop and shoot for the big payoff.

Pro and Con Decision Trees

Any cash-flow forecast rests on some assumption about the firm's future investment and operating strategy. Often that assumption is implicit. Decision trees force the underlying strategy into the open. By displaying the links between today's and tomorrow's decisions, they help the financial manager to find the strategy with the highest net present value.

The trouble with decision trees is that they get so _____ complex so _____ quickly (insert your own expletives). What will Air Coromondal do if demand is neither high nor low but just middling?

In that event Mr. Talwar might sell the turboprop and buy a piston-engine plane, or he might defer expansion and abandonment decisions until year 2. Perhaps middling demand requires a decision about a price cut or an intensified sales campaign.

We could draw a new decision tree covering this expanded set of events and decisions. Try it if you like: you will see how fast the circles, squares, and branches accumulate.

Life is complex, and there is very little we can do about it. It is therefore unfair to criticize decision trees because they can become complex. Our criticism is reserved for analysts who let the complexity become overwhelming. The point of decision trees is to allow explicit analysis of possible future events and decisions. They should be judged not on their comprehensiveness but on whether they show the most important links between today's and tomorrow's decisions. Decision trees used in real life will be more complex than Figure 10.7, but they will nevertheless display only a small fraction of possible future events and decisions. Decision trees are like grapevines: They are productive only if they are vigorously pruned.

Decision trees can help identify the future choices available to the manager and can give a clearer view of the cash flows and risks of a project. However, our analysis of the Air Coromondal project begged an important question. The option to expand enlarged the spread of possible outcomes and therefore increased the risk of investing in a piston aircraft. Conversely, the option to bail out would narrow the spread of possible outcomes, reducing the risk of investment. We finessed this problem by interpreting all the cash-flow figures in Figure 10.7 as the certainty-equivalent cash flows, which could then be discounted at the risk-free interest rate. When we come to the issue of option pricing in Chapter 21, we will explain how investment options can be valued by calculating the certainty-equivalent cash flows.

Decision Trees and Monte Carlo Simulation

We have said that any cash-flow forecast rests on assumptions about future investment and operating strategy. Think back to the Monte Carlo simulation model that we constructed for Otobai's electric scooter project. What strategy was that based on? We don't know. Inevitably Otobai will face decisions about pricing, production, expansion, and abandonment, but the model builder's assumptions about these decisions are buried in the model's equations. The model builder may have implicitly identified a future strategy for Otobai, but it is clearly not the optimal one. There will be some runs of the model when nearly everything goes wrong and when in real life Otobai would abandon to cut its losses. Yet the model goes on period after period, heedless of the drain on Otobai's cash resources. The most unfavorable outcomes reported by the simulation model would never be encountered in real life.

On the other hand, the simulation model probably understates the project's potential value if nearly everything goes right: There is no provision for expanding to take advantage of good luck.

Most simulation models incorporate a business-as-usual strategy, which is fine as long as there are no major surprises. The greater the divergence from expected levels of market growth, market share, cost, etc., the less realistic is the simulation. Therefore the extreme high and low simulated values—the "tails" of the simulated distributions—should be treated with caution. Do not take the area under the tails as realistic probabilities of disaster or bonanza.

SUMMARY

There is more to capital budgeting than grinding out calculations of net present value. If you can identify the major uncertainties, you may find that it is worth undertaking some additional preliminary research that will *confirm* whether the project is worthwhile. And even if you decide that you have done all you can to resolve the uncertainties, you still want to be aware of the potential problems. You do not want to be caught by surprise if things go wrong: You want to be ready to take corrective action.

There are three ways in which companies try to identify the principal threats to a project's success. The simplest is *sensitivity analysis*. In this case the manager considers in turn each of the determinants of the project's success and recalculates NPV at very optimistic and very pessimistic levels of that variable. This establishes a range of possible values. The project is "sensitive to" the variable if the range is wide, especially on the pessimistic side.

Sensitivity analysis of this kind is easy, but it is not always helpful. Variables do not usually change one at a time. If costs are higher than you expect, it is a good bet that prices will be higher also. And if prices are higher, it is a good bet that sales volume will be lower. If you do not allow for the dependencies between the swings and the merry-go-rounds, you may get a false idea of the hazards of the fairground business. Many companies try to cope with this problem by examining the effect on the project of alternative plausible combinations of variables. In other words, they will estimate the net present value of the project under different *scenarios* and compare these estimates with the base case.

In a sensitivity analysis you change variables one at a time: When you analyze scenarios, you look at a limited number of alternative combinations of variables. If you want to go whole hog and look at *all* possible combinations of variables, then you will probably use *Monte Carlo simulation* to cope with the complexity. In that case you must construct a complete model of the project and specify the probability distribution of each of the determinants of cash flow. You can then ask the computer to select a random number for each of these determinants and work out the cash flows that would result. After the computer has repeated this process a few thousand times, you should have a fair idea of the expected cash flow in each year and the spread of possible cash flows.

Simulation can be a useful tool. The discipline of building a model of the project can in itself lead you to a deeper understanding of the project. And once you have constructed your model, it is a simple matter to see how the outcomes would be affected by altering the scope of the project or the distribution of any of the variables.

Elementary treatises on capital budgeting sometimes create the impression that, once the manager has made an investment decision, there is nothing to do but sit back and watch the cash flows unfold. In practice, companies are constantly modifying their operations. If cash flows are better than anticipated, the project may be expanded; if they are worse, it may be contracted or abandoned altogether. Options to modify projects are known as *real options*. In this chapter we introduced the main categories of real options: *expansion* options, *abandonment* options, *timing* options, and options providing *flexibility in production*.

Good managers take account of real options when they value a project. One convenient way to summarize real options and their cash-flow consequences is to create a *decision tree*. You identify the things that could happen to the project and the main counteractions that you might take. Then, working back from the future to the present, you can consider which action you *should* take in each case.

Decision trees can help to identify the possible impact of real options on project cash flows, but we largely skirted the issue of how to value real options. We will return to this topic in Chapter 22, after we have covered option-valuation methods in the previous two chapters.

FURTHER READING

Merck's use of Monte Carlo simulation is discussed in:

N. A. Nichols: "Scientific Management at Merck: An Interview with Judy Lewent," *Harvard Business Review,* 72 (January–February 1994), pp. 89–99.

Three not-too-technical references on real options are listed below. Additional references follow Chapter 22.

M. Amram and N. Kulatilaka: *Real Options: Managing Strategic Investments in an Uncertain World,* Harvard Business School Press, Boston, 1999.

A. Dixit and R. Pindyck: "The Options Approach to Capital Investment," *Harvard Business Review,* 73 (May–June 1995), pp. 105–115.

W. C. Kester: "Today's Options for Tomorrow's Growth," *Harvard Business Review,* 62 (March–April 1984), pp. 153–160.

CONCEPT REVIEW QUESTIONS

1. There are three ways that a manager can try to identify the principal threats to a project's success—sensitivity analysis, scenario analysis, and Monte Carlo simulation. Briefly describe how you would use each technique. (pages 248–258)
2. Can you derive optimistic and pessimistic values for total project flows from sensitivity analysis? Why or why not? (page 250)
3. What are the advantages of scenario analysis compared with sensitivity analysis? (page 250)

For additional Concept Review Questions, please visit us at www.mhhe.com/bmam8e or refer to your Student CD.

QUIZ

1. Define and briefly explain each of the following terms or procedures:
   a. Sensitivity analysis
   b. Scenario analysis
   c. Break-even analysis
   d. Monte Carlo simulation
   e. Decision tree
   f. Real option
   g. Abandonment value
   h. Expansion value
2. True or false?
   a. Sensitivity analysis is unnecessary for projects with asset betas that are equal to 0.
   b. Sensitivity analysis can be used to identify the variables most crucial to a project's success.
   c. If only one variable is uncertain, sensitivity analysis gives "optimistic" and "pessimistic" values for project cash flow and NPV.
   d. The break-even sales level of a project is higher when *breakeven* is defined in terms of NPV rather than accounting income.
   e. Monte Carlo simulation can be used to help forecast cash flows.
   f. Monte Carlo simulation eliminates the need to estimate a project's opportunity cost of capital.
3. Suppose a manager has already estimated a project's cash flows, calculated its NPV, and done a sensitivity analysis like the one shown in Table 10.2. List the additional steps required to carry out a Monte Carlo simulation of project cash flows.
4. True or false?
   a. Decision trees can help identify and describe real options.
   b. The option to expand increases NPV
   c. High abandonment value decreases NPV.
   d. If a project has positive NPV, the firm should always invest immediately.

PRACTICE QUESTIONS

1. What is the NPV of the electric scooter project under the following scenario?

Market size	1.1 million
Market share	.1
Unit price	¥400,000
Unit variable cost	¥360,000
Fixed cost	¥2 billion

Please visit us at www.mhhe.com/bmam8e or refer to your Student CD.

2. Otobai's staff has come up with the following revised estimates for the electric scooter project:

	Pessimistic	Expected	Optimistic
Market size	.8 million	1.0 million	1.2 million
Market share	.04	.1	.16
Unit price	¥300,000	¥375,000	¥400,000
Unit variable cost	¥350,000	¥300,000	¥275,000
Fixed cost	¥5 billion	¥3 billion	¥1 billion

Conduct a sensitivity analysis using the "live" spreadsheets (available on this book's CD or at **www.mhhe.com/bmam8e**). What are the principal uncertainties in the project?

3. Otobai is considering still another production method for its electric scooter. It would require an additional investment of ¥15 billion but would reduce variable costs by ¥40,000 per unit. Other assumptions follow Table 10.1.
   a. What is the NPV of this alternative scheme?
   b. Draw break-even charts for this alternative scheme along the lines of Figure 10.1.
   c. Explain how you would interpret the break-even figure.
   d. Now suppose Otobai's management would like to know the figure for variable cost per unit at which the electric scooter project in Section 10.1 would break even. Calculate the level of costs at which the project would earn zero profit and at which it would have zero NPV. Assume that the initial investment is ¥15 billion.

4. The Rustic Welt Company is proposing to replace its old welt-making machinery with more modern equipment. The new equipment costs Rs. 9 million (the existing equipment has zero salvage value). The attraction of the new machinery is that it is expected to cut manufacturing costs from their current level of Rs. 8 a welt to Rs. 4. However, as the following table shows, there is some uncertainty both about future sales and about the performance of the new machinery:

	Pessimistic	Expected	Optimistic
Sales, millions of welts	.4	.5	.7
Manufacturing cost with new machinery, dollars per welt	6	4	3
Economic life of new machinery, years	7	10	13

Please visit us at www.mhhe.com/bmam8e or refer to your Student CD.

Conduct a sensitivity analysis of the replacement decision, assuming a discount rate of 12 percent. Rustic Welt does not pay taxes.

5. Rustic Welt could commission engineering tests to determine the actual improvement in manufacturing costs generated by the proposed new welt machines. (See Practice Question 4 above.) The study would cost Rs. 450,000. Would you advise the company to go ahead with the study?

6. Operating leverage is often measured as the percentage increase in pretax profits after depreciation for a 1 percent increase in sales.
   a. Calculate the operating leverage for the electric scooter project assuming unit sales are 100,000 (see Section 10.1).
   b. Now show that this figure is equal to 1 + (fixed costs including depreciation divided by pretax profits).
   c. Would operating leverage be higher or lower if sales were 200,000 scooters?

excel

Please visit us at www.mhhe.com/bmam8e or refer to your Student CD.

7. Look back at the Vegetron electric mop project in Section 9.4. Assume that if tests fail and Vegetron continues to go ahead with the project, the Rs. 1 million investment would generate only Rs. 75,000 a year. Display Vegetron's problem as a decision tree.
8. The CD that accompanies this book and our Web site **www.mhhe.com/bmam8e** contain an Excel program for simulating the cash flows from the Otobai project. Use this program to examine which are the principal uncertainties surrounding the project. Suppose that some more analysis could effectively remove uncertainty about *one* of the variables. Suggest where it could be most usefully applied.
9. Describe the real option in each of the following cases:
   a. Deutsche Metall postpones a major plant expansion. The expansion has positive NPV on a discounted-cash-flow basis but top management wants to get a better fix on product demand before proceeding.
   b. Western Telecom commits to production of digital switching equipment specially designed for the European market. The project has a negative NPV, but it is justified on strategic grounds by the need for a strong market position in the rapidly growing, and potentially very profitable, market.
   c. Western Telecom vetoes a fully integrated, automated production line for the new digital switches. It relies on standard, less-expensive equipment. The automated production line is more efficient overall, according to a discounted-cash-flow calculation.
   d. Mount Fuji Airways buys a jumbo jet with special equipment that allows the plane to be switched quickly from freight to passenger use or vice versa.
   e. The British–French treaty giving a concession to build a railroad link under the English Channel also required the concessionaire to propose by the year 2000 to build a "drive-through link" if "technical and economic conditions permit . . . and the decrease in traffic shall justify it without undermining the expected return on the first [rail] link." Other companies will not be permitted to build a link before the year 2020.
10. An auto plant that costs Rs. 100 million to build can produce a new line of cars that will generate cash flows with a present value of Rs. 140 million if the line is successful, but only Rs. 50 million if it is unsuccessful. You believe that the probability of success is only about 50 percent.
    a. Would you build the plant?
    b. Suppose that the plant can be sold for Rs. 90 million to another automaker if the line is not successful. Now would you build the plant?
    c. Illustrate this option to abandon using a decision tree.
11. Rajesh Talwar has found some errors in his data (see Section 10.3). The corrected figures are as follows:

Price of turbo, year 0	Rs.350,000
Price of piston, year 0	Rs. 180,000
Discount rate	8 percent

Redraw the decision tree with the changed data. Calculate the value of the option to expand. Which plane should Mr. Talwar buy?

12. Following discovery of the errors in her data (see Practice Question 11), Mr. Talwar has thought of another possibility. He could abandon the venture entirely by selling the plane at the end of the first year. Suppose that the piston-engine plane can be sold for Rs. 150,000 and the turboprop can be sold for Rs. 500,000. .
    a. In what circumstances would it pay for Mr. Talwar to sell either plane?
    b. Redraw the decision tree in Figure 10.7 to recongnize that there will be circumstances in which Mr.Talwar will choose to take the money and bail out.
    c. Recalculate the value of the project recognizing the abandonment option.
    d. How much does the option to abandon add to the value of the piston-engine project? How much does it add to the value of the turboprop project?

CHALLENGE QUESTIONS

1. You own an unused gold mine that will cost Rs. 100,000 to reopen. If you open the mine, you expect to be able to extract 1,000 ounces of gold a year for each of three years. After that, the deposit will be exhausted. The gold price is currently Rs. 500 an ounce, and each year the price is equally likely to rise or fall by Rs. 50 from its level at the start of the year. The extraction cost is Rs. 460 an ounce and the discount rate is 10 percent.
    a. Should you open the mine now or delay one year in the hope of a rise in the gold price?
    b. What difference would it make to your decision if you could costlessly (but irreversibly) shut down the mine at any stage?
2. Look back at the guano project in Section 6.2. Use the Crystal Ball™ software to simulate how uncertainty about inflation could affect the project's cash flows.

MINI-CASE

Waldo County

Waldo County, the well-known real estate developer, worked long hours, and he expected his staff to do the same. So George Chavez was not surprised to receive a call from the boss just as George was about to leave for a long summer's weekend.

Mr. County's success had been built on a remarkable instinct for a good site. He would exclaim "Location! Location! Location!" at some point in every planning meeting. Yet finance was not his strong suit. On this occasion he wanted George to go over the figures for a new $90 million outlet mall designed to intercept tourists heading downeast toward Maine. "First thing Monday will do just fine," he said as he handed George the file. "I'll be in my house in Bar Harbor if you need me."

George's first task was to draw up a summary of the projected revenues and costs. The results are shown in Table 10.7. Note that the mall's revenues would come from two sources: The company would charge retailers an annual rent for the space they occupied and in addition it would receive 5 percent of each store's gross sales.

Construction of the mall was likely to take three years. The construction costs could be depreciated straight-line over 15 years starting in year 3. As in the case of the company's other developments, the mall would be built to the highest specifications and would not need to be rebuilt until year 17. The land was expected to retain its value, but could not be depreciated for tax purposes.

Construction costs, revenues, operating and maintenance costs, and real estate taxes were all likely to rise in line with inflation, which was forecasted at 2 percent a year. The company's tax rate was 35 percent and the cost of capital was 9 percent in nominal terms.

George decided first to check that the project made financial sense. He then proposed to look at some of the things that might go wrong. His boss certainly had a nose for a good retail project, but he was not infallible. The Salome project had been a disaster because store sales had turned out to be 40 percent below fore-

	Year					
	0	1	2	3	4	5–17
Investment:						
Land	30					
Construction	20	30	10			
Operations:						
Rentals				12	12	12
Share of retail sales				24	24	24
Operating and maintenance costs	2	4	4	10	10	10
Real estate taxes	2	2	3	4	4	4

TABLE 10.7

Projected revenues and costs in real terms for the Downeast Tourist Mall (figures in $ millions).

cast. What if that happened here? George wondered just how far sales could fall short of forecast before the project would be underwater.

Inflation was another source of uncertainty. Some people were talking about a zero long-term inflation rate, but George also wondered what would happen if inflation jumped to, say, 10 percent.

A third concern was possible construction cost overruns and delays due to required zoning changes and environmental approvals. George had seen cases of 25 percent construction cost overruns and delays up to 12 months between purchase of the land and the start of construction. He decided that he should examine the effect that this scenario would have on the project's profitability.

"Hey, this might be fun," George exclaimed to Mr. Waldo's secretary, Fifi, who was heading for Old Orchard Beach for the weekend. "I might even try Monte Carlo."

"Waldo went to Monte Carlo once," Fifi replied. "Lost a bundle at the roulette table. I wouldn't remind him. Just show him the bottom line. Will it make money or lose money? That's the bottom line."

"OK, no Monte Carlo," George agreed. But he realized that building a spreadsheet and running scenarios was not enough. He had to figure out how to summarize and present his results to Mr. County.

QUESTIONS

1. What is the project's NPV, given the projections in Table 10.7?
2. Conduct a sensitivity and a scenario analysis of the project. What do these analyses reveal about the project's risks and potential value?

CHAPTER [11]

STRATEGY AND THE CAPITAL INVESTMENT DECISION

WHY IS A manager who has learned about DCF like a baby with a hammer? Answer: Because to a baby with a hammer, everything looks like a nail.

Our point is that you should not focus on the arithmetic of DCF and thereby ignore the forecasts that are the basis of every investment decision. Senior managers are continuously bombarded with requests for funds for capital expenditures. All these requests are supported with detailed DCF analyses showing that the projects have positive NPVs.[1] How, then, can managers distinguish the NPVs that are truly positive from those that are merely the result of forecasting errors? We suggest that they should ask some probing questions about the possible sources of economic gain.

To make good investment decisions, you need to understand your firm's competitive advantages. This is where corporate strategy and finance come together. Good strategy positions the firm to generate the most value from its assets and growth opportunities. The search for good strategy starts with understanding how your firm stacks up versus your competitors, and how they will respond to your initiatives. Are your cash-flow forecasts realistic in your competitive environment? What effects will your competitors' actions have on the NPVs of your investments?

The first section in this chapter reviews certain common pitfalls in capital budgeting, notably the tendency to apply DCF when market values are already available and no DCF calculations are needed. The second section covers the *economic rents* that underlie all positive-NPV investments. The third section presents a case study describing how Marvin Enterprises, the gargle blaster company, analyzed the introduction of a radically new product.

[1]Here is another riddle. Are projects proposed because they have positive NPVs, or do they have positive NPVs because they are proposed? No prizes for the correct answer.

11.1 LOOK FIRST TO MARKET VALUES

Let us suppose that you have persuaded all your project sponsors to give honest forecasts. Although those forecasts are unbiased, they are still likely to contain errors, some positive and others negative. The average error will be zero, but that is little consolation because you want to accept only projects with *truly* superior profitability.

Think, for example, of what would happen if you were to jot down your estimates of the cash flows from operating various lines of business. You would probably find that about half *appeared* to have positive NPVs. This may not be because you personally possess any superior skill in operating jumbo jets or running a chain of laundromats but because you have inadvertently introduced large errors into your estimates of the cash flows. The more projects you contemplate, the more likely you are to uncover projects that *appear* to be extremely worthwhile. Indeed, if you were to extend your activities to making cash-flow estimates for various companies, you would also find a number of *apparently* attractive takeover candidates. In some of these cases you might have genuine information and the proposed investment really might have a positive NPV. But in many other cases the investment would look good only because you made a forecasting error.

What can you do to prevent forecast errors from swamping genuine information? We suggest that you begin by looking at market values.

The Cadillac and the Movie Star

The following parable should help to illustrate what we mean. Your local Cadillac dealer is announcing a special offer. For $ 45,001 you get not only a brand new Cadillac but also the chance to shake hands with your favorite movie star. You wonder how much you are paying for that handshake.

There are two possible approaches to the problem. You could evaluate the worth of the Cadillac's power steering, disappearing windshield wipers, and other features and conclude that the Cadillac is worth $ 46,000. This would seem to suggest that the dealership is willing to pay $ 999 to have a movie star shake hands with you. Alternatively, you might note that the market price for Cadillacs is $ 45,000, so that you are paying $ 1 for the handshake. As long as there is a competitive market for Cadillacs, the latter approach is more appropriate.

Security analysts face a similar problem whenever they value a company's stock. They must consider the information that is already known to the market about a company, *and* they must evaluate the information that is known only to them. The information that is known to the market is the Cadillac; the private information is the handshake with the movie star. Investors have already evaluated the information that is generally known. Security analysts do not need to evaluate this information again. They can *start* with the market price of the stock and concentrate on valuing their private information.

While lesser mortals would instinctively accept the Cadillac's market value of $ 45,000, the financial manager is trained to enumerate and value all the costs and benefits from an investment and is therefore tempted to substitute his or her own opinion for the market's. Unfortunately this approach increases the chance of error. Many capital assets are traded in a competitive market, so it makes sense to *start* with the market price and then ask why these assets should earn more in your hands than in your rivals'.

Example: Investing in a New Department Store

We encountered a department store chain that estimated the present value of the expected cash flows from each proposed store, including the price at which it could eventually sell the store. Although the firm took considerable care with these estimates, it was disturbed to find that its conclusions were heavily influenced by the forecasted selling price of each store. Management disclaimed any particular real estate expertise, but it discovered that its investment decisions were unintentionally dominated by its assumptions about future real estate prices.

Once the financial managers realized this, they always checked the decision to open a new store by asking the following question: "Let us assume that the property is fairly priced. What is the evidence that it is best suited to one of our department stores rather than to some other use? In other words, *if an asset is worth more to others than it is to you, then beware of bidding for the asset against them.*

Let us take the department store problem a little further. Suppose that the new store costs Rs. 100 million.[2] You forecast that it will generate after-tax cash flow of Rs. 8 million a year for 10 years. Real estate prices are estimated to grow by 3 percent a year, so the expected value of the real estate at the end of 10 years is $100 \times (1.03)^{10}$ = Rs. 134 million. At a discount rate of 10 percent, your proposed department store has an NPV of Rs. 1 million:

$$\text{NPV} = -100 + \frac{8}{1.10} + \frac{8}{(1.10)^2} + \cdots + \frac{8+134}{(1.10)^{10}} = \text{Rs. 1 million}$$

Notice how sensitive this NPV is to the ending value of the real estate. For example, an ending value of Rs. 120 million implies an NPV of −Rs. 5 million.

---

[2]For simplicity we assume the Rs. 100 million goes entirely to real estate. In real life there would also be substantial investments in fixtures, information systems, training, and start-up costs.

FIGURE 11.1

Beginning in year 6, the department store's income fails to cover the rental charge.

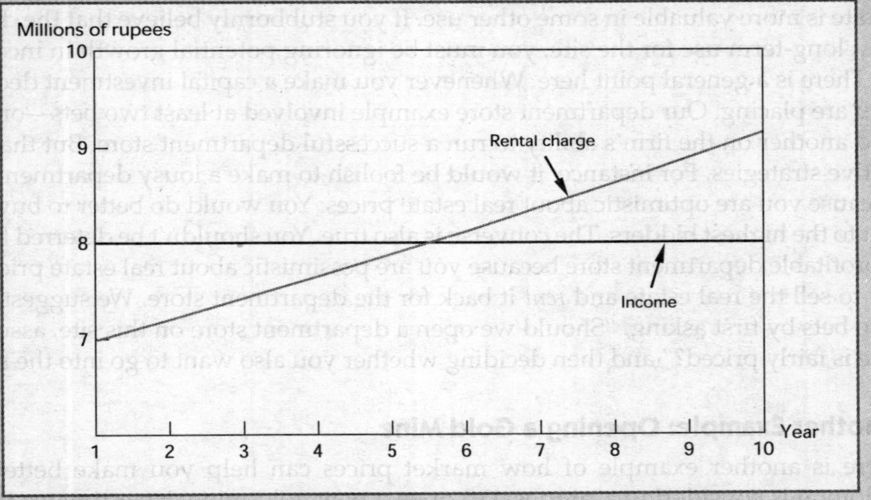

It is helpful to imagine such a business as divided into two parts—a real estate subsidiary which buys the building and a retailing subsidiary which rents and operates it. Then figure out how much rent the real estate subsidiary would have to charge, and ask whether the retailing subsidiary could afford to pay the rent.

In some cases a fair market rental can be estimated from real estate transactions. For example, we might observe that similar retail space recently rented for Rs. 10 million a year. In that case we would conclude that our department store was an unattractive use for the site. Once the site had been acquired, it would be better to rent it out at Rs. 10 million than to use it for a store generating only Rs. 8 million.

Suppose, on the other hand, that the property could be rented for only Rs. 7 million per year. The department store could pay this amount to the real estate subsidiary and still earn a net operating cash flow of $8 - 7 =$ Rs. 1 million. It is therefore the best *current* use for the real estate.[3]

Will it also be the best *future* use? Maybe not, depending on whether retail profits keep pace with any rent increases. Suppose that real estate prices and rents are expected to increase by 3 percent per year. The real estate subsidiary must charge $7 \times 1.03 =$ Rs. 7.21 million in year 2, $7.21 \times 1.03 =$ Rs. 7.43 million in year 3, and so on.[4] Figure 11.1 shows that the store's income fails to cover the rental after year 5.

---

[3]The fair market rent equals the profit generated by the real estate's *second*-best use.

[4]This rental stream yields a 10 percent rate of return to the real estate subsidiary. Each year it gets a 7 percent "dividend" and 3 percent capital gain. Growth at 3 percent would bring the value of the property to Rs. 134 million by year 10.

The present value (at $r = .10$) of the growing stream of rents is

$$PV = \frac{7}{r - g} = \frac{7}{.10 - .03} = \text{Rs. 100 million}$$

This PV is the initial market value of the property.

If these forecasts are right, the store has only a five-year economic life; from that point on the real estate is more valuable in some other use. If you stubbornly believe that the department store is the best long-term use for the site, you must be ignoring potential growth in income from the store.[5]

There is a general point here. Whenever you make a capital investment decision, think what bets you are placing. Our department store example involved at least two bets—one on real estate prices and another on the firm's ability to run a successful department store. But that suggests some alternative strategies. For instance, it would be foolish to make a lousy department store investment just because you are optimistic about real estate prices. You would do better to buy real estate and rent it out to the highest bidders. The converse is also true. You shouldn't be deterred from going ahead with a profitable department store because you are pessimistic about real estate prices. You would do better to sell the real estate and *rent* it back for the department store. We suggest that you separate the two bets by first asking, "Should we open a department store on this site, assuming that the real estate is fairly priced?" and then deciding whether you also want to go into the real estate business.

Another Example: Opening a Gold Mine

Here is another example of how market prices can help you make better decisions. Kingsley Solomon is considering a proposal to open a new gold mine. He estimates that the mine will cost Rs. 200 million to develop and that in each of the next 10 years it will produce .1 million ounces of gold at a cost, after mining and refining, of Rs. 200 an ounce. Although the extraction costs can be predicted with reasonable accuracy, Mr. Solomon is much less confident about future gold prices. His best guess is that the price will rise by 5 percent per year from its current level of Rs. 400 an ounce. At a discount rate of 10 percent, this gives the mine an NPV of −Rs. 10 million:

$$\text{NPV} = -200 + \frac{.1(420-200)}{1.10} + \frac{.1(441-200)}{(1.10)^2} + \cdots + \frac{.1(652-200)}{(1.10)^{10}}$$

$$= -\text{Rs. } 10 \text{ million}$$

Therefore the gold mine project is rejected.

Unfortunately, Mr. Solomon did not look at what the market was telling him. What is the PV of an ounce of gold? Clearly, if the gold market is functioning properly, it is the current price—Rs. 400 an ounce. Gold does not produce any income, so Rs. 400 is the discounted value of the expected future gold price.[6] Since the mine is expected to produce a total of 1 million ounces (.1 million ounces

[5]Another possibility is that real estate rents and values are expected to grow at less than 3 percent a year. But in that case the real estate subsidiary would have to charge more than Rs. 7 million rent in year 1 to justify its Rs. 100 million real estate investment (see footnote 4). That would make the department store even less attractive.

[6]Investing in an ounce of gold is like investing in a stock that pays no dividends: The investor's return comes entirely as capital gains. Look back at Section 4.4, where we showed that P_0, the price of the stock today, depends on DIV_1 and P_1, the expected dividend and price for next year, and the opportunity cost of capital r:

$$P_0 = \frac{\text{DIV}_1 + P_1}{1+r}$$

But for gold $\text{DIV}_1 = 0$, so

$$P_0 = \frac{P_1}{1+r}$$

per year for 10 years), the present value of the revenue stream is 1 × 400 = Rs. 400 million.[7] We assume that 10 percent is an appropriate discount rate for the relatively certain extraction costs. Thus

$$\text{NPV} = -\text{initial investment} + \text{PV revenues} - \text{PV costs}$$
$$= -200 + 400 - \sum_{t=1}^{10} \frac{.1 \times 200}{(1.10)^t} = \text{Rs. 77 million}$$

It looks as if Kingsley Solomon's mine is not such a bad bet after all.[8]

Mr. Solomon's gold was just like anyone else's gold. So there was no point in trying to value it separately. By taking the PV of the gold sales as given, Mr. Solomon was able to focus on the crucial issue: Were the extraction costs sufficiently low to make the venture worthwhile? That brings us to another of those fundamental truths: If others are producing an article profitably and (like Mr. Solomon) you can make it more cheaply, then you don't need any NPV calculations to know that you are probably onto a good thing.

We confess that our example of Kingsley Solomon's mine is somewhat special. Unlike gold, most commodities are not kept solely for investment purposes, and therefore you cannot automatically assume that today's price is equal to the present value of the future price.[9]

In words, *today's price is the present value of next year's price*. Therefore, we don't have to know either P_1 or r to find the present value. Also since $DIV_2 = 0$,

$$P_1 = \frac{P_2}{1+r}$$

and we can express P_0 as

$$P_0 = \frac{P_1}{1+r} = \frac{1}{1+r}\left(\frac{P_2}{1+r}\right) = \frac{P_2}{(1+r)^2}$$

In general,

$$P_0 = \frac{P_t}{(1+r)^t}$$

This holds for any asset which pays no dividends, is traded in a competitive market, and costs nothing to store. Storage costs for gold or common stocks are very small compared to asset value.

We also assume that guaranteed future delivery of gold is just as good as having gold in hand today. This is not quite right. As we will see in Chapter 27, gold in hand can generate a small "convenience yield."

[7]We assume that the extraction rate does not vary. If it can vary, Mr. Solomon has a valuable operating option to increase output when gold prices are high or to cut back when prices fall. Option pricing techniques are needed to value the mine when operating options are important. See Chapters 21 and 22.

[8]As in the case of our department store example, Mr. Solomon is placing two bets: one on his ability to mine gold at a low cost and the other on the price of gold. Suppose that he really does believe that gold is overvalued. That should not deter him from running a low-cost gold mine as long as he can place separate bets on gold prices. For example, he might be able to enter into a long-term contract to sell the mine's output or he could sell gold futures. (We explain *futures* in Chapter 27.)

[9]A more general guide to the relationship of current and future commodity prices was provided by Hotelling, who pointed out that if there are constant returns to scale in mining any mineral, the expected rise in the price of the mineral *less* extraction costs should equal the cost of capital. If the expected growth were faster, everyone would want to postpone extraction; if it were slower, everyone would want to exploit the resource today. In this case the value of a mine would be independent of when it was exploited, and you could value it by calculating the value of the mineral at today's price less the current cost of extraction. If (as is usually the case) there are declining returns to scale, then the expected price rise net of costs must be less than the cost of capital. For a review of Hotelling's principle, see S. Devarajan and A. C. Fisher, "Hotelling's 'Economics of Exhaustible Resources': Fifty Years Later," *Journal of Economic Literature* 19 (March 1981), pp. 65–73. And for an application, see M. H. Miller and C. W. Upton, "A Test of the Hotelling Valuation Principle," *Journal of Political Economy* 93 (1985), pp. 1–25.

However, here is another way that you may be able to tackle the problem. Suppose that you are considering investment in a new copper mine and that someone offers to buy the mine's future output at a fixed price. If you accept the offer—and the buyer is completely creditworthy—the revenues from the mine are certain and can be discounted at the risk-free interest rate.[10] That takes us back to Chapter 9, where we explained that there are two ways to calculate PV:

- Estimate the expected cash flows and discount at a rate that reflects the risk of those flows.
- Estimate what sure-fire cash flows would have the same values as the risky cash flows. Then discount these *certainty-equivalent* cash flows at the risk-free interest rate.

When you discount the fixed-price revenues at the risk-free rate, you are using the certainty-equivalent method to value the mine's output. By doing so, you gain in two ways: You don't need to estimate future mineral prices, and you don't need to worry about the appropriate discount rate for risky cash flows.

But here's the question: What is the minimum fixed price at which you could agree today to sell your future output? In other words, what is the certainty-equivalent price? Fortunately, for many commodities there is an active market in which firms fix today the price at which they will buy or sell copper and other commodities in the future. This market is known as the *futures market*, which we will cover in Chapter 27. Futures prices are certainty equivalents, and you can look them up in the daily newspaper. So you don't need to make elaborate forecasts of copper prices to work out the PV of the mine's output. The market has already done the work for you; you simply calculate future revenues using the price in the newspaper of copper futures and discount these revenues at the risk-free interest rate.

Of course, things are never as easy as textbooks suggest. Trades in organized futures exchanges are largely confined to deliveries over the next year or so, and therefore your newspaper won't show the price at which you could sell output beyond this period. But financial economists have developed techniques for using the prices in the futures market to estimate the amount that buyers would agree to pay for more-distant deliveries.[11]

Our two examples of gold and copper producers are illustrations of a universal principle of finance:

> When you have the market value of an asset, *use it*, at least as a starting point in your analysis.

11.2 ECONOMIC RENTS AND COMPETITIVE ADVANTAGE

Profits that more than cover the cost of capital are known as *economic rents*. Business strategy experts stress that firms can generate economic rents both by their choice of industry and by the way that they position themselves within that industry. Michael Porter identifies five aspects of industry

---

[10] We assume that the *volume* of output is certain (or does not have any market risk).

[11] After reading Chapter 27, check out E. S. Schwartz, "The Stochastic Behavior of Commodity Prices: Implications for Valuation and Hedging," *Journal of Finance* 52 (July 1997), pp. 923–973; and A. J. Neuberger, "Hedging Long-Term Exposures with Multiple Short-Term Contracts," *Review of Financial Studies* 12 (1999), pp. 429–459.

structure (or "five forces") that determine which industries are able to provide sustained economic rents.[12] These are the rivalry among existing competitors, the likelihood of new competition, the threat of substitutes, and the bargaining power both of suppliers and customers.

With increasing global competition, firms cannot rely so easily on industry structure to provide high returns. Therefore, managers also need to ensure that the firm is positioned *within* its industry so as to secure a competitive advantage. Michael Porter suggests three ways that this can be done—by cost leadership, by product differentiation, and by focus on a particular market niche.[13]

In today's world, successful strategies that combine different mixes of cost leadership, product differentiation, and focus appear to be the key to developing a unique position in an industry.[14] Think, for example, of Maruti Udyog Limited. It blends elements of all three strategies. It is one of the low-cost manufacturer of passenger cars in India. It differentiates itself from its competitors by its distinct Japanese design. It provides insurance with delivery to customers. It makes funds available in the showrooms so that customers buying its cars can get instant credit. It also provides third and fourth year warranty on its cars. It has a clear focus on a group of customers, who belong to the middle class and are price-conscious.

You can see how business strategy and finance reinforce each other. Managers who have a clear understanding of their firm's competitive strengths are better placed to separate those projects that truly have a positive NPV from those that do not. Therefore when you are presented with a project that appears to have a positive NPV, do not just accept the calculations at face value. They may reflect simple estimation errors in forecasting cash flows. Probe behind the cash-flow estimates, and *try to identify the source of economic rents.* A positive NPV for a new project is believable only if you believe that your company has some special advantage.

Thinking about competitive advantage can also help ferret out negative-NPV calculations that are negative by mistake. For example, if you are the lowest-cost producer of a profitable product in a growing market, then you should invest to expand along with the market. If your calculations show a negative NPV for such an expansion, then you have probably made a mistake.

We will work through shortly an extended example that shows how a firm's analysis of its competitive position confirmed that its investment had a positive NPV. But first we look at an example in which the analysis helped a firm to ferret out a negative-NPV transaction and avoid a costly mistake.

How One Company Avoided a $100 Million Mistake

A U.S. chemical producer was about to modify an existing plant to produce a specialty product, polyzone, which was in short supply on world markets.[15] At prevailing raw material and finished-product prices the expansion would have been strongly profitable. Table 11.1 shows a simplified version of management's analysis. Note the NPV of about $64 million at the company's 8 percent real cost of capital—not bad for a $100 million outlay.

[12]See M. E. Porter, *Competitive Strategy: Techniques for Analyzing Industries and Competitors* (New York: The Free Press, 1980).

[13]See M. E. Porter, *Competitive Advantage: Creating and Sustaining Superior Advantage* (New York: The Free Press, 1985).

[14]See page 248 of R. M. Grant, *Contemporary Strategy Analysis*, 4th ed. (Oxford: Blackwell, 2002).

[15]This is a true story, but names and details have been changed to protect the innocent.

	Year 0	Year 1	Year 2	Years 3-10
Investment	100			
Production, millions of pounds per year[a]	0	0	40	80
Spread, dollars per pound	1.20	1.20	1.20	1.20
Net revenues	0	0	48	96
Production costs[b]	0	0	30	30
Transport[c]	0	0	4	8
Other costs	0	20	20	20
Cash flow	-100	-20	-6	38
NPV (at r = 8%) = $63.6 million				

excel

Please visit us at www.mhhe.com/bmam8e or refer to your Student CD.

TABLE 11.1

NPV calculation for proposed investment in polyzone production by a U.S. chemical company (figures in $ millions except as noted).

Note: For simplicity, we assume no inflation and no taxes. Plant and equipment have no salvage value after 10 years.
[a]Production capacity is 80 million pounds per year.
[b]Production costs are $.375 per pound after start-up ($.75 per pound in year 2, when production is only 40 million pounds).
[c]Transportation costs are $.10 per pound to European ports.

Then doubt began to creep in. Notice the outlay for transportation costs. Some of the project's raw materials were commodity chemicals, largely imported from Europe, and much of the polyzone production would be exported back to Europe. Moreover, the U.S. company had no long-run technological edge over potential European competitors. It had a head start perhaps, but was that really enough to generate a positive NPV?

Notice the importance of the price spread between raw materials and finished product. The analysis in Table 11.1 forecasted the spread at a constant $1.20 per pound of polyzone for 10 years. That had to be wrong: European producers, who did not face the U.S. company's transportation costs, would see an even larger NPV and expand capacity. Increased competition would almost surely squeeze the spread. The U.S. company decided to calculate the *competitive* spread—the spread at which a European competitor would see polyzone capacity as zero NPV. Table 11.2 shows management's analysis. The resulting spread of about $.95 per pound was the best *long-run* forecast for the polyzone market, other things constant of course.

How much of a head start did the U.S. producer have? How long before competitors forced the spread down to $.95? Management's best guess was five years. It prepared Table 11.3, which is identical to Table 11.1 except for the forecasted spread, which would shrink to $.95 by the start of year 5. Now the NPV was negative.

The project might have been saved if production could have been started in year 1 rather than 2 or if local markets could have been expanded, thus reducing transportation costs. But these changes were not feasible, so management canceled the project, albeit with a sigh of relief that its analysis had not stopped at Table 11.1.

This is a perfect example of the importance of thinking through sources of economic rents. Positive NPVs are suspect without some long-run competitive advantage. When a company contemplates investing in a new product or expanding production of an existing product, it should specifically identify its advantages or disadvantages over its most dangerous competitors. It should

	Year 0	Year 1	Year 2	Years 3-10
Investment	100			
Production, millions of pounds per year	0	0	40	80
Spread, dollars per pound	.95	.95	.95	.95
Net revenues	0	0	38	76
Production costs	0	0	30	30
Transport	0	0	0	0
Other costs	0	20	20	20
Cash flow	-100	-20	-12	+26
NPV (at r = 8%) = 0				

TABLE 11.2

What is the competitive spread to a European producer? About $.95 per pound of polyzone. Note that European producers face no transportation costs. Compare Table 11.1 (figures in $ millions except as noted).

excel

Please visit us at www.mhhe.com/bmam8e or refer to your Student CD .

	Year					
	0	1	2	3	4	5-10
Investment	100					
Production (mn. pounds p.a.)	0	0	40	80	80	80
Spread ($ per pound)	1.20	1.20	1.20	1.20	1.10	.95
Net revenues	0	0	48	96	88	76
Production costs	0	0	30	30	30	30
Transport	0	0	4	8	8	8
Other costs	0	20	20	20	20	20
Cash flow	-100	-20	-6	38	30	18
NPV (at r = 8%) = -9.8						

TABLE 11.3

Recalculation of NPV for polyzone investment by U.S. company (figures in $ millions except as noted). If expansion by European producers forces competitive spreads by year 5, the U.S. producer's NPV falls to −$9.8 million. Compare Table 11.1.

excel

Please visit us at www.mhhe.com/bmam8e or refer to your Student CD .

calculate NPV from those competitors' points of view. If competitors' NPVs come out strongly positive, the company had better expect decreasing prices (or spreads) and evaluate the proposed investment accordingly.

11.3 EXAMPLE—MARVIN ENTERPRISES DECIDES TO EXPLOIT A NEW TECHNOLOGY

To illustrate some of the problems involved in predicting economic rents, let us leap forward several years and look at the decision by Marvin Enterprises to exploit a new technology.[16]

One of the most unexpected developments of these years was the remarkable growth of a completely new industry. By 2026 annual sales of gargle blasters totaled $1.68 billion, or 240 million units. Although it controlled only 10 percent of the market, Marvin Enterprises was among the most exciting growth companies of the decade. Marvin had come late into the business, but it had pioneered the use of integrated microcircuits to control the genetic engineering processes used to manufacture gargle blasters. This development had enabled producers to cut the price of gargle blasters from $9 to $7 and had thereby contributed to the dramatic growth in the size of the market. The estimated demand curve in Figure 11.2 shows just how responsive demand is to such price reductions.

Table 11.4 summarizes the cost structure of the old and new technologies. While companies with the new technology were earning 20 percent on their initial investment, those with first-generation equipment had been hit by the successive price cuts. Since all Marvin's investment was in the 2022 technology, it had been particularly well placed during this period.

Rumors of new developments at Marvin had been circulating for some time, and the total market value of Marvin's stock had risen to $460 million by January 2027. At that point Marvin called a press conference to announce another technological breakthrough. Management claimed that its new third-generation process involving mutant neurons enabled the firm to reduce capital costs to $10 and manufacturing costs to $3 per unit. Marvin proposed to capitalize on this invention by embarking on a huge $1 billion expansion program that would add 100 million units to capacity. The company expected to be in full operation within 12 months.

Before deciding to go ahead with this development, Marvin had undertaken extensive calculations on the effect of the new investment. The basic assumptions were as follows:

1. The cost of capital was 20 percent.
2. The production facilities had an indefinite physical life.
3. The demand curve and the costs of each technology would not change.
4. There was no chance of a fourth-generation technology in the foreseeable future.
5. The corporate income tax, which had been abolished in 2017, was not likely to be reintroduced.

Marvin's competitors greeted the news with varying degrees of concern. There was general agreement that it would be five years before any of them would have access to the new technology.

[16]We thank Stewart Hodges for permission to adapt this example from a case prepared by him, and we thank the BBC for permission to use the term *gargle blasters*.

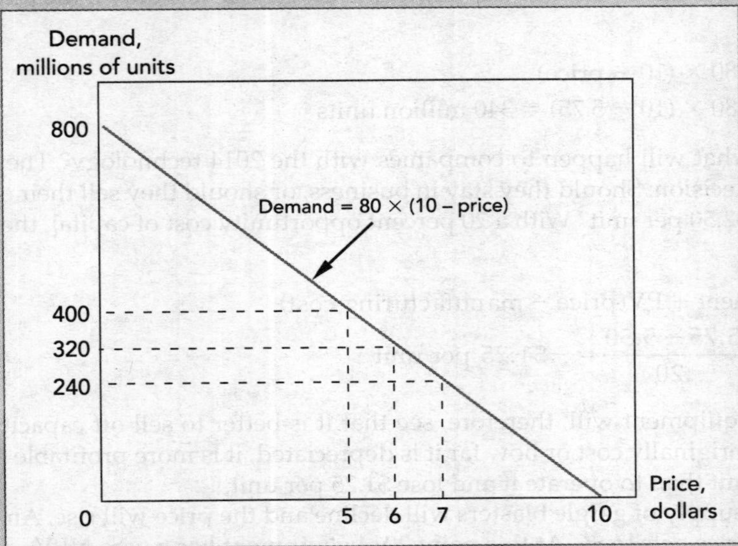

FIGURE 11.2

The demand "curve" for gargle blasters shows that for each $1 cut in price there is an increase in demand of 80 million units.

Technology	Capacity, Millions of Units: Industry	Capacity, Millions of Units: Marvin	Capital Cost per Unit ($)	Manufacturing Cost per Unit ($)	Salvage Value per Unit ($)
First generation (2014)	120	—	17.50	5.50	2.50
Second generation (2022)	120	24	17.50	3.50	2.50

TABLE 11.4

Size and cost structure of the gargle blaster industry before Marvin announced its expansion plans.

Note: Selling price is $7 per unit. One unit means one gargle blaster.

On the other hand, many consoled themselves with the reflection that Marvin's new plant could not compete with an existing plant that had been fully depreciated.

Suppose that you were Marvin's financial manager. Would you have agreed with the decision to expand? Do you think it would have been better to go for a larger or smaller expansion? How do you think Marvin's announcement is likely to affect the price of its stock?

You have a choice. You can go on *immediately* to read *our* solution to these questions. But you will learn much more if you stop and work out your own answer first. Try it.

Forecasting Prices of Gargle Blasters

Up to this point in any capital budgeting problem we have always given you the set of cash-flow forecasts. In the present case you have to *derive* those forecasts.

The first problem is to decide what is going to happen to the price of gargle blasters. Marvin's new venture will increase industry capacity to 340 million units. From the demand curve in

Figure 11.2, you can see that the industry can sell this number of gargle blasters only if the price declines to \$5.75:

$$\begin{aligned}\text{Demand} &= 80 \times (10 - \text{price}) \\ &= 80 \times (10 - 5.75) = 340 \text{ million units}\end{aligned}$$

If the price falls to \$5.75, what will happen to companies with the 2014 technology? They also have to make an investment decision: Should they stay in business, or should they sell their equipment for its salvage value of \$2.50 per unit? With a 20 percent opportunity cost of capital, the NPV of staying in business is

$$\begin{aligned}\text{NPV} &= -\text{investment} + \text{PV(price} - \text{manufacturing cost)} \\ &= -2.50 + \frac{5.75 - 5.50}{.20} = -\$1.25 \text{ per unit}\end{aligned}$$

Smart companies with 2014 equipment will, therefore, see that it is better to sell off capacity. No matter what their equipment originally cost or how far it is depreciated, it is more profitable to sell the equipment for \$2.50 per unit than to operate it and lose \$1.25 per unit.

As capacity is sold off, the supply of gargle blasters will decline and the price will rise. An equilibrium is reached when the price gets to \$6. At this point 2014 equipment has a zero NPV:

$$\text{NPV} = -2.50 + \frac{6.00 - 5.50}{.20} = \$0 \text{ per unit}$$

How much capacity will have to be sold off before the price reaches \$6? You can check that by going back to the demand curve:

$$\begin{aligned}\text{Demand} &= 80 \times (10 - \text{price}) \\ &= 80 \times (10 - 6) = 320 \text{ million units}\end{aligned}$$

Therefore Marvin's expansion will cause the price to settle down at \$6 a unit and will induce first-generation producers to withdraw 20 million units of capacity.

But after five years Marvin's competitors will also be in a position to build third-generation plants. As long as these plants have positive NPVs, companies will increase their capacity and force prices down once again. A new equilibrium will be reached when the price reaches \$5. At this point, the NPV of new third-generation plants is zero, and there is no incentive for companies to expand further:

$$\text{NPV} = -10 + \frac{5.00 - 3.00}{.20} = \$0 \text{ per unit}$$

Looking back once more at our demand curve, you can see that with a price of \$5 the industry can sell a total of 400 million gargle blasters:

$$\text{Demand} = 80 \times (10 - \text{price}) = 80 \times (10 - 5) = 400 \text{ million units}$$

The effect of the third-generation technology is, therefore, to cause industry sales to expand from 240 million units in 2026 to 400 million five years later. But that rapid growth is no protection against failure. By the end of five years any company that has only first-generation equipment will no longer be able to cover its manufacturing costs and will be *forced* out of business.

The Value of Marvin's New Expansion

We have shown that the introduction of third-generation technology is likely to cause gargle blaster prices to decline to \$6 for the next five years and to \$5 thereafter. We can now set down the expected cash flows from Marvin's new plant:

	Year 0 (Investment)	Years 1–5 (Revenue − Manufacturing Cost)	Year 6, 7, 8, . . . (Revenue − Manufacturing Cost)
Cash flow per unit (\$)	−10	6 − 3 = 3	5 − 3 = 2
Cash flow, 100 million units (\$ millions)	−1,000	600 − 300 = 300	500 − 300 = 200

Discounting these cash flows at 20 percent gives us

$$\text{NPV} = -1{,}000 + \sum_{t=1}^{5} \frac{300}{(1.20)^t} + \frac{1}{(1.20)^5}\left(\frac{200}{.20}\right) = \$299 \text{ million}$$

It looks as if Marvin's decision to go ahead was correct. But there is something we have forgotten. When we evaluate an investment, we must consider *all* incremental cash flows. One effect of Marvin's decision to expand is to reduce the value of its existing 2022 plant. If Marvin decided not to go ahead with the new technology, the \$7 price of gargle blasters would hold until Marvin's competitors started to cut prices in five years' time. Marvin's decision, therefore, leads to an immediate \$1 cut in price. This reduces the present value of its 2022 equipment by

$$24 \text{ million} \times \sum_{t=1}^{5} \frac{1.00}{(1.20)^t} = \$72 \text{ million}$$

Considered in isolation, Marvin's decision has an NPV of \$299 million. But it also reduces the value of existing plant by \$72 million. The net present value of Marvin's venture is, therefore, 299 − 72 = \$227 million.

Alternative Expansion Plans

Marvin's expansion has a positive NPV, but perhaps Marvin would do better to build a larger or smaller plant. You can check that by going through the same calculations as above. First you need to estimate how the additional capacity will affect gargle blaster prices. Then you can calculate the net present value of the new plant and the change in the present value of the existing plant. The total NPV of Marvin's expansion plan is

$$\text{Total NPV} = \text{NPV of new plant} + \text{change in PV of existing plant}$$

We have undertaken these calculations and plotted the results in Figure 11.3. You can see how total NPV would be affected by a smaller or larger expansion.

FIGURE 11.3

Effect on net present value of alternative expansion plans. Marvin's 100-million-unit expansion has a total NPV of $227 million (total NPV = NPV new plant + change in PV existing plant = 299 − 72 = 227). Total NPV is maximized if Marvin builds 200 million units of new capacity. If Marvin builds 280 million units of new capacity, total NPV is −$144 million.

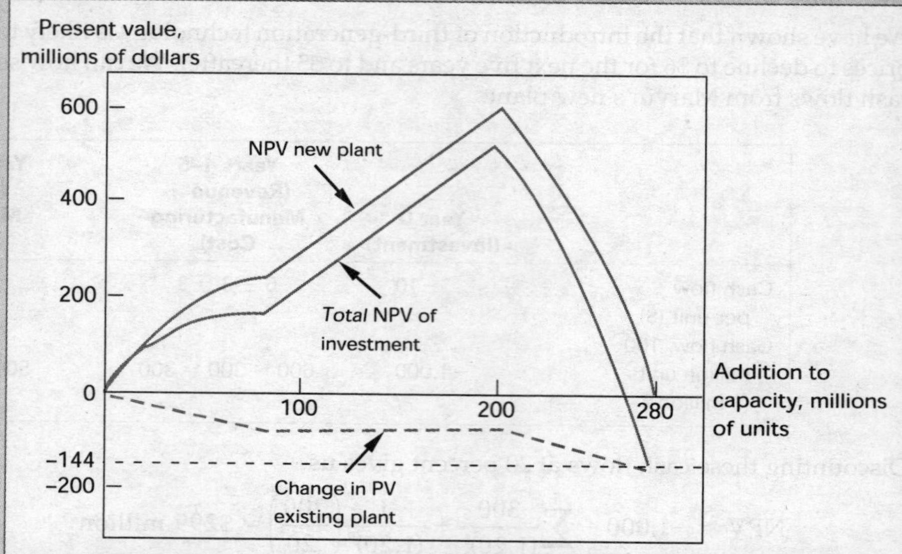

When the new technology becomes generally available in 2032, firms will construct a total of 280 million units of new capacity.[17] But Figure 11.3 shows that it would be foolish for Marvin to go that far. If Marvin added 280 million units of new capacity in 2027, the discounted value of the cash flows from the new plant would be zero *and* the company would have reduced the value of its old plant by $144 million. To maximize NPV, Marvin should construct 200 million units of new capacity and set the price just below $6 to drive out the 2014 manufacturers. Output is, therefore, less and price is higher than either would be under free competition.[18]

The Value of Marvin Stock

Let us think about the effect of Marvin's announcement on the value of its common stock. Marvin has 24 million units of second-generation capacity. In the absence of any third-generation technology, gargle blaster prices would hold at $7 and Marvin's existing plant would be worth

$$\text{PV} = 24 \text{ million} \times \frac{7.00 - 3.50}{.20}$$
$$= \$420 \text{ million}$$

Marvin's new technology reduces the price of gargle blasters initially to $6 and after five years to $5. Therefore the value of existing plant declines to

[17]Total industry capacity in 2032 will be 400 million units. Of this, 120 million units are second-generation capacity, and the remaining 280 million units are third-generation capacity.

[18]Notice that we are assuming that all customers have to pay the same price for their gargle blasters. If Marvin could charge each customer the maximum price which that customer would be willing to pay, output would be the same as under free competition. Such direct price discrimination is illegal and in any case difficult to enforce. But firms do search for indirect ways to differentiate between customers. For example, stores often offer free delivery which is equivalent to a price discount for customers who live at an inconvenient distance.

$$\text{PV} = 24 \text{ million} \times \left[\sum_{t=1}^{5} \frac{6.00 - 3.50}{(1.20)^t} + \frac{5.00 - 3.50}{.20 \times (1.20)^5}\right]$$
$$= \$252 \text{ million}$$

But the *new* plant makes a net addition to shareholders' wealth of $299 million. So after Marvin's announcement its stock will be worth

$$252 + 299 = \$551 \text{ million}^{19}$$

Now here is an illustration of something we talked about in Chapter 4: Before the announcement, Marvin's stock was valued in the market at $460 million. The difference between this figure and the value of the existing plant represented the present value of Marvin's growth opportunities (PVGO). The market valued Marvin's ability to stay ahead of the game at $40 million even before the announcement. After the announcement PVGO rose to $299 million.[20]

The Lessons of Marvin Enterprises

Marvin Enterprises may be just a piece of science fiction, but the problems that it confronts are very real. Whenever Intel considers developing a new microprocessor or Biogen considers developing a new drug, these firms must face up to exactly the same issues as Marvin. We have tried to illustrate the *kind* of questions that you should be asking when presented with a set of cash-flow forecasts. Of course, no economic model is going to predict the future with accuracy. Perhaps Marvin can hold the price above $6. Perhaps competitors will not appreciate the rich pickings to be had in the year 2032. In that case, Marvin's expansion would be even more profitable. But would you want to bet $1 billion on such possibilities? We don't think so.

Investments often turn out to earn far more than the cost of capital because of a favorable surprise. This surprise may in turn create a temporary opportunity for further investments earning more than the cost of capital. But anticipated and more prolonged rents will naturally lead to the entry of rival producers. That is why you should be suspicious of any investment proposal that predicts a stream of economic rents into the indefinite future. Try to estimate *when* competition will drive the NPV down to zero, and think what that implies for the price of your product.

Many companies try to identify the major growth areas in the economy and then concentrate their investment in these areas. But the sad fate of first-generation gargle blaster manufacturers illustrates how rapidly existing plants can be made obsolete by changes in technology. It is fun being in a growth industry when you are at the forefront of the new technology, but a growth industry has no mercy on technological laggards.

You can expect to earn economic rents only if you have some superior resource such as management, sales force, design team, or production facilities. Therefore, rather than trying to move into growth areas, you would do better to identify your firm's comparative advantages and try to capitalize on them. These issues came to the fore during the boom in New Economy stocks in the

---

19 To finance the expansion, Marvin is going to have to sell $1,000 million of new stock. Therefore the *total* value of Marvin's stock will rise to $1,551 million. But investors who put up the new money will receive shares worth $1,000 million. The value of Marvin's old shares after the announcement is therefore $551 million.

20 Notice that the market value of Marvin stock will be greater than $551 million if investors expect the company to expand again within the five-year period. In other words, PVGO after the expansion may still be positive. Investors may expect Marvin to stay one step ahead of its competitors or to successfully apply its special technology in other areas.

late 1990s. The optimists argued that the information revolution was opening up opportunities for companies to grow at unprecedented rates. The pessimists pointed out that competition in e-commerce was likely to be intense and that competition would ensure that the benefits of the information revolution would go largely to consumers. The Finance in the News box, which contains an extract from an article by Warren Buffett, emphasizes the point that rapid growth is no guarantee of superior profits.

We do not wish to imply that good investment opportunities don't exist. For example, such opportunities frequently arise because the firm has invested money in the past which gives it the option to expand cheaply in the future. Perhaps the firm can increase its output just by adding an extra production line, whereas its rivals would need to construct an entirely new factory. In such cases, you must take into account not only *whether* it is profitable to exercise your option but also *when* it is best to do so.

Marvin also reminded us of project interactions, which we first discussed in Chapter 6. When you estimate the incremental cash flows from a project, you must remember to include the project's impact on the rest of the business. By introducing the new technology immediately, Marvin reduced the value of its existing plant by $72 million.

Sometimes the losses on existing plants may completely offset the gains from a new technology. That is why we may see established, technologically advanced companies deliberately slowing down the rate at which they introduce new products. But this can be a dangerous game to play if it opens up opportunities for competitors. For example, for many years Bausch & Lomb was the dominant producer of contact lenses and earned large profits from glass contact lenses that needed to be sterilized every night. Because its existing business generated high returns, the company was slow to introduce disposable lenses. This delay opened up an opportunity for competitors and enabled Johnson & Johnson to enter the disposable lens market and take away business from Bausch & Lomb.

Notice that Marvin's economic rents were equal to the difference between its costs and those of the marginal producer. The costs of the marginal 2014-generation plant consisted of the manufacturing costs plus the opportunity cost of not selling the equipment. Therefore, if the salvage value of the 2014 equipment were higher, Marvin's competitors would incur higher costs and Marvin could earn higher rents. We took the salvage value as given, but it in turn depends on the cost savings from substituting outdated gargle blaster equipment for some other asset. In a well-functioning economy, assets will be used so as to minimize the *total* cost of producing the chosen set of outputs. The economic rents earned by any asset are equal to the total extra costs that would be incurred if that asset were withdrawn.

Here is another point about salvage value which takes us back to our discussion of Air Coromondal in the last chapter: A high salvage value gives the firm an option to abandon a project if things start to go wrong. However, if competitors *know* that you can bail out easily, they are more likely to enter your market. If it is clear that you have no alternative but to stay and fight, they will be more cautious about competing.

When Marvin announced its expansion plans, many owners of first-generation equipment took comfort in the belief that Marvin could not compete with their fully depreciated plant. Their comfort was misplaced. Regardless of past depreciation policy, it paid to scrap first-generation equipment rather than keep it in production. Do not expect that numbers in your balance sheet can protect you from harsh economic reality.

FINANCE IN THE NEWS

WARREN BUFFETT ON GROWTH AND PROFITABILITY

I thought it would be instructive to go back and look at a couple of industries that transformed this country much earlier in this century: automobiles and aviation. Take automobiles first: I have here one page, out of 70 in total, of car and truck manufacturers that have operated in this country. At one time, there was a Berkshire car and an Omaha car. Naturally I noticed those. But there was also a telephone book of others.

All told, there appear to have been at least 2,000 car makes, in an industry that had an incredible impact on people's lives. If you had foreseen in the early days of cars how this industry would develop, you would have said, "Here is the road to riches." So what did we progress to by the 1990s? After corporate carnage that never let up, we came down to three U.S. car companies—themselves no lollapaloozas for investors. So here is an industry that had an enormous impact on America—and also an enormous impact, though not the anticipated one, on investors. Sometimes, incidentally, it's much easier in these transforming events to figure out the losers. You could have grasped the importance of the auto when it came along but still found it hard to pick companies that would make you money. But there was one obvious decision you could have made back then—it's better sometimes to turn these things upside down—and that was to short horses. Frankly, I'm disappointed that the Buffett family was not short horses through this entire period. And we really had no excuse: Living in Nebraska, we would have found it super-easy to borrow horses and avoid a "short squeeze."

U.S. Horse Population
1900: 21 million
1998: 5 million

The other truly transforming business invention of the first quarter of the century, besides the car, was the airplane—another industry whose plainly brilliant future would have caused investors to salivate. So I went back to check out aircraft manufacturers and found that in the 1919–39 period, there were about 300 companies, only a handful still breathing today. Among the planes made then—we must have been the Silicon Valley of that age—were both the Nebraska and the Omaha, two aircraft that even the most loyal Nebraskan no longer relies upon.

Move on to failures of airlines. Here's a list of 129 airlines that in the past 20 years filed for bankruptcy. Continental was smart enough to make that list twice. As of 1992, in fact—though the picture would have improved since then—the money that had been made since the dawn of aviation by all of this country's airline companies was zero. Absolutely zero.

Sizing all this up, I like to think that if I'd been at Kitty Hawk in 1903 when Orville Wright took off, I would have been farsighted enough, and public-spirited enough—I owed this to future capitalists—to shoot him down. I mean, Karl Marx couldn't have done as much damage to capitalists as Orville did.

I won't dwell on other glamorous businesses that dramatically changed our lives but concurrently failed to deliver rewards to U.S. investors: the manufacture of radios and televisions, for example. But I will draw a lesson from these businesses: The key to investing is not assessing how much an industry is going to affect society, or how much it will grow, but rather determining the competitive advantage of any given company and, above all, the durability of that advantage. The products or services that have wide, sustainable moats around them are the ones that deliver rewards to investors.

Source: C. Loomis, "Mr. Buffett on the Stock Market," *Fortune* (November 22, 1999), pp. 110–115. © 1999 Time Inc. Reprinted with permission.

SUMMARY

It helps to use present value when you are making investment decisions, but that is not the whole story. Good investment decisions depend both on a sensible criterion and on sensible forecasts. In this chapter we have looked at the problem of forecasting.

Projects may look attractive for two reasons: (1) There may be some errors in the sponsor's forecasts, or (2) the company can genuinely expect to earn excess profit from the project. Good managers, therefore, try to ensure that the odds are stacked in their favor by expanding in areas in which the company has a comparative advantage. We like to put this another way by saying that good managers try to understand the relationship between finance and strategy. They carefully avoid expansion when competitive advantages are absent and economic rents are unlikely. They do not project favorable current product prices into the future without checking whether entry or expansion by competitors will drive future prices down.

Our story of Marvin Enterprises illustrates the origin of rents and how they determine a project's cash flows and net present value.

Any present value calculation, including our calculation for Marvin Enterprises, is subject to error. That's life: There's no other sensible way to value most capital investment projects. But some assets, such as gold, real estate, crude oil, ships, and airplanes, and financial assets, such as stocks and bonds, are traded in reasonably competitive markets. When you have the market value of such an asset, *use it*, at least as a starting point for your analysis.

FURTHER READING

P. Barwise, P. Marsh, and R. Wensley: "Must Finance and Strategy Clash?" *Harvard Business Review*, (September–October 1989), pp. 2–7.

M. Porter: "What Is Strategy?" *Harvard Business Review*, (November–December 1996), pp. 61–78.

R. M. Grant, *Contemporary Strategy Analysis*, 4th ed., Blackwell Publisher, Oxford, 2002.

CONCEPT REVIEW QUESTIONS

1. We described a manager who has just learned about DCF as like a baby with a hammer. What is the point of our analogy? (page 277)
2. Michael Porter observes that firms can generate economic rents both by their choice of industry and by the way that they position themselves within that industry. What are the three ways that they can usefully position themselves within their industry? (page 283)
3. A new leaching process allows your company to recover some gold as a by-product of its aluminum mining operations. How would you calculate the PV of the future cash flows from gold sales? (page 280)

For additional Concept Review Questions, please visit us at www.mhhe.com/bmam8e or refer to your Student CD.

QUIZ

1. True or false?
   a. A firm that earns the opportunity cost of capital is earning economic rents.
   b. A firm that invests in positive-NPV ventures expects to earn economic rents.
   c. Financial managers should try to identify areas where their firms can earn economic rents, because it is there that positive-NPV projects are likely to be found.
   d. Economic rent is the equivalent annual cost of operating capital equipment.

2. Demand for concave utility meters is expanding rapidly, but the industry is highly competitive. A utility meter plant costs Rs. 50 million to set up, and it has an annual capacity of 500,000 meters. The production cost is Rs. 5 per meter, and this cost is not expected to change. The machines have an indefinite physical life and the cost of capital is 10 percent. What is the competitive price of a utility meter?
   a. Rs. 5
   b. Rs. 10
   c. Rs. 15

3. Your brother-in-law wants you to join him in purchasing a building on the outskirts of town. You and he would then develop and run a Taco Palace restaurant. Both of you are extremely optimistic about future real estate prices in this area, and your brother-in-law has prepared a cash-flow forecast that implies a large positive NPV. This calculation assumes sale of the property after 10 years.

   What further calculations should you do before going ahead?

4. On the London Metals Exchange the price for copper to be delivered in one year is $ 1,600 a ton. *Note:* Payment is made when the copper is delivered. The risk-free interest rate is 5 percent and the expected market return is 12 percent.
   a. Suppose that you expect to produce and sell 100,000 tons of copper next year. What is the PV of this output? Assume that the sale occurs at the end of the year.
   b. If copper has a beta of 1.2, what is the expected price of copper at the end of the year? What is the certainty-equivalent price?

5. New-model commercial airplanes are much more fuel-efficient than older models. How is it possible for airlines flying older models to make money when its competitors are flying newer planes? Explain briefly.

PRACTICE QUESTIONS

1. Suppose that you are considering investing in an asset for which there is a reasonably good secondary market. Specifically, your company is Jet Airways, and the asset is a Boeing 757, a widely used airplane. How does the presence of a secondary market simplify your problem in principle? Do you think these simplifications could be realized in practice? Explain.

2. There is an active, competitive leasing (i.e., rental) market for most standard types of commercial jets. Many of the planes flown by the major domestic and international airlines are not owned by them but leased for periods ranging from a few months to several years.

   Coromondal Airlines, however, owns two long range DC-11s just withdrawn from Singapore operations. Coromondal is considering using these planes to develop the potentially lucrative new route from Jamshedpur to Bangalore. A considerable investment in terminal facilities, training, and advertising will be required. Once committed, Coromondal will have to operate the route for at least three years. One further complication: the manager of Coromondal's international division is opposing commitment of the planes to the Jamshedpur–Bangalore route because of the anticipated future growth in traffic through Coromondal's new hub in Bangkok.

   How would you evaluate the proposed Jamshedpur-Bangalore project? Give a detailed list of the necessary steps in your analysis. Explain how the airline leasing market would be taken into account. If the project is attractive, how would you respond to the manager of the international division?

3. Suppose that the current price of gold is Rs. 10,200 per 10 grams. Yellow-Gold Consultants advises you that gold prices will increase at an average rate of 12 percent for the next two year. After that the growth rate will fall to a long-run trend of 3 percent per year. What is the price of 1 kg of gold produced in eight years? Assume that gold prices have a beta of 0 and that the risk-free rate is 6.2 percent.

   eXcel

   Please visit us at www.mhhe.com/bmam8e or refer to your Student CD.

4. Thanks to the acquisition of a new patent, your company now has exclusive production rights for barkelgassers (BGs) in India. Production facilities for 200,000 BGs per year will require a Rs. 25 million immediate capital expenditure. Production

costs are estimated at Rs. 65 per BG. The BG marketing manager is confident that all 200,000 units can be sold for Rs. 100 per unit (in real terms) until the patent runs out five years hence. After that the marketing manager hasn't a clue about what the selling price will be.

What is the NPV of the BG project? Assume the real cost of capital is 9 percent. To keep things simple, also make the following assumptions:

- The technology for making BGs will not change. Capital and production costs will stay the same in real terms.
- Competitors know the technology and can enter as soon as the patent expires, that is, in year 6.
- If your company invests immediately, full production begins after 12 months, that is, in year 1.
- There are no taxes.
- BG production facilities last 12 years. They have no salvage value at the end of their useful life.

5. How would your answer to question 4 change if:

- Technological improvements reduce the cost of new BG production facilities by 3 percent per year?

Thus a new plant built in year 1 would cost only 25 (1 − .03) = Rs. 24.25 million; a plant built in year 2 would cost Rs. 23.52 million; and so on. Assume that production costs per unit remain at Rs. 65.

6. Go to the "live" Excel spreadsheets versions of Tables 11.1 to 11.3 on this book's CD or at **www.mhhe.com/bmam8e.** Reevaluate the NPV of the proposed polyzone project under each of the following assumptions. What's the right management decision in each case?

Please visit us at www.mhhe.com/bmam8e or refer to your Student CD.

a. Spread in year 4 holds at $1.20 per pound.
b. The U.S. chemical company can start up polyzone production at 40 million pounds in year 1 rather than year 2.
c. The U.S. company makes a technological advance that reduces its annual production costs to $25 million. Competitors' production costs do not change.

7. Photographic laboratories recover and recycle the silver used in photographic film. Riverside Photo is considering purchase of improved equipment for their laboratory at Kolkata. Here is the information they have:

- The equipment costs Rs. 1000,000 and will cost Rs. 800,000 per year to run.
- It has an economic life of 10 years but can be depreciated over five years by the written-down value method (see Section 6.2).
- It will recover an additional 5,000 grams of silver per year.
- Silver is selling for Rs. 19,122 per kg. Over the past 10 years, the price of silver has appreciated by 4.5 percent per year in real terms. Silver is traded in an active, competitive market.
- The marginal tax rate is 3.5 percent. Assume Indian tax law.
- The company cost of capital is 8 percent in real terms.
- The nominal interest rate is 6.2 percent.

What is the NPV of the new equipment? Make additional assumptions as necessary.

8. The Dracula Dramatic Association has come up with a unique prize for its December 2009 fund-raising ball: twenty prizes will be distributed, each one a ticket entitling the bearer to receive a cash-award from its association on December 31, 2010. The cash award is to be determined by calculating the ratio of the level of S&P CNX Nifty Index of stock prices on December 31, 2010, to its level on June 30, 2010, and multiplying it by Rs.1000. Thus if the index turns out to be 1,000 on June 30, 2010, and 1200 on December 31, 2010 the payoff will be 1000 × (1,200/1,000) = Rs. 1200

After the ball, a black market springs up in which tickets are traded. What will tickets sell for on January 1, 2010? On June 30, 2010? Assume that the risk-free rate is 10 percent per year. Also assume that the Dracula Dramatic Association will be solvent at year-end 2010 and will, in fact, pay off on the tickets. Make other assumptions as necessary.

Would ticket values be different if the tickets' payoffs depended on Sensex rather than on Nifty?

9. You are asked to value a large building in northern New Jersey. The valuation is needed for a bankruptcy settlement. Here are the facts:

- The settlement *requires* that the building's value equal the PV value of the *net cash proceeds* the railroad would receive if it cleared the building and sold it for its highest and best nonrailroad use, which is as a warehouse.
- The building has been appraised at $1 million. This figure is based on actual recent selling prices of a sample of similar New Jersey buildings used as, or available for use as, warehouses.
- If rented today as a warehouse, the building could generate $80,000 per year. This cash flow is calculated *after* out-of-pocket operating expenses and *after* real estate taxes of $50,000 per year:

Gross rents	$180,000
Operating expenses	50,000
Real estate taxes	50,000
Net	$80,000

Gross rents, operating expenses, and real estate taxes are uncertain but are expected to grow with inflation.
- However, it would take one year and $200,000 to clear out the railroad equipment and prepare the building for use as a warehouse. This expenditure would be spread evenly over the next year.
- The property will be put on the market when ready for use as a warehouse. Your real estate adviser says that properties of this type take, on average, one year to sell after they are put on the market. However, the railroad could rent the building as a warehouse while waiting for it to sell.
- The opportunity cost of capital for investment in real estate is 8 percent in *real* terms.
- Your real estate adviser notes that selling prices of comparable buildings in northern New Jersey have declined, in real terms, at an average rate of 2 percent per year over the last 10 years.
- A 5 percent sales commission would be paid by the railroad at the time of the sale.
- The railroad pays no income taxes. It would have to pay property taxes.

CHALLENGE QUESTIONS

1. The manufacture of polysyllabic acid is a competitive industry. Most plants have an annual output of 100,000 tons. Operating costs are Rs. 90 a ton, and the sales price is Re. 1 a ton. A 100,000-ton plant costs Rs. 100,000 and has an indefinite life. Its current scrap value of Re. 60,000 is expected to decline to Rs. 57,900 over the next two years.

eXcel
Please visit us at www.mhhe.com/bmam8e or refer to your Student CD

Phlogiston, Inc., proposes to invest Rs. 100,000 in a plant that employs a new low-cost process to manufacture polysyllabic acid. The plant has the same capacity as existing units, but operating costs are Rs. 85 a ton. Phlogiston estimates that it has two years' lead over each of its rivals in use of the process but is unable to build any more plants itself before year 2. Also it believes that demand over the next two years is likely to be sluggish and that its new plant will therefore cause temporary over capacity.

You can assume that there are no taxes and that the cost of capital is 10 percent.

a. By the end of year 2, the prospective increase in acid demand will require the construction of several new plants using the Phlogiston process. What is the likely NPV of such plants?
b. What does that imply for the price of polysyllabic acid in year 3 and beyond?
c. Would you expect existing plant to be scrapped in year 2? How would your answer differ if scrap value were Rs. 40,000 or Rs. 80,000?
d. The acid plants of United Alchemists, Inc., have been fully depreciated. Can it operate them profitably after year 2?

e. Acidosis, Inc., purchased a new plant last year for Rs. 100,000 and is writing it down by Rs. 10,000 a year. Should it scrap this plant in year 2?

f. What would be the NPV of Phlogiston's venture?

2. The world airline system is composed of the routes X and Y, each of which requires 10 aircraft. These routes can be serviced by three types of aircraft—A, B, and C. There are 5 type A aircraft available, 10 type B, and 10 type C. These aircraft are identical except for their operating costs, which are as follows:

	Annual Operating Cost (Rs. millions)	
Aircraft Type	**Route X**	**Route Y**
A	1.5	1.5
B	2.5	2.0
C	4.5	3.5

The aircraft have a useful life of five years and a salvage value of Rs. 1 million.

The aircraft owners do not operate the aircraft themselves but rent them to the operators. Owners act competitively to maximize their rental income, and operators attempt to minimize their operating costs. Airfares are also competitively determined.

Assume the cost of capital is 10 percent.

a. Which aircraft would be used on which route, and how much would each aircraft be worth?

b. What would happen to usage and prices of each aircraft if the number of type A aircraft increased to 10?

c. What would happen if the number of type A aircraft increased to 15?

d. What would happen if the number of type A aircraft increased to 20?

State any additional assumptions you need to make.

3. Taxes are a cost, and, therefore, changes in tax rates can affect consumer prices, project lives, and the value of existing firms. The following problem illustrates this. It also illustrates that tax changes that appear to be "good for business" do not always increase the value of existing firms. Indeed, unless new investment incentives increase consumer demand, they can work only by rendering existing equipment obsolete.

The manufacture of bucolic acid is a competitive business. Demand is steadily expanding, and new plants are constantly being opened. Expected cash flows from an investment in a new plant are as follows:

	0	1	2	3
1. Initial investment	100			
2. Revenues		100	100	100
3. Cash operating costs		50	50	50
4. Tax depreciation		33.33	33.33	33.33
5. Income pretax		16.67	16.67	16.67
6. Tax at 40%		6.67	6.67	6.67
7. Net income		10	10	10
8. After-tax salvage				15
9. Cash flow (7 + 8 + 4 − 1)	−100	+43.33	+43.33	+58.33
NPV at 20% = 0				

Assumptions:
1. Tax depreciation is straight-line over three years.
2. Pretax salvage value is 25 in year 3 and 50 if the asset is scrapped in year 2.
3. Tax on salvage value is 40 percent of the difference between salvage value and depreciated investment.
4. The cost of capital is 20 percent.

a. What is the value of a one-year-old plant? Of a two-year-old plant?
b. Suppose that the government now changes tax depreciation to allow a 100 percent writeoff in year 1. How does this affect the value of existing one- and two-year-old plants? Existing plants must continue using the original tax depreciation schedule.
c. Would it now make sense to scrap existing plants when they are two rather than three years old?
d. How would your answers change if the corporate income tax were abolished entirely?

MINI-CASE

Ecsy-Cola[21]

Libby Flannery, the regional manager of Ecsy-Cola, the international soft drinks empire, was reviewing her investment plans for Central Asia. She had contemplated launching Ecsy-Cola in the ex-Soviet republic of Inglistan in 2007. This would involve a capital outlay of $20 million in 2006 to build a bottling plant and set up a distribution system there. Fixed costs (for manufacturing, distribution, and marketing) would then be $3 million per year from 2006 onward. This would be sufficient to make and sell 200 million liters per year—enough for every man, woman, and child in Inglistan to drink four bottles per week! But there would be few savings from building a smaller plant, and import tariffs and transport costs in the region would keep all production within national borders.

The variable costs of production and distribution would be 12 cents per liter. Company policy requires a rate of return of 25 percent in nominal dollar terms, after local taxes but before deducting any costs of financing. The sales revenue is forecasted to be 35 cents per liter.

Bottling plants last almost forever, and all unit costs and revenues were expected to remain constant in nominal terms. Tax would be payable at a rate of 30 percent, and under the Inglistan corporate tax code, capital expenditures can be written off on a straight-line basis over four years.

All these inputs were reasonably clear. But Ms. Flannery racked her brain trying to forecast sales. Ecsy-Cola found that the "1–2–4" rule works in most new markets. Sales typically double in the second year, double again in the third year, and after that remain roughly constant. Libby's best guess was that, if she went ahead immediately, initial sales in Inglistan would be 12.5 million liters in 2008, ramping up to 50 million in 2010 and onward.

Ms. Flannery also worried whether it would be better to wait a year. The soft drink market was developing rapidly in neighboring countries, and in a year's time she should have a much better idea whether Ecsy-Cola would be likely to catch on in Inglistan. If it didn't catch on and sales stalled below 20 million liters, a large investment probably would not be justified.

Ms. Flannery had assumed that Ecsy-Cola's keen rival, Sparky-Cola, would not also enter the market. But last week she received a shock when in the lobby of the Kapitaliste Hotel she bumped into her opposite number at Sparky-Cola. Sparky-Cola would face costs similar to Ecsy-Cola. How would Sparky-Cola respond if Ecsy-Cola entered the market? Would it decide to enter also? If so, how would that affect the profitability of Ecsy-Cola's project?

Ms. Flannery thought again about postponing investment for a year. Suppose Sparky-Cola was interested in the Inglistan market. Would that favor delay or immediate action? Maybe Ecsy-Cola should announce its plans before Sparky-Cola had a chance to develop its own proposals. It seemed that the Inglistan project was becoming more complicated by the day.

QUESTIONS

1. Calculate the NPV of the proposed investment, using the inputs suggested in this case. How sensitive is this NPV to future sales volume?
2. What are the pros and cons of waiting for a year before deciding whether to invest? *Hint:* What happens if demand turns out high and Sparky-Cola also invests? What if Ecsy-Cola invests right away and gains a one-year head start on Sparky-Cola?

[21]We thank Anthony Neuberger for suggesting this topic.

CHAPTER [12]

AGENCY PROBLEMS, MANAGEMENT COMPENSATION AND THE MEASUREMENT OF PERFORMANCE

SO FAR WE'VE concentrated on criteria and procedures for identifying capital investments with positive NPVs. If a firm takes all (and only) positive-NPV projects, it maximizes the firm's value. But do the firm's managers want to maximize value?

Managers have no special gene or chromosome that automatically aligns their personal interests with outside investors' financial objectives. So how do shareholders ensure that top managers do not feather their own nests or grind their own axes? And how do top managers ensure that middle managers and employees try as hard as they can to find positive-NPV projects?

Here we circle back to the principal–agent problems first raised in Chapters 1 and 2. Shareholders are the ultimate principals; top managers are the stockholders' agents. But middle managers and employees are in turn agents of top management. Thus senior managers, including the chief financial officer, are simultaneously agents vis-à-vis shareholders and principals vis-à-vis the rest of the firm. The problem is to get everyone working together to maximize value.

This chapter summarizes how corporations grapple with that problem as they identify and commit to capital investment projects. We start with basic facts and trade-offs and end with difficult problems in performance measurement. The main topics are as follows:

- Process: How companies develop plans and budgets for capital investments, how they authorize specific projects, and how they check whether projects perform as promised.
- Information: Getting accurate information and good forecasts to decision makers.
- Incentives: Making sure managers and employees are rewarded appropriately when they add value to the firm.
- Performance Measurement: You can't reward value added unless you can measure it. Since you get what you reward, and reward what you measure, you get what you measure. Make sure you are measuring the right thing.

In each case we will summarize standard practice and warn against common mistakes. The section on incentives probes more deeply into principal–agent relationships. The last two sections of the chapter describe performance measures, including residual income and economic value added. We also uncover the biases lurking in accounting measures of performance. The pitfalls in measuring profitability are serious but are not as widely recognized as they should be.

12.1 THE CAPITAL INVESTMENT PROCESS

For most large firms, the investment process starts with preparation of an annual **capital budget,** which is a list of investment projects planned for the coming year.

Most firms let project proposals bubble up from plants for review by divisional management and then from divisions for review by senior management and their planning staff. Of course middle managers cannot identify all worthwhile projects. For example, the managers of plants A and B cannot be expected to see the potential economies of closing their plants and consolidating production at a new plant C. Divisional managers would propose plant C.

Preparation of the capital budget is not a rigid, bureaucratic exercise. There is plenty of give-and-take and back-and-forth. Divisional managers negotiate with plant managers and fine-tune the division's list of projects. The final capital budget must also reflect the corporation's strategic planning. Strategic planning takes a top-down view of the company. It attempts to identify businesses in which the company has a competitive advantage. It also attempts to identify businesses to sell or that should be allowed to run down.

In other words, a firm's capital investment choices should reflect both bottom-up and top-down processes—capital budgeting and strategic planning, respectively. The two processes should complement each other. Plant and division managers, who do most of the work in bottom-up capital budgeting, may not see the forest for the trees. Strategic planners may have a mistaken view of the forest because they do not look at the trees one by one.

Project Authorizations

Once the capital budget has been approved by top management and the board of directors, it is the official plan for the ensuing year. However, it is not the final sign-off for specific projects. Most companies require **appropriation requests** for each proposal. These requests include detailed forecasts, discounted-cash-flow analyses, and backup information.

Because investment decisions are so important to the value of the firm, final approval of appropriation requests tends to be reserved for top management. Companies set ceilings on the size of projects that divisional managers can authorize. Often these ceilings are surprisingly low. For example, a large company, investing Rs 400 crores per year, might require top management approval of all projects over Rs 50 lack.

Some Investments May Not Show Up in the Capital Budget

The boundaries of capital expenditure are often imprecise. Consider the investments in information technology, or IT (computers, software and systems, training, and telecommunications), made by large banks. These investments soak up *hundreds* of millions of rupees annually, and some multi-year IT projects have costs well over Rs 10 billion. Yet much of this expenditure goes to intangibles such as system design, testing, or training. Such outlays often bypass capital expenditure controls, particularly if the outlays are made piecemeal rather than as large, discrete commitments. Investments in IT may not appear in the capital budget, but for financial institutions they are much more important than outlays for plant and equipment.

Here are some further examples of important investments that rarely appear in the capital budget.

Research and Development For many companies, the most important asset is technology. The technology is embodied in patents, unique products, or special production methods. It is generated by investment in research and development (R&D).

R&D budgets for major pharmaceutical companies are huge. Ranbaxy Laboratories, the largest spender on new-drug research in India, spent Rs.399.65 crores on R&D in 2004-05. In fact a PHARMABIZ study shows that the R&D expenditure of 25 drug companies in India increased by 42 percent from Rs.1278 crores in 2003-04 to Rs.1814.65 crores in 2004-05.[1] These figures pale into insignificance compared to the R&D expenditures of the pharmaceutical giants like Pfizer that spent more than $7 billion in 2003 itself. The R&D cost of bringing one new prescription drug to market has been estimated at $800 million (approximately Rs.3680 crores.)[2]

Marketing In 1998 Gillette launched the Mach3 safety razor. It had invested $750 million in new, custom machinery and renovated production facilities. It planned to spend $300 million on the

[1]See http://www.pharmabiz.com/

[2]The figure represents the average pretax cost of development of 68 randomly selected new drugs, including the cost of the capital employed. See J. A. DiMasi, R. W. Hansen, and H. G. Grabowski, "The Price of Innovation: New Estimates of Drug Development Costs," *Journal of Health Economics* 22 (2003), pp.151–185.

initial marketing program. Its goal was to make the Mach3 a long-lived, brand-name, cash-cow consumer product. This marketing outlay was clearly a capital investment, because it was cash spent to generate future cash inflows. In India, Maruti Udyog Limited plans to spend Rs.2718 crores (about $590 million) by 2008 for new product launches, R&D and technology upgradation. The company wants to launch five new car models in the next five years[3].

Training and Personnel Development By launch of the Mach3, Gillette had hired 160 new workers and paid for 30,000 hours of training.

Small Decisions Add Up Operating managers make investment decisions every day. They may carry extra inventories of raw materials just to be sure they won't be caught short. Operating managers...be caught short. Managers at the Regent Hotel, Delhi, may decide they need one more car or a rice cooking machine for the cafeteria. They may hold on to an idle machine tool or an extra car that could have been sold. These are not big investments (Rs.40,000 here, Rs.50,000 there) but they add up.

How can the financial manager ensure that small investments are made for the right reasons? Financial staff can't second-guess every operating decision. They can't demand a discounted-cash-flow analysis of a cappuccino machine. Instead they have to make operating managers conscious of the cost of investment and alert for investments that add value. We return to this problem later in the chapter.

Our general point is this: The financial manager has to consider all investments, regardless of whether they appear in the formal capital budget. The financial manager in a pharmaceutical company should be deeply involved in decisions about R&D. In a consumer goods company, the financial manager should play a key role in marketing decisions to develop and launch new products.

Postaudits

Most firms keep a check on the progress of large projects by conducting postaudits shortly after the projects have begun to operate. Postaudits identify problems that need fixing, check the accuracy of forecasts, and suggest questions that should have been asked before the project was undertaken. Postaudits pay off mainly by helping managers to do a better job when it comes to the next round of investments. After a postaudit the controller may say, "We should have anticipated the extra working capital needed to support the project." When the next proposal arrives, working capital will get the attention it deserves.

Postaudits may not be able to measure all cash flows generated by a project. It may be impossible to split the project away from the rest of the business. Suppose that you have just taken over a trucking firm that operates a merchandise delivery service for local stores. You decide to revitalize the business by cutting costs and improving service. This requires three investments:

1. Buying five new diesel trucks.
2. Constructing a dispatching center.
3. Buying a computer and special software to keep track of packages and schedule trucks.

A year later you try a postaudit of the computer. You verify that it is working properly and check actual costs of purchase, installation, and training against projections. But how do you identify the incremental cash inflows generated by the computer? No one has kept records of the extra diesel fuel that *would have been* used or the extra shipments that *would have been* lost had the computer not been installed. You may be able to verify that service is better, but how much of the improvement comes

[3]See Motorindia, February 28, 2006, Page 56.

from the new trucks, how much comes from the dispatching center, and how much comes from the new computer? It is impossible to say. The only meaningful way to judge the success or failure of your revitalization program is to examine the delivery business as a whole.

12.2 DECISION MAKERS NEED GOOD INFORMATION

Good investment decisions require good information. Decision makers get such information only if other managers are encouraged to supply it. Here are four information problems that financial managers need to think about.

Establishing Consistent Forecasts

Inconsistent assumptions often creep into investment proposals. Suppose the manager of your furniture division is bullish on housing starts but the manager of your appliance division is bearish. This inconsistency makes the furniture division's projects look better than the appliance division's. Senior management ought to negotiate a consensus estimate and make sure that all NPVs are recomputed using that joint estimate. Then projects can be evaluated consistently.

This is why many firms begin the capital budgeting process by establishing forecasts of economic indicators, such as inflation and growth in gross national product, as well as forecasts of particular items that are important to the firm's business, such as housing starts or the price of raw materials. These forecasts can then be used as the basis for all project analyses.

Reducing Forecast Bias

Anyone who is keen to get a project accepted is likely to look on the bright side when forecasting the project's cash flows. Such overoptimism seems to be a common feature in financial forecasts. Overoptimism afflicts governments too, probably more than private businesses. How often have you heard of a new dam, highway, or military aircraft that actually cost *less* than was originally forecasted?

You will probably never be able to eliminate bias completely, but if you are aware of why bias occurs, you are at least part of the way there. Project sponsors are likely to overstate their case deliberately only if you, the manager, encourage them to do so. For example, if they believe that success depends on having the largest division rather than the most profitable one, they will propose large expansion projects that they do not truly believe have positive NPVs. Or if you invite each division to compete for limited resources, you will find that each attempts to outbid the other for those resources. The fault in such cases is your own—if you hold up the hoop, others will try to jump through it.

Getting Senior Management the Information That It Needs

Valuing capital investment opportunities is hard enough when you can do the entire job yourself. In real life it is a cooperative effort. Although cooperation brings more knowledge to bear, it has its own problems. Some are unavoidable, just another cost of doing business. Others can be alleviated by adding checks and balances to the investment process.

Many of the problems stem from sponsors' eagerness to obtain approval for their favorite projects. As a proposal travels up the organization, alliances are formed. Preparation of the request inevitably involves compromises. But, once a division has agreed on its plants' proposals, the plants unite in competing against outsiders.

The competition among divisions can be put to good use if it forces division managers to develop a well-thought-out case for what they want to do. But the competition has its costs as well. Several thousand appropriation requests may reach the senior management level each year, all essentially sales documents presented by united fronts and designed to persuade. Alternative schemes have been filtered out at an earlier stage. The danger is that senior management cannot obtain (let alone absorb) the information to evaluate each project rationally.

The dangers are illustrated by the following practical question: Should we announce a definite opportunity cost of capital for computing the NPV of projects in our furniture division? The answer in theory is a clear yes, providing that the projects of the division are all in the same risk class. Remember that most project analysis is done at the plant or divisional level. Plant and division managers cannot judge projects correctly unless they know the true opportunity cost of capital.

Suppose that senior management settles on 12 percent. That helps plant managers make rational decisions. But it also tells them exactly how optimistic they have to be to get their pet project accepted. Brealey, Myers, and Allen's Second Law states: *The proportion of proposed projects having a positive NPV at the official corporate hurdle rate is independent of the hurdle rate.*[4]

This is not a facetious conjecture. The law was tested in a large oil company, whose capital budgeting staff kept careful statistics on forecasted profitability of proposed projects. One year top management announced a big push to conserve cash. It imposed discipline on capital expenditures by increasing the corporate hurdle rate by several percentage points. But staff statistics showed that the fraction of proposals with positive NPVs stayed rock-steady at about 85 percent of all proposals. Top management's tighter discipline was repaid with expanded optimism.

A firm that accepts poor information at the top faces two consequences. First, senior management cannot evaluate individual projects. So projects that have the approval of division general managers are seldom turned down by their group of divisions, and those reaching top management are almost never rejected.[5] Second, since managers have limited control over project-by-project decisions, capital investment decisions are effectively decentralized regardless of what formal procedures specify.

Some senior managers try to impose discipline and offset optimism by setting rigid capital expenditure limits. This artificial capital rationing forces plant or division managers to set priorities. The firm ends up using capital rationing not because capital is truly unobtainable but as a way of decentralizing decisions.

Eliminating Conflicts of Interest

Plant and divisional managers are concerned about their own futures. Sometimes their interests conflict with stockholders' and that may lead to investment decisions that do not maximize shareholder wealth. For example, new plant managers naturally want to demonstrate good performance

[4]There is no First Law; we thought that "Second Law" sounded better. There *is* a Third Law, but that is for another chapter.

[5]See J. L. Bower, *Managing the Resource Allocation Process: A Study of Corporate Planning and Investment*, Division of Research, Graduate School of Business Administration, Harvard University, Boston, 1970.

right away, in order to move up the corporate ladder, so they are tempted to propose quick-payback projects even if NPV is sacrificed. And if their performance is judged on book earnings, they will also be attracted by projects whose accounting results look good. That leads us to the next topic: how to motivate managers.

12.3 INCENTIVES

Managers will act in shareholders' interests only if they have the right incentives. Good capital investment decisions therefore depend on how managers' performance is measured and rewarded.

We start this section with an overview of agency problems encountered in capital investment, and then we look at how top management is actually compensated. Finally we consider how top management can set incentives for the middle managers and other employees who actually operate the business.

Overview: Agency Problems in Capital Budgeting

As you have surely guessed, there is no perfect system of incentives. But it's easy to see what *won't* work. Suppose shareholders decide to pay the financial managers a fixed salary—no bonuses, no stock options, just RsX per month. The manager, as the stockholders' agent, is instructed to find and invest in all positive-NPV projects open to the firm. The manager may sincerely try to do so, but will face various tempting alternatives:

Reduced effort. Finding and implementing investment in truly valuable projects is a high-effort, high-pressure activity. The financial manager will be tempted to slack off.

Perks. Our hypothetical financial manager gets no bonuses. Only RsX per month. But he or she may take a bonus anyway, not in cash, but in tickets to sporting events, lavish office accommodations, planning meetings scheduled at luxury resorts, and so on. Economists refer to these nonpecuniary rewards as *private benefits.* Ordinary people call them *perks* (short for perquisites).

Empire building. Other things equal, managers prefer to run large businesses rather than small ones. Getting from small to large may not be a positive-NPV undertaking.

Entrenching investment. Suppose manager Q considers two expansion plans. One plan will require a manager with special skills that manager Q just happens to have. The other plan requires only a general-purpose manager. Guess which plan Q will favor. Projects designed to require or reward the skills of existing managers are called *entrenching investments*.[6]

Entrenching investments and empire building are typical symptoms of overinvestment, that is, investing beyond the point where NPV falls to zero. The temptation to overinvest is highest

[6] A. Shleifer and R. W. Vishny, "Management Entrenchment: The Case of Manager-Specific Investments," *Journal of Financial Economics* 25 (November 1989), pp. 123–140.

when the firm has plenty of cash but limited investment opportunities. Michael Jensen calls this a *free-cash-flow* problem.[7]

Avoiding risk. If the manager receives only a fixed salary, she cannot share in the upside of risky projects. But, if the risky project turns out to be a loser, her job may be on the line. In this case safe projects are from the manager's viewpoint better than risky ones. But risky projects can sometimes have large, positive NPVs.

A manager on a fixed salary could hardly avoid all these temptations all of the time. The resulting loss in value is an agency cost.

Monitoring

Agency costs can be reduced in two ways: by *monitoring* the managers' effort and actions and by giving them the right *incentives* to maximize value.

Monitoring can prevent the more obvious agency costs, such as blatant perks. It can confirm that the manager is putting sufficient time on the job. But monitoring requires time and money. Some monitoring is almost always worthwhile, but a limit is soon reached at which an extra rupee spent on monitoring would not return an extra rupee of value from reduced agency costs. Like all investments, monitoring encounters diminishing returns.

Some agency costs can't be prevented even with spendthrift monitoring. Suppose a shareholder undertakes to monitor capital investment decisions. How could he or she ever know for sure whether a capital budget approved by top management includes (1) *all* the positive-NPV opportunities open to the firm and (2) *no* projects with negative NPVs due to empire-building or entrenching investments? The managers obviously know more about the firm's prospects than outsiders ever can. If the shareholder could list all projects and their NPVs, then the managers would hardly be needed!

Who actually does the monitoring? Ultimately it is the shareholders' responsibility, but in large, public companies, monitoring is *delegated* to the board of directors, who are elected by shareholders and are supposed to represent their interests. The board meets regularly, both formally and informally, with top management. Attentive directors come to know a great deal about the firm's prospects and performance and the strengths and weaknesses of its top management.

The board also hires independent accountants to audit the firm's financial statements. If the audit uncovers no problems, the auditors issue an opinion that the financial statements fairly represent the company's financial condition and are consistent with generally accepted accounting principles (GAAP, for short).

If problems are found, the auditors will negotiate changes in assumptions or procedures. Managers almost always agree, because if acceptable changes are not made, the auditors will issue a *qualified opinion*, which is bad news for the company and its shareholders. A qualified opinion suggests that managers are covering something up and undermines investors' confidence that they can monitor effectively.

A qualified audit opinion may be bad news, but when investors learn of accounting irregularities that have escaped detection by auditors, there can be hell to pay. In January 2004 Adecco, the giant Swiss employment agency, announced that it had discovered material accounting irregularities in its North American operations. The next day Adecco's share price fell by 40 percent, wiping $5 billion off the market value of the company.

---

[7]M. C. Jensen, "Agency Costs of Free Cash Flow, Corporate Finance and Takeovers," *American Economic Review* 76 (May 1986), pp. 323–329.

Lenders also monitor. If a company takes out a large bank loan, the bank will track the company's assets, earnings, and cash flow. By monitoring to protect its loan, the bank protects shareholders' interests also.[8]

Delegated monitoring is especially important when ownership is widely dispersed. If there is a dominant shareholder, he or she will generally keep a close eye on top management. But when the number of stockholders is large, and each stock-holding is small, individual investors cannot justify much time and expense for monitoring. Each is tempted to leave the task to others, taking a free ride on others' efforts. But if everybody prefers to let somebody else do it, then it will not get done; that is, monitoring by shareholders will not be strong or effective. Economists call this the *free-rider problem.*[9]

If the free-rider problem is severe, delegated monitoring may be the only solution. But delegation brings its own agency problems. For example, many board members may be long-standing friends of the CEO and may be indebted to the CEO for help or advice. Understandably, they may be reluctant to fire the CEO or enquire too deeply into his or her conduct. Auditing firms may also have conflicts of interest. For example, many believed that Enron's auditors, Arthur Andersen, might have been tougher on the company had it not also earned substantial fees from providing Enron with consulting services. As a result, auditing firms are no longer allowed to provide both auditing and consulting services to the same company.[10]

Providing Incentives for Managers

Because monitoring is necessarily imperfect, compensation plans must be designed to give managers the right incentive.

Compensation can be based on input (for example, the manager's effort) or on output (actual return or value added as a result of the manager's decisions). But input is difficult to measure. For example, how do outside investors observe effort? They can check that the manager clocks in on time but not how hard he is thinking. Therefore, incentives are almost always based on output. The trouble is that output depends not just on the manager's decisions, but also on many other factors outside his or her control. So unless you can separate out the manager's contribution, you face a dilemma. You want to provide managers with a high-powered incentive, so that they capture the benefits of their contribution to the firm, but you don't want to load onto the managers the risk of those changes in the firm's value that are outside their control.

The result is a compromise. Firms do link managers' pay to performance, but fluctuations in firm value are shared by managers and shareholders. Managers bear some of the risks that are beyond their control and shareholders bear some of the agency costs if managers shirk, empire build, or otherwise fail to maximize firm value. Thus some agency costs are inevitable. For example, since managers split the gains from hard work with the stockholders but reap all the personal benefits of an idle or indulgent life, they will be tempted to put in less effort than if shareholders could reward their contribution perfectly.

---

[8]Lenders' and shareholders' interests are not always aligned—see Chapter 18. But a company's ability to satisfy lenders is normally good news for stockholders, particularly when lenders are well placed to monitor. See C. James "Some Evidence on the Uniqueness of Bank Loans," *Journal of Financial Economics* 19 (December 1987), pp. 217–235.

[9]The free-rider problem might seem to drive out all monitoring by dispersed shareholders. But investors have another reason to investigate: They want to make money on their common stock portfolios by buying undervalued companies and selling overvalued ones. To do this they must investigate companies' performance.

[10]The Sarbanes-Oxley Act forbids auditing firms from providing their clients with fairness opinions, actuarial services, investment banking services, management functions, legal services, or any other services proscribed by the Public Company Accounting Oversight Board.

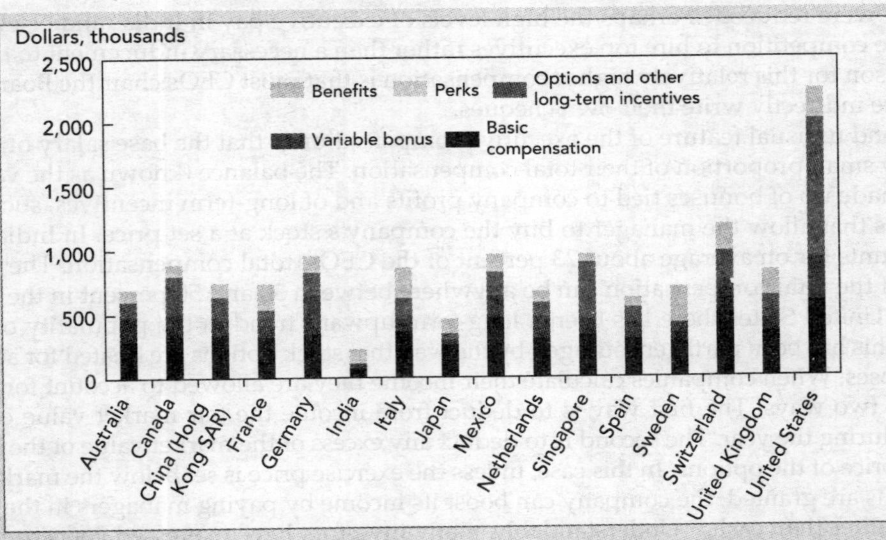

FIGURE 12.1

CEO compensation around the world.

Note: Benefits include contributions for pensions, life insurance, etc. They exclude accruals for unfunded pension plans.
Source: Towers Perrin, *Worldwide Total Remuneration, 2003–2004* © 2004 Towers Perrin. All rights reserved.

Management Compensation

Figure 12.1 compares the level of management compensation in different countries. Notice that the United States has unusually high levels of executive pay. For example, in 2002 the average compensation for the chief executives of companies in Standard & Poor's Composite Index averaged $9.4 million, or about 500 times the amount received by the typical production worker.[11] The record amount of compensation, according to *BusinessWeek's* rankings, went to Larry Ellison, the CEO of Oracle Corporation, who received $706 million in 2001.[12]

From Figure 12.1, you will notice that India stands at the bottom in terms of CEO compensation among the sixteen countries. In fact in 2001, ex-Mr. Dhirubhai Ambani[13], the then-CEO of RIL got an annual compensation of $1.92 million (Rs.8.85 crores). This can be partly explained by the fact that the Companies Act limits the total compensation packages of directors of profit making public limited companies to 11 percent of net profit. However, now the Government of India is proposing to amend this provision and plans to empower the shareholders to decide the remuneration, commission and compensation packages of managing directors and other directors[14]. We believe after another five years, Indian CEOs will definitely catch up with their western counterparts in terms of total compensation.

Such high levels of executive pay undoubtedly encourage CEOs to work hard and (equally important) offer an attractive carrot to those who aspire to become CEOs. But did Mr. Ambani really need Rs.8.85 crores to make him work hard, or would Indian managers put in much less effort if

[11]B. J. Hall and K. J. Murphy, "The Trouble with Stock Options," *Journal of Economic Perspectives* 17 (Summer 2003), pp. 49–70.

[12]There is always room for argument about how compensation should be calculated. *BusinessWeek* included the value of stock options exercised during the year, but not the value of options granted.

[13]As per a Business Today survey in 2001, Mr. Ambani topped the list of CEOs in terms of annual compensation. See Business Today, 28 October, 2001.

[14]See Financial Express, May 8, 2006.

their pay were reduced? Perhaps the high levels of executive pay in India (and elsewhere) simply reflect the competition to hire top executives rather than a necessary inducement to try harder. Another reason for this relatively higher compensation is that most CEOs chair the Board of Directors and hence indirectly write their own cheques.

A second unusual feature of the executive compensation is that the base salary of CEOs forms a relatively small proportion of their total compensation. The balance (known as the variable pay) is largely made up of bonuses tied to company profits and of long-term incentives, such as stock-option plans that allow the manager to buy the company's stock at a set price. In India, the variable pay accounts for on average about 23 percent of the CEOs' total compensation. The variable component of the total compensation can be anywhere between 30 and 50 percent in the U.S.

In the United States there has been a long-term upward trend in the popularity of stock option plans.[15] This has been partly encouraged by the way that stock options are treated for accounting and tax purposes. When companies calculate their income they are allowed to account for option grants in one of two ways. The first way is to deduct from income the fair market value of any options granted during the year. The second is to deduct any excess of the market value of the stock over the exercise price of the options. In this case, unless the exercise price is set below the market price when the options are granted, the company can boost its income by paying managers in the form of stock options rather than cash.[16] Understandably, many investors have expressed concern that, if a company adopts this second method, a potentially major compensation expense will not show up in the company's income statement. Some major companies have therefore moved to the first method and deduct from income the fair value of any options granted. If this becomes common practice or (as seems likely) compulsory, managers and investors may become more aware of the cost of their stock option programs.

In India stock options were very popular during the late 90's. However, their popularity has come down now. Infosys decided to shut down its employee stock options plan in March 2004. Infosys cited two reasons for this: the lack of a model to account for ESOP, and the conflicting norms on pricing laid down by the Indian and the U.S. regulators.[17]

You can see the merits of tying managers' compensation to the value of the firm's stock. When the manager, who owns stock options, works hard to maximize firm value, she is helping both the firm's shareholders and herself. How well this serves as an incentive may depend on several issues. For example, we pointed out earlier that with the ideal incentive scheme management should bear all the consequences of their own actions, but should not be exposed to fluctuations in firm value over which they have no control. But that raises a question: Since managers are not responsible for fluctuations in the general level of the market, why do companies not tie top management's compensation to stock returns relative to the market or to the firm's close competitors? This would link managers' compensation more closely to their own contributions.

In fact in the early 2000's, after the poor performance of the IT sector, the average compensation of the CEOs in the IT sector came down. In 2001, the average compensation of the CEOs from the IT sector was Rs.60 lakhs as against the all-India average of Rs.99 lakhs.

Tying management compensation to stock prices raises another difficult issue. The market value of a company's shares reflects investors' expectations. The stockholder's return depends on how

[15]Hall and Murphy calculate that the real (inflation-adjusted) value of options granted by large U.S. firms to managers and other employees increased from an average of $22 million per company in 1992 to $238 million per company in 2000, before falling back to $141 million in 2002. See Hall and Murphy, op. cit.

[16]However, companies are obliged to provide detailed information on option grants in a footnote to the accounts. Aboody and others argue that investors take this information into account when valuing the stock. See D. Aboody, M. E. Barth, and R. Kasznik, "SFAS 123 Stock-Based Compensation Expense and Equity Market Values," Graduate School of Business, Stanford University, 2003.

[17]See Economic Times, March 15, 2004

well the company performs relative to expectations. For example, suppose a company announces the appointment of an outstanding new manager. The stock price leaps up in anticipation of improved performance. Thenceforth, if the new manager delivers exactly the good performance that investors expected, the stock will earn only a normal, average rate of return. In this case a compensation scheme linked to the stock return after the manager starts would fail to recognize the manager's special contribution.

If we want managers to maximize shareholder value, it makes sense to reward them when they do so. But the accounting scandals at companies such as Enron and WorldCom have led to worries that managers holding stock or options may be tempted to manipulate their earnings and pump up the price of their shares. The problem here is that management compensation that is tied to the stock price will work *only* if there is openness and transparency, so that managers cannot take advantage of important inside information about the true state of the company's affairs.[18]

12.4 MEASURING AND REWARDING PERFORMANCE: RESIDUAL INCOME AND EVA

Almost all top executives of firms with publicly traded shares have compensation packages that depend in part on their firms' stock price performance. But their compensation also includes a bonus that depends on increases in earnings or on other accounting measures of performance. For lower-level managers, compensation packages usually depend more on accounting measures and less on stock returns.

Accounting measures of performance have two advantages:

- They are based on absolute performance, rather than on performance relative to investors' expectations.
- They make it possible to measure the performance of junior managers whose responsibility extends to only a single division or plant.

Tying compensation to accounting profits also creates some obvious problems. First, accounting profits are partly within the control of management. For example, managers whose pay depends on near-term earnings may cut maintenance or staff training. This is not a recipe for adding value, but an ambitious manager hoping for a quick promotion will be tempted to pump up short-term profits, leaving longer-run problems to his or her successors.

Second, accounting earnings and rates of return can be severely biased measures of true profitability. We ignore this problem for now, but return to it in the next section.

Third, growth in earnings does not necessarily mean that shareholders are better off. Any investment with a positive rate of return (1 or 2 percent will do) will eventually increase earnings.

[18]The Sarbanes-Oxley Act in the US has attempted to address this problem by requiring that managers must pay back any profits from bonuses and stock sales obtained during the 12-month period following a financial report that is subsequently restated because of "misconduct."

Therefore, if managers are told to maximize growth in earnings, they will dutifully invest in projects offering 1 or 2 percent rates of return—projects that destroy value. But shareholders do not want growth in earnings for its own sake, and they are not content with 1 or 2 percent returns. They want positive-NPV investments, and *only* positive-NPV investments. They want the company to invest only if the expected rate of return exceeds the cost of capital. In short, managers ought not to forget the cost of capital. In judging their performance, the focus should be on value added, that is, on returns over and above the cost of capital.

Look at Table 12.1, which contains a simplified income statement and balance sheet for your company's Bangalore City confabulator plant. There are two methods for judging whether the plant has increased shareholder value.

Net Return on Investment Book return on investment (ROI) is just the ratio of after-tax operating income to the net (depreciated) book value of assets. In Chapter 5 we rejected book ROI as a capital investment criterion, and in fact few companies now use it for that purpose. However, managers frequently assess the performance of a division or a plant by comparing its ROI with the cost of capital.

Suppose you need to assess the performance of the Bangalore City plant. As you can see from Table 12.1, the corporation has Rs. 1,000 million invested in the plant, which is generating earnings of Rs. 130 million. Therefore the firm is earning an ROI of $130/1{,}000 = .13$ or 13 percent.[19] If the cost of capital is (say) 10 percent, then the firm's activities are adding to shareholder value. The *net* return is $13 - 10 = 3$ percent. If the cost of capital is (say) 20 percent, then shareholders would have been better off investing Rs. 1 billion somewhere else. In this case the net return is negative, at $13 - 20 = -7$ percent.

Residual Income or Economic Value Added (EVA ®)[20] The second method calculates a net rupee return to shareholders. It asks, what are earnings after deducting a charge for the cost of capital?

When firms calculate income, they start with revenues and then deduct costs, such as wages, raw material costs, overhead, and taxes. But there is one cost that they do not commonly deduct: the cost of capital. True, they allow for depreciation of the assets financed by investors' capital, but investors also expect a positive return on their investment. As we pointed out in Chapter 10, a business that breaks even in terms of accounting profits is really making a loss; it is failing to cover the cost of capital.

To judge the net contribution to value, we need to deduct the cost of capital contributed to the plant by the parent company and its stockholders. For example, suppose that the cost of capital is 10 percent. Then the rupee cost of capital for the Bangalore City plant is $.10 \times$ Rs. 1,000 = Rs. 100 million. The net gain is therefore $130 - 100 =$ Rs. 30 million. This is the addition to shareholder wealth due to management's hard work (or good luck).

---

[19]Notice that earnings are calculated after tax but with no deductions for interest paid. The plant is evaluated as if it were all-equity financed. This is standard practice (see Chapter 6). It helps to separate investment and financing decisions. The tax advantages of debt financing supported by the plant are picked up not in the plant's earnings or cash flows but in the discount rate. The cost of capital is the after-tax weighted average cost of capital, or WACC. WACC is explained in Chapters 17 and 19.

[20]EVA is the term used by the consulting firm Stern–Stewart, which has done much to popularize and implement this measure of residual income. With Stern–Stewart's permission, we omit the copyright symbol in what follows.

TABLE 12.1

Simplified statements of income and assets for the Bangalore City confabulator plant (figures in Rs. millions).

*Includes depreciation expense.

†Current assets less current liabilities.

Income		Assets	
Sales	Rs. 550	Net working capital†	Rs. 80
Cost of goods sold*	275	Property, plant, and equipment investment	1,170
Selling, general, and administrative expenses	75	Less cumulative depreciation	360
	200	Net investment	810
Taxes at 35%	70	Other assets	110
Net income	Rs.130	Total assets	Rs.1,000

Net income after deducting the dollar return required by investors is called *residual income, economic value added*, or *EVA*. The formula is

$$\text{EVA} = \text{residual income} = \text{income earned} - \text{income required}$$
$$= \text{income earned} - \text{cost of capital} \times \text{investment}$$

For our example, the calculation is

$$\text{EVA} = \text{residual income} = 130 - (.10 \times 1{,}000) = +\text{Rs. } 30 \text{ million}$$

But if the cost of capital were 20 percent, EVA would be negative by Rs. 70 million.

Net return on investment and EVA are focusing on the same question. When return on investment equals the cost of capital, net return and EVA are both zero. But the net return is a percentage and ignores the scale of the company. EVA recognizes the amount of capital employed and the number of rupees of additional wealth created.

A growing number of firms now calculate EVA and tie management compensation to it.[21] They believe that a focus on EVA can help managers concentrate on increasing shareholder wealth. One example is Quaker Oats:

> Until Quaker adopted [EVA] in 1991, its businesses had one overriding goal—increasing quarterly earnings. To do it, they guzzled capital. They offered sharp price discounts at the end of each quarter, so plants ran overtime turning out huge shipments of Gatorade, Rice-A-Roni, 100% Natural Cereal, and other products. Managers led the late rush, since their bonuses depended on raising profits each quarter.
>
> This is the pernicious practice known as trade loading (because it loads up the trade, or retailers, with product) and many consumer product companies are finally admitting it damages long-run returns. An important reason is that it demands so much capital. Pumping up sales requires many warehouses (capital) to hold vast temporary inventories (more capital). But who cared? Quaker's operating businesses paid no charge for capital in internal accounting, so they barely noticed. It took EVA to spot the problem.[22]

[21]It can be shown that compensation plans that are linked to economic value added can induce a manager to choose the efficient investment level. See W. P. Rogerson, "Intertemporal Cost Allocation and Managerial Incentives: A Theory Explaining the Use of Economic Value Added as a Performance Measure," *Journal of Political Economy* 4 (August 1997), pp. 770–795.

[22]Shawn Tully, "The Real Key to Creating Shareholder Wealth," *Fortune* (September 20, 1993), p. 48.

When Quaker Oats implemented EVA, most of the capital-guzzling stopped.

The term *EVA* has been popularized by the consulting firm Stern–Stewart. But the concept of residual income has been around for some time,[23] and many companies that are not Stern–Stewart clients use this concept to measure and reward managers' performance.

Other consulting firms have their own versions of residual income. McKinsey & Company uses *economic profit (EP)*, defined as capital invested multiplied by the spread between return on investment and the cost of capital. This is another expression of the concept of residual income. For the Bangalore City plant, with a 10 percent cost of capital, economic profit is the same as EVA:

$$\text{Economic profit} = \text{EP} = (\text{ROI} - r) \times \text{capital invested}$$
$$= (0.13 - 0.10) \times 1{,}000 = \text{Rs. } 30 \text{ million}$$

EVA's most important use is in measuring and rewarding performance inside the firm. But it can also be applied to firms as a whole. Business periodicals regularly report EVAs for companies and industries. Table 12.2 shows the economic value added in 2003 for a sample of U.S. companies. Notice that the firms with the highest return on capital did not necessarily add the most economic value. For example, Wal-Mart was top of the class in terms of economic value added, but its return on capital was less than half that of Microsoft. This is partly because Wal-Mart has more capital invested and partly because it is less risky than Microsoft and its cost of capital is correspondingly lower.

Pros and Cons of EVA

Let us start with the pros. EVA, economic profit, and other residual income measures are clearly better than earnings or earnings growth for measuring performance. A plant that is generating lots of EVA should generate accolades for its managers as well as value for shareholders. EVA may also highlight parts of the business that are not performing up to scratch. If a division is failing to earn a positive EVA, its management is likely to face some pointed questions about whether the division's assets could be better employed elsewhere.

EVA sends a message to managers: Invest if and only if the increase in earnings is enough to cover the cost of capital. For managers who are used to tracking earnings or growth in earnings, this is a relatively easy message to grasp. Therefore EVA can be used down deep in the organization as an incentive compensation system. It is a substitute for explicit monitoring by top management. Instead of *telling* plant and divisional managers not to waste capital and then trying to figure out whether they are complying, EVA rewards them for careful and thoughtful investment decisions. Of course, if you tie junior managers' compensation to their economic value added, you must also give them power over those decisions that affect EVA. Thus the use of EVA implies delegated decision making.

[23]EVA is conceptually the same as the residual income measure long advocated by some accounting scholars. See, for example, R. Anthony, "Accounting for the Cost of Equity," *Harvard Business Review* 51 (1973), pp. 88–102 and "Equity Interest—Its Time Has Come," *Journal of Accountancy* 154 (1982), pp. 76–93.

TABLE 12.2

EVA performance of selected Indian companies, 2005.

	Economic Value Added (EVA)	Capital Invested	Return on Capital	Cost of Capital
Reliance Industries Ltd.	Rs. 1930.41 Crores	Rs. 54673.82 Crores	16.1%	12.6%
ITC Limited	1356.10	7912.16	28.1	11.0
Infosys Technologies Ltd.	905.02	5241.73	36.9	19.6
Larsen & Toubro Ltd.	591.63	4592.99	26.3	13.4
Grasim Industries Ltd.	314.78	6039.74	16.2	11.0
Bharti Airtel Ltd.	149.51	9311.37	16.0	14.3
Dr. Reddy's Laboratories Ltd.	-192.26	2084.69	3.8	13.0
Tata Power Co. Ltd.	-288.42	7950.68	8.7	12.3
Reliance Energy Ltd.	-378.16	8005.09	6.3	11.1
HDFC	-1159.22	37755.85	7.0	10.1

Note: Economic value added is the rate of return on capital less the cost of capital times the amount of capital invested: for ITC, EVA = (0.281 − 0.11) × 7912.16 = Rs. 1356.1 crores

Source: Own teaching notes

EVA makes the cost of capital *visible* to operating managers. A plant manager can improve EVA by (a) increasing earnings or (b) *reducing* capital employed. Therefore underutilized assets tend to be flushed out and disposed of. Working capital may be reduced, or at least not added to casually, as Quaker Oats did by trade loading in its pre-EVA era. The plant managers in Bangalore City may decide to do without that cappuccino machine or extra forklift.

Introduction of residual income measures often leads to surprising reductions in assets employed—not from one or two big capital disinvestment decisions, but from many small ones. Ehrbar quotes a sewing machine operator at Herman Miller Corporation:

> [EVA] lets you realize that even assets have a cost. . . . we used to have these stacks of fabric sitting here on the tables until we needed them. . . . We were going to use the fabric anyway, so who cares that we're buying it and stacking it up there? Now no one has excess fabric. They only have the stuff we're working on today. And it's changed the way we connect with suppliers, and we're having [them] deliver fabric more often.[24]

If you propose to tie a manager's remuneration to her business' profitability, it is clearly better to use EVA than accounting income which takes no account of the cost of the capital employed. But what are the limitations of EVA? Here we return to the same question that bedevils stock-based measures of performance. How can you judge whether a low EVA is a consequence of bad management or stems from factors outside the manager's control? The deeper you go in the organization, the less independence that managers have and therefore the greater the problem in measuring their contribution.

The second limitation with any accounting measure of performance lies in the data on which it is based. We will explore this issue in the next section.

[24] A. Ehrbar, *EVA: The Real Key to Creating Wealth* (New York: John Wiley & Sons, Inc., 1998), pp. 130–131.

12.5 BIASES IN ACCOUNTING MEASURES OF PERFORMANCE

Anyone using accounting measures of performance had better hope that the accounting numbers are accurate. Unfortunately, they are often not accurate, but biased. Applying EVA or any other accounting measure of performance therefore requires major adjustments to the income statements and balance sheets.[25]

For example, think of the difficulties in measuring the profitability of a pharmaceutical research program, where it typically takes 10 to 12 years to bring a new drug from discovery to final regulatory approval and the drug's first revenues. That means 10 to 12 years of guaranteed losses, even if the managers in charge do everything right. Similar problems occur in startup ventures, where there may be heavy capital outlays but low or negative earnings in the first years of operation. This does not imply negative NPV, so long as operating earnings and cash flows are sufficiently high later on. But EVA and ROI would be negative in the startup years, even if the project were on track to a strong positive NPV.

The problem in these cases is not with EVA or ROI, but with the accounting data. The pharmaceutical R&D program may be showing accounting losses, because generally accepted accounting principles require that outlays for R&D be written off as a current expense. But from an economic point of view, those outlays are an investment, not an expense. If a proposal for a new business predicts accounting losses during a startup period, but the proposal nevertheless shows a positive NPV, then the startup losses are really an investment—cash outlays made to generate larger cash flows when the business hits its stride. A more accurate measure of EVA or ROI would need to adjust the income and assets to recognize this.[26]

Example: Measuring the Profitability of the Jamshedpur Supermarket

Supermarket chains invest heavily in building and equipping new stores. The regional manager of a chain is about to propose investing Rs. 1 million in a new store in Jamshedpur. Projected cash flows are

	Year						
	1	2	3	4	5	6	after 6
Cash flow (Rs thousands)	100	200	250	298	298	298	0

Of course, real supermarkets last more than six years. But these numbers are realistic in one important sense: it may take two or three years for a new store to catch on—that is, to build up a substantial, habitual clientele. Thus cash flow is low for the first few years even in the best locations.

[25] In calculating the measures of EVA and ROI, Stern-Stewart makes a number of adjustments to income and assets. But it is impossible to include the value of all assets. For example, did Infosys really earn a true economic return of 36.9 percent? We suspect that the value of its assets is understated. The value of its intellectual property – the fruits of its investment over the years in software and operating systems – is not shown on the balance sheet. If the denominator in a return on investment calculation is too low, the resulting profitability measure is too high.

[26] For example, R&D should not be treated as an immediate expense but as an investment to be added to the balance sheet and written off over a reasonable period.

	Year					
	1	2	3	4	5	6
1. Cash flow	100	200	250	298	298	298
2. Book value at start of year, straight-line depreciation	1,000	833	667	500	333	167
3. Book value at end of year, straight-line depreciation	833	667	500	333	167	0
4. Book depreciation	167	167	167	167	167	167
5. Book income (1 - 4)	-67	+33	+83	+131	+131	+131
6. Book ROI	-.067	+.04	+.124	+.262	0.393	+.787
7. EVA	-167	-50	+17	+81	+98	+115

TABLE 12.3

Forecasted book income, ROI, and EVA for the proposed Jamshedpur store. Book ROI and EVA are underestimated for the first two years and overestimated thereafter.

eXcel

Please visit us at www.mhhe.com/bmam8e or refer to your Student CD .

We will assume the opportunity cost of capital is 10 percent. The Jamshedpur store's NPV at 10 percent is zero. It is an acceptable project, but not an unusually good one:

$$\text{NPV} = -1{,}000 + \frac{100}{1.10} + \frac{200}{(1.10)^2} + \frac{250}{(1.10)^3} + \frac{298}{(1.10)^4} + \frac{298}{(1.10)^5} + \frac{298}{(1.10)^6} = 0$$

With NPV = 0, the true (internal) rate of return of this cash-flow stream is also 10 percent.

Table 12.3 shows the store's forecasted *book* profitability, assuming straight-line depreciation over its six-year life. The book ROI is lower than the true return for the first two years and higher afterward.[27] This is the typical outcome: accounting profitability measures are too low when a project or business is young and are too high as it matures.

At this point the regional manager steps up on stage for the following soliloquy:

> The Jamshedpur store's a decent investment. I really should propose it. But if we go ahead, I won't look very good at next year's performance review. And what if I also go ahead with the new stores in Ranchi, Bhubaneswar and Cuttack? Their cash-flow patterns are pretty much the same. I could actually appear to lose money next year. The stores I've got won't earn enough to cover the initial losses on four new ones.
>
> Of course, everyone knows new supermarkets lose money at first. The loss would be in the budget. My boss will understand—I think. But what about her boss? What if the board of directors starts asking pointed questions about profitability in my region? I'm under a lot of pressure to generate better earnings. Saraswati Majumdar, the upstate manager, got a bonus for generating a 40 percent increase in book ROI. She didn't spend much on expansion.

The regional manager is getting conflicting signals. On the one hand, he is told to find and propose good investment projects. *Good* is defined by discounted cash flow. On the other hand, he is also urged to increase book earnings. But the two goals conflict because book earnings do not

[27]The errors in book ROI always catch up with you in the end. If the firm chooses a depreciation schedule that overstates a project's return in some years, it must also understate the return in other years. In fact, you can think of a project's IRR as a kind of average of the book returns. It is not a simple average, however. The weights are the project's book values discounted at the IRR. See J. A. Kay, "Accountants, Too, Could Be Happy in a Golden Age: The Accountant's Rate of Profit and the Internal Rate of Return," *Oxford Economic Papers* 28 (1976), pp. 447–460.

measure true earnings. The greater the pressure for immediate book profits, the more the regional manager is tempted to forgo good investments or to favor quick-payback projects over longer-lived projects, even if the latter have higher NPVs.

Would EVA solve this problem? No, EVA would also be biased. It would be negative in the first two years of the Jamshedpur store. In year 2, for example,

$$\text{Forecasted EVA} = 33 - (.10 \times 833) = -50, \text{ or } -\text{Rs. } 50{,}000$$

This calculation risks reinforcing the regional manager's qualms about the new Jamshedpur store.

Again, the fault here is not in the principle of EVA but in the measurement of income. If the project performs as projected in Table 12.3, the apparent negative EVA in year 2 is really an investment.

12.6 MEASURING ECONOMIC PROFITABILITY

Let us think for a moment about how profitability should be measured in principle. It is easy enough to compute the true, or economic, rate of return for a common stock that is continuously traded. We just record cash receipts (dividends) for the year, add the change in price over the year, and divide by the beginning price:

$$\text{Rate of return} = \frac{\text{cash receipts} + \text{change in price}}{\text{beginning price}}$$

$$= \frac{C_1 + (P_1 - P_0)}{P_0}$$

The numerator of the expression for rate of return (cash flow plus change in value) is called **economic income:**

$$\text{Economic income} = \text{cash flow} + \text{change in present value}$$

Any reduction in present value represents **economic depreciation;** any increase in present value represents *negative* economic depreciation. Therefore

$$\text{Economic depreciation} = \text{reduction in present value}$$

and

$$\text{Economic income} = \text{cash flow} - \text{economic depreciation}$$

The concept works for any asset. Rate of return equals cash flow plus change in value divided by starting value:

$$\text{Rate of return} = \frac{C_1 + (\text{PV}_1 - \text{PV}_0)}{\text{PV}_0}$$

where PV_0 and PV_1 indicate the present values of the business at the ends of years 0 and 1.

The only hard part in measuring economic income and return is calculating present value. You can observe market value if shares in the asset are actively traded, but few plants, divisions, or

		Year					
		1	2	3	4	5	6
1.	Cash flow	100	200	250	298	298	298
2.	PV at start of year, 10 percent discount rate	1,000	1,000	901	741	517	271
3.	PV at end of year 10 percent discount rate	1,000	901	741	517	271	0
4.	Economic depreciation	0	100	160	224	246	271
5.	Economic income (1 - 4)	100	100	90	74	52	27
6.	Rate of return	.10	.10	.10	.10	.10	.10
7.	Forecasted EVA	0	0	0	0	0	0

TABLE 12.4

Forecasted economic income, rate of return, and EVA for the proposed Jamshedpur store. Economic income equals cash flow minus economic depreciation. Rate of return equals economic income divided by value at start of year. EVA equals income minus cost of capital times value at start of year.

Note: There are minor rounding errors in some annual figures.

excel

Please visit us at www.mhhe.com/bmam8e or refer to your Student CD

capital projects have shares traded in the stock market. You can observe the present market value of *all* the firm's assets but not of any one of them taken separately.

Accountants rarely even attempt to measure present value. Instead they give us net book value (BV), which is original cost less depreciation computed according to some arbitrary schedule. Companies use the book value to calculate the book return on investment:

$$\text{Book income} = \text{cash flow} - \text{book depreciation}$$
$$= C_1 + (BV_1 - BV_0)$$

Therefore

$$\text{Book ROI} = \frac{C_1 + (BV_1 - BV_0)}{BV_0}$$

If book depreciation and economic depreciation are different (they are rarely the same), then the book profitability measures will be wrong; that is, they will not measure true profitability. (In fact, it is not clear that accountants should even *try* to measure true profitability. They could not do so without heavy reliance on subjective estimates of value. Perhaps they should stick to supplying objective information and leave the estimation of value to managers and investors.)

It is not hard to forecast economic income and rate of return. Table 12.4 shows the calculations. From the cash-flow forecasts we can forecast present value at the start of periods 1 to 6. Cash flow minus economic depreciation equals economic income. Rate of return equals economic income divided by start-of-period value.

Of course, these are forecasts. Actual future cash flows and values will be higher or lower. Table 12.4 shows that investors *expect* to earn 10 percent in each year of the store's six-year life. In other words, investors expect to earn the opportunity cost of capital each year from holding this asset.

Notice that EVA calculated using present value and economic income is zero in each year of the Jamshedpur project's life. For year 2, for example,

$$\text{EVA} = 100 - (.10 \times 100) = 0$$

EVA *should* be zero, because the project's true rate of return is only equal to the cost of capital. EVA will always give the right signal if income equals economic income and asset values are measured accurately.

Do the Biases Wash Out in the Long Run?

Some people downplay the problem we have just described. Is a temporary dip in book profits a major problem? Do the errors not wash out in the long run, when the region settles down to a steady state with an even mix of old and new stores?

It turns out that the errors diminish but do *not* exactly offset. The simplest steady-state condition occurs when the firm does not grow, but reinvests just enough each year to maintain earnings and asset values. Table 12.5 shows steady-state book ROIs and forecasted EVAs for the supermarket chain if it opens one store a year. For simplicity we assume that the company starts from scratch and that each store's cash flows are carbon copies of the Jamshedpur store. The true rate of return on each store is, therefore, 10 percent and the true EVA is zero. But as Table 12.5 demonstrates, steady-state book ROI and estimated EVA *overstate* the true profitability. Therefore, you cannot assume that biases in accounting measures of performance will wash out in the long run.

Thus we still have a problem even in the long run. The extent of the error depends on how fast the business grows. We have just considered one steady state with a zero growth rate. Think of another firm with a 5 percent steady-state growth rate. Such a firm would invest Rs. 1,000 the first year, Rs. 1,050 the second, Rs. 1,102.50 the third, and so on. Clearly the faster growth means more new projects relative to old ones. The greater weight given to young projects, which have low book ROIs and negative apparent EVAs, the lower the business's apparent profitability. Figure 12.2 shows how this works out for a business composed of projects like the Jamshedpur store. Book ROI and EVA will either overestimate or underestimate true profitability unless the amount that the firm invests each year grows at the same rate as the true rate of return.[28]

You can imagine the problems that this can cause. Think of our supermarket chain with its mix of old and new stores. While the regional manager is worrying about the low initial return on his new store, analysts who just see the profitability of the company as a whole are likely to be misled into *over*estimating its true profitability. Managers of other companies may see juicy pickings to be had in the supermarket business, while antitrust regulators may launch an inquiry into why supermarkets are able to earn such high returns.

What Can We Do about Biases in Accounting Profitability Measures?

The dangers in judging profitability by accounting measures are clear from this chapter's discussion and examples. To be forewarned is to be forearmed. But we can say something beyond just "be careful."

It is natural for firms to set a standard of profitability for plants or divisions. Ideally that standard should be the opportunity cost of capital for investment in the plant or division. That is the whole point of EVA: to compare actual profits with the cost of capital. But if performance is measured by return on investment or EVA, then these measures need to recognize accounting biases. Ideally, the financial manager should identify and eliminate accounting biases before judging or rewarding performance.

[28]This also is a general result. Biases in steady-state book ROIs disappear when the growth rate equals the true rate of return.

TABLE 12.5

Book ROI for a group of stores like the Jamshedpur store. The steady-state book ROI overstates the 10 percent *economic rate* of return. The steady-state EVA is also biased upwards.

	Year 1	2	3	4	5	6
Book income for store[a]						
1	-67	+33	+83	+131	+131	+131
2		-67	+33	+83	+131	+131
3			-67	+33	+83	+131
4				-67	+33	+83
5					-67	+33
6						-67
Total book income	-67	-34	+49	+180	+311	+442
Book value for store						
1	1,000	833	667	500	333	167
2		1,000	833	667	500	333
3			1,000	833	667	500
4				1,000	833	667
5					1,000	833
6						1,000
Total book value	1,000	1,833	2,500	3,000	3,333	3,500
Book ROI for all stores = (total book income)/ (total book value)	-0.067	-0.019	+.020	+.060	+.093	+.126[b]
EVA for all stores = (total book income) - (.10 x total book value)	-167	-217	-201	-120	-22	+92[c]

[a] Book income = cash flow − book depreciation.
[b] Steady-state book ROI.
[c] Steady-state EVA.
Note: There are minor rounding errors in some annual figures.

Please visit us at www.mhhe.com/bmam8e or refer to your Student CD.

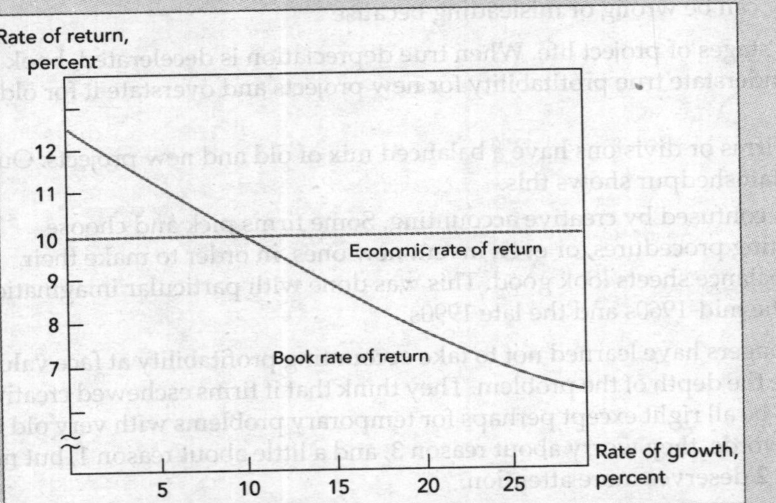

FIGURE 12.2

The faster Jamshedpur grows, the lower its book rate of return is, providing true profitability is constant and cash flows are constant or increasing over project life. This graph is drawn for a firm composed of identical projects, all like the Jamshedpur store (Table 12.3), but growing at a constant compound rate. A similar graph drawn for EVA would show that EVA also declines as growth increases.

Please visit us at www.mhhe.com/bmam8e or refer to your Student CD.

This is easier said than done. Accounting biases are notoriously hard to get rid of. Thus, many firms end up asking not "Did the widget division earn more than its cost of capital last year?" but "Was the widget division's book ROI typical of a successful firm in the widget industry?" The underlying assumptions are that (1) similar accounting procedures are used by other widget manufacturers and (2) successful widget companies earn their cost of capital.

There are some simple accounting changes that could reduce biases in perfor-mance measures. Remember that the biases all stem from *not* using economic depreciation. Therefore why not switch to economic depreciation? The main reason is that each asset's present value would have to be reestimated every year. Imagine the confusion if this were attempted. You can understand why accountants set up a depreciation schedule when an investment is made and then stick to it apart from exceptional circumstances. But why restrict the choice of depreciation schedules to the old standbys, such as straight-line? Why not specify a depreciation pattern that at least matches *expected* economic depreciation? For example, the Jamshedpur store could be depreciated according to the expected economic depreciation schedule shown in Table 12.4. This would avoid any systematic biases.[29] It would break no law or accounting standard. This step seems so simple and effective that we are at a loss to explain why firms have not adopted it.[30]

One final comment: suppose that you *do* conclude that a project has earned less than its cost of capital. This indicates that you made a mistake in taking on the project and, if you could have your time over again, you would not accept it. But does that mean you should bail out now? Not necessarily. That depends on how much the assets would be worth if you sold them or put them to an alternative use. A plant that produces low profits may still be worth operating if it has few alternative uses. Conversely, on some occasions it may pay to sell or redeploy a highly profitable plant.

Do Managers Worry Too Much about Book Profitability?

Book measures of profitability can be wrong or misleading because

1. Errors occur at different stages of project life. When true depreciation is decelerated, book measures are likely to understate true profitability for new projects and overstate it for old ones.
2. Errors also occur when firms or divisions have a balanced mix of old and new projects. Our steady-state analysis of Jamshedpur shows this.
3. Book measures are often confused by creative accounting. Some firms pick and choose among available accounting procedures, or even invent new ones, in order to make their income statements and balance sheets look good. This was done with particular imagination in the "go-go years" of the mid-1960s and the late 1990s.

Investors and financial managers have learned not to take accounting profitability at face value. Yet many people do not realize the depth of the problem. They think that if firms eschewed creative accounting, everything would be all right except perhaps for temporary problems with very old or very young projects. In other words, they worry about reason 3, and a little about reason 1, but not at all about 2. We think reason 2 deserves more attention.

---

[29]Using expected economic depreciation will not generate book ROIs that are exactly right unless realized cash flows exactly match forecasted flows. But we expect forecasts to be right, on average.

[30]This procedure has been suggested by several authors, for example by Zvi Bodie in "Compound Interest Depreciation in Capital Investment," *Harvard Business Review* 60 (May–June 1982), pp. 58–60.

SUMMARY

We began this chapter by describing how capital budgeting is organized and ended by exposing serious biases in accounting measures of financial performance. Inevitably such discussions stress the mechanics of organization, control, accounting, and performance measurement. It is harder to talk about the informal procedures that reinforce the formal ones. But remember that it takes informal communication and personal initiative to make capital budgeting work. Also, the accounting biases are partly or wholly alleviated because managers and stockholders are smart enough to look behind book earnings.

Formal capital budgeting systems usually have three stages:

1. A *capital budget* for the firm is prepared. This is a plan for capital expenditure by plant, division, or other business unit.
2. *Project authorizations* are approved to give authority to go ahead with specific projects.
3. *Postaudits* are conducted to check on the progress of recent investments.

Capital budgeting is not entirely a bottom-up process. Strategic planners practice capital budgeting on a grand scale by attempting to identify those businesses in which the firm has a special advantage. Project proposals that support the firm's accepted overall strategy are much more likely to have clear sailing as they come up through the organization.

But do not assume that all important capital outlays appear as projects in the capital budgeting process. Many important investment decisions may never receive formal financial analysis. First, plant or division managers decide which projects to propose. Top management and financial staff may never see the alternatives. Second, investments in intangible assets, for example, marketing and R&D outlays, may bypass the capital budget. Third, there are countless routine investment decisions that must be made by middle management. These outlays are small if looked at one by one, but they add up.

Capital investment decisions must be decentralized to a large extent. Consequently, agency problems are inevitable. Plant or divisional managers may be tempted to slack, to avoid risk, or to propose empire-building or entrenching investments. Of course, top management is also exposed to similar temptations.

Agency problems are mitigated by a combination of monitoring and incentives. For example, shareholders delegate the task of monitoring top management to the board of directors and to the accountants who audit the company's books.

To encourage managers to maximize shareholder value, a large part of their compensation is usually tied to company performance. Typically, this performance-related pay consists of a mixture of stock or stock options, and bonuses that depend on accounting measures of profitability. The United States is unusual both in the high levels of compensation for top executives and the extent to which pay is performance-related.

If you want to align the interests of the manager and the shareholder, it makes sense to give the manager common stock or stock options. But this is not a complete solution. The performance of the stock depends on events outside management's control, and today's stock price already reflects investors' expectations of management's performance. Also, since the scandals at Enron, WorldCom, and other companies, many worry that the award of executive stock options may tempt unscrupulous managers to pump up the price of their stock and disguise the true state of the firm.

The further you go down in the organization, the more tenuous the link between a manager's actions and the performance of the stock price. Therefore, for junior managers a higher proportion of pay is likely to be related to accounting measures of profitability. Many large companies have implemented sophisticated bonus schemes based on residual income or economic value added (EVA). In these schemes, managers' bonuses depend on earnings minus a charge for capital employed. This creates a strong incentive to dispose of unneeded assets and to acquire new ones only if the additional returns exceed the cost of capital.

Of course, any accounting measure of profitability, such as EVA or the book return on investment (ROI), depends on accurate measures of earnings and capital employed. Unless adjustments are made to accounting data, these measures may underestimate the true profitability of new assets and overestimate that of old assets.

In principle, the solution is easy. EVA and ROI should be calculated using true or economic income. Economic income is equal to the cash flow less economic depreciation (that is, the decline in the present value of the asset). Unfortunately, we can't ask accountants to recalculate each asset's present value each time income is calculated. But it does seem fair to ask why they don't at least try to match book depreciation schedules to typical patterns of economic depreciation.

FURTHER READING

Current practices in management remuneration are discussed in:

K. J. Murphy: "Executive Compensation," in O. Ashenfelter and D. Cards (eds.), *Handbook of Labor Economics*, North-Holland, 1999.

B. J. Hall and K. J. Murphy: "The Trouble with Stock Options," *Journal of Economic Perspectives*, 17 (Summer 2003), pp. 49–70.

J. E. Core, W. R. Guay, and D. F. Larcker: "Executive Equity Compensation and Incentives: A Survey," *Federal Reserve Bank of New York Economic Policy Review*, 9 (April 2003), pp. 27–50; **www.ny.frb.org/research.**

For easy-to-read descriptions of EVA, see:

A. Ehrbar: *EVA: The Real Key to Creating Wealth*, John Wiley & Sons, Inc., New York, 1998.

J. M. Stern and J. S. Shiely: *The EVA Challenge—Implementing Value-added Change in an Organization*, John Wiley & Sons, Inc., New York, 2001.

Biases in book ROI and procedures for reducing the biases are discussed by:

F. M. Fisher and J. I. McGowan: "On the Misuse of Accounting Rates of Return to Infer Monopoly Profits," *American Economic Review*, 73 (March 1983), pp. 82–97.

Z. Bodie: "Compound Interest Depreciation in Capital Investment," *Harvard Business Review*, 60 (May–June 1982),pp. 58–60.

CONCEPT REVIEW QUESTIONS

1. What is meant by agency costs? (pages 306–307)
2. What are the two broad ways that agency costs are mitigated? (page 307)
3. What is meant when people say that monitoring by shareholders suffers from a free-riding problem? (page 308)

For additional Concept Review Questions, please visit us at www.mhhe.com/bmam8e or refer to your Student CD.

QUIZ

1. True or false?
   a. The approval of a capital budget allows managers to go ahead with any project included in the budget.
   b. Capital budgets and project authorizations are mostly developed "bottom up." Strategic planning is a "top-down" process.
   c. Project sponsors are likely to be overoptimistic.
   d. Investments in marketing (for new products) and R&D are not capital outlays.
   e. Many capital investments are not included in the company's capital budget. (If true, give some examples.)
   f. Postaudits are typically undertaken about five years after project completion.
2. Explain how each of the following actions or problems can distort or disrupt the capital budgeting process.
   a. Overoptimism by project sponsors.
   b. Inconsistent forecasts of industry and macroeconomic variables.
   c. Capital budgeting organized solely as a bottom-up process.
   d. A demand for quick results from operating managers, e.g., requiring new capital expenditures to meet a payback constraint.
3. Define the following: **(a)** Agency costs in capital investment, **(b)** private benefits, **(c)** empire building, **(d)** free-rider problem, **(e)** entrenching investment, **(f)** delegated monitoring.
4. Monitoring alone can never completely eliminate agency costs in capital investment. Briefly explain why.
5. Here are several questions about economic value added or EVA.
   a. Is EVA expressed as a percentage or a rupee amount?
   b. Write down the formula for calculating EVA.
   c. What is the difference, if any, between EVA and residual income?
   d. What is the point of EVA? Why do firms use it?
   e. Does the effectiveness of EVA depend on accurate measures of accounting income and assets?
6. The Modern Language Corporation earned Rs. 1.6 million on net assets of Rs. 20 million. The cost of capital is 11.5 percent. Calculate the net percentage return on investment and EVA.
7. Fill in the blanks:
   "A project's economic income for a given year equals the project's ______ less its ______ depreciation. New projects may take several years to reach full profitability. In these cases book income is ______ than economic income early in the project's life and ______ than economic income later in its life."
8. Consider the following project:

	Period			
	0	1	2	3
Net cash flow	−100	0	78.55	78.55

The internal rate of return is 20 percent. The NPV, assuming a 20 percent opportunity cost of capital, is exactly zero. Calculate the expected *economic* income and economic depreciation in each year.

PRACTICE QUESTIONS

1. Draw up an outline or flowchart tracing the capital budgeting process from the initial idea for a new investment project to the completion of the project and the start of operations. Assume the idea for a new obfuscator machine comes from a plant manager in the Deconstruction Division of the Modern Language Corporation.

   Here are some questions your outline or flowchart should consider: Who will prepare the original proposal? What information will the proposal contain? Who will evaluate it? What approvals will be needed, and who will give them? What happens if the machine costs 40 percent more to purchase and install than originally forecasted? What will happen when the machine is finally up and running?

2. Compare typical compensation and incentive arrangements for **(a)** top management, for example, the CEO or CFO, and **(b)** plant or division managers. What are the chief differences? Can you explain them?

3. Suppose all plant and division managers were paid only a fixed salary—no other incentives or bonuses.
   a. Describe the agency problems that would appear in capital investment decisions.
   b. How would tying the managers' compensation to EVA alleviate these problems?

Please visit us at www.mhhe.com/bmam8e or refer to your Student CD.

4. Table 12.6 shows a condensed profit and loss account and balance sheet for Indian Potash Limited.
   a. Calculate the company's EVA. Assume the cost of capital is 11 percent.
   b. As Table 12.6 shows, the fixed assets are carried on Indian Potash's books at Rs.19 crores. However, the fixed assets can be sold to another potash manufacturing company for Rs.59 crores. How should this fact change your calculation of EVA?

5. Here are a few questions about compensation schemes that tie top management's compensation to the rate of return earned on the company's common stock.
   a. Today's stock price depends on investors' expectations of future performance. What problems does this create?
   b. Stock returns depend on factors outside the managers' control, for example, changes in interest rates or prices of raw materials. Could this be a serious problem? If so, can you suggest a partial solution?
   c. Compensation schemes that depend on stock returns do *not* depend on accounting data. Is that an advantage? Why or why not?

6. Herbal Resources is a small but profitable producer of dietary supplements for pets. This is not a high-tech business, but Herbal's earnings have averaged around Rs. 1.2 million after tax, largely on the strength of its patented enzyme for making cats nonallergenic. The patent has eight years to run, and Herbal has been offered Rs. 4 million for the patent rights.

   Herbal's assets include Rs. 2 million of working capital and Rs. 8 million of property, plant, and equipment. The patent is not shown on Herbal's books. Suppose Herbal's cost of capital is 15 percent. What is its EVA?

TABLE 12.6

Condensed financial statements for Indian Potash Limited. See Practice Question 4 (figures in Rs. Crores).

P & L Account for 2004-05		Assets, March 31, 2005	
Revenue	Rs. 3289	Net Working Capital	Rs. 174
Raw Material Costs	2997		
Operating Costs	240	Gross Block	28
Depreciation	1	*Less: Accumulated Depreciation*	11
Interest	11	Net Block	17
Pretax Income	40	Capital Work in Progress	2
Tax at 37%	14.8	Investments	6
Net Income	Rs. 25.2	Total Assets	Rs. 199

7. True or false? Explain briefly.
   a. Book profitability measures are biased measures of true profitability for individual assets. However, these biases "wash out" when firms hold a balanced mix of old and new assets.
   b. Systematic biases in book profitability would be avoided if companies used depreciation schedules that matched expected economic depreciation. However, few, if any, firms have done this.

excel — Please visit us at www.mhhe.com/bmam8e or refer to your Student CD.

8. Calculate the year-by-year book and economic profitability for investment in polyzone production, as described in Chapter 11. Use the cash flows and competitive spreads shown in Table 11.2, and assume straight-line depreciation over 10 years. What is the steady-state book rate of return (ROI) for a mature company producing polyzone? Assume no growth and competitive spreads.

excel — Please visit us at www.mhhe.com/bmam8e or refer to your Student CD.

9. The website of this book contains an Excel program for calculating the profitability of the Nodhead project (similar to the Jamshedpur project we discussed in this chapter). Now suppose that the cash flows from Nodhead's new supermarket are as follows:

	Year						
	0	1	2	3	4	5	6
Cash flows ($ thousands)	−1,000	+298	+298	+298	+138	+138	+138

   a. Recalculate economic depreciation. Is it accelerated or decelerated?
   b. Rework Tables 12.3 and 12.4 to show the relationship between (i) the "true" rate of return and book ROI and (ii) true EVA and forecasted EVA in each year of the project's life.

excel — Please visit us at www.mhhe.com/bmam8e or refer to your Student CD.

10. Using the Excel program discussed on Q9 above, construct a table (similar to Table 12.5 for the Jamshedpur project) assuming a steady-state growth rate of 10 percent per year. Your answer will illustrate a fascinating theorem, namely, that book rate of return equals the economic rate of return when the economic rate of return and the steady-state growth rate are the same.

STANDARD &POOR'S

11. From the website of icicidirect.com (http://icicidirect.com/research/researchcomplist_snapshot.asp?fwdfile=companysnapshot.asp), download financial data for any three companies and then estimate the EVA for these three companies. What problems did you encounter in doing this?

CHALLENGE QUESTIONS

1. Consider an asset with the following cash flows:

excel — Please visit us at www.mhhe.com/bmam8e or refer to your Student CD.

	Year			
	0	1	2	3
Cash flows (Rs. millions)	−12	+5.20	+4.80	+4.40

The firm uses straight-line depreciation. Thus, for this project, it writes off Rs. 4 million per year in years 1, 2, and 3. The discount rate is 10 percent.
   a. Show that economic depreciation equals book depreciation.
   b. Show that the book rate of return is the same in each year.
   c. Show that the project's book profitability is its true profitability.

You've just illustrated another interesting theorem. If the book rate of return is the same in each year of a project's life, the book rate of return equals the IRR.

TABLE 12.7

Estimated market values of a Boeing 737 in January 1987 as a function of age, plus the cash flows needed to provide a 10 percent true rate of return (figures in Rs. millions).

Start of Year	Market Value	Cash Flow
1	19.69	
2	17.99	Rs. 3.67
3	16.79	3.00
4	15.78	2.69
5	14.89	2.47
6	14.09	2.29
7	13.36	2.14
8	12.68	2.02
9	12.05	1.90
10	11.46	1.80
11	10.91	1.70
12	10.39	1.61
13	9.91	1.52
14	9.44	1.46
15	9.01	1.37
16	8.59	1.32

excel

Please visit us at www.mhhe.com/bmam8e or refer to your Student CD.

2. In our Jamshedpur store example, true depreciation was decelerated. That is not always the case. For instance, Table 12.7 shows how on average the market value of a Boeing 737 has varied with its age[31] and the cash flow needed in each year to provide a 10 percent return. (For example, if you bought a 737 for $19.69 million at the start of year 1 and sold it a year later, your total profit would be 17.99 + 3.67 − 19.69 = $1.97 million, 10 percent of the purchase cost.)

Many airlines write off their aircraft straight-line over 15 years to a salvage value equal to 20 percent of the original cost.

a. Calculate economic and book depreciation for each year of the plane's life.

b. Compare the true and book rates of return in each year.

c. Suppose an airline invested in a fixed number of Boeing 737s each year. Would steady-state book return overstate or understate true return?

[31] We are grateful to Mike Staunton for providing us with these estimates.

PART FOUR RELATED WEB SITES

Chapter 14 provides an overview of corporate financing. Useful sources of data on financing for U.S. corporations include:

www.census.gov/csd/qfr (balance sheet and income data)

www.federalreserve.gov/releases (flow of funds accounts; includes data on asset holdings by class of investor)

Chapter 15 discusses venture capital financing. Relevant sites include:

www.redherring.com

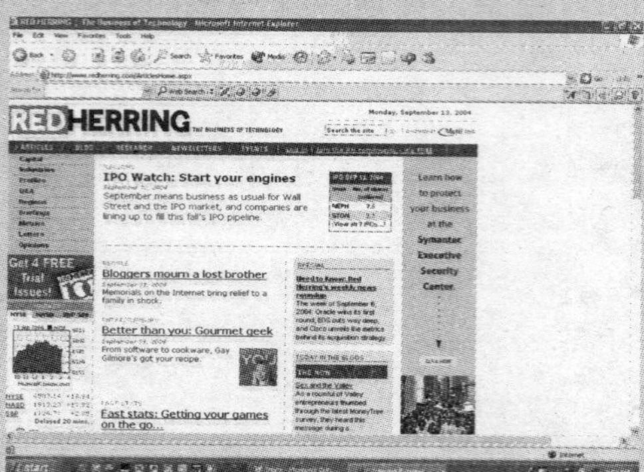

www.nvca.org (Web site of the National Venture Capital Association)

www.evca.com (Web site of the European Venture Capital Association)

www.asianfn.com (Web site of the Asian Venture Capital Journal)

www.ventureeconomics.com (includes statistics on venture capital activity)

www.pwcmoneytree.com (includes results of quarterly survey of venture capital activity)

www.v1.com (includes statistics on venture capital activity)

www.vnpartners.com/primer.htm (a useful primer on venture capital)

Sites on initial public offerings include:

www.hoovers.com

www.ipodata.com

cbs.marketwatch.com

www.redherring.com

biz.yahoo.com/ipo

www.edgar-online.com/ipoexpress

bear.cba.ufl.edu/ritter (Jay Ritter's home page is a mine of data on the performance of IPOs)

Nasdaq provides a useful explanation of how to go public together with some data on new listings:

www.nasdaq.com

Underwriter league tables are published on:

www.tfibcm.com

There are several routes for accessing the SEC's huge database of prospectuses and registration statements:

www.sec.gov/edgar.shtml

edgarscan.pwcglobal.com

www.edgar-online.com

PART [4]

FINANCING DECISIONS AND MARKET EFFICIENCY

SO FAR OUR focus has been on the investment decision. Now we turn to the problem of paying for these investments. This can be a challenging task. For example, suppose that you are the finance director of BP. You need to ensure that there is cash to pay for capital expenditures that are forecasted at $12–12.5 billion a year. These investments are scattered across the world, including major developments in Angola, Azerbaijan, and Russia. BP has a variety of possible financing choices. For example, it can plow back part of its earnings, borrow from the banks, or make a public issue of stock or long-term bonds.

Later chapters will describe in detail the principal sources of finance, but Part 4 sets the scene. We begin in Chapter 13 with a fundamental question: Can managers be confident that investors will pay a fair price for the firm's securities? Many scholars believe that securities are competitively priced, but we will also encounter some conflicting evidence.

Chapter 14 takes a first look at the firm's securities and their relative importance. It shows how they differ in their rights to payment and in the control that their holders can exercise.

Part 4 concludes with Chapter 15, where we show how infant companies finance themselves and how, after reaching adulthood, they sell their securities to the public.

CHAPTER [13]

CORPORATE FINANCING AND THE SIX LESSONS OF MARKET EFFICIENCY

UP TO THIS point we have concentrated almost exclusively on the left-hand side of the balance sheet—the firm's capital expenditure decision. Now we move to the right-hand side and to the problems involved in financing the capital expenditures. To put it crudely, you've learned how to spend money, now learn how to raise it.

Of course, we haven't totally ignored financing in our discussion of capital budgeting. But we made the simplest possible assumption: all-equity financing. That means we assumed the firm raises its money by selling stock and then invests the proceeds in real assets. Later, when those assets generate cash flows, the cash is returned to the stockholders. Stockholders supply all the firm's capital, bear all the business risks, and receive all the rewards.

Now we are turning the problem around. We take the firm's present portfolio of real assets and its future investment strategy as given, and then we determine the best financing strategy. For example,

- Should the firm reinvest most of its earnings in the business, or distribute the cash to shareholders?
- If the firm needs more money, should it issue more stock or should it borrow?
- Should it borrow short-term or long-term?
- Should it borrow by issuing a normal long-term bond or a convertible bond (i.e., a bond which can be exchanged for stock by the bondholders)?

There are countless other financing trade-offs, as you will see.

The purpose of holding the firm's capital budgeting decision constant is to separate that decision from the financing decision. Strictly speaking, this assumes that capital budgeting and financing decisions are *independent*. In many circumstances this is a reasonable assumption. The firm is generally free to change its capital structure by repurchasing one security and issuing another. In that case there is no need to associate a particular investment project with a particular source of cash. The firm can think, first, about which projects to accept and, second, about how they should be financed.

Sometimes decisions about capital structure depend on project choice or vice versa, and in those cases the investment and financing decisions have to be considered jointly. However, we defer discussion of such interactions of financing and investment decisions until later in the book.

We start this chapter by contrasting investment and financing decisions. The objective in each case is the same—to maximize NPV. However, it may be harder to find positive-NPV financing opportunities. The reason it is difficult to add value by clever financing decisions is that capital markets are efficient. By this we mean that fierce competition between investors eliminates profit opportunities and causes debt and equity issues to be fairly priced. If you think that sounds like a sweeping statement, you are right. That is why we have devoted this chapter to explaining and evaluating the efficient-market hypothesis.

You may ask why we start our discussion of financing issues with this conceptual point, before you have even the most basic knowledge about securities and issue procedures. We do it this way because financing decisions seem overwhelmingly complex if you don't learn to ask the right questions. We are afraid you might flee from confusion to the myths that often dominate popular discussion of corporate financing. You need to understand the efficient-market hypothesis not because it is *universally* true but because it leads you to ask the right questions.

We define the efficient-market hypothesis more carefully in Section 13.2. The hypothesis comes in different strengths, depending on the information available to investors. Sections 13.2 and 13.3 review the evidence for and against efficient markets. The evidence "for" is considerable, but over the years a number of puzzling anomalies have accumulated. To explain these anomalies, scholars have turned to evidence of irrational behavior that has been well documented by behavioral psychologists. We describe the main features of behavioral finance and of the challenge that it poses to the efficient-market hypothesis.

The chapter closes with the *six lessons of market efficiency.*

13.1 WE ALWAYS COME BACK TO NPV

Although it is helpful to separate investment and financing decisions, there are basic similarities in the criteria for making them. The decisions to purchase a machine tool and to sell a bond each involve valuation of a risky asset. The fact that one asset is real and the other is financial doesn't matter. In both cases we end up computing net present value.

The phrase *net present value of borrowing* may seem odd to you. But the following example should help to explain what we mean: as part of its policy of encouraging industrialization in Tamil Nadu, the Tamil Nadu Government allows the companies to defer the payment of sales tax (with certain exceptions, of course[1]) to the State Government for a period of 14 years. That is, the companies can collect the sales tax from the customers at the time of sale and retain the sales tax collected as an interest-free loan from the government for a period of 14 years. The sales tax deferred in year 1 will be repayable in five equal annual installments from year 15 to 19; sales tax deferred in year 2 will be repayable in five equal annual installments from year 16 to 20, and so on and finally the sales tax collected in year 14 will be repayable in five equal annual installments from year 28 to 32.

Let's assume that your company sets up a new plant in Tamil Nadu and that you expect to collect Rs. 5 million of sales tax every year. This means that for each of the next 14 years, your company will receive Rs. 5 million as an interest-free loan from the Tamil Nadu Government. In year 15, the company will refund Rs. 1 million; In Year 16, the company will refund Rs.2 million (1 million from year 1 and 1 million from year 2), and so on and so forth. We show the repayment schedule in the nearby table. Should you accept the offer?

We can compute the NPV of the loan agreement in the usual way. The one difference is that the first few cash flows are *positive* and the subsequent cash flows are *negative*.

NPV = sales tax collected - present value of sales tax payments[2] =

$$\sum_{t=1}^{14}\frac{5}{(1+r)^t}-\frac{1}{(1+r)^{15}}-\frac{2}{(1+r)^{16}}-\frac{3}{(1+r)^{17}}-\frac{4}{(1+r)^{18}}$$

$$-\sum_{t=19}^{28}\frac{5}{(1+r)^t}-\frac{4}{(1+r)^{29}}-\frac{3}{(1+r)^{30}}-\frac{2}{(1+r)^{31}}-\frac{1}{(1+r)^{32}}$$

The only missing variable is r, the opportunity cost of capital. You need that to value the liability created by this deferred sales tax benefits. We reason this way: The deferred sales tax benefit to you is a financial asset: a piece of paper representing your promise to pay the sales tax collected back to the government after the 14th year. How much would that paper sell for if freely traded in the capital market? It would sell for the present value of those cash flows, discounted at r, the rate of return offered by other securities issued by your firm. All you have to do to determine r is to answer the question, what interest rate would my firm have to pay to borrow money directly from the capital markets rather than the government?

Suppose that this rate is 10 percent. Then

[1]See http://www.indiainbusiness.nic.in/indian-states/tamilnadu/ITPol.htm for details.

[2]Here, we assume that the entire sales tax will be paid at the end of the year. Actually, Tamil Nadu Government expects you to pay the money in four equal quarterly installments. We ignore that here.

Deferred Sales Tax Example															
	Payments Made in Year—														
	1	2	3	4	5	6	7	8	9	10	11	12	13	14	Total Payments
Total Sales Tax >>	5	5	5	5	5	5	5	5	5	5	5	5	5	5	
15	1														1
16	1	1													2
17	1	1	1												3
18	1	1	1	1											4
19	1	1	1	1	1										5
20		1	1	1	1	1									5
21			1	1	1	1	1								5
22				1	1	1	1	1							5
23					1	1	1	1	1						5
24						1	1	1	1	1					5
25							1	1	1	1	1				5
26								1	1	1	1	1			5
27									1	1	1	1	1		5
28										1	1	1	1	1	5
29											1	1	1	1	4
30												1	1	1	3
31													1	1	2
32														1	1

$$\text{NPV} = \sum_{t=1}^{14} \frac{5}{(1+0.1)^t} - \frac{1}{(1+0.1)^{15}} - \frac{2}{(1+0.1)^{16}} - \frac{3}{(1+0.1)^{17}} - \frac{4}{(1+0.1)^{18}}$$

$$-\sum_{t=19}^{28} \frac{5}{(1+0.1)^t} - \frac{4}{(1+0.1)^{29}} - \frac{3}{(1+0.1)^{30}} - \frac{2}{(1+0.1)^{31}} - \frac{1}{(1+0.1)^{32}}$$

$$= \text{Rs. } 28.74 \text{ million}$$

Of course, you do not need any arithmetic to tell you that getting an interest-free loan for 14 years is a good deal when the fair rate is 10 percent. But the NPV calculations tell you just how much that opportunity is worth (Rs. 28.74 million)[3]. It also brings out the essential similarity of investment and financing decisions.

Differences between Investment and Financing Decisions

In some ways investment decisions are simpler than financing decisions. The number of different financing decisions (i.e., securities) is continually expanding. You will have to learn the major families, genera, and species. You will also need to become familiar with the vocabulary of financing. You will learn about such matters as caps, strips, swaps, and bookrunners; behind each of these terms lies an interesting story.

[3]We ignore here any tax consequences of borrowing. These are discussed in Chapter 18.

There are also ways in which financing decisions are much easier than investment decisions. First, financing decisions do not have the same degree of finality as investment decisions. They are easier to reverse. That is, their abandonment value is higher. Second, it's harder to make or lose money by smart or stupid financing strategies. That is, it is difficult to find financing schemes with NPVs significantly different from zero. This reflects the nature of the competition.

When the firm looks at capital investment decisions, it does *not* assume that it is facing perfect, competitive markets. It may have only a few competitors that specialize in the same line of business in the same geographical area. And it may own some unique assets that give it an edge over its competitors. Often these assets are intangible, such as patents, expertise, or reputation. All this opens up the opportunity to make superior profits and find projects with positive NPVs.

In financial markets your competition is all other corporations seeking funds, to say nothing of the state, local, and central governments that go to Mumbai, New York, London, and other financial centers to raise money. The investors who supply financing are comparably numerous, and they are smart: Money attracts brains. The financial amateur often views capital markets as *segmented*, that is, broken down into distinct sectors. But money moves between those sectors, and it moves fast.

Remember that a good financing decision generates a positive NPV. It is one in which the amount of cash raised exceeds the value of the liability created. But turn that statement around. If selling a security generates a positive NPV for the seller, it must generate a negative NPV for the buyer. Thus, the deferred sales tax loan we discussed was a good deal for your firm but a negative NPV from the Tamil Nadu government's point of view. By giving interest free deferred sales tax loan, it offered a subsidy of Rs. 28.74 million.

What are the chances that your firm could consistently trick or persuade investors into purchasing securities with negative NPVs to them? Pretty low. In general, firms should assume that the securities they issue are fairly priced. That takes us into the main topic of this chapter: efficient capital markets.

13.2 WHAT IS AN EFFICIENT MARKET?

A Startling Discovery: Price Changes Are Random

As is so often the case with important ideas, the concept of efficient capital markets stemmed from a chance discovery. In 1953 Maurice Kendall, a British statistician, presented a controversial paper to the Royal Statistical Society on the behavior of stock and commodity prices.[4] Kendall had expected to find regular price cycles, but to his surprise they did not seem to exist. Each series appeared to be "a 'wandering' one, almost as if once a week the Demon of Chance drew a random number . . . and added it to the current price to determine the next week's price." In other words, the prices of stocks and commodities seemed to follow a *random walk*.

[4]See M. G. Kendall, "The Analysis of Economic Time Series, Part I. Prices," *Journal of the Royal Statistical Society* 96 (1953), pp. 11–25. Kendall's idea was not wholly new. It had been proposed in an almost forgotten thesis written 53 years earlier by a French doctoral student, Louis Bachelier. Bachelier's accompanying development of the mathematical theory of random processes anticipated by five years Einstein's famous work on the random Brownian motion of colliding gas molecules. See L. Bachelier, *Theorie de la Speculation* (Paris: Gauthiers-Villars, 1900). Reprinted in English (A. J. Boness, trans.) in P. H. Cootner (ed.), *The Random Character of Stock Market Prices* (Cambridge, MA: MIT Press, 1964), pp. 17–78.

If you are not sure what we mean by "random walk," you might like to think of the following example: You are given Rs. 100 to play a game. At the end of each week a coin is tossed. If it comes up heads, you win 3 percent of your investment; if it is tails, you lose 2.5 percent. Therefore, your capital at the end of the first week is either Rs. 103.00 or Rs. 97.50. At the end of the second week the coin is tossed again. Now the possible outcomes are:

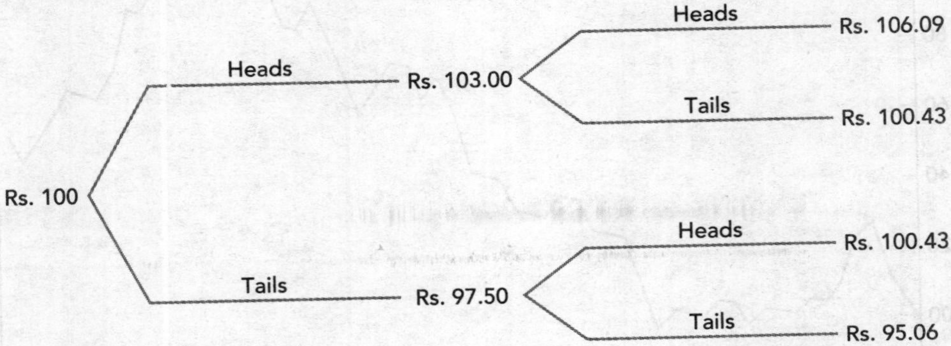

This process is a random walk with a positive drift of .25 percent per week.[5] It is a random walk because successive changes in value are independent. That is, the odds each week are the same, regardless of the value at the start of the week or of the pattern of heads and tails in the previous weeks.

If you find it difficult to believe that there are no patterns in share price changes, look at the two charts in Figure 13.1. One of these charts shows the outcome from playing our game for five years; the other shows the actual performance of the Sensex Index for a five-year period. Can you tell which one is which?[6]

When Maurice Kendall suggested that stock prices follow a random walk, he was implying that the price changes are independent of one another just as the gains and losses in our coin-tossing game were independent. Figure 13.2 illustrates this. Each dot shows the change in the price of Infosys stock on successive days. The diamond-marked point in the south-east quadrant refers to a pair of days in which a 4 percent increase was followed by an 8 percent decrease. If there was a systematic tendency for increases to be followed by decreases, there would be many dots in the south-east quadrant and a few in the north-east quadrant. It is obvious from a glance that there is very little pattern in the price movements, but we can test this more precisely by calculating the coefficient of correlation between each day's price change and the next. If price movements persisted, the correlation would be positive; if there was no relationship, it would be 0. In our example, the correlation between successive price changes is Infosys stock was –0.0218; there was a negligible tendency for price rises to be followed by subsequent price decreases.[7]

[5]The drift is equal to the expected outcome: $(1/2)(3) + (1/2)(-2.5) = .25\%$.

[6]The bottom chart in Figure 13.1 shows the real Sensex for April 1996 - March 2001; the top chart is a series of cumulative random numbers. Of course, 50 percent of you are likely to have guessed right, but we bet it was just a guess. A similar comparison between cumulated random numbers and actual price series was first suggested by H. V. Roberts, "Stock Market 'Patterns' and Financial Analysis: Methodological Suggestions," *Journal of Finance* 14 (March 1959), pp. 1–10.

[7]The correlation coefficient between successive observations is known as the *autocorrelation coefficient*. An autocorrelation of - 0.0218 implies that, if Infosys price rose by 1 percent more than average yesterday, your best forecast of today's price change would be an increase of 2.18 percent less than average.

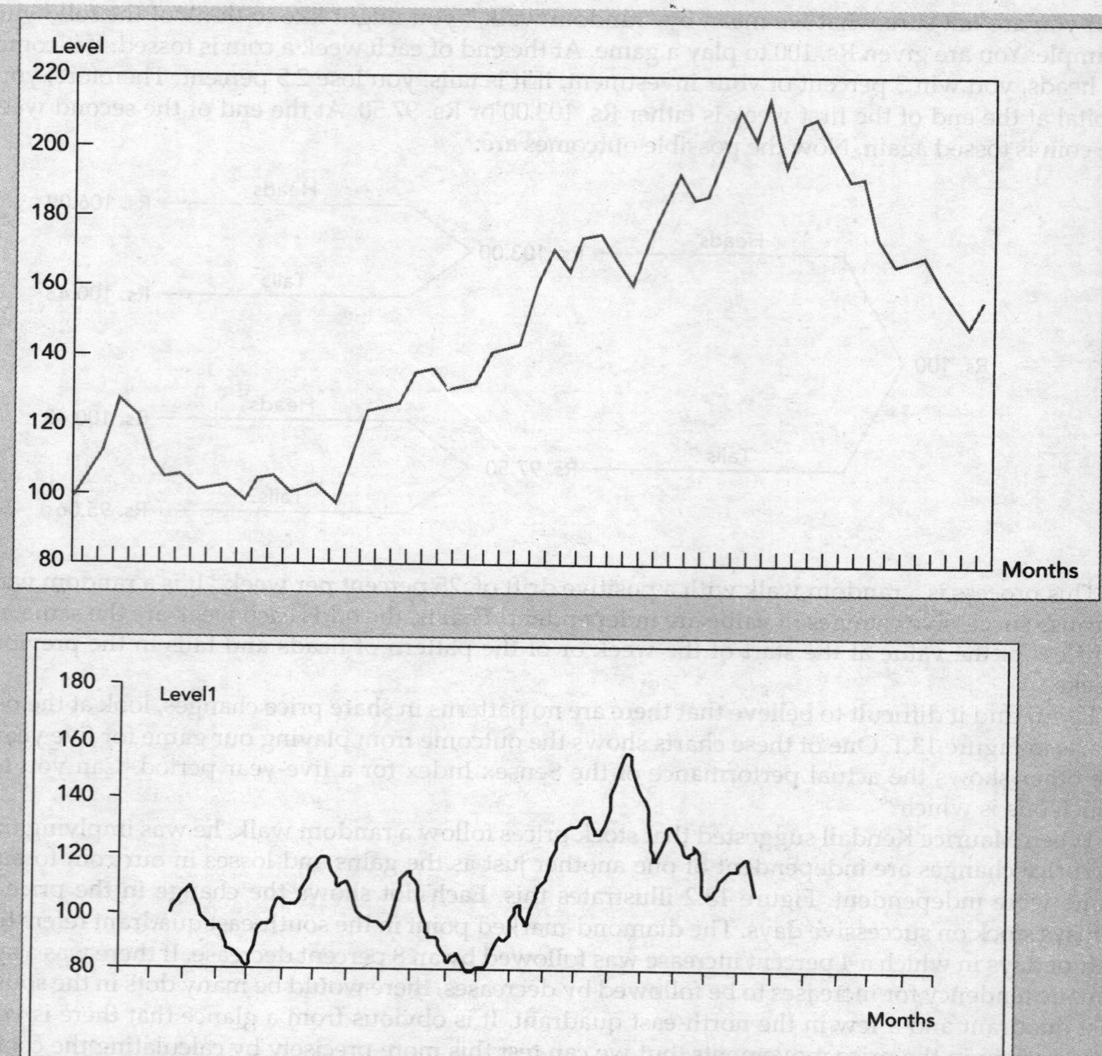

FIGURE 13.1

One of these charts shows the Sensex Index for a five-year period. The other shows the results of playing our coin-tossing game for five years. Can you tell which is which?

Figure 13.2 suggests that Infosys' price changes were effectively uncorrelated. Today's price change gave investors almost no clue as to the likely change tomorrow. Does that surprise you? If so, imagine that it were not the case and that changes in Infosys' stock price were expected to persist for several months. Figure 13.3 provides an example of such a predictable cycle. You can see

FIGURE 13.2

Each dot shows a pair of returns for Infosys stock on two consecutive days between November 1994 and March 2006. The diamond sized-dot in the southest quadrant records a daily return of +4 percent and then -8 percent on the next day. The scatter diagram shows no significant relationship between returns on successive days.

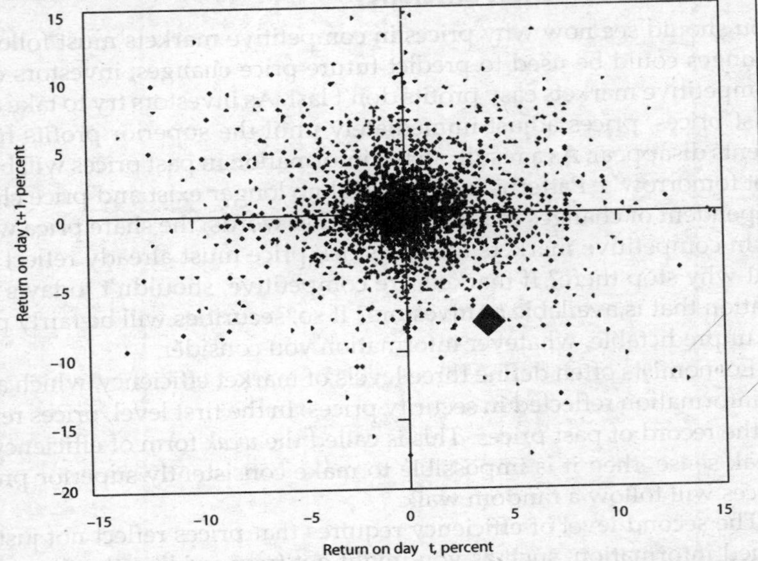

FIGURE 13.3

Cycles self-destruct as soon as they are recognized by investors. The stock price instantaneously jumps to the present value of the expected future price.

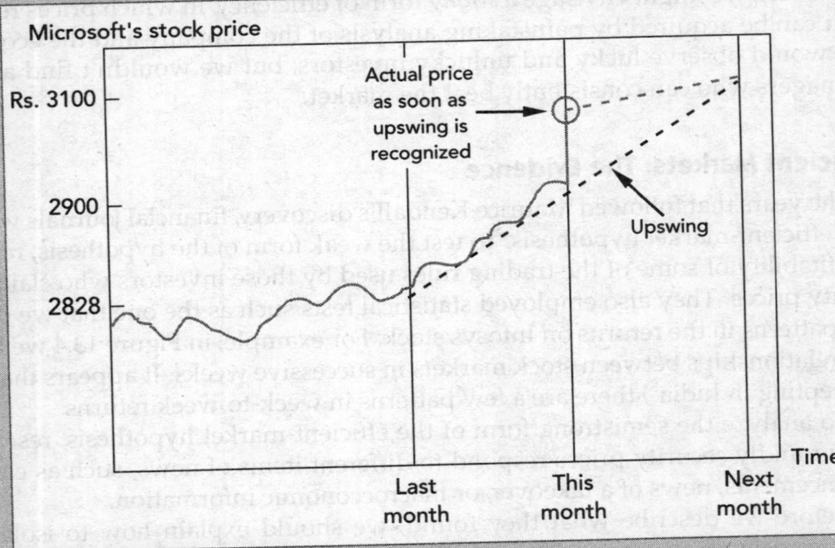

that an upswing in Infosys's stock price started last month, when the price was Rs. 2828, and it is expected to carry the price to Rs. 3100 next month. What will happen when investors perceive this bonanza? Since Infosys's stock price is a bargain at Rs. 2900, investors will rush to buy. They will stop buying only when the stock offers a normal rate of return. Therefore, as soon as a cycle becomes apparent to investors, they immediately eliminate it by their trading.

Three Forms of Market Efficiency

You should see now why prices in competitive markets must follow a random walk. If past price changes could be used to predict future price changes, investors could make easy profits. But in competitive markets easy profits don't last. As investors try to take advantage of the information in past prices, prices adjust immediately until the superior profits from studying past price movements disappear. As a result, all the information in past prices will be reflected in *today's* stock price, not tomorrow's. Patterns in prices will no longer exist and price changes in one period will be independent of changes in the next. In other words, the share price will follow a random walk.

In competitive markets today's stock price must already reflect the information in past prices. But why stop there? If markets are competitive, shouldn't today's stock price reflect *all* the information that is available to investors? If so, securities will be fairly priced and security returns will be unpredictable, whatever information you consider.

Economists often define three levels of market efficiency, which are distinguished by the degree of information reflected in security prices. In the first level, prices reflect the information contained in the record of past prices. This is called the *weak* form of efficiency. If markets are efficient in the weak sense, then it is impossible to make consistently superior profits by studying past returns. Prices will follow a random walk.

The second level of efficiency requires that prices reflect not just past prices but all other published information, such as you might get from reading the financial press. This is known as the *semistrong* form of market efficiency. If markets are efficient in this sense, then prices will adjust immediately to public information such as the announcement of the last quarter's earnings, a new issue of stock, a proposal to merge two companies, and so on.

Finally, we might envisage a *strong* form of efficiency, in which prices reflect all the information that can be acquired by painstaking analysis of the company and the economy. In such a market we would observe lucky and unlucky investors, but we wouldn't find any superior investment managers who can consistently beat the market.

Efficient Markets: The Evidence

In the years that followed Maurice Kendall's discovery, financial journals were packed with tests of the efficient-market hypothesis. To test the weak form of the hypothesis, researchers measured the profitability of some of the trading rules used by those investors who claim to find patterns in security prices. They also employed statistical tests such as the one that we described when looking for patterns in the returns on Infosys stock. For example, in Figure 13.4 we have used the same test for relationships between stock markets in successive weeks. It appears that throughout the world (excepting in India[8]) there are a few patterns in week-to-week returns.

To analyze the semistrong form of the efficient-market hypothesis, researchers have measured how rapidly security prices respond to different items of news, such as earnings or dividend announcements, news of a takeover, or macroeconomic information.

Before we describe what they found, we should explain how to isolate the effect of an announcement on the price of a stock. Suppose, for example, that you need to know how the stock

[8]The correlation coefficient continues to remain positive (in fact, increases marginally) even when we ignore the pre-1992 time period for India.

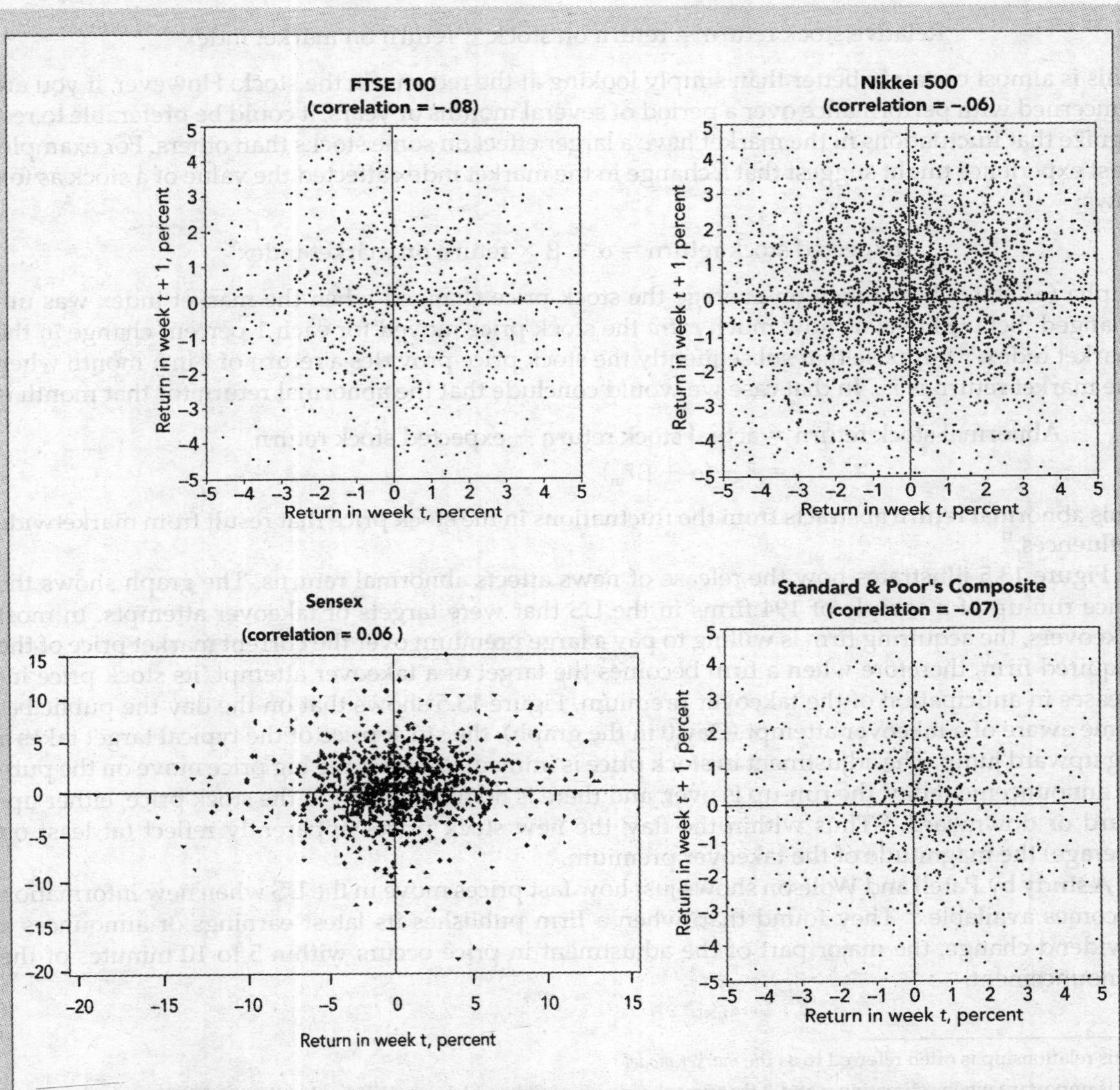

FIGURE 13.4

Each point in these scatter diagrams shows the return in successive weeks on four stock market indexes between May 1984 and May 2004. The wider scatter of points shows that there is almost no correlation between the return in one week and the next. The four indexes are FTSE 100 (UK), the Nikkei 500 (Japan), Sensex 30 (India), and Standard & Poor's Composite (USA).

price responds to news of a takeover. As a first stab, you could look at the returns on the stock in the months surrounding the announcement. But that would provide a very noisy measure, for the price would reflect among other things what was happening to the market as a whole. A second possibility would be to calculate a measure of relative performance:

$$\text{Relative stock return} = \text{return on stock} - \text{return on market index}$$

This is almost certainly better than simply looking at the returns on the stock. However, if you are concerned with performance over a period of several months or years, it could be preferable to recognize that fluctuations in the market have a larger effect on some stocks than others. For example, past experience might suggest that a change in the market index affected the value of a stock as follows:

$$\text{Expected stock return} = \alpha + \beta \times \text{return on market index}$$[9]

Alpha (α) states how much on average the stock price changed when the market index was unchanged. Beta (β) tells us how much *extra* the stock price moved for each 1 percent change in the market index.[10] Suppose that subsequently the stock price provides a return of $\tilde{r}$ in a month when the market return is $\tilde{r}_m$. In that case we would conclude that the abnormal return for that month is

$$\begin{aligned}\text{Abnormal stock return} &= \text{actual stock return} - \text{expected stock return}\\ &= \tilde{r} - (\alpha + \beta\tilde{r}_m)\end{aligned}$$

This abnormal return abstracts from the fluctuations in the stock price that result from marketwide influences.[11]

Figure 13.5 illustrates how the release of news affects abnormal returns. The graph shows the price run-up of a sample of 194 firms in the US that were targets of takeover attempts. In most takeovers, the acquiring firm is willing to pay a large premium over the current market price of the acquired firm; therefore when a firm becomes the target of a takeover attempt, its stock price increases in anticipation of the takeover premium. Figure 13.5 shows that on the day the public become aware of a takeover attempt (Day 0 in the graph), the stock price of the typical target takes a big upward jump. The adjustment in stock price is immediate: After the big price move on the public announcement day, the run-up is over, and there is no further drift in the stock price, either upward or downward.[12] Thus within the day, the new stock prices apparently reflect (at least on average) the magnitude of the takeover premium.

A study by Patell and Wolfson shows just how fast prices move in the US when new information becomes available.[13] They found that, when a firm publishes its latest earnings or announces a dividend change, the major part of the adjustment in price occurs within 5 to 10 minutes of the announcement.

---

[9]This relationship is often referred to as the *market model.*

[10]It is important when estimating α and β that you choose a period in which you believe that the stock behaved normally. If its performance was abnormal, then estimates of α and β cannot be used to measure the returns that investors expected. As a precaution, ask yourself whether your estimates of expected returns look sensible. Methods for estimating abnormal returns are analyzed in A. C. MacKinlay, "Event Studies in Economics and Finance," *Journal of Economic Literature* 35 (1997), pp. 13–39.

[11]The market is not the only common influence on stock prices. For example, in Section 8.4 we described the Fama–French three-factor model, which states that a stock's return is influenced by three common factors—the market factor, a size factor, and a book-to-market factor. In this case we would calculate the expected stock return as $a + b_{\text{market}}(\tilde{r}_{\text{market factor}}) + b_{\text{size}}(\tilde{r}_{\text{size factor}}) + b_{\text{book-to-market}}(\tilde{r}_{\text{book-to-market factor}})$.

[12]See A. Keown and J. Pinkerton, "Merger Announcements and Insider Trading Activity," *Journal of Finance* 36 (September 1981), pp. 855–869. Note that prices on the days *before* the public announcement do show evidence of a sustained upward drift. This is evidence of a gradual leakage of information about a possible takeover attempt.

[13]See J. M. Patell and M. A. Wolfson, "The Intraday Speed of Adjustment of Stock Prices to Earnings and Dividend Announcements," *Journal of Financial Economics* 13 (June 1984), pp. 223–252.

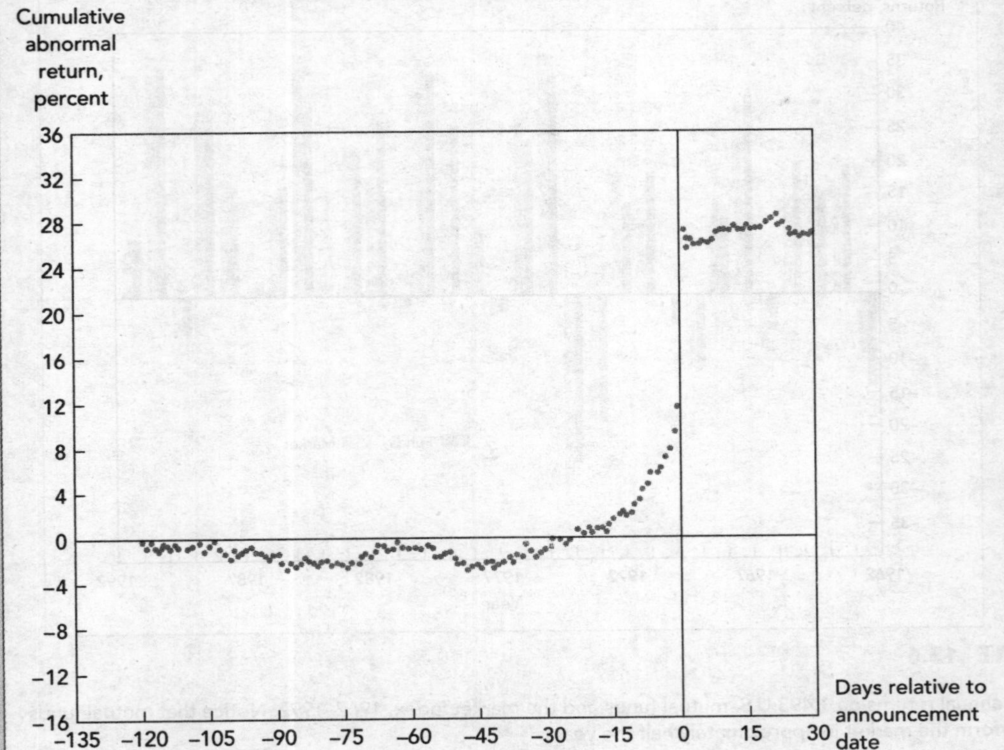

FIGURE 13.5

The performance of the stocks of target companies compared with that of the market. The prices of target stocks jump up on the announcement day, but from then on, there are no unusual price movements. The announcement of the takeover attempt seems to be fully reflected in the stock price on the announcement day.

Source: A. Keown and J. Pinkerton, "Merger Announcements and Insider Trading Activity," *Journal of Finance* 36 (September 1981), pp. 855–869. Reprinted with permission of Blackwell Publishers Journal Rights.

Tests of the strong form of the hypothesis have examined the recommendations of professional security analysts and have looked for mutual funds or pension funds that could predictably outperform the market. Some researchers have found a slight persistent outperformance, but just as many have concluded that professionally managed funds fail to recoup the costs of management. Look, for example, at Figure 13.6, which is taken from a study by Mark Carhart of the average return on nearly 1,500 U.S. mutual funds. You can see that in some years the mutual funds beat the market, but as often as not it was the other way around. Figure 13.6 provides a fairly crude comparison, for mutual funds have tended to specialize in particular sectors of the market, such as low-beta stocks or large-firm stocks, that may have given below-average returns. To control for such differences, each fund needs to be compared with a benchmark portfolio of similar securities. The study by Mark Carhart did this, but the message was unchanged: The funds earned a lower return than the benchmark portfolios *after* expenses and roughly matched the benchmarks *before* expenses.

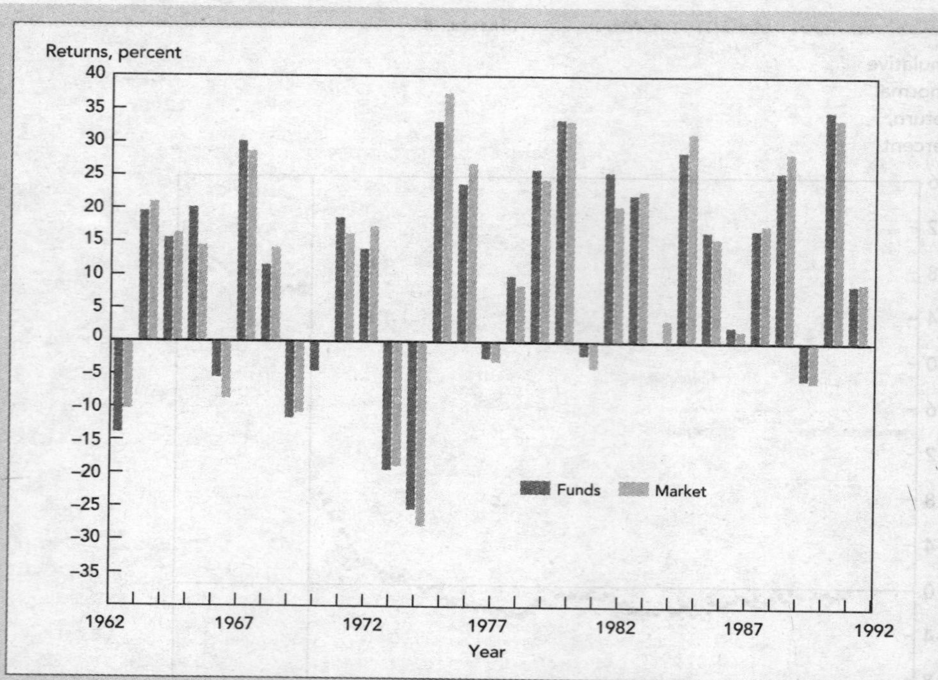

FIGURE 13.6

Average annual returns on 1,493 U.S. mutual funds and the market index, 1962–1992. Notice that mutual funds underperform the market in approximately half the years.

Source: M. M. Carhart, "On Persistence in Mutual Fund Performance," *Journal of Finance* 52 (March 1997), pp. 57–82. Reprinted with permission of Blackwell Publishers Journal Rights.

It would be surprising if some managers were not smarter than others and could earn superior returns. But it seems difficult to spot the smart ones, and the top-performing managers one year have about an average chance of falling on their face the next year.[14]

Such evidence on strong-form efficiency has proved to be sufficiently convincing that many professionally managed funds have given up the pursuit of superior performance. They simply "buy the index," which maximizes diversification and minimizes the costs of managing the portfolio. Corporate pension plans now invest over a quarter of their U.S. equity holdings in index funds.

13.3 PUZZLES AND ANOMALIES—WHAT DO THEY MEAN FOR THE FINANCIAL MANAGER?

Almost without exception, early researchers concluded that the efficient-market hypothesis was a remarkably good description of reality. So powerful was the evidence that any dissenting research

[14]See, for example, B. G. Malkiel, "Returns from Investing in Equity Mutual Funds 1971 to 1991," *Journal of Finance* 50 (June 1995), pp. 549–572. Some contrary evidence that good performance does persist is provided in E. J. Elton, M. J. Gruber, and C. R. Blake, "The Persistence of Risk-Adjusted Mutual Fund Performance," *Journal of Business* 69 (April 1996), pp. 133–157.

was regarded with suspicion. But eventually the readers of finance journals grew weary of hearing the same message. The interesting articles became those that turned up some puzzle. Soon the journals were packed with evidence of anomalies that investors have apparently failed to exploit.

We have already referred to one such puzzle—the abnormally high returns on the stocks of small firms. For example, look back at Figure 8.11, which shows the cumulative difference between the returns on small-firm stocks and large-firm stocks in the US. You can see that since 1926 the stocks of the firms with the lowest market capitalizations have performed substantially better than those with the highest capitalizations.

Now this may mean one (or more) of several things. First, it could be that investors have demanded a higher expected return from small firms to compensate for some extra risk factor that is not captured in the simple capital asset pricing model. That is why we asked in Chapter 8 whether the small-firm effect is evidence against the CAPM.

Second, the superior performance of small firms could simply be a coincidence, a finding that stems from the efforts of many researchers to find interesting patterns in the data. There is evidence for and against the coincidence theory. Those who believe that the small-firm effect is a pervasive phenomenon can point to the fact that small-firm stocks have provided a higher return in many other countries. On the other hand, you can see from Figure 8.11 that the small-firm effect seems to have disappeared as soon as it was first documented in 1981.[15]

The third possibility is that we have here an important exception to the efficient-market theory, one that provided investors with an opportunity to make predictably superior profits over a period of two decades. If such anomalies offer easy pickings, you would expect to find a number of investors eager to take advantage of them. It turns out that, while many investors do try to exploit such anomalies, it is surprisingly difficult to get rich by doing so. For example, Professor Richard Roll, who probably knows as much as anyone about market anomalies, confesses

> Over the past decade, I have attempted to exploit many of the seemingly most promising "inefficiencies" by actually trading significant amounts of money according to a trading rule suggested by the "inefficiencies" . . . I have never yet found one that worked in practice, in the sense that it returned more after cost than a buy-and-hold strategy.[16]

Do Investors Respond Slowly to New Information?

We have dwelt on the small-firm effect, but there is no shortage of other puzzles and anomalies. Some of them relate to the short-term behavior of stock prices. For example, returns appear to be higher in January than in other months, they seem to be lower on a Monday than on other days of the week, and most of the daily return comes at the beginning and end of the day. A study by Prof. IM Pandey[17] shows statistically negative returns in the month of March in India. The same study also documents negative returns (though statistically insignificant) in the month of April.

To have any chance of making money from such short-term patterns, you need to be a professional trader, with one eye on the computer screen and the other on your annual bonus. If you are a corporate financial manager, these short-term patterns in stock prices may be intriguing conundrums, but they are unlikely to change the major financial decisions about which projects to invest in and how they should be financed. The more troubling concern for the corporate finan-

[15]This might also imply that investors *did* underestimate the attractions of small-firm stocks before 1981, but as soon as the mispricing was documented, practitioners moved to eliminate the profit opportunities.

[16]R. Roll, "What Every CFO Should Know about Scientific Progress in Financial Economics: What Is Known and What Remains to Be Resolved," *Financial Management* 23 (Summer 1994), pp. 69–75.

[17]Pandey, I.M., "The monthly effect in Stock Returns: The Indian Evidence". ICFAI Journal of Applied Finance, November 2002.

cial manager is the possibility that it may be several years before investors fully appreciate the significance of new information. The studies of daily and hourly price movements that we referred to above may not pick up this long-term mispricing, but here are two examples of an apparent long-term delay in the reaction to news.

The Earnings Announcement Puzzle The earnings announcement puzzle is summarized in Figure 13.7, which shows stock performance following the announcement of unexpectedly good or bad earnings during the years 1974 to 1986 in the US.[18] The 10 percent of the stocks of firms with the best earnings news outperform those with the worst news by more than 4 percent over the two months following the announcement. It seems that investors underreact to the earnings announcement and become aware of the full significance only as further information arrives. Using data for 90 stocks for the sample period January 1990 to March 1996, Prof. Hari Om Chaturvedi[19] reports similar results from India. Within a span of 40 days after the announcement of the earnings, the 20 percent of the stocks of firms with the best earnings news outperform those with the worst news by 26 percent.

The New-Issue Puzzle When firms issue stock to the public, investors typically rush to buy. On average those lucky enough to receive stock receive an immediate capital gain. However, researchers have found that these early gains often turn into losses. For example, suppose that you bought stock immediately following each initial public offering and then held that stock for five years. Over the period 1970–2002 your average annual return would have been 4.2 percent less than the return on a portfolio of similar-sized stocks in the US. Madhusoodanan and Thiripalraju, and Baral and Obaidullah report positive abnormal return on the first day of listing of IPOs in India[20]. Both the studies also report negative *risk-adjusted returns* in the one-year period after the listing of IPOs. The study by Baral and Obaidullah document another interesting results about the Indian IPOs. They find the average return from the day of listing till the 20th day after listing, is 11.5 percent. This means even if an investor does not apply (or does not get the allotment) for the IPOs, he can still make excess return by buying on the day of listing and selling it on the 20th day. However, the same study also documents lower liquidity on the first day of the listing.

The jury is still out on these studies of longer-term anomalies. Take, for example, the new-issue puzzle. Most new issues during the past 30 years have involved growth stocks with high market values and limited book assets. When the long-run performance of new issues is compared with a portfolio that is matched in terms of both size and book-to-market, the difference in performance almost halves.[21] So the new-issue puzzle could well turn out to be just the book-to-market puzzle in disguise.

---

[18]V. L. Bernard and J. K. Thomas, "Post-Earnings Announcement Drift: Delayed Price Response or Risk Premium?" *Journal of Accounting Research* 27 (Supplement 1989), pp. 1–36.

[19]Chaturvedi, H.O., "is SUE and Effective Discriminator? Evidence from the Indian Capital Market - It does Discriminate!", ICFAI Journal of Applied Finance, January, 1999.

[20]See Madhusoodanan, T.P., and M. T. Thiripalraju, "Underpricing in Initial Public Offerings: The Indian Evidence", Vikalpa, 1997.

See also Baral, S K., and M. Obaidullah, "Short-run Price Behavior of IPOs in India: Some Empirical Findings", paper presented in the First Capital Markets Conference held at the Indian Institute of Capital Markets, 1997.

[21]The long-run underperformance of new issues was described in R. Loughran and J. R. Ritter, "The New Issues Puzzle," *Journal of Finance* 50 (1995), pp. 23–51. The figures are updated on Jay Ritter's Web site and the returns compared with those of a portfolio which is matched in terms of size and book-to-market. (See **bear.cba.ufl.edu/ritter.**)

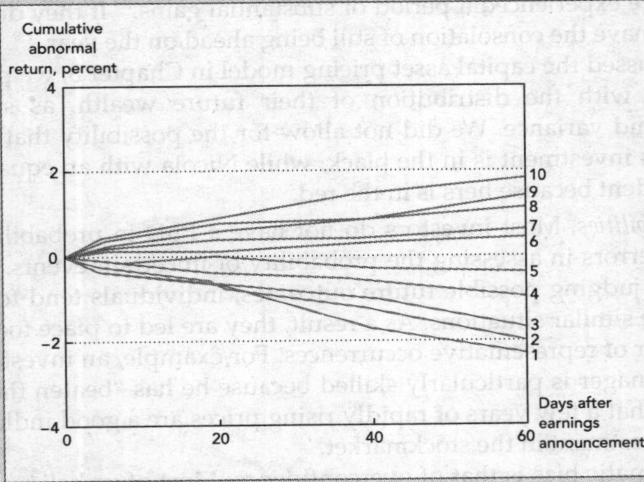

FIGURE 13.7

The cumulative abnormal returns of stocks of firms over the 60 days following an announcement of quarterly earnings. The 10 percent of the stocks with the best earnings news (Group 10) outperformed those with the worst news (Group 1) by more than 4 percent.

Source: V. L. Bernard and J. K. Thomas, "Post-Earnings-Announcement Drift: Delayed Price Response or Risk Premium?" *Journal of Accounting Research* 27 (Supplement 1989), pp. 1–36. Reprinted with permission of Blackwell Publishers Journal Rights.

Stock Market Anomalies and Behavioral Finance

In the meantime, some scholars are casting around for an alternative theory that might explain these apparent anomalies. Some argue that the answers lie in behavioral psychology. People are not 100 percent rational 100 percent of the time. This shows up in two broad areas—their attitudes to risk and the way that they assess probabilities.

1. *Attitudes toward risk.* Psychologists have observed that, when making risky decisions, people are particularly loath to incur losses. It seems that investors do not focus solely on the *current* value of their holdings, but look back at whether their investments are showing a profit or a loss. For example, if I sell my holding of HLL for Rs. 50,000, I may gain considerable satisfaction if it had cost me only Rs. 5,000, but I would be much less happy if it had cost Rs. 75,000. This observation is the basis for *prospect theory.*[22] Prospect theory states that (a) the value investors place on a particular outcome is determined by the gains or losses that they have made since the asset was acquired or the holding last reviewed, and (b) investors are particularly averse to the possibility of even a very small loss and need a correspondingly higher return to compensate for it.

   The pain of a loss seems also to depend on whether it comes on the heels of earlier losses, so that, once investors have suffered a loss, they may be even more concerned not to risk a further loss. Conversely, just as gamblers are known to be more willing to make large bets when they are ahead, so investors may be more prepared to run the risk of a stock market

[22]Prospect theory was first set out in D. Kahneman and A. Tversky, "Prospect Theory: An Analysis of Decision under Risk," *Econometrica* 47 (1979), pp. 263–291.

dip after they have experienced a period of substantial gains.[23] If they do then suffer a small loss, they at least have the consolation of still being ahead on the year.

When we discussed the capital asset pricing model in Chapter 8, we pictured investors as concerned solely with the distribution of their future wealth, as summarized by the expected return and variance. We did not allow for the possibility that Nicholas would be elated because his investment is in the black, while Nicola with an equal amount of wealth would be despondent because hers is in the red.

2. *Beliefs about probabilities*. Most investors do not have a PhD in probability theory and may make systematic errors in assessing the probability of uncertain events. Psychologists have found that, when judging possible future outcomes, individuals tend to look back at what happened in some similar situations. As a result, they are led to place too much weight on a very small number of representative occurrences. For example, an investor might judge that an investment manager is particularly skilled because he has "beaten the market" for three years in a row or that a few years of rapidly rising prices are a good indication of the profits to be had from investment in the stockmarket.

   A second systematic bias is that of overconfidence. Most of us believe that we are better-than-average drivers, and most investors think that they are better-than-average stock pickers. Two speculators who trade with each other cannot both make money from the deal; for every winner there must be a loser. But presumably investors are prepared to continue trading because each is confident that it is the other one who is the patsy. Overconfidence also shows up in the certainty that people express in their judgments. They consistently underestimate the chances of an unlikely event occurring.

Now these behavioral tendencies have been well documented by psychologists, and there is plenty of evidence that private investors are not paragons of rationality. For example, most individuals are reluctant to sell stocks that show a loss. They also seem to be overconfident in their views and to trade excessively.[24] But this raises a question. It may well be true that many of us are not wholly rational in our investment decisions. However, hard-headed pros are constantly on the lookout for possible biases that may be a source of future profits. So it is not enough to refer to irrationality on the part of individual investors; we also need to explain why financial institutions do not compete away the profit opportunities that may arise.

Take, for example, the Dutch company Royal Dutch Petroleum and the British company Shell Transport & Trading. Before Shell decided to merge the two companies, they were effectively Siamese twins that shared in the profits of the oil giant. Royal Dutch was entitled to 60 percent of the cash flow of the joint company and Shell T&T was entitled to 40 percent. So you would expect

[23] The effect is described in R. H. Thaler and E. J. Johnson, "Gambling with the House Money and Trying to Break Even: The Effects of Prior Outcomes on Risky Choice," *Management Science* 36 (1990), pp. 643–660. The implications of prospect theory for stock returns are explored in N. Barberis, M. Huang, and T. Santos, "Prospect Theory and Asset Prices," *Quarterly Journal of Economics* 116 (February 2001), pp. 1–53.

[24] See T. Odean, "Are Investors Reluctant to Realize their Losses?" *Journal of Finance* 53 (October 1998), pp. 1775–1798; and T. Odean, "Boys Will Be Boys: Gender, Overconfidence, and Common Stock Investment," *Quarterly Journal of Economics* 116 (February 2001), pp. 261–292.

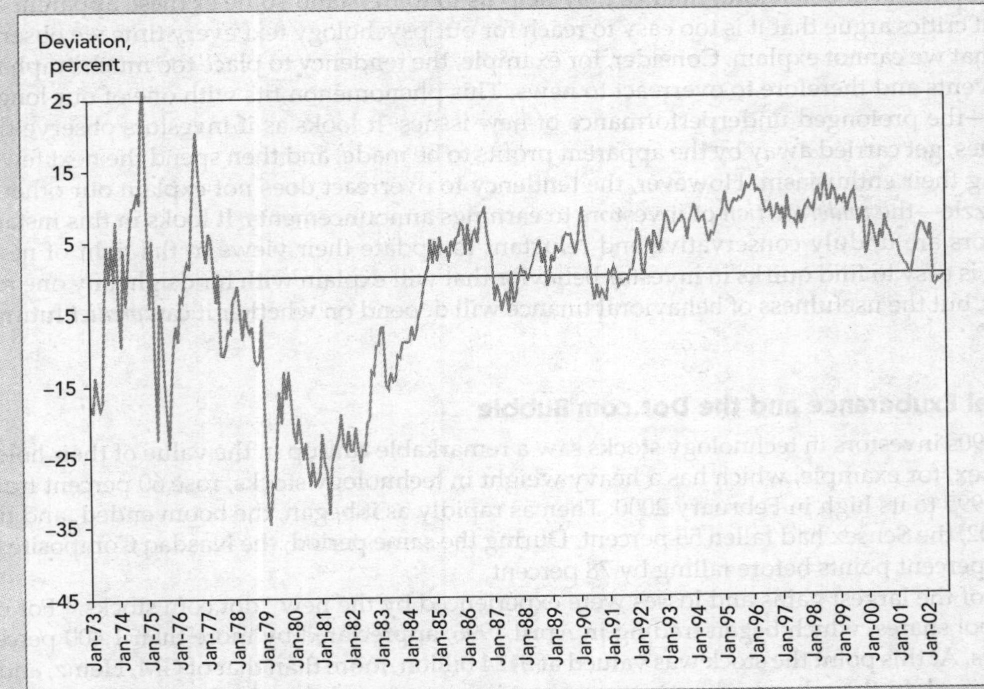

FIGURE 13.8

Log deviations from Royal Dutch Shell/Shell T&T parity.

Source: The plot extends and updates the original plot in K. Froot and E. Dabora, "How Are Stock Prices Affected by the Location of Trade," *Journal of Financial Economics*, 53 (1999), pp.189–216.

that the market value of Royal Dutch would always be equal to 60/40 = 1.5 times that of Shell T&T. But, as you can see from Figure 13.8, in practice the values of the two shares often traded away from parity for long periods.

This would appear to suggest an opportunity for easy profits—just buy the stock that is relatively cheap and sell the other one. Of course, some arbitrageurs do seek to profit from such discrepancies, but there are no easy profits here. The main problem is that the undervalued share may become even more undervalued in the future. For example, suppose that you were a professional money manager in December 1978 when Royal Dutch was 15 percent below parity. Would you have been tempted to sell Shell T&T and buy Royal Dutch? If you did, you would have had to wait nearly two years before you saw any profit on your position and in the meantime you would have had to watch while the stock moved to 35 percent below parity (and probably while a new investment manager was appointed in your stead).[25]

[25]Of course, an arbitrageur would also have had to bear some transaction costs. The deviations from parity for the two Shell companies are analyzed in K. A. Froot and E. M. Dabora, "How Are Stock Prices Affected by the Location of Trade?" *Journal of Financial Economics* 53 (August 1999), pp. 189–216. See also A. Shleifer and R. W. Vishny, "The Limits to Arbitrage," *Journal of Finance* 52 (March 1997), pp. 35–55.

Developments in behavioral finance may help us to understand some of these apparent anomalies. But critics argue that it is too easy to reach for our psychology text every time we observe behavior that we cannot explain. Consider, for example, the tendency to place too much emphasis on recent events and therefore to overreact to news. This phenomenon fits with one of our long-term puzzles—the prolonged underperformance of new issues. It looks as if investors observe the hot new issues, get carried away by the apparent profits to be made, and then spend the next few years regretting their enthusiasm. However, the tendency to overreact does not explain our other long-term puzzle—the *underreaction* of investors to earnings announcements. It looks in this instance as if investors are unduly conservative and reluctant to update their views in the light of new evidence. It is easy to find quirks in investor behavior that will explain with hindsight any one market anomaly, but the usefulness of behavioral finance will depend on whether it can *predict* future mispricing.[26]

Irrational Exuberance and the Dot.com Bubble

In the 1990s investors in technology stocks saw a remarkable run-up in the value of their holdings. The Sensex, for example, which has a heavy weight in technology stocks, rose 60 percent from the start of 1995 to its high in February 2000. Then as rapidly as it began, the boom ended, and by October 2002, the Sensex had fallen 55 percent. During the same period, the Nasdaq Composite index rose 580 percent points before falling by 78 percent.

Some of the largest gains and losses were experienced by the new "dot.com stocks." For example, Yahoo! shares, which began trading in April 1996, appreciated by more than 1,400 percent in four years. At this point the stock was valued at $124 billion, more than that of GM, Heinz, and Boeing combined. In these heady days some companies even found that they could boost their stock price simply by adding "dot-com" to the company name.[27]

What caused the extraordinary boom in these stocks? It is difficult to believe that future earnings growth would ever be sufficient to provide investors with a reasonable return.[28] For behavioral finance scholars the dot.com boom seemed to provide an irrefutable demonstration that markets are liable to be swayed by irrational crazes. In his book *Irrational Exuberance* Robert Shiller argued that, as the bull market developed, it generated optimism about the future and stimulated further demand for shares.[29] Moreover, as individuals racked up profits on their investments, they became even more confident of their opinions.

But why didn't smart professional investors step in, sell high-tech stocks, and force their prices down to fair value? Perhaps the reason was that it was too difficult to predict when the boom would end and that their jobs would be at risk if they moved into cash while others were raking up profits.

---

[26]This point is made in E. F. Fama, "Market Efficiency, Long-Term Returns, and Behavioral Finance," *Journal of Financial Economics* 49 (September 1998), pp. 283–306. One paper that does seek to model why investors may both underreact and overreact is N. Barberis, A. Shleifer, and R. Vishny, "A Model of Investor Sentiment," *Journal of Financial Economics* 49 (September 1998), pp. 307–343.

[27]P. R. Rau, O. Dimitrov, and M. Cooper, "A Rose.com by Any Other Name," *Journal of Finance* 56 (2001), pp. 2371–2388.

[28]See, for example, E. Ofek and M. Richardson, "The Valuation and Market Rationality of Internet Stock Prices," *Oxford Review of Economic Policy,* 18 (Autumn 2002), pp. 265–287.

[29]See R. J. Shiller, *Irrational Exuberance* (New York: Broadway Books, 2001). The term "irrational exuberance" was coined by Alan Greenspan, chairman of the Federal Reserve, in a commentary on the dot.com boom.

The Dot.com Boom and Relative Efficiency

The dot.com boom and crash remind us how exceptionally difficult it is to value common stocks. For example, imagine that at the market's peak in the year 2000 you wanted to check whether the stocks forming S&P CNX 500 Index were fairly valued. As a first step you might use the constant-growth formula that we introduced in Chapter 4[30]. In 2000, the annual dividends paid by the companies in the index totaled about Rs.9728.14 crores. Suppose that these dividends were expected to grow at a steady rate of 13.8 percent a year and that investors required a return of 15 percent. Then the constant-growth formula gives a value for the common stocks of

$$\text{PV(common stocks)} = \frac{\text{DIV}}{r - g} = \frac{9728.14 \times (1 + 13.8\%)}{(15\% - 13.8\%)} = \text{Rs. } 922{,}552 \text{ crores}$$

which was roughly their total value (equal to Rs. 892,490 crores). But how confident could anyone have been about these figures? Perhaps the likely dividend growth was only 12.8 percent per year. In that case the value of the common stocks would decline to

$$\text{PV(common stocks)} = \frac{\text{DIV}}{r - g} = \frac{9728.14 \times (1 + 12.8\%)}{(15\% - 12.8\%)} = \text{Rs. } 498{,}788 \text{ crores}$$

which was the value of these stocks in October 2002. In other words, the 46 percent decline in the S&P CNX 500 index could have been caused simply by investors revising their forecast of dividend growth by 1 percentage points.

The extreme difficulty of valuing common stocks from scratch has two important consequences. First, investors find it easier to price a common stock relative to yesterday's price or relative to today's price of comparable securities. In other words, they generally take yesterday's price as correct, adjusting upward or downward on the basis of today's information. If information arrives smoothly, then as time passes, investors become increasingly confident that today's price level is correct. But, when investors lose confidence in the benchmark of yesterday's price, there may be a period of confused trading and volatile prices before a new benchmark is established.

Second, most of the tests of market efficiency are concerned with *relative* prices and focus on whether there are easy profits to be made. It is almost impossible to test whether stocks are *correctly valued*, because no one can measure true value with any precision. Take, for example, SBI stock, which was sold for Rs.870 in May 2006. Could we prove that this was its true value? Of course, not, but we could be more confident that the price of SBI should be nearly three times that of Corporation Bank (Rs.299) since SBI's earnings per share were nearly three times that of Corporation Bank and the two banks had similar growth prospects.

Market Anomalies and the Financial Manager

The financial manager needs to be confident that, when the firm issues new securities, it can do so at a fair price. There are two reasons that this might sometimes not be the case. First, the strong form of the efficient-market hypothesis may not be 100 percent true, so that the financial manager may have information that other investors do not have. Alternatively, investors may have the same information as management, but may be subject to irrational biases or slow to react to the informa-

[30] You would not want to use the formula to value a dot.com start-up.But most of the companies represented in S&P CNX 500 index are mature firms for which the assumption of constant growth is more plausible.

tion. For example, we described above some evidence that new issues of stock tend to be followed by a prolonged period of low stock returns.

You sometimes hear managers say something along the following lines:

> Great! Our stock is clearly overpriced. This means we can raise capital cheaply and invest in Project X. Our high stock price gives us a big advantage over our competitors who could not possibly justify investing in Project X.

But that doesn't make sense. If your stock is truly overpriced, you can help your current shareholders by selling additional stock and using the cash to invest in other capital market securities. But you should *never* issue stock to invest in a project that offers a lower rate of return than you could earn elsewhere in the capital market. Such a project would have a negative NPV. You can always do better than investing in a negative-NPV project: Your company can go out and buy common stocks. In an efficient market, such purchases are always *zero* NPV.

What about the reverse? Suppose you know that your stock is *underpriced*. In that case, it certainly would not help your current shareholders to sell additional "cheap" stock to invest in other fairly priced stocks. If your stock is sufficiently underpriced, it may even pay to forego an opportunity to invest in a positive-NPV project rather than to allow new investors to buy into your firm at a low price. Financial managers who believe that their firm's stock is underpriced may be justifiably reluctant to issue more stock, but they may instead be able to finance their investment program by an issue of debt. In this case the market inefficiency would affect the firm's choice of financing but not its real investment decisions. In Chapter 15 we will have more to say about the financing choice when managers believe their stock is mispriced.

13.4 THE SIX LESSONS OF MARKET EFFICIENCY

The efficient-market hypothesis emphasizes that arbitrage will rapidly eliminate any profit opportunities and drive market prices back to fair value. Behavioral-finance specialists may concede that there are no easy profits, but argue that arbitrage is costly and sometimes slow-working, so that deviations from fair value may persist.

Sorting out the puzzles will take time, but we suggest that financial managers should assume, at least as a starting point, that there are no free lunches to be had on *Wall Street*. This has some important implications.

Lesson 1: Markets Have No Memory

The weak form of the efficient-market hypothesis states that the sequence of past price changes contains no information about future changes. Economists express the same idea more concisely when they say that the market has no memory. Sometimes financial managers *seem* to act as if this were not the case. For example, after an abnormal market rise, managers prefer to issue equity rather than debt.[31] The idea is to catch the market while it is high. Similarly, they are often reluctant to

[31]See, for example, P. Asquith and D. W. Mullins, Jr., "Equity Issues and Offering Dilution," *Journal of Financial Economics* 15 (January–February 1986), pp. 16–89; and (for the UK) P. R. Marsh, "The Choice between Debt and Equity: An Empirical Study," *Journal of Finance* 37 (March 1982), pp. 121–144.

issue stock after a fall in price. They are inclined to wait for a rebound. But we know that the market has no memory and the cycles that financial managers seem to rely on do not exist.[32]

Sometimes a financial manager will have inside information indicating that the firm's stock is overpriced or underpriced.[33] Suppose, for example, that there is some good news which the market does not know but you do. The stock price will rise sharply when the news is revealed. Therefore, if the company sold shares at the current price, it would be offering a bargain to new investors at the expense of present stockholders.

Naturally, managers are reluctant to sell new shares when they have favorable inside information. But such information has nothing to do with the history of the stock price. Your firm's stock could be selling at half its price of a year ago, and yet you could have special information suggesting that it is *still* grossly overvalued. Or it may be undervalued at twice last year's price.

Lesson 2: Trust Market Prices

In an efficient market you can trust prices, for they impound all available information about the value of each security. This means that in an efficient market, there is no way for most investors to achieve consistently superior rates of return. To do so, you not only need to know more than *anyone* else; you also need to know more than *everyone* else. This message is important for the financial manager who is responsible for the firm's exchange-rate policy or for its purchases and sales of debt. If you operate on the basis that you are smarter than others at predicting currency changes or interest-rate moves, you will trade a consistent financial policy for an elusive will-o'-the-wisp.

The company's assets may also be directly affected by management's faith in its investment skills. For example, one company may purchase another simply because its management thinks that the stock is undervalued. On approximately half the occasions the stock of the acquired firm will with hindsight turn out to be undervalued. But on the other half it will be overvalued. On average the value will be correct, so the acquiring company is playing a fair game except for the costs of the acquisition.

Lesson 3: Read the Entrails

If the market is efficient, prices impound all available information. Therefore, if we can only learn to read the entrails, security prices can tell us a lot about the future. For example, in Chapter 24 we will show how information in a company's financial statements can help the financial manager to estimate the probability of bankruptcy. But the market's assessment of the company's securities can also provide important information about the firm's prospects. Thus, if the company's bonds are offering a much higher yield than the average, you can deduce that the firm is probably in trouble.

---

[32]If high stock prices signal expanded investment opportunities and the need to finance these new investments, we would expect to see firms raise more money *in total* when stock prices are historically high. But this does not explain why firms prefer to raise the extra cash at these times by an issue of equity rather than debt.

[33]For evidence that managers do successfully time equity issues, see M. Baker and J. Wurgler, "The Equity Share in New Issues and Aggregate Stock Returns," *Journal of Finance* 55 (October 2000), pp. 2219–2257.

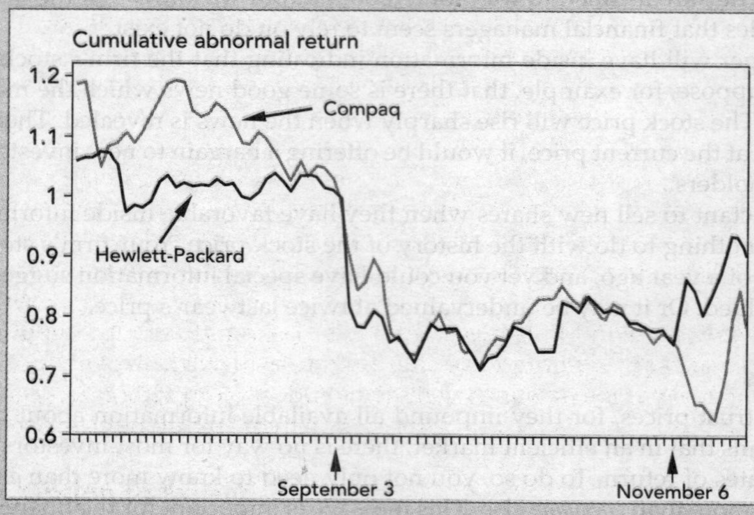

FIGURE 13.9

Cumulative abnormal returns on Hewlett Packard and Compaq stocks during four-month period surrounding the announcement on September 3, 2001, of a proposed merger. Hewlett Packard stock recovered after the Hewlett family announced on November 6 that it would vote against the merger.

Here is another example: Suppose that investors are confident that interest rates are set to rise over the next year. In that case, they will prefer to wait before they make long-term loans, and any firm that wants to borrow long-term money today will have to offer the inducement of a higher rate of interest. In other words, the long-term rate of interest will have to be higher than the one-year rate. Differences between the long-term interest rate and the short-term rate tell you something about what investors expect to happen to short-term rates in the future.[34]

Example—Hewlett Packard Proposes to Merge with Compaq On September 3, 2001, two computer companies, Hewlett Packard and Compaq, revealed plans to merge. Announcing the proposal, Carly Fiorina, the chief executive of Hewlett Packard, stated: "This combination vaults us into a leadership role" and creates "substantial shareowner value through significant cost structure improvements and access to new growth opportunities." But investors and analysts gave the proposal a big thumbs-down. Figure 13.9 shows that over the following two days the shares of Hewlett Packard underperformed the market by 21 percent, while Compaq shares underperformed by 16 percent. Investors, it seems, believed that the merger had a negative net present value of $13 billion. When on November 6 the Hewlett family announced that it would vote against the proposal, investors took heart, and the next day Hewlett Packard shares gained 16 percent.[35] We do not wish to imply that investor concerns about the merger were justified, for management may have had important information that investors lacked. Our point is simply that the price reaction of the two stocks provided a potentially valuable summary of investor opinion about the effect of the merger on firm value.

[34]We will discuss the relationship between short-term and long-term interest rates in Chapter 23. Notice, however, that in an efficient market the difference between the prices of *any* short-term and long-term contracts always says something about how participants expect prices to move.

[35]The stock of Compaq, which was thought to be less badly affected by the merger, fell on the news, before also rising.

Lesson 4: There Are No Financial Illusions

In an efficient market there are no financial illusions. Investors are unromantically concerned with the firm's cash flows and the portion of those cash flows to which they are entitled. However, there are occasions on which managers seem to assume that investors suffer from financial illusion.

Example—Accounting Changes Some firms devote considerable ingenuity to the task of manipulating earnings reported to stockholders. This is done by "creative accounting," that is, by choosing accounting methods that stabilize and increase reported earnings. Presumably firms go to this trouble because management believes that stockholders take the figures at face value.[36]

One way that companies can affect their reported earnings is through the way that they cost the goods taken out of inventory. As per the Accounting Standard 2 (AS 2) prescribed by ICAI, India, companies can choose between two methods. Under the FIFO (first-in, first-out) method, the firm deducts the cost of the first goods to have been placed in the inventory. Under the weighted-average cost method companies deduct the weighted average cost of the latest goods to arrive in the warehouse. When inflation is high, the cost of the goods that were brought first is likely to be lower than the cost of those that were brought last (and hence likely to be lower than the weighted average cost). So earnings calculated by FIFO appear higher than those calculated under the weighted average cost method.

Now, if it were just a matter of presentation, there would be no harm in switching from weighted average cost method to FIFO. Section 145A of the Income Tax Act does not prescribe any method of inventory valuation. It merely states that the valuation of inventory shall be in accordance with the method of accounting regularly employed by the company. In an inflationary environment, the weighted average cost method will reduce the tax liability of a company. So the lower apparent earnings from using the weighted average cost method also bring lower immediate tax payments.

Though AS 2 in India does not allow LIFO, the US GAAP accepts LIFO as a legitimate way of valuing inventories. Under LIFO (last-in, first-out), a firm reports still lower earnings as compared to FIFO and weighted-average cost method under inflationary environment. In the U.S., the IRS insists that the same method that is used to report to shareholders also be used to calculate the firm's taxes.

If markets are efficient, investors should welcome a change to LIFO accounting, even though it reduces earnings. Biddle and Lindahl, who studied the matter, concluded that this is exactly what happens, so that the move to LIFO is associated with an abnormal rise in the stock price.[37] It seems that shareholders look behind the figures and focus on the amount of the tax savings.

Lesson 5: The Do-It-Yourself Alternative

In an efficient market investors will not pay others for what they can do equally well themselves. As we shall see, many of the controversies in corporate financing center on how well individuals can replicate corporate financial decisions. For example, companies often justify mergers on the grounds that they produce a more diversified and hence more stable firm. But if investors can hold the stocks of both companies why should they thank the companies for diversifying? It is much easier and cheaper for them to diversify than it is for the firm.

---

[36]For a discussion of the evidence that investors are not fooled by earnings manipulation, see R. Watts, "Does It Pay to Manipulate EPS?" in J. M. Stern and D. H. Chew, Jr. (eds.), *The Revolution in Corporate Finance* (Oxford: Basil Blackwell, 1992).

[37]G. C. Biddle and F. W. Lindahl, "Stock Price Reactions to LIFO Adoptions: The Association between Excess Returns and LIFO Tax Savings," *Journal of Accounting Research* 20 (Autumn 1982, Part 2), pp. 551–588.

The financial manager needs to ask the same question when considering whether it is better to issue debt or common stock. If the firm issues debt, it will create financial leverage. As a result, the stock will be more risky and it will offer a higher expected return. But stockholders can obtain financial leverage without the firm's issuing debt; they can borrow on their own accounts. The problem for the financial manager is, therefore, to decide whether the company can issue debt more cheaply than the individual shareholder.

Lesson 6: Seen One Stock, Seen Them All

The elasticity of demand for any article measures the percentage change in the quantity demanded for each percentage addition to the price. If the article has close substitutes, the elasticity will be strongly negative; if not, it will be near zero. For example, coffee, which is a staple commodity, has a demand elasticity of about $-.2$. This means that a 5 percent increase in the price of coffee changes sales by $-.2 \times .05 = -.01$; in other words, it reduces demand by only 1 percent. Consumers are likely to regard different *brands* of coffee as much closer substitutes for each other. Therefore, the demand elasticity for a particular brand could be in the region of, say, -2.0. A 5 percent increase in the price of Nescafe relative to that of Bru would in this case reduce demand by 10 percent.

Investors don't buy a stock for its unique qualities; they buy it because it offers the prospect of a fair return for its risk. This means that stocks should be like *very* similar brands of coffee, almost perfect substitutes. Therefore, the demand for a company's stock should be highly elastic. If its prospective return is too low relative to its risk, *nobody* will want to hold that stock. If the reverse is true, *everybody* will scramble to buy.

Suppose that you want to sell a large block of stock. Since demand is elastic, you naturally conclude that you need to cut the offering price only very slightly to sell your stock. Unfortunately, that doesn't necessarily follow. When you come to sell your stock, other investors may suspect that you want to get rid of it because you know something they don't. Therefore, they will revise their assessment of the stock's value downward. Demand is still elastic, but the whole demand curve moves down. Elastic demand does not imply that stock prices never change when a large sale or purchase occurs; it *does* imply that you can sell large blocks of stock at close to the market price *as long as you can convince other investors that you have no private information.*

Here is one case that supports this view: In June 1977 the Bank of England offered its holding of BP shares for sale at 845 pence each. The Bank owned nearly 67 million shares of BP, so the total value of the holding was £564 million, or about $970 million. It was a huge sum to ask the public to find.

Anyone who wished to apply for BP stock had nearly two weeks within which to do so. Just before the Bank's announcement the price of BP stock was 912 pence. Over the next two weeks the price drifted down to 898 pence, largely in line with the British equity market. Therefore, by the final application date, the discount being offered by the Bank was only 6 percent. In return for this discount, any applicant had to raise the necessary cash, taking the risk that the price of BP would decline before the result of the application was known, and had to pass over to the Bank of England the next dividend on BP.

If Nescafe coffee is offered at a discount of 6 percent, the demand is unlikely to be overwhelming. But the discount on BP stock was enough to bring in applications for $4.6 billion worth of stock, 4.7 times the amount on offer.

Here again we encounter an apparent contradiction with practice. Many corporations seem to believe not only that the demand elasticity is low but also that it varies with the stock price, so that when the price is relatively low, new stock can be sold only at a substantial discount. State and federal regulatory commissions, which set the prices charged by local telephone companies, electric companies, and other utilities, have sometimes allowed significantly higher earnings to compensate the firm for price "pressure." This pressure is the decline in the firm's stock price that is supposed to occur when new shares are offered to investors. Yet Paul Asquith and David Mullins, who searched for evidence of pressure, found that new stock issues by utilities drove down their stock prices on average by only .9 percent.[38] We will come back to the subject of pressure when we discuss stock issues in Chapter 15.

[38]See P. Asquith and D. W. Mullins, "Equity Issues and Offering Dilution," *Journal of Financial Economics* 15 (January–February 1986), pp. 61–89.

SUMMARY

The patron saint of the Bolsa (stock exchange) in Barcelona, Spain, is Nuestra Señora de la Esperanza—Our Lady of Hope. She is the perfect patroness, for we all hope for superior returns when we invest. But competition between investors will tend to produce an efficient market. In such a market, prices will rapidly impound any new information, and it will be difficult to make consistently superior returns. We may indeed hope, but all we can rationally *expect* in an efficient market is a return just sufficient to compensate us for the time value of money and for the risks we bear.

The efficient-market hypothesis comes in three different flavors. The weak form of the hypothesis states that prices efficiently reflect all the information in the past series of stock prices. In this case it is impossible to earn superior returns simply by looking for patterns in stock prices; in other words, price changes are random. The semistrong form of the hypothesis states that prices reflect all published information. That means it is impossible to make consistently superior returns just by reading the newspaper, looking at the company's annual accounts, and so on. The strong form of the hypothesis states that stock prices effectively impound all available information. It tells us that superior information is hard to find because in pursuing it you are in competition with thousands, perhaps millions, of active, intelligent, and greedy investors. The best you can do in this case is to assume that securities are fairly priced and to hope that one day Nuestra Señora will reward your humility.

For many years every article on the topic seemed to provide additional evidence that financial markets are efficient. But then readers became tired of hearing the same message and wanted to read about the possible exceptions. A succession of studies began to document a long list of apparent anomalies. One task has been to separate out the genuine puzzles and to discard those anomalies that vanished as soon as they were discovered. A second task has been to devise a theory that can explain how anomalies might arise and persist. One result has been the development of behavioral finance. Behavioral finance rests on two arguments. First, it stresses that individual investors may be irrational in their attitudes to risk and the way that they assess probabilities. Irrationality on the part of these investors may cause prices to deviate from fair value. Second, it assumes that it can be costly for professional investors to profit from (and thereby eliminate) these price discrepancies. Not everyone is convinced by this view, and we will need to wait and see whether behavioral finance has a central role to play in understanding security prices.

For the corporate treasurer who is concerned with issuing or purchasing securities, the efficient-market theory has obvious implications. In one sense, however, it raises more questions than it answers. The existence of efficient markets does not mean that the financial manager can let financing take care of itself. It provides only a starting point for analysis. It is time to get down to details about securities and issue procedures. We start in Chapter 14.

FURTHER READING

Malkiel's book is an-easy-to-read book on market efficiency, while Fama has written two classic review articles on the topic:

B. G. Malkiel: *A Random Walk Down Wall Street*, 8th ed., W.W. Norton & Company, New York, 2004.

E. F. Fama: "Efficient Capital Markets: A Review of Theory and Empirical Work," *Journal of Finance*, 25 (May 1970), pp. 383–417.

E. F. Fama: "Efficient Capital Markets: II," *Journal of Finance*, 46 (December 1991), pp. 1575–1617.

There are a number of useful works on behavioral finance, including an excellent survey by Barberis and Thaler:

N. Barberis and R. H. Thaler: "A Survey of Behavioral Finance," in G. M. Constantinides, M. Harris, and R. M. Stulz (eds.), *Handbook of the Economics of Finance*, Elsevier Science, 2003.

R. J. Shiller: "Human Behavior and the Efficiency of the Financial System," in J. B. Taylor and M. Woodford (eds.), *Handbook of Macroeconomics*, North-Holland, Amsterdam, 1999.

A. Shleifer: *Inefficient Markets: An Introduction to Behavioral Finance*, Oxford University Press, Oxford, 2000.

R. H. Thaler (ed.): *Advances in Behavioral Finance*, Russell Sage Foundation, New York, 1993.

Some conflicting views on market efficiency are provided by:

G. W. Schwert: "Anomalies and Market Efficiency," in G. M. Constantinides, M. Harris, and R. M. Stulz (eds.), *Handbook of the Economics of Finance*, Elsevier Science, 2003.

M. Rubinstein: "Rational Markets: Yes or No? The Affirmative Case?" *Financial Analysts Journal*, 57 (May–June 2001), pp. 15–29.

B. G. Malkiel: "The Efficient Market Hypothesis and Its Critics," *Journal of Economic Perspectives*, 17 (Winter 2003), pp. 59–82.

R. J. Shiller: "From Efficient Markets Theory to Behavioral Finance," *Journal of Economic Perspectives*, 17 (Winter 2003), pp. 83–104.

CONCEPT REVIEW QUESTIONS

1. What is meant by a "random walk"? Explain why prices in an efficient market should follow something like a random walk. (pages 336–339)
2. Describe the three forms of the efficient-market hypothesis and give an example of the evidence for each. (pages 340–344)
3. Give three examples of apparent exceptions to the efficient-market hypothesis. (pages 345–346)

For additional Concept Review Questions, please visit us at www.mhhe.com/bmam8e or refer to your Student CD.

QUIZ

1. Which (if any) of these statements are true? Stock prices appear to behave as though successive values **(a)** are random numbers, **(b)** follow regular cycles, **(c)** differ by a random number.

2. Supply the missing words:
"There are three forms of the efficient-market hypothesis. Tests of randomness in stock returns provide evidence for the ________ form of the hypothesis. Tests of stock price reaction to well-publicized news provide evidence for the ________ form, and tests of the performance of professionally managed funds provide evidence for the ________ form. Market efficiency results from competition between investors. Many investors search for new information about the company's business that would help them to value the stock more accurately. Such research helps to ensure that prices reflect all available information; in other words, it helps to keep the market efficient in the ________ form. Other investors study past stock prices for recurrent patterns that would allow them to make superior profits. Such research helps to ensure that prices reflect all the information contained in past stock prices; in other words, it helps to keep the market efficient in the ________ form."

3. True or false? The efficient-market hypothesis assumes that
   a. There are no taxes.
   b. There is perfect foresight.
   c. Successive price changes are independent.
   d. Investors are irrational.
   e. There are no transaction costs.
   f. Forecasts are unbiased.

4. True or false?
   a. Financing decisions are less easily reversed than investment decisions.
   b. Tests have shown that there is almost perfect negative correlation between successive price changes.
   c. The semistrong form of the efficient-market hypothesis states that prices reflect all publicly available information.
   d. In efficient markets the expected return on each stock is the same.

5. Analysis of 60 monthly rates of return on ITC common stock indicates a beta of 0.83 and an alpha of 1.49 percent per month. A month later, the market is up by 5 percent, and ITC is up by 6 percent. What is ITC's abnormal return ?

6. True or false?
   a. Analysis by security analysts and investors helps keep markets efficient.
   b. Psychologists have found that, once people have suffered a loss, they are more relaxed about the possibility of incurring further losses.
   c. Psychologists have observed that people tend to regard recent events as representative of what might happen in the future.
   d. If the efficient-market hypothesis is correct, managers will not be able to increase stock prices by creative accounting that boosts reported earnings.

7. Geothermal Corporation has just received good news: its earnings increased by 20 percent from last year's value. Most investors are anticipating an increase of 25 percent. Will Geothermal's stock price increase or decrease when the announcement is made?

8. Here again are the six lessons of market efficiency. For each lesson give an example showing the lesson's relevance to financial managers.
   a. Markets have no memory.
   b. Trust market prices.
   c. Read the entrails.
   d. There are no financial illusions.
   e. The do-it-yourself alternative.
   f. Seen one stock, seen them all.

PRACTICE QUESTIONS

1. How would you respond to the following comments?
   a. "Efficient market, my eye! I know lots of investors who do crazy things."
   b. "Efficient market? Balderdash! I know at least a dozen people who have made a bundle in the stock market."
   c. "The trouble with the efficient-market theory is that it ignores investors' psychology."
   d. "Despite all the limitations, the best guide to a company's value is its written-down book value. It is much more stable than market value, which depends on temporary fashions."
2. Respond to the following comments:
   a. "The random-walk theory, with its implication that investing in stocks is like playing roulette, is a powerful indictment of our capital markets."
   b. "If everyone believes you can make money by charting stock prices, then price changes won't be random."
   c. "The random-walk theory implies that events are random, but many events are not random. If it rains today, there's a fair bet that it will rain again tomorrow."
3. Which of the following observations *appear* to indicate market inefficiency? Explain whether the observation appears to contradict the weak, semistrong, or strong form of the efficient-market hypothesis.
   a. Tax-exempt municipal bonds offer lower pretax returns than taxable government bonds.
   b. Managers make superior returns on their purchases of their company's stock.
   c. There is a positive relationship between the return on the market in one quarter and the change in aggregate profits in the next quarter.
   d. There is disputed evidence that stocks which have appreciated unusually in the recent past continue to do so in the future.
   e. The stock of an acquired firm tends to appreciate in the period before the merger announcement.
   f. Stocks of companies with unexpectedly high earnings *appear* to offer high returns for several months after the earnings announcement.
   g. Very risky stocks on average give higher returns than safe stocks.
4. Here are alphas and betas for HLL and SBI for the 60 months ending August 2002. Alpha is expressed as a percent per month.

	Alpha	Beta
HLL	0.012	0.74
SBI	0.001	1.24

   Explain how these estimates would be used to calculate an abnormal return.
5. It is sometimes suggested that stocks with low price–earnings ratios tend to be underpriced. Describe a possible test of this view. Be as precise as possible.
6. "If the efficient-market hypothesis is true, the pension fund manager might as well select a portfolio with a pin." Explain why this is not so.
7. The bottom graph in Figure 13.1 shows the actual performance of Sensex for a five-year period. Two financial managers, Alpha and Beta, are contemplating this chart. Each manager's company needs to issue new shares of common stock sometime in the next year.

   Alpha: My company's going to issue right away. The stock market cycle has obviously topped out, and the next move is almost surely down. Better to issue now and get a decent price for the shares.

   Beta: You're too nervous; we're waiting. It's true that the market's been going nowhere for the past year or so, but the figure clearly shows a basic upward trend. The market's on the way up to a new plateau.

   What would you say to Alpha and Beta?

TABLE 13.1

See Practice Question 10. Rates of return in percent per month:

Month	(A) Market Return	(B) Infosys Return	(C) Ranbaxy Labs Return
Jul-03.	5.01	9.59	3.25
Aug-03	11.26	8.46	21.09
Sep-03	4.80	14.58	−3.75
Oct-03	9.70	4.69	1.93
Nov-03	2.77	3.79	3.89
Dec-03	14.62	12.20	7.18
Jan-04	−2.48	−6.85	−9.98
Feb-04	−0.50	−2.40	−5.50
Mar-04	−1.37	−2.67	0.11
Apr-04	1.15	4.14	12.07
May-04	−17.24	1.20	−7.24
Jun-04	0.75	5.85	−8.32
Jul-04	7.53	11.81	3.43
Aug-04	0.42	1.35	1.77
Sep-04	7.27	7.36	12.96
Oct-04	1.58	11.74	0.72
Nov-04	9.45	11.95	2.32
Dec-04	5.74	−2.80	10.71
Jan-05	−0.71	−1.05	−14.27
Feb-05	2.38	7.90	−6.19
Mar-05	−3.35	0.69	−1.58
Apr-05	−5.35	−17.69	−9.50

Excel

Please visit us at www.mhhe.com/bmam8e or refer to your Student CD.

8. What does the efficient-market hypothesis have to say about these two statements?
   a. "I notice that short-term interest rates are about 1 percent below long-term rates. We should borrow short-term."
   b. "I notice that interest rates in Japan are lower than rates in India. We would do better to borrow Japanese yen rather than Indian rupees."

9. We suggested that there are three possible interpretations of the small-firm effect: a required return for some unidentified risk factor, a coincidence, or market inefficiency. Write three brief memos, arguing each point of view.

10. Column (A) in Table 13.1 shows the monthly returns on Sensex from July 2003 through April 2005. Columns (B) and (C) show returns on the stocks of two firms–Infosys Technologies and Ranbaxy Laboratories. Both firms announced their earnings in April 2005. Calculate the average abnormal return of the two stocks during the month of the earnings announcement.

11. On May 15, 1997, the government of Kuwait offered to sell 170 million BP shares, worth about $2 billion. Goldman Sachs was contacted after the stock market closed in London and given one hour to decide whether to bid on the stock. They decided to offer 710.5 pence ($11.59) per share, and Kuwait accepted. Then Goldman Sachs went looking for buyers. They lined up 500 institutional and individual investors worldwide, and resold all the shares at 716 pence ($11.70). The resale was complete before the London Stock Exchange opened the next morning. Goldman Sachs made $15 million overnight.[38]

    What does this deal say about market efficiency? Discuss.

[38] "Goldman Sachs Earns a Quick $15 Million Sale of BP Shares," *The Wall Street Journal*, May 16, 1997, p. A4.

CHALLENGE QUESTIONS

1. "The strong-form of the efficient-market hypothesis is nonsense. Look at mutual fund X; it has had superior performance for each of the last 10 years." Does the speaker have a point? Suppose that there is a 50 percent probability that X will obtain superior performance in any year simply by chance.
   a. If X is the only fund, calculate the probability that it will have achieved superior performance for each of the past 10 years.
   b. Now recognize that there are over 420 mutual funds in India. What is the probability that by chance there is at least 1 out of 420 funds that obtained 10 successive years of superior performance?
2. "An analysis of the behavior of exchange rates and bond prices around the time of international assistance for countries in balance of payments difficulties suggests that on average prices decline sharply for a number of months before the announcement of the assistance and are largely stable after the announcement. This suggests that the assistance is effective but comes too late." Does this follow?
3. From the website of NSE (www.nseindia.com) download daily prices for five stocks for the recent 12 months period. Avoid any stock that has announced a bonus issue, stock split or rights issue in the last 12 months period. For each stock construct a scatter diagram of successive returns as in Figure 13.2. Then calculate the correlation coefficient between the returns on successive days. Do you find any consistent patterns?

CHAPTER [14]

AN OVERVIEW OF CORPORATE FINANCING

WE NOW BEGIN our analysis of long-term financing decisions—an undertaking we will not complete until Chapter 26. This chapter provides an introduction to corporate financing. It reviews with a broad brush several topics that will be explored more carefully later on.

We start the chapter by looking at aggregate data on the sources of financing for Indian corporations. Much of the money for new investment comes from profits that companies retain and reinvest. The remainder comes from selling new debt or equity securities. These financing patterns raise several interesting questions. Do companies rely too heavily on internal financing rather than on external equity financing? Are debt ratios of Indian corporations dangerously high? How do patterns of financing differ across the major industrialized and emerging economies?

Our second task in the chapter is to review some of the essential features of debt and equity. Lenders and stockholders have different *cash flow rights* and also different *control rights*. The lenders have first claim on cash flow, because they are promised definite cash payments for interest and principal. The stockholder receives whatever cash is left over after the lenders are paid. Stockholders, on the other hand, have complete control of the firm, providing that they keep their promises to lenders. As owners of the business, stockholders have the ultimate control over what assets the company buys, how the assets are financed, and how they are used. Of course, in large public corporations the stockholders delegate these decisions to the board of directors, who in turn appoint senior management. In these cases *effective* control often ends up with the company's management.

The simple division of sources of cash into debt and equity glosses over the many different types of debt that companies issue. Therefore, we close our discussion of debt and equity with a brief canter through the main categories of debt. We also pause to describe certain less common forms of equity, particularly preferred stock.

Financial institutions play an important role in supplying finance to companies. For example, banks provide short- and medium-term debt, help to arrange new public issues of securities, buy and sell foreign currencies, and so on. We introduce you to the major financial institutions and look at the roles that they play in corporate financing and in the economy at large.

14.1 PATTERNS OF CORPORATE FINANCING

Companies invest in long-term assets (mainly property, plant, and equipment) and net working capital. Figure 14.1 shows where they get the cash to pay for these investments. You can see that by far the greater part of the money is generated internally. In other words, it comes from cash that the company has set aside as depreciation and from retained earnings (earnings not paid out as dividends).[1] Shareholders are happy for companies to plow back this money into the firm, so long as it goes to positive-NPV investments. Every positive-NPV investment generates a higher price for their shares.

In most years there is a gap between the cash that companies need and the cash that they generate internally. This gap is the financial deficit. To make up the deficit, companies must either sell new equity or borrow. So companies face two basic financing decisions: How much profit should be plowed back into the business rather than paid out to shareholders? and What pro-

[1]In Figure 14.1, internally generated cash was calculated by adding depreciation to retained earnings. Depreciation is a noncash expense. Thus, retained earnings understate the cash flow available for reinvestment.

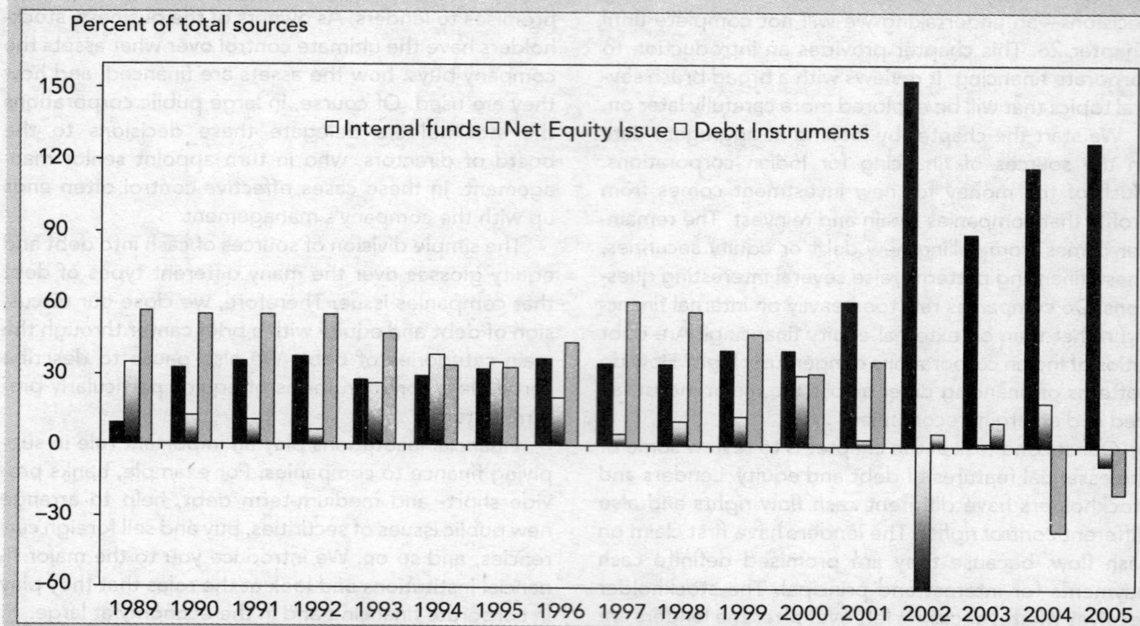

FIGURE 14.1

Sources of funds for Indian nonfinancial corporations expressed as a fraction of the total.

Source: Data compiled from Prowess Database of CMIE. The figures are based on a sample size of 5235 companies

portion of the deficit should be financed by borrowing rather than by an issue of equity? To answer the first question the firm requires a payout policy (we discuss this in Chapter 16); and to answer the second it needs a debt policy (this is the topic of Chapters 17 and 18).

Notice that net stock issues were negative in 2002 and again in 2005. This means that the amount of new money raised by companies issuing equity was more than offset by the amount of money returned to shareholders by repurchases of previously outstanding shares. (Companies can buy back their own shares, or they may repurchase and retire other companies' shares in the course of mergers and acquisitions.) We discuss share repurchases in Chapter 16 and mergers and acquisitions in Chapter 32.

From Figure 14.1 you will see that the net debt issues were negative in both 2004 and 2005. This means that the amount of new money raised by companies issuing debt was more than offset by the amount of money returned to debt holders by redemption of the previously outstanding debt. The companies paid down debt in 2004 and 2005 primarily from the high internal profits generated.

You will notice from Figure 14.1 that Indian companies started becoming more dependent on internal funds only after 2000. Till 1999, new debt issues were the primary sources of funds for the Indian companies. Internal funds make up more than two-thirds of corporate financing in Germany, Japan, the U.S. and the United Kingdom.[2]

[2]See, for example, J. Corbett and T. Jenkinson, "How Is Investment Financed? A Study of Germany, Japan, the United Kingdom and the United States," *The Manchester School* 65 (Supplement 1997), pp. 69–93.

Liabilities and Net Worth	Rs. Crores	Assets	Rs. Crores
Current Liability	537064.5	Current Assets	764391.8
Secured Loans	396057.8	Fixed Assets	848268.6
Unsecured Loans	251213.1		
Total Liabilities	1184335		
Net Worth	605227.9	Investments	176902.9
Total Liabilities	1789563	Total Assets	1789563

TABLE 14.1

Aggregate Balance Sheet for non-finance corporations in India, as on 31st March, 2005.

Source: Data compiled from prowess database of CMIE

Do Firms Rely Too Much on Internal Funds?

We have seen that on average internal funds (retained earnings plus depreciation) cover most of the cash needed for investment. During the period 1989-2005, 51 percent of the total funds of the manufacturing companies in India came from internal funds. New issue of debt and equity contributed 34 percent and 15 percent respectively. In the post-2000 period, internal funds contributed as much as 93 percent of the total required funds[3]. New issues of debt and equity contributed 2 percent and 5 percent respectively. It seems that internal financing is more convenient than external financing by stock and debt issues. But some observers worry that managers have an irrational or self-serving aversion to external finance. A manager seeking comfortable employment could be tempted to forego a risky but positive-NPV project if it involved launching a new stock issue and facing awkward questions from potential investors. Perhaps managers take the line of least resistance and dodge the "discipline of capital markets."

But there are also some good reasons for relying on internally generated funds. The cost of issuing new securities is avoided, for example. Moreover, the announcement of a new equity issue is usually bad news for investors, who worry that the decision signals lower future profits or higher risk.[4] If issues of shares are costly and send a bad-news signal to investors, companies may be justified in looking more carefully at those projects that would require a new stock issue.

How Much Do Firms Borrow?

It is difficult to generalize about how much firms borrow, because financing policy varies so much from industry to industry and from firm to firm. But a few statistics will do no harm as long as you keep these difficulties in mind.

Table 14.1 shows the aggregate balance sheet of all Indian non-financial corporations. If all these businesses were merged into one single gigantic firm, Table 14.1 would be its balance sheet[5]. Assets and liabilities are entered at book value, that is, accounting values. These do not generally equate

[3]New issue of debt, however, remained the primary mode of financing during the pre-2000 era, with a contribution of 49 percent to the total funds required. Internal funds and new equity issues contributed 31 and 20 percent respectively.

[4]Managers do have insiders' insights and naturally are tempted to issue stock when the price looks good to them, that is, when they are less optimistic than outside investors. The outside investors realize this and will buy a new issue only at a discount from the pre-announcement price. More on stock issues in Chapter 15.

[5]This ignores all the adjustments that need to the made while combining the balance sheets of different companies. Thus for example, investments of one company will be share capital of another.

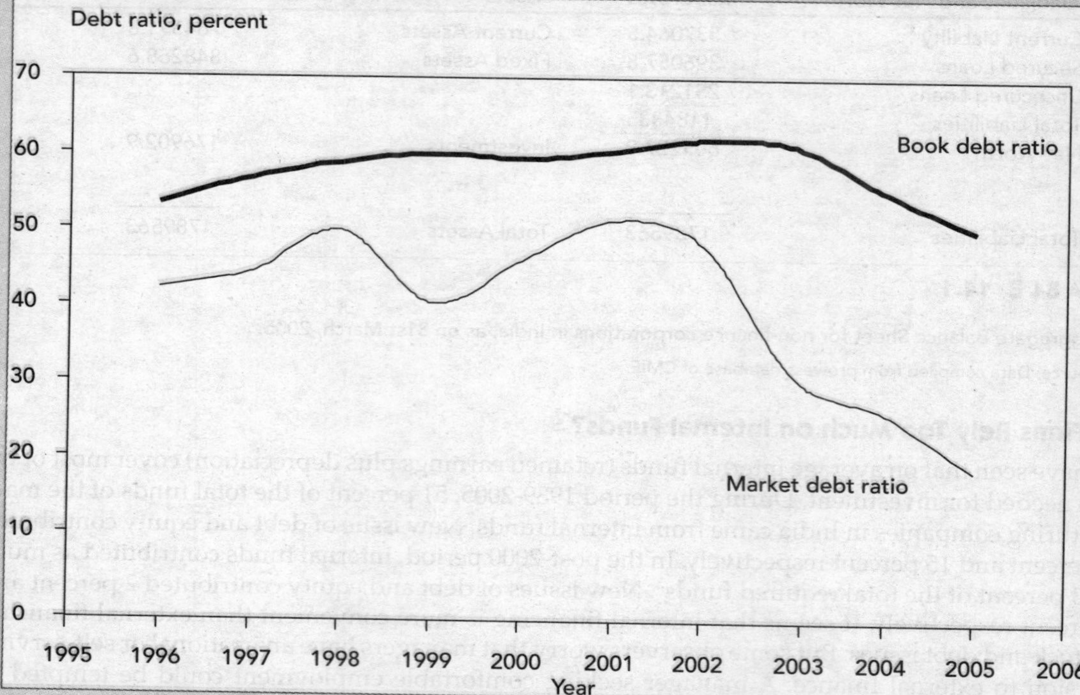

FIGURE 14.2

The ratio of debt to debt plus equity for the manufacturing corporate sector, India.

Source: Data compiled from Prowess database

market values. The numbers are nevertheless instructive. Notice that firms had long-term debt of Rs.647271 crores and equity of Rs.605228 crores. The ratio of long-term debt to long-term debt plus equity was, therefore, Rs.647271/(Rs.647271 + Rs.605228) = 0.52.

The book debt ratio has historically fluctuated between 0.5 and 0.6[6]. However, in the recent years, there is a distinct tendency on the part of the Indian firms to be less dependent on debt. This trend becomes more obvious, when we measure the market debt ratio. Figure 14.2 shows that the booming stock prices in the post-2002 period ensured that the market debt ratio remains below 0.3.

Is the declining debt ratio a reason to celebrate? It is true that higher debt ratios mean that more companies will fall into financial distress if a serious recession hits the economy. But all companies live with this risk to some degree, and it does not follow that less risk is better. Finding the optimal debt ratio is like finding the optimal speed limit. We can agree that accidents at 30 miles per hour

[6]Using a much smaller sample size, the website of the Reserve Bank of India gives the book debt figures for the post 1970 period for the non-finance corporate sector in India. The book debt ratio used to hover between 0.5 and 0.7 before 1990. It however came down after 1990. The average book ratio during the 1970-90 period was 0.6. It came down to 0.44 in the post-1990 period. These results are not surprising as this period also coincides with the emergence of the so-called equity-cult in India.

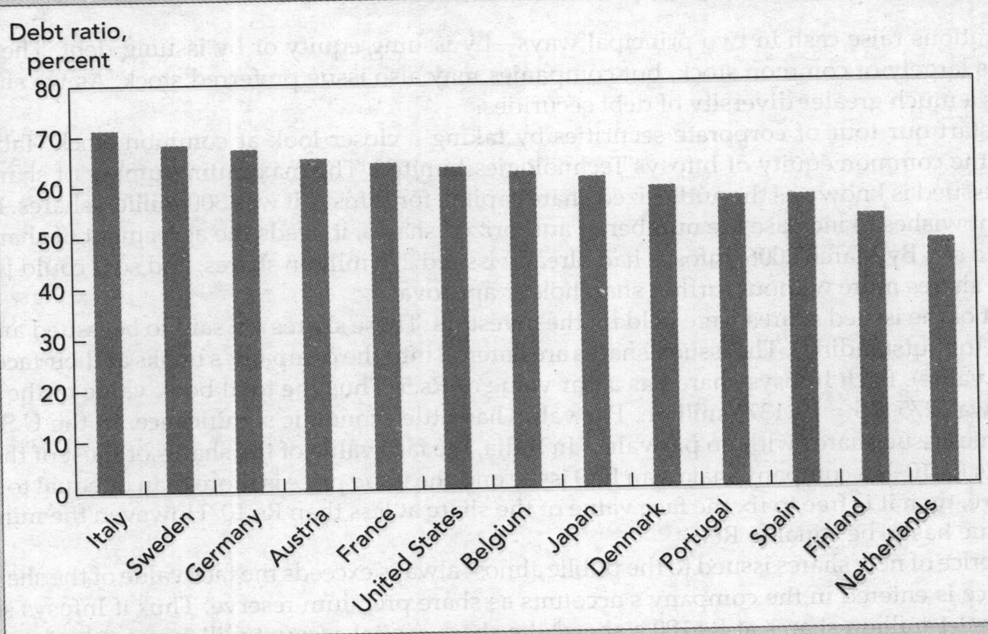

FIGURE 14.3

Ratios of total liabilities to total liabilities plus equity for manufacturing industry, 2001.

Source: European Union *Bach* database of harmonized company accounts. © European Communities, 1995–2003.

are generally less dangerous than accidents at 60 miles per hour, but we do not therefore set the speed limit on all roads at 30. Speed has benefits as well as risks. So does debt, as we will see in Chapter 18. So the decline in debt ratios that we find need not necessarily mean that we should celebrate now.

There is no God-given, correct debt ratio, and if there were, it would change. It may be that some of the new tools that allow firms to manage their risks have made higher debt ratios practicable.

International Comparisons International comparisons of corporate debt ratios are always muddies by differences in accounting standards. However, by comparing Indian debt ratio with the debt ratios of the other countries, we can at least get a rough indication of where India ranks in the debt-ratio league. Figure 14.3 compares the average ratio of total liabilities to total liabilities plus equity for manufacturing industry in a sample of countries. The debt-ratio of the U.S. (not given in Figure 14.3) is 0.35. You can see that the debt ratio in most of the countries (with the exceptions of U.S., Netherlands and Finland) is greater than that of India.

14.2 COMMON STOCK

Corporations raise cash in two principal ways—by issuing equity or by issuing debt. The equity consists largely of common stock, but companies may also issue preferred stock. As we shall see, there is a much greater diversity of debt securities.

We start our tour of corporate securities by taking a closer look at common stock. Table 14.2 shows the common equity of Infosys Technologies Limited. The maximum number of shares that can be issued is known as the authorized share capital; for Infosys it was 300 million shares. If management wishes to increase the number of authorized shares, it needs the agreement of shareholders to do so[7]. By March 2006, Infosys had already issued 275 million shares, and so it could issue 25 million shares more without further shareholder approval.

Most of the issued shares were held by the investors. These shares are said to be issued and subscribed (or outstanding). The issued shares are entered into the company's books at their face value (or par value). Each Infosys share has a par value of Rs.5. Thus the total book value of the issued shares was 275 x 5 = Rs.1375 million. Par value has little economic significance. In the U.S. some companies issue shares with no par value. In India, the face value of the shares of most of the companies is Rs.10. If a company makes an IPO issue and the issue price is more than or equal to Rs.500 per share, then it is free to fix the face value of the share at less than Rs.10. However, the minimum face value has to be equal to Re.1.

The price of new shares issued to the public almost always exceeds the face value of the share. The difference is entered in the company's accounts as share premium reserve. Thus if Infosys sold an additional 1 million shares at Rs.100 a share[8] the share capital account will increase by 1 million x Rs.5 = Rs.5 million, and the share premium account will increase by 1 million x Rs.95 = Rs.95 million.

Infosys distributed part of its earnings as dividends. The remainder was retained in the business and used to finance new investments. The cumulative amount of retained earnings (that was not transferred to general reserve) was Rs. 21950 million.

Infosys's shares had a book value (also known as net worth) in March 2006 of Rs. 68970 million. That works out to 68970 / 275 = Rs.251 per share. But in March 2006, Infosys' shares were priced at about Rs.2900 each. So the market value of the outstanding shares was 275 million x Rs.2900 = Rs.797500 million, over Rs.72 billion higher than book.

Ownership of the Corporation

A corporation is held by its ordinary shareholders. Some of the ordinary shares are held by individual investors and promoters. The remaining shares are held by the institutional investors including financial institutions, mutual funds, foreign institutional investors, pension funds, and the banks. For example, look at Figure 14.4. You can see that in India, about 50% of the total shares are held by the promoters. The individual investors hold 31 percent of the total shares. Private corporate bodies hold 11 percent of the total shares. The remaining shares are held by the institutional investors.

The institutional investors usually avoid the illiquid stocks. If we consider the 30 companies that are part of Sensex, we will observe that about 35.94 percent of the shares are owned by the institutional investors. The promoters own 39 percent of the shares. If we consider the 500 stocks that are part of S&P CNX 500, then the stake of the institutional investors drops to 18.51 percent, whereas the stake of the promoters increases to 50.31 percent.

[7]The memorandum of association of a company mentions the authorized capital. If a company wants to increase the authorized capital, then it need shareholders' permission to amend the capital clause in the memorandum of association.

[8]We will be more than happy to buy the shares at this price!

TABLE 14.2

Book Value of Common shareholders' equity of Infosys Technologies Limited, March 31, 2006

Sources: Annual Reports of Infosys.

Authorized Shares (Rs.5 face value per share) 30,00,00,000 equity shares		Rs. 150 crores
Issued, Subscribed and paid-up 27,55,54,980 shares[a]		Rs. 138 crores
Reserves and Surpluses		
Capital Reserve	Rs. 6 crores	
Share Premium Reserves[b]	Rs. 1543 crores	
General Reserve	Rs. 3015 crores	
Balance in P & L Account	Rs. 2195 crores	
Total Reserves and Surpluses		Rs. 6759 Crores
Total Shareholders' Funds		Rs. 6897 Crores

[a] Of the above 258 million shares have been issued as bonus shares

[b] Includes receipts on exercise of employee stock options and income tac benefits therefrom

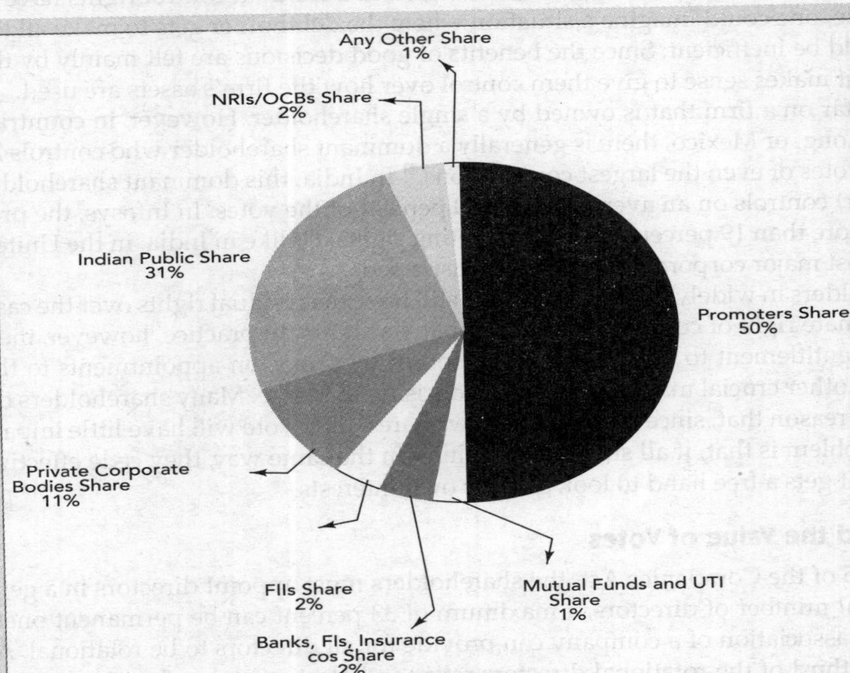

FIGURE 14.4

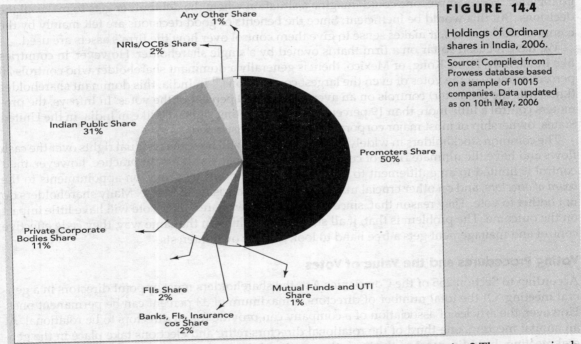

Holdings of Ordinary shares in India, 2006.

Source: Compiled from Prowess database based on a sample of 10015 companies. Data updated as on 10th May, 2006

What do we mean when we say that these stockholders *own* the corporation? The answer is obvious if the company has issued no other securities. Consider the simplest possible case of a corporation financed solely by common stock, all of which is owned by the firm's chief executive officer (CEO). This lucky owner–manager receives all the cash flows and makes all investment and operating decisions. She has complete *cash-flow* rights and also complete *control rights.*

These rights are split up and reallocated as soon as the company borrows money. If it takes out a bank loan, it enters into a contract with the bank promising to pay interest and eventually repay the principal. The bank gets a privileged, but limited, right to cash flows; the residual cash-flow rights are left with the stockholder.

The bank will typically protect its claim by imposing restrictions on what the firm can or cannot do. For example, it may require the firm to limit future borrowing, and it may forbid the firm to sell off assets or to pay excessive dividends. The stockholders' control rights are thereby limited. However, the contract with the bank can never restrict or determine all the operating and investment decisions necessary to run the firm efficiently. (No team of lawyers, no matter how long they scribbled, could ever write a contract covering all possible contingencies.[9]) The owner of the common stock retains the residual rights of control over these decisions. For example, she may choose to increase the selling price of the firm's products, to hire temporary rather than permanent employees, or to construct a new plant in Miami Beach rather than Hollywood.[10]

Ownership of the firm can of course change. If the firm fails to make the promised payments to the bank, it may be forced into bankruptcy. Once the firm is under the "protection" of a bankruptcy court, shareholders' cash-flow and control rights are tightly restricted and may be extinguished altogether. Unless some rescue or reorganization plan can be implemented, the bank will become the new owner of the firm and will acquire the cash-flow and control rights of ownership. (We discuss bankruptcy in Chapter 33.)

There is no law of nature that says residual cash-flow rights and residual control rights have to go together. For example, one could imagine a situation where the debtholder gets to make all the decisions. But this would be inefficient. Since the benefits of good decisions are felt mainly by the common stockholders, it makes sense to give them control over how the firm's assets are used.

We have focused so far on a firm that is owned by a single shareholder. However, in countries like India, Italy, Hong Kong, or Mexico, there is generally a dominant shareholder who controls 20 percent or more of the votes of even the largest corporations.[11] In India, this dominant shareholder (known as the promoter) controls on an average about 50 percent of the votes. In Infosys, the promoters control a little more than 19 percent of the total voting rights. Unlike in India, in the United States, ownership of most major corporations is widely dispersed.

The common stockholders in widely held corporations still have the residual rights over the cash flows and have the ultimate right of control over the company's affairs. In practice, however, their control is limited to an entitlement to vote, either in person or by proxy, on appointments to the *board of directors,* and on other crucial matters such as the decision to merge. Many shareholders do not bother to vote. They reason that, since they own so few shares, their vote will have little impact on the outcome. The problem is that, if all shareholders think in the same way, they cede effective control and management gets a free hand to look after its own interests.

Voting Procedures and the Value of Votes

According to Section 255 of the Companies Act, the shareholders must appoint directors in a general meeting. Of the total number of directors, a maximum of 33 percent can be permanent ones. However, the articles of association of a company can provide for all directors to be rotational. At an annual meeting, one-third of the rotational directors retire and elections take place in the general meeting. In India, most of the time, the rotational directors contest the election again and reelect themselves.

Usually, the articles of associations provide for election of directors by a simple majority (also known as *majority voting* system). As per the majority voting system, all the directors of a company

---

[9]Theoretical economists therefore stress the importance of *incomplete contracts.* Their point is that contracts pertaining to the management of the firm *must* be incomplete and that someone must exercise residual rights of control. See O. Hart, *Firms, Contracts, and Financial Structure* (Oxford: Clarendon Press, 1995).

[10]Of course, the bank manager may suggest that a particular decision is unwise, or even threaten to cut off future lending, but the bank does not have any *right* to make these decisions.

[11]See R. La Porta, F. Lopez-de-Silanes, and A. Shleifer, "Corporate Ownership around the World," *Journal of Finance* 54 (1999), pp. 471–517.

can be elected by a simple majority and the minority shareholders will not be able to elect a single director. Let's assume that the promoter of a company has 51 percent of the shares. Then the promoter, under the majority voting system, can elect all the directors. Even with the remaining 49 percent shares, the minority shareholders will not be able to appoint a single director. According to Section 265 of the Companies Act, a company can, however, provide for the system of proportional representation (also known as the cumulative voting system) in its articles of association. Under this system, the minority shareholders may be able to elect a director to the board, provided they act intelligently. Let's assume that in the above case, there are five directors to be elected to the board. Then the promoter has 51 x 5 = 255 votes and the minority shareholder has 49 x 5 = 245 votes. Then the minority shareholders (with 49 percent stake) can elect two members by casting 123 votes for the first candidate and 122 votes for the second.

The issues on which stockholders are asked to vote are rarely contested, particularly in the case of large, publicly traded firms. Occasionally, there are *proxy contests* in which the firm's existing management and directors compete with outsiders for effective control of the corporation. But the odds are stacked against the outsiders, for the insiders can get the firm to pay all the costs of presenting their case and obtaining votes.

Usually companies have one class of common stock and each share has one vote. The Companies Amendment Act, 2000 has, however, allowed companies in India to issue shares with differential rights. This Act came into effect on 9 March, 2001. Usually, differential shares have different voting rights. However, the Companies Amendment Act, 2000 allows companies to issue shares with differential rights to vote, dividends, or otherwise, provided they satisfy certain conditions. We find many instances of companies based in the U.S. to issue shares with differential voting rights. For example, when Google made its first issue of common stock, the founders were reluctant to give up control of the company. Therefore, the company created two classes of share. The A shares, which were sold to the public, had one vote each, while the B shares that were owned by the founders had 10 votes each. Both classes of share had the same cash-flow rights, but they had different control rights.

When there are two classes of stock, shareholders with the extra voting power may sometimes use it to toss out bad management or to force management to adopt policies that enhance shareholder value. But, as long as both classes of share have identical cash-flow rights, all shareholders benefit equally from such changes. So here is the question: If everyone gains equally from better management, why do shares with superior voting power typically sell at a premium? The only plausible reason is that there are *private benefits* captured by the owners of these shares. For example, a holder of a block of voting shares might be able to obtain a seat on the board of directors or access to perquisites provided by the company. (How about a ride to Bermuda on the corporate jet?) The shares might have extra bargaining power in an acquisition. Or they might be held by another company, which could use its voting power and influence to secure a business advantage. These are some of the reasons why the superior voting shares usually sell for a higher price.

These private benefits of control seem to be much larger in some countries than others. For example, Tatiana Nenova has looked at a number of countries in which firms may have two classes of stock.[12] In the United States the premium that an investor needed to pay to gain voting control amounted to only 2 percent of firm value, but in Italy it was over 29 percent and in Mexico it was

[12]T. Nenova, "The Value of Corporate Voting Rights and Control: A Cross-Country Analysis," *Journal of Financial Economics* 68 (June 2003) pp. 325–352.

FINANCE IN THE NEWS

A CONTEST OVER VOTING RIGHTS

"Not so long ago," wrote *The Economist* magazine, "shareholder friendly companies in Switzerland were as rare as Swiss admirals. Safe behind anti-takeover defences, most managers treated their shareholders with disdain." However, *The Economist* perceived one encouraging sign that these attitudes were changing. This was a proposal by the Union Bank of Switzerland (UBS) to change the rights of its equity holders.

UBS had two classes of shares—bearer shares, which are anonymous, and registered shares, which are not. In Switzerland, where anonymity is prized, bearer shares usually traded at a premium. UBS's bearer shares had sold at a premium for many years. However, there was another important distinction between the two share classes. The registered shares carried five times as many votes as an equivalent investment in the bearer shares. Presumably attracted by this feature, an investment company, BK Vision, began to accumulate a large position in the registered shares, and their price rose to a 38 percent premium over the bearer shares.

At this point UBS announced its plan to merge the two classes of share, so that the registered shares would become bearer shares and would lose their superior voting rights. Since all UBS's shares would then sell for the same price, UBS's announcement led to a rise in the price of the bearer shares and a fall in the price of the registered.

Martin Ebner, the president of BK Vision, objected to the change, complaining that it stripped the registered shareholders of some of their voting rights without providing compensation. The dispute highlighted the question of the value of superior voting stock. If the votes are used to secure benefits for *all* shareholders, then the stock should not sell at a premium. However, a premium would arise if holders of the superior voting stock expected to secure benefits for themselves alone.

To many observers UBS's proposal was a welcome attempt to prevent one group of shareholders from profiting at the expense of others and to unite all shareholders in the common aim of maximizing firm value. To others it represented an attempt to take away their rights. In any event, the debate over the proposal was never fully resolved, for UBS shortly afterward agreed to merge with SBC, another Swiss bank.

36 percent. It appears that in these two countries majority investors are able to secure large private benefits for themselves. The Finance in the News box describes a major dispute in Switzerland over the value of superior voting rights.

Even when there is only one class of shares, minority stockholders may be at a disadvantage; the company's cash flow and potential value may be diverted to management or to one or a few dominant stockholders holding large blocks of shares. In the United States, the law protects minority stockholders from exploitation, but minority stockholders in other countries (including India) do not always fare so well.[13]

Example Financial economists sometimes refer to the exploitation of minority shareholders as *tunneling;* the majority shareholder tunnels into the firm and acquires control of the assets for himself. Let us look at an example of tunneling Russian-style.

To grasp how the scam works, you first need to understand *reverse stock splits.* These are often used by companies with a large number of low-priced shares. The company making the reverse split simply combines its existing shares into a smaller (and, hopefully, more convenient) number of new shares. For example, the shareholders might be given 2 new shares in place of the 3 shares

[13]International differences in the opportunities for dominant shareholders to exploit their position is discussed in S. Johnson et al., "Tunnelling," *American Economic Review* 90 (May 2000), pp. 22–27.

that they currently own. As long as all shareholdings are reduced by the same proportion, nobody gains or loses by such a move.

However, the majority shareholder of one Russian company realized that the reverse stock split could be used to loot the company's assets. He therefore proposed that existing shareholders receive 1 new share in place of every 136,000 shares they currently held.[14]

Why did the majority shareholder pick the number "136,000"? Answer: because the two minority shareholders owned less than 136,000 shares and therefore did not have the right to *any* shares. Instead they were simply paid off with the par value of their shares and the majority shareholder was left owning the entire company. The majority shareholders of several other companies were so impressed with this device that they also proposed similar reverse stock splits to squeeze out their minority shareholders.

Preferred Stock

Usually when investors talk about equity or stock, they are referring to what is known as common stock or ordinary shares. But some companies also issue preferred stock or preference shares. Thus for example, Titan Industries Limited has issued Rs.40 crore of preference shares, and this is usually considered as part of the equity of the company. Despite its name, preferred stock provides only a small part of most companies' cash needs and it will occupy less time in later chapters. However, it can be a useful method of financing in mergers and certain other special situations.

Like debt, preferred stock offers a series of fixed payments to the investor. The company can choose *not* to pay a preferred dividend, but in that case it may not pay a dividend to its common stockholders. Most issues of preferred are known as *cumulative preferred stock.* This means that the firm must pay *all* past preferred dividends before common stockholders get a paisa. If the company does miss a preferred dividend, the preferred stockholders generally gain some voting rights, so that the common stockholders are obliged to share control of the company with the preferred holders. Directors are also aware that failure to pay the preferred dividend earns the company a black mark with investors, so they do not take such a decision lightly.

14.3 DEBT

When companies borrow money, they promise to make regular interest payments and to repay the principal. However, this liability is limited. Stockholders have the right to default on the debt if they are willing to hand over the corporation's assets to the lenders. Clearly, they will choose to do this only if the value of the assets is less than the amount of the debt.[15]

Because lenders are considered to be owners of the firm, they do not normally have any voting power. The company's payments of interest are regarded as a cost and are deducted from taxable income. Thus interest is paid from *before-tax* income, whereas dividends on common and preferred stock are paid from *after-tax* income. Therefore the government provides a tax subsidy on the use of debt which it does not provide on equity. We will discuss debt and taxes in detail in Chapter 18.

We have seen that financial institutions (including insurance companies, banks, and mutual funds) own a substantial portion of the total equity of the Indian companies. Figure 14.5 shows that this is also true of the company's bonds. In fact, they own majority of the debt instruments issued by the companies. The promoters contribute hardly 0.4 percent of the total debt of the Indian companies.

[14] Since a reverse stock split required only the approval of a simple majority of the shareholders, the proposal was voted through.

[15] In practice this handover of assets is far from straightforward. Sometimes there may be thousands of lenders with different claims on the firm. Administration of the handover is usually left to the bankruptcy court (see Chapter 33).

Debt Comes in Many Forms

The financial manager is faced with an almost bewildering choice of debt securities. For example, look at Table 14.3, which shows the many ways that H. J. Heinz in the US has borrowed money. Heinz in the US has also entered into a number of other arrangements that are not shown on the balance sheet. For example, it has arranged lines of credit that allow it to take out further short-term

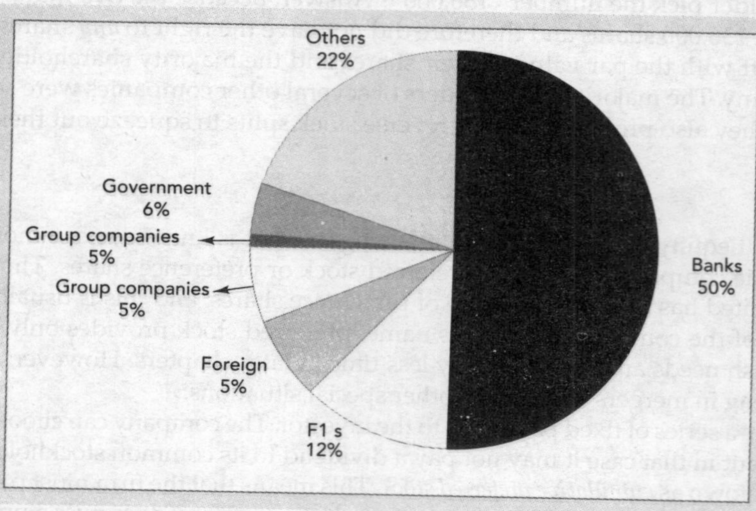

FIGURE 14.5

Holdings of different debt securities issued in India by different non-finance companies in 2005.

Source: Compiled from Prowess Database of CMIE.

U.S. Dollar Debt	Foreign Currency Debt
Bank loans	Euro notes
Notes	New Zealand dollar notes
Guaranteed notes	Sterling notes
Unsecured debentures	
Revenue bonds	
Remarketable securities	
Eurodollar notes	
Senior eurobonds	

TABLE 14.3

Large firms issue many different securities. This table shows some of the debt securities on Heinz's balance sheet in April 2003.

bank loans. Also it has entered into a swap that converts some of its fixed-rate debt into floating-rate debt.

You are probably wondering what a swap or floating-rate debt is. Relax—later in the book we will spend several chapters explaining the various features of corporate debt. For the moment, simply notice that the mixture of loans that each company issues reflects the financial manager's response to a number of questions:

1. *Should the company borrow short-term or long-term?* If your company simply needs to finance a temporary increase in inventories ahead of the Christmas season, then it may make sense to take out a short-term bank loan. But suppose that the cash is needed to pay for expansion of an oil refinery. Refinery facilities can operate more or less continuously for 15 or 20 years. In that case it would be more appropriate to issue a long-term bond.[16]

[16]A company might choose to finance a long-term project with short-term debt if it wished to signal its confidence in the future. Investors would deduce that, if the company anticipated declining profits, it would not take the risk of being unable to take out a fresh loan when the first one matured. See D. Diamond, "Debt Maturity Structure and Liquidity Risk," *Quarterly Journal of Economics* 106 (1991), pp. 709–737.

Some loans are repaid in a steady regular way; in other cases the entire loan is repaid at maturity. Occasionally either the borrower or the lender has the option to terminate the loan early and to demand that it be repaid immediately.

2. *Should the debt be fixed or floating rate*? The interest payment, or coupon, on long-term bond is commonly fixed at the time of issue. If a Rs.1,000 bond is issued when long-term interest rates are 10 percent, the firm continues to pay Rs.100 per year regardless of how interest rates fluctuate.

   Most bank loans and some bonds offer a variable, or *floating*, rate. For example, the interest rate in each period may be set at 1 percent above MIBOR (Mumbai Interbank Offer Rate). When MIBOR changes, the interest rate on your loan also changes.

3. *Should you borrow rupees or some other currency*? Many firms in India borrow from within India only. As can be seen from Figure 14.5, foreign currency loans account for only 5 percent of the total loans issued by the Indian companies.

   Because these international bonds have usually been marketed by the London branches of international banks they have traditionally been known as **eurobonds** and the debt is called **eurocurrency** debt. A eurobond may be denominated in dollars, yen, or any other currency. Unfortunately, when the single European currency was established, it was called the *euro*. It is, therefore, easy to confuse a *eurobond* (a bond that is sold internationally) with a bond that is denominated in euros. (Notice that Heinz has issued both eurodollar debt and euro debt.)

4. *What promises should you make to the lender*? Lenders want to make sure that their debt is as safe as possible. Therefore, they may demand that their debt is senior to other debt. If default occurs, *senior* debt is first in line to be repaid. The *junior*, or *subordinated*, debtholders are paid only after all senior debtholders are satisfied (though all debtholders rank ahead of the preferred and common stockholders).

   The firm may also set aside some of its assets specifically for the protection of particular creditors. Such debt is said to be **secured** and the assets that are set aside are known as **collateral.** Thus a retailer might offer inventory or accounts receivable as collateral for a bank loan. If the retailer defaults on the loan, the bank can seize the collateral and use it to help pay off the debt.

   Usually the firm also provides assurances to the lender that it will use the money well and not take unreasonable risks. For example, a firm that borrows in moderation is less likely to get into difficulties than one that is up to its gunwales in debt. So the borrower may agree to limit the amount of extra debt that it can issue. Lenders are also concerned that, if trouble occurs, others will push ahead of them in the queue. Therefore, the firm may agree not to create new debt that is senior to existing debtholders or to put aside assets for other lenders.

5. *Should you issue straight or convertible bonds*? Companies often issue securities that give the owner an option to convert them into other securities. These options may have a substantial effect on value. The most dramatic example is provided by a **warrant,** which is *nothing but* an option. The owner of a warrant can purchase a set number of the company's shares at a set price before a set date. Warrants and bonds are often sold together as a package.

A **convertible bond** gives its owner the option to exchange the bond for a predetermined number of shares. The convertible bondholder hopes that the issuing company's share price will zoom up so that the bond can be converted at a big profit. But if the shares zoom down, there is no obligation to convert; the bondholder remains a bondholder.[17]

Variety's the Very Spice of Life

We have indicated several dimensions along which corporate securities can be classified. That gives the financial manager plenty of choice in designing securities. As long as you can convince investors of its attractions, you can issue a convertible, subordinated, floating-rate bond denominated in Swedish kronor. Rather than combining features of existing securities, you may create an entirely new one. We can imagine a coal mining company issuing convertible bonds on which the payment fluctuates with coal prices. We know of no such security, but it is perfectly legal to issue it—and who knows?—it might generate considerable interest among investors.

14.4 FINANCIAL MARKETS AND INSTITUTIONS

That completes our tour of corporate securities. You may feel like the tourist who has just seen 12 cathedrals in five days. But there will be plenty of time in later chapters for reflection and analysis. It is now time to move on and to look briefly at the markets in which the firm's securities are traded and at the financial institutions that hold them.

We have explained that corporations raise money by selling financial assets such as stocks and bonds. This increases the amount of cash held by the company and the amount of stocks and bonds held by the public. Such an issue of securities is known as a *primary issue* and it is sold in the **primary market.** But in addition to helping companies to raise cash, financial markets also allow investors to trade stocks or bonds between themselves. For example, Ms. Sundarrajan might decide to raise some cash by selling her ACC stock at the same time that Mr. Sharma invests his savings in ACC. So they make a trade. The result is simply a transfer of ownership from one person to another, which has no effect on the company's cash, assets, or operations. Such purchases and sales are known as *secondary transactions* and they take place in the **secondary market.**

Some financial assets have less active secondary markets than others. For example, when a company borrows money from the bank, the bank acquires a financial asset (the company's promise to repay the loan with interest). Banks do sometimes sell packages of loans to other banks, but usually they retain the loan until it is repaid by the borrower. Other financial assets are regularly traded and their prices are shown each day in the newspaper. Some, such as shares of stock, are traded on organized exchanges like the Mumbai, New York, London, or Tokyo stock exchanges. In other cases there is no organized exchange and the financial assets are traded by a network of dealers. For example, if Reliance Industries needs to buy foreign currency for an overseas investment, it will do so from one of the major banks that deals regularly in currency. Markets where there is no organized exchange are known as *over-the-counter (OTC)* markets.

Financial Institutions

We have referred to the fact that a large proportion of the company's equity and debt is owned by financial institutions. Since we will be meeting some of these financial institutions in the following chapters, we should introduce them to you here and explain what functions they serve.

[17]Companies may also issue convertible preferred stock. The Heinz preferred stock that we mentioned earlier is convertible.

Financial institutions act as *financial intermediaries* that gather the savings of many individuals and reinvest them in the financial markets. For example, banks raise money by taking deposits and by selling debt and common stock to investors. They then lend the money to companies and individuals. Of course banks must charge sufficient interest to cover their costs and to compensate depositors and other investors.

Banks are the most familiar intermediaries. But there are many others, such as financial institutions, insurance companies, and mutual funds. In the United States insurance companies are more important than banks for the long-term financing of business. Prior to 1990s, the Development Financial Institutions (DFIs) were the main financers of the long-term financing to the corporate sector in India. The DFIs had access to low-cost funds. They were allowed to issue bonds with government guarantee, and were given funds through budgetary allocations. IDBI, the largest DFI, was also allocated a sizeable portion of RBI's National Industrial Credit (Long Term Operations) funds.[18] The interest rate on the long-term finance was also kept lower as compared to the working capital loans provided by the commercial banks. The commercial banks were not allowed to provide the long-term finance to the corporate sector. The corporate sector also did not have any incentive in financing long-term projects by issuing debentures because of three reasons. The interest rates on bonds were much higher than the interest charged by the DFIs. The Finance Ministry never allowed companies to go for bond issues when the debt-equity ratio (after the bond issue) exceeded 2:1. However, the DFIs were allowed to extend long-term finance that raised the debt-equity ratio to 3:1. Finally, the state governments used to charge high stamp duties on the secondary market transactions in bonds. These factors ensured that the DFIs remained virtually the only source of funds for the companies in India till the early 1990s.

However, after the liberalization process started, the DFIs started loosing their importance. After 1991, they had to compete with the commercial banks while extending long-term finances to the companies. While the commercial banks had access to cheaper sources of funds, the DFIs stopped getting budgetary support and were not allowed to issue bonds with government guarantee. Both ICICI and IDBI got merged with their own banking subsidiaries. So after the late 1990s, the banks started dominating the long-term finance market.

Why are financial intermediaries different from a manufacturing corporation? First, the financial intermediary may raise money in special ways, for example, by taking deposits or by selling insurance policies. Second, the financial intermediary invests in *financial assets*, such as stocks, bonds, or loans to businesses or individuals. By contrast, the manufacturing company's main investments are in *real* assets, such as plant and equipment. Thus the intermediary receives cash flows from its investment in one set of financial assets (stocks, bonds, etc.) and repackages those flows as a different set of financial assets (bank deposits, insurance policies, etc.). The intermediary hopes that investors will find the cash flows on this new package more attractive than those provided by the original security.

Financial intermediaries contribute in many ways to our individual well-being and the smooth functioning of the economy. Here are some examples.

The Payment Mechanism Think how inconvenient life would be if all payments had to be made in cash. Fortunately, checking accounts, credit cards, and electronic transfers allow individuals and firms to send and receive payments quickly and safely over long distances. Banks are the obvious providers of payments services, but they are not alone. For example, if you buy shares in a money-market mutual fund, your money is pooled with that of other investors and is used to buy safe, short-term securities. You can then write checks on this mutual fund investment, just as if you had a bank deposit.

[18]See Patil, R.H., "Broadbasing and Deepening the Bond Market in India," Wharton Financial Institutions Centre, University of Pennsylvania, 2001.

Borrowing and Lending Almost all financial institutions are involved in channeling savings toward those who can best use them. Thus, if Ms. Jones has more money now than she needs and wishes to save for a rainy day, she can put the money in a bank savings deposit. If Mr. Smith wants to buy a car now and pay for it later, he can borrow money from the bank. Both the lender and borrower are happier than if they were forced to spend cash as it arrived. Of course, individuals are not alone in needing to raise cash. Companies with profitable investment opportunities may wish to borrow from the bank, or they may raise the finance by selling new shares or bonds. Governments also often run at a deficit, which they fund by issuing large quantities of debt.

In principle, individuals or firms with cash surpluses could take out newspaper advertisements or surf the Net looking for those with cash shortages. But it can be cheaper and more convenient to use a financial intermediary, such as a bank, to link up the borrower and lender. For example, banks are equipped to check out the would-be borrower's creditworthiness and to monitor the use of cash lent out. Would you lend money to a stranger contacted over the Internet? You would be safer lending the money to the bank and letting the bank decide what to do with it.

Notice that banks promise their checking account customers instant access to their money and at the same time make long-term loans to companies and individuals. Since there is no marketplace in which bank loans are regularly bought and sold, most of the loans that banks make are illiquid. This mismatch between the liquidity of the bank's liabilities (the deposits) and most of its assets (the loans) is possible only because the number of depositors is sufficiently large that the bank can be fairly sure that they will not all want to withdraw their money simultaneously.

Pooling Risk Financial markets and institutions allow firms and individuals to pool their risks. For instance, insurance companies make it possible to share the risk of an automobile accident or a household fire. Here is another example. Suppose that you have only a small sum to invest. You could buy the stock of a single company, but then you would be wiped out if that company went belly-up. It is generally better to buy shares in a mutual fund that invests in a diversified portfolio of common stocks or other securities. In this case you are exposed only to the risk that security prices as a whole will fall.

The basic functions of financial markets are the same the world over. So it is not surprising that similar institutions have emerged to perform these functions. In almost every country you will find banks accepting deposits, making loans, and looking after the payments system. You will also encounter insurance companies offering life insurance and protection against accident. If the country is relatively prosperous, other institutions, such as pension funds and mutual funds, will also have been established to help manage people's savings.

Of course there are differences in institutional structure. Take banks, for example. In many countries where securities markets are relatively undeveloped, banks play a much more dominant role in financing industry. Often the banks undertake a wider range of activities than they do in the United States. For example, they may take large equity stakes in industrial companies; this would not generally be allowed in the United States.[19] In India the banks control 2.33 percent of the total equity shares of the non-financial companies.

[19]U.S. banks are permitted to acquire temporary equity holdings as a result of company bankruptcy.

SUMMARY

Financial managers are faced with two broad financing decisions:

1. What proportion of profits should the corporation reinvest in the business rather than distribute to its shareholders?
2. What proportion of the deficit should be financed by borrowing rather than by an issue of equity?

The answer to the first question reflects the firm's payout policy and the answer to the second depends on its debt policy.

Figure 14.1 summarized the ways that companies raise and spend money. Have another look at it and try to get a feel for the numbers. Notice that

1. Internally generated cash is the principal source of funds. Some people worry about this; they think that if management does not have to go to the trouble of raising the money, it won't think so hard when it comes to spending it.
2. The mix of financing changes from year to year. Sometimes companies prefer to issue equity and pay back part of their debt. At other times, they raise more debt than they need for investment and they use the balance to repurchase equity.

Common stock is the simplest form of finance. The common stockholders own the corporation. They are therefore entitled to whatever earnings are left over after all the firm's debts are paid. Stockholders also have the ultimate control over how the firm's assets are used. They exercise this control by voting on important matters, such as membership of the board of directors.

The second source of finance is preferred stock. Preferred is like debt in that it promises a fixed dividend, but preferred dividends are within the discretion of the board of directors. The firm must pay any dividends on the preferred before it is allowed to pay a dividend on the common stock. Lawyers and tax experts treat preferred stock as part of the company's equity. This means that preferred dividends are not tax-deductible. That is one reason that preferred is less popular than debt.

The third important source of finance is debt. Debtholders are entitled to a regular payment of interest and the final repayment of principal. If the company cannot make these payments, it can file for bankruptcy. The usual result is that the debtholders then take over and either sell the company's assets or continue to operate them under new management.

Note that the tax authorities treat interest payments as a cost and therefore the company can deduct interest when calculating its taxable income. Interest is paid from pretax income, whereas dividends and retained earnings come from after-tax income.

Debt ratios in the United States have generally increased over the post–World War II period. However, they are not appreciably higher than the ratios in the other major industrialized countries.

The variety of debt instruments is almost endless. The instruments differ by maturity, interest rate (fixed or floating), currency, seniority, security, and whether the debt can be converted into equity.

The majority of the firm's debt and equity is owned by financial institutions—notably banks, insurance companies, pension funds, and mutual funds. These institutions provide a variety of services. They run the payment system, channel savings to those who can best use them, and help firms to manage their risk. These basic functions do not change but the ways that financial markets and institutions perform these functions is constantly changing.

FURTHER READING

A useful article for comparing financial structure in the United States and other major industrial countries is:

R. G. Rajan and L. Zingales: "What Do We Know about Capital Structure? Some Evidence from International Data," *Journal of Finance*, 50 (December 1995), pp. 1421–1460.

For a discussion of the allocation of control rights and cash-flow rights between stockholders and debtholders, see:

O. Hart: *Firms, Contracts, and Financial Structure*, Oxford University Press, Oxford, 1995.

Robert Merton gives an excellent overview of the functions of financial institutions in:

R. Merton: "A Functional Perspective of Financial Intermediation," *Financial Management*, 24 (Summer 1995), 23–41.

For a more extensive description of financial institutions, see:

A. Saunders and M. Cornett: *Financial Markets and Institutions*, McGraw-Hill, New York, 2003.

WEB EXERCISES

1. The Web site **www. federalreserve.gov/releases/zl/current/data.htm** provides data on sources of funds and an aggregate balance sheet for nonfarm nonfinancial corporations. Look at Table F.102 for the latest year. What proportion of the funds that companies needed was generated internally and how much had to be raised on the financial markets? Is this the usual pattern? Now look at "new equity issues." Were companies on average issuing new equity or buying their shares back?

2. An aggregate balance sheet for U.S. manufacturing corporations can be found on **www.census.gov/csd/qfr.** Find the balance sheet for the latest year. What was the ratio of long-term debt to long-term debt plus equity? What about the ratio of all long-term liabilities to long-term liabilities plus equity?

CONCEPT REVIEW QUESTIONS

1. What is the main source of funds for most companies? What is meant by the company's *financial deficit*? (page 365)
2. How is it possible for issues of shares to be negative? (page 366)
3. What are treasury shares? (page 370)

For additional Concept Review Questions, please visit us at www.mhhe.com/bmam8e or refer to your Student CD

QUIZ

1. True or false?
   a) Net stock issues by indian non-financial corporations are in most years small but positive.
   b) Most capital investment by Indian companies is funded by retained earnings and reinvested depreciation.
   c) Debt ratios in India have generally increased in the last five years.
2. The authorized share capital of Reliance Industries Limited is 2,500,000,000 equity shares and 500,000,000 preference shares. The equity was shown in the company's books as on 31st March, 2005 as follows:

Ordinary Shares (Rs. 10 face value)	Rs. 1393.09 crores
Share Premium Account	Rs. 15465.41 crores
Profit and Loss Account Balances	Rs. 8967.86 crores
Other Reserves	Rs. 14576.96 crores
Net Worth	Rs. 40403.32 crores

   a) How many shares are issued?

b) How many shares are outstanding?
c) When will your answers to a) and b) above will be different?
d) How many more equity shares can be issued without the approval of the shareholders?
e) What is the book value per share?
f) Suppose that Reliance issues 1 million preference shares at Rs.10. each. What will be the book value per equity share?
g) How will the book value per share change if Reliance buys back 1 million equity shares by paying Rs.100 per share?

3. There are 10 directors to be elected. A shareholder owns 80 shares. What is the maximum number of votes that he or she can cast for a favorite candidate under (a) majority voting? (b) cumulative voting?

4. Fill in the blanks, using the following terms: floating rate, common stock, convertible, subordinated, preferred stock, senior, warrant.
   a. If a lender ranks behind the firm's general creditors in the event of default, his or her loan is said to be ________.
   b. Interest on many bank loans is based on a ________ of interest.
   c. A(n) ________ bond can be exchanged for shares of the issuing corporation.
   d. A(n) ________ gives its owner the right to buy shares in the issuing company at a predetermined price.
   e. Dividends on ________ cannot be paid unless the firm has also paid any dividends on its ________.

5. True or false?
   a. In India most ordinary shares are owned by individual investors.
   b. An insurance company is a financial intermediary.

PRACTICE QUESTIONS

1. Inbox Software was founded in 2005. Its founder put up Rs.20 million for 2 million shares of ordinary shares. Each stock has a face value of Rs.10.
   a. Construct an equity account (like the one in Table 14.2) for Inbox on the day after its incorporation. Ignore any legal and administrative costs of setting up the company.
   b. After two years of operation, Inbox generated earnings of Rs.0.12 million and paid no dividends. What was the equity account at this point?
   c. After three years the company sold 1 million additional shares for Rs.50 per share. It earned Rs.0.25 million during the year and paid no dividends. What was the equity account?

2. Look back at Table 14.2.
   a) Suppose that Infosys issued an additional 50 million shares at Rs.2000 a share. Rework Table 14.2 to show the company's equity after the issue.
   b) Suppose that Infosys *subsequently* repurchased 20 million shares at Rs. 2050 a share. Rework Table 14.2 to show the effect of this further change.

3. Suppose that East Corporation has issued voting and nonvoting stock. Investors hope that holders of the voting stock will use their power to vote out the company's incompetent management. Would you expect the voting stock to sell for a higher price? Explain.

4. In 2004 Beta Corporation earned gross profits of Rs. 760,000.
   a. Suppose that it is financed by a combination of common stock and Rs. 1 million of debt. The interest rate on the debt is 10 percent, and the corporate tax rate is 35 percent. How much profit is available for common stockholders after payment of interest and corporate taxes?
   b. Now suppose that instead of issuing debt Beta is financed by a combination of common stock and Rs. 1 million of preferred stock. The dividend yield on the preferred is 8 percent and the corporate tax rate is still 35 percent. How much profit is now available for common stockholders after payment of preferred dividends and corporate taxes?

5. Look up the financial statements for an Indian company on the Internet and construct a Table like Table 14.3 showing the types of debt that the company has issued. What arrangements has it made that would allow it to borrow more in the future? (You will need to look at the notes to accounts to answer this.)
6. Which of the following features would increase the value of a corporate bond? Which would reduce its value?
   - a. The borrower has the option to repay the loan before maturity.
   - b. The bond is convertible into shares.
   - c. The bond is secured by a mortgage on real estate.
   - d. The bond is subordinated.

CHALLENGE QUESTION

1. The shareholders of the Pickwick Paper Company need to elect five directors. There are 200,000 shares outstanding. How many shares do you need to own to *ensure* that you can elect at least one director if (a) the company has majority voting? (b) it has cumulative voting?

CHAPTER [15]

HOW CORPORATIONS ISSUE SECURITIES

IN CHAPTER 11 we encountered Marvin Enterprises, one of the most remarkable growth companies of the twenty-first century. It was founded by George and Mildred Marvin, two high-school dropouts, together with their chum Charles P. (Chip) Norton. To get the company off the ground the three entrepreneurs relied on their own savings together with personal loans from a bank. However, the company's rapid growth meant that they had soon borrowed to the hilt and needed more equity capital. Equity investment in young private companies is generally known as **venture capital.** Such venture capital may be provided by investment institutions or by wealthy individuals who are prepared to back an untried company in return for a piece of the action. In the first part of this chapter we will explain how companies like Marvin go about raising venture capital.

Venture capital organizations aim to help growing firms over that awkward adolescent period before they are large enough to go public. For a successful firm such as Marvin, there is likely to come a time when it needs to tap a wider source of capital and therefore decides to make its first public issue of common stock. The next section of the chapter describes what is involved in such an issue. We will explain the process for registering the offering with the Securities and Exchange Board of India and we will introduce you to the underwriters who buy the issue and resell it to the public. We will also see that new issues are generally sold below the price at which they subsequently trade. To understand why that is so, we will need to make a brief sortie into the field of auction procedures.

A company's first issue of stock is seldom its last. In Chapter 14 we saw that corporations face a persistent financial deficit which they meet by selling securities. We will therefore look at how established corporations go about raising more capital. In the process we will encounter another puzzle: When companies announce a new issue of stock, the stock price generally falls. We suggest that the explanation lies in the information that investors read into the announcement.

If a stock or bond is sold publicly, it can then be traded on the securities markets. But sometimes investors intend to hold onto their securities and are not concerned about whether they can sell them. In these cases there is little advantage to a public issue, and the firm may prefer to place the securities directly with one or two financial institutions. At the end of this chapter we will explain how companies arrange a private placement.

15.1 VENTURE CAPITAL

On April 1, 2016, George and Mildred Marvin met with Chip Norton in their research lab (which also doubled as a bicycle shed) to celebrate the incorporation of Marvin Enterprises. The three entrepreneurs had raised $100,000 from savings and personal bank loans and had purchased one million shares in the new company. At this *zero-stage* investment, the company's assets were $90,000 in the bank ($10,000 had been spent for legal and other expenses of setting up the company), plus the *idea* for a new product, the household gargle blaster. George Marvin was the first to see that the gargle blaster, up to that point an expensive curiosity, could be commercially produced using microgenetic refenestrators.

Marvin Enterprises' bank account steadily drained away as design and testing proceeded. Local banks did not see Marvin's idea as adequate collateral, so a transfusion of equity capital was clearly needed. Preparation of a *business plan* was a necessary first step. The plan was a confidential document describing the proposed product, its potential market, the underlying technology, and the resources (time, money, employees, plant, and equipment) needed for success.

Most entrepreneurs are able to spin a plausible yarn about their company. But it is as hard to convince a venture capitalist that your business plan is sound as to get a first novel published. Marvin's managers were able to point to the fact that they were prepared to put their money where their mouths were. Not only had they staked all their savings in the company but they were mortgaged to the hilt. This *signaled* their faith in the business.[1]

First Meriam Venture Partners was impressed with Marvin's presentation and agreed to buy one million new shares for $1 each. After this *first-stage* financing, the company's market-value balance sheet looked like this:

Marvin Enterprises' First-Stage Balance Sheet (Market Values in $ Millions)

Cash from new equity	$1	$1	New equity from venture capital
Other assets, mostly intangible	1	1	Original equity held by entrepreneurs
Value	$2	$2	Value

By accepting a $2 million *after-the-money* valuation, First Meriam implicitly put a $1 million value on the entrepreneurs' idea and their commitment to the enterprise. It also handed the entrepreneurs a $900,000 paper gain over their original $100,000 investment. In exchange, the entrepreneurs gave up half their company and accepted First Meriam's representatives to the board of directors.[2]

The success of a new business depends critically on the effort put in by the managers. Therefore venture capital firms try to structure a deal so that management has a strong incentive to work hard. That takes us back to Chapters 1 and 12, where we showed how the shareholders of a firm (who are the principals) need to provide incentives for the managers (who are their agents) to work to maximize firm value.

If Marvin's management had demanded watertight employment contracts and fat salaries, they would not have found it easy to raise venture capital. Instead the Marvin team agreed to put up with modest salaries. They could cash in only from appreciation of their stock. If Marvin failed they would get nothing, because First Meriam actually bought *preferred* stock designed to convert automatically into common stock when and if Marvin Enterprises succeeded in an initial public offering or consistently generated more than a target level of earnings. But if Marvin Enterprises had failed, First Meriam would have been first in line to claim any salvageable assets. This raised even further the stakes for the company's management.[3]

[1] For a formal analysis of how management's investment in the business can provide a reliable signal of the company's value, see H. E. Leland and D. H. Pyle, "Informational Asymmetries, Financial Structure, and Financial Intermediation," *Journal of Finance* 32 (May 1977), pp. 371–387.

[2] Venture capital investors do not necessarily demand a majority on the board of directors. Whether they do depends, for example, on how mature the business is and on what fraction they own. A common compromise gives an equal number of seats to the founders and to outside investors; the two parties then agree to one or more additional directors to serve as tie-breakers in case a conflict arises. Regardless of whether they have a majority of directors, venture capital companies are seldom silent partners; their judgment and contacts can often prove useful to a relatively inexperienced management team.

[3] Notice the trade-off here. Marvin's management is being asked to put all its eggs into one basket. That creates pressure for managers to work hard, but it also means that they take on risk that could have been diversified away.

Venture capitalists rarely give a young company all the money it will need all at once. At each stage they give enough to reach the next major checkpoint. Thus in spring 2018, having designed and tested a prototype, Marvin Enterprises was back asking for more money for pilot production and test marketing. Its *second-stage* financing was $4 million, of which $1.5 million came from First Meriam, its original backers, and $2.5 million came from two other venture capital partnerships and wealthy individual investors. The balance sheet just after the second stage was as follows:

Marvin Enterprises' Second-Stage Balance Sheet (Market Values in $ Millions)

Cash from new equity	$4	$4	New equity, second stage
Fixed assets	1	5	Equity from first stage
Other assets, mostly intangible	9	5	Original equity held by entrepreneurs
Value	$14	$14	Value

Now the after-the-money valuation was $14 million. First Meriam marked up its original investment to $5 million, and the founders noted an additional $4 million paper gain.

Does this begin to sound like a (paper) money machine? It was so only with hindsight. At stage 1 it wasn't clear whether Marvin would ever get to stage 2; if the prototype hadn't worked, First Meriam could have refused to put up more funds and effectively closed the business down.[4] Or it could have advanced stage 2 money in a smaller amount on less favorable terms. The board of directors could also have fired George, Mildred, and Chip and gotten someone else to try to develop the business.

In Chapter 14 we pointed out that stockholders and lenders differ in their cash-flow rights and control rights. The stockholders are entitled to whatever cash flows remain after paying off the other security holders. They also have control over how the company uses its money, and it is only if the company defaults that the lenders can step in and take control of the company. When a new business raises venture capital, these cash-flow rights and control rights are usually negotiated separately. The venture capital firm will want a say in how that business is run and will demand representation on the board and a significant number of votes. The venture capitalist may agree that it will relinquish some of these rights if the business subsequently performs well. However, if performance turns out to be poor, the venture capitalist may automatically get a greater say in how the business is run and whether the existing management should be replaced.

For Marvin, fortunately, everything went like clockwork. Third-stage *mezzanine financing* was arranged,[5] full-scale production began on schedule, and gargle blasters were acclaimed by music critics worldwide. Marvin Enterprises went public on February 3, 2022. Once its shares were traded, the paper gains earned by First Meriam and the company's founders turned into fungible wealth. Before we go on to this initial public offering, let us look briefly at the venture capital markets today.

[4] If First Meriam had refused to invest at stage 2, it would have been an exceptionally hard sell convincing another investor to step in its place. The other outside investors knew they had less information about Marvin than First Meriam and would have read its refusal as a bad omen for Marvin's prospects.

[5] Mezzanine financing does not necessarily come in the third stage; there may be four or five stages. The point is that mezzanine investors come in late, in contrast to venture capitalists who get in on the ground floor.

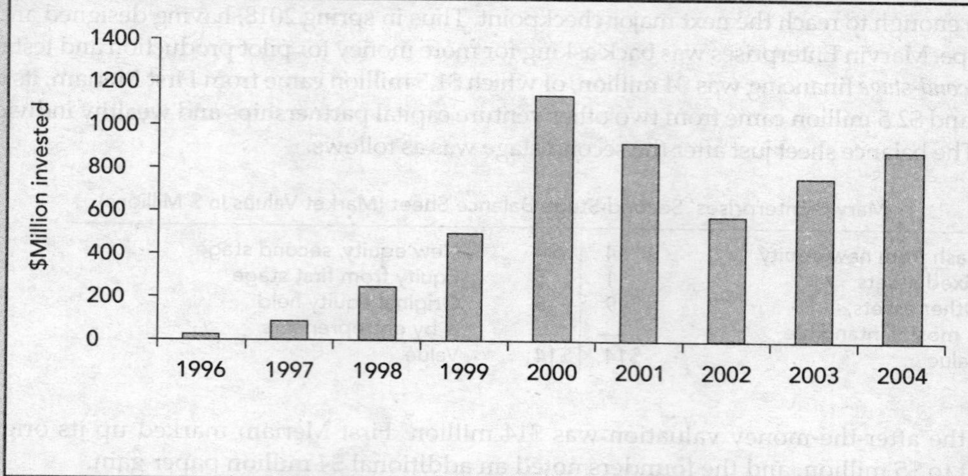

FIGURE 15.1

Venture capital investment in India (Figures in $ millions; the exchange rate during this time was approximately Rs. 46 per 1 $)

Sources: India Venture Capital Association (see www.indiavca.org)

The Venture Capital Market

Most new companies rely initially on family funds and bank loans. Some of them continue to grow with the aid of equity investment provided by wealthy individuals known as *angel investors*. However, like Marvin, many adolescent companies raise capital from specialist venture-capital firms, which pool funds from a variety of investors, seek out fledgling companies to invest in, and then work with these companies as they try to grow. In addition, some large technology firms, such as Intel, General Electric, and Sun Microsystems, act as *corporate venturers* by providing equity capital to new innovative companies.

The Indian Government issued the guidelines to legalize the operations of the venture capital in November 1988[6]. More or less at the same time four state-owned financial institutions established venture capital subsidiaries (including Technology Development and Information Company of India[7] (now ICICI Ventures), subsidiary of ICICI, with the active help of the World Bank. In 1996, international and private domestic venture capitalists started investing in India. Draper International, Walden International Investment Group, etc entered India in 1996. Walden International Investment Group of U.S. and Nikko Capital of Japan started the first VC fund, named, Walden - Nikko India Fund. As of now there are multiple legal bodies that monitor the activities of the venture capitalists in India. The Department of Economic Affairs (in Ministry of Finance), the Central Board of Direct Taxes, and the Security Exchange Board of India are the three regulators that regulate the different activities of the venture capitalists in India. On the top of it, the foreign venture capitalists are also monitored by two additional regulatory bodies, namely the Foreign Investment Promotion Board and the Reserve Bank of India.

[6]For an excellent discussion on the history of venture capital financing in India, read Dossani and Kenney (2002), "Creating an Environment: Developing Venture Capital in India," Berkeley Roundtable on International Economy, Working paper No. 143.

[7]Actually TDICI was set up in August 1988.

Figure 15.1 shows the changing level of venture capital investment in India. During the heydays of the year 2000 funds invested over $1 billion, but with the end of the dot.com boom, venture capital investments slumped. However, it has started increasing again and in 2004, reached the $900 million figure. These figures however pale into insignificance when compared with the venture capital investments in the developed countries. In the United States, for example, the venture capital companies invested more than $100 billion in 2000 itself.

In the U.S. most venture capital funds are organized as limited private partnerships with a fixed life of about 10 years. In India, the regulations, however, do not recognize limited life funds. Since it is easier to terminate a trust in India, most funds were set up as trusts. However, when a trust is closed, the entire firm was closed rather than a particular fund within the firm. So initially each fund was created as a trust.

You will find that these venture capital firms are often lumped together with similar firms that provide funds for companies in distress or that buy out whole companies or divisions of companies and then take them private. The general term for these activities is *private equity investing*.

Venture capital firms are not passive investors. They provide ongoing advice to the firms that they invest in and often play a major role in recruiting the senior management team. This advice can be valuable to businesses in their early years and helps them to bring their products more quickly to market.[8]

Venture capitalists may cash in on their investment in two ways. Sometimes, once the new business has established a track record, it may be sold out to a larger firm. However, many entrepreneurs do not fit easily into a corporate bureaucracy and would prefer instead to remain the boss. In this case, the company may decide, like Marvin, to go public and so provide the original backers with an opportunity to "cash out," selling their stock and leaving the original entrepreneurs in control. A thriving venture capital market therefore needs an active stock exchange, such as Nasdaq, that specializes in trading the shares of young, rapidly growing firms.[9]

During the late 1990s the venture capital market in Europe was helped by the formation of new European stock exchanges that modeled themselves on Nasdaq and specialized in trading the stocks of young fast-growing firms. In three years the Neuer Markt exchange in Frankfurt listed over 300 new companies, more than half of which were backed by venture capital firms. But then the exchange was hit by scandal as one high-tech firm, Comroad, revealed that most of its claimed $94 million of revenue was fictitious. As the dot.com boom fizzled out, stock prices on the Neuer Markt fell by 95 percent and the exchange was finally closed down.

For every 10 first-stage venture capital investments, only two or three may survive as successful, self-sufficient businesses, and rarely will they pay off as big as Marvin Enterprises. From these statistics come two rules for success in venture capital investment. First, don't shy away from uncertainty; accept a low probability of success. But don't buy into a business unless you can see the *chance* of a big, public company in a profitable market. There's no sense taking a long shot unless it pays off handsomely if you win. Second, cut your losses; identify losers early, and if you can't fix the problem—by replacing management, for example—throw no good money after bad.

How successful is venture capital investment? Since you can't look up the value of new start-up businesses in *The Economic Times,* it is difficult to say with confidence. However, *Venture Economics,* which tracks the performance of a large sample of venture capital funds in the US, calculated that from 1980 to 2002 investors in these funds would have earned an average annual return of over 18 percent after expenses.[10] That is nearly 5 percent a year more than they would have earned from investing in the stocks of large public corporations.

[8]For evidence on the role of venture capitalists in assisting new businesses, see T. Hellman and Manju Puri, "The Interaction between Product Market and Financial Strategy: The Role of Venture Capital," *Review of Financial Studies* 13 (2000), pp. 959–984; and S. N. Kaplan and P. Stromberg, "Contracts, Characteristics and Actions: Evidence from Venture Capitalist Analyses," *Journal of Finance* 59 (October 2004), pp. 2177–2210.

[9]This argument is developed in B. Black and R. Gilson, "Venture Capital and the Structure of Capital Markets: Banks versus Stock Markets," *Journal of Financial Economics* 47 (March 1998), pp. 243–277.

[10]See **www.ventureeconomics.com/news.** Gompers and Lerner, who studied the period 1979–1997, found somewhat higher returns (see P. A. Gompers and J. Lerner, "Risk and Reward in Private Equity Investments: The Challenge of Performance Assessment," *Journal of Private Equity,* Winter 1997, pp. 5–12).

15.2 THE INITIAL PUBLIC OFFERING

Very few new businesses make it big, but venture capitalists keep sane by forgetting about the many failures and reminding themselves of the success stories—the investors who got in on the ground floor of firms like Federal Express, Genentech, Compaq, Intel, and Sun Microsystems. When First Meriam invested in Marvin Enterprises, it was not looking for cash dividends from its investment; instead it was hoping for rapid growth that would allow Marvin to go public and give First Meriam an opportunity to cash in on some of its gains.

By 2022 Marvin had grown to the point at which it needed still more capital to implement its second-generation production technology. At this point it decided to make an **initial public offering** of stock or **IPO.** This was to be partly a *primary* offering; that is, new shares were to be sold to raise additional cash for the company. It was also to be partly a *secondary* offering; that is, the venture capitalists and the company's founders were looking to sell some of their existing shares.

Often when companies go public, the issue is solely intended to raise new capital for the company. But there are also occasions when no new capital is raised and all the shares on offer are being sold as a secondary offering by existing shareholders. For example, in 1998 Du Pont sold off a large part of its holding in Conoco for $4.4 billion.[11]

Some of the biggest IPOs occur when governments sell off their shareholdings in companies. For example, the Indian government raised Rs.994 crores while selling 7.94 crores shares in Maruti Udyog Limited. Similarly, the British Government raised $9 billion from its sale of British Gas stock.

For Marvin there were other benefits from going public. The market value of its stock would provide a readily available measure of the company's performance and would allow Marvin to reward its management team with stock options. Because information about the company would become more widely available, Marvin could diversify its sources of finance and reduce its costs of borrowing. These benefits outweighed the expense of the public issue and the continuing costs of administering a public company and communicating with its shareholders.

Instead of going public, many successful entrepreneurs may continue to operate successfully as private, unlisted companies. In the United States some very large companies, such as Bechtel, Cargill, and Levi Strauss, have chosen to remain private. In India, most of the successful unlisted (though not necessarily private) companies are either group holding companies like Tata Sons and TV Sundaram Iyengar & Sons or public sector units like Bharat Sanchar Nigam Limited. Tata Consultancy Services, one of the most successful IT companies in India was unlisted till 2004. In certain other countries, it is more common for large businesses to remain privately owned. For example, in Italy, there are only about 250 listed companies. The U.K. has almost 10 times that number and the USA nearly 20 times. By April 2006, in India, about 4800 companies' stocks were listed in BSE alone.

Arranging an Initial Public Offering[12]

Once Marvin had made the decision to go public, its first task was to select the *underwriters*. Underwriters act as financial midwives to a new issue. Usually they play a triple role: First they provide the company with procedural and financial advice, then they buy the issue, and finally they resell it to the public.

After some discussion Marvin settled on Klein Merrick as the managing underwriter and Goldman Stanley as the co-manager. Klein Merrick then formed a syndicate of underwriters who would buy the entire issue and reoffer it to the public.

---

[11]The Conoco issue was a record U.S. IPO, but it is dwarfed by the Japanese telecom company NTT DoCoMo, which sold $18 billion of stock in 1998 and handed out $500 million in fees to the underwriters.

[12]For an excellent case study of how one company went public, see B. Uttal, "Inside the Deal That Made Bill Gates $350,000,000," *Fortune*, July 21, 1986.

Together with Klein Merrick and firms of lawyers and accountants, Marvin prepared a **registration statement** for the approval of the Securities and Exchange Commission (SEC).[13] This statement is a detailed and somewhat cumbersome document that presents information about the proposed financing and the firm's history, existing business, and plans for the future.

The most important sections of the registration statement are distributed to investors in the form of a **prospectus.**[14] In the appendix to this chapter we have reproduced the prospectus for Marvin's first public issue of stock. Real prospectuses would go into much more detail on each topic, but this example should give you some feel for the mixture of valuable information and redundant qualification that characterizes these documents. The Marvin prospectus also illustrates how the SEC insists that investors' eyes are opened to the dangers of purchase (see "Certain Considerations" of the prospectus). Some investors have joked that if they read each prospectus carefully, they would not dare buy any new issue.

In addition to registering the issue with the SEC, Marvin needed to check that the issue complied with the so-called *blue-sky laws* of each state that regulate sales of securities within the state.[15] It also arranged for its newly issued shares to be traded on the Nasdaq exchange.

The Sale of Marvin Stock

While the registration statement was awaiting approval, Marvin and its underwriters began to firm up the issue price. First they looked at the price–earnings ratios of the shares of Marvin's principal competitors. Then they worked through a number of discounted-cash-flow calculations like the ones we described in Chapters 4 and 11. Most of the evidence pointed to a market price in the region of $74 to $76 a share and the company therefore included this provisional figure in the preliminary version of the prospectus.

Marvin and Klein Merrick arranged a *road show* to talk to potential investors. Mostly these were institutional investors, such as managers of mutual funds and pension funds. The investors gave their reactions to the issue and indicated to the underwriters how much stock they wished to buy. Some stated the maximum price that they were prepared to pay, but others said that they just wanted to invest so many dollars in Marvin at whatever issue price was chosen. These discussions with fund managers allowed Klein Merrick to build up a book of potential orders.[16] Although the managers were not bound by their responses, they knew that, if they wanted to keep in the underwriters' good books, they should be careful not to go back on their expressions of interest. The underwriters also were not bound to treat all investors equally. Some investors who were keen to buy Marvin stock were disappointed in the allotment that they subsequently received.

---

[13]The rules governing the sale of securities derive principally from the Securities Act of 1933. The SEC is concerned solely with disclosure and it has no power to prevent an issue as long as there has been proper disclosure. Some public issues are exempt from registration. These include issues by small businesses and loans maturing within nine months.

[14]The company is allowed to circulate a preliminary version of the prospectus (known as a *red herring*) before the SEC has approved the registration statement.

[15]In 1980, when Apple Computer Inc. went public, the Massachusetts state government decided the offering was too risky and barred the sale of the shares to individual investors in the state. The state relented later after the issue was out and the price had risen. Needless to say, this action was not acclaimed by Massachusetts investors.

States do not usually reject security issues by honest firms through established underwriters. We cite the example to illustrate the potential power of state securities laws and to show why underwriters keep careful track of them.

[16]The managing underwriter is therefore often known as the *bookrunner*.

Immediately after it received clearance from the SEC, Marvin and the underwriters met to fix the issue price. Investors had been enthusiastic about the story that the company had to tell and it was clear that they were prepared to pay more than $75 for the stock. Marvin's managers were tempted to go for the highest possible price, but the underwriters were more cautious. Not only would they be left with any unsold stock if they overestimated investor demand but they also argued that some degree of underpricing was needed to tempt investors to buy the stock. Marvin and the underwriters therefore compromised on an issue price of $80. Potential investors were encouraged by the fact that the offer price was higher than the $74 to $76 proposed in the preliminary prospectus and decided that the underwriters must have encountered considerable enthusiasm for the issue.

Although Marvin's underwriters were committed to buy only 900,000 shares from the company, they chose to sell 1,035,000 shares to investors. This left the underwriters short of 135,000 shares or 15 percent of the issue. If Marvin's stock had proved unpopular with investors and traded below the issue price, the underwriters could have bought back these shares in the marketplace. This would have helped to stabilize the price and would have given the underwriters a profit on these extra shares that they sold. As it turned out, investors fell over themselves to buy Marvin stock and by the end of the first day the stock was trading at $105. The underwriters would have incurred a heavy loss if they had been obliged to buy back the shares at $105. However, Marvin had provided underwriters with a *greenshoe* option which allowed them to buy an additional 135,000 shares from the company. This ensured that the underwriters were able to sell the extra shares to investors without fear of loss.

In choosing Klein Merrick to manage its IPO, Marvin was influenced by Merrick's proposals for making an active market in the stock in the weeks after the issue.[17] Merrick also planned to generate continuing investor interest in the stock by distributing a major research report on Marvin's prospects.[18] Marvin hoped that this report would encourage investors to hold its stock.

The Underwriters

Marvin's underwriters were prepared to enter into a firm commitment to buy the stock and then offer it to the public. Thus they took the risk that the issue might flop and they would be left with unwanted stock. Occasionally, where the sale of common stock is regarded as particularly risky, the underwriters may be prepared to handle the sale only on a best-efforts basis. In this case the underwriters promise to sell as much of the issue as possible but do not guarantee to sell the entire amount.[19]

In India, for the normal public issues underwriting is not compulsory. However, underwriting is mandatory if the issue price is determined by the bookbuilding method. In India, the underwriter comes to picture after the issue is over. If the issue devolves, then the underwriter buys the unsubscribed portion of the shares (up to the underwriting obligations limit). If the company does not receive 90 percent of the net offer including the devolvement of underwriters within 60 days from the date of closure of the issue, the company has to return the entire money collected from the investors.

Successful underwriting requires financial muscle and considerable experience. The names of Marvin's underwriters are of course fictitious, but Table 15.1 shows that underwriting in the United

[17]On average the managing underwriter accounts for 40 to 60 percent of trading volume in the stock during the first 60 days after an IPO. See K. Ellis, R. Michaely, and M. O'Hara, "When the Underwriter Is the Market Maker: An Examination of Trading in the IPO Aftermarket," *Journal of Finance* 55 (June 2000), pp. 1039–1074.

[18]The 25 days after the offer is designated as a *quiet period*. Merrick is obliged to wait until after this period before commenting on the valuation of the company. Survey evidence suggests that, in choosing an underwriter, firms place considerable importance on its ability to provide follow-up research reports. See L. Krigman, W. H. Shaw, and K. L. Womack, "Why Do Firms Switch Underwriters?" *Journal of Financial Economics* 60 (May–June 2001), pp. 245–284.

[19]The alternative is to enter into an *all-or-none* arrangement. In this case, either the entire issue is sold at the offering price or the deal is called off and the issuing company receives nothing.

Underwriter	Value of Issues ($ billions)	Number of Issues
Citigroup	$543	1,872
Morgan Stanley	395	1,365
Merrill Lynch	380	1,914
Lehman Brothers	354	1,264
J.P. Morgan	354	1,417

TABLE 15.1

The top managing underwriters January 2003 to December 2003. Values include global debt and equity issues. Figures in billions.

Source: Thomson Financial Investment Banking/Capital Markets (**www.tfibcm.com**). © 2004 Thomson Financial.

States is dominated by the major investment banks and large commercial banks. Foreign players are also heavily involved in underwriting securities that are sold internationally.

Underwriting is not always fun. On October 15, 1987, the British government finalized arrangements to sell its holding of BP shares at £3.30 a share.[20] This huge issue involved more than $12 billion and was underwritten by an international group of underwriters who marketed it in a number of countries. Four days after the underwriting was agreed, the October crash caused stock prices around the world to nose-dive. The underwriters appealed to the British government to cancel the issue but without success. By the closing date of the offer, the price of BP stock had fallen to £2.96, and the underwriters had lost more than a billion dollars.

Companies get to make only one IPO, but underwriters are in the business all the time. Wise underwriters, therefore, realize that their reputation is on the line and will not handle an issue unless they believe the facts have been presented fairly to investors. So, when a new issue goes wrong, the underwriters may be blamed for overhyping the issue and failing in their "due diligence." For example, in December 1999 the software company Va Linux went public at $30 a share. The next day trading opened at $299 a share, but then the price began to sag. Within two years it had fallen below $2. Disgruntled Va Linux investors sued the underwriters, complaining that the prospectus was "materially false." These underwriters had plenty of company, for following the collapse of the "new economy" stocks in 2000, investors in many other high-tech IPOs sued the underwriters. There was further embarrassment when it emerged that several well-known underwriters had engaged in "spinning"—that is, allocating stock in popular new issues to managers of their important corporate clients. The underwriter's seal of approval for a new issue no longer seemed as valuable as it once had.

Costs of a New Issue

We have described Marvin's underwriters as filling a triple role—providing advice, buying the new issue, and reselling it to the public. In return they received payment in the form of a *spread*[21]; that is, they were allowed to buy the shares for less than the *offering price* at which the shares were sold to investors.[22] Klein Merrick as syndicate manager kept 20 percent of this spread. A further 25 percent of the spread was used to pay those underwriters who bought the issue. The remaining 55 percent went to the firms that provided the salesforce.

[20]The issue was partly a secondary issue (the sale of the British government's shares) and partly a primary issue (BP took the opportunity to raise additional capital by selling new shares). The government's only concession was to put a floor on the underwriters' losses by giving them the opportunity to resell their stock to the government at £2.80 a share.

[21]In India, underwriters typically receive their payment in the form of a commision based on the issue price and the amount underwritten.

[22]In the more risky cases the underwriter usually receives some extra noncash compensation, such as warrants to buy additional common stock in the future.

The underwriting spread on the Marvin issue amounted to 7 percent of the total sum raised from investors. Since many of the costs incurred by underwriters are fixed, you would expect that the percentage spread would decline with issue size. This in part is what we find. For example, a $5 million IPO might carry a spread of 10 percent, while the spread on a $300 million issue might be only 5 percent. However, Chen and Ritter found that with almost every IPO between $20 and $80 million the spread was exactly 7 percent.[23] Since it is difficult to believe that all these issues were equally costly to underwrite, this clustering at 7 percent is a puzzle.[24]

In addition to the underwriting fee, Marvin's new issue entailed substantial administrative costs. Preparation of the registration statement and prospectus involved management, legal counsel, and accountants, as well as the underwriters and their advisers. In addition, the firm had to pay fees for registering the new securities, printing and mailing costs, and so on. You can see from the first page of the Marvin prospectus (see this chapter's appendix) that these administrative costs totaled $820,000.

Underpricing of IPOs

Marvin's issue was costly in yet another way. Since the offering price was less than the true value of the issued securities, investors who bought the issue got a bargain at the expense of the firm's original shareholders.

These costs of *underpricing* are hidden but nevertheless real. For IPOs they generally exceed all other issue costs. Whenever any company goes public, it is very difficult to judge how much investors will be prepared to pay for the stock. Sometimes they misjudge dramatically. For example, when the prospectus for the IPO of eBay was first published, the underwriters indicated that the company would sell 3.5 million shares at a price between $14 and $16 each. However, the enthusiasm for eBay's Web-based auction system was such that the underwriters increased the issue price to $18. The next morning dealers were flooded with orders to buy eBay; over 4.5 million shares traded and the stock closed the day at a price of $47.375.

We admit that the eBay issue was unusual.[25] But researchers have found that investors who buy at the issue price on average realize very high returns over the following days. For example, one study of nearly 15,000 U.S. IPOs from 1960 to 2003 found average underpricing of 19.1 percent.[26] During the dot.com boom of the late 1990s the average first-day return on IPOs reached nearly 70 percent but as the number of new issues slumped in 2001, so did the amount of underpricing.

---

[23] H.C. Chen and J.R. Ritter, "The Seven Percent Solution," *Journal of Finance* 55 (June 2000), pp. 1105–1132.

[24] Chen and Ritter argue that the fixed spread suggests the underwriting market is not competitive and the Justice Department was led to investigate whether the spread constituted evidence of price-fixing. Robert Hansen disagrees that the market is not competitive. See R. Hansen, "Do Investment Banks Compete in IPOs?: The Advent of the Seven Percent Plus Contract," *Journal of Financial Economics* 59 (2001) pp. 313–346.

[25] It does not, however, hold the record. That honor goes to Va Linux.

[26] R. G. Ibbotson, J. L. Sindelar, and J. R. Ritter, "The Market's Problems with the Pricing of Initial Public Offerings," *Journal of Applied Corporate Finance* 7 (Spring 1994), pp. 66–74. Our figure is an equally weighted average of first-day returns and is calculated from updated data on **bear.cba.ufl.edu/ritter.** As we saw in Chapter 13, there is some evidence that these early gains are not maintained and in the five years following an IPO the shares underperform the market.

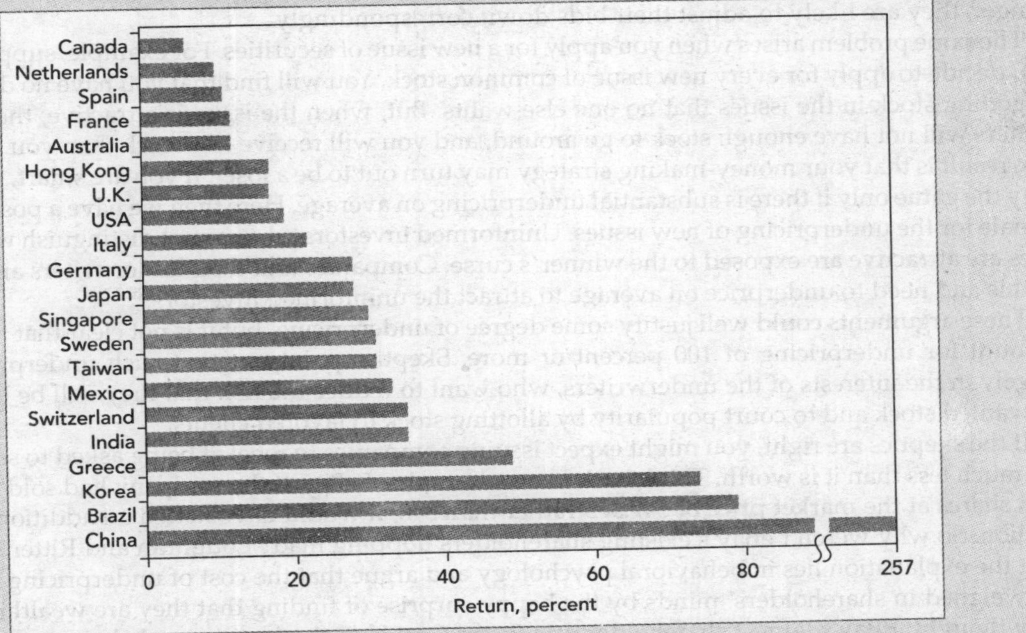

FIGURE 15.2

Average initial returns from investing in IPOs in different countries.

Source: T. Loughran, J. R. Ritter, and K. Rydqvist, "Initial Public Offerings: International Insights," *Pacific Basin Finance Journal* 2 (1994), pp. 165–199, extended and updated on **bear.cba.ufl.edu/ritter.** © 1994 Elsevier Science. Reprinted with permission.

Figure 15.2 shows that the United States is not the only country in which IPOs are underpriced. In China the gains from buying IPOs have averaged over 250 percent.[27]

You might think that shareholders would prefer not to sell stock in their company for less than its market price, but many investment bankers and institutional investors argue that underpricing is in the interests of the issuing firm. They say that a low offering price on an IPO raises the price when it is subsequently traded in the market and enhances the firm's ability to raise further capital.[28]

There is another possible reason that it may make sense to underprice new issues. Suppose that you successfully bid for a painting at an art auction. Should you be pleased? It is true that you now own the painting, which was presumably what you wanted, but everybody else at the auction apparently thought that the painting was worth less than you did. In other words, your success suggests that you may have overpaid. This problem is known as the *winner's curse*. The highest bidder in an auction is most likely to have overestimated the object's value and, unless

[27]The Chinese returns are for A shares, which are traded domestically.

[28]For an analysis of how a firm could rationally underprice to facilitate subsequent stock issues, see I. Welch, "Seasoned Offerings, Imitation Costs and the Underpricing of Initial Public Offerings," *Journal of Finance* 44 (June 1989), pp. 421–449.

bidders recognize this in their bids, the buyer will on average overpay. If bidders are aware of the danger, they are likely to adjust their bids down correspondingly.

The same problem arises when you apply for a new issue of securities. For example, suppose that you decide to apply for every new issue of common stock. You will find that you have no difficulty in getting stock in the issues that no one else wants. But, when the issue is attractive, the underwriters will not have enough stock to go around, and you will receive less stock than you wanted. The result is that your money-making strategy may turn out to be a loser. If you are smart, you will play the game only if there is substantial underpricing on average. Here then we have a possible rationale for the underpricing of new issues. Uninformed investors who cannot distinguish which issues are attractive are exposed to the winner's curse. Companies and their underwriters are aware of this and need to underprice on average to attract the uninformed investors.[29]

These arguments could well justify some degree of underpricing, but it is not clear that they can account for underpricing of 100 percent or more. Skeptics point out that such underpricing is largely in the interests of the underwriters, who want to reduce the risk that they will be left with unwanted stock and to court popularity by allotting stock to favored clients.

If the skeptics are right, you might expect issuing companies to rebel at being asked to sell stock for much less than it is worth. Think back to our example of eBay. If the company had sold 3.5 million shares at the market price of $47.375 rather than $18, it would have netted an additional $103 million. So why weren't eBay's existing shareholders hopping mad? Loughran and Ritter suggest that the explanation lies in behavioral psychology and argue that the cost of underpricing may be outweighed in shareholders' minds by the happy surprise of finding that they are wealthier than they thought. EBay's largest shareholder was Pierre Omidyar, the founder and chairman, who retained his entire holding of 15.2 million shares. The initial jump in the stock price from $18 to $47.375 added $447 million to Mr Omidyar's wealth. This may well have pushed the cost of underpricing to the back of his mind.[30]

15.3 OTHER NEW-ISSUE PROCEDURES

Table 15.2 summarizes the main steps involved in making an initial public offering of stocks in India. Of late most IPOs in India use the book-building method in which the book runner builds a book of likely orders and uses this information to set the issue price.

Although bookbuilding is rapidly gaining in popularity throughout the world,[31] firms and governments in different countries employ a variety of techniques for selling their securities. The main alternatives to bookbuilding are a fixed price offer or an auction. The fixed price offer is often used for IPOs in the U.K. In this case the firm fixes the selling price and then advertises the number of shares on offer. If the price is set too high, investors will not apply for all the shares on offer and the underwriters will be obliged to buy the unsold shares. If the price is set too low, the applications will exceed the number of shares on offer and investors will receive only a proportion of the shares

[29]Notice that the winner's curse would disappear if only investors knew what the market price was going to be. One response is to allow trading in a security before it has been issued. This is known as a *gray market* and is most common for debt issues. Investors can observe the price in the gray market and can be more confident that they are not overbidding when the actual issue takes place.

[30]T. Loughran and J. Ritter, "Why Don't Issuers Get Upset about Leaving Money on the Table in IPOs?" *Review of Financial Studies* 15 (2002), pp. 413–443.

[31]The growth in bookbuilding is discussed in A. E. Sherman, "Global Trends in IPO Methods: Book Building vs. Auctions," working paper, Department of Finance and Business Economics, University of Notre Dame, 2003.

TABLE 15.2

The key steps involved in making an initial public offering of stocks in India.

Source: www.sebi.gov.in

1. Company appoints merchant banker(s), registrars, brokers, and other intermediaries to the issue.
2. If there are more than one merchant bankers,[32] then appropriate distribution of responsibilities must be carried out and the same should be communicated to SEBI in the prescribed format.
3. The company files draft prospectus with SEBI through the Merchant Banker at least 21 days prior to filing of Prospectus with the Registrar of Companies (ROC). The lead merchant banker must also file the draft offer document with the stock exchanges where the securities are proposed to be listed.
4. Roadshow arranged to market the issue to potential investors. The book runner(s) build(s) book of potential demand.
5. SEBI approves registration. The company and the book runners agree on issue price.
6. The subscription list for public issues is kept open for at least 3 days and for a maximum period of 10 days (21 days for infrastructure companies).
7. The post-issue lead manager shall actively associate himself with the post-issue activities, namely, allotment of shares, refund of application money, dispatch of relevant documents, and shall regularly monitor redressal of investor grievances. It should also release an ad (giving details of subscription, basis of allotment, etc.) in at least an English national daily, one Hindi national paper, and a regional language daily circulated at the place where the registered office of the issuer company is located.
8. In case there is devolvement on the underwriters, the lead merchant banker shall ensure that the underwriters honor their commitments within 60 days from the date of closure of the issue.
9. In August 2003, SEBI introduced the system of Green Shoe option in India. An issuing company can avail of this facility to stabilize the post-listing prices of its shares. It must appoint one of the issue managers as the stabilization agent (SA), who will be responsible for the price stabilization process.

that they applied for. Since the most underpriced offers are likely to be heavily oversubscribed, the fixed price offer leaves investors very exposed to the winner's curse.[33]

The alternative is to sell new securities by auction. In this case investors are invited to submit their bids, stating both how many securities they wish to buy and the price. The securities are then sold to the highest bidders. Most governments, including the Reserve Bank of India sell their bonds by auction. In the United States auctions of IPOs have been largely restricted to a few firms, such as Google, that have auctioned common stock on the Internet. However, in France and Japan the method is quite commonly used to sell new issues of stock with apparently less of an underpricing problem.[34]

Notice that the bookbuilding method is in some ways like an auction, since potential buyers state how many shares they are prepared to buy at given prices. However, the bids are not binding and are used only as a guide to fix the price of the issue. Thus the issue price is commonly set below the price that is needed to sell the issue, and the underwriters are more likely to allot stock to their favorite clients and to those investors whose bids are most helpful in setting the issue price.[35]

---

[32]In case the issue price is determined by the bookbuilding route, then the merchant bankers also play the role of the book runners and hence are called the book-running lead managers (BRLMs).

[33]Mario Levis found that, though IPOs in the U.K. offered an average first-day return of nearly 9 percent in the period 1985–1988, an investor who applied for an equal amount of each IPO would have done little better than break even. See M. Levis, "The Winner's Curse Problem, Interest Costs and the Underpricing of Initial Public Offerings," *Economic Journal* 100 (1990), pp. 76–89.

[34]The evidence on the underpricing of auctioned stock in France and Japan is summarized in J. R. Ritter, "Investment Banking and Securities Issuance," in G. M. Constantinides, M. Harris, and R. Stulz (eds), *Handbook of the Economics of Finance* (Amsterdam: Elsevier Science, 2003).

[35]F. Cornelli and D. Goldreich, "Bookbuilding and Strategic Allocation," *Journal of Finance* 56 (December 2001),pp. 2337–2369.

Types of Auction

Suppose that a government wishes to auction four million bonds and three would-be buyers submit bids. Investor A bids Rs. 1,020 each for one million bonds, B bids Rs. 1,000 for three million bonds, and C bids Rs. 980 for two million bonds. The bids of the two highest bidders (A and B) absorb all the bonds on offer and C is left empty-handed. What price do the winning bidders, A and B, pay?

The answer depends on whether the sale is a *discriminatory auction* or a *uniform-price auction*. In a discriminatory auction every winner is required to pay the price that he or she bid. In this case A would pay Rs. 1,020 and B would pay Rs. 1,000. In a uniform-price auction both would pay Rs. 1,000, which is the price of the lowest winning bidder (investor B).

It might seem from our example that the proceeds from a uniform-price auction would be lower than from a discriminatory auction. But this ignores the fact that the uniform-price auction provides better protection against the winner's curse. Wise bidders know that there is little cost to overbidding in a uniform-price auction, but there is potentially a very high cost to doing so in a discriminatory auction.[36] Economists therefore often argue that the uniform-price auction should result in higher proceeds.[37]

In India, both types of auctions are used by the RBI for the issue of G-Secs. The Reserve Bank of India announces in the notification of the auction itself whether the auction is a uniform price auction or discriminatory auction.

Sales of bonds by the U.S. Treasury used to take the form of discriminatory auctions so that successful buyers paid their bid. However, governments do occasionally listen to economists, and the Treasury has now switched to a uniform-price auction. The Mexican government has also been sufficiently convinced to change from a discriminatory auction to a uniform-price auction.[38]

15.4 SECURITY SALES BY PUBLIC COMPANIES

For most companies their first public issue of stock is seldom their last. As they grow, they are likely to make further issues of debt and equity. Public companies can issue securities either by offering them to investors at large or by making a rights issue that is limited to existing stockholders. We begin by describing general cash offers, which are now used for almost all debt and equity issues in the United States. We then describe rights issues, which are widely used in other countries for issues of common stock.

General Cash Offers

When a company makes a general cash offer of debt or equity in India, it goes through much the same procedure as when it first went public. In other words, it registers the issue with SEBI and then the issue remains open for the specified time period. If the issue price is determined through the bookbuilding route, then the lead book runner builds up a book of likely demand for the securities.

---

[36]In addition, the price in the uniform-price auction depends not only on the views of B but also on those of A (for example, if A had bid Rs. 990 rather than Rs. 1,020, then both A and B would have paid Rs. 990 for each bond). Since the uniform-price auction takes advantage of the views of both A and B, it reduces the winner's curse.

[37]Sometimes auctions reduce the winner's curse by allowing uninformed bidders to enter noncompetitive bids, whereby they submit a quantity but not a price. In India, noncompetitive bids upto 5 percent of the notified amount are accepted in the auction of dated G.Secs.

[38]Experience in the United States and Mexico with uniform-price auctions suggests that they do indeed reduce the winner's curse problem and realize higher prices for the seller. See K. G. Nyborg and S. Sundaresan, "Discriminatory versus Uniform Treasury Auctions: Evidence from When-Issued Transactions," *Journal of Financial Economics* 42 (1996), pp. 63–105; and S. Umlauf, "An Empirical Study of the Mexican Treasury Bill Auction," *Journal of Financial Economics* 33 (1993), pp. 313–340.

In the U.S., the SEC allows large companies to file a single registration statement covering financing plans for up to two years into the future. In India, SEBI has extended this facility only to the public sector banks, scheduled commercial banks and public financial institutions. The bank or institution proposing to take advantage of this has to first file, what is known as a *shelf prospectus* with SEBI. The shelf prospectus must disclose, among other things, the aggregate amount proposed to be raised through all the stages of offers of securities made under the shelf prospectus. Once the shelf prospectus is filed and approved, the actual issue can then be done with scant additional paperwork, whenever the firm needs the cash or thinks it can issue securities at an attractive price. This is known as *shelf registration* – the registration statement is "put on the shelf", to be taken down and used as needed.

Think of how you as a financial manager might use shelf registration. Suppose your company is likely to need up to Rs. 200 million of new long-term debt over the next year or so. It can file a registration statement for that amount. It then has prior approval to issue up to Rs. 200 million of debt, but it isn't obligated to issue a paisa. Nor is it required to work through any particular underwriters; the registration statement may name one or more underwriters the firm thinks it may work with, but others can be substituted later.

Now you can sit back and issue debt as needed, in bits and pieces if you like. Suppose Citi Bank comes across an insurance company with Rs. 10 million ready to invest in corporate bonds. Your phone rings. It's Citi Bank offering to buy Rs. 10 million of your bonds, priced to yield, say, 8½ percent. If you think that's a good price, you say OK and the deal is done, subject only to a little additional paperwork. Citi Bank then resells the bonds to the insurance company, it hopes at a higher price than it paid for them, thus earning an intermediary's profit.

Here is another possible deal: Suppose that you perceive a window of opportunity in which interest rates are temporarily low. You invite bids for Rs. 100 million of bonds. Some bids may come from large investment banks acting alone; others may come from ad hoc syndicates. But that's not your problem; if the price is right, you just take the best deal offered.

Not all companies eligible for shelf registration actually use it for all their public issues. Sometimes they believe they can get a better deal by making one large issue through traditional channels, especially when the security to be issued has some unusual feature or when the firm believes that it needs the investment banker's counsel or stamp of approval on the issue. Consequently, shelf registration is less often used for issues of common stock or convertible securities than for garden-variety corporate bonds. In India, shelf registration can be used only for the issue of debt securities.

International Security Issues

Well-established companies are not restricted to the capital market in India; they can also sell securities in the international capital markets. The procedures for such issues are broadly similar to those used in the United States. The Department of Economic Affairs (Investment Division) of the Ministry of Finance has framed certain guidelines for American Depository Issues (ADR) and Global Depository Issues (GDR) by the Indian Companies. Here are a few points to note[39]:

1. Indian companies raising money through ADRs/GDRs through registered exchanges can freely access the ADR/GDR markets without the prior approval of the Ministry of Finance, Department of Economic Affairs[40]. Private placement of ADRs/GDRs would also be eligible

[39]Source: http://finmin.nic.in/the_ministry/dept_eco_affairs/investment_div/addr_gdr_sec2.htm.

[40]However, the issuer company will require the following approvals: i) mandatory approval requirement under FDI policy, ii) approvals as required under the Companies Act, iii) approvals for overseas investments/business acquistion (where ADR/GDR proceeds are utilized for overseas investments). The issuer company will also need to obtain RBI approval under the provisions FERA/FEMA prior to the overseas issue.

for the automatic approval provided the issue is lead managed by an investment banker. Here, an Investment Banker is defined as one registered with the Securities and Exchange Commission in the USA, or under Financial Services Act in U.K., or the appropriate regulatory authority in Europe, Singapore or in Japan.

2. The retention and deployment of funds will be governed by the RBI. However, the companies will not be allowed to invest the money in the stock market and in the real estate.
3. The issue related expenses (including underwriting commissions, lead managers charges, legal expenses and other reimbursable expenses) will be subject to a ceiling of 4 percent in case of GDRs and 7 percent in case of ADRs. However, a company can incur higher issue expenses with the approval of the RBI.

In May 1992, Reliance Industries raised $150 million in the first-ever GDR issue by any Indian company. Most of the Indian companies that have issued GDRs prefer Luxembourg stock exchange because deals can be closed very fast at Luxembourg. In fact the highest number of foreign companies listed in Luxembourg exchange are of Indian origin. Till 1999, Indian companies used to prefer the GDR route mainly because of the stringent disclosure requirements (and adherence to US Accounting Standards) required in case of ADR issues.

BPL Cellular is the first Indian company to have issued its ADRs in the US and it got its shares listed in NASDAQ in May 1997[41]. In December 1996, BPL cellular attempted to issue ADRs. However, the company pulled out the issue hours before it went on offer. The lead underwriters found it difficult to find enough takers at the initially-proposed issue price of $16. Even when the underwriters reduced the price to $10, there was not enough interest in the stock and hence BPL Cellular had to pull out in the last moment. VSNL also had to go through two failed attempts in 1994 before successfully issuing its GDRs in March 1997.

The shares of many companies are now listed and traded on major international exchanges. British Telecom trades on the New York Stock Exchange, as do Sony, Fiat, Telefonos de Mexico, and so on.[42] Several of these companies also trade on overseas exchanges. Citigroup, one of the largest banks in the United States, trades in New York, London, Amsterdam, Tokyo, Zurich, Toronto, and Frankfurt, as well as several smaller exchanges.

Some companies' stocks do not trade at all in their home country. For example, in 2000 AsiaInfo, a software company from the People's Republic of China raised $120 million by an IPO in the United States. Its stock was not traded in China. The company thought it could get a better price and more active follow-on trading in New York.

The Costs of a General Cash Offer

Whenever a firm makes a cash offer of securities, it incurs substantial administrative costs. The expenses include fees payable to lead managers and co-lead managers (if any), fees payable to co-managers and other merchant bankers, fees payable to registrars to the issue, fees payable to issue advisors, fees payable to bankers to the issue, fees payable to trustees (in case of debenture issues), underwriting commissions, brokerage commissions and selling commissions. Table 15.3 lists issue expenses for a few issues in 2006 in India.

[41]ICICI is the first Indian company to list on NYSE through an issue of ADRs.

[42]Rather than issuing shares directly in the United States, foreign companies generally issue *American depository receipts (ADRs)*. These are simply claims to the shares of the foreign company that are held by a bank on behalf of the ADR owners.

Issuing Company	Issue Size (Rs. Million)	Issue Expenses (Rs. Million)	Issue Expenses as % of Issue size
Gangotri Textile Limited	550	40	7%
Unity Infraprojects Limited	232.4	19.3	8%
D S Kulkarni Developers	2117.5	114.87	5%
Opto Circuits (India) Limited	1080	70.6	7%
Plathico Pharmaceuticals	1100	78.9	7%
Lokesh Machines Limited	420	30	7%
Emkay Shares and Stock Brokers Limited	750	38.5	5%
R Systems International Limited	1102.09	113	10%
Kewal Kiran Clothing	806	72.55	9%
Uttam Sugar Mills	1360	70.5	5%
Adhunik Metalics	1000	88	9%

TABLE 15.3

Issue expenses as percentage of total issue size of selected issues, 2006

Source: www.sebi.org.in

In the U.S., since the issuing company directly sells to the underwriters, it compensates the underwriters by selling them securities below the price (the difference is known as underwriting spreads) that they expect to receive from investors. The underwriting spreads for debt securities are lower than for common stocks, less than 1 percent for many issues. Larger issues tend to have lower spreads than smaller issues. This may partly stem from the fact that there are fixed costs to selling securities, but large issues are generally made by large companies, which are better known and easier for the underwriter to monitor. So do not assume that a small company could make a jumbo issue at a negligible percentage spread.[43]

Figure 15.3 summarizes a study by Lee, Lochhead, Ritter, and Zhao of total issue costs (spreads plus administrative costs) for several thousand issues between 1990 and 1994 in the US.

Market Reaction to Stock Issues

Economists who have studied seasoned issues of common stock have generally found that announcement of the issue results in a decline in the stock price. For industrial issues in the United States this decline amounts to about 3 percent.[44] While this may not sound overwhelming, the fall in market value is equivalent, on average, to nearly a third of the new money raised by the issue.

What's going on here? One view is that the price of the stock is simply depressed by the prospect of the additional supply. On the other hand, there is little sign that the extent of the price fall increases with the size of the stock issue. There is an alternative explanation that seems to fit the facts better.

Suppose that the CFO of a restaurant chain is strongly optimistic about its prospects. From her point of view, the company's stock price is too low. Yet the company wants to issue shares to finance expansion into the new state of Northern California.[45] What is she to do? All the choices have

[43]This point is emphasized in O. Altinkilic and R. S. Hansen, "Are There Economies of Scale in Underwriting Fees? Evidence of Rising External Financing Costs," *Review of Financial Studies* 13 (Spring 2000), pp. 191–218.

[44]See, for example, P. Asquith and D. W. Mullins, "Equity Issues and Offering Dilution," *Journal of Financial Economics* 15 (January–February 1986), pp. 61–90.

[45]Northern California seceded from California and became the fifty-second state in 2010.

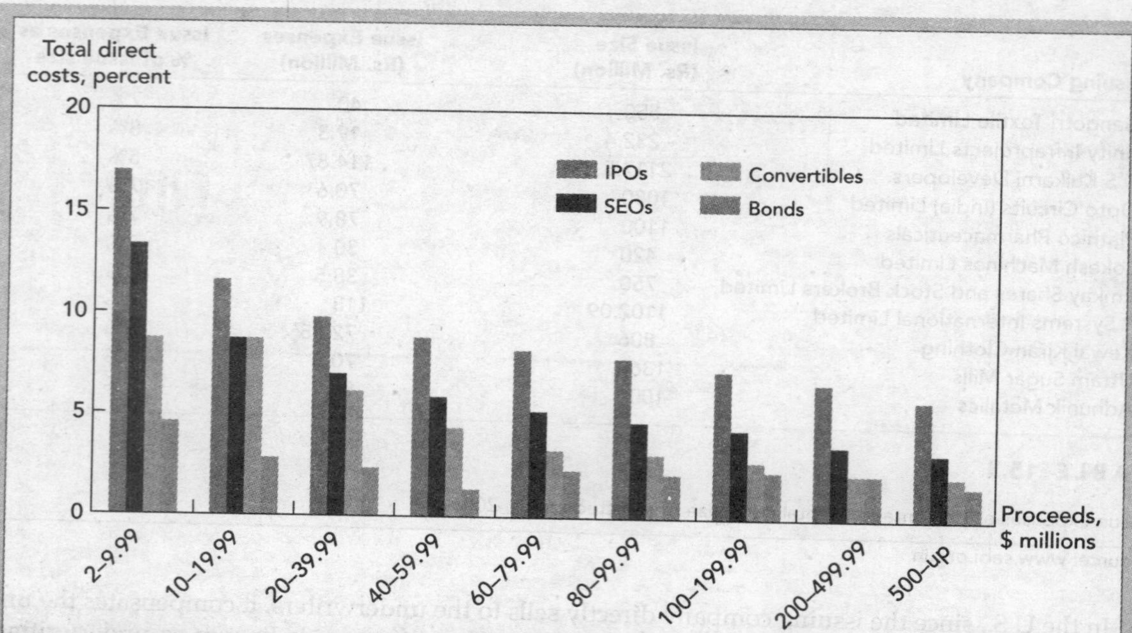

FIGURE 15.3

Total direct costs as a percentage of gross proceeds. The total direct costs for initial public offerings (IPOs), seasoned equity offerings (SEOs), convertible bonds, and straight bonds are composed of underwriter spreads and other direct expenses.

Source: I. Lee, S. Lochhead, J. R. Ritter, and Q. Zhao, "The Costs of Raising Capital," *Journal of Financial Research* 19 (Spring 1996), pp. 59–74. Reprinted with permission of Blackwell Publishers Journal Rights.

drawbacks. If the chain sells common stock, it will favor new investors at the expense of old shareholders. When investors come to share the CFO's optimism, the share price will rise, and the bargain price to the new investors will be evident.

If the CFO could convince investors to accept her rosy view of the future, then new shares could be sold at a fair price. But this is not so easy. CEOs and CFOs always take care to *sound* upbeat, so just announcing "I'm optimistic" has little effect. But supplying detailed information about business plans and profit forecasts is costly and is also of great assistance to competitors.

The CFO could scale back or delay the expansion until the company's stock price recovers. That too is costly, but it may be rational if the stock price is severely undervalued and a stock issue is the only source of financing.

If a CFO knows that the company's stock is *over*valued, the position is reversed. If the firm sells new shares at the high price, it will help existing shareholders at the expense of the new ones. Managers might be prepared to issue stock even if the new cash was just put in the bank.

Of course, investors are not stupid. They can predict that managers are more likely to issue stock when they think it is overvalued and that optimistic managers may cancel or defer issues. Therefore, when an equity issue is announced, they mark down the price of the stock accordingly. Thus the decline in the price of the stock at the time of the new issue may have nothing to do with the increased supply but simply with the information that the issue provides.[46]

Cornett and Tehranian devised a natural experiment which pretty much proves this point.[47] They examined a sample of stock issues by commercial banks. Some of these issues were necessary to meet capital standards set by banking regulators. The rest were ordinary, voluntary stock issues designed to raise money for various corporate purposes. The necessary issues caused a much smaller drop in stock prices than the voluntary ones, which makes perfect sense. If the issue is outside the manager's discretion, announcement of the issue conveys no information about the manager's view of the company's prospects.[48]

Most financial economists now interpret the stock price drop on equity issue announcements as an information effect and not a result of the additional supply.[49] But what about an issue of preferred stock or debt? Are they equally likely to provide information to investors about company prospects? A pessimistic manager might be tempted to get a debt issue out before investors become aware of the bad news, but how much profit can you make for your shareholders by selling overpriced debt? Perhaps 1 or 2 percent. Investors know that a pessimistic manager has a much greater incentive to issue equity rather than preferred stock or debt. Therefore, when companies announce an issue of preferred or debt, there is a barely perceptible fall in the stock price.[50]

There is, however, at least one puzzle left. As we saw in Chapter 13, it appears that the long-run performance of companies that issue shares is substandard. Investors who bought these companies' shares *after* the stock issue earned lower returns than they would have if they had bought into similar companies. This result holds for both IPOs and seasoned issues.[51] It seems that investors fail to appreciate fully the issuing companies' information advantage. If so, we have an exception to the efficient-market theory.

Rights Issues

Instead of making an issue of stock to investors at large, companies sometimes give their existing shareholders the right of first refusal. In India, when a company wants to make further issue of equity shares, Sec 81 of the Companies Act of India makes it mandatory for the companies to offer the

[46]This explanation was developed in S. C. Myers and N. S. Majluf, "Corporate Financing and Investment Decisions When Firms Have Information That Investors Do Not Have," *Journal of Financial Economics* 35 (1994), pp. 99–122.

[47]M. M. Cornett and H. Tehranian, "An Examination of Voluntary versus Involuntary Issuances by Commercial Banks," *Journal of Financial Economics* 35 (1994), pp. 99–122.

[48]The "involuntary issuers" did make a choice: they could have foregone the stock issue and run the risk of failing to meet the regulatory capital standards. The banks that were more concerned with this risk were more likely to issue. Thus it is no surprise that Cornett and Tehranian found some drop in stock price even for the involuntary issues.

[49]There is another possible information effect. Just as an unexpected increase in the dividend suggests to investors that the company is generating more cash than they thought, the announcement of a new issue may have the reverse implication. However, this effect cannot explain why the announcement of an issue of debt does not result in a similar fall in the stock price.

[50]See L. Shyam-Sunder, "The Stock Price Effect of Risky vs. Safe Debt," *Journal of Financial and Quantitative Analysis* 26 (December 1991), pp. 549–558. Evidence on the price impact of issues of different types of security is summarized in C. Smith, "Investment Banking and the Capital Acquisition Process," *Journal of Financial Economics* 15 (January–February 1986), pp. 3–29.

[51]See, for example, T. Loughran and J. R. Ritter, "The New Issues Puzzle," *Journal of Finance* 50 (March 1995), pp. 23–51; and Jay Ritter's Web site **bear.cba.ufl.edu/ritter**.

shares to the existing equity shareholders. However, as per Sec 81(1A) of the Companies Act, a company can issue new shares to outsiders to the total exclusion of the existing shareholders if the company has passed a special resolution to this effect. Alternatively, after passing a general resolution, the Board of Directors of a company can directly appeal to the Central Government and issue additional shares to outsiders. Indian law with regard to rights issue is very similar to the practice followed by the European countries, where seasoned issues of common stock (a non-IPO public issue) must generally be sold by rights. In the United States, however, rights issues are largely confined to closed-end investment companies.

Here is an example of rights issue. In July 2005, the Board of Kinetic Engineering needed to raise Rs.32.55 crores of new equity. It did so by offering to its existing shareholders the right to buy 2 shares for every 1 that they currently held. The new shares were prices at Rs.40 each (Rs.10 face value + Rs.30 premium per share), nearly 60 percent below the preannouncement price of Rs.102.

Imagine that you hold 1 share of Kinetic just prior to the rights issue. Your holding is worth Rs.102. Kinetic gives you the opportunity to buy 2 additional shares for Rs.40 each. If you buy the new share, your holding increases to 3 shares, and the value of your holding increases by the extra cash to 102 + (2 x 40) = Rs.182. Therefore, after the issue, the value of each share is no longer Rs.102 but lower at Rs. 60.67.

How much is your right to buy each new share for Rs. 40 worth? The answer is Rs. 60.67 – 40 = Rs. 20.67. An investor, who could buy a share worth Rs. 60.67 for Rs.40, would be willing to pay Rs. 20.67 for the right to do so.[52]

It should be clear on reflection that Kinetic could have raised the same amount of money on a variety of terms. For example, instead of a 2-for-1 at Rs.40, it could have made an 4-for-1 issue at Rs.20. In this case it would have sold twice as many shares at half the price. If you held 1 share of Kinetic before the issue, you could subscribe for 4 new shares at Rs.20 each. This could give you 5 shares in total worth 102 + (4 x 20) = Rs.182. After the issue, the value of each share would be 182/5 = Rs. 36.4. This is less than in the case of the 2-for-1 issue, but then you would have the compensation of owning 5 rather than 3 shares. Suppose that you wanted to sell your right to buy one new share for Rs.20. Investors would be prepared to pay you Rs. 16.4 for this right. They would then pay Rs. 20 to Kinetic and receive a share worth Rs. 36.4.

Our example illustrates that as long as the company successfully sells the new shares, the issue price in a rights offering is irrelevant. That is not the case in a general cash offer. If the company sells stock to new shareholders for less than the market will bear, the buyer makes a profit at the expense of existing shareholders. General cash offers are typically sold at a small discount of about 3 percent on the previous day's closing price,[53] so underpricing is not a major worry. But, since this cost can be avoided completely by using a rights issue, we are puzzled by the apparent preference of companies for general cash offers.

15.5 PRIVATE PLACEMENTS AND PUBLIC ISSUES

As we saw earlier, public issue of shares is a costly affair. A company could avoid this costly process by selling the securities privately. All private placements are governed by Section 81 (1A) of the Companies Act, SEBI guidelines and RBI Guidelines (in case of private placement of shares with the FIIs).

---

[52]In fact he should be prepared to pay slightly more, because he is not compelled to buy the stock and can choose not to do so. In practice, since the option is usually well in the money and its time to expiration is short, its value is usually negligible.

[53]See S. A. Corwin, "The Determinants of Underpricing for Seasoned Equity Offers," *Journal of Finance* 58 (October 1993), pp. 2249–2279; and S. Mola and T. Loughran, "Discounting and Clustering in Seasoned Equity Offering Price," *Journal of Financial and Quantitative Analysis* 39 (March 2004), pp. 1–23.

As per the SEBI guidelines, the securities issued under the private placement route will be subject to a 1-year lock-in period from the date of their allotment[54].

An Indian company can also make what is known as *Qualified Institutions Placement* (private placement of shares with qualified institutional buyers) if its shares are listed on a stock exchange having nation-wide trading terminals and if it has got the prescribed minimum shareholding requirement of the listing agreement[55]. As per the SEBI guidelines, a minimum of 10% of the total issue should be reserved for the mutual funds. The company should file a placement document (containing all material information regarding the issue) with SEBI within 30 days of the allotment of the securities. As per the SEBI guidelines, if the issue size is less than or equal to Rs.250 crores, then there must be at least 2 allottees of the securities. Else the minimum number of allottees is 5[56]. This issue, like a public issue, is also managed by a merchant banker.

One of the drawbacks of a private placement is that the investor cannot easily resell the security. However, institutions such as life insurance companies invest huge amounts in corporate debt for the long haul and are less concerned about its marketability. Consequently, an active private placement market has evolved for corporate debt.

As you would expect, it costs less to arrange a private placement than to make a public issue. This is a particular advantage for companies making smaller issues.

In 1990 the SEC in the US relaxed its restrictions on who can buy and trade unregistered securities. The new rule, Rule 144A, allows large financial institutions (known as *qualified institutional buyers*) to trade unregistered securities among themselves. Rule 144A was intended to increase liquidity and reduce interest rates and issue costs for private placements. It was aimed largely at foreign corporations deterred by registration requirements in the United States. The SEC argued that such firms would welcome the opportunity to issue unregistered stocks and bonds which could then be freely traded by large U.S. financial institutions.

Rule 144A issues have proved very popular, particularly with foreign issuers. There has also been an increasing volume of secondary trading in Rule 144A issues.

SUMMARY

In this chapter we have summarized the various procedures for issuing corporate securities. We first looked at how infant companies raise venture capital to carry them through to the point at which they can make their first public issue of stock. We then looked at how companies can make further public issues of securities by a general cash offer. Finally, we reviewed the procedures for a private placement.

It is always difficult to summarize a summary. Instead we will remind you of some of the most important implications for the financial manager who must decide how to issue capital.

Larger is cheaper There are economies of scale in issuing securities. It is cheaper to go to the market once for $100 million than to make two trips for $50 million each. Consequently firms bunch security issues. That may often mean relying on short-term financing until a large issue is justified. Or it may mean issuing more than is needed at the moment in order to avoid another issue later.

Watch out for underpricing Underpricing is a hidden cost to the existing shareholders. Fortunately, it is usually serious only for companies that are selling stock to the public for the first time.

[54]If a company makes preferential allotment of shares to the promoters of the company under the private placement route, then the shares shall be subject to a 3-year lock-in period.

[55]This is very similar to Rule 144a of SEC.

[56]In the U.S. the SEC has insisted that the security should be sold to no more than a dozen or so knowledgeable investors.

The winner's curse may be a serious problem with IPOs Would-be investors in an initial public offering (IPO) do not know how other investors will value the stock and they worry that they are likely to receive a larger allocation of the overpriced issues. Careful design of issue procedure may reduce the winner's curse.

New stock issues may depress the price The extent of this price pressure varies, but for industrial issues in the United States the fall in the value of the existing stock may amount to a significant proportion of the money raised. This pressure is due to the information that the market reads into the company's decision to issue stock.

Shelf registration often makes sense for debt issues by blue-chip firms Shelf registration reduces the time taken to arrange a new issue, it increases flexibility, and it may cut underwriting costs. It seems best suited for debt issues by large firms that are happy to switch between investment banks. It seems less suited for issues of unusually risky or complex securities or for issues by small companies that are likely to benefit from a close relationship with an investment bank.

APPENDIX

Marvin's New-Issue Prospectus[57]

PROSPECTUS
900,000 Shares
Marvin Enterprises Inc.
Common Stock ($.10 par value)

Of the 900,000 shares of Common Stock offered hereby, 500,000 shares are being sold by the Company and 400,000 shares are being sold by the Selling Stockholders. See "Principal and Selling Stockholders." The Company will not receive any of the proceeds from the sale of shares by the Selling Stockholders.

Before this offering there has been no public market for the Common Stock. **These securities involve a high degree of risk. See "Certain Considerations."**

THESE SECURITIES HAVE NOT BEEN APPROVED OR DISAPPROVED BY THE SECURITIES AND EXCHANGE COMMISSION NOR HAS THE COMMISSION PASSED ON THE ACCURACY OR ADEQUACY OF THIS PROSPECTUS. ANY REPRESENTATION TO THE CONTRARY IS A CRIMINAL OFFENSE.

	Price to Public	Underwriting Discount	Proceeds to Company[1]	Proceeds to Selling Stockholders[1]
Per share	$80.00	$5.60	$74.40	$74.40
Total[2]	$72,000,000	$5,040,000	$37,200,000	$29,760,000

[1]Before deducting expenses payable by the Company estimated at $820,000, of which $455,555 will be paid by the Company and $364,445 will be paid by the Selling Stockholders.

[2]The Company has granted to the Underwriters an option to purchase up to an additional 135,000 shares at the initial public offering price, less the underwriting discount, solely to cover overallotment.

The Common Stock is offered subject to receipt and acceptance by the Underwriters, to prior sale, and to the Underwriters' right to reject any order in whole or in part and to withdraw, cancel, or modify the offer without notice.

[57]Most prospectuses have content similar to that of the Marvin prospectus but go into considerably more detail. Also we have omitted Marvin's financial statements.

Klein Merrick Inc. **February 3, 2022**

No person has been authorized to give any information or to make any representations, other than as contained therein, in connection with the offer contained in this Prospectus, and, if given or made, such information or representations must not be relied upon. This Prospectus does not constitute an offer of any securities other than the registered securities to which it relates or an offer to any person in any jurisdiction where such an offer would be unlawful. The delivery of this Prospectus at any time does not imply that information herein is correct as of any time subsequent to its date.

IN CONNECTION WITH THIS OFFERING, THE UNDERWRITERS MAY OVERALLOT OR EFFECT TRANSACTIONS WHICH STABILIZE OR MAINTAIN THE MARKET PRICE OF THE COMMON STOCK OF THE COMPANY AT A LEVEL ABOVE THAT WHICH MIGHT OTHERWISE PREVAIL IN THE OPEN MARKET. SUCH STABILIZING, IF COMMENCED, MAY BE DISCONTINUED AT ANY TIME.

Prospectus Summary

The following summary information is qualified in its entirety by the detailed information and financial statements appearing elsewhere in this Prospectus.

The Offering

Common Stock offered by the Company ....500,000 shares
Common Stock offered by the Selling Stockholders ....400,000 shares
Common Stock to be outstanding after this offering ....4,100,000 shares

Use of Proceeds

For the construction of new manufacturing facilities and to provide working capital.

The Company

Marvin Enterprises Inc. designs, manufactures, and markets gargle blasters for domestic use. Its manufacturing facilities employ integrated microcircuits to control the genetic engineering processes used to manufacture gargle blasters.

The Company was organized in Delaware in 2016.

Use of Proceeds

The net proceeds of this offering are expected to be $36,744,445. Of the net proceeds, approximately $27.0 million will be used to finance expansion of the Company's principal manufacturing facilities. The balance will be used for working capital.

Certain Considerations

Investment in the Common Stock involves a high degree of risk. The following factors should be carefully considered in evaluating the Company:

Substantial Capital Needs The Company will require additional financing to continue its expansion policy. The Company believes that its relations with its lenders are good, but there can be no assurance that additional financing will be available in the future.

Licensing The expanded manufacturing facilities are to be used for the production of a new imploding gargle blaster. An advisory panel to the U.S. Food and Drug Administration (FDA) has recommended approval of this product for the U.S. market but no decision has yet been reached by the full FDA committee.

Dividend Policy

The company has not paid cash dividends on its Common Stock and does not anticipate that dividends will be paid on the Common Stock in the foreseeable future.

Management

The following table sets forth information regarding the Company's directors, executive officers, and key employees.

Name	Age	Position
George Marvin	32	President, Chief Executive Officer, & Director
Mildred Marvin	28	Treasurer & Director
Chip Norton	30	General Manager

George Marvin—George Marvin established the Company in 2016 and has been its Chief Executive Officer since that date. He is a past president of the Institute of Gargle Blasters and has recently been inducted into the Confrèrie des gargarisateurs.

Mildred Marvin—Mildred Marvin has been employed by the Company since 2016.

Chip Norton—Mr. Norton has been General Manager of the Company since 2016. He is a former vice-president of Amalgamated Blasters, Inc.

Executive Compensation

The following table sets forth the cash compensation paid for services rendered for the year 2021 by the executive officers:

Name	Capacity	Cash Compensation
George Marvin	President and Chief Executive Officer	$300,000
Mildred Marvin	Treasurer	220,000
Chip Norton	General Manager	220,000

Certain Transactions

At various times between 2017 and 2020 First Meriam Venture Partners invested a total of $8.5 million in the Company. In connection with this investment, First Meriam Venture Partners was granted certain rights to registration under the Securities Act of 1933, including the right to have their shares of Common Stock registered at the Company's expense with the Securities and Exchange Commission.

Principal and Selling Stockholders

The following table sets forth certain information regarding the beneficial ownership of the Company's voting Common Stock as of the date of this prospectus by (i) each person known by the Company to be the beneficial owner of more than 5 percent of its voting Common Stock, and (ii) each director of the Company who beneficially owns voting Common Stock. Unless otherwise indicated, each owner has sole voting and dispositive power over his or her shares.

	Common Stock				
	Shares Beneficially Owned Prior to Offering			Shares Beneficially Owned After Offer[1]	
Name of Beneficial Owner	Number	Percent	Shares to Be Sold	Number	Percent
George Marvin	375,000	10.4	60,000	315,000	7.7
Mildred Marvin	375,000	10.4	60,000	315,000	7.7
Chip Norton	250,000	6.9	80,000	170,000	4.1
First Meriam Venture Partners	1,700,000	47.2	—	1,700,000	41.5
TFS Investors	260,000	7.2	—	260,000	6.3
Centri-Venture Partnership	260,000	7.2	—	260,000	6.3
Henry Pobble	180,000	5.0	—	180,000	4.4
Georgina Sloberg	200,000	5.6	200,000	—	—

[1]Assuming no exercise of the Underwriters' overallotment option.

Lock-up Agreements

The holders of the common stock have agreed with the underwriters not to sell, pledge or otherwise dispose of their shares, other than as specified in this prospectus, for a period of 180 days after the date of the prospectus without the prior consent of Klein Merrick.

Description of Capital Stock

The Company's authorized capital stock consists of 10,000,000 shares of voting Common Stock.

As of the date of this Prospectus, there are 10 holders of record of the Common Stock.

Under the terms of one of the Company's loan agreements, the Company may not pay cash dividends on Common Stock except from net profits without the written consent of the lender.

Underwriting

Subject to the terms and conditions set forth in the Underwriting Agreement, the Company has agreed to sell to each of the Underwriters named below, and each of the Underwriters, for whom Klein Merrick Inc. are acting as Representatives, has severally agreed to purchase from the Company, the number of shares set forth opposite its name below.

Underwriters	Number of Shares to Be Purchased
Klein Merrick, Inc.	300,000
Goldman Stanley, Inc.	300,000
Salomon, Buffett & Co.	100,000
Orange County Securities	100,000
Bank of New England	100,000

In the Underwriting Agreement, the several Underwriters have agreed, subject to the terms and conditions set forth therein, to purchase all shares offered hereby if any such shares are purchased. In the event of a default by any Underwriter, the Underwriting Agreement provides that, in certain circumstances, purchase commitments of the nondefaulting Underwriters may be increased or the Underwriting Agreement may be terminated.

There is no public market for the Common Stock. The price to the public for the Common Stock was determined by negotiation between the Company and the Underwriters and was based on, among other things, the Company's financial and operating history and condition, its prospects and the prospects for its industry in general, the management of the Company, and the market prices of securities for companies in businesses similar to that of the Company.

Legal Matters

The validity of the shares of Common Stock offered by the Prospectus is being passed on for the Company by Dodson and Fogg and for the Underwriters by Kenge and Carboy.

Experts

The consolidated financial statements of the Company have been so included in reliance on the reports of Hooper Firebrand, independent accountants, given on the authority of that firm as experts in auditing and accounting.

Financial Statements

[*Text and tables omitted.*]

FURTHER READING

Megginson, Fenn et al., and Gompers and Lerner provide an overview of the venture capital industry, while Sahlman looks at the form of the venture capital contract:

W. L. Megginson, "Toward a Global Model of Venture Capital?" *Journal of Applied Corporate Finance* 16 (Winter 2004), pp. 89–107.

G. W. Fenn, N. Liang, and S. Prowse, "The Economics of the Private Equity Market," Staff Studies, No. 168, Board of Governors of the Federal Reserve System, (December 1995), pp. 1–69 (**www.federalreserve.gov/pubs.staffstudies/1990-99/ss168.pdf**).

P. Gompers and J. Lerner, "The Venture Capital Revolution," *Journal of Economic Perspectives* 15 (Spring 2001), pp. 145–168.

W. A. Sahlman, "Aspects of Financial Contracting in Venture Capital," *Journal of Applied Corporate Finance* (Summer 1988), pp. 23–26.

Ritter reviews both IPOs and seasoned issues, while the other three readings focus on IPOs:

J. R. Ritter, "Investment Banking and Securities Issuance," in G. M. Constantinides, M. Harris, and R. Stulz (eds.), *Handbook of the Economics of Finance* (Amsterdam: Elsevier Science, 2003).

T. Jenkinson and A. Ljungqvist, *Going Public: The Theory and Evidence on How Companies Raise Equity Finance*, 2nd ed. (Oxford: Oxford University Press, 2001).

R. G. Ibbotson, J. L. Sindelar, and J. R. Ritter: "The Market's Problems with the Pricing of Initial Public Offerings," *Journal of Applied Corporate Finance* 7 (Spring 1994), pp. 66–74.

L. M. Benveniste and W. J. Wilhelm, Jr.: "Initial Public Offerings: Going by the Book," *Journal of Applied Corporate Finance* 10 (Spring 1997) pp. 98–108.

A useful introduction to the design of auctions is:

P. Milgrom, "Auctions and Bidding: A Primer," *Journal of Economic Perspectives* 2 (1989), pp. 3–22.

WEB EXERCISE

Find a recent IPO by using one of the Web sites listed in the Related Web sites section and then use the Edgar database to find the prospectus. (You may find it easiest to look up the company on **finance.yahoo** and use the link to SEC filings. In any case finding the final prospectus can be a matter of trial and error.) Compare the IPO with that of Marvin. For example, Who were the existing shareholders? Was the company raising more capital or were existing shareholders selling? Were existing shareholders prevented by a lock-up agreement from selling more shares? How did the underwriting and other costs compare with those of Marvin? Did the underwriters have a greenshoe option? Did the issue turn out to be underpriced (the Yahoo! Web site should help here)? If so, how much money was left on the table?

CONCEPT REVIEW QUESTIONS

1. Vocabulary check. Define
   a. angel investors
   b. corporate venturers
   c. carried interest
   d. private equity
   e. bookbuilding
   f. shelf registration
   g. Rule 144A (pages 390–407)
2. How are venture capital funds organized? (page 391)
3. How is venture capital financing structured so as to ensure that the new business is a success? (pages 388–389)

For additional Concept Review Questions, please visit us at www.mhhe.com/bmam8e or refer to your Student CD.

QUIZ

1. After each of the following issue methods we have listed two types of issue. Choose the one more likely to employ that method.
   a. Rights issue (*initial public offer/further sale of an already publicly traded stock*)
   b. Rule 144A issue (*international bond issue/U.S. bond issue by a foreign corporation*)
   c. Private placement (*issue of existing stock/bond issue by an industrial company*)
   d. Shelf registration (*initial public offer/bond issue by a large financial institution*)
2. Each of the following terms is associated with one of the events beneath. Can you match them up?
   a. Bookbuilding
   b. Shelf registration
   c. Rule 144A

   Events:
   a. Investors indicate to the underwriter how many shares they would like to buy in a new issue and these indications are used to help set the price.
   b. Some issues are not registered but can be traded freely among qualified institutional buyers.
   c. Several tranches of the same security may be sold under the same registration. (A "tranche" is a batch, a fraction of a larger issue.)
3. Explain what each of the following terms or phrases means:
   a. Venture capital
   b. Primary offering
   c. Secondary offering
   d. Registration statement
   e. Winner's curse
4. For each of the following pairs of issues, which is likely to involve the lower proportionate underwriting and administrative costs?
   a. A large issue/a small issue.
   b. A bond issue/a common stock issue.
   c. Initial public offering/subsequent issue of stock.
   d. A small private placement of bonds/a small general cash offer of bonds.
5. True or false?
   a. Venture capitalists typically provide first-stage financing sufficient to cover all development expenses. Second-stage financing is provided by stock issued in an IPO.
   b. Large international companies' stocks may be listed and traded on several different international exchanges.
   c. Stock price generally falls when the company announces a new issue of shares. This is attributable to the information released by the decision to issue.
6. Look back at the prospectus for Marvin's IPO (Appendix):
   a. If there is unexpectedly heavy demand for the issue, how many extra shares can the underwriter buy?
   b. How many shares are to be sold in the primary offering? How many will be sold in the secondary offering?
   c. One day post-IPO, Marvin shares traded at $105. What was the degree of underpricing? How does that compare with the average degree of underpricing for IPOs in the United States?
   d. There are three kinds of cost to Marvin's new issue—underwriting expense, administrative costs, and underpricing. What was the *total* dollar cost of the Marvin issue?

7. You need to choose between making a public offering and arranging a private placement. In each case the issue involves Rs. 10 million face value of 10-year debt. You have the following data for each:
   - *A public issue:* The interest rate on the debt would be 8.5 percent, and the debt would be issued at face value. The underwriting spread would be 1.5 percent, and other expenses would be Rs. 80,000.
   - *A private placement:* The interest rate on the private placement would be 9 percent, but the total issuing expenses would be only Rs. 30,000.

   a. What is the difference in the proceeds to the company net of expenses?
   b. Other things being equal, which is the better deal?
   c. What other factors beyond the interest rate and issue costs would you wish to consider before deciding between the two offers?
8. Associated Breweries is planning to market unleaded beer. To finance the venture it proposes to make a rights issue at Rs. 10 of one new share for each two shares held. (The company currently has outstanding 100,000 shares priced at Rs. 40 a share.) Assuming that the new money is invested to earn a fair return, give values for the following:
   a. Number of new shares.
   b. Amount of new investment.
   c. Total value of company after issue.
   d. Total number of shares after issue.
   e. Stock price after the issue.
   f. Price of the right to buy one new share.

PRACTICE QUESTIONS

1. Here is a further vocabulary quiz. Briefly explain each of the following:
   a. Zero-stage vs. first- or second-stage financing.
   b. After-the-money valuation.
   c. Mezzanine financing.
   d. Road show.
   e. Qualified institutional buyer.
2. a. "A signal is credible only if it is costly." Explain why management's willingness to invest in Marvin's equity was a credible signal. Was its willingness to accept only part of the venture capital that would eventually be needed also a credible signal?
   b. "When managers take their reward in the form of increased leisure or executive jets, the cost is borne by the shareholders." Explain how First Meriam's financing package tackled this problem.
3. In the U.K. initial public offerings of common stock are usually sold by an *offer for sale*. Mr. Bean has observed that on average these stocks are underpriced by about 9 percent and for some years has followed a policy of applying for a constant proportion of each issue. He is therefore disappointed and puzzled to find that this policy has not resulted in a profit. Explain to him why this is so.
4. Find the prospectus of a recent Indian IPO. How do the issue costs compare with those shown in Table 15.3? Can you suggest reasons for the differences?
5. Why are the costs of debt issues less than those of equity issues? List the possible reasons.
6. There are three reasons that a common stock issue might cause a fall in price: (a) the price fall is needed to absorb the extra supply, (b) the issue causes temporary price pressure until it has been digested, and (c) management has information that stockholders do not have. Explain these reasons more fully. Which do you find most plausible? Is there any way that you could seek to test whether you are right?
7. Construct a simple example to show the following:
   a. Existing shareholders are made worse off when a company makes a cash offer of new stock below the market price.

b. Existing shareholders are not made worse off when a company makes a rights issue of new stock below the market price even if the new stockholders do not wish to take up their rights.

8. In 1998 the Pandora Box Company made a rights issue at Rs. 5 a share of one new share for every four shares held. Before the issue there were 10 million shares outstanding and the share price was Rs. 6.
   a. What was the total amount of new money raised?
   b. What was the value of the right to buy one new share?
   c. What was the prospective stock price after the issue?
   d. How far could the total value of the company fall before shareholders would be unwilling to take up their rights?

9. Practice Question 8 contains details of a rights offering by Pandora Box. Suppose that the company had decided to issue new stock at Rs. 4. How many new shares would it have needed to sell to raise the same sum of money? Recalculate the answers to questions (b) to (d) in question 8. Show that the shareholders are just as well off if the company issues the shares at Rs. 4 rather than Rs. 5.

10. Suppose that the management of Marvin want to issue Indian Depository Receipts (IDRs) in India rather than in the U.S[58]. What are the differences in the public issue procedures between India and U.S.? Do you think it would have made any difference to Marvin?

CHALLENGE QUESTIONS

1. a. Why do venture capital companies prefer to advance money in stages? If you were the management of Marvin Enterprises, would you have been happy with such an arrangement? With the benefit of hindsight did First Meriam gain or lose by advancing money in stages?
   b. The price at which First Meriam would invest more money in Marvin was not fixed in advance. But Marvin could have given First Meriam an *option* to buy more shares at a preset price. Would this have been better?
   c. At the second stage Marvin could have tried to raise money from another venture capital company in preference to First Meriam. To protect themselves against this, venture capital firms sometimes demand first refusal on new capital issues. Would you recommend this arrangement?

2. Explain the difference between a uniform-price auction and a discriminatory auction. Why might you prefer to sell securities by one method rather than another?

3. Here is recent financial data on Pisa Construction, Inc.

Stock price	Rs. 40	Market value of firm	Rs. 400,000
Number of shares	10,000	Earnings per share	Rs. 4
Book net worth	Rs. 500,000	Return on investment	8%

Pisa has not performed spectacularly to date. However, it wishes to issue new shares to obtain Rs. 80,000 to finance expansion into a promising market. Pisa's financial advisers think a stock issue is a poor choice because, among other reasons, "sale of stock at a price below book value per share can only depress the stock price and decrease shareholders' wealth." To prove the point they construct the following example: "Suppose 2,000 new shares are issued at Rs. 40 and the proceeds are invested. (Neglect issue costs.) Suppose return on investment does not change. Then

Book net worth = Rs. 580,000

Total earnings = .08(580,000) = Rs. 46,400

$$\text{Earnings per share} = \frac{46,400}{12,000} = \text{Rs. } 3.87$$

Thus, EPS declines, book value per share declines, and share price will decline proportionately to Rs. 38.70."

Evaluate this argument with particular attention to the assumptions implicit in the numerical example.

[58]http www.sebi.gov.in to know the details of IDR issue.

PART FIVE RELATED WEB SITES

Dividend policy and leverage decisions may be influenced by tax rates. Here are some sites with information on tax rates:

www.taxsites.com (includes links to sites providing tax rates for a variety of countries)

finance.yahoo.com (information on personal tax rates)

www.quicken.com (information on personal tax rates)

You can get information on recent dividend announcements on:

www.fulldisclosure.com

aol.ccbn.com

www.ex-dividend.com

For information on the capital structure of individual firms as well as industries:

finance.yahoo.com

ValuePro provides software and data for estimating WACCs:

www.valuepro.net

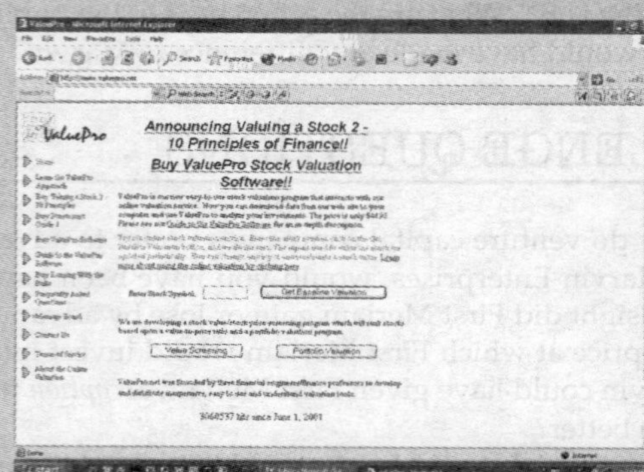

PART [5]

PAYOUT POLICY AND CAPITAL STRUCTURE

MANY ENERGY COMPANIES have been large borrowers and for many years Westar Energy, the Kansas utility company, was no exception. However, in 2003 Westar set about reducing its large mountain of debt and regaining an investment-grade rating for its bonds. It sold off some unwanted businesses, cut its dividend from $1.20 a share to $.76, and issued $250 million of common stock. By early 2004 Westar had reduced its burden of debt by $1.4 billion.

Westar's managers faced two basic financing decisions. One was how much cash it should distribute to shareholders. In cutting the dividend, the company stated that it planned to pay out in the future 60–75 percent of earnings. But the company could have chosen instead to maintain the dividend and to raise the cash by making a larger issue of common stock. Chapter 16 discusses the choice of how much a company should pay out.

Westar's second decision was to reduce its borrowing and to substitute equity. A company's mix of debt and equity is termed its *capital structure.* Chapters 17 through 19 examine the choice of capital structure and its implications for the cost of capital.

There are no simple answers to the dividend or capital structure decisions; for example, more debt can be good or bad, depending on the circumstances. But Part 5 will supply the concepts and facts needed for assessing how much the company should pay out to its shareholders and what is a sensible capital structure.

CHAPTER [16]

PAYOUT POLICY

COMPANIES CAN HAND back cash to their shareholders either by paying a dividend or by buying back their stock. In this chapter we explain how companies decide on the amount and form of this payout, and we discuss the controversial question of how payout policy affects the value of the firm.

The first step toward understanding payout policy is to recognize that the phrase means different things to different people. Therefore, we must start by defining what we mean by it.

A firm's decision about how much cash to distribute is often mixed up with other financing and investment decisions. Some firms pay out little cash because management is optimistic about the firm's future and wishes to retain earnings for expansion. Suppose, however, that the future investment opportunities evaporate, that a dividend increase is announced, and the stock price falls. How do we separate the impact of the dividend increase from the impact of investor's disappointment at the lost growth opportunities?

Another firm might finance capital expenditures largely by borrowing. This releases cash that can be distributed to shareholders. In this case the payout is a by-product of the borrowing decision.

We must isolate payout policy from other financial decisions. The precise question we should ask is, What is the effect of a change in payout policy, *given the firm's capital budgeting and borrowing decisions*? Suppose that the firm proposes to increase its dividend. The cash for that payment must come from somewhere. If we fix the firm's investment outlays and borrowing, there is only one possible source—an issue of stock. What if the firm decides to *reduce* its dividend? In that case it will have extra cash. If investment outlays and borrowing are fixed, there is only one possible way that this cash can be used—to repurchase stock. Thus payout policy implies a trade-off between higher or lower cash dividends and the issue or repurchase of common stock.

We start the chapter with some basic institutional material on dividends and stock repurchases. We then look at how companies decide on the level and method of payment and we show how both dividends and stock repurchases provide information to investors about company prospects. We then come to the central question, How does the decision to pay a dividend or repurchase stock affect firm value?

16.1 THE CHOICE OF PAYOUT POLICY

Companies can pay out cash to their shareholders in two ways. They can pay a dividend or they can buy back some of the outstanding shares. Figure 16.1 shows that dividend payments in India amount to about 40 percent of earnings. In fact the dividend payout ratio has increased from 21 percent in 1990 to a little more than 40 percent in 2001. These figures compare favorably with the U.S. dividend payout ratio. Between 1998 and 2002, the dividend payout ratio in U.S. averaged 42 percent.

Indian companies were allowed to buyback shares from 1998.[1] In 2004, a total of 10 companies went ahead with buyback of shares. Among them were Godrej Consumer Products Limited (Rs. 8.4 crores), Britannia Industries (Rs. 78 crores), and Reliance Industries Limited (Rs.2999 crores). Once the Board of Directors approves the company's decision to buyback shares, the companies inform SEBI of the decision. However, it is always possible that the company does not actually buyback any share even after filing a copy of the resolution passed by the Board with SEBI. Reliance Energy wanted to buyback shares worth Rs. 350 crores at a maximum share price of Rs. 525 each and informed SEBI of its decision on 16 June, 2004. However, on 27 June 2005, it informed SEBI that during the buyback period it did not buyback any share.

[1]Share Buyback in India is regulated by Secs. 77A, 77AA, and 77B of the Companies Act and SEBI (Buy Back of Securities) Regulations, 1998. The three sections in the Companies Act were inserted by the Companies (Amendment) Act in 1999 and apply with retrospective effect from 31st October, 1998.

FIGURE 16.1

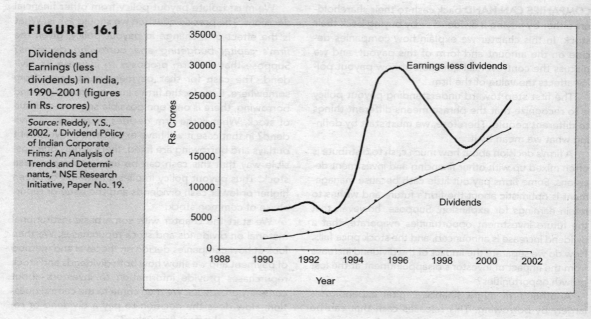

Dividends and Earnings (less dividends) in India, 1990–2001 (figures in Rs. crores)

Source: Reddy, Y.S., 2002, " Dividend Policy of Indian Corporate Frims: An Analysis of Trends and Determinants," NSE Research Initiative, Paper No. 19.

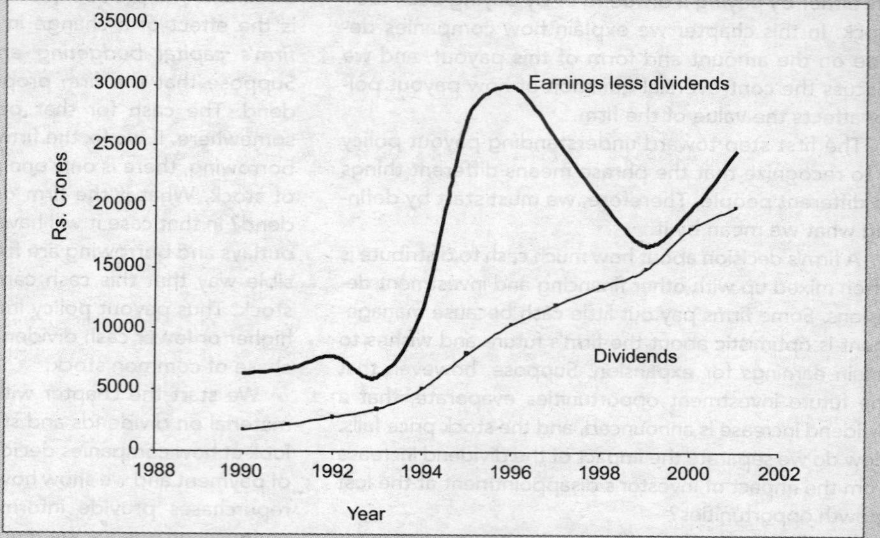

Till 1998, dividends were the principal way that corporate India returned cash to shareholders. Dividends continue to remain as the pre-dominant form of cash distribution even after share buybacks were legalized in India. Nevertheless, Reddy (2002) finds that only about a third of companies paid dividends in India in 2001. Some of the remainder had paid dividends in the past but they fell on hard times and were forced to conserve cash. A large part of the non-dividend paying companies never paid any dividends. According to Reddy, 34 percent of the companies in his sample never paid any dividends. In the U.S. some of the growth companies, like Sun Microsystems, Cisco, and Oracle do not pay any dividends and invest their total profit in the business itself.

As you can see from Figure 16.1, total dividend payments have increased fairly steadily. However, the proportion of companies paying a dividend has declined sharply from 60.5 percent in 1990 to 32.1 percent in 2001. You will also notice from Figure 16.1 that the fluctuation in earnings is much more than that of the level of dividends.

16.2 DIVIDEND PAYMENTS AND STOCK REPURCHASES

Before we look at the choice between dividends and stock repurchase, we need to review how these payments to shareholders take place.

How Dividends Are Paid

A company's dividend is set by the board of directors. The announcement of the dividend states that the payment will be made to all those stockholders who are registered on a particular *record date*. Then about two weeks later dividend checks are mailed to stockholders.

Stocks are normally bought and sold *with dividend* or *cum dividend* until a few weeks before the record date, and then they trade *ex dividend*. Investors who buy with dividend need not worry if their shares are not registered in time. The dividend must be paid over to them by the seller.

The company is not free to declare whatever dividend it chooses. Dividend payments by Indian companies are regulated by Sec. 205 of the Companies Act. As per the Act, a company can pay dividends out of profits for that year arrived at after providing for depreciation (Sec. 205 (1)) to the extent specified in Sec. 350 of the Companies Act[2] and after transferring to the reserves (Sec. 205 (2A)) of the company at least 10 percent of its profits for that year. However, the Central Government may allow a company to pay dividend in public interest even if the company fails to provide for depreciation in any year. A company can, for example, pay dividends out of past years' profits (when its current year's profits are either negative or inadequate to pay dividends) in accordance with the Companies (Declaration of Dividends out of Reserves) Rules, 1975.

Most companies pay regular dividends each year, but occasionally this is supplemented by a one-off *extra* or *special dividend*. Videsh Sanchar Nigam Limited (VSNL), for example, offered its shareholders 750% special dividend before its divestment in December 2001.[3] Government of India, having controlled about 53 percent of the shares of VSNL, was the largest beneficiary of this dividend payment. Many companies in the U.S. offer shareholders automatic dividend reinvestment plans (DRIPs). Often the new shares are issued at a 5 percent discount from the market price. Sometimes 10 percent or more of total dividends will be reinvested under such plans.[4]

Dividends are not always in the form of cash.[5] Frequently companies also declare *stock dividends*.[6] For example, if a company announces a 1:2 bonus issue (50% stock dividends), it sends each shareholder 1 extra share for every 2 shares currently held. Practically a bonus issue is equivalent to a stock split. Both increase the number of shares but do not affect the company's assets, profits, or total value. So both reduce value *per share*.[7] Our focus in this chapter will be on cash dividends.

Importance of Bonus Issues in India

Bonus issues (stock dividends) play a vital role in India. To understand the role of the bonus issues, one should know the way Indian companies announce the dividends. When an Indian company announces a 20 percent dividend, it pays 20% ¥ Rs.10 = Rs.2 of dividend per share (with face value of Rs.10 per share). Internationally, when a company announces 20 percent dividend, it actually distributes 20 percent of the total profit after tax to the shareholders as dividends. Since the face value of share does not change after a bonus issue, the shareholders receive more cash from the company after a bonus issue if the company does not proportionately reduce the dividend rate.

To illustrate, let's assume that a company announces 1:1 bonus to the shareholders. The shareholders now possess two shares for every one share they had before the bonus issue. If the company continues to pay 20 percent dividends to the shareholders, then the cash flow to the shareholders get doubled after the bonus issue. Of course, a company has the option of reducing the dividend rate to 10 percent after the bonus issue and keeping the total dividends constant.

---

[2]A company can also charge depreciation using a different method. However, it must ensure that 95% of the original cost of the asset is depreciated over the *specified period*. Here, specified period refers to the number of years after which at least 95 percent of the original cost of that asset to the company will have been provided for by way of depreciation if depreciation were to be calculated in accordance with the provisions of Sec. 350 of the Companies Act.

[3]In July 2001, VSNL had already distributed a 400% special dividend to the shareholders.

[4]Sometimes companies not only allow shareholders to reinvest dividends but also allow them to buy additional shares at a discount. For an amusing and true rags-to-riches story, see M. S. Scholes and M. A. Wolfson, "Decentralized Investment Banking: The Case of Dividend-Reinvestment and Stock-Purchase Plans," *Journal of Financial Economics* 24 (September 1989), pp. 7–36.

[5]Of course, Sec. 205 (3) prohibits companies from paying dividends in any form other than cash. However, the same section allows companies to capitalize profits and reserves as fully paid-up bonus shares.

[6]This is the same as issue of bonus shares.

[7]The distinction between bonus issue and stock split is technical. A bonus issue is shown in the accounts as a transfer from retained earnings to share capital, whereas a split is shown as a reduction in the par value of each share.

Mohanty finds that Indian companies do not reduce the dividend rate proportionately after the bonus issues.[8] During the 1982-96 sample period, only 9 percent of the companies reduced the dividend proportionately (or more than proportionately) after a bonus issue. In the remaining 91 percent of the cases, the shareholders received higher dividends from the companies.

How Firms Repurchase Buyback Stock

Instead of paying a dividend to its stockholders, the firm can use the cash to repurchase stock. As per the SEBI (Buy Back of Securities) Regulations, 1998, a company can buyback its shares by the tender offer (on a proportionate basis), from open market either through the bookbuilding process or stock exchanges, or from odd-lot holders. Companies in India mostly use the open market route to buyback shares. Out of the 22 buyback offers made by the Indian companies during 2004–06 (for which information is available in the website of SEBI), only 7 offers are tender offers. The remaining 15 offers have been made through the open market route. In the U.S. a company is also allowed to buyback shares by employing Dutch auction. In this case the firm states a series of prices at which it is prepared to repurchase stock. Shareholders submit offers declaring how many shares they wish to sell at each price and the company calculates the lowest price at which it can buy the desired number of shares.[9] A company cannot buyback shares through negotiated deals. However, in the U.S. a company can buy back shares by direct negotiation with a major shareholder. The most notorious instances are *greenmail* transactions, in which the target of an attempted takeover buys off the hostile bidder by repurchasing any shares that it has acquired. "Greenmail" means that these shares are repurchased at a price that makes the bidder happy to leave the target alone. This price does not always make the target's shareholders happy, as we point out in Chapter 32.

16.3 HOW DO COMPANIES DECIDE ON THE PAYOUT?

In the mid-1950s John Lintner held a classic series of interviews with corporate managers about their payout policies.[10] His conclusions can be summarized in four stylized facts:[11]

1. Firms have long-run target dividend payout ratios. Mature companies with stable businesses generally pay out a high proportion of earnings; growth companies have low payouts (if they pay any dividends at all).
2. Managers focus more on dividend changes than on absolute levels. Thus paying a $2.00 dividend is an important financial decision if last year's dividend was $1.00, but no big deal if last year's dividend was $2.00.
3. Dividend changes follow shifts in long-run sustainable earnings. Managers "smooth" dividends. Transitory earnings changes are unlikely to affect dividend payouts.
4. Managers are reluctant to make dividend changes that may have to be reversed. They are particularly worried about having to rescind a dividend increase.

When Lintner conducted his interviews, dividends were effectively the only means of distributing cash. More recent work on payout policy since the dramatic increase in repurchases suggests a fifth stylized fact.[12]

5. Firms repurchase stock when they have accumulated a large amount of unwanted cash or wish to change their capital structure by replacing equity with debt.

[8]Mohanty, P., 1999 Dividend and Bonus Policies of Indian Companies: An Analysis, Vikalpa, pp 35-42.

[9]This is another example of the uniform-price auction described in Section 15.3.

[10]See J. Lintner, "Distribution of Incomes of Corporations among Dividends, Retained Earnings, and Taxes," *American Economic Review* 46 (May 1956), pp. 97–113; and, for example, E. F. Fama and H. Babiak, "Dividend Policy: An Empirical Analysis," *Journal of the American Statistical Association* 63 (December 1968), pp. 1132–1161.

[11]The stylized facts are given by T. A. Marsh and R. C. Merton, "Dividend Behavior for the Aggregate Stock Market," *Journal of Business* 60 (January 1987), pp. 1–40. See especially pp. 5–6. We have paraphrased and embellished.

[12]See M. Jagannathan, C. P. Stephens, and M. S. Weisbach, "Financial Flexibility and the Choice between Dividends and Stock Repurchases," *Journal of Financial Economics* 57 (September 2000), pp. 355–384.

While stock repurchases are like bumper dividends, they do not typically *substitute* for dividends. Many companies that repurchase stock are mature, profitable companies that also pay dividends. Consider the case of U.S. banks. In 1997 large bank holding companies paid out just under 40 percent of their earnings as dividends. There were few profitable investment opportunities for the remaining income, but the banks did not want to commit themselves in the long run to any larger dividend payments. They therefore returned the cash to shareholders not by upping the dividend rate, but by repurchasing $16 billion of stock.[13]

Given these differences in the way that dividends and repurchases are used, it is not surprising to find that repurchases are much more volatile than dividends. Repurchases generally mushroom during boom times as firms accumulate excess cash and wither in recessions.

In recent years a number of countries, just like India such as Japan and Sweden, have allowed repurchases for the first time.[14] Some countries, however, continue to ban them entirely or to tax them as dividends. In these countries firms that have amassed large amounts of cash may be tempted to invest it at very low rates of return rather than hand it back to shareholders, who could reinvest it in firms that are short of cash.

16.4 THE INFORMATION IN DIVIDENDS AND STOCK REPURCHASES

In some countries you cannot rely on the information that companies provide. Passion for secrecy and a tendency to construct multilayered corporate organizations produce asset and earnings figures that are next to meaningless.

How does an investor in such a world separate marginally profitable firms from the real money makers? One clue is dividends. Investors can't read managers' minds, but they can learn from managers' actions. They know that a firm which reports good earnings and pays a generous dividend is putting its money where its mouth is. We can understand, therefore, why investors would value the information content of dividends and would refuse to believe a firm's reported earnings unless they were backed up by an appropriate dividend policy.

Of course, firms can cheat in the short run by overstating earnings and scraping up cash to pay a generous dividend. But it is hard to cheat in the long run, for a firm that is not making enough money will not have enough cash to pay out. If a firm chooses a high dividend payout without the cash flow to back it up, that firm will ultimately have to reduce its investment plans or turn to investors for additional debt or equity financing. All of these consequences are costly. Therefore, most managers don't increase dividends until they are confident that sufficient cash will flow in to pay them.

Researchers, who have attempted to measure the information in dividend changes, have come up with mixed evidence. Some have found that dividend changes have little or no ability to predict future earnings. Reddy finds that Indian companies that paid dividends for the first time in four years, had positive and increasing past earnings. These companies also experienced 216 percent growth in standardized earnings in the year the dividend was paid. Healey and Palepu similarly find that companies in the U.S. that paid dividends for the first time, experience an increase of 43 percent earnings growth in the year a dividend is paid. If managers thought that this was a temporary windfall, they might have been cautious about committing themselves to paying out cash. But it looks as if these managers had good reason to be confident about prospects, for earnings continued to rise in the following years.[15]

[13]B. Hirtle, "Bank Holding Company Capital Ratios and Shareholder Payouts," *Federal Reserve Bank of New York: Current Issues in Economics and Finance* 4 (September 1998), pp. 1–6 (**www.ny.frb.org/research/current_issues/ci4-9.pdf**).

[14]Repurchases have been permitted in Japan since 1995 and in Sweden since 2000.

[15]See P. Healy and K. Palepu, "Earnings Information Conveyed by Dividend Initiations and Omissions," *Journal of Financial Economics* 21 (1988), pp. 149–175. For an example of a study which finds no information in the announcement, see G. Grullon, R. Michaely, and B. Swaminathan, "Are Dividend Changes a Sign of Firm Maturity?" *Journal of Business,* 75 (July 2002), pp. 387–424.

Investors certainly appear to take comfort from an increase in dividends. When the increase is announced, analysts generally up their forecast of the current year's earnings.[16] It is no surprise, therefore, to find that a higher dividend prompts a rise in the stock price, whereas a dividend cut results in a fall in price. For example, in the case of the dividend initiations studied by Healy and Palepu, the dividend announcement resulted in an abnormal rise of 4 percent in the stock price.[17]

Notice that investors do not get excited about the *level* of a company's dividend; they worry about the *change*, which they view as an important indicator of the sustainability of earnings. In Finance in the News we illustrate how an unexpected change in dividends can cause the stock price to bounce back and forth as investors struggle to interpret the significance of the change.

It seems that in some other countries investors are less preoccupied with dividend changes. For example, in Japan there is a much closer relationship between corporations and major stockholders, and therefore information may be more easily shared with investors. Consequently, Japanese corporations are more prone to cut their dividends when there is a drop in earnings, but investors do not mark the stocks down as sharply as in the United States.[18]

The Information Content of Share Repurchase

Share repurchases, like dividends, are a way to hand cash back to shareholders. But unlike dividends, share repurchases are frequently a one-off event. So a company that announces a repurchase program is not making a long-term commitment to earn and distribute more cash. The information in the announcement of a share repurchase program is therefore likely to be different from the information in a dividend payment.

Companies repurchase shares when they have accumulated more cash than they can invest profitably or when they wish to increase their debt levels. Neither circumstance is good news in itself, but shareholders are frequently relieved to see companies paying out the excess cash rather than frittering it away on unprofitable investments. Shareholders also know that firms with large quantities of debt to service are less likely to squander cash. A study by Comment and Jarrell, who looked at the announcements of open-market repurchase programs, found that on average they resulted in an abnormal price rise of 2 percent.[19]

Stock repurchases may also be used to signal a manager's confidence in the future. Suppose that you, the manager, believe that your stock is substantially undervalued. You announce that the company is prepared to buy back a fifth of its stock at a price that is 20 percent above the current

[16]A. R. Ofer and D. R. Siegel, "Corporate Financial Policy, Information, and Market Expectations: An Empirical Investigation of Dividends," *Journal of Finance* 42 (September 1987) pp. 889–911.

[17]Healy and Palepu also looked at companies that *stopped* paying a dividend. In this case the stock price on average declined by an abnormal 9.5 percent on the announcement and earnings fell over the next four quarters.

[18]The dividend policies of Japanese *keiretsus* are analyzed in K. L. Dewenter and V. A. Warther, "Dividends, Asymmetric Information, and Agency Conflicts: Evidence from a Comparison of the Dividend Policies of Japanese and U.S. Firms," *Journal of Finance* 53 (June 1998), pp. 879–904.

[19]See R. Comment and G. Jarrell, "The Relative Signalling Power of Dutch-Auction and Fixed Price Self-Tender Offers and Open-Market Share Repurchases," *Journal of Finance* 46 (September 1991), pp. 1243–1271. There is also evidence of continuing superior performance during the years following a repurchase announcement. See D. Ikenberry, J. Lakonishok, and T. Vermaelen, "Market Underreaction to Open Market Share Repurchases," *Journal of Financial Economics* 39 (October 1995), pp. 181–208.

FINANCE IN THE NEWS

THE DIVIDEND CUT HEARD ROUND THE WORLD

On May 9, 1994, FPL Group, the parent company of Florida Power & Light Company, announced a 32 percent reduction in its quarterly dividend payout, from 62 cents per share to 42 cents. In its announcement, FPL did its best to spell out to investors why it had taken such an unusual step. It stressed that it had studied the situation carefully and that, given the prospect of increased competition in the electric utility industry, the company's high dividend payout ratio (which had averaged 90 percent in the past 4 years) was no longer in the shareholders' best interests. The new policy resulted in a payout of about 60 percent of the previous year's earnings. Management also announced that, starting in 1995, the dividend payout would be reviewed in February instead of May to reinforce the linkage between dividends and annual earnings. In doing so, the company wanted to minimize unintended "signaling effects" from any future changes in dividends.

At the same time that it announced this change in dividend policy, FPL Group's board authorized the repurchase of up to 10 million shares of common stock over the next 3 years. In adopting this strategy, the company noted that changes in the U.S. tax code since 1990 had made capital gains more attractive than dividends to shareholders.

Besides providing a more tax-efficient means of distributing excess cash to its stockholders, FPL's substitution of stock repurchases for dividends was also designed to increase the company's financial flexibility in preparation for a new era of heightened competition among utilities. Although much of the cash savings from the dividend cut would be returned to shareholders in the form of stock repurchases, the rest would be used to retire debt and so reduce the company's leverage ratio. This deleveraging was intended to prepare the company for the likely increase in business risk and to provide some slack that would allow the company to take advantage of future business opportunities.

All this sounded logical, but investors' first reaction was dismay. On the day of the announcement, the stock price fell nearly 14 percent. But, as analysts digested the news and considered the reasons for the reduction, they concluded that the action was not a signal of financial distress but a well-considered strategic decision. This view spread throughout the financial community, and FPL's stock price began to recover. By the middle of the following month at least 15 major brokerage houses had placed FPL's common stock on their "buy" lists and the price had largely recovered from its earlier fall.

Source: Modified from D. Soter, E. Brigham, and P. Evanson, "The Dividend Cut 'Heard 'Round the World': The Case of FPL," *Journal of Applied Corporate Finance* 9 (Spring 1996), pp. 4–15.

market price. But (you say) you are certainly not going to sell any of your own stock at that price. Investors jump to the obvious conclusion—you must believe that the stock is good value even at 20 percent above the current price.

When companies offer to repurchase their stock at a premium, senior management and directors usually commit to hold on to their stock.[20] So it is not surprising that researchers have found that announcements of offers to buy back shares above the market price have prompted a larger rise in the stock price, averaging about 11 percent.[21]

[20]Not only do managers hold on to their stock; on average they also add to their holdings *before* the announcement of a repurchase. See D. S. Lee, W. Mikkelson, and M. M. Partch, "Managers' Trading around Stock Repurchases," *Journal of Finance* 47 (December 1992), pp. 1947–1961.

[21]See R. Comment and G. Jarrell, *op. cit.*

16.5 THE PAYOUT CONTROVERSY

We have seen that a change in payout may provide information about management's confidence in the future and so affect the stock price. But eventually this change in the stock price would happen anyway as information about future earnings seeps out through other channels. But does the payout policy *change* the value of the stock, rather than simply providing a signal of its value?

On this issue economists fall into three groups. On the right, there is a conservative group which believes that an increase in the dividend payment increases firm value. On the left, there is a radical group which believes that a higher dividend payout reduces value. And in the center, there is a middle-of-the-road party which claims that payout policy makes no difference.

The middle-of-the-road party was founded in 1961 by Miller and Modigliani (always referred to as "MM" or "M and M"), when they published a theoretical paper showing the irrelevance of dividend policy in a world without taxes, transaction costs, or other market imperfections.[22] By the standards of 1961 MM were leftist radicals, because at that time most people believed that even under idealized assumptions increased dividends made shareholders better off.[23] But now MM's proof is generally accepted as correct, and the argument has shifted to whether taxes or other market imperfections alter the situation. In the process MM have been pushed toward the center by a new leftist party which argues for *low* dividends. The leftists' position is based on MM's argument modified to take account of taxes and costs of issuing securities.

Why should you care about this debate? Of course, if you help to decide your company's dividend payment or stock repurchase, you will want to know how it affects value. But there is a more general reason than that. We have up to this point assumed that the company's investment decision is independent of its financing policy. In that case a good project is a good project is a good project, no matter who undertakes it or how it is ultimately financed. If dividend policy does not affect value, that is still true. But perhaps it *does* affect value. In that case the attractiveness of a new project may depend on where the money is coming from. For example, if investors prefer companies with high payouts, companies might be reluctant to take on investments financed by retained earnings.

We begin our discussion of dividend policy with a presentation of MM's original argument. Then we will undertake a critical appraisal of the positions of the three parties.

---

[22] M. H. Miller and F. Modigliani: "Dividend Policy, Growth and the Valuation of Shares," *Journal of Business* 34 (October 1961), pp. 411–433.

[23] Not *everybody* believed dividends make shareholders better off. MM's arguments were anticipated in 1938 in J. B. Williams, *The Theory of Investment Value,* Harvard University Press, Cambridge, MA, 1938. Also, a proof very similar to MM's was developed by J. Lintner in "Dividends, Earnings, Leverage, Stock Prices and the Supply of Capital to Corporations," *Review of Economics and Statistics* 44 (August 1962), pp. 243–269.

Dividend Policy Is Irrelevant in Perfect Capital Markets

In their classic 1961 article MM argued as follows: Suppose your firm has settled on its investment program. You have worked out how much of this program can be financed from borrowing, and you plan to meet the remaining funds requirement from retained earnings. Any surplus money is to be paid out as dividends.

Now think what happens if you want to increase the total payout by upping the dividend without also changing the investment and borrowing policy. The extra money must come from somewhere. If the firm fixes its borrowing, the only way it can finance the extra dividend is to print some more shares and sell them. The new stockholders are going to part with their money only if you can offer them shares that are worth as much as they cost. But how can the firm do this when its assets, earnings, investment opportunities, and, therefore, market value are all unchanged? The answer is that there must be a *transfer of value* from the old to the new stockholders. The new ones get the newly printed shares, each one worth less than before the dividend change was announced, and the old ones suffer a capital loss on their shares. The capital loss borne by the old shareholders just offsets the extra cash dividend they receive.

Figure 16.2 shows how this transfer of value occurs. Our hypothetical company pays out a third of its total value as a dividend and it raises the money to do so by selling new shares. The capital loss suffered by the old stockholders is represented by the reduction in the size of the green boxes. But that capital loss is exactly offset by the fact that the new money raised (the blue boxes) is paid over to them as dividends.

Does it make any difference to the old stockholders that they receive an extra dividend payment plus an offsetting capital loss? It might if that were the only way they could get their hands on cash. But as long as there are efficient capital markets, they can raise the cash by selling shares. Thus the old shareholders can cash in either by persuading the management to pay a higher dividend or by selling some of their shares. In either case there will be a transfer of value from old to new shareholders. The only difference is that in the former case this transfer is caused by a dilution in the value of each of the firm's shares, and in the latter case it is caused by a reduction in the number of shares held by the old shareholders. The two alternatives are compared in Figure 16.3.

Because investors do not need dividends to get their hands on cash, they will not pay higher prices for the shares of firms with high payouts. Therefore firms ought not to worry about dividend policy. They can let dividends fluctuate as a by-product of their investment and financing decisions.

Dividend Irrelevance—An Illustration

Consider the case of Rational Demiconductor, which at this moment has the following balance sheet:

Rational Demiconductor's Balance Sheet (Market Values)

Cash (Rs. 1,000 held for investment)	1,000	0	Debt
Fixed assets	9,000	10,000 + NPV	Equity
Investment opportunity (Rs. 1,000 investment required)	NPV		
Total asset value	Rs. 10,000 + NPV	Rs. 10,000 + NPV	Value of firm

FIGURE 16.2

This firm pays out a third of its worth as a dividend and raises the money by selling new shares. The transfer of value to the new stockholders is equal to the dividend payment. The total value of the firm is unaffected.

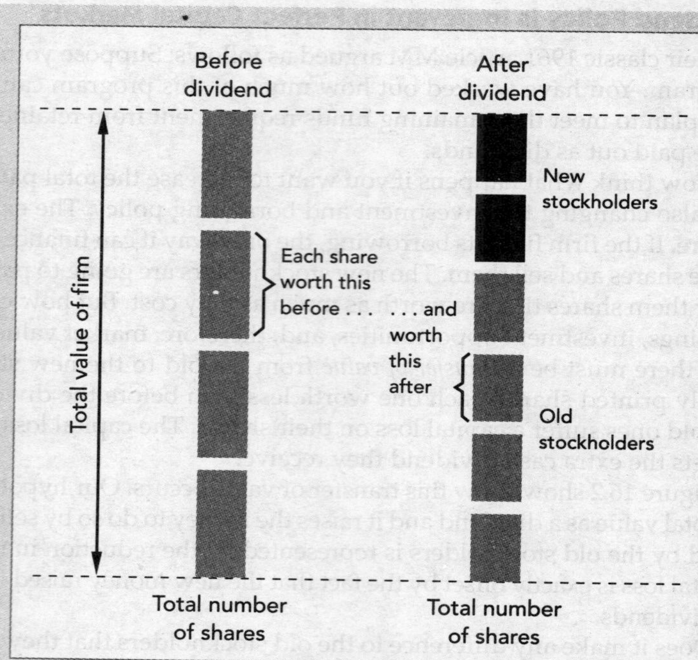

FIGURE 16.3

Two ways of raising cash for the firm's original shareholders. In each case the cash received is offset by a decline in the value of the old stockholders' claim on the firm. If the firm pays a dividend, each share is worth less because more shares have to be issued against the firm's assets. If the old stockholders sell some of their shares, each share is worth the same but the old stockholders have fewer shares.

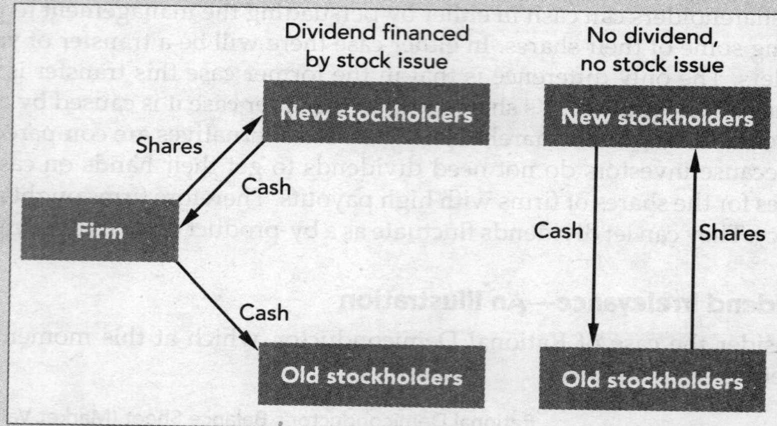

Rational Demiconductor has Rs. 1,000 cash earmarked for a project requiring Rs. 1,000 investment. We do not know how attractive the project is, and so we enter it at NPV; after the project is undertaken it will be worth Rs. 1,000 + NPV. Note that the balance sheet is constructed with market values; equity equals the market value of the firm's outstanding shares (price per share times number of shares outstanding). It is not necessarily equal to book net worth.

Now Rational Demiconductor uses the cash to pay a Rs. 1,000 dividend to its stockholders. The benefit to them is obvious: Rs. 1,000 of spendable cash. It is also obvious that there must be a cost. The cash is not free.

Where does the money for the dividend come from? Of course, the immediate source of funds is Rational Demiconductor's cash account. But this cash was earmarked for the investment project. Since we want to isolate the effects of dividend policy on shareholders' wealth, we assume that the company *continues* with the investment project. That means that Rs. 1,000 in cash must be raised by new financing. This could consist of an issue of either debt or stock. Again, we just want to look at dividend policy for now, and we defer discussion of the debt-equity choice until Chapters 17 and 18. Thus Rational Demiconductor ends up financing the dividend with a Rs. 1,000 stock issue.

Now we examine the balance sheet after the dividend is paid, the new stock is sold, and the investment is undertaken. Because Rational Demiconductor's investment and borrowing policies are unaffected by the dividend payment, its *overall* market value must be unchanged at Rs. 10,000 + NPV.[24] We know also that if the new stockholders pay a fair price, their stock is worth Rs. 1,000. That leaves us with only one missing number—the value of the stock held by the original stockholders. It is easy to see that this must be

$$\begin{aligned}\text{Value of original stockholders' shares} &= \text{value of company} - \text{value of new shares}\\ &= (10{,}000 + \text{NPV}) - 1{,}000\\ &= \text{Rs. } 9{,}000 + \text{NPV}\end{aligned}$$

The old shareholders have received a Rs. 1,000 cash dividend and incurred a Rs. 1,000 capital loss. Dividend policy doesn't matter.

By paying out Rs. 1,000 with one hand and taking it back with the other, Rational Demiconductor is recycling cash. To suggest that this makes shareholders better off is like advising a cook to cool the kitchen by leaving the refrigerator door open.

Of course, our proof ignores taxes, issue costs, and a variety of other complications. We will turn to those items in a moment. The really crucial assumption in our proof is that the new shares are sold at a fair price. The shares sold to raise Rs. 1,000 must actually be *worth* Rs. 1,000.[25] In other words, we have assumed efficient capital markets.

Calculating Share Price

We have assumed that Rational Demiconductor's new shares can be sold at a fair price, but what is that price and how many new shares are issued?

Suppose that before this dividend payout the company had 1,000 shares outstanding and that the project had an NPV of Rs. 2,000. Then the old stock was worth in total Rs. 10,000 + NPV = Rs. 12,000, which works out at Rs. 12,000/1,000 = Rs. 12 per share. After the company has paid the dividend and completed the financing, this old stock is worth Rs. 9,000 + NPV = Rs. 11,000. That works out at Rs. 11,000/1,000 = Rs. 11 per share. In other words, the price of the old stock falls by the amount of the Re. 1 per share dividend payment.

Now let us look at the new stock. Clearly, after the issue this must sell at the same price as the rest of the stock. In other words, it must be valued at Rs. 11. If the new stockholders get fair value, the company must issue Rs. 1,000/Rs. 11 or 91 new shares in order to raise the Rs. 1,000 that it needs.

---

[24] All other factors that might affect Rational Demiconductor's value are assumed constant. This is not a necessary assumption, but it simplifies the proof of MM's theory.

[25] The "old" shareholders get all the benefit of the positive NPV project. The new shareholders require only a fair rate of return. They are making a zero-NPV investment.

Share Repurchase

We have seen that any increased cash dividend payment must be offset by a stock issue if the firm's investment and borrowing policies are held constant. In effect the stockholders finance the extra dividend by selling off part of their ownership of the firm. Consequently, the stock price falls by just enough to offset the extra dividend.

This process can also be run backward. With investment and borrowing policy given, any *reduction* in dividends must be balanced by a reduction in the number of shares issued or by repurchase of previously outstanding stock. But if the process has no effect on stockholders' wealth when run forward, it must likewise have no effect when run in reverse. We will confirm this by another numerical example.

Suppose that a technical discovery reveals that Rational Demiconductor's new project is not a positive-NPV venture but a sure loser. Management announces that the project is to be discarded and that the Rs. 1,000 earmarked for it will be paid out as an extra dividend of Re. 1 per share. After the dividend payout, the balance sheet is

Rational Demiconductor's Balance Sheet (Market Values)

Cash	Rs. 0	Rs. 0	Debt
Existing fixed assets	9,000	9,000	Equity
New project	0		
Total asset value	Rs. 9,000	Rs. 9,000	Total firm value

Since there are 1,000 shares outstanding, the stock price is Rs. 10,000/1,000 = Rs. 10 before the dividend payment and Rs. 9,000/1,000 = Rs. 9 *after* the payment.

What if Rational Demiconductor uses the Rs.1,000 to repurchase stock instead? As long as the company pays a fair price for the stock, the Rs. 1,000 buys Rs. 1,000/Rs. 10 = 100 shares. That leaves 900 shares worth 900 × Rs. 10 = Rs. 9,000.

As expected, we find that switching from cash dividends to share repurchase has no effect on shareholders' wealth. They forgo a Re. 1 cash dividend but end up holding shares worth Rs. 10 instead of Rs. 9.

Note that when shares are repurchased the transfer of value is in favor of those stockholders who do not sell. They forgo any cash dividend but end up owning a larger slice of the firm. In effect they are using their share of Rational Demiconductor's Rs.1,000 distribution to buy out some of their fellow shareholders.

Stock Repurchase and Valuation

Valuing the equity of a firm that repurchases its own stock can be confusing. Let's work through a simple example.

Company X has 100 shares outstanding. It earns Rs. 1,000 a year, all of which is paid out as a dividend. The dividend per share is, therefore, Rs. 1,000/100 = Rs. 10. Suppose that investors expect the dividend to be maintained indefinitely and that they require a return of 10 percent. In this case the value of each share is PV_{share} = Rs. 10/.10 = Rs. 100. Since there are 100 shares outstanding, the *total* market value of the equity is PV_{equity} = 100 × Rs. 100 = Rs. 10,000. Note that we could reach the same conclusion by discounting the *total* dividend payments to shareholders (PV_{equity} = Rs. 1,000/.10 = Rs. 10,000).[26]

Now suppose the company announces that instead of paying a cash dividend in year 1, it will spend the same money repurchasing its shares in the open market. The total expected cash flows to shareholders (dividends and cash from stock repurchase) are unchanged at Rs. 1,000. So the total value of the equity also remains at Rs. 1,000/.10 = Rs. 10,000. This is made up of the value of the Rs. 1,000 received from the stock repurchase in year 1 ($PV_{repurchase}$ = Rs. 1,000/1.1 = Rs. 909.1) and the value of the Rs. 1,000-a-year dividend starting in year 2 [$PV_{dividends}$ = Rs.1,000/(.10 × 1.1) = Rs. 9,091]. Each share continues to be worth Rs. 10,000/100 = Rs. 100 just as before.

Think now about those shareholders who plan to sell their stock back to the company. They will demand a 10 percent return on their investment. So the price at which the firm buys back shares must be 10 percent higher than today's price, or Rs. 110. The company spends Rs. 1,000 buying back its stock, which is sufficient to buy Rs. 1,000/Rs. 110 = 9.09 shares.

The company starts with 100 shares, it buys back 9.09, and therefore 90.91 shares remain outstanding. Each of these shares can look forward to a dividend stream of Rs. 1,000/90.91 = Rs. 11 per share. So after the repurchase shareholders have 10 percent fewer shares, but earnings and dividends per share are 10 percent higher. An investor who owns one share today that is not repurchased will receive no dividends in year 1 but can look forward to Rs. 11 a year thereafter. The value of each share is therefore 11/(.1 × 1.1) = Rs. 100.

Our example illustrates several points. First, other things equal, company value is unaffected by the decision to repurchase stock rather than to pay a cash dividend. Second, when valuing the entire equity you need to include both the cash that is paid out as dividends and the cash that is used to repurchase stock. Third, when calculating the cash flow *per share*, it is double counting to include both the forecasted dividends per share *and* the cash received from repurchase (if you sell back your share, you don't get any subsequent dividends). Fourth, a firm that repurchases stock instead of paying dividends reduces the number of shares outstanding but produces an offsetting increase in earnings and dividends per share.

16.6 THE RIGHTISTS

MM's argument implies that the value of the company is determined by the company's assets and the cash flows that they generate. If the company increases the total amount of the payout, the extra cash must be clawed back from the shareholders by a new issue of stock. And if the company chooses to hold the total payout constant, any increase in the dividend payment must be offset by a corresponding reduction in the cash that shareholders receive by a repurchase of their shares. Hence MM's conclusion that firm value cannot be increased by changing the amount or the form of the distribution.

[26]When valuing the entire equity, remember that if the company is expected to issue additional shares in the future, we should include the dividend payments on these shares only if we also include the amount that investors pay for them. See Chapter 19.

Before MM published their paper, much of the finance literature had advocated high payout ratios. Here, for example, is a statement of the rightist position made by Graham and Dodd in 1951:

> The considered and continuous verdict of the stock market is overwhelmingly in favor of liberal dividends as against niggardly ones. The common stock investor must take this judgment into account in the valuation of common stock for purchase. It is now becoming standard practice to evaluate common stock by applying one multiplier to that portion of earnings paid out in dividends and a much smaller multiplier to the undistributed balance.[27]

Those who favor large payouts point out that there is a natural clientele for high-payout stocks. For example, some financial institutions in the U.S. are legally restricted from holding stocks lacking established dividend records. In India, the Insurance Regulatory and Development Authority (IRDA) has not specified any clear guidelines about the stocks in which an insurance company can invest. However, it has made its apparent bias towards dividend paying companies clear when its prudential norms for debentures recommend insurance companies to buy only those fully and partly convertible debentures where dividends are likely to be received.

There is also a natural clientele of investors who look to their stock portfolios for a steady source of cash to live on. In principle, this cash could be easily generated from stocks paying no dividends at all; the investor could just sell off a small fraction of his or her holdings from time to time. But it is simpler and cheaper for the company to send a quarterly check than for its shareholders to sell, say, one share every three months. Regular dividends relieve many of its shareholders of transaction costs and considerable inconvenience.[28]

Some observers have appealed to behavioral psychology to explain why we may prefer to receive those regular dividends rather than sell small amounts of stock.[29] We are all, they point out, liable to succumb to temptation. Some of us may hanker after fattening foods, while others may be dying for a drink. We could seek to control these cravings by willpower, but that can be a painful struggle. Instead, it may be easier to set simple rules for ourselves ("cut out chocolate," or "wine with meals only"). In just the same way, we may welcome the self-discipline that comes from spending only dividend income, and thereby sidestep the difficult decision of how much we should dip into capital.

Payout Policy, Investment Policy, and Management Incentives

There is another reason that shareholders often clamor for more generous payouts. Suppose a company has plenty of free cash flow but few profitable investment opportunities. Shareholders may not trust the managers to spend retained earnings wisely and may fear that the money will be plowed back into building a larger empire rather than a more profitable one. In such cases investors may

---

[27]These authors later qualified this statement, recognizing the willingness of investors to pay high price–earnings multiples for growth stocks. But otherwise they stuck to their position. We quoted their 1951 statement because of its historical importance. Compare B. Graham and D. L. Dodd, *Security Analysis: Principles and Techniques*, 3rd ed. (New York: McGraw-Hill, 1951), p. 432, with B. Graham, D. L. Dodd, and S. Cottle, *Security Analysis: Principles and Techniques*, 4th ed. (New York: McGraw-Hill, 1962), p. 480.

[28]Those advocating generous dividends might go on to argue that a regular cash dividend relieves stockholders of the risk of having to sell shares at "temporarily depressed" prices. Of course, the firm will have to issue shares eventually to finance the dividend, but (the argument goes) the firm can pick the *right time* to sell. If firms really try to do this and if they are successful—two big *ifs*—then stockholders of high-payout firms might indeed get something for nothing.

[29]See H. Shefrin and M. Statman, "Explaining Investor Preference for Cash Dividends," *Journal of Financial Economics* 13 (June 1984), pp. 253–282.

FINANCE IN THE NEWS

MICROSOFT'S PAYOUT BONANZA

There is a point at which hoarding money becomes embarrassing. . . . Microsoft, which grew into the world's largest software company . . . and which has been generating cash at the rate of $1 billion a month passed that point years ago. On July 20th, it finally addressed the issue.

Its solution was to give back to its shareholders, in various forms, an unprecedented $75 billion. One dollop, to the tune of $32 billion, will be a one time dividend to be paid in December. Another will be share buy-backs worth $30 billion over four years. The third will be a doubling of Microsoft's ongoing dividend to 32 cents a share annually, payable in quarterly installments. Not bad for a company that has not even turned 30 yet, and that only declared its first dividend in January 2003.

The decision is impressive for the mature analysis by Microsoft of its role in the industry and the prospects for the future that it implies.

Source: "An End to Growth?" *The Economist*, July 24, 2004, p. 61.

clamor for higher dividends or a stock repurchase not because these are valuable in themselves, but because they encourage a more careful, value-oriented investment policy.[30]

The nearby box describes how Microsoft announced the largest cash distribution in corporate history. By 2004 the company's investment opportunities had diminished, and investors were, therefore, happy to see Microsoft distribute its cash mountain rather than invest it in negative-NPV projects.

16.7 TAXES AND THE RADICAL LEFT

The left-wing dividend creed is simple: Whenever dividends are taxed more heavily than capital gains, firms should pay the lowest cash dividend they can get away with. Available cash should be retained or used to repurchase shares.

By shifting their distribution policies in this way, corporations can transmute dividends into capital gains. If this financial alchemy results in lower taxes, it should be welcomed by any taxpaying investor. That is the basic point made by the leftist party when it argues for low-dividend payout.

If dividends are taxed more heavily than capital gains, investors should pay more for stocks with low dividend yields. In other words, they should accept a lower *pretax* rate of return from securities offering returns in the form of capital gains rather than dividends. Table 16.1 illustrates this. The stocks of firms A and B are equally risky. Investors expect A to be worth Rs. 112.50 per share next year. The share price of B is expected to be only Rs. 102.50, but a Rs.10 dividend is also forecasted, and so the total pretax payoff is the same, Rs. 112.50.

[30]La Porta et al. argue that in countries such as the United States shareholders are able to pressure companies to disgorge cash and this prevents managers from using too high a proportion of earnings to benefit themselves. By contrast, companies pay out a smaller proportion of earnings in those countries where the law is more relaxed about overinvestment and empire building. See R. La Porta, F. Lopez-de-Silanes, A. Shleifer, and R. W. Vishny, "Agency Problems and Dividend Policies around the World," *Journal of Finance* 55 (February 2000), pp. 1–34.

	Firm A (No Dividend)	Firm B (High Dividend)
Next year's price	Rs. 112.50	Rs. 102.50
Dividend	Rs. 0	Rs. 10.00
Total pretax payoff	Rs. 112.50	Rs. 112.50
Today's stock price	Rs. 100	Rs. 97.78
Capital gain	Rs. 12.50	Rs. 4.72
Before-tax rate of return	$100\times\left(\frac{12.5}{100}\right)=12.5\%$	$100\times\left(\frac{14.72}{97.78}\right)=15.05\%$
Tax on dividend at 40%	Rs. 0	.40 × 10 = Rs. 4.00
Tax on capital gains at 20%	.20 × 12.50 = Rs. 2.50	.20 × 4.72 = Rs. 94
Total after-tax income (dividends plus capital gains less taxes)	(0 + 12.50) − 2.50 = Rs. 10.00	(10.00 + 4.72) − (4.00 + .94) = Rs. 9.78
After-tax rate of return	$100\times\left(\frac{10}{100}\right)=10.0\%$	$100\times\left(\frac{9.78}{97.78}\right)=10.0\%$

TABLE 16.1

Effects of a shift in dividend policy when dividends are taxed more heavily than capital gains. The high-payout stock (firm B) must sell at a lower price to provide the same after-tax return.

Yet we find B's stock selling for less than A's and therefore offering a higher pretax rate of return. The reason is obvious: Investors prefer A because its return comes in the form of capital gains. Table 16.1 shows that A and B are equally attractive to investors who, we assume, pay a 40 percent tax on dividends and a 20 percent tax on capital gains. Each offers a 10 percent return after all taxes. The difference between the stock prices of A and B is exactly the present value of the extra taxes the investors face if they buy B.[31]

The management of B could save these extra taxes by eliminating the Rs. 10 dividend and using the released funds to repurchase stock instead. Its stock price should rise to Rs. 100 as soon as the new policy is announced.

Dividend Tax Policy in India

In India, when a company announces dividends, it also pays the *dividend distribution* tax directly to the Government of India and the shareholders do not have to pay any tax on the dividends they receive. Before the introduction of the dividend distribution tax in India in 1997, dividends were taxed in the hands of the shareholders.[32] Shareholders used to disclose the dividend income under the head 'Income from Other Sources' and then used to pay tax on dividend at a rate that depended on their individual tax bracket. The Finance Act, 1997 introduced the dividend distribution tax for the first time in India and under this system, companies used to pay dividend distribution tax directly at the rate of 10 percent. Such dividend was exempt in the hands of the shareholders and this benefited those shareholders who fell in the higher-than-10-percent tax bracket.

The 2002–03 Budget reverted back to the earlier system for one year where dividends were again taxed in the hands of the shareholders. However, the 2003–04 Budget reintroduced the dividend distribution tax rate in India (albeit at a higher rate of 12.5 percent plus the surcharges). Currently the effective dividend distribution tax rate in India works out to 14.03 percent.

[31] Michael Brennan has modeled what happens when you introduce taxes into an otherwise perfect market. He found that the capital asset pricing model continues to hold, but on an *after-tax* basis. Thus, if A and B have the same beta, they should offer the same after-tax rate of return. The spread between pretax and post-tax returns is determined by a weighted average of investors' tax rates. See M. J. Brennan, "Taxes, Market Valuation and Corporate Financial Policy," *National Tax Journal* 23 (December 1970), pp. 417–427.

[32] The actual system was very complicated where the companies used to deduct taxes directly and issue a withholding tax certificate to the shareholders. The shareholders used to pay taxes on this dividend using the applicable rate and claim credit based on the withholding tax certificates provided by the company.

The Finance Bill No 22 in 2004 introduced a securities transaction tax (STT) of 0.15 percent on the total turnover[33] and removed the long-term capital gains tax on sale of shares listed in recognized stock exchanges altogether. The short term capital gains tax rate (on sell of equity shares) has been reduced to 10 percent in the same bill. Prior to this the long-term capital gains tax rate depended on the type of tax payer. The individual tax payers and the companies (both domestic and MNCs) were subject to a long-term capital gains tax rate of 20 percent; the foreign institutional investors, however, were subject to a 10 percent long term capital gains tax rate.

Why Pay Any Dividends at All?

So the current tax system in India favors low dividend payments by the companies. This raises a very interesting question: if dividends attract more tax than capital gains, why should any firm ever pay a cash dividend? If cash is to be distributed to stockholders, isn't share repurchase always the best channel for doing so?

The answer is 'no'. Buyback transactions are not recognized as taxable securities transactions because they do not take place in a recognized stock exchange. So in case of buyback, the normal capital gains tax rates (20 percent for most investors, and 10 percent for FIIs) apply.

So if an Indian company pays more dividends, then the company pays 14.025 percent dividend distribution tax. If the company buys back shares instead, then individual investors pay 20 percent capital gains tax (assuming they sell the shares back after a year of purchase and hence are subject to long-term capital gains tax) whereas the FIIs pay 10 percent capital gains tax. So in most cases the individual investors will prefer high dividends in India, whereas the FIIs will prefer buyback of shares.[34]

Empirical Evidence on Dividends and Taxes

It is hard to deny that taxes are important to investors. You can see that in the bond market. RBI issues two types of relief bonds in India. In the first type of bond, the interest rate is 6.5 percent and interest is tax free; in the second type of bond, the interest rate is 8 percent and interest is taxable. It does not seem likely that investors in bonds just forget about taxes when they enter the stock market.

So in companies in which FII holding is high, we should expect high dividend stocks to sell at lower prices and therefore to offer higher returns. Similarly, in companies in which the FII holding is low and the public holding is high, we should expect in most cases high dividend stocks to sell at higher prices and to offer lower returns.

Unfortunately, there are difficulties in measuring this effect. For example, suppose that stock A is priced at Rs. 100 and is expected to pay a Rs. 5 dividend. The *expected* yield is, therefore, 5/100 = .05, or 5 percent. The company now announces bumper earnings and a Rs. 10 dividend. Thus with the benefit of hindsight, A's *actual* dividend yield is 10/100 = .10, or 10 percent. If the unexpected increase in earnings causes a rise in A's stock price, we will observe that a high actual yield is accompanied by a high actual return. But that would not tell us anything about whether a high *expected* yield was accompanied by a high *expected* return. In order to measure the effect of dividend policy, we need to estimate the dividends that investors expected.

A second problem is that nobody is quite sure what is meant by high dividend yield. Did the high divident stocks have a high yield all year, or only in months or on days that dividends were paid? Perhaps for most of the year, they had zero yields and were perfect holdings for the highly taxed individuals.[35]

---

[33]It has been hiked by 25 percent with effect from 1 July 2006.

[34]See the discussion in Section 16.8 for a numerical example.

[35]Suppose there are 250 trading days in a year. Think of a stock paying quarterly dividends. We could say that the stock offers a high dividend yield on 4 days but a zero dividend yield on the remaining 246 days.

A number of researchers have attempted to tackle these problems and to measure whether investors demand a higher return from high-yielding stocks. Their findings offer some limited comfort to the dividends-are-bad school, for most of the researchers have suggested that high-yielding stocks have provided higher returns. However, the estimated tax rates differ substantially from one study to another. For example, while Litzenberger and Ramaswamy concluded that investors have priced stocks as if dividend income attracted an extra 14 to 23 percent rate of tax, Miller and Scholes using a different methodology came up with a negligible 4 percent difference in the rate of tax.[36] In India, Narasimhan and Asha find that after the change in dividend tax system in India in 1998, investors demand changed in favor of the high payout companies.[37]

Here, we have assumed that the companies will adopt that dividend policy that reduces the tax liability of their investors. But do the companies care? Reddy finds that the tax regime changes have not influenced the dividend behavior of Indian corporate firms in the post-1997 period.

16.8 THE MIDDLE-OF-THE-ROADERS

The middle-of-the-road party, principally represented by Miller, Black, and Scholes,[38] maintains that a company's value is not affected by its dividend policy. Unlike the other two parties, they emphasize that the supply of dividends is free to adjust to the demand. Therefore, if companies could increase their stock price by changing their dividend payout, they would surely have done so. Presumably, dividends are where they are because no company believes that it could add value simply by upping or reducing its dividend payout.

This "supply argument" is not inconsistent with the existence of a clientele of investors who prefer low-payout stocks. If necessary, these investors would be prepared to pay a premium for low-payout stocks. But perhaps they do not have to. Enough firms may have already noticed the existence of this clientele and switched to low-payout policies. If so, there is no incentive for *additional* firms to switch to low-payout policies. Similarly, there may well be some investors who prefer high dividends, but these investors too already have a wide choice of suitable stocks. A third group of investors, such as pension funds and other tax-exempt institutions, may have no reason to prefer dividends to capital gains. These investors will be happy to hold both low- and high-payout stocks, and the value that they place on each stock will be unaffected by the company's dividend policy. In that case we are back in an MM world where dividend policy is irrelevant.

The middle-of-the-roaders stress that companies would not supply such a large quantity of dividends unless they believed that this was what investors wanted. But that still leaves a puzzle. Even in the days when there was a large tax disadvantage to dividends in the US, many investors were apparently happy to hold high-payout stocks. Why? The response of the middle-of-the-roaders has been to argue that there are always plenty of wrinkles in the tax system which shareholders can use to avoid paying taxes on dividends. For example, instead of investing directly in common stocks,

[36]See R. H. Litzenberger and K. Ramaswamy, "The Effects of Dividends on Common Stock Prices: Tax Effects or Information Effects," *Journal of Finance* 37 (May 1982), pp. 429–443; and M. H. Miller and M. Scholes, "Dividends and Taxes: Some Empirical Evidence," *Journal of Political Economy* 90 (1982), pp. 1118–1141. Merton Miller provides a broad review of the empirical literature in "Behavioral Rationality in Finance: The Case of Dividends," *Journal of Business* 59 (October 1986), pp. S451–S468.

[37]See Narasimhan, M.S., and C Asha, 1997, "Implications of Dividend Tax on Corporate Financial Policies", The ICFAI Journal of Applied Finance, July, pp 11-28.

[38]F. Black and M. S. Scholes, "The Effects of Dividend Yield and Dividend Policy on Common Stock Prices and Returns," *Journal of Financial Economics* 1 (May 1974), pp. 1–22; M. H. Miller and M. S. Scholes, "Dividends and Taxes," *Journal of Financial Economics* 6 (December 1978), pp. 333–364; and M. H. Miller, "Behavioral Rationality in Finance: The Case of Dividends," *Journal of Business* 59 (October 1986), pp. S451–S468.

they can do so through a pension fund or insurance company, which receives more favorable tax treatment. However, it is not clear that this is the whole story, for a high proportion of dividends are regularly paid out to wealthy individuals and included in their taxable income.[39]

There is another possible reason that U.S. companies may pay dividends even when these dividends result in higher tax bills. Companies that pay *low* dividends will be more attractive to highly taxed individuals; those that pay *high* dividends will have a greater proportion of pension funds or other tax-exempt institutions as their stockholders. These financial institutions are sophisticated investors; they monitor carefully the companies that they invest in and they bring pressure on poor managers to perform. Successful, well-managed companies are happy to have financial institutions as investors, but their poorly managed brethren would prefer unsophisticated and more docile stockholders.

You can probably see now where the argument is heading. Well-managed companies want to signal their worth. They can do so by having a high proportion of demanding institutions among their stockholders. How do they achieve this? By paying high dividends. Those shareholders who pay tax do not object to these high dividends as long as the effect is to encourage institutional investors who are prepared to put the time and effort into monitoring the management.[40]

Alternative Tax Systems

In India shareholders' returns are taxed twice. They are taxed at the corporate level, both when the company earns profit (corporate tax) and when it distributes dividend (dividend distribution tax). These two tiers of tax are illustrated in Table 16.2, which shows the after-tax return to the shareholder if the company distributes all its income as dividends. We assume the company earns Rs. 100 a share before tax and therefore pays corporate tax of 0.3366 × 100 = Rs. 33.66. This leaves Rs. 66.34 a share to be paid out as a dividend, which is then subject to second layer of tax. Since the effective dividend distribution tax rate in India is 14.025 percent, the company can at best give Rs. 58.18 a share as dividends. This dividend will be subject to a dividend distribution tax of Rs. 8.16 a share. Instead of distribution Rs. 66.34 as dividends, the company can buyback shares worth Rs. 66.34. In that case, the individual shareholders will have to pay capital gains tax on the difference between Rs. 66.34 and the cost of acquisition of the proportionate number of shares. Let's assume that the cost of acquiring the necessary number of shares (that the company is able to buy back today by offering Rs. 66.34) is Rs. 25.54. Then the shareholder will have to pay capital gains tax equal to 0.2 × (Rs. 66.34 – Rs. 25.54) = Rs. 8.16. So the net payoff to the shareholder will be Rs. 66.34 – Rs. 8.16 = Rs. 58.18. This is the same payoff that the individual shareholder will receive if the company pays off the entire income as dividends. Therefore, whether the individual shareholders prefer dividends to share buyback or not will depend on the actual capital gains. We can similarly show that the foreign institutional investors will always prefer share buyback to dividends irrespective of the actual cost of acquiring the shares.

Of course, dividends are regularly paid by companies that operate under very different tax systems. In fact, the two-tier Indian system (or for that matter the U.S. system) is relatively rare. Some countries tax investors at a higher rate on dividends than on capital gains, but they offset this by having a split-rate system of corporate taxes. Profits that are retained in the business attract a higher rate of corporate tax than profits that are distributed. Under this split-rate system, tax-exempt investors prefer that the company pay high dividends, whereas millionaires might vote to retain profits.

[39]See, for example, F. Allen and R. Michaely, "Payout Policy," in G. Constantinides, M. Harris, and R. Stulz (eds.), *Handbook of the Economics of Finance: Corporate Finance* (Amsterdam: North-Holland, 2003).

[40]This signaling argument is developed in F. Allen, A. E. Bernardo, and I. Welch, "A Theory of Dividends Based on Tax Clienteles," *Journal of Finance* 55 (December 2000), pp. 2499–2536.

Operating income	Rs. 100	
Corporate tax at 33.66%	33.66 ←	Corporate tax
After-tax income	66.34	
Distributed as Dividends	58.18	
Dividend Distribution tax paid	8.16 ←	Dividend distribution tax paid by companies

TABLE 16.2

In India, returns to shareholders are taxed twice. This example assumes dividends are distributed in such a manner that the dividends and the dividend distribution tax exhaust the total after-tax income.

	Rate of Income Tax		
	15%	30%	47%
Operating income	100	100	100
Corporate tax (T_c = .30)	30	30	30
After-tax income	70	70	70
Grossed-up dividend	100	100	100
Income tax	15	30	47
Tax credit for corporate payment	−30	−30	−30
Tax due from shareholder	−15	0	17
Available to shareholder	85	70	53

TABLE 16.3

Under imputation tax systems, such as that in Australia, shareholders receive a tax credit for the corporate tax that the firm has paid (figures in Australian dollars per share).

In some other countries, shareholders' returns are not taxed twice. For example, in Australia shareholders are taxed on dividends, but they may deduct from this tax bill their share of the corporate tax that the company has paid. This is known as an *imputation tax system.* Table 16.3 shows how the imputation system works. Suppose that an Australian company earns pretax profits of $A100 a share. After it pays corporate tax at 30 percent, the profit is $A70 a share. The company now declares a net dividend of $A70 and sends each shareholder a check for this amount. This dividend is accompanied by a tax credit saying that the company has already paid $A30 of tax on the shareholder's behalf. Thus shareholders are treated as if each received a total, or gross, dividend of 70 + 30 = $A100 and paid tax of $A30. If the shareholder's tax rate is 30 percent, there is no more tax to pay and the shareholder retains the net dividend of $A70. If the shareholder pays tax at the top personal rate of 47 percent, then he or she is required to pay an additional $17 of tax; if the tax rate is 15 percent (the rate at which Australian pension funds are taxed), then the shareholder receives a *refund* of 30 − 15 = $A15.[41]

Under an imputation tax system, millionaires have to cough up the extra personal tax on dividends. If this is more than the tax that they would pay on capital gains, then millionaires would prefer that the company does not distribute earnings. If it is the other way around, they would prefer dividends.[42] Investors with low tax rates have no doubts about the matter. If the company pays a dividend, these investors receive a check from the revenue service for the excess tax that the company has paid, and therefore they prefer high payout rates.

Look once again at Table 16.3 and think what would happen if the corporate tax rate was zero. The shareholder with a 15 percent tax rate would still end up with $A85, and the shareholder with the 47 percent rate would still receive $A53. Thus, under an imputation tax system, when a company pays out all its earnings, there is effectively only one layer of tax—the tax on the shareholder. The revenue service collects this tax through the company and then sends a demand to the shareholder for any excess tax or makes a refund for any overpayment.[43]

[41] In Australia, shareholders receive a credit for the full amount of corporate tax that has been paid on their behalf. In other countries the tax credit is less than the corporate tax rate. You can think of the tax system in these countries as lying between the Australian and U.S. systems.

[42] In the case of Australia the tax rate on capital gains is the same as the tax rate on dividends. However, for securities that are held for more than 12 months only half of the gain is taxed.

[43] This is only true for earnings that are paid out as dividends. Retained earnings are subject to corporate tax. Shareholders get the benefit of retained earnings in the form of capital gains.

SUMMARY

When managers decide on the dividend, their primary concern seems to be to give shareholders a "fair" payment on their investment. Most managers have a conscious or subconscious long-term target payout rate. But if firms simply applied the target payout rate to each year's earnings, dividends could fluctuate wildly. Managers therefore try to ensure that any dividend payment is sustainable by moving only partway toward the target in each year.

As an alternative to dividend payments, the company can repurchase its own stock. In recent years companies have bought back their stock in large quantities, but repurchases do not generally substitute for dividends. Instead they are used to return unwanted cash to shareholders or to retire equity and replace it with debt. Investors usually interpret stock repurchases as an indication of managers' optimism.

If we hold the company's investment decision and capital structure constant, then payout policy is a trade-off between cash dividends and the issue or repurchase of common stock. Should firms retain whatever earnings are necessary to finance growth and pay out any residual as cash dividends? Or should they increase dividends and then (sooner or later) issue stock to make up the shortfall of equity capital? Or should they reduce dividends and use the released cash to repurchase stock?

If we lived in an ideally simple and perfect world, there would be no problem, for the choice would have no effect on market value. The controversy centers on the effects of dividend policy in our flawed world. Many investors believe that a high dividend payout enhances share price. Perhaps they welcome the self-discipline that comes from spending only dividend income rather than having to decide whether they should dip into capital. We suspect also that investors often pressure companies to increase dividends when they do not trust management to spend free cash flow wisely. In this case a dividend increase may lead to a rise in the stock price not because investors like dividends as such but because they want managers to run a tighter ship.

The most obvious and serious market imperfection has been the different tax treatment of dividends and capital gains. In the past, dividends in the United States have often been much more heavily taxed than capital gains. In 2003 the maximum tax rate was set at 15 percent on both dividends and gains, though capital gains continued to enjoy one advantage—the tax payment is not due until any gain was realized. If dividends are more heavily taxed, highly taxed investors should hold mostly low-payout stocks, and we would expect high-payout stocks to offer investors the compensation of greater pretax returns.

This view has a respectable theoretical basis. It is supported by some evidence that, when dividends were at a significant tax disadvantage in the United States, gross returns did reflect the tax differential. The weak link is the theory's silence on the question of why companies continued to distribute such large dividends when they landed investors with such large tax bills.

The third view of dividend policy starts with the notion that the actions of companies do reflect investors' preferences; thus the fact that companies pay substantial dividends is the best evidence that investors want them. If the supply of dividends exactly meets the demand, no single company could improve its market value by changing its payout policy. Unfortunately, this third view does not say why dividends are what they are and not some other amount.

It is difficult to be dogmatic over these controversies. If investment policy and borrowing are held constant, then the arguments over payout policy are largely about shuffling money from one pocket to another. Unless there are substantial tax consequences to these shuffles, it is unlikely that firm value is greatly affected either by the total amount of the payout or the choice between dividends and repurchase. Investors' concern with payout decisions seems to stem mainly from the information that they read into managers' actions.

If dividend policy doesn't affect firm value, then you don't need to worry about it when estimating the cost of capital. But if (say) you believe that tax effects are important, then in principle you should recognize that investors demand higher returns from high-payout stocks. Some financial managers do take dividend policy into account when estimating the cost of capital, but most become de facto middle-of-the-roaders. It seems that the effects of dividend policy are too uncertain to justify fine-tuning such estimates.

FURTHER READING

The two classic papers on payout policy are:

J. Lintner, "Distribution of Incomes of Corporations among Dividends, Retained Earnings, and Taxes," *American Economic Review* 46: (May 1956), pp. 97–113.

M. H. Miller and F. Modigliani, "Dividend Policy, Growth, and the Valuation of Shares," *Journal of Business*, 34: (October 1961), pp. 411–433.

For a comprehensive review of the literature on payout policy, see:

F. Allen and R. Michaely, "Payout Policy," in G. Constantinides, M. Harris, and R. Stulz, (eds.), *Handbook of the Economics of Finance: Corporate Finance* (Amsterdam: North-Holland, 2003).

CONCEPT REVIEW QUESTIONS

1. What are the two ways that firms pay out cash to shareholders? Which method has grown most rapidly in popularity? (page 419)
2. Are companies free to declare whatever dividends they choose? Why or why not? (page 421)
3. What are the four main ways to repurchase stock? (page 422)

For additional Concept Review Questions, please visit us at www.mhhe.com/bmam8e or refer to your Student CD.

QUIZ

1. In 2004 IBM paid a regular quarterly dividend of $.18 a share.
   a. Match each of the following sets of dates:

(A1) 27 April 2004	(B1) Record date
(A2) 5 May 2004	(B2) Payment date
(A3) 6 May 2004	(B3) Ex-dividend date
(A4) 10 May 2004	(B4) Last with-dividend date
(A5) 10 June 2004	(B5) Declaration date

   b. On one of these dates the stock price is likely to fall by about the value of the dividend. Which date? Why?
   c. IBM's stock price at the end of April was $88.17. What was the dividend yield?
   d. If earnings per share for 2004 are $4.95, what is the percentage payout rate?
   e. Suppose that in 2004 the company paid a 10 percent stock dividend. What would be the expected fall in price?

2. Here are several "facts" about typical corporate dividend policies. Which are true and which false?
   a. Companies decide each year's dividend by looking at their capital expenditure requirements and then distributing whatever cash is left over.
   b. Most companies have some notion of a target payout ratio.
   c. They set each year's dividend equal to the target payout ratio times that year's earnings.
   d. Managers and investors seem more concerned with dividend changes than with dividend levels.
   e. Managers often increase dividends temporarily when earnings are unexpectedly high for a year or two.
   f. Companies undertaking substantial share repurchases usually finance them with an offsetting reduction in cash dividends.
3. a. Wotan owns 1,000 shares of a firm that has just announced an increase in its dividend from Rs. 2.00 to Rs. 2.50 a share. The share price is currently Rs. 150. If Wotan does not wish to spend the extra cash, what should he do to offset the dividend increase?
   b. Brunhilde owns 1,000 shares of a firm that has just announced a dividend cut from Rs. 8.00 a share to Rs. 5.00. The share price is currently Rs. 200. If Brunhilde wishes to maintain her consumption, what should she do to offset the dividend cut?
4. Patriot Games has 5 million shares outstanding. The president has proposed that, given the firm's large cash holdings, the annual dividend should be increased from Rs. 6.00 a share to Rs. 8.00. If you agree with the president's plans for investment and capital structure, what else must the company do as a consequence of the dividend increase?
5. House of Haddock has 5,000 shares outstanding and the stock price is $140. The company is expected to pay a dividend of $20 per share next year and thereafter the dividend is expected to grow indefinitely by 5 percent a year. The President, George Mullet, now makes a surprise announcement: He says that the company will henceforth distribute half the cash in the form of dividends and the remainder will be used to repurchase stock.
   a. What is the total value of the company before and after the announcement? What is the value of one share?
   b. What is the expected stream of dividends per share for an investor who plans to retain his shares rather than sell them back to the company? Check your estimate of share value by discounting this stream of dividends per share.
6. Here are key financial data for House of Herring, Inc.:

Earnings per share for 2012	$5.50
Number of shares outstanding	40 million
Target payout ratio	50%
Planned dividend per share	$2.75
Stock price, year-end 2012	$130

   House of Herring plans to pay the entire dividend early in January 2013. All corporate and personal taxes were repealed in 2011.
   a. Other things equal, what will be House of Herring's stock price after the planned dividend payout?
   b. Suppose the company cancels the dividend and announces that it will use the money saved to repurchase shares. What happens to the stock price on the announcement date? Assume that investors learn nothing about the company's prospects from the announcement. How many shares will the company need to repurchase?
   c. Suppose the company increases dividends to $5.50 per share and then issues new shares to recoup the extra cash paid out as dividends. What happens to the with- and ex-dividend share prices? How many shares will need to be issued? Again, assume investors learn nothing from the announcement about House of Herring's prospects.

7. Answer the following question twice, once assuming current tax law and once assuming that dividends are taxed at the hands of the shareholders at the rate of 30% and the capital gains tax rate is 20%.

Suppose all investments offered the same expected return before tax. Consider two equally risky shares, Hi and Lo. Hi shares pay a generous dividend and offer low expected capital gains. Lo shares pay low dividends and offer high expected capital gains. Which of the following investors would prefer Lo shares? Which would prefer the Hi shares? Which should not care? (Assume that any stock purchased will be sold after one year.)
   a. A high net worth individual
   b. An FII
   c. LIC
   d. An NRI
   e. An MNC
   f. An Indian company

PRACTICE QUESTIONS

1. Find out an Indian company that has announced an interim dividend recently.
   a. How frequently does the company pay a regular dividend?
   b. What is the amount of the dividend?
   c. By what amount must your stock be registered for you to receive the dividend? (Visit the website of any of the online brokerage houses to get this information)
   d. How many weeks later is the dividend paid?
   e. Look up the stock price and calculate the annual yield on the stock.
2. Which types of companies would you expect to distribute a relatively high or low proportion of current earnings? Which would you expect to have a relatively high or low price–earnings ratio?
   a. High-risk companies.
   b. Companies that have experienced an unexpected decline in profits.
   c. Companies that *expect* to experience a decline in profits.
   d. Growth companies with valuable future investment opportunities.
3. Little Oil has outstanding 1 million shares with a total market value of Rs. 20 million. The firm is expected to pay Rs. 1 million of dividends next year, and thereafter the amount paid out is expected to grow by 5 percent a year in perpetuity. Thus the expected dividend is Rs. 1.05 million in year 2, Rs. 1.105 million in year 3, and so on. However, the company has heard that the value of a share depends on the flow of dividends, and therefore it announces that next year's dividend will be increased to Rs. 2 million and that the extra cash will be raised immediately by an issue of shares. After that, the total amount paid out each year will be as previously forecasted, that is, Rs. 1.05 million in year 2 and increasing by 5 percent in each subsequent year.
   a. At what price will the new shares be issued in year 1?
   b. How many shares will the firm need to issue?
   c. What will be the expected dividend payments on these new shares, and what therefore will be paid out to the *old* shareholders after year 1?
   d. Show that the present value of the cash flows to current shareholders remains Rs. 20 million.
4. We stated in Section 16.5 that MM's proof of dividend irrelevance assumes that new shares are sold at a fair price. Look back at Practice Question 3. Assume that new shares are issued in year 1 at Rs. 10 a share. Show who gains and who loses. Is dividend policy still irrelevant? Why or why not?
5. Respond to the following comment: "It's all very well saying that I can sell shares to cover cash needs, but that may mean selling at the bottom of the market. If the company pays a regular cash dividend, investors avoid that risk."

6. Refer to the first balance sheet prepared for Rational Demiconductor in Section 16.5. Again it uses cash to pay a Rs. 1,000 cash dividend, planning to issue stock to recover the cash required for investment. But this time catastrophe hits before the stock can be issued. A new pollution control regulation increases manufacturing costs to the extent that the value of Rational Demiconductor's existing business is cut in half, to Rs. 4,500. The NPV of the new investment opportunity is unaffected, however. Show that dividend policy is still irrelevant.

7. "Many companies use stock repurchases to increase earnings per share. For example, suppose that a company is in the following position:

Net profit	Rs. 10 million
Number of shares before repurchase	1 million
Earnings per share	Rs. 10
Price–earnings ratio	20
Share price	Rs. 200

The company now repurchases 200,000 shares at Rs. 200 a share. The number of shares declines to 800,000 shares and earnings per share increase to Rs. 12.50. Assuming the price–earnings ratio stays at 20, the share price must rise to Rs. 250." Discuss.

8. Hors d'Age Cheeseworks has been paying a regular cash dividend of $4 per share each year for over a decade. The company is paying out all its earnings as dividends and is not expected to grow. There are 100,000 shares outstanding selling for $80 per share. The company has sufficient cash on hand to pay the next annual dividend.

   Suppose that Hors d'Age decides to cut its cash dividend to zero and announces that it will repurchase shares instead.

   a. What is the immediate stock price reaction? Ignore taxes, and assume that the repurchase program conveys no information about operating profitability or business risk.
   b. How many shares will Hors d'Age purchase?
   c. Project and compare future stock prices for the old and new policies. Do this for at least years 1, 2, and 3.

9. An article on stock repurchase in the *Los Angeles Times* noted: "An increasing number of companies are finding that the best investment they can make these days is in themselves." Discuss this view. How is the desirability of repurchase affected by company prospects and the price of its stock?

10. Comment briefly on each of the following statements:
    a. "Unlike American firms, which are always being pressured by their shareholders to increase dividends, Japanese companies pay out a much smaller proportion of earnings and so enjoy a lower cost of capital."
    b. "Unlike new capital, which needs a stream of new dividends to service it, retained earnings have zero cost."
    c. "If a company repurchases stock instead of paying a dividend, the number of shares falls and earnings per share rise. Thus stock repurchase must always be preferred to paying dividends."

11. Formaggio Vecchio has just announced its regular quarterly cash dividend of $1 per share.
    a. When will the stock price fall to reflect this dividend payment—on the record date, the ex-dividend date, or the payment date?
    b. Assume that there are no taxes. By how much is the stock price likely to fall?
    c. Now assume that *all* investors pay tax of 30 percent on dividends and nothing on capital gains. What is the likely fall in the stock price?
    d. Suppose, finally, that everything is the same as in part (c), except that security dealers pay tax on *both* dividends and capital gains. How would you expect your answer to (c) to change? Explain.

12. Refer back to Practice Question 11. Assume no taxes and a stock price immediately after the dividend announcement of $. 100.
    a. If you own 100 shares, what is the value of your investment? How does the dividend payment affect your wealth?
    b. Now suppose that Formaggio Vecchio cancels the dividend payment and announces that it will repurchase 1 percent of its stock at $100. Do you rejoice or yawn? Explain.
13. The shares of A and B both sell for Rs. 100 and offer a pretax return of 10 percent. However, in the case of company A the return is entirely in the form of dividend yield (the company pays a regular annual dividend of Rs. 10 a share), while in the case of B the return comes entirely as capital gain (the shares appreciate by 10 percent a year). Suppose that dividends and capital gains are both taxed at 30 percent. What is the after-tax return on share A? What is the after-tax return on share B to an investor who sells after two years? What about an investor who sells after 10 years?
14. **a.** The Horner Pie Company pays a quarterly dividend of $1. Suppose that the stock price is expected to fall on the ex-dividend date by $.90. Would you prefer to buy on the with-dividend date or the ex-dividend date if you were (i) a tax-free investor, (ii) an investor with a marginal tax rate of 40 percent on income and 16 percent on capital gains?
    b. In a study of ex-dividend behavior, Elton and Gruber[44] estimate that the stock price fell on the average by 85 percent of the dividend. Assuming that the tax rate on capital gains was 40 percent of the rate on income tax, what did Elton and Gruber's result imply about investors' marginal rate of income tax?
    c. Elton and Gruber also observed that the ex-dividend price fall was different for high-payout stocks and for low-payout stocks. Which group would you expect to show the larger price fall as a proportion of the dividend?
    d. Would the fact that investors can trade stocks freely around the ex-dividend date alter your interpretation of Elton and Gruber's study?
    e. Suppose Elton and Gruber repeat their tests for 2004, when the tax rate was the same on dividends and capital gains. How would you expect their results to change?
15. The middle-of-the-road party holds that dividend policy doesn't matter because the *supply* of high-, medium-, and low-payout stocks has already adjusted to satisfy investors' demands. Investors who like generous dividends hold stocks which give them all the dividends that they want. Investors who want capital gains see a surfeit of low-payout stocks to choose from. Thus, high-payout firms cannot gain by transforming to low-payout firms, or vice versa.

    Suppose the government reduces the tax rate on dividends. Suppose that before this change the supply of dividends matched investor needs. How would you expect the tax change to affect the total cash dividends paid by Indian corporations and the proportion of high- versus low-payout companies? Would dividend policy still be irrelevant after any dividend supply adjustments are completed? Explain.
16. Suppose, in the 2007–08 Budget, the Finance Minister of India reduces the securities transaction tax to 0.1%. Will it have any effect on the decision of the FIIs to buy the shares of a company that pays high dividend vis-à-vis another company that prefers to buy back shares.

CHALLENGE QUESTIONS

1. Consider the following two statements: "Dividend policy is irrelevant," and "Stock price is the present value of expected future dividends." (See Chapter 4.) They *sound* contradictory. This question is designed to show that they are fully consistent.

    The current price of the shares of Charles River Mining Corporation is Rs. 50. Next year's earnings and dividends per share are Rs. 4 and Rs. 2, respectively. Investors expect perpetual growth at 8 percent per year. The expected rate of return demanded by investors is $r = 12$ percent.

[44] E. J. Elton and M. J. Gruber, "Marginal Stockholders' Tax Rates and the Clientele Effect," *Review of Economics and Statistics* 52 (1970), pp. 68–74.

We can use the perpetual-growth model to calculate stock price.

$$P_0 = \frac{\text{DIV}}{r - g} = \frac{2}{.12 - .08} = 50$$

Suppose that Charles River Mining announces that it will switch to a 100 percent payout policy, issuing shares as necessary to finance growth. Use the perpetual-growth model to show that current stock price is unchanged.

2. "If a company pays a dividend, the investor is liable for tax on the total value of the dividend. If instead the company distributes the cash by stock repurchase, the investor is liable for tax only on any capital gain rather than on the entire amount. Therefore, even if the tax rates on dividend income and capital gains are the same, stock repurchase is always preferable to a dividend payment." Explain with a simple example why this is not the case. (Ignore the fact that capital gains may be postponed.)
3. Adherents of the "dividends-are-good" school sometimes point to the fact that stocks with high yields tend to have above-average price–earnings multiples. Is this evidence convincing? Discuss.
4. Suppose that there are just three types of investor with the following tax rates:

	Individuals	Corporations	Institutions
Dividends	50%	5%	0%
Capital gains	15	35	0

Individuals invest a total of Rs. 80 billion in stock and corporations invest Rs. 10 billion. The remaining stock is held by the institutions. All three groups simply seek to maximize their after-tax income.

These investors can choose from three types of stock offering the following pretax payouts:

	Low Payout	Medium Payout	High Payout
Dividends	Rs. 5	Rs. 5	Rs.30
Capital gains	15	5	0

These payoffs are expected to persist in perpetuity. The low-payout stocks have a total market value of Rs. 100 billion, the medium-payout stocks have a value of Rs. 50 billion, and the high-payout stocks have a value of Rs. 120 billion.

a. Who are the marginal investors that determine the prices of the stocks?
b. Suppose that this marginal group of investors requires a 12 percent after-tax return. What are the prices of the low-, medium-, and high-payout stocks?
c. Calculate the after-tax returns of the three types of stock for each investor group.
d. What are the dollar amounts of the three types of stock held by each investor group?

CHAPTER [17]

DOES DEBT POLICY MATTER?

A FIRM'S BASIC resource is the stream of cash flows produced by its assets. When the firm is financed entirely by common stock, all those cash flows belong to the stockholders. When it issues both debt and equity securities, it splits the cash flows into two streams, a relatively safe stream that goes to the debtholders and a riskier stream that goes to the stockholders.

The firm's mix of debt and equity financing is called its **capital structure.** Of course capital structure is not just "debt versus equity." There are many different flavors of debt, at least two flavors of equity (common versus preferred), plus hybrids such as convertible bonds. The firm can issue dozens of distinct securities in countless combinations. It attempts to find the particular combination that maximizes the overall market value of the firm.

Are such attempts worthwhile? We must consider the possibility that *no* combination has any greater appeal than any other. Perhaps the really important decisions concern the company's assets, and decisions about capital structure are mere details—matters to be attended to but not worried about.

Modigliani and Miller (MM), who showed that payout policy doesn't matter in perfect capital markets, also showed that financing decisions don't matter in perfect markets. Their famous "proposition 1" states that a firm cannot change the total value of its securities just by splitting its cash flows into different streams: The firm's value is determined by its real assets, not by the securities it issues. Thus capital structure is irrelevant as long as the firm's investment decisions are taken as given.

MM's proposition 1 allows complete separation of investment and financing decisions. It implies that any firm could use the capital budgeting procedures presented in Chapters 2 through 12 without worrying about where the money for capital expenditures comes from. In those chapters, we assumed all-equity financing without really thinking about it. If MM are right, that is exactly the right approach. If the firm uses a mix of debt and equity financing, its overall cost of capital will be exactly the same as its cost of equity with all-equity financing.

We believe that in practice capital structure does matter, but we nevertheless devote all of this chapter to MM's argument. If you don't fully understand the conditions under which MM's theory holds, you won't fully understand why one capital structure is better than another. The financial manager needs to know what kinds of market imperfection to look for.

For example, the firm may invent some new security that a particular clientele of investors is willing to buy at a premium price, thereby increasing the overall market value of the firm. (We will argue, however, that such financial innovations are easily copied and that any gains in value will be confined to the first few issuers.)

In Chapter 18 we undertake a detailed analysis of the imperfections that are most likely to make a difference, including taxes, the costs of bankruptcy and financial distress, the costs of writing and enforcing complicated debt contracts, differences created by imperfect information, and the effects of debt on incentives for management. In Chapter 19 we show how such imperfections (especially taxes) affect the weighted-average cost of capital and the value of the firm.

17.1 THE EFFECT OF FINANCIAL LEVERAGE IN A COMPETITIVE TAX-FREE ECONOMY

Financial managers try to find the combination of securities that has the greatest overall appeal to investors—the combination that maximizes the market value of the firm. Before tackling this problem, we should check whether a policy which maximizes firm value also maximizes the wealth of the shareholders.

Let D and E denote the market values of the outstanding debt and equity of the Wapshot Mining Company. Wapshot's 1,000 shares sell for Rs. 50 apiece. Thus

$$E = 1{,}000 \times 50 = \text{Rs. } 50{,}000$$

Wapshot has also borrowed Rs. 25,000, and so V, the aggregate market value of all Wapshot's outstanding securities, is

$$V = D + E = \text{Rs. } 75{,}000$$

Wapshot's stock is known as *levered equity*. Its stockholders face the benefits and costs of **financial leverage**, or *gearing*. Suppose that Wapshot "levers up" still further by borrowing an additional Rs. 10,000 and paying the proceeds out to shareholders as a special dividend of Rs. 10 per share. This substitutes debt for equity capital with no impact on Wapshot's assets.

What will Wapshot's equity be worth after the special dividend is paid? We have two unknowns, E and V:

Old debt	Rs. 25,000	Rs. 35,000 = D
New debt	Rs. 10,000	
Equity		? = E
Firm value		? = V

If V is Rs. 75,000 as before, then E must be $V - D = 75{,}000 - 35{,}000 = $ Rs. 40,000. Stockholders have suffered a capital loss which exactly offsets the Rs. 10,000 special dividend. But if V *increases* to, say, Rs. 80,000 as a result of the change in capital structure, then $E =$ Rs. 45,000 and the stockholders are Rs. 5,000 ahead. In general, any increase or decrease in V caused by a shift in capital structure accrues to the firm's stockholders. We conclude that a policy which maximizes the market value of the firm is also best for the firm's stockholders.

This conclusion rests on two important assumptions: first, that Wapshot can ignore payout policy and, second, that after the change in capital structure the old and new debt is *worth* Rs. 35,000.

Payout policy may or may not be relevant, but there is no need to repeat the discussion of Chapter 16. We need only note that shifts in capital structure sometimes force important decisions about payout policy. Perhaps Wapshot's cash dividend has costs or benefits which should be considered in addition to any benefits achieved by its increased financial leverage.

Our second assumption that old and new debt ends up worth Rs. 35,000 seems innocuous. But it could be wrong. Perhaps the new borrowing has increased the risk of the old bonds. If the holders of old bonds cannot demand a higher rate of interest to compensate for the increased risk, the value of their investment is reduced. In this case Wapshot's stockholders gain at the expense of the holders of old bonds even though the overall value of the debt and equity is unchanged.

But this anticipates issues better left to Chapter 18. In this chapter we will assume that any issue of debt has no effect on the market value of existing debt.

Enter Modigliani and Miller

Let us accept that the financial manager would like to find the combination of securities that maximizes the value of the firm. How is this done? MM's answer is that the financial manager should stop worrying: In a perfect market any combination of securities is as good as another. The value of the firm is unaffected by its choice of capital structure.[1]

You can see this by imagining two firms that generate the same stream of operating income and differ only in their capital structure. Firm U is unlevered. Therefore the total value of its equity E_U is the same as the total value of the firm V_U. Firm, L, on the other hand, is levered. The value of its stock is, therefore, equal to the value of the firm less the value of the debt: $E_L = V_L - D_L$.

Now think which of these firms you would prefer to invest in. If you don't want to take much risk, you can buy common stock in the unlevered firm U. For example, if you buy 1 percent of firm U's shares, your investment is $.01V_U$ and you are entitled to 1 percent of the gross profits:

Rupee Investment	Rupee Return
$.01V_U$	$.01 \times$ Profits

Now compare this with an alternative strategy. This is to purchase the same fraction of *both* the debt and the equity of firm L. Your investment and return would then be as follows:

	Rupee Investment	Rupee Return
Debt	$.01D_L$	$.01 \times$ Interest
Equity	$.01E_L$	$.01 \times$ (Profits − interest)
Total	$.01\,(D_L + E_L)$ $= .01V_L$	$.01 \times$ Profits

Both strategies offer the same payoff: 1 percent of the firm's profits. In well-functioning markets two investments that offer the same payoff must have the same cost. Therefore, $.01V_U$ must equal $.01V_L$: The value of the unlevered firm must equal the value of the levered firm.

Suppose that you are willing to run a little more risk. You decide to buy 1 percent of the outstanding shares in the *levered* firm. Your investment and return are now as follows:

Rupee Investment	Rupee Return
$.01E_L$ $= .01(V_L - D_L)$	$.01 \times$ (Profits − interest)

But there is an alternative strategy. This is to borrow $.01D_L$ on your own account and purchase 1 percent of the stock of the *unlevered* firm. In this case, your borrowing gives you an immediate cash *inflow* of $.01D_L$, but you have to pay interest on your loan equal to 1 percent of the interest that is paid by firm L. Your total investment and return are, therefore, as follows:

[1]F. Modigliani and M. H. Miller, "The Cost of Capital, Corporation Finance and the Theory of Investment," *American Economic Review* 48 (June 1958), pp. 261–297. MM's basic argument was anticipated in 1938 by J. B. Williams and to some extent by David Durand. See J. B. Williams, *The Theory of Investment Value*, Harvard University Press, Cambridge, MA, 1938; and D. Durand, "Cost of Debt and Equity Funds for Business: Trends and Problems of Measurement," in *Conference on Research in Business Finance*, National Bureau of Economic Research, New York, 1952.

Again both strategies offer the same payoff: 1 percent of profits after interest. Therefore, both investments must have the same cost. The payoff $.01(V_U - D_L)$ must equal $.01(V_L - D_L)$ and V_U must equal V_L.

	Rupee Investment	Rupee Return
Borrowing	$-.01D_L$	$-.01 \times$ Interest
Equity	$.01V_U$	$.01 \times$ Profits
Total	$.01(V_U - D_L)$	$.01 \times$ (Profits − interest)

It does not matter whether the world is full of risk-averse chickens or venturesome lions. All would agree that the value of the unlevered firm U must be equal to the value of the levered firm L. As long as investors can borrow or lend on their own account on the same terms as the firm, they can "undo" the effect of any changes in the firm's capital structure. This is the basis for MM's famous proposition 1: "The market value of any firm is independent of its capital structure."

The Law of Conservation of Value

MM's argument that debt policy is irrelevant is an application of an astonishingly simple idea. If we have two streams of cash flow, *A* and *B*, then the present value of *A* + *B* is equal to the present value of *A* plus the present value of *B*. We met this principle of *value additivity* in our discussion of capital budgeting, where we saw that the present value of two assets combined is equal to the sum of their present values considered separately.

In the present context we are not combining assets but splitting them up. But value additivity works just as well in reverse. We can slice a cash flow into as many parts as we like; the values of the parts will always sum back to the value of the unsliced stream. (Of course, we have to make sure that none of the stream is lost in the slicing. We cannot say, "The value of a pie is independent of how it is sliced," if the slicer is also a nibbler.)

This is really a *law of conservation of value*. The value of an asset is preserved regardless of the nature of the claims against it. Thus proposition 1: Firm value is determined on the *left-hand* side of the balance sheet by real assets—not by the proportions of debt and equity securities issued to buy the assets.

The simplest ideas often have the widest application. For example, we could apply the law of conservation of value to the choice between issuing preferred stock, common stock, or some combination. The law implies that the choice is irrelevant, assuming perfect capital markets and providing that the choice does not affect the firm's investment, borrowing, and operating policies. If the total value of the equity "pie" (preferred and common combined) is fixed, the firm's owners (its common stockholders) do not care how this pie is sliced.

The law also applies to the *mix* of debt securities issued by the firm. The choices of long-term versus short-term, secured versus unsecured, senior versus subordinated, and convertible versus nonconvertible debt all should have no effect on the overall value of the firm.

Combining assets and splitting them up will not affect values as long as they do not affect an investor's choice. When we showed that capital structure does not affect choice, we implicitly

TABLE 17.1 Macbeth Spot Removers is entirely equity-financed. Although it expects to have an income of Rs. 1,500 a year in perpetuity, this income is not certain. This table shows the return to the stockholder under different assumptions about operating income. We assume no taxes.

Data				
Number of shares	1,000			
Price per share	Rs. 10			
Market value of shares	Rs. 10,000			
	Outcomes			
Operating income (Rs.)	500	1,000	**1,500**	2,000
Earnings per share (Rs.)	.50	1.00	**1.50**	2.00
Return on shares (%)	5	10	**15**	20
			Expected outcome	

assumed that both companies and individuals can borrow and lend at the same risk-free rate of interest. As long as this is so, individuals can undo the effect of any changes in the firm's capital structure.

In practice corporate debt is not risk-free and firms cannot escape with rates of interest appropriate to a government security. Some people's initial reaction is that this alone invalidates MM's proposition. It is a natural mistake, but capital structure can be irrelevant even when debt is risky.

If a company borrows money, it does not *guarantee* repayment: It repays the debt in full only if its assets are worth more than the debt obligation. The shareholders in the company, therefore, have limited liability.

Many individuals would like to borrow with limited liability. They might, therefore, be prepared to pay a small premium for levered shares *if the supply of levered shares were insufficient to meet their needs.*[2] But there are literally thousands of common stocks of companies that borrow. Therefore it is unlikely that an issue of debt would induce them to pay a premium for *your* shares.[3]

An Example of Proposition 1

Macbeth Spot Removers is reviewing its capital structure. Table 17.1 shows its current position. The company has no leverage and all the operating income is paid as dividends to the common stockholders (we assume still that there are no taxes). The expected earnings and dividends per share are Rs. 1.50, but this figure is by no means certain—it could turn out to be more or less than Rs. 1.50. The price of each share is Rs. 10. Since the firm expects to produce a level stream of earnings in perpetuity, the expected return on the share is equal to the earnings–price ratio, 1.50/10.00 = .15, or 15 percent.

[2]Of course, individuals could *create* limited liability if they chose. In other words, the lender could agree that borrowers need repay their debt in full only if the assets of company X are worth more than a certain amount. Presumably individuals don't enter into such arrangements because they can obtain limited liability more simply by investing in the stocks of levered companies.

[3]Capital structure is also irrelevant if each investor holds a fully diversified portfolio. In that case he or she owns *all* the risky securities offered by a company (both debt and equity). But anybody who owns *all* the risky securities doesn't care about how the cash flows are divided between different securities.

TABLE 17.2

Macbeth Spot Removers is wondering whether to issue Rs. 5,000 of debt at an interest rate of 10 percent and repurchase 500 shares. This table shows the return to the shareholder under different assumptions about operating income.

Data				
Number of shares	500			
Price per share	Rs.10			
Market value of shares	Rs.5,000			
Market value of debt	Rs.5,000			
Interest at 10%	Rs.500			
			Outcomes	
Operating income (Rs.)	500	1,000	**1,500**	2,000
Interest (Rs.)	500	500	**500**	500
Equity earnings (Rs.)	0	500	**1,000**	1,500
Earnings per share (Rs.)	0	1	**2**	3
Return on shares (%)	0	10	**20**	30
			Expected outcome	

Ms. Macbeth, the firm's president, has come to the conclusion that shareholders would be better off if the company had equal proportions of debt and equity. She therefore proposes to issue Rs. 5,000 of debt at an interest rate of 10 percent and use the proceeds to repurchase 500 shares. To support her proposal, Ms. Macbeth has analyzed the situation under different assumptions about operating income. The results of her calculations are shown in Table 17.2.

In order to see more clearly how leverage would affect earnings per share, Ms. Macbeth has also produced Figure 17.1. The green line shows how earnings per share would vary with operating income under the firm's current all-equity financing. It is, therefore, simply a plot of the data in Table 17.1. The blue line shows how earnings per share would vary given equal proportions of debt and equity. It is, therefore, a plot of the data in Table 17.2.

Ms. Macbeth reasons as follows: "It is clear that the effect of leverage depends on the company's income. If income is greater than Rs. 1,000, the return to the equity-holder is *increased* by leverage. If it is less than Rs. 1,000, the return is *reduced* by leverage. The return is unaffected when operating income is exactly Rs. 1,000. At this point the return on the market value of the assets is 10 percent, which is exactly equal to the interest rate on the debt. Our capital structure decision, therefore, boils down to what we think about income prospects. Since we expect operating income to be above the Rs. 1,000 break-even point, I believe we can best help our shareholders by going ahead with the Rs. 5,000 debt issue."

As financial manager of Macbeth Spot Removers, you reply as follows: "I agree that leverage will help the shareholder as long as our income is greater than Rs. 1,000. But your argument ignores the fact that Macbeth's shareholders have the alternative of borrowing on their own account. For example, suppose that an investor borrows Rs. 10 and then invests Rs. 20 in two unlevered Macbeth shares. This person has to put up only Rs. 10 of his or her own money. The payoff on the investment varies with Macbeth's operating income, as shown in Table 17.3. This is exactly the same

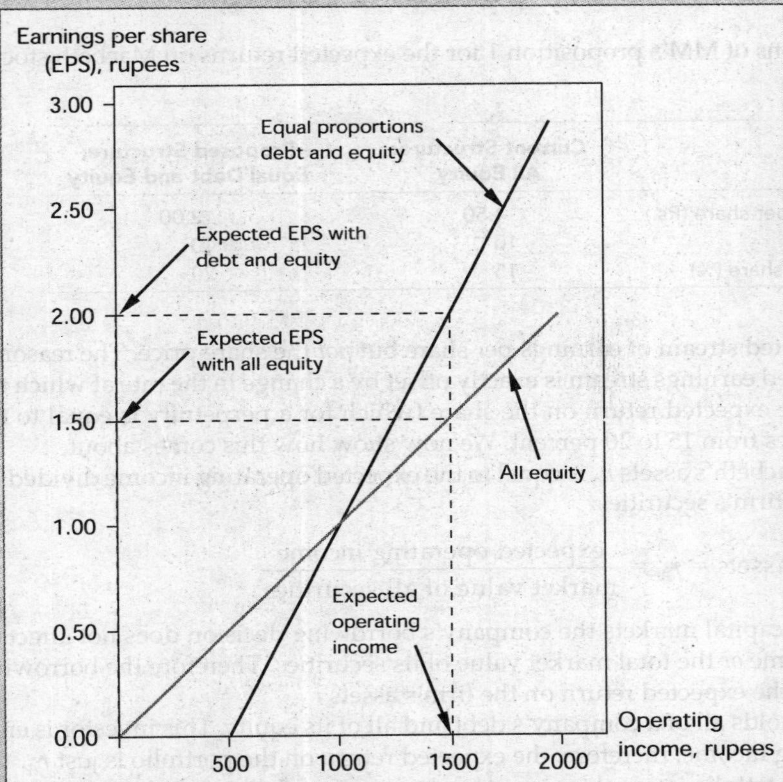

FIGURE 17.1

Borrowing increases Macbeth's EPS (earnings per share) when operating income is greater than Rs. 1,000 and reduces EPS when operating income is less than Rs. 1,000. Expected EPS rises from Rs. 1.50 to Rs. 2.

	Operating Income (Rs.)			
	500	**1,000**	**1,500**	**2,000**
Earnings on two shares (Rs.)	1	2	**3**	4
Less interest at 10% (Rs.)	1	1	**1**	1
Net earnings on investment (Rs.)	0	1	**2**	3
Return on Rs. 10 investment (%)	0	10	**20**	30
			Expected outcome	

TABLE 17.3

Individual investors can replicate Macbeth's leverage.

set of payoffs as the investor would get by buying one share in the levered company. (Compare the last two lines of Tables 17.2 and 17.3.) Therefore, a share in the levered company must also sell for Rs. 10. If Macbeth goes ahead and borrows, it will not allow investors to do anything that they could not do already, and so it will not increase value."

The argument that you are using is exactly the same as the one MM used to prove proposition 1.

17.2 FINANCIAL RISK AND EXPECTED RETURNS

Consider now the implications of MM's proposition 1 for the expected returns on Macbeth stock:

	Current Structure: All Equity	Proposed Structure: Equal Debt and Equity
Expected earnings per share (Rs.)	1.50	2.00
Price per share (Rs.)	10	10
Expected return on share (%)	15	20

Leverage increases the expected stream of earnings per share but *not* the share price. The reason is that the change in the expected earnings stream is exactly offset by a change in the rate at which the earnings are discounted. The expected return on the share (which for a perpetuity is equal to the earnings–price ratio) increases from 15 to 20 percent. We now show how this comes about.

The expected return on Macbeth's assets r_A is equal to the expected operating income divided by the total market value of the firm's securities:

$$\text{Expected return on assets} = r_A = \frac{\text{expected operating income}}{\text{market value of all securities}}$$

We have seen that in perfect capital markets the company's borrowing decision does not affect *either* the firm's operating income *or* the total market value of its securities. Therefore the borrowing decision also does not affect the expected return on the firm's assets r_A.

Suppose that an investor holds all of a company's debt and all of its equity. This investor is entitled to all the firm's operating income; therefore, the expected return on the portfolio is just r_A.

The expected return on a portfolio is equal to a weighted average of the expected returns on the individual holdings. Therefore the expected return on a portfolio consisting of *all* the firm's securities is

$$\begin{aligned}\text{Expected return on assets} &= (\text{proportion in debt} \times \text{expected return on debt})\\ &\quad + (\text{proportion in equity} \times \text{expected return on equity})\end{aligned}$$

$$r_A = \left(\frac{D}{D+E} \times r_D\right) + \left(\frac{E}{D+E} \times r_E\right)$$

This formula is of course an old friend from Chapter 9. The overall expected return r_A is called the *company cost of capital* or the *weighted-average cost of capital* (WACC).

We can turn the formula around to solve for r_E, the expected return to equity for a levered firm:

$$\begin{aligned}\text{Expected return on equity} &= \text{expected return on assets}\\ &\quad + (\text{expected return on assets} - \text{expected return on debt})\\ &\quad \times \text{debt–equity ratio}\end{aligned}$$

$$r_E = r_A + (r_A - r_D)\frac{D}{E}$$

Proposition 2

This is MM's proposition 2: The expected rate of return on the common stock of a levered firm increases in proportion to the debt–equity ratio (D/E), expressed in market values; the rate of increase depends on the spread between r_A, the expected rate of return on a portfolio of all the firm's securities, and r_D, the expected return on the debt. Note that $r_E = r_A$ if the firm has no debt.

We can check out this formula for Macbeth Spot Removers. Before the decision to borrow

$$r_E = r_A = \frac{\text{expected operating income}}{\text{market value of all securities}}$$
$$= \frac{1{,}500}{10{,}000} = .15, \text{ or } 15\%$$

If the firm goes ahead with its plan to borrow, the expected return on assets r_A is still 15 percent. The expected return on equity is

$$r_E = r_A + (r_A - r_D)\frac{D}{E}$$
$$= .15 + (.15 - .10)\frac{5{,}000}{5{,}000} = .20, \text{ or } 20\%$$

MM's Proposition 1 says that financial leverage has no effect on shareholders' wealth. Proposition 2 says that the rate of return they can expect to receive on their shares increases as the firm's debt–equity ratio increases. How can shareholders be indifferent to increased leverage when it increases expected return? The answer is that any increase in expected return is exactly offset by an increase in risk and therefore in shareholders' *required* rate of return.

Look at what happens to the risk of Macbeth shares if it moves to equal debt–equity proportions. Table 17.4 shows how a shortfall in operating income affects the payoff to the shareholders.

The debt–equity proportion does not affect the *dollar* risk borne by equity-holders. Suppose operating income drops from Rs. 1,500 to Rs. 500. Under all-equity financing, equity earnings drop by Rs. 1 per share. There are 1,000 outstanding shares, and so *total* equity earnings fall by Rs. 1 × 1,000 = Rs. 1,000. With 50 percent debt, the same drop in operating income reduces earnings per share by Rs. 2. But there are only 500 shares outstanding, and so total equity income drops by Rs. 2 × 500 = Rs. 1,000, just as in the all-equity case.

However, the debt–equity choice does amplify the spread of *percentage* returns. If the firm is all-equity-financed, a decline of Rs. 1,000 in the operating income reduces the return on the shares by 10 percent. If the firm issues risk-free debt with a fixed interest payment of Rs. 500 a year, then a decline of Rs. 1,000 in the operating income reduces the return on the shares by 20 percent. In other words, the effect of leverage is to double the amplitude of the swings in Macbeth's shares. Whatever the beta of the firm's shares before the refinancing, it would be twice as high afterward.

Now you can see why investors require higher returns on levered equity. The required return simply rises to match the increased risk.

TABLE 17.4

Financial leverage increases the risk of Macbeth shares. A Rs.1,000 drop in operating income reduces earnings per share by Rs.1 with all-equity financing, but by Rs.2 with 50 percent debt.

If operating income falls from		Rs.1,500	to Rs.500	Change
No debt:	Earnings per share	Rs.1.50	Rs.50	−Rs.1.00
	Return	15%	5%	−10%
50% debt:	Earnings per share	Rs.2.00	0	−Rs.2.00
	Return	20%	0	−20%

Example Let us revisit a numerical example from Chapter 9. We looked at a company with the following market-value balance sheet:

Asset value	100	Debt (D)	30	at $r_D = 7.5\%$
		Equity (E)	70	at $r_E = 15\%$
Asset value	100	Firm value (V)	100	

and an overall cost of capital of:

$$r_A = r_D\frac{D}{V} + r_E\frac{E}{V}$$

$$= \left(7.5 \times \frac{30}{100}\right) + \left(15 \times \frac{70}{100}\right) = 12.75\%$$

If the firm is contemplating investment in a project that has the same risk as the firm's existing business, the opportunity cost of capital for this project is the same as the firm's cost of capital; in other words, it is 12.75 percent.

What would happen if the firm issued an additional 10 of debt and used the cash to repurchase 10 of its equity? The revised market-value balance sheet is

Asset value	100	Debt value (D)	40
		Equity value (E)	60
Asset value	100	Firm value (V)	100

The change in financial structure does not affect the amount or risk of the cash flows on the total package of debt and equity. Therefore, if investors required a return of 12.75 percent on the total package before the refinancing, they must require a 12.75 percent return on the firm's assets afterward.

Although the required return on the *package* of debt and equity is unaffected, the change in financial structure does affect the required return on the individual securities. Since the company has more debt than before, the debtholders are likely to demand a higher interest rate. We will suppose that the expected return on the debt rises to 7.875 percent. Now you can write down the basic equation for the return on assets.

$$r_A = r_D\frac{D}{V} + r_E\frac{E}{V}$$

$$= \left(7.875 \times \frac{40}{100}\right) + \left(r_E \times \frac{60}{100}\right) = 12.75\%$$

and solve for the return on equity $r_E = 16.0\%$.

Increasing the amount of debt increased debtholder risk and led to a rise in the return that debtholders required (r_{debt} rose from 7.5 to 7.875 percent). The higher leverage also made the equity riskier and increased the return that shareholders required (r_E rose from 15 to 16 percent). The weighted-average return on debt and equity remained at 12.75 percent:

$$\begin{aligned} r_A &= (r_D \times .4) + (r_E \times .6) \\ &= (7.875 \times .4) + (16 \times .6) = 12.75\% \end{aligned}$$

Suppose that the company decided instead to repay all its debt and to replace it with equity. In that case all the cash flows would go to the equity holders. The company cost of capital, r_A, would stay at 12.75 percent, and r_E would also be 12.75 percent.

How Changing Capital Structure Affects Beta

We have looked at how changes in financial structure affect expected return. Let us now look at the effect on beta.

The stockholders and debtholders both receive a share of the firm's cash flows, and both bear part of the risk. For example, if the firm's assets turn out to be worthless, there will be no cash to pay stockholders or debtholders. But debtholders usually bear much less risk than stockholders. Debt betas of large blue-chip firms are typically in the range of .1 to .3.

If you owned a portfolio of all the firm's securities, you wouldn't share the cash flows with anyone. You wouldn't share the risks with anyone either; you would bear them all. Thus the firm's asset beta is equal to the beta of a portfolio of all the firm's debt and its equity.

The beta of this hypothetical portfolio is just a weighted average of the debt and equity betas:

$$\beta_A = \beta_{portfolio} = \beta_D \frac{D}{V} + \beta_E \frac{E}{V}$$

Think back to our example. If the debt before the refinancing has a beta of .1 and the equity has a beta of 1.1, then

$$\beta_A = (.1 \times .3) + (1.1 \times .7) = .8$$

What happens after the refinancing? The risk of the total package is unaffected, but both the debt and the equity are now more risky. Suppose that the debt beta increases to .2. We can work out the new equity beta:

$$\begin{aligned} \beta_A &= \beta_{portfolio} = \beta_D \frac{D}{V} + \beta_E \frac{E}{V} \\ .8 &= (.2 \times .4) + (\beta_E \times .6) \\ \beta_E &= 1.2 \end{aligned}$$

You can see why borrowing is said to create financial leverage or gearing. Financial leverage does not affect the risk or the expected return on the firm's assets, but it does push up the risk of the common stock. Shareholders demand a correspondingly higher return because of this *financial risk.*

Now you can see how to *unlever* betas, that is, how to go from an observed β_E to β_A. You have the equity beta, say, 1.2. You also need the debt beta, say, .2, and the relative market values of debt (D/V) and equity (E/V). If debt accounts for 40 percent of overall value V,

$$\beta_A = (.2 \times .4) + (1.2 \times .6) = .8$$

This runs the previous example in reverse. Just remember the basic relationship:

$$\beta_A = \beta_{\text{portfolio}} = \beta_D\left(\frac{D}{V}\right) + \beta_E\left(\frac{E}{V}\right)$$

17.3 THE WEIGHTED-AVERAGE COST OF CAPITAL

What did financial experts think about debt policy before MM? It is not easy to say because with hindsight we see that they did not think too clearly.[4] However, a "traditional" position has emerged in response to MM. In order to understand it, we have to return to the weighted-average cost of capital.

Figure 17.2 sums up the implications of MM's propositions for the costs of debt and equity and the weighted-average cost of capital. The figure assumes that the firm's bonds are essentially risk-free at low debt levels. Thus r_D is independent of D/E, and r_E increases linearly as D/E increases. As the firm borrows more, the risk of default increases and the firm is required to pay higher rates of interest. Proposition 2 predicts that when this occurs the rate of increase in r_E slows down. This is also shown in Figure 17.2. The more debt the firm has, the less sensitive r_E is to further borrowing.

Why does the slope of the r_E line in Figure 17.2 taper off as D/E increases? Essentially because holders of risky debt bear some of the firm's business risk. As the firm borrows more, more of that risk is transferred from stockholders to bondholders.

Two Warnings

Sometimes the objective in financing decisions is stated not as "maximize overall market value" but as "minimize the weighted-average cost of capital." If MM's proposition 1 holds, then these are equivalent objectives. If MM's proposition 1 does *not* hold, then the capital structure that maximizes the value of the firm also minimizes the weighted-average cost of capital, *provided* that operating income is independent of capital structure. Remember that the weighted-average cost of capital is the expected rate of return on the market value of all of the firm's securities. Anything that increases the value of the firm reduces the weighted-average cost of capital if operating income is constant. But if operating income is varying too, all bets are off.

In Chapter 18 we will show that financial leverage can affect operating income in several ways. Therefore maximizing the value of the firm is *not* always equivalent to minimizing the weighted-average cost of capital.

Warning 1 Shareholders want management to increase the firm's value. They are more interested in being rich than in owning a firm with a low weighted-average cost of capital.

[4] Financial economists in 20 years may remark on Brealey, Myers, and Allen's blind spots and clumsy reasoning. On the other hand, they may not remember us at all.

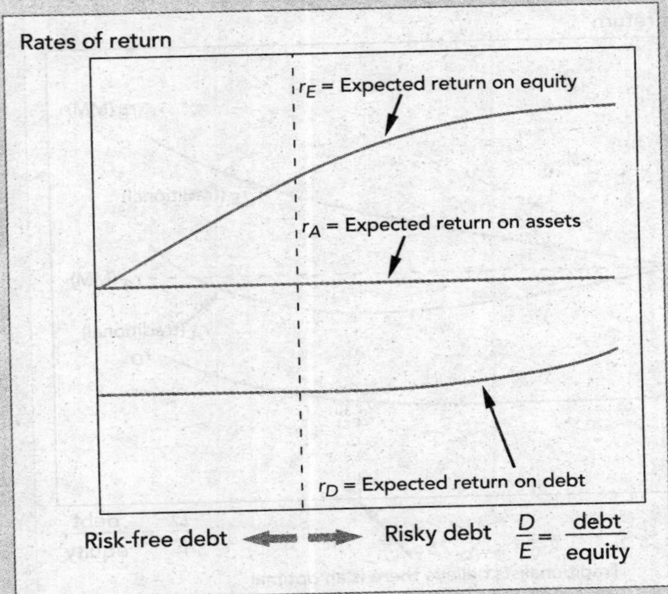

FIGURE 17.2
MM's proposition 2. The expected return on equity r_E increases linearly with the debt–equity ratio so long as debt is risk-free. But if leverage increases the risk of the debt, debtholders demand a higher return on the debt. This causes the rate of increase in r_E to slow down.

Warning 2 Trying to minimize the weighted-average cost of capital seems to encourage logical short circuits like the following. Suppose that someone says, "Shareholders demand—and deserve—higher expected rates of return than bondholders do. Therefore debt is the cheaper capital source. We can reduce the weighted-average cost of capital by borrowing more." But this doesn't follow if the extra borrowing leads stockholders to demand a still higher expected rate of return. According to MM's proposition 2 the cost of equity capital r_E increases by just enough to keep the weighted-average cost of capital constant.

This is not the only logical short circuit you are likely to encounter. We have cited two more in Practice Question 7 at the end of this chapter.

Rates of Return on Levered Equity—The Traditional Position

You may ask why we have even mentioned the aim of minimizing the weighted-average cost of capital if it is often wrong or confusing. We had to because the traditionalists accept this objective and argue their case in terms of it.

The logical short circuit we just described rested on the assumption that r_E, the expected rate of return demanded by stockholders, does not rise, or rises very slowly, as the firm borrows more. Suppose, just for the sake of argument, that this is true. Then r_A, the weighted-average cost of capital, must decline as the debt–equity ratio rises.

The traditionalists' position is shown in Figure 17.3. They say that a moderate degree of financial leverage may increase the expected equity return r_E, but not as much as predicted by MM's proposition 2. But irresponsible firms that borrow *excessively* find r_E shooting up *faster* than MM predict. Therefore the weighted-average cost of capital declines at first, then rises. It reaches a minimum at some intermediate debt ratio. Remember that minimizing the weighted-average cost of capital is equivalent to maximizing firm value if operating income is not affected by borrowing.

FIGURE 17.3

The dashed lines show MM's view of the effect of leverage on the expected return on equity r_E and the weighted-average cost of capital r_A. (See Figure 17.2.) The solid lines show the traditional view. Traditionalists say that borrowing at first increases r_E more slowly than MM predict but that r_E shoots up with excessive borrowing. If so, the weighted-average cost of capital can be minimized if you use just the right amount of debt.

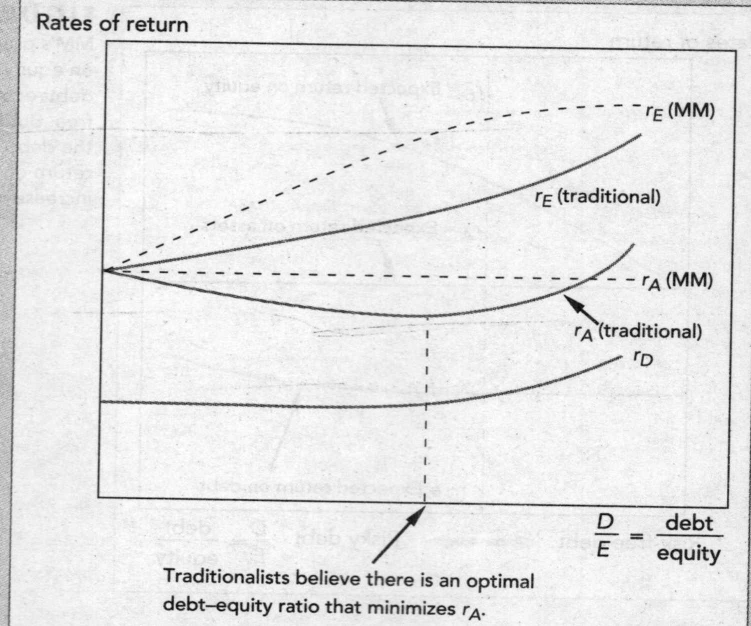

Two arguments could be advanced in support of this position. First, perhaps investors do not notice or appreciate the financial risk created by moderate borrowing, although they wake up when debt is "excessive." If so, stockholders in moderately leveraged firms may accept a lower rate of return than they really should.

That seems naive.[5] The second argument is better. It accepts MM's reasoning as applied to perfect capital markets but holds that actual markets are imperfect. Imperfections may allow firms that borrow to provide a valuable service for investors. If so, levered shares might trade at premium prices compared to their theoretical values in perfect markets.

Suppose that corporations can borrow more cheaply than individuals. Then it would pay investors who want to borrow to do so indirectly by holding the stock of levered firms. They would be willing to live with expected rates of return that do not fully compensate them for the business and financial risk they bear.

Is corporate borrowing really cheaper? It's hard to say. Interest rates on home mortgages are not too different from rates on high-grade corporate bonds.[6] Rates on margin debt (borrowing from a

[5]This first argument may reflect a confusion between financial risk and the risk of default. Default is not a serious threat when borrowing is moderate; stockholders worry about it only when the firm goes "too far." But stockholders bear financial risk—in the form of increased volatility of rate of return and higher beta—even when the chance of default is nil.

[6]One of the authors once obtained a home mortgage at a rate 1/2 percentage point *less* than the contemporaneous yield on long-term AAA bonds.

stockbroker with the investor's shares tendered as security) are not too different from the rates firms pay banks for short-term loans.

There are some individuals who face relatively high interest rates, largely because of the costs lenders incur in making and servicing small loans. There are economies of scale in borrowing. A group of small investors could do better by borrowing via a corporation, in effect pooling their loans and saving transaction costs.[7]

But suppose that this class of investors is large, both in number and in the aggregate wealth it brings to capital markets. That creates a clientele for whom corporate borrowing is better than personal borrowing. That clientele would, in principle, be willing to pay a premium for the shares of a levered firm.

But maybe it doesn't *have* to pay a premium. Perhaps smart financial managers long ago recognized this clientele and shifted the capital structures of their firms to meet its needs. The shifts would not have been difficult or costly to make. But if the clientele is now satisfied, it no longer needs to pay a premium for levered shares. Only the financial managers who *first* recognized the clientele extracted any advantage from it.

Maybe the market for corporate leverage is like the market for automobiles. Americans need millions of automobiles and are willing to pay thousands of dollars apiece for them. But that doesn't mean that you could strike it rich by going into the automobile business. You're at least 50 years too late.

Today's Unsatisfied Clienteles Are Probably Interested in Exotic Securities

So far we have made little progress in identifying cases where firm value might plausibly depend on financing. But our examples illustrate what smart financial managers look for. They look for an *unsatisfied* clientele, investors who want a particular kind of financial instrument but because of market imperfections can't get it or can't get it cheaply.

MM's proposition 1 is violated when the firm, by imaginative design of its capital structure, can offer some *financial service* that meets the needs of such a clientele. Either the service must be new and unique or the firm must find a way to provide some old service more cheaply than other firms or financial intermediaries can.

Now, is there an unsatisfied clientele for garden-variety debt or levered equity? We doubt it. But perhaps you can invent an exotic security and uncover a latent demand for it.

In the next several chapters we will encounter a number of new securities that have been invented by companies and advisers. These securities take the company's basic cash flows and repackage them in ways that are thought to be more attractive to investors. However, while inventing these new securities is easy, it is more difficult to find investors who will rush to buy them.

[7]Even here there are alternatives to borrowing on personal account. Investors can draw down their savings accounts or sell a portion of their investment in bonds. The impact of reductions in lending on the investor's balance sheet and risk position is exactly the same as increases in borrowing.

Imperfections and Opportunities

The most serious capital market imperfections are often those created by government. An imperfection which supports a violation of MM's proposition 1 *also* creates a money-making opportunity. Firms and intermediaries will find some way to reach the clientele of investors frustrated by the imperfection.

For many years the U.S. government imposed a limit on the rate of interest that could be paid on savings accounts. It did so to protect savings institutions by limiting competition for their depositors' money. The fear was that depositors would run off in search of higher yields, causing a cash drain that savings institutions would not be able to meet.

These regulations created an opportunity for firms and financial institutions to design new savings schemes that were not subject to the interest-rate ceilings. One invention was the *floating-rate note,* first issued in 1974 by Citicorp, and with terms designed to appeal to individual investors. Floating-rate notes are medium-term debt securities whose interest payments "float" with short-term interest rates. On the Citicorp issue, for example, the coupon rate used to calculate each semiannual interest payment was set at 1 percentage point above the contemporaneous yield on Treasury bills. The holder of the Citicorp note was therefore protected against fluctuating interest rates, because Citicorp sent a larger check when interest rates rose (and, of course, a smaller check when rates fell).

In India, floating rate notes (or floaters as they are popularly known) were, however, introduced for entirely different reasons. The spread between the deposit rate and the borrowing rate in India was very high before 1994. The Governor of the RBI therefore proposed the banks to issue floating rate bonds to reduce the above spread. In 1994, SBI became the first company in India to issue floating rate bonds in India with an interest rate that was 3 percent higher than the maximum deposit rate ruling every six months.

Long before interest-rate ceilings were finally removed in U.S., most of the gains had gone out of issuing the new securities to individual investors. Once the clientele was finally satisfied, MM's proposition 1 was restored (until the government creates a new imperfection). The moral of the story is this: If you ever find an unsatisfied clientele, do something right away, or capital markets will evolve and steal it from you.

This is actually an encouraging message for the economy as a whole. If MM are right, investors' demands for different types of securities are satisfied at minimal cost. The cost of capital will reflect only business risk. Capital will flow to companies with positive-NPV investments, regardless of the companies' capital structures. This is the efficient outcome.

17.4 A FINAL WORD ON THE AFTER-TAX WEIGHTED-AVERAGE COST OF CAPITAL

MM left us a simple message. When the firm changes its mix of debt and equity securities, the risk and expected returns of these securities change, but the company's overall cost of capital does not change.

Now if you think that message is too neat and simple, you're right. The complications are spelled out in the next two chapters. But we must note one complication here: Interest paid on a firm's borrowing can be deducted from taxable income. Thus the *after-tax* cost of debt is $r_D(1 - T_c)$, where T_c is the marginal corporate tax rate. When companies discount an average-risk project, they do not use the company cost of capital as we have computed it. They use the after-tax cost of debt to compute the after-tax weighted-average cost of capital or WACC:

$$\text{After-tax WACC} = r_D(1 - T_c)\frac{D}{V} + r_E\frac{E}{V}$$

Titan Industries Limited's WACC

We already know two ways of estimating the cost of equity for any company. The discounted cash flow method (discussed in Section 4.4) gives a cost of equity of 18 percent for Titan. If we use the capital asset pricing model, we obtain 24.28 percent as the cost of equity. Let's compromise with γ_E = 20 percent.[8] Titan's long-term borrowing rate was r_D = 8.48 percent.[9] The company has also issued preference shares of Rs. 40 crores. We assume 12 percent to be the cost of preference shares (r_P). The company's capital structure, using market values of equity, debt, and preference shares, was[10] :

Debt (D)	Rs. 318 crores	at r_D	8.48%
Equity (E)	2443.8	at r_E	20.0%
Preference Capital (P)	40	at r_P	12.0%
Firm value (V)	Rs. 2802 million		

The market-value debt ratio is D/V = 318 / 2802 = 0.11, the market value preference shares ratio is 40 / 2802 = 0.02, and the equity ratio is E / V = 0.87. We will assume that Titan's marginal tax rate is the statutory rate of T_C = 0.3366. Therefore the after-tax cost of debt is 0.0848 × (1 – 0.3366) = 0.0563, and the after-tax WACC is

$$\text{After-tax WACC} = 0.0848 \times (1 - 0.3366) \times 0.11 + 0.12 \times 0.02 + 0.2 \times 0.87$$
$$= 0.1825, \text{ or } 18.25\%$$

[8]The difference between the DCF and CAPM estimates is, admittedly, unusally large.

[9]The debentures issued by Titan are rated 'A' by CRISIL. As per FIMMDA, the yield on A_rated debentures was about 1.9 percent above the risk free rate of return.

[10]Here, we assume that the market values of debt and preference capital are equal to their respective book values.

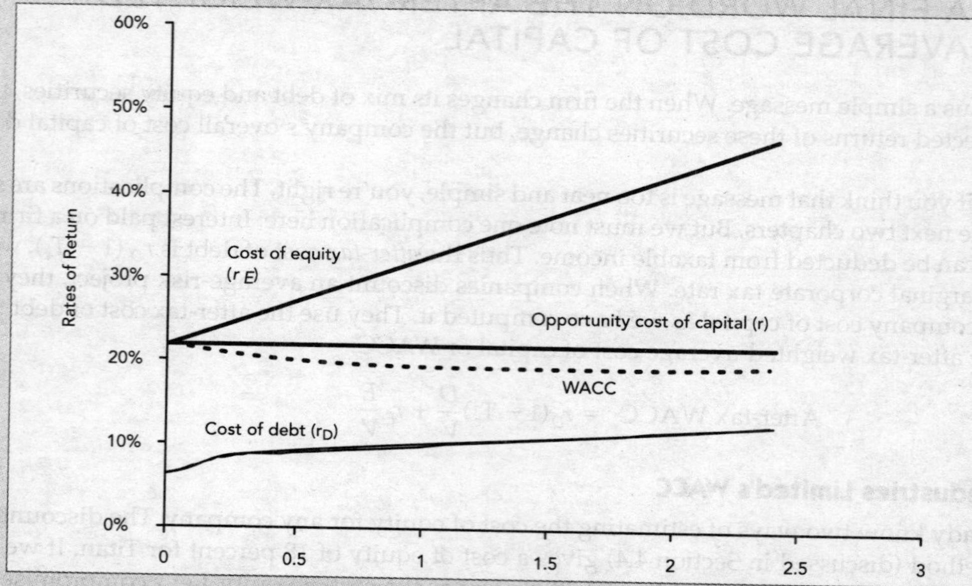

FIGURE 17.4

Estimated after-tax WACC for Titan at different debt-equity ratios. The figure assumes $r_E = 24.28$ percent at a 13 percent debt ratio and a borrowing rate of $r_D = 8.48$ percent. Notice that the debt interest rate is assumed to increase with the debt-equity ratio. Here, we ignore preference capital because it constitutes only 2 percent of the total capital for Titan.

Figure 17.4 shows how the after-tax WACC falls as debt increases. In this example it falls *only* because debt interest is tax-deductible. Note that the opportunity cost of capital r is still plotted as a straight horizontal line.

SUMMARY

Think of the financial manager as taking all of the firm's real assets and selling them to investors as a package of securities. Some financial managers choose the simplest package possible: all-equity financing. Some end up issuing dozens of debt and equity securities. The problem is to find the particular combination that maximizes the market value of the firm.

Modigliani and Miller's (MM's) famous proposition 1 states that no combination is better than any other—that the firm's overall market value (the value of all its securities) is independent of capital structure. Firms that borrow do offer investors a more complex menu of securities, but investors yawn in response. The menu is redundant. Any shift in capital structure can be duplicated or "undone" by investors. Why should they pay extra for borrowing indirectly (by holding shares in a levered firm) when they can borrow just as easily and cheaply on their own accounts?

MM agree that borrowing increases the expected rate of return on shareholders' investments. But it also increases the risk of the firm's shares. MM show that the risk increase exactly offsets the increase in expected return, leaving stockholders no better or worse off.

Proposition 1 is an extremely general result. It applies not just to the debt–equity trade-off but to *any* choice of financing instruments. For example, MM would say that the choice between long-term and short-term debt has no effect on firm value.

The formal proofs of proposition 1 all depend on the assumption of perfect capital markets. MM's opponents, the "traditionalists," argue that market imperfections make personal borrowing excessively costly, risky, and inconvenient for some investors. This creates a natural clientele willing to pay a premium for shares of levered firms. The traditionalists say that firms should borrow to realize the premium.

But this argument is incomplete. There may be a clientele for levered equity, but that is not enough; the clientele has to be *unsatisfied*. There are already thousands of levered firms available for investment. Is there still an unsatiated clientele for garden-variety debt and equity? We doubt it.

Proposition 1 is violated when financial managers find an untapped demand and satisfy it by issuing something new and different. The argument between MM and the traditionalists finally boils down to whether this is difficult or easy. We lean toward MM's view: Finding unsatisfied clienteles and designing exotic securities to meet their needs is a game that's fun to play but hard to win.

If MM are right, the overall cost of capital—the expected rate of return on a portfolio of all the firm's outstanding securities—is the same regardless of the mix of securities issued to finance the firm. The overall cost of capital is usually called the company cost of capital or the weighted-average cost of capital (WACC). MM say that WACC doesn't depend on capital structure. But MM assume away lots of complications. The first complication is taxes. When we recognize that debt interest is tax-deductible, and compute WACC with the after-tax interest rate, WACC declines as the debt ratio increases. There is more—lots more—on taxes and other complications in the next two chapters.

FURTHER READING

The pioneering work on the theory of capital structure is:

F. Modigliani and M. H. Miller, "The Cost of Capital, Corporation Finance and the Theory of Investment," *American Economic Review* 48 (June 1958), pp. 261–297.

However, Durand deserves credit for setting out the issues that MM later solved:

D. Durand, "Cost of Debt and Equity Funds for Business: Trends and Problems in Measurement," in *Conference on Research in Business Finance* (New York: National Bureau of Economic Research, 1952), pp. 215–247.

The fall 1988 issue of the Journal of Economic Perspectives *contains an anniversary collection of articles, including one by Modigliani and Miller, which review and assess the MM propositions. The summer 1989 issue of* Financial Management *contains three more articles under the heading "Reflections on the MM Propositions 30 Years Later."*

The Winter 1992 edition of the Journal of Applied Corporate Finance *contains several interesting surveys of financial innovation. Other articles include:*

K. A. Karow, G. R. Erwin, and J. J. McConnell: "Survey of U.S. Corporate Financing Innovations: 1970–1997," *Journal of Applied Corporate Finance* 12 (Spring 1999), pp. 55–69.

P. Tufano: "Financial Innovation," in G. M. Constantinides, M. Harris, and R. Stulz (eds.), *Handbook of the Economics of Finance*, Vol 1A (Amsterdam: Elsevier North-Holland, 2003).

Miller reviews the MM propositions in:

M. H. Miller: "The Modigliani-Miller Propositions after Thirty Years," *Journal of Applied Corporate Finance* 2 (Spring 1989), pp. 6–18.

For a skeptic's view of MM's arguments see:

S. Titman: "The Modigliani-Miller Theorem and the Integration of Financial Markets," *Financial Management* 31 (Spring 2002), pp. 101–115.

CONCEPT REVIEW QUESTIONS

1. "Financial managers try to find the combination of securities . . . that maximizes the market value of the firm." Why does pursuit of this goal benefit *shareholders*? (page 448)
2. MM's proposition 1 says that financing with debt instead of equity does *not* affect:
   a. The price–earnings ratio for the firm's stock.
   b. The total market value of the firm's shares (price per share × number of shares outstanding).
   c. The total market value of the firm.
   d. The beta of the firm's stock.
   e. The interest rate on the firm's debt.
   f. The cost of equity.
   g. The firm's overall (weighted-average) cost of capital.

   Which statements are correct? (pages 451–458)
3. What is *financial risk*? How does it depend on the firm's capital structure? (page 455)

For additional Concept Review Questions, please visit us at www.mhhe.com/bmam8e or refer to your Student CD.

QUIZ

1. Ms. Pooja owns 50,000 shares of the common stock of Copper Corporation with a market value of Rs.20 per share. The company is currently financed as follows:

	Book Value
Share Capital (8 million shares)	Rs.20 million
Short-term loans	Rs.2 million

   Copper Corporation now announces that it is replacing Rs.10 million of short-term debt with an issue of Shares. What action can Ms. Pooja take to ensure that she is entitled to exactly the same proportion of profits as before?
2. Spam Corp. is financed entirely by equity and has a beta of 1.0. The firm is expected to generate a level, perpetual stream of earnings and dividends. The stock has a price-earnings ratio of 8 and a cost of equity of 12.5 percent. The company's stock is selling for Rs. 50. Now the firm decides to repurchase half of its shares and substitute an equal value of debt. The debt is risk-free, with a 5 percent interest rate. The company is exempt from corporate income taxes. Assuming MM are correct, calculate the following items after the refinancing:
   a. The cost of equity.
   b. The overall cost of capital (WACC).
   c. The price–earnings ratio.
   d. The stock price.
   e. The stock's beta.
3. The equity and debt of N.S. Limited are valued at Rs. 50 million and Rs. 30 million, respectively. Investors currently require a 16 percent return on the equity and an 8 percent return on the debt. If N.S. Limited issues an additional Rs. 10 million of equity and uses this money to retire debt, what happens to the expected return on the stock? Assume that the change in capital structure does not affect the risk of the debt and that there are no taxes.
4. Suppose that Macbeth Spot Removers issues only Rs. 2,500 of debt and uses the proceeds to repurchase 250 shares.
   a. Rework Table 17.2 to show how earnings per share and share return now vary with operating income.

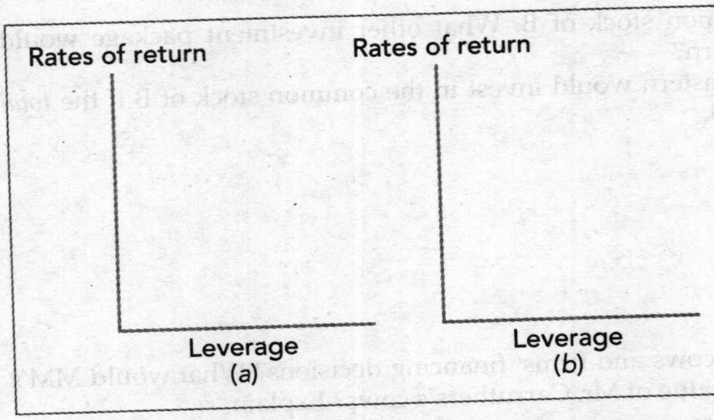

FIGURE 17.5

See Quiz Question 7.

b. If the beta of Macbeth's assets is .8 and its debt is risk-free, what would be the beta of the equity after the debt issue?

5. True or false?
   a. MM's propositions assume perfect financial markets, with no distorting taxes or other imperfections.
   b. MM's proposition 1 says that corporate borrowing increases earnings per share but reduces the price–earnings ratio.
   c. MM's proposition 2 says that the cost of equity increases with borrowing and that the increase is proportional to *D*/*V*, the ratio of debt to firm value.
   d. MM's proposition 2 assumes that increased borrowing does not affect the interest rate on the firm's debt.
   e. Borrowing does not increase financial risk and the cost of equity if there is no risk of bankruptcy.
   f. Borrowing increases firm value if there is a clientele of investors with a reason to prefer debt.

6. Look back to Section 17.1. Suppose that Ms. Macbeth's investment bankers have informed her that since the new issue of debt is risky, debtholders will demand a return of 12.5 percent, which is 2.5 percent above the risk-free interest rate.
   a. What are r_A and r_E?
   b. Suppose that the beta of the unlevered stock was .6. What will β_A, β_E, and β_D be after the change to the capital structure?

7. Note the two blank graphs in Figure 17.5. On graph (*a*), assume MM are right, and plot the relationship between financial leverage and (i) the rates of return on debt and equity and (ii) the weighted-average cost of capital. Then fill in graph (*b*), assuming the traditionalists are right.

8. Gaucho Services starts life with all-equity financing and a cost of equity of 14 percent. Suppose it refinances to the following market-value capital structure:

Debt (*D*)	45%	at $r_D = 9.5\%$
Equity (*E*)	55%	

Gaucho pays taxes at a marginal rate of $T_C = 40$ percent. Calculate Gaucho's after-tax weighted-average cost of capital. Use MM's proposition 2 to calculate the new cost of equity.

PRACTICE QUESTIONS

1. Companies A and B differ only in their capital structure. A is financed 30 percent debt and 70 percent equity; B is financed 10 percent debt and 90 percent equity. The debt of both companies is risk-free.
   a. Rosencrantz owns 1 percent of the common stock of A. What other investment package would produce identical cash flows for Rosencrantz?

b. Guildenstern owns 2 percent of the common stock of B. What other investment package would produce identical cash flows for Guildenstern?

c. Show that neither Rosencrantz nor Guildenstern would invest in the common stock of B if the *total* value of company A were less than that of B.

2. Here is a limerick:

There once was a man named Carruthers,
Who kept cows with miraculous udders.
He said, "Isn't this neat?
They give cream from one teat,
And skim milk from each of the others!"

What is the analogy between Mr. Carruthers's cows and firms' financing decisions? What would MM's proposition 1, suitably adapted, say about the value of Mr. Carruthers's cows? Explain.

3. Executive Chalk is financed solely by equity and has outstanding 25 million shares with a market price of Rs. 10 a share. It now announces that it intends to issue Rs. 160 million of debt and to use the proceeds to buy back equity.

a. How is the market price of the stock affected by the announcement?
b. How many shares can the company buy back with the Rs. 160 million of new debt that it issues?
c. What is the market value of the firm (equity plus debt) after the change in capital structure?
d. What is the debt ratio after the change in structure?
e. Who (if anyone) gains or loses?

Now try the next question.

4. Executive Cheese has issued debt with a market value of Rs.100 million and has outstanding 15 million shares with a market price of Rs. 10 a share. It now announces that it intends to issue a further Rs.60 million of debt and to use the proceeds to buy back equity. Debtholders, seeing the extra risk, mark the value of the existing debt down to Rs. 70 million.

a. How is the market price of the stock affected by the announcement?
b. How many shares can the company buy back with the Rs. 60 million of new debt that it issues?
c. What is the market value of the firm (equity plus debt) after the change in capital structure?
d. What is the debt ratio after the change in structure?
e. Who (if anyone) gains or loses?

5. Hubbard's Pet Foods is financed 80 percent by common stock and 20 percent by bonds. The expected return on the common stock is 12 percent and the rate of interest on the bonds is 6 percent. Assuming that the bonds are default-risk free, draw a graph that shows the expected return of Hubbard's common stock (r_E) and the expected return on the package of common stock and bonds (r_A) for different debt–equity ratios.

6. "MM totally ignore the fact that as you borrow more, you have to pay higher rates of interest." Explain carefully whether this is a valid objection.

7. Indicate what's wrong with the following arguments:

a. "As the firm borrows more and debt becomes risky, both stockholders and bondholders demand higher rates of return. Thus by *reducing* the debt ratio we can reduce *both* the cost of debt and the cost of equity, making everybody better off."

b. "Moderate borrowing doesn't significantly affect the probability of financial distress or bankruptcy. Consequently moderate borrowing won't increase the expected rate of return demanded by stockholders."

8. Each of the following statements is false or at least misleading. Explain why in each case.

a. "A capital investment opportunity offering a 10 percent DCF rate of return is an attractive project if it can be 100 percent debt-financed at an 8 percent interest rate."

b. "The more debt the firm issues, the higher the interest rate it must pay. That is one important reason why firms should operate at conservative debt levels."

9. Can you invent any new kinds of debt that might be attractive to investors? Why do you think they have not been issued?

10. Imagine a firm that is expected to produce a level stream of operating profits. As leverage is increased, what happens to
    a. The ratio of the market value of the equity to income after interest?
    b. The ratio of the market value of the *firm* to income before interest if (i) MM are right and (ii) the traditionalists are right?

11. Archimedes Levers is financed by a mixture of debt and equity. You have the following information about its cost of capital:

r_E = —	$r_D = 12\%$	r_A = ___
$\beta_E = 1.5$	β_D = ___	β_A = ___
$r_f = 10\%$	$r_m = 18\%$	$D/V = .5$

    Can you fill in the blanks?

12. Look back to Practice Question 11. Suppose now that Archimedes repurchases debt and issues equity so that $D/V = .3$. The reduced borrowing causes r_D to fall to 11 percent. How do the other variables change?

13. Omega Corporation has 10 million shares outstanding, now trading at Rs. 55 per share. The firm has estimated the expected rate of return to shareholders at about 12 percent. It has also issued long-term bonds at an interest rate of 7 percent. It pays tax at a marginal rate of 35 percent.
    a. What is Omega's after-tax WACC?
    b. How much higher would WACC be if Omega used no debt at all? *Hint:* For this problem you can assume that the firm's overall beta (β_A) is not affected by its capital structure or the taxes saved because debt interest is tax-deductible.

14. Gamma Airlines has an asset beta of 1.5. The risk-free interest rate is 6 percent, and the market risk premium is 8 percent. Assume the capital asset pricing model is correct. Gamma pays taxes at a marginal rate of 35 percent. Draw a graph plotting Gamma's cost of equity and after-tax WACC as a function of its debt-to-equity ratio D/E, from no debt to $D/E = 1.0$. Assume that Gamma's debt is risk-free up to $D/E = .25$. Then the interest rate increases to 6.5 percent at $D/E = .5$, 7 percent at $D/E = .8$, and 8 percent at $D/E = 1.0$. As in problem 13, you can assume that the firm's overall beta (β_A) is not affected by its capital structure or the taxes saved because debt interest is tax-deductible.

CHALLENGE QUESTIONS

1. Consider the following three tickets: ticket A pays Rs. 10 if _____ is elected as president, ticket B pays Rs. 10 if _____ is elected, and ticket C pays Rs. 10 if neither is elected. (Fill in the blanks yourself.) Could the three tickets sell for less than the present value of Rs. 10? Could they sell for more? Try auctioning off the tickets. What are the implications for MM's proposition 1?

2. People often convey the idea behind MM's proposition 1 by various supermarket analogies, for example, "The value of a pie should not depend on how it is sliced," or, "The cost of a whole chicken should equal the cost of assembling one by buying two drumsticks, two wings, two breasts, and so on."

    Actually proposition 1 doesn't work in the supermarket. You'll pay less for an uncut whole pie than for a pie assembled from pieces purchased separately. Supermarkets charge more for chickens after they are cut up. Why? What costs or imperfections cause proposition 1 to fail in the supermarket? Are these costs or imperfections likely to be important for corporations issuing securities in India? Explain.

3. Suppose that new security designs could be patented.[12] The patent holder could restrict use of the new design or charge other firms royalties for using it. What effect would such patents have on MM's capital-structure irrelevance theory?

[12]So far security designs cannot be patented, but other financial applications have received patent protection. See J. Lerner, "Where Does State Street Lead? A First Look at Finance Patents," *Journal of Finance* 57 (April 2002), pp. 901–930.

CHAPTER [18]

HOW MUCH SHOULD A FIRM BORROW?

IN CHAPTER 17 we found that debt policy rarely matters in well-functioning capital markets with no taxes. Few financial managers would accept that conclusion as a practical guideline. If debt policy doesn't matter, then they shouldn't worry about it—financing decisions should be delegated to underlings. Yet financial managers do worry about debt policy. This chapter explains why.

If debt policy were completely irrelevant, then actual debt ratios should vary randomly from firm to firm and industry to industry. Yet almost all airlines, utilities, banks, and real estate development companies rely heavily on debt. And so do many firms in capital-intensive industries like steel, aluminum, chemicals, petroleum, and mining. On the other hand, it is rare to find a pharmaceutical company or advertising agency that is not predominantly equity-financed. Glamorous growth companies rarely use much debt despite rapid expansion and often heavy requirements for capital.

The explanation of these patterns lies partly in the things we left out of the last chapter. We mostly ignored taxes. We assumed bankruptcy was cheap, quick, and painless. It isn't, and there are costs associated with financial distress even if legal bankruptcy is ultimately avoided. We ignored potential conflicts of interest between the firm's security holders. For example, we did not consider what happens to the firm's "old" creditors when new debt is issued or when a shift in investment strategy takes the firm into a riskier business. We ignored the information problems that favor debt over equity when cash must be raised from new security issues. We ignored the incentive effects of financial leverage on management's investment and payout decisions.

Now we will put all these things back in: taxes first, then the costs of bankruptcy and financial distress. This will lead us to conflicts of interest and to information and incentive problems. In the end we will have to admit that debt policy does matter.

However, we will not throw away the MM theory we developed so carefully in Chapter 17. We're shooting for a theory combining MM's insights plus the effects of taxes, costs of bankruptcy and financial distress, and various other complications. We're not dropping back to a theory based on inefficiencies in the capital market. Instead, we want to see how well-functioning capital markets respond to taxes and the other things covered in this chapter.

18.1 CORPORATE TAXES

Debt financing has one important advantage under the corporate income tax system in India. The interest that the company pays is a tax-deductible expense. Thus the return to bondholders escapes taxation at the corporate level.

Table 18.1 shows simple income statements for firm U, which has no debt, and firm L, which has borrowed Rs. 1,000 at 8 percent. The tax bill of L is Rs. 28 less than that of U. This is the *tax shield* provided by the debt of L. In effect the government pays 35 percent of the interest expense of L. The total income that L can pay out to its bondholders and stockholders increases by that amount.

Tax shields can be valuable assets. Suppose that the debt of L is fixed and permanent. (That is, the company commits to refinance its present debt obligations when they mature and to keep rolling over its debt obligations indefinitely.) Then L can look forward to a permanent stream of cash flows of Rs. 28 per year. The risk of these flows is likely to be less than the risk of the

TABLE 18.1

The tax deductibility of interest increases the total income that can be paid out to bondholders and stockholders.

	Income Statement of Firm U	Income Statement of Firm L
Earnings before interest and taxes	Rs. 1,000	Rs. 1,000
Interest paid to bondholders	0	80
Pretax income	1,000	920
Tax at 35%	350	322
Net income to stockholders	Rs. 650	Rs. 598
Total income to both bondholders and stockholders	Rs. 0 + 650 = Rs. 650	Rs. 80 + 598 = Rs. 678
Interest tax shield (.35 × interest)	Rs. 0	Rs. 28

operating assets of L. The tax shields depend only on the corporate tax rate[1] and on the ability of L to earn enough to cover interest payments. The corporate tax rate has been pretty stable. And the ability of L to earn its interest payments must be reasonably sure; otherwise it could not have borrowed at 8 percent. Therefore we should discount the interest tax shields at a relatively low rate.

But what rate? One common assumption is that the risk of the tax shields is the same as that of the interest payments generating them. Thus we discount at 8 percent, the expected rate of return demanded by investors who are holding the firm's debt:

$$\text{PV(tax shield)} = \frac{28}{.08} = \text{Rs. } 350$$

In effect the government itself assumes 35 percent of the Rs. 1,000 debt obligation of L.

Under these assumptions, the present value of the tax shield is independent of the return on the debt r_D. It equals the corporate tax rate T_c times the amount borrowed D:

$$\text{Interest payment} = \text{return on debt} \times \text{amount borrowed}$$
$$= r_D \times D$$

$$\text{PV(tax shield)} = \frac{\text{corporate tax rate} \times \text{interest payment}}{\text{expected return on debt}}$$
$$= \frac{T_c(r_D D)}{r_D} = T_c D$$

Of course, PV(tax shield) is less if the firm does not plan to borrow a permanent fixed amount,[2] or if it may not have enough taxable income to use the interest tax shields.[3]

[1] "Always use the marginal corporate tax rate, not the average rate. Average rates are often much lower than marginal rates because of difference in depreciation method (written down value method vis-à-vis straight line method) and other tax adjustments. For large corporations, the marginal rate is usually taken as the statutory rate, which was 33.66 percent for the Indian companies when this chapter was written (2006). It was 41.82 percent for the foreign companies. However, effective marginal rates can be less than the statutory rate, especially for smaller, riskier companies which cannot be sure that they will earn taxable income in the future."

[2] In this example, we assume that the amount of debt is fixed and stable over time. The natural alternative assumption is a fixed *ratio* of debt to firm value. If the ratio is fixed, then the level of debt and the amount of interest tax shields will fluctuate as firm value fluctuates. In that case projected interest tax shields can't be discounted at the cost of debt. We cover this point in detail in the next chapter.

[3] If the income of L does not cover interest in some future year, the tax shield is not necessarily lost. L can carry back the loss and receive a tax refund up to the amount of taxes paid in the previous two years. If L has a string of losses, and thus no prior tax payments that can be refunded, then losses can be carried forward and used to shield income in subsequent years.

Normal Balance Sheet (Market Values)	
Asset value (present value of after-tax cash flows)	Debt
	Equity
Total assets	Total value

Expanded Balance Sheet (Market Values)	
Pretax asset value (present value of *pretax* cash flows)	Debt
	Government's claim (present value of future taxes)
	Equity
Total pretax assets	Total pretax value

TABLE 18.2

Normal and expanded market value balance sheets. In a normal balance sheet, assets are valued after tax. In the expanded balance sheet, assets are valued pretax, and the value of the government's tax claim is recognized on the right-hand side. Interest tax shields are valuable because they reduce the government's claim.

How Do Interest Tax Shields Contribute to the Value of Stockholders' Equity?

MM's proposition 1 amounts to saying that the value of a pie does not depend on how it is sliced. The pie is the firm's assets, and the slices are the debt and equity claims. If we hold the pie constant, then a dollar more of debt means a dollar less of equity value.

But there is really a third slice, the government's. Look at Table 18.2. It shows an *expanded* balance sheet with *pretax* asset value on the left and the value of the government's tax claim recognized as a liability on the right. MM would still say that the value of the pie—in this case *pretax* asset value—is not changed by slicing. But anything the firm can do to reduce the size of the government's slice obviously makes stockholders better off. One thing it can do is borrow money, which reduces its tax bill and, as we saw in Table 18.1, increases the cash flows to debt and equity investors. The *after-tax* value of the firm (the sum of its debt and equity values as shown in a normal market value balance sheet) goes up by PV(tax shield).

Recasting Asian Paints' Capital Structure

Asian Paints, is a large, successful firm that uses relatively little long-term debt. Table 18.3(a) shows simplified book and market value balance sheets for Asian Paints in March 2005.

Suppose that you were Asian Paints' financial manager with complete responsibility for its capital structure. You decide to borrow Rs.50 crores on a permanent basis and use the proceeds to repurchase shares.

Table 18.3(b) shows the new balance sheets. The book version simply has Rs.50 crores more long-term debt and Rs.50 crores less equity. But we know Asian Paints' assets must be worth more because its tax bill has been reduced by 33.66 percent of the interest on the new debt. In other words, Asian Paints has an increase in PV(tax shield), which is worth $T_cD = 0.3366 \times$ Rs.50 crores = Rs. 16.83 crores. If the MM theory holds except for taxes, firm value must increase by Rs. 16.83 crores to Rs. 3882.67 crores. Asian Paints' equity ends up worth Rs. 3768.25 crores.

TABLE 18.3(a)

Simplified balance sheets for Asian Paints Limited, March 2005 (figures in crores).

Notes:

1. Market value is equal to book value for net current assets, secured and unsecured loans. Market value of equity = number of shares times closing price for March 2005. The difference between the market and book values of long-term assets is equal to the difference between the market and book value of equity.
2. PV of interest tax shield assumes fixed, perpetual debt, with a 33.66% tax rate.

Book Values			
Secured and Unsecured Loans	Rs. 83.88	Rs. 108.7	Net current Assets
Deferred Tax Liability	30.54		
Equity	572.22	577.94	Long term Assets
Total Value	Rs. 686.64	Rs. 686.64	Total Assets
Market Values			
Secured and Unsecured Loans	Rs. 83.88	Rs. 108.7	Net Current Assets
Deferred Tax Liability	30.54	28.23	PV of interest tax shield
Equity	3751.42	3728.91	Long term Assets
Total Value	Rs. 3865.84	Rs. 3865.84	Total Assets

TABLE 18.3(b)

Balance Sheets for Asian Paints with additional Rs. 50 crores of long-term debt substituted for shareholders' equity (figures in crores).

Book Values			
Secured and Unsecured Loans	Rs. 133.88	Rs. 108.7	Net current Assets
Deferred Tax Liability	30.54		
Equity	522.22	577.94	Long term Assets
Total Value	Rs. 686.64	Rs. 686.64	Total Assets
Market Values			
Secured and Unsecured Loans	Rs. 133.88	Rs. 108.7	Net Current Assets
Deferred Tax Liability	30.54	61.89	PV of interest tax shield
Equity	3718.25	3712.08	Long term Assets
Total Value	Rs. 3882.67	Rs. 3882.67	Total Assets

Now you have repurchased Rs. 50 crores worth of shares, but Asian Paints' equity value has dropped by only Rs. 33.17 crores. Therefore, Asian Paints' shareholders must be Rs. 16.83 crores ahead. Not a bad day's work.[4]

MM and Taxes

We have just developed a version of MM's proposition 1 as corrected by them to reflect corporate income taxes.[5] The new proposition is

$$\text{Value of firm} = \text{value if all-equity-financed} + \text{PV(tax shield)}$$

In the special case of permanent debt,

$$\text{Value of firm} = \text{value if all-equity-financed} + T_c D$$

[4]Notice that as long as the bonds are sold at a fair price, all the benefits from the tax shield go to the shareholders.

[5]Interest tax shields are recognized in MM's original article, F. Modigliani and M. H. Miller, "The Cost of Capital, Corporation Finance and the Theory of Investment," *American Economic Review* 48 (June 1958), pp. 261–296. The valuation procedure used in Table 18.3(*b*) is presented in their 1963 article "Corporate Income Taxes and the Cost of Capital: A Correction," *American Economic Review* 53 (June 1963), pp. 433–443.

Our imaginary financial surgery on Asian Paints provides the perfect illustration of the problems inherent in this "corrected" theory. That Rs.16.83 crores came too easily; it seems to violate the law that there is no such thing as a money machine. And if Asian Paints' shareholders would be richer with Rs.50 crores of corporate debt, why not Rs.60 crores or Rs.100 crores? At what level should Asian Paints stop borrowing? Our formula implies that firm value and shareholders' wealth continue to go up as D increases. The optimal debt policy appears to be embarrassingly extreme. All firms should be 100 percent debt-financed.

MM were not that fanatical about it. No one would expect the formula to apply at extreme debt ratios. There are several reasons why our calculations overstate the value of interest tax shields. First, it's wrong to think of debt as fixed and perpetual; a firm's ability to carry debt changes over time as profits and firm value fluctuate. Second, many firms face marginal tax rates less than 33.66 percent. Third, you can't use interest tax shields unless there will be future profits to shield—and no firm can be absolutely sure of that.

But none of these qualifications explains why firms like Asian Paints not only exist but also thrive with scarcely any debt at all. It is hard to believe that the management of Asian Paints is simply missing the boat.

Therefore we have argued ourselves into a corner. There are just two ways out:

1. Perhaps a fuller examination of the Indian system of corporate *and personal* taxation will uncover a tax disadvantage of corporate borrowing, offsetting the present value of the interest tax shield.
2. Perhaps firms that borrow incur other costs—bankruptcy costs, for example.

We will now explore these two escape routes.

18.2 CORPORATE AND PERSONAL TAXES

When personal taxes are introduced, the firm's objective is no longer to minimize the *corporate* tax bill; the firm should try to minimize the present value of *all* taxes paid on corporate income. "All taxes" include *personal* taxes paid by bondholders and stockholders.

Figure 18.1 illustrates how corporate and personal taxes are affected by leverage. Depending on the firm's capital structure, a rupee of operating income will accrue to investors either as debt interest or equity income (dividends or capital gains). That is, the rupee can go down either branch of Figure 18.1.

Notice that Figure 18.1 distinguishes between T_p, the personal tax rate on interest, and T_pE, the effective personal tax rate on equity income. As of now (2006), companies pay dividend distribution tax (effective rate = 14.03%) before distributing the dividends. The investors pay securities transaction tax of 0.125 percent on any purchase or sale of shares. The short-term capital gains tax rate is 10 percent now and the long term capital gains tax rate is nil provided, securities transaction tax has been paid. So the effective personal tax rate on equity income is much lower than 14.03 percent. The personal tax rate on interest depends on the personal tax bracket of the tax payer and can be as high as 33.66 percent. Tp_E can be well below T_p, depending on the mix of dividends and capital gains realized by shareholders. In fact, since the marginal tax rate is 20.4 percent for income exceeding Rs.150,000, for most of the investors Tp_E will be lower than T_p.

The firm's objective should be to arrange its capital structure so as to maximize after-tax income. You can see from Figure 18.1 that corporate borrowing is better if $(1 - T_p)$ is more than $(1 - T_{pE}) \times (1 - T_c)$; otherwise it is worse. The *relative tax* advantage of debt over equity is

$$\text{Relative tax advantage of debt} = \frac{1 - T_p}{(1 - T_{pE})(1 - T_c)}$$

FIGURE 18.1

The firm's capital structure determines whether operating income is paid out as interest or equity income. Interest is taxed only at the personal level. Equity income is taxed at both the corporate and the personal levels. However, T_{pE}, the personal tax rate on equity income, can be less than T_p, the personal tax rate on interest income.

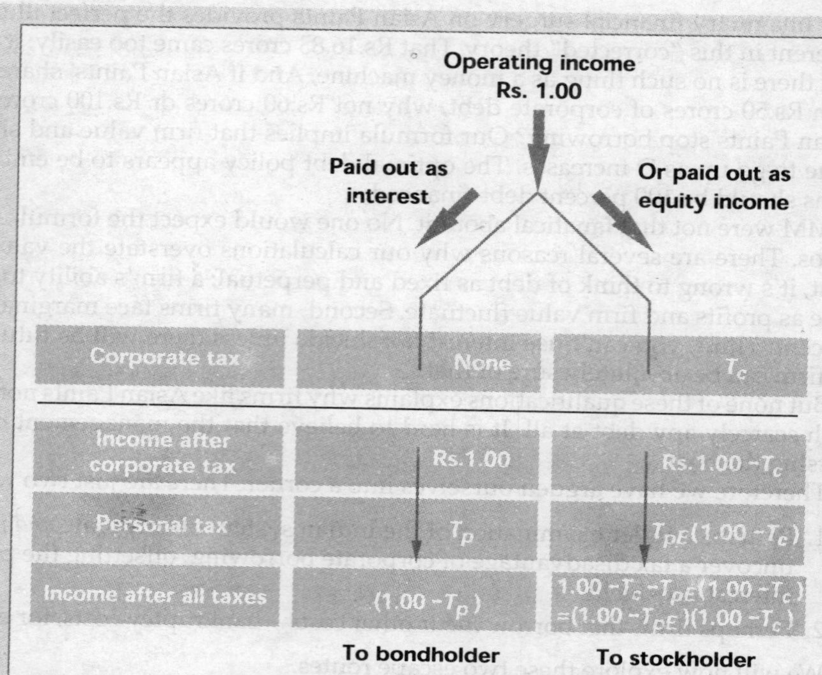

This suggests two special cases. First, suppose that debt and equity income were taxed at the same effective personal rate. But with $T_{pE} = T_p$, the relative advantage depends only on the *corporate rate:*

$$\text{Relative advantage} = \frac{1 - T_p}{(1 - T_{pE})(1 - T_c)} = \frac{1}{1 - T_c}$$

In this case, we can forget about personal taxes. The tax advantage of corporate borrowing is exactly as MM calculated it.[6] They do not have to assume away personal taxes. Their theory of debt and taxes requires only that debt and equity be taxed at the same rate.

The second special case occurs when corporate and personal taxes cancel to make debt policy irrelevant. This requires

$$1 - T_p = (1 - T_{pE})(1 - T_c)$$

[6]Of course, personal taxes reduce the rupee amount of corporate interest tax shields, but the appropriate discount rate for cash flows after personal tax is also lower. If investors are willing to lend at a prospective return *before* personal taxes of r_D, then they must also be willing to accept a return *after* personal taxes of $r_D(1 - T_p)$, where T_p is the marginal rate of personal tax. Thus we can compute the value after personal taxes of the tax shield on permanent debt:

$$\text{PV(tax shield)} = \frac{T_c \times r_D D \times (1 - T_p)}{r_D \times (1 - T_p)} = T_c D$$

This brings us back to our previous formula for firm value:

$$\text{Value of firm} = \text{value if all-equity-financed} + T_c D$$

This case can happen only if T_c, the corporate rate, is less than the personal rate T_p *and* if T_{pE}, the effective rate on equity income, is small. Merton Miller explored this situation at a time when U.S. tax rates on interest and dividends were much higher than now, but we won't go into the details of his analysis here.[7]

In any event we seem to have a simple, practical decision rule. Arrange the firm's capital structure to shunt operating income down that branch of Figure 18.1 where the tax is least. Unfortunately that is not as simple as it sounds. What's T_{pE}, for example? The list of shareholders of any large company is likely to include foreign institutional investors (who get certain tax advantages in India in case they are tax residents of countries with which India has entered into a Double Taxation Avoidance Agreement), NRIs, and other investors. However, in most cases, the effective tax rate on equity income will be the same for most shareholders in India for a particular company. It is however, difficult to find Tp, the personal tax rate on interest as it depends on the tax bracket of the investor. The FIIs pay interest tax at the rate of 20 percent. (It may be 10 percent, if the FII is a tax resident of Cyprus.)

Some investors may be much happier to buy your debt than others. For example, you should have no problems inducing a tax resident of Cyprus to lend. But a high net worth investor in India may be more reluctant to hold debt and will be prepared to do so only if he is compensated by a high rate of interest. Investors paying tax at the top rate of 33.66 percent may be particularly reluctant to hold debt. They will prefer to hold common stock.

To determine the net tax advantage of debt, companies would need to know the tax rates faced by the marginal investor – that is an investor who is equally happy to hold debt or equity. This makes it hard to put a precise figure on the tax benefit, but we can nevertheless provide a back-of-the envelope calculation. Let's consider a large, dividend-paying company like Tata Steel. Tata Steel's dividend payout ratio is 20 percent, so for each Rs.1 of income, 20 paise is received as dividends and 80 paise as capital gains. Suppose that the marginal investor is in the top tax bracket paying 33.66 percent on interest income. Let's assume that the investor sells the shares after one year and hence pays only the securities transaction tax. Since he can defer the payment of the securities transaction tax, let's assume that the effective securities transaction tax rate is 0.0625 percent. Therefore, if the investor invests in Tata Steel's shares, the tax on each Rs.1 of equity income is TpE = $(0.1403 \times 0.2) + (0.000625 \times 0.8) =$ 2.856 percent.

Now we can calculate the effect of shunting a rupee income down each of the two branches in Figure 18.1:

	Interest	Equity Income
Income before tax	Rs. 1	Rs. 1
Less corporate tax at $T_c = 0.3366$	0	0.35
Income after corporate tax	1	0.66
Personal tax at $T_p = 0.3366$ and $T_{pE} = 0.02856$	0.34	0.02
Income after all taxes	Rs. 0.66	Rs. 0.64
	Advantage to debt = Rs. 0.02	

The advantage of debt financing appears to be about 2 paise on the rupee.

We would emphasize that our back-of-the-envelope calculation is just that. But it's interesting to see how debt's tax advantage shrinks when we account for the relatively low personal tax rate on equity. This reflects a tax-law change in this decade when the securities transaction tax was intro-

[7]See M. H. Miller, "Debt and Taxes," *Journal of Finance* 32 (May 1977), pp. 261–276.

duced. Before that change, the capital gains tax rate was 10 percent for the FIIs and NRIs and 20 percent for the most of the other investors. The advantage to debt is about 6 paise if we use these prior rates in our back-of-the envelope calculation.

Notice that borrowing is not the only way to shield income against tax. Firms use written down value method to depreciate assets. There are also many other provisions in the Income Tax Act in India that allow firms to report lower taxable income. The more that firms shield income in these ways, the lower is the expected shield from corporate borrowing. Even if the firm is confident that it will earn a taxable profit with the current level of debt, it is unlikely to be so positive if the amount of debt is increased.[8]

Despite these qualifications, most financial managers believe that there is a moderate tax advantage to corporate borrowing, at least for companies that are reasonably sure they can use the corporate tax shields. For companies that cannot benefit from corporate tax shields there is probably a moderate tax disadvantage.

Do companies make full use of interest tax shields? John Graham argues that they don't. His estimates suggest that a typical tax-paying corporation could add 7.5 percent to firm value by levering up to a still-conservative debt ratio.[9] Nevertheless, it appears that financial managers have passed by some easy tax savings. Perhaps they saw some offsetting disadvantage to increased borrowing. We will now explore this second escape route.

18.3 COSTS OF FINANCIAL DISTRESS

Financial distress occurs when promises to creditors are broken or honored with difficulty. Sometimes financial distress leads to bankruptcy. Sometimes it only means skating on thin ice.

As we will see, financial distress is costly. Investors know that levered firms may fall into financial distress, and they worry about it. That worry is reflected in the current market value of the levered firm's securities. Thus, the value of the firm can be broken down into three parts:

$$\begin{matrix}\text{Value} \\ \text{of firm}\end{matrix} = \begin{matrix}\text{value if} \\ \text{all-equity-financed}\end{matrix} + \text{PV(tax shield)} - \begin{matrix}\text{PV(costs of} \\ \text{financial distress)}\end{matrix}$$

The costs of financial distress depend on the probability of distress and the magnitude of costs encountered if distress occurs.

[8]For some evidence on the average marginal tax rate of U.S. firms, see J. R. Graham, "Debt and the Marginal Tax Rate," *Journal of Financial Economics* 41 (May 1996), pp. 41–73, and "Proxies for the Corporate Marginal Tax Rate," *Journal of Financial Economics* 42 (October 1996), pp. 187–221.

[9]Graham's estimates for individual firms recognize both the uncertainty in future profits and the existence of noninterest tax shields. See J. R. Graham, "How Big Are the Tax Benefits of Debt?" *Journal of Finance* 55 (October 2000), pp. 1901–1941.

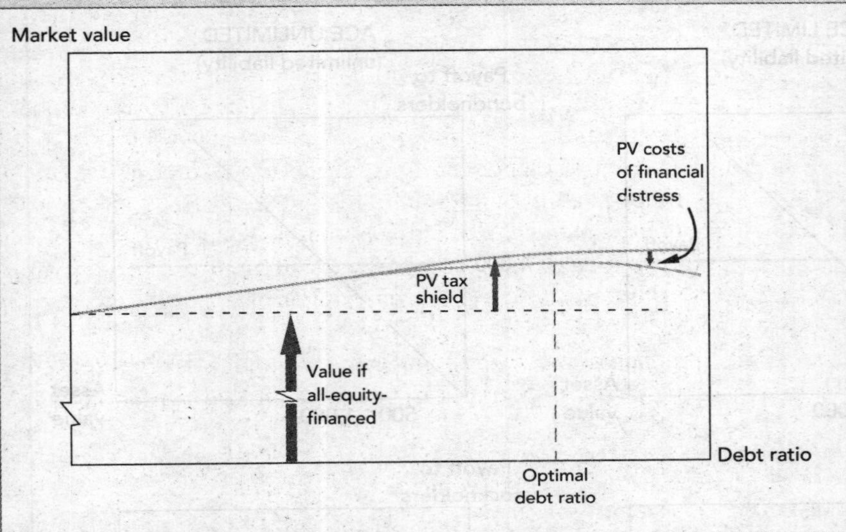

FIGURE 18.2

The value of the firm is equal to its value if all-equity-financed plus PV tax shield minus PV costs of financial distress. According to the trade-off theory of capital structure, the manager should choose the debt ratio that maximizes firm value.

Figure 18.2 shows how the trade-off between the tax benefits and the costs of distress determines optimal capital structure. PV(tax shield) initially increases as the firm borrows more. At moderate debt levels the probability of financial distress is trivial, and so PV(cost of financial distress) is small and tax advantages dominate. But at some point the probability of financial distress increases rapidly with additional borrowing; the costs of distress begin to take a substantial bite out of firm value. Also, if the firm can't be sure of profiting from the corporate tax shield, the tax advantage of additional debt is likely to dwindle and eventually disappear. The theoretical optimum is reached when the present value of tax savings due to further borrowing is just offset by increases in the present value of costs of distress. This is called the *trade-off theory* of capital structure.

Costs of financial distress cover several specific items. Now we identify these costs and try to understand what causes them.

Bankruptcy Costs

You rarely hear anything nice said about corporate bankruptcy. But there is some good in almost everything. Corporate bankruptcies occur when stockholders exercise their *right to default*. That right is valuable; when a firm gets into trouble, limited liability allows stockholders simply to walk away from it, leaving all its troubles to its creditors. The former creditors become the new stockholders, and the old stockholders are left with nothing.

In our legal system all stockholders in corporations automatically enjoy limited liability. But suppose that this were not so. Suppose that there are two firms with identical assets and operations. Each firm has debt outstanding, and each has promised to repay Rs. 1,000 (principal and interest) next year. But only one of the firms, Ace Limited, enjoys limited liability. The other firm, Ace Unlimited, does not; its stockholders are personally liable for its debt.

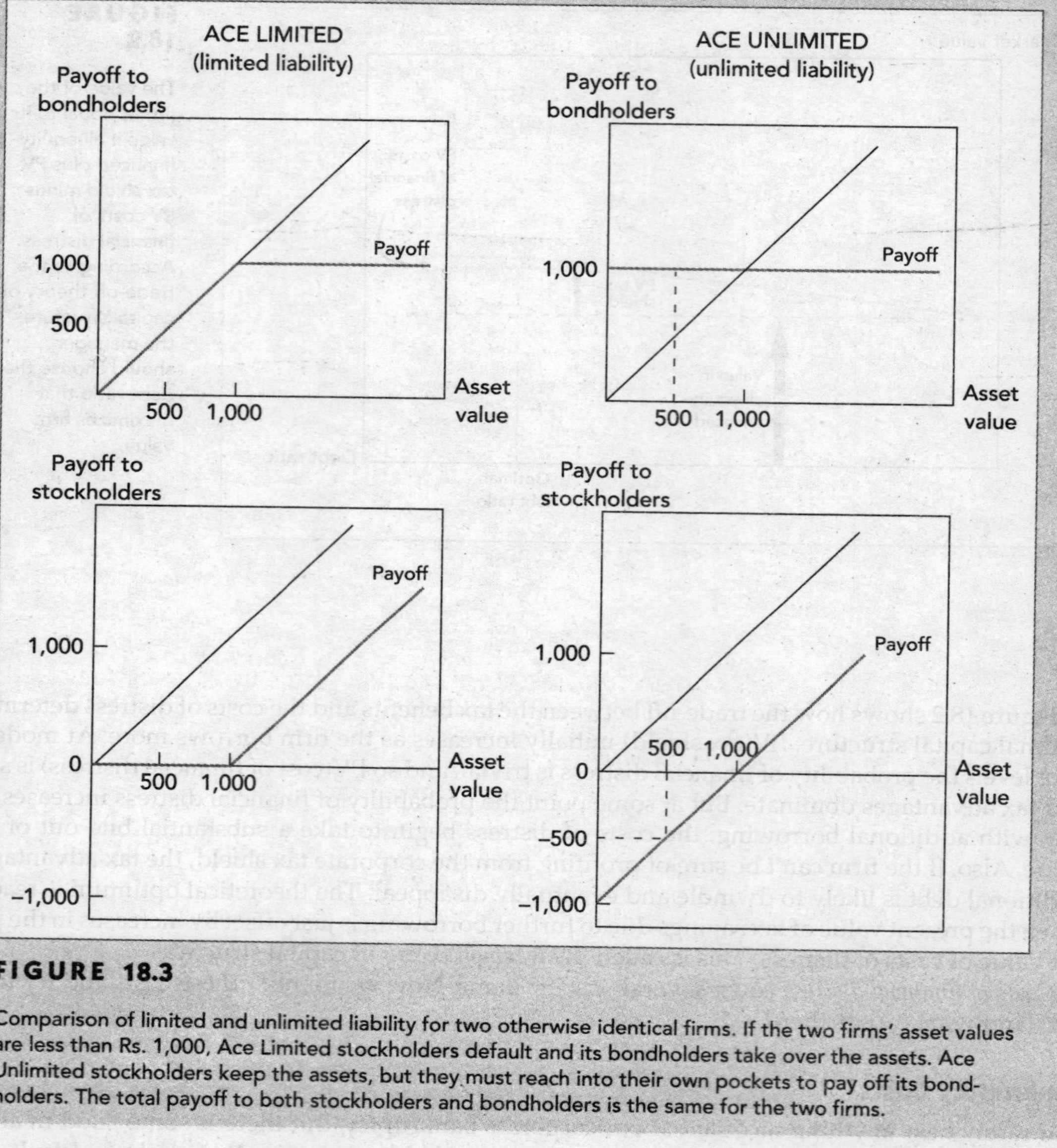

FIGURE 18.3

Comparison of limited and unlimited liability for two otherwise identical firms. If the two firms' asset values are less than Rs. 1,000, Ace Limited stockholders default and its bondholders take over the assets. Ace Unlimited stockholders keep the assets, but they must reach into their own pockets to pay off its bondholders. The total payoff to both stockholders and bondholders is the same for the two firms.

Figure 18.3 compares next year's possible payoffs to the creditors and stockholders of these two firms. The only differences occur when next year's asset value turns out to be less than Rs. 1,000. Suppose that next year the assets of each company are worth only Rs. 500. In this case Ace Limited defaults. Its stockholders walk away; their payoff is zero. Bondholders get the assets worth Rs. 500. But Ace Unlimited's stockholders can't walk away. They have to cough up Rs. 500, the difference between asset value and the bondholders' claim. The debt is paid whatever happens.

Suppose that Ace Limited does go bankrupt. Of course, its stockholders are disappointed that their firm is worth so little, but that is an operating problem having nothing to do with financing. Given poor operating performance, the right to go bankrupt—the right to default—is a valuable

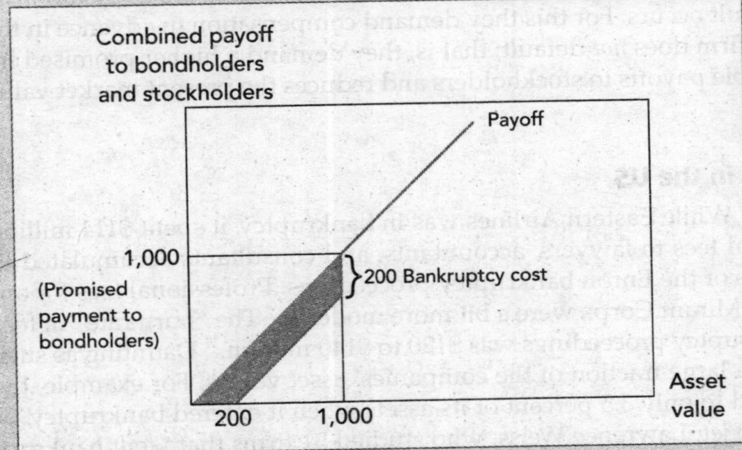

FIGURE 18.4

Total payoff to Ace Limited security holders. There is a Rs. 200 bankruptcy cost in the event of default (shaded area).

privilege. As Figure 18.3 shows, Ace Limited's stockholders are in better shape than Unlimited's are.

The example illuminates a mistake people often make in thinking about the costs of bankruptcy. Bankruptcies are thought of as corporate funerals. The mourners (creditors and especially shareholders) look at their firm's present sad state. They think of how valuable their securities used to be and how little is left. Moreover, they think of the lost value as a cost of bankruptcy. That is the mistake. The decline in the value of assets is what the mourning is really about. That has no necessary connection with financing. The bankruptcy is merely a legal mechanism for allowing creditors to take over when the decline in the value of assets triggers a default. Bankruptcy is not the *cause* of the decline in value. It is the result.

Be careful not to get cause and effect reversed. When a person dies, we do not cite the implementation of his or her will as the cause of death.

We said that bankruptcy is a legal mechanism allowing creditors to take over when a firm defaults. *Bankruptcy costs* are the costs of using this mechanism. There are no bankruptcy costs at all shown in Figure 18.3. Note that only Ace Limited can default and go bankrupt. But, regardless of what happens to asset value, the *combined* payoff to the bondholders and stockholders of Ace Limited is always the same as the *combined* payoff to the bondholders and stockholders of Ace Unlimited. Thus the overall market values of the two firms now (this year) must be identical. Of course, Ace Limited's stock is worth more than Ace Unlimited's stock because of Ace Limited's right to default. Ace Limited's debt is worth correspondingly less.

Our example was not intended to be strictly realistic. Anything involving courts and lawyers cannot be free. Suppose that court and legal fees are Rs. 200 if Ace Limited defaults. The fees are paid out of the remaining value of Ace's assets. Thus if asset value turns out to be Rs. 500, creditors end up with only Rs. 300. Figure 18.4 shows next year's *total* payoff to bondholders and stockholders net of this bankruptcy cost. Ace Limited, by issuing risky debt, has given lawyers and the court system a claim on the firm if it defaults. The market value of the firm is reduced by the present value of this claim.

It is easy to see how increased leverage affects the present value of the costs of financial distress. If Ace Limited borrows more, it increases the probability of default and the value of the lawyers' claim. It increases PV (costs of financial distress) and reduces Ace's present market value.

The costs of bankruptcy come out of stockholders' pockets. Creditors foresee the costs and foresee that *they* will pay them if default occurs. For this they demand compensation in advance in the form of higher payoffs when the firm does *not* default; that is, they demand a higher promised interest rate. This reduces the possible payoffs to stockholders and reduces the present market value of their shares.

Evidence on Bankruptcy Costs in the US

Bankruptcy costs can add up fast. While Eastern Airlines was in bankruptcy, it spent $114 million on professional fees.[10] Professional fees to lawyers, accountants, and consultants accumulated to $306 million in the first 13 months of the Enron bankruptcy proceedings. Professional fees for another distressed energy company, Mirant Corp., were a bit more moderate. The "burn rate" of fees for the first year of Mirant's bankruptcy proceedings was $120 to $140 million.[11] Daunting as such numbers may seem, they are not a large fraction of the companies' asset values. For example, the fees incurred by Eastern amounted to only 3.5 percent of its assets when it entered bankruptcy, or about the equivalent of one jumbo jet. Lawrence Weiss, who studied 31 firms that went bankrupt between 1980 and 1986, found average costs of about 3 percent of total book assets and 20 percent of the market value of equity in the year prior to bankruptcy. A study by Edward Altman found that costs were similar for retail companies but higher for industrial companies. Also, bankruptcy eats up a larger fraction of asset value for small companies than for large ones. There are significant economies of scale in going bankrupt.[12] Finally, a study by Andrade and Kaplan of a sample of troubled and highly leveraged firms estimated costs of financial distress amounting to 10 to 20 percent of predistress market value, although they found it hard to decide whether these costs were caused by financial distress or by the business setbacks that led to distress.[13]

Direct versus Indirect Costs of Bankruptcy

So far we have discussed the *direct* (that is, legal and administrative) costs of bankruptcy. There are indirect costs too, which are nearly impossible to measure. But we have circumstantial evidence indicating their importance.

Managing a bankrupt firm is not easy. Consent of the bankruptcy court is required for many routine business decisions, such as the sale of assets or investment in new equipment. At best this

[10]L. Gibbs and A. Boardman, "A Billion Later, Eastern's Finally Gone," *American Lawyer Newspaper Groups*, February 6, 1995.

[11]M. Orey, "Group of Enron Creditors Say Court Costs Grow Unwieldy," *The Wall Street Journal*, November 4, 2002, p. B3; and "Mirant Bankruptcy Legal Fees Seen Topping $120 Million," Reuters, January 20, 2004.

[12]The pioneering study of bankruptcy costs is J. B. Warner, "Bankruptcy Costs: Some Evidence," *Journal of Finance* 26 (May 1977), pp. 337–348. The Weiss and Altman papers are L. A. Weiss, "Bankruptcy Resolution: Direct Costs and Violation of Priority of Claims," *Journal of Financial Economics* 27 (October 1990), pp. 285–314; and E. I. Altman, "A Further Investigation of the Bankruptcy Cost Question," *Journal of Finance* 39 (September 1984), pp. 1067–1089.

[13]G. Andrade and S. N. Kaplan, "How Costly Is Financial (not Economic) Distress? Evidence from Highly Leveraged Transactions That Became Distressed," *Journal of Finance* 53 (October 1998), pp. 1443–1493.

involves time and effort; at worst the proposals are thwarted by the firm's creditors, who have little interest in the firm's long-term prosperity and would prefer the cash to be paid out to them.

Sometimes the problem is reversed: The bankruptcy court is so anxious to maintain the firm as a going concern that it allows the firm to engage in negative-NPV activities. When Eastern Airlines entered the "protection" of the bankruptcy court in 1989, it still had some valuable, profit-making routes and saleable assets such as planes and terminal facilities. The creditors would have been best served by a prompt liquidation, which probably would have generated enough cash to pay off all debt and preferred stockholders. But the bankruptcy judge was keen to keep Eastern's planes flying at all costs, so he allowed the company to sell many of its assets to fund hefty operating losses. When Eastern finally closed down after two years, it was not just bankrupt, but *administratively* insolvent: There was almost nothing for creditors, and the company was running out of cash to pay legal expenses.[14]

We do not know what the sum of direct and indirect costs of bankruptcy amounts to. We suspect it is a significant number, particularly for large firms for which proceedings would be lengthy and complex. Perhaps the best evidence is the reluctance of creditors to force bankruptcy. In principle, they would be better off to end the agony and seize the assets as soon as possible. Instead, creditors often overlook defaults in the hope of nursing the firm over a difficult period. They do this in part to avoid costs of bankruptcy.[15] There is an old financial saying, "Borrow $1,000 and you've got a banker. Borrow $10,000,000 and you've got a partner."

In all this discussion of bankruptcy costs we have said very little about bankruptcy *procedures*. These are described in Chapter 33.

Financial Distress without Bankruptcy

Not every firm that gets into trouble goes bankrupt. As long as the firm can scrape up enough cash to pay the interest on its debt, it may be able to postpone bankruptcy for many years. Eventually the firm may recover, pay off its debt, and escape bankruptcy altogether.

But the mere threat of financial distress can be costly to the threatened firm. Customers and suppliers are extra cautious about doing business with a firm that may not be around for long. Customers worry about resale value and the availability of service and replacement parts. (Would you buy a new car from a manufacturer that is driving down the road to bankruptcy?) Suppliers are disinclined to put effort into servicing the distressed firm's account and may demand cash on the nail for their products. Potential employees are unwilling to sign on and existing staff keep slipping away from their desks for job interviews.

[14]The bankruptcy of Eastern Airlines is analyzed in L. A. Weiss and K. H. Wruck, "Information Problems, Conflicts of Interest, and Asset Stripping: Chapter 11's Failure in the Case of Eastern Airlines," *Journal of Financial Economics* 48 (1998), pp. 55–97.

[15]There is another reason. Creditors are not always given absolute priority in bankruptcy. *Absolute priority* means that creditors must be paid in full before stockholders receive a cent. Sometimes reorganizations are negotiated which provide something for everyone, even though creditors are *not* paid in full. Thus creditors can never be sure how they will fare in bankruptcy.

High debt, and thus high financial risk, also appears to reduce firms' appetites for business risk. For example, Luigi Zingales looked at the fortunes of U.S. trucking companies after the trucking industry was deregulated in the late 1970s.[16] The deregulation sparked a wave of competition and restructuring. Survival required new investment and improvements in operating efficiency. Zingales found that conservatively financed trucking companies were more likely to survive in the new competitive environment. High-debt firms were more likely to drop out of the game.

Debt and Incentives

When a firm is in trouble, both bondholders and stockholders want it to recover, but in other respects their interests may be in conflict. In times of financial distress the security holders are like many political parties—united on generalities but threatened by squabbling on any specific issue.

Financial distress is costly when these conflicts of interest get in the way of proper operating, investment, and financing decisions. Stockholders are tempted to forsake the usual objective of maximizing the overall market value of the firm and to pursue narrower self-interest instead. They are tempted to play games at the expense of their creditors. We will now illustrate how such games can lead to costs of financial distress.

Here is the Circular File Company's book balance sheet:

Circular File Company (Book Values)

Net current assets	Rs. 20	Rs. 50	Bonds outstanding
Fixed assets	80	50	Shareholders' funds
Total assets	Rs. 100	Rs. 100	Total value

We will assume there is only one share and one bond outstanding. The stockholder is also the manager. The bondholder is somebody else.

Here is its balance sheet in market values—a clear case of financial distress, since the face value of Circular's debt (Rs. 50) exceeds the firm's total market value (Rs. 30):

Circular File Company (Market Values)

Net current assets	Rs. 20	Rs. 25	Bonds outstanding
Fixed assets	10	5	Shareholders' funds
Total assets	Rs. 30	Rs. 30	Total value

If the debt matured today, Circular's owner would default, leaving the firm bankrupt. But suppose that the bond actually matures one year hence, that there is enough cash for Circular to limp along for one year, and that the bondholder cannot "call the question" and force bankruptcy before then.

The one-year grace period explains why the Circular share still has value. Its owner is betting on a stroke of luck that will rescue the firm, allowing it to pay off the debt with something left over. The bet is a long shot—the owner wins only if firm value increases from Rs. 30 to more than Rs. 50.[17] But the owner has a secret weapon: He controls investment and operating strategy.

---

[16] L. Zingales, "Survival of the Fittest or the Fattest? Exit and Financing in the Trucking Industry," *Journal of Finance* 53 (June 1998), pp. 905–938.

[17] We are not concerned here with how to work out whether $5 is a fair price for stockholders to pay for the bet. We will come to that in Chapter 24 when we discuss risky debt.

Risk Shifting: The First Game

Suppose that Circular has Rs. 10 cash. The following investment opportunity comes up:

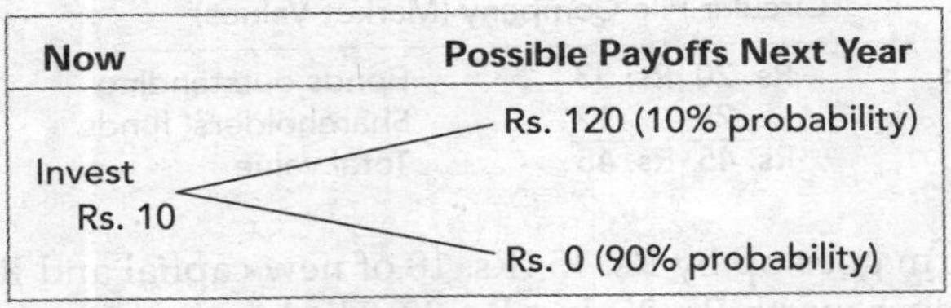

This is a wild gamble and probably a lousy project. But you can see why the owner would be tempted to take it anyway. Why not go for broke? Circular will probably go under anyway, so the owner is essentially betting with the bondholder's money. But the owner gets most of the loot if the project pays off.

Suppose that the project's NPV is −Rs. 2 but that it is undertaken anyway, thus depressing firm value by Rs. 2. Circular's new balance sheet might look like this:

Circular File Company (Market Values)

Net current assets	Rs. 10	Rs. 20	Bonds outstanding
Fixed assets	18	8	Shareholders' funds
Total assets	Rs. 28	Rs. 28	Total value

Firm value falls by Rs. 2, but the owner is Rs. 3 ahead because the bond's value has fallen by Rs. 5.[18] The Rs. 10 cash that used to stand behind the bond has been replaced by a very risky asset worth only Rs. 8.

Thus a game has been played at the expense of Circular's bondholder. The game illustrates the following general point: Stockholders of levered firms gain when business risk increases. Financial managers who act strictly in their shareholders' interests (and *against* the interests of creditors) will favor risky projects over safe ones. They may even take risky projects with negative NPVs.

This warped strategy for capital budgeting clearly is costly to the firm and to the economy as a whole. Why do we associate the costs with financial distress? Because the temptation to play is strongest when the odds of default are high. A blue-chip company like ExxonMobil would never invest in our negative-NPV gamble. Its creditors are not vulnerable to this type of game.

Refusing to Contribute Equity Capital: The Second Game

We have seen how stockholders, acting in their immediate, narrow self-interest, may take projects that reduce the overall market value of their firm. These are errors of commission. Conflicts of interest may also lead to errors of omission.

Assume that Circular cannot scrape up any cash, and therefore cannot take that wild gamble. Instead a *good* opportunity comes up: a relatively safe asset costing Rs. 10 with a present value of Rs. 15 and NPV = +Rs. 5.

This project will not in itself rescue Circular, but it is a step in the right direction. We might therefore expect Circular to issue Rs. 10 of new stock and to go ahead with the investment. Suppose that

[18]We are not calculating this Rs. 5 drop. We are simply using it as a plausible assumption. The tools necessary for a calculation come in Chapter 24.

two new shares are issued to the original owner for Rs. 10 cash. The project is taken. The new balance sheet might look like this:

Circular File Company (Market Values)

Net current assets	Rs. 20	Rs. 33	Bonds outstanding
Fixed assets	25	12	Shareholders' funds
Total assets	Rs. 45	Rs. 45	Total value

The total value of the firm goes up by Rs. 15 (Rs. 10 of new capital and Rs. 5 NPV). Notice that the Circular bond is no longer worth Rs. 25, but Rs. 33. The bondholder receives a capital gain of Rs. 8 because the firm's assets include a new, safe asset worth Rs. 15. The probability of default is less, and the payoff to the bondholder if default occurs is larger.

The stockholder loses what the bondholder gains. Equity value goes up not by Rs. 15 but by Rs. 15 − Rs. 8 = Rs. 7. The owner puts in Rs. 10 of fresh equity capital but gains only Rs. 7 in market value. Going ahead is in the firm's interest but not the owner's.

Again, our example illustrates a general point. If we hold business risk constant, any increase in firm value is shared among bondholders and stockholders. The value of any investment opportunity to the firm's *stockholders* is reduced because project benefits must be shared with bondholders. Thus it may not be in the stockholders' self-interest to contribute fresh equity capital even if that means forgoing positive-NPV investment opportunities.

This problem theoretically affects all levered firms, but it is most serious when firms land in financial distress. The greater the probability of default, the more bondholders have to gain from investments that increase firm value.

And Three More Games, Briefly

As with other games, the temptation to play the next three games is particularly strong in financial distress.

Cash In and Run Stockholders may be reluctant to put money into a firm in financial distress, but they are happy to take the money out—in the form of a cash dividend, for example. The market value of the firm's stock goes down by less than the amount of the dividend paid, because the decline in *firm* value is shared with creditors. This game is just "refusing to contribute equity capital" run in reverse.

Playing for Time When the firm is in financial distress, creditors would like to salvage what they can by forcing the firm to settle up. Naturally, stockholders want to delay this as long as they can. There are various devious ways of doing this, for example, through accounting changes designed to conceal the true extent of trouble, by encouraging false hopes of spontaneous recovery, or by cutting corners on maintenance, research and development, and so on, in order to make this year's operating performance look better.

Bait and Switch This game is not always played in financial distress, but it is a quick way to get *into* distress. You start with a conservative policy, issuing a limited amount of relatively safe debt. Then you suddenly switch and issue a lot more. That makes all your debt risky, imposing a capital loss on the "old" bondholders. Their capital loss is the stockholders' gain.

The most dramatic example of bait and switch occurred in October 1988, when the management of RJR Nabisco announced its intention to acquire the company in a *leveraged buy-out* (LBO). This put the company "in play" for a transaction in which existing shareholders would be bought out and the company would be "taken private." The cost of the buy-out would be almost entirely debt-financed. The new private company would start life with an extremely high debt ratio.

RJR Nabisco had debt outstanding with a market value of about Rs. 2.4 billion. The announcement of the coming LBO drove down this market value by Rs. 298 million.[19]

What the Games Cost

Why should anyone object to these games so long as they are played by consenting adults? Because playing them means poor decisions about investments and operations. These poor decisions are *agency costs* of borrowing.

The more the firm borrows, the greater is the temptation to play the games (assuming the financial manager acts in the stockholders' interest). The increased odds of poor decisions in the future prompt investors to mark down the present market value of the firm. The fall in value comes out of the shareholders' pockets. Therefore it is ultimately in their interest to avoid temptation. The easiest way to do this is to limit borrowing to levels at which the firm's debt is safe or close to it.

Banks and other corporate lenders are also not financial innocents. They realize that games may be played at their expense and so protect themselves by rationing the amount that they will lend or by imposing restrictions on the company's actions. For example, consider the case of Henrietta Ketchup, a budding entrepreneur with two possible investment projects that offer the following payoffs:

	Investment	Payoff	Probability of Payoff
Project 1	−12	+15	1.0
Project 2	−12	+24	.5
		0	.5

Project 1 is surefire and very profitable; project 2 is risky and a rotten project. Ms. Ketchup now approaches her bank and asks to borrow the present value of Rs. 10 (she will find the remaining money out of her own purse). The bank calculates that the payoff will be split as follows:

	Expected Payoff to Bank	Expected Payoff to Ms. Ketchup
Project 1	+10	+5
Project 2	(.5 × 10) + (.5 × 0) = +5	.5 × (24 − 10) = +7

If Ms. Ketchup accepts project 1, the bank's debt is certain to be paid in full; if she accepts project 2, there is only a 50 percent chance of payment and the expected payoff to the bank is only Rs. 5. Unfortunately, Ms. Ketchup will prefer to take project 2, for if things go well, she gets most

[19]We thank Paul Asquith for these figures. RJR Nabisco was finally taken private not by its management but by another LBO partnership. We discuss this LBO in Chapter 33.

of the profit, and if they go badly, the bank bears most of the loss. Unless Ms. Ketchup can convince the bank that she will not gamble with its money, the bank will limit the amount that it is prepared to lend.[20]

How can Ms. Ketchup reassure the bank of her intentions? The obvious answer is to give it veto power over potentially dangerous decisions. There we have the ultimate economic rationale for all that fine print backing up corporate debt. Debt contracts frequently limit dividends or equivalent transfers of wealth to stockholders; the firm may not be allowed to pay out more than it earns, for example. Additional borrowing is almost always limited. For example, many companies are prevented by existing bond indentures from issuing any additional long-term debt unless their ratio of earnings to interest charges exceeds 2.0.[21]

Sometimes firms are restricted from selling assets or making major investment outlays except with the lenders' consent. The risks of playing for time are reduced by specifying accounting procedures and by giving lenders access to the firm's books and its financial forecasts.

Of course, fine print cannot be a complete solution for firms that insist on issuing risky debt. The fine print has its own costs; you have to spend money to save money. Obviously a complex debt contract costs more to negotiate than a simple one. Afterward it costs the lender more to monitor the firm's performance. Lenders anticipate monitoring costs and demand compensation in the form of higher interest rates; thus the monitoring costs—another agency cost of debt—are ultimately paid by stockholders.

Perhaps the most severe costs of the fine print stem from the constraints it places on operating and investment decisions. For example, an attempt to prevent the risk-shifting game may also prevent the firm from pursuing *good* investment opportunities. At the minimum there are delays in clearing major investments with lenders. In some cases lenders may veto high-risk investments even if net present value is positive. The lenders are tempted to play a game of their own, forcing the firm to stay in cash or low-risk assets even if good projects are forgone.

Debt contracts cannot cover every possible manifestation of the games we have just discussed. Any attempt to do so would be hopelessly expensive and doomed to failure in any event. Human imagination is insufficient to conceive of all the possible things that could go wrong. Therefore contracts are always *incomplete.* We will always find surprises coming at us on dimensions we never thought to think about.

We hope we have not left the impression that managers and stockholders always succumb to temptation unless restrained. Usually they refrain voluntarily, not only from a sense of fair play but also on pragmatic grounds: A firm or individual that makes a killing today at the expense of a creditor will be coldly received when the time comes to borrow again. Aggressive game playing is done only by out-and-out crooks and by firms in extreme financial distress. Firms limit borrowing precisely because they don't wish to land in distress and be exposed to the temptation to play.

---

[20]You might think that, if the bank suspects Ms. Ketchup will undertake project 2, it should just raise the interest rate on its loan. In this case Ms. Ketchup will not want to take on project 2 (they can't both be happy with a lousy project). But Ms. Ketchup also would not want to pay a high rate of interest if she is going to take on project 1 (she would do better to borrow less money at the risk-free rate). So simply raising the interest rate is not the answer.

[21]We discuss covenants and the rest of the fine print in debt contracts in Section 25.5.

Costs of Distress Vary with Type of Asset

Suppose your firm's only asset is a large downtown hotel, mortgaged to the hilt. The recession hits, occupancy rates fall, and the mortgage payments cannot be met. The lender takes over and sells the hotel to a new owner and operator. You use your firm's stock certificates for wallpaper.

What is the cost of bankruptcy? In this example, probably very little. The value of the hotel is, of course, much less than you hoped, but that is due to the lack of guests, not to the bankruptcy. Bankruptcy doesn't damage the hotel itself. The direct bankruptcy costs are restricted to items such as legal and court fees, real estate commissions, and the time the lender spends sorting things out.

Suppose we repeat the story of Heartbreak Hotel for Fledgling Electronics. Everything is the same, except for the underlying real assets—not real estate but a high-tech going concern, a growth company whose most valuable assets are technology, investment opportunities, and its employees' human capital.

If Fledgling gets into trouble, the stockholders may be reluctant to put up money to cash in on its growth opportunities. Failure to invest is likely to be much more serious for Fledgling than for a company like Heartbreak Hotel.

If Fledgling finally defaults on its debt, the lender will find it much more difficult to cash in by selling off the assets. Many of them are intangibles which have value only as a part of a going concern.

Could Fledgling be kept as a going concern through default and reorganization? It may not be as hopeless as putting a wedding cake through a car wash, but there are a number of serious difficulties. First, the odds of defections by key employees are higher than they would be if the firm had never gotten into financial trouble. Special guarantees may have to be given to customers who have doubts about whether the firm will be around to service its products. Aggressive investment in new products and technology will be difficult; each class of creditors will have to be convinced that it is in its interest for the firm to invest new money in risky ventures.

Some assets, like good commercial real estate, can pass through bankruptcy and reorganization largely unscathed;[22] the values of other assets are likely to be considerably diminished. The losses are greatest for the intangible assets that are linked to the health of the firm as a going concern—for example, technology, human capital, and brand image. That may be why debt ratios are low in the pharmaceutical industry, where value depends on continued success in research and development, and in many service industries where value depends on human capital. We can also understand why highly profitable growth companies, such as Infosys or HLL, use mostly equity finance.

The moral of these examples is this: *Do not think only about the probability that borrowing will bring trouble. Think also of the value that may be lost if trouble comes.*

Heartbreak Hotel for Enron? Enron was one of the most glamorous, fast-growing, and (apparently) profitable companies of the 1990s. It played a lead role in the deregulation of electric power markets, both in the United States and internationally. It invested in electric power generation and distribution,

[22]In 1989 the Rockefeller family sold 80 percent of Rockefeller Center—several acres of extremely valuable Manhattan real estate—to Mitsubishi Estate Company for $1.4 billion. A REIT, Rockefeller Center Properties, held a $1.3 billion mortgage loan (the REIT's only asset) secured by this real estate. But rents and occupancy rates did not meet forecasts, and by 1995 Mitsubishi had incurred losses of about $600 million. Then Mitsubishi quit, and Rockefeller Center was bankrupt. That triggered a complicated series of maneuvers and negotiations. But did this damage the value of the Rockefeller Center properties? Was Radio City Music Hall, one of the properties, any less valuable because of the bankruptcy? We doubt it.

gas pipelines, telecommunications networks, and various other ventures. It also built up an active energy trading business. At the start of 2000, the aggregate market value of Enron's common stock exceeded $60 billion. By the end of 2000, Enron was in bankruptcy and its shares were worthless.

With hindsight we see that Enron was playing many of the games that we described earlier in this section. It was borrowing aggressively and hiding the debt in "special purpose entities" (SPEs). The SPEs also allowed it to pump up its reported earnings, playing for time while making more and more risky investments. When the bubble burst, there was hardly any value left.

The collapse of Enron didn't really destroy $60 billion in value, because that $60 billion wasn't there in the first place. But there were genuine costs of financial distress. Let's focus on Enron's energy trading business. That business was not as profitable as it appeared, but it was nevertheless a valuable asset. It provided an important service for wholesale energy customers and suppliers who wanted to buy or sell contracts that locked in the future prices and quantities of electricity, natural gas, and other commodities.

What happened to this business when it became clear that Enron was in financial distress and probably headed for bankruptcy? It disappeared. Trading volume went to zero immediately. None of its customers were willing to make a new trade with Enron, because it was far from clear that Enron would be around to honor its side of the bargain. With no trading volume, there was no trading business. As it turned out, Enron's trading business more resembled Fledgling Electronics than a tangible asset like Heartbreak Hotel.

The value of Enron's trading business depended on Enron's creditworthiness. The value should have been protected by conservative financing. Most of the lost value can be traced back to Enron's aggressive borrowing. This loss of value was therefore a cost of financial distress.

The Trade-off Theory of Capital Structure

Financial managers often think of the firm's debt–equity decision as a trade-off between interest tax shields and the costs of financial distress. Of course, there is controversy about how valuable interest tax shields are and what kinds of financial trouble are most threatening, but these disagreements are only variations on a theme. Thus, Figure 18.2 illustrates the debt–equity trade-off.

This *trade-off theory* of capital structure recognizes that target debt ratios may vary from firm to firm. Companies with safe, tangible assets and plenty of taxable income to shield ought to have high target ratios. Unprofitable companies with risky, intangible assets ought to rely primarily on equity financing.

If there were no costs of adjusting capital structure, then each firm should always be at its target debt ratio. However, there are costs, and therefore delays, in adjusting to the optimum. Firms cannot immediately offset the random events that bump them away from their capital structure targets, so we should see random differences in actual debt ratios among firms having the same target debt ratio.

All in all, this trade-off theory of capital structure choice tells a comforting story. Unlike MM's theory, which seemed to say that firms should take on as much debt as possible, it avoids extreme predictions and rationalizes moderate debt ratios. Also, if you ask financial managers whether their firms have target debt ratios, they will usually say yes.[23] This is consistent with the trade-off theory.

But what are the facts? Can the trade-off theory of capital structure explain how companies actually behave?

The answer is "yes and no." On the "yes" side, the trade-off theory successfully explains many industry differences in capital structure. High-tech growth companies, for example, whose assets are risky and mostly intangible, normally use relatively little debt. Airlines can and do borrow heavily because their assets are tangible and relatively safe.[24]

On the "no" side, there are a few things the trade-off theory cannot explain. It cannot explain why some of the most successful companies thrive with little debt. Think of Asian Paints, which as Table 18.3(a) shows is almost all-equity financed. Granted, Asian Paints' most valuable assets are intangible, its brand name and its distribution network. We know that intangible assets and conservative capital structures go together. But Asian Paints also has a very large corporate income tax bill (about Rs.970 crores in 2005) and the highest possible credit rating (CRISIL rating: AAA). It could borrow enough to save crores of rupees without raising a whisker of concern about possible financial distress.

Asian Paints illustrates an odd fact about real-life capital structures: The most profitable companies commonly borrow the least.[25] Here the trade-off theory fails, for it predicts exactly the reverse. Under the trade-off theory, high profits should mean more debt-servicing capacity and more taxable income to shield and so should give a *higher* target debt ratio.[26]

In general it appears that public companies rarely make major shifts in capital structure just because of taxes,[27] and it is hard to detect the present value of interest tax shields in firms' market values.[28]

---

[23]See J. Graham and C. Harvey, "The Theory and Practice of Corporate Finance: Evidence from the Field," *Journal of Financial Economics* 60 (May/June 2001), pp. 187–244.

[24]We are not suggesting that all airline companies are safe; many are not. But air*craft* can support debt where air*lines* cannot. If Fly-by-Night Airlines fails, its planes retain their value in another airline's operations. There's a good secondary market in used aircraft, so a loan secured by aircraft can be well protected even if made to an airline flying on thin ice (and in the dark).

[25]For example, in an international comparison Wald found that profitability was the single largest determinant of firm capital structure. See J. K. Wald, "How Firm Characteristics Affect Capital Structure: An International Comparison," *Journal of Financial Research* 22 (Summer 1999), pp. 161–187.

[26]Here we mean debt as a fraction of the book or replacement value of the company's assets. Profitable companies might not borrow a greater fraction of their market value. Higher profits imply higher market value as well as stronger incentives to borrow.

[27]Mackie-Mason found that taxpaying companies are more likely to issue debt (vs. equity) than nontaxpaying companies. This shows that taxes do affect financing choices. However, it is not necessarily evidence for the trade-off theory. Look back to Section 18.2, and note the special case where corporate and personal taxes cancel to make debt policy irrelevant. In that case, taxpaying firms would see no net tax advantage to debt: corporate interest tax shields would be offset by the taxes paid by investors in the firm's debt. But the balance would tip in favor of equity for a firm that was losing money and reaping no benefits from interest tax shields. See J. Mackie-Mason, "Do Taxes Affect Corporate Financing Decisions?" *Journal of Finance* 45 (December 1990), pp. 1471–1493.

[28]A study by E. F. Fama and K. R. French, covering over 2,000 firms from 1965 to 1992, failed to find any evidence that interest tax shields contributed to firm value. See "Taxes, Financing Decisions and Firm Value," *Journal of Finance* 53 (June 1998), pp. 819–843.

A final point on the "no" side for the trade-off theory: The average debt ratio in India has remained stable at 60 percent in most of the last 16 years (1990-2005) despite huge declines in both corporate and personal tax rates. Similarly, in the U.S., the debt ratios have remained stable despite an increase in the income tax rates. Debt ratios in many other countries are equal to or higher than those in India. Many of these countries have imputation tax system, which should eliminate the value of the interest tax shields.[29]

None of this disproves the trade-off theory. As George Stigler emphasized, theories are not rejected by circumstantial evidence; it takes a theory to beat a theory. So we now turn to a completely different theory of financing.

18.4 THE PECKING ORDER OF FINANCING CHOICES

The pecking-order theory starts with *asymmetric information*—a fancy term indicating that managers know more about their companies' prospects, risks, and values than do outside investors.

Managers obviously know more than investors. We can prove that by observing stock price changes caused by announcements by managers. When a company announces an increased regular dividend, stock price typically rises, because investors interpret the increase as a sign of management's confidence in future earnings. In other words, the dividend increase transfers information from managers to investors. This can happen only if managers know more in the first place.

Asymmetric information affects the choice between internal and external financing and between new issues of debt and equity securities. This leads to a *pecking order*, in which investment is financed first with internal funds, reinvested earnings primarily; then by new issues of debt; and finally with new issues of equity. New equity issues are a last resort when the company runs out of debt capacity, that is, when the threat of costs of financial distress brings regular insomnia to existing creditors and to the financial manager.

We will take a closer look at the pecking order in a moment. First, you must appreciate how asymmetric information can force the financial manager to issue debt rather than common stock.

Debt and Equity Issues with Asymmetric Information

To the outside world Om & Company and Jai, Inc., our two example companies, are identical. Each runs a successful business with good growth opportunities. The two businesses are risky, however, and investors have learned from experience that current expectations are frequently bettered or disappointed. Current expectations price each company's stock at Rs. 100 per share, but the true values could be higher or lower:

---

[29]We described the Australian imputation tax system in Section 16.8. Look again at Table 16.3, supposing that an Australian corporation pays $A10 of interest. This reduces the corporate tax by $A3.00; it also reduces the tax credit taken by the shareholders by $A3.00. The final tax does not depend on whether the corporation or the shareholder borrows.

You can check this by redrawing Figure 18.1 for the Australian system. The corporate tax rate T_c will cancel out. Since income after all taxes depends only on investors' tax rates, there is no special advantage to corporate borrowing.

	Om & Co.	Jai, Inc.
True value could be higher, say	Rs. 120	Rs. 120
Best current estimate	100	100
True value could be lower, say	80	80

Now suppose that both companies need to raise new money from investors to fund capital investment. They can do this either by issuing bonds or by issuing new shares of common stock. How would the choice be made? One financial manager—we will not tell you which one—might reason as follows:

> Sell stock for Rs. 100 per share? Ridiculous! It's worth at least Rs. 120. A stock issue now would hand a free gift to new investors. I just wish those stupid, skeptical shareholders would appreciate the true value of this company. Our new factories will make us the world's lowest-cost producer. We've painted a rosy picture for the press and security analysts, but it just doesn't seem to be working. Oh well, the decision is obvious: we'll issue debt, not underpriced equity. A debt issue will save underwriting fees too.

The other financial manager is in a different mood:

> Beefalo burgers were a hit for a while, but it looks like the fad is fading. The fast-food division's gotta find some good new products or it's all downhill from here. Export markets are OK for now, but how are we going to compete with those new Siberian ranches? Fortunately the stock price has held up pretty well—we've had some good short-run news for the press and security analysts. Now's the time to issue stock. We have major investments underway, and why add increased debt service to my other worries?

Of course, outside investors can't read the financial managers' minds. If they could, one stock might trade at Rs. 120 and the other at Rs. 80.

Why doesn't the optimistic financial manager simply educate investors? Then the company could sell stock on fair terms, and there would be no reason to favor debt over equity or vice versa.

This is not so easy. (Note that both companies are issuing upbeat press releases.) Investors can't be told what to think; they have to be convinced. That takes a detailed layout of the company's plans and prospects, including the inside scoop on new technology, product design, marketing plans, and so on. Getting this across is expensive for the company and also valuable to its competitors. Why go to the trouble? Investors will learn soon enough, as revenues and earnings evolve. In the meantime the optimistic financial manager can finance growth by issuing debt.

Now suppose there are two press releases:

> Jai, Inc., will issue Rs. 120 million of five-year senior notes.
>
> Om & Co. announced plans today to issue 1.2 million new shares of common stock. The company expects to raise Rs. 120 million.

As a rational investor, you immediately learn two things. First, Jai's financial manager is optimistic and Om's is pessimistic. Second, Om's financial manager is also stupid to think that investors would pay Rs. 100 per share. The *attempt* to sell stock shows that it must be worth less. Om might sell stock at Rs. 80 per share, but certainly not at Rs. 100.[30]

[30] An Om stock issue might not succeed even at Rs. 80. Persistence in trying to sell at Rs. 80 could convince investors that the stock is worth even less!

Smart financial managers think this through ahead of time. The end result? Both Om and Jai end up issuing debt. Jai, Inc., issues debt because its financial manager is optimistic and doesn't want to issue undervalued equity. A smart, but pessimistic, financial manager at Om issues debt because an attempt to issue equity would force the stock price down and eliminate any advantage from doing so. (Issuing equity also reveals the manager's pessimism immediately. Most managers prefer to wait. A debt issue lets bad news come out later through other channels.)

The story of Om and Jai illustrates how asymmetric information favors debt issues over equity issues. If managers are better informed than investors and both groups are rational, then any company that can borrow will do so rather than issuing fresh equity. In other words, debt issues will be higher in the pecking order.

Taken literally this reasoning seems to rule out any issue of equity. That's not right, because asymmetric information is not always important and there are other forces at work. For example, if Om had already borrowed heavily, and would risk financial distress by borrowing more, then it would have a good reason to issue common stock. In this case announcement of a stock issue would not be entirely bad news. The announcement would still depress the stock price—it would highlight managers' concerns about financial distress—but the fall in price would not necessarily make the issue unwise or infeasible.

High-tech, high-growth companies can also be credible issuers of common stock. Such companies' assets are mostly intangible, and bankruptcy or financial distress would be especially costly. This calls for conservative financing. The only way to grow rapidly and keep a conservative debt ratio is to issue equity. If investors see equity issued for these reasons, problems of the sort encountered by Om's financial manager become much less serious.

With such exceptions noted, asymmetric information can explain the dominance of debt financing over new equity issues in practice. Debt issues are frequent; equity issues, rare. The bulk of external financing comes from debt, even in the United States, where equity markets are highly information-efficient. Equity issues are even more difficult in countries with less well developed stock markets.

None of this says that firms ought to strive for high debt ratios—just that it's better to raise equity by plowing back earnings than issuing stock. In fact, a firm with ample internally generated funds doesn't have to sell any kind of security and thus avoids issue costs and information problems completely.[31]

Implications of the Pecking Order

The pecking-order theory of corporate financing goes like this.[32]

1. Firms prefer internal finance.
2. They adapt their target dividend payout ratios to their investment opportunities, while trying to avoid sudden changes in dividends.

[31]Even debt issues can create information problems if the odds of default are significant. A pessimistic manager may try to issue debt quickly, before bad news gets out. An optimistic manager will delay pending good news, perhaps arranging a short-term bank loan in the meantime. Rational investors will take this behavior into account in pricing the risky debt issue.

[32]The description is paraphrased from S. C. Myers, "The Capital Structure Puzzle," *Journal of Finance* 39 (July 1984), pp. 581–582.

3. Sticky dividend policies, plus unpredictable fluctuations in profitability and investment opportunities, mean that internally generated cash flow is sometimes more than capital expenditures and other times less. If it is more, the firm pays off debt or invests in marketable securities. If it is less, the firm first draws down its cash balance or sells its marketable securities.
4. If external finance is required, firms issue the safest security first. That is, they start with debt, then possibly hybrid securities such as convertible bonds, then perhaps equity as a last resort.

In this theory, there is no well-defined target debt–equity mix, because there are two kinds of equity, internal and external, one at the top of the pecking order and one at the bottom. Each firm's observed debt ratio reflects its cumulative requirements for external finance.

The pecking order explains why the most profitable firms generally borrow less—not because they have low target debt ratios but because they don't need outside money. Less profitable firms issue debt because they do not have internal funds sufficient for their capital investment programs and because debt financing is first on the pecking order of *external* financing.

In the pecking-order theory, the attraction of interest tax shields is assumed to be a second-order effect. Debt ratios change when there is an imbalance of internal cash flow, net of dividends, and real investment opportunities. Highly profitable firms with limited investment opportunities work down to low debt ratios. Firms whose investment opportunities outrun internally generated funds are driven to borrow more and more.

This theory explains the inverse intraindustry relationship between profitability and financial leverage. Suppose firms generally invest to keep up with the growth of their industries. Then rates of investment will be similar within an industry. Given sticky dividend payouts, the least profitable firms will have less internal funds and will end up borrowing more.

The Trade-off Theory vs. The Pecking-Order Theory—Some Recent Tests

In 1995 Rajan and Zingales published a study of debt versus equity choices by large firms in Canada, France, Germany, Italy, Japan, the United Kingdom, and the United States. Rajan and Zingales found that the debt ratios of individual companies seemed to depend on four main factors:[33]

1. *Size.* Large firms tend to have higher debt ratios.
2. *Tangible assets.* Firms with high ratios of fixed assets to total assets have higher debt ratios.
3. *Profitability.* More profitable firms have lower debt ratios.
4. *Market to book.* Firms with higher ratios of market-to-book value have lower debt ratios.

[33]R. G. Rajan and L. Zingales, "What Do We Know about Capital Structure? Some Evidence from International Data," *Journal of Finance* 50 (December 1995), pp. 1421–1460. The same four factors seem to work in developing economies. See L. Booth, V. Aivazian, A. Demirguc-Kunt, and V. Maksimovic, "Capital Structure in Developing Countries," *Journal of Finance* 56 (February 2001), pp. 87–130.

These results convey good news for both the trade-off and pecking-order theories. Trade-off enthusiasts note that large companies with tangible assets are less exposed to costs of financial distress and would be expected to borrow more. They interpret the market-to-book ratio as a measure of growth opportunities and argue that growth companies could face high costs of financial distress and would be expected to borrow less. Pecking-order advocates stress the importance of profitability, arguing that profitable firms use less debt because they can rely on internal financing. They interpret the market-to-book ratio as just another measure of profitability.

It seems that we have two competing theories, and they're both right! That's not a comfortable conclusion. So recent research has tried to run horse races between the two theories in order to find the circumstances in which one or the other wins. It seems that the pecking order works best for large, mature firms that have access to public bond markets. These firms rarely issue equity. They prefer internal financing, but turn to debt markets if needed to finance investment. Smaller, younger, growth firms are more likely to rely on equity issues when external financing is required. Here the pecking-order theory stumbles.[34]

The trade-off theory still retains some explanatory power once pecking-order motives are accounted for. The theory is particularly helpful in explaining differences in capital structure across industries. Debt ratios are higher in relatively safe industries and those with tangible assets. Debt ratios are lower in riskier industries where value depends on intangible assets and growth opportunities.

The Bright Side and the Dark Side of Financial Slack

Other things equal, it's better to be at the top of the pecking order than at the bottom. Firms that have worked down the pecking order and need external equity may end up living with excessive debt or passing by good investments because shares can't be sold at what managers consider a fair price.

In other words, *financial slack* is valuable. Having financial slack means having cash, marketable securities, readily saleable real assets, and ready access to the debt markets or to bank financing. Ready access basically requires conservative financing so that potential lenders see the company's debt as a safe investment.

In the long run, a company's value rests more on its capital investment and operating decisions than on financing. Therefore, you want to make sure your firm has sufficient financial slack so that financing is quickly available for good investments. Financial slack is most valuable to firms with plenty of positive-NPV growth opportunities. That is another reason why growth companies usually aspire to conservative capital structures.

There is also a dark side to financial slack. Too much of it may encourage managers to take it easy, expand their perks, or empire-build with cash that should be paid back to stockholders. In other words, slack can make agency problems worse.

Michael Jensen has stressed the tendency of managers with ample free cash flow (or unnecessary financial slack) to plow too much cash into mature businesses or ill-advised acquisitions. "The

---

[34] L. Shyam-Sunder and S. C. Myers, "Testing Static Trade-off against Pecking-Order Models of Capital Structure," *Journal of Financial Economics* 51 (February 1999), pp. 219–244; M. Frank and V. Goyal, "Testing the Pecking Order Theory of Capital Structure," *Journal of Financial Economics* 67 (February 2003), pp. 217–248; and M. L. Lemmon and J. F. Zender, "Debt Capacity and Tests of Capital Structure Theories," working paper, University of Utah, 2002.

problem," Jensen says, "is how to motivate managers to disgorge the cash rather than investing it below the cost of capital or wasting it in organizational inefficiencies."[35]

If that's the problem, then maybe debt is an answer. Scheduled interest and principal payments are contractual obligations of the firm. Debt forces the firm to pay out cash. Perhaps the best debt level would leave just enough cash in the bank, after debt service, to finance all positive-NPV projects, with not a penny left over.

We do not recommend this degree of fine-tuning, but the idea is valid and important. Debt can discipline managers who are tempted to invest too much. It can also provide the pressure to force improvements in operating efficiency. We pick up this theme again in Chapter 33.

---

[35]M. C. Jensen, "Agency Costs of Free Cash Flow, Corporate Finance and Takeovers," *American Economic Review* 26 (May 1986), p. 323.

SUMMARY

Our task in this chapter was to show why capital structure matters. We did not throw away MM's proposition 1, that capital structure is irrelevant; we added to it. However, we did not arrive at any simple, universal theory of optimal capital structure.

The trade-off theory emphasizes taxes and financial distress. The value of the firm is broken down as

$$\text{Value if all-equity-financed} + \text{PV(tax shield)} - \text{PV(costs of financial distress)}$$

According to this theory, the firm should increase debt until the value from PV(tax shield) is just offset, at the margin, by increases in PV(costs of financial distress).

The costs of financial distress can be broken down as follows:

1. Bankruptcy costs
   a. Direct costs such as court fees.
   b. Indirect costs reflecting the difficulty of managing a company undergoing liquidation or reorganization.
2. Costs of financial distress short of bankruptcy
   a. Doubts about a firm's creditworthiness can hobble its operations. Customers and suppliers will be reluctant to deal with a firm that may not be around next year. Key employees will be tempted to leave. We noted evidence that highly leveraged firms seem to be less vigorous product-market competitors.
   b. Conflicts of interest between bondholders and stockholders of firms in financial distress may lead to poor operating and investment decisions. Stockholders acting in their narrow self-interest can gain at the expense of creditors by playing "games" that reduce the overall value of the firm.
   c. The fine print in debt contracts is designed to prevent these games. But fine print increases the costs of writing, monitoring, and enforcing the debt contract.

The value of the tax shield is more controversial. It would be easy to compute if we had only corporate taxes to worry about. In that case the net tax saving from borrowing would be just the marginal corporate tax rate T_c times $r_D D$, the interest payment. This tax shield is usually valued by discounting at the borrowing rate r_D. In the special case of fixed, permanent debt

$$\text{PV(tax shield)} = \frac{T_c(r_D D)}{r_D} = T_c D$$

However, corporate taxes are only part of the story. If investors pay higher taxes on interest income than on equity income (dividends and capital gains), then interest tax shields to the corporation will be partly offset by higher taxes paid by investors. The recent (2003) reductions in U.S. tax rates on dividends and capital gains have reduced the tax advantage to corporate borrowing.

We suggest that borrowing may make sense for some firms but not for others. If a firm can be fairly sure of earning a profit, there is likely to be a net tax saving from borrowing. However, for firms that are unlikely to earn sufficient profits to benefit from the corporate tax shield, there is little, if any, net tax advantage to borrowing. For these firms the net tax saving could even be negative.

The trade-off theory balances the tax advantages of borrowing against the costs of financial distress. Corporations are supposed to pick a target capital structure that maximizes firm value. Firms with safe, tangible assets and plenty of taxable income to shield ought to have high targets. Unprofitable companies with risky, intangible assets ought to rely primarily on equity financing.

This theory of capital structure successfully explains many industry differences in capital structure, but it does not explain why the most profitable firms *within* an industry generally have the most conservative capital structures. Under the trade-off theory, high profitability should mean high debt capacity *and* a strong corporate tax incentive to use that capacity.

There is a competing, pecking-order theory, which states that firms use internal financing when available and choose debt over equity when external financing is required. This explains why the less profitable firms in an industry borrow more—not because they have higher target debt ratios but because they need more external financing and because debt is next on the pecking order when internal funds are exhausted.

The pecking order is a consequence of asymmetric information. Managers know more about their firms than outside investors do, and they are reluctant to issue stock when they believe the price is too low. They try to time issues when shares are fairly priced or overpriced. Investors understand this, and interpret a decision to issue shares as bad news. That explains why stock price usually falls when a stock issue is announced.

Debt is better than equity when these information problems are important. Optimistic managers will prefer debt to undervalued equity, and pessimistic managers will be pressed to follow suit. The pecking-order theory says that equity will be issued only when debt capacity is running out and financial distress threatens.

The pecking-order theory is clearly not 100 percent right. There are many examples of equity issued by companies that could easily have borrowed. But the theory does explain why most external financing comes from debt, and it explains why changes in debt ratios tend to follow requirements for external financing.

The pecking-order theory stresses the value of financial slack. Without sufficient slack, the firm may be caught at the bottom of the pecking order and be forced to choose between issuing undervalued shares, borrowing and risking financial distress, or passing up positive-NPV investment opportunities.

There is, however, a dark side to financial slack. Surplus cash or credit tempts managers to overinvest or to indulge an easy and glamorous corporate lifestyle. When temptation wins, or threatens to win, a high debt ratio can help: It forces the company to disgorge cash and prods managers and organizations to try harder to be more efficient.

FURTHER READING

Modigliani and Miller's analysis of the present value of interest tax shields at the corporate level is in:

F. Modigliani and M. H. Miller: "Corporate Income Taxes and the Cost of Capital: A Correction," *American Economic Review,* 53 (June 1963), pp. 433–443.

F. Modigliani and M. H. Miller, "Some Estimates of the Cost of Capital to the Electric Utility Industry, 1954–57," *American Economic Review* 56 (June 1966), pp. 333–391.

Miller extends the MM model to personal as well as corporate taxes. Graham's estimates of the tax benefits of debt recognize the possibility that firms will not earn taxable profits in the future:

M. H. Miller, "Debt and Taxes," *Journal of Finance* 32 (May 1977), pp. 261–276.

J. R. Graham, "How Big Are the Tax Benefits of Debt?" *Journal of Finance* 55 (October 2000), pp. 1901–1941.

The following articles analyze the conflicts of interest between bondholders and stockholders and their implications for financing policy:

M. C. Jensen and W. H. Meckling, "Theory of the Firm: Managerial Behavior, Agency Costs and Ownership Structure," *Journal of Financial Economics* 3 (October 1976), pp. 305–360.

S. C. Myers, "Determinants of Corporate Borrowing," *Journal of Financial Economics* 5 (1977), pp. 146–175.

Myers's 1984 paper describes the pecking-order theory and the following three papers test it:

S. C. Myers, "The Capital Structure Puzzle," *Journal of Finance* 39 (July 1984), pp. 575–592.

L. Shyam-Sunder and S. C. Myers, "Testing Static Trade-Off against Pecking-Order Models of Capital Structure," *Journal of Financial Economics* 51 (February 1999), pp. 219–244.

E. F. Fama and K. R. French, "Testing Trade-off and Pecking-Order Predictions about Dividends and Debt," *Review of Financial Studies* 15 (Spring 2002), pp. 1–33.

M. Frank and V. Goyal, "Testing the Pecking-Order Theory of Capital Structure," *Journal of Financial Economics* 67 (February 2003), pp. 217–248.

The following paper surveys chief financial officers' views about capital structure:

J. Graham and C. Harvey, "How Do CFOs Make Capital Budgeting and Capital Structure Decisions?" *Journal of Applied Corporate Finance* 15 (Spring 2002), pp. 8–23.

Finally, here are two review articles on capital structure:

S. C. Myers, "Still Searching for Optimal Capital Structure," *Journal of Applied Corporate Finance* 6 (Spring 1993), pp. 4–14.

S. C. Myers, "Financing of Corporations," in G. M. Constantinides, M. Harris, and R. Stulz (eds.), *Handbook of the Economics of Finance* (Amsterdam: Elsevier North-Holland, 2003).

The Spring 1993 and Winter 1995 issues of the Journal of Applied Corporate Finance *contain several articles on the incentive effects of capital structure.*

CONCEPT REVIEW QUESTIONS

1. Suppose a company borrows Rs. 1 million at an interest rate of 6 percent and the corporate tax rate is 30 percent. What is the annual interest tax shield? If the debt is permanent, what is the value of the tax shield? (page 472)
2. Why might the existence of personal taxes partly offset the benefit of the corporate tax shield on interest payments? (pages 475–477)
3. List the direct and indirect costs of bankruptcy. Would you expect the indirect costs to be above or below average for firms with lots of intangible assets? (pages 481–483)

For additional Concept Review Questions, please visit us at www.mhhe.com/bmam8e or refer to your Student CD.

QUIZ

1. Compute the present value of interest tax shields generated by these three debt issues. Consider corporate taxes only. The marginal tax rate is $T_c = .35$.
   a. A Rs. 1,000, one-year loan at 8 percent.
   b. A five-year loan of Rs.1,000 at 8 percent. Assume no principal is repaid until maturity.
   c. A Rs. 1,000 perpetuity at 7 percent.
2. Here are book and market value balance sheets of the United Frypan Company (UF):

Book

Net current assets	Rs. 20	Debt	Rs. 40
Long-term assets	80	Equity	60
	Rs. 100		Rs. 100

Market

Net current assets	Rs. 20	Debt	Rs. 40
Long-term assets	140	Equity	120
	Rs. 160		Rs. 160

   Assume that MM's theory holds with taxes. There is no growth, and the Rs. 40 of debt is expected to be permanent. Assume a 40 percent corporate tax rate.
   a. How much of the firm's value is accounted for by the debt-generated tax shield?
   b. How much better off will UF's shareholders be if the firm borrows Rs. 20 more and uses it to repurchase stock?
3. What is the relative tax advantage of corporate debt if the corporate tax rate is $T_c = .35$, the personal tax rate is $T_p = .35$, but all equity income is received as capital gains and escapes tax entirely ($T_{pE} = 0$)? How does the relative tax advantage change if the company decides to pay out all equity income as cash dividends which are taxed at 15 percent?
4. "The firm can't use interest tax shields unless it has (taxable) income to shield." What does this statement imply for the debt policy? Explain briefly.
5. This question tests your understanding of financial distress.
   a. What are the costs of going bankrupt? Define these costs carefully.
   b. "A company can incur costs of financial distress without ever going bankrupt." Explain how this can happen.
   c. Explain how conflicts of interest between bondholders and stockholders can lead to costs of financial distress.
6. On February 29, 2003, when PDQ Computers announced bankruptcy, its share price fell from \$3.00 to \$.50 per share. There were 10 million shares outstanding. Does that imply bankruptcy costs of 10 × (3.00 − .50) = \$25 million? Explain.
7. Let us go back to Circular File's market value balance sheet:

Net current assets	Rs. 20	Rs. 25	Bonds outstanding
Fixed assets	10	5	Shareholders' funds
Total assets	Rs. 30	Rs. 30	Total value

   Who gains and who loses from the following maneuvers?
   a. Circular scrapes up Rs. 5 in cash and pays a cash dividend.
   b. Circular halts operations, sells its fixed assets, and converts net working capital into Rs. 20 cash. Unfortunately the fixed assets fetch only Rs. 6 on the secondhand market. The Rs. 26 cash is invested in Treasury bills.
   c. Circular encounters an acceptable investment opportunity, NPV = 0, requiring an investment of Rs. 10. The firm borrows to finance the project. The new debt has the same security, seniority, etc., as the old.
   d. Suppose that the new project has NPV = +Rs. 2 and is financed by an issue of preferred stock.
   e. The lenders agree to extend the maturity of their loan from one year to two in order to give Circular a chance to recover.

8. The traditional theory of optimal capital structure states that firms trade off corporate interest tax shields against the possible costs of financial distress due to borrowing. What does this theory predict about the relationship between book profitability and target book debt ratios? Is the theory's prediction consistent with the facts?
9. Why does asymmetric information push companies to raise external funds by borrowing rather than by issuing common stock?
10. For what kinds of companies is financial slack most valuable? Are there situations in which financial slack should be reduced by borrowing and paying out the proceeds to the stockholders? Explain.

PRACTICE QUESTIONS

1. Suppose that, in an effort to increase the tax collections, the Finance Minister of India increases the top personal tax rate from 30 percent to 35 percent, but retains the securities transaction tax at its current level of 0.125 percent. The corporate tax rate stays at 33.66 percent. Compute the total corporate plus personal taxes paid on debt versus equity income if **(a)** all capital gains are realized immediately and the short term capital gains tax (paid over and above the securities transaction tax) is 10 percent and **(b)** sell of shares is deferred forever. Assume capital gains are half of equity income. The effective dividend distribution tax is 14 percent.
2. "The trouble with MM's argument is that it ignores the fact that individuals can deduct interest for personal income tax." Show why this is not an objection if personal tax rates on interest and equity income are the same.
3. Look back at the Asian Paints example in Section 18.1. Suppose that Asian Paints moves to a 40 percent book debt ratio by issuing debt and using the proceeds to repurchase shares. Consider only corporate taxes. Now reconstruct Table 18.3(b) to reflect the new capital structure. How much additional value is created if the assumptions in the table are correct?
4. Visit the website of Asian Paints (http://www.apaints.com/AsianPaints.jsp).
   a. Recalculate the book- and market-value balance sheets using the most recent available financial information.
   b. Track Asian Paints' long-term debt and debt ratio over the last five years. How have they changed? Does it appear that Asian Paints has a stable target debt ratio? Do you see any incidence of pecking-order financing?
   c. Would the trade-off theory predict share repurchases for a conservatively financed company like Asian Paints?
5. In Section 18.3, we briefly referred to three games: Playing for time, cash in and run, and bait and switch. For each game, construct a simple numerical example (like the example for the risk-shifting game) showing how shareholders can gain at the expense of creditors. Then explain how the temptation to play these games could lead to costs of financial distress.
6. Look at some real companies with different types of assets. What operating problems would each encounter in the event of financial distress? How well would the assets keep their value?
7. The Salad Oil Storage (SOS) Company has financed a large part of its facilities with long-term debt. There is a significant risk of default, but the company is not on the ropes yet. Explain:
   a. Why SOS stockholders could lose by investing in a positive-NPV project financed by an equity issue.
   b. Why SOS stockholders could gain by investing in a negative-NPV project financed by cash.
   c. Why SOS stockholders could gain from paying out a large cash dividend.

   How might the firm's adherence to a target debt ratio mitigate some or all of the problems noted above?

8. a. Who benefits from the fine print in bond contracts when the firm gets into financial trouble? Give a one-sentence answer.

b. Who benefits from the fine print when the bonds are issued? Suppose the firm is offered the choice of issuing (i) a bond with standard restrictions on dividend payout, additional borrowing, etc., and (ii) a bond with minimal restrictions but a much higher interest rate? Suppose the interest rates on both (i) and (ii) are fair from the viewpoint of lenders. Which bond would you expect the firm to issue? Why?

9. "I was amazed to find that the announcement of a stock issue drives down the value of the issuing firm by *30 percent*, on average, of the proceeds of the issue. That issue cost dwarfs the underwriter's spread and the administrative costs of the issue. It makes common stock issues prohibitively expensive."

a. You are contemplating a Rs. 100 million stock issue. On past evidence, you anticipate that announcement of this issue will drive down stock price by 3 percent and that the market value of your firm will fall by 30 percent of the amount to be raised. On the other hand, additional equity funds are necessary to fund an investment project which you believe has a positive NPV of Rs. 40 million. Should you proceed with the issue?

b. Is the fall in market value on announcement of a stock issue an *issue cost* in the same sense as an underwriter's spread? Respond to the quote that begins this question.

Use your answer to (a) as a numerical example to explain your response to (b).

10. Ronald Masulis[36] has analyzed the stock price impact of *exchange offers* of debt for equity or vice versa. In an exchange offer, the firm offers to trade freshly issued securities for seasoned securities in the hands of investors. Thus, a firm that wanted to move to a higher debt ratio could offer to trade new debt for outstanding shares. A firm that wanted to move to a more conservative capital structure could offer to trade new shares for outstanding debt securities.

Masulis found that debt for equity exchanges were good news (stock price increased on announcement) and equity for debt exchanges were bad news.

a. Are these results consistent with the trade-off theory of capital structure?

b. Are the results consistent with the evidence that investors regard announcements of (i) stock issues as bad news, (ii) stock repurchases as good news, and (iii) debt issues as no news, or at most trifling disappointments?

c. How could Masulis's results be explained?

11. The possible payoffs from Ms. Ketchup's projects (see Section 18.3) have not changed but there is now a 40 percent chance that project 2 will pay off Rs. 24 and a 60 percent chance that it will pay off Rs. 0.

a. Recalculate the expected payoffs to the bank and Ms. Ketchup if the bank lends the present value of Rs. 10. Which project would Ms. Ketchup undertake?

b. What is the maximum amount the bank could lend that would induce Ms. Ketchup to take project 1?

12. Select six companies that are part of Nifty. Estimate how much more these companies could borrow before they would exhaust taxable profits.

13. Estimate the debt ratios for a few of the largest company from the following industries and find the average debt ratio within the industry. Can you explain the differences between these industry-average ratios?

---

[36]R. W. Masulis, "The Effects of Capital Structure Change on Security Prices: A Study of Exchange Offers," *Journal of Financial Economics* 8 (June 1980), pp. 139–177, and "The Impact of Capital Structure Change on Firm Value," *Journal of Finance* 38 (March 1983), pp. 107–126.

CHALLENGE QUESTIONS

1. Most financial managers measure debt ratios from their companies' book balance sheets. Financial economists tend to emphasize ratios from market-value balance sheets. Which is the right measure in principle? Does the trade-off theory propose to explain book or market leverage? How about the pecking-order theory?
2. From some financial database, estimate the book- and market-debt ratios of 100 large manufacturing companies in India. Find out how well differences in company leverage seem to support the trade-off theory and the pecking order theory.

CHAPTER [19]

FINANCING AND VALUATION

IN CHAPTERS 5 and 6 we showed how to value a capital investment project by a four-step procedure:

1. Forecast after-tax cash flows, assuming all-equity financing.
2. Assess the project's risk.
3. Estimate the opportunity cost of capital.
4. Calculate NPV, using the opportunity cost of capital as the discount rate.

There's nothing wrong with this procedure, but now we're going to extend it to include value contributed by financing decisions. There are two ways to do this:

1. *Adjust the discount rate.* The adjustment is typically downward, to account for the value of interest tax shields. This is the most common approach, which is usually implemented via the after-tax weighted-average cost of capital (WACC). We introduced the after-tax WACC in Chapter 17, but here we will provide a lot more guidance on how it is calculated and used.
2. *Adjust the present value.* That is, start by estimating the firm or project's base-case value, assuming it is all-equity-financed, and then adjust this base-case value to account for financing.

Adjusted present value (APV)
= base-case value + value of financing side effects

Once you identify and value the financing side effects, calculating APV is no more than addition or subtraction.

This is a how-to-do-it chapter. In the first section, we explain and derive the after-tax WACC and use it to value a project and business. Then in Section 19.2 we work through a more complex and realistic valuation problem. Section 19.3 covers some tricks of the trade: helpful hints on how to estimate inputs and on how to adjust WACC when business risk or capital structure changes. Section 19.4 turns to the APV method. The idea behind APV is simple enough, but tracing through all the financing side effects can be tricky. We conclude the chapter with a question-and-answer section designed to clarify points that managers and students often find confusing. The Appendix covers an important special case, namely, the after-tax valuation of safe cash flows.

19.1 THE AFTER-TAX WEIGHTED-AVERAGE COST OF CAPITAL

We first addressed problems of valuation and capital budgeting in Chapters 2 to 6. In those early chapters we said hardly a word about financing decisions. In fact we proceeded under the simplest possible financing assumption, namely, all-equity financing. We were really assuming a Modigliani–Miller (MM) world in which all financing decisions are irrelevant. In a strict MM world, firms can analyze real investments as if they are all-equity-financed; the actual financing plan is a mere detail to be worked out later.

Under MM assumptions, decisions to spend money can be separated from decisions to raise money. Now we reconsider the capital budgeting decision when investment and financing decisions interact and cannot be wholly separated.

One reason that financing and investment decisions interact is taxes. Interest is a tax-deductible expense. Think back to Chapter 17 where we introduced the *after-tax* weighted-average cost of capital:

$$\text{WACC} = r_D(1-T_C)\frac{D}{V} + r_E\frac{E}{V}$$

Here D and E are the market values of the firm's debt and equity, $V = D + E$ is the total market value of the firm, r_D and r_E are the costs of debt and equity, and T_C is the marginal corporate tax rate.

Notice that $r_D(1 - T_C)$, the *after-tax* cost of debt, is used in the WACC formula. That is how the after-tax WACC captures the value of interest tax shields. Notice too that all the variables in the WACC formula refer to the firm as a whole. As a result, the formula gives the right discount rate only for projects that are just like the firm undertaking them. The formula works for the "average" project. It is incorrect for projects that are safer or riskier than the average of the firm's existing assets. It is incorrect for projects whose acceptance would lead to an increase or decrease in the firm's target debt ratio.

The WACC is based on the firm's *current* characteristics, but managers use it to discount *future* cash flows. That's fine as long as the firm's business risk and debt ratio are expected to remain constant, but when the business risk and debt ratio are expected to change, discounting cash flows by the WACC is only approximately correct.

Example: Sangria Corporation

Sangria is an Indian company whose products aim to promote happy, low-stress lifestyles. Let's calculate Sangria's WACC. Its book and market-value balance sheets are:

Sangria Corporation (Book Values, Rs. millions)

Asset value	Rs. 1,000	Rs. 500	Debt
		500	Equity
	Rs. 1,000	Rs. 1,000	

Sangria Corporation (Market Values, Rs. millions)

Asset value	Rs. 1,250	Rs. 500	Debt
		750	Equity
	Rs. 1,250	Rs. 1,250	

We calculated the market value of equity on Sangria's balance sheet by multiplying its current stock price (Rs. 7.50) by 100 million, the number of its outstanding shares. The company's future prospects are good, so the stock is trading above book value (Rs. 7.50 vs. Rs. 5.00 per share). However, interest rates have been stable since the firm's debt was issued and the book and market values of debt are in this case equal.

Sangria's cost of debt (the market interest rate on its existing debt and on any new borrowing[1]) is 6 percent. Its cost of equity (the expected rate of return demanded by investors in Sangria's stock) is 12.4 percent.

The market-value balance sheet shows assets worth Rs. 1,250 million. Of course we can't observe this value directly, because the assets themselves are not traded. But we know what they are worth to debt and equity investors (Rs. 500 + 750 = Rs. 1,250 million). This value is entered on the left of the market-value balance sheet.

Why did we show the book balance sheet? Only so you could draw a big X through it. Do so now.

[1]Always use an up-to-date interest rate (yield to maturity), not the interest rate when the firm's debt was first issued and not the coupon rate on the debt's book value.

When estimating the weighted-average cost of capital, you are not interested in past investments but in current values and expectations for the future. Sangria's true debt ratio is not 50 percent, the book ratio, but 40 percent, because its assets are worth Rs. 1,250 million. The cost of equity, $r_E = .124$, is the expected rate of return from purchase of stock at Rs. 7.50 per share, the current market price. It is not the return on book value per share. You can't buy shares in Sangria for Rs. 5 anymore.

Sangria is consistently profitable and pays taxes at the marginal rate of 35 percent. This tax rate is the final input for Sangria's WACC. The inputs are summarized here:

Cost of debt (r_D)	.06
Cost of equity (r_E)	.124
Marginal tax rate (T_C)	.35
Debt ratio (D/V)	500/1,250 = .4
Equity ratio (E/V)	750/1,250 = .6

The company's after-tax WACC is

$$\text{WACC} = .06 \times (1 - .35) \times .4 + .124 \times .6 = .090, \text{ or } 9.0\%$$

That's how you calculate the weighted-average cost of capital. Now let's see how Sangria would *use* it.

Example Sangria's enologists have proposed investing Rs. 12.5 million in the construction of a perpetual crushing machine, which (conveniently for us) never depreciates and generates a perpetual stream of earnings and cash flow of Rs. 1.731 million per year pretax. The project is average risk, so we can use WACC. The after-tax cash flow is:

Pretax cash flow	Rs. 1.731 million
Tax at 35%	.606
After-tax cash flow	C = Rs. 1.125 million

Notice: This after-tax cash flow takes no account of interest tax shields on debt supported by the perpetual crusher project. As we explained in Chapter 6, standard capital budgeting practice calculates after-tax cash flows as if the project were all-equity-financed. However, the interest tax shields will not be ignored: We are about to discount the project's cash flows by Sangria's WACC, in which the cost of debt is entered after tax. The value of interest tax shields is picked up not as higher after-tax cash flows, but in a lower discount rate.

The crusher generates a perpetual after-tax cash flow of C = Rs. 1.125 million, so NPV is

$$\text{NPV} = -12.5 + \frac{1.125}{0.09} = 0$$

NPV = 0 means a barely acceptable investment. The annual cash flow of Rs. 1.125 million per year amounts to a 9 percent rate of return on investment (1.125/12.5 = .09), exactly equal to Sangria's WACC.

If project NPV is exactly zero, the return to equity investors must exactly equal the cost of equity, 12.4 percent. Let's confirm that Sangria shareholders can actually look forward to a 12.4 percent return on their investment in the perpetual crusher project.

Suppose Sangria sets up this project as a mini-firm. Its market-value balance sheet looks like this:

Perpetual Crusher (Market Values, Rs. millions)

Asset value	Rs. 12.5	Rs. 5.0	Debt
		7.5	Equity
	Rs. 12.5	Rs. 12.5	

Calculate the expected rupee return to shareholders:

$$\text{After-tax interest} = r_D(1 - T_C)D = 0.06 \times (1 - .35) \times 5 = .195$$

$$\text{Expected equity income} = C - r_D(1 - T_C)D = 1.125 - .195 = 0.93$$

The project's earnings are level and perpetual, so the expected rate of return on equity is equal to the expected equity income divided by the equity value:

$$\text{Expected equity return} = r_E = \frac{\text{expected equity income}}{\text{equity value}}$$

$$= \frac{0.93}{7.5} = .124, \text{ or } 12.4\%$$

The expected return on equity equals the cost of equity, so it makes sense that the project's NPV is zero.

Review of Assumptions

When discounting the perpetual crusher's cash flows at Sangria's WACC, we assume that:

- The project's business risks are the same as those of Sangria's other assets and remain so for the life of the project.
- The project supports the same fraction of debt to value as in Sangria's overall capital structure, which remains constant for the life of the project.

You can see the importance of these two assumptions: If the perpetual crusher had greater business risk than Sangria's other assets, or if the acceptance of the project would lead to a permanent, material change in Sangria's debt ratio,[2] then Sangria's shareholders would not be content with a 12.4 percent expected return on their equity investment in the project.

[2]Users of WACC need not worry about small or temporary fluctuations in debt-to-value ratios. Suppose that Sangria management decides for convenience to borrow Rs. 12.5 million to allow immediate construction of the crusher. This does not necessarily change Sangria's long-term financing policy. If the crusher supports only Rs. 5.0 million of debt, Sangria would have to pay down debt to restore its overall debt ratio to 40 percent. For example, it could fund later projects with less debt and more equity.

We have illustrated the WACC formula only for a project offering perpetual cash flows. But the formula works for any cash-flow pattern if the firm adjusts its borrowing to maintain a constant debt ratio over time.[3] When the firm departs from this borrowing policy, WACC is only approximately correct.

19.2 VALUING BUSINESSES

On most workdays the financial manager concentrates on valuing projects, arranging financing, and helping run the firm more effectively. The valuation of the business as a whole is left to investors and financial markets. But on some days the financial manager has to take a stand on what an entire business is worth. When this happens, a *big* decision is typically in the offing. For example:

- If firm A is about to make a takeover offer for firm B, then A's financial managers have to decide how much the combined business A + B is worth under A's management. This task is particularly difficult if B is a private company with no observable share price.
- If firm C is considering the sale of one of its divisions, it has to decide what the division is worth in order to negotiate with potential buyers.
- When a firm goes public, the investment bank must evaluate how much the firm is worth in order to set the issue price.

---

[3]We can prove this statement as follows. Denote expected after-tax cash flows (assuming all-equity financing) as $C_1, C_2, \ldots, C_T$. With all-equity financing, these flows would be discounted at the opportunity cost of capital r. But we need to value the cash flows for a firm that is financed partly with debt.

Start with value in the next to last period: $V_{T-1} = D_{T-1} + E_{T-1}$. The total cash payoff to debt and equity investors is the cash flow plus the interest tax shield. The expected total return to debt and equity investors is:

$$\text{Expected cash payoff in } T = C_T + T_C r_D D_{T-1} \quad (1)$$

$$= V_{T-1}\left(1 + r_D \frac{D_{T-1}}{V_{T-1}} + r_E \frac{E_{T-1}}{V_{T-1}}\right) \quad (2)$$

Assume the debt ratio is constant at $L = D/V$. Equate (1) and (2) and solve for V_{T-1}:

$$V_{T-1} = \frac{C_T}{1 + (1 - T_C)r_D L + r_E(1 - L)} = \frac{C_T}{1 + \text{WACC}}$$

The logic repeats for V_{T-2}. Note that the next period's payoff includes V_{T-1}:

$$\text{Expected cash payoff in } T - 1 = C_{T-1} + T_C r_D D_{T-2} + V_{T-1}$$

$$= V_{T-2}\left(1 + r_D \frac{D_{T-2}}{V_{T-2}} + r_E \frac{E_{T-2}}{V_{T-2}}\right)$$

$$V_{T-2} = \frac{C_{T-1} + V_{T-1}}{1 + (1 - T_C)r_D L + r_E(1 - L)} = \frac{C_{T-1} + V_{T-1}}{1 + \text{WACC}} = \frac{C_{T-1}}{1 + \text{WACC}} + \frac{C_T}{(1 + \text{WACC})^2}$$

We can continue all the way back to date 0:

$$V_0 = \sum_{t=1}^{T} \frac{C_t}{(1 + \text{WACC})^t}$$

In addition, thousands of analysts in stockbrokers' offices and investment firms spend every workday burrowing away in the hope of finding undervalued firms. Many of these analysts use the valuation tools we are about to cover.

We have seen how WACC can be used to value a capital investment project. But you can also use it to value an entire company as long as the debt ratio is expected to remain approximately constant. You just treat the company as if it were one big project. You forecast the company's cash flows (the hardest part of the exercise) and discount back to present value. But be sure to remember three important points:

1. If you discount at WACC, cash flows have to be projected just as you would for a capital investment project. Do not deduct interest. Calculate taxes as if the company were all-equity-financed. (The value of interest tax shields is not ignored, because the after-tax cost of debt is used in the WACC formula.)
2. Unlike most projects, companies are potentially immortal. But that does not mean that you need to forecast every year's cash flow from now to eternity. Financial managers usually forecast to a medium-term horizon and add a terminal value to the cash flows in the horizon year. The terminal value is the present value at the horizon of all subsequent cash flows. Estimating the terminal value requires careful attention because it often accounts for the majority of the company's value.
3. Discounting at WACC values the assets and operations of the company. If the object is to value the company's equity, that is, its common stock, don't forget to subtract the value of the company's outstanding debt.

Here's an example.

Valuing Geo Corporation

Sangria is tempted to acquire the Geo Corporation, which is also in the business of promoting relaxed, happy life styles. Geo has developed a special weight-loss program called the Goan Diet, based on barbecues, red wine, and sunshine. The firm guarantees that within three months you will have a figure that will allow you to fit right in at Baga or Vagator beach in Goa. But before you head for the beach, you've got the job of working out how much Sangria should pay for Geo.

Geo is an Indian company. It is privately held, so Sangria has no stock-market price to rely on. Geo has 1.5 million shares outstanding and debt with a market and book value of Rs. 36 million. Geo is in the same line of business as Sangria, so we will assume that it has the same business risk as Sangria and can support the same proportion of debt. Therefore we can use Sangria's WACC.

Your first task is to forecast Geo's *free cash flow* (FCF). Free cash flow is the amount of cash that the firm can pay out to investors after making all investments necessary for growth. Free cash flow is calculated assuming the firm is all-equity-financed. Discounting the free cash flows at the after-tax WACC gives the total value of Geo (debt *plus* equity). To find the value of its equity, you will need to subtract the Rs. 36 million of debt.

We will forecast each year's free cash flow out to a *valuation horizon* (H) and predict the business's value at that horizon (PV_H). The cash flows and horizon value are then discounted back to the present:

$$PV = \underbrace{\frac{FCF_1}{1 + WACC} + \frac{FCF_2}{(1 + WACC)^2} + \cdots + \frac{FCF_H}{(1 + WACC)^H}}_{\text{PV(free cash flow)}} + \underbrace{\frac{PV_H}{(1 + WACC)^H}}_{\text{PV(horizon value)}}$$

Of course, the business will continue after the horizon, but it's not practical to forecast free cash flow year by year to infinity. PV_H stands in for the value in year H of free cash flow in periods $H + 1$, $H + 2$, etc.

Free cash flow and net income are not the same. They differ in several important ways:

- Income is the return to shareholders, calculated after interest expense. Free cash flow is calculated before interest.
- Income is calculated after various noncash expenses, including depreciation. Therefore we will add back depreciation when we calculate free cash flow.
- Capital expenditures and investments in working capital do not appear as expenses on the income statement, but they do reduce free cash flow.

Free cash flow can be negative for rapidly growing firms, even if the firms are profitable, because investment exceeds cash flow from operations. Negative free cash flow is normally temporary, fortunately for the firm and its stockholders. Free cash flow turns positive as growth slows down and the payoffs from prior investments start to roll in.

Table 19.1 sets out the information that you need to forecast Geo's free cash flows. We will follow common practice and start with a projection of sales. In the year just ended Geo had sales of Rs. 83.6 million. In recent years sales have grown by between 5 and 8 percent a year. You forecast that sales will grow by about 7 percent a year for the next three years. Growth will then slow to 4 percent for years 4 to 6 and to 3 percent starting in year 7.

The other components of cash flow in Table 19.1 are driven by these sales forecasts. For example, you can see that costs are forecasted at 74 percent of sales in the first year with a gradual increase to 76 percent of sales in later years, reflecting increased marketing costs as Geo's competitors gradually catch up.

Increasing sales are likely to require further investment in fixed assets and working capital. Geo's net fixed assets are currently about Rs. 0.79 for each rupee of sales. Unless Geo has surplus capacity or can squeeze more output from its existing plant and equipment, its investment in fixed assets will need to grow along with sales. Therefore we assume that every rupee of sales growth requires an increase of Rs. 0.79 in net fixed assets. We also assume that working capital grows in proportion to sales.

Geo's free cash flow is calculated in Table 19.1 as profit after tax, plus depreciation, minus investment. Investment is the change in the stock of (gross) fixed assets and working capital from the previous year. For example, in year 1:

$$\begin{aligned}\text{Free cash flow} &= \text{Profit after tax} + \text{depreciation} + \text{investment in fixed assets}\\ &\quad + \text{investment in working capital}\\ &= 8.7 + 9.9 - (109.6 - 95.0) - (11.6 - 11.1) = \text{Rs. } 3.5 \text{ million}\end{aligned}$$

Estimating Horizon Value

Valuation horizons are often chosen arbitrarily. Sometimes the boss tells everybody to use 10 years because that's a round number. We will use year 6, because Geo's sales are expected to settle down to stable, long-term growth starting in year 7. To find the present value of the cash flows in years 1 to 6, we discount at the 9 percent WACC:

$$PV = \frac{3.5}{1.09} + \frac{3.2}{1.09^2} + \frac{3.4}{1.09^3} + \frac{5.9}{1.09^4} + \frac{6.1}{1.09^5} + \frac{6.0}{1.09^6} = \text{Rs. } 20.3 \text{ million}$$

	Latest year	Forecast						
	0	1	2	3	4	5	6	7
1. Sales	83.6	89.5	95.8	102.5	106.6	110.8	115.2	118.7
2. Cost of goods sold	63.1	66.2	71.3	76.3	79.9	83.1	87.0	90.2
3. EBITDA (1 - 2)	20.5	23.3	24.4	26.1	26.6	27.7	28.2	28.5
4. Depreciation	3.3	9.9	10.6	11.3	11.8	12.3	12.7	13.1
5. Profit before tax (EBIT) (3 - 4)	17.2	13.4	13.8	14.8	14.9	15.4	15.5	15.4
6. Tax	6.0	4.7	4.8	5.2	5.2	5.4	5.4	5.4
7. Profit after tax (5 - 6)	11.2	8.7	9.0	9.6	9.7	10.0	10.1	10.0
8. Investment in fixed assets	11.0	14.6	15.5	16.6	15.0	15.6	16.2	15.9
9. Investment in working capital	1.0	0.5	0.8	0.9	0.5	0.6	0.6	0.4
10. Free cash flow (7 + 4 - 8 - 9)	2.5	3.5	3.2	3.4	5.9	6.1	6.0	6.8
PV Free cash flow, years 1-6	**20.3**							
PV Horizon value	**67.6**				(Horizon value in year 6)		113.4	
PV of company	**87.9**							
Assumptions:								
Sales growth (percent)	6.7	7.0	7.0	7.0	4.0	4.0	4.0	3.0
Costs (percent of sales)	75.5	74.0	74.5	74.5	75.0	75.0	75.5	76.0
Working capital (percent of sales)	13.3	13.0	13.0	13.0	13.0	13.0	13.0	13.0
Net fixed assets (percent of sales)	79.2	79.0	79.0	79.0	79.0	79.0	79.0	79.0
Depreciation (percent of net fixed assets)	5.0	14.0	14.0	14.0	14.0	14.0	14.0	14.0
Tax rate, percent	35.0							
WACC, percent	9.0							
Long-term growth forecast, percent	3.0							
Fixed assets and working capital								
Gross fixed assets	95.0	109.6	125.1	141.8	156.8	172.4	188.6	204.5
Less accumulated depreciation	29.0	38.9	49.5	60.8	72.6	84.9	97.6	110.7
Net fixed assets	66.0	70.7	75.6	80.9	84.2	87.5	91.0	93.8
Net working capital	11.1	11.6	12.4	13.3	13.9	14.4	15.0	15.4

TABLE 19.1

Free-cash-flow projections and company value for Geo Corporation (Rs. millions).

eXcel

Please visit us at www.mhhe.com/bmam8e or refer to your Student CD .

Now we need to find the value of the cash flows from year 7 onward.

There are several formulas or rules of thumb for estimating horizon value. First let's try the constant-growth DCF formula. This requires a forecast of the free cash flow for year 7, which we have worked out in the final column of Table 19.1, assuming a long-run growth rate of 3 percent per year.[4] The free cash flow is Rs. 6.8 million, so

$$PV_H = \frac{FCF_{H+1}}{WACC - g} = \frac{6.8}{.09 - .03} = \text{Rs. } 113.4 \text{ million}$$

$$\text{PV at year } 0 = \frac{1}{1.09^6} \times 113.4 = \text{Rs. } 67.6 \text{ million}$$

[4]Notice that expected free cash flow increases by about 14 percent from year 6 to year 7 because the transition from 4 to 3 percent sales growth reduces required investment. But sales, investment, and free cash flow will all increase at 3 percent once the company settles into stable growth. Recall that the first cash flow in the constant-growth DCF formula occurs in the next year, year 7 in this case. Growth progresses at a steady-state 3 percent from year 7 onward. Therefore it's OK to use the 3 percent growth rate in the horizon-value formula.

We now have all we need to value the business:

$$\begin{aligned}\text{PV(company)} &= \text{PV(cash flow years 1–6)} + \text{PV(horizon value)}\\ &= \text{Rs. } 20.3 + 67.6 = \text{Rs. } 87.9 \text{ million}\end{aligned}$$

This is the total value of Geo. To find the value of the equity, we simply subtract the value of the debt:

$$\text{Total value of equity} = \text{Rs. } 87.9 - 36.0 = \text{Rs. } 51.9 \text{ million}$$

And to find the value per share, we divide by the total number of shares outstanding:

$$\text{Value per share} = 51.9/1.5 = \text{Rs. } 34.60$$

Thus Sangria could afford to pay up to Rs. 34.60 per share for Geo.

Now, are we done? Well, the mechanics of this calculation are perfect. But doesn't it make you just a little nervous to find that about three-quarters of the value of Geo rests on its horizon value? Moreover, a little checking shows how the horizon value can change in response to apparently minor changes in assumptions. For example, if the long-run growth rate is 4 percent rather than 3 percent, Geo needs to invest more to support the higher growth, but firm value increases from Rs. 87.9 million to Rs. 89.9 million.

In other words, it's easy for a discounted-cash-flow calculation to be mechanically perfect and practically wrong. Smart financial managers try to check their results by calculating horizon value in several different ways. One common approach uses *multiples* of earnings before interest, taxes, depreciation, and amortization (EBITDA) or earnings before interest and taxes (EBIT). Suppose you can find mature, public companies whose scale, risk, and growth prospects today roughly match those projected for Geo at the investment horizon. You discover that these companies tend to sell at multiples of 4.5 times EBITDA and 7.5 times EBIT.[5] Then you can reasonably guess that Geo's value in year 6 will be about 4.5 times forecasted EBITDA, that is, 4.5×28.5 = Rs. 128 million. Using EBIT the horizon value is 7.5×15.4 = Rs. 115.5 million. These results are not too far off the Rs. 113.4 million horizon value that we obtained by using the constant-growth DCF formula in Table 19.1.

Investors and security analysts may use other multiples. For example, oil companies' market values can be expressed as a multiple of barrels of oil reserves. In regulated industries, where allowed profits are based on book asset values, market-to-book multiples are often used. In the late 1990s, when dot.com companies were growing rapidly but losing lots of money, multiples were based on the number of subscribers or Web site visits.

It's easy to poke holes in these rules of thumb. Book value, for example, is often a poor measure of the true value of a company's assets. It can fall far behind actual asset values when there is rapid inflation, and it misses intangible assets, such as trademarks or patents. Finally, even if book value multiples make sense, you never know when you have found a sample of truly similar companies.

---

[5] An EBITDA multiple of 4.5 means that the *total* market value of the firm, debt and equity combined, is 4.5 times EBITDA. EBIT multiples are also based on total market value.

Given all these problems, you may be tempted to stick with discounted cash flow as the most detailed and "scientific" valuation method. But remember, the purpose of discounted cash flow is to estimate market value—to estimate what investors would pay for a stock or a business. When you can *observe* what they actually pay for similar companies, you gain valuable evidence. Try to figure a way to use it. One way to do so is through valuation rules of thumb based on multiples. A rule of thumb, artfully employed, sometimes beats a complex discounted-cash-flow calculation hands-down.

When you forecast cash flows, it is easy to become mesmerized by the numbers and just do it mechanically. As we pointed out in Chapter 11, it is important to take a strategic view. Are the revenue figures consistent with what you expect your competitors to do? Are the costs you have predicted realistic? Probe the assumptions behind the numbers to make sure they are sensible. Be particularly careful about the growth rates and profitability assumptions that drive horizon values. Don't assume that the business you are valuing will grow and earn more than the cost of capital in perpetuity.[6] This would be a nice outcome for the business, but not an outcome that competition will tolerate.

You should also check whether the business is worth more dead than alive. Sometimes a company's *liquidation value* exceeds its value as a going concern. Smart financial analysts sometimes ferret out idle or underexploited assets that would be worth much more if sold to someone else. You may end up counting these assets at their likely sale price and valuing the rest of the business without them.

WACC vs. the Flow-to-Equity Method

When valuing Geo we forecast the cash flows assuming all-equity financing and we used the WACC to discount these cash flows. The WACC formula picked up the value of the interest tax shields. Then to find equity value, we subtracted the value of debt from the total value of the firm.

If our task is to value a firm's equity, there's an obvious alternative to discounting company cash flows at the firm's WACC: Discount cash flows to *equity*, after interest and after taxes, at the cost of equity capital. This is called the *flow-to-equity* method. If the company's debt ratio is constant over time, the flow-to equity method should give the same answer as discounting cash flows at the WACC and then subtracting debt.

The flow-to-equity method seems simple, and it is simple if the proportions of debt and equity financing stay reasonably close to constant for the life of the company. But the cost of equity depends on financial leverage; in other words, it depends on financial risk as well as business risk. If financial leverage is expected to change significantly, discounting flows to equity at today's cost of equity will not give the right answer.

[6]Table 19.1 is too optimistic in this respect, because the horizon value increases with the assumed long-run growth rate. This implies that Geo has valuable growth opportunities (PVGO) even after the horizon in year 6. A more sophisticated spreadsheet would add an intermediate growth stage, say from years 7 through 10, and gradually reduce profitability to competitive levels. See Challenge Question 3 at the end of this chapter.

19.3 USING WACC IN PRACTICE

Some Tricks of the Trade

Sangria had just one asset and two sources of financing. A real company's market-value balance sheet has many more entries, for example:[7]

Current assets, including cash, inventory, and accounts receivable	Current liabilities, including accounts payable and short-term debt
Property, plant, and equipment (PP&E)	Long-term debt (D)
	Preferred stock (P)
Growth opportunities	Equity (E)
Total assets	Total liabilities plus equity

Several questions immediately arise:

How does the formula change when there are more than two sources of financing? Easy: There is one cost for each element. The weight for each element is proportional to its market value. For example, if the capital structure includes both preferred and common shares,

$$\text{WACC} = r_D(1 - T_C)\frac{D}{V} + r_P\frac{P}{V} + r_E\frac{E}{V}$$

where r_P is investors' expected rate of return on the preferred stock, P is the amount of preferred stock outstanding, and $V = D + P + E$.

What about short-term debt? Many companies consider only long-term financing when calculating WACC. They leave out the cost of short-term debt. In principle this is incorrect. The lenders who hold short-term debt are investors who can claim their share of operating earnings. A company that ignores this claim will misstate the required return on capital investments.

But "zeroing out" short-term debt is not a serious error if the debt is only temporary, seasonal, or incidental financing or if it is offset by holdings of cash and marketable securities. Suppose, for example, that one of your foreign subsidiaries takes out a six-month loan to finance its inventory and accounts receivable. The rupee equivalent of this loan will show up as a short-term debt. At the same time headquarters may be lending money by investing surplus rupees in short-term securities.

[7]This balance sheet is for exposition and should not be confused with a real company's books. It includes the value of growth opportunities, which accountants do not recognize, though investors do. It excludes certain accounting entries, for example, deferred taxes.

Deferred taxes arise when a company uses faster depreciation for tax purposes than it uses in reports to investors. That means the company reports more in taxes than it pays. The difference is accumulated as a liability for deferred taxes. In a sense there is a liability, because the Internal Revenue Service "catches up," collecting extra taxes, as assets age. But this is irrelevant in capital investment analysis, which focuses on actual after-tax cash flows and uses accelerated tax depreciation.

Deferred taxes should not be regarded as a source of financing or an element of the weighted-average cost of capital formula. The liability for deferred taxes is not a security held by investors. It is a balance sheet entry created for accounting purposes.

Deferred taxes can be important in regulated industries, however. Regulators take deferred taxes into account in calculating allowed rates of return and the time patterns of revenues and consumer prices.

If this lending and borrowing offset, there is no point in including the cost of short-term debt in the weighted-average cost of capital, because the company is not a *net* short-term borrower.

What about other current liabilities? Current liabilities are usually "netted out" by subtracting them from current assets. The difference is entered as net working capital on the left-hand side of the balance sheet. The sum of long-term financing on the right is called *total capitalization*.

Net working capital = current assets − current liabilities	Long-term debt (D)
Property, plant, and equipment	Preferred stock (P)
Growth opportunities	Equity (E)
	Total capitalization (V)

When net working capital is treated as an asset, forecasts of cash flows for capital investment projects must treat increases in net working capital as a cash outflow and decreases as in inflow. This is standard practice, which we followed in Section 6.2. We also did so when we estimated the future investments that Geo would need to make in working capital.

Since current liabilities include short-term debt, netting them out against current assets excludes the cost of short-term debt from the weighted-average cost of capital. We have just explained why this can be an acceptable approximation. But when short-term debt is an important, permanent source of financing—as is common for small firms and firms outside the India—it should be shown explicitly on the right-hand side of the balance sheet, not netted out against current assets.[8] A quick glance at the financing pattern of 8059 companies in India shows that short term borrowings constitute at least 50 percent of the total borrowings in 2504 companies (31 percent). Short term borrowings constitute at least 25 percent of the total borrowings in 4059 companies (about 50 percent). The interest cost of short term debt is then one element of the weighted average cost of capital of such companies.

How are the costs of financing calculated? You can often use stock market data to get an estimate of r_E, the expected rate of return demanded by investors in the company's stock. With that estimate, WACC is not too hard to calculate, because the borrowing rate r_D and the debt and equity ratios D/V and E/V can be directly observed or estimated without too much trouble.[9] Estimating the value and required return for preferred shares is likewise usually not too complicated.

Estimating the required return on other security types can be troublesome. Convertible debt, where the investors' return comes partly from an option to exchange the debt for the company's stock, is one example. We will leave convertibles to Chapter 25.

Junk debt, where the risk of default is high, is likewise difficult. The higher the odds of default, the lower the market price of the debt, and the higher is the *promised* rate of interest. But the weighted-average cost of capital is an *expected*, that is average, rate of return, not a promised one. For example, in June 2004, Delta Airline bonds maturing in 2016 sold at only 42 percent of face value and

[8]Financial practitioners have rules of thumb for deciding whether short-term debt is worth including in WACC. One rule checks whether short-term debt is at least 10 percent of total liabilities and net working capital is negative. If so, then short-term debt is almost surely being used to finance long-term assets and is explicitly included in WACC.

[9]Most corporate debt is not actively traded, so its market value cannot be observed directly. But you can usually value a non-traded debt security by looking to securities that *are* traded and that have approximately the same default risk and maturity. See Chapter 24.

For healthy firms the market value of debt is usually not too far from book value, so many managers and analysts use book value for D in the weighted-average cost of capital formula. However, be sure to use *market*, not book, values for E.

offered a 24 percent promised yield, about 19 percentage points above yields on the highest-quality debt issues maturing at the same time. The price and yield on the Delta bond demonstrated investors' concern about the company's chronic financial ill-health. But the 24 percent yield was not an expected return, because it did not average in the losses to be incurred if Delta defaults. Including 24 percent as a "cost of debt" in a calculation of WACC would therefore overstate Delta's true cost of capital.

This is bad news: There is no easy or tractable way of estimating the expected rate of return on most junk debt issues.[10] The good news is that for most debt the odds of default are small. That means the promised and expected rates of return are close, and the promised rate can be used as an approximation in the weighted-average cost of capital.

Company vs. Industry WACCs Of course you want to know what your company's WACC is. Yet industry WACCs are sometimes more useful. Here's an example. Grasim Industries is primarily into the manufacturing of viscose staple fibre, cement, and sponge iron. Almost 94 percent of the total revenue of Grasim comes from these three business segments. Grasim's overall WACC is not right for any of the three business segments. The company will be well advised to use a VSF industry WACC for its VSF division, cement industry WACC for its cement division, and sponge iron WACC for its sponge iron division.

Industry WACCs are less exposed to random noise and estimation errors. Fortunately, for Grasim, there are several large, pure-play (almost) Indian companies that are exclusively into the manufacturing of cement or sponge iron. Of course, use of an industry WACC for a particular company's investments assumes that the company and industry have approximately the same business risk and financing.

Mistakes People Make in Using the Weighted-Average Formula

The weighted-average formula is very useful but also dangerous. It tempts people to make logical errors. For example, manager Q, who is campaigning for a pet project, might look at the formula

$$\text{WACC} = r_D(1 - T_c)\frac{D}{V} + r_E\frac{E}{V}$$

and think, "Aha! My firm has a good credit rating. It could borrow, say, 90 percent of the project's cost if it likes. That means $D/V = .9$ and $E/V = .1$. My firm's borrowing rate r_D is 8 percent, and the required return on equity, r_E, is 15 percent. Therefore

$$\text{WACC} = .08(1 - .35)(.9) + .15(.1) = .062$$

or 6.2 percent. When I discount at that rate, my project looks great."

[10]When betas can be estimated for the junk issue or for a sample of similar issues, the expected return can be calculated from the capital asset pricing model. Otherwise the yield should be adjusted for the probability of default. Evidence on historical default rates on junk bonds is described in Chapter 24.

Manager Q is wrong on several counts. First, the weighted-average formula works only for projects that are carbon copies of the firm. The firm isn't 90 percent debt-financed.

Second, the immediate source of funds for a project has no necessary connection with the hurdle rate for the project. What matters is the project's overall contribution to the firm's borrowing power. A dollar invested in Q's pet project will not increase the firm's debt capacity by Rs. 90. If the firm borrows 90 percent of the project's cost, it is really borrowing in part against its *existing* assets. Any advantage from financing the new project with more debt than normal should be attributed to the old projects, not to the new one.

Third, even if the firm were willing and able to lever up to 90 percent debt, its cost of capital would not decline to 6.2 percent (as Q's naive calculation predicts). You cannot increase the debt ratio without creating financial risk for stockholders and thereby increasing r_E, the expected rate of return they demand from the firm's common stock. Going to 90 percent debt would certainly increase the borrowing rate, too.

Adjusting WACC when Debt Ratios and Business Risks Differ

The WACC formula assumes that the project or business to be valued will be financed in the same debt–equity proportions as the company (or industry) as a whole. What if that is not true? For example, what if Sangria's perpetual crusher project supports only 20 percent debt, versus 40 percent for Sangria overall?

Moving from 40 to 20 percent debt changes all the inputs to the WACC formula.[11] Obviously the financing weights change. But the cost of equity r_E is less, because financial risk is reduced. The cost of debt may be lower too.

Take another look at Figure 17.4 on page 464, which plots WACC and the costs of debt and equity as a function of the debt–equity ratio. The flat line is r, the opportunity cost of capital. Remember, this is the expected rate of return that investors would want from the project if it were all-equity-financed. The opportunity cost of capital depends only on business risk and is the natural reference point.

Suppose Sangria or the perpetual crusher project were all-equity-financed ($D/V = 0$). At that point WACC equals cost of equity, and both equal the opportunity cost of capital. Start from that point in Figure 19.1. As the debt ratio increases, the cost of equity increases, because of financial risk, but notice that WACC declines. The decline is *not* caused by use of "cheap" debt in place of "expensive" equity. It falls because of the tax shields on debt interest payments. If there were no corporate income taxes, the weighted-average cost of capital would be constant, and equal to the opportunity cost of capital, at all debt ratios. We showed this in Chapter 17.

Figure 19.1 shows the *shape* of the relationship between financing and WACC, but initially we have numbers only for Sangria's current 40 percent debt ratio. We want to recalculate WACC at a 20 percent ratio.

---

[11]Even the tax rate could change. For example, Sangria might have enough taxable income to cover interest payments at 20 percent debt but not at 40 percent debt. In that case the effective marginal tax rate would be higher at 20 than 40 percent debt.

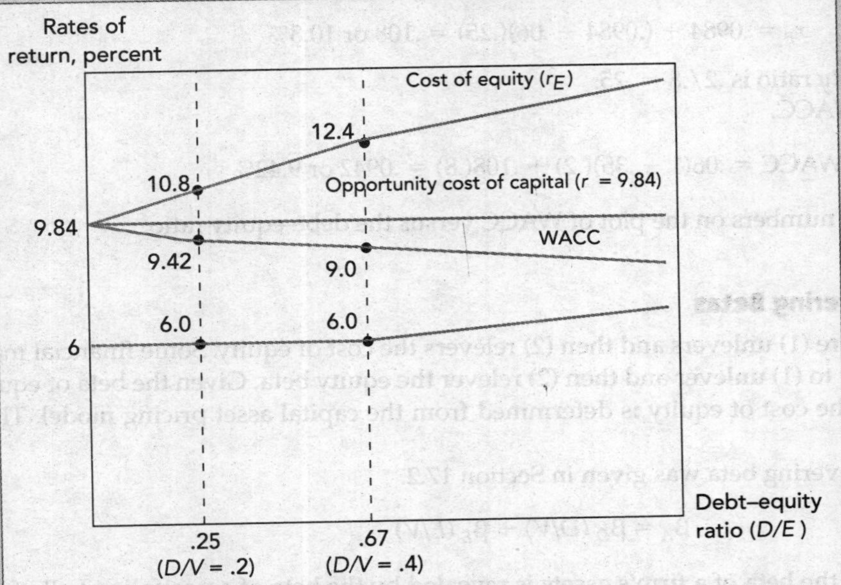

FIGURE 19.1

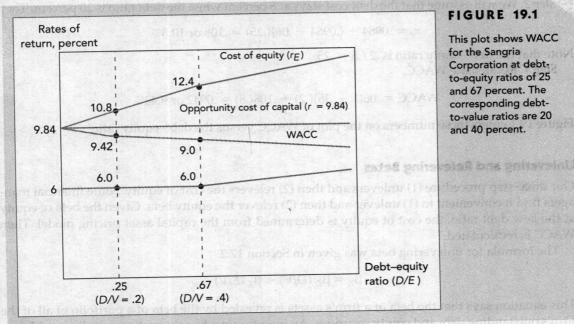

This plot shows WACC for the Sangria Corporation at debt-to-equity ratios of 25 and 67 percent. The corresponding debt-to-value ratios are 20 and 40 percent.

Here is the simplest way to do it. There are three steps.

Step 1 Calculate the opportunity cost of capital. In other words, calculate WACC and the cost of equity at zero debt. This step is called *unlevering* the WACC. The simplest unlevering formula is

$$\text{Opportunity cost of capital} = r = r_D D/V + r_E E/V$$

This formula comes directly from Modigliani and Miller's proposition 1 (see Section 17.1). If taxes are left out, the weighted-average cost of capital equals the opportunity cost of capital and is independent of leverage.

Step 2 Estimate the cost of debt, r_D, at the new debt ratio, and calculate the new cost of equity.

$$r_E = r + (r - r_D)D/E$$

This formula is Modigliani and Miller's proposition 2 (see Section 17.2). It calls for D/E, the ratio of debt to *equity*, not debt to value.

Step 3 Recalculate the weighted-average cost of capital at the new financing weights.

Let's do the numbers for Sangria at $D/V = .20$ or 20 percent.

Step 1. Sangria's current debt ratio is $D/V = .4$. So

$$r = .06(.4) + .124(.6) = .0984 \text{ or } 9.84\%$$

Step 2. We will assume that the debt cost stays at 6 percent when the debt ratio is 20 percent. Then

$$r_E = .0984 + (.0984 - .06)(.25) = .108 \text{ or } 10.8\%$$

Note that the debt–*equity* ratio is .2/.8 = .25.

Step 3. Recalculate WACC.

$$\text{WACC} = .06(1 - .35)(.2) + .108(.8) = .0942 \text{ or } 9.42\%$$

Figure 19.1 enters these numbers on the plot of WACC versus the debt–equity ratio.

Unlevering and Relevering Betas

Our three-step procedure (1) unlevers and then (2) relevers the cost of equity. Some financial managers find it convenient to (1) unlever and then (2) relever the equity beta. Given the beta of equity at the new debt ratio, the cost of equity is determined from the capital asset pricing model. Then WACC is recalculated.

The formula for unlevering beta was given in Section 17.2.

$$\beta_A = \beta_D\,(D/V) + \beta_E\,(E/V)$$

This equation says that the beta of a firm's assets is revealed by the beta of a portfolio of all of the firm's outstanding debt and equity securities. An investor who bought such a portfolio would own the assets free and clear and absorb only business risks.

The formula for relevering beta closely resembles MM's proposition 2, except that betas are substituted for rates of return:

$$\beta_E = \beta_A + (\beta_A - \beta_D)\,D/E$$

Use this formula to recalculate β_E when D/E changes.

The Importance of Rebalancing

The formulas for WACC and for unlevering and relevering expected returns are simple, but we must be careful to remember underlying assumptions. The most important point is *rebalancing*.

Calculating WACC for a company at its existing capital structure requires that the capital structure *not* change; in other words, the company must rebalance its capital structure to maintain the same market-value debt ratio for the relevant future. Take Sangria Corporation as an example. It starts with a debt-to-value ratio of 40 percent and a market value of Rs. 1,250 million. Suppose that Sangria's products do unexpectedly well in the marketplace and that market value increases to Rs. 1,500 million. Rebalancing means that it will then increase debt to .4 × 1,500 = Rs. 600 million,[12] thus regaining a 40 percent ratio. If market value instead falls, Sangria would have to pay down debt proportionally.

[12]The proceeds of the additional borrowing would be paid out to shareholders or used, along with additional equity investment, to finance Sangria's growth.

Of course real companies do not rebalance capital structure in such a mechanical and compulsive way. For practical purposes, it's sufficient to assume gradual but steady adjustment toward a long-run target. But if the firm plans significant changes in capital structure (for example, if it plans to pay off its debt), the WACC formula won't work. In such cases, you should turn to the APV method, which we describe in the next section.

Our three-step procedure for recalculating WACC makes a similar rebalancing assumption.[13] Whatever the starting debt ratio, the firm is assumed to rebalance to maintain that ratio in the future.[14]

The Modigliani–Miller Formula, Plus Some Final Advice

What if the firm does not rebalance to keep its debt ratio constant? In this case the only general approach is adjusted present value, which we cover in the next section. But sometimes financial managers turn to other discount-rate formulas, including one derived by Modigliani and Miller

[13]Similar, but not identical. The basic WACC formula is correct whether rebalancing occurs at the end of each period or continuously. The unlevering and relevering formulas used in steps 1 and 2 of our three-step procedure are exact only if rebalancing is continuous so that the debt ratio stays constant day-to-day and week-to-week. However, the errors introduced from annual rebalancing are very small and can be ignored for practical purposes.

[14]Here's why the formulas work with continuous rebalancing. Think of a market-value balance sheet with assets and interest tax shields on the left and debt and equity on the right, with $D + E = \text{PV(assets)} + \text{PV(tax shield)}$. The total risk (beta) of the firm's debt and equity equals the blended risk of PV(assets) and PV(tax shield)

$$\beta_D \frac{D}{V} + \beta_E \frac{E}{V} = \alpha\beta_A + (1-\alpha)\beta_{\text{tax shield}} \tag{1}$$

where α is the proportion of the total firm value from its assets and $1 - \alpha$ is the proportion from interest tax shields. If the firm readjusts its capital structure to keep D/V constant, then the beta of the tax shield must be the same as the beta of the assets. With rebalancing, an x percent change in firm value V changes debt D by x percent; the interest tax shield $T_C r_D D$ will change by x percent as well. Thus the risk of the tax shield must be the same as the risk of the firm as a whole:

$$\beta_{\text{tax shield}} = \beta_A = \beta_D \frac{D}{V} + \beta_E \frac{E}{V} \tag{2}$$

This is our unlevering formula expressed in terms of beta. Since expected returns depend on beta:

$$r_A = r_D \frac{D}{V} + r_E \frac{E}{V} \tag{3}$$

Rearrange formulas (2) and (3) to get the relevering formulas for β_E and r_E.

$$\beta_E = \beta_A + (\beta_A - \beta_D)D/E$$

$$r_E = r_A + (r_A - r_D)D/E$$

All this assumes continuous rebalancing. Suppose instead that the firm rebalances once a year, so that the next year's interest tax shield, which depends on this year's debt, is known. Then you can use a formula developed by Miles and Ezzell:

$$r_{\text{Miles-Ezzell}} = r_A - (D/V)r_D T_C \left(\frac{1 + r_A}{1 + r_D}\right)$$

See J. Miles and J. Ezzell, "The Weighted Average Cost of Capital, Perfect Capital Markets, and Project Life: A Clarification," *Journal of Financial and Quantitative Analysis* 15 (September 1980), pp. 719–730.

(MM). MM considered a company or project generating a level, perpetual stream of cash flows financed with fixed, perpetual debt, and derived a simple after-tax discount rate:[15]

$$r_{MM} = r(1 - T_C D/V),$$

Here it's easy to unlever: just set the debt-capacity parameter (D/V) equal to zero.[16]

MM's formula is still used in practice, but the formula is exact only in the special case where there is a level, perpetual stream of cash flows and fixed, perpetual debt. However, the formula is not a bad approximation for shorter-lived projects when debt is issued in a fixed amount.[17]

So which team do you want to play with, the fixed-debt team or the rebalancers? If you join the fixed-debt team you will be outnumbered. Most financial managers use the plain, after-tax WACC, which assumes constant market-value debt ratios and therefore assumes rebalancing. That makes sense, because the debt *capacity* of a firm or project must depend on its future value, which will fluctuate.

At the same time, we must admit that the typical financial manager doesn't care much if his or her firm's debt ratio drifts up or down within a reasonable range of moderate financial leverage. The typical financial manager acts as if a plot of WACC against the debt ratio is "flat" (constant) over this range. This too makes sense, if we just remember that interest tax shields are the *only* reason why the after-tax WACC declines in Figure 17.4 or 19.1. The WACC formula doesn't explicity capture costs of financial distress or any of the other nontax complications discussed in Chapter 18.[18] All these complications may roughly cancel the value added by interest tax shields (within a range of moderate leverage). If so, the financial manager is wise to focus on the firm's operating and investment decisions, rather than on fine-tuning its debt ratio.

---

[15]The formula first appeared in F. Modigliani and M. H. Miller, "Corporate Income Taxes and the Cost of Capital: A Correction," *American Economic Review* 53 (June 1963) pp. 433–443. It is explained more fully in M. H. Miller and F. Modigliani: "Some Estimates of the Cost of Capital to the Electric Utility Industry: 1954–1957," *American Economic Review* 56 (June 1966), pp. 333–391.

Given perpetual fixed debt,

$$V = \frac{C}{r} + T_C D$$

$$V = \frac{C}{r(1 - T_C D / V)} = \frac{C}{r_{MM}}$$

[16]In this case the relevering formula for the cost of equity is:

$$r_E = r_A + (1 - T_C)(r_A - r_D)D/E$$

See R. Hamada: "The Effect of a Firm's Capital Structure on the Systematic Risk of Common Stocks," *Journal of Finance* 27 (May 1972), pp. 435–452.

[17]See S. C. Myers, "Interactions of Corporate Financing and Investment Decisions—Implications for Capital Budgeting," *Journal of Finance* 29 (March 1974), pp. 1–25.

[18]Costs of financial distress can show up as rapidly increasing costs of debt and equity, especially at high debt ratios. The costs of financial distress could "flatten out" the WACC curve in Figures 17.4 and 19.1, and finally increase WACC as leverage climbs. Thus some practitioners calculate an industry WACC and take it as constant, at least within the range of debt ratios observed for healthy companies in the industry.

Personal taxes could also generate a flatter curve for after-tax WACC as a function of leverage. See Section 18.2.

19.4 ADJUSTED PRESENT VALUE

The idea behind **adjusted present value (APV)** is to divide and conquer. APV does not attempt to capture taxes or other effects of financing in a WACC or adjusted discount rate. A series of present value calculations is made instead. The first establishes a base-case value for the project or firm: its value as a separate, all-equity-financed venture. The discount rate for the base-case value is just the opportunity cost of capital. Once the base-case value is set, then each financing side effect is traced out, and the present value of its cost or benefit to the firm is calculated. Finally, all the present values are added together to estimate the project's total contribution to the value of the firm:

$$\text{APV} = \text{base-case NPV} + \text{sum of PVs of financing side effects}$$

The most important financing side effect is the interest tax shield on the debt supported by the project (a plus). Other possible side effects are the issue costs of securities (a minus) or financing packages subsidized by a supplier or government (a plus).

APV gives the financial manager an explicit view of the factors that are adding or subtracting value. APV can prompt the manager to ask the right follow-up questions. For example, suppose that base-case NPV is positive but less than the costs of issuing shares to finance the project. That should prompt the manager to look around to see if the project can be rescued by an alternative financing plan.

APV for the Perpetual Crusher

APV is easiest to understand in simple numerical examples. Let's apply it to Sangria's perpetual crusher project. We start by showing that APV is equivalent to discounting at WACC if we make the same assumptions about debt policy.

We used Sangria's WACC (9 percent) as the discount rate for the crusher's projected cash flows. The WACC calculation assumed that debt will be maintained at a constant 40 percent of the future value of the project or firm. In this case, the risk of interest tax shields is the same as the risk of the project.[19] Therefore we will discount the tax shields at the opportunity cost of capital (r). We calculated the opportunity cost of capital in the last section by unlevering Sangria's WACC to obtain $r =$ 9.84 percent.

The first step is to calculate base-case NPV. We discount after-tax project cash flows of Rs. 1.125 million at the opportunity cost of capital of 9.84 percent and subtract the Rs. 12.5 million outlay. The cash flows are perpetual, so

$$\text{Base-case NPV} = -12.5 + \frac{1.125}{.0984} = -\text{Rs. } 1.067 \text{ million}$$

Thus the project would not be worthwhile with all-equity financing. But it actually supports debt of Rs. 5 million. At a 6 percent borrowing rate ($r_D = .06$) and a 35 percent tax rate ($T_C = .35$), annual tax shields are $.35 \times .06 \times 5 = .105$, or Rs. 105,000.

[19]That is, $\beta_A = \beta_{\text{tax shields}}$. See footnote 14 above.

What are those tax shields worth? If the firm is constantly rebalancing its debt, we discount at r = 9.84 percent:

$$\text{PV(interest tax shields, debt rebalanced)} = \frac{105{,}000}{.0984} = \text{Rs}\,1.067\text{ million}$$

APV is the sum of base-case value and PV(interest tax shields)

$$\text{APV} = -1.067\text{ million} + 1.067\text{ million} = 0$$

This is exactly the same as we obtained by one-step discounting with WACC. The perpetual crusher is a breakeven project by either valuation method.

But with APV, we don't have to hold debt at a constant proportion of value. Suppose Sangria plans to keep project debt fixed at Rs. 5 million. In this case we assume the risk of the tax shields is the same as the risk of the debt and we discount at the 6 percent rate on debt:

$$\text{PV(tax shields, debt fixed)} = \frac{105{,}000}{.06} = \text{Rs 1.75 million}$$

$$\text{APV} = -1.067 + 1.75 = \text{Rs. 683 million}$$

Now the project is more attractive. With fixed debt, the interest tax shields are safe and therefore worth more. (Whether the fixed debt is safer for Sangria is another matter. If the perpetual crusher project fails, the Rs. 5 million of fixed debt may end up as a burden on Sangria's other assets.)

Other Financing Side Effects

Suppose Sangria has to finance the perpetual crusher by issuing debt and equity. It issues Rs. 7.5 million of equity with issue costs of 7 percent (Rs. 525,000) and Rs. 5 million of debt with issue costs of 2 percent (Rs. 100,000). Assume the debt is fixed once issued, so that interest tax shields are worth Rs. 1.75 million. Now we can recalculate APV, taking care to subtract the issue costs:

$$\text{APV} = -1.067 + 1.75 - .525 - .100 = .058\text{ million, or Rs. 58,000}$$

The issue costs would reduce APV to nearly zero.

Sometimes there are favorable financing side effects that have nothing to do with taxes. For example, suppose that a potential manufacturer of crusher machinery offers to sweeten the deal by leasing it to Sangria on favorable terms. Then you could calculate APV as the sum of base-case NPV plus the NPV of the lease. Or suppose that a local government offers to lend Sangria Rs. 5 million at a very low interest rate if the crusher is built and operated locally. The NPV of the subsidized loan could be added in to APV. (We cover leases in Chapter 26 and subsidized loans in the Appendix to this chapter.)

APV for Businesses

APV can also be used to value businesses. Let's take another look at the valuation of Geo. In Table 19.1, we assumed a constant 40 percent debt ratio and discounted free cash flow at Sangria's WACC. Table 19.2 runs the same analysis, but with a fixed debt schedule.

We'll suppose that Sangria has decided to make an offer for Geo. If successful, it plans to finance the purchase with Rs. 51 million of debt. It intends to pay down the debt to Rs. 45 million in year 6.

	Latest year	Forecast						
	0	1	2	3	4	5	6	7
Free cash flow	2.5	3.5	3.2	3.4	5.9	6.1	6.0	6.8
PV Free cash flow, years 1-6	**19.7**							
PV Horizon value	**64.6**			(Horizon value in year 6)			113.4	
Base-Case PV of company	**84.3**							
Debt	51.0	50.0	49.0	48.0	47.0	46.0	45.0	
Interest		3.06	3.00	2.94	2.88	2.82	2.76	
Interest tax shield		1.07	1.05	1.03	1.01	0.99	0.97	
PV Interest tax shields	**5.0**							
APV	**89.3**							
Tax rate, percent	35.0							
Opportunity cost of capital, percent	9.84							
WACC, percent (to discount horizon value to year 6)	9.0							
Long-term growth forecast, percent	3.0							
Interest rate, percent (years 1 - 6)	6.0							
After-tax debt service		2.99	2.95	2.91	2.87	2.83	2.79	

TABLE 19.2

APV valuation of Geo Corporation (Rs. millions).

Please visit us at www.mhhe.com/bmam8e or refer to your Student CD .

Recall Geo's horizon value of Rs. 113.4 million, which is calculated in Table 19.1 and shown again in Table 19.2. The debt ratio at the horizon is therefore projected at 45/133.4 = .397, about 40 percent. Thus Sangria plans to take Geo back to a normal 40 percent debt ratio at the horizon.[20] But Geo will be carrying a heavier debt load before the horizon. For example, the Rs. 51 million of initial debt is about 58 percent of company value as calculated in Table 19.1.

Let's see how Geo's APV is affected by this more aggressive borrowing schedule. Table 19.2 shows projections of free cash flows from Table 19.1.[21] Now we need Geo's base-case value, so we discount these flows at the opportunity cost of capital (9.84 percent), not at WACC. The resulting base-case value for Geo is Rs. 84.3 million. Table 19.2 also projects debt levels, interest, and interest tax shields. If the debt levels are taken as fixed, then the tax shields should be discounted back at the 6 percent borrowing rate. The resulting PV of interest tax shields is Rs. 5.0 million. Thus,

$$\begin{aligned} \text{APV} &= \text{base-case NPV} + \text{PV(interest tax shields)} \\ &= \text{Rs. } 84.3 + 5.0 = \text{Rs. } 89.3 \text{ million} \end{aligned}$$

an increase of Rs. 1.4 million from NPV in Table 19.1.The increase can be traced to the higher early debt levels and to the assumption that the debt levels and interest tax shields are fixed and relatively safe.[22]

[20]Therefore we still calculate the horizon value in year 6 by discounting subsequent free cash flows at WACC. The horizon value in year 6 is discounted back to year 0 at the opportunity cost of capital, however.

[21]Many of the assumptions and calculations in Table 19.1 have been hidden in Table 19.2. The hidden rows can be recalled in the "live" version of Table 19.2, which is available on this book's CD and Web site **(www.mhhe.com/bmam8e)**.

[22]But will Geo really *support* debt at the levels shown in Table 19.2? If not, then the debt must be partly supported by Sangria's other assets, and only part of the Rs. 5 million in PV(interest tax shields) can be attributed to Geo itself.

Now a difference of Rs. 1.4 million is not a big deal, considering all the lurking risks and pitfalls in forecasting Geo's free cash flows. But you can see the advantage of the flexibility that APV provides. The APV spreadsheet allows you to explore the implications of different financing strategies without locking into a fixed debt ratio or having to calculate a new WACC for every scenario.

APV is particularly useful when the debt for a project or business is tied to book value or has to be repaid on a fixed schedule. For example, Kaplan and Ruback used APV to analyze the prices paid for a sample of leveraged buyouts (LBOs). LBOs are takeovers, typically of mature companies, financed almost entirely with debt. However, the new debt is not intended to be permanent. LBO business plans call for generating extra cash by selling assets, shaving costs, and improving profit margins. The extra cash is used to pay down the LBO debt. Therefore you can't use WACC as a discount rate to evaluate an LBO because its debt ratio will not be constant.

APV works fine for LBOs. The company is first evaluated as if it were all-equity-financed. That means that cash flows are projected after tax, but without any interest tax shields generated by the LBO's debt. The tax shields are then valued separately and added to the all-equity value. Any other financing side effects are added also. The result is an APV valuation for the company.[23] Kaplan and Ruback found that APV did a pretty good job explaining prices paid in these hotly contested takeovers, considering that not all the information available to bidders had percolated into the public domain. Kaplan and Ruback were restricted to publicly available data.

APV for International Investments

APV is most useful when financing side effects are numerous and important. This is frequently the case for large international investments, which may have custom-tailored *project financing* and special contracts with suppliers, customers, and governments. Here are a few examples of financing side effects encountered in international finance.[24]

We explain project finance in Chapter 25. It typically means very high debt ratios to start, with most or all of a project's early cash flows committed to debt service. Equity investors have to wait. Since the debt ratio will not be constant, you have to turn to APV.

Project financing may include debt available at favorable interest rates. Most governments subsidize exports by making special financing packages available, and manufacturers of industrial equipment may stand ready to lend money to help close a sale. Suppose, for example, that your project requires construction of an on-site electricity generating plant. You solicit bids from suppliers in various countries. Don't be surprised if the competing suppliers sweeten their bids with offers of low interest rate project loans or if they offer to lease the plant on favorable terms. You should then calculate the NPVs of these loans or leases and include them in your project analysis.

---

[23]Kaplan and Ruback actually used "compressed" APV, in which all cash flows, including interest tax shields, are discounted at the opportunity cost of capital. S. N. Kaplan and R. S. Ruback, "The Valuation of Cash Flow Forecasts: An Empirical Analysis," *Journal of Finance* 50 (September 1995), pp. 1059–1093.

[24]Use of APV for international projects was first advocated by D. L. Lessard, "Valuing Foreign Cash Flows: An Adjusted Present Value Approach," in D. L. Lessard, (ed), *International Financial Management: Theory and Application* (Boston: Warren, Gorham and Lamont, 1979).

Sometimes international projects are supported by contracts with suppliers or customers. Suppose a manufacturer wants to line up a reliable supply of a crucial raw material—powdered magnoosium, say. The manufacturer could subsidize a new magnoosium smelter by agreeing to buy 75 percent of production and guaranteeing a minimum purchase price. The guarantee is clearly a valuable addition to project APV: If the world price of powdered magnoosium falls below the minimum, the project doesn't suffer. You would calculate the value of this guarantee (by the methods explained in Chapters 20 to 22) and add it to APV.

Sometimes local governments impose costs or restrictions on investment or disinvestment. For example, Chile, in an attempt to slow down a flood of short-term capital inflows in the 1990s, required investors to "park" part of their incoming money in non-interest-bearing accounts for a period of two years. An investor in Chile during this period would calculate the cost of this requirement and subtract it from APV.

19.5 YOUR QUESTIONS ANSWERED

Question: All these cost of capital formulas—which ones do financial managers actually use?

Answer: The after-tax weighted-average cost of capital, most of the time. WACC is estimated for the company, or sometimes for an industry. We recommend industry WACCs when data are available for firms with similar assets, operations, business risks, and growth opportunities.

Of course, conglomerate companies, with divisions operating in two or more unrelated industries, should not use a single company or industry WACC. Such firms should try to estimate a different industry WACC for each operating division.

Question: But WACC is the correct discount rate only for "average" projects. What if the project's financing differs from the company's or industry's?

Answer: Remember, investment projects are usually not separately financed. Even when they are, you should focus on the project's contribution to the firm's overall debt capacity, not on its immediate financing. (Suppose it's convenient to raise all the money for a particular project with a bank loan. That doesn't mean the project itself supports 100 percent debt financing. The company is borrowing against its existing assets as well as the project.)

But if the project's debt capacity is materially different from the company's existing assets, or if the company's overall debt policy changes, WACC should be adjusted. The adjustment can be done by the three-step procedure explained in Section 19.3.

Question: Could we do one more numerical example?

Answer: Sure. Suppose that WACC has been estimated as follows at a 30 percent debt ratio:

$$\begin{aligned}\text{WACC} &= r_D(1 - T_c)\frac{D}{V} + r_E\frac{E}{V} \\ &= .09(1 - .35)(.3) + .15(.7) = .1226, \text{ or } 12.26\%\end{aligned}$$

What is the correct discount rate at a 50 percent debt ratio?

Step 1. Calculate the opportunity cost of capital.

$$r = r_D D/V + r_E E/V$$
$$= .09(.3) + .15(.7) = .132, \text{ or } 13.2\%$$

Step 2. Calculate the new costs of debt and equity. The cost of debt will be higher at 50 percent debt than 30 percent. Say it is $r_D = .095$. The new cost of equity is

$$r_E = r + (r - r_D)D/E$$
$$= .132 + (.132 - .095)\ 50/50$$
$$= .169, \text{ or } 16.9\%$$

Step 3. Recalculate WACC.

$$\text{WACC} = r_D(1 - T_C)D/V + r_E E/V$$
$$= .095(1 - .35)(0.5) + .169(.5) = .1154, \text{ or about } 11.5\%$$

Question: How do I use the capital asset pricing model to calculate the after-tax weighted-average cost of capital?

Answer: First plug the equity beta into the capital asset pricing formula to calculate r_E, the expected return to equity. Then use this figure, along with the after-tax cost of debt and the debt-to-value and equity-to-value ratios, in the WACC formula.

Of course the CAPM is not the only way to estimate the cost of equity. For example, you might be able to use the dividend-discount model (see Section 4.3).

Question: But suppose I do use the CAPM? What if I have to recalculate the equity beta for a different debt ratio?

Answer: The formula for the equity beta is

$$\beta_E = \beta_A + (\beta_A - \beta_D)\ D/E$$

where β_E is the equity beta, β_A is the asset beta, and β_D is the beta of the company's debt. The asset beta is a weighted average of the debt and equity betas:

$$\beta_A = \beta_D\ (D/V) + \beta_E\ (E/V)$$

Suppose you needed the opportunity cost of capital r. You could calculate β_A and then r from the capital asset pricing model.

Question: I think I understand how to adjust for differences in debt capacity or debt policy. How about differences in business risk?

Answer: If business risk is different, then r, the opportunity cost of capital, is different.

Figuring out the right r for an unusually safe or risky project is never easy. Sometimes the financial manager can use estimates of risk and expected return for companies similar to the project. Suppose, for example, that a traditional pharmaceutical company is considering a major commitment to biotech research. The financial manager could pick a sample of biotech companies, estimate their average beta and cost of capital, and use these estimates as benchmarks for the biotech investment.

But in many cases it's difficult to find a good sample of matching companies for an unusually safe or risky project. Then the financial manager has to adjust the opportunity cost of capital by judgment. Section 9.3 may be helpful in such cases.

Question: When do I need adjusted present value (APV)?

Answer: The WACC formula picks up only one financing side effect: the value of interest tax shields on debt supported by a project. If there are other side effects—subsidized financing tied to a project, for example—you should use APV.

You can also use APV to break out the value of interest tax shields:

$$\text{APV} = \text{base-case NPV} + \text{PV(tax shield)}$$

Suppose, for example, that you are analyzing a company just after a leveraged buyout. The company has a very high initial debt level but plans to pay down the debt as rapidly as possible. APV could be used to obtain an accurate valuation.

Question: When should personal taxes be incorporated into the analysis?

Answer: Always use T_C, the marginal corporate tax rate, when calculating WACC as a weighted average of the costs of debt and equity. The discount rate is adjusted *only* for corporate taxes. Any effects of personal taxes are reflected in r_D and r_E, the rates of return demanded by debt and equity investors.

In principle, APV can be adjusted for personal taxes by replacing the marginal corporate rate T_C with an effective tax rate that combines corporate and personal taxes and reflects the net tax advantage per rupee of interest paid by the firm. We provided back-of-the-envelope calculations of this advantage in Section 18.2. The effective tax rate is almost surely less than T_C, but it is very difficult to pin down the numerical difference. Therefore, in practice T_C is almost always used as an approximation.

Question: Are taxes really that important? Do financial managers really fine-tune the debt ratio to minimize WACC?

Answer: As we saw in Chapter 18, financing decisions reflect many forces beyond taxes, including costs of financial distress, differences in information, and incentives for managers. There may not be a sharply defined optimal capital structure. Therefore most financial managers don't fine-tune their companies' debt ratios, and they don't rebalance financing to keep debt ratios strictly constant. In effect they assume that a plot of WACC for different debt ratios is "flat" over a reasonable range of moderate leverage.

SUMMARY

This chapter has considered how financing can be incorporated into the valuation of projects and ongoing businesses. There are two ways to take financing into account. The first is to calculate NPV by discounting at an adjusted discount rate, usually the after-tax weighted-average cost of capital (WACC). The second approach discounts at the opportunity cost of capital and then adds or subtracts the present values of financing side effects. The second approach is called adjusted present value, or APV.

The formula for the after-tax WACC is:

$$\text{WACC} = r_D(1 - T_C)\frac{D}{V} + r_E\frac{E}{V}$$

where r_D and r_E are the expected rates of return demanded by investors in the firm's debt and equity securities, D and E are the current *market values* of debt and equity, and V is the total market value of the firm ($V = D + E$). Of course, the WACC formula expands if there are other sources of financing, for example, preferred stock.

Strictly speaking, discounting at WACC works only for projects that are carbon copies of the existing firm—projects with the same business risk that will be financed to maintain the firm's current, market debt ratio. But firms can use WACC as a benchmark rate to be adjusted for differences in business risk or financing. We gave a three-step procedure for adjusting WACC for different debt ratios.

Discounting cash flows at the WACC assumes that debt is rebalanced to keep a constant ratio of debt to market value. The amount of debt supported by a project is assumed to rise or fall with the project's after-the-fact success or failure. The WACC formula also assumes that financing matters *only* because of interest tax shields. When this or other assumptions are violated, only APV will give an absolutely correct answer.

APV is, in concept at least, simple. First calculate the base-case NPV of the project or business on the assumption that financing *doesn't* matter. (The discount rate is not WACC, but the opportunity cost of capital.) Then calculate the present values of any relevant financing side effects and add or subtract from base-case value. A capital investment project is worthwhile if

$$\text{APV} = \text{base-case NPV} + \text{PV(financing side effects)}$$

is positive. Common financing side effects include interest tax shields, issue costs, and special financing packages offered by suppliers or governments.

For firms or going-concern businesses, value depends on free cash flow. Free cash flow is the amount of cash that can be paid out to all investors, debt as well as equity, after deducting cash needed for new investment or increases in working capital. Free cash flow does not include the value of interest tax shields, however. The WACC formula accounts for interest tax shields by using the after-tax cost of debt. APV adds PV(interest tax shields) to base-case value.

Businesses are usually valued in two steps. First free cash flow is forecasted out to a valuation horizon and discounted back to present value. Then a horizon value is calculated and also discounted back. The horizon value is usually estimated by using the perpetual-growth DCF formula or by multiplying forecasted EBIT or EBITDA[25] by multiples observed for similar firms. Be particularly careful to avoid unrealistically high horizon values. By the time the horizon arrives, competitors will have had several years to catch up. Also, when you are done valuing the business, don't forget to subtract its debt to get the value of the firm's equity.

All of this chapter's examples reflect assumptions about the amount of debt supported by a project or business. Remember not to confuse "supported by" with the immediate source of funds for investment. For example, a firm might, as a matter of convenience, borrow Rs. 1 million for a Rs. 1 million research program. But the research is unlikely to contribute Rs. 1 million in debt capacity; a large part of the Rs. 1 million new debt would be supported by the firm's other assets.

Also remember that *debt capacity* is not meant to imply an absolute limit on how much the firm *can* borrow. The phrase refers to how much it *chooses* to borrow against a project or ongoing business.

[25]Recall that EBIT = earnings before interest and taxes and EBITDA = EBIT plus depreciation and amortization.

APPENDIX

Discounting Safe, Nominal Cash Flows

Suppose you're considering purchase of a Rs. 100,000 machine. The manufacturer sweetens the deal by offering to finance the purchase by lending you Rs. 100,000 for five years, with annual interest payments of 5 percent. You would have to pay 13 percent to borrow from a bank. Your marginal tax rate is 35 percent ($T_C = .35$).

How much is this loan worth? If you take it, the cash flows, in thousands of Rupees, are

	Period					
	0	1	2	3	4	5
Cash flow	100	−5	−5	−5	−5	−105
Tax shield		+1.75	+1.75	+1.75	+1.75	+1.75
After-tax cash flow	100	−3.25	−3.25	−3.25	−3.25	−103.25

What is the right discount rate?

Here you are discounting *safe, nominal* cash flows—safe because your company must commit to pay if it takes the loan,[26] and nominal because the payments would be fixed regardless of future inflation. Now, the correct discount rate for safe, nominal cash flows is your company's *after-tax*, unsubsidized borrowing rate,[27] $r_D(1 - T_C) = .13(1 - .35) = .0845$. Therefore

$$\text{NPV} = +100 - \frac{3.25}{1.0845} - \frac{3.25}{(1.0845)^2} - \frac{3.25}{(1.0845)^3} - \frac{3.25}{(1.0845)^4} - \frac{103.25}{(1.0845)^5}$$
$$= +20.52, \text{ or Rs } 20{,}520$$

The manufacturer has effectively cut the machine's purchase price from Rs. 100,000 to Rs. 100,000 − Rs. 20,520 = Rs. 79,480. You can now go back and recalculate the machine's NPV using this fire-sale price, or you can use the NPV of the subsidized loan as one element of the machine's adjusted present value.

A General Rule

Clearly, we owe an explanation of why $r_D(1 - T_C)$ is the right discount rate for safe, nominal cash flows. It's no surprise that the rate depends on r_D, the unsubsidized borrowing rate, for that is investors' opportunity cost of capital, the rate they would demand from your company's debt. But why should r_D be converted to an *after-tax* figure?

Let's simplify by taking a *one-year* subsidized loan of Rs. 100,000 at 5 percent. The cash flows, in thousands of rupees, are

	Period 0	Period 1
Cash flow	100	−105
Tax shield		+1.75
After-tax cash flow	100	−103.25

[26]In theory, *safe* means literally "risk-free," like the cash returns on a Treasury bond. In practice, it means that the risk of not paying or receiving a cash flow is small.

[27]In Section 13.1 we calculated the NPV of subsidized financing using the *pretax* borrowing rate. Now you can see that was a mistake. Using the pretax rate implicitly defines the loan in terms of its pretax cash flows, violating a rule promulgated way back in Section 6.1: *Always* estimate cash flows on an after-tax basis.

Now ask, What is the maximum amount X that could be borrowed for one year through regular channels if Rs. 103,250 is set aside to service the loan?

"Regular channels" means borrowing at 13 percent pretax and 8.45 percent after tax. Therefore you will need 108.45 percent of the amount borrowed to pay back principal plus after-tax interest charges. If $1.0845X = 103{,}250$, then $X = 95{,}205$. Now if you can borrow Rs. 100,000 by a subsidized loan, but only Rs. 95,205 through normal channels, the difference (Rs. 4,795) is money in the bank. Therefore, it must also be the NPV of this one-period subsidized loan.

When you discount a safe, nominal cash flow at an after-tax borrowing rate, you are implicitly calculating the *equivalent loan*, the amount you could borrow through normal channels, using the cash flow as debt service. Note that

$$\text{Equivalent loan} = \text{PV}\left(\begin{matrix}\text{cash flow available}\\ \text{for debt service}\end{matrix}\right) = \frac{103{,}250}{1.0845} = 95{,}205$$

In some cases, it may be easier to think of taking the lender's side of the equivalent loan rather than the borrower's. For example, you could ask, How much would my company have to invest today in order to cover next year's debt service on the subsidized loan? The answer is Rs. 95,205: If you lend that amount at 13 percent, you will earn 8.45 percent after tax, and therefore have 95,205(1.0845) = Rs. 103,250. By this transaction, you can in effect cancel, or "zero out," the future obligation. If you can borrow Rs. 100,000 and then set aside only Rs. 95,205 to cover all the required debt service, you clearly have Rs. 4,795 to spend as you please. That amount is the NPV of the subsidized loan.

Therefore, regardless of whether it's easier to think of borrowing or lending, the correct discount rate for safe, nominal cash flows is an after-tax interest rate.[28]

In some ways, this is an obvious result once you think about it. Companies are free to borrow or lend money. If they *lend*, they receive the after-tax interest rate on their investment; if they *borrow* in the capital market, they pay the after-tax interest rate. Thus, the opportunity cost to companies of investing in debt-equivalent cash flows is the after-tax interest rate. This is the adjusted cost of capital for debt-equivalent cash flows.[29]

Some Further Examples

Here are some further examples of debt-equivalent cash flows.

Payout Fixed by Contract Suppose you sign a maintenance contract with a truck leasing firm, which agrees to keep your leased trucks in good working order for the next two years in exchange for 24 fixed monthly payments. These payments are debt-equivalent flows.

---

[28]Borrowing and lending rates should not differ by much if the cash flows are truly safe, that is, if the chance of default is small. Usually your decision will not hinge on the rate used. If it does, ask which offsetting transaction—borrowing or lending—seems most natural and reasonable for the problem at hand. Then use the corresponding interest rate.

[29]All the examples in this section are forward-looking; they call for the value today of a stream of future debt-equivalent cash flows. But similar issues arise in legal and contractual disputes when a *past* cash flow has to be brought forward in time to a present value today. Suppose it's determined that company A should have paid B Rs. 1 million 10 years ago. B clearly deserves more than Rs. 1 million today, because it has lost the time value of money. The time value of money should be expressed as an after-tax borrowing or lending rate, or if no risk enters, as the after-tax risk-free rate. The time value of money is *not* equal to B's overall cost of capital. Allowing B to "earn" its overall cost of capital on the payment allows it to earn a risk premium without bearing risk. For a broader discussion of these issues, see F. Fisher and C. Romaine, "Janis Joplin's Yearbook and Theory of Damages," *Journal of Accounting, Auditing & Finance* 5 (Winter/Spring 1990), pp. 145–157.

Depreciation Tax Shields Capital projects are normally valued by discounting the total after-tax cash flows they are expected to generate. Depreciation tax shields contribute to project cash flow, but they are not valued separately; they are just folded into project cash flows along with dozens, or hundreds, of other specific inflows and outflows. The project's opportunity cost of capital reflects the average risk of the resulting aggregate.

However, suppose we ask what depreciation tax shields are worth *by themselves*. For a firm that's sure to pay taxes, depreciation tax shields are a safe, nominal flow. Therefore, they should be discounted at the firm's after-tax borrowing rate.

Suppose we buy an asset with a depreciable basis of Rs. 200,000, which can be depreciated by the five-year tax depreciation schedule (see Table 6.4). The resulting tax shields are

	Period					
	1	2	3	4	5	6
Percentage deductions	20	32	19.2	11.5	11.5	5.8
Rupee deductions (thousands)	Rs. 40	Rs. 64	Rs. 38.4	Rs. 23	Rs. 23	Rs. 11.6
Tax shields at T_c = .35 (thousands)	Rs. 14	Rs. 22.4	Rs. 13.4	Rs. 8.1	Rs. 8.1	Rs. 4.0

The after-tax discount rate is $r_D(1 - T_C) = .13(1 - .35) = .0845$. (We continue to assume a 13 percent pretax borrowing rate and a 35 percent marginal tax rate.) The present value of these shields is

$$PV = \frac{14}{1.0845} + \frac{22.4}{(1.0845)^2} + \frac{13.4}{(1.0845)^3} + \frac{8.1}{(1.0845)^4} + \frac{8.1}{(1.0845)^5} + \frac{4.0}{(1.0845)^6}$$

$= +56.2$, or Rs 56,200

A Consistency Check

You may have wondered whether our procedure for valuing debt-equivalent cash flows is consistent with the WACC and APV approaches presented earlier in this chapter. Yes, it is consistent, as we will now illustrate.

Let's look at another very simple numerical example. You are asked to value a Rs. 1 million payment to be received from a blue-chip company one year hence. After taxes at 35 percent, the cash inflow is Rs. 650,000. The payment is fixed by contract.

Since the contract generates a debt-equivalent flow, the opportunity cost of capital is the rate investors would demand on a one-year note issued by the blue-chip company, which happens to be 8 percent. For simplicity, we'll assume this is your company's borrowing rate too. Our valuation rule for debt-equivalent flows is therefore to discount at $r_D(1 - T_C) = .08(1 - .35) = .052$:

$$PV = \frac{650,000}{1.052} = \text{Rs. } 617,900$$

What is the *debt capacity* of this Rs. 650,000 payment? Exactly Rs. 617,900. Your company could borrow that amount and pay off the loan completely—principal and after-tax interest—with the Rs. 650,000 cash inflow. The debt capacity is 100 percent of the PV of the debt-equivalent cash flow.

If you think of it that way, our discount rate $r_D(1 - T_C)$ is just a special case of WACC with a 100 percent debt ratio ($D/V = 1$).

$$\text{WACC} = r_D(1 - T_C)D/V + r_E E/V$$
$$= r_D(1 - T_C) \text{ if } D/V = 1 \text{ and } E/V = 0$$

Now let's try an APV calculation. This is a two-part valuation. First, the Rs. 650,000 inflow is discounted at the opportunity cost of capital, 8 percent. Second, we add the present value of interest tax shields on debt supported by the project. Since the firm can borrow 100 percent of the cash flow's value, the tax shield is $r_D T_C$ APV, and APV is

$$\text{APV} = \frac{650{,}000}{1.08} + \frac{.08(.35)\text{APV}}{1.08}$$

Solving for APV, we get Rs. 617,900, the same answer we obtained by discounting at the after-tax borrowing rate. Thus our valuation rule for debt-equivalent flows is a special case of APV.

FURTHER READING

The adjusted-present-value rule was developed in:

S. C. Myers: "Interactions of Corporate Financing and Investment Decisions—Implications for Capital Budgeting," *Journal of Finance* 29 (March 1974), pp. 1–25.

The Harvard Business Review *has published a popular account of APV:*

T. A. Luehrman, "Using APV: A Better Tool for Valuing Operations," *Harvard Business Review* 75 (May–June 1997), pp. 145–154.

There have been dozens of articles on the weighted-average cost of capital and other issues discussed in this chapter. Here are three:

J. Miles and R. Ezzell, "The Weighted Average Cost of Capital, Perfect Capital Markets, and Project Life: A Clarification," *Journal of Financial and Quantitative Analysis* 15 (September 1980), pp. 719–730.

R. A. Taggart, Jr., "Consistent Valuation and Cost of Capital Expressions with Corporate and Personal Taxes," *Financial Management* 20 (Autumn 1991), pp. 8–20.

R. S. Ruback, "Capital Cash Flows: A Simple Approach to Valuing Risky Cash Flows," *Financial Management*, 31 (Summer 2002), pp. 85–103.

Two books that provide detailed explanations of how to value companies are:

T. Copeland, T. Koller, and J. Murrin, *Valuation: Measuring and Managing the Value of Companies*, 3rd ed. (New York: Wiley, 2000).

S. P. Pratt, R. F. Reilly, and R. P. Schweihs, *Valuing a Business: The Analysis and Appraisal of Closely Held Companies*, 4th ed. (New York: McGraw-Hill, 2000).

The valuation rule for safe, nominal cash flows is developed in:

R. S. Ruback, "Calculating the Market Value of Risk-Free Cash Flows," *Journal of Financial Economics* 15 (March 1986), pp. 323–339.

CONCEPT REVIEW QUESTIONS

1. Write down the formula for the after-tax WACC. Why is WACC usually less than the opportunity cost of capital? (page 505)
2. What assumptions does WACC rely on? (page 508)
3. a. In the Sangria example in Section 19.1, how would the WACC change if the *book* values were Rs. 300 million debt and Rs. 700 million equity?

b. How would the WACC change if instead the *market* values were Rs. 300 million debt and Rs. 950 million equity? (pages 506–508)

For additional Concept Review Questions, please visit us at www.mhhe.com/bmam8e or refer to your Student CD.

QUIZ

1. Calculate the weighted-average cost of capital (WACC) of Junkyards of India, using the following information:
   - Debt: Rs. 75,000,000 book value outstanding. The debt is trading at 90 percent of book value. The yield to maturity is 9 percent.
   - Equity: 2,5000,000 shares selling at Rs.42 per share. Assume the expected rate of return on Junkyard's stock is 18 percent.
   - Taxes: Junkyard's marginal tax rate is $T_C = 0.3366$
2. Suppose Junkyards of India decides to move to a more conservative debt policy. A year later its debt ratio is down to 15 percent ($D/V = 0.15$). Interest rate has dropped to 8.6 percent. Recalculate Junkyard's WACC under these new assumptions. The company's business risk, opportunity cost of capital, and tax rate have not changed. Use the three-step procedure explained in Section 19.3.
3. True or false? Use of the WACC formula assumes
   a. A project supports a fixed amount of debt over the project's economic life.
   b. The *ratio* of the debt supported by a project to project value is constant over the project's economic life.
   c. The firm rebalances debt each period, keeping the debt-to-value ratio constant.
4. What is meant by the flow-to-equity valuation method? What discount rate is used in this method? What assumptions are necessary for this method to give an accurate valuation?
5. True or false? The APV method
   a. Starts with a base-case value for the project.
   b. Calculates the base-case value by discounting project cash flows, forecasted assuming all-equity financing, at the WACC for the project.
   c. Is especially useful when debt is to be paid down on a fixed schedule.
6. A project costs Rs. 1 million and has a base-case NPV of exactly zero (NPV = 0). What is the project's APV in the following cases?
   a. If the firm invests, it has to raise Rs. 500,000 by a stock issue. Issue costs are 15 percent of *net* proceeds.
   b. If the firm invests, its debt capacity increases by Rs. 500,000. The present value of interest tax shields on this debt is Rs. 76,000.
7. Whispering Pines Limited is all-equity financed. The expected rate of return on the company's shares is 12 percent.
   a. What is the opportunity cost of capital for an average-risk Whispering Pines investment?
   b. Suppose the company issues debt, buys back shares, and moves to a 30 percent debt-to-value ratio ($D/V = 0.30$). What will the company's weighted-average cost of capital be at the new capital structure? The borrowing rate is 7.5 percent and the tax rate is 35 percent.
8. Consider a project lasting one year only. The initial outlay is Rs. 1,000 and the expected inflow is Rs. 1,200. The opportunity cost of capital is $r = .20$. The borrowing rate is $r_D = .10$, and the tax shield per rupee of interest is $T_C = .35$.
   a. What is the project's base-case NPV?
   b. What is its APV if the firm borrows 30 percent of the project's required investment?
9. The WACC formula seems to imply that debt is "cheaper" than equity—that is, that a firm with more debt could use a lower discount rate. Does this make sense? Explain briefly.

10. Suppose Kolkata Motors Limited buys out Howrah Trucking, a privately owned business, for Rs. 50 million. Kolkata Motors has only Rs. 5 million of cash in hand, so it arranges a Rs. 45 million bank loan. A normal debt-to-value ratio for a trucking company would be 50 percent at most, but the bank is satisfied with Kolkata Motor's credit rating.

Suppose you were valuing Howrah Trucking by APV in the same format as Table 19.2. How much debt would you include? Explain briefly.

PRACTICE QUESTIONS

1. Table 19.3 shows a *book* balance sheet for the Wishing Well Motel chain. The company's long-term debt is secured by its real estate assets, but it also uses short-term bank financing. It pays 10 percent interest on the bank debt and 9 percent interest on the secured debt. Wishing Well has 10 million shares of stock outstanding, trading at Rs. 90 per share. The expected return on Wishing Well's common stock is 18 percent.

   Calculate Wishing Well's WACC. Assume that the book and market values of Wishing Well's debt are the same. The marginal tax rate is 35 percent.
2. Suppose Wishing Well is evaluating a new motel and resort on a romantic site near Baga Beach, Goa. Explain how you would forecast the after-tax cash flows for this project. (Hints: How would you treat taxes? Interest expenses? Changes in working capital?)
3. To finance the Baga Beach project, Wishing Well will have to arrange an additional Rs. 80 million of long-term debt and make a Rs. 20 million of equity issue. Underwriting fees, spreads, and other costs of this financing will total Rs. 4 million. How would you take this into account in valuing the proposed investment?
4. Table 19.4 shows a simplified balance sheet for Divinity Felt. Calculate this company's weighted-average cost of capital. The debt has just been refinanced at an interest rate of 6 percent (short term) and 8 percent (long term). The expected rate of return on the company's shares is 15 percent. There are 7.46 million shares outstanding, and the shares are trading at Rs. 46. The tax rate is 35 percent.
5. How will Divinity Felt's WACC and cost of equity change if it issues Rs. 50 million in new equity and uses the proceeds to retire long-term debt? Assume the company's borrowing rates are unchanged. Use the three-step procedure from Section 19.3.
6. Digital Organics (DO) has the opportunity to invest Rs. 1 million now ($t = 0$) and expects after-tax returns of Rs. 600,000 in $t = 1$ and Rs. 700,000 in $t = 2$. The project will last for two years only. The appropriate cost of capital is 12 percent with all-equity financing, the borrowing rate is 8 percent, and DO will borrow Rs. 300,000 against the project. This debt must be repaid in two equal installments. Assume debt tax shields have a net value of Rs. 30 per rupee of interest paid. Calculate the project's APV using the procedure followed in Table 19.2.

TABLE 19.3

Balance sheet for Wishing Well, Ltd. (figures in Rs. millions).

Cash and marketable securities	100	Bank loan	280
Inventory	50	Accounts payable	120
Accounts receivable	200	Current liabilities	400
Current assets	350		
Real estate	2,100	Long-term debt	1,800
Other assets	150	Equity	400
Total	2,600	Total	2,600

TABLE 19.4

Simplified balance sheet for Divinity Felt (figures in Rs. thousands).

Cash and marketable securities	1,500	Short-term debt	75,600
Accounts receivable	120,000	Accounts payable	62,000
Inventories	125,000	Current liabilities	137,600
Current assets	246,500		
		Long-term debt	208,600
Fixed Assets	302,000	Deferred taxes	45,000
Other assets	89,000	Shareholders' equity	246,300
Total	637,500	Total	637,500

7. Consider another perpetual project like the crusher described in Section 19.1. Its initial investment is Rs. 1,000,000, and the expected cash inflow is Rs. 95,000 a year in perpetuity. The opportunity cost of capital with all-equity financing is 10 percent, and the project allows the firm to borrow at 7 percent. The tax rate is 35 percent.
   Use APV to calculate this project's value.
   a. Assume first that the project will be partly financed with Rs. 400,000 of debt and that the debt amount is to be fixed and perpetual.
   b. Then assume that the initial borrowing will be increased or reduced in proportion to changes in the future market value of this project.
   Explain the difference between your answers to (a) and (b).

8. Suppose the project described in Practice Question 7 is to be undertaken by a university. Funds for the project will be withdrawn from the university's endowment, which is invested in a widely diversified portfolio of stocks and bonds. However, the university can also borrow at 7 percent. The university is tax exempt.
   The university treasurer proposes to finance the project by issuing Rs. 400,000 of perpetual bonds at 7 percent and by selling Rs. 600,000 worth of common stocks from the endowment. The expected return on the common stocks is 10 percent. He therefore proposes to evaluate the project by discounting at a weighted-average cost of capital, calculated as

$$r = r_D \frac{D}{V} + r_E \frac{E}{V}$$

$$= .07\left(\frac{400,000}{1,000,000}\right) + .10\left(\frac{600,000}{1,000,000}\right)$$

$$= .088, \text{ or } 8.8\%$$

excel Please visit us at www.mhhe.com/bmam8e or refer to your Student CD.

   What's right or wrong with the treasurer's approach? Should the university invest? Should it borrow? Would the project's value to the university change if the treasurer financed the project entirely by selling common stocks from the endowment?

9. Consider a project to produce solar water heaters. It requires a Rs. 10 million investment and offers a level after-tax cash flow of Rs. 1.75 million per year for 10 years. The opportunity cost of capital is 12 percent, which reflects the project's business risk.
   a. Suppose the project is financed with Rs. 5 million of debt and Rs. 5 million of equity. The interest rate is 8 percent and the marginal tax rate is 35 percent. The debt will be paid off in equal annual installments over the project's 10-year life. Calculate APV.
   b. How does APV change if the firm incurs issue costs of Rs. 400,000 to raise the Rs. 5 million of required equity?

10. Take another look at the valuations of Geo in Tables 19.1 and 19.2. Use a spreadsheet to show how the valuations depend on:
   a. The forecasted long-term growth rate.
   b. The required amounts of investment in fixed assets and working capital.
   c. The opportunity cost of capital. Note you can also vary the opportunity cost of capital in Table 19.1.
   d. Profitability, that is, cost of goods sold as a percentage of sales.
   e. The assumed amount of debt financing.

11. The Bunsen Chemical Company is currently at its target debt ratio of 40 percent. It is contemplating a Rs. 1 million expansion of its existing business. This expansion is expected to produce a cash inflow of Rs. 130,000 a year in perpetuity.
   The company is uncertain whether to undertake this expansion and how to finance it. The two options are a Rs. 1 million issue of common stock or a Rs. 1 million issue of 20-year debt. The flotation costs of a stock issue would be around 5 percent of the amount raised, and the flotation costs of a debt issue would be around 1½ percent.

Bunsen's financial manager, Miss Polly Ethylene, estimates that the required return on the company's equity is 14 percent, but she argues that the flotation costs increase the cost of new equity to 19 percent. On this basis, the project does not appear viable.

On the other hand, she points out that the company can raise new debt on a 7 percent yield which would make the cost of new debt 8½ percent. She therefore recommends that Bunsen should go ahead with the project and finance it with an issue of long-term debt.

Is Miss Ethylene right? How would you evaluate the project?

12. Hyderabad Hydro is 40 percent debt-financed and has a weighted-average cost of capital of 9.7 percent:

$$\text{WACC} = (1 - T_c)r_D\frac{D}{V} + r_E\frac{E}{V}$$
$$= (1 - .35)(.085)(.40) + .125(.60) = .097$$

Banker's Tryst Company is advising Hyderabad Hydro to issue Rs. 75 million of preferred stock at a dividend yield of 9 percent. The proceeds would be used to repurchase and retire common stock. The preferred issue would account for 10 percent of the preissue market value of the firm.

Banker's Tryst argues that these transactions would reduce Hyderabad Hydro's WACC to 9.4 percent:

$$\text{WACC} = (1 - .35)(.085)(.40) + .09(.10) + .125(.50)$$
$$= .094, \text{ or } 9.4\%$$

Do you agree with this calculation? Explain.

13. Table 19.5 is a simplified book balance sheet for Jet Airways as on 31st March 2005. Here is some further information:

Number of outstanding shares (N)	86.33 million
Price per share (P)	Rs. 1211
Beta	0.78
Treasury bill rate	5.61%
20-year G-Sec rate	7.11%
Cost of debt (r_D)	8.36%
Marginal tax rate	33.66%

a. Calculate Jet's WACC. Use the capital asset pricing model and the additional information given above. Make additional assumptions and approximations as necessary.
b. What is Jet's opportunity cost of capital?
c. Now go to the website of www.myiris.com, www.nseindia.com and www.fimmda.org and get the relevant information to update your answers to questions (a) and (b).

TABLE 19.5

Simplified book balance sheet for Jet Airways, 31st March, 2005 (figures in Rs. millions).

Current assets	36401.3	Current liabilities	13057.8
Fixed assets	23466.5	Long-term debt	29648.4
		Shareholders' equity	17161.6
Total	59867.8	Total	59867.8

Source: *www.myiris.com*

	Historical			Forecast				
Year:	−2	−1	0	1	2	3	4	5
1. Sales	35,348	39,357	40,123	36,351	30,155	28,345	29,982	30,450
2. Cost of goods sold	17,834	18,564	22,879	21,678	17,560	16,459	15,631	14,987
3. Other costs	6,968	7,645	8,025	6,797	5,078	4,678	4,987	5,134
4. EBITDA (1 - 2 - 3)	10,546	13,148	9,219	7,876	7,517	7,208	9,364	10,329
5. Depreciation	5,671	5,745	5,678	5,890	5,670	5,908	6,107	5,908
6. EBIT (Pretax profit) (4 - 5)	4,875	7,403	3,541	1,986	1,847	1,300	3,257	4,421
7. Tax at 35%	1,706	2,591	1,239	695	646	455	1,140	1,547
8. Profit after tax (6 - 7)	3,169	4,812	2,302	1,291	1,201	845	2,117	2,874
9. Change in working capital	325	566	784	−54	−342	−245	127	235
10. Investment (change in gross fixed assets)	5,235	6,467	6,547	7,345	5,398	5,470	6,420	6,598

TABLE 19.6

Cash flow projections for Chiara Corp. (Rs. thousands)

excel

Please visit us at www.mhhe.com/bmam8e or refer to your Student CD.

14. Chiara Company's management has made the projections shown in Table 19.6. Use this Excel spreadsheet as a starting point to value the company as a whole. The WACC for Chiara is 12 percent and the long-run growth rate after year 5 is 4 percent. The company has Rs. 5 million debt and 865,000 shares outstanding. What is the value per share?

The following problems refer to the Appendix to this chapter.

15. The Indian government has settled a dispute with your company for Rs. 16 million. It is committed to pay this amount in exactly 12 months. However, your company will have to pay tax on the award at a marginal tax rate of 35 percent. What is the award worth? The one-year Treasury rate is 5.5 percent.

16. You are considering a five-year lease of office space for R&D personnel. Once signed, the lease cannot be canceled. It would commit your firm to six annual Rs. 100,000 payments, with the first payment due immediately. What is the present value of the lease if your company's borrowing rate is 9 percent and its tax rate is 35 percent? *Note:* The lease payments would be tax-deductible.

CHALLENGE QUESTIONS

1. In footnote 15 we referred to the Miles–Ezzell discount rate formula, which assumes that debt is not rebalanced continuously, but at one-year intervals. Derive this formula. Then use it to unlever Sangria's WACC and calculate Sangria's opportunity cost of capital. Your answer will be slightly different from the opportunity cost that we calculated in Section 19.3. Can you explain why?

2. The WACC formula assumes that debt is rebalanced to maintain a constant debt ratio D/V. Rebalancing ties the level of future interest tax shields to the future value of the company. This makes the tax shields risky. Does that mean that fixed debt levels (no rebalancing) are better for stockholders?

3. Modify Table 19.1 on the assumption that competition eliminates any opportunities to earn more than WACC on new investment after year 7 (PVGO = 0). How does the valuation of Geo change?

PART SIX RELATED WEB SITES

The options exchanges contain explanations of options markets and lots of data:

www.cboe.com

www.iseoptions.com

Here are two other useful sources of options data:

finance.yahoo.com

www.pcquote.com/options

Campbell Harvey's home page contains demonstrations of how option values are affected by changing volatility, etc.:

www.duke.edu/~charvey

There are a number of good options sites, many of which provide data and calculators for Black–Scholes values and implied standard deviations:

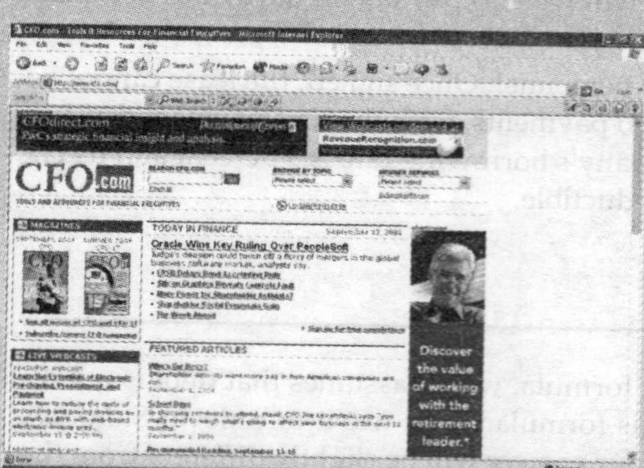

www.cfo.com

www.fintools.com

www.numa.com

www.optionscentral.com

www.pcquote.com/options

www.pmpublishing.com (includes historical implied volatilities)

www.schaeffersresearch.com

The following sites are concerned with the real options discussed in Chapter 22:

www.puc-rio.br/marco.ind

www.crystalball.com (also includes attractive software for Black–Scholes and binomial calculations)

PART [6]

OPTIONS

POP QUIZ: What do the following events have in common?

- Flatiron offers its president a bonus if the company's stock price exceeds $120.
- As part of a private placement of debt, Amerigon issues 2.2 million warrants that give the holder the right to buy its common stock for $17.80 each.
- Amazon.com issues a $1.25 billion convertible bond that can be exchanged in the future for common stock.
- Blitzen Computer dips a toe in the water and enters a new market.
- Malted Herring postpones investment in a positive-NPV plant.
- Hewlett-Packard exports partially assembled printers even though it would be cheaper to ship the finished product.
- An investment uses standard machinery rather than efficient custom-designed machinery.

Answers: (1) each of these events involves an option, and (2) each is analyzed in subsequent chapters. But you must walk before you can run. Therefore we start by focusing on a simple option to buy the stock of Amgen. Chapter 20 examines the payoffs from this option and Chapter 21 shows how it is valued.

Chapter 22 looks at the real options that arise in capital budgeting decisions. We encountered these in Chapter 10, when we used decision trees to set out future opportunities to modify a project. Now we place a value on this flexibility.

In later chapters we will look at warrants, convertible bonds, and a variety of other securities that include a built-in option.

CHAPTER [20]

UNDERSTANDING OPTIONS

THIS AND THE following two chapters are concerned with options. But why should the financial manager of an industrial company be interested? There are several reasons. First, companies regularly use commodity, currency, and interest-rate options to reduce risk. For example, a meatpacking company that wishes to put a ceiling on the cost of beef might take out an option to buy live cattle at a fixed price. A company that wishes to limit its future borrowing costs might take out an option to sell long-term bonds at a fixed price. And so on. In Chapter 27 we will explain how firms employ options to limit their risk.

Second, many capital investments include an embedded option to expand in the future. For instance, the company may invest in a patent that allows it to exploit a new technology or it may purchase adjoining land that gives it the option in the future to increase capacity. In each case the company is paying money today for the opportunity to make a further investment. To put it another way, the company is acquiring *growth opportunities*.

Here is another disguised option to invest: You are considering the purchase of a tract of desert land that is known to contain gold deposits. Unfortunately, the cost of extraction is higher than the current price of gold. Does this mean the land is almost worthless? Not at all. You are not obliged to mine the gold, but ownership of the land gives you the option to do so. Of course, if you know that the gold price will remain below the extraction cost, then the option is worthless. But if there is uncertainty about future gold prices, you could be lucky and make a killing.[1]

If the option to expand has value, what about the option to bail out? Projects don't usually go on until the equipment disintegrates. The decision to terminate a project is usually taken by management, not by nature. Once the project is no longer profitable, the company will cut its losses and exercise its option to abandon the project. Some projects have higher abandonment value than others. Those that use standardized equipment may offer a valuable abandonment option. Others may actually cost money to discontinue. For example, it is very costly to decommission an offshore oil rig.

We took a peek at investment options in Chapter 10, and we showed there how to use decision trees to analyze Magna Charter's options to expand its airline operation or abandon it. In Chapter 22 we will take a more thorough look at these *real* options.

The other important reason why financial managers need to understand options is that they are often tacked on to an issue of corporate securities and so provide the investor or the company with the flexibility to change the terms of the issue. For example, in Chapter 25 we will show how warrants and convertibles give their holders an option to buy common stock in exchange for cash or bonds.

In fact, we shall see in Chapter 24 that whenever a company borrows, it gains an option to walk away from its debts and surrender its assets to the bondholders. If the value of the company's assets is less than the amount of the debt, the company will choose to default on the payment and the bondholders will get to keep the company's assets. Thus, when the firm borrows, the lender effectively acquires the company and the shareholders obtain the option to buy it back by paying off the debt. This is an extremely important insight. It means that anything that we can learn about traded options applies equally to corporate liabilities.

In this chapter we use traded stock options to explain how options work, but we hope that our brief survey has convinced you that the interest of financial managers in options goes far beyond traded stock options. That is why we are asking you to invest here to acquire several important ideas for use later.

If you are unfamiliar with the wonderful world of options, it may seem baffling on first encounter. We will therefore divide this chapter into three bite-sized pieces. Our first task is to introduce you to call and put options and to show you how the payoff on these

[1]In Chapter 11 we valued Kingsley Solomon's gold mine by calculating the value of the gold in the ground and then subtracting the value of the extraction costs. That is correct only if we *know* that the gold will be mined. Otherwise, the value of the mine is increased by the value of the option to leave the gold in the ground if its price is less than the extraction cost.

options depends on the price of the underlying asset. We will then show how financial alchemists can combine options to produce a variety of interesting strategies.

We conclude the chapter by identifying the variables that determine option values. Here you will encounter some surprising and counterintuitive effects. For example, investors are used to thinking that increased risk reduces present value. But for options it is the other way around.

20.1 CALLS, PUTS, AND SHARES

Investors regularly trade options on common stocks.[2] For example, Table 20.1 reproduces quotes from the National Stock Exchange of India (NSE) for options on the stock of Arvind Mills. You can see that there are two types of options – calls and puts. We will explain each in turn.

Call Options and Position Diagrams

A **call option** gives its owner the right to buy stock at a specified *exercise* or *strike price* on or before a specified exercise date. If the option can be exercised only on one particular day, it is conventionally known as a *European call;* in other cases (such as the Arvind Mills options shown in Table 20.1), the option can be exercised on or at any time before that day, and it is then known as an *American call.*

The third column of Table 20.1 sets out the prices of Arvind Mills call options with different exercise prices and exercise dates. Look at the options maturing in July 2006.[3] The first entry says that for Rs.18 you could acquire an option to buy one share[4] of Arvind Mills stock for Rs. 40 on or before July 2006. Moving down to the next row, you can see that an option to buy for Rs. 5 more (Rs. 45 vs. Rs. 40) costs Rs. 4.55 less, that is Rs. 13.45. In general, the value of a call option goes down as the exercise price goes up.

Now look at the quotes for options maturing in August 2006 and September 2006. Notice how the option price increases as option maturity is extended. For example, at an exercise price of Rs. 60, the July 2006 call option costs Rs. 3.15, the August 2006 option costs Rs. 6.55 and the September option costs Rs. 8.15.

In Chapter 13 we met Louis Bachelier, who in 1900 first suggested that security prices follow a random walk. Bachelier also devised a very convenient shorthand to illustrate the effects of investing in different options.[5] We will use this shorthand to compare a call option and a put option on Arvind Mills stock.

The *position diagram* in Figure 20.1(a) shows the possible consequences of investing in Arvind Mills August 2006 call options with an exercise price of Rs. 60 (boldfaced in Table 20.1). The outcome from investing in Arvind Mills calls depends on what happens to the stock price. If the stock price at the end of this two-month period turns out to be less than the Rs. 60 exercise price, nobody will pay Rs. 60 to

---

[2]The two principal options exchanges in India are the National Exchange of India and the Mumbai Stock Exchange.

[3]In the NSE, options mature on the last Thursday of a month.

[4]You can't actually buy an option on a single share. Trades are in multiples of 2150. The minimum order would be for 2150 options on 2150 Arvind Mills shares. The lot size in the NSE is different for different underlying asset.

[5]L. Bachelier, *Théorie de la Speculation* (Paris: Gauthier-Villars, 1900). Reprinted in English in P. H. Cootner (ed.), *The Random Character of Stock Market Prices* (Cambridge, MA: M.I.T. Press, 1964).

TABLE 20.1

Selected prices of put and call options on Arvind Mills stock, June 2006, when the closing price was about Rs. 60.

Source: Settlement price as reported at the National Stock Exchange (www.nseindia.com)

Option Maturity	Exercise Price	Price of Call Option	Price of Put Option
July-06	Rs. 40	Rs. 18	Rs. 0
	45	13.45	0.6
	50	9.5	1.6
	55	5.6	3.35
	60	3.15	5.25
	65	1.65	9.35
	70	0.85	13.3
Aug-06	Rs. 40	Rs. 19	Re. 1
	45	15.05	1.85
	50	11.6	3.35
	55	8.8	5.5
	60	6.55	8.15
	65	4.8	11.35
	70	3.45	15
Sep-06	Rs. 40	Rs. 20	Rs. 2
	45	16.15	2.75
	50	13	4.5
	55	10.35	6.75
	60	8.15	9.45
	65	6.35	12.6
	70	4.95	16.1

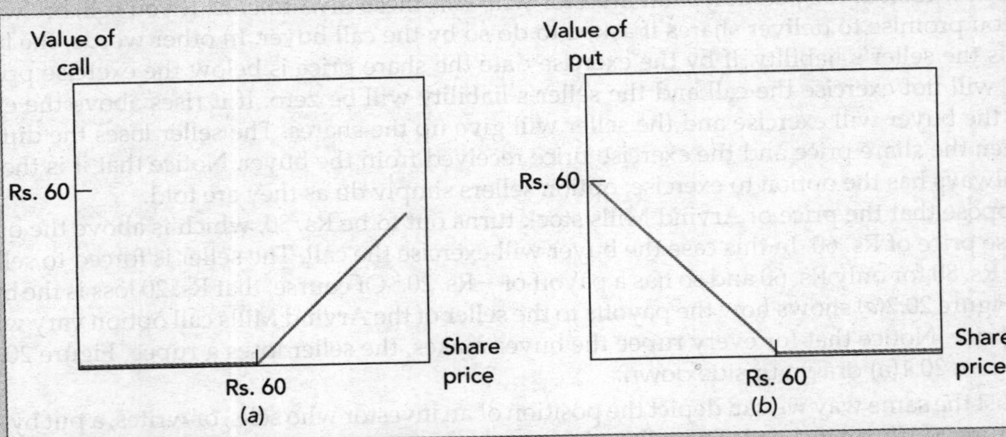

FIGURE 20.1

Position diagrams show how payoffs to owners of Arvind Mills calls, puts, and shares (shown by the colored lines) depend on the share price. (*a*) Result of buying Arvind Mills call exercisable at Rs. 60. (*b*) Result of buying Arvind Mills put exercisable at Rs. 60.

obtain the share via the call option. Your call will in that case be valueless, and you will throw it away. On the other hand, if the stock price turns out to be greater than Rs. 60, it will pay to exercise your option to buy the share. In this case the call will be worth the market price of the share minus the Rs. 60 that you must pay to acquire it. For example, suppose that the price of Arvind Mills stock rises to Rs. 100. Your call will then be worth Rs. 100 − Rs. 60 = Rs. 40. That is your payoff, but of course it is not all profit. Table 20.1 shows that you had to pay Rs. 6.55 to buy the call.

Put Options

Now let us look at the Arvind Mills put options in the right-hand column of Table 20.1. Whereas the call option gives you the right to *buy* a share for a specified exercise price, the comparable put gives you the right to *sell* the share. For example, the boldfaced entry in the right-hand column of table 20.1 shows that for Rs. 8.15 you could acquire an option to sell Arvind Mills stock for a price of Rs. 60 anytime before August 2006. The circumstances in which the put turns out to be profitable are just the opposite of those in which the call is profitable. You can see this from the position diagram in Figure 20.1(b). If Arvind Mills' share price *immediately* before expiration turns out to be *greater* than Rs. 60, you won't want to sell stock at that price. You would do better to sell the share in the market, and your put option will be worthless. Conversely, if the share price turns out to be less than Rs. 60, it will pay to buy the stock at the low price and then take advantage of the option to sell it for Rs. 60. In this case, the value of the put option on the exercise date is the difference between the Rs. 60 proceeds of the sale and the market price of the share. For example, if the share is worth Rs. 40, the put is worth Rs. 20:

$$\text{Value of put option at expiration} = \text{exercise price} - \text{market price of the share}$$
$$= \text{Rs. } 60 - \text{Rs. } 40 = \text{Rs. } 20$$

Table 20.1 confirms that the value of a put *increases* when the exercise price is raised. However, extending the maturity date makes *both* puts and calls more valuable.

Selling Calls, Puts, and Shares

Let us now look at the position of an investor who *sells* these investments. If you sell, or "write," a call, you promise to deliver shares if asked to do so by the call buyer. In other words, the buyer's asset is the seller's liability. If by the exercise date the share price is below the exercise price, the buyer will not exercise the call and the seller's liability will be zero. If it rises above the exercise price, the buyer will exercise and the seller will give up the shares. The seller loses the difference between the share price and the exercise price received from the buyer. Notice that it is the buyer who always has the option to exercise; option sellers simply do as they are told.

Suppose that the price of Arvind Mills stock turns out to be Rs. 80, which is above the option's exercise price of Rs. 60. In this case the buyer will exercise the call. The seller is forced to sell stock worth Rs. 80 for only Rs. 60 and so has a payoff of −Rs. 20.[6] Of course, that Rs. 20 loss is the buyer's gain. Figure 20.2(*a*) shows how the payoffs to the seller of the Arvind Mills call option vary with the stock price. Notice that for every rupee the buyer makes, the seller loses a rupee. Figure 20.2(*a*) is just Figure 20.1(a) drawn upside down.

In just the same way we can depict the position of an investor who sells, or writes, a put by standing Figure 20.1(*b*) on its head. The seller of the put has agreed to pay the exercise price of Rs. 60 for the share if the buyer of the put should request it. Clearly the seller will be safe as long as the share price remains above Rs. 60 but will lose money if the share price falls below this figure. The worst thing that can happen is that the stock becomes worthless. The seller would then be obliged to pay Rs. 60 for a stock worth Rs. 0. The "value" of the option position would be −Rs. 60.

[6]The seller has some consolation, for he or she was paid Rs. 6.55 in June for selling the call.

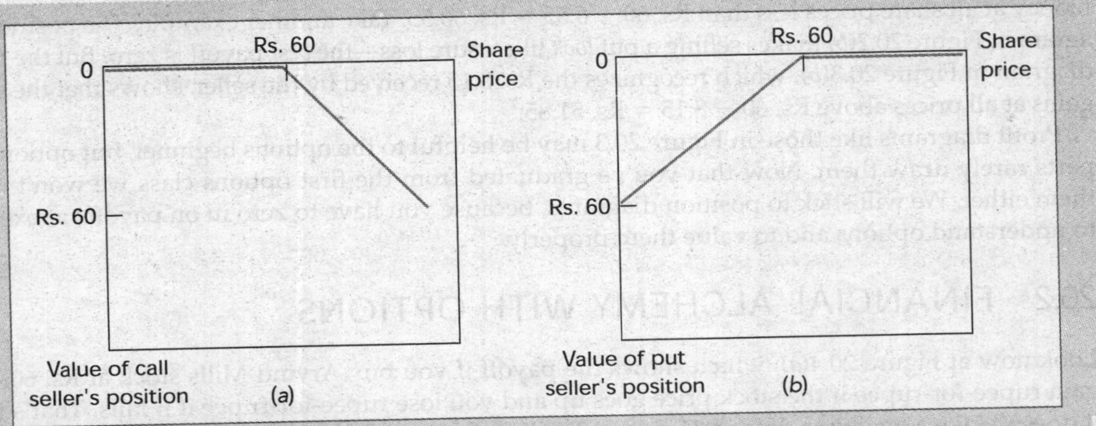

FIGURE 20.2

Payoffs to *sellers* of Arvind Mills calls, puts, and shares (shown by the colored lines) depend on the share price. (*a*) Result of selling Arvind Mills call exercisable at Rs. 60. (*b*) Result of selling Arvind Mills put exercisable at Rs. 60.

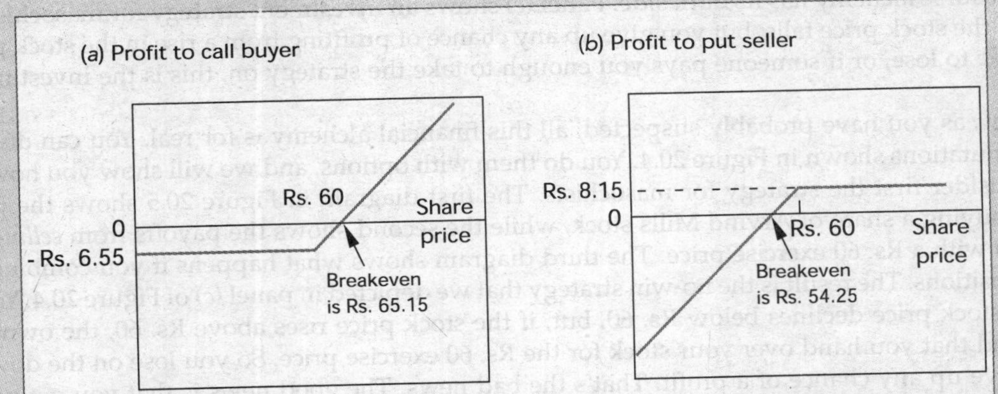

FIGURE 20.3

Profit diagrams incorporate the costs of buying an option or the proceeds from selling one. In panel (*a*), we substract Rs. 5.15 cost of the Arvind Mills call from the payoffs plotted in Figure 20.1(*a*). In panel (*b*), we add the Rs. 5.75 proceeds from selling the Arvind Mills put to the payoffs in Figure 20.2(*b*).

Position Diagrams Are Not Profit Diagrams

Position diagrams show *only* the payoffs at option exercise; they do not account for the initial cost of buying the option or the initial proceeds from selling it.

This is a common point of confusion. For example, the position diagram in Figure 20.1(*a*) makes purchase of a call *look* like a sure thing—the payoff is at worst zero, with plenty of "upside" if Arvind Mills, stock price goes above Rs. 60 by July 2004. But compare the *profit diagram* in Figure 20.3(*a*), which subtracts the Rs. 6.55 *cost* of the call from the payoff at maturity. The call buyer loses money at all share prices less than Rs. 60 + 6.55 = Rs. 66.55. Take another example: The position diagram in Figure 20.2(*b*) makes selling a put *look* like a sure loss—the *best* payoff is zero. But the profit diagram in Figure 20.3(*b*), which recognizes the Rs. 8.15 received by the seller, shows that the seller gains at all prices above Rs. 60 − 8.15 = Rs. 51.85.[7]

Profit diagrams like those in Figure 20.3 may be helpful to the options beginner, but options experts rarely draw them. Now that you've graduated from the first options class we won't draw them either. We will stick to position diagrams, because you have to zero in on payoffs at exercise to understand options and to value them properly.

20.2 FINANCIAL ALCHEMY WITH OPTIONS

Look now at Figure 20.4(*a*), which shows the payoff if you buy Arvind Mills stock at Rs. 60. You gain rupee-for-rupee if the stock price goes up and you lose rupee-for-rupee if it falls. That's trite; it doesn't take a genius to draw a 45-degree line.

Look now at panel (*b*), which shows the payoffs from an investment strategy that retains the upside potential of Arvind Mills stock but gives complete downside protection. In this case your payoff stays at Rs. 60 even if the Arvind Mills stock price falls to Rs. 50, Rs. 40, or zero. Panel (*b*)'s payoffs are clearly better than panel (*a*)'s. If a financial alchemist could turn panel (*a*) into panel (*b*), you'd be willing to pay for the service.

Of course alchemy has its dark side. Panel (*c*) shows an investment strategy for masochists. You lose if the stock price falls, but you give up any chance of profiting from a rise in the stock price. If you *like* to lose, or if someone pays you enough to take the strategy on, this is the investment for you.

Now, as you have probably suspected, all this financial alchemy is for real. You can do all the transmutations shown in Figure 20.4. You do them with options, and we will show you how.

Consider first the strategy for masochists. The first diagram in Figure 20.5 shows the payoffs from buying a share of Arvind Mills stock, while the second shows the payoffs from *selling* a call option with a Rs. 60 exercise price. The third diagram shows what happens if you combine these two positions. The result is the no-win strategy that we depicted in panel (*c*) of Figure 20.4. You lose if the stock price declines below Rs. 60, but, if the stock price rises above Rs. 60, the owner will demand that you hand over your stock for the Rs. 60 exercise price. So you lose on the downside and give up any chance of a profit. That's the bad news. The good news is that you get paid for taking on this liability. In June 2006 you would have been paid Rs. 6.55, the price of one-month call option.

Now, we'll create the downside protection shown in Figure 20.4(*b*). Look at row 1 of Figure 20.6. The first diagram again shows the payoff from buying a share of Arvind Mills stock, while the next diagram in row 1 shows the payoffs from buying an Arvind Mills put option with an exercise price of Rs. 60. The third diagram shows the effect of combining these two positions. You can see that, if Arvind Mills stock price rises above Rs. 60, your put option is valueless, so you simply receive the gains from your investment in the share. However, if the stock price falls below Rs. 60, you can exercise your put option and sell your stock for Rs. 60. Thus, by adding a put option to your invest-

[7]The fact that you have made a profit on your position is not necessarily a cause for rejoicing. The profit needs to compensate you for the time value of money and the risk that you took.

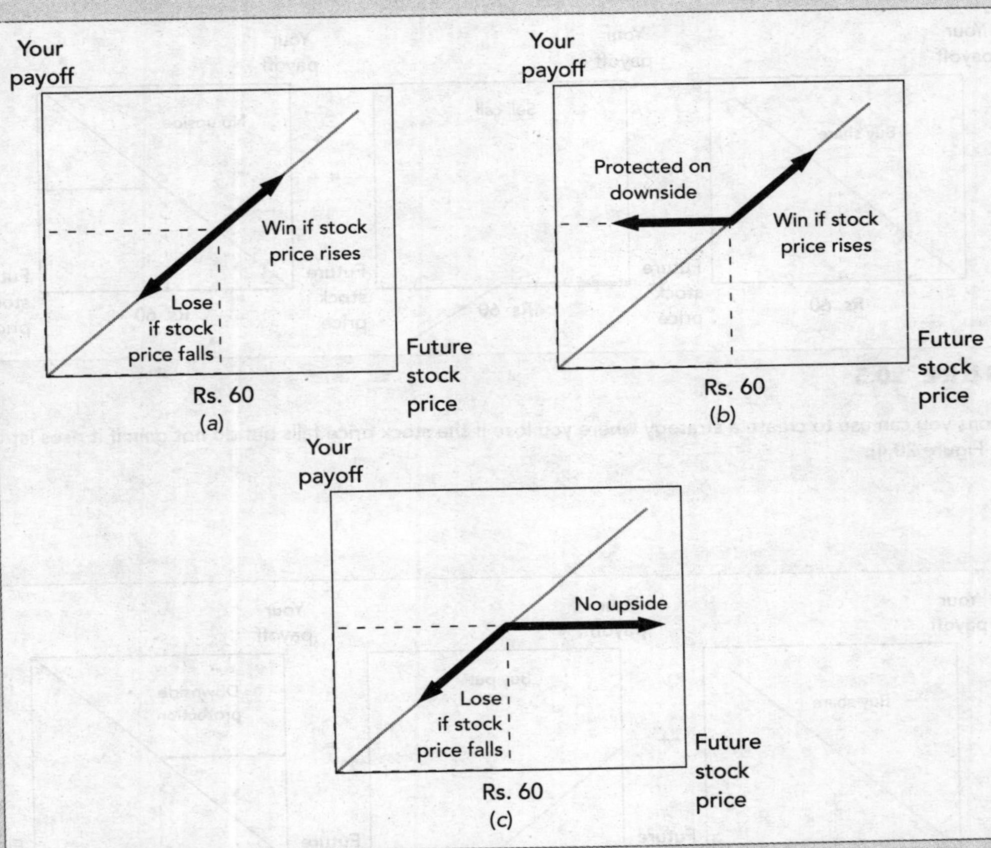

FIGURE 20.4

Payoffs to three investment strategies for Arvind Mills stock. (*a*) You buy one share for Rs. 60. (*b*) No downside. If stock price falls, your payoff stays at Rs. 60. (*c*) A strategy for masochists? You lose if stock price falls, but you don't gain if it rises.

ment in the stock, you have protected yourself against loss.[8] This is the strategy that we depicted in panel (*b*) of Figure 20.4. Of course, there is no gain without pain. The *cost* of insuring yourself against loss is the amount that you pay for a put option on Arvind Mills stock with an exercise price of Rs. 60. In June 2006 the price of this put was Rs. 8.15. This was the going rate for financial alchemists.

We have just seen how put options can be used to provide downside protection. We will now show you how call options can be used to get the same result. This is illustrated in row 2 of Figure 20.6. The first diagram shows the payoff from placing the present value of Rs. 60 in a bank deposit. Regardless of what happens to the price of Arvind Mills stock, your bank deposit will pay off

[8]This combination of a stock and a put option is known as a *protective put*.

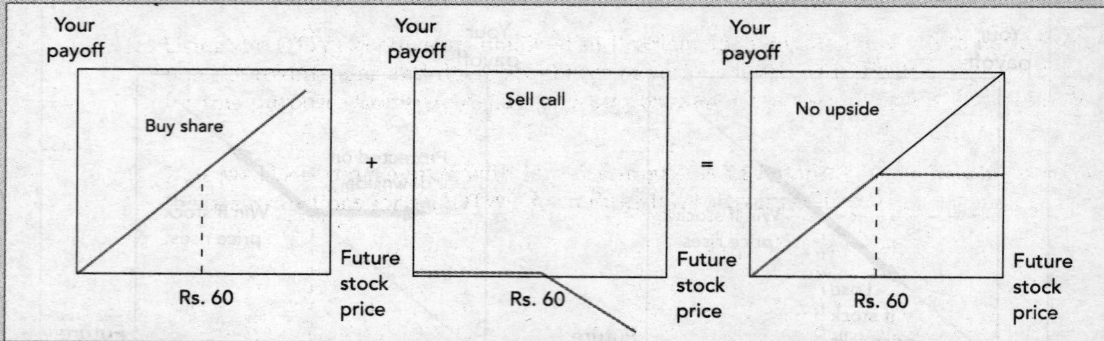

FIGURE 20.5

Options you can use to create a strategy where you lose if the stock price falls but do not gain if it rises [strategy (*c*) in Figure 20.4].

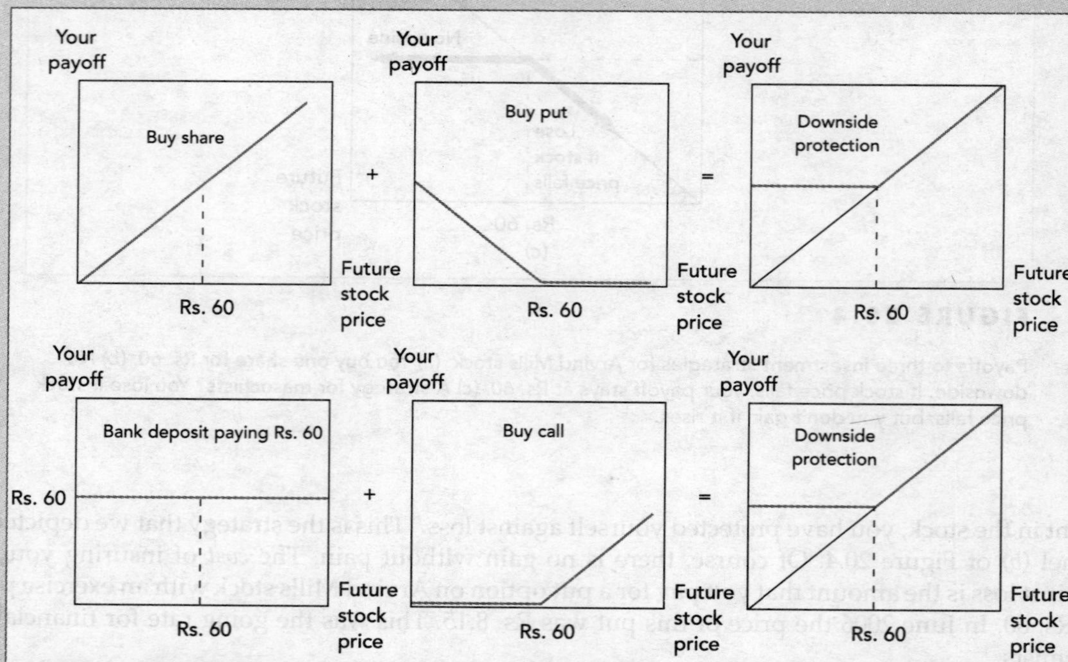

FIGURE 20.6

Each row in the figure shows a different way to create a strategy where you gain if the stock price rises but are protected on the downside [strategy (*b*) in Figure 20.4].

Rs. 60. The second diagram in row 2 shows the payoff from a call option on Arvind Mills stock with an exercise price of Rs. 60, and the third diagram shows the effect of combining these two positions. Notice that, if the price of Arvind Mills stock falls, your call is worthless, but you still have your Rs. 60 in the bank. For every rupee that Arvind Mills stock price rises above Rs. 60, your investment in the call option pays off an extra rupee. For example, if the stock price rises to Rs. 100, you will have Rs. 60 in the bank and a call worth Rs. 40. Thus you participate fully in any rise in the price of the stock, while being fully protected against any fall. So we have just found another way to provide the downside protection depicted in panel (*b*) of Figure 20.4.

These last two rows of Figure 20.6 tell us something about the relationship between a call option and a put option. Regardless of the future stock price, both investment strategies provide identical payoffs. In other words, if you buy the share and a put option to sell it after one month for Rs. 60, you receive the same payoff as from buying a call option and setting enough money aside to pay the Rs. 60 exercise price. Therefore, if you are committed to holding the two packages until the options expire, the two packages should sell for the same price today. This gives us a fundamental relationship for European options:

Value of call + present value of exercise price = value of put + share price

To repeat, this relationship holds because the payoff of

[Buy call, invest present value of exercise price in safe asset[9]]

is identical to the payoff from

[Buy put, buy share]

This basic relationship among share price, call and put values, and the present value of the exercise price is called **put–call parity.**[10]

The relationship can be expressed in several ways. Each expression implies two investment strategies that give identical results. For example, suppose that you want to solve for the value of a put. You simply need to twist the put–call parity formula around to give

Value of put = value of call + present value of exercise price − share price

From this expression you can deduce that

[buy put]

is identical to

[Buy call, invest present value of exercise price in safe asset, sell share]

---

[9]The present value is calculated at the *risk-free* rate of interest. It is the amount that you would have to invest today in a bank deposit or Treasury bills to realize the exercise price on the option's expiration date.

[10]Put-call parity holds only if you are committed to holding the options until the final exercise date. It therefore does not hold for American options, which you can exercise *before* the final date. We discuss possible reasons for early exercise in Chapter 21. Also if the stock makes a dividend payment before the final exercise date, you need to recognize that the investor who buys the call misses out on this dividend. In this case the relationship is

Value of call + present value of exercise price = value of put + share price − present value of dividend

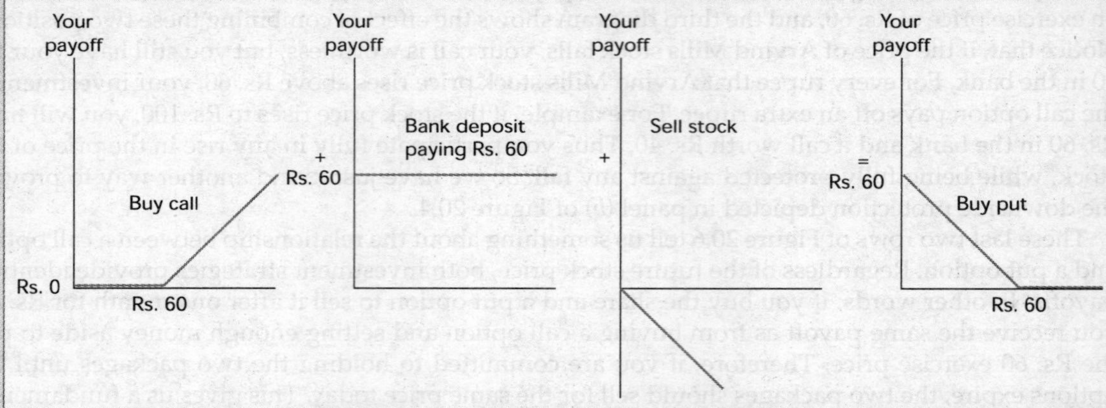

FIGURE 20.7

A strategy of buying a call, depositing the present value of the exercise price in the bank, and selling the stock is equivalent to buying a put.

In other words, if puts are not available, you can create them by buying calls, putting cash in the bank, and selling shares.

If you find this difficult to believe, look at Figure 20.7, which shows the possible payoffs from each position. The diagram on the left shows the payoffs from a call option on Arvind Mills stock with an exercise price of Rs. 60. The second diagram shows the payoffs from placing the present value of Rs. 60 in the bank. Regardless of what happens to the share price, this investment will pay off Rs. 60. The third diagram shows the payoffs from selling Arvind Mills stock. When you sell a share that you don't own, you have a liability—you must sometime buy it back. As they say on Dalal Street:

He who sells what isn't his'n
Buys it back or goes to pris'n

Therefore the best that can happen to you is that the share price falls to zero. In that case it costs you nothing to buy the share back. But for every extra rupee on the future share price, you will need to spend an extra rupee to buy the share. The final diagram in Figure 20.7 shows that the *total* payoff from these three positions is the same as if you had bought a put option. For example, suppose that when the option matures the stock price is Rs. 30. Your call will be worthless, your bank deposit will be worth Rs. 60, and it will cost you Rs. 30 to repurchase the share. Your total payoff is 0 + 60 − 30 = Rs. 30, exactly the same as the payoff from the put.

Spotting the Option

Options rarely come with a large label attached. Often the trickiest part of the problem is to identify the option. When you are not sure whether you are dealing with a put or a call or a complicated blend of the two, it is a good precaution to draw a position diagram. Here is an example.

OLP Limited has offered its president, Ms. Laxmi, the following incentive scheme: At the end of the year Ms. Laxmi will be paid a bonus of Rs. 50,000 for every rupee that the price of OLP stock

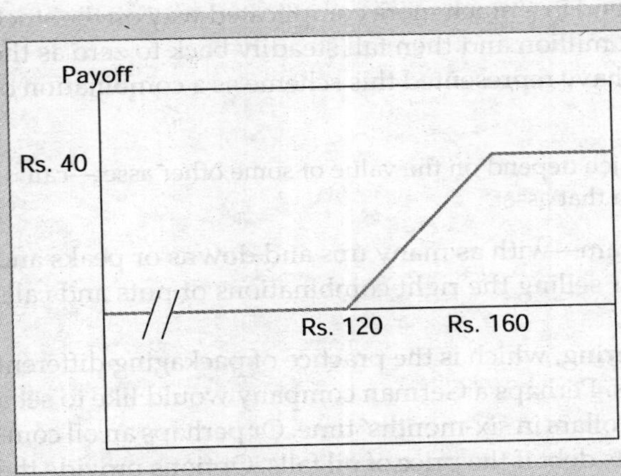

FIGURE 20.8

The payoff from one of Ms. Laxmi's " tickets" depends on OLP stock price.

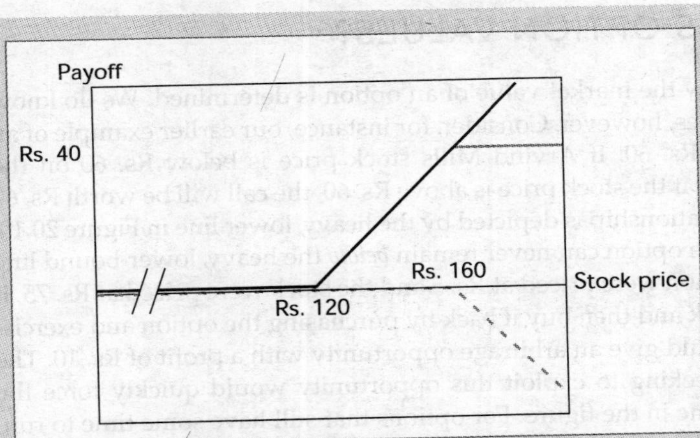

FIGURE 20.9

The solid black line shows the payoff from buying a call with an exercise price of Rs. 120. The dotted line shows the sale of a call with an exercise price of Rs. 160. The combined purchase and sale (shown by the colored line) is identical to one of Ms. Laxmi's " tickets."

exceeds its current figure of Rs. 120. However, the maximum bonus that she can receive is set as Rs. 2 million.

You can think of Ms. Laxmi as owning 50,000 tickets, each of which pays nothing if the stock price fails to beat Rs. 120. The value of each ticket then rises by Re. 1 for each rupee rise in the stock price up to the maximum of Rs. 2,000,000/50,000 = Rs. 40. Figure 20.8 shows the payoffs from just one of these tickets. The payoffs are not the same as those of the simple put and call options that we drew in Figure 20.1, but it is possible to find a combination of options that exactly replicates Figure 20.8. Before going on to read the answer, see if you can spot it yourself. (If you are someone who enjoys puzzles of the make-a-triangle-from-just-two-matchsticks type, this one should be a walkover.)

The answer is in Figure 20.9. The solid black line represents the purchase of a call option with an exercise price of Rs. 120, and the dotted line shows the sale of another call option with an exercise price of Rs. 160. The colored line shows the payoffs from a combination of the purchase and the sale—exactly the same as the payoffs from one of Ms. Laxmi's tickets.

Thus, if we wish to know how much the incentive scheme is costing the company, we need to calculate the difference between the value of 50,000 call options with an exercise price of Rs. 120 and the value of 50,000 calls with an exercise price of Rs. 160.

We could have made the incentive scheme depend in a much more complicated way on the stock price. For example, the bonus could peak at Rs. 2 million and then fall steadily back to zero as the stock price climbs above Rs. 160.[11] You could still have represented this scheme as a combination of options. In fact, we can state a general theorem:

> Any set of contingent payoffs—that is, payoffs which depend on the value of some other asset—can be constructed with a mixture of simple options on that asset.

In other words, you can create any position diagram—with as many ups and downs or peaks and valleys as your imagination allows—by buying or selling the right combinations of puts and calls with different exercise prices.[12]

Finance pros often talk about **financial engineering,** which is the practice of packaging different investments to create new tailor-made instruments. Perhaps a German company would like to set a minimum and maximum cost at which it can buy dollars in six-months' time. Or perhaps an oil company would like to pay a lower rate of interest on its debt if the price of oil falls. Options provide the building blocks that financial engineers use to create these interesting payoff structures.

20.3 WHAT DETERMINES OPTION VALUES?

So far we have said nothing about how the market value of an option is determined. We do know what an option is worth when it matures, however. Consider, for instance, our earlier example of an option to buy Arvind Mills stock at Rs. 60. If Arvind Mills stock price is below Rs. 60 on the exercise date, the call will be worthless; if the stock price is above Rs. 60, the call will be worth Rs. 60 less than the value of the stock. This relationship is depicted by the heavy, lower line in Figure 20.10.

Even before maturity the price of the option can never remain *below* the heavy, lower-bound line in Figure 20.10. For example, if our option were priced at Rs. 5 and the stock were priced at Rs. 75, it would pay any investor to sell the stock and then buy it back by purchasing the option and exercising it for an additional Rs. 60. That would give an arbitrage opportunity with a profit of Rs. 10. The demand for options from investors seeking to exploit this opportunity would quickly force the option price up, at least to the heavy line in the figure. For options that still have some time to run, the heavy line is therefore a *lower bound* on the market price of the option.

The diagonal line in Figure 20.10 is the *upper bound* to the option price. Why? Because the stock gives a higher ultimate payoff than the option. If at the option's expiration the stock price ends up *above* the exercise price, the option is worth the stock price *less* the exercise price. If the stock price ends up *below* the exercise price, the option is worthless, but the stock's owner still has a valuable

[11]This is not as nutty a bonus scheme as it may sound. Maybe Ms. Laxmi's hard work can lift the value of the stock by so much and the only way she can hope to increase it further is by taking on extra risk. You can deter her from doing this by making her bonus start to decline beyond some point. We are reminded here of a senior investment banker, who commented that the first time a trader made unusually large profits he would be warned; the second time, he would be fired. It was a good bet that such a trader was taking excessive risks.

[12]In some cases you may also have to borrow or lend money to generate a position diagram with your desired pattern. Lending raises the payoff line in position diagrams, as in the bottom row of Figure 20.6. Borrowing lowers the payoff line.

security. Let P be the stock price at the option's expiration date, and assume the option's exercise price is Rs. 60. Then the extra rupee returns realized by stockholders are shown in the following table:

	Stock Payoff	Option Payoff	Extra Payoff from Holding Stock Instead of Option
Option exercised (P greater than Rs. 60)	P	$P - 60$	Rs. 60
Option expires unexercised (P less than or equal to Rs. 60)	P	0	P

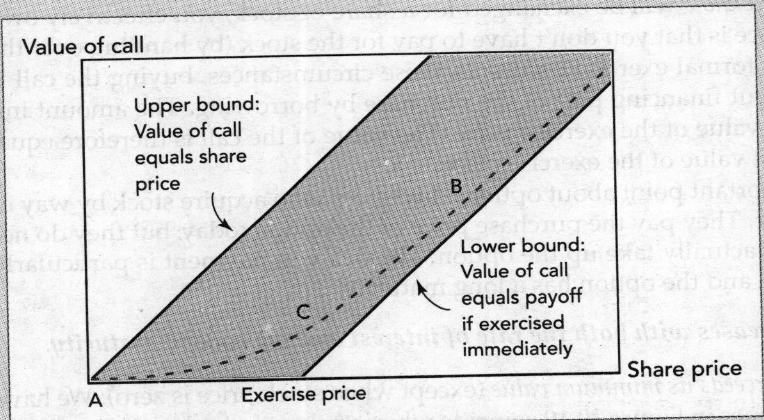

FIGURE 20.10

Value of a call before its expiration date (dashed line). The value depends on the stock price. It is always worth more than its value if exercised now (heavy line). It is never worth more than the stock price itself.

If the stock and the option have the same price, everyone will rush to sell the option and buy the stock. Therefore, the option price must be somewhere in the shaded region of Figure 20.10. In fact, it will lie on a curved, upward-sloping line like the dashed curve shown in the figure. This line begins its travels where the upper and lower bounds meet (at zero). Then it rises, gradually becoming parallel to the upward-sloping part of the lower bound.

But let us look more carefully at the shape and location of the dashed line. Three points, *A*, *B*, and *C*, are marked on the dashed line. As we explain each point you will see why the option price has to behave as the dashed line predicts.

Point A *When the stock is worthless, the option is worthless:* A stock price of zero means that there is no possibility the stock will ever have any future value.[13] If so, the option is sure to expire unexercised and worthless, and it is worthless today.

That brings us to our first important point about option value:

The value of an option increases as stock price increases, if the exercise price is held constant.

[13]If a stock *can* be worth something in the future, then investors will pay *something* for it today, although possibly a very small amount.

That should be no surprise. Owners of call options clearly hope for the stock price to rise and are happy when it does.

Point B *When the stock price becomes large, the option price approaches the stock price less the present value of the exercise price:* Notice that the dashed line representing the option price in Figure 20.10 eventually becomes parallel to the ascending heavy line representing the lower bound on the option price. The reason is as follows: The higher the stock price is, the higher is the probability that the option will eventually be exercised. If the stock price is high enough, exercise becomes a virtual certainty; the probability that the stock price will fall below the exercise price before the option expires becomes trivially small.

If you own an option that you *know* will be exchanged for a share of stock, you effectively own the stock now. The only difference is that you don't have to pay for the stock (by handing over the exercise price) until later, when formal exercise occurs. In these circumstances, buying the call is equivalent to buying the stock but financing part of the purchase by borrowing. The amount implicitly borrowed is the present value of the exercise price. The value of the call is therefore equal to the stock price less the present value of the exercise price.

This brings us to another important point about options. Investors who acquire stock by way of a call option are buying on credit. They pay the purchase price of the option today, but they do not pay the exercise price until they actually take up the option. The delay in payment is particularly valuable if interest rates are high and the option has a long maturity.

Thus, the value of an option increases with both the rate of interest and the time to maturity.

Point C *The option price always exceeds its minimum value* (except when stock price is zero): We have seen that the dashed and heavy lines in Figure 20.10 coincide when stock price is zero (point *A*), but elsewhere the lines diverge; that is, the option price must exceed the minimum value given by the heavy line. The reason for this can be understood by examining point *C*.

At point *C*, the stock price exactly equals the exercise price. The option is therefore worthless if exercised today. However, suppose that the option will not expire until three months hence. Of course we do not know what the stock price will be at the expiration date. There is roughly a 50 percent chance that it will be higher than the exercise price and a 50 percent chance that it will be lower. The possible payoffs to the option are therefore

Outcome	Payoff
Stock price rises (50 percent probability)	Stock price less exercise price (option is exercised)
Stock price falls (50 percent probability)	Zero (option expires worthless)

If there is a positive probability of a positive payoff, and if the worst payoff is zero, then the option must be valuable. That means the option price at point C exceeds its lower bound, which at point

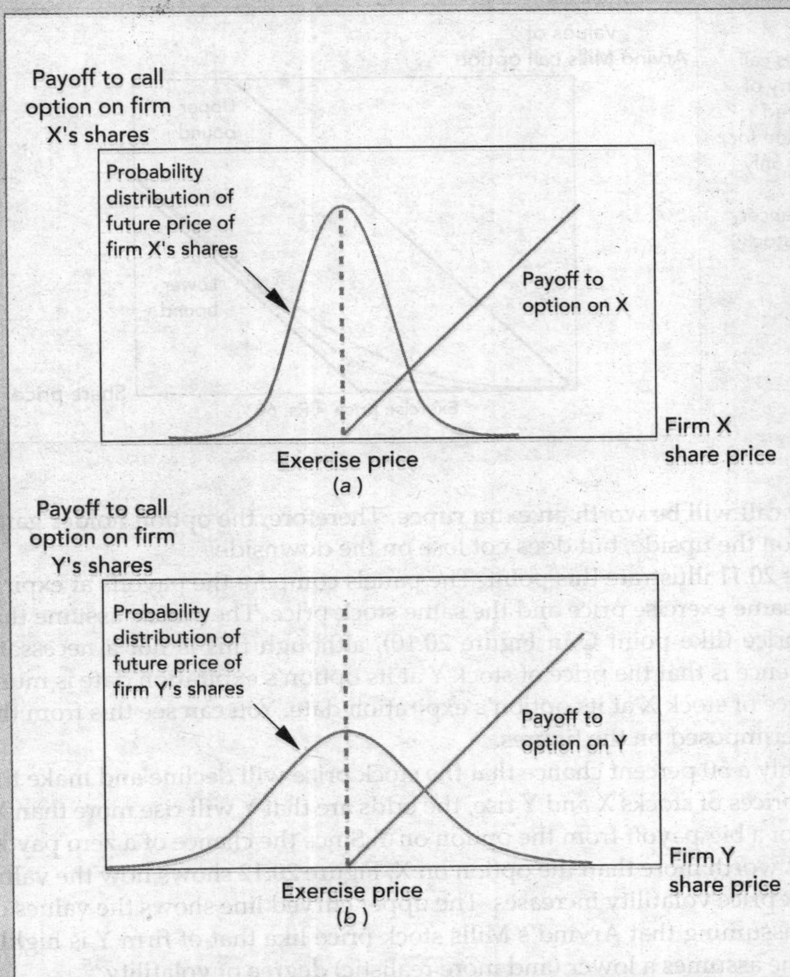

FIGURE 20.11

Call options on the shares of (*a*) firm X and (*b*) firm Y. In each case, the current share price equals the exercise price, so each option has a 50 percent chance of ending up worthless (if the share price falls) and a 50 percent chance of ending up "in the money" (if the share price rises). However, the chance of a large payoff is greater for the option on firm Y's shares because Y's stock price is more volatile and therefore has more upside potential.

C is zero. In general, the option prices will exceed their lower-bound values as long as there is time left before expiration.

One of the most important determinants of the *height* of the dashed curve (i.e., of the difference between actual and lower-bound value) is the likelihood of substantial movements in the stock price. An option on a stock whose price is unlikely to change by more than 1 or 2 percent is not worth much; an option on a stock whose price may halve or double is very valuable.

As an option holder, you gain from volatility because the payoffs are not symmetric. If the stock price falls *below* the exercise price, your call option will be worthless, regardless of whether the shortfall is a few paise or many rupees. On the other hand, for every rupee that the stock price rises

FIGURE 20.12

How the value of the Arvind Mills call option increases with the volatility of the stock price. Each of the curved lines shows the value of the option for different initial stock prices. The only difference is that the upper line assumes a much higher level of uncertainty about Arvind Mills future stock price.

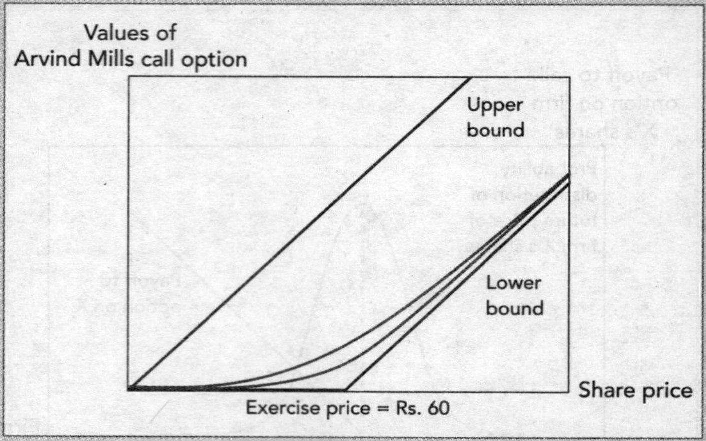

above the exercise price, your call will be worth an extra rupee. Therefore, the option holder gains from the increased volatility on the upside, but does not lose on the downside.

Panels (*a*) and (*b*) in Figure 20.11 illustrate this point. The panels compare the payoffs at expiration of two options with the same exercise price and the same stock price. The panels assume that stock price equals exercise price (like point *C* in Figure 20.10), although this is not a necessary assumption.[14] The only difference is that the price of stock Y at its option's expiration date is much harder to predict than the price of stock X at its option's expiration date. You can see this from the probability distributions superimposed on the figures.

In both cases there is roughly a 50 percent chance that the stock price will decline and make the options worthless, but if the prices of stocks X and Y rise, the odds are that Y will rise more than X. Thus there is a larger chance of a big payoff from the option on Y. Since the chance of a zero payoff is the same, the option on Y is worth more than the option on X. Figure 20.12 shows how the value of an option increases as stock price volatility increases. The upper curved line shows the values of the Arvind Mills call option assuming that Arvind's Mills stock price like that of firm Y is highly variable. The lower curved line assumes a lower (and more realistic) degree of volatility.[15]

The probability of large stock price changes during the remaining life of an option depends on two things: (1) the variance (i.e., volatility) of the stock price *per period* and (2) the number of periods until the option expires. If there are *t* remaining periods, and the variance per period is σ^2, the

[14]In drawing Figure 20.11 we have assumed that the distribution of possible stock prices is symmetric. This also is not a necessary assumption, and we will look more carefully at the distribution of price changes in the next chapter.

[15]The option values shown in Figure 20.12 were calculated by using the Black-Scholes option-valuation model. We explain this model in Chapter 21 and use it to value the Arvind Mills option.

1. If there is an *increase* in:	The change in the call option price is:	The change in the put option price is:
Stock price (P)	Positive	Negative
Exercise price (EX)	Negative	Positive
Interest rate (r_f)	Positive*	Negative
Time to expiration (t)	Positive	Positive
Volatility of stock price (σ)	Positive*	Positive

2. Other properties of call options:
   a. *Upper bound.* The option price is always less than the stock price.
   b. *Lower bound.* The call price never falls below the payoff to immediate exercise ($P - EX$ or zero, whichever is larger).
   c. If the stock is worthless, the call is worthless.
   d. As the stock price becomes very large, the call price approaches the stock price less the present value of the exercise price.

TABLE 20.2

What the price of a call option depends on.

*The *direct* effects of increases in r_f or σ on option price are positive. There may also be *indirect* effects. For example, an increase in r_f could reduce stock price P. This in turn could affect option price.

value of the option should depend on cumulative variability $\sigma^2 t$.[16] Other things equal, you would like to hold an option on a volatile stock (high σ^2). Given volatility, you would like to hold an option with a long life ahead of it (large t).

Thus the value of an option increases with both the volatility of the share price and the time to maturity.

It's a rare person who can keep all these properties straight at first reading. Therefore, we have summed them up in Table 20.2. For reference, the table also shows the effect of a change in each variable on the price of a put.

Risk and Option Values

In most financial settings, risk is a bad thing; you have to be paid to bear it. Investors in risky (high-beta) stocks demand higher expected rates of return. High-risk capital investment projects have correspondingly high costs of capital and have to beat higher hurdle rates to achieve positive NPV.

For options it's the other way around. As we have just seen, options written on volatile assets are worth *more* than options written on safe assets. If you can understand and remember that one fact about options, you've come a long way.

Example. Suppose you have to choose between two job offers, as CFO of either Establishment Industries or Digital Organics. Establishment Industries' compensation package includes a grant of the stock options described on the left side of Table 20.3. You demand a similar package from Digital Organics, and they comply. In fact they match the Establishment Industries options in every respect, as you can see on the right side of Table 20.3. (The two companies' current stock prices just happen to be the same.) The only difference is that Digital Organics' stock is half again as volatile as Establishment Industries' stock (36 percent annual standard deviation vs. 24 percent for Establishment Industries).

[16]Here is an intuitive explanation: If the stock price follows a random walk (see Section 13.2), successive price changes are statistically independent. The cumulative price change before expiration is the sum of t random variables. The variance of a sum of independent random variables is the sum of the variances of those variables. Thus, if σ^2 is the variance of the daily price change, and there are t days until expiration, the variance of the cumulative price change is $\sigma^2 t$.

TABLE 20.3

Which package of executive stock options would you choose? The package offered by Digital Organics is more valuable, because the volatility of that company's stock is higher.

	Establishment Industries	Digital Organics
Number of options	100,000	100,000
Exercise price	Rs. 25	Rs. 25
Maturity	5 years	5 years
Current stock price	Rs. 22	Rs. 22
Stock price volatility (standard deviation of return)	24%	36%

If your job choice hinges on the value of the executive stock options, you should take the Digital Organics offer. The Digital Organics options are written on the more volatile asset and therefore are worth more. We will value the two stock-option packages in the next chapter.

SUMMARY

If you have managed to reach this point, you are probably in need of a rest and a stiff gin and tonic. So we will summarize what we have learned so far and take up the subject of options again in the next chapter when you are rested (or drunk).

There are two types of option. An American call is an option to buy an asset at a specified exercise price on or before a specified exercise date. Similarly, an American put is an option to sell the asset at a specified price on or before a specified date. European calls and puts are exactly the same except that they cannot be exercised before the specified exercise date. Calls and puts are the basic building blocks that can be combined to give any pattern of payoffs.

What determines the value of a call option? Common sense tells us that it ought to depend on three things:

1. To exercise an option you have to pay the exercise price. Other things being equal, the less you are obliged to pay, the better. Therefore, the value of a call option increases with the ratio of the asset price to the exercise price.
2. You do not have to pay the exercise price until you decide to exercise the option. Therefore, a call option gives you a free loan. The higher the rate of interest and the longer the time to maturity, the more this free loan is worth. So the value of a call option increases with the interest rate and time to maturity.
3. If the price of the asset falls short of the exercise price, you won't exercise the call option. You will, therefore, lose 100 percent of your investment in the option no matter how far the asset depreciates below the exercise price. On the other hand, the more the price rises *above* the exercise price, the more profit you will make. Therefore the option holder does not lose from increased volatility if things go wrong, but gains if they go right. The value of an option increases with the variance per period of the stock return multiplied by the number of periods to maturity.

Always remember that an option written on a risky (high-variance) asset is worth more than an option on a safe asset. It's easy to forget, because in most other financial contexts increases in risk reduce present value.

FURTHER READING

See Further Readings for Chapter 21.

CONCEPT REVIEW QUESTIONS

1. Explain the difference between an American and a European option. (page 544)
2. "Someone who sells an option can only lose money." True or false? (page 548)
3. Draw the position diagram for the buyer of a put option. What is the maximum possible payoff? (page 545)

For additional Concept Review Questions, please visit us at www.mhhe.com/bmam8e or refer to your Student CD.

QUIZ

1. Complete the following passage:

   A __________ option gives its owner the opportunity to buy a stock at a specified price which is generally called the __________ price. A __________ option gives its owner the opportunity to sell stock at a specified price. Options that can be exercised only at maturity are called __________ options.
2. Note Figure 20.13. Match each diagram, *(a)* and *(b)*, with one of the following positions:
   - Call buyer
   - Call seller
   - Put buyer
   - Put seller
3. Suppose that you hold a share of stock and a put option on that share. What is the payoff when the option expires if **(a)** the stock price is below the exercise price? **(b)** the stock price is above the exercise price?

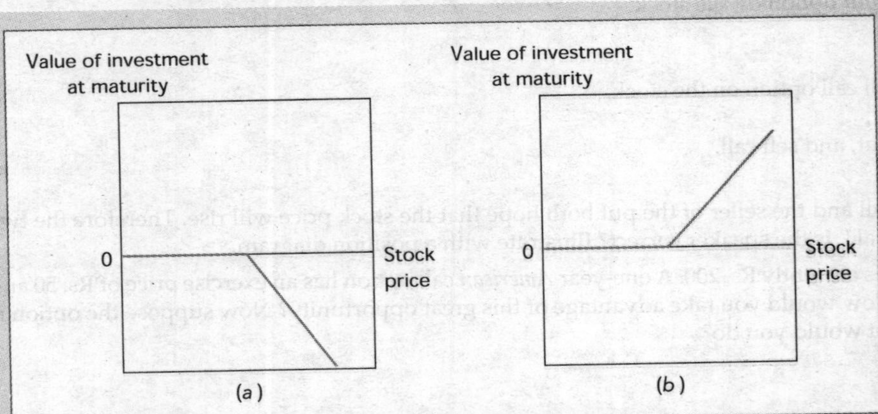

FIGURE 20.13

See Quiz Question 2.

4. What is put–call parity and why does it hold? Could you apply the parity formula to a call and put with different exercise prices?
5. There is another strategy involving calls and borrowing and lending that gives the same payoffs as the strategy described in Quiz Question 3. What is the alternative strategy?
6. Dr. Livingstone I. Presume holds £600,000 in East African gold stocks. Bullish as he is on gold mining, he requires absolute assurance that at least £500,000 will be available in six months to fund an expedition. Describe two ways for Dr. Presume to achieve this goal. There is an active market for puts and calls on East African gold stocks, and the rate of interest is 6 percent per year.
7. Suppose you buy a one-year European call option on Wombat stock with an exercise price of Rs. 100 and sell a one-year European put option with the same exercise price. The current stock price is Rs. 100, and the interest rate is 10 percent.
   a. Draw a position diagram showing the payoffs from your investments.
   b. How much will the combined position cost you? Explain.
8. Look again at Figure 20.13. It appears that the call buyer in panel (b) can't lose and the call seller in panel (a) can't win. Is that correct? Explain. *Hint:* Draw a profit diagram for each panel.
9. What is a call option worth if (a) the stock price is zero? (b) the stock price is extremely high relative to the exercise price?
10. How does the price of a call option respond to the following changes, other things equal? Does the call price go up or down?
    a. Stock price increases.
    b. Exercise price is increased.
    c. Risk-free rate increases.
    d. Expiration date of the option is extended.
    e. Volatility of the stock price falls.
    f. Time passes, so the option's expiration date comes closer.
11. Respond to the following statements.
    a. "I'm a conservative investor. I'd much rather hold a call option on a safe stock like ExxonMobil than a volatile stock like Arvind Mills."
    b. "When a company lands in financial distress, stockholders are better off if the financial manager shifts to safer assets and operating strategies."

PRACTICE QUESTIONS

1. Discuss briefly the risks and payoffs of the following positions:
   a. Buy stock and a put option on the stock.
   b. Buy stock.
   c. Buy call.
   d. Buy stock and sell call option on the stock.
   e. Buy bond.
   f. Buy stock, buy put, and sell call.
   g. Sell put.
2. "The buyer of the call and the seller of the put both hope that the stock price will rise. Therefore the two positions are identical." Is the speaker correct? Illustrate with a position diagram.
3. Pintail's stock price is currently Rs. 200. A one-year *American* call option has an exercise price of Rs. 50 and is priced at Rs. 75. How would you take advantage of this great opportunity? Now suppose the option is a *European* call. What would you do?

4. It is possible to buy three-month call options and three-month puts on stock Q. Both options have an exercise price of Rs. 60 and both are worth Rs. 10. Is a six-month call with an exercise price of Rs. 60 more or less valuable than a similar six-month put? *Hint:* Use put–call parity.
5. In June 2006, a three-month call on the stock of Alok Textiles, with an exercise price of Rs. 60, was sold for Rs. 8. The stock price was Rs. 62. The risk-free interest rate was 7 percent. How much would you be willing to pay for a put on Alok Textile stock with the same maturity and exercise price? Assume that Alok Textiles options are European options.
6. Go to the website of NSE at www.nseindia.com. Check out the delayed quotes for Arvind Mills for different exercise prices and maturities.
   a. Confirm that higher exercise prices mean lower call prices and higher put prices.
   b. Confirm that longer maturity means higher prices for both puts and calls.
   c. Choose an Arvind Mills put and call with the same exercise price and maturity. Confirm that put-call parity holds (approximately). Note: You will have to use an up-to-date risk-free interest rate.
7. The Great Indian Bank has succeeded in hiring ace foreign exchange trader, Rakesh Vyas. His remuneration package reportedly includes an annual bonus of 20 percent of the profits that he generates in excess of Rs. 100 million. Does Mr. Vyas have an option? Does it provide him with an appropriate incentive?
8. Suppose that Mr. Palaniappan borrows the present value of Rs. 100, buys a six-month put option on stock Y with an exercise price of Rs. 150, and sells a six-month put option on Y with an exercise price of Rs. 50.
   a. Draw a position diagram showing the payoffs when the options expire.
   b. Suggest two other combinations of loans, options, and the underlying stock that would give Mr. Palaniappan the same payoffs.
9. Which *one* of the following statements is correct?
   a. Value of put + present value of exercise price = value of call + share price.
   b. Value of put + share price = value of call + present value of exercise price.
   c. Value of put − share price = present value of exercise price − value of call.
   d. Value of put + value of call = share price − present value of exercise price.

   The correct statement equates the value of two investment strategies. Plot the payoffs to each strategy as a function of the stock price. Show that the two strategies give identical payoffs.
10. Test the formula linking put and call prices by using it to explain the relative prices of actual traded puts and calls. (Note that the formula is exact only for European options. Most traded puts and calls are American.)
11. a. If you can't sell a share short, you can achieve exactly the same final payoff by a combination of options and borrowing or lending. What is this combination?
    b. Now work out the mixture of stock and options that gives the same final payoff as investment in a risk-free loan.
12. The common stock of Triangular File Company is selling at Rs. 90. A 26-week call option written on Triangular File's stock is selling for Rs. 8. The call's exercise price is Rs. 100. The risk-free interest rate is 10 percent per year.
    a. Suppose that puts on Triangular stock are not traded, but you want to buy one. How would you do it?
    b. Suppose that puts *are* traded. What should a 26-week put with an exercise price of Rs. 100 sell for?
13. Digital Organics has 10 million outstanding shares trading at Rs. 25 per share. It also has a large amount of debt outstanding, all coming due in one year. The debt pays interest at 8 percent. It has a par (face) value of Rs. 350 million, but is trading at a market value of only Rs. 280 million. The one-year risk-free interest rate is 6 percent.
    a. Write out the put–call parity formula for Digital Organics' stock, debt, and assets.
    b. What is the value of the default put given up by Digital Organics' creditors?

TABLE 20.4

Prices of options on common stocks (in dollars). See Practice Question 17.

Stock	Time to Exercise (months)	Exercise Price	Stock Price	Put Price	Call Price
Drongo Corp.	6	50	80	20	52
Ragwort, Inc.	6	100	80	10	15
Wombat Corp.	3	40	50	7	18
	6	40	50	5	17
	6	50	50	8	10

14. Option traders often refer to "straddles" and "butterflies." Here is an example of each:
    - *Straddle:* Buy call with exercise price of Rs. 100 and simultaneously buy put with exercise price of Rs. 100.
    - *Butterfly:* Simultaneously buy one call with exercise price of Rs. 100, sell two calls with exercise price of Rs. 110, and buy one call with exercise price of Rs. 120.

    Draw position diagrams for the straddle and butterfly, showing the payoffs from the investor's net position. Each strategy is a bet on variability. Explain briefly the nature of each bet.

15. Look at actual trading prices of call options on stocks to check whether they behave as the theory presented in this chapter predicts. For example,
    a. Follow several options as they approach maturity. How would you expect their prices to behave? Do they actually behave that way?
    b. Compare two call options written on the same stock with the same maturity but different exercise prices.
    c. Compare two call options written on the same stock with the same exercise price but different maturities.

16. Is it more valuable to own an option to buy a portfolio of stocks or to own a portfolio of options to buy each of the individual stocks? Say briefly why.

17. Table 20.4 lists some prices of options on common stocks (prices are quoted to the nearest rupee). The interest rate is 10 percent a year. Can you spot any mispricing? What would you do to take advantage of it?

18. You've just completed a month-long study of energy markets and conclude that energy prices will be *much* more volatile in the next year than historically. Assuming you're right, what types of option strategies should you undertake? *Note:* You can buy or sell options on oil-company stocks or on the price of future deliveries of crude oil, natural gas, fuel oil, etc.

CHALLENGE QUESTIONS

1. Figure 20.14 shows some complicated position diagrams. Work out the combination of stocks, bonds, and options that produces each of these positions.

2. In 1988 the Australian firm Bond Corporation sold a share in some land that it owned near Rome for $110 million and as a result boosted its 1988 earnings by $74 million. In 1989 a television program revealed that the buyer was given a put option to sell its share in the land back to Bond for $110 million and that Bond had paid $ 20 million for a call option to repurchase the share in the land for the same price.[17]

[17]See *Sydney Morning Herald*, March 14, 1989, p. 27. The options were subsequently renegotiated.

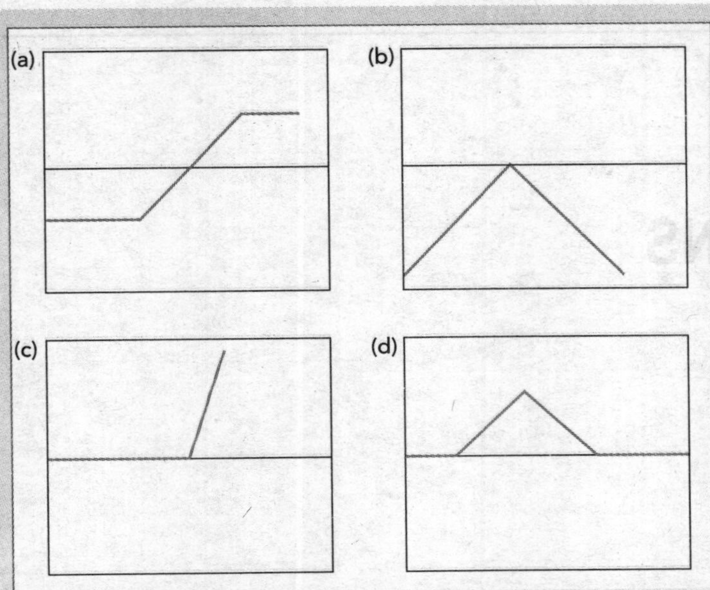

FIGURE 20.14

Some complicated position diagrams. See Challenge Question 1.

a. What happens if the land is worth more than $110 million when the options expire? What if it is worth less than $110 million?
b. Use position diagrams to show the net effect of the land sale and the option transactions.
c. Assume a one-year maturity on the options. Can you deduce the interest rate?
d. The television program argued that it was misleading to record a profit on the sale of land. What do you think?

3. Three six-month call options are traded on Hogswill stock:

Exercise Price	Call Option Price
Rs. 90	Rs. 5
100	11
110	15

How would you make money by trading in Hogswill options? (*Hint:* Draw a graph with the option price on the vertical axis and the ratio of stock price to exercise price on the horizontal axis. Plot the three Hogswill options on your graph. Does this fit with what you know about how option prices should vary with the ratio of stock price to exercise price?) Now look in the newspaper at options with the same maturity but different exercise prices. Can you find any money-making opportunities?

4. Ms. Laxmi has been offered yet another incentive scheme (see Section 20.2). She will receive a bonus of Rs. 500,000 if the stock price at the end of the year is Rs. 120 or more; otherwise she will receive nothing. (Don't ask why anyone should want to offer such an arrangement. Maybe there's some tax angle.)
   a. Draw a position diagram illustrating the payoffs from such a scheme.
   b. What combination of options would provide these payoffs? (*Hint:* You need to buy a large number of options with one exercise price and sell a similar number with a different exercise price.)

CHAPTER [21]

VALUING OPTIONS

IN THE LAST chapter we introduced you to call and put options. Call options give the owner the right to buy an asset at a specified exercise price; put options give the right to sell. We also took the first step toward understanding how options are valued. The value of a call option depends on five variables:

1. The higher the price of the asset, the more valuable an option to buy it.
2. The lower the price that you must pay to exercise the call, the more valuable the option.
3. You do not need to pay the exercise price until the option expires. This delay is most valuable when the interest rate is high.
4. If the stock price is below the exercise price at maturity, the call is valueless regardless of whether the price is Re. 1 below or Rs. 100 below. However, for every rupee that the stock price rises above the exercise price, the option holder gains an additional rupee Thus, the value of the call option increases with the volatility of the stock price.
5. Finally, a long-term option is more valuable than a short-term option. A distant maturity delays the point at which the holder needs to pay the exercise price and increases the chance of a large jump in the stock price before the option matures.

In this chapter we show how these variables can be combined into an exact option-valuation model—a formula we can plug numbers into to get a definite answer. We first describe a simple way to value options, known as the binomial model. We then introduce the Black–Scholes formula for valuing options. Finally, we provide a checklist showing how these two methods can be used to solve a number of practical option problems.

The only feasible way to value most options is to use a computer. But in this chapter we will work through some simple examples by hand. We do so because unless you understand the basic principles behind option valuation, you are likely to make mistakes in setting up an option problem and you won't know how to interpret the computer's answer and explain it to others.

In the last chapter we introduced you to the put and call options on Arvind Mills stock. In this chapter we will stick with that example and show you how to value the Arvind Mills options. But remember *why* you need to understand option valuation. It is not to make a quick buck trading on an options exchange. It is because many capital budgeting and financing decisions have options embedded in them. We will discuss a variety of these options in subsequent chapters.

21.1 A SIMPLE OPTION-VALUATION MODEL

Why Discounted Cash Flow Won't Work for Options

For many years economists searched for a practical formula to value options until Fisher Black and Myron Scholes finally hit upon the solution. Later we will show you what they found, but first we should explain why the search was so difficult.

Our standard procedure for valuing an asset is to (1) figure out expected cash flows and (2) discount them at the opportunity cost of capital. Unfortunately, this is not practical for options. The first step is messy but feasible, but finding *the* opportunity cost of capital is impossible, because the risk of an option changes every time the stock price moves, and we know it *will* move along a random walk through the option's lifetime.

When you buy a call, you are taking a position in the stock but putting up less of your own money than if you had bought the stock directly. Thus, an option is always riskier than the underlying stock. It has a higher beta and a higher standard deviation of return.

How much riskier the option is depends on the stock price relative to the exercise price. A call option that is in the money (stock price greater than exercise price) is safer than one that is out of the money (stock price less than exercise price). Thus a stock price increase raises the option's price *and* reduces its risk. When the stock price falls, the option's price falls *and* its risk increases. That is why the expected rate of return investors demand from an option changes day by day, or hour by hour, every time the stock price moves.

We repeat the general rule: The higher the stock price is relative to the exercise price, the safer is the call option, although the option is always riskier than the stock. The option's risk changes every time the stock price changes.

Constructing Option Equivalents from Common Stocks and Borrowing

If you've digested what we've said so far, you can appreciate why options are hard to value by standard discounted-cash-flow formulas and why a rigorous option-valuation technique eluded economists for many years. The breakthrough came when Black and Scholes exclaimed, "Eureka! We have found it![1] The trick is to set up an *option equivalent* by combining common stock investment and borrowing. The net cost of buying the option equivalent must equal the value of the option."

We shall show you how this works with a simple numerical example. We will travel back to June 2006 and consider a three-month call option on Arvind Mills with an exercise price of Rs. 60. We will pick a day when Arvind Mills stock was also trading at Rs. 60, so that this option is *at the money*. The short term, risk-free interest rate is assumed to be about 4 percent per year, or about 1 percent for three months.

To keep the example as simple as possible, we assume that Arvind Mills stock can do only two things over the option's three-month life: either the price will fall by a quarter to Rs. 45 or rise by one-third to Rs. 80.

If Arvind Mills stock price falls to Rs. 45, the call option will be worthless, but if the price rises to Rs. 80, the option will be worth 80 − 60 = Rs. 20. The possible payoffs to the option are therefore

	Stock Price = Rs. 45	**Stock Price = Rs. 80**
1 call option	Rs. 0	Rs. 20

Now compare these payoffs with what you would get if you bought 4/7 Arvind Mills shares and borrowed Rs. 25.46 from the bank:[2]

	Stock Price = Rs. 45	**Stock Price = Rs. 80**
4/7 shares	Rs. 25.71	Rs. 45.71
Repayment of loan + interest	−25.71	−25.71
Total payoff	Rs. 0	Rs. 20.00

[1]We do not know whether Black and Scholes, like Archimedes, were sitting in bathtubs at the time.

[2]The amount that you need to borrow from the bank is simply the present value of the difference between the payoffs from the option and the payoffs from 4/7 shares. This figure is the same if the stock price falls or rises. In our example, amount borrowed = ((4/7) × 45 − 0)/1.01 = ((4/7) × 80 − 20)/1.01 = Rs. 25.46.

Notice that the payoffs from the levered investment in the stock are identical to the payoffs from the call option. Therefore, both investments must have the same value:

$$\text{Value of call} = \text{value of } (4/7) \text{ shares} - \text{Rs. } 25.46 \text{ bank loan}$$
$$= 60 \times (4/7) - 25.46 = \text{Rs. } 8.83$$

Presto! You've valued a call option.

To value the Arvind Mills option, we borrowed money and bought stock in such a way that we exactly replicated the payoff from a call option. This is called a **replicating portfolio.** The number of shares needed to replicate one call is called the **hedge ratio** or **option delta.** In our Arvind Mills example one call is replicated by a levered position in 4/7 shares. The option delta is, therefore, 4/7, or about .571.

How did we know that Arvind Mills call option was equivalent to a levered position in 4/7 shares? We used a simple formula that says

$$\text{Option delta} = \frac{\text{spread of possible option prices}}{\text{spread of possible share prices}} = \frac{20-0}{80-45} = \frac{20}{35} = \frac{4}{7}$$

You have learned not only to value a simple option but also that you can replicate an investment in the option by a levered investment in the underlying asset. Thus, if you can't buy or sell an option on an asset, you can create a homemade option by a replicating strategy—that is, you buy or sell delta shares and borrow or lend the balance.

Risk-Neutral Valuation Notice why the Arvind Mills call option should sell for Rs. 8.83. If the option price is higher than Rs. 8.83, you could make a certain profit by buying 4/7 shares of stock, selling a call option, and borrowing Rs. 25.46. Similarly, if the option price is less than Rs. 8.83, you could make an equally certain profit by selling 4/7 shares, buying a call, and lending the balance. In either case there would be an arbitrage opportunity.[3]

If there's a possible arbitrage profit, everyone scurries to take advantage of it. So when we said that the option price had to be Rs. 8.83 or there would be an arbitrage opportunity, we did not have to know anything about investor attitudes to risk. The option price cannot depend on whether investors detest risk or do not care a jot.

This suggests an alternative way to value the option. We can *pretend* that all investors are *indifferent* about risk, work out the expected future value of the option in such a world, and discount it back at the risk-free interest rate to give the current value. Let us check that this method gives the same answer.

If investors are indifferent to risk, the expected return on the stock must be equal to the risk-free rate of interest:

$$\text{Expected return on Arvind Mills stock} = 1.0\% \text{ per three months}$$

We know that Arvind Mills stock can either rise by 33.3 percent to Rs. 80 or fall by 25 percent to Rs. 45. We can, therefore, calculate the probability of a price rise in our hypothetical risk-neutral world:

$$\text{Expected return} = [\text{probability of rise} \times 33.3]$$
$$+ [(1 - \text{probability of rise}) \times (-25)]$$
$$= 1.0 \text{ percent.}$$

[3]Of course, you don't get seriously rich by dealing in 4/7 shares. But if you multiply each of our transactions by a million, it begins to look like real money.

Therefore,

$$\text{Probability of rise} = .446, \text{ or } 44.6\%$$

Notice that this is not the *true* probability that Arvind Mills stock will rise. Since investors dislike risk, they will almost surely require a higher expected return than the risk-free interest rate from Arvind Mills stock. Therefore the true probability is greater than .446.

The general formula for calculating the risk-neutral probability of a rise in value is

$$p = \frac{\text{interest rate} - \text{downside change}}{\text{upside change} - \text{downside change}}$$

In the case of Arvind Mills stock

$$p = \frac{.01 - (-.25)}{.333 - (-.25)} = .446$$

We know that if the stock price rises, the call option will be worth Rs. 20; if it falls, the call will be worth nothing. Therefore, if investors are risk-neutral, the expected value of the call option is

$$[\text{Probability of rise} \times 20] + [(1 - \text{probability of rise}) \times 0]$$
$$= (.446 \times 20) + (.554 \times 0)$$
$$= \text{Rs. } 8.92$$

And the current value of the call is

$$\frac{\text{Expected future value}}{1 + \text{interest rate}} = \frac{8.92}{1.01} = \text{Rs. } 8.83$$

Exactly the same answer that we got earlier!

We now have two ways to calculate the value of an option:

1. Find the combination of stock and loan that replicates an investment in the option. Since the two strategies give identical payoffs in the future, they must sell for the same price today.
2. Pretend that investors do not care about risk, so that the expected return on the stock is equal to the interest rate. Calculate the expected future value of the option in this hypothetical *risk-neutral* world and discount it at the risk-free interest rate. This idea may seem familiar to you. In Chapter 9 we showed how you can value an investment either by discounting the expected cash flows at a risk-adjusted discount rate or by adjusting the expected cash flows for risk and then discounting these *certainty-equivalent* flows at the risk-free interest rate. We have just used this second method to value the Arvind Mills option. The certainty-equivalent cash flows on the stock and option are the cash flows that would be expected in a risk-neutral world.

Valuing the Arvind Mills Put Option

Valuing the Arvind Mills call option may well have seemed like pulling a rabbit out of a hat. To give you a second chance to watch how it is done, we will use the same method to value another option—this time, the three-month Arvind Mills put option with a Rs. 60 exercise price.[4] We continue to assume that the stock price will either rise to Rs. 80 or fall to Rs. 45.

[4]When valuing *American* put options, you need to recognize the possibility that it will pay to exercise early. We discuss this complication later in the chapter, but it is unimportant for valuing the Arvind Mills put and we ignore it here.

If Arvind Mills' stock price rises to Rs. 80, the option to sell for Rs. 60 will be worthless. If the price falls to Rs. 45, the put option will be worth Rs. 60 − 45 = Rs. 15. Thus the payoffs to the put are

	Stock Price = Rs. 45	Stock Price = Rs. 80
1 put option	Rs. 15	Rs. 0

We start by calculating the option delta using the formula that we presented above:[5]

$$\text{Option delta} = \frac{\text{spread of possible option prices}}{\text{spread of possible stock prices}} = \frac{0-15}{80-45} = -\frac{3}{7}, \text{ or about } -.429$$

Notice that the delta of a put option is always negative; that is, you need to *sell* delta shares of stock to replicate the put. In the case of the Arvind Mills put you can replicate the option payoffs by *selling* 3/7 Arvind Mills shares and *lending* Rs. 33.95. Since you have sold the share short, you will need to lay out money at the end of three months to buy it back, but you will have money coming in from the loan. Your net payoffs are exactly the same as the payoffs you would get if you bought the put option:

	Stock Price = Rs. 45	Stock Price = Rs. 80
Sale of 3/7 shares	−Rs. 19.29	−Rs. 34.29
Repayment of loan + interest	+34.29	+34.29
Total payoff	Rs. 15	Rs. 0

Since the two investments have the same payoffs, they must have the same value:

$$\begin{aligned}\text{Value of put} &= -(3/7)\text{ shares} + \text{Rs. } 33.95 \text{ bank loan}\\ &= -(3/7)\times 60 + 33.95 = 8.23\end{aligned}$$

Valuing the Put Option by the Risk-Neutral Method Valuing the Arvind Mills put option with the risk-neutral method is a cinch. We already know that the probability of a rise in the stock price is .446. Therefore the expected value of the put option in a risk-neutral world is

$$\begin{aligned}&[\text{Probability of rise} \times 0] + [(1 - \text{probability of rise}) \times 15]\\ &= (.446 \times 0) + (.554 \times 15)\\ &= \text{Rs. } 8.31\end{aligned}$$

And therefore the current value of the put is

$$\frac{\text{Expected future value}}{1+\text{interest rate}} = \frac{8.31}{1.01} = \text{Rs. } 8.23$$

[5]The delta of a put option is always equal to the delta of a call option with the same exercise price minus one. In our example, delta of put = (4/7) − 1 = −(3/7).

The Relationship between Call and Put Prices We pointed out earlier that for European options there is a simple relationship between the value of the call and that of the put.[6]

$$\text{Value of put} = \text{value of call} - \text{share price} + \text{present value of exercise price}$$

Since we had already calculated the value of the Arvind Mills call, we could also have used this relationship to find the value of the put:

$$\text{Value of put} = 8.83 - 60 + \frac{60}{1.01} = \text{Rs. } 8.23$$

Everything checks.

21.2 THE BINOMIAL METHOD FOR VALUING OPTIONS

The essential trick in pricing any option is to set up a package of investments in the stock and the loan that will exactly replicate the payoffs from the option. If we can price the stock and the loan, then we can also price the option. Equivalently, we can pretend that investors are risk-neutral, calculate the expected payoff on the option in this fictitious risk-neutral world, and discount by the rate of interest to find the option's present value.

These *concepts* are completely general, but there are several ways to find the replicating package of investments. The example in the last section used a simplified version of what is known as the **binomial method.** The method starts by reducing the possible changes in next period's stock price to two, an "up" move and a "down" move. This assumption that there are just two possible prices for Arvind Mills stock at the end of three months is clearly fanciful.

We could make the Arvind Mills problem a trifle more realistic by assuming that there are two possible price changes in each of one-and-half-month period. This would give a wider variety of three-month prices. And there is no reason to stop at one-and-half-month periods. We could go on to take shorter and shorter intervals, with each interval showing two possible changes in Arvind Mills' stock price and giving an even wider selection of three-month prices.

This is illustrated in Figure 21.1. The two left-hand diagrams show our starting assumption: just two possible prices at the end of three months. Moving to the right, you can see what happens when there are two possible price changes every one-and-half months. This gives three possible stock prices when the option matures. In Figure 21.a(c), we have gone on to divide the three-month period into 17 two-day periods (2.33 days to be exact), in each of which the price can make one of two small moves. The distribution of prices at the end of three months is now looking more realistic.

We could continue in this way to chop the period into shorter and shorter intervals, until eventually we would reach a situation in which the stock price is changing continuously and there is a continuum of possible future stock prices.

Example: The Two-Stage Binomial Method

Dividing the period into shorter intervals doesn't alter the basic method for valuing a call option. We can still replicate the call by a levered investment in the stock, but we need to adjust the degree

[6] *Reminder:* This formula applies only when the two options have the same exercise price and exercise date.

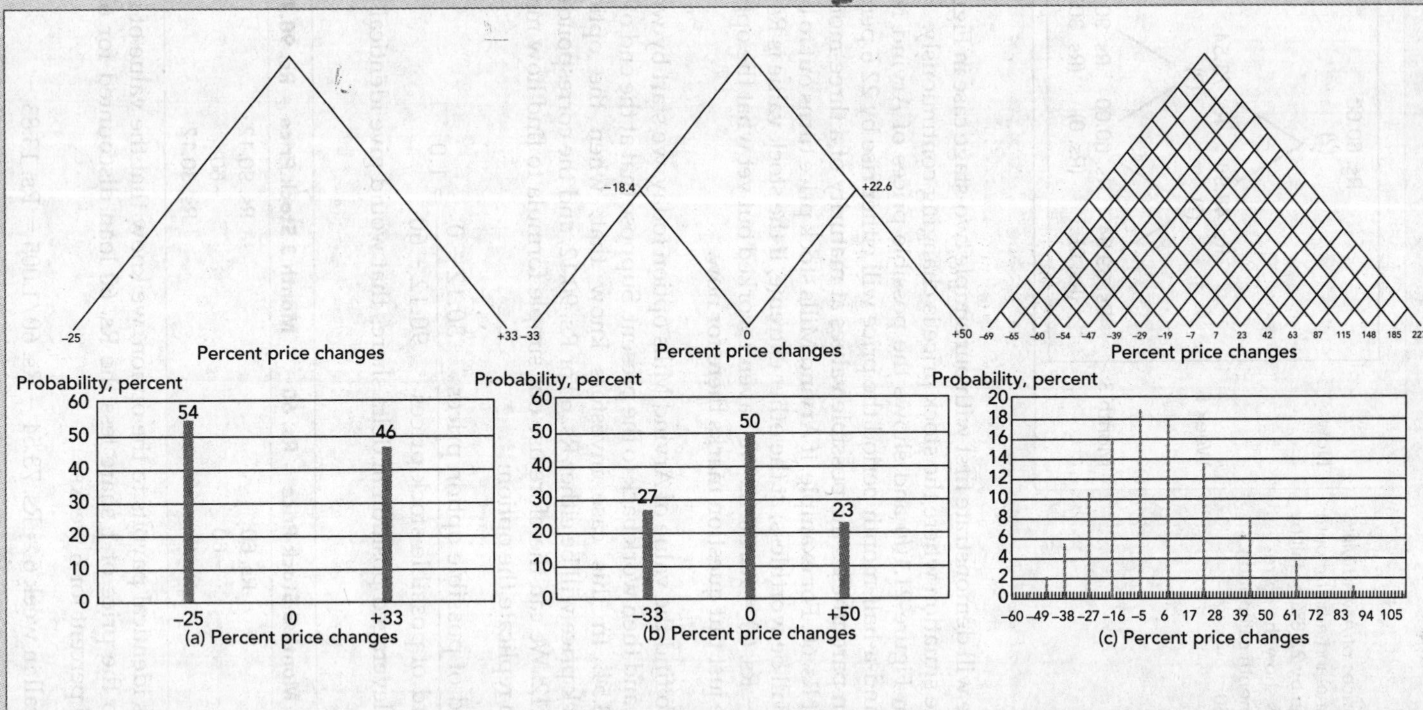

FIGURE 21.1

"This Figure shows the possible three-month price changes for Arvind Mills stock assuming that the stock makes a single up or down move each three-months [Fig.21.1(a)], two moves, one every one-and-half months [Fig21.1(b)], or 17 moves, one about every second day [Figure 21.1(c)]. Beneath each tree we show a histogram of the possible three-month price changes, assuming investors are risk neutral."

FIGURE 21.2

Present and possible future prices of Arvind Mills stock assuming that in each one-and-a-half-month period the price will either rise by 22.6% or fall by 18.4%. Figures in parentheses show the corresponding values of an three-month call option with an exercise price of Rs. 60.

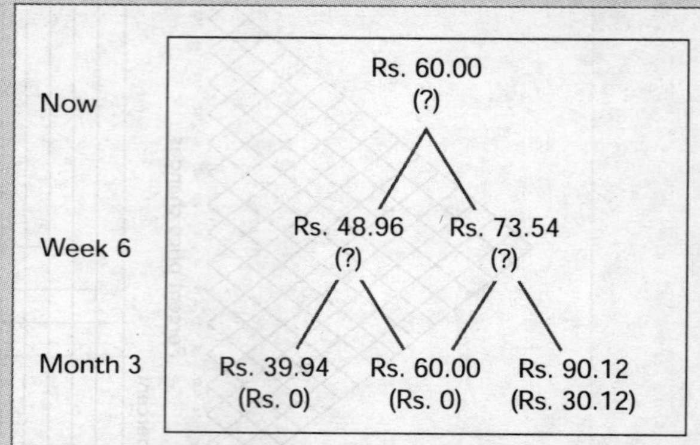

of leverage at each stage. We will demonstrate first with our simple two-stage case in Figure 21.1(*b*). Then we will work up to the situation where the stock price is changing continuously.

Figure 21.2 is taken from Figure 21.1(*b*) and shows the possible prices of Arvind Mills stock, assuming that in each one-and-a-half-month period the price will either rise by 22.6 percent or fall by 18.4 percent.[7] We show in parentheses the possible values at maturity of a three-month call option with an exercise price of Rs. 60. For example, if Arvind Mills stock price turns out to be Rs. 39.94 in month 3, the call option will be worthless; at the other extreme, if the stock value is Rs. 90.12, the call will be worth Rs. 90.12 − Rs. 60 = Rs. 30.12. We haven't worked out yet what the option will be worth *before* maturity, so we just put question marks there for now.

Option Value in Week 6 To find the value of Arvind Mills option today, we start by working out its possible values in week 6 and then work back to the present. Suppose that at the end of six weeks the stock price is Rs. 73.54. In this case investors know that, when the option finally matures in month 3, the stock price will be either Rs. 60 or Rs. 90.12, and the corresponding option price will be Rs. 0 or Rs. 30.12. We can therefore use our simple formula to find how many shares we need to buy in week 6 to replicate the option:

$$\text{Option delta} = \frac{\text{spread of possible option prices}}{\text{spread of possible stock prices}} = \frac{30.12 - 0}{90.12 - 60} = 1.0$$

Now we can construct a leveraged position in delta shares that would give identical payoffs to the option:

	Month 3 Stock Price = Rs. 60	Month 3 Stock Price = Rs. 90.12
Buy 1.0 shares	Rs. 60	Rs. 90.12
Borrow PV(60)	−60	−60
Total payoff	Rs. 0	Rs. 30.12

Since this portfolio provides identical payoffs to the option, we know that the value of the option in week 6 must be equal to the price of 1 share less the Rs. 60 loan discounted for 6 weeks at 4 percent per year, about 0.5 percent for 6 weeks:

$$\text{Value of call in week 6} = \text{Rs. } 73.54 - \text{Rs. } 60/1.005 = \text{Rs. } 13.83$$

[7]We will explain shortly why we picked these figures.

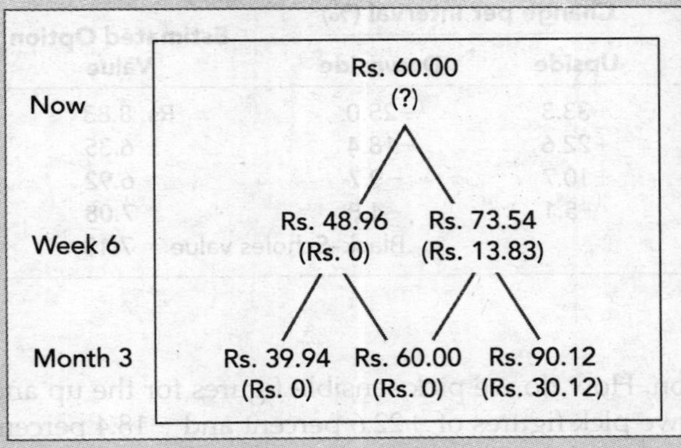

FIGURE 21.3

Present and possible future prices of Arvind Mills-stock. Figures in parentheses show the corresponding values of a three-month call option with an exercise price of Rs. 60.

Therefore, if the share price rises in the first six weeks, the option will be worth Rs. 13.83. But what if the share price falls to Rs. 48.96? In that case the most that you can hope for is that the share price will recover to Rs. 60. Therefore the option is bound to be worthless when it matures and must be worthless at week 6.

Option Value Today We can now get rid of two of the question marks in Figure 21.2. Figure 21.3 shows that if the stock price in week 6 is Rs. 73.54, the option value is Rs. 13.83 and, if the stock price is Rs. 48.96, the option value is zero. It only remains to work back to the option value today.

We again begin by calculating the option delta:

$$\text{Option delta} = \frac{\text{spread of possible option prices}}{\text{spread of possible stock prices}} = \frac{13.83 - 0}{73.54 - 48.96} = .563$$

We can now find the leveraged position in delta shares that would give identical payoffs to the option:

	Week 6 Stock Price = Rs. 48.96	**Week 6 Stock Price = Rs. 73.54**
Buy .563 shares	Rs. 27.55	Rs. 41.39
Borrow PV(27.55)	−27.55	−27.55
Total payoff	Rs. 0	Rs. 13.83

The value of the Arvind Mills option today is equal to the value of this leveraged position:

$$\text{PV option} = \text{PV}(.563 \text{ shares}) - \text{PV}(\text{Rs. } 27.55)$$
$$= .563 \times \text{Rs. } 60 - \text{Rs. } 27.55/1.005 = \text{Rs. } 6.35$$

The General Binomial Method

Moving to two steps when valuing the Arvind Mills call probably added extra realism. But there is no reason to stop there. We could go on, as in Figure 21.1, to chop the period into smaller and smaller intervals. We could still use the binomial method to work back from the final date to the present. Of course, it would be tedious to do the calculations by hand, but simple to do so with a computer.

Since a stock can usually take on an almost limitless number of future values, the binomial method gives a more realistic and accurate measure of the option's value if we work with a large number of

TABLE 21.1

As the number of steps is increased, you must adjust the range of possible changes in the value of the asset to keep the same standard deviation. But you will get increasingly close to the Black–Scholes value of the Arvind Mills call option.

Note: The standard deviation is $\sigma = 0.5755$

Number of Steps	Change per Interval (%)		Estimated Option Value
	Upside	Downside	
1	+33.3	−25.0	Rs. 8.83
2	+22.6	−18.4	6.35
8	+10.7	−9.7	6.92
34	+5.1	−4.8	7.08
		Black–Scholes value =	7.13

subperiods. But that raises an important question. How do we pick sensible figures for the up and down changes in value? For example, why did we pick figures of +22.6 percent and −18.4 percent when we revalued Arvind Mills option with two subperiods? Fortunately, there is a neat little formula that relates the up and down changes to the standard deviation of stock returns:

$$1 + \text{upside change} = u = e^{\sigma\sqrt{h}}$$

$$1 + \text{downside change} = d = 1/u$$

where

e = base for natural logarithms = 2.718
σ = standard deviation of (continuously compounded) stock returns
h = interval as fraction of a year

When we said that Arvind Mills' stock could either rise by 33.3 percent or fall by 25 percent over three months (h = 0.25), our figures were consistent with a figure of 57.55 percent of the standard deviation of annual returns:[8]

$$1 + \text{upside change (3-month interval)} = u = e^{0.5755\sqrt{0.25}} = 1.333$$

$$1 + \text{downside change} = d = 1/u = 1/1.333 = 0.75$$

To work out the equivalent upside and downside changes when we divide the period into two one-and-half-month intervals (h = 0.125), we use the same formula:

$$1 + \text{upside change (4-month interval)} = u = e^{0.5755\sqrt{0.25}} = 1.226$$

$$1 + \text{downside change} = d = 1/u = 1/1.226 = 0.816$$

The centre columns in Table 21.1 show the equivalent up and down moves in the value of the firm if we chop the period into eight and-and-half-week or 34 two-day periods, and the final column shows the effect on the estimated option value. (We will explain the Black-Scholes value shortly.)

[8] To find the standard deviation given u, we turn the formula around:

$$\sigma = \log(u)/\sqrt{h}$$

where

log = natural logarithm

In our example:

$$\sigma = \log(1.333)/\sqrt{0.25} = 0.2877/\sqrt{.25} = 5755$$

The Binomial Method and Decision Trees

Calculating option values by the binomial method is basically a process of solving decision trees. You start at some future date and work back through the tree to the present. Eventually the possible cash flows generated by future events and actions are folded back to a present value.

Is the binomial method *merely* another application of decision trees, a tool of analysis that you learned about in Chapter 10? The answer is no, for at least two reasons. First, option pricing theory is absolutely essential for discounting within decision trees. Standard discounting doesn't work within decision trees for the same reason that it doesn't work for puts and calls. As we pointed out in Section 21.1, there is no single, constant discount rate for options because the risk of the option changes as time and the price of the underlying asset change. There is no single discount rate inside a decision tree, because if the tree contains meaningful future decisions, it also contains options. The market value of the future cash flows described by the decision tree has to be calculated by option pricing methods.

Second, option theory gives a simple, powerful framework for describing complex decision trees. For example, suppose that you have the option to postpone an investment for many years. The complete decision tree would overflow the largest classroom chalkboard. But now that you know about options, the opportunity to postpone investment might be summarized as "an American call on a perpetuity with a constant dividend yield." Of course, not all real problems have such easy option analogies, but we can often approximate complex decision trees by some simple package of assets and options. A custom decision tree may get closer to reality, but the time and expense may not be worth it. Most men buy their suits off the rack even though a custom-made Armani suit would fit better and look nicer.

21.3 THE BLACK–SCHOLES FORMULA

Look back at Figure 21.1, which showed what happens to the distribution of possible Arvind Mills stock price changes as we divide the option's life into a larger and larger number of increasingly small subperiods. You can see that the distribution of price changes becomes increasingly smooth.

If we continued to chop up the option's life in this way, we would eventually reach the situation shown in Figure 21.4, where there is a continuum of possible stock price changes at maturity. Figure 21.4 is an example of a lognormal distribution. The lognormal distribution is often used to summarize the probability of different stock price changes.[9] It has a number of good commonsense features. For example, it recognizes the fact that the stock price can never fall by more than 100 percent, but that there is some, perhaps small, chance that it could rise by much more than 100 percent.

Subdividing the option life into indefinitely small slices does not affect the principle of option valuation. We could still replicate the call option by a levered investment in the stock, but we would need to adjust the degree of leverage continuously as time went by. Calculating option value when there is

[9]When we first looked at the distribution of stock price changes in Chapter 8, we assumed that these changes were normally distributed. We pointed out at the time that this is an acceptable approximation for very short intervals, but the distribution of changes over longer intervals is better approximated by the lognormal.

FIGURE 21.4

As the option's life is divided into more and more sub-periods, the distribution of possible stock price changes approaches a lognormal distribution.

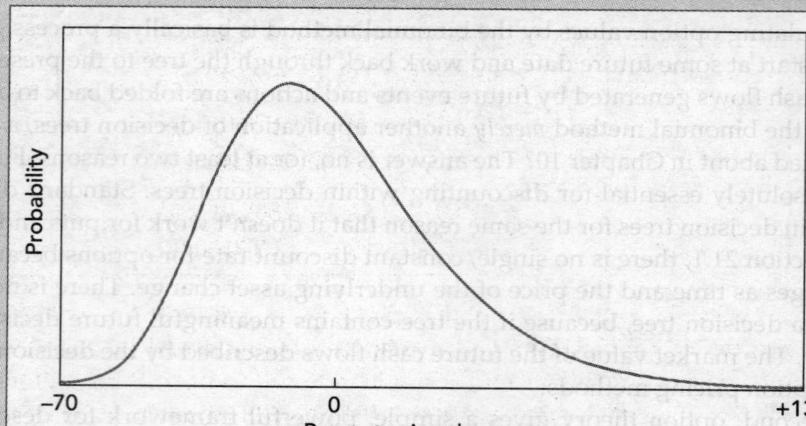

an infinite number of subperiods may sound a hopeless task. Fortunately, Black and Scholes derived a formula that does the trick.[10] It is an unpleasant-looking formula, but on closer acquaintance you will find it exceptionally elegant and useful. The formula is

$$\text{Value of call option} = [\text{delta} \times \text{share price}] - [\text{bank loan}]$$

$$\uparrow \qquad\qquad \uparrow \qquad\qquad \uparrow$$

$$[N(d_1) \times P] - [N(d_2) \times \text{PV(EX)}]$$

where

$$d_1 = \frac{\log[P / \text{PV(EX)}]}{\sigma\sqrt{t}} + \frac{\sigma\sqrt{t}}{2}$$

$$d_2 = d_1 - \sigma\sqrt{t}$$

$N(d)$ = cumulative normal probability density function[11]

EX = exercise price of option; PV(EX) is calculated by discounting at the risk-free interest rate r_f

t = number of periods to exercise date

P = price of stock now

σ = standard deviation per period of (continuously compounded) rate of return on stock

[10] The important assumptions of the Black–Scholes formula are that (a) the price of the underlying asset follows a lognormal random walk, (b) investors can adjust their hedge continuously and costlessly, (c) the risk-free rate is known, and (d) the underlying asset does not pay dividends.

[11] That is, $N(d)$ is the probability that a normally distributed random variable $\tilde{x}$ will be less than or equal to d. $N(d_1)$ in the Black–Scholes formula is the option delta. Thus the formula tells us that the value of a call is equal to an investment of $N(d_1)$ in the common stock less borrowing of $N(d_2) \times \text{PV(EX)}$.

Notice that the value of the call in the Black–Scholes formula has the same properties that we identified earlier. It increases with the level of the stock price P and decreases with the present value of the exercise price PV(EX), which in turn depends on the interest rate and time to maturity. It also increases with the time to maturity and the stock's variability $(\sigma\sqrt{t})$.

To derive their formula Black and Scholes assumed that there is a continuum of stock prices, and therefore to replicate an option investors must continuously adjust their holding in the stock. Of course this is not literally possible, but even so the formula performs remarkably well in the real world, where stocks trade only intermittently and prices jump from one level to another. The Black–Scholes model has also proved very flexible; it can be adapted to value options on a variety of assets with special features, such as foreign currency, bonds, and commodities. It is not surprising, therefore, that it has been extremely influential and has become the standard model for valuing options. Every day dealers on the options exchanges use this formula to make huge trades. These dealers are not for the most part trained in the formula's mathematical derivation; they just use a computer or a specially programmed calculator to find the value of the option.

Using the Black–Scholes Formula

The Black–Scholes formula may look difficult, but it is very straightforward to apply. Let us practice using it to value the Arvind Mills call.

Here are the data that you need:

- Price of stock now = P = Rs. 60
- Exercise price = EX = Rs. 60
- Standard deviation of continuously compounded annual returns = σ = 0.5755
- Years to maturity = t = 0.25
- Interest rate per annum = r_f = 4 percent (equivalent to 0.98534 percent for three months).[12]

Remember that the Black–Scholes formula for the value of a call is

$$[N(d_1) \times P] - [N(d_2) \times \text{PV(EX)}]$$

where

$$d_1 = \log[P / \text{PV(EX)}] / \sigma\sqrt{t} + \sigma\sqrt{t} / 2$$
$$d_2 = d_1 - \sigma\sqrt{t}$$

$$N(d) = \text{cumulative normal probability function}$$

[12]If the annually compounded rate of interest is 4 percent, the equivalent rate for three months is 0.98534 percent. This will give PV(EX) = $60/(1.04)^{0.25}$ = Rs. 59.41. (In our earlier binomial examples, we used a 1percent three-month rate.)

While valuing options, it is more common to use continuously compounded rates (see Section 3.3). If the annual rate is 4 percent, the equivalent continuously compounded rate is 3.922 percent. (The natural log of 1.04 is 0.03922, and $e^{0.03922} = 1.04$.) using continuous compounding, $60 \times e^{-0.25 \times 0.03922}$ = Rs. 59.41.

There is only one trick here: If you are using a spreadsheet or computer program that calls for a continuously compounded interest rate, make sure that you enter a continuously compounded rate. The error is you use the wrong rate will usually be small, but you can waste a lot of time trying to trace it.

There are three steps to using the formula to value the Arvind Mills call:

Step 1 Calculate d_1 and d_2. This is just a matter of plugging numbers into the formula (noting that "log" means *natural* log):

$$d_1 = \log[P / PV(EX)] / \sigma\sqrt{t} + \sigma\sqrt{t} / 2$$
$$= \log[59.41] / \left(0.5755 \times \sqrt{0.25}\right) + 0.5755 \times \sqrt{0.25} / 2$$
$$= .1783$$
$$d_2 = d_1 - \sigma\sqrt{t} = 0.1783 - 0.5755\sqrt{0.25} = -0.1093$$

Step 2 Find $N(d_1)$ and $N(d_2)$. $N(d_1)$ is the probability that a normally distributed variable will be less than d_1 standard deviations above the mean. If d_1 is large, $N(d_1)$ is close to 1.0 (i.e., you can be almost certain that the variable will be less than d_1 standard deviations above the mean). If d_1 is zero, $N(d_1)$ is .5 (i.e., there is a 50 percent chance that a normally distributed variable will be below the average).

The simplest way to find $N(d_1)$ is to use the Excel function NORMSDIST. For example, if you enter NORMSDIST(.1783) into an Excel spreadsheet, you will see that there is a .5708 probability that a normally distributed variable will be less than .1783 standard deviations above the mean. Alternatively, you can use a set of normal probability tables such as those in Appendix Table 6, in which case you need to interpolate between the cumulative probabilities for $d_1 = .17$ and $d_1 = .18$.

Again you can use the Excel function to find $N(d_2)$. If you enter NORMSDIST(−.1093) into an Excel spreadsheet, you should get the answer .4565. In other words, there is a probability of .4565 that a normally distributed variable will be less than .1093 standard deviations *below* the mean. Alternatively, if you use Appendix Table 6, you need to look up the value for +.1093 and subtract it from 1.0:

$$N(d_2) = N(-.1093) = 1 - N(+.1093)$$
$$= 1 - .5435 = .4565$$

Step 3 Plug these numbers into the Black–Scholes formula. You can now calculate the value of the Arvind Mills call:

$$[\text{Delta} \times \text{price}] - [\text{bank loan}]$$
$$= [N(d_1) \times P] - [N(d_2) \times PV(EX)]$$
$$= [0.5708 \times 60] - [0.4566 \times 60/(1.04)^{0.25}] = \text{Rs. } 7.13.$$

Some More Practice Suppose you repeated the calculations for the Arvind Mills call for a wide range of stock prices. The result is shown in Figure 21.5. You can see that the option values lie along an upward-sloping curve that starts its travels in the bottom left-hand corner of the diagram. As the stock price increases, the option value rises and gradually becomes parallel to the lower bound for the option value. This is exactly the shape we deduced in Chapter 20 (see Figure 20.10).

The height of this curve of course depends on risk and time to maturity. For example, if the risk of Arvind Mills stock had suddenly decreased, the curve shown in Figure 21.5 would drop at every possible stock price.

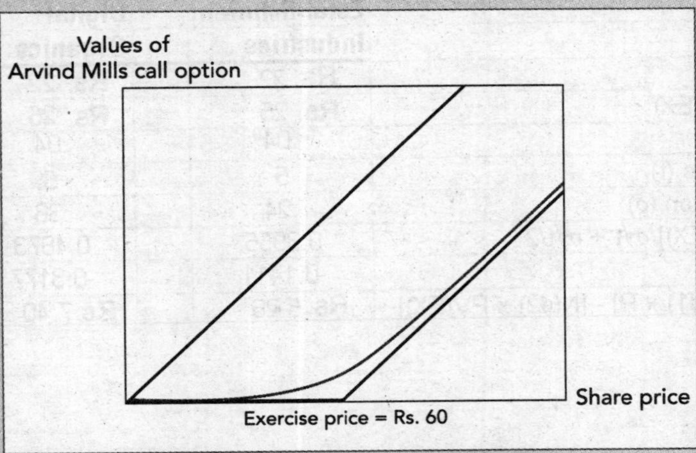

FIGURE 21.5

The curved line shows how the value of the Arvind Mills call option changes as the price of Arvind Mills stock changes.

The Black–Scholes Formula and the Binomial Method

Look back at Table 21.1 where we used the binomial method to calculate the value of the Arvind Mills call. Notice that, as the number of intervals is increased, the values that you obtain from the binomial method begin to snuggle up to the Black–Scholes value of Rs. 7.13.

The Black–Scholes formula recognizes a continuum of possible outcomes. This is usually more realistic than the limited number of outcomes assumed in the binomial method. The formula is also more accurate and quicker to use than the binomial method. So why use the binomial method at all? The answer is that there are many circumstances in which you cannot use the Black–Scholes formula but the binomial method will still give you a good measure of the option's value. We will look at several such cases in Section 21.5.

21.4 BLACK–SCHOLES IN ACTION

To illustrate the principles of option valuation, we focused on the example of Arvind Mills options. But financial managers turn to the Black–Scholes model to estimate the value of a variety of different options. Here are four examples.

Executive Stock Options

In 2000, companies in the Standard & Poor's 500-share index gave their key employees stock options worth a total of \$. 119 billion.[13] Although these options involve a cost just like salaries and wages, businesses have successfully argued that they should not be obliged to report this cost in their financial statements. Some companies have voluntarily reported the cost of their stock option programs. For example, in the year ending June 2003 the directors of Microsoft were granted 7-year options to buy 254 million shares with an average exercise price of \$ 24.27 a share. These options

[13]Option grants in 2000 were unusually high. See B. J. Hall and K. J. Murphy, "The Trouble with Stock Options," *Journal of Economic Perspectives* 17 (Summer 2003), pp. 49–70.

TABLE 21.2

Using the Black-Scholes formula to value the executive stock options for Establishment Industries and Digital Organics (see Table 20.3).

eXcel

Please visit us at www.mhhe.com/bmam8e or refer to your Student CD.

	Establishment Industries	Digital Organics
Stock price (P)	Rs. 22	Rs. 22
Exercise price (EX)	Rs. 25	Rs. 25
Interest rate (r_f)	.04	.04
Maturity in years (t)	5	5
Standard deviation (σ)	.24	.36
d1 = $\log[P/PV(EX)]/\sigma\sqrt{t} + \sigma\sqrt{t}/2$	0.3955	0.4873
d2 = d1 - $\sigma\sqrt{t}$	-0.1411	-0.3177
Call value = [N(d1) x P] - [N(d2) x PV(EX)]	Rs. 5.26	Rs. 7.40

were at-the-money; in other words, their exercise price was equal to the current stock price. The total value of these options was $3.07 billion, according to the company's financial statements. How did the company come up with this figure? It used the Black–Scholes model assuming a standard deviation of 42 percent and an interest rate of 3.9 percent.[14]

Speaking of executive stock options, we can now use the Black–Scholes formula to value the option packages you were offered in Section 20.3 (see Table 20.3). Table 21.2 calculates the value of the options from the safe-and-stodgy Establishment Industries at Rs. 5.26 each. The options from risky-and-glamorous Digital Organics are worth Rs. 7.40 each. Congratulations.[15]

Warrants

When Kindred Healthcare emerged from bankruptcy in 2001, its junior debtholders were paid off with a mixture of common stock and 5-year warrants. The Series A warrants gave holders the option to buy the common stock for $30 a share, and the Series B warrants gave holders an option to buy the stock for $33.33. You can be sure that, when the debtholders were asked to agree to this plan of reorganization, they calculated the value of the warrants under different assumptions about the volatility of Kindred Healthcare's stock. The Black–Scholes formula is tailor-made for such calculations.

Portfolio Insurance

Your company's pension fund owns an $800 million diversified portfolio of common stocks that moves closely in line with the market index. The pension plan is currently fully funded, but you are concerned that a 20 percent fall in prices could put it underwater. Suppose that your bank offers to

[14]Microsoft subsequently changed its compensation plan and no longer offers executive stock options.

[15]The Black–Scholes formula tells us the *cost* of your options to the company. If the options oblige you to hold a less diversified portfolio than you would wish, you might place a lower value on them. Note also that for this reason you may wish to exercise your options earlier than you otherwise would.

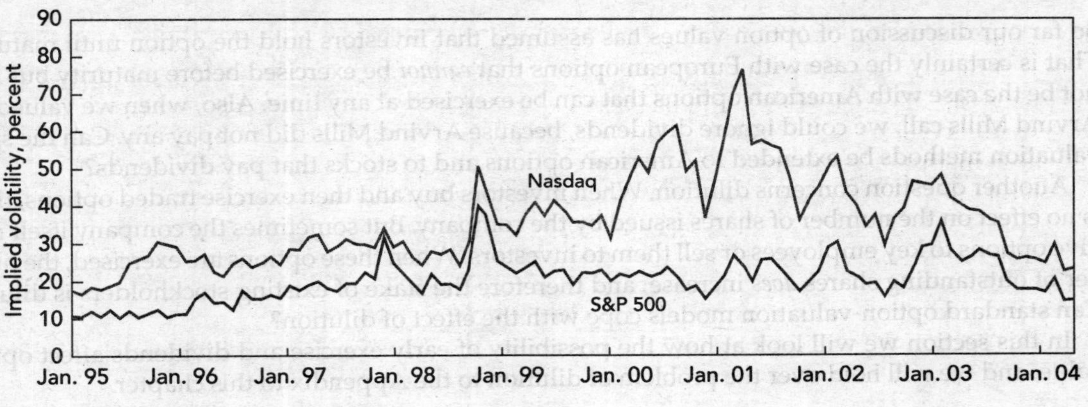

FIGURE 21.6

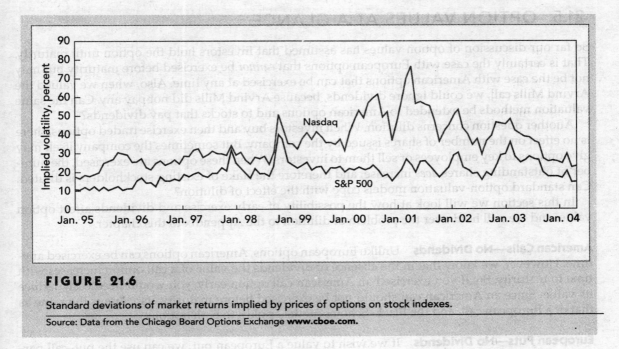

Standard deviations of market returns implied by prices of options on stock indexes.

Source: Data from the Chicago Board Options Exchange **www.cboe.com.**

insure you for one year against this possibility. What would you be prepared to pay for this insurance? Think back to Section 20.2 (Figure 20.6), where we showed that you can shield against a fall in asset prices by buying a protective put option. In the present case the bank would be selling you a one-year put option on U.S. stock prices with an exercise price 20 percent below their current level. The Black–Scholes formula tells you the value of that option.

Calculating Implied Volatilities

So far we have used our option pricing model to calculate the value of an option given the standard deviation of the asset's returns. Sometimes it is useful to turn the problem around and ask what the option price is telling us about the asset's variability. For example, the Chicago Board Options Exchange trades options on several market indexes. As we write this, the Standard and Poor's 500-share index is 1050, while a seven-month at-the-money call option on the index is priced at 55.50. If the Black–Scholes formula is correct, then an option value of 55.50 makes sense only if investors believe that the standard deviation of index returns is about 16 percent a year. You may be interested to compare this number with Figure 21.6, which shows the stock market volatility that was implied by the price of index options in earlier years. Notice the sharp increase in investor uncertainty about the value of Nasdaq stocks during the crash of the dot.com stocks in late 2000. This uncertainty showed up in the high price that investors were prepared to pay for options.

21.5 OPTION VALUES AT A GLANCE

So far our discussion of option values has assumed that investors hold the option until maturity. That is certainly the case with European options that *cannot* be exercised before maturity but may not be the case with American options that can be exercised at any time. Also, when we valued the Arvind Mills call, we could ignore dividends, because Arvind Mills did not pay any. Can the same valuation methods be extended to American options and to stocks that pay dividends?

Another question concerns dilution. When investors buy and then exercise traded options, there is no effect on the number of shares issued by the company. But sometimes the company itself may give options to key employees or sell them to investors. When these options are exercised, the number of outstanding shares *does* increase, and therefore the stake of existing stockholders is diluted. Can standard option-valuation models cope with the effect of dilution?

In this section we will look at how the possibility of early exercise and dividends affect option value, and we will hold over the problem of dilution to the Appendix to this chapter.

American Calls—No Dividends Unlike European options, American options can be exercised anytime. However, we know that in the absence of dividends the value of a call option increases with time to maturity. So, if you exercised an American call option early, you would needlessly reduce its value. Since an American call should not be exercised before maturity, its value is the same as that of a European call, and the Black–Scholes model applies to both options.

European Puts—No Dividends If we wish to value a European put, we can use the put–call parity formula from Chapter 20:

$$\text{Value of put} = \text{value of call} - \text{value of stock} + \text{PV(exercise price)}$$

American Puts—No Dividends It can sometimes pay to exercise an American put before maturity to reinvest the exercise price. For example, suppose that immediately after you buy an American put, the stock price falls to zero. In this case there is no advantage to holding onto the option since it *cannot* become more valuable. It is better to exercise the put and invest the exercise money. Thus an American put is always more valuable than a European put. In our extreme example, the difference is equal to the present value of the interest that you could earn on the exercise price. In all other cases the difference is less.

Because the Black–Scholes formula does not allow for early exercise, it cannot be used to value an American put exactly. But you can use the step-by-step binomial method as long as you check at each point whether the option is worth more dead than alive and then use the higher of the two values.

European Calls and Puts on Dividend-Paying Stocks Part of the share value comprises the present value of dividends. The option holder is not entitled to dividends. Therefore, when using the Black–Scholes model to value a European option on a dividend-paying stock, you should reduce the price of the stock by the present value of the dividends paid before the option's maturity.

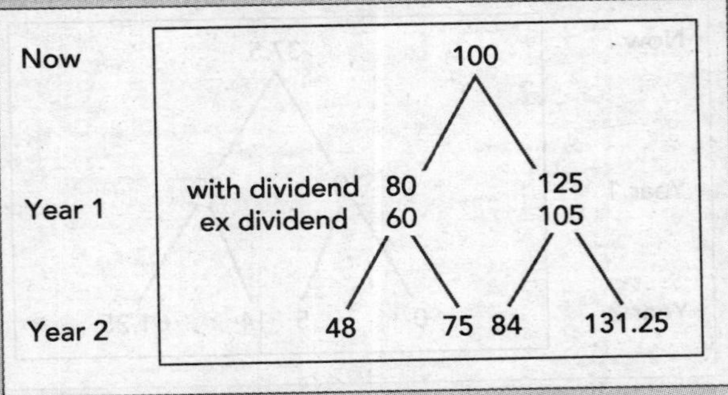

FIGURE 21.7

Possible values of Consolidated Pork Bellies stock.

Dividends don't always come with a big label attached, so look out for instances where the asset holder gets a benefit and the option holder does not. For example, when you buy foreign currency, you can invest it to earn interest; but if you own an option to buy foreign currency, you miss out on this income. Therefore, when valuing an option to buy foreign currency, you need to deduct the present value of this foreign interest from the current price of the currency.[16]

American Calls on Dividend-Paying Stocks We have seen that when the stock does not pay dividends, an American call option is *always* worth more alive than dead. By holding onto the option, you not only keep your option open but also earn interest on the exercise money. Even when there are dividends, you should never exercise early if the dividend you gain is less than the interest you lose by having to pay the exercise price early. However, if the dividend is sufficiently large, you might want to capture it by exercising the option just before the ex-dividend date.

The only general method for valuing an American call on a dividend-paying stock is to use the step-by-step binomial method. In this case you must check at each stage to see whether the option is more valuable if exercised just before the ex-dividend date than if held for at least one more period.

Example. Here is a last chance to practice your option valuation skills by valuing an American call on a dividend-paying stock. Figure 21.7 summarizes the possible price movements in Consolidated Pork Bellies stock. The stock price is currently Rs. 100, but over the next year it could either fall by 20 percent to Rs. 80 or rise by 25 percent to Rs. 125. In either case the company will then pay its regular dividend of Rs. 20. Immediately after payment of this dividend the stock price will fall to 80 − 20 = Rs. 60, or 125 − 20 = Rs. 105. Over the second year the price will again either fall by 20 percent from the ex-dividend price or rise by 25 percent.[17]

---

[16]For example, suppose that it currently costs \$2 to buy £1 and that this pound can be invested to earn interest of 5 percent. The option holder misses out on interest of .05 × \$2 = \$10. So, before using the Black–Scholes formula to value an option to buy sterling, you must adjust the current price of sterling:

$$\text{Adjusted price of sterling} = \text{current price} - \text{PV(interest)}$$
$$= \$2 - .10/1.05 = \$1.905.$$

[17]Notice that the payment of a fixed dividend in year 1 results in four possible stock prices at the end of year 2. In other words, 60 × 1.25 does not equal 105 × .8. Don't let that put you off. You still start from the end and work back one step at a time to find the possible option values at each date.

FIGURE 21.8

Values of a two-year call option on Consolidated Pork Bellies stock. Exercise price is Rs. 70. Although we show option values for year 2, the option will not be alive then. It will be exercised in year 1.

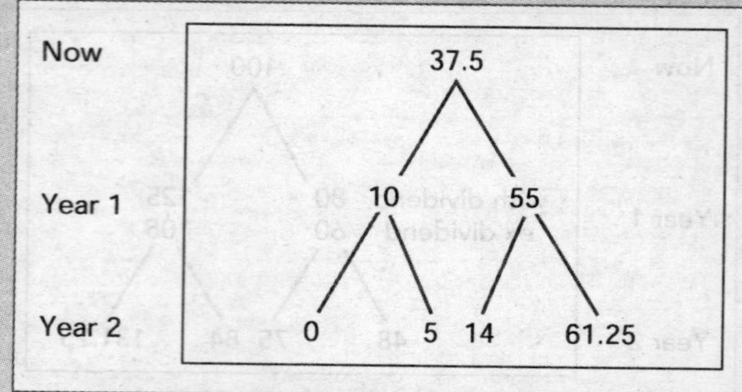

Suppose that you wish to value a two-year American call option on Consolidated stock. Figure 21.8 shows the possible option values at each point, assuming an exercise price of Rs. 70 and an interest rate of 12 percent. We won't go through all the calculations behind these figures, but we will focus on the option values at the end of year 1.

Suppose that the stock price has fallen in the first year. What is the option worth if you hold onto it for a further period? You should be used to this problem by now. First pretend that investors are risk-neutral and calculate the probability that the stock will rise in price. This probability turns out to be 71 percent.[18] Now calculate the expected payoff on the option and discount at 12 percent:

$$\text{Option value if not exercisedin year 1} = \frac{(.71 \times 5) + (.29 \times 0)}{1.12} = \text{Rs. } 3.18$$

Thus, if you hold onto the option, it is worth Rs. 3.18. However, if you exercise the option just before the ex-dividend date, you pay an exercise price of Rs. 70 for a stock worth Rs. 80. This Rs. 10 value from exercising is greater than the Rs. 3.18 from holding onto the option. Therefore in Figure 21.8 we put in an option value of Rs. 10 if the stock price falls in year 1.

You will also want to exercise if the stock price *rises* in year 1. The option is worth Rs. 42.45 if you hold onto it but Rs. 55 if you exercise. Therefore in Figure 21.8 we put in a value of Rs. 55 if the stock price rises.

The rest of the calculation is routine. Calculate the expected option payoff in year 1 and discount by 12 percent to give the option value today:

$$\text{Option value today} = \frac{(.71 \times 55) + (.29 \times 10)}{1.12} = \text{Rs. } 37.50$$

[18]Using the formula given in Section 21.1,

$$p = \frac{\text{interest rate} - \text{downside change}}{\text{upside change} - \text{downside change}} = \frac{12 - (-20)}{25 - (-20)} = .71$$

SUMMARY

In this chapter we introduced the basic principles of option valuation by considering a call option on a stock that could take on one of two possible values at the option's maturity. We showed that it is possible to construct a package of the stock and a loan that would provide exactly the same payoff as the option *regardless* of whether the stock price rises or falls. Therefore the value of the option must be the same as the value of this replicating portfolio.

We arrived at the same answer by pretending that investors are risk-neutral, so that the expected return on every asset is equal to the interest rate. We calculated the expected future value of the option in this imaginary risk-neutral world and then discounted this figure at the interest rate to find the option's present value.

The general binomial method adds realism by dividing the option's life into a number of subperiods in each of which the stock price can make one of two possible moves. Chopping the period into these shorter intervals doesn't alter the basic method for valuing a call option. We can still replicate the call by a package of the stock and a loan, but the package changes at each stage.

Finally, we introduced the Black–Scholes formula. This calculates the option's value when the stock price is constantly changing and takes on a continuum of possible future values.

When valuing options in practical situations there are a number of features to look out for. For example, you may need to recognize that the option value is reduced by the fact that the holder is not entitled to any dividends.

APPENDIX

How Dilution Affects Option Value

If you buy a call option on an options exchange and then exercise it, you have no effect on the number of outstanding shares. The investor who sold the call simply hands over to you his or her shares. However, sometimes the company itself may issue options to buy its own shares. For example, we saw in Section 21.4 that in 2003 Microsoft granted its directors options to buy 254 million shares of common stock.

Companies also issue convertible bonds, which give investors the option to exchange their bonds in the future for common stock. Therefore, a convertible bond resembles a package of a straight bond and an option to buy the stock. Alternatively, the company may sell a package of bonds and warrants. These warrants are long-term call options to buy the company's stock. Presumably the company hopes that the warrants will serve as a "sweetener," so that by including options in the package investors will be induced to pay a much higher price. If the holders of the convertible bonds or the warrants decide to exercise their option, the company must issue the additional shares to them.

Options that are issued by the company are somewhat trickier to value than exchange-traded options. When these options are exercised, the firm's assets and profits are spread over a larger number of shares. Sometimes this dilution is negligible and can safely be ignored. But, if the number of shares can increase substantially, you need to take it into account when valuing the options. To illustrate how you can do so, we will work through the example of United Glue's warrants.

TABLE 21A.1

United Glue's market value balance sheet (in Rs. millions).

Before the Issue			
Existing assets	Rs. 16	Rs. 4	Existing loans
		12	Common stock (1 million shares at Rs. 12 a share)
Total	Rs. 16	Rs. 16	Total
After the Issue			
Existing assets	Rs. 16	Rs. 4	Existing loans
New assets financed by debt and warrants	2	1.5	New loan without warrants
		5.5	Total debt
		.5	Warrants
		12	Common stock
		12.5	Total equity
Total	Rs. 18	Rs. 18.0	Total

Example: Valuing United Glue's Warrants

United Glue has just issued a Rs. 2 million package of debt and warrants. Here are some basic data that we can use to value the warrants:

Number of shares outstanding (*N*)	1 million
Current stock price (*P*)	Rs. 12
Number of warrants issued per share outstanding (*q*)	.10
Total number of warrants issued (*Nq*)	100,000
Exercise price of warrants (EX)	Rs. 10
Time to expiration of warrants (*t*)	4 years
Annual standard deviation of stock price changes (σ)	.40
Rate of interest (*r*)	10%
United stock pays no dividends	

Suppose that without the warrants the debt is worth Rs. 1.5 million. Then investors must be paying Rs. 5 million for the warrants:

$$\text{Cost of warrants} = \text{total amount of financing} - \text{value of loan without warrants}$$

$$\text{Rs. } 500{,}000 = \text{Rs. } 2{,}000{,}000 - \text{Rs. } 1{,}500{,}000$$

$$\text{Each warrantcosts investors} = \frac{500{,}000}{100{,}000} = \text{Rs. } 5$$

Table 21A.1 shows the market value of United's assets and liabilities both before and after the issue.

Now let us take a stab at checking whether the warrants are really worth the Rs. 500,000 that investors are paying for them. Since the warrant is a call option to buy the United stock, we can use the Black–Scholes formula to value the warrant. It turns out that a four-year call to buy United stock at Rs. 10 is worth Rs. 6.15.[19] Thus the warrant issue looks like a good deal for investors and a bad

[19] Plugging the data for United into the Black–Scholes formula gives

$$d_1 = \log[12 / (10 / 1.1^4)] / \left(.40 \times \sqrt{4}\right) + .40 \times \sqrt{4} / 2 = 1.104 \text{ and } d_2 = 1.104 - .40 \times \sqrt{4} = .304$$

Appendix Table 6 shows that $N(d_1) = .865$, and $N(d_2) = .620$. Therefore, estimated warrant value = $.865 \times 12 - .620 \times (10/1.1^4) = \text{Rs. } 6.15$.

deal for United. Investors are paying Rs. 5 a share for warrants that are worth Rs. 6.15.

How the Value of United Warrants Is Affected by Dilution

Unfortunately, our calculations for United warrants do not tell the whole story. Remember that when investors exercise a traded call or put option, there is no change in either the company's assets or the number of shares outstanding. But, if United's warrants are exercised, the number of shares outstanding will increase by $Nq = 100{,}000$. Also the assets will increase by the amount of the exercise money ($Nq \times \text{EX} = 100{,}000 \times$ Rs. 10 = Rs. 1 million). In other words, there will be dilution. We need to allow for this dilution when we value the warrants.

Let us call the value of United's equity V:

$$\text{Value of equity} = V = \text{value of United's total assets} - \text{value of debt}$$

If the warrants are exercised, equity value will increase by the amount of the exercise money to $V + Nq\text{EX}$. At the same time the number of shares will increase to $N + Nq$. So the share price after the warrants are exercised will be

$$\text{Share price after exercise} = \frac{V + Nq\text{EX}}{N + Nq}$$

At maturity the warrant holder can choose to let the warrants lapse or to exercise them and receive the share price less the exercise price. Thus the value of the warrants will be the share price minus the exercise price or zero, whichever is the higher. Another way to write this is

$$\begin{aligned}\text{Warrant value at maturity} &= \text{maximum (share price} - \text{exercise price, zero)} \\ &= \text{maximum}\left(\frac{V + Nq\text{EX}}{N + Nq} - \text{EX}, 0\right) \\ &= \text{maximum}\left(\frac{V/N - \text{EX}}{1+q}, 0\right) \\ &= \frac{1}{1+q}\text{maximum}\left(\frac{V}{N} - \text{EX}, 0\right)\end{aligned}$$

This tells us the effect of dilution on the value of United's warrants. The warrant value is the value of $1/(1 + q)$ call options written on the stock of an alternative firm with the same total equity value V, *but with no outstanding warrants*. The alternative firm's stock price would be equal to V/N—that is, the total value of United's equity (V) divided by the number of shares outstanding (N).[20] The stock price of this alternative firm is more variable than United's stock price. So when we value the call option on the alternative firm, we must remember to use the standard deviation of the changes in V/N.

[20]The modifications to allow for dilution when valuing warrants were originally proposed in F. Black and M. Scholes, "The Pricing of Options and Corporate Liabilities," *Journal of Political Economy* 81 (May–June 1973), pp. 637–654. Our exposition follows a discussion in D. Galai and M. I. Schneller, "Pricing of Warrants and the Valuation of the Firm," *Journal of Finance* 33 (December 1978), pp. 1333–1342.

Now we can recalculate the value of United's warrants allowing for dilution. First we find the stock price of the alternative firm:

$$\text{Current equity value of alternative firm} = V = \text{value of United's total assets} - \text{value of loans}$$
$$= 18 - 5.5 = \$12.5 \text{ millon}$$

$$\text{Current share price of alternative firm} = \frac{V}{N} = \frac{12.5 \text{ millon}}{1 \text{ millon}} = \$12.50$$

Also, suppose the standard deviation of the share price changes of this alternative firm is $\sigma^* = .41$.[21]

The Black–Scholes formula gives a value of \$6.64 for a call option on a stock with a price of \$12.50 and a standard deviation of .41. The value of United warrants is equal to the value of $1/(1 + q)$ call options on the stock of this alternative firm. Thus warrant value is

$$\frac{1}{1+q} \times \text{value of call on alternative firm} = \frac{1}{1.1} \times 6.64 = \$6.04$$

This is a somewhat lower value than the one we computed when we ignored dilution but still a bad deal for United.

It may sound from all this as if you need to know the value of United warrants to compute their value. This is not so. The formula does not call for warrant value but for V, the value of United's equity (that is, the shares *plus* warrants). Given equity value, the formula calculates how the overall value of equity should be split up between stock and warrants. Thus, suppose that United's underwriter advises that \$500,000 extra can be raised by issuing a package of bonds and warrants rather than bonds alone. Is this a fair price? You can check using the Black–Scholes formula with the adjustment for dilution.

Finally, notice that these modifications are necessary to apply the Black–Scholes formula to value a warrant. They are not needed by the warrant holder, who must decide whether to exercise at maturity. If at maturity the price of the stock exceeds the exercise price of the warrant, the warrant holder will of course exercise.

---

[21]How in practice could we compute σ^*? It would be easy if we could wait until the warrants had been trading for some time. In that case σ^* could be computed from the returns on a package of *all* the company's shares and warrants. In the present case we need to value the warrants *before* they start trading. We argue as follows: The standard deviation of the *assets* before the issue is equal to the standard deviation of a package of the common stock and the existing loans. For example, suppose that the company's debt is risk-free and that the standard deviation of stock returns *before* the bond-warrant issue is 38 percent. Then we calculate the standard deviation of the initial assets as follows:

$$\begin{array}{c}\text{Standard deviation}\\ \text{of initial assets}\end{array} = \begin{array}{c}\text{proportion in}\\ \text{common stock}\end{array} \times \begin{array}{c}\text{standard deviation}\\ \text{of common stock}\end{array}$$
$$= \frac{12}{16} \times 38 = 28.5\%$$

Now suppose that the assets after the issue are equally risky. Then

$$\begin{array}{c}\text{Standard deviation}\\ \text{of assets after issue}\end{array} = \begin{array}{c}\text{proportion of equity}\\ \text{after issue}\end{array} \times \begin{array}{c}\text{standard deviation}\\ \text{of equity}(\sigma^*)\end{array}$$
$$28.5 = \frac{12.5}{18} \times \text{standard deviation of equity}(\sigma^*)$$
$$\text{Standard deviation of equity}(\sigma^*) = 41\%$$

Notice that in our example the standard deviation of the stock returns *before* the warrant issue was slightly lower than the standard deviation of the package of stock and warrants. However, the warrant holders bear proportionately more of this risk than do the stockholders; so the bond-warrant package could either increase or reduce the risk of the stock.

FURTHER READING

The classic articles on option valuation are:

F. Black and M. Scholes: "The Pricing of Options and Corporate Liabilities," *Journal of Political Economy* 81 (May–June 1973), pp. 637–654.

R. C. Merton, "Theory of Rational Option Pricing," *Bell Journal of Economics and Management Science* 4 (Spring 1973), pp. 141–183.

Two readable articles about the Black–Scholes model are:

F. Black, "How We Came up with the Option Formula," *Journal of Portfolio Management* 15 (1989), pp. 4–8.

F. Black, "The Holes in Black–Scholes," *RISK* Magazine 1 (1988), pp. 27–29.

There are a number of good books on option valuation. They include:

J. Hull, *Options, Futures and Other Derivatives*, 5th ed. (Englewood Cliffs, NJ: Prentice-Hall, Inc., 2003).

R. Jarrow and S. Turnbull, *Derivative Securities*, 2nd ed. (Cincinnati, OH: South-Western 1999).

R. L. McDonald, *Derivatives Markets* (Reading, MA: Pearson Addison Wesley, 2002).

P. Wilmott, *Paul Wilmott on Quantitative Finance* (New York: John Wiley & Sons, 2000).

CONCEPT REVIEW QUESTIONS

1. Why won't discounted cash flow work for options? (page 567)
2. There are two equivalent ways to value an option. One is to create a replicating portfolio. What is the other? (pages 569–570)
3. Explain what is meant by an option's delta. (page 569)

For additional Concept Review Questions, please visit us at www.mhhe.com/bmam8e or refer to your Student CD.

QUIZ

1. The stock price of Heavy Metal (HM) changes only once a month: either it goes up by 20 percent or it falls by 16.7 percent. Its price now is Rs. 40. The interest rate is 12.7 percent per year, or about 1 percent per month.
   - **a.** What is the value of a one-month call option with an exercise price of Rs. 40?
   - **b.** What is the option delta?
   - **c.** Show how the payoffs of this call option can be replicated by buying HM's stock and borrowing.
   - **d.** What is the value of a two-month call option with an exercise price of Rs. 40?
   - **e.** What is the option delta of the two-month call over the first one-month period?
2. **a.** Can the delta of a call option be greater than 1.0? Explain.
   - **b.** Can it be less than zero?
   - **c.** How does the delta of a call change if the stock price rises?
   - **d.** How does it change if the risk of the stock increases?
3. Use either the replicating-portfolio approach or the risk-neutral method to value the three-month call and put options on Arvind Mills stock with an exercise price of Rs. 55 (see Table 20.1). Assume Arvind Mills stock price = Rs. 60 and the risk-free rate of return = 7 percent per annum.
4. Imagine that Arvind Mills' stock price will either increase by 25 percent or fall by 20 percent over the next three months (see Section 21.1). Recalculate the value of the call option (exercise price = Rs. 60) using (a) the replicating portfolio method and (b) the risk-neutral method. Explain intuitively why the option value falls from the value computed in Section 21.1.

5. Over the coming year Ragwort's stock price will halve to Rs. 50 from its current level of Rs. 100 or it will rise to Rs. 200. The one-year interest rate is 10 percent.
   a. What is the delta of a one-year call option on Ragwort stock with an exercise price of Rs. 100?
   b. Use the replicating-portfolio method to value this call.
   c. In a risk-neutral world what is the probability that Ragwort stock will rise in price?
   d. Use the risk-neutral method to check your valuation of the Ragwort option.
   e. If someone told you that in reality there is a 60 percent chance that Ragwort's stock price will rise to Rs. 200, would you change your view about the value of the option? Explain.
6. Use the Black–Scholes formula with Appendix A: Present Value Table 6 to value the following options:
   a. A call option written on a stock selling for Rs. 60 per share with a Rs. 60 exercise price. The stock's standard deviation is 6 percent per month. The option matures in three months. The risk-free interest rate is 1 percent per month.
   b. A put option written on the same stock at the same time, with the same exercise price and expiration date.

   Now for each of these options find the combination of stock and risk-free asset that would replicate the option.
7. "An option is always riskier than the stock it is written on." True or false? How does the risk of an option change when the stock price changes?
8. For which of the following options *might* it be rational to exercise before maturity? Explain briefly why or why not.
   a. American put on a non-dividend-paying stock.
   b. American call—the dividend payment is Rs. 5 per annum, the exercise price is Rs. 100 pesos, and the interest rate is 10 percent.
   c. American call—the interest rate is 10 percent, and the dividend payment is 5 percent of future stock price. *Hint:* The dividend depends on the stock price, which could either rise or fall.

PRACTICE QUESTIONS

1. Johnny Jones's high school derivatives homework asks for a binomial valuation of a 12-month call option on the common stock of the Overland Railroad. The stock is now selling for $45 per share and has a standard deviation of 24 percent. Johnny first constructs a binomial tree like Figure 21.2, in which stock price moves up or down every six months. Then he constructs a more realistic tree, assuming that the stock price moves up or down once every three months, or four times per year.
   a. Construct these two binomial trees.
   b. How would these trees change if Overland's standard deviation were 30 percent? *Hint:* Make sure to specify the right up and down percentage changes.
2. Suppose a stock price can go up by 15 percent or down by 13 percent over the next year. You own a one-year put on the stock. The interest rate is 10 percent, and the current stock price is Rs. 60.
   a. What exercise price leaves you indifferent between holding the put or exercising it now?
   b. How does this break-even exercise price change if the interest rate is increased?
3. The price of Rakha Mining stock is Rs. 100. During each of the next two six-month periods the price may either rise by 25 percent or fall by 20 percent (equivalent to a standard deviation of 31.5 percent a year). At month 6 the company will pay a dividend of Rs. 20. The interest rate is 10 percent per six-month period. What is the value of a one-year American call option with an exercise price of Rs. 80? Now recalculate the option value, assuming that the dividend is equal to 20 percent of the with-dividend stock price.

4. Buffelhead's stock price is Rs. 220 and could halve or double in each six-month period (equivalent to a standard deviation of 98 percent). A one-year call option on Buffelhead has an exercise price of Rs. 165. The interest rate is 21 percent a year.
   a. What is the value of the Buffelhead call?
   b. Now calculate the option delta for the second six months if (i) the stock price rises to Rs. 440 and (ii) the stock price falls to Rs. 110.
   c. How does the call option delta vary with the level of the stock price? Explain intuitively why.
   d. Suppose that in month 6 the Buffelhead stock price is Rs. 110. How at that point could you replicate an investment in the stock by a combination of call options and risk-free lending? Show that your strategy does indeed produce the same returns as those from an investment in the stock.
5. Suppose that you own an American put option on Buffelhead stock (see question 4) with an exercise price of Rs. 220.
   a. Would you ever want to exercise the put early?
   b. Calculate the value of the put.
   c. Now compare the value with that of an equivalent European put option.
6. Recalculate the value of the Buffelhead call option (see question 4), assuming that the option is American and that at the end of the first six months the company pays a dividend of Rs. 25. (Thus the price at the end of the year is either double or half the *ex*-dividend price in month 6.) How would your answer change if the option were European?
7. Suppose that you have an option which allows you to sell Buffelhead stock (see question 4) in month 6 for Rs. 165 *or* to buy it in month 12 for Rs. 165. What is the value of this unusual option?
8. The current price of the stock of Mont Tremblant Air is C$100. During each six-month period it will either rise by 11.1 percent or fall by 10 percent (equivalent to an annual standard deviation of 14.9 percent). The interest rate is 5 percent per six-month period.
   a. Calculate the value of a one-year European put option on Mont Tremblant's stock with an exercise price of C$102.
   b. Recalculate the value of the Mont Tremblant put option, assuming that it is an American option.
9. The current price of United Carbon (UC) stock is Rs. 200. The standard deviation is 22.3 percent a year, and the interest rate is 21 percent a year. A one-year call option on UC has an exercise price of Rs. 180.
   a. Use the Black–Scholes model to value the call option on UC. You may find it helpful to use the "live" spreadsheet in Table 21.2 on the book's CD or Web site **www.mhhe.com/bmam8e.**
   b. Use the formula given in Section 21.2 to calculate the up and down moves that you would use if you valued the UC option with the one-period binomial method. Now value the option by using that method.
   c. Recalculate the up and down moves and revalue the option by using the two-period binomial method.
   d. Use your answer to part (c) to calculate the option delta (i) today; (ii) next period if the stock price rises; and (iii) next period if the stock price falls. Show at each point how you would replicate a call option with a levered investment in the company's stock.
10. Suppose you construct an option hedge by buying a levered position in delta shares of stock and selling one call option. As the share price changes, the option delta changes, and you will need to adjust your hedge. You can minimize the cost of adjustments if changes in the stock price have only a small effect on the option delta. Construct an example to show whether the option delta is likely to vary more if you hedge with an in-the-money option, an at-the-money option, or an out-of-the-money option.
11. Other things equal, which of these American options are you most likely to want to exercise early?
    a. A put option on a stock with a large dividend or a call on the same stock.
    b. A put option on a stock that is selling below exercise price or a call on the same stock.
    c. A put option when the interest rate is high or the same put option when the interest rate is low.

    Illustrate your answer with examples.
12. Is it better to exercise a call option on the with-dividend date or on the ex-dividend date? How about a put option? Explain.

13. Look back at the companies listed in Table 7.3. Download the daily stock price data from the website of NSE (www.nseindia.com). For each company compute the monthly adjusted prices and save it in an Excel spreadsheet. Calculate each company's standard deviation from the monthly returns given on the spreadsheet. The Excel function is STDEV. Convert the standard deviations from monthly to annual units by multiplying by the square root of 12.
    a. Use the Black-Scholes formula to value 1,2, and 3 month call options on each stock. Assume the exercise price equals the current stock price, and use a current risk-free annual interest rate.
    b. For each stock, pick a traded option with an exercise price approximately equal to the current stock price. Use the Black–Scholes formula and your estimate of standard deviation to value the option. How close is your calculated value to the traded price of the option?
    c. Your answer to part (b) will not exactly match the traded price. Experiment with different values for standard deviation until your calculations match the traded options prices as closely as possible. What are these implied volatilites? What do the implied volatilities say about investors' forecasts of future volatility?
14. Here is a question about dilution. The Electric Bassoon Company has outstanding 2,000 shares with a total market value of Rs. 20,000 *plus* 1,000 warrants with a total market value of Rs. 5,000. Each warrant gives its holder the option to buy one share at Rs. 20.
    a. To value the warrants, you first need to value a call option on an alternative share. How might you calculate its standard deviation?
    b. Suppose that the value of a call option on this alternative share was Rs. 6. Calculate whether the Electric Bassoon warrants were undervalued or overvalued.
15. Look back at Section 21.4. Now use the "live" Black–Scholes program on this book's CD or at **www.mhhe.com/bmam8e** to
    a. Check the value of Microsoft's executive stock options.
    b. Estimate the value of Kindred Healthcare's Series A and Series B warrants, assuming an annual standard deviation of 60 percent and an (annually compounded) interest rate of 3.5 percent.

CHALLENGE QUESTIONS

1. Use the formula that relates the value of the call and the put (see Section 20.2) and the one-period binomial model to show that the option delta for a put option is equal to the option delta for a call option minus 1.
2. Show how the option delta changes as the stock price rises relative to the exercise price. Explain intuitively why this is the case. (What happens to the option delta if the exercise price of an option is zero? What happens if the exercise price becomes indefinitely large?)
3. Your company has just awarded you a generous stock option scheme. You suspect that the board will either decide to increase the dividend or announce a stock repurchase program. Which do you secretly hope they will decide? Explain. (You may find it helpful to refer back to Chapter 16.)
4. Some corporations have issued *perpetual* warrants. Warrants are call options issued by a firm, allowing the warrant holder to buy the firm's stock. We discuss warrants in Chapter 25. For now, just consider a perpetual call.
    a. What does the Black-Scholes formula predict for the value of an infinite-lived call option on a non-dividend-paying stock? Explain the value you obtain. (*Hint:* what happens to the present value of the exercise price of a long-maturity option?)
    b. Do you think this prediction is realistic? If not, explain carefully why. (*Hint:* for one of several reasons: if a company's stock price followed the exact time-series process assumed by Black and Scholes, could the company ever be bankrupt, with a stock price of zero?)

MINI-CASE
Bruce Honiball's Invention

It was another disappointing year for Bruce Honiball, the manager of retail services at the Gibb River Bank. Sure, the retail side of Gibb River was making money, but it didn't grow at all in 2003. Gibb River had plenty of loyal depositors, but few new ones. Bruce had to figure out some new product or financial service—something that would generate some excitement and attention.

Bruce had been musing on one idea for some time. How about making it easy *and safe* for Gibb River's customers to put money in the stock market? How about giving them the upside of investing in equities—at least *some* of the upside—but none of the downside?

Bruce could see the advertisements now:

> How would you like to invest in Australian stocks completely risk-free? You can with the new Gibb River Bank *Equity-Linked Deposit*. You share in the good years; we take care of the bad ones.
>
> Here's how it works. Deposit \$A100 with us for one year. At the end of that period you get back your \$A100 *plus* \$A5 for every 10 percent rise in the value of the Australian All Ordinaries stock index. But, if the market index falls during this period, the Bank will still refund your \$A100 deposit in full.
>
> There's no risk of loss. Gibbs River Bank is your safety net.

Bruce had floated the idea before and encountered immediate skepticism, even derision: "Heads they win, tails we lose—is that what you're proposing, Mr. Honiball?" Bruce had no ready answer. Could the bank really afford to make such an attractive offer? How should it invest the money that would come in from customers? The bank had no appetite for major new risks.

Year	Interest Rate	Market Return	End-Year Dividend Yield	Year	Interest Rate	Market Return	End-Year Dividend Yield
1984	11.0%	−2.3%	5.1%	1994	5.4%	−8.7%	4.1%
1985	15.0	44.1	4.6	1995	8.0	20.2	3.9
1986	17.1	52.2	3.9	1996	7.4	14.6	3.6
1987	14.1	−7.9	4.8	1997	5.5	12.2	3.6
1988	11.7	17.9	5.4	1998	5.0	11.6	3.8
1989	17.3	17.4	5.5	1999	4.9	19.3	3.5
1990	15.9	−17.5	6.0	2000	4.9	5.0	3.2
1991	11.1	34.2	3.8	2001	4.8	10.1	3.3
1992	6.8	−2.3	3.8	2002	4.8	−8.1	4.0
1993	5.3	45.4	3.2	2003	4.9	15.9	3.5

TABLE 21.3

Australian interest rates and equity returns, 1984- 2003.

Bruce has puzzled over these questions for the past two weeks but has been unable to come up with a satisfactory answer. He believes that the Australian equity market is currently fully valued, but he realizes that some of his colleagues are more bullish than he is about equity prices.

Fortunately, the bank had just recruited a smart new MBA graduate, Sheila Liu. Sheila was sure that she could find the answers to Bruce Honiball's questions. First she collected data on the Australian market to get a preliminary idea of whether equity-linked deposits could work. These data are shown in Table 21.3. She was just about to undertake some quick calculations when she received the following further memo from Bruce:

> Sheila, I've got another idea. A lot of our customers probably share my view that the market is overvalued. Why don't we also offer them a chance to make some money by offering a "bear market deposit"? If the market goes up, they would just get back their $A100 deposit. If it goes down, they get their $A100 back plus $5 for each 10 percent that the market falls. Can you figure out whether we could do something like this? Bruce.

QUESTIONS

1. What kinds of options is Bruce proposing? How much would the options be worth? Would the equity-linked and bear-market deposits generate positive NPV for Gibb River Bank?

CHAPTER [22]

REAL OPTIONS

WHEN YOU USE discounted cash flow (DCF) to value a project, you implicitly assume that your firm will hold the project passively. In other words, you are ignoring the *real options* attached to the project—options that sophisticated managers can take advantage of. You could say that DCF does not reflect the value of management. Managers who hold real options do not have to be passive; they can make decisions to capitalize on good fortune or to mitigate loss. The opportunity to make such decisions clearly adds value whenever project outcomes are uncertain.

Chapter 10 introduced the four main types of real options:

- The option to expand if the immediate investment project succeeds.
- The option to wait (and learn) before investing.
- The option to shrink or abandon a project.
- The option to vary the mix of output or the firm's production methods.

Chapter 10 gave several simple examples of real options. We also showed you how to use decision trees to set out possible future outcomes and decisions. But we did not show you how to value real options. That is our task in this chapter. We will apply the concepts and valuation principles you learned in Chapter 21.

For the most part we will work with simple numerical examples. The art and science of valuing real options are illustrated just as well with simple calculations as complex ones. But we will also describe several more complex examples, including:

- A strategic investment in the computer business.
- The valuation of an aircraft purchase option.
- The option to develop commercial real estate.
- The decision to operate or mothball an oil tanker.

These examples show how financial managers can value real options in real life.

22.1 THE VALUE OF FOLLOW-ON INVESTMENT OPPORTUNITIES

It is 1982. You are assistant to the chief financial officer (CFO) of Blitzen Computers, an established computer manufacturer casting a profit-hungry eye on the rapidly developing personal computer market. You are helping the CFO evaluate the proposed introduction of the Blitzen Mark I Micro.

The Mark I's forecasted cash flows and NPV are shown in Table 22.1. Unfortunately the Mark I can't meet Blitzen's customary 20 percent hurdle rate and has a Rs. 46 million negative NPV, contrary to top management's strong gut feeling that Blitzen ought to be in the personal computer market.

The CFO has called you in to discuss the project:

"The Mark I just can't make it on financial grounds," the CFO says. "But we've got to do it for strategic reasons. I'm recommending we go ahead."

"But you're missing the all-important financial advantage, Chief," you reply.

"Don't call me 'Chief.' What financial advantage?"

"If we don't launch the Mark I, it will probably be too expensive to enter the micro market later, when Apple, IBM, and others are firmly established. If we go ahead, we have the opportunity to make follow-on investments that could be extremely profitable. The Mark I gives not only its own cash flows but also a call option to go on with a Mark II micro. That call option is the real source of strategic value."

"So it's strategic value by another name. That doesn't tell me what the Mark II investment's worth. The Mark II could be a great investment or a lousy one—we haven't got a clue."

TABLE 22.1

Summary of cash flows and financial analysis of the Mark I microcomputer (Rs. millions).

	Year					
	1982	1983	1984	1985	1986	1987
After-tax operating cash flow (1)		+110	+159	+295	+185	0
Capital investment (2)	450	0	0	0	0	0
Increase in working capital (3)	0	50	100	100	−125	−125
Net cash flow (1) − (2) − (3)	−450	+60	+59	+195	+310	+125
NPV at 20% = −Rs. 46.45, or about − Rs. 46 million						

"That's exactly when a call option is worth the most," you point out perceptively. "The call lets us invest in the Mark II if it's great and walk away from it if it's lousy."

"So what's it worth?"

"Hard to say precisely, but I've done a back-of-the-envelope calculation, which suggests that the value of the option to invest in the Mark II could more than offset the Mark I's Rs. 46 million negative NPV. [The calculations are shown in Table 22.2.] If the option to invest is worth Rs. 55 million, the total value of the Mark I is its own NPV, −Rs. 46 million, plus the Rs. 55 million option attached to it, or +Rs. 9 million."

"You're just overestimating the Mark II," the CFO says gruffly. "It's easy to be optimistic when an investment is three years away."

"No, no," you reply patiently. "The Mark II is expected to be no more profitable than the Mark I—just twice as big and therefore twice as bad in terms of discounted cash flow. I'm forecasting it to have a negative NPV of about Rs. 100 million. But there's a chance the Mark II could be extremely valuable. The call option allows Blitzen to cash in on those upside outcomes. The chance to cash in could be worth Rs. 55 million.

"Of course, the Rs. 55 million is only a trial calculation, but it illustrates how valuable follow-on investment opportunities can be, especially when uncertainty is high and the product market is growing rapidly. Moreover, the Mark II will give us a call on the Mark III, the Mark III on the Mark IV, and so on. My calculations don't take subsequent calls into account."

"I think I'm beginning to understand a little bit of corporate strategy," mumbles the CFO.

Questions and Answers about Blitzen's Mark II

Question: I know how to use the Black–Scholes formula to value traded call options, but this case seems harder. What number do I use for the stock price? I don't see any traded shares.

Answer: With traded call options, you can see the value of the *underlying asset* that the call is written on. Here the option is to buy a nontraded real asset, the Mark II. We can't observe the Mark II's value; we have to compute it.

The Mark II's forecasted cash flows are set out in Table 22.3. The project involves an initial outlay of Rs. 900 million in 1985. The cash inflows start in the following year and have a present value of Rs. 807 million in 1985, equivalent to Rs. 467 million in 1982 as shown in Table 22.3. So the real option to invest in the Mark II amounts to a three-year call on an underlying asset worth Rs. 467 million, with a Rs. 900 million exercise price.

TABLE 22.2

Valuing the option to invest in the Mark II microcomputer.

Assumptions

1. The decision to invest in the Mark II must be made after 3 years, in 1985.
2. The Mark II investment is double the scale of the Mark I (note the expected rapid growth of the industry). Investment required is Rs. 900 million (the exercise price), which is taken as fixed.
3. Forecasted cash inflows of the Mark II are also double those of the Mark I, with present value of Rs. 807 million in 1985 and $807/(1.2)^3$ = Rs. 467 million in 1982.
4. The future value of the Mark II cash flows is highly uncertain. This value evolves as a stock price does with a standard deviation of 35 percent per year. (Many high-technology stocks have standard deviations higher than 35 percent.)
5. The annual interest rate is 10 percent.

Interpretation

The opportunity to invest in the Mark II is a three-year call option on an asset worth Rs. 467 million with a Rs. 900 million exercise price.

Valuation

$$\text{PV(exercise price)} = \frac{900}{(1.1)^3} = 676$$

$$\text{Call value} = [N(d_1) \times P] - [N(d_2) \times \text{PV(EX)}]$$

$$d_1 = \log[P/\text{PV(EX)}]/\sigma\sqrt{t} + \sigma\sqrt{t}/2$$

$$= \log[.691]/.606 + .606/2 = -.3072$$

$$d_2 = d_1 - \sigma\sqrt{t} = -.3072 - .606 = -.9134$$

$$N(d_1) = .3793, \; N(d_2) = .1805$$

$$\text{Call value} = [.3793 \times 467] - [.1805 \times 676] = \text{Rs. } 55.1 \text{ million}$$

Notice that real options analysis does *not* replace DCF. You typically need DCF to value the underlying asset.

Question: Table 22.2 uses a standard deviation of 35 percent per year. Where does that number come from?

Answer: We recommend you look for *comparables,* that is, traded stocks with business risks similar to the investment opportunity.[1] For the Mark II, the ideal comparables would be growth stocks in the personal computer business, or perhaps a broader sample of high-tech growth stocks. Use the average standard deviation of the comparable companies' returns as the benchmark for judging the risk of the investment opportunity.[2]

Question: Table 22.3 discounts the Mark II's cash flows at 20 percent. I understand the high discount rate, because the Mark II is risky. But why is the Rs. 900 million investment discounted at the risk-free interest rate of 10 percent? Table 22.3 shows the present value of the investment in 1982 of Rs. 676 million.

---

[1]You could also use scenario analysis, which we described in Chapter 10. Work out "best" and "worst" scenarios to establish a range of possible future values. Then find the annual standard deviation that would generate this range over the life of the option. For the Mark II, a range from Rs. 300 million to Rs. 2 billion would cover about 90 percent of the possible outcomes. This range, shown in Figure 22.1, is consistent with an annual standard deviation of 35 percent.

[2]Be sure to "unlever" the standard deviations, thereby eliminating volatility created by debt financing. Chapter 17 covered unlevering procedures for beta. The same principles apply for standard deviation: You want the standard deviation of a portfolio of all the debt and equity securities issued by the comparable firm.

		Year				
	1982	**1985**	**1986**	**1987**	**1988**	**1989**	**1990**
After-tax operating cash flow			+220	+318	+590	+370	0
Increase in working capital			100	200	200	−250	−250
Net cash flow			+120	+118	+390	+620	+250
Present value at 20%	+467 ←	+807					
Investment, PV at 10%	676 ← (PV in 1982)	900					
Forecasted NPV in 1985		−93					

TABLE 22.3

Cash flows of the Mark II microcomputer, as forecasted from 1982 (Rs. millions).

Answer: Black and Scholes assumed that the exercise price is a fixed, certain amount. We wanted to stick with their basic formula. If the exercise price is uncertain, you can switch to a slightly more complicated valuation formula.[3]

Question: Nevertheless, if I had to decide in 1982, once and for all, whether to invest in the Mark II, I wouldn't do it. Right?

Answer: Right. The NPV of a commitment to invest in the Mark II is negative:

$$\text{NPV(1982)} = \text{PV(cash inflows)} - \text{PV(investment)} = \text{Rs. } 467 - 676 = -\text{Rs. } 209 \text{ million}$$

The option to invest in the Mark II is "out of the money" because the Mark II's value is far less than the required investment. Nevertheless, the option is worth +Rs. 55 million. It is especially valuable because the Mark II is a risky project with lots of upside potential. Figure 22.1 shows the probability distribution of the possible present values of the Mark II in 1985. The expected (i.e., mean or average) outcome is our forecast of Rs. 807,[4] but the actual value could exceed Rs. 2 billion.

Question: Could it also be far below Rs. 807 million—Rs. 500 million or less?

Answer: The downside is irrelevant, because Blitzen won't invest unless the Mark II's actual value turns out higher than Rs. 900 million. The net option payoffs for all values less than Rs. 900 million are zero.

---

[3]If the required investment is uncertain, you have, in effect, an option to exchange one risky asset (the future value of the exercise price) for another (the future value of the Mark II's cash inflows). See W. Margrabe, "The Value of an Option to Exchange One Asset for Another," *Journal of Finance* 33 (March 1978), pp. 177–186.

[4]We have drawn the future values of the Mark II as a lognormal distribution, consistent with the assumptions of the Black–Scholes formula. Lognormal distributions are skewed to the right, so the average outcome is greater than the most likely outcome. (The most likely outcome is the highest point on the probability distribution.)

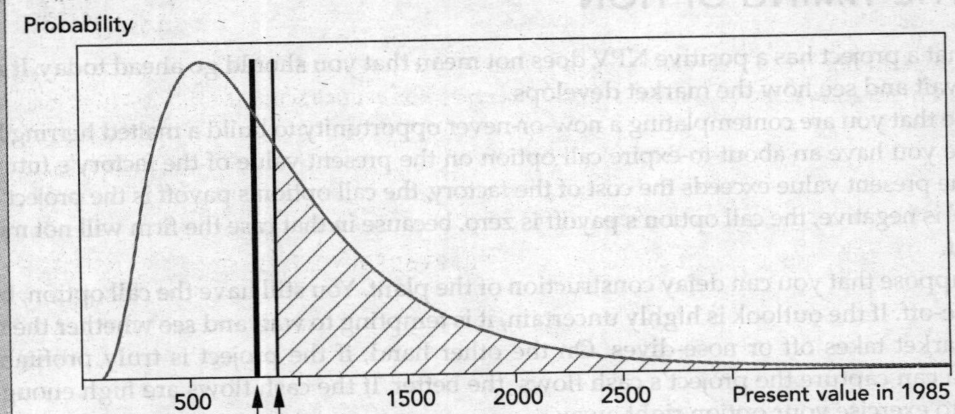

FIGURE 22.1

This distribution shows the range of possible present values for the Mark II project in 1985. The expected value is about Rs. 800 million, less than the required investment of Rs. 900 million. The option to invest pays off in the shaded area above Rs. 900 million.

In a DCF analysis, you discount the expected outcome (Rs. 807 million), which averages the downside against the upside, the bad outcomes against the good. The value of a call option depends only on the upside. You can see the danger of trying to value a future investment option with DCF.

Question: What's the decision rule?
Answer: Adjusted present value. The Mark I project costs Rs. 46 million (NPV = −Rs. 46 million), but accepting it creates the expansion option for the Mark II. The expansion option is worth Rs. 55 million, so:

$$\text{APV} = -46 + 55 = +\text{Rs. } 9 \text{ million}$$

Of course we haven't counted other follow-on opportunities. If the Mark I and Mark II are successes, there will be an option to invest in the Mark III, possibly the Mark IV, and so on.

Other Expansion Options

You can probably think of many other cases where companies spend money today to create opportunities to expand in the future. A mining company may acquire rights to an ore body that is not worth developing today but could be very profitable if product prices increase. A real estate developer may invest in worn-out farmland that could be turned into a shopping mall if a new highway is built. A pharmaceutical company may acquire a patent that gives the right but not the obligation to market a new drug. In each case the company is acquiring a real option to expand.

22.2 THE TIMING OPTION

The fact that a project has a positive NPV does not mean that you should go ahead today. It may be better to wait and see how the market develops.

Suppose that you are contemplating a now-or-never opportunity to build a malted herring factory. In this case you have an about-to-expire call option on the present value of the factory's future cash flows. If the present value exceeds the cost of the factory, the call option's payoff is the project's NPV. But if NPV is negative, the call option's payoff is zero, because in that case the firm will not make the investment.

Now suppose that you can delay construction of the plant. You still have the call option, but you face a trade-off. If the outlook is highly uncertain, it is tempting to wait and see whether the malted herring market takes off or nose-dives. On the other hand, if the project is truly profitable, the sooner you can capture the project's cash flows, the better. If the cash flows are high enough, you will want to exercise your option right away.

The cash flows from an investment project play the same role as dividend payments on a stock. When a stock pays no dividends, an American call is always worth more alive than dead and should never be exercised early. But payment of a dividend before the option matures reduces the ex-dividend price and the possible payoffs to the call option at maturity. Think of the extreme case: If a company pays out all its assets in one bumper dividend, the stock price must be zero and the call worthless. Therefore, any in-the-money call would be exercised just before this liquidating dividend.

Dividends do not always prompt early exercise, but if they are sufficiently large, call option holders capture them by exercising just before the ex-dividend date. We see managers acting in the same way: When a project's forecasted cash flows are sufficiently large, managers capture the cash flows by investing right away.[5] But when forecasted cash flows are small, managers are inclined to hold onto their call rather than to invest, even when project NPV is positive.[6] This explains why managers are sometimes reluctant to commit to positive-NPV projects. This caution is rational as long as the option to wait is open and sufficiently valuable.

Valuing the Malted Herring Option

Figure 22.2 shows the possible cash flows and end-of-year values for the malted herring project. If you commit and invest Rs. 180 million, you have a project worth Rs. 200 million. If demand turns out to be low in year 1, the cash flow is only Rs. 16 million and the value of the project falls to Rs. 160 million. But if demand is high in year 1, the cash flow is Rs. 25 million and value rises to Rs. 250 million. Although the project lasts indefinitely, we assume that investment cannot be

[5]In this case the call's value equals its lower-bound value because it is exercised immediately.

[6]We have been a bit vague about forecasted project cash flows. If competitors can enter and take away cash that you could have earned, the meaning is clear. But what about the decision to, say, develop an oil well? Here delay doesn't waste barrels of oil in the ground; it simply postpones production and the associated cash flow. The cost of waiting is the decline in today's *present value* of revenues from production. Present value declines if the future rate of increase in oil prices is not sufficiently high, that is, if the discounted price of oil is less than the current price.

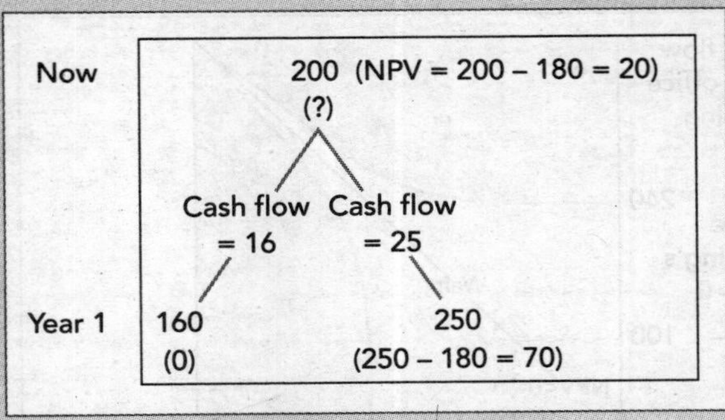

FIGURE 22.2

Possible cash flows and end-of-period values for the malted herring project are shown in blue. The project costs Rs. 180 million, either now or later. The green figures in parentheses show payoffs from the option to wait and to invest later if the project is positive-NPV at year 1. Waiting means loss of the first year's cash flows. The problem is to figure out the current value of the option.

postponed beyond the end of the first year, and therefore we show only the cash flows for the first year and the possible values at the end of the year. Notice that if you undertake the investment right away, you capture the first year's cash flow (Rs. 16 million or Rs. 25 million); if you delay, you miss out on this cash flow, but you will have more information on how the project is likely to work out.

We can use the binomial method to value this option. The first step is to pretend that investors are risk neutral and to calculate the probabilities of high and low demand in this risk-neutral world. If demand is high in the first year, the malted herring plant has a cash flow of Rs. 25 million and a year-end value of Rs. 250 million. The total return is (25 + 250)/200 − 1 = .375, or 37.5 percent. If demand is low, the plant has a cash flow of Rs. 16 million and a year-end value of Rs. 160 million. Total return is (16 + 160)/200 − 1 = −.12, or −12 percent. In a *risk-neutral* world, the expected return would be equal to the interest rate, which we assume is 5 percent:

$$\text{Expected return} = \left(\begin{array}{c}\text{Probability of}\\ \text{high demand}\end{array}\right) \times 37.5 + \left(\begin{array}{c}1 - \text{probability of}\\ \text{high demand}\end{array}\right) \times (-12) = 5\%$$

Therefore the (pretend) probability of high demand is 34.3 percent.

We want to value a call option on the malted herring project with an exercise price of Rs. 180 million. We begin as usual at the end and work backward. The bottom row of Figure 22.2 shows the possible values of this option at the end of the year. If project value is Rs. 160 million, the option to invest is worthless. At the other extreme, if project value is Rs. 250 million, option value is 250 − 180 = Rs. 70 million.

To calculate the value of the option today, we work out the expected payoffs in a risk-neutral world and discount at the interest rate of 5 percent. Thus, the value of your option to invest in the malted herring plant is

$$\frac{(.343 \times 70) + (.657 \times 0)}{1.05} = \text{Rs. 22.9 million}$$

But here is where we need to recognize the opportunity to exercise the option immediately. The option is worth Rs. 22.9 million if you keep it open, and it is worth the project's immediate NPV (200 − 180 = Rs. 20 million) if exercised now. Thus the fact that the malted herring project has a positive NPV is not sufficient reason for investing. There is a still better strategy: Wait and see.

FIGURE 22.3

Development option for vacant land, assuming two mutually exclusive uses, either hotel or office building. The developer should "wait and see" unless the hotel's and office building's cash flows end up in one of the shaded areas.

Source: Adapted from Figure 1 in P. D. Childs, T. J. Riddiough, and A. J. Triantis, "Mixed Uses and the Redevelopment Option," *Real Estate Economics* 24 (Fall 1996), pp. 317–339.

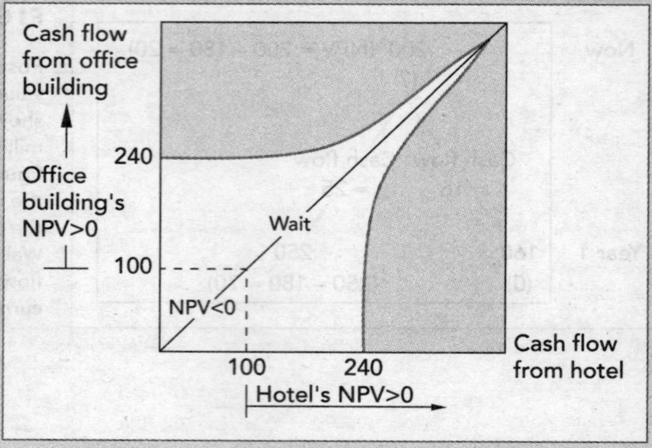

Optimal Timing for Real Estate Development

Sometimes it pays to wait for a long time, even for projects with large positive NPVs. Suppose you own a plot of vacant land in the suburbs.[7] The land can be used for a hotel or an office building, but not for both. A hotel could be later converted to an office building, or an office building to a hotel, but only at significant cost. You are therefore reluctant to invest, even if both investments have positive NPVs.

In this case you have two options to invest, but only one can be exercised. You therefore learn two things by waiting. First, you learn about the general *level* of cash flows from development, for example, by observing changes in the value of developed properties near your land. Second, you can update your estimates of the *relative* size of the hotel's future cash flows versus the office building's.

Figure 22.3 shows the conditions in which you would finally commit to build either the hotel or the office building. The horizontal axis shows the current cash flows that a hotel would generate. The vertical axis shows current cash flows for an office building. For simplicity, we will assume that each investment would have an NPV of exactly zero at a current cash flow of 100. Thus, if you were forced to invest today, you would choose the building with the higher cash flow, assuming the cash flow is greater than 100. (What if you were forced to decide today and each building could generate the same cash flow, say, 150? You would flip a coin.)

If the two buildings' cash flows plot in the colored area at the lower right of Figure 22.3, you build the hotel. To fall in this area, the hotel's cash flows have to beat two hurdles. First, they must exceed a minimum level of about 240. Second, they must exceed the office building's cash flows by a sufficient amount. If the situation is reversed, with office building cash flows above the minimum level of 240, and also sufficiently above the hotel's, then you build the office building. In this case, the cash flows plot in the colored area at the top left of the figure.

Notice how the "Wait and see" region extends upward along the 45-degree line in Figure 22.3. When the cash flows from the hotel and office building are nearly the same, you become *very* cautious before choosing one over the other.

[7] The following example is based on P. D. Childs, T. J. Riddiough, and A. J. Triantis, "Mixed Uses and the Redevelopment Option," *Real Estate Economics* 24 (Fall 1996), pp. 317–339.

You may be surprised at how high cash flows have to be in Figure 22.3 to justify investment. There are three reasons. First, building the office building means not building the hotel, and vice versa. Second, the calculations underlying Figure 22.3 assumed cash flows that were small, but growing; therefore, the costs of waiting to invest were small. Third, the calculations did not consider the threat that someone might build a competing hotel or office building right next door. In that case the "relax and wait" area of Figure 22.3 would shrink dramatically.

22.3 THE ABANDONMENT OPTION

Expansion value is important. When investments turn out well, the quicker and easier the business can be expanded, the better. But suppose bad news arrives, and cash flows are far below expectations. In that case it is useful to have the option to bail out and recover the value of the project's plant, equipment, or other assets. The option to abandon is equivalent to a put option. You exercise that abandonment option if the value recovered from the project's assets is greater than the present value of continuing the project for at least one more period.

The binomial method is tailor-made for most abandonment options. Here is an example.

The Zircon Subductor Project

Dawn East, the chief financial officer of Maine Subductor Corp., has to decide whether to start production of zircon subductors. The investment required is $12 million— $2 million for roads and site preparation and $10 million for equipment. The equipment costs $700,000 per year ($.7 million) to operate (a fixed cost). For simplicity, we will ignore other costs and taxes.

At today's prices, the project would generate revenues of $2.5 million per year. Annual output will be constant, so revenue is proportional to price. If the mine were operating today, cash flow would be $2.5 − .7 = $1.8 million.

Calculate the Present Value of the Project The first step in a real options analysis is to value the underlying asset, that is, the project if it had no options attached. Usually this is done by discounted cash flow (DCF). In this case the chief source of uncertainty is the future selling price of zircon subductors. Therefore Ms. East starts by calculating the present value of future revenues. She perceives no upward trend in subductor prices, and ends up forecasting stable prices for the next 10 years. Fixed costs are constant at $.7 million. The top panel of Figure 22.4 shows these cash-flow forecasts and calculates present values: about $16 million for revenues, after discounting at a risk-adjusted rate of 9 percent, and $5.15 million for fixed costs, after discounting at a risk-free rate of 6 percent.[8] The NPV of the project, assuming no salvage value or abandonment over its 10-year life, is

$$\begin{aligned}\text{NPV} &= \text{PV(revenues)} - \text{PV(fixed costs)} - \text{investment required}\\ &= \$16.044 - 5.152 - 12.00 = -\$1.108 \text{ million}\end{aligned}$$

This NPV is slightly negative, but Ms. East has so far made no provision for abandonment.

[8]Why calculate present values for revenues and fixed costs separately? Because it's easier to construct a binomial tree for revenues, which can be assumed to follow a random walk with constant standard deviation. We will subtract fixed costs after the binomial tree is constructed.

FIGURE 22.4

Binomial tree for the Subductor project. Cash flow (top number) and end-of-period present value are shown for each node in millions of dollars. Abandonment occurs if cash flows drop into the shaded boxes. Beginning present value is about \$14.7 million.

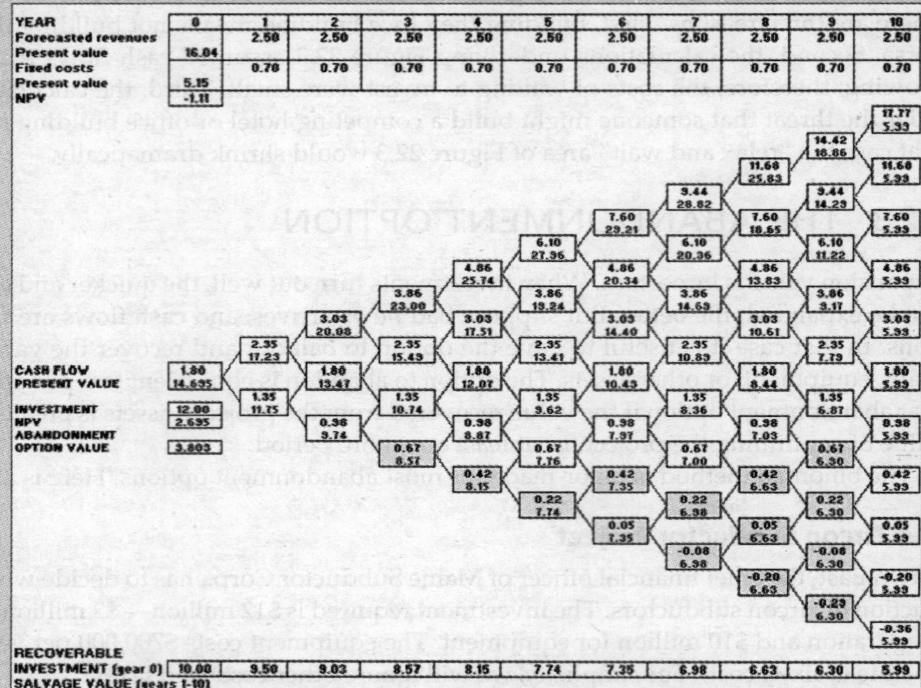

eXcel

Please visit us at www.mhhe.com/bmam8e or refer to your Student CD.

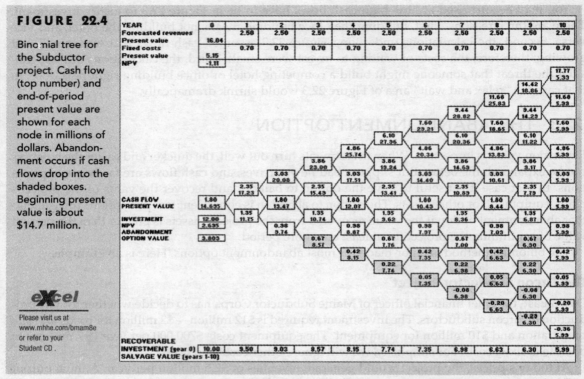

Build a Binomial Tree Now Ms. East constructs a binomial tree for revenues and PV(revenues). She notes that subductor prices have followed a random walk with an annual standard deviation of about 20 percent. She constructs a binomial tree with one step per year. The "up" values for revenues are 122 percent of the prior year's revenues. The "down" values are 82 percent of prior revenues.[9] Thus, the up and down revenues for year 1 are \$2.5 × 1.22 = \$3.05 and \$2.5 × .82 = \$2.05 million, respectively. After deduction of fixed costs, the up and down cash flows are \$2.35 and \$1.35 million, respectively. The first two years of the resulting tree are shown below (figures in millions of dollars).

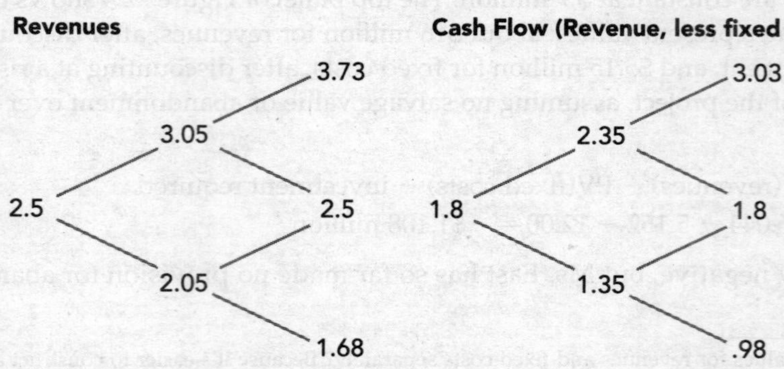

[9]The formula (given in Section 21.2) for the up percentage is $u = e^{\sigma\sqrt{h}}$ where σ is the standard deviation per year and h is the interval as a fraction of a year. In this case, $h = 1$ and $e^{\sigma} = e^{.2} = 1.22$. The down value is $d = 1/u = .82$.

Figure 22.4 shows the whole tree, starting with cash flows in year 1. (Maine Subductor can't generate any revenues in year 0 because it hasn't started production yet.) The top number at each node is cash flow. The bottom number is the *end*-of-year present value of *all* subsequent cash flows, including the value of the production equipment when the project ends or is abandoned. We will see in a moment how these present values are calculated.

Finally, Ms. East calculates the risk-neutral probabilities of up and down changes in revenues, p and $1 - p$, respectively. Here she must pause to make sure that each year's revenue is valued properly. Remember that we have discounted revenues at a risk-adjusted rate of 9 percent. Thus the present value of year 1 revenues is not \$2.5 million, but only

$$\text{PV} = \frac{2.5}{1.09} = \$2.29 \text{ million}$$

Therefore, Ms. East needs to calculate the risk-neutral probabilities that generate an expected return equal to the 6 percent risk-fee rate.[10]

$$\text{Expected return} = \frac{3.05p + 2.05(1-p)}{2.29} = .06$$

$$\text{Probability of up change} = .382$$

$$\text{Probability of down change} = .618$$

Ms. East can use these probabilities at every node of the binomial tree, because the proportional up and down moves are the same at each node.

Solve for Optimal Abandonment and Project Value Ms. East has assumed a project life of 10 years. At that time the production equipment, which normally depreciates by about 5 percent per year, should be worth \$5.99 million. This salvage value represents what the equipment could be sold for, or its value to Maine Subrductor if shifted to another use. Forecasted salvage values are shown year-by-year at the bottom of Figure 22.4.

Now let's calculate this project's value in the binomial tree. We start at the far right of Figure 22.4 (year 10) and work back to the present. The company will abandon for sure in year 10, when the ore body is exhausted. Thus we enter the ending salvage value (\$5.99 million) as the end-of-year value in year 10. Then we step back to year 9.

Suppose that Maine Subductor ends up in the best possible place in that year, where cash flow is \$14.42 million. The upside payoff if the company does not abandon is the "up" node in year 10: 17.77 + 5.99 = \$23.76 million. The downside payoff is 11.68 + 5.99 = \$17.67 million. The present value, using the risk-neutral probabilities, is

$$\text{PV} = \frac{(.382 \times 23.76) + (.618 \times 17.67)}{1.06} = \$18.86 \text{ million}$$

The company could abandon at the end of year 9, realizing salvage value of \$6.30 million, but continuing is better. We therefore enter \$18.86 million as the end-of-year value at the top node for year 9 in Figure 22.4.

---

[10]Notice that the "up" revenues are 122 percent of today's revenue level, but 133 percent of the present value of next year's forecasted revenues. Thus the "up" probability required to generate a 6 percent average return is relatively small.

We can fill in the end-of-period values for the other nodes in year 9 by the same procedure. But at some point, as we step down to lower and lower cash flows, there will come a node where it's better to bail out than continue. This occurs when cash flow is \$.67 million. The present value of continuing is only

$$PV = \frac{.382 \times (.98 + 5.99) + .618 \times (.42 + 5.99)}{1.06} = \$6.25 \text{ million}$$

The payoff to abandonment is \$6.30 million, so that payoff is entered as the value in year 9 at all nodes with cash flows equal to or less than \$.67 million.

The cash flows and end-of-year values for year 9 are the payoffs to continuing from year 8. We then calculate values in year 8, checking at each node whether to abandon, for year 7, and so on back to year 0. In this example, Maine Subductor should abandon the project if cash flows drop to \$.67 million in year 3, \$.42 million in year 4, \$.22 million in year 5, or \$.42 million or less in years 6 to 8. We have colored the nodes in Figure 22.4 where abandonment occurs.

Solving back through the binomial tree, we get a present value of \$14.965 million at year 0, and net present value of \$14.695 − 12.0 = \$2.695 million.[11] The DCF valuation at the top right of Figure 22.4 is − \$1.108 million.[12] Therefore the option to abandon is worth \$2.695 + 1.108 = \$3.803 million.[13] In an APV format,

$$\text{APV} = \text{NPV with no abandonment} + \text{abandonment option value}$$
$$= -1.108 + 3.803 = +\$2.695 \text{ million}$$

The project looks good, although Ms. East may wish to check out the timing option. She could decide to wait.

Abandonment Value and Project Life

Ms. East assumed that the zircon subductor project had a definite 10-year life. But most projects' economic lives are not known at the start. Cash flows from a new product may last only a year or so if the product fails in the marketplace. But if it succeeds, that product, or variations or improvements of it, could be produced for decades.

A project's economic life can be just as hard to predict as the project's cash flows. Yet in standard DCF capital-budgeting analysis, that life is assumed to end at a fixed future date. Real options analysis allows us to relax that assumption. Here is the procedure.[14]

1. Forecast the range of possible cash flows well beyond your best guess of the project's economic life. Suppose, for example, that your guess is 10 years. You could prepare a binomial tree like Figure 22.4 stretching out 25 years into the future.

---

[11] We will spare you the calculations. You can check them, however. The "live" spreadsheet for Figure 22.4 is on this book's CD and Web site **(www.mhhe.com/bmam8e)**.

[12] You could also revalue the binomial tree with all salvage values set to zero. The present value in year 0 then falls to \$10.902 million, implying NPV = \$10.902 − 12.00 = −\$1.098 million. You can do this calculation in the spreadsheet program on the CD and Web site. Just set "Salvage $t = 0$" equal to zero.

[13] It turns out, however, that the value of *early* abandonment in this example is relatively small. Suppose that Maine Subductor could recover salvage value of \$5.99 million in year 10, but not before. The present value of this recovery in year 0, using a 6 percent discount rate, is \$3.34 million. APV in this case is −1.108 + 3.34 = \$2.23 million, only slightly less than the APV of \$2.695 million with early abandonment allowed.

[14] See S. C. Myers and S. Majd, "Abandonment Value and Project Life," in F. J. Fabozzi (ed.), *Advances in Futures and Options Research*, (Greenwich, CT: JAI Press, 1990).

2. Then value the project, including its abandonment value. In the best upside scenarios, project life will be 25 years—it will never make sense to abandon before year 25. In the worst downside scenarios, project life will be much shorter, because the project will be more valuable dead than alive. If your original guess about project life is right, then in intermediate scenarios, where actual cash flows match expectations, abandonment will occur around year 10.

This procedure links project life to the performance of the project. It does not impose an arbitrary ending date, except in the far distant future.

Temporary Abandonment

Companies are often faced with complex options that allow them to abandon a project *temporarily*, that is, to mothball it until conditions improve. Suppose you own an oil tanker operating in the short-term spot market. (In other words, you charter the tanker voyage by voyage, at whatever short-term charter rates prevail at the start of the voyage.) The tanker costs $5 million a year to operate and at current tanker rates it produces charter revenues of $5.25 million per year. The tanker is therefore profitable but scarcely cause for celebration. Now tanker rates dip by about 10 percent, forcing revenues down to $4.7 million. Do you immediately lay off the crew and mothball the tanker until prices recover? The answer is clearly yes if the tanker business can be turned on and off like a faucet. But that is unrealistic. There is a fixed cost to mothballing the tanker. You don't want to incur this cost only to regret your decision next month if rates rebound to their earlier level. The higher the costs of mothballing and the more variable the level of charter rates, the greater the loss that you will be prepared to bear before you call it quits and lay up the boat.

Suppose that eventually you do decide to take the boat off the market. You lay up the tanker temporarily.[15] Two years later your faith is rewarded; charter rates rise, and the revenues from operating the tanker creep above the operating cost of $5 million. Do you reactivate immediately? Not if there are costs to doing so. It makes more sense to wait until the project is well in the black and you can be fairly confident that you will not regret the cost of bringing the tanker back into operation.

These choices are illustrated in Figure 22.5. The green line shows how the value of an operating tanker varies with the level of charter rates. The blue line shows the value of the tanker when mothballed.[16] The level of rates at which it pays to mothball is given by M and the level at which it pays to reactivate is given by R. The higher the costs of mothballing and reactivating and the greater the variability in tanker rates, the further apart these points will be. You can see that it will pay for you to mothball as soon as the value of a mothballed tanker reaches the value of an operating tanker plus the costs of mothballing. It will pay to reactivate as soon as the value of a

[15]We assume it makes sense to keep the tanker in mothballs. If rates fall sufficiently, it will pay to scrap the tanker.

[16]Dixit and Pindyck estimate these thresholds for a medium-sized tanker and show how they depend on costs and the volatility of freight rates. See A. K. Dixit and R. S. Pindyck, *Investment under Uncertainty* (Princeton, NJ: Princeton University Press, 1994), Chapter 7. Brennan and Schwartz provide an analysis of a mining investment that also includes an option to shut down temporarily. See M. Brennan and E. Schwartz, "Evaluating Natural Resource Investments," *Journal of Business* 58 (April 1985), pp. 135–157.

FIGURE 22.5

An oil tanker should be mothballed when tanker rates fall to M, where the tanker's value if mothballed is enough above its value in operation to cover mothballing costs. The tanker is reactivated when rates recover to R.

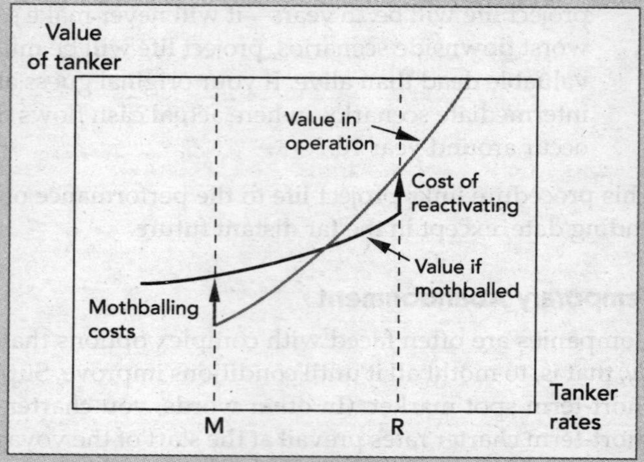

tanker that is operating in the spot market reaches the value of a mothballed tanker plus the costs of reactivating. If the level of rates falls below M, the value of the tanker is given by the blue line; if the level is greater than R, value is given by the green line. If rates lie between M and R, the tanker's value depends on whether it happens to be mothballed or operating.

22.4 FLEXIBLE PRODUCTION—AND ANOTHER LOOK AT AIRCRAFT PURCHASE OPTIONS

Companies often have an option to vary either the inputs in the production process or the outputs. For example, an electric utility plant may be designed to operate on either oil or natural gas. Or a manufacturer may invest in computer-integrated manufacturing (CIM) systems that allow it to vary the production mix.

In such cases the firm has the option to acquire one asset in exchange for another. Consider the electric utility's decision to build an oil-fired generating plant that can be converted to run on natural gas. You can think of the utility as having an option to "buy" a gas-fired plant in exchange for the oil-fired plant. If oil prices were certain, this would be a simple call option on a gas-fired plant with a fixed exercise price (the value of an oil-fired plant plus the cost of conversion). If the price of gas is sufficiently low, it pays to exercise the option and switch to gas.

In practice both oil and gas prices are likely to vary. This means that the exercise price of the utility's call option changes as the price of oil changes. Uncertainty about this exercise price could reduce or enhance the value of the option, depending on the correlation between the prices of the two fuels. If oil prices and gas prices moved together dollar for dollar, your option to switch fuels would be valueless. The benefit of a rise in the value of the underlying asset (the gas-fired plant) would be

FINANCE IN THE NEWS

VALUING FLEXIBILITY

With the help of faculty from Stanford University, Hewlett-Packard has experimented with real options since the beginning of the 1990s. Example: In the '80s, HP customized inkjet printers for foreign markets at the factory, then shipped them in finished form to warehouses. Customizing at the factory is cheaper than customizing in the field. But HP kept guessing wrong on demand and ending up with, say, too many printers configured for French customers but not enough for Germans.

Executives realized that it would be smarter to ship partially assembled printers and then customize them at the warehouse, once it had firm orders. True, local customization costs more. But even though production costs rose, HP saved $3 million a month by more effectively matching supply to demand, says Corey A. Billington, a former Stanford professor who directs HP's Strategic Planning & Modeling group.

Common sense? Sure. But you can also view it as a neat solution of a real-options problem. Increasing the cost of production—anathema to your average engineer—was in effect the price HP paid for the option to delay configuration choices until the optimal time.

Source: P. Coy, "Exploiting Uncertainty," *Business Week*, June 7, 1999. Reprinted with permission from The McGraw-Hill Companies, Inc.

exactly offset by a rise in the option's exercise price (the value of the oil-fired plant). The best of all worlds would occur if the prices of the two fuels were negatively correlated. In this case whenever oil became expensive, the gas would become cheap. In these (unlikely) circumstances the option to switch between the two fuels would be particularly valuable.

In this example, the output is the same (electricity); option value comes from flexibility in raw materials (gas or oil). In other cases, option value comes from the flexibility to switch from product to product using the same production facilities. For example, textile firms have invested heavily in computer-controlled knitting machines, which allow production to shift from product to product, or from design to design, as demand and fashion dictate.

Flexibility in *procurement* can also have option value. For example, a computer manufacturer planning next year's production must also plan to buy components, such as disk drives and microprocessors, in large quantities. Should it strike a deal today with the component manufacturer? This locks in the quantity, price, and delivery dates. But it also gives up flexibility, for example, the ability to switch suppliers next year or buy at a "spot" price if next year's prices are lower.

The Finance in the News box features another example of the value of flexibility in production or procurement.

Another Look at Aircraft Purchase Options

For our final example, we return to the problem confronting airlines that order new airplanes for future use. In this industry "lead times" between an order and delivery can extend to several years. Long lead times mean that airlines that order planes today may end up not needing them. You can see why an airline might negotiate for an aircraft purchase *option*.

	Year 0	Year 3	Year 4	Year 5 or later
Buy option	Airline and manufacturer set price and delivery date	Exercise? (Yes or no)	Aircraft delivered if option exercised	
Wait	Wait	Buy now? If yes, negotiate price and wait for delivery.		Aircraft delivered if purchased at year 3.

FIGURE 22.6

This aircraft purchase option, if exercised at year 3, guarantees delivery at year 4 at a fixed price. Without the option, the airline can still order the plane at year 3, but the price is uncertain and the wait for delivery longer.

Source: Adapted from Figure 17–17 in J. Stonier, "What is an Aircraft Purchase Option Worth? Quantifying Asset Flexibility Created through Manufacturer Lead-Time Reductions and Product Commonality," in G. F. Butler and M. R. Keller (eds.), *Handbook of Airline Finance*. Copyright 1999 Aviation Week Books; reprinted with permission from The McGraw-Hill Companies, Inc.

In Section 10.3, we used aircraft purchase option to illustrate the option to expand. What we said there was the truth, but not the whole buth. Let's take another look. Soppose an airline forecasts a need for a new Airbus A320 four years hence.[17] It has at least three choices.

- *Commit now.* It can commit now to buy the plane, in exchange for Airbus's offer of locked-in price and delivery date.
- *Acquire option.* It can seek a purchase option from Airbus, allowing the airline to decide later whether to buy. A purchase option fixes the price and delivery date if the option is exercised.
- *Wait and decide later.* Airbus will be happy to sell another A320 at any time in the future if the airline wants to buy one. However, the airline may have to pay a higher price and wait longer for delivery, especially if the airline industry is flying high and many planes are on order.

The top half of Figure 22.6 shows the terms of a typical purchase option for an Airbus A320. The option must be exercised at year 3, when final assembly of the plane will begin. The option fixes the purchase price and the delivery date in year 4. The bottom half of the figure shows the consequences of "wait and decide later." We assume that the decision will come at year 3. If the decision is "buy," the airline pays the year-3 price and joins the queue for delivery in year 5 or later.

The payoffs from "wait and decide later" can never be better than the payoffs from an aircraft purchase option, since the airline can discard the option and negotiate afresh with Airbus if it wishes. In most cases the airline will be better off in the future with the option than without it; the airline is at least guaranteed a place in the production line, and it may have locked in a favorable purchase price. But how much are these advantages worth today, compared to the wait-and-see strategy?

[17]The following example is based on J. E. Stonier, "What is an Aircraft Purchase Option Worth? Quantifying Asset Flexibility Created through Manufacturer Lead-Time Reductions and Product Commonality," in G. F. Butler and M. R. Keller (eds.), *Handbook of Airline Finance*. © 1999 Aviation Week Books; reprinted with permission from The McGraw-Hill Companies, Inc.

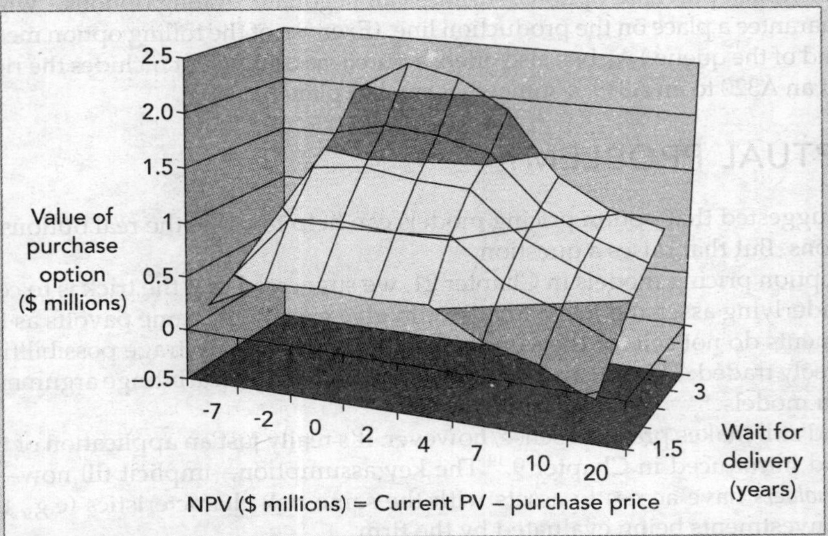

FIGURE 22.7

Value of aircraft purchase option—the extra value of the option versus waiting and possibly negotiating a purchase later. (See Figure 22.6.) The purchase option is worth most when NPV of purchase now is about zero and the forecasted wait for delivery is long.

Source: Adapted from Fig. 17–20 in J. Stonier, "What Is an Aircraft Purchase Option Worth? Quantifying Asset Flexibility Created Through Manufacturer Lead-Time Reductions and Product Commonality," in G. F. Butler and M. R. Keller (eds.), *Handbook of Aviation Finance*. © 1999 Aviation Week Books; reprinted with permission from The McGraw-Hill Companies, Inc.

Figure 22.7 illustrates Airbus's answers to this problem. It assumes a three-year purchase option with an exercise price equal to the current A320 price of $45 million. The present value of the purchase option depends on both the NPV of purchasing an A320 at that price and on the forecasted wait for delivery if the airline does *not* have a purchase option but nevertheless decides to place an order in year 3. The longer the wait in year 3, the more valuable it is to have the purchase option today. (Remember that the purchase option holds a place in the A320 production line and guarantees delivery in year 4.)

If the NPV of buying an A320 today is very high (the right-hand side of Figure 22.7), future NPV will probably be high as well, and the airline will want to buy regardless of whether it has a purchase option. In this case the value of the purchase option comes mostly from the value of guaranteed delivery in year 4.[18] If the NPV is very low, then the option has low value because the airline is unlikely to exercise it. (Low NPV today probably means low NPV in year 3.) The purchase option is worth the most, compared to the wait-and-decide-later strategy, when NPV is around zero. In this case the airline can exercise the option, getting a good price and early delivery, if future NPV is higher than expected, and walk away from the option if NPV disappoints. Of course, if it walks away, it may still wish to negotiate with Airbus for delivery at a price lower than the option's exercise price.

We have cruised by many of the technical details of Airbus's valuation model for purchase options. But the example does illustrate how real-options models are being built and used. By the way, Airbus

[18]The Airbus real-options model assumes that future A320 prices will be increased when demand is high, but only to an upper bound. Thus the airline that waits and decides later may still have a positive-NPV investment opportunity if future demand and NPV are high. Figure 22.7 plots the *difference* between the value of the purchase option and this wait-and-see opportunity. This difference can shrink when NPV is high, especially if forecasted waiting times are short.

offers more than just plain-vanilla purchase options. Airlines can negotiate "rolling options," which lock in price but do not guarantee a place on the production line. (Exercise of the rolling option means that the airline joins the end of the queue.) Airbus also offers a purchase option that includes the right to switch from delivery of an A320 to an A319, a somewhat smaller plane.

22.5 A CONCEPTUAL PROBLEM?

In this chapter we have suggested that option pricing models can help to value the real options in capital investment decisions. But that raises a question.

When we introduced option pricing models in Chapter 21, we suggested that the trick is to construct a package of the underlying asset and a loan that would give exactly the same payoffs as the option. If the two investments do not sell for the same price, then there are arbitrage possibilities. But many assets are not freely traded. This means that we can no longer rely on arbitrage arguments to justify the use of option models.

The risk-neutral method still makes practical sense, however. It's really just an application of the *certainty-equivalent* method introduced in Chapter 9.[19] The key assumption—implicit till now—is that the company's *shareholders* have access to assets with the same risk characteristics (e.g., the same beta) as the capital investments being evaluated by the firm.

Think of each real investment opportunity as having a "double," a security or portfolio with identical risk. Then the expected rate of return offered by the double is also the cost of capital for the real investment and the discount rate for a DCF valuation of the investment project. Now what would investors pay for a real *option* based on the project? The same as for an identical traded option written on the double. This traded option does not have to exist; it is enough to know how it would be valued by investors, who could employ either the arbitrage or the risk-neutral method. The two methods give the same answer, of course.

When we value a real option by the risk-neutral method, we are calculating the option's value if it could be traded. This exactly parallels standard capital budgeting. If shareholders can buy traded securities or portfolios with the same risk characteristics as the real investments being evaluated by the firm, they would vote unanimous endorsement for any real investment whose market value if traded would exceed the investment required. This key assumption supports the use of both DCF and real-option valuation methods.

Practical Challenges

The challenges in applying real-options analysis are not conceptual but practical. It isn't always easy. We can tick off some of the reasons why.

First, real options can be complex, and valuing them can absorb a lot of analytical and computational horsepower. Whether you want to invest in that horsepower is a matter for business judgment. Sometimes an approximate answer now is more useful than a "perfect" answer later, particularly if the perfect answer comes from a complicated model that other managers will regard

[19]Use of risk-neutral probabilities converts future cash flows to certainty equivalents, which are then discounted to present value at a risk-free rate.

as a black box. One advantage of real options analysis, if you keep it simple, is that it's relatively easy to explain. Complex decision trees can often be described as the payoffs to one or two simple call options.

The second problem is lack of *structure*. To quantify the value of a real option, you have to specify its possible payoffs, which depend on the range of possible values of the underlying asset, exercise prices, timing of exercise, etc. In this chapter we have taken well-structured examples where it is easy to see the road map of possible outcomes. In other cases you may not have a road map. For example, reading this book can enhance your personal call option to work in financial management, yet we suspect that you would find it hard to write down how that option would change the binomial tree of your entire future career.

A third problem can arise when your *competitors* have real options. This is not a problem in industries where products are standardized and no single competitor can shift demand and prices. But when you face just a few key competitors, all with real options, then the options can interact. If so, you can't value your options without thinking of your competitors' moves. Your competitors will be thinking in the same fashion.

An analysis of competitive interactions would take us into other branches of economics, including game theory. But you can see the danger of assuming passive competitors. Think of the timing option. A simple real-options analysis will often tell you to wait and learn before investing in a new market. Be careful that you don't wait and learn that a competitor has moved first.[20]

But understanding real options pays off even when quantification is difficult. If you can identify real options, you will be a more sophisticated consumer of discounted-cash-flow analysis and better equipped to invest your company's money wisely.

[20]Being the first mover into a new market is not always the best strategy, of course. Sometimes later movers win. For a survey of real options and product-market competition, see H. Smit and L. Trigeorgis, *Strategic Investment, Real Options and Games* (Princeton, NJ: Princeton University Press, 2004).

SUMMARY

In Chapter 21 you learned the basics of option valuation. In this chapter we described four important real options:

1. *The option to make follow-on investments.* Companies often cite "strategic" value when taking on negative-NPV projects. A close look at the projects' payoffs reveals call options on follow-on projects in addition to the immediate projects' cash flows. Today's investments can generate tomorrow's opportunities.
2. *The option to wait (and learn) before investing.* This is equivalent to owning a call option on the investment project. The call is exercised when the firm commits to the project. But often it's better to defer a positive-NPV project in order to keep the call alive. Deferral is most attractive when uncertainty is great and immediate project cash flows—which are lost or postponed by waiting—are small.
3. *The option to abandon.* The option to abandon a project provides partial insurance against failure. This is a put option; the put's exercise price is the value of the project's assets if sold or shifted to a more valuable use.
4. *The option to vary the firm's output or its production methods.* Firms often build flexibility into their production facilities so that they can use the cheapest raw materials or produce the most valuable set of outputs. In this case they effectively acquire the option to exchange one asset for another.

We should offer here a healthy warning: The real options encountered in practice are often complex. Each real option brings its own issues and trade-offs. Nevertheless the tools that you have learned in this and previous chapters can be used in practice. The Black–Scholes formula often suffices to value expansion options. Problems of investment timing and optimal abandonment can be tackled with binomial trees.

Binomial trees are cousins of decision trees. You work back through binomial trees from future payoffs to present value. Whenever a future decision needs to be made, you figure out the value-maximizing choice, using the principles of option pricing theory, and record the resulting value at the appropriate node of the tree.

Don't jump to the conclusion that real-option-valuation methods can replace discounted cash flow (DCF). First, DCF works fine for safe cash flows. It also works fine for "cash cow" assets—that is, for assets or businesses whose value depends primarily on forecasted cash flows, not on real options. Second, the starting point in most real-option analyses is the present value of an underlying asset. To value the underlying asset, you typically have to use DCF.

Real options are rarely traded assets. When we value a real option, we are estimating its value if it could be traded. This is the standard approach in corporate finance, the same approach taken in DCF valuations. The key assumption is that shareholders can buy traded securities or portfolios with the same risk characteristics as the real investments being evaluated by the firm. If so, they would vote unanimously for any real investment whose market value if traded would exceed the investment required. This key assumption supports the use of both DCF and real-option valuation methods.

FURTHER READING

Further reading for Chapter 10 lists several introductory articles on real options. The Summer 2001 issue of the Journal of Applied Corporate Finance *contains additional articles, including the following survey of how real options are used in practice:*

A. Triantis and A. Borison, "Real Options: State of the Practice," *Journal of Applied Corporate Finance* 14 (Summer 2001), pp. 8–24.

The standard texts on real options include:

M. Amran and N. Kulatilaka, *Real Options: Managing Strategic Investments in an Uncertain World* (Boston: Harvard Business School Press, 1999).

T. Copeland and V. Antikarov, *Real Options: A Practitioner's Guide* (New York: Texere, 2001).

A. K. Dixit and R. S. Pindyck: *Investment under Uncertainty* (Princeton, NJ: Princeton University Press, 1994).

H. Smit and L. Trigeorgis, *Strategic Investment, Real Options and Games* (Princeton, NJ: Princeton University Press, 2004).

L. Trigeorgis: *Real Options* (Cambridge, MA: MIT Press, 1996).

The Autumn 1993 issue of Financial Management *includes six articles on real options, including a description of how to value an industrial facility that can be fueled with gas or oil:*

N. Kulatilaka, "The Value of Flexibility: The Case of a Dual-Fuel Industrial Steam Boiler," *Financial Management* 22 (Autumn 1993), pp. 271–280.

Mason and Merton review a range of option applications to corporate finance:

S. P. Mason and R. C. Merton, "The Role of Contingent Claims Analysis in Corporate Finance," in E. I. Altman and M. G. Subrahmanyan (eds.), *Recent Advances in Corporate Finance* (Homewood, IL: Richard D. Irwin, Inc., 1985).

Brennan and Schwartz have worked out an interesting application to natural resource investments:

M. J. Brennan and E. S. Schwartz, "Evaluating Natural Resource Investments," *Journal of Business* 58 (April 1985), pp. 135–157.

CONCEPT REVIEW QUESTIONS

1. What are the four types of real option? (page 599)
2. Describe the real options in each of the following cases: (page 599)
   a. Icarus Airlines pays Boeing for the option to purchase ten 7E7 jets in 2008.
   b. Icarus buys Boeing 767 passenger jets with reinforced floors, larger doors, and other features that would allow quick conversion to a cargo plane.
   c. ExxonMobil pays $75 million for drilling rights in central Costaguana. The Costaguanan fields are too costly to develop now but development could be profitable if oil prices rise.
   d. Forest Investors purchases a remote stand of Northern hardwoods. Harvest is positive-NPV now but the company postpones logging.

For additional Concept Review Questions, please visit us at www.mhhe.com/bmam8e or refer to your Student CD.

QUIZ

1. Look again at the valuation in Table 22.2 of the option to invest in the Mark II project. Consider a change in each of the following inputs. Would the change increase or decrease the value of the expansion option?
   a. Increased uncertainty (higher standard deviation).
   b. More optimistic forecast (higher expected value) of the Mark II in 1985.
   c. Increase in the required investment in 1985.
2. Respond to the following comments.
   a. "You don't need option pricing theories to value flexibility. Just use a decision tree. Discount the cash flows in the tree at the company cost of capital."
   b. "These option pricing methods are just plain nutty. They say that real options on risky assets are worth more than options on safe assets."
   c. "Real-options methods eliminate the need for DCF valuation of investment projects."
3. You own a parcel of vacant land. You can develop it now, or wait.
   a. What is the advantage of waiting?
   b. Why might you decide to develop the property immediately?

PRACTICE QUESTIONS

1. Describe each of the following situations in the language of options:
   a. Drilling rights to undeveloped heavy crude oil in Bombay High. Development and production of the oil is a negative-NPV endeavor. The break-even oil price is Rs. 3000 per barrel, versus a spot price of Rs. 2500. However, the decision to develop can be put off up to five years. Development costs are expected to increase by 5 percent per year.
   b. A restaurant is producing net cash flows, after all out-of-pocket expenses, of Rs. 700,000 per year. There is no upward or downward trend in the cash flows, but they fluctuate, with an annual standard deviation of 15 percent. The real estate occupied by the restaurant is owned, not leased, and could be sold for Rs. 5 million. Ignore taxes.
   c. A variation on part (b): Assume the restaurant faces known fixed costs of Rs. 300,000 per year, incurred as long as the restaurant is operating. Thus

$$\text{Net cash flow} = \text{revenue less variable costs} - \text{fixed costs}$$

$$\text{Rs. } 700{,}000 = 1{,}000{,}000 - 300{,}000$$

   The annual standard deviation of the forecast error of revenue less variable costs is 10.5 percent. The interest rate is 10 percent. Ignore taxes.

d. A paper mill can be shut down in periods of low demand and restarted if demand improves sufficiently. The costs of closing and reopening the mill are fixed.

e. A real estate developer uses a parcel of urban land as a parking lot, although construction of either a hotel or an apartment building on the land would be a positive-NPV investment.

f. Air India negotiates a purchase option for the first 10 Dreamliners produced by Boeing. Air India must confirm its order in 2009. Otherwise, Boeing will be free to sell the aircraft to other airlines.

excel

Please visit us at www.mhhe.com/bmam8e or refer to your Student CD.

2. Look again at Table 22.2. How does the value in 1982 of the option to invest in the Mark II change if:

a. The investment required for the Mark II is Rs. 800 million (vs. Rs. 900 million)?

b. The present value of the Mark II in 1982 is Rs. 500 million (vs. Rs. 467 million)?

c. The standard deviation of the Mark II's present value is only 20 percent (vs. 35 percent)?

excel

Please visit us at www.mhhe.com/bmam8e or refer to your Student CD.

3. You own a 1-year call option on 1 acre of Mumbai real estate. The exercise price is Rs. 200 crores, and the current appraised market value of the land is Rs. 170 crores. The land is currently used as a parking lot, generating just enough money to cover real estate taxes. The annual standard deviation is 20 percent and the interest rate is 8 percent. How much is your call worth?

excel

Please visit us at www.mhhe.com/bmam8e or refer to your Student CD.

4. A variation on Practice Question 3: Suppose the land is occupied by a warehouse generating rents of Rs. 150,000 after real estate taxes and all other out-of-pocket costs. The value of the land plus warehouse is again Rs. 1.7 million. Other facts are as in Practice Question 3. You have a European call option. What is it worth?

5. In Section 22.4 we described the problem faced by a utility that was contemplating an investment in equipment that would allow it to burn either oil or gas. How would the value of the option to cofire be affected if (a) the prices of both oil and gas were very variable, but (b) the prices of oil and gas were highly correlated?

excel

Please visit us at www.mhhe.com/bmam8e or refer to your Student CD.

6. You have an option to purchase all of the assets of the Overland Railroad for \$2.5 billion. The option expires in 9 months. You estimate Overland's current (month 0) present value (PV) as \$2.7 billion. Overland generates after-tax free cash flow (FCF) of \$50 million at the end of each quarter (i.e., at the end of each three-month period). If you exercise your option at the start of the quarter, that quarter's cash flow is paid out to you. If you do not exercise, the cash flow goes to Overland's current owners.

In each quarter, Overland's PV either increases by 10 percent or decreases by 9.09 percent. This PV includes the quarterly FCF of \$50 million. After the \$50 million is paid out, PV drops by \$50 million. Thus the binomial tree for the first quarter is (figures in millions):

Month 0 (now)

Month 3 (end of quarter)
PV before payout − FCF = end-of-quarter PV

PV = \$2,700 → \$2,970 − 50 = \$2,920 (+10%)

PV = \$2,700 → \$2,455 − 50 = \$2,405 (−9.09%)

The risk-free interest rate is 2 percent per quarter.

a. Build a binomial tree for Overland, with one up or down change for each 3-month period (three steps to cover your 9-month option).

b. Suppose you can only exercise your option now, or after 9 months (not at month 3 or 6). Would you exercise now?

c. Suppose you can exercise now, or at month 3, 6, or 9. What is your option worth today? Should you exercise today, or wait?

excel

Please visit us at www.mhhe.com/bmam8e or refer to your Student CD

7. In Section 10.3 we considered two production technologies for a new Wankel-engined outboard motor. Technology A was the most efficient but had no salvage value if the new outboards failed to sell. Technology B was less efficient but offered a salvage value of $10 million.

Figure 10.6 shows the present value of the project as either $18.5 or 8.5 million in year 1 if Technology A is used. Assume that the present value of these payoffs is $11.5 million at year 0.

a. With Technology B, the payoffs at year 1 are $18 or 8 million. What is the present value in year 0 if Technology B is used? (*Hint:* The payoffs with Technology B vs. A differ by a constant $.5 million.) The risk-free rate is 7 percent.

b. Technology B allows abandonment in year 1 for $10 million salvage value. Calculate abandonment value.

excel

Please visit us at www.mhhe.com/bmam8e or refer to your Student CD .

8. Look again at Practice Question 7. We will assume that Technology A has a salvage value of $7 million, rather than zero. The present value of the project with Technology A is $11.5 million at year 0, assuming no abandonment. The risk-free rate is 7 percent.

excel

Please visit us at www.mhhe.com/bmam8e or refer to your Student CD .

a. Construct a one-year binomial tree for this project, with one up or down step every three months (four steps total). The up steps are +25 percent, the down steps are −16.7 percent.

b. Suppose abandonment can only occur at year 1. In what circumstances would you abandon then? What is abandonment value at year 0?

9. Ravi Jacob, who has only read part of Chapter 10, decides to value a real option by (1) setting out a decision tree, with cash flows and probabilities forecasted for each future outcome; (2) deciding what to do at each decision point in the tree; and (3) discounting the resulting expected cash flows at the company cost of capital. Will this procedure give the right answer? Why or why not?

CHALLENGE QUESTIONS

1. Suppose you expect to need a new plant that will be ready to produce turbo-encabulators in 36 months. If design A is chosen, construction must begin immediately. Design B is more expensive, but you can wait 12 months before breaking ground. Figure 22.8 shows the cumulative present value of construction costs for the two designs up to the 36-month deadline. Assume that the designs, once built, will be equally efficient and have equal production capacity.

A standard discounted-cash-flow analysis ranks design A ahead of design B. But suppose the demand for turbo-encabulators falls and the new factory is not needed; then, as Figure 22.8 shows, the firm is better off with design B, provided the project is abandoned before month 24.

Describe this situation as the choice between two (complex) call options. Then describe the same situation in terms of (complex) abandonment options. The two descriptions should imply identical payoffs, given optimal exercise strategies.

FIGURE 22.8

Cumulative construction cost of the two plant designs. Plant A takes 36 months to build; plant B, only 24. But plant B costs more.

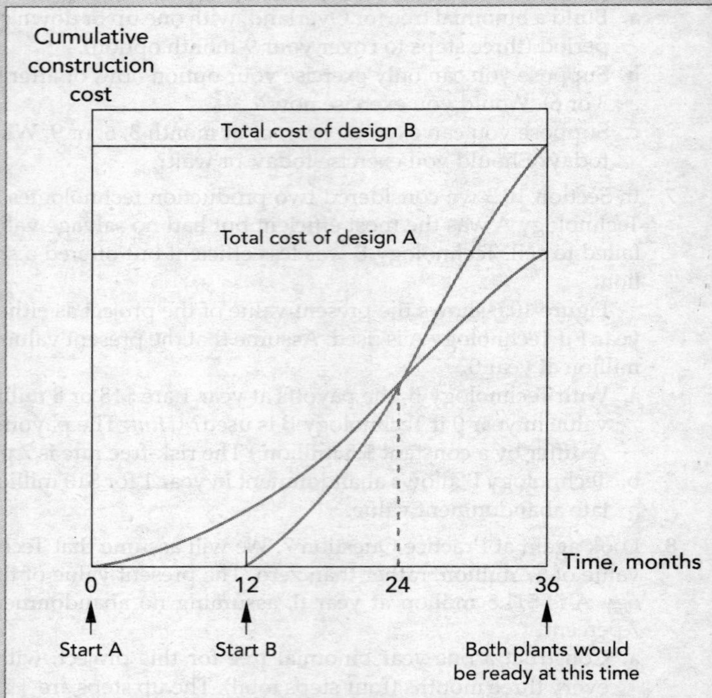

2. In Chapter 4, we expressed the value of a share of stock as

$$P_0 = \frac{EPS_1}{r} + PVGO$$

where EPS_1 is earnings per share from existing assets, r is the expected rate of return required by investors, and PVGO is the present value of growth opportunities. PVGO really consists of a portfolio of expansion options.

a. What is the effect of an increase in PVGO on the standard deviation or beta of the stock's rate of return?

b. Suppose the CAPM is used to calculate the cost of capital for a growth (high-PVGO) firm. Assume all-equity financing. Will this cost of capital be the correct hurdle rate for investments to expand the firm's plant and equipment, or to introduce new products?

PART SEVEN RELATED WEB SITES

Part 1 introduced the basics of bond valuation and we listed there several Web sites. Here are a few further sites:

www.fintools.com (has a somewhat more advanced bond calculator)

www.loanpricing.com (includes data on bond issuance volumes)

For some nice illustrations of changes in the term structure over time, see:

www.smartmoney.com

www.stockcharts.com/charts/yieldcurve.html

Chapters 24 and 25 focus on risky corporate bonds. The Web sites of the rating agencies provide lots of information on default risk and corporate bond yields:

www.moodys.com

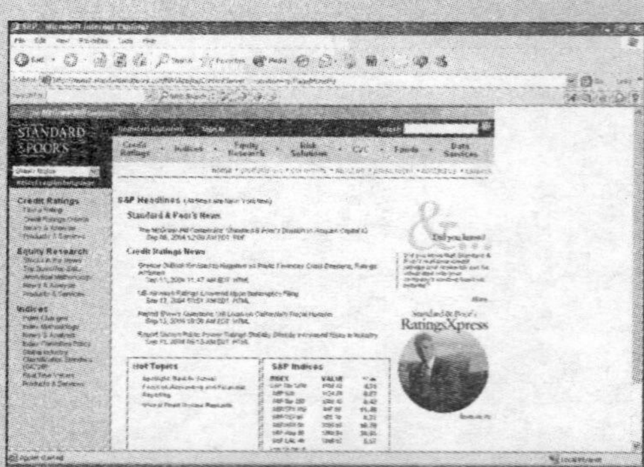

www.standardandpoors.com

www.fitchibca.com

www.bondsonline.com (mainly a subscription service but includes data on bond spreads)

For material on the estimation of default probabilities, see:

www.moodyskmv.com (Moody's KMV)

www.riskmetrics.com (includes a detailed description of Creditmetrics risk analysis)

Some sites that focus on project finance:

www.ipfa.org (International Project Finance Association)

www.hbs.edu/projfinportal (maintained by Benjamin Esty with excellent links including links to specific large projects)

The following sites contain material on leasing, which is covered in Chapter 26:

www.elaonline.com (Equipment Leasing Association)

www.chooseleasing.org

PART [7]

DEBT FINANCING

A RUSH BY CORPORATIONS to take advantage of some of the lowest interest rates in 40 years made 2003 a boom year for corporate borrowing. The largest issue that year was a record-breaking $17 billion bond offering by General Motors.

GM's offering consisted of a package of different types of bond. The dollar debt included bonds with different maturities, varying from 3 to 30 years. The 3-year bonds offered a yield of about 4.5 percent, while the 30-year bonds paid nearly 7.5 percent or 4 percentage points above the rate on long-term government bonds.

Why did GM issue 30-year bonds, when the interest rate was lower on 3-year debt? Were the 3-year bonds cheap and the 30-year bonds expensive? And why did the company have to pay so much more interest than the U.S. government? Part 7 first explains how government bonds are priced and why short-term interest rates may differ from long-term rates. Chapter 24 proceeds to consider default risk and looks at why GM and other corporations need to pay higher rates of interest than the U.S. government. We also look at how to measure the risk of corporate debt. We think first how to measure the probability that the company will default on its debt and then we look at the value at risk if the probability of default changes.

Companies have an enormous choice as to how they borrow. For example, although the bulk of the GM issue consisted of dollar debt, the package also included about $6 billion of euro and sterling bonds. Most of the bonds paid a fixed rate of interest, but some offered a floating rate that rises and falls with the general level of interest rates. Also some of the bonds that GM sold gave investors the right to convert the debt into GM shares. Chapter 25 explains these and the many other choices that borrowers face.

Finally, Chapter 26 explains leases and shows how they are valued. Leases have many of the characteristics of bonds.

CHAPTER [23]

VALUING GOVERNMENT BONDS

HOW DO YOU estimate the present value of a bond? The answer is simple: You take the cash flows and discount them at the opportunity cost of capital. Therefore, if a bond produces cash flows of C rupees per year for N years and is then repaid at its face value (Rs. 1,000), the present value is

$$PV = \frac{C}{1+r_1} + \frac{C}{(1+r_2)^2} + \cdots + \frac{C}{(1+r_N)^N} + \frac{\text{Rs. }1{,}000}{(1+r_N)^N}$$

where $r_1, r_2, \ldots, r_N$ are the appropriate discount rates for the cash flows to be received by the bond owners in periods 1, 2, . . . , N.

That is correct as far as it goes but it does not tell us anything about what determines the discount rate. For example,

- In 2004-05, 91-day Indian Treasury Bills offered a return of 4.36 percent: At their 1996-97 peak they offered a return of over 13.5 percent. Why does the same security offer radically different yields at different times?
- In June 2006 the RBI could borrow for one year at an interest rate of 7 percent, but it had to pay 8.5 percent for a 20-year loan. Why do bonds maturing at different dates offer different rates of interest? In other words, why is there a *term structure* of interest rate?
- In June 2006 Government of India could issue long-term bonds at a rate of 8.5 percent. But even the most blue-chip corporate issuers had to pay at least 68 basis points (0.68 percent) more on their long-term borrowing. What explains the premium that firms have to pay?

These questions lead to deep issues that will keep economists simmering for years. But we can give general answers and at the same time present some fundamental ideas.

Why should the financial manager care about these ideas? Who needs to know how bonds are priced as long as the bond market is active and efficient? Efficient markets protect the ignorant trader. If it is necessary to know whether the price is right for a proposed bond issue, you can check the prices of similar bonds. There is no need to worry about the historical behavior of interest rates, about the term structure, or about the other issues discussed in this chapter.

We do not believe that ignorance is desirable even when it is harmless. At least you ought to be able to read the bond tables in *The Business Line* and talk to investment bankers about the prices of recently issued bonds. More important, you will encounter many problems of bond pricing where there are no similar instruments already traded. How do you evaluate a private placement with a custom-tailored repayment schedule? How about financial leases? In Chapter 26 we will see that they are essentially debt contracts, but often extremely complicated ones, for which traded bonds are not close substitutes. Many companies, notably banks and insurance firms, are exposed to the risk of interest rate fluctuations. To control their exposure, these companies need to understand how interest rates change.[1] You will find that the terms, concepts, and facts presented in this chapter are essential to the analysis of these and other practical problems.

Our focus in this chapter is on government bonds and we will postpone the issue of default risk. We start with our first question: Why does the general level of interest rates change over time? Next we turn to the relationship between short- and long-term interest rates. We consider three issues:

- Each period's cash flow on a bond potentially needs to be discounted at a different interest rate, but bond investors often calculate the yield to maturity as a summary measure of the interest rate on the bond. We first explain how these measures are related.
- Second, we show why a change in interest rates has a greater impact on the price of long-term loans than on short-term loans.
- Finally, we look at some theories that explain why short- and long-term interest rates differ.

When you buy a Government of India bond, you can be confident that the loan will be repaid. But an investor who buys a corporate bond faces the risk that the company will fall on hard times and will not be able to repay its debts. In the next chapter we will shift the focus to corporate bonds and examine the risk of default and its effect on bond prices.

[1] We discuss in Chapter 27 how firms protect themselves against interest rate risk.

23.1 REAL AND NOMINAL RATES OF INTEREST

Indexed Bonds and the Real Rate of Interest

In Chapter 3 we drew the distinction between the real and nominal rate of interest. Most bonds promise a fixed *nominal* rate of interest. The *real* interest rate that you receive depends on the inflation rate. For example, if a one-year bond promises you a return of 10 percent and the expected inflation rate is 4 percent, the expected real return on your bond is $1.10/1.04 - 1 = .058$, or 5.8 percent. Since future inflation rates are uncertain, the real return on a bond is also uncertain. For example, if inflation turns out to be higher than the expected 4 percent, the real return will be *lower* than 5.8 percent.

You can nail down a real return; you do so by buying an indexed bond whose payments are linked to inflation. Indexed bonds have been around in many countries for decades, but they were almost unknown in India until December 1997 when the Reserve Bank of India issued the 6 percent Capital Indexed Bond, 2002. The inflation indexed bonds were introduced in the U.S. in 1997.

Unlike the inflation-indexed bonds issued in other countries, the capital indexed bonds (CIB) issued by the RBI protected only the principal and not the interest against the inflation rate. The real cash flows on the capital indexed bonds are fixed. But the nominal cash flows (interest and principal) are increased as the Wholesale Price Index (WPI) increases. However, there was no further issue of the capital indexed bonds by the RBI due to a lack of enthusiasm by the market for this instrument.

In May 2004, the RBI proposed to issue the capital indexed bonds again in the market. The proposed bonds would offer inflation-linked returns on both the principal and interest. The coupon rates on the bonds would also be issued in real terms. For example, suppose that the RBI issues 3 percent 20-year CIB at a price of Rs.100. If during the first year, the WPI for all commodities (1993-94 = 100) rises by (say) 10 percent, then the coupon payment on the bond would be increased by 10 percent to $(1.1 \times 3) = 3.3$ percent. And the final payment of the principal would also be increased in the same proportion to $(1.1 \times 100) = 110$ percent. Thus an investor who buys the bond at issue price and holds it to maturity can be assured of a real yield of 3 percent.[2] The RBI is yet to issue CIB however.

In the spring of 2004, long-term Treasury Inflation-protected Securities (TIP, as they are popularly known in the USA) offer a yield of 2.2 percent. This yield is a real yield: it measures how much extra goods your investment would allow you to buy.

The 2.2 percent yield on TIPs was about 2.8 percent less than on nominal Treasury bonds. If the annual inflation rate proves to be higher than 2.8 percent, you will earn a higher return by holding long-term TIPs; if the inflation rate is lower than 2.8 percent, the reverse will be true.

What determines the real interest rate that investors demand? The classical economist's answer to this question is summed up in the title of Irving Fisher's great book: *The Theory of Interest: As Determined by Impatience to Spend Income and Opportunity to Invest It.*[3] The real interest rate, according to Fisher, is the price which equates the supply and demand for capital. The supply depends on people's willingness to save.[4] The demand depends on the opportunities for productive investment.

For example, suppose that investment opportunities generally improve. Firms have more good projects, so they are willing to invest more than previously at any interest rate. Therefore, the rate

[2]For details refer to http://www.rbi.org.in/scripts/PublicationReportDetails.aspx?UrlPage=&ID=381.

[3]New York: August M. Kelley, 1965; originally published in 1930.

[4]Some of this saving is done indirectly. For example, if you hold 100 shares of GM stock, and GM retains earnings of Re. 1 per share, GM is saving Rs. 100 on your behalf.

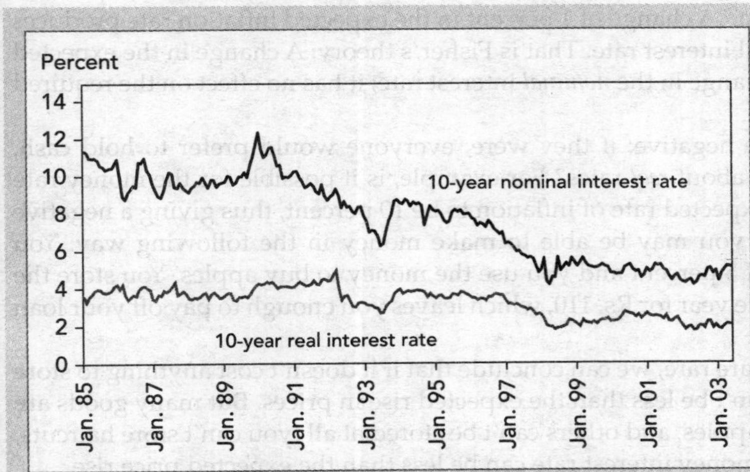

FIGURE 23.1

The green line shows the real yield on long-term indexed bonds issued by the U.K. government. The blue line shows the yield on U.K. government long-term nominal bonds. Notice that the real yield has been much more stable than the nominal yield.

has to rise to induce individuals to save the additional amount that firms want to invest.[5] Conversely, if investment opportunities deteriorate, there will be a fall in the real interest rate.

Fisher's theory emphasizes that the required real rate of interest depends on real phenomena. A high aggregate willingness to save may be associated with high aggregate wealth (because wealthy people usually save more), an uneven distribution of wealth (an even distribution would mean fewer rich people, who do most of the saving), and a high proportion of middle-aged people (the young don't need to save and the old don't want to—"You can't take it with you"). Correspondingly, a high propensity to invest may be associated with a high level of industrial activity or major technological advances.

Real interest rates do change but they do so gradually. We can see this by looking at the U.K., where the government has issued indexed bonds since 1982. The green line in Figure 23.1 shows that the (real) yield on these bonds has fluctuated within a relatively narrow range, while the yield on nominal government bonds has declined dramatically.

Inflation and Nominal Interest Rates

Now let us see what Irving Fisher had to say about inflation and interest rates. Suppose that consumers are equally happy with 100 apples today or 105 apples in a year's time. In this case the real or "apple" interest rate is 5 percent. Suppose also that I know the price of apples will increase over the year by 10 percent. Then I will part with Rs. 100 today if I am repaid Rs. 115 at the end of the year. That Rs. 115 is needed to buy me 5 percent more apples than I can get for my Rs. 100 today. In other words, the nominal, or "money," rate of interest must equal the required real, or "apple," rate

[5]We assume that investors save more as interest rates rise. It doesn't have to be that way; here is an example of how a higher interest rate could mean *less* saving: Suppose that 20 years hence you will need Rs. 50,000 at current prices for your children's college expenses. How much will you have to set aside today to cover this obligation? The answer is the present value of a real expenditure of Rs. 50,000 after 20 years, or 50,000/(1 + real interest rate)^{20}. The higher the real interest rate, the lower the present value and the less you have to set aside.

plus the prospective rate of inflation.[6] A change of 1 percent in the expected inflation rate produces a change of 1 percent in the nominal interest rate. That is Fisher's theory: A change in the expected inflation rate will cause the same change in the *nominal* interest rate; it has no effect on the required real interest rate.[7]

Nominal interest rates cannot be negative; if they were, everyone would prefer to hold cash, which pays zero interest. But what about *real* rates? For example, is it possible for the money rate of interest to be 5 percent and the expected rate of inflation to be 10 percent, thus giving a negative real interest rate? If this happens, you may be able to make money in the following way: You borrow Rs. 100 at an interest rate of 5 percent and you use the money to buy apples. You store the apples and sell them at the end of the year for Rs. 110, which leaves you enough to pay off your loan plus Rs. 5 for yourself.

Since easy ways to make money are rare, we can conclude that if it doesn't cost anything to store goods, the money rate of interest can't be less than the expected rise in prices. But many goods are even more expensive to store than apples, and others can't be stored at all (you can't store haircuts, for example). For these goods, the money interest rate can be less than the expected price rise.

How Well Does Fisher's Theory Explain Interest Rates?

Not all economists would agree with Fisher that the real rate of interest is unaffected by the inflation rate. For example, if changes in prices are associated with changes in the level of industrial activity, then in inflationary conditions I might want more or less than 105 apples in a year's time to compensate me for the loss of 100 today.

We wish we could show you the past behavior of interest rates and expected inflation. Instead we have done the next best thing and plotted in Figure 23.2 the yields on 1-year G-Secs against *actual* inflation. Notice that the yield on G-secs has generally been a little above the rate of inflation. Investors in Government securities earned an average real return of just over 2 percent during this period.

Look at the relationship between the rate of inflation and the yield on G-sec. Figure 23.2 shows that when inflation has been high, investors have generally demanded a higher rate of interest. So it looks as if Fisher's theory provides a useful rule of thumb for financial managers.

If the expected inflation rate changes, it is a good bet that there will be a corresponding change in the interest rate.

[6] We oversimplify. If apples cost Re. 1.00 a piece today and Rs. 1.10 next year, you need 1.10 × 105 = Rs. 115.50 next year to buy 105 apples. The money rate of interest is 15.5 percent, not 15. Remember, the exact formula relating real and money rates is

$$1 + r_{money} = (1 + r_{real})\,(1 + i)$$

where i is the expected inflation rate. Thus

$$r_{money} = r_{real} + i + i(r_{real})$$

In our example, the money rate should be

$$r_{money} = .05 + .10 + .10(.05) = .155$$

When we said the money rate should be 15 percent, we ignored the cross-product term $i\,(r_{real})$. This is a common rule of thumb because the cross-product term is usually small. But there are countries where i is large (sometimes 100 percent or more). In such cases it pays to use the full formula.

[7] The apple example was taken from R. Roll, "Interest Rates on Monetary Assets and Commodity Price Index Changes," *Journal of Finance* 27 (May 1972), pp. 251–278.

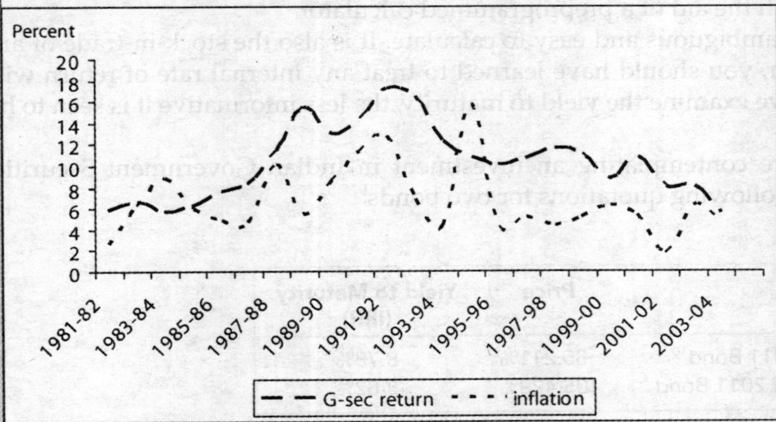

FIGURE 23.2

The return on 1-year Indian Government Securities and the rate of inflation 1981-2005.

Source: Data compiled from www.rbi.org.in

23.2 TERM STRUCTURE AND YIELDS TO MATURITY

We turn now to the relationship between short- and long-term rates of interest. Suppose that we have a simple loan that pays Rs. 1 at time 1. The present value of this loan is

$$PV = \frac{1}{1 + r_1}$$

Thus we discount the cash flow at r_1, the rate appropriate for a one-period loan. This rate, which is fixed today, is often called today's one-period **spot rate.**

If we have a loan that pays Rs. 1 at both time 1 and time 2, present value is

$$PV = \frac{1}{1 + r_1} + \frac{1}{(1 + r_2)^2}$$

Thus the first period's cash flow is discounted at today's one-period spot rate and the second period's flow is discounted at today's two-period spot rate. The series of spot rates r_1, r_2, etc., is one way of expressing the **term structure** of interest rates.

Yield to Maturity

Rather than discounting each of the payments at a different rate of interest, we could find a single rate of discount that would produce the same present value. Such a rate is known as the **yield to maturity,** though it is in fact no more than our old acquaintance, the internal rate of return (IRR), masquerading under another name. If we call the yield to maturity y, we can write the present value of the two-year loan as

$$PV = \frac{1}{1 + y} + \frac{1}{(1 + y)^2}$$

All you need to calculate y is the price of a bond, its annual payment, and its maturity. You can then rapidly work out the yield with the aid of a preprogrammed calculator.

The yield to maturity is unambiguous and easy to calculate. It is also the stock-in-trade of any bond dealer. By now, however, you should have learned to treat any internal rate of return with suspicion.[8] The more closely we examine the yield to maturity, the less informative it is seen to be. Here is an example.

Example. It is 2006. You are contemplating an investment in Indian Government Securities (G-Secs) and come across the following quotations for two bonds[9]:

Bond	Price	Yield to Maturity (IRR)
5%, 2011 Bond[10]	85.211%	8.78%
10% of 2011 Bond	105.429%	8.62%

The phrase "5%, 2011 Bond" refers to a bond maturing in 2011, paying an annual interest of 5 percent of the bond's face value. The interest payment is called the *coupon* payment. In continental Europe, coupons are usually paid annually; in India and U.S. they are usually paid every six months, so the 5% 2011 bond would pay 2.5 percent of face value every six months. To simplify the arithmetic, we will pretend throughout this chapter that all coupon payments are annual. When the bonds mature in 2011, bondholders receive the bond's face value in addition to the final interest payment.

Most of the time, the price of each bond is quoted as a percent of face value. Therefore, if face value is quoted as 85.21 percent, and the face value is Rs.1000, then you would have to pay Rs. 852.11 to buy the bond and your yield would be 8.78 percent. Letting 2006 be t = 0, 2007 be t = 1, etc., we have the following discounted-cash-flow calculation:

Bond	Cash Flows						Yield
	C_0	C_1	C_2	C_3	C_4	C_5	
5%, 2011 Bond	−852.11	+50	+50	+50	+50	+1,050	8.78%
10%, 2011 Bond	−1,054.29	+100	+100	+100	+100	+1,100	8.62%

Although the two bonds mature at the same time, they presumably were issued at different times – the 5%, 2011 bonds when interest rates were low and the 10%, 2011 bonds when interest rates were high.

Are the 5%, 2011 bonds a better buy? Is the market making a mistake by pricing these two issues at different yields? The only way you will know for sure is to calculate the bonds' present values by using spot rates of interest: r_1 for 2007, r_2 for 2008, etc. This is done in Table 23.1.

The important assumption in Table 23.1 is that long-term interest rates are higher than short-term interest rates. We have assumed that the one-year interest rate is r_1 = 0.05, the two-year rate is

[8]See Section 5.3.

[9]The quoted bond price is known as the *flat* (or *clean*) price. The price that the bond buyer pays (sometimes called the *dirty* price) is equal to the flat price *plus* the interest that the seller has already earned on the bond since the last interest payment date. You need to use the flat price to calculate yields to maturity.

[10]Sometimes this is also written as "5s of 11"

TABLE 23.1

Calculating present value of two bonds when long-term interest rates are higher than short-term rates.

		Present Value Calculations			
		5% 2011 bond		10% 2011 bond	
Period	Interest Rate	C_t	PV at r_t	C_t	PV at r_t
t = 1	$r_1 = .05$	Rs. 50	Rs. 47.62	Rs. 100	Rs. 95.24
t = 2	$r_2 = .06$	50	44.50	100	89.00
t = 3	$r_3 = .07$	50	40.81	100	81.63
t = 4	$r_4 = .08$	50	36.75	100	73.50
t = 5	$r_5 = .09$	1,050	682.43	1,100	714.92
	Totals		Rs. 852.11		Rs. 1,054.29

$r_2 = 0.06$, and so on. When each year's cash flow is discounted at the rate appropriate to that year, we see that each bond's present value is exactly equal to the quoted price. Thus each bond is fairly priced.

Why do the 5% bonds have a higher yield? Because for each rupee that you invest in the 5% bonds you receive relatively little cash inflow in the first four years and a relatively high cash inflow in the final year. Therefore, although the two bonds have identical maturity dates, the 5% bonds provide a greater proportion of their cash flows in 2011. In this sense the 5% bonds are a longer-term investment than the 10% bonds. Their higher yield to maturity just reflects the fact that long-term interest rates are higher than short-term rates.

Notice why the yield to maturity can be misleading. When the yield is calculated, the *same* rate is used to discount *all* payments on the bond. But in our example bondholders actually demanded different rates of return (r_1, r_2, etc.) for cash flows that occurred at different times. Since the cash flows on the two bonds were not identical, the bonds had different yields to maturity. Therefore, the yield to maturity on the 5%, 2011 bonds offered only a rough guide to the appropriate yield on the 10%, 2011 bonds.[11]

Measuring the Term Structure

Financial managers who just want a quick, summary measure of interest rates look in the financial press at the yields to maturity on government bonds. Thus managers will make broad generalizations such as "If we borrow money today, we will have to pay an interest rate of 8 percent." But if you wish to understand why different bonds sell at different prices, you must dig deeper and look at the separate interest rates for one-year cash flows, for two-year cash flows, and so on. In other words, you must look at the spot rates of interest.

To find the spot interest rate, you need the price of a bond that simply makes one future payment. Such bonds do exist in the US. They are known as *stripped bonds* or *strips*. Strips originated in 1982 when several investment bankers came up with a novel idea. They bought U.S. Treasury bonds and reissued their own separate mini-bonds, each of which made only one payment. The idea proved to be popular with investors, who welcomed the opportunity to buy the mini-bonds rather

[11]For a good analysis of the relationship between the yield to maturity and spot interest rates, see S. M. Schaefer, "The Problem with Redemption Yields," *Financial Analysts Journal* 33 (July–August 1977), pp. 59–67.

FIGURE 23.3

Spot rates on U.S. Treasury strips, February 2004.

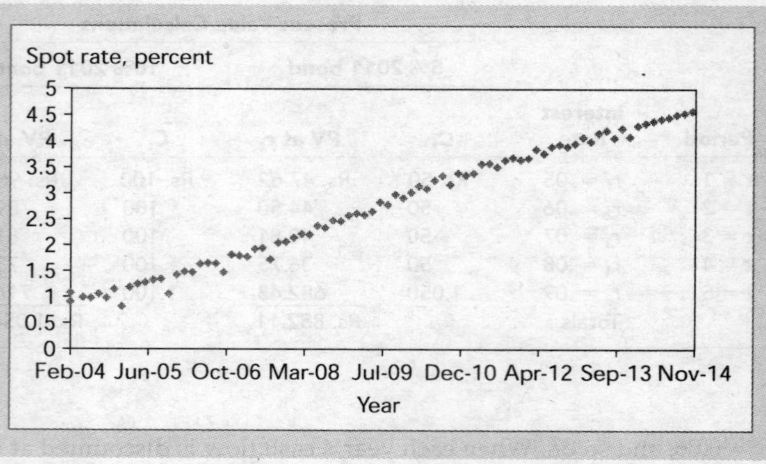

than the complete package. If you've got a smart idea, you can be sure that others will soon clamber onto your bandwagon. It was therefore not long before the Treasury issued its own mini-bonds.[12] The prices of these bonds are shown each day in the daily press. For example, in early 2004, a strip maturing in February 2014 cost $647.02 and 10 years later will give the investors a single payment of $1,000. Thus the 10-year spot rate was $(1000/647.02)^{1/10} - 1 = .0445$, or 4.45 percent.[13]

In Figure 23.3 we have used the prices of strips with different maturities to plot the term structure of spot rates from 1 to 10 years. You can see that investors required an interest rate of 1.2 percent from a bond that made a payment only at the end of one year and a rate of about 4.5 percent from a bond that paid off only at the end of 10 years.

23.3 HOW INTEREST RATE CHANGES AFFECT BOND PRICES

Duration and Bond Volatility

In Chapter 7 we reviewed the historical performance of different security classes. We showed that since 1900 long-term government bonds in the US have provided a higher average return than short-term bills, but have also been more variable. The standard deviation of annual returns on a portfolio of long-term bonds was 8.2 percent compared with a standard deviation of 2.8 percent for bills.

Figure 23.4 illustrates why long-term bonds are more variable. Each line shows how the price of a 5 percent bond changes with the level of interest rates. You can see that the price of a longer-term bond is more sensitive to interest rate fluctuations than that of a shorter bond.[14]

[12]The Treasury continued to auction coupon bonds in the normal way, but investors could exchange them at the Federal Reserve Bank for stripped bonds.

[13]This is an annually compounded rate. The yields quoted by investment dealers are semiannually compounded rates.

[14]Notice also that, particularly for long bonds, the relationship between the bond price and the interest rate is *convex*. In other words, the increase in price resulting from a 1 percent *fall* in the interest rate is greater than the decline from a 1 percent *rise* in the rate.

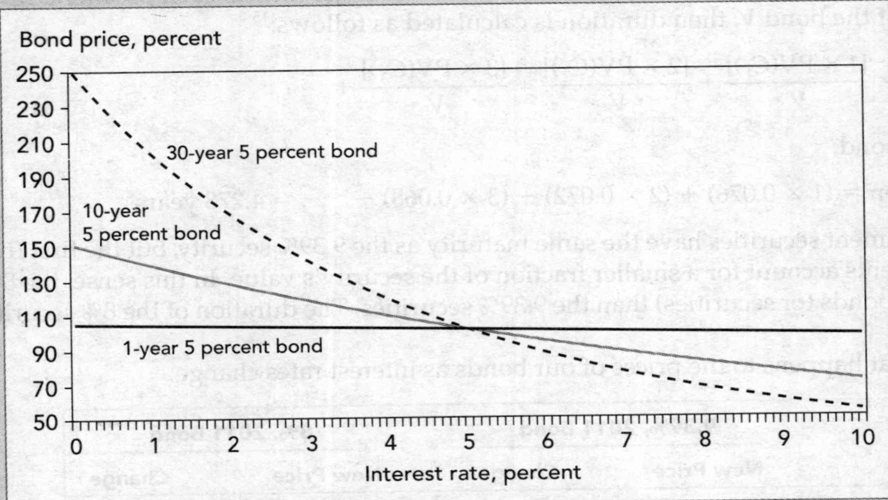

FIGURE 23.4

How bond prices change as interest rates change. Note that longer-term bonds are more sensitive to interest rate changes.

Year	Ct	PV(Ct)	Proportion of Total Value [PV(Ct)/V]	Proportion of Total Value × time
1	9.39	8.92	0.076	0.076
2	9.39	8.47	0.072	0.144
3	9.39	8.04	0.068	0.205
4	9.39	7.63	0.065	0.260
5	109.39	84.42	0.719	3.593
		V = 117.47	1.000	Duration = 4.278 years

TABLE 23.2

The first four columns show that the cash flow in year 5 accounts' for just under 72 percent of the present value of the 9.39% of 2011 bond. The final column shows how to calculate a weighted average of the time to each cash flow. This average is the bond's duration.

Excel

Please visit us at www.mhhe.com/bmam8e or refer to your Student CD .

But what do we mean by long-term and short-term bonds? It is obvious in the case of strips that make payments in only one year. However, a coupon bond that matures in year 10 makes payments in *each* of years 1 through 10. Therefore, it is somewhat misleading to describe the bond as a 10-year bond; the average time to each cash flow is less than 10 years.

Consider the 9.39% Government security, maturing on 2nd July, 2011. In July 2006, it had a present value of 117.47 percent of face value and yielded about 5.32 percent. The third and fourth columns in Table 23.2 show where this present value comes from. Notice that each cash flow in year 5 accounts for only 71.9 percent of the bond's value. The remaining 28.1 percent of the value comes from the earlier cash flows.

Bond analysts often use the term **duration** to describe the average time to each payment. If we call the total value of the bond V, then duration is calculated as follows:[15]

$$\text{Duration} = \frac{[1 \times PV(C_1)]}{V} + \frac{[2 \times PV(C_2)]}{V} + \frac{[3 \times PV(C_3)]}{V} + \cdots$$

For the 9.39%, 2011 bond,

$$\text{Duration} = (1 \times 0.076) + (2 \times 0.072) + (3 \times 0.068) + \ldots = 4.278 \text{ years}$$

The 8%, 2011 Government securities have the same maturity as the 9.39% security, but the first five years' coupon payments account for a smaller fraction of the security's value. In this sense, the 8% securities are longer bonds (or securities) than the 9.39% securities. The duration of the 8% security is 4.35 years.

Consider now what happens to the prices of our bonds as interest rates change:

	9.39%, 2011 Bond		8%, 2011 Bond	
	New Price	**Change**	**New Price**	**Change**
Yield falls 0.5%	Rs. 119.88	2.06%	Rs. 113.84	2.09%
Yield rises 0.5%	115.11	−2.00%	109.23	−2.04%
Difference		4.06		4.13

Thus, a 1 percentage point variation in yield causes the price of the 9.39% bond to change by 4.06 percent. We can say that the 9.39% bonds have a volatility of 4.06 percent, while the 8% bonds have a volatility of 4.13 percent.

Notice that the 8 percent bonds have a greater volatility and that they also have the longer duration. In fact, a bond's volatility is directly related to its duration:[16]

$$\text{Volatility(percent)} = \frac{\text{duration}}{1 + \text{yield}}$$

In the case of the 9.39% bond,

$$\text{Volatility(percent)} = \frac{4.278}{1.0532} = 4.06$$

In Figure 23.4 we showed how bond prices vary with the level of interest rates. Each bond's volatility is simply the slope of the line relating the bond price to the interest rate. You can see this more clearly in Figure 23.5, where the convex curve shows the price of the 5 percent 30-year bond for different interest rates. The bond's volatility is measured by the slope of a tangent to this curve. For example, the figure shows that, if the interest rate is 5 percent, the curve has a slope of 15.4. At this point the change in bond price is 15.4 times a change in the interest rate. Notice that the bond's volatility changes as the interest rate changes. Volatility is higher at lower interest rates (the curve is steeper), and it is lower at higher rates (the curve is flatter).

[15]This measure is also known as *Macaulay duration* after its inventor. See F. Macaulay, *Some Theoretical Problems Suggested by the Movements of Interest Rates, Bond Yields, and Stock Prices in the United States since 1856* (New York: National Bureau of Economic Research, 1938).

[16]For this reason volatility is also called *modified duration*.

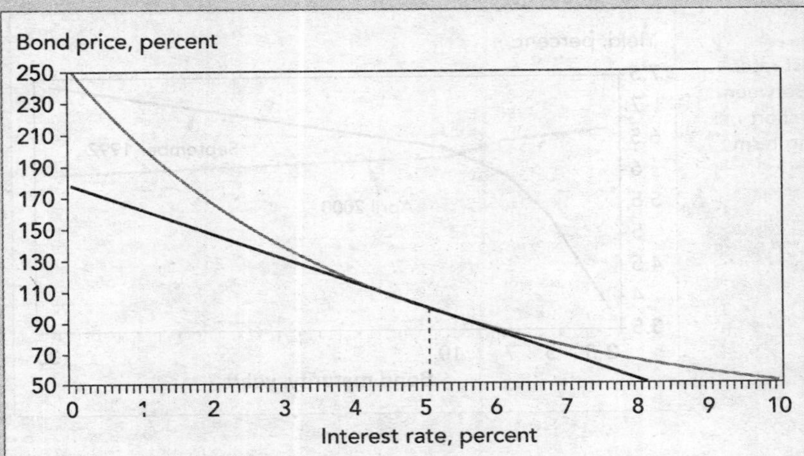

FIGURE 23.5

Volatility is the slope of the curve relating the bond price to the interest rate. For example, a 30-year 5 percent bond has a volatility of 15.4 when the interest rate is 5 percent. At this point the change in price is 15.4 times the change in the interest rate. Its volatility is higher at lower interest rates (the curve is steeper) and lower at higher rates (the curve is flatter).

Managing Interest Rate Risk

Volatility is a useful, summary measure of the likely effect of a change in interest rates on the value of a bond. The longer a bond's duration, the greater is its volatility. In Chapter 27 we will make use of this relationship between duration and volatility to describe how firms can protect themselves against interest rate changes. Here is an example that should give you a flavor of things to come.

Suppose your firm has promised to make pension payments to retired employees. The discounted value of these pension payments is Rs. 1 million; therefore, the firm puts aside Rs. 1 million in the pension fund and invests the money in government bonds. So the firm has a liability of Rs. 1 million and (through the pension fund) an offsetting asset of Rs. 1 million. But, as interest rates fluctuate, the value of the pension liability will change and so will the value of the bonds in the pension fund. How can the firm ensure that the value of the bonds in the fund is always sufficient to meet the liabilities? Answer: By making sure that the duration of the bonds is always the same as the duration of the pension liability.

A Cautionary Note

Bond volatility measures the effect on bond prices of a shift in interest rates. For example, we calculated that the 9.39% bond had volatility of 4.06. This means a 1 percentage point change in interest rates leads to a 4.06 percent change in bond price:

$$\text{Change in bond price} = 4.06 \times \text{change in interest rates}$$

This relationship is sometimes called a *one-factor model* of bond returns; it tells us how each bond's price changes in response to one factor—a change in the overall level of interest rates. One-factor models have proved very useful in helping firms to understand how they are affected by interest-rate changes and how they can protect themselves against these risks.

If the yield on all G-Secs moves in precise lockstep, then changes in the price of each bond would be exactly proportional to the bond's duration. For example, the price of a long-term bond with a duration of 20 years would always rise or fall twice as much as the price of a medium term bond with a duration of 10 years. However, Figure 23.6 illustrates that short- and long-term interest rates

FIGURE 23.6

Short-term and long-term interest rates do not always move in parallel. Between September 1992 and April 2000 short-term rates rose sharply while long-term rates declined.

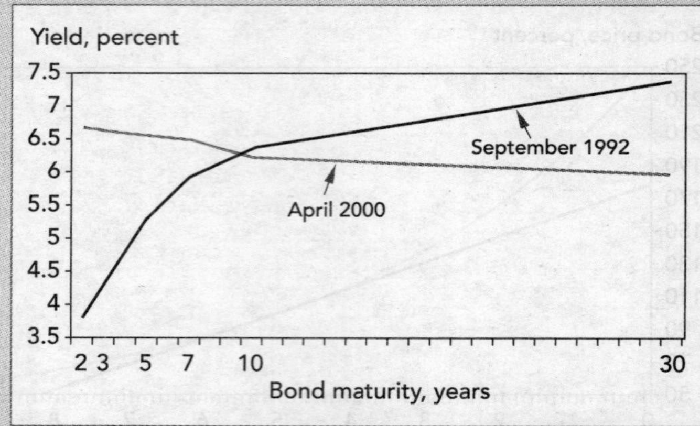

do not always move in perfect unison. Between 1992 and 2002 short-term interest rates in the U.S. nearly doubled while long-term rates declined. As a result, the term structure, which initially sloped steeply upward, shifted to a downward slope. Because short- and long-term yields do not move in parallel, one-factor models cannot be the whole story, and managers need to worry not just about the risks of an overall change in interest rates but also about shifts in the term structure.

23.4 EXPLAINING THE TERM STRUCTURE

The term structure that we showed in Figure 23.3 was upward-sloping. In other words, long rates of interest are higher than short rates. This is the more common pattern but sometimes it is the other way around, with short rates higher than long rates. Why do we get these shifts in term structure?

Let us look at a simple example. Figure 23.3 showed that in the February 2004 the one-year spot rate (r_1) was about 1.2 percent. The two-year spot rate (r_2) was higher at 1.8 percent. Suppose that in 2004 you invest in a one-year U.S. Treasury strip. You would earn the one-year spot rate of interest and by the end of the year each dollar that you invested would have grown to $\$(1 + r_1) = \$1.012$. If instead you were prepared to invest for two years, you would earn the two-year spot rate of r_2 and by the end of the two years each dollar would have grown to $\$(1 + r_2)^2 = \$1.018^2 = \$1.0363$. By keeping your money invested for a further year, your savings grow from \$1.012 to \$1.0363, an increase of 2.40 percent. This extra 2.40 percent that you earn by keeping your money invested for two years rather than one is termed the **forward interest rate** or f_2.

Notice how we calculated the forward rate. When you invest for one year, each dollar grows to $\$(1 + r_1)$. When you invest for two years, each dollar grows to $\$(1 + r_2)^2$. Therefore, the extra return that you earn for that second year is $f_2 = (1 + r_2)^2/(1 + r_1) - 1$. In our example,

$$f_2 = (1 + r_2)^2/(1 + r_1) - 1 = (1.018)^2/(1.012) - 1 = .024, \text{ or } 2.4\%$$

If you twist this equation around, you obtain an expression for the two-year spot rate, r_2, in terms of the one-year spot rate, r_1, and the forward rate, f_2:

$$(1 + r_2)^2 = (1 + r_1) \times (1 + f_2)$$

(*a*) The future value of $1 invested in a two-year loan

Period 0 → Period 2

$$(1 + r_2)^2 = (1 + r_1) \times (1 + f_2)$$

(*b*) The future value of $1 invested in two successive one-year loans

Period 0 → Period 1 → Period 2

$$(1 + r_1) \quad \times \quad (1 + {}_1r_2)$$

FIGURE 23.7

An investor can invest either in a two-year loan (*a*) or in two successive one-year loans (*b*). The expectations theory says that in equilibrium the expected payoffs from these two strategies must be equal. In other words, the forward rate, f_2, must equal the expected spot rate, r_2.

In other words, you can think of the two-year investment as earning the one-year spot rate for the first year and the extra return, or forward rate, for the second year.

The Expectations Theory

Would you have been happy in 2004 to earn an extra 2.4 percent for investing for two years rather than one? The answer depends on how you expected interest rates to change over the coming year. Suppose, for example, that you were confident that interest rates would rise sharply, so that at the end of the year the one-year rate would be 4 percent. In that case rather than investing in a two-year bond and earning the extra 2.4 percent for the second year, you would do better to invest in a one-year bond and, when that matured, to reinvest the money for a further year at 4 percent. If other investors shared your view, no one would be prepared to hold the two-year bond and its price would fall. It would stop falling only when the extra return from holding the two-year bond equalled the expected future one-year rate. Let us call this expected rate ${}_1r_2$—that is, the spot rate of interest at year 1 on a loan maturing at the end of year 2.[17] Figure 23.7 shows that at that point investors would earn the same expected return from investing in a two-year loan as from investing in two successive one-year loans.

This is known as the **expectations theory** of term structure.[18] It states that in equilibrium the forward interest rate, f_2, must equal the expected one-year spot rate, ${}_1r_2$. The expectations theory implies that the *only* reason for an upward-sloping term structure, such as existed in 2004, is that investors expect short-term interest rates to rise; the *only* reason for a declining term structure is that investors expect short-term rates to fall.[19] The expectations theory also implies that investing in a succession of short-term bonds gives exactly the same expected return as investing in long-term bonds.

If short-term interest rates are significantly lower than long-term rates, it is often tempting to borrow short-term rather than long-term. The expectations theory implies that such naïve strategies

[17] Be careful to distinguish ${}_1r_2$ from r_2, the spot interest rate on a two-year bond held from time 0 to time 2. The quantity ${}_1r_2$ is a one-year spot rate established at time 1.

[18] The expectations theory is usually attributed to Lutz and Lutz. See F. A. Lutz and V. C. Lutz, *The Theory of Investment in the Firm* (Princeton, NJ: Princeton University Press, 1951).

[19] This follows from our example. If the two-year spot rate, r_2, exceeds the one-year rate, r_1, then the forward rate, f_2, also exceeds r_1. If the forward rate equals the expected spot rate, ${}_1r_2$, then ${}_1r_2$ must also exceed r_1. The converse is likewise true.

won't work. If short rates are lower than long rates, then investors must be expecting interest rates to rise. When the term structure is upward-sloping, you are likely to make money by borrowing short only if investors are *overestimating* future increases in interest rates.

Even on a casual glance the expectations theory does not seem to be the complete explanation of term structure. For example, if we look back over the period 1900–2003, we find that the return on long-term U.S. Treasury bonds was on average 1.2 percent higher than the return on short-term Treasury bills. Perhaps short-term interest rates did not go up as much as investors expected, but it seems more likely that investors wanted a higher expected return for holding long bonds and that on the average they got it. If so, the expectations theory is wrong.

The expectations theory has few strict adherents, but most economists believe that expectations about future interest rates have an important effect on term structure. For example, the expectations theory implies that if the forward rate of interest is 1 percent above the spot rate of interest, then your best estimate is that the spot rate of interest will rise by 1 percent. In a study of the U.S. Treasury bill market between 1959 and 1982, Eugene Fama found that a forward premium does on average precede a rise in the spot rate but the rise is less than the expectations theory would predict.[20]

The Liquidity-Preference Theory

What does the expectations theory leave out? The most obvious answer is "risk." If you are confident about the future level of interest rates, you will simply choose the strategy that offers the highest return. But, if you are not sure of your forecast, you may well opt for the less risky strategy even if it offers a lower expected return.

Remember that the prices of long-duration bonds are more volatile than those of short-term bonds. For some investors this extra volatility may not be a concern. For example, pension funds and life insurance companies with long-term liabilities may prefer to lock in future returns by investing in long-term bonds. However, the volatility of long-term bonds *does* create extra risk for investors who do not have such long-term fixed obligations.

Here we have the basis for the **liquidity-preference theory** of the term structure.[21] If investors incur extra risk from holding long-term bonds, they will demand the compensation of a higher expected return. In this case the forward rate must be higher than the expected spot rate. This difference between the forward rate and the expected spot rate is usually called the **liquidity premium.** If the liquidity-preference theory is right, the term structure should be upward-sloping more often than not. Of course, if future spot rates are expected to fall, the term structure could be downward-sloping and *still* reward investors for lending long. But the liquidity-preference theory would predict a less dramatic downward slope than the expectations theory.

[20]See E. F. Fama, "The Information in the Term Structure," *Journal of Financial Economics* 13 (December 1984), pp. 509–528. Evidence from the Treasury bond market that the forward premium has some power to predict changes in spot rates is provided in J. Y. Campbell, A. W. Lo, and A. C. MacKinlay, *The Econometrics of Financial Markets* (Princeton, NJ: Princeton University Press, 1997), pp. 421–422.

[21]The liquidity-preference hypothesis is usually attributed to Hicks. See J. R. Hicks, *Value and Capital: An Inquiry into Some Fundamental Principles of Economic Theory*, 2nd ed. (Oxford: Oxford University Press, 1946).

Introducing Inflation

The money cash flows on a U.S. Treasury bond are certain, but the real cash flows are not. In other words, Treasury bonds are still subject to inflation risk. Let us look therefore at how uncertainty about inflation affects the risk of bonds with different maturities.[22]

Suppose that Irving Fisher is right and short rates of interest always incorporate fully the market's latest views about inflation. Suppose also that the market learns more as time passes about the likely inflation rate in a particular year. Perhaps today investors have only a very hazy idea about inflation in year 2, but in a year's time they expect to be able to make a much better prediction. Since investors expect to learn a good deal about the inflation rate in year 2 from experience in year 1, next year they will be in a much better position to judge the appropriate interest rate in year 2.

You are saving for your retirement. Which of the following strategies is the more risky? Invest in a succession of one-year Treasury bonds or invest in a 20-year bond?

If you buy the 20-year bond, you know what money you will have at the end of 20 years, but you will be making a long-term bet on inflation. Inflation may seem benign now, but who knows what it will be in 10 or 20 years? This uncertainty about inflation makes it more risky for you to fix today the rates at which you will lend in the distant future.

You can reduce this uncertainty by investing in successive short-term bonds. You do not know the interest rate at which you will be able to reinvest your money at the end of each year, but at least you know that it will incorporate the latest information about inflation in the coming year. So, if the prospects for inflation deteriorate, it is likely that you will be able to reinvest your money at a higher interest rate.

Inflation uncertainty may help to explain why long-term bonds provide a liquidity premium. If inflation creates additional risks for long-term lenders, borrowers must offer some incentive if they want investors to lend long. Therefore, the forward rate of interest f_2 must be greater than the expected spot rate $E({}_1r_2)$ by an amount that compensates investors for the extra risk of inflation.

Relationships between Bond Returns

These term structure theories tell us how bond prices may be determined at a point in time. More recently, financial economists have proposed some important theories of how price *movements* are related. These theories take advantage of the fact that the returns on bonds with different maturities tend to move together. For example, if short-term interest rates are high, it is a good bet that long-term rates will also be high. If short-term rates fall, long-term rates usually keep them company. Such linkages between interest rate movements can tell us something about relationships between bond prices.

The models that bond traders use to exploit these relationships can be quite complex and we can't get deeply into the subject here. However, the following example will give you a flavor of how the models work.

Suppose that you can invest in three possible government loans: a three-month Treasury bill, a medium-term bond, and a long-term bond. The return on the Treasury bill over the next three

[22]See R. A. Brealey and S. M. Schaefer, "Term Structure and Uncertain Inflation," *Journal of Finance* 32 (May 1977), pp. 277–290.

TABLE 23.3

Illustrative payoffs from three government securities. Note the wider range of outcomes from the longer-duration loans. We don't know what the medium-term bond sells for; we need to figure it out from how its value *changes* when interest rates rise or fall.

		Change in Value		
	Beginning Price	If Interest Rates Rise	If Interest Rates Fall	Ending Value
Treasury bill	98	+2	+2	100
Medium-term bond	?	−6.5	+10	?
Long-term bond	105	−15	+18	90 or 123

months is certain; we will assume it yields a 2 percent quarterly rate. The return on each of the other bonds depends on what happens to interest rates. Suppose that you foresee only two possible outcomes—a sharp rise in interest rates or a sharp fall. Table 23.3 summarizes how the prices of the three investments would be affected. Notice that the long-term bond has a longer duration and therefore a wider range of possible outcomes.

Here's the puzzle. You know the price of the Treasury bill and the long-term bond. But can you get rid of the two question marks in Table 23.3 and figure out what the medium-term bond should sell for?

Suppose that you start with Rs. 100. You invest half of this money in the Treasury bill and half in the long-term bond. In this case the change in the value of your portfolio will be $(.5 \times 2) + [.5 \times (-15)] = -$Rs. 6.5 if interest rates rise and $(.5 \times 2) + (.5 \times 18) = +$Rs. 10 if interest rates fall. Thus, regardless of whether interest rates rise or fall, your portfolio will provide exactly the same payoffs as an investment in the medium-term bond. Since the two investments provide identical payoffs, they must sell for the same price or there will be a money machine. So, the value of the medium-term bond must be halfway between the value of a three-month bill and that of the long-term bond, that is, $(98 + 105)/2 = 101.5$. Knowing this, you can calculate what the yield to maturity on the medium-term bond has to be. You can also calculate its value next year, either $101.5 - 6.5 = 95$ or $101.5 + 10 = 111.5$.

Everything now checks; regardless of whether interest rates rise or fall, the medium-term bond will provide the same payoff as the package of Treasury bill and long-term bond and therefore it must cost the same:

		Ending Value	
	Initial Outlay	If Interest Rates Rise	If Interest Rates Fall
Equal holdings of Treasury bill & long-term bond	(.5 × 98) + (.5 × 105) = 101.5	(.5 × 100) + (.5 × 90) = 95	(.5 × 100) + (.5 × 123) = 111.5
Medium-term bond	101.5	101.5 − 6.5 = 95	101.5 + 10 = 111.5

Our example is grossly oversimplified, but you have probably already noticed that the basic idea is the same that we used when valuing an option. To value an option on a share, we constructed a portfolio of a risk-free loan and the common stock that would exactly replicate the payoffs from the option. That allowed us to price the option *given* the price of the risk-free loan and the share. Here we value a bond by constructing a portfolio of two or more other bonds that will provide exactly the same payoffs.[23] That allows us to value one bond *given* the prices of the other bonds.

Our example carries three messages. First, bond traders focus on *changes* in bond prices and on how the changes for different bonds are linked. Second, changes in bond prices can be related to a small number of factors (in our example, the change in the overall level of interest rates completely defined the change in the price of each bond). Third, once the linkages between bond prices can be pinned down, then each bond can be priced relative to a package of other bonds.

[23]Two early examples of models that use no-arbitrage conditions to model the term structure are O. Vasicek, "An Equilibrium Characterization of the Term Structure," *Journal of Financial Economics* 5 (November 1977), pp. 177–188; and J. C. Cox, J. E. Ingersoll, and S. A. Ross, "A Theory of the Term Structure of Interest Rates," *Econometrica* 53 (May 1985), pp. 385–407.

SUMMARY

Efficient debt management presupposes that you understand how bonds are valued. That means you need to consider three problems:

1. What determines the general level of interest rates?
2. What determines the difference between long-term and short-term rates?
3. What determines the difference between the interest rates on company and government debt?

In this chapter we addressed the first two of these questions.

Here are some things to remember. The rate of interest depends on the demand for savings and the supply. The *demand* comes from firms who wish to invest in new plant and equipment. The supply of savings comes from individuals who are willing to consume tomorrow rather than today. The equilibrium interest rate is the rate that produces a *balance* between the demand and supply.

The best-known theory about the effect of inflation on interest rates was suggested by Irving Fisher. He argued that the nominal, or money, rate of interest is equal to the expected real rate plus the expected (and unrelated) inflation rate. If the expected inflation rate increases by 1 percent, so too will the money rate of interest. During the last 25 years Fisher's simple theory has not done a bad job of explaining changes in short-term interest rates in India.

The value of any bond is equal to the cash payments discounted at the spot rates of interest. For example, the value of a 10-year bond with a 5 percent coupon equals

$$\text{PV(percent of face value)} = \frac{5}{1 + r_1} + \frac{5}{(1 + r_2)^2} + \cdots + \frac{105}{(1 + r_{10})^{10}}$$

Bond dealers generally look at the yield to maturity on a bond. This is simply the internal rate of return y, the discount rate at which

$$\text{Bond price} = \frac{5}{1 + y} + \frac{5}{(1 + y)^2} + \cdots + \frac{105}{(1 + y)^{10}}$$

The yield to maturity y is a complex average of the spot interest rates r_1, r_2, etc. Like most averages it can be a useful summary measure, but it can also hide a lot of interesting information. We suggest you refer to yields on stripped bonds as measures of the spot rates of interest.

When you invest in a bond you usually receive a regular interest payment and then the final principal payment. Duration measures the *average* time to each payment. It is a useful summary measure of the length of a loan. It is also important because there is a direct relationship between the duration of a bond and its volatility. A change in interest rates has a greater effect on the price of a bond with a longer duration.

The one-period spot rate r_1 may be very different from the two-period spot rate r_2. In other words, investors often want a different annual rate of interest for lending for one year than for two years. Why is this? The *expectations theory* says that bonds are priced so that the expected rate of return from investing in bonds over any period is independent of the maturity of the bonds held by the investor. The expectations theory predicts that r_2 will exceed r_1 only if next year's one-period interest rate is expected to rise.

The expectations theory cannot be a complete explanation of the term structure if investors are worried about risk. Long bonds may be a safe haven for investors with long-term fixed liabilities. But other investors may not like the extra volatility of long-term bonds and may be concerned that a sudden burst in inflation could largely wipe out the real value of these bonds. Such investors will be prepared to hold long-term bonds only if they offer a liquidity premium—that is, a higher rate of interest.

We mentioned that the financial manager must also understand why company debt commands a higher rate of interest than government debt. The simple answer is that the higher interest is needed to compensate investors for the risk that companies may default. But how do you measure the risk of default and how do you factor this risk into the price of a bond? You'll find out in the next chapter.

FURTHER READING

A good general text on debt markets is:

A. Sundaresan and S. Sundaresan, *Fixed Income Markets and Their Derivatives*, 2nd ed. (Cincinnati, OH: South-Western College Publishing, 2001).

Empirical tests of term structure theories are provided by Fama and Shiller, Campbell, and Schoenholtz:

E. F. Fama, "The Information in the Term Structure," *Journal of Financial Economics* 13 (December 1984), pp. 509–528.

E. F. Fama, "Term Premiums in Bond Returns," *Journal of Financial Economics* 13 (December 1984), pp. 529–546.

R. J. Shiller, J. Y. Campbell, and K. L. Schoenholtz, "Forward Rates and Future Policy: Interpreting the Term Structure of Interest Rates," *Brookings Papers on Economic Activity* 1 (1983), pp. 173–217.

The following paper by Schaefer is a good review of duration and of how it is used to hedge fixed liabilities:

S. M. Schaefer, "Immunisation and Duration: A Review of Theory, Performance and Application," *Midland Corporate Finance Journal* 3 (Autumn 1984), pp. 41–58.

WEB EXERCISE

1. Log on to www.nseindia.com and find the zero coupon yield curve (ZCYC) for the day. How does today's yield curve compare with that of yesterday? Obtain the ZCYC for the last one month. You will find the link in ZCYC Time Series. Do short-term interest rates move more or less than long-term rates? Why do you think this is the case?

CONCEPT REVIEW QUESTIONS

1. Explain the difference between a conventional bond and an indexed bond. Why can't you directly compare the yields on the two bonds? (pages 628–629)
2. What does the real rate of interest depend on? (page 629)
3. What did Fisher say about the relationship between inflation and interest rates? (pages 629–630)

For additional Concept Review Questions, please visit us at www.mhhe.com/bmam8e or refer to your Student CD.

QUIZ

1. In June 2006, 11.03%, 2012 bonds offered a semiannually compounded yield of 5.434 percent. Recognizing that coupons are paid semiannually, calculate the bond's price.
2. Here are the prices in 2006 of four G-Secs with similar maturities:

G-Sec	Price (%)
6.72%, 2014	113.87
7.37%, 2014	119.25
10%, 2014	135.6
10.50%, 2014	141.9

   a. If coupons are paid annually, which bond offered the highest yield to maturity? Which had the lowest?
   b. Which bonds had the longest and shortest durations?
3. a. What is the formula for the value of a two-year, 5 percent bond in terms of spot rates?
   b. What is the formula for its value in terms of yield to maturity?
   c. If the two-year spot rate is higher than the one-year rate, is the yield to maturity greater or less than the two-year spot rate?
   d. In each of the following sentences choose the correct term from within the parentheses:
   "The (yield-to-maturity/spot-rate) formula discounts all cash flows from one bond at the same rate even though they occur at different points in time."
   "The (yield-to-maturity/spot-rate) formula discounts all cash flows received at the same point in time at the same rate even though the cash flows may come from different bonds."
4. Construct some simple examples to illustrate your answers to the following:
   a. If interest rates rise, do bond prices rise or fall?
   b. If the bond yield is greater than the coupon, is the price of the bond greater or less than 100?
   c. If the price of a bond exceeds 100, is the yield greater or less than the coupon?
   d. Do high-coupon bonds sell at higher or lower prices than low-coupon bonds?
   e. If interest rates change, does the price of high-coupon bonds change proportionately more than that of low-coupon bonds?
5. The following table shows the prices of a sample of U.S. Treasury strips in August 2004. Each strip makes a single payment of $1000 at maturity.

Maturity	Price (%)
August 2006	95.56
August 2007	92.30
August 2008	88.62
August 2014	64.42

a. Calculate the annually compounded, spot interest rate for each year.

b. Is the term structure upward- or downward-sloping?

c. Would you expect the yield on a *coupon* bond maturing in August 2014 to be higher or lower than the yield on the 2014 strip?

d. Calculate the annually compounded, one-year forward rate of interest for August 2006. Now do the same for August 2007.

eXcel

Please visit us at www.mhhe.com/bmam8e or refer to your Student CD.

6. a. An 8 percent, five-year bond yields 6 percent. If the yield remains unchanged, what will be its price one year hence? Assume annual coupon payments.

b. What is the total return to an investor who held the bond over this year?

c. What can you deduce about the relationship between the bond return over a particular period and the yields to maturity at the start and end of that period?

eXcel

Please visit us at www.mhhe.com/bmam8e or refer to your Student CD.

7. True or false? Explain.

a. Longer-maturity bonds necessarily have longer durations.

b. The longer a bond's duration, the lower its volatility.

c. Other things equal, the lower the bond coupon, the higher its volatility.

d. If interest rates rise, bond durations rise also.

8. Calculate the durations and volatilities of securities A, B, and C. Their cash flows are shown below. The interest rate is 8 percent.

	Period 1	Period 2	Period 3
A	40	40	40
B	20	20	120
C	10	10	110

9. a. Suppose that the one-year spot rate of interest at time 0 is 1 percent and the two-year spot rate is 3 percent. What is the forward rate of interest for year 2?

b. What does the expectations theory of term structure say about the relationship between the forward rate and the one-year spot rate at time 1?

c. Over a very long period of time, the term structure in India has been on average upward-sloping. Is this evidence for or against the expectations theory?

d. What does the liquidity-preference theory say about the relationship between the forward rate and the one-year spot rate at time 1?

e. If the liquidity-preference theory is a good approximation and you have to meet long-term liabilities (college tuition for your children, for example), is it safer to invest in long- or short-term bonds? Assume inflation is predictable.

f. If inflation is very uncertain and you have to meet long-term real liabilities, is it safer to invest in long- or short-term bonds?

PRACTICE QUESTIONS

1. A 6 percent six-year bond yields 12 percent and a 10 percent six-year bond yields 8 percent. Calculate the six-year spot rate. (Assume annual coupon payments.)

2. Is the yield on high-coupon bonds more likely to be higher than that on low-coupon bonds when the term structure is upward-sloping or when it is downward-sloping?

3. The one-year spot rate is $r_1 = 6$ percent, and the forward rate for a one-year loan maturing in year 2 is $f_2 = 6.4$ percent. Similarly, $f_3 = 7.1$ percent, $f_4 = 7.3$ percent, and $f_5 = 8.2$ percent. What are the spot rates r_2, r_3, r_4, and r_5? If the expectations hypothesis holds, what can you say about expected future interest rates?

4. Suppose your company will receive Rs. 100 million at $t = 4$ but must make a Rs. 107 million payment at $t = 5$. Assume the spot and forward rates from Practice Question 3. Show how the company can lock in the interest rate at which it will invest at $t = 4$. Will the Rs. 100 million, invested at this locked-in rate, be sufficient to cover the Rs. 107 million liability?

5. Use the rates from Practice Question 3 one more time. Consider the following bonds, each with a five-year maturity. Calculate the yield to maturity for each. Which is the better investment (or are they equally attractive)? Each has Rs. 1,000 face value and pays coupons annually.

Coupon	Price
5	92.07%
7	100.31
12	120.92

6. You have estimated spot rates as follows:

Year	Spot Rate
1	$r_1 = 5.00\%$
2	$r_2 = 5.40$
3	$r_3 = 5.70$
4	$r_4 = 5.90$
5	$r_5 = 6.00$

excel

Please visit us at www.mhhe.com/bmam8e or refer to your Student CD.

a. What are the discount factors for each date (that is, the present value of Rs. 1 paid in year t)?
b. What are the forward rates for each period?
c. Calculate the PV of the following G-Secs assuming annual coupons:
 i. 5 percent, two-year note.
 ii. 5 percent, five-year note.
 iii. 10 percent, five-year note.
d. Explain intuitively why the yield to maturity on the 10 percent bond is less than that on the 5 percent bond.
e. What should be the yield to maturity on a five-year zero-coupon bond?
f. Show that the correct yield to maturity on a five-year annuity is 5.75 percent.
g. Explain intuitively why the yield on the five-year G-Secs described in part (c) must lie between the yield on a five-year zero-coupon bond and a five-year annuity.

7. Look at the spot interest rates shown in question 6. Suppose that someone told you that the six-year spot interest rate was 4.80 percent. Why would you not believe him? How could you make money if he was right? What is the minimum sensible value for the six-year spot rate?

8. Look again at the spot interest rates shown in question 6. What can you deduce about the one-year spot interest rate in four years if
a. The expectations theory of term structure is right?
b. The liquidity-preference theory of term structure is right?
c. The term structure contains an inflation uncertainty premium?

excel

Please visit us at www.mhhe.com/bmam8e or refer to your Student CD.

9. Look up prices of 10 Government securities with different coupons and different maturities. Calculate how their prices would change if their yields to maturity increased by one percentage point. Are long- or short-term bonds most affected by the change in yields? Are high- or low-coupon bonds most affected?

excel

Please visit us at www.mhhe.com/bmam8e or refer to your Student CD.

10. In Section 23.3 we stated that in 2006 the duration of the 8%, 2011 bond was 4.35 years. Construct a table like Table 23.2 to show that this is so.

11. Prepare a spreadsheet for table 23.2 of this book. Show how duration and volatility change if (a) the bond's coupon is 7 percent of face value and (b) the bond's yield is 5 percent. Explain your finding.
12. The formula for the duration of a perpetual bond which makes an equal payment each year in perpetuity is (1 + yield)/yield. If bonds yield 5 percent, which has the longer duration—a perpetual bond or a 15-year zero-coupon bond? What if the yield is 10 percent?
13. You have just been fired as CEO. As consolation the board of directors gives you a five-year consulting contract at Rs. 150,000 per year. What is the duration of this contract if your personal borrowing rate is 9 percent? Use duration to calculate the change in the contract's present value for a .5 percent increase in your borrowing rate.
14. Look at the example in Section 23.4 of the Treasury bill and the medium- and long-term bonds. Now assume that the price of the medium-term bond can either fall by Rs. 10.75 or rise by Rs. 14.0. What can you say now about the relationship between the value of the three bonds?

CHALLENGE QUESTIONS

1. Find the arbitrage opportunity (opportunities?). Assume for simplicity that coupons are paid annually. In each case the face value of the bond is Rs. 1,000.

Bond	Maturity (years)	Coupon (Rs.)	Price (Rs.)
A	3	zero	751.30
B	4	50	842.30
C	4	120	1,065.28
D	4	100	980.57
E	3	140	1,120.12
F	3	70	1,001.62
G	2	zero	834.00

2. The duration of a bond that makes an equal payment each year in perpetuity is (1 + yield)/yield. Prove it.
3. What is the duration of a common stock whose dividends are expected to grow at a constant rate in perpetuity?
4. a. What spot and forward rates are embedded in the following G-Secs? The price of 364-days T-bills is 93.46 percent. Assume for simplicity that G-Secs make only annual payments. Hint: Can you devise a mixture of long and short positions in these bonds that gives a cash payoff only in year 2? In year 3?

Coupon (%)	Maturity (years)	Price (%)
4	2	94.92
8	3	103.64

   b. A three-year bond with a 4 percent coupon is selling at 95.00 percent. Is there a profit opportunity here? If so, how would you take advantage of it?
5. Look back at our example in Section 23.4 of the short-, medium-, and long-term bonds. Remember that we said that the prices must stand in a particular relationship or there would be an arbitrage opportunity. This means that we can take advantage of the risk-neutral trick that we used to value options. Pretend that investors are risk-neutral. Now answer the following questions:

a. Suppose that the price of the short bond is 98 and the price of the medium is 83. What is the price of the long bond?
b. What are the possible future prices of these three bonds at the end of three months if rates rise and if they fall?
c. What would be the expected return over the three months on each bond?
d. What is the probability of an interest rate rise?
e. Show that the expected return on each bond is equal.

CHAPTER [24]

CREDIT RISK

WHEN Government of India borrows money, you can be confident that the debt will be repaid in full and on time. That is not the case with corporate borrowing. For example, in 2002 companies worldwide defaulted on a record $190 billion of rated debt.[1] Lenders are aware of the danger that they will not get repaid and so demand a higher rate of interest when they lend to companies rather than to governments.

We begin this chapter by looking at how the value of corporate debt is affected by the risk of default. We go on to look at bond ratings and some of the techniques that are used by banks and bond investors to estimate the chance that the borrower will default. Finally, in Section 24.5 we discuss how to measure the likely losses on a single loan or a portfolio of loans.

[1]Standard & Poor's 2003 Annual Corporate Default Study, **www.standardandpoors.com.**

24.1 THE VALUE OF CORPORATE DEBT

In 2003 Avado Brands, owners of Don Pablo's Mexican Kitchen restaurants, was a company in trouble. Its 11.75 percent bonds maturing in 2009 were priced at 13 and offered a yield of 92 percent. A naïve investor who compared this with the 3 percent yield on G-Sec might have concluded that the Avado Brands debt was a good investment. But the investor would not earn a return of 92 percent unless the company managed to scrape up the cash to repay the bonds in full. Since there was a substantial risk that the company would default, the *expected* return on the bonds was less than 92 percent.

Corporate bonds, such as the Avado Brands bond, offer a higher *promised* yield than government bonds, but do they necessarily offer a higher *expected* yield? We can answer this question with a simple numerical example. Suppose that the interest rate on one-year *risk-free* bonds is 5 percent. Backwoods Chemical Company has issued 5 percent notes with a face value of Rs. 1,000, maturing in one year. What will the Backwoods notes sell for?

If the notes are risk-free, the answer is easy—just discount principal (Rs. 1,000) and interest (Rs. 50) at 5 percent:

$$\text{PV of notes} = \frac{\text{Rs. } 1{,}000 + 50}{1.05} = \text{Rs. } 1{,}000$$

Suppose, however, that there is a 20 percent chance that Backwoods will default and that, if default does occur, holders of its notes receive half the face value of the notes, or Rs. 500. In this case, the possible payoffs to the noteholders are

	Payoff	Probability
Full payment	Rs. 1,050	.8
No payment	500	.2

The expected payment is .8(Rs. 1,050) + .2(Rs. 500) = Rs. 940.

We can value the Backwoods notes like any other risky asset, by discounting their expected payoff (Rs. 940) at the appropriate opportunity cost of capital. We might discount at the risk-free interest rate (5 percent) if Backwoods's possible default is totally unrelated to other events in the economy. In this case default risk is wholly diversifiable, and the beta of the notes is zero. The notes would sell for

$$\text{PV of notes} = \frac{\text{Rs. }940}{1.05} = \text{Rs. }895$$

An investor who purchased the notes for Rs. 895 would receive a *promised* yield of 17.3 percent:

$$\text{Promised yield} = \frac{\text{Rs. }1050}{\text{Rs. }895} - 1 = .173$$

That is, an investor who purchased the notes for Rs. 895 would earn a return of 17.3 percent if Backwoods does not default. Bond traders therefore might say that the Backwoods notes "yield 17.3 percent." But the smart investor would realize that the notes' expected yield is only 5 percent, the same as on risk-free bonds.

This of course assumes that the risk of default with these notes is wholly diversifiable, so that they have no market risk. In general, risky bonds do have market risk (that is, positive betas) because default is more likely to occur in recessions when all businesses are doing poorly. Suppose that investors demand a 3 percent risk premium and an 8 percent expected rate of return. Then the Backwoods notes will sell for 940/1.08 = Rs. 870 and offer a promised yield of (1,050/870) − 1 = .207, or 20.7 percent.

The Difference Between Safe and Risky Debt

The difference between a corporate bond and a comparable G-Sec is that the company has the option to default whereas the government supposedly doesn't.[2] That is a valuable option. If you don't believe us think about whether (other things equal) you would prefer to be a shareholder in a company with limited liability or in a company with unlimited liability. Of course, you would prefer to have the option to walk away from your company's debts. Unfortunately, every silver lining has its cloud, and the drawback to having a default option is that corporate bondholders expect to be compensated for giving it to you. That is why corporate bonds sell at lower prices and offer higher yields than government bonds.

We can illustrate the nature of the default option by returning to the plight of Circular File Company, which we discussed in Chapter 18. Circular File borrowed Rs. 50 per share, but then the firm fell on hard times and the market value of its assets fell to Rs. 30. Circular's bond and stock prices fell to Rs. 25 and Rs. 5, respectively. Thus Circular's *market-value* balance sheet is:

Circular File Company (Market Values)

Asset value	Rs. 30	Rs. 25	Bonds
		5	Stock
	Rs. 30	Rs. 30	Firm value

If Circular's debt were due and payable now, the firm could not repay the Rs. 50 it originally borrowed. It would default, leaving bondholders with assets worth Rs. 30 and shareholders with

[2]But governments cannot print the currencies of other countries. Therefore, they may be forced into default on their foreign currency debt. For example, in December 2001 Argentina defaulted on $155 billion of foreign currency debt. Very occasionally governments have even defaulted on their own currency's debt. After World War II the West German government could have printed money to pay off its bonds, but it chose to default rather than run the risk of hyperinflation.

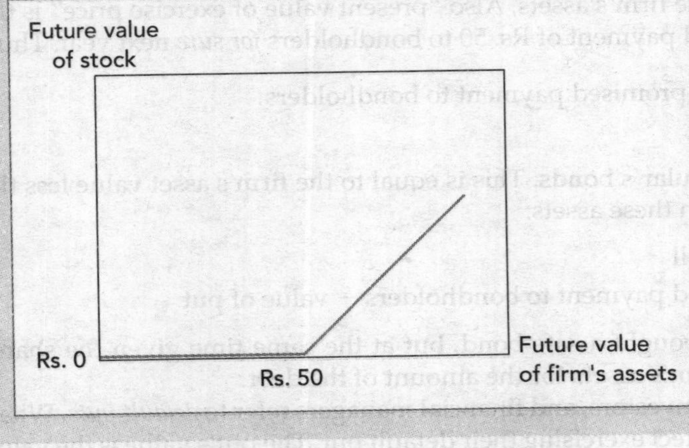

FIGURE 24.1

The value of Circular's common stock is the value of a call option on the firm's assets with an exercise price of Rs. 50.

nothing. The reason that Circular stock has a market value of Rs. 5 is that the debt is *not* due now, but rather a year from now. A stroke of good fortune could increase firm value enough to pay off the bondholders in full, with something left over for the stockholders.

When Circular File borrowed, it acquired an option to default. In other words, it is not compelled to repay the debt at maturity. If the value of its assets is less than the Rs. 50 that it owes, it will choose to default on the debt and the bondholders will get to keep the assets. To put it another way, when Circular borrowed, the bondholders effectively acquired the company's assets and the shareholders gained an option to buy them back by paying off the debt. In effect, the stockholders purchased a call option on the assets of the firm. Thus the balance sheet of Circular File can be expressed as follows:

Circular File Company (Market Values)

Asset value	Rs. 30	Rs. 25	Bond value = asset value − value of call
		5	Stock value = value of call
	Rs. 30	Rs. 30	Firm value = asset value

Figure 24.1 shows the possible payoffs to Circular File's shareholders when the bonds mature at the end of the year. If the future value of the assets is less than Rs. 50, Circular will default and the stock will be worthless. If the value of the assets exceeds Rs. 50, the stockholders will receive asset value *less* the Rs. 50 paid over to the bondholders. Does Figure 24.1 look familiar to you? It should if you have read Chapter 20 on options. The payoffs in Figure 24.1 are identical to those of a call option on the firm's assets with an exercise price of Rs. 50.

In Chapter 20 we also set out the basic relationship between calls and puts:

$$\text{Value of call} + \text{present value of exercise price} = \text{value of put} + \text{value of share}$$

To apply this to Circular File, we need to interpret "value of share" as "asset value," because the common stock is a call option on the firm's assets. Also "present value of exercise price" is the present value of receiving the promised payment of Rs. 50 to bondholders *for sure* next year. Thus

$$\text{Value of call} + \text{present value of promised payment to bondholders}$$
$$= \text{value of put} + \text{asset value}$$

Now we can solve for the value of Circular's bonds. This is equal to the firm's asset value less the value of the shareholders' call option on these assets:

$$\text{Bond value} = \text{asset value} - \text{value of call}$$
$$= \text{present value of promised payment to bondholders} - \text{value of put}$$

Circular's bondholders have in effect bought a safe bond, but at the same time given the shareholders a put option to sell them the firm's assets for the amount of the debt.

Now you can see why bond traders, investors, and financial managers refer to *default puts*. When a firm defaults, its stockholders are in effect exercising their default put. The put's value is the value of limited liability—the value of the stockholders' right to walk away from their firm's debts in exchange for handing over the firm's assets to its creditors. In the case of Circular File this option to default is extremely valuable because default is likely to occur. At the other extreme, the value of Reliance's option to default is trivial compared with the value of Reliance's assets. Default on Reliance bonds is possible but extremely unlikely. Option traders would say that for Circular File the put option is "deep in the money" because today's asset value (Rs. 30) is well below the exercise price (Rs. 50). For Reliance the put option is far "out of the money" because the value of Reliance's assets substantially exceeds the amount of Reliance's debt.

Valuing corporate bonds should be a two-step process:

$$\text{Bond value} = \begin{matrix}\text{bond value assuming} \\ \text{no chance of default}\end{matrix} - \begin{matrix}\text{value of put} \\ \text{option on assets}\end{matrix}$$

The first step is easy: Calculate the bond's value assuming no default risk. (Discount promised interest and principal payments at the rates offered by G-Sec issues.) Second, calculate the value of a put written on the firm's assets, where the maturity of the put equals the maturity of the bond and the exercise price of the put equals the promised payment to bondholders.

Owning a corporate bond is also equivalent to owning the firm's assets but giving a call option on these assets to the firm's stockholders:

$$\text{Bond value} = \text{asset value} - \text{value of call option on assets}$$

Thus you can also calculate a bond's value, given the value of the firm's assets, by valuing a call option on these assets and subtracting the value of this call from that of the assets. (Remember: The call value is just the value of the firm's common stock.) Therefore, if you can value puts and calls on the firm's assets, you can value its debt.[3]

[3]However, option-valuation procedures cannot value the *assets* of the firm. Puts and calls must be valued as a proportion of asset value. For example, note that the Black–Scholes formula (Section 21.3) requires stock price to compute the value of a call option.

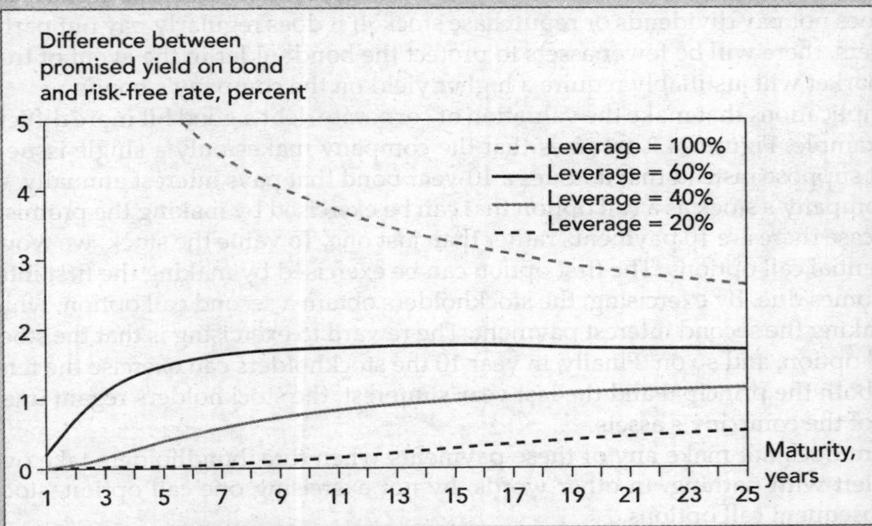

FIGURE 24.2

How the interest rate on risky corporate debt changes with leverage and maturity. These curves are calculated using option pricing theory under the following simplified assumptions: (1) the risk-free interest rate is constant for all maturities; (2) the standard deviation of the returns on the company's assets is 25 percent per annum; (3) debt is in the form of zero-coupon bonds; and (4) leverage is the ratio *D/V*, where *D* is the face value of the debt discounted at the risk-free interest rate and *V* is the market value of the assets.

Valuing the Default Option

Figure 24.2 shows a simple application of option theory to pricing corporate debt. It takes a company with average operating risk and shows how the promised interest rate on its debt should vary with the leverage and the maturity of the debt.[4] For example, if the company has a 20 percent debt ratio and all its debt matures in 25 years, then it should pay about one-half percentage point above the government borrowing rate to compensate for default risk. Companies with more leverage ought to pay higher premiums. Notice that except in the case of very high debt ratios, promised yields increase with maturity. This makes sense, for the longer you have to wait for repayment, the greater is the chance that things will go wrong. However, if the company is already in distress and its assets are worth less than the face value of the debt, then promised yields are higher at *low* maturities. (In our example, they run off the top of the graph for maturities of less than five years.) In these cases the longer that you wait, the greater is the chance that the company will recover and avoid default.[5]

[4]Note that in Figure 24.2 leverage is defined as the face value of the debt discounted at the risk-free interest rate as a proportion of the market value of the firm's assets.

[5]Sarig and Warga plot the difference between corporate bond yields and the yields on U.S. Treasuries. They confirm that the yield difference increases with maturity for high-grade bonds and declines for low-grade bonds. See O. Sarig and A. Warga, "Bond Price Data and Bond Market Liquidity," *Journal of Financial and Quantitative Analysis* 44 (1989), pp. 1351–1360. Incidentally, the shape of the curves in Figure 24.2 depends on how leverage is defined. If we had plotted curves for a constant ratio of the *market* value of debt to debt plus equity, the curves would all have started at zero.

Notice that in constructing Figure 24.2 we made several artificial assumptions. One assumption is that the company does not pay dividends or repurchase stock. If it does regularly pay out part of its assets to stockholders, there will be fewer assets to protect the bondholder in the event of trouble. In this case, the market will justifiably require a higher yield on the company's bonds.

There are other complications that make the valuation of corporate debt a good bit more difficult than it sounds. For example, Figure 24.2 assumes that the company makes only a single issue of zero-coupon debt. But suppose instead that it issues a 10-year bond that pays interest annually. We can still think of the company's stock as a call option that can be exercised by making the promised payments. But in this case there are 10 payments rather than just one. To value the stock, we would need to value 10 sequential call options. The first option can be exercised by making the first interest payment when it comes due. By exercising, the stockholders obtain a second call option, which can be exercised by making the second interest payment. The reward to exercising is that the stockholders get a third call option, and so on. Finally, in year 10 the stockholders can exercise the tenth option. By paying off both the principal and the last year's interest, the stockholders regain unencumbered ownership of the company's assets.

Of course, if the firm does not make any of these payments when due, bondholders take over and stockholders are left with nothing. In other words, by not exercising one call option, stockholders give up all subsequent call options.

Valuing the equity when the 10-year bond is issued is equivalent to valuing the first of the 10 call options. But you cannot value the first option without valuing the nine that follow.[6] Even this example understates the practical difficulties, because large firms may have dozens of outstanding debt issues with different interest rates and maturities, and before the current debt matures they may make further issues. But do not lose heart. Computers can solve these problems, more or less by brute force, even in the absence of simple, exact valuation formulas.

In practice, interest rate differentials tend to be much greater than those shown in Figure 24.2. High-grade corporate bonds typically offer promised yields about 1 percentage point higher than Indian Government securities. It is very difficult to justify differentials of this magnitude simply in terms of default risk.[7] So what is going on? It could be that companies are paying too much for their debt, but it seems likely that the high yields on corporate bonds stem in part from some other drawback. One possibility is that investors demand the additional yield to compensate for the illiquidity of corporate debt.[8] There is little doubt that investors prefer bonds that are easily bought and sold. We can even see small yield differences in the Treasury bond market, where the latest bonds to have been issued (known as "on-the-run" bonds) are traded much more heavily and typically yield a few basis points less than more seasoned issues.

---

[6]The other approach to valuing the company's debt (subtracting the value of a put option from risk-free bond value) is no easier. The analyst would be confronted by not one simple put option but a package of 10 sequential puts.

[7]See, for example, J. Huang and M. Huang, "How Much of the Corporate-Treasury Yield Spread Is Due to Credit Risk? Results from a New Calibration Approach," working paper, Pennsylvania State University, May 2003.

[8]For evidence that the more liquid corporate bonds have lower yields than less liquid bonds, see E. J. Elton, M. J. Gruber, D. Agrawal, and C. Mann, "Factors Affecting the Valuation of Corporate Bonds," working paper, Stern School of Business, New York University, February 2002.

Valuing Government Loan Guarantees

In 2002 America West Airlines was in desperate need of cash. The decline in traffic that followed the terrorist attacks of September 11 had caused a sharp fall in AWA's revenues, and the company's banks were reluctant to extend their exposure to such a high-risk company. To help keep the airline flying, the government agreed to guarantee $380 million of new loans to AWA. If the company defaulted on these loans, investors could get their money back directly from the government.

The loan guarantee was a helping hand to bring America West through a difficult period. If the company is subsequently unable to repay its debt, the U.S. government will have to step in and make up any shortfall. The government recognized this possibility and to calculate the cost of its loan guarantee to America West it estimated the probability that it would have to pay out on the guarantee and discounted the expected cash payment by the interest rate on Treasury bonds. This procedure suggests that the cost of the guarantee was about $85 million.

Unfortunately, the government's calculations ignore the fact that by providing the guarantee, it has taken on the risk that would otherwise have been borne by the bondholders. The guarantee changed AWA's loans from risky debt to safe debt. Its present value was therefore the difference between the value of a risk-free Treasury loan and the value of a loan with a chance of default. This value can be substantial when the loan is large and the chance of default is high.

It turns out that a loan guarantee can be valued as a put option on the firm's assets, where the put's maturity equals the loan's maturity and its exercise price equals the interest and principal payments promised to lenders. We can easily show the equivalence by starting with the definition of the value of the guarantee.

$$\text{Value of guarantee} = \begin{array}{c}\text{loan value with}\\ \text{the guarantee}\end{array} - \begin{array}{c}\text{loan value without}\\ \text{the guarantee}\end{array}$$

With the guarantee the debt is as safe as a loan to the U.S. government; *without* the guarantee it is an ordinary debt obligation of the firm. We already know what the difference is between the value of safe government debt and risky corporate debt. It is the value of the stockholders' right to walk away from their firm's debts in exchange for handing over the firm's assets to its creditors. Thus the value of the loan guarantee is the value of this put option.[9]

In a study prepared for the Congressional Budget Office Deborah Lucas, Marvin Phaup, and Ravi Prasad use the example of America West to show how option pricing models can be used to give better measures of the cost of loan guarantees.[10] Their estimates suggest that the true cost of the AWA guarantee was $133 million, or $48 million more than the government's estimate.[11]

---

[9]Now you can see why the government's calculations underestimate the cost of the guarantee. We know from our discussion of the risk-neutral method in Chapter 21 that when valuing an option, it is the *certainty-equivalent* cash flows that need to be discounted at the rate of interest.

[10]"Estimating the value of subsidies for Federal Loans and Loan Guarantees," Congress of the United States, Congressional Budget Office, Washington, DC, August 2004.

[11]This cost was partly offset by the fact that the government charged America West a fee for providing the guarantee and in addition received long-term options to buy the company's common stock. Lucas, Phaup, and Prasad estimated that the net cost to the government was $26 million.

Option pricing should lead to a better way of calculating the cost of the government's many loan guarantee programs. This will be a healthy thing. The government's possible liability under existing guarantee programs is enormous. For example, in 2003 the government guaranteed $365 billion of new loans. Many guaranteed loans are for housing, but they also include loans to airlines, shipowners and shipyards, steel companies, and oil and gas companies.

24.2 BOND RATINGS AND THE PROBABILITY OF DEFAULT

Banks and other financial institutions not only want to know the value of the loans that they have made but they also need to know the risk that they are incurring. Some rely on the judgments of specialized bond rating services. Others have developed their own models for measuring the probability that the borrower will default. We will describe bond ratings first, and then discuss two models for predicting default.

The relative quality of most traded bonds can be judged by bond ratings. There are three principal rating services in India – Credit Rating Information Services of India Limited (CRISIL), Investment Information and Credit Rating Agency of India Limited (ICRA), and Credit Analysis and Research Limited (CARE).[12] Table 24.1 summarizes these ratings. For example, the highest-quality bonds are rated triple-A (AAA) by CRISIL, then come double-A (AA) bonds, and so on. Bonds rated BBB or above are known as investment-grade bonds.[13] As per the IRDA regulations, insurance companies are not allowed to invest in any bonds with a rating below AA.

TABLE 24.1

Key to bond ratings. The highest quality bonds are rated triple-A. Investment-grade bonds have to be the equivalent of triple-B or higher. Bonds that do not make this cut are called "high-yield" or "junk" bonds.

CRISIL	ICRA
Investment-grade bonds:	
AAA	LAAA
AA	LAA
A	LA
BBB	LBBB
Junk bonds:	
BB	LBB
B	LB
C	LC
D	LD

[12]As per Indiainfoline.com survey, these three rating agencies enjoy a combined market share of 96 percent in India.

[13]Rating services also provide a finer breakdown. Thus a bond might be rated AA$^+$, AA, or AA$^-$ (the lowest AA rating). In addition, the rating service may announce that it has put an issue on its watch list for a possible upgrade or downgrade.

Ratio	AAA	AA	A	BBB	BB	B	C	D
Retained Earnings to Total Assets	0.06	0.04	0.04	0.03	0.01	–0.01	0.00	–0.02
Total Assets (natural Logarithms of)*	7.71	5.69	4.71	4.88	4.74	5.12	4.74	4.97
Market value of equity to book debt	4.51	1.95	1.19	0.58	0.51	0.24	0.26	0.18

TABLE 24.2

How financial ratios differ according to a firm's bond rating. *Total assets measured in Rs. crores.

Source: Sahoo, B.K., and P Mohany, 2002, "An Alternative to CRISIL Credit rating using discriminant Analysis", The ICFAI Journal of Applied Finance, January.

	Percentage Defaulting within		
Rating at the Time of Issue	**1 Year after Issue**	**2 Years after Issue**	**3 Years after Issue**
AAA	0.00	0.00	0.00
AA	0.00	0.44	1.45
A	1.00	4.29	9.00
BBB	3.40	9.49	17.26
Investment Grade (BBB to AAA)	0.91	3.19	6.39
Speculative Grade	18.85	31.69	41.38

TABLE 24.3

Default rates of corporate bonds, 1992–2005, by CRISIL rating at time of issue.

Source: CRISIL's Insight in Risk: CRISIL Default Study (http://www.crisil.com/credit-ratings-risk-assessment/crisil-rating-default-study-2005.pdf) Reprinted by permission of CRISIL.

Bond ratings are judgments about firms' financial and business prospects. There is no fixed formula by which ratings are calculated. Nevertheless, investment bankers, bond portfolio managers, and others who follow the bond market closely can get a fairly good idea of how a bond will be rated by looking at a few key numbers such as the firm's debt ratio, the ratio of earnings to interest, book value of total assets, return on assets, retained earnings to total assets, etc. Table 24.2 shows how these ratios vary with the firm's bond rating (as rated by CRISIL).

Table 24.3 shows that bond ratings do reflect the probability of default. Since 1992 no bond that was initially rated triple-A by CRISIL has defaulted in the next three years after issue. At the other extreme, about 40% of the speculative-grade bonds defaulted within three years of the issue. Of course, bonds do not usually fall suddenly from grace. As time passes and the company becomes progressively more shaky, the agencies revise downward the bond's rating to reflect the increasing probability of default.

Rating agencies don't always get it right. When Enron went belly-up in 2001, investors protested that only two months earlier the company's debt had an investment-grade rating. As the nearby box illustrates, rating bonds can be a lonely and friendless task.

FINANCE IN THE NEWS

DIFFICULT TIMES FOR RATING AGENCIES

THE big credit-rating agencies are under the spotlight again. Their failure to detect early signs of trouble at Enron, WorldCom and other once high-flying companies has left regulators wondering where the agencies get their information, how they analyse it, and whether their opinions are worth the paper they are written on. During two days of public hearings in Washington, DC, on November 15th and 21st, the SEC is asking out loud if the three biggest agencies—Standard & Poor's (S&P), Moody's Investors Service, and Fitch Ratings—have become too big for their own (and everybody else's) good.

S&P, Moody's and their smaller rival, Fitch, owe their special status to the SEC's decision in 1934 to introduce a net capital rule for broker dealers operating in the capital markets.

This determined that the dealers must have a "haircut" (reduce the value of securities they can trade) if their capital were depleted by a fall in the value of bonds held on their books. The SEC decided that the haircuts could be less severe if the securities were rated by nationally recognized and respected agencies. Since then, the agencies have taken on other quasi-regulatory roles. For example, the SEC insists that the bulk of the billions of dollars held in money-market funds—savings products not guaranteed by the government—carry top or near-top ratings from at least one approved agency.

When things go wrong, the agencies get it in the neck from both sides. Investors caught holding Enron's investment-grade bonds as their price sank to below that of junk say that the agencies are just too slow to spot companies' declining health. A better guide, say some, are the spreads (above Treasury bonds of a similar maturity) at which the bonds trade. Others argue that the agencies are now acting too quickly to downgrade companies' ratings in order to avoid further accusations that they fail to spot problems. And that, say the critics, is a classic case of slamming the stable door shut after the horse has bolted. This week, the bosses of several large French companies lashed out at the rating agencies, accusing them of unjustified downgrades that have precipitated several debt crises. Alcatel's chief executive, Serge Tchuruk, likened the agencies to "pyromaniac firemen", while Vivendi Universal's boss, Jean-Rene Fourtou, called them "the executioner".

Source: Excerpt from "Global Agenda", *The Economist Online*, **(www.economist.com)**, November 20, 2002, p. 1. Reprinted with permission of The Economist Newspaper Group, Inc. Further reproduction is prohibited.

Since bond ratings generally reflect the probability of default, it is not surprising that there is a close correspondence between a bond's rating and its promised yield. Figure 24.3 shows the yields of corporate bonds relative to those of Government securities. On average, triple-A bonds have yielded about 1 percent more than Government securities and BBB- bonds have yielded 7 percent more. However, the spreads vary considerably from year to year. When times are hard and bankruptcies begin to multiply, investors scurry to high-quality debt and the promised yield on junk bonds can rise to more than 10 percent above that of Treasuries.

Remember, these are promised yields and companies don't always keep their promises. Many high-yielding bonds have defaulted, while some of the more successful issuers have called their debt, thus depriving their holders of the prospect of a continuing stream of high coupon payments. So, while *promised yield* on BBB-bonds has averaged 7 percent more than G-Sec yields, the annual *realized return* would be much lower.

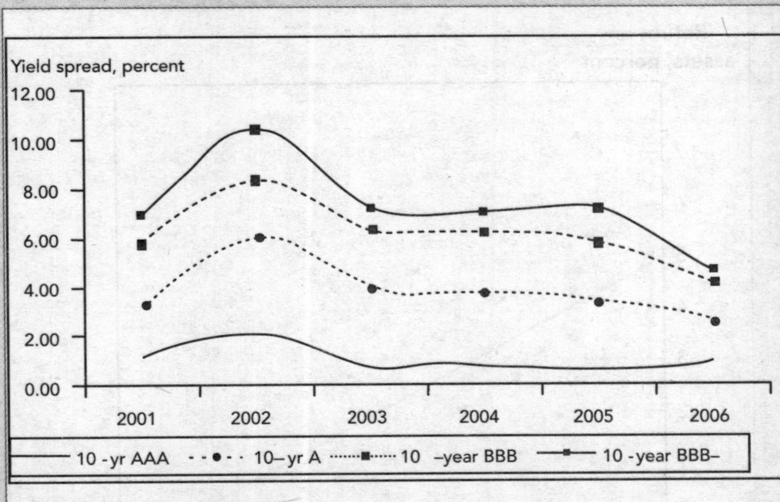

FIGURE 24.3

Yield spreads between corporate and 10-year G-Sec yields.

Source: Compiled from www.fimmda.org.

24.3 PREDICTING THE PROBABILITY OF DEFAULT

Credit Scoring

If you apply for a credit card or a bank loan, you will probably be asked to complete a questionnaire that provides details about your job, home, and financial position. This information is then used to calculate an overall credit score. Applicants who do not make the grade on the score are likely to be refused credit or subjected to a more detailed analysis.

Banks also employ mechanical credit scoring systems to assess the risk of their corporate loans. For example, suppose that you want to construct a scoring system that will be used to decide whether to extend credit to small businesses. You believe that there is an above-average probability that firms with a low return on assets and a low interest cover will default.

Your next step is to combine these two measures into a single yardstick of the likelihood of default. One way to do this is to take a sample of past loans and construct a scatter diagram showing for each borrower the return on assets and the interest cover (see Figure 24.4). Those businesses that repaid their loans are shown by a blue x; the ones that defaulted are shown in green. Now try to draw a straight dividing line between the two groups. You can't completely separate them, but the line in our diagram keeps the two groups as far apart as possible. (Note that there are only three blue x's below the line and three green +'s above it.) This line tells us that if you wish to *discriminate* between the good and the bad risks, you should give 5 times as much weight to the interest cover as you give to the return on assets. The index of creditworthiness is

$$\text{Index of creditworthiness} = Z = \text{return on assets} + 5\ (\text{interest cover})$$

You minimize the degree of misclassification if you predict that applicants with Z-scores over 5 will repay their debts and that those with Z-scores below 5 will not repay.[14]

[14]The quantity 5 is an arbitrary constant. We could just as well have used 50, in which case the Z-score is Z = 10(return on assets, percent) + 50(interest cover)

FIGURE 24.4

The blue x's represent a hypothetical group of firms that subsequently repaid their loans; the green+'s represent those that defaulted. The sloping line discriminates between the two groups on the basis of return on assets and interest cover. The line represents the equation *Z* = return on assets + 5(interest cover) = 5. Firms that plot above the line have *Z*-scores greater than 5.

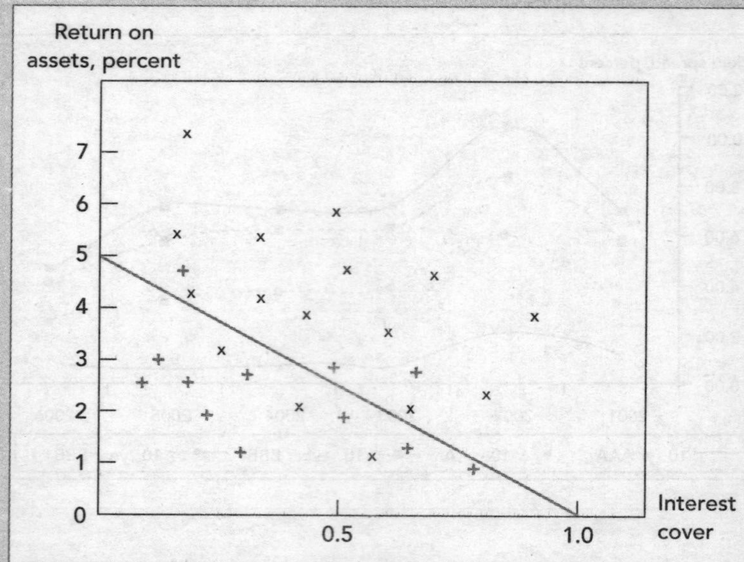

In practice you are not restricted to considering only two variables, nor do you need to estimate the equation by eye. *Multiple discriminant analysis (MDA)* is a straightforward statistical technique for calculating how much weight to put on each variable to separate the creditworthy sheep from the impecunious goats.

Edward Altman has used discriminant analysis to come up with the following index of creditworthiness:[15]

$$Z = .72\frac{\text{(net working capital)}}{\text{total assets}} + .85\frac{\text{(retained earnings)}}{\text{total assets}} + 3.1\frac{\text{(EBIT)}}{\text{total assets}}$$
$$+ .42\frac{\text{(shareholders' equity)}}{\text{total liabilities}} + 1.0\frac{\text{(sales)}}{\text{total assets}}$$

Those companies with a *Z*-score of less than 1.20 were predicted to go bankrupt. Companies with *Z*-scores between 1.20 and 2.90 were hovering in the grey area between decline and recovery.

Updated versions and variants of Altman's *Z*-score model are regularly used by banks and finance companies. We wish we could show you one of these recent measures, but they are all top-secret. A company with a superior method for identifying good and bad borrowers has a significant leg-up on the competition.

Credit scoring systems should carry a health warning. When you construct a risk index, it is tempting to experiment with many different combinations of variables until you find the equation that would have worked best in the past. Unfortunately, if you "mine" the data in this way, you are likely to find that the system works less well in the future than it did previously. If you are misled by the past successes into placing too much faith in your model, you may refuse credit to a number

[15]EBIT is earnings before interest and taxes. *Z*-score models for predicting bankruptcy were originally developed by E. I. Altman, "Financial Ratios and the Prediction of Corporate Bankruptcy," *Journal of Finance* 23 (September 1968), pp. 589–609. The equation cited here comes from E. I. Altman, *Corporate and Bankruptcy Financial Distress*, 2nd ed., (New York: John Wiley, 1993), p. 29.

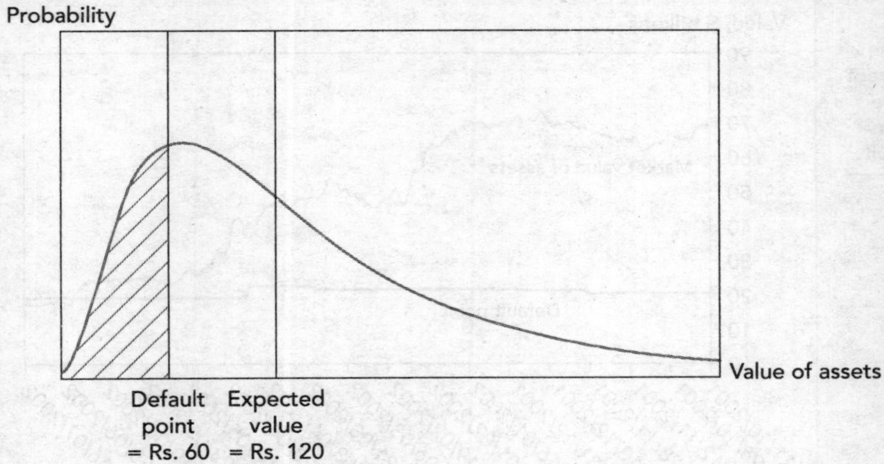

FIGURE 24.5

Backwoods Chemical has issued five-year debt with a face value of Rs. 60. The shaded area shows that there is a 20 percent probability that the value of the company's assets in year 5 with be less than Rs. 60, in which case the company will choose to default.

of potentially good customers. The profits that you lose by turning away these customers could more than offset the gains that you make by avoiding a few bad eggs. As a result, you could be worse off than if you had pretended that you could not tell one would-be borrower from another and extended credit to all of them.

Does this mean that banks should not use credit scoring systems? Not a bit. It merely implies that it is not sufficient to have a good system; you also need to know how much to rely on it.

Market-Based Risk Models

Credit scoring systems rely primarily on the companies' financial statements to estimate which firms are most likely to become bankrupt and default on their debts. For small businesses there may be little alternative to the use of accounting data, but for large, publicly traded firms it is also possible to take advantage of the information in security prices. These techniques build on the idea that stockholders will exercise their option to default if the market value of the assets falls below the payments that must be made on the debt.

Suppose that the assets of Backwoods Chemical have a current market value of Rs. 100 and its debt has a face value of Rs. 60 (i.e., 60 percent leverage), all of which is due to be repaid at the end of five years. Figure 24.5 shows the range of possible values of Backwoods's assets when the loan becomes due. The expected value of the assets is Rs. 120, but this value is by no means certain. There is a probability of 20 percent that the asset value could fall below Rs. 60, in which case the company will default on its debt. This probability is shown by the shaded area in Figure 24.5.

To calculate the probability that Backwoods will default, we need to know the expected growth in the market value of its assets, the face value and maturity of the debt, and the variability of future asset values. Real-world cases are likely to be more complex than our Backwoods example. For example, firms may have several classes of debt maturing on different dates. If so, it may pay the stockholders to put up more money to pay off the short-term debt and thus keep alive the chance that the firm's fortunes will recover before the rest of the debt becomes due.

However, banks and consulting firms are now finding that they can use these ideas to measure the risk of actual loans. Consider the case of WorldCom. In July 2002 WorldCom became America's largest

FIGURE 24.6

The market value of the assets of WorldCom crept closer and closer to the point at which the firm would choose to default.

Source: Moody's KMV.

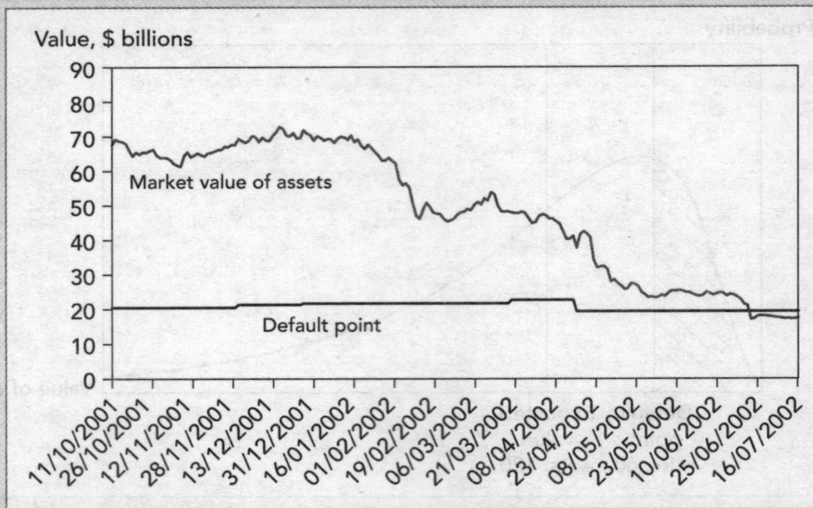

FIGURE 24.7

Estimates by Moody's KMV of the probability that WorldCom would default on its debt within a year.

Note: KMV's probabilities range from a low of 0.02 percent to a high of 20 percent.

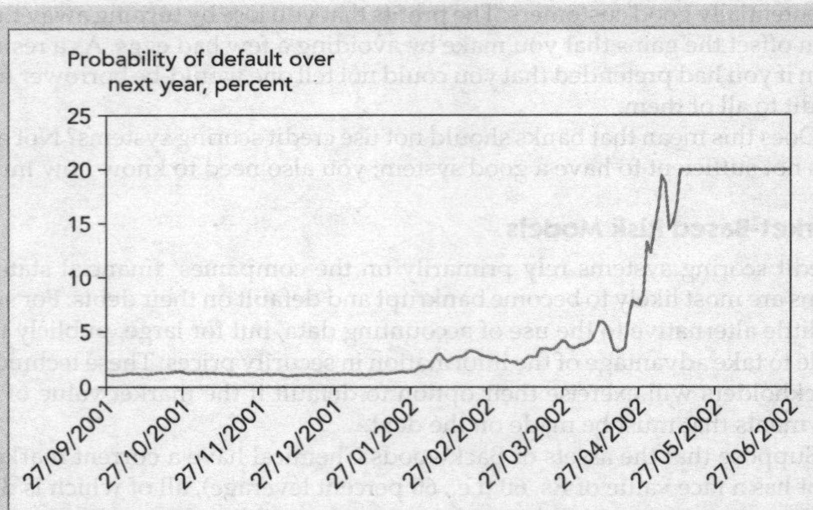

bankruptcy with over $100 billion of book assets. The extent of the company's problems had been partly obscured by a huge accounting fraud, but the company could not hide from investors its burden of debt or the problems posed by the industry glut in fiber-optic capacity.

How close was WorldCom to default? Figure 24.6 provides an answer. One top line shows the market value of its assets, and the other line shows the asset value at which the company would choose to default on its debts. You can see that, as 2002 progressed, the value of the company's assets crept closer and closer to the default point.

Of course, nobody had a crystal ball to foresee what would happen to WorldCom, but Moody's KMV, which specializes in credit models, estimated the *probability* at each point that the company would default in the next year. For any company the probability provided by KMV may range from

0.02 percent to 20 percent. Figure 24.7 shows how KMV progressively increased its assessment of the probability that WorldCom would default, until by May 2002 the probability of default was at the top of the range.

24.4 VALUE AT RISK

It is July 2006 and you own 7.27 percent bonds of Apollo Hospitals maturing in July 2008. The bonds are rated AA- by CRISIL and are currently priced at Rs. 97.8 to give a promised yield of 8.51 percent.[16] If you plan to hold the bonds for the next 12 months, what is your expected return and how much risk are you taking?

You may be tempted to look back at past default rates for AA- rated bonds and conclude that there is a negligible chance that the bonds will default during the next year and therefore your investment is almost as safe as Indian T-bills. But of course this ignores the possibility that, although default is unlikely in the short run, Apollo's prospects may not be as good as the end of the year as they are now. If so, the bonds would be downgraded and their value would fall.

Banks and consulting firms have developed a variety of ways to measure the risks that lenders face from a deterioration in credit quality. For example, one of the most popular, the *Creditmetrics* system, looks at the possible impact of changes in the bond rating.[17] Table 24.4 shows how frequently bonds were rerated in the years 1992-2005 by CRISIL. Since Apollo bonds were AA- rated, we will focus on the second row of the table.[18] You can see that in the past 89.66 percent of AA-rated bonds were still AA-rated after one year and a few were even upgraded to AAA. However, 7.42 percent of the bonds moved down one notch to BBB and some moved into the junk bond category.

Now we can ask how these possible changes in rating would be likely to affect the yield on Apollo's bonds and their price. In July 2006 AAA bonds offered an average yield of 8.22 percent. Suppose that by July 2007 Apollo's bonds were upgraded to triple-A and as a result the yield has fallen to 8.22 percent. In this case the price of the bond rises to Rs.98.31:[19]

$$\frac{7.27}{1.0822} + \frac{107.27}{(1.0822)^2} = 98.31$$

This suggests that the best that can happen to you is that your Apollo bonds are rerated to triple-A, in which case the value of your investment would appreciate by (98.31/97.80) – 1 = 0.0052, or 0.52 percent.[20]

Table 24.5 shows the average bond yields in July 2006 for different ratings and calculates what a rating change would imply for the value of your Apollo bonds. The news is certainly not all good, for there is the possibility of some large losses. In the unlikely event that the bonds are downgraded to BB and investors demand a yield of 10.77 percent, you would realize a return of a mere 3.53 percent. The very worst that can happen to you is that the company defaults on its debt. History in the U.S. suggests that if that were to occur, you would recover only 46 percent of the face value of your loan.[21] Since the market price of Apollo is currently Rs.97.80, in the even of default the expected fall in the value of your investments is 52.9 percent (46 / 97.80 –1 = –0.53).

---

[16] *Here, we valued the bond by using the yield that AA- rated bonds were giving in July 2006.*

[17] *Creditmetrics* was originally developed by J. P. Morgan. For a dscription of *Creditmetrics*, see the manuals provided by **www.riskmetrics.com.**

[18] Table 24.4 does not show the figures for AA- rated bonds separately. Here, we assume that AA- bonds were rerated as frequently as the AA and the AA+ rated bonds.

[19] For simplicity we assume annual interest payments.

[20] In addition, you would receive the 7.27 percent coupon, so that your total return over the year would be (98.31 +7.27)/97.80 – 1 = 0.07955, or 7.96 percent.

[21] We provide more detail on how recovery rates with the type of debt in Section 25.3.

TABLE 24.4

Proportion of bonds changing from one rating to another, 1992–2005.

Source: CRISIL's Insight in Risk: CRISIL Default Study. (http://www.crisil.com/credit-ratings-risk-assessment/crisil-rating-default-study-2005.pdf) Reprinted with permission of CRISIL.

Rating at start of year (%)	Rating at year-end (%)							
	AAA	AA	A	BBB	BB	B	C	D
AAA	97.24	2.76	0.00	0.00	0.00	0.00	0.00	0.00
AA	2.45	89.66	6.74	0.61	0.38	0.15	0.00	0.00
A	0.00	3.78	82.37	7.42	4.50	0.21	0.71	1.00
BBB	0.00	0.32	5.67	73.26	14.10	1.30	1.94	3.40
BB	0.00	0.60	0.00	1.79	75.00	1.79	5.36	15.48
B	0.00	0.00	0.00	5.88	0.00	55.88	8.82	29.41
CCC	0.00	0.00	0.00	1.23	0.00	0.00	70.37	28.40

TABLE 24.5

How bond yields vary with rating and the likely effect of a change in rating on the price of Apollo bonds.

*Obtained from the website of FIMMDA (www.fimmda.org). The yield for BBB-rated bonds has been used for BB rated bonds here.

**Based on average recovery rate for defaulted unsecured bonds in the U.S., 1988–2002.

Rating after One Year	Percent Yield for Given Rating*	Implied Percentage Change in Price for Alcan Bonds
AAA	0.0822	0.52
AA	0.0851	0.00
A	0.0908	−1.01
BBB	0.103	−3.11
BB	0.1077	−3.90
B	NA	NA
C	NA	NA
Default	—	−53.00**

The downside from holding a corporate bond is much larger than the upside. Even if the bonds are upgraded to triple-A, your gains are quite modest, whereas if the company's prospects deteriorate sharply, you could lose a large part of your investment. To calculate the expected effect of credit risk on the value of Apollo's bonds, we need to weight each possible outcome by the likelihood of its occurrence. The expected outcome is a capital loss of 0.52% × 2.45%] + [–0.0% × 89.66%] +... +[–53% × 0.15%] = –0.17 percent.[22]

Bankers and bond investors often refer to a loan's **value at risk** (or **VAR**). For example, holders of the Apollo bond might say that at the 5 percent confidence level, the value at risk is roughly 1 percent. By this they mean that there is about a 5 percent chance (precisely a 7.88 percent chance according to Table 24.4[23]) that holders will lose 1 percent or more over the coming year.

[22]Here, we assumed that the probability of default is 0.15 percent.

[23]From Table 24.4 the probability of a fall of at least 1 percent is 6.74 + 0.61 + 0.38 + 0.15 = 7.88 percent.

There are a number of ways that we might be able to improve our estimate of the value at risk. For example, we assumed that the probability of default and the likely recovery rate are constant. But in practice in a recession bonds are much more likely to default and the bondholders are likely to receive a smaller proportion of what they are owed.[24] Notice also that when we calculated the value at risk from investing in the Apollo bond, we looked only at how the price of the bonds would be affected if the bond's rating changed or Apollo defaulted. In other words, we focused solely on the credit risk. If we wanted a comprehensive measure of value at risk, we would need to recognize that risk-free interest rates may also change over the coming year.

Banks and bond investors are not just interested in the risk of individual loans; they would also like to know the risk of their entire portfolio. Therefore, specialists in credit risk need to recognize the correlation between the outcomes. A portfolio of loans, all of which are to factory outlets in suburban Hyderabad, is likely to be more risky than a portfolio with a variety of different borrowers.[25]

Banks have been to the forefront in developing models of the value at risk from loan portfolios. Their interest in the topic has been boosted by changes in bank regulation. Regulators require each bank to keep an equity cushion against possible losses on its portfolio. The higher the risk of the loan portfolio, the greater the cushion that is needed to ensure that the bank does not fail. For many years regulators used relatively crude rules of thumb for estimating this risk. But in recent years they have recognized that most large banks have developed their own sophisticated models for measuring the risk of their loan portfolios, and they have allowed these banks to use these risk measures when determining how much equity they must hold.

[24]See V. V. Acharya, S. T. Bharath, and A. Srinivasan, "Understanding the Recovery Rates on Defaulted Securities," working paper, London Business School, April 2004.

[25]A diversified loan portfolio may not be less risky if the lender cannot monitor the borrowers. See V. V. Acharya, I. Hasan, and A. Saunders, "Should Banks Be Diversified? Evidence from Individual Bank Loan Portfolio," Working Paper No. 118, Bank of International Settlements, September 2002.

SUMMARY

Corporations have limited liability. If companies are unable to pay their debts, they can file for bankruptcy. Lenders are aware that they may receive less than they are owed, and that the *expected* yield on a corporate bond is less than the *promised yield*.

The company's option to default is equivalent to a put option. If the value of the firm's assets is less than the amount of the debt, it will pay for the company to default and to allow the lenders to take over the assets in settlement of the debt. Unfortunately, most companies have several loans outstanding with payments due at different times. This considerably complicates the task of valuing the put option.

When investors want a measure of the risk of a company's bonds, they usually look at the rating that has been assigned by *CRISIL, CARE, or ICRA*. They know that bonds with a triple-A rating are much less likely to default than bonds with a junk rating.

Banks, rating services, and consulting firms have also developed a number of models for estimating the likelihood of default. Credit scoring systems, such as the famous Z-score model, take a variety of accounting ratios or other indicators of corporate health and weight them to produce a single measure of default. *CRISIL's* KMV takes a different tack and seeks to measure the probability that the market value of the firm's assets will fall to the point that the firm will choose to default rather than try to keep up with its debt payments.

Don't assume that there is no risk just because there is no immediate prospect of default If the quality of the bonds deteriorates, investors will demand a higher yield and the bond price will fall. One way to calculate the value at risk is to look at the probability of possible ratings changes and to estimate the likely effect of these changes for the bond's price.

FURTHER READING

The classic paper on the valuation of the option to default on corporate debt is:

R. Merton, "On the Pricing of Corporate Debt: The Risk Structure of Interest Rates," *Journal of Finance* 29 (May 1974), pp. 449–470.

The Web sites of the main credit scoring agencies and of CRISIL's KMV contain a variety of useful reports on credit risk. Altman provides a review of credit scoring models in:

E. I. Altman, *Corporate Financial Distress and Bankruptcy*, 2nd ed. (New York: John Wiley, 1993).

There are a number of books about modeling credit risk. Look, for example, at:

A. Saunders, *Credit Risk Measurement* (New York: John Wiley, 1999).

D. Duffie and K. J. Singleton, *Credit Risk Pricing, Measurement and Management*, (Princeton, NJ: Princeton University Press, 2003).

CONCEPT REVIEW QUESTIONS

1. Why does the expected yield on a corporate bond differ from its promised yield? (page 651)
2. Explain why you can think of equity as a call option on the assets of the firm. What is the call's exercise price? (pages 652–653)
3. Why do bond coupons make it much more difficult to value a risky corporate bond? (page 656)

For additional Concept Review Questions, please visit us at www.mhhe.com/bmam8e or refer to your Student CD.

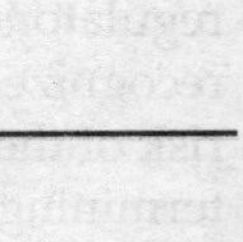

QUIZ

1. You own a 5 percent bond maturing in two years and priced at 87%. Suppose that there is a 10 percent chance that at maturity the bond will default and you will receive only 40 percent of the promised payment. What is the bond's promised yield? What is its expected yield?
2. Other things equal, would you expect the difference between the price of a G-Sec and a corporate bond to increase or decrease with
   a. The company's business risk?
   b. The degree of leverage?
3. The difference between the value of a G-Sec and a simple corporate bond is equal to the value of an option. What is this option and what is its exercise price?
4. The following table shows some financial data for two companies:

	A	B
Total assets	Rs. 1,552.1	Rs. 1,565.7
Net working capital	861.5	−58.5
Retained earnings	105.1	7.3
EBIT	182.6	41.3
Shareholder's equity	738.1	28.6
Total liabilities	814.0	1,537.1
Sales	260.9	778.0

Use the formula shown in Section 24.3 to calculate which has the higher Z-score. Is either predicted to go bankrupt or is either in the grey area?

5. What variables are required to use a market-based approach to calculate the probability that a company will default on its debt?
6. You have an AAA-rated bond. On past evidence, what is the probability that it will continue to be rated AAA in one year's time? What is the probability that it will have a lower rating?
7. You have an A-rated bond. Is a rise in rating more likely than a fall? Would your answer be the same if the bond were B-rated?
8. Why is it more difficult to estimate the value at risk for a portfolio of loans rather than for a single loan?

PRACTICE QUESTIONS

STANDARD & POOR'S

1. Company A has issued a single zero-coupon bond maturing in 10 years. Company B has issued a coupon bond maturing in 10 years. Explain why it is more complicated to value B's debt than A's.
2. Company X has borrowed Rs. 150 maturing this year and Rs. 50 maturing in 10 years. Company Y has borrowed Rs. 200 maturing in five years. In both cases asset value is Rs. 140. Why might company X not default while Y does?
3. Discuss the problems with developing a numerical credit scoring system for evaluating personal loans. You can only test your system using data for applicants who have in the past been granted credit. Is this a potential problem?
4. Select any three industrial companies. Calculate Z-score for each, using the formula shown in Section 24.3. Now look at each company's bond rating. Do these two measures provide consistent message?
5. What problems are you likely to encounter when using a market-based approach for estimating the probability that a company will default?
6. Suppose that in 2006 you owned a 10-year A-rated bond with a coupon of 9.08 percent and a price of Rs. 100. Use the data in Tables 24.4 and 24.5 to measure the value at risk.

CHALLENGE QUESTIONS

1. Look back to the first Backwoods Chemical example at the start of Section 24.1. Suppose that the firm's book balance sheet is

Backwoods Chemical Company (Book Values)

Net working capital	Rs. 400	Rs. 1,000	Debt
Net fixed assets	1,600	1,000	Equity (net worth)
Total assets	Rs. 2,000	Rs. 2,000	Total value

excel

Please visit us at www.mhhe.com/bmam8e or refer to your Student CD.

The debt has a one-year maturity and a promised interest payment of 9 percent. Thus, the promised payment to Backwoods's creditors is Rs. 1,000. The market value of the assets is Rs. 1,200 and the standard deviation of asset value is 45 percent per year. The risk-free interest rate is 9 percent. Calculate the value of Backwoods debt and equity.

2. Use the Black–Scholes model and redraw Figure 24.1 assuming that the standard deviation of the return on the firm's assets is 40 percent a year. Do the calculations only for 60 percent and 100 percent leverage. (Hint: It is simplest to assume that the risk-free interest rate is zero.) What does this tell you about the effect of changing risk on the spread between high-grade and low-grade corporate bonds?

CHAPTER [25]

THE MANY DIFFERENT KINDS OF DEBT

IN CHAPTERS 17 and 18 we discussed how much a company should borrow. But companies also need to think about what type of debt to issue. They can choose to issue short- or long-term debt, straight or convertible bonds; they can issue in India or in the international debt market; and they can sell the debt publicly or place it privately with a few large investors.

As a financial manager, you need to choose the type of debt that makes sense for your company. For example, if a firm has only a temporary need for funds, it may make sense to issue short-term debt. Firms with a substantial overseas business may prefer to issue foreign currency debt. Sometimes competition between lenders opens a window of opportunity in a particular sector of the debt market. The effect may be only a few basis points reduction in yield, but on a large issue that can translate into savings of several million dollars. Remember the saying, "A million dollars here and a million there—pretty soon it begins to add up to real money."[1]

Our focus in this chapter is on long-term debt.[2] We begin our discussion by looking at different types of bond. We examine the differences between senior and junior bonds and between secured and unsecured bonds. Then we describe how bonds may be repaid by means of a sinking fund and how the borrower or the lender may have an option for early repayment. In Section 25.6 we look at convertible bonds and at their close relative, the package of bonds and warrants.

Debt may be sold to the public or placed privately with large financial institutions. Because privately placed bonds are broadly similar to public issues, we will not discuss them at length. However, we will discuss another form of private placement known as project finance. This is the glamorous part of the debt market. The words *project finance* conjure up images of multi-million-dollar loans to finance huge ventures in exotic parts of the world. You'll find there's something to the popular image, but it's not the whole story.

We conclude with a look at a few unusual bonds and consider the reasons for innovation in the debt market.

As we look at these different features of corporate debt, we will try to explain why sinking funds, repayment options, convertible securities, and the like exist. They are not simply matters of custom or neutral mutations; there are generally good reasons for their use.

We should point out that not all debt is shown on the company's balance sheet. For example, companies may be able to disguise the debt by establishing *special purpose entities (SPEs),* which raise cash by a mixture of equity and debt and then use that cash to help fund the parent company. By making use of SPEs, Enron kept a large amount of its debt off-balance-sheet, but that did not stop the company from going bankrupt. Since the Enron scandal accountants have moved to tighten up the rules on disclosing SPE debt.

Companies have other important long-term liabilities that we do *not* discuss in this chapter. For instance, long-term leases are very similar to debt. The user of the equipment agrees to make a series of lease payments and, if it defaults, it may be forced into bankruptcy. We discuss leases in Chapter 26.

Post-retirement health benefits and pension promises can also be huge liabilities. For example, in 1993 General Motors had a pension deficit of $19 billion. To reduce this deficit, GM made a large issue of bonds and invested the majority of the proceeds in its pension fund. You could say that the effect was to increase the company's debt, but the economic reality was that it substituted one long-term obligation (the new debt) for another (its pension obligation). Management of pension plans is outside the scope of this book, but financial managers spend a good deal of time worrying about the pension "debt."

---

[1]The remark was made by the late Senator Everett Dirksen. However, he was talking billions.

[2]Short-term debt is discussed in Chapter 31.

25.1 DOMESTIC BONDS, FOREIGN BONDS, AND EUROBONDS

A firm can issue a bond either in its home country or in another country. Bonds that are sold to local investors in another country's bond market are known as *foreign bonds*. The United States is by far the largest market for foreign bonds, but Japan and Switzerland are substantial markets as well. Foreign bonds have a variety of nicknames: A bond sold by a foreign company in the United States is known as a *yankee bond;* a bond sold by a foreign firm in Japan is a *samurai.*

Of course, any firm that raises money in a foreign country is subject to the rules of the country in which it does so. For example, any issue in the United States of publicly traded bonds needs to be registered with the SEC. However, foreign firms commonly avoid registration by complying with the SEC's Rule 144A for bond issues in the United States. Rule 144A bonds can be bought and sold only by large financial institutions.[3]

There is also a large international market for long-term bonds. These international bond issues are sold throughout the world by syndicates of underwriters, mainly located in London. They include the London branches of large U.S., European, and Japanese banks and security dealers. International issues are usually made in one of the major currencies, such as the U.S. dollar or the euro.

The international bond market arose during the 1960s because the U.S. government imposed an interest-equalization tax on the purchase of foreign securities and discouraged American corporations from exporting capital. Therefore both European and American multinationals were forced to tap an international market for capital.[4] This market came to be known as the *eurobond market*, but be careful not to confuse a eurobond (which may be in any currency) with a bond denominated in euros.

The interest-equalization tax was removed in 1974, and there are no longer any controls on capital exports from the United States. Since firms can now choose whether to borrow in New York or London, the interest rates in the two markets are usually similar. However, the eurobond market is not directly subject to regulation by the U.S. authorities, and therefore the financial manager needs to be alert to small differences in the cost of borrowing in one market rather than another.

25.2 THE BOND CONTRACT

To give you some feel for the bond contract (and for some of the language in which it is couched), we have summarized in Table 25.1 the terms of an issue of 5-year bonds by ICICI Bank. We will look at the principal items in turn.

Indenture, or Trust Deed

The ICICI Bank bond offering was a public issue of bonds, which was registered with the SEBI.[5] In the case of a public issue, the bond agreement is in the form of an **indenture, or trust deed,** between the bondholder and a trust company[6]. The Western India Trustee and Executor Company, which is the trust company for the issue, represents the bondholders. It must see that the terms of the indenture are observed and look after the bondholders in the event of default. The bond indenture is a turgid legal document. A copy of it is included in the registration statement and the main provisions are summarized in the prospectus to the issue.

[3]We described Rule 144A in Section 15.5.

[4]Also, until 1984 the United States imposed a withholding tax on interest payments to foreign investors. Investors could avoid this tax by buying a eurobond issued in London rather than a similar bond issued in New York.

[5]All offer documents can be downloaded from the website of SEBI (www.sebi.gov.in)

[6]In the case of a eurobond issue, there is a *fiscal agent*, who carries out some of the same functions as the bond trustee.

TABLE 25.1

Summary of terms of 5.8 percent 5-year bond issued by ICICI Bank.

Trustee	The Western India Trustee and Executor Company Limited
Rights on default	Bondholders can approach Trustees or SEBI or the Department of Company Affairs. The trustees may appoint a nominee director in case of default
Registered	Yes
Denomination	Rs. 5000
Amount issued	Rs. 350 crores with a right to retain an additional Rs. 350 crores
Issue date	26-March-05
Offered	at par
Interest	5.8 percent payable on March 1 every year
Seniority	Ranks pari passu with other unsecured unsubordinated debt
Security	Not secured
Maturity	5 year from date of issue
Debenture Redemption Reserve	Not there as Banks need not create debenture redemption reserve while issuing debenture
Callable	No
Puttable	No
Rating	ICRA LAAA and CARE's CARE-AAA

Moving down Table 25.1, you will see that the ICICI Bank bonds are *registered*. This means that the company's registrar records the ownership of each bond and the company pays the interest and final principal amount directly to each owner.[7]

Most of the bonds in India are issued in registered form, but in many countries bonds may be issued in *bearer* form. In this case the certificate constitutes the primary evidence of ownership, so the bondholder must send the certificate itself to claim the final payment of principal. Eurobonds almost invariably allow the owner to hold them in bearer form.

[7]Often, investors do not physically hold the security; instead their ownership is represented by a book entry. The "book" is in practice a computer.

The Bond Terms

The face value of the bonds issued by ICICI Bank was Rs. 5000. Though the ICICI Bank bonds were issued to the public at par, the Bank received Rs. 4912.5 for every bond issued. The difference represents the issue expenses. The issue expenses would typically include the management fees paid to the lead-managers and the co-managers of the issue, brokerage fees, fees payable to the registrars, and fees payable to the trustees.

The annual interest or *coupon* payments on each bond is 5.8 percent, or Rs. 290 per bond. The interest is payable annually, and will be paid on 1st of March every year. The regular interest payments is a hurdle that the company must keep jumping. If the company ever fails to pay the coupon, lenders can demand their money back instead of waiting until matters may deteriorate further. Thus coupon payments provide added protection for lenders.[8]

Sometimes bonds are sold with a lower coupon payment but at a larger discount on their face value, so investors receive a significant part of their return in the form of capital appreciation.[9] The ultimate is the zero-coupon bond, which pays no interest at all; in this case the entire return consists of capital appreciation. Along with the above 5.8 percent issue, ICICI Bank also issued another series of bonds as deep discount bonds. These bonds had a face value of Rs. 6630 and were issued at a discounted price of Rs. 5000.

The ICICI Bank bond interest payment is fixed for the life of the bond, but in some issues, the payment varies with the general level of interest rates. For example, the payment may be set at 1 percent over the 91-day T-Bill rate or over the Mumbai Interbank Offer Rate (MIBOR). Sometimes these floating-rate bonds specify a minimum (or floor) interest rate or they may specify a maximum (or cap) on the rate.[10] You may also come across "collars", which stipulate both a maximum and a minimum payment.

25.3 SECURITY AND SENIORITY

Almost all debt issues by Government of India, state governments, undertakings owned by governments, and development financial institutions are generally unsecured obligations and are called bonds. All debt issues made by private entities are usually secured obligations and are called debentures.[11] This means that if a company defaults on its debt, the trustee or lender may take possession of the relevant assets. If these are insufficient to satisfy them, the remaining debt will have a general claim, alongside any unsecured debt, on the other assets of the firm.

[8]See F. Black and J. C. Cox, "Valuing Corporate Securities: Some Effects of Bond Indenture Provisions," *Journal of Finance* 31 (May 1976), pp. 351–367. Black and Cox point out that the interest payments would be a trivial hurdle if the company could sell assets to make the payment. Such sales are therefore restricted.

[9]Any bond that is issued at a discount is known as an *original issue discount bond*. A zero-coupon bond is often called a "pure discount bond."

[10]Instead of issuing a capped floating-rate loan, a company will sometimes issue an uncapped loan and at the same time buy a cap from a bank. The bank pays the interest in excess of the specified level.

[11]Another important difference between bond and debenture in India is that the stamp duty on debentures is a state subject, whereas the stamp duties on bonds come under Indian Stamp Act, 1899.

In the case of secured debt issue (debentures), the issuing company will provides security in the form of a first mortgage or charge on the fixed assets on a pari-passu basis with other fixed charge holders. Usually the charge is created on behalf of all the debenture holders by a trustee appointed for this purpose by the issuing company.

Under Section 117C of the Companies Act (introduced through the Companies Amendment Act, 2000), all companies that have issued debentures and are making profits must mandatorily create a debenture redemption reserve out of the profits. This fund is created to protect the interests of the debenture holders and is to be maintained by the company till the debentures are redeemed. However, financial institutions and the non-banking financial institutions are not required to create this reserve. Thus for example, ICICI Bank has not created any debenture redemption reserve for the above bond.[12]

Bonds may be senior claims or they may be subordinated to the senior bonds or to *all* other creditors.[13] If the firm defaults, the senior bonds come first in the pecking order. The subordinated lender gets in line behind the general creditors but ahead of the preferred stockholder and the common stockholder.

As you can see from Figure 25.1, (that is based on US research) if default does occur, it pays to hold senior secured bonds. On average, investors in these bonds can expect to recover over half of the amount of the loan. At the other extreme, recovery rates for junior unsecured bondholders are less than 20 percent of the face value of the debt.

Asset-Backed Securities

Instead of borrowing money directly, companies sometimes bundle up a group of assets and then sell the cash flows from these assets. These issues are known as **asset-backed securities.**

Suppose your company has made a large number of mortgage loans to buyers of homes or commercial real estate. However, you don't want to wait until the loans are paid off; you would like to get your hands on the money now. Here is what you do. You establish a separate company that buys a package of the mortgage loans. To finance this purchase, the company sells *mortgage pass-through certificates.*[14] The holders of these certificates simply receive a share of the mortgage payments. For example, if interest rates fall and the mortgages are repaid early, holders of the pass-through certificates are also repaid early. That is not generally popular with these holders, for they get their money back just when they don't want it—when interest rates are low.[15]

---

[12]The Government of India, Ministry of Company Affairs has vide General Circular No. 9/2002 No.6/3/2001-CL.V dated April 18,2002 clarified that banks need not create Debenture Redemption Reserve as specified under section 117C of the Companies Act, 1956.

[13]If a bond does not specifically state that it is junior, you can assume that it is senior.

[14]Mortgage-backed loans for commercial real estate are called (not surprisingly) *commercial mortgage-backed securities* or *CMBS.*

[15]Sometimes, instead of issuing one class of pass-through certificates, the company will issue several different classes of security, known as *collateralized mortgage obligations* or *CMOs.* For example, any mortgage payments might be used first to pay off one class of security holders and only then will other classes start to be repaid.

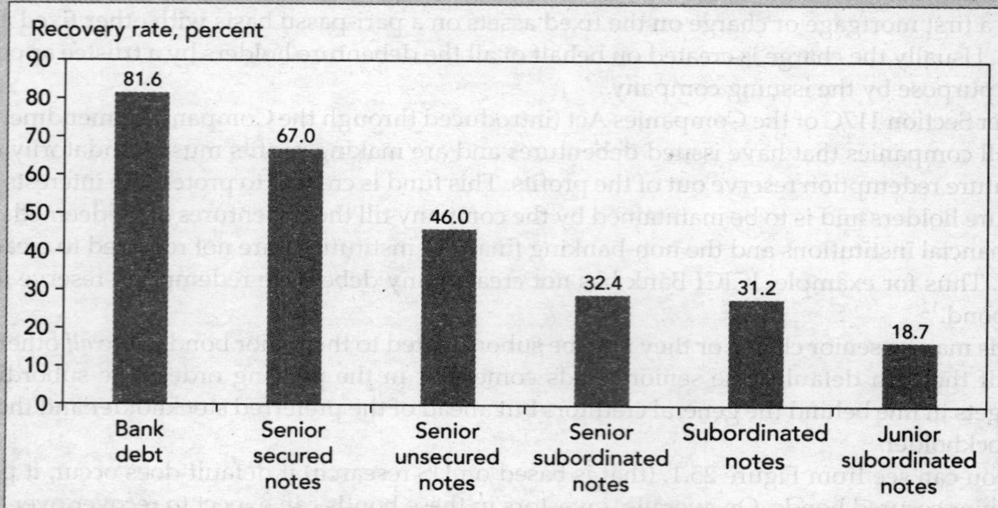

FIGURE 25.1

Ultimate percentage recovery rates on defaulting debt by seniority and security, 1988–2002.

Source: Standard & Poor's, "Ratings Performance 2002: Default, Transition, Recovery and Spreads," **www.standardandpoors.com.**

Real estate companies are not unique in wanting to turn future cash receipts into up-front cash. Automobile loans, student loans, and credit card receivables are also often bundled and remarketed as a bond. Indeed, investment bankers seem able to repackage any set of cash flows into a loan. In 1997 David Bowie, the British rock star, established a company that then purchased the royalties from his current albums. The company financed the purchase by selling $55 million of 10-year notes. The royalty receipts were used to make the principal and interest payments on the notes. When asked about the singer's reaction to the idea, his manager replied, "He kind of looked at me cross-eyed and said 'What?' "[16]

25.4 REPAYMENT PROVISIONS

Sinking Funds

In the US companies start repaying the principle on a regular basis even before the maturity date. To do this, the company makes repayment into a sinking fund. If the payment is in the form of cash, the trustee selects bonds by lottery and uses the cash to redeem them at their face value.[17] Alterna-

[16]See J. Matthews, "David Bowie Reinvents Himself, This Time as a Bond Issue," *Washington Post*, February 7, 1997.

[17]Every investor dreams of buying up the entire supply of a sinking-fund bond that is selling way below face value and then forcing the company to buy the bonds back at face value. Cornering the market in this way is fun to dream about but difficult to do. For a discussion, see K. B. Dunn and C. S. Spatt, "A Strategic Analysis of Sinking Fund Bonds," *Journal of Financial Economics* 13 (September 1984), pp. 399–424.

tively, the company can buy bonds in the marketplace and pay these into the fund.[18] This is a valuable option for the company. If the bond price is low, the firm will buy the bonds in the market and hand them to the sinking fund; if the price is high, it will call the bonds by lottery.

Call Provisions

Corporate bonds occasionally include a call option that allows the company to pay back the debt early. Sometimes you come across bonds that give the *investor* the repayment option. Retractable (or puttable) bonds give investors the right to demand early repayment; extendible bonds give them the option to extend the bond's life.

For some companies callable bonds offer a natural form of insurance. For example, Fannie Mae and Freddie Mac of the US are federal agencies that offer fixed-rate mortgages to home buyers. When interest rates fall, home owners are likely to repay their fixed-rate mortgage and take out a new mortgage at the lower interest rate. This can severely dent the income of the two agencies. Therefore, to protect themselves against the effect of falling interest rates, they issue large quantities of long-term callable debt. When interest rates fall, the agencies can reduce their funding costs by calling their bonds and replacing them with new bonds at a lower rate. Ideally, the fall in bond interest payments should exactly offset the reduction in mortgage income.

How does a company know when to call its bonds? The answer is simple: Other things equal, if it wishes to maximize the value of its stock, it must minimize the value of its bonds. Therefore, a company should never call the bonds if their market value is less than the call price, for that would just be giving a present to the bondholders. Equally, a company *should* call the bond if it is worth *more* than the call price.

Of course, investors take the call option into account when they buy or sell the bond. They know that the company will call the bond as soon as it is worth more than the call price, so no investor will be willing to pay more than the call price for the bond. The market price of the bond may, therefore, reach the call price, but it will not rise above it. This gives the company the following rule for calling its bonds: *Call the bond when, and only when, the market price reaches the call price.*[19]

---

[18]If the bonds are privately placed, the company cannot repurchase them in the marketplace; it must call them at their face value.

[19]See M. J. Brennan and E. S. Schwartz, "Savings Bonds, Retractable Bonds, and Callable Bonds," *Journal of Financial Economics* 5 (1997), pp. 67–88. Of course, this assumes that the bond is correctly priced, that investors are behaving rationally, and that investors expect the *firm* to behave rationally. Also we ignore some complications. First, you may not wish to call a bond if you are prevented by a nonrefunding clause from issuing new debt. Second, the call premium is a tax-deductible expense for the company but is taxed as a capital gain to the bondholder. Third, there are other possible tax consequences to both the company and the investor from replacing a low-coupon bond with a higher-coupon bond. Fourth, there are costs and delays to calling and reissuing debt.

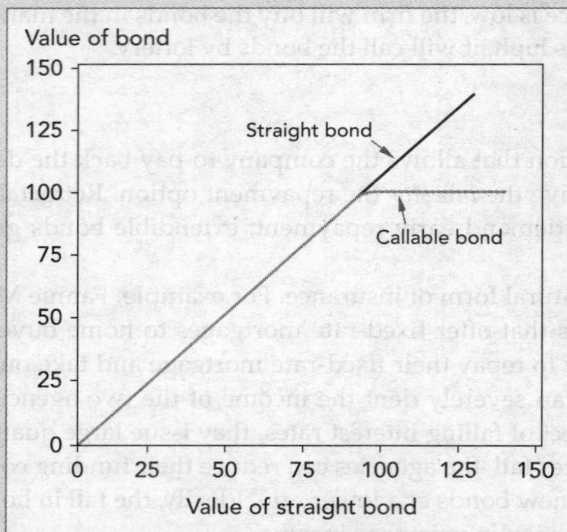

FIGURE 25.2

Relationship between the value of a callable bond and that of a straight (noncallable) bond. Assumptions: (1) Both bonds have an 8 percent coupon and a five-year maturity; (2) the callable bond may be called at face value any time before maturity; (3) the short-term interest rate follows a random walk, and the expected returns on bonds of all maturities are equal.

Source: M. J. Brennan and E. S. Schwartz, "Savings Bonds, Retractable Bonds, and Callable Bonds," *Journal of Financial Economics* 5 (1977), pp. 67–88.

If we know how bond prices behave over time, we can modify the basic option-valuation model of Chapter 21 to find the value of the callable bond, *given* that investors know that the company will call the issue as soon as the market price reaches the call price. For example, look at Figure 25.2. It illustrates the relationship between the value of a straight 8 percent five-year bond and the value of a comparable callable bond. Suppose that the value of the straight bond is very low. In this case there is little likelihood that the company will ever wish to call its bonds. (Remember that it will call the bonds only when their price equals the call price.) Therefore the value of the callable bond will be almost identical to the value of the straight bond. Now suppose that the straight bond is worth exactly 100. In this case there is a good chance that at some time the company will wish to call its bonds. Therefore the value of our callable bond will be slightly less than that of the straight bond. If interest rates decline further, the price of the straight bond will continue to rise, but nobody will ever pay more than the call price for the callable bond.

A call provision is not a free lunch. It provides the issuer with a valuable option, but that is recognized in a lower issue price. So why do companies bother with a call provision? One reason is that bond indentures often place a number of restrictions on what the company can do. Companies are happy to agree to these restrictions as long as they know that they can escape from them if the restrictions prove too inhibiting. The call provision provides the escape route.

We mentioned earlier that some bonds also provide the investor with an option to demand early repayment. *Puttable* bonds exist largely because bond indentures cannot anticipate every action the company may take that could harm the bondholder. If the value of the bonds is reduced, the put option allows the bondholders to demand repayment.

Puttable loans can sometimes get their issuers into BIG trouble. During the 1990s many loans to Asian companies gave their lenders a repayment option. Consequently, when the Asian crisis struck in 1997, these companies were faced by a flood of lenders demanding their money back.

25.5 DEBT COVENANTS

Investors in corporate bonds know that there is a risk of default. But they still want to make sure that the company plays fair. They don't want it to gamble with their money. Therefore, the loan agreement usually includes a number of *debt covenants* that prevent the company from purposely increasing the value of its default option.[20]

Lenders worry that after they have made the loan, the company may pile up more debt and so increase the chance of default. They protect themselves against this risk by prohibiting the company from making further debt issues unless the ratio of debt to equity is below a specified limit.

Not all debts are created equal. If the firm defaults, the senior debt comes first in the pecking order and must be paid off in full before the junior debtholders get a cent.[21] Therefore, when a company issues senior debt, the lenders will place limits on further issues of senior debt. But they won't restrict the amount of *junior* debt that the company can issue. Because the senior lenders are at the front of the queue, they view the junior debt in the same way that they view equity: They would be happy to see an issue of either. Of course, the converse is not true. Holders of the junior debt *do* care both about the total amount of debt and the proportion that is senior to their claim. As a result, an issue of junior debt generally includes a restriction on both total debt and senior debt.

All bondholders worry that the company may issue more secured debt. An issue of mortgage bonds often imposes a limit on the amount of secured debt. This is not necessary when you are issuing unsecured debentures. As long as the debenture holders are given an equal claim, they don't care how much you mortgage your assets. Therefore, unsecured bonds usually include a so-called *negative-pledge clause*, in which the unsecured holders simply say, "Me too."[22]

Instead of borrowing money to buy an asset, companies may enter into a long-term agreement to rent or lease it. For the debtholder this is very similar to secured borrowing. Therefore debt agreements also include limitations on leasing.

We have talked about how an unscrupulous borrower can try to increase the value of the default option by issuing more debt. But that is not the only way that such a company can exploit its existing bondholders. For example, we know that the value of an option is reduced when the company pays out some of its assets to stockholders. In the extreme case a company could sell all its assets and pay out the proceeds to shareholders as a bumper dividend. That would leave nothing for the lenders. To guard against such dangers, many debt issues restrict the amount that the company may pay out in the form of dividends or repurchases of stock.[23]

Debt covenants *do* matter. Asquith and Wizman, who studied the effect of leveraged buyouts on the value of the company's debt, found that when there were no restrictions on further debt issues,

[20]We described in Section 18.3 some of the games that managers can play at the expense of bondholders.

[21]In practice the courts do not always observe the strict rules of precedence (see Section 33.4). Therefore the subordinated debtholder may receive *some* payment even when the senior debtholder is not fully paid off.

[22]"Me too" is not acceptable legal jargon. Instead the bond agreement may state that the company "will not consent to any lien on its assets without securing the existing bonds equally and ratably."

[23]See A. Kalay, "Stockholder-Bondholder Conflict and Dividend Constraints," *Journal of Financial Economics* 10 (1982), pp. 211–233. A dividend restriction might typically prohibit the company from paying dividends if their cumulative amount would exceed the sum of (1) cumulative net income, (2) the proceeds from the sale of stock or conversion of debt, and (3) a dollar amount equal to one year's dividend.

FINANCE IN THE NEWS

U.S. SHOE'S OWNER RILES BONDHOLDERS WITH ITS DEBT MOVES

Imagine a company trying to push its bonds into technical default just so it can redeem them before maturity. Some bond analysts assert that this is exactly what Luxottica Group SpA of Italy—the new owner of U.S. Shoe Corp.—is doing with U.S. Shoe's 8 5/8% note issue.

Luxottica's strategy, which the company asserts wasn't deliberately designed to hurt bondholders, is shaping to be the newest wrinkle in corporate America's scramble to pry high-interest-bearing bonds from the hands of investors before they mature, some analysts say. As interest rates have fallen, a host of corporate issuers—from stodgy utilities to fleet-footed finance companies—have rushed to redeem their high-interest bonds with lower coupon issues. As long as the bonds are "callable," or redeemable, there is usually no problem. Increasingly, however, corporate issuers are trying to redeem noncallable bonds—securities that can't be wrested from investors before maturity—using unusual tactics.

Bond analysts say Luxottica has been trying to put U.S. Shoe's 8 5/8% note issue, maturing in 2002, in technical default by piling $1.4 billion of secured debt onto the company earlier this year. That's because a little-noticed covenant in U.S. Shoe's bond indenture says its bonds are in technical default if it adds secured debt to its financial ledger without simultaneously adding collateral to back the 8 5/8% securities so they're on the same level as the bank debt.

What's riling bondholders is that Luxottica hasn't been willing to secure its 8 5/8% notes even though it took on a load of secured debt earlier this year. Now Luxottica is trying to redeem its bonds early, which the company says it can do under the covenants when the issue is in technical default.

"This action is 10 times worse than Marriott on its worst day, because Marriott never violated an explicit covenant," contends Max Holmes, a securities analyst at Salomon Brothers Inc.

Source: Extracted from Anita Raghaven, "U.S. Shoe's owner Riles Bondholders with Its Debt Moves," *The Wall Street Journal*, October 18, 1995, p. C1. Eastern Edition (Staff-produced copy only). © 1995 by Dow Jones & Co., Inc., in the format textbook, via Copyright Clearance Center.

dividend payments, or mergers, the buyout led to a 5.2 percent fall in the value of existing bonds.[24] Those bonds that were protected by strong covenants against excessive borrowing increased in price by 2.6 percent.

Unfortunately, it is not always easy to cover all loopholes, as the bondholders of Marriott Corporation discovered in 1992. They hit the roof when the company announced plans to divide its operations into two separate businesses. One business, Marriott International, would manage Marriott's hotel chain and receive most of the revenues, while the other, Host Marriott, would own all the company's real estate and be responsible for servicing essentially all of the old company's $3 billion of debt. As a result the price of Marriott's bonds plunged nearly 30 percent, and investors began to think about how they could protect themselves against such *event risks*.[25] For example, some bondholders started to insert *poison-put* clauses that oblige the borrower to repay the debt if there is a change of control and the bonds are downrated.

Unfortunately, there are always nasty surprises round the next corner. The nearby box describes one such surprise for bond investors of U.S. Shoe.

[24] P. Asquith and T. Wizman "Event Risk, Covenants, and Bondholder Returns in Leveraged Buyouts," *Journal of Financial Economics* 27 (September 1990), pp. 195–213. Leveraged buyouts (LBOs) are company acquisitions that are financed by large issues of (usually unsecured) debt. We describe LBOs in Chapter 33.

[25] A bondholder group with more than Rs. 100 million of Marriott's senior debt unsuccessfully sued the company for damages.

25.6 CONVERTIBLE BONDS AND WARRANTS

What Is a Convertible Bond?

Unlike the common or garden bond, a convertible security can change its spots. It starts life as a bond (or preferred stock), but subsequently may turn into a common stock. For example, in 1999 Amazon.com issued $1.25 billion of 4.75 percent convertible subordinated notes due in 2009. Each bond could be converted at any time into 12.82 shares of common stock.[26] In other words, the owner had a 10-year option to return the bond to the company and receive 12.82 shares of stock in exchange. The number of shares into which each bond can be converted is called the bond's **conversion ratio.** The conversion ratio of the Amazon.com bond was 12.82.

To receive 12.82 shares of Amazon stock, the owner had to surrender bonds with a face value of $1,000. This means that to receive *one* share, the owner had to surrender a face amount of 1,000/12.82 = $78.03. This figure is called the **conversion price.** Anybody who bought the bond at $1,000 to convert it into 12.82 shares paid the equivalent of $78.03 a share, about 30 percent above the stock price at the time of the convertible issue.

You can think of a convertible bond as equivalent to a straight bond plus an option to acquire common stock. When convertible bondholders exercise this option, they do not pay cash; instead they give up their bonds in exchange for shares. In 1999 the Amazon bonds would probably have sold for about $600 if they had not been convertible. This was the exercise price of the conversion option.

The difference between the price of a convertible bond and the price of an equivalent straight bond represents the value that investors place on the conversion option. For example, an investor who paid $1,000 in 1999 for the Amazon convertible would have paid $1,000 − $600 = $400 for the option to acquire 12.82 shares.

The Value of a Convertible at Maturity

By the time that the Amazon convertible matures investors need to choose whether to stay with the bond or convert to common stock. Figure 25.3(*a*) shows the possible bond values at maturity. Notice that the bond value is simply the face value as long as Amazon does not default. However, if the value of Amazon's assets is sufficiently low, the bondholders will receive *less* than the face value. In the extreme case that the assets are worthless, the bondholders will receive nothing.[27]

You can think of the bond value as a lower bound, or "floor," to the price of the convertible. But that floor has a nasty slope and, when the company falls on hard times, the bond may not be worth much. For example, by fall 2001 the price of Amazon stock had slumped to $6, well below the conversion price of $78.03. Convertible bondholders might have hoped that the bond value would provide a secure floor to the value of their investment. Unfortunately, at that point Amazon's bonds no longer looked as safe as they once had and the price of the convertible fell to about $400.

[26] When the bond was issued investors were entitled to convert it into 6.41 shares of common stock. The figure was subsequently adjusted when the company split its stock 2-for-1 and the value of each share halved.

[27] You may recognize this as the position diagram for a default-free bond *minus* a put option on the assets with an exercise price equal to the face value of the bonds. See Section 24.1.

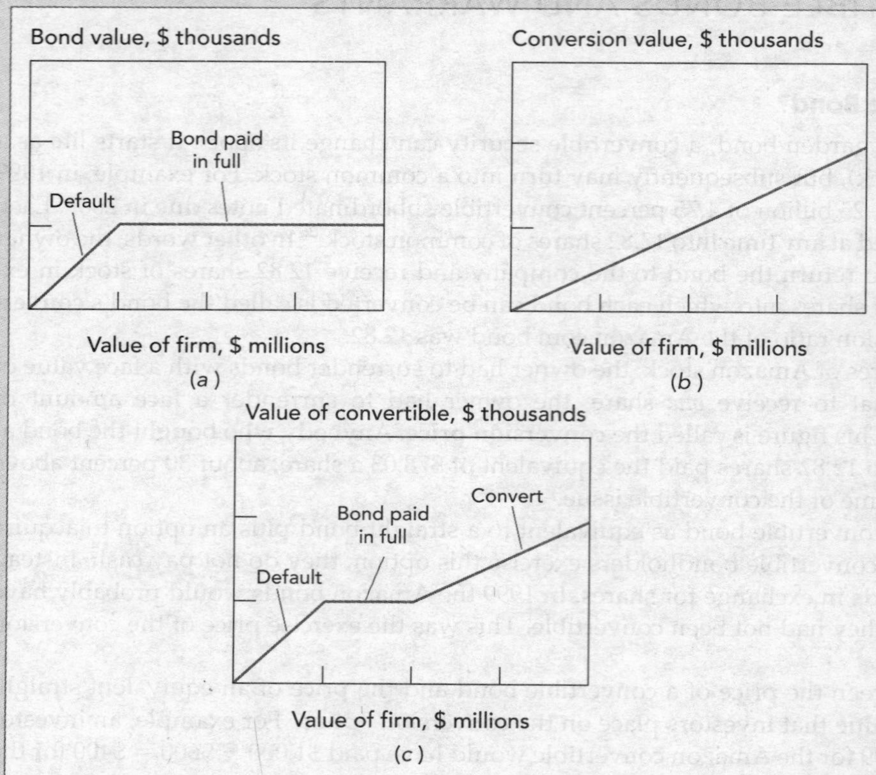

FIGURE 25.3

(a) The bond value when Amazon.com's convertible bond matures. If firm value is at least equal to the face value of Amazon's debt, the bond is paid off at face value. (b) The conversion value at maturity. If converted, the value of the convertible rises in proportion to firm value. (c) At maturity the convertible bondholder can choose to receive the payment on the bond or convert to common stock. The value of the convertible bond is therefore the higher of its bond value and its conversion value.

The possible conversion values at maturity are shown in Figure 25.3(*b*). If Amazon's assets are worthless, the shares into which the convertible can be exchanged are also worthless. But, as the value of the assets rises, so does the conversion value.

Amazon's convertible cannot sell for less than its conversion value. If it did, investors would buy the convertible, exchange it rapidly for stock, and sell the stock. Their profit would be equal to the difference between the conversion value and the price of the convertible. Therefore, there are two lower bounds to the price of the convertible; its bond value and its conversion value. Investors will not convert if bond value exceeds conversion value; they *will* do so if conversion value exceeds bond value. In other words, the price of the convertible at maturity is represented by the higher of the two lines in Figure 25.3(*a*) and (*b*). This is shown in Figure 25.3(*c*).

Forcing Conversion

Beginning in 2002 Amazon has an option to buy back (or *call*) its convertible bonds at a small premium over their face value. In this case, the owners can choose to surrender their bonds or convert them. If the amount that they are offered is higher than conversion value, they will take the cash. Otherwise, they will prefer to convert. Thus a call can *force conversion* if the stock price is high enough.

Before 2002 Amazon could not have called its convertible except in one special circumstance. It could have called the issue before the end of the call protection period if the stock price had exceeded $117, in which case investors would have had a nice conversion profit.

As we saw earlier, calling a bond does not affect the total size of the company pie, but it can affect the size of the individual slices. The company maximizes the shareholders' slice if

1. It does not give the bondholders an unnecessary profit by calling the bonds when they are *less* than the call price.
2. It does not allow the bonds to remain uncalled if their value is *above* the call price.

Think what this implies for Amazon. When call protection on the Amazon convertible ended in 2002, the price of the convertible was still well below the call price. Since calling the bond would have given the convertible holders a free gift, Amazon decided not to do so.

On the other hand, suppose that when the period of call protection ended in 2002, the price of Amazon's stock had been $100, so that the bonds could have been converted into stock worth 12.82 × $100 = $1,282. In this case it would have paid the company to have called the bonds immediately. The holders could no longer wait to decide whether to convert. They would have been forced to exercise their option and convert into stock.[28]

What if call protection had ended with the conversion value only marginally above the call price? If Amazon had announced a call, bondholders would have had a 30-day period in which to decide whether to convert or hand in their bonds. During this period the conversion value could easily have fallen below the call price, forcing the company to redeem the bonds for cash. Therefore, Amazon's financial manager would probably have waited. Usually calls are not announced until the stock price is about 20 percent above the call price. This provides a safety margin to ensure conversion.[29]

Do companies follow our simple guidelines? On the surface they don't, for there are many instances of convertible bonds selling well above the call price. But the explanation seems to lie in the call-protection period, during which companies are not allowed to call their bonds. Paul Asquith found that most convertible bonds that are worth calling are called soon after this period ends.[30] The typical delay for bonds that can be called is less than four months after the conversion value first exceeds the call price.

Why Do Companies Issue Convertibles?

You are approached by an investment banker who is anxious to persuade you that your company should issue a convertible bond with a conversion price set somewhat above the current stock price. She points out that investors would be prepared to accept a lower yield on the convertible, so that

[28]The financial manager might delay calling if interest payments on the convertible are less than the extra dividends that would be paid after conversion. This delay would reduce cash payments to bondholders. Nothing is lost if the financial manager calls on the way down. Note that investors may convert voluntarily if they would thereby increase their income.

[29]See P. Asquith and D. Mullins, "Convertible Debt: Corporate Call Policy," *Journal of Finance* 46 (September 1991), pp. 1273–1290.

[30]See P. Asquith, "Convertible Bonds Are Not Called Late," *Journal of Finance* 50 (September 1995), pp. 1275–1289.

it is "cheaper" debt than a straight bond.[31] You observe that if your company's stock performs as well as you expect, investors will convert the bond. "Great," she replies, "in that case you will have sold shares at a much better price than you could sell them for today. It's a win-win opportunity."

Is the investment banker right? Are convertibles "cheap debt"? Of course not. They are a package of a straight bond and an option. The higher price that investors are prepared to pay for the convertible represents the value that they place on the option. The convertible is "cheap" only if this price overvalues the option.

What then of the other argument, that the issue represents a deferred sale of common stock at an attractive price? The convertible gives investors the right to buy stock by giving up a bond.[32] Bondholders may decide to do this, but then again they may not. Thus issue of a convertible bond *may* amount to a deferred stock issue. But if the firm needs equity capital, a convertible issue is an unreliable way of getting it.

A survey of companies in the US that had seriously considered issuing convertibles found that in 58 percent of the cases management considered convertibles an inexpensive way to issue "delayed" common stock. Forty-two percent of the firms viewed convertibles as less expensive than straight debt.[33] Taken at their face value, these arguments don't make sense. But we suspect that these phrases encapsulate some more complex and rational motives.

Notice that convertibles tend to be issued by the smaller and more speculative firms. They are almost invariably unsecured and generally subordinated. Now put yourself in the position of a potential investor. You are approached by a firm with an untried product line that wants to issue some junior unsecured debt. You know that if things go well, you will get your money back, but if they do not, you could easily be left with nothing. Since the firm is in a new line of business, it is difficult to assess the chances of trouble. Therefore you don't know what the fair rate of interest is. Also, you may be worried that once you have made the loan, management will be tempted to run extra risks. It may take on additional senior debt, or it may decide to expand its operations and go for broke on your money. In fact, if you charge a very high rate of interest, you could be encouraging this to happen.

What can management do to protect you against a wrong estimate of the risk and to assure you that its intentions are honorable? In crude terms, it can give you a piece of the action. You don't mind the company running unanticipated risks as long as you share in the gains as well as the losses.[34] Convertible securities make sense whenever it is unusually costly to assess the risk of debt or whenever investors are worried that management may not act in the bondholders' interest.[35]

---

[31]She might even point out to you that in 2002 several Japanese companies were able to issue convertible bonds at a negative yield. You actually *paid them* to hold their debt.

[32]That is much the same as already having the stock together with the right to sell it for the convertible's bond value. In other words, instead of thinking of a convertible as a bond plus a call option, you could think of it as the stock plus a put option. Now you can see why it is wrong to think of a convertible as equivalent to the sale of stock; it is equivalent to the sale of both stock and a put option. If there is any possibility that investors will want to hold onto their bond, that put option has value.

[33]See J. R. Graham and C. R. Harvey, "The Theory and Practice of Finance: Evidence from the Field," *Journal of Financial Economics* 61 (2001), pp. 187–243.

[34]See M. J. Brennan and E. S. Schwartz, "The Case for Convertibles," *Journal of Applied Corporate Finance* 1 (Summer 1988), pp. 55–64. In the survey referred to above a further 44 percent of the respondents reported that an important factor in their decision was the fact that convertibles were attractive to investors who were unsure about the riskiness of the company.

[35]Changes in risk ought to be more likely when the firm is small and its debt is low-grade. If so, we should find that convertible bonds of such firms offer their owners a larger potential ownership share. This is indeed the case. See C. M. Lewis, R. J. Rogalski, and J. K. Seward, "Understanding the Design of Convertible Debt," *Journal of Applied Corporate Finance* 11 (Spring 1998), pp. 45–53.

The relatively low coupon rate on convertible bonds may also be a convenience for rapidly growing firms facing heavy capital expenditures.[36] They may be willing to provide the conversion option to reduce immediate cash requirements for debt service. Without that option, lenders might demand extremely high (promised) interest rates to compensate for the probability of default. This would not only force the firm to raise still more capital for debt service but also increase the risk of financial distress. Paradoxically, lenders' attempts to protect themselves against default may actually increase the probability of financial distress by increasing the burden of debt service on the firm.

Valuing Convertible Bonds

We have seen that a convertible bond is equivalent to a package of a bond and an option to buy stock. This means that the option-valuation models that we described in Chapter 21 can also be used to value the option to convert. We don't want to repeat that material here, but we should note three wrinkles that you need to look out for when valuing a convertible:

1. *Dividends*. If you hold the common stock, you may receive dividends. The investor who holds an option to convert into common stock misses out on these dividends. In fact the convertible holder loses out every time a cash dividend is paid because the dividend reduces the stock price and thus reduces the value of the conversion option. If the dividends are high enough, it may even pay to convert before maturity to capture the extra income. We showed how dividend payments affect option value in Section 21.5.

2. *Dilution*. The second complication arises because conversion increases the number of outstanding shares. Therefore, exercise means that each shareholder is entitled to a smaller proportion of the firm's assets and profits.[37] This problem of *dilution* never arises with traded options. If you buy an option through an option exchange and subsequently exercise it, you have no effect on the number of shares outstanding. We showed how dilution affects option value in the Appendix to Chapter 21.

3. *Changing bond value*. When investors convert to shares, they give up their bond. The exercise price of the option is therefore the value of the bond that they are relinquishing. But this bond value is not constant. If the bond value at issue is less than the face value (and it usually is less), it is likely to change as maturity approaches. Also the bond value varies as interest rates change and as the company's credit standing changes. If there is some possibility of default, investors cannot even be certain of what the bond will be worth at maturity. In Chapter 21 we did not get into the complication of uncertain exercise prices.

[36]Of course, the firm could also make an equity issue rather than an issue of straight debt or convertibles. However, a convertible issue sends a better signal to investors than an issue of common stock. As we explained in Chapter 15, announcement of a stock issue prompts worries of overvaluation and usually depresses the stock price. Convertibles are hybrids of debt and equity and send a less negative signal. If the company is likely to need equity, its willingness to issue a convertible and take the chance that the stock price will rise enough to lead to conversion also signals management's confidence in the future. See J. Stein, "Convertible Bonds as Backdoor Equity Financing," *Journal of Financial Economics* 32 (1992), pp. 3–21.

[37]In their financial statements companies recognize the possibility of dilution by showing how earnings would be affected by the issue of the extra shares.

Some Variations on Convertible Bonds: Compulsorily Convertible Bonds (Debentures) and Reverse Convertibles

The Amazon convertible bond is a fairly typical issue, but there are a number of variants on this common or garden convertible. Later in the chapter we will describe two exotic variants, but there are also some more mundane variations. For example, in recent years a number of companies have issued a bond or preferred stock that is *automatically* converted into equity after several years. Investors in these *compulsorily convertible debentures* receive the benefit of a higher current income than common stockholders, but there is usually a limit on the value of the common stock that they ultimately receive. Thus they share in the appreciation of the common stock only up to this limit. As the stock price rises further, the number of shares that the convertible holder receives is reduced proportionately.

A rather different type of convertible bond is common in Germany and Switzerland. The *reverse convertible* gives the conversion option to the company rather than to the investor. Suppose that trouble strikes and the stock price slumps. Then, rather than repaying cash when the bond matures, the company can pay off the bond with low-value stock. Effectively, the reverse convertible allows the company to reduce its debt burden as distress threatens.[38]

A Third Variation on Convertible Bonds: The Bond–Warrant Package

Instead of issuing a convertible bond, companies sometimes sell a package of straight bonds and warrants. Warrants are simply long-term call options that give the investor the right to buy the firm's common stock. For example, each warrant might allow the holder to buy a share of stock for Rs. 50 at any time during the next five years. Obviously, the warrant holders hope that the company's stock will zoom up, so that they can exercise their warrants at a profit. But, if the company's stock price remains below Rs. 50, holders will choose not to exercise, and the warrants will expire worthless.

Convertible bonds consist of a package of a straight bond and an option. An issue of bonds and warrants also contains a straight bond and an option. But there are some differences:

1. *Warrants are usually issued privately.* Packages of bonds with warrants tend to be more common in private placements. By contrast, most convertible bonds are issued publicly.
2. *Warrants can be detached.* When you buy a convertible, the bond and the option are bundled together. You cannot sell them separately. This may be inconvenient. If your tax position or attitude to risk inclines you to bonds, you may not want to hold options as well. Warrants are sometimes also "nondetachable," but usually you can keep the bond and sell the warrant.
3. *Warrants are exercised for cash.* When you convert a bond, you simply exchange your bond for common stock. When you exercise warrants, you generally put up extra cash, though occasionally you have to surrender the bond or can choose to do so. This means that the bond-warrant package and the convertible bond have different effects on the company's cash flow and on its capital structure.

[38]Reverse convertibles are described in C. Culp, "Contingent Capital: Integrating Corporate Financing and Risk Management Decisions," *Journal of Applied Corporate Finance* 15 (Spring 2002), pp. 46–56.

4. *Warrants may be issued on their own*. Warrants do not have to be issued in conjunction with other securities. Often they are used to compensate investment bankers for underwriting services. Many companies also give their executives long-term options to buy stock. These executive stock options are not usually called warrants, but that is exactly what they are. Companies can also sell warrants on their own directly to investors, though they rarely do so.

25.7 PRIVATE PLACEMENTS AND PROJECT FINANCE

The ICICI Bonds were registered with the SEBI and sold to the public. However, debt is often placed privately with a small number of financial institutions.[39] As we saw in Section 15.5, it costs less to arrange a private placement than to make a public debt issue. But there are three other ways in which the private placement bond may differ from its public counterpart.

First, if you place an issue privately with one or two financial institutions, it may be necessary to sign only a simple promissory note. This is just an IOU which lays down certain conditions that the borrower must observe. However, when you make a public issue of debt, you must worry about who is supposed to represent the bondholders in any subsequent negotiations and what procedures are needed for paying interest and principal. Therefore, the contract has to be somewhat more complicated.

The second characteristic of publicly issued bonds is that they are highly standardized products. They *have* to be—investors are constantly buying and selling without checking the fine print in the agreement. This is not so necessary in private placements and so the debt can be custom-tailored for firms with special problems or opportunities. The relationship between borrower and lender is much more intimate. Imagine a Rs. 20 million debt issue privately placed with an insurance company, and compare it with an equivalent public issue held by 200 anonymous investors. The insurance company can justify a more thorough investigation of the company's prospects and therefore may be more willing to accept unusual terms or conditions.[40]

As we saw earlier, all bond agreements seek to protect the lender by imposing a number of conditions on the borrower. These conditions tend to be more severe in the case of privately placed debt. For example, the loan agreement may state that the borrower will be in default if interest payments ever exceed a certain multiple of earnings or if the company fails to maintain a minimum level of liquid assets.[41] Borrowers are willing to agree to such stringent conditions because they know that if the debt is privately placed, the conditions can be modified later if it makes sense. In the case of a public issue, it can be cumbersome to get the permission of all the existing bondholders.

Covenants in privately placed debt do get modified as conditions change. In Chapter 31 we will describe how the fashion company, LA Gear, went belly up. As LA Gear's creditworthiness steadily deteriorated, Bank of America made 14 successive amendments to the line of credit that it extended

[39] As per a BSE study, in the year 2002, around 92 percent of the total corporate debt issues were made through the private placement route. (www.bseindia.com)

[40] Of course debt with the same terms could be offered publicly, but then 200 separate investigations would be required—a much more expensive proposition.

[41] For example, the covenant might specify a minimum current ratio (the ratio of current assets to current liabilities) or a minimum quick ratio (the ratio of cash plus short-term securities plus receivables to current liabilities).

to the company. The amount that LA Gear was permitted to borrow was progressively reduced from $360 million to $25 million and the company was required to agree to increasingly tough conditions.[42]

These features of private placements give them a particular niche in the corporate debt market, namely, loans to small- and medium-sized firms. These are the firms that face the highest costs in public issues, that require the most detailed investigation, and that may require specialized, flexible loan arrangements. However, many large companies also use private placements.

Of course, the advantages of private placements are not free, for the lenders demand a higher rate of interest to compensate them for holding an illiquid asset. It is difficult to generalize about the difference in interest rates between private placements and public issues, but a typical differential is on the order of 50 basis points, or .50 percentage points.

Project Finance

We are not going to dwell further on the topic of private placement bonds, because the greater part of what we have had to say about public issues is also true of private placements. However, we do need to discuss a different form of private loan, one that is tied as closely as possible to the fortunes of a particular project and that minimizes the exposure of the parent. Such a loan is usually referred to as **project finance** and is a specialty of large international banks.

Project finance means debt supported by the project, not by the project's sponsoring companies. Debt ratios are nevertheless very high for most project financings. They can be high because the debt is supported not just by the project's assets but also by a variety of contracts and guarantees provided by customers, suppliers, and local governments as well as by the project's owners.

Example Here is how project finance was used to construct a large new oil-fired power plant in Pakistan. First, a separate firm, the Hub Power Company (Hubco) was established to own the power station. Hubco then engaged a consortium of companies, headed by the Japanese company Mitsui & Co., to build the power station, while the British company, International Power, became responsible for managing and running it. Hubco agreed to buy the fuel from the Pakistan State Oil Company and to sell the power station's output to another government body, the Water and Power Development Authority (WAPDA).

Hubco's lawyers drew up a complex series of contracts to make certain that each of these parties came up to scratch. For example, the contractors agreed to deliver the plant on time and to ensure that it would operate to specifications. International Power, the plant manager, agreed to maintain the plant and operate it efficiently. Pakistan State Oil Company entered into a long-term contract to supply oil to Hubco and WAPDA agreed to buy Hubco's output for the next 30 years.[43] Since WAPDA would pay

[42]The changes in LA Gear's line of credit agreements are described in H. DeAngelo, L. DeAngelo, and K. H. Wruck, "Asset Liquidity, Debt Covenants, and Managerial Discretions in Financial Distress," *Journal of Financial Economics* 64 (2002), pp. 3–34.

[43]WAPDA entered into a *take-or-pay* agreement with Hubco; if it did not take the electricity, it still had to pay for it. In the case of pipeline projects the contract with the customer is often in the form of a *throughput* agreement, whereby the customer agrees to make a minimum use of the pipeline. Another arrangement for transferring revenue risk to a customer is the *tolling contract*, whereby the customer agrees to deliver to the project company materials that the company is to process and return to the customer. One purpose of transferring revenue risk to customers is to encourage them to estimate their demand for the project's output thoroughly.

for the electricity with rupees, Hubco was concerned about the possibility of a fall in the value of the rupee. The State Bank of Pakistan therefore arranged to provide Hubco with foreign exchange at guaranteed exchange rates.

The effect of these contracts was to ensure that each risk was borne by the party that was best able to measure and control it. For example, the contractors were best placed to ensure that the plant was completed on time, so it made sense to ask them to bear the risk of construction delays. Similarly, the plant operator was best placed to operate the plant efficiently and would be penalized if it failed to do so. The contractors and the plant manager were prepared to take on these risks because the project involved an established technology and there was relatively little chance of unpleasant surprises.

While these contracts sought to be as precise as possible about each party's responsibilities, they could not cover every eventuality; inevitably the contracts were incomplete. Therefore, to buttress the formal legal agreements, the contractors and the plant manager became major shareholders in Hubco. This meant that if they cut corners in building and running the plant, they would share in the losses.

The equity in Hubco was highly levered. Over 75 percent of the $1.6 billion investment in the project was financed by debt. Some of this was junior debt provided by a fund that was set up by the World Bank and Western and Japanese government aid agencies. The bulk of the debt was senior debt provided in a mixture of currencies by a group of major international banks.[44] The banks were encouraged to invest because they knew that the World Bank and several governments were in the frontline and would take a hit if the project were to fail. But they were still concerned that the government of Pakistan might prevent Hubco from paying out foreign currency or it might impose a special tax or prevent the company from bringing in the specialist staff it needed. Therefore, to protect Hubco against these political risks, the government promised to pay compensation if it interfered in such ways with the operation of the project. Of course, the government could not be prevented from tearing up that agreement, but, if it did, Hubco was able to call on a $360 million guarantee by the World Bank and the Japan Bank for International Cooperation. This was supposed to keep the Pakistan government honest once the plant was built and operating. Governments can be surprisingly relaxed in the face of the wrath of a private corporation but are usually reluctant to break an agreement that lands the World Bank with a large bill.

The arrangements for the Hubco project were complex, costly, and time-consuming. Not everything was plain sailing. The project was suspended for over a year by a Pakistani court ruling that the interest on the loans contravened Islamic law. Ten years after the start of the discussions the final agreement on financing the project was signed and within a short time Hubco was producing a fifth of all Pakistan's electricity.

[44]Notice that, although most of the debt had a maturity of 12 years, the project was not financed by a public bond issue. The concentrated ownership of bank debt induces the lenders to evaluate the project carefully and to monitor its subsequent progress. It also facilitates the renegotiation of the debt if the project company runs into difficulties.

That was not the end of the Hubco story. After the fall of Benazir Bhutto's government in Pakistan, the new government terminated the contract with Hubco and announced a 30 percent cut in electricity tariffs. After three years of painful dispute, which threatened Pakistan's relationships with the World Bank, Hubco finally agreed to a new tariff. The feud with the government appeared to be finally over.

Project Finance—Some Common Features

No two project financings are alike, but they have some common features:

- The project is established as a separate company.
- The contractors and the plant manager become major shareholders in the project and thus share in the risk of the project's failure.
- The project company enters into a complex series of contracts that distributes risk among the contractors, the plant manager, the suppliers, and the customers.
- The government may guarantee that it will provide the necessary permits, allow the purchase of foreign exchange, and so on.
- The detailed contractual arrangements and the government guarantees allow a large part of the capital for the project to be provided in the form of bank debt or other privately placed borrowing.

The Role of Project Finance

Project finance is widely used in developing countries to fund power, telecommunications, and transportation projects, but it is also used in the major industrialized countries. In the United States project finance has been most commonly used to fund power plants. For example, an electric utility company may get together with an industrial company to construct a cogeneration plant that provides electricity to the utility and waste heat to a nearby industrial plant. The utility stands behind the cogeneration project and guarantees its revenue stream. Banks are happy to lend as much as 90 percent of the cost of the project because they know that once the project is up and running, the cash flow is insulated from most of the risks facing normal businesses.[45]

As lenders have gained experience in providing project finance, they have been prepared to widen the range of assets that they will consider and to provide support for more risky projects. In such cases

[45]There are some interesting regulatory implications to this arrangement. When a utility builds a power plant, it is entitled to a fair return on its investment: Regulators are supposed to set customer charges that will allow the utility to earn its cost of capital. Unfortunately, the cost of capital is not easily measured and is a natural focus for argument in regulatory hearings. But when a utility buys electric power, the cost of capital is rolled into the contract price and treated as an operating cost. In this case the pass-through to the customer may be less controversial.

lenders have reduced the amounts that they are willing to lend or have looked for some recourse to the parent in the event of default.[46]

25.8 INNOVATION IN THE BOND MARKET

Domestic bonds and eurobonds, fixed- and floating-rate bonds, coupon bonds and zeros, callable and puttable bonds, privately placed bonds and project finance—you might think that this would give you as much choice as you need. Yet almost every day some new type of bond seems to be issued.

Table 25.2 lists some of the more interesting bonds that have been invented in recent years.[47] Earlier in the chapter we cited the "Bowie bonds" as an example of asset-backed securities, and in Chapter 27 we will discuss catastrophe bonds whose payoffs are linked to the occurrence of natural disasters.

Since we have recently been discussing convertible bonds, let us look at a couple of examples of exotic convertibles. Consider Motorola's liquid yield option note, or LYON. A LYON is a callable and puttable, zero-coupon convertible bond (and you can't get much more complicated than that). Motorola's LYON was a 20-year zero-coupon bond, convertible at any time into 54.8 shares. The bonds were issued in 1989 at a price of $306.56. At that time, the bonds would probably have sold for less than $200 if they had not been convertible. This was the cost to investors of exercising their option in 1989. Investors who waited 20 years to convert would be relinquishing a bond worth $1,000 (as long as the firm is still solvent). So the cost of exercising the conversion option for the Motorola LYON rises as the bond approaches maturity.

The Motorola LYON contains two other options. Since 1990 the company has had the right to call the bond for cash. The exercise price of this option started at $325.23 and rose each year until it reaches $1,000 in 2009. The bondholders also had an option, for there were three occasions between 1994 and 2004 when they could have demanded repayment of the bonds. The repayment price started at $412 in 1994 and increased to $744 in 2004. These put prices help to provide a more solid floor to the issue. Even if interest rates had risen and prices of other bonds had fallen, LYON holders on these three days had a guaranteed price at which they could have sold their bonds.[48] Obviously, investors who exercised the put gave up the opportunity to convert their bonds into stock; so it was worth taking advantage of the guarantee only if the conversion price of the bonds was well below the exercise price of the put.[49]

---

[46]These trends in project finance are discussed in B. Esty, "Returns on Project-Financed Investments: Evolution and Managerial Implications," *Journal of Applied Corporate Finance* 15 (Spring 2002), pp. 71–86.

[47]For a more comprehensive list of innovations, see K. A. Carrow and J. J. McConnell, "A Survey of U.S. Corporate Financing Innovations: 1970–1997," *Journal of Applied Corporate Finance* 12 (Spring 1999), pp. 55–69.

[48]Of course, this guarantee would not be worth much if the company was in financial distress and couldn't buy back the bonds.

[49]The reasons for issuing LYONs are discussed in J. J. McConnell and E. S. Schwartz, "The Origin of LYONs: A Case Study in Financial Innovation," *Journal of Applied Corporate Finance* 4 (Winter 1992), pp. 40–47. For a discussion of how to value LYONs, see J. J. McConnell and E. S. Schwartz, "Taming LYONs," *Journal of Finance* 41 (July 1986), pp. 561–576.

TABLE 25.2 Some examples of innovation in bond design.

Liquid yield option notes (LYONs)	Puttable, callable, convertible, zero-coupon debt.
Floating-price (death-spiral) convertibles	Convertible debt where the bondholder can convert into a fixed *value* of shares.
Asset-backed securities	Many small loans are packaged together and resold as a bond.
Catastrophe (CAT) bonds	Payments are reduced in the event of a specified natural disaster.
Reverse floaters (yield-curve notes)	Floating-rate bonds that pay a higher rate of interest when other interest rates fall and a lower rate when other rates rise.
Equity-linked bonds	Payments are linked to the performance of a stock market index.
Pay-in-kind bonds (PIKs)	Issuer can choose to make interest payments either in cash or in more bonds with an equivalent face value.
Rate-sensitive bonds	Coupon rate changes as company's credit rating changes.
Longevity bonds	Bonds whose payments are linked to the proportion of the population surviving to a particular age.

Now for our second type of exotic convertible. Toward the end of the 1990s there was a flurry of new issues of *floating-price convertibles,* or as they were more commonly called "death-spiral," or "toxic," convertibles.[50] When death-spiral convertibles are issued, the conversion price is set below the current stock price. Moreover, each bond is convertible not into a fixed *number* of shares but into shares with a fixed *value*. Therefore, the more the share price falls, the more shares that the convertible bondholder is entitled to. With a normal convertible, the value of the conversion option falls whenever the value of the firm's assets falls; so the convertible holder shares part of the pain with the stockholders. With a death-spiral convertible, the holder is entitled to shares with a fixed value; so the entire effect of the fall in asset value falls on the common stockholders. Death-spiral convertibles were issued largely by companies that were already in desperate straits and many of the firms performed very poorly. After the initial flurry of issues, death-spiral convertibles seem to have been consigned to the garbage heap of unsuccessful innovations.

Some financial innovations are stimulated by changes in government regulation or taxes. We have already seen how the eurobond market was a response to the U.S. government's imposition of a tax on purchases of foreign securities. At other times new financial instruments succeed because they widen investor choice. Economists refer to such securities as helping to "complete the market." For example, the unusual weather in 1997–1998 resulting from El Niño encouraged a number of firms to market financial contracts that would pay off in unusual weather conditions. These firms hoped that *weather derivatives* would prove popular with the newly deregulated energy companies, the agricultural community, and many other businesses that might wish to protect themselves against the vagaries of the weather. The demand for weather derivatives proved sufficiently popular that the futures exchanges soon leapt on the bandwagon and started to trade weather futures.

[50]The performance of death spirals is analyzed in P. Hillion and T. Vermaelen, "Death Spiral Convertibles," *Journal of Financial Economics* 71 (February 2004), pp. 381–416.

SUMMARY

You should now have a fair idea of what you are letting yourself in for when you make an issue of bonds. You can issue bonds in the domestic Indian market, in a foreign bond market, or in the international bond market. International bonds (also called eurobonds) are marketed simultaneously in a number of foreign countries, usually by the London branches of international banks and security dealers.

The detailed bond agreement is set out in the indenture between your company and a trustee, but the main provisions are summarized in the prospectus to the issue. The indenture states whether the bonds are senior or subordinated, and whether they are secured or unsecured. Most bonds are unsecured debentures or notes. This means that they are general claims on the corporation. The principal exceptions are utility mortgage bonds, collateral trust bonds, and equipment trust certificates. In the event of default, the trustee to these issues can repossess the company's assets to pay off the debt.

Some long-term bond issues have a sinking fund. This means that the company must set aside enough money each year to retire a specified number of bonds. A sinking fund reduces the average life of the bond, and it provides a yearly test of the company's ability to service its debt. It therefore helps to protect the bondholders against the risk of default.

Long-dated bonds may be callable before maturity. The option to call the bond may be very valuable. If interest rates decline and bond value rises, you may be able to call a bond that would be worth substantially more than the call price. Of course, if investors know that you may call the bond, the call price will act as a ceiling on the market price. Your best strategy, therefore, is to call the bond as soon as the market price hits the call price. You are unlikely to do better than that.

Lenders usually seek to prevent the borrower from taking actions that would damage the value of their loans. Here are some examples of debt covenants:

1. The loan agreement may limit the amount of additional borrowing by the company.
2. Unsecured loans may incorporate a negative pledge clause, which prohibits the company from securing additional debt without giving equal treatment to the existing unsecured bonds.
3. Lenders may place a limit on the company's dividend payments or repurchases of stock.

Bank loans and other privately placed debt tend to impose more restrictive conditions, but these conditions are more easily changed if it makes sense to do so.

Most bonds start and finish their lives as bonds, but convertible bonds give their owner the option to exchange the bond for common stock. The *conversion ratio* measures the number of shares into which each bond can be exchanged. You can think of a convertible bond as equivalent to a straight bond plus a call option on the stock. Sometimes, instead of issuing a convertible, companies may decide to issue a package of bonds and options (or *warrants*) to buy the stock. If the stock price rises above the exercise price, the investor may then keep the bond and exercise the warrants for cash.

Private placements are less standardized than public issues, but otherwise they are generally close counterparts of publicly issued bonds. Sometimes private debt takes the form of project finance. In this case the loan is tied to the fortunes of a particular project.

There is an enormous variety of bond issues and new forms of bonds are spawned almost daily. By a process of natural selection, some of these new instruments become popular and may even replace existing species. Others are ephemeral curiosities. Some innovations succeed because they widen investor choice and allow investors to manage their risks better. Others owe their origin to tax rules and government regulation.

FURTHER READING

A useful general work on debt securities is:

F. J. Fabozzi (ed.), *The Handbook of Fixed Income Securities*, 6th ed. (New York: McGraw-Hill, 2000).

For nontechnical discussions of the pricing of convertible bonds and the reasons for their use, see:

M. J. Brennan and E. S. Schwartz, "The Case for Convertibles," *Journal of Applied Corporate Finance* 1 (Summer 1988), pp. 55–64.

C. M. Lewis, R. J. Rogalski, and J. K. Seward, "Understanding the Design of Convertible Debt," *Journal of Applied Corporate Finance* 11 (Spring 1998), pp. 45–53.

Discussions of project finance include:

B. C. Esty, *Modern Project Finance: A Casebook* (NewYork: John Wiley, 2003).

B. C. Esty, "Returns on Project-Financed Investments: Evolution and Managerial Implications," *Journal of Applied Corporate Finance* 15 (Spring 2002), pp. 71–86.

R. A. Brealey, I. A. Cooper, and M. Habib, "Using Project Finance to Fund Infrastructure Investments," *Journal of Applied Corporate Finance* 9 (Fall 1996), pp. 25–38.

The readings listed at the end of Chapter 17 include several articles on financial innovation.

CONCEPT REVIEW QUESTIONS

1. *Vocabulary check.* Define the following terms: Indenture or trust deed, subordinated bond, call provision, sinking fund, foreign bond, negative pledge clause. (pages 672–679)
2. Explain the difference between a senior bond and a secured bond. (page 675)
3. What is the difference between a bearer bond and a registered bond? (pages 673–674)

For additional Concept Review Questions, please visit us at www.mhhe.com/bmam8e or refer to your Student CD.

QUIZ

1. Select the most appropriate term from within the parentheses:
   a. (Bonds/debentures) are usually unsecured debt instruments.
   b. Public Sector Units in India raise debt capital by issue of (bonds/debentures)
   c. Mortgage pass-through certificate is an example of (an asset-backed security/project finance)
   d. Dhabol Power Project is an example of (project finance/private placement)
2. a. As a senior bondholder, would you like the company to issue more junior debt, would you prefer it not to do so, or would you not care?
   b. You hold debt secured on the company's existing property. Would you like the company to issue more unsecured debt, would you prefer it not to do so, or would you not care?
3. Use Table 25.1 (but not the text) to answer the following questions:
   a. Who is the trustee of the issue?
   b. Is the bond "bearer" or "registered"?
   c. What is the maximum interest that ICICI Bank has to pay to the bondholders every year?
4. Look at Table 25.1:
   a. When is the first interest payment due on the bond, and what is the amount of the payment? Assume that ICICI Bank has not exercised the Green Shoe option.
   b. On what date do the bonds finally mature? Assume that ICICI Bank does not pay any interest to the bondholders. It rather reinvests the interest in the bond itself. How much money will the bondholders get from ICICI Bank on the maturity date for every bond held?

c. Suppose that the bond is callable and that the market price of the bond rises to Rs. 5100 and thereafter does not change. When should the Bank call the issue? Assume that the bank has the right to call back the bond at Rs. 5200 in March 2006, at Rs. 5150 in March 2007, at Rs. 5100 in March 2008, and at Rs. 5000 thereafter.

5. Explain the three principal ways in which the terms of private placement bonds commonly differ from those of public issues.

6. True or false? Briefly explain in each case.
   a. Lenders in project financings rarely have any recourse against the project's owners if the project fails.
   b. Many new and exotic debt securities are triggered by government policies or regulations.
   c. Call provisions give a valuable option to debt investors.
   d. Restrictive covenants have been shown to protect debt investors when takeovers are financed with large amounts of debt.
   e. Privately placed debt issues often include stricter covenants than public debt. However, public debt covenants are more difficult and expensive to renegotiate.

7. Maple Aircraft has issued a 4 ¾ percent convertible subordinated debenture due 2011. The conversion price is Rs. 47.00 and the debenture is callable at 102.75 percent of face value. The market price of the convertible is 91 percent of face value, and the price of the share is Rs. 41.50. Assume that the value of the bond in the absence of a conversion feature is about 65 percent of face value.
   a. What is the conversion ratio of the debenture?
   b. If the conversion ratio were 50, what would be the conversion price?
   c. What is the conversion value?
   d. At what stock price is the conversion value equal to the bond value?
   e. Can the market price be less than the conversion value?
   f. How much is the convertible holder paying for the option to buy one share of share stock?
   g. By how much does the share have to rise by 2011 to justify conversion?
   h. When should Maple call the debenture?

8. True or false?
   a. Convertible bonds are usually senior claims on the firm.
   b. The higher the conversion ratio, the more valuable the convertible.
   c. The higher the conversion price, the more valuable the convertible.
   d. Convertible bonds do not share fully in the price of the common stock, but they provide some protection against a decline.

PRACTICE QUESTIONS

1. Suppose that the ICICI Bank bond was issued at Rs. 4900 (discount to the face value). Sketch what you think would happen to the bond price as the first interest payment date approaches and then passes. What about the price of the bond plus the accrued interest?

2. Visit the website of SEBI (www.sebi.gov.in) and find out the terms and conditions of Flexi-bond issues made by IDBI and compare them with those of the ICICI Bank bond issue.

3. Bond prices can fall either because of a change in the general level of interest rates or because of an increased risk of default. To what extent do floating-rate bonds and put-table bonds protect the investor against each of these risks?

4. Proctor Power has fixed assets worth Rs. 200 million and net working capital worth Rs. 100 million. It is financed partly by equity and partly by three issues of debt. These consist of Rs. 250 million of First Mortgage Bonds secured only on the company's fixed assets, Rs. 100 million of senior debentures, and Rs. 120 million of subordinated debentures. If the debt were due today, how much would each debtholder be entitled to receive?

5. Elixir Corporation has just filed for bankruptcy. Elixir is a holding company whose assets consist of real estate worth Rs. 80 million and 100 percent of the equity of its two operating subsidiaries. It is financed partly by equity and partly by an issue of Rs. 400 million of senior collateral trust bonds that are just about to

mature. Subsidiary A has issued directly Rs. 320 million of debentures and Rs. 15 million of preferred stock. Subsidiary B has issued Rs. 180 million of senior debentures and Rs. 60 million of subordinated debentures. A's assets have a market value of Rs. 500 million and B's have a value of Rs. 220 million. How much will each security holder receive if the assets are sold and distributed strictly according to precedence?

6. a. Residential mortgages may stipulate either a fixed rate or a variable rate. As a *borrower*, what considerations might cause you to prefer one rather than the other?
   b. Why might holders of mortgage pass-through certificates wish the mortgages to have a floating rate?
7. After a sharp change in interest rates, newly issued bonds generally sell at yields different from those of outstanding bonds of the same quality. One suggested explanation is that there is a difference in the value of the call provisions. Explain how this could arise.
8. Suppose that a company simultaneously issues a zero-coupon bond and a coupon bond with identical maturities. Both are callable at any time at their face values. Other things equal, which is likely to offer the higher yield? Why?
9. a. If interest rates rise, will callable or noncallable bonds fall more in price?
   b. Sometimes you encounter bonds that can be repaid after a fixed interval at the option of *either* the issuer or the bondholder. If the exercise price of each option is the same and both the issuer and bondholder act rationally, what will happen when the options can be exercised? (Ignore refinements such as transactions or issue costs.)
10. A puttable bond is a bond which may be repaid before maturity at the investor's option. Sketch a diagram similar to Figure 25.2 showing the relationship between the value of a straight bond and that of a puttable bond.
11. Alpha Corp. is prohibited from issuing more senior debt unless net tangible assets exceed 200 percent of senior debt. Currently the company has outstanding Rs. 100 million of senior debt and has net tangible assets of Rs. 250 million. How much more senior debt can Alpha Corp. issue?
12. Explain carefully why bond indentures place limitations on the following actions:
    a. Sale of the company's assets.
    b. Payment of dividends to shareholders.
    c. Issue of additional senior debt.
13. Explain when it makes sense to use project finance rather than a direct debt issue by the parent company.
14. The Surplus Value Company had Rs. 10 million (face value) of convertible bonds outstanding in 2004. Each bond has the following features.

Face value	Rs. 1000
Conversion price	Rs. 25
Current call price	105 (percent of face value)
Current trading price	130 (percent of face value)
Maturity	2014
Current stock price	Rs. 30 (per share)
Interest rate	10 (coupon as percent of face value)

    a. What is the bond's conversion value?
    b. Can you explain why the bond is selling above conversion value?
    c. Should Surplus call? What will happen if it does so?
15. Piglet Pies has issued a zero-coupon 10-year bond that can be converted into 10 Piglet shares. Comparable straight bonds are yielding 8 percent. Piglet stock is priced at $50 a share.

a. Suppose that you had to make a now-or-never decision on whether to convert or to stay with the bond. Which would you do?
b. If the convertible bond is priced at $550, how much are investors paying for the option to buy Piglet shares?
c. If after one year the value of the conversion option is unchanged, what is the value of the convertible bond?

16. Iota Microsystems' 10 percent convertible is about to mature. The conversion ratio is 27.
a. What is the conversion price?
b. The stock price is Rs. 47. What is the conversion value?
c. Should you convert?

17. In 1996 Marriott International made an issue of LYONS. The bond matured in 2011, had a zero coupon, and was issued at $532.15. It could be converted into 8.76 shares. Beginning in 1999 the bonds could be called by Marriott. The call price was $603.71 in 1999 and increased by 4.3 percent a year thereafter. Holders had an option to put the bond back to Marriott in 1999 at $603.71 and in 2006 at $810.36. At the time of issue the price of the common stock was about $50.50.
a. What was the yield to maturity on the bond?
b. Assuming that comparable nonconvertible bonds yielded 10 percent, how much were investors paying for the conversion option?
c. What was the conversion value of the bonds at the time of issue?
d. What was the initial conversion price of the bonds?
e. What is the conversion price in 2005? Why does it change?
f. If the price of the bond in 2006 is less than $810.36, would you put the bond back to Marriott?
g. At what price can Marriott call the bonds in 2006? If the price of the bond in 2006 is more than this, should Marriott call them?

CHALLENGE QUESTIONS

1. Dorlcote Milling has outstanding a $1 million 3 percent mortgage bond maturing in 10 years. The coupon on any new debt issued by the company is 10 percent. The finance director, Mr. Tulliver, cannot decide whether there is a tax benefit to repurchasing the existing bonds in the marketplace and replacing them with new 10 percent bonds. What do you think? Does it matter whether bond investors are taxed?
2. Refer back to the Hub Power project in Section 25.7. There were many other ways that the Hubco project could have been financed. For example, a government agency could have invested in the power plant and hired National Power to run it. Alternatively, National Power could have owned the power plant directly and funded its cost by a mixture of new borrowing and the sale of shares. What do you think were the advantages of setting up a separately financed company to undertake the project?
3. This question illustrates that when there is scope for the firm to vary its risk, lenders may be more prepared to lend if they are offered a piece of the action through the issue of a convertible bond. Ms. Blavatsky is proposing to form a new start-up firm with initial assets of $10 million. She can invest this money in one of two projects. Each has the same expected payoff, but one has more risk than the other. The relatively safe project offers a 40 percent chance of a $12.5 million payoff and a 60 percent chance of an $8 million payoff. The risky project offers a 40 percent chance of a $20 million payoff and a 60 percent chance of a $5 million payoff.

   Ms. Blavatsky initially proposes to finance the firm by an issue of straight debt with a promised payoff of $7 million. Ms. Blavatsky will receive any remaining payoff. Show the possible payoffs to the lender and to Ms. Blavatsky if (a) she chooses the safe project and (b) she chooses the risky project. Which project is Ms. Blavatsky likely to choose? Which will the lender want her to choose?

   Suppose now that Ms. Blavatsky offers to make the debt convertible into 50 percent of the value of the firm. Show that in this case the lender receives the same expected payoff from the two projects.

4. Occasionally it is said that issuing convertible bonds is better than issuing stock when the firm's shares are undervalued. Suppose that the financial manager of the Butternut Furniture Company does have inside information indicating that the Butternut stock price is too low. Butternut's future earnings will in fact be higher than investors expect. Suppose further that the inside information cannot be released without giving away a valuable competitive secret. Clearly, selling shares at the present low price would harm Butternut's existing shareholders. Will they also lose if convertible bonds are issued? If they do lose in this case, is the loss more or less than it would be if common stock were issued?

Now suppose that investors forecast earnings accurately, but still undervalue the stock because they overestimate Butternut's actual business risk. Does this change your answers to the questions posed in the preceding paragraph? Explain.

MINI-CASE

The Shocking Demise of Mr. Thorndike

It was one of Morse's most puzzling cases. That morning Rupert Thorndike, the autocratic CEO of Thorndike Oil, was found dead in a pool of blood on his bedroom floor. He had been shot through the head, but the door and windows were bolted on the inside and there was no sign of the murder weapon.

Morse looked in vain for clues in Thorndike's office. He had to take another tack. He decided to investigate the financial circumstances surrounding Thorndike's demise. The company's capital structure was as follows:

- 5% debentures: $250 million face value. The bonds matured in 10 years and offered a yield of 12 percent.
- Stock: 30 million shares, which closed at $9 a share the day before the murder.
- 10% subordinated convertible notes: The notes mature in one year and are convertible at any time at a conversion ratio of 110. The day before the murder these notes were priced at 5 percent more than their conversion value.

Yesterday Thorndike had flatly rejected an offer by T. Spoone Dickens to buy all of the common stock for $10 a share. With Thorndike out of the way, it appeared that Dickens's offer would be accepted, much to the profit of Thorndike Oil's other shareholders.[51]

Thorndike's two nieces, Doris and Patsy, and his nephew John all had substantial investments in Thorndike Oil and had bitterly disagreed with Thorndike's dismissal of Dickens's offer. Their stakes are shown in the following table:

	5% Debentures (Face Value)	(Number of Shares Stock in Millions)	10% Convertible Notes (Face Value)
Doris	$4 million	1.2	$0 million
John	0	.5	5
Patsy	0	1.5	3

All debt issued by Thorndike Oil would be paid off at face value if Dickens's offer went through. Holders of the convertible notes could choose to convert and tender their shares to Dickens.

Morse kept coming back to the problem of motive. Which niece or nephew, he wondered, stood to gain most by eliminating Thorndike and allowing Dickens's offer to succeed?

QUESTION

1. Help Morse solve the case. Which of Thorndike's relatives stood to gain most from his death?

[51]Rupert Thorndike's shares would go to a charitable foundation formed to advance the study of financial engineering and its crucial role in world peace and progress. The managers of the foundation's endowment were not expected to oppose the takeover.

CHAPTER [26]

LEASING

MOST OF US occasionally rent a car, bicycle, or boat. Usually such personal rentals are short-lived; we may rent a car for a day or week. But in corporate finance longer-term rentals are common. A rental agreement that extends for a year or more and involves a series of fixed payments is called a **lease.**

Firms lease as an alternative to buying capital equipment. Computers are often leased; so are trucks, railroad cars, aircraft, and ships. Just about every kind of asset has been leased sometime by somebody, including electric power plants, nuclear fuel, handball courts, and zoo animals.

Every lease involves two parties. The *user* of the asset is called the *lessee.* The lessee makes periodic payments to the *owner* of the asset, who is called the *lessor.* For example, if you sign an agreement to rent an apartment for a year, you are the lessee and the owner is the lessor.

You often see references to the *leasing industry.* This refers to lessors. (Almost all firms are lessees to at least a minor extent.) Who are the lessors?

Some of the largest lessors are equipment manufacturers. For example, IBM is a large lessor of computers, and Deere is a large lessor of agricultural and construction equipment.

The other two major groups of lessors are banks and independent leasing companies. Leasing companies play an enormous role in the airline business. For example, in 2004 GE Capital Aviation Services, a subsidiary of GE Capital, owned and leased out 1,100 commercial aircraft. A large fraction of the world's airlines rely entirely on leasing to finance their fleets.

Leasing companies offer a variety of services. Some act as lease brokers (arranging lease deals) as well as lessors. Others specialize in leasing automobiles, trucks, and standardized industrial equipment; they succeed because they can buy equipment in quantity, service it efficiently, and if necessary resell it at a good price.

We begin this chapter by cataloging the different kinds of leases and some of the reasons for their use. Then we show how short-term, or cancelable, lease payments can be interpreted as equivalent annual costs. The remainder of the chapter analyzes long-term leases used as alternatives to debt financing.

26.1 WHAT IS A LEASE?

Leases come in many forms, but in all cases the lessee (user) promises to make a series of payments to the lessor (owner). The lease contract specifies the monthly or semiannual payments, with the first payment usually due as soon as the contract is signed. The payments are usually level, but their time pattern can be tailored to the user's needs. For example, suppose that a manufacturer leases a machine to produce a complex new product. There will be a year's "shakedown" period before volume production starts. In this case, it might be possible to arrange for lower payments during the first year of the lease.

When a lease is terminated, the leased equipment reverts to the lessor. However, the lease agreement often gives the user the option to purchase the equipment or take out a new lease.

Some leases are short-term or cancelable during the contract period at the option of the lessee. These are generally known as *operating leases.* Others extend over most of the estimated economic life of the asset and cannot be canceled or can be canceled only if the lessor is reimbursed for any losses. These are called *capital, financial,* or *full-payout leases.*

Financial leases are a *source of financing.* Signing a financial lease contract is like borrowing money. There is an immediate cash inflow because the lessee is relieved of having to pay for the asset. But the lessee also assumes a binding obligation to make the payments specified in the lease contract. The user could have borrowed the full purchase price of the asset by accepting a binding obligation to make interest and principal payments to the lender. Thus the cash-flow consequences of leasing and borrowing are similar. In either case, the firm raises cash now and pays it back later. A large part of this chapter will be devoted to comparing leasing and borrowing as financing alternatives.

Leases also differ in the services provided by the lessor. Under a *full-service*, or *rental*, lease, the lessor promises to maintain and insure the equipment and to pay any property taxes due on it. In a *net* lease, the lessee agrees to maintain the asset, insure it, and pay any property taxes. Financial leases are usually net leases.

Most financial leases are arranged for brand new assets. The lessee identifies the equipment, arranges for the leasing company to buy it from the manufacturer, and signs a contract with the leasing company. This is called a *direct* lease. In other cases, the firm sells an asset it already owns and leases it back from the buyer. These sale and lease-back arrangements are common on real estate and civil aviation industry. For example, firm X may wish to raise cash by selling an aircraft but still retain use of the aircraft. Thus for example, in 2005–06, Jet Airways sold and leased back five aircrafts and reported an additional book income of Rs. 271 crores. Legal ownership of the aircrafts passed to the leasing company, but the right to use it stayed with Jet Airways.

You may also encounter *leveraged* leases. These are financial leases in which the lessor borrows part of the purchase price of the leased asset, using the lease contract as security for the loan. This does not change the lessee's obligations, but it can complicate the lessor's analysis considerably.

26.2 WHY LEASE?

You hear many suggestions about why companies should lease equipment rather than buy it. Let us look at some sensible reasons and then at four more dubious ones.

Sensible Reasons for Leasing

Short-Term Leases Are Convenient Suppose you want the use of a car for a week. You could buy one and sell it seven days later, but that would be silly. Quite apart from the fact that registering ownership is a nuisance, you would spend some time selecting a car, negotiating purchase, and arranging insurance. Then at the end of the week you would negotiate resale and cancel the registration and insurance. When you need a car only for a short time, it clearly makes sense to rent it. You save the trouble of registering ownership, and you know the effective cost. In the same way, it pays a company to lease equipment that it needs for only a year or two. Of course, this kind of lease is always an operating lease.

Sometimes the cost of short-term rentals may seem prohibitively high, or you may find it difficult to rent at any price. This can happen for equipment that is easily damaged by careless use. The owner knows that short-term users are unlikely to take the same care they would with their own equipment. When the danger of abuse becomes too high, short-term rental markets do not survive. Thus, it is easy enough to buy a Lamborghini Gallardo, provided your pockets are deep enough, but nearly impossible to rent one.

Cancellation Options Are Valuable Some leases that *appear* expensive really are fairly priced once the option to cancel is recognized. We return to this point in the next section.

Maintenance Is Provided Under a full-service lease, the user receives maintenance and other services. Many lessors are well equipped to provide efficient maintenance. However, bear in mind that these benefits will be reflected in higher lease payments.

Standardization Leads to Low Administrative and Transaction Costs Suppose that you operate a leasing company that specializes in financial leases for trucks. You are effectively lending money to a large number of firms (the lessees) which may differ considerably in size and risk. But, because the underlying asset is in each case the same saleable item (a truck), you can safely "lend" the money (lease the truck) without conducting a detailed analysis of each firm's business. You can also use a simple, standard lease contract. This standardization makes it possible to "lend" small sums of money without incurring large investigative, administrative, or legal costs.

For these reasons leasing is often a relatively cheap source of cash for the small company. It offers financing on a flexible, piecemeal basis, with lower transaction costs than in a bond or stock issue.

Tax Shields Can Be Used The lessor owns the leased asset and deducts its depreciation from taxable income. If the lessor can make better use of depreciation tax shields than an asset's user can, it may make sense for the leasing company to own the equipment and pass on some of the tax benefits to the lessee in the form of low lease payments.

Avoiding the Alternative Minimum Tax Red-blooded financial managers want to earn lots of money for their shareholders but *report* low profits to the tax authorities. Tax law in the United States allows this. A firm may use straight-line depreciation in its annual report but choose accelerated depreciation (and the shortest possible asset life) for its tax books. By this and other perfectly legal and ethical devices, profitable companies have occasionally managed to escape tax entirely. Almost all companies pay less tax than their public income statements suggest.[1]

But there is a trap for companies that shield too much income: the alternative minimum tax (*AMT*). Corporations must pay the AMT whenever it is higher than their tax computed in the regular way.

Here is how the AMT works: It requires a second calculation of taxable income, in which part of the benefit of accelerated depreciation and other tax-reducing items[2] is added back. The AMT is 20 percent of the result.

Suppose Yuppytech Services would have $10 million in taxable income but for the AMT, which forces it to add back $9 million of tax privileges:

[1]Year-by-year differences between reported tax expense and taxes actually paid are explained in footnotes to the financial statements. The cumulative difference is shown on the balance sheet as a deferred tax liability. (Note that accelerated depreciation *postpones* taxes; it does not eliminate taxes.)

[2]Other items include some interest receipts from tax-exempt municipal securities and taxes deferred by use of completed contract accounting. (The completed contract method allows a manufacturer to postpone reporting taxable profits until a production contract is completed. Since contracts may span several years, this deferral can have a substantial positive NPV.)

	Regular Tax	Alternative Minimum Tax
Income	$10	10 + 9 = 19
Tax rate	.35	.20
Tax	$3.5	$3.8

Yuppytech must pay $3.8 million, not $3.5.[3]

How can this painful payment be avoided? How about leasing? Lease payments are *not* on the list of items added back in calculating the AMT. If you lease rather than buy, tax depreciation is less and the AMT is less. There is a net gain if the *lessor* is not subject to the AMT and can pass back depreciation tax shields in the form of lower lease payments.

In India, however, only the excess depreciation relating to the revalued assets is added back to the book profit. Secondly, the lessee deducts lease rentals while calculating taxable income, whereas it deducts apportioned interest (on lease rentals) and depreciation while calculating the book profit (following AS 19 issued by the ICAI). If lease rental is equal to the apportioned interest plus depreciation, then the difference between book profit and taxable income will be entirely due to factors not related to the leasing transaction. So minimum alternative tax (MAT) cannot be a sensible reason for leasing in India.

Some Dubious Reasons for Leasing

Leasing Avoids Capital Expenditure Controls In many companies lease proposals are scrutinized as carefully as capital expenditure proposals, but in others leasing may enable an operating manager to avoid the approval procedures needed to buy an asset. Although this is a dubious reason for leasing, it may be influential, particularly in the public sector. For example, city hospitals have sometimes found it politically more convenient to lease their medical equipment than to ask the city government to provide funds for purchase.

Leasing Preserves Capital Leasing companies provide "100 percent financing"; they advance the full cost of the leased asset. Consequently, they often claim that leasing preserves capital, allowing the firm to save its cash for other things.

But the firm can also "preserve capital" by borrowing money. If Blueline Bus leases a Rs. 800,000 bus rather than buying it, it does conserve Rs. 800,000 cash. It could also (1) buy the bus for cash and (2) borrow Rs. 800,000, using the bus as security. Its bank balance ends up the same whether it leases or buys and borrows. It has the bus in either case, and it incurs a Rs. 800,000 liability in either case. What's so special about leasing?

Leases May Be Off-Balance-Sheet Financing In some countries financial leases are off-balance-sheet financing; that is, a firm can acquire an asset, finance it through a financial lease, and show neither the asset nor the lease contract on its balance sheet.

In India, Accounting Standard 19 issued by ICAI requires that all financial leases (capital leases) be capitalized. This means that the present value of the lease payments must be calculated and shown alongside debt on the right-hand side of the balance sheet. The same amount must be shown as an asset on the left-hand side.[4]

[3]But Yuppytech can carry forward the $3 million difference. If later years' AMTs are *lower* than regular taxes, the difference can be used as a tax credit. Suppose the AMT next year is $4 million and the regular tax is $5 million. Then Yuppytech pays only 5 − .3 = $4.7 million.

[4]This "asset" is then amortized over the life of the lease. The amortization is deducted from book income, just as depreciation is deducted for a purchased asset.

The AS19 defines financial leases as leases which meet *any one* of the following requirements:

1. The lease agreement transfers ownership to the lessee before the lease expires.
2. The lessee can purchase the asset for a bargain price when the lease expires.
3. The lease lasts for at least 75 percent of the asset's estimated economic life.
4. The present value of the lease payments is at least 90 percent of the asset's value.

All other leases are operating leases as far as the accountants are concerned.

Many financial managers have tried to take advantage of this arbitrary boundary between operating and financial leases. Suppose that you want to finance a computer-controlled machine tool costing Rs. 1 million. The machine tool's life is expected to be 12 years. You could sign a lease contract for 8 years, 11 months (just missing requirement 3) with lease payments having a present value of Rs. 899,000 (just missing requirement 4). You could also make sure the lease contract avoids requirements 1 and 2. Result? You have off-balance-sheet financing. This lease would not have to be capitalized, although it is clearly a long-term, fixed obligation.

Now we come to the Rs. 64,000 question: Why should anyone *care* whether financing is off balance sheet or on balance sheet? Shouldn't the financial manager worry about substance rather than appearance?

When a firm obtains off-balance-sheet financing, the conventional measures of financial leverage, such as the debt–equity ratio, understate the true degree of financial leverage. Some believe that financial analysts do not always notice off-balance-sheet lease obligations (which are still referred to in footnotes) or the greater volatility of earnings that results from the fixed lease payments. They may be right, but we would not expect such an imperfection to be widespread.

Leasing Affects Book Income Leasing can make the firm's balance sheet and income statement *look* better by increasing book income or decreasing book asset value, or both.

A lease that qualifies as off-balance-sheet financing affects book income in only one way: The lease payments are an expense. If the firm buys the asset instead and borrows to finance it, both depreciation and interest expense are deducted. Leases are usually set up so that payments in the early years are less than depreciation plus interest under the buy-and-borrow alternative. Consequently, leasing increases book income in the early years of an asset's life. The book rate of return can increase even more dramatically, because the book value of assets (the denominator in the book-rate-of-return calculation) is understated if the leased asset never appears on the firm's balance sheet.

Leasing's impact on book income should in itself have no effect on firm value. In efficient capital markets investors will look through the firm's accounting results to the true value of the asset and the liability incurred to finance it.

26.3 OPERATING LEASES

Remember our discussion of *equivalent annual* costs in Chapter 6? We defined the equivalent annual cost of, say, a machine as the annual rental payment sufficient to cover the present value of all the costs of owning and operating it.

In Chapter 6's examples, the rental payments were hypothetical—just a way of converting a present value to an annual cost. But in the leasing business the payments are real. Suppose you decide to lease a machine tool for one year. What will the rental payment be in a competitive leasing industry? The lessor's equivalent annual cost, of course.

Example of an Operating Lease

The boyfriend of the daughter of the CEO of Establishment Industries takes her to the college party in a pearly white stretch limo. The CEO is impressed. He decides Establishment Industries ought to have one for VIP transportation. Establishment's CFO prudently suggests a one-year operating lease instead and approaches Sriram Limolease for a quote.

Table 26.1 shows Sriram's analysis. Suppose it buys a new limo for Rs. 34.5 lakhs which it plans to lease out for seven years (years 0 through 6). The table gives Sriram's forecasts of operating, maintenance, and administrative costs, the latter including the costs of negotiating the lease, keeping track of payments and paperwork, and finding a replacement lease when Establishment's year is up. For simplicity we assume zero inflation and use a 7% real cost of capital. We also assume that the limo will have zero salvage value at the end of year 6. The present value of all costs, partially offset by the value of depreciation tax shields,[5] is Rs. 46.77 lakhs. Now how much does Shriram have to charge to break-even?

Sriram can afford to buy and lease out the limo only if the rental payments forecasted over six years have a present value of at least Rs. 46.77 lakhs. The problem, then, is to calculate a six-year annuity with a present value of Rs. 46.77 lakhs. We will follow common leasing practice and assume rental payments in advance[6].

As Table 26.1 shows, the required annuity is Rs. 13.47 lakhs, that is, about Rs. 13.5 lakhs.[7] This annuity's present value (after taxes) exactly equals the present value of the after-tax costs of owning and operating the limo. The annuity provides Sriram with a competitive expected rate of return (7 percent) on its investment. Sriram could try to charge Establishment Industries more than Rs. 13.5 lakhs, but if the CFO is smart enough to ask for bids from Sriram's competitors, the winning lessor will end up receiving this amount.

Remember that Establishment Industries is not obligated to continue using the limo for more than one year. Sriram may have to find several new lessees over the limo's economic life. Even if Establishment continues, it can renegotiate a new lease at whatever rates prevail in the future. Thus Sriram does not know what it can charge in year 1 or afterward. If pearly white falls out of favor with teenagers and CEOs, Sriram is probably out of luck.

---

[5]The depreciation tax shields are safe cash flows if the tax rate does not change and Sriram is sure to pay taxes. If 7 percent is the right discount rate for the other flows in Table 26.1, the depreciation tax shields deserve a lower rate. A more refined analysis would discount safe depreciation tax shields at an after-tax borrowing or lending rate. See the Appendix to Chapter 19 or the next section of this chapter.

[6]In Section 6.3 the hypothetical rentals were paid *in arrears*.

[7]This is a level annuity because we are assuming that (1) there is no inflation and (2) the services of a six-year-old limo are no different than a brand-new limo's. If users of aging limos see them as obsolete or unfashionable, or if new limos are cheaper, then lease rates for older limos would have to be cut. This would give a *declining* annuity: initial users would pay more than the amount shown in Table 26.1, later users, less.

	A	B	C	D	E	F	G	H
1		Year						
2		0	1	2	3	4	5	6
3	Initial cost	-3450						
4	Maintenance costs, etc	-552	-552	-552	-552	-552	-552	-552
5	Tax shield on costs	+185.80	+185.80	+185.80	+185.80	+185.80	+185.80	+185.80
7	Depreciation tax shield[a]		+174.19	+148.06	+125.85	+106.97	+90.93	+515.26
8	Total	-3,816.20	-192.01	-218.13	-240.34	-259.22	-275.27	149.06
10	PV at 7% = -4677.05[b]							
11								
12	Break-even rent (level)	-1,346.66	-1,346.66	-1,346.66	-1,346.66	-1,346.66	-1,346.66	-1,346.66
13	Tax	+535.59	+535.59	+535.59	+535.59	+535.59	+535.59	+535.59
14	Breakeven rent after tax	-811.07	-811.07	-811.07	-811.07	-811.07	-811.07	-811.07
16	PV at 7% = -4677.05[b]							

TABLE 26.1

Calculating the zero-NPV rental value (or equivalent annual cost) for Establishment Industries's pearly white stretch limo (figures in Rs. thousands).

Note: We assume no inflation and a 7 percent real cost of capital. The tax rate is 33.66%

[a]Depreciation tax shields are calculated using 15 percent written down value rate and by assuming that scrap value of limo is zero.

[b]Note that the first payment of these annuities comes immediately. The standard annuity factor must be multiplied by 1 + r = 1.07.

eXcel

Please visit us at www.mhhe.com/bmam8e or refer to your Student CD.

In real life Sriram would have several further things to worry about. For example, how long will the limo stand idle when it is returned at year 1? If idle time is likely before a new lessee is found, then lease rates have to be higher to compensate.[8]

In an operating lease, the *lessor* absorbs these risks, not the lessee. The discount rate used by the lessor must include a premium sufficient to compensate its shareholders for the risks of buying and holding the leased asset. In other words, Sriram's 7 percent real discount rate must cover the risks of investing in stretch limos. (As we will see in the next section, risk bearing in *financial* leases is fundamentally different.)

Lease or Buy?

If you need a car or limo for only a day or a week you will surely rent it; if you need one for five years you will probably buy it. In between there is a gray region in which the choice of lease or buy is not obvious. The decision rule should be clear in concept, however: If you need an asset for your business, *buy it if the equivalent annual cost of ownership and operation is less than the best lease rate you can get from an outsider.* In other words, buy if you can "rent to yourself" cheaper than you can rent from others. (Again we stress that this rule applies to *operating* leases.)

If you plan to use the asset for an extended period, your equivalent annual cost of owning the asset will usually be less than the operating lease rate. The lessor has to mark up the lease rate to cover the costs of negotiating and administering the lease, the foregone revenues when the asset is off-lease and idle, and so on. These costs are avoided when the company buys and rents to itself.

[8]If, say, limos were off-lease and idle 20 percent of the time, lease rates would have to be 25 percent above those shown in Table 26.1.

There are two cases in which operating leases may make sense even when the company plans to use an asset for an extended period. First, the lessor may be able to buy and manage the asset at less expense than the lessee. For example, the major truck leasing companies buy thousands of new vehicles every year. That puts them in an excellent bargaining position with truck manufacturers. These companies also run very efficient service operations, and they know how to extract the most salvage value when trucks wear out and it is time to sell them. A small business, or a small division of a larger one, cannot achieve these economies and often finds it cheaper to lease trucks than to buy them.

Second, operating leases often contain useful options. Suppose Sriram offers Establishment Industries the following two leases:

1. A one-year lease for Rs. 26,000.
2. A six-year lease for Rs. 28,000, *with the option to cancel the lease* at any time from year 1 on.[9]

The second lease has obvious attractions. Suppose Establishment's CEO becomes fond of the limo and wants to use it for a second year. If rates increase, lease 2 allows Establishment to continue at the old rate. If rates decrease, Establishment can cancel lease 2 and negotiate a lower rate with Sriram or one of its competitors.

Of course, lease 2 is a more costly proposition for Sriram: In effect it gives Establishment an insurance policy protecting it from increases in future lease rates. The difference between the costs of leases 1 and 2 is the annual insurance premium. But lessees may happily pay for insurance if they have no special knowledge of future asset values or lease rates. A leasing company acquires such knowledge in the course of its business and can generally sell such insurance at a profit.

Airlines face fluctuating demand for their services and the mix of planes that they need is constantly changing. Most airlines, therefore, lease a proportion of their fleet on a short-term cancelable basis and are willing to pay a premium to lessors for bearing the cancelation risk. Specialist aircraft lessors are well-placed to bear this risk, for they will hope to find new customers for any aircraft that are returned to them.

Be sure to check out the options before you sign (or reject) an operating lease.[10]

26.4 VALUING FINANCIAL LEASES

For operating leases the decision centers on "lease versus buy." For *financial* leases the decision amounts to "lease versus borrow." Financial leases extend over most of the economic life of the leased equipment. They are *not* cancelable. The lease payments are fixed obligations equivalent to debt service.

Financial leases make sense when the company is prepared to take on the business risks of owning and operating the leased asset. If Establishment Industries signs a *financial* lease for the stretch

[9]Sriram might also offer a one-year lease for Rs. 28,000 but give the lessee an option to *extend* the lease on the same terms for up to five additional years. This is, of course, identical to lease 2. It doesn't matter whether the lessee has the (put) option to cancel or the (call) option to continue.

[10]McConnell and Schallheim calculate the value of options in operating leases under various assumptions about asset risk, depreciation rates, etc. See J. J. McConnell and J. S. Schallheim, "Valuation of Asset Leasing Contracts," *Journal of Financial Economics* 12 (August 1983), pp. 237–261.

limo, it is stuck with that asset. The financial lease is just another way of borrowing money to pay for the limo.

Financial leases do offer special advantages to some firms in some circumstances. However, there is no point in further discussion of these advantages until you know how to value financial lease contracts.

Example of a Financial Lease

Imagine yourself in the position of Haridas Pai, president of Bluelines Bus. Your firm was established by your grandfather, who was quick to capitalize on the growing demand for transportation between Mangalore and Mumbai. The company has owned all its vehicles from the time the company was formed; you are now reconsidering that policy. Your operating manager wants to buy new bus consisting Rs. 46 lakhs. The bus will last only eight years before going to the scrap yard. You are convinced that investment in the additional equipment is worthwhile. However, the representative of the bus manufacturer has pointed out that his firm would also be willing to lease the bus to you for eight annual payments of Rs. 7.83 lakhs. Bluelines would remain responsible for all maintenance, insurance, and operating expenses.

Table 26.2 shows the direct cash-flow consequences of the signing of the lease contract. (An important indirect effect is considered later.) The consequences are:

1. Bluelines does not have to pay for the bus. This is equivalent to a cash inflow of Rs. 46 lakhs.
2. Bluelines no more owns the bus, and so it cannot depreciate it. Therefore it gives up a valuable depreciation tax shield. In Table 26.2, we have assumed depreciation would be calculated using written down value method. The WDV rate is 25 percent. The net book value of the bus at the end of year 6 has been written off in year 7.
3. Bluelines must pay Rs. 7.83 lakhs per year for eight years to the lessor. The first payment is due immediately.
4. However, these lease payments are fully-tax-deductible. At a 33.66 percent marginal tax rate, the lease payments generate tax shields of about Rs. 2.64 lakhs per year. You would say that the after-tax cost of the lease payment is 7.83 – 2.64 = Rs. 5.19 lakhs.

	A	B	C	D	E	F	G	H	I
1		Year							
2		0	1	2	3	4	5	6	7
3	Cost of new bus	+4600.00							
5	Lost depreciation tax shield		-387.09	-290.32	-217.74	-163.30	-122.48	-91.86	-275.57
6	Lease payments	-783.00	-783.00	-783.00	-783.00	-783.00	-783.00	-783.00	-783.00
7	Tax shield on lease payments	+263.56	+263.56	+263.56	+263.56	+263.56	+263.56	+263.56	+263.56
8	cash flow from lease	+4080.56	-906.53	-809.76	-737.18	-682.75	-641.92	-611.30	-795.02

TABLE 26.2

Cash-flow consequences of the lease contract offered to Bluelines Bus (figures in Rs. thousands; some columns do not add due to rounding).

eXcel

Please visit us at www.mhhe.com/bmam8e or refer to your Student CD .

We must emphasize that Table 26.2 assumes that Bluelines will pay taxes at the full 33.66 percent marginal tax rate. If the firm were sure to lose money, and therefore pay no taxes, lines 2 and 4 would be left blank. The depreciation tax shields are worth nothing to a firm that pays no tax, for example.

Table 26.2 also assumes the bus will be worthless when it goes to the scrap yard at the end of year 7. Otherwise there would be an entry for salvage value lost.

Who Really Owns the Leased Asset?

To a lawyer or a tax accountant, that would be a silly question: The lessor is clearly the *legal* owner of the leased asset. That is why the lessor is allowed to deduct depreciation from taxable income.

From an *economic* point of view, you might say that the *user* is the real owner, because in a *financial* lease, the user faces the risks and receives the rewards of ownership. Bluelines cannot cancel a financial lease. If the new bus turns out to be hopelessly costly and unsuited for Blueline's routes, that is Blueline's problem, not the lessor's. If it turns out to be a great success, the profit goes to Bluelines, not the lessor. The success or failure of the firm's business operations does not depend on whether the buses are financed by leasing or some other financial instrument.

In many respects, a financial lease is equivalent to a secured loan. The lessee must make a series of fixed payments; if the lessee fails to do so, the lessor can repossess the asset. Thus we can think of a balance sheet like this

Bluelines Bus (Figures in Rs. Thousands)

Bus	4600	4600	Loan secured by bus
All other assets	46000	20700	Other loans
		25300	Equity
Total assets	50600	50600	Total liabilities

as being economically equivalent to a balance sheet like this

Bluelines Bus (Figures in Rs. Thousands)

Bus	4600	4600	Financial lease
All other assets	46000	20700	Other loans
		25300	Equity
Total assets	50600	50600	Total liabilities

Having said this, we must immediately add two qualifications. First, legal ownership can make a big difference when a financial lease expires because the lessor gets the salvage value of the asset. Once a secured loan is paid off, the user owns the asset free and clear.

Second, lessors and secured creditors may be treated differently in bankruptcy. If a company defaults on a lease payment, you might think that the lessor could pick up the leased asset and take it home. But if the bankruptcy court decides the asset is "essential" to the lessee's business, it "affirms" the lease. Then the bankrupt firm can continue to use the asset, *but* it must also continue to make the lease payments. This can be *good* news for the lessor: It is paid cash while other creditors cool their heels. Even secured creditors are not paid until the bankruptcy process works itself out.

If the lease is not affirmed but "rejected," the lessor can of course recover the leased asset. If it is worth less than the future payments the lessee had promised, the lessor can try to recoup this loss. But in this case the lender must get in line with the unsecured creditors.

Of course, neither the lessor nor the secured lender can be sure it will come out whole. Our point is that lessors and secured creditors have different rights when the asset user gets into trouble.

Leasing and the Internal Revenue Service

We have already noted that the lessee loses the tax depreciation of the leased asset but can deduct the lease payment in full. The *lessor,* as legal owner, uses the depreciation tax shield but must report the lease payments as taxable rental income.

However, the Income Tax department is suspicious by nature and will not allow the lessor to charge the entire depreciation expenses unless it is satisfied that the arrangement is a genuine lease. The Central Board of Direct Taxes (CBDT) in a circular issued on February 9, 2001 raises concerns about leases on assets that do not exist and sale and leaseback transactions. Some companies, for example, show a water purifier as a pollution preventing equipment and claim 100 percent depreciation on such assets in the very first year of its purchase. The CBDT circular has asked the assessing officers to be very careful before granting depreciation benefits to the lessor on such assets. In case of a sale and lease back transaction, the depreciation is estimated at the depreciated book value of the asset and not on the sale price. Thus for example, if Come Airlines sells an aircraft valued at Rs. 10 crores to a leasing company at Rs. 15 crores and leases it back, then the leasing company can claim depreciation only on Rs. 10 crores and not on Rs. 15 crores.

A First Pass at Valuing a Lease Contract

When we left Haridas Pai, president of Bluelines Bus, he had just set down in Table 26.2 the cash flows of the financial lease proposed by the bus manufacturer.

These cash flows are typically assumed to be about as safe as the interest and principal payments on a secured loan issued by the lessee. This assumption is reasonable for the lease payments because the lessor is effectively lending money to the lessee. But the various tax shields might carry enough risk to deserve a higher discount rate. For example, Bluelines might be confident that it could make the lease payments but not confident that it could earn enough taxable income to use these tax shields. In that case the cash flows generated by the tax shields would probably deserve a higher discount rate than the borrowing rate used for the lease payments.

A lessee might, in principle, end up using a separate discount rate for each line of Table 26.2, each rate chosen to fit the risk of that line's cash flow. But established, profitable firms usually find it reasonable to simplify by discounting the types of flows shown in Table 26.2 at a single rate based on the rate of interest the firm would pay if it borrowed rather than leased. We will assume Blueline's borrowing rate is 10 percent.

At this point we must go back to our discussion in the Appendix to Chapter 19 of debt-equivalent flows. When a company lends money, it pays tax on the interest it receives. Its net return is the after-tax interest rate. When a company borrows money, it can *deduct* interest payments from its taxable income. The net cost of borrowing is the after-tax interest rate. Thus the after-tax interest rate is the effective rate at which a company can transfer debt-equivalent flows from one time period to another. Therefore, to value the incremental cash flows stemming from the lease, we need to discount them at the after-tax interest rate.

Since Bluelines can borrow at 10 percent, we should discount the lease cash flows at $r_D(1 - T_C)$ = 0.10 × (1–0.3366) = 0.6634, or 6.634 percent. Thus gives

$$\text{NPV lease} = +4080.56 - \frac{906.53}{1.06634} - \frac{809.76}{(1.06634)^2} - \frac{737.18}{(1.06634)^3}$$
$$- \frac{682.75}{(1.06634)^4} - \frac{641.92}{(1.06634)^5} - \frac{611.3}{(1.06634)^6} - \frac{795.02}{(1.06634)^7}$$
$$= -6.24 \text{ or } - \text{Rs.}6.24 \text{ thousands}$$

Since the lease has a negative NPV, Bluelines is better off buying the bus.

A positive or negative NPV is not an abstract concept; in this case Bluelines' shareholders really are Rs. 6.24 thousands poorer if the company leases. Let us now check how this situation comes about.

Look once more at Table 26.2. The lease cash flows are

	Year							
	0	1	2	3	4	5	6	7
Cash flows from lease (Rs. thousands)	+4080.56	−906.53	−809.76	−737.18	−682.75	−641.92	−641.92	−795.02

The lease payments are contractual obligations like the principal and interest payments on secured debt. Thus you can think of the incremental lease cash flows in years 1 through 7 as the "debt service" of the lease. Table 26.3 shows a loan with exactly the same debt service as the lease. The initial amount of the loan is Rs. 40.86 lakhs. If Bluelines borrowed this sum, it would need to pay interest in the first year of 0.1 × 40.86 = 4.086 and would receive a tax shield on this interest of 0.3366 × 4.086 = 1.37. Bluelines could then repay 6.35 of the loan, leaving a net cash flow of 9.06 (exactly the same as for the lease) in year 1 and an outstanding debt at the start of year 2 of 34.51.

As you walk through the calculations in Table 26.3, you see that it costs exactly the same to service a loan that brings an immediate cash flow of Rs. 40.86 lakhs as it does to service the lease, which brings Rs. 40.80 lakhs. This is why we say that the lease has a net present value of 40.80 – 40.86 = – 0.06, or Rs. 0.06 lakhs. If Bluelines leases the bus rather than raising an equivalent loan,[11] there will be Rs. 6 thousands less in the bank account.

Our example illustrates two general points about leases and equivalent loans. First, if you can devise a borrowing plan that gives the same cash flow as the lease in every future period but a higher immediate cash flow, then you should not lease. If, however, the equivalent loan provides the same future cash outflows as the lease but a lower immediate inflow, then leasing is the better choice.

Second, our example suggests two ways to value a lease:

1. *Hard way.* Construct a table like Table 26.3 showing the equivalent loan.
2. *Easy way.* Discount the lease cash flows at the *after-tax* interest rate that the firm would pay on an equivalent loan. Both methods give the same answer—in our case an NPV of −Rs. 0.06 lakhs.

[11]When we compare the lease to its equivalent loan, we do not mean to imply that the bus alone could support all of that loan. Some part of the loan would be supported by Blueline's other assets. Some part of the lease would likewise be supported by the other assets.

	A	B	C	D	E	F	G	H	I
1		Year							
2		0	1	2	3	4	5	6	7
3	Amount borrowed at year-end	4086.80	3451.39	2870.59	2323.85	1795.27	1272.44	745.56	0.00
4	Interest paid at 10%		-408.68	-345.14	-287.06	-232.38	-179.53	-127.24	-74.56
5	Interest tax shield at 33.66%		137.56	116.17	96.62	78.22	60.43	42.83	25.10
6	Interest paid after tax		-271.12	-228.97	-190.44	-154.16	-119.10	-84.41	-49.46
7	Principal repaid		-635.41	-580.79	-546.75	-528.58	-522.82	-526.89	-745.56
8	Net cash flow of equivalent loan	4086.80	-906.53	-809.76	-737.18	-682.75	-641.92	-611.30	-795.02

TABLE 26.3

Details of the equivalent loan to the lease offered to Bluelines Bus (figures in Rs. thousands; cash outflows shown with negative sign).

excel

Please visit us at www.mhhe.com/bmam8e or refer to your Student CD.

The Story So Far

We concluded that the lease contract offered to Bluelines Bus was *not* attractive because the lease provided Rs. 0.06 lakhs less financing that the equivalent loan. The underlying principle is as follows. A financial lease is superior to buying and borrowing if the financing provided by the lease exceeds the financing generated by the equivalent loan.

The principle implies this formula

$$\text{Net value of lease} = \text{initial financing provided} - \sum_{t=1}^{N} \frac{\text{lease cash flow}}{[1 + r_D(1 - T_c)]^t}$$

where N is the length of the lease. Initial financing provided equals the cost of the leased asset minus any immediate lease payment or other cash outflow attributable to the lease.

Notice that the value of the lease is its incremental value relative to borrowing via an equivalent loan. A positive lease value means that *if* you acquire the asset, lease financing is advantageous. It does not prove you should acquire the asset.

Sometimes favorable lease terms rescue a capital investment project. Suppose Bluelines has decided against buying a new bus because the NPV of the Rs. 46 lakhs investment was – Rs. 1 lakh assuming normal financing. The bus manufacturer could rescue the deal by offering a lease with a value of, say, Rs. 2 lakhs. By offering such a lease, the manufacturer would in effect cut the price of the bus to Rs. 44 lakhs, giving the bus-lease package a still higher positive value to Bluelines. We could express this formally by treating the lease's NPV as a favorable financing side effect that adds to project adjusted present value:[12]

$$\begin{aligned} \text{APV} &= \text{NPV of project} + \text{NPV of lease} \\ &= -1 + 2 = \text{Rs. 1 lakh} \end{aligned}$$

Notice also that our formula applies to net financial leases. Any insurance, maintenance, and other operating costs picked up by the lessor have to be evaluated separately and added to the value of the lease. If the asset has salvage value at the end of the lease, that value should be taken into account also.

[12]See Chapter 19 for the general definition and discussion of APV.

Suppose, for example, that the bus manufacturer offers to provide routine maintenance that would otherwise cost Rs. 92,000 per year after tax. However, Mr. Haridas Pai reconsiders and decides that the bus will probably be worth Rs. 4.6 lakhs after eight years. (Previously he assumed the bus would be worthless at the end of the lease.) Then the value of the lease increases by the present value of the maintenance savings and decreases by the present value of the lost salvage value.

Maintenance and salvage value are harder to predict than the cash flows shown in Table 26.2, and normally deserve a higher discount rate. Suppose that Mr. Pai uses 12 percent. Then the maintenance savings are worth

$$\sum_{10}^{7} \frac{92000}{(1.12)^t} = \text{Rs. } 5.12 \text{ lakhs}$$

The lost salvage value is worth Rs. 4.6 lakhs / $(1.12)^8$ = Rs. 1.86 lakhs. Remember that we previously calculated the value of the lease as +Rs. 0.7 lakhs. The revised value is therefore +0.7 + 5.12 – 1.86 = Rs. 3.96 lakhs. Now the lease looks much better.

26.5 WHEN DO FINANCIAL LEASES PAY?

We have examined the value of a lease from the viewpoint of the lessee. However, the lessor's criterion is simply the reverse. As long as lessor and lessee are in the same tax bracket, every cash outflow to the lessee is an inflow to the lessor, and vice versa. In our numerical example, the bus manufacturer would project cash flows in a table like Table 26.2, but with the signs reversed. The value of the lease to the bus manufacturer would be

$$\begin{aligned} \text{NPV lease} &= -4080.56 + \frac{906.53}{1.06634} + \frac{809.76}{(1.06634)^2} + \frac{737.18}{(1.06634)^3} \\ &\quad + \frac{682.75}{(1.06634)^4} + \frac{641.91}{(1.06634)^5} \frac{611.3}{(1.06634)^6} \frac{795.02}{(1.06634)^7} \\ &= +6.24, \text{ or} + \text{Rs. } 6.24 \text{ thousands} \end{aligned}$$

In this case, the values to lessee and lessor exactly offset (– Rs. 0.0624 + Rs. 0.0624 = 0). The lessor can win only at the lessee's expense.

But both the lessee and the lessor can win of their tax rates differ. Suppose that Bluelines paid no tax ($T_C = 0$). Then the only cash flows of the bus lease would be

	Year							
	0	1	2	3	4	5	6	7
Cost of new bus	+4600.00							
Lease payment	−783.00	−783.00	−783.00	−783.00	−783.00	−783.00	−783.00	−783.00
Cash flow from lease	+3817.00	−783.00	−783.00	−783.00	−783.00	−783.00	−783.00	−783.00

These flows would be discounted at 10 percent, because $r_D(1–T_C) = r_D$ when $T_C = 0$. The value of the lease is

$$\begin{aligned} \text{Value of lease} &= +4600 - \sum_{t=1}^{7} \frac{783}{(1.1)^t} \\ &= 4600 - 4594.97 = +5.03, \text{ or Rs. } 5.03 \text{ thousands} \end{aligned}$$

In this case there is a net gain of Rs. 6.24 thousands to the lessor (who has the 33.66 percent tax rate) and a net gain of Rs. 5.03 thousands to the lessee (who pays zero tax). The mutual gain is at the expense of the government. On the one hand, the government gains from the lease contract because it can tax the lease payments. On the other hand, the contract allows the lessor to take advantage of depreciation and interest tax shields which are of no use to the lessee. However, because the depreciation is written-down-value based and the interest rate is positive, the government suffers a net loss in the present value of its tax receipts as a result of the lease.

Now you should begin to understand the circumstances in which the government incurs a loss on the lease and the other two parties gain. Other things being equal, the potential gains to lessor and lessee are highest when

- The lessor's tax rate is substantially higher than the lessee's.
- The depreciation tax shield is received mostly early in the lease period
- The lease period is long and the lease payments are concentrated toward the end of the period.
- The interest rate r_D is high—if it were zero, there would be no advantage in present value terms to postponing tax.

Lessors are constantly on the lookout for arrangements that increase the potential gains from leasing. Some of the most ingenious arrangements involve cross-border leases and take advantage of the fact that different tax authorities define "ownership" in different ways. For example, suppose that an asset is bought by a company in Switzerland, which then "leases" the asset to a firm in the United States. As the legal owner, the company can depreciate the asset for tax purposes in Switzerland. But the terms of the lease may be such that in the United States the user of the asset is regarded as the *effective* owner and therefore gets to depreciate it for tax purposes. Needless to say, the tax authorities are keen to prevent such "double-dipping," but, as soon as one opportunity is blocked off, another seems to arise.

SUMMARY

A lease is just an extended rental agreement. The owner of the equipment (the *lessor*) allows the user (the *lessee*) to operate the equipment in exchange for regular lease payments.

There is a wide variety of possible arrangements. Short-term, cancelable leases are known as *operating leases*. In these leases the lessor bears the risks of ownership. Long-term, noncancelable leases are called *full-payout*, *financial*, or *capital* leases. In these leases the lessee bears the risks. Financial leases are *sources of financing* for assets the firm wishes to acquire and use for an extended period.

The key to understanding operating leases is equivalent annual cost. In a competitive leasing market, the annual operating lease payment will be forced down to the lessor's equivalent annual cost. Operating leases are attractive to equipment users if the lease payment is less than the *user's* equivalent annual cost of buying the equipment. Operating leases make sense when the user needs the equipment only for a short time, when the lessor is better able to bear the risks of obsolescence, or when the lessor can offer a good deal on maintenance. Remember too that operating leases often have valuable options attached.

A financial lease extends over most of the economic life of the leased asset and cannot be canceled by the lessee. Signing a financial lease is like signing a secured loan to finance purchase of the leased asset. With financial leases, the choice is not "lease versus buy" but "lease versus borrow."

Many companies have sound reasons for financing via leases. For example, companies that are not paying taxes can usually strike a favorable deal with a tax- paying lessor. Also, it may be less costly and time-consuming to sign a standardized lease contract than to negotiate a long-term secured loan.

When a firm borrows money, it pays the after-tax rate of interest on its debt. Therefore, the opportunity cost of lease financing is the after-tax rate of interest on the firm's bonds. To value a financial lease, we need to discount the incremental cash flows from leasing by the after-tax interest rate.

An equivalent loan is one that commits the firm to exactly the same future cash flows as a financial lease. When we calculate the net present value of the lease, we are measuring the difference between the amount of financing provided by the lease and the financing provided by the equivalent loan:

$$\text{Value of lease} = \text{financing provided by lease} - \text{value of equivalent loan}$$

We can also analyze leases from the lessor's side of the transaction, using the same approaches we developed for the lessee. If lessee and lessor are in the same tax bracket, they will receive exactly the same cash flows but with signs reversed. Thus, the lessee can gain only at the lessor's expense, and vice versa. However, if the lessee's tax rate is lower than the lessor's, then both can gain at the federal government's expense.

FURTHER READING

Two useful general references on leasing are:

J. S. Schallheim, *Lease or Buy? Principles for Sound Decision Making* (Boston: Harvard Business School Press, 1994).

P. K. Nevitt and F. J. Fabozzi, *Equipment Leasing*, 4th ed. (New Hope, PA: Frank Fabozzi Associates, 2000).

The approach to valuing financial leases presented in this chapter is based on:

S. C. Myers, D. A. Dill and A. J. Bautista, "Valuation of Financial Lease Contracts," *Journal of Finance* 31 (June 1976), pp. 799–819.

J. R. Franks and S. D. Hodges, "Valuation of Financial Lease Contracts: A Note," *Journal of Finance* 33 (May 1978), pp. 647–669.

Other useful works include the theoretical discussions of Miller and Upton and of Lewellen, Long, and McConnell:

M. H. Miller and C. W. Upton, "Leasing, Buying and the Cost of Capital Services," *Journal of Finance* 31 (June 1976), pp. 761–786.

W. G. Lewellen, M. S. Long, and J. J. McConnell, "Asset Leasing in Competitive Capital Markets," *Journal of Finance* 31 (June 1976), pp. 787–798.

The options embedded in many operating leases are discussed in:

T. E. Copeland and J. E. Weston, "A Note on the Evaluation of Cancelable Operating Leases," *Financial Management* 11 (Summer 1982), pp. 68–72.

J. J. McConnell and J. S. Schallheim, "Valuation of Asset Leasing Contracts," *Journal of Financial Economics* 12 (August 1983), pp. 237–261.

S. R. Grenadier, "Valuing Lease Contracts: A Real Options Approach," *Journal of Financial Economics* 38 (July 1995), pp. 297–331.

CONCEPT REVIEW QUESTIONS

1. Explain the difference between an operating lease and a financial lease. (pages 701–702)
2. List some good reasons for leasing and some dubious ones. (pages 702–705)
3. How should a financial manager calculate the net present value of an operating lease? (page 707)

For additional Concept Review Questions, please visit us at www.mhhe.com/bmam8e or refer to your Student CD.

QUIZ

1. The following terms are often used to describe leases:
   a. Direct
   b. Full-service
   c. Operating
   d. Financial
   e. Rental
   f. Net
   g. Leveraged
   h. Sale and lease-back
   i. Full-payout

   Match one or more of these terms with each of the following statements:
   A. The initial lease period is shorter than the economic life of the asset.
   B. The initial lease period is long enough for the lessor to recover the cost of the asset.
   C. The lessor provides maintenance and insurance.
   D. The lessee provides maintenance and insurance.
   E. The lessor buys the equipment from the manufacturer.
   F. The lessor buys the equipment from the prospective lessee.
   G. The lessor finances the lease contract by issuing debt and equity claims against it.
2. Some of the following reasons for leasing are rational. Others are irrational or assume imperfect or inefficient capital markets. Which of the following reasons are the rational ones?
   a. The lessee's need for the leased asset is only temporary.
   b. Specialized lessors are better able to bear the risk of obsolescence.
   c. Leasing provides 100 percent financing and thus preserves capital.
   d. Leasing allows firms with low marginal tax rates to "sell" depreciation tax shields.
   e. Leasing increases earnings per share.
   f. Leasing reduces the transaction cost of obtaining external financing.
   g. Leasing avoids restrictions on capital expenditures.
   h. Leasing can reduce the alternative minimum tax.
3. Explain why the following statements are true:
   a. In a competitive leasing market, the annual operating lease payment equals the lessor's equivalent annual cost.
   b. Operating leases are attractive to equipment users if the lease payment is less than the *user's* equivalent annual cost.
4. True or false?
   a. Lease payments are usually made at the start of each period. Thus the first payment is usually made as soon as the lease contract is signed.
   b. Financial leases can still provide off-balance-sheet financing.
   c. The cost of capital for a financial lease is the interest rate the company would pay on a bank loan.
   d. An equivalent loan's principal plus after-tax interest payments exactly match the after-tax cash flows of the lease.
   e. A financial lease should not be undertaken unless it provides more financing than the equivalent loan.
   f. It makes sense for firms that pay no taxes to lease from firms that do.
   g. Other things equal, the net tax advantage of leasing increases as nominal interest rates increase.
5. Sriram Leasing has branched out to rentals of office furniture to start-up companies. Consider a Rs. 75,000 desk. Desks last for six years and can be depreciated over a six-year period using the WDV rate of 20 percent. What is the break-even operating lease rate for a new desk? Assume that lease rates for old and new desks are the same and that Sriram's pre-tax administrative costs are Rs. 1000 per desk per year. The cost of capital is 9 percent and the tax rate is 35 percent. Lease payments are made in advance, that is, at the start of each year. The inflation rate is zero.

6. Refer again to Quiz Question 5. Suppose a blue-chip company requests a six-year financial lease for a Rs. 75,000 desk. The company has just issued five-year debentures at an interest rate of 6 percent per year. What is the break-even rate in this case? Assume administrative costs drop to Rs. 500 per year. Explain why your answers to Question 5 and this question differ.
7. Suppose that National Waferonics has before it a proposal for a four-year financial lease. The firm constructs a table like Table 26.2. The bottom line of its table shows the lease cash flows:

	Year 0	Year 1	Year 2	Year 3
Lease cash flow	+62,000	−26,800	−22,200	−17,600

These flows reflect the cost of the machine, depreciation tax shields, and the after-tax lease payments. Ignore salvage value. Assume the firm could borrow at 10 percent and faces a 35 percent marginal tax rate.
   a. What is the value of the equivalent loan?
   b. What is the value of the lease?
   c. Suppose the machine's NPV under normal financing is −Rs. 5,000. Should National Waferonics invest? Should it sign the lease?

PRACTICE QUESTIONS

1. In Quiz Question 5 we assumed identical lease rates for old and new desks.
   a. How does the initial break-even lease rate change if the expected inflation rate is 5 percent per year? Assume that the *real* cost of capital does not change. *Hint:* Look at the discussion of equivalent annual costs in Chapter 6.
   b. How does your answer to part (a) change if wear and tear force Sriram to cut lease rates by 10 percent in real terms for every year of a desk's age?
2. Look at Table 26.1. How would the initial break-even operating lease rate change if rapid technological change in limo manufacturing reduces the costs of new limos by 5 percent per year? *Hint:* We discussed technological change and equivalent annual costs in Chapter 6.

The following questions all apply to financial leases. To answer Practice Questions 3 to 7 you may find it helpful to use the "live" Excel spreadsheets on this book's CD or at www.mhhe.com/bmam8e.

3. Look again at the bus lease described in Table 26.2.
   a. What is the value of the lease if Bluelines' marginal tax rate is $T_C = 0.20$?
   b. What would the lease value be if Bluelines had to use 15 percent WDV rate to depreciate the bus?
4. In Section 26.4 we showed that the lease offered to Bluelines Bus had a positive NPV of Rs. 0.05 lakhs if Bluelines paid no tax and a Rs. 0.0624 lakhs to a lessor paying 33.66 percent tax. What is the minimum lease payment the lessor could accept under these assumptions? What is the maximum amount that Bluelines could pay?
5. In Section 26.5 we listed four circumstances in which there are potential gains from leasing. Check them out by conducting a sensitivity analysis on the Bluelines Bus lease assuming that Bluelines does not pay tax. Try in turn, (a) a lessor tax rate of 40 percent (rather than 33.66 percent), (b) immediate 100 percent depreciation in year 0 (rather than 25 percent WDV), (c) a three-year lease with four annual rentals (rather than an eight-year lease), and (d) an interest rate of 20 percent (rather than 10 percent). In each case, find the minimum rental that would satisfy the lessor and calculate the NPV to the lessee.
6. In Section 26.5 we stated that if the interest rate were zero, there would be no advantage in postponing tax and therefore no advantage in leasing. Value the Bluelines Bus lease with an interest rate of zero. Assume that Bluelines does not pay tax. Can you devise any lease terms that would make both a lessee and a lessor happy? (If you can, we would like to hear from you.)

7. A lease with a varying rental schedule is known as a *structured lease*. Try structuring the Bluelines Bus lease to increase value to the lessee while preserving the value to the lessor. Assume that Bluelines does not pay tax.

excel

Please visit us at www.mhhe.com/bmam8e or refer to your Student CD.

8. Nodhead College needs a new computer. It can either buy it for $250,000 or lease it from Compulease. The lease terms require Nodhead to make six annual payments (prepaid) of $62,000. Nodhead pays no tax. Compulease pays tax at 35 percent. Compulease can depreciate the computer for tax purposes over five years. The computer will have no residual value at the end of year 5. The interest rate is 8 percent.
   a. What is the NPV of the lease for Nodhead College?
   b. What is the NPV for Compulease?
   c. What is the overall gain from leasing?

excel

Please visit us at www.mhhe.com/bmam8e or refer to your Student CD.

9. The Safety Razor Company has a large tax-loss carry-forward and does not expect to pay taxes for another 10 years. The company is therefore proposing to lease Rs. 50 lakhs of new machinery. The lease terms consist of eight equal lease payments prepaid annually. The lessor can write the machinery off over seven years using 20 percent WDV method. There is no salvage value at the end of the machinery's economic life. The tax rate is 33.66 percent, and the rate of interest is 10 percent. Mr. Rahul Birani, the president of Safety Razor, wants to know the maximum lease payment that his company should be willing to make and the minimum payment that the lessor is likely to accept. Can you help him? How would your answer differ if the lessor was allowed to use straight-line depreciation for tax purpose? (Assume that it is allowed in India).

10. Many companies calculate the internal rate of return of the incremental after-tax cash flows from financial leases. What problems do you think this may give rise to? To what rate should the IRR be compared?

CHALLENGE QUESTIONS

1. Pooja Charter has been asked to operate a Beaver bush plane for a mining company exploring north and west of Orissa. Pooja will have a firm one-year contract with the mining company and expects that the contract will be renewed for the five-year duration of the exploration program. If the mining company renews at year 1, it will commit to use the plane for four more years.

   Pooja has the following choices.
   - Buy the plane for Rs. 2.5 crores.
   - Take a one-year operating lease for the plane. The lease rate is Rs. 59 lakhs, paid in advance.
   - Arrange a five-year, non-cancelable financial lease at a rate of Rs. 37.5 lakhs per year, paid in advance.

   These are net leases: all operating costs are absorbed by Pooja Charter.

   How would you advise Pooja Varma, the charter company's CEO? For simplicity assume 25 percent WDV depreciation for tax purposes. The company will depreciate the asset over a period of five years. The company's tax rate is 33.66 percent. The weighted-average cost of capital for the bush-plane business is 14 percent, but Pooja can borrow at 9 percent. The expected inflation rate is 4 percent.

   Ms. Pooja thinks the plane will be worth Rs. 1.5 crores after five years. But if the contract with the mining company is not renewed (there is a 20 percent probability of this outcome at year 1), the plane will have to be sold on short notice for Rs. 2 crores.

   If Pooja Charter takes the five-year financial lease and the mining company cancels at year 1, Pooja can sublet the plane, that is, rent it out to another user.

   Make additional assumptions as necessary.

excel

Please visit us at www.mhhe.com/bmam8e or refer to your Student CD.

excel

Please visit us at www.mhhe.com/bmam8e or refer to your Student CD.

2. Here is a variation on Challenge Question 1. Suppose Pooja Charter is offered a five-year cancelable lease at an annual rate of Rs. 62.5 lakhs, paid in advance. How would you go about analyzing this lease? You do not have enough information to do a full option pricing analysis, but you can calculate costs and present values for different scenarios.

PART EIGHT RELATED WEB SITES

Chapter 27 discusses futures markets. The major futures exchanges have useful sites that provide data and explain how futures markets work:

www.cbot.com (Chicago Board of Trade)

www.cme.com (Chicago Mercantile Exchange)

www.nymex.com (New York Mercantile Exchange)

www.lme.com (London Metal Exchange)

www.eurexchange.com (Eurex)

www.liffe.com (London International Financial Futures and Options Exchange)

The site for the Bank for International Settlements includes periodic surveys of derivative and currency markets:

www.bis.org

Commodity and futures quotes and comments are available on:

www.commoditytrader.net

ISDA is the trade association for swap dealers:

www.isda.org

There are numerous sites with spot currency rates. They include official sites and more user-friendly commercial ones:

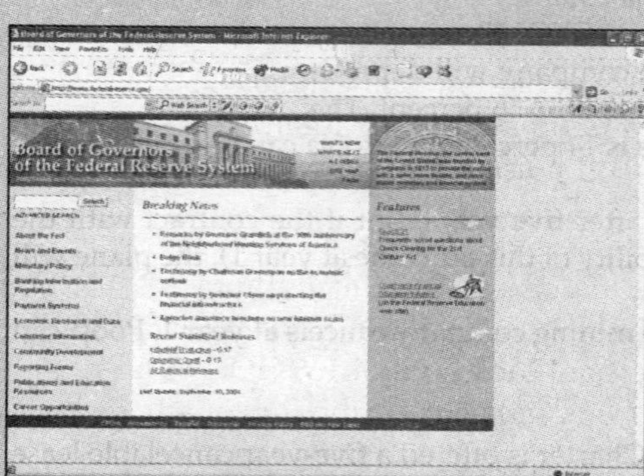

www.federalreserve.gov

www.stls.frb.org

www.ny.frb.org (the New York Fed, also includes a good description of the foreign exchange market)

www.oecd.org (the OECD, also includes "effective" or "real" exchange rates)

www.bankofengland.co.uk (includes "effective" or "real" exchange rates and, for sterling only, forward exchange rates)

www.ecb.int (the European Central Bank, includes nominal and "effective" or "real" exchange rates for the euro)

www.oanda.com

www.x-rates.com

www.economist.com/markets/currency/map.cfm (map of the world allowing you to find cross-rates between two countries and change in rate)

www.globalfindata.com (this marvelous site includes some very long-term exchange rate data)

The OECD Web site is a good source of short- and long-term interest rates by country:

www.oecd.org

The following sites provide useful financial information for a variety of countries:

www.corporateinformation.com (company data and links to finance-related sites for each country)

www.emgmkts.com (data and commentary on emerging markets)

www.securities.com (news on emerging markets)

For sample rankings of countries by political risk, see:

www.prsgroup.com

PART [8]

RISK MANAGEMENT

TO ADD VALUE, companies need to take risks. But they try to avoid those risks that carry no compensating gains. Consider, for example, Green Mountain Coffee, which buys and roasts each year about 11 million pounds of coffee. The price of raw coffee beans is extremely volatile. Between 1997 and 2001 prices slumped by 87 percent before jumping nearly 80 percent in the next three years.[1] Such fluctuations could knock Green Mountain badly off course. The company therefore enters into long-term contracts that fix the price of a large proportion of its future coffee requirements and it uses coffee futures and options to reduce even further the risk of sudden price hikes.

No two companies are exposed to the same risks. Some financial managers lie awake worrying about the price of oil or copper;

others may sweat about changes in interest rates or exchange rates. Part 8 explains how each can achieve peace of mind. We start our discussion in Chapter 27 by asking why shareholders should care whether managers have peaceful minds, and we look at when it does and doesn't make sense for companies to hedge or insure their risks. The rest of the chapter focuses on the risk of changes in commodity prices and interest rates. You will discover there how commodity and financial futures work.

Chapter 28 turns to the special risks of doing business internationally. These follow largely from fluctuations in exchange rates, so we explain how exchange rates are related to international differences in interest rates and inflation.

[1]Data is from **www.nybot.com.**

CHAPTER [27]

MANAGING RISK

MOST OF THE TIME we take risk as God-given. A project has its beta, and that's that. Its cash flow is exposed to changes in demand, raw material costs, technology, and a seemingly endless list of other uncertainties. There's nothing the manager can do about it.

That's not wholly true. The manager can avoid some risks. We have already come across one way to do so: firms use *real options* to provide flexibility. For example, a petrochemical plant that is designed to use either oil or natural gas as a feedstock reduces the risk of an unfavorable shift in the price of raw materials. As another example, think of a company that employs standard machine tools rather than custom machinery and thereby lowers the cost of bailing out if its products do not sell. In other words, the standard machinery provides the firm with a valuable abandonment option.

We covered real options in Chapter 22. This chapter explains how companies use financial contracts to protect against various hazards. We discuss the pros and cons of corporate insurance policies that protect against specific risks, such as fire, floods, or environmental damage. We describe forward and futures contracts, which can be used to lock in the future price of commodities such as oil, copper, or soybeans. *Financial* forward and futures contracts allow the firm to lock in the prices of financial assets such as interest rates or foreign exchange rates. We also describe swaps, which are packages of forward contracts.

Most of this chapter describes how to reduce business risks. But why bother? Why should *shareholders* care whether the company's future profits are linked to future changes in interest rates, exchange rates, or commodity prices? We start the chapter with that question.

27.1 WHY MANAGE RISK?

Risk reduction does not come free. Transactions undertaken *solely* to reduce risk do not add value. Why not? There are two basic reasons.

- *Reason 1: Hedging is a zero-sum game.* A corporation that insures or hedges a risk does not eliminate it. It simply passes the risk to someone else. For example, suppose that a heating-oil distributor contracts with a refiner to buy all of next winter's heating oil deliveries at a fixed price. This contract is a *zero-sum game,* because the refiner loses what the distributor gains, and vice versa.[2] If next winter's price of heating-oil turns out to be unusually high, the distributor wins from having locked in a below-market price, but the refiner is forced to sell below the market. Conversely, if the price of heating-oil is unusually *low,* the refiner wins, because the distributor is forced to buy at the high fixed price. Of course, neither party knows next winter's price at the time that the deal is struck, but they consider the range of possible prices, and in an efficient market they negotiate terms that are fair (zero-NPV) on both sides of the bargain.
- *Reason 2: Investors' do-it-yourself alternative.* Corporations cannot increase the value of their shares by undertaking transactions that investors can easily do on their own. When the shareholders in the heating-oil distributor made their investment, they were presumably aware of the risks of the business. If they did not want to be exposed to the ups and downs of energy prices, they could have protected themselves in several ways. Perhaps they bought shares in both the distributor and refiner, and do not care whether one wins next winter at the other's expense.

[2] In game theory, "zero-sum" means that the payoffs to all players add up to zero, so that one player can win only at the others' expense.

Of course, shareholders can adjust their exposure only when companies keep investors fully informed of the transactions that they have made. For example, when a group of European central banks announced in 1999 that they would limit their sales of gold, the gold price immediately shot up. Investors in gold-mining shares rubbed their hands at the prospect of rising profits. But when they discovered that some mining companies had protected themselves against price fluctuations and would *not* benefit from the price rise, the hand-rubbing by investors turned to hand-wringing.[3]

Some stockholders of these gold-mining companies wanted to make a bet on rising gold prices; others didn't. But all of them gave the same message to management. The first group said, "Don't hedge! I'm happy to bear the risk of fluctuating gold prices, because I think gold prices will increase." The second group said, "Don't hedge! I'd rather do it myself." We have seen this do-it-yourself principle before. Think of other ways that the firm could reduce risk. It could do so by diversifying, for example, by acquiring another firm in an unrelated industry. But we know that investors can diversify on their own, and so diversification by corporations is redundant.[4]

Corporations can also lessen risk by borrowing less. But we showed in Chapter 17 that just reducing financial leverage does not make shareholders any better or worse off, because they can instead reduce financial risk by borrowing less (or lending more) in their personal accounts. Modigliani and Miller (MM) proved that a corporation's debt policy is irrelevant in perfect financial markets. We could extend their proof to say that risk management is also irrelevant in perfect financial markets.

Of course, in Chapter 18 we decided that debt policy *is* relevant, not because MM were wrong, but because of other things, such as taxes, agency problems, and costs of financial distress. The same line of argument applies here. If risk management affects the value of the firm, it must be because of "other things," not because risk reduction is inherently valuable.

Let's review the reasons that risk-reducing transactions can make sense in practice.[5]

Reducing the Risk of Cash Shortfalls or Financial Distress

Transactions that reduce risk make financial planning simpler and reduce the odds of an embarrassing cash shortfall. This shortfall might mean only an unexpected trip to the bank, but a financial manager's worst nightmare is landing in a financial pickle and having to pass up a valuable investment opportunity for lack of funds. In extreme cases an unhedged setback could trigger financial distress or even bankruptcy.

[3]The news was worst for the shareholders of Ashanti Goldfields, the huge Ghanaian mining company. Ashanti had gone to the opposite extreme and placed a bet that gold prices would fall. The 1999 price rise nearly drove Ashanti into bankruptcy.

[4]See Section 7.5 and also our discussion of diversifying mergers in Chapter 32. Note that diversification reduces overall risk, but not necessarily market risk.

[5]There may be other, special reasons not covered here. For example, governments are quick to tax profits, but may be slow to rebate taxes when there are losses. In the United States, losses can only be set against tax payments in the last two years. Any losses that cannot be offset in this way can be carried forward and used to shield future profits. Thus a firm with volatile income and more frequent losses has a higher effective tax rate. A firm can reduce the fluctuations in its income by hedging. For most firms this motive for risk reduction is not a big deal. See J. R. Graham and C. W. Smith, Jr., "Tax Incentives to Hedge," *Journal of Finance* 54 (December 1999), pp. 2241–2262.

Banks and bondholders recognize these dangers. They try to keep track of the firm's risks, and before lending they may require the firm to carry insurance or to implement hedging programs. Risk management and conservative financing are therefore substitutes, not complements. Thus a firm might hedge part of its risk in order to operate safely at a higher debt ratio.

Smart financial managers make sure that cash (or ready financing) will be available if investment opportunities expand. That happy match of cash and investment opportunities does not necessarily require hedging, however. Let's contrast two examples.

Cirrus Oil produces from several oil fields and also invests to find and develop new fields. Should it lock in future revenues from its existing fields by hedging oil prices? Probably not, because its investment opportunities expand when oil prices rise and contract when they fall. Locking in oil prices could leave it with too much cash when oil prices fall and too little, relative to its investment opportunities, when prices rise.

Banroxy Pharmaceuticals sells worldwide and half of its revenues are received in foreign currencies. Most of its R&D is done in India. Should it hedge at least some of its foreign exchange exposure? Probably yes, because pharmaceutical R&D programs are very expensive, long-term investments. Banroxy can't turn its R&D program on or off depending on a particular year's earnings, so it may wish to stabilize cash flows by hedging against fluctuations in exchange rates.

Agency Costs May Be Mitigated by Risk Management

In some cases hedging can make it easier to monitor and motivate managers. Suppose your confectionery division delivers a 60 percent profit increase in a year when cocoa prices fall by 12 percent. Does the division manager deserve a stern lecture or a pat on the back? How much of the profit increase is due to good management and how much to lower cocoa prices? If the cocoa prices were hedged, it's probably good management. If they were not hedged, you will have to sort things out with hindsight, probably by asking, "What would profits have been if cocoa prices had been hedged?"

The fluctuations in cocoa prices are outside the manager's control. But she will surely worry about cocoa prices if her bottom line and bonus depend on them. Hedging prices ties her bonus more closely to risks that she can control and allows her to spend worrying time on these risks.[6]

Hedging external risks that would affect individual managers does not necessarily mean that the *firm* ends up hedging. Some large firms allow their operating divisions to hedge away risks in an internal "market." The internal market operates with real (external) market prices, transferring risks from the division to the central treasurer's office. The treasurer then decides whether to hedge the firm's aggregate exposure.

This sort of internal market makes sense for two reasons. First, divisional risks may cancel out. For example, your refining division may benefit from an increase in heating-oil prices at the same time that your distribution division suffers. Second, because operating managers do not trade actual financial contracts, there is no danger that the managers will cause the firm to take speculative positions. For example, suppose that profits are down late in the year, and hope for end-year

[6]A Texas oilman who lost hundreds of millions in ill-fated deals protested, "Why should I worry? Worry is for strong minds and weak characters." If there are any financial managers with weak minds and strong characters, we especially advise them to hedge when they can.

bonuses is fading. Could you be tempted to make up the shortfall with a quick score in the cocoa futures market? Well . . . not you, of course, but you can probably think of some acquaintances who would try just one speculative fling.

The dangers of permitting operating managers to make real speculative trades should be obvious. The manager of your confectionery division is an amateur in the cocoa futures market. If she were a skilled professional trader, she would probably not be running chocolate factories.[7]

The Evidence on Risk Management

Which firms manage risk? Almost all do to some extent. Most take out insurance policies against fire, accidents, and theft, and from time to time they will hedge currency, commodity, or interest-rate risk. Many firms have contracts that fix prices of raw materials or output, at least for the near future.

Some natural resource companies work hard to hedge their exposure to price fluctuations; others shrug their shoulders and let prices wander as they may. Explaining why some hedge and others don't is not easy. Peter Tufano's study of the gold-mining industry suggests that managers' personal risk aversion may have something to do with it. Hedging of gold prices appears to be more common when top management has large personal shareholdings in the company. It is less common when top management holds lots of stock options. (Remember that the value of an option falls when the risk of the underlying security is reduced.) David Haushalter's study of oil and gas producers found the firms that hedged the most had high debt ratios, no debt ratings, and low dividend payouts. It seems that for these firms hedging programs were designed to improve the firms' access to debt finance and to reduce the likelihood of financial distress.[8]

27.2 INSURANCE

Most businesses buy insurance against a variety of hazards—the risk that their plants will be damaged by fire; that their ships, planes, or vehicles will be involved in accidents; that the firm will be held liable for environmental damage; and so on.

When a firm takes out insurance, it is simply transferring the risk to the insurance company. Insurance companies have some advantages in bearing risk. First, they may have considerable experience in insuring similar risks, so they are well placed to estimate the probability of loss and price the risk accurately. Second, they may be skilled at providing advice on measures that the firm can take to reduce the risk, and they may offer lower premiums to firms that take this advice. Third, an insurance company can *pool* risks by holding a large, diversified portfolio of policies. The claims on any individual policy can be highly uncertain, yet the claims on a portfolio of policies may be very stable. Of course, insurance companies cannot diversify away market or macroeconomic risks;

---

[7]Amateur speculation is doubly dangerous when the manager's initial trades are losers. At that point the manager is already in deep trouble and has nothing more to lose by going for broke.

[8]See P. Tufano, "The Determinants of Stock Price Exposure: Financial Engineering and the Gold Mining Industry," *Journal of Finance* 53 (June 1998), 1014–1052; and G. D. Haushalter, "Financing Policy, Basis Risk and Corporate Hedging," *Journal of Finance* 55 (February 2000), pp. 107–152.

firms use insurance policies to reduce their specific risk, and they find other ways to avoid macro risks.

Insurance companies also suffer some *disadvantages* in bearing risk, and these are reflected in the prices they charge. Suppose your firm owns a $1 billion offshore oil platform. A meteorologist has advised you that there is a 1-in-10,000 chance that in any year the platform will be destroyed as a result of a storm. Thus the *expected* loss from storm damage is $1 billion/10,000 = $100,000.

The risk of storm damage is almost certainly not a macroeconomic risk and can potentially be diversified away. So you might expect that an insurance company would be prepared to insure the platform against such destruction as long as the premium was sufficient to cover the expected loss. In other words, a fair premium for insuring the platform should be $ 100,000 a year.[9] Such a premium would make insurance a zero-NPV deal for your company. Unfortunately, no insurance company would offer a policy for only $ 100,000. Why not?

- *Reason 1: Administrative costs.* An insurance company, like any other business, incurs a variety of costs in arranging the insurance and handling any claims. For example, disputes about the liability for environmental damage can eat up millions of dollars in legal fees. Insurance companies need to recognize these costs when they set their premiums.
- *Reason 2: Adverse selection.* Suppose that an insurer offers life insurance policies with "no medical exam needed, no questions asked." There are no prizes for guessing who will be most tempted to buy this insurance. Our example is an extreme case of the problem of *adverse selection*. Unless the insurance company can distinguish between good and bad risks, the latter will always be most eager to take out insurance. Insurers increase premiums to compensate.
- *Reason 3: Moral hazard.* Two farmers met on the road to town. "George," said one, "I was sorry to hear about your barn burning down." "Shh," replied the other, "that's tomorrow night." The story is an example of another problem for insurers, known as *moral hazard*. Once a risk has been insured, the owner may be less careful to take proper precautions against damage. Insurance companies are aware of this and factor it into their pricing.

The extreme forms of adverse selection and moral hazard (like the fire in the farmer's barn) are rarely encountered in professional corporate finance. But these problems arise in more subtle ways. That oil platform may not be a "bad risk," but the oil company knows more about the platform's weaknesses than the insurance company does. The oil company will not purposely scuttle the platform, but once insured it could be tempted to save on maintenance or structural reinforcements. Thus, the insurance company may end up paying for engineering studies or for a program to monitor maintenance. All these costs are rolled into the insurance premium.

When the costs of administration, adverse selection, and moral hazard are small, insurance may be close to a zero-NPV transaction. When they are large, insurance is a costly way to protect against risk.

Many insurance risks are *jump risks;* one day there is not a cloud on the horizon and the next day the hurricane hits. The risks can also be huge. For example, Hurricane Andrew, which

[9] If the premium is paid at the beginning of the year and the claim is not settled until the end, then the zero-NPV premium equals the discounted value of the expected claim or $100,000/(1 + r).

devastated Florida, cost insurance companies $17 billion; the attack on the World Trade Center on September 11, 2001, is likely to involve payments of nearly $35 billion. Insurance companies have been looking for ways to share catastrophic risks with investors. One solution is for the insurance company to issue *catastrophe bonds* (or *Cat bonds*). The payment on a Cat bond depends on whether a catastrophe occurs and how much is lost.[10]

The first public issue of a Cat bond was made by the Swiss insurance giant, Winterthur. As a major provider of automobile insurance, Winterthur wanted to protect itself against the risk that storm damage could lead to an unusually large number of claims. Therefore, when it issued its bond, the company stated that it would not pay the annual interest if ever there was a hailstorm in Switzerland which damaged at least 6,000 cars that it had insured. In effect, owners of the Winterthur Cat bonds coinsured the company's risks.

How British Petroleum (BP) Changed Its Insurance Strategy[11]

Major public companies typically buy insurance against large potential losses and self-insure against routine ones. The idea is that large losses can trigger financial distress. On the other hand, routine losses for a corporation are predictable, so there is little point paying premiums to an insurance company and receiving back a fairly constant proportion as claims.

BP has challenged this conventional wisdom. Like all oil companies, BP is exposed to a variety of potential losses. Some arise from routine events such as vehicle accidents and industrial injuries. At the other extreme, they may result from catastrophes such as a major oil spill or the loss of an offshore oil rig. In the past BP purchased considerable external insurance.[12] During the 1980s it paid out an average of $115 million a year in insurance premiums and recovered $25 million a year in claims.

BP then took a hard look at its insurance strategy. It decided to allow local managers to insure against routine risks, where insurance companies have an advantage in assessing and pricing risk and compete vigorously against one another. BP decided that the insurance companies could do these tasks more efficiently than its own managers. But BP decided not to insure against most losses over $10 million. For these larger, more specialized risks BP felt that insurance companies had less ability to assess risk and were less well placed to advise on safety measures. As a result, BP concluded, insurance against large risks was not competitively priced.

How much extra risk did BP assume by its decision not to insure against major losses? BP estimated that large losses of above $500 million could be expected to occur once in 30 years. But BP is a huge company with equity worth about $200 billion. So even a $500 million loss, which could throw most companies into bankruptcy, would translate after tax into a fall of less than 1 percent in

[10]For a discussion of Cat bonds and other techniques to spread insurance risk, see N. A. Doherty, "Financial Innovation in the Management of Catastrophe Risk," *Journal of Applied Corporate Finance* 10 (Fall 1997), pp. 84–95; and K. Froot, "The Market for Catastrophe Risk: A Clinical Examination," *Journal of Financial Economics* 60 (2001), pp. 529–571.

[11]Our description of BP's insurance strategy draws heavily on N. A. Doherty and C. W. Smith, Jr., "Corporate Insurance Strategy: The Case of British Petroleum," *Journal of Applied Corporate Finance* 6 (Fall 1993), pp. 4–15.

[12]However, with one or two exceptions insurance has not been available for the very largest losses of $500 million or more.

the value of BP's equity. BP concluded that this was a risk worth taking. In other words, it concluded that for large, low-probability risks the stock market was a more efficient risk-absorber than the insurance industry.

27.3 FORWARD AND FUTURES CONTRACTS

Hedging involves taking on one risk to offset another. We will explain shortly how to set up a hedge, but first we will give some examples and describe some tools that are specially designed for hedging. These are forwards, futures, and swaps. Together with options, they are known as *derivative instruments* or *derivatives* because their value depends on the value of another asset.

A Simple Forward Contract

We start with an example of a simple **forward contract**. Agarwal Jewellery, a leading gold ornament designer from India, requires 100 kilogram of gold to deliver gold jewellery to the Duty-Free Shopping Arcade of Dubai before next Christmas. Agarwal worries about high gold prices and wants to lock in the cost of buying its supply. Shah Gold Mines of Kollar is in the opposite position. It will extract gold before next Christmas, but does not know what the gold can be sold for. So the two firms strike a deal: Agarwal Jewellery agrees in August to buy 100 kg gold from Shah Gold Mines at Rs. 9000 per 10 grams, to be paid on delivery in November. Shah Gold Mines agrees to sell and deliver 100 kg gold to Agarwal Jewellery in November at Rs. 9000 per 10 grams.

Agarwal and Shah are now the two *counterparties* in a forward contract. The **forward price** is Rs. 9000 per 10 grams. This price is fixed today, in August in our example, but payment and delivery occur later. (The price for immediate delivery is called the **spot price**). Agarwal Jewellery, which has agreed to buy in November, has the long position in the contract. Shah Gold Mines, which has agreed to sell in November, has the short position. Both companies have eliminated a business risk: Agarwal has locked in its costs, and Shah has locked in its revenues for 100 kg of output.[13]

Do not confuse this forward contract with an option. Agarwal does not have the option not to buy. It has committed to buy, even if spot prices in November turn out to be much lower than Rs. 9000 per 10 grams. Shah does not have the option not to sell. It cannot back away from the deal, even if spot prices in November turn out to be much higher than Rs. 9000 per 10 grams. Note, however, that both Agarwal and Shah have to worry about counterparty risk, that is, the risk that the other party will not perform as promised.

Futures Exchanges

Agarwal Jewellery and Shah Gold Mines do not have to negotiate a one-off bilateral contract. Each can go to an exchange where standardized contracts on gold are traded. Agarwal would buy contracts and Shah would sell.

[13]For now we are ignoring several complications. Suppose, for example, that retail gold prices move up and down with wholesale prices. In that case the gold distributor is naturally hedged, because costs and revenues move together. Locking in costs with a forward contract could actually make the distributor's profits more volatile. See A. C. Shapiro and S. Titman, "An Integrated Approach to Risk Management," *Midland Corporate Finance Journal* 3 (Summer 1985), pp. 41–56.

Future	Exchange	Future	Exchange
Aluminium	MCX, NCDEX	Cardamom	NMCE
Cashew	NCDEX	Coffee	NMCE, NCDEX
Coconut Oil Cake	MCX, NMCE	Castor Seed	NMCE, NCDEX
Chana	MCX, NCDEX, NMCE	Chilli	NCDEX
Gold	MCX, NCDEX	Jeera	MCX, NCDEX, NMCE
Masoor	MCX, NCDEX	Peper	MCX, NCDEX, NMCE
Potato	MCX, NCDEX	PVC	MCX
Raw Jute	NMCX, NCDEX	Rubber	NMCE, NCDEX
Sponge Iron	NCDEX	Sugar	MCX, NCDEX, NMCE
Turmeric	NCDEX	Urad Dal	MCX, NCDEX
Wheat	MCX, NCDEX, NMCE	Zinc	MCX, NCDEX

TABLE 27.1

Some commodity futures in India and some of the exchanges in which they are traded.

Key to abbreviations:

NCDEX	National Commodity & Derivatives Exchange Limited
MCX	Multi Commodity Exchange of India Limited
NMCE	National Multi-Commodity Exchange of India Limited

Here we encounter some tricky vocabulary. When a standardized forward contract is traded on an exchange, it is called a **futures contract**—same contract, but a different label. The exchange is called a **futures exchange.** The distinction between "futures" and "forward" does not apply to the contract, but to how the contract is traded. We will describe futures trading in a moment.

Table 27.1 lists some of the important commodity futures contracts and the exchanges on which they are traded in India. Agarwal and Shah can trade on the Multi Commodity Exchange of India Limited (MCX). A wheat farmer and a miller can trade wheat futures on the National Multi-Commodity Exchange of India Limited (NMCE). A chilli farmer and a chilli powder manufacturer can trade on the National Commodity & Derivatives Exchange Limited (NCDEX).

For many firms the wide fluctuations in interest rates and exchange rates have become at least as important a source of risk as changes in commodity prices. Financial futures are similar to commodity futures, but instead of placing an order to buy or sell a commodity at a future date, you place an order to buy or sell a financial asset at a future date. Table 27.2 lists some important financial futures. Like Table 27.1 it is far from complete. You can also trade futures on the Thai stock market index, the Hungarian forint, Finnish government bonds, and many other financial assets.

Financial futures have been a remarkably successful innovation. They were invented in 1972 in the U.S; within a few years, trading in financial futures far outspaced trading in commodity futures. In India trading in futures started in 2000–01. Within a span of five years, the total turnover in Index futures in NSE alone has increased by more than 639 times.

Future	Exchange	Future	Exchange
U.S. Treasury bonds	CBT	Euroyen deposits	CME, Simex, TIFFE
U.S. Treasury notes	CBT		
German government bonds (bunds)	CBT, Eurex	S&P 500 Index	CME
Japanese government bonds (JGBs)	CME, Simex, TSE	French equity index (CAC)	MATIF
British government bonds (gilts)	LIFFE	German equity index (DAX)	Eurex
U.S. Treasury bills	CME	Japanese equity index (Nikkei)	CME, OSE, Simex
		U.K. equity index (FTSE)	LIFFE
LIBOR	CME	Euro	CME
EURIBOR	LIFFE	Japanese yen	CME
Eurodollar deposits	CME		
BSE Sensex	BSE	BSE PSU Index	BSE
S&P CNX Nifty	NSE		

TABLE 27.2

Some financial futures and some of the exchanges on which they are traded.

Key to abbreviations:

CBT	Chicago Board of Trade	OSE	Osaka Securities Exchange
CME	Chicago Mercantile Exchange	Simex	Singapore International Monetary Exchange
LIFFE	Euronext LIFFE	TIFFE	Tokyo International Financial Futures Exchange
MATIF	Euronext MATIF	TSE	Tokyo Stock Exchange
BSE	Mumbai Stock Exchange	NSE	National Stock Exchange

The Mechanics of Futures Trading

When you buy or sell futures contract, the price is fixed today but payment is not made until later. You will, however, be asked to put up **margin** in the form of either (a) cash, or (b) bank guarantee issued by any of the approved commercial banks, or (c) fixed deposits issued by any one or more of the approved commercial banks, or (d) deposit of approved securities in dematerialized form to demonstrate that you have the money to honor your side of the bargain. As long as you earn interest on the margined securities, there is no cost to you.

In addition, futures contract are **marked to market**. This means that each day any profits or losses on the contract are calculated, you pay the exchange any losses and receive any profits. For example, suppose that in August Agarwal Jewellery buys 100 November gold futures contract at a futures price of Rs. 9 lakhs per kg.[14] The next day the price of the November contract increases to Rs. 9.2 lakhs per kg. Agarwal now has a profit of Rs. 0.2 lakhs × 100 = Rs. 2 lakhs. The exchange's clearing house therefore pays Rs. 1 lakhs into Agarwal's margin account. If the price then drops back to Rs. 9.1 lakhs, Agarwal's margin account pays Rs. 1 lakh back to the clearing house. It is as if Agarwal closes out its position every day and then opens a new position at the new futures price.

Of course Shah Gold Mines is in the opposite position. Suppose it sells 100 November gold futures contract at a futures price of Rs. 9 lakhs per kg. If the price increases to Rs. 9.2 lakhs per kg, it loses Rs. 0.2 lakhs × 100 = Rs. 2 lakhs and must pay this amount into the clearinghouse. In effect the

[14]In NCDEX, the unity of trading for gold futures is 1 kg. So when one buys one gold futures contract, one effectively agrees to buy 1 kg of gold at same future date. So when Agarwal Jewellery buys 100 gold futures contract, it agrees to buy 100 kg of gold.

goldmine closes out its position at a loss of Rs. 0.2 lakhs per kg and opens a new contract to deliver in November at Rs. 9.2 lakhs per kg. Notice that neither Agarwal nor Shah has to worry about whether the other party will honor the other side of the bargain. The futures exchange guarantees the contracts and protects itself by setting up profits and losses each day. Futures trading eliminates counterparty risk.

Now consider what happens over the life of the futures contract. We're assuming that Agarwal and Shah take offsetting short and long positions in the November contract (not directly with each other, but with the exchange). Suppose that a sudden increase in demand of gold pushes the spot price of gold in November to Rs. 10 lakhs per kg. Then the futures price at the end of the contract will also be Rs. 10 lakhs per kg.[15] So Agarwal gets a cumulative profit of $(10 - 9) \times 100$ = Rs. 100 lakhs. It can take delivery of 100 kg of gold, paying Rs. 10 lakhs per kg, or Rs. 1000 lakhs. Its net cost, counting the profits on the futures contract is Rs. 1000 lakhs – Rs. 100 lakhs = Rs. 900 lakhs, or Rs. 9 lakhs per kg of gold. Thus it has locked in the Rs. 9 lakhs per kg price quoted in August when it first brought the futures contract. You can easily check that Agarwal's net cost always ends up at Rs. 9 lakhs per kg, regardless of the spot price and the ending futures price in November.

Shah Gold Mines suffers a cumulative loss of Rs. 100 lakhs, if the November price is Rs. 10 lakhs. That's bad news; the good news is that it can sell and deliver gold for Rs. 10 lakhs per kg. Its net revenues are Rs. 1000 lakhs – Rs. 100 lakhs = Rs. 900 lakhs, or Rs. 9 lakhs per kg, the futures price in August. Again you can easily check that Shah's net selling price always ends up at Rs. 9 lakhs per 1 kg.

Agarwal does not have to take delivery directly from the futures exchange, and Shah does not have to deliver to the exchange. They will probably close out their futures positions just before the end of the contract, take their profits and losses, and buy or sell in the spot market.[16] In the previous two paragraphs, this is what we have assumed.

Taking delivery directly from an exchange can be costly and inconvenient. For example, the NCDEX gold futures contract calls for delivery in Mumbai or Ahmedabad. Agarwal will be better off taking delivery from a local source such as Jaipur. Shah will likewise be better off delivering gold locally rather than sending it to Mumbai from Karnataka. Both parties can nevertheless use the NCDEX futures contract to hedge their risk.

The effectiveness of this hedge depends on the correlation between changes in gold prices locally and in Mumbai or Ahmedabad. Prices in both locations will be highly positively correlated because of a common dependence on world gold prices. But the correlation need not be perfect. In that case the hedging will not be perfect.

Trading and Pricing Financial Futures Contracts

Financial futures trade in the same way as commodity futures. Suppose you work with a U.S. firm in New York after your MBA from India. Your firm's pension fund manager thinks that the German stock market will outperform other European markets over the next six months. She

[15] Recall that the spot price is the price for immediate delivery. The futures contract also calls for immediate delivery when the contract ends in January. Therefore, the ending price of a futures or forward contract must converge to the spot price at the end of the contract.

[16] Some financial futures exchanges *prohibit* delivery. All positions are closed out at the spot price at contract maturity.

forecasts a 10 percent six-year return. How can she place a bet? She can buy German stocks, of course. But she could also buy futures contracts on the DAX index of German stocks, which are traded on the Eurex exchange . Suppose she buys 10 six-month futures contracts at 4,000. Each contract pays off 25 times the level of the index, so she has a long position of 10 × 25 × 4,000 = €1,000,000. This position is marked to market daily. If the DAX goes up, Eurex puts the profits into your fund's margin account; if the DAX falls, the margin account falls too. If your pension manager is right about the German market, and the DAX ends up at 4,600 after six months, then your fund's cumulative profit on the futures position is 10 × (4,600 − 4,000) × 25 = €150,000. The pension manager can use these profits to offset the cost of purchasing German stocks at that time.

If you want to buy a security, you have a choice. You can buy for immediate delivery at the spot price or you can "buy forward" by placing an order for future delivery at the futures price. You end up with the same security either way, but there are two differences. First, if you buy forward, you don't pay up front, and so you can earn interest on the purchase price. Second, you miss out on any interest or dividend that is paid in the meantime. This tells us the relationship between spot and futures prices:

$$F_t = S_0\,(1 + r_f - y)^t$$

where F_t is the futures price for a contract lasting t periods, S_0 is today's spot price, r_f is the risk-free interest rate, and y is the dividend yield or interest rate.[17] The following example shows how and why this formula works.

Example Suppose the six-month DAX futures contract trades at 4,000 when the current (spot) DAX index is 3,970.22. The interest rate is 3.5 percent per year (about 1.75 percent over six months) and the dividend yield on the index is 2 percent (about 1 percent over six months). These numbers fit the formula because

$$F_t = 3{,}970.22 \times (1 + .0175 - .01) = 4{,}000$$

but why are the numbers consistent?

Suppose you just buy the DAX index for 3,970.22 today. Then in six months you will own the index and also have dividends of .01 × 3,970 = 39.70. But you decide to buy a futures contract for 4,000 instead, and you put €3,970.22 in the bank. After six months, the bank account has earned interest at 1.75 percent, so you have 3,970.22 × 1.0075 = €4,039.70, enough to buy the index for 4,000 with €39.70 left over, just enough to cover the dividend you missed by buying futures rather than spot. You get what you pay for.[18]

---

[17] This formula is strictly true only for forward contracts that are not marked to market. Otherwise the value of the future depends on the path of interest rates over the life of the contract. In practice this qualification is usually not important, and the formula works for futures as well as forward contracts. See J. C. Cox, J. E. Ingersoll and S. A. Ross, "The Relationship between Forward and Futures Prices," *Journal of Financial Economics* 9 (1981), pp. 321–346.

[18] We can derive our formula as follows. Let S_6 be the value of the index after six months. Today S_6 is unknown. You can invest S_0 in the index today and get $S_6 + yS_0$ after six months. You can also buy the futures contract, put S_0 in the bank, and use your bank balance to pay the futures price F_6 in six months. In the latter strategy you get $S_6 - F_6 + S_0\,(1 + r_f)$ after six months. Since the investment is the same, and you get S_6 with either strategy, the payoffs must be the same:

$$S_6 + yS_0 = S_6 - F_6 + S_0\,(1 + r_f)$$
$$F_6 = S_0\,(1 + r_f - y)$$

Here we assume that r_f and y are six-month rates. If they are monthly rates, the general formula is $F_t = S_0(1 + r_f - y)^t$, where t is the number of months. If they are annual rates, the formula is $F_t = S_0(1 + r_f - y)^{t/12}$.

Spot and Futures Prices—Commodities

The difference between buying *commodities* today and buying commodity futures is more complicated. First, because payment is again delayed, the buyer of the future earns interest on her money. Second, she does not need to store the commodities and, therefore, saves warehouse costs, wastage, and so on. On the other hand, the futures contract gives no *convenience yield,* which is the value of being able to get your hands on the real thing. The manager of a supermarket can't burn heating oil futures if there's a sudden cold snap, and he can't stock the shelves with orange juice futures if he runs out of inventory at 1 P.M. on a Saturday.

Let's express storage costs and convenience yield as fractions of the spot price. For commodities, the futures price for t periods ahead is[19]

$$F_t = S_0\,(1 + r_f + \text{storage costs} - \text{convenience yield})^t$$

It's interesting to compare this formula with the formula for a financial future. Convenience yield plays the same role as dividends or interest foregone (y) on securities. But financial assets cost nothing to store, and storage costs do not appear in the formula for financial futures.

Usually you can't observe storage cost or convenience yield, but you can infer the difference between them by comparing spot and futures prices. This difference—that is convenience yield less storage cost—is called *net convenience yield* (net convenience yield = convenience yield − storage costs).

Example In January 2006, the spot price of coffee was Rs. 102 pr kg and the 3-month futures price was Rs. 98 per kg in NCDEX. The interest rate was about 6 percent, or 1.5 percent over 3 months. Thus

$$F_t = S_0\,(1 + r_f + \text{storage costs} - \text{convenience yield})$$
$$98 = 102(1.015 - \text{net convenience yield})$$

So net convenience yield was negative, that is, net convenience yield = convenience yield – storage costs = 0.054, or 5.4 percent over 3 months. Evidently the cost of holding coffee inventories was greater than the convenience yield provided by those inventories.

Figure 27.1 plots the annualized net convenience yield for coffee in the U.S. over a 10-year period. Notice how much the spread between the spot and futures price can bounce around. When there are shortages or fears of an interruption of supply, traders may be prepared to pay a premium of 50 percent per year for the convenience of having beans in the warehouse rather than the promise of future delivery.

There is one further complication that we should note. There are some commodities that cannot be stored at all. You can't store electricity, for example. As a result, electricity supplied in, say, six-months' time is effectively a different commodity from electricity available now, and there is no simple link between today's price and that of a futures contract to buy or sell at the end of six

[19]This formula could overstate the futures price if no one is willing to hold the commodity, that is, if inventories fall to zero or some absolute minimum.

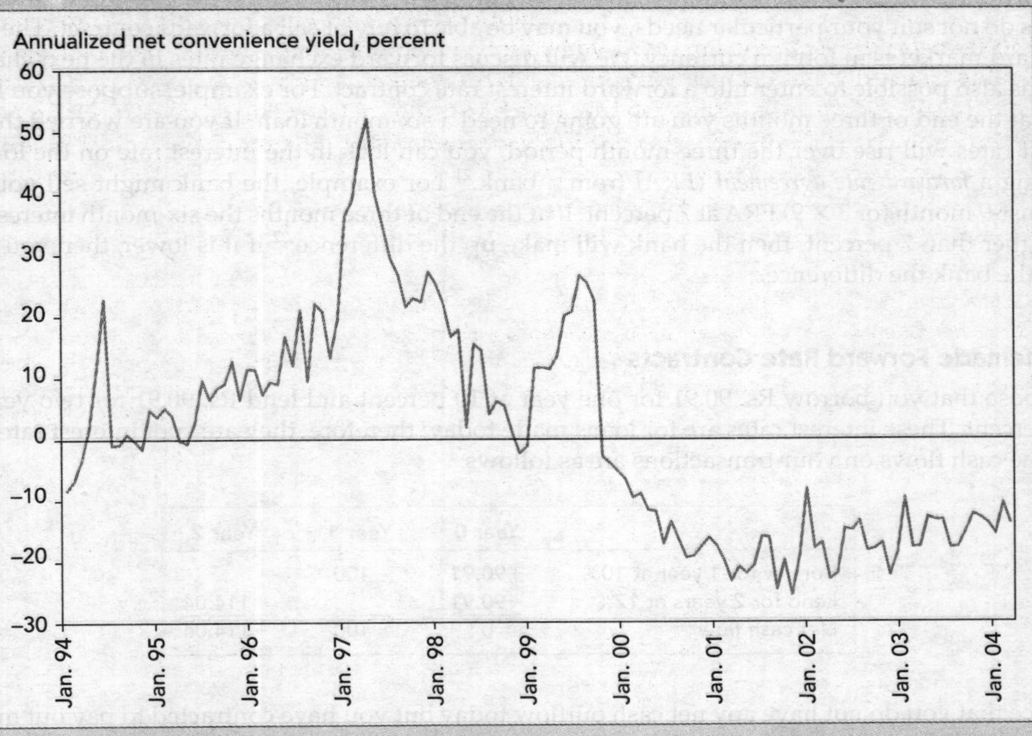

FIGURE 27.1

Annualized percentage net convenience yield (convenience yield *less* storage costs) for coffee.

months. Of course, generators and electricity users will have their own views of what the spot price is likely to be, and the futures price will reveal these views to some extent.[20]

More about Forward Contracts

Each day billions of dollars of futures contracts are bought and sold. This liquidity is possible only because futures contracts are standardized and mature on a limited number of dates each year.

[20]Critics and proponents of futures markets sometimes argue about whether the markets provide "price discovery." That is, they argue about whether futures prices reveal traders' forecasts of spot prices when the futures contract matures. If one of these fractious personalities comes your way, we suggest that you respond with a different question: "Do futures prices reveal information about spot prices that is not already in *today's* spot price?" Our formulas reveal the answer to this question. There is useful information in futures prices, but it is information about convenience yields and storage costs, or about dividend or interest payments in the case of financial futures. Futures prices reveal information about spot prices only when a commodity is not stored or cannot be stored. Then the link between spot and futures prices is broken, and futures prices can assist with price discovery.

Fortunately there is usually more than one way to skin a financial cat. If the terms of futures contracts do not suit your particular needs, you may be able to buy or sell a forward contract. The main forward market is in foreign currency. We will discuss forward exchange rates in the next chapter.

It is also possible to enter into a forward interest rate contract. For example, suppose you know that at the end of three months you are going to need a six-month loan. If you are worried that interest rates will rise over the three-month period, you can lock in the interest rate on the loan by buying a *forward rate agreement (FRA)* from a bank.[21] For example, the bank might sell you a 3-against-9 month (or 3×9) FRA at 7 percent. If at the end of three months the six-month interest rate is higher than 7 percent, then the bank will make up the difference;[22] if it is lower, then you must pay the bank the difference.[23]

Homemade Forward Rate Contracts

Suppose that you borrow Rs. 90.91 for one year at 10 percent and lend Rs. 90.91 for two years at 12 percent. These interest rates are for loans made today; therefore, they are spot interest rates.

The cash flows on your transactions are as follows:

	Year 0	Year 1	Year 2
Borrow for 1 year at 10%	+90.91	−100	
Lend for 2 years at 12%	−90.91		+114.04
Net cash flow	0	−100	+114.04

Notice that you do not have any net cash outflow today but you have contracted to pay out money in year 1. The interest rate on this forward commitment is 14.04 percent. To calculate this forward interest rate, we simply worked out the extra return for lending for two years rather than one:

$$\text{Forward interest rate} = \frac{(1 + \text{2-year spot rate})^2}{1 + \text{1-year spot rate}} - 1$$

$$= \frac{(1.12)^2}{1.10} - 1 = .1404, \text{ or } 14.04\%$$

In our example you manufactured a forward loan by borrowing short-term and lending long. But you can also run the process in reverse. If you wish to fix today the rate at which you borrow next year, you borrow long and lend the money until you need it next year.

[21]Note that the party that profits from a rise in rates is described as the "buyer." In our example you would be said to "buy three against nine months" money, meaning that the forward rate agreement is for a six-month loan in three months' time.

[22]The interest rate is usually measured by LIBOR. LIBOR (London interbank offered rate) is the interest rate at which major international banks in London send each other dollars.

[23]These payments would be made when the loan matures nine months from now.

27.4 SWAPS

Some company cash flows are fixed. Others vary with the level of interest rates, rates of exchange, prices of commodities, and so on. These characteristics may not always result in the desired risk profile. For example, a company that pays a fixed rate of interest on its debt might prefer to pay a floating rate, while another company that receives cash flows in euros might prefer to receive them in yen. Swaps allow them to change their risk in these ways.

The market for swaps is huge. In 2003 the total notional amount of swaps outstanding was about $120 trillion. By far the major part of this figure consisted of interest rate swaps, but it is also possible to swap different currencies, equity indexes, and commodities.[24] We will show first how interest rate swaps work, and then describe a currency swap. We conclude with a brief look at *default swaps*. The default swap is an example of a *credit derivative*, a relatively new box of tools for managing risk.

Interest Rate Swaps

Friendly Bancorp has made a five-year, Rs. 50 million loan to fund part of the construction cost of a large cogeneration project. The loan carries a fixed interest rate of 8 percent. Annual interest payments are therefore Rs. 4 million. Interest payments are made annually, and all the principal will be repaid at year 5.

Suppose that instead of receiving fixed interest payments of Rs. 4 million a year, the bank would prefer to receive floating-rate payments. It can do so by swapping the Rs. 4 million, five-year annuity (the fixed interest payments) into a five-year floating-rate annuity. We will show first how Friendly Bancorp can make its own homemade swap. Then we will describe a simpler procedure.

The bank can borrow at a 6 percent fixed rate for five years.[25] Therefore, the Rs. 4 million interest it receives can support a fixed-rate loan of $4/.06$ = Rs. 66.67 million. The bank can now construct the homemade swap as follows: it borrows Rs. 66.67 million at a fixed interest rate of 6 percent for five years and simultaneously lends the same amount at MIBOR. We assume that MIBOR is initially 5 percent.[26] MIBOR is a short-term interest rate, so future interest receipts will fluctuate as the bank's investment is rolled over.

The net cash flows to this strategy are shown in the top portion of Table 27.3. Notice that there is no net cash flow in year 0 and that in year 5 the principal amount of the short-term investment is used to pay off the Rs. 66.67 million loan. What's left? A cash flow equal to the *difference* between the interest earned (MIBOR $\times$ 66.67) and the Rs. 4 million outlay on the fixed loan. The bank also

[24]Data on swaps are provided by the Bank for International Settlements **(see www.bis.org/statistics)**. Equity swaps typically involve one party receiving the dividends and capital gains on an equity index, while the other party receives a fixed or floating rate of interest. Similarly, in a commodity swap one party receives a payment linked to the commodity price and the other receives the interest rate.

[25]The spread between the bank's 6 percent borrowing rate and the 8 percent lending rate is the bank's profit on the project financing.

[26]Maybe the short-term interest rate is below the five-year interest rate because investors expect interest rates to rise.

	Year					
	0	1	2	3	4	5
Homemade swap:						
1. Borrow Rs. 66.67 at 6% fixed rate	+66.67	−4	−4	−4	−4	−(4 + 66.67)
2. Lend Rs. 66.67 at MIBOR floating rate	−66.67	+.05 × 66.67	+$MIBOR_1$ × 66.67	+$MIBOR_2$ × 66.67	+$MIBOR_3$ × 66.67	+$MIBOR_4$ × 66.67 + 66.67
Net cash flow	0	−4 +.05 × 66.67	−4 + $MIBOR_1$ × 66.67	−4 + $MIBOR_2$ × 66.67	−4 + $MIBOR_3$ × 66.67	−4 + $MIBOR_4$ × 66.67
Standard fixed-to-floating swap:						
Net cash flow	0	−4 + .05 × 66.67	−4 + $MIBOR_1$ × 66.67	−4 + $MIBOR_2$ × 66.67	−4 + $MIBOR_3$ × 66.67	−4 + $MIBOR_4$ × 66.67

TABLE 27.3

The top panel shows the cash flows in millions of rupees to a homemade fixed-to-floating interest rate swap. The bottom panel shows the cash flows to a standard swap transaction.

has Rs. 4 million per year coming in from the project financing, so it has transformed that fixed payment into a floating payment keyed to MIBOR.

Of course, there's an easier way to do this, shown in the bottom portion of Table 27.3. The bank can just enter into a five-year swap.[27] Naturally, Friendly Bancorp takes this easier route. Let's see what happens.

Friendly Bancorp calls a swap dealer, which is typically a large commercial or investment bank, and agrees to *swap* the payments on a Rs. 66.67 million fixed-rate loan for the payments on an equivalent floating-rate loan. The swap is known as a fixed-to-floating interest rate swap and the Rs. 66.67 million is termed the *notional principal* amount of the swap. Friendly Bancorp and the dealer are the counterparties to the swap.

The dealer is quoting a rate for five-year swaps of 6 percent against MIBOR.[28] This figure is sometimes quoted as a spread over the yield on Government securities. For example, if the yield on five-year G-Sec is 5.25 percent, the swap spread is .75 percent.[29]

The first payment on the swap occurs at the end of year 1 and is based on the starting MIBOR rate of 5 percent.[30] The dealer (who pays floating) owes the bank 5 percent of Rs. 66.67 million, while

[27]Both strategies are equivalent to a series of forward contracts on MIBOR. The forward prices are Rs. 4 million each for $MIBOR_1$ × Rs. 66.67, $MIBOR_2$ × Rs. 66.67, and so on. Separately negotiated forward prices would not be Rs. 4 million for any one year, but the PVs of the "annuities" of forward prices would be identical.

[28]Notice that the swap rate always refers to the interest rate on the fixed leg of the swap. Rates are generally quoted against MIBOR, though dealers will also be prepared to quote rates against other shortterm debt.

[29]Swap spreads fluctuate. After Russia defaulted on its debt in 1998 and the U.S. hedge fund Long Term Capital Management (LTCM) came close to collapse, five-year swap spreads increased from 0.5 percent to 0.8 percent.

[30]More commonly, interest rate swaps are based on three-month MIBOR and involve quarterly cash payments.

the bank (which pays fixed) owes the dealer Rs. 4 million (6 percent of Rs. 66.67 million). The bank therefore makes a net payment to the dealer of 4 – (.05 × 66.67) = Rs. 67 million:

Bank	←	.05 × Rs. 66.67 = Rs. 3.33	←	Counterparty
Bank	→	Rs. 4	→	Counterparty
Bank	→	Net = Rs. 67	→	Counterparty

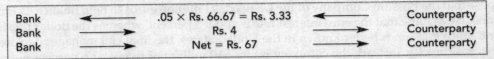

The second payment is based on MIBOR at year 1. Suppose it increases to 6 percent. Then the net payment is zero:

Bank	←	.06 × Rs. 66.67 = Rs. 4	←	Counterparty
Bank	→	Rs. 4	→	Counterparty
Bank	→	Net = 0	→	Counterparty

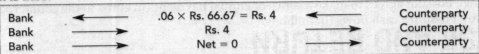

The third payment depends on MIBOR at year 2, and so on.

Notice that, when the two counterparties entered into the swap, the deal was fairly valued. In other words, the net cash flows had zero present value. What happens to the value of the swap as time passes? That depends on long-term interest rates. For example, suppose that after two years interest rates are unchanged, so a 6 percent note issued by the bank would continue to trade at its face value. In this case the swap still has zero value. (You can confirm this by checking that the NPV of a new three-year homemade swap is zero.) But if long rates increase over the two years to 7 percent (say), the value of a three-year note falls to

$$\text{PV} = \frac{4}{1.07} + \frac{4}{(1.07)^2} + \frac{4 + 66.67}{(1.07)^3} = \text{Rs. } 64.92 \text{ million}$$

Now the fixed payments that the bank has agreed to make are less valuable and the swap is worth 66.67 – 64.92 = Rs. 1.75 million.

How do we know the swap is worth Rs. 1.75 million? Consider the following strategy:

1. The bank can enter a new three-year swap deal in which it agrees to *pay* MIBOR on the same notional principal of Rs. 66.67 million.
2. In return it receives fixed payments at the new 7 percent interest rate, that is, .07 × 66.67 = Rs. 4.67 per year.

The new swap cancels the cash flows of the old one, but it generates an extra. Rs. 0.67 million for three years. This extra cash flow is worth

$$\text{PV} = \sum_{t=1}^{3} \frac{.67}{(1.07)^t} = \text{Rs. } 1.75 \text{ million}$$

Remember, ordinary interest rate swaps have no initial cost or value (NPV = 0), but their value drifts away from zero as time passes and long-term interest rates change. One counterparty wins as the other loses.

In our example, the swap dealer loses from the rise in interest rates. Dealers will try to hedge the risk of interest rate movements by engaging in a series of futures or forward contracts or by entering into an offsetting swap with a third party. As long as Friendly Bancorp and the other counterparty honor their promises, the dealer is fully protected against risk. The recurring nightmare for swap managers is that one party will default, leaving the dealer with a large unmatched position. This is another example of counterparty risk.

Currency Swaps

We now look briefly at an example of a currency swap.

Suppose that the Possum Company of the US needs 11 million euros to help finance its European operations. We assume that the euro interest rate is about 5 percent, whereas the dollar rate is about 6 percent. Since Possum is better known in the United States, the financial manager decides not to borrow euros directly. Instead, the company issues $10 million of five-year 6 percent notes in the United States. Then it arranges with a counterparty to swap this dollar loan into euros. Under this arrangement the counterparty agrees to pay Possum sufficient dollars to service its dollar loan, and in exchange Possum agrees to make a series of annual payments in euros to the counterparty.

Here are Possum's cash flows (in millions):

	Year 0		Years 1–4		Year 5	
	Dollars	Euros	Dollars	Euros	Dollars	Euros
1. Issue dollar loan	+10		−.6		−10.6	
2. Swap dollars for euros	−10	+8	+.6	−.4	+10.6	−8.4
3. Net cash flow	0	+8	0	−.4	0	−8.4

Look first at the cash flows in year 0. Possum receives $10 million from its issue of dollar notes, which it then pays over to the swap counterparty. In return the counterparty sends Possum a check for €8 million. (We assume that at current rates of exchange $10 million is worth €8 million.)

Now move to years 1 through 4. Possum needs to pay interest of 6 percent on its debt issue, which works out at $.06 \times 10 = \$6$ million. The swap counterparty agrees to provide Possum each year with sufficient cash to pay this interest and in return Possum makes an annual payment to the counterparty of 5 percent of €8 million, or €.4 million. Finally, in year 5 the swap counterparty pays Possum enough to make the final payment of interest and principal on its dollar notes ($10.6 million), while Possum pays the counterparty €8.4 million.

The combined effect of Possum's two steps (line 3) is to convert a 6 percent dollar loan into a 5 percent euro loan. You can think of the cash flows for the swap (line 2) as a series of contracts to buy euros in years 1 through 5. In each of years 1 through 4 Possum agrees to purchase $6 million at a cost of .4 million euros; in year 5 it agrees to buy $10.6 million at a cost of 8.4 million euros.[31]

Credit Derivatives

In recent years there has been considerable growth in the use of **credit derivatives,** which protect lenders against the risk that a borrower will default. For example, bank A may be reluctant to refuse a loan to a major customer (customer X) but may be concerned about the total size of its exposure to that customer. Bank A can go ahead with the loan, but use credit derivatives to shuffle off the risk to bank B.

The most common credit derivative is known as a **default swap.** It works as follows. Bank A promises to pay a fixed sum each year to B as long as company X has not defaulted on its debts. If

[31] Usually in a currency swap the two parties make an initial payment to each other (i.e., Possum pays the bank $10 million and receives €8 million). However, this is not necessary and Possum might prefer to buy the €8 million from another bank.

X defaults, B compensates A for the loss, but otherwise pays nothing. Thus you can think of B as providing A with long-term insurance against default in return for an annual insurance premium.[32]

Banks that have a portfolio of loans may be more concerned with the possibility of widespread defaults than with the risk of a single loan. In principle, they could negotiate a default swap on each individual loan. In practice, it is generally simpler to enter into a portfolio default swap that provides protection on the entire loan portfolio.

27.5 HOW TO SET UP A HEDGE

To hedge risk the firm buys one asset and sells an equal amount of another asset. Suppose a farmer owns 100 metric tons (MT) of potato and sells 10 potato futures in NCDEX (the unit of trading for potato futures in NCDEX is 10 MT). As long as the potato that the farmer owns is identical to the potato that he has promised to deliver, this strategy minimizes risk.

In practice the potato the farmer owns and the potato he sells in the futures market are unlikely to be identical. For example, if he sells potato futures on the NCDEX, he agrees to deliver potatoes with width between 40 mm and 75 mm, potatoes with a maximum of 2kg soil in a 51 kg bag, and a maximum of 15 percent damaged potatoes (dull, skin blemishes, black scars, cut, cracked, and green potatoes). If the potatoes he grows are different then the prices of the two potatoes will not exactly move together.

Figure 27.2 shows how changes in the prices of the two types of potatoes may have been related in the past. Notice two things about this figure. First, the scatter of points suggests that the price changes are imperfectly related. If so, it is not possible to construct a hedge that eliminates all risk. Some basis risk will remain. Second, the slope of the fitted line shows that a 1 percent change in the price of potatoes specified by NCDEX was on average associated with a 0.8 percent change in the price of the farmer's potato. Because the price of the farmer's potato is relatively insensitive to changes in NCDEX-specified potato prices, he needs to sell $0.8 \times 10 = 8$ potato futures to minimize risk.

Let us generalize. Suppose that you already own an asset, A (e.g., potato), and that you wish to hedge against changes in the value of A by making an offsetting sale of another asset, B (e.g., potato futures). Suppose also that percentage changes in the value of A are related in the following way to percentage changes in the value of B:

$$\text{Expected change in value of A} = a + \delta\ (\text{change in value of B})$$

Delta (δ) measures the sensitivity of A to changes in the value of B. It is also equal to the *hedge ratio*—that is, the number of units of B which should be sold to hedge the purchase of A. You minimize risk if you offset your position in A by the sale of delta units of B.[33]

The trick in setting up a hedge is to estimate the delta or hedge ratio. This often calls for a strong dose of judgment. For example, suppose that Antarctic Air would like to protect itself against a hike

[32]Another form of credit derivative is the credit option. In this case A would pay an up-front premium and B would assume the obligation to pay A in the event of X's default.

[33]Notice that A, the item that you wish to hedge, is the dependent variable. Delta measures the sensitivity of A to changes in B.

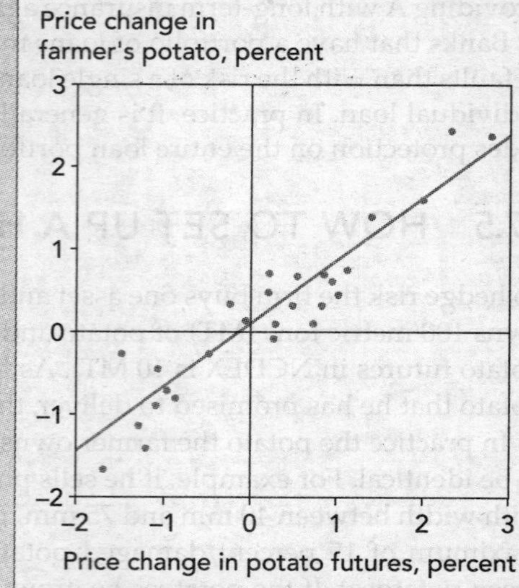

FIGURE 27.2

Hypothetical plot of past changes in the price of the farmer's potato against changes in the price of NCDEX-specified potato futures. A 1 percent change in the futures price implies, on average, a 0.8 percent change in the price of the farmer's potato.

in oil prices. As the financial manager, you need to decide how much a rise in oil prices would affect firm value. Suppose the company spent \$200 million on fuel last year. Other things equal, a 10 percent increase in the price of oil will cost the company an extra $.1 \times 200 =$ \$20 million. But perhaps you can partially offset the higher costs by higher ticket prices, in which case earnings will fall by *less* than \$20 million. Or perhaps an oil price rise will lead to a slowdown in business activity and therefore lower passenger numbers. In that case earnings will decline by *more* than \$20 million. Working out the likely effect on firm *value* is even more tricky, because that depends on whether the rise is likely to be permanent. Perhaps the price rise will induce an increase in production or encourage consumers to economize on energy usage.

Sometimes in such cases some history may help. For example, you could look at how firm value changed in the past as oil prices changed. In other cases it may be possible to call on a little theory to set up the hedge.

Using Theory to Set Up the Hedge: An Example

OLP Leasing has just purchased some equipment and arranged to rent it out for Rs. 2 million a year over eight years. At an interest rate of 12 percent, OLP's rental income has a present value of Rs. 9.94 million:[34]

$$\text{PV} = \frac{2}{1.12} + \frac{2}{(1.12)^2} + \cdots + \frac{2}{(1.12)^8} = \text{Rs. } 9.94 \text{ million}$$

OLP proposes to finance the deal by issuing a package of Rs. 1.91 million of one-year debt and Rs. 8.03 million of six-year debt, each with a 12 percent coupon. Think of its new asset (the stream of rental income) and the new liability (the issue of debt) as a package. Does OLP stand to gain or lose on this package if interest rates change?

[34]We ignore taxes in this example.

To answer this question, it is helpful to go back to the concept of duration that we introduced in Chapter 23. Duration, you may remember, is the weighted-average time to each cash flow. Duration is important because it is directly related to volatility. If two assets have the same duration, their prices will be equally affected by any change in interest rates. If we call the total value of OLP's rental income V, then the duration of OLP's rental income is calculated as follows:

$$\text{Duration} = \frac{1}{V}\{[PV(C_1)\times 1] + [PV(C_2)\times 2] + [PV(C_3)\times 3] + \cdots\}$$

$$= \frac{1}{9.94}\left\{\left[\frac{2}{1.12}\times 1\right] + \left[\frac{2}{(1.12)^2}\times 2\right] + \cdots + \left[\frac{2}{(1.12)^8}\times 8\right]\right\}$$

$$= 3.9 \text{ years}$$

We can also calculate the duration of OLP's new liabilities. The duration of the 1-year debt is 1 year, and the duration of the 6-year debt is 4.6 years. The duration of the package of 1- and 6-year debt is a weighted average of the durations of the individual issues:

$$\text{Duration of liability} = (1.91/9.94) \times \text{duration of 1-year debt}$$
$$+ (8.03/9.94) \times \text{duration of 6-year debt}$$
$$= (.192 \times 1) + (.808 \times 4.6) = 3.9 \text{ years}$$

Thus, both the asset (the lease) and the liability (the debt package) have a duration of 3.9 years. Therefore, both are affected equally by a change in interest rates. If rates rise, the present value of OLP's rental income will decline, but the value of its debt obligation will also decline by the same amount. By equalizing the duration of the asset and that of the liability, OLP has *immunized* itself against any change in interest rates. It looks as if OLP's financial manager knows a thing or two about hedging.

When OLP set up the hedge, it needed to find a package of loans that had a present value of Rs. 9.94 million and a duration of 3.9 years. Call the proportion of the proceeds raised by the six-year loan x and the proportion raised by the one-year loan $(1 - x)$. Then

$$\text{Duration of package} = (x \times \text{duration of 6-year loan})$$
$$+ [(1 - x) \times \text{duration of 1-year loan}]$$
$$3.9 \text{ years} = (x \times 4.6 \text{ years}) + [(1 - x) \times 1 \text{ year}]$$
$$x = .808$$

Since the package of loans must raise Rs. 9.94 million, OLP needs to issue .808 × 9.94 = Rs. 8.03 million of the six-year loan.

An important feature of this hedge is that it is dynamic. As interest rates change and time passes, the duration of OLP's asset may no longer be the same as that of its liability. Thus, to remain hedged against interest rate changes, OLP must be prepared to keep adjusting the duration of its debt.

If OLP is not disposed to follow this dynamic hedging strategy, it has an alternative. It can devise a debt issue whose cash flows exactly match the rental income from the lease. For example, suppose that it issues an eight-year sinking fund bond; the amount of the sinking fund is Rs. 810,000 in year 1, and the payment increases by 12 percent annually. Table 27.4 shows that the debt service (interest plus sinking fund) is Rs. 2 million in each year.

	Cash Flows (Rs. millions)							
	Year							
	1	2	3	4	5	6	7	8
Balance at start of year	9.94	9.13	8.23	7.22	6.08	4.81	3.39	1.79
Interest at 12%	1.19	1.10	.99	.87	.73	.58	.40	.21
Sinking fund payment	.81	.90	1.01	1.13	1.27	1.42	1.60	1.79
Interest plus sinking fund payment	2.00	2.00	2.00	2.00	2.00	2.00	2.00	2.00

TABLE 27.4

OLP can hedge by issuing this sinking fund bond that pays out Rs. 2 million each year.

Since the cash flows from the lease exactly match the debt service, OLP's financial manager can now relax. Each year the manager simply collects the Rs. 2 million rental income and hands it to the bondholders. Whatever happens to interest rates, the firm is always perfectly hedged.

Why wouldn't OLP's financial manager *always* prefer to construct matching assets and liabilities? One reason is that it may be relatively costly to devise a bond with a specially tailored pattern of cash flows. Another may be that OLP is continually entering into new lease agreements and issuing new debt. In this case the manager can never relax; it may be simpler to keep the durations of the assets and liabilities equal than to maintain an exact match between the cash flows.

Options, Deltas, and Betas

Here's another case where some theory can help you set up a hedge. In Chapter 20 we came across options. These give you the right, but not the obligation, to buy or sell an asset. Options are derivatives; their value depends only on what happens to the price of the underlying asset.

The *option delta* summarizes the link between the option and the asset. For example, if you own an option to buy a share of Infosys stock, the change in the value of your investment will be the same as it would be if you held delta shares of Infosys.

Since the option price is tied to the asset price, options can be used for hedging. Thus, if you own an option to buy a share of Infosys and at the same time you sell delta shares of Infosys, any change in the value of your position in the stock will be exactly offset by the change in the value of your option position.[35] In other words, you will be perfectly hedged—hedged, that is, for the next short period of time. Option deltas change as the stock price changes and time passes. Therefore, option-based hedges need to be adjusted frequently.

Options can be used to hedge commodities too. A farmer could offset changes in the price of future wheat sales by selling call options on wheat (or options on wheat futures). But this is not the simplest way to lock in the proceeds from the sale of the farmer's harvest. The farmer would have

[35]We are assuming that you hold one option and hedge by selling δ shares. If you owned one share and wanted to hedge by selling options, you would need to sell $1/\delta$ options.

to check the option delta to see how many options to sell, and then would have to track changes in the delta and reset the hedge as necessary.[36]

It's the same for financial assets. Suppose you hold a well-diversified portfolio of stocks with a beta of 1.0 and near-perfect correlation with the market return. You want to lock in the portfolio's value at year-end. You could accomplish this by selling call options on the index, but to maintain the hedge, the option position would have to be adjusted frequently. It's simpler just to sell index futures maturing at year-end.

Speaking of betas . . . what if your portfolio has a beta of .60, not 1.0? Then your hedge will require 40 percent fewer index futures contracts. And since your low-beta portfolio is probably not perfectly correlated with the market, there will be some basis risk as well. In this context our old friend beta (β) and the hedge ratio (δ) are one and the same. Remember, to hedge A with B, you need to know δ because

$$\text{Expected change in value of A} = a + \delta(\text{change in value of B})$$

When A is a stock or portfolio, and B is the market, we estimate beta from the same relationship:

$$\text{Expected change in stock or portfolio value} = a + \beta(\text{change in market index})$$

27.6 IS "DERIVATIVE" A FOUR-LETTER WORD?

A wheat farmer can sell wheat futures to reduce business risk. But if you were to copy the farmer and sell futures without an offsetting holding of wheat, you would increase risk, not reduce it. You would be *speculating*.

Speculators in search of large profits (and prepared to tolerate large losses) are attracted by the leverage that derivatives provide. By this we mean that it is not necessary to lay out much money up front and the profits or losses may be many times the initial outlay. "Speculation" has an ugly ring, but a successful derivatives market needs speculators who are prepared to take on risk and provide more cautious people like our farmer and miller with the protection they need. For example, if an excess of farmers wish to sell wheat futures, the price of futures will be forced down until enough speculators are tempted to buy in the hope of a profit. If there is a surplus of millers wishing to buy wheat futures, the reverse will happen. The price of wheat futures will be forced *up* until speculators are drawn in to sell.

Speculation may be necessary to a thriving derivatives market, but it can get companies into serious trouble. Finance in the News describes how the German metals and oil trading company, Metallgesellschaft, took a $1 billion bath on its positions in oil futures. Metallgesellschaft had plenty of company. The Japanese company, Showa Shell, reported a loss of $1.5 billion on positions in foreign exchange futures. And in 1995 Baring Brothers, a blue-chip British merchant bank with a 200-year history, became insolvent. The reason: Nick Leeson, a trader in Baring's Singapore office, had placed very large bets on the Japanese stock market index resulting in losses of $1.4 billion.

[36]Quiz: What is the farmer's position if he sells call options on wheat and simply holds them until maturity?

FINANCE IN THE NEWS

THE DEBACLE AT METALLGESELLSCHAFT

In January 1994 the German industrial giant Metallgesellschaft shocked investors with news of huge losses in its U.S. oil subsidiary, MGRM. These losses, later estimated at over $1 billion, brought the firm to the brink of bankruptcy and it was saved only, by a $1.9 billion rescue package from 120 banks.

The previous year MGRM had embarked on what looked like a sure-fire way to make money. It offered its customers forward contracts on deliveries of gasoline, heating oil, and diesel fuel for up to 10 years. These price guarantees proved extremely popular. By September 1993, MGRM had sold forward over 150 million barrels of oil at prices that were $3 to $5 a barrel over the prevailing spot prices.

As long as oil prices did not rise appreciably, MGRM stood to make a handsome profit from its forward sales, but if oil prices did return to their level of earlier years the result would be a calamitous loss. MGRM therefore sought to avoid such an outcome by buying energy futures. Unfortunately, the long-term futures contracts that were needed to offset MGRM's price guarantees did not exist. MGRM's solution was to enter into what is known as a "stack-and-roll" hedge. In other words, it bought a stack of short-dated futures contracts and, as these were about to expire, it rolled them over into a fresh stack of short-dated contracts.

MGRM was relaxed about the mismatch between the long-term maturity of its price guarantees and the much shorter maturity of its futures contracts. It could point to past history to justify its confidence, for in most years energy traders have placed a high value on owning the oil rather than having a promise of future delivery. In other words, the net convenience yield on oil has generally been positive. As long as that continued to be the case, then each time that MGRM rolled over its futures contracts, it would be selling its maturing contracts at a higher price than it would need to pay for the stack of new contracts. However, if the net convenience yield were to become negative, the maturing futures contracts would sell for *less* than more distant ones. Unfortunately, this is what occurred in 1993. In that year there was a glut of oil, the storage tanks were full, and nobody was prepared to pay extra to get their hands on oil. The result was that MGRM was forced to pay a premium to roll over each stack of maturing contracts.

The fall in oil prices had another unfortunate consequence for MGRM. Futures contracts are marked to market. This means that the investor settles up the profits and losses on each contract as they arise. Therefore, as oil prices continued to fall in 1993, MGRM incurred losses on its purchases of oil futures. This resulted in huge margin calls.* The offsetting good news was that the fall in oil prices meant that its long-term forward contracts were looking increasingly profitable, but this profit was not money in the bank.

When Metallgesellschaft's board learned of these problems, it fired the chief executive and instructed the company to cease all hedging activities and to start negotiations with customers to cancel the long-term contracts. Almost immediately the fall in oil prices reversed. Within eight months the price had risen about 40 percent. If only MGRM had been able to hold on, it would have enjoyed a huge cash inflow.

Observers have continued to argue about the Metallgesellschaft debacle. Was the company's belief that the net convenience yield would remain positive a reasonable assumption or a gigantic speculation? How much did the company anticipate its cash needs and could it have financed them by borrowing on the strength of its long-term forward contracts? Did senior management mistake the margin calls for losses and just lose its nerve when it decided to liquidate the company's positions?

---

*In addition to buying futures contracts, MGRM also bought short-term over-the-counter forward contracts and commodity swaps. As these matured, MGRM had to make good the loss on them, even though it did not receive the gains on the price guarantees.

These tales of woe have some cautionary messages for corporations. During the 1970s and 1980s many firms turned their treasury operations into profit centers and proudly announced their profits from trading in financial instruments. But it is not possible to make large profits in financial markets without also taking large risks, so these profits should have served as a warning rather than a matter for congratulation.

A Boeing 747 weighs 400 tons, flies at nearly 600 miles per hour, and is inherently very dangerous. But we don't ground 747s; we just take precautions to ensure that they are flown with care. Similarly, it is foolish to suggest that firms should ban the use of derivatives, but it makes obvious sense to take precautions against their misuse. Here are two bits of horse sense:

- *Precaution 1: Don't be taken by surprise.* By this we mean that senior management needs to monitor regularly the value of the firm's derivatives positions and to know what bets the firm has placed. At its simplest, this might involve asking what would happen if interest rates or exchange rates were to change by 1 percent. But large banks and consultants have also developed sophisticated models for measuring the risk of derivatives positions.
- *Precaution 2: Place bets only when you have some comparative advantage that ensures the odds are in your favor.* If a bank were to announce that it was drilling for oil or launching a new soap powder, you would rightly be suspicious about whether it had what it takes to succeed.

Imprudent speculation in derivatives is undoubtedly an issue of concern for the company's shareholders, but is it a matter for more general concern? Some people believe so. They point to the huge volume of trading in derivatives and argue that speculative losses could lead to major defaults that might threaten the whole financial system. These worries have led to calls for increased regulation of derivatives markets.

Now, this is not the place for a discussion of regulation, but we should warn you about careless measures of the size of the derivatives markets and the possible losses. In December 2003 the notional value of outstanding derivative contracts was about $235 trillion.[37] This is a very large sum, but it tells you *nothing* about the money that was being put at risk. For example, suppose that a bank enters into a $10 million interest rate swap and the other party goes bankrupt the next day. How much has the bank lost? Nothing. It hasn't paid anything up front; the two parties simply promised to pay sums to each other in the future. Now the deal is off.

Suppose that the other party does not go bankrupt until a year after the bank entered into the swap. In the meantime interest rates have moved in the bank's favor, so it should be receiving more money from the swap than it is paying out. When the other side defaults on the deal, the bank loses the difference between the interest that it is due to receive and the interest that it should pay. But it doesn't lose $10 million.[38]

The only meaningful measure of the potential loss from default is the amount that it would cost firms showing a profit to replace their swap positions. This figure is only about one percent of the principal amount of swaps outstanding.

---

[37]Bank of International Settlements, *Derivatives Statistics* **(www.bis.org/statistics/derstats.htm).**

[38]This does not mean that firms don't worry about the possibility of default, and there are a variety of ways that they try to protect themselves. In the case of swaps, firms are reluctant to deal with banks that do not have the highest credit rating.

SUMMARY

As a manager, you are paid to take risks, but you are not paid to take just any risks. Some risks are simply bad bets, and others could jeopardize the value of the firm. Hedging risks, when it is practical to do so, can make sense if it reduces the chance of cash shortfalls or financial distress. In some cases, hedging can also make it easier to monitor and motivate operating managers. Relieving managers of risk outside their control helps them concentrate on what can be controlled.

Most businesses insure against possible losses. Insurance companies specialize in assessing risks and can pool risks by holding a diversified portfolio of policies. Insurance works less well when policies are taken up by those companies which are most at risk (*adverse selection*) or when the insured company is tempted to skip on maintenance or safety procedures (*moral hazard*).

Firms can also hedge with forward and futures contracts. A forward contract is an advance order to buy or sell an asset. The forward price is fixed today, but payment is not made until the delivery date at the end of the contract. Forward contracts traded on organized futures exchanges are called futures contracts. Futures contracts are standardized and traded in huge volumes. The futures markets allow firms to lock in future prices for dozens of different commodities, securities, and currencies.

Instead of buying or selling a standardized futures contract, you may be able to arrange a tailor-made forward contract with a bank. Firms can protect against changes in foreign exchange rates by buying or selling forward currency contracts. Forward rate agreements (FRAs) provide protection against changes in interest rates. You can also construct homemade forward contracts. For example, if you borrow for two years and at the same time lend for one year, you have effectively taken out a forward loan.

Firms also hedge with swap contracts. For example, a firm can make a deal to pay interest to a bank at a fixed long-term rate and receive interest from the bank at a floating short-term rate. The firm swaps a fixed for a floating rate. Such a swap could make sense if the firm has relatively easy access to short-term borrowing but dislikes the exposure to fluctuating short-term interest rates. Swap contracts can also be used to hedge currency, credit, and a variety of other risks.

The theory of hedging is straightforward. You find two closely related assets. You then buy one and sell the other in proportions that minimize the risk of your net position. If the assets are *perfectly* correlated, you can make the net position risk-free. If they are less than perfectly correlated, you will have to absorb some basis risk.

The trick is to find the hedge ratio or delta—that is, the number of units of one asset that is needed to offset changes in the value of the other asset. Sometimes the best solution is to look at how the prices of the two assets have moved together in the past. For example, suppose you observe that a 1 percent change in the value of B has been accompanied on average by a 2 percent change in the value of A. Then delta equals 2.0; to hedge each dollar invested in A, you need to sell two dollars of B.

On other occasions theory can help to set up the hedge. For example, the effect of a change in interest rates on an asset's value depends on the asset's duration. If two assets have the same duration, they will be equally affected by fluctuations in interest rates.

Many of the hedges described in this chapter are static. Once you have set up the hedge, you can take a long vacation, confident that the firm is well protected. However, some hedges, such as those that match durations, are dynamic. As time passes and prices change, you need to rebalance your position to maintain the hedge.

Hedging and risk reduction sound as wholesome as mom's apple pie. But remember that hedging solely to reduce risk, with no other business purpose, cannot add value. It is a zero-sum game: risks aren't eliminated, just shifted to some counterparty. And remember that investors can also hedge by adjusting the composition of their portfolios or by trading in futures or other derivatives. Investors won't reward the firm for doing something that they can do perfectly well for themselves.

Some companies have decided that speculation is much more fun than hedging. This view can lead to serious trouble. We do not believe that speculation makes sense for an industrial company, but we caution against the view that derivatives are a threat to the financial system.

FURTHER READING

Two general articles on corporate risk management are:

C. W. Smith and R. M. Stulz, "The Determinants of Firms' Hedging Policies," *Journal of Financial and Quantitative Analysis* 20 (December 1985), pp. 391–405.

K. A. Froot, D. Scharfstein, and J. C. Stein, "A Framework for Risk Management," *Harvard Business Review* 72 (November–December 1994), pp. 59–71.

The following two papers investigate risk management and hedging policies in the gold-mining and oil industries:

P. Tufano, "The Determinants of Stock Price Exposure: Financial Engineering and the Gold Mining Industry," *Journal of Finance* 53 (June 1998), pp. 1014–1052.

G. D. Haushalter, "Financing Policy, Basis Risk and Corporate Hedging: Evidence from Oil and Gas Producers," *Journal of Finance* 55 (February 2000), pp. 107–152.

Risk magazine covers current news and developments in risk management. You may also wish to refer to the following texts:

C. W. Smith, Jr., C. H. Smithson, and D. S. Wilford, *Managing Financial Risk*, 3rd ed. (New York: McGraw-Hill, 1998).

R. M. Stulz, *Risk Management and Derivatives* (Cincinnati, OH: Thompson-Southwestern Publishing, 2003).

Schaefer's paper is a useful review of how duration measures are used to immunize fixed liabilities:

S. M. Schaefer, "Immunisation and Duration: A Review of Theory, Performance and Applications," *Midland Corporate Finance Journal* 3 (Autumn 1984), pp. 41–58.

The Metallgesellschaft debacle makes fascinating reading. See, for example:

F. Edwards, "The Collapse of Metallgesellschaft: Unhedgeable Risks, Poor Hedging Strategy, or Just Bad Luck?" *Journal of Futures Markets* 15 (May 1995), pp. 211–264.

CONCEPT REVIEW QUESTIONS

1. Why might a firm undertake risk-reducing financial transactions, for example, a hedge against fluctuations in raw materials prices? Give two good reasons. (pages 724–726)
2. Which of the following companies would be more likely to hedge its raw materials prices?
   a. A mature firm with no debt outstanding.
   b. A growth firm that will rely on debt to finance future capital investments. (page 725)
3. Why did BP decide to insure against routine risks, such as vehicle accidents and workplace injuries, but not against major risks, such as loss of an offshore oil platform? (pages 728–729)

For additional Concept Review Questions, please visit us at www.mhhe.com/bmam8e or refer to your Student CD.

QUIZ

1. Vocabulary Check. Define the following terms:
   a. Spot price
   b. Forward vs. futures contract
   c. Long vs. short position
   d. Basis risk
   e. Mark to market
   f. Net convenience yield
2. True or false?
   a. Hedging transactions in an active futures market have zero or slightly negative NPVs.
   b. When you buy a futures contract, you pay now for delivery at a future date.
   c. The holder of a financial futures contract misses out on any dividend or interest payments made on the underlying security.
   d. The holder of a commodities futures contract does not have to pay for storage costs, but foregoes convenience yield.
3. Yesterday you sold six-month futures contract on the Nifty index at a price of Rs. 3250. Today the Nifty closed at 3255 and Nifty futures closed at 3260. You get a call from your broker, who reminds that your futures position is marked to the market each day. Is he asking you to pay money, or is he about to offer to pay you?
4. Calculate the value of a six-month futures contract on a G-Sec. You have the following information:
   - Six-month interest rate: 10 percent per year, or a 4.9 percent for six months.
   - Spot price of security: 95.
   - The security pays an 8 percent coupon, 4 percent every six months.
5. "The farmer does not avoid risk by selling wheat futures. If spot wheat prices stay about Rs. 821 per quintal (100 kg), then he will actually have lost by selling wheat futures at Rs. 800 per quintal." Is this a fair comment?
6. Calculate convenience yield for aluminum from the following information:
   - Spot price Rs. 116 per kg
   - Futures price: Rs. 110 for a 6 months contract
   - Interest rate: 6 percent
   - Storage costs: Re. 1 per year per kg
7. Residents of the northeastern United States suffered record-setting low temperatures throughout November and December 2015. Spot prices of heating oil rose 25 percent, to over $2 a gallon.
   a. What effect did this have on the net convenience yield and on the relationship between futures and spot prices?
   b. In late 2016 refiners and distributors were surprised by record-setting *high* temperatures. What was the effect on net convenience yield and spot and futures prices for heating oil?
8. After a record harvest, grain silos are full to the brim. Are storage costs likely to be high or low? What does this imply for the *net* convenience yield?
9. A year ago a bank entered into a Rs. 50 million five-year interest rate swap. It agreed to pay company A each year a fixed rate of 6 percent and to receive in return MIBOR plus 1 percent. When the bank entered into this swap, MIBOR was 5 percent, but now interest rates have risen, so on a four-year interest rate swap the bank could expect to pay 6 1/2 percent and receive MIBOR plus 1 percent.
   a. Is the swap showing a profit or loss to the bank?
   b. Suppose that at this point company A approaches the bank and asks to terminate the swap. If there are four annual payments still remaining, how much should the bank charge A to terminate?

10. What is basis risk? In which of the following cases would you expect basis risk to be most serious?
    a. A broker owning a large block of Tata Motors common stock hedges by selling index futures.
    b. A Kerala farmer hedges the selling price of raw rice of his crop by selling MCX Basmati rice futures.
    c. An importer must pay 900 million euros in six months. He hedges by buying euros forward.
11. You own a Rs. 1 million portfolio of software stocks with a beta of 1.2. You are very enthusiastic about IT but uncertain about the prospects for the overall stock market. Explain how you could hedge out your market exposure by selling the market short. How much would you sell? How in practice would you go about "selling the market"?
12. a. Marshall Arts has just invested $1 million in long-term Treasury bonds. Marshall is concerned about increasing volatility in interest rates. He decides to hedge using bond futures contracts. Should he buy or sell such contracts?
    b. The treasurer of Zeta Corporation plans to issue bonds in three months. She is also concerned about interest rate volatility and wants to lock in the price at which her company could sell 5 percent coupon bonds. How would she use bond futures contracts to hedge?

PRACTICE QUESTIONS

1. Large businesses spend millions of rupees annually on insurance. Why? Should they insure against all risks or does insurance make more sense for some risks than others?
2. On some catastrophe bonds, payments are reduced if the claims against the issuer exceed a specified sum. In other cases payments are reduced only if claims against the entire industry exceed some sum. What are the advantages and disadvantages of the two structures? Which involves more basis risk? Which may create a problem of moral hazard?
3. List some of the commodity futures contracts that are traded on exchanges. Who do you think could usefully reduce risk by buying each of these contracts? Who do you think might wish to sell each contract?
4. Bata Motors wants to lock in the cost of 2000 kg of aluminum to be used in next quarter's production of Mindica cars. It buys three-month futures contracts for 2000 kg of aluminum at a price of Rs. 115 per kg.
    a. Suppose the spot price of aluminum falls to Rs. 110 in three months' time. Does Bata have a profit or loss on the futures contract? Has it locked in the cost of purchasing the aluminum it needs?
    b. How do your answers change if the spot price of aluminum increases to Rs. 150 per kg after three months?
5. In July 2004, three-month futures on the Brazilian Ibovespa stock index traded at 21,950. Spot was 21,317. The interest rate was 16 percent and the dividend yield was about 4 percent. Were the futures fairly priced?
6. If you buy a nine-month T-bill future, you undertake to buy a three-month bill in nine months' time. Suppose that Treasury bills and notes currently offer the following yields:

Months to Maturity	Annual Yield
3	6%
6	6.5
9	7
12	8

What is the value of a nine-month bill future?

Commodity	Spot Price	Futures Price	Comments
Magnoosium	$2,550 per ton	$2,728.50 per ton	Monthly storage cost = monthly convenience yield
Frozen quiche	$.50 per pound	$.514 per pound	Six months' storage costs = $.10 per pound; six months' convenience yield = $.05 per pound.
Nevada Hydro 8s of 2002	77	78.39	4% semiannual coupon payment is due just before futures contract expires.
Costaguanan pulgas (currency)	9,300 pulgas = $1	6,900 pulgas = $1	Costaguanan interest rate is 95% per year.
Establishment Industries common stock	$95	$97.54	Establishment pays dividends of $2 per quarter. Next dividend is paid two months from now.
Cheap white wine	$12,500 per 10,000-gal. tank	$14,200 per 10,000-gal. tank	Six months' convenience yield = $250 per tank. Your company has surplus storage and can store 50,000 gallons at no cost.

TABLE 27.5

Spot and six-month futures prices for selected commodities and securities. See Practice Problem 7.

7. Table 27.5 contains spot and six-month futures prices for several commodities and financial instruments. There may be some money-making opportunities. See if you can find them, and explain how you would trade to take advantage of them. The interest rate is 14.5 percent; or 7 percent over the six-month life of the contracts.

8. The following table shows gold futures prices for varying contract lengths. Gold is predominantly an investment good, not an industrial commodity. Investors hold gold because it diversifies their portfolios and because they hope its price will rise. They do not hold it for its convenience yield.

   Calculate the interest rate faced by traders in gold futures for each of the contract lengths shown below. The spot price is $295.2 per ounce.

	Contract Length (months)				
	1	3	9	15	21
Futures price	$296.49	$300.11	$312.32	$325.57	$339.65

9. In September 2008 swap dealers were quoting a rate for five-year euro interest-rate swaps of 4.5 percent against Euribor (the short-term interest rate for euro loans). Euribor at the time was 4.1 percent. Suppose that A arranges with a dealer to swap a €10 million five-year fixed-rate loan for an equivalent floating-rate loan in euros.
   a. What is the value of this swap at the time that it is entered into?
   b. Suppose that immediately after A has entered into the swap, the long-term interest rate rises by 1 percent. Who gains and who loses?
   c. What is now the value of the swap?

10. Securities A, B, and C have the following cash flows:

	Period 1	Period 2	Period 3
A	Rs. 40	Rs. 40	Rs. 40
B	Rs. 120	—	—
C	Rs. 10	Rs. 10	Rs. 110

a. Calculate their durations if the interest rate is 8 percent.
b. Suppose that you have an investment of Rs. 10 million in A. What combination of B and C would immunize this investment against interest rate changes?
c. Now suppose that you have a Rs. 10 million investment in B. How would you immunize?

11. What is meant by "delta" (δ) in the context of hedging? Give examples of how delta can be estimated or calculated.

12. A gold-mining firm is concerned about short-term volatility in its revenues. Gold currently sells for Rs. 8000 per 10 gm, but the price is extremely volatile and could fall as low to Rs. 6000 or rise as high as Rs. 11000 in the next month. The company will bring 10000 kg of gold to the market next month.
a. What will be the total revenues if the firm remains unhedged for gold prices of Rs. 7000, Rs. 8000, and Rs. 9000 per 10 gm?
b. The future price of gold for delivery one month ahead is Rs. 8080. What will be the firm's total revenues at each gold price if the firm enters into a one-month futures contract to deliver 10000 kg of gold?
c. What will total revenues be if the firm buys one-month put option to sell gold for Rs. 8000 per 10 gm? The put option costs Rs. 100 per 10 gm.

13. Har-Jeet Securities owns shares in UTI's Sensex fund worth Rs. 10 millions on September 15. (This is an index that tracks the BSE Sensitivity Index.) It wants to cash in now, but his accountant advises him to wait six months so as to defer a large capital gains tax. Explain to Har-Jeet how he can use stock index futures to hedge out his exposure to market movements over the next six months. Could Har-Jeet 'cash in' without actually selling his shares?

14. Your investment bank has an investment of $100 million in the stock of the Swiss Roll Corporation and a short position in the stock of the Frankfurter Sausage Company. Here is the recent price history of the two stocks:

Percentage Price Change		
Month	**Frankfurter Sausage**	**Swiss Roll**
January	−10	−10
February	−10	−5
March	−10	0
April	+10	0
May	+10	+5
June	+10	+10

On the evidence of these six months, how large would your short position in Frankfurter Sausage need to be to hedge you as far as possible against movements in the price of Swiss Roll?

15. Price changes on two gold-mining stocks have shown strong positive correlation. Their historical relationship is

Average percentage change in A = .001 + .75 (percentage change in B)

Changes in B explain 60 percent of the variation of the changes in A ($R^2 = .6$).
a. Suppose you own Rs. 100,000 of A. How much of B should you sell to minimize the risk of your net position?
b. What is the hedge ratio?
c. Here is the historical relationship between stock A and gold prices.

Average percentage change in A = −.002 + 1.2 (percentage change in gold price)

If $R^2 = .5$, can you lower the risk of your net position by hedging with gold (or gold futures) rather than with stock B? Explain.

TABLE 27.6

Spot prices for selected commodities and financial assets. See Practice Question 18.

Asset	Spot Price	Comments
Magnoosium	$2,800 per ton	Net convenience yield = 4% per year
Oat bran	$44 per bushel	Net convenience yield = .5% per month
Biotech stock index	140.2	Dividend = 0
Allen Wrench Co. common stock	$58.00	Cash dividend= $2.4 per year
5-year Treasury note	108.93	8% coupon
Westonian ruple	3.1 ruples= $1	12% interest rate in ruples

16. In Section 27.5, we stated that the duration of OLP's lease equals the duration of its debt.
    a. Show that this is so.
    b. Now suppose that the interest rate falls to 3 percent. Show how the value of the lease and the debt package are now affected by a .5 percent rise or fall in the interest rate. What would OLP need to do to reestablish the interest rate hedge?
17. Petrochemical Parfum (PP) is concerned about a possible increase in the price of heavy fuel oil, which is one of its major inputs. Show how PP can use either options or futures contracts to protect itself against a rise in the price of crude oil. Show how the payoffs in each case would vary if the oil price were $24, $26, or $28 a barrel. What are the advantages and disadvantages for PP of using futures rather than options to reduce risk?
18. Consider the commodities and financial assets listed in Table 27.6. The risk-free interest rate is 6 percent a year, and the term structure is flat.
    a. Calculate the six-month futures price for each case.
    b. Explain how a magnoosium producer would use a futures market to lock in the selling price of a planned shipment of 1,000 tons of magnoosium six months from now.
    c. Suppose the producer takes the actions recommended in your answer to (b), but after one month magnoosium prices have fallen to $2,200. What happens? Will the producer have to undertake additional futures market trades to restore its hedged position?
    d. Does the biotech index futures price provide useful information about the expected future performance of biotech stocks?
    e. Suppose Allen Wrench stock falls suddenly by $10 per share. Investors are confident that the cash dividend will not be reduced. What happens to the futures price?
    f. Suppose interest rates suddenly fall to 4 percent. The term structure remains flat. What happens to the six-month futures price on the five-year Treasury note? What happens to a trader who shorted 100 notes at the futures price calculated in part (a)?
    g. An importer must make a payment of one million ruples three months from now. Explain *two* strategies the importer could use to hedge against unfavorable shifts in the ruple—dollar exchange rate.
19. "Speculators want futures contracts to be incorrectly priced; hedgers want them to be correctly priced." Why?

CHALLENGE QUESTIONS

1. Phillip's Screwdriver Company has borrowed Rs. 20 million from a bank at a floating interest rate of 2 percentage points above three-month G-Secs; which now yield 5 percent. Assume that interest payments are made quarterly and, that the entire principal of the loan is repaid after five years.

   Phillip's wants to convert the bank loan to fixed-rate debt. It could have issued a fixed-rate five-year debentures at a yield to maturity of 9 percent. Such a note would now trade at par. The five-year G-Secs yield to maturity is 7 percent.

   a. Is Phillip's stupid to want long-term debt at an interest rate of 9 percent? It is borrowing from the bank at 7 percent.

   b. Explain how the conversion could be carried out by an interest rate swap. What will be the initial terms of the swap? (Ignore transaction costs and the swap dealer's profit.)

   One year from now short- and medium-term Treasury yields *decrease* to 6 percent, so the term structure then is flat. (The changes actually occur in month 5.) Phillip's credit standing is unchanged; it can still borrow at 2 percentage points over Treasury rates.

   c. What net swap payment will Phillip's make or receive?

   d. Suppose that Phillip's now wants to cancel the swap. How much would it need to pay the swap dealer? Or would the dealer pay Phillip's? Explain.

CHAPTER [28]

MANAGING INTERNATIONAL RISKS

IN THE LAST chapter we considered the risks that flow from changes in interest rates and commodity prices. But companies with substantial overseas interests encounter a variety of other hazards, including political risks and currency fluctuations. *Political risk* means the possibility that a hostile foreign government will expropriate your business without compensation or not allow profits to be taken out of the country.

To understand currency risk, you first need to understand how the foreign exchange market works and how prices for foreign currency are determined. We therefore start this chapter with some basic institutional detail about the foreign exchange market and we will look at some simple theories that link exchange rates, interest rates, and inflation. We will use these theories to show how firms assess and hedge their foreign currency exposure.

When we discussed investment decisions in Chapter 6, we showed that financial managers do not need to forecast exchange rates in order to evaluate overseas investment proposals. They can simply forecast the foreign currency cash flows and discount these flows at the foreign currency cost of capital. In this chapter we will explain why this rule makes sense. It turns out that it is the ability to hedge foreign exchange risk that allows companies to ignore future exchange rates when making investment decisions.

We conclude the chapter with a discussion of political risk. We show that, while companies cannot restrain a determined foreign government, they can structure their operations to reduce the risk of hostile actions.

28.1 THE FOREIGN EXCHANGE MARKET

An Indian company that imports goods from the U.S. may need to buy dollars to pay for the purchase. An Indian company exporting to the U.S. may receive dollars, which it sells for exchange of rupees. Both firms make use of the foreign exchange market.

The foreign exchange market has no central marketplace. Business is conducted electronically. The principal dealers are the larger commercial banks and investment banks. A corporation that wants to buy or sell currency usually does so through a commercial bank. Turnover in the foreign exchange market is huge. In London in April 2004 $753 billion of currency changed hands each day. That is equivalent to an annual turnover of about $200 trillion ($200,000,000,000,000). New York and Tokyo together accounted for a further $400 billion turnover per day.[1] The total turnover in India in April 2004 was $125 billion per month. This is equivalent to an annual turnover of $1500 billion per annum.[2]

Table 28.1 is adapted from the table of exchange rates in the *Business Line*. Exchange rates are generally expressed in terms of the number of Indian rupees needed to buy one unit of foreign currency. This is named a *direct quote*. In the first column of Table 28.1, the direct quote for the Euro shows you can buy 1 Euro (€) for Rs. 59.915. This is often written as Rs. 59.915/€.

An *indirect* exchange quote states the number of units of foreign currency needed to buy one Indian rupee. In the U.S. currency rates are usually quoted as indirect quotes. For example, Table 28.1 shows that 1$ is equivalent to Rs. 46.4750 rupees or, more concisely, Rs. 46.4750/$. It can also be stated as an indirect quote: $0.02152/Rupee.

[1]The results of the triennial survey of foreign exchange business are published on **www.bis.org/publ.**

[2]Source:www.rbi.org.in

TABLE 28.1

Spot and Forward Exchange rates, August 9, 2006.

*Rates show number of Indian Rupees per unit of foreign currency, except for Yen, which show the number of Indian Rupees per 100 Japanese Yen. Rates mentioned above are the averages of bid and ask rates.

Source: *Business Line, August 9, 2006*

		Forward Rate		
	Spot Rate*	**1 Month**	**3 Months**	**6 Months**
US Dollar	46.475	46.52	46.585	46.73
Euro	59.915	59.99	60.245	60.685
Pound Sterling	88.72	88.785	88.975	89.33
Deutsche Mark	30.635	30.67	30.8	31.03
Japanese Yen**	40.445	40.55	40.875	41.43
French Franc	9.13	9.145	9.185	9.25
Swiss Franc	38.04	38.105	38.355	38.765
Dutch Guilder	27.19	27.22	27.335	27.535
Danish Kroner	8.03	8.045	8.075	8.14
Singapore Dollar	29.55	29.58	29.695	29.9
Hong Kong Dollar	5.975	5.985	6	6.035
Australian Dollar	35.55	35.63	35.645	35.705

The exchange rates in the first column of Table 28.1 are the prices of currency for immediate delivery. They are known as **spot rates of exchange**. The spot rate for Australian dollar is Rs. 35.55/AUD, and the spot rate for Japanese Yen is Rs. 40.445/100Yen.

In addition to the spot exchange market, there is a *forward market*. In the forward market you buy and sell currency for future delivery. If you know that you are going to pay out or receive foreign currency at some future date, you can insure yourself against loss by buying or selling forward. Thus, if you need one million U.S. dollars in three months, you can enter into a three-month *forward contract*. The **forward rate** on this contract is the price you agree to pay in three months when the one million U.S. dollars are delivered. If you look again at Table 28.1, you will see that the three-month forward rate for the U.S. dollar is quoted at Rs. 46.585/\$. If you buy U.S. dollars for three months' delivery, you get fewer dollars for your rupee than if you buy them spot. In this case the dollar is said to trade at a forward premium relative to the rupee, because forward rates are expensive than the spot rates. Expressed as an annual rate, the forward premium is[3]

$$4 \times \left(\frac{46.585}{46.475} - 1 \right) = +0.009, \text{ or } +0.9\%$$

You could also say that *rupee* was selling at a *forward discount*.

A forward purchase or sale is a made-to-measure transaction between you and the bank. It can be for any currency, any amount, and any delivery day. You could buy, say, 99,999 Vietnamese dong or Haitian gourdes for a year and a day forward as long as you can find a bank ready to deal. Most forward transactions are for six months or less, but the long-term currency swaps that we described

[3]Here is an occasional point of confusion. Since the quote is a direct quote, we calculate the premium by talking the ratio of the forward rate to the spot rate, If we use indirect quotes, then we need to calculate the ratio of the spot rate to the forward rate. In the case of U.S. dollars, the forward premium with direct quotes is $4 \times [(1/46.475) / (1/46.585)\text{-}1] = +0.009$, or +0.9 percent.

in Chapter 27 are equivalent to a bundle of forward transactions. When firms want to enter into long-term forward contracts, they usually do so through a currency swap.[4]

There is also an organized market for currency for future delivery known as the currency *futures* market. Futures contracts are highly standardized; they are for specified amounts and for a limited choice of delivery dates.[5]

When you buy a forward or futures contract, you are committed to taking delivery of the currency. As an alternative, you can take out an *option* to buy or sell currency in the future at a price that is fixed today. Made-to-measure currency options can be bought from the major banks, and standardized options are traded on the options exchanges.

28.2 SOME BASIC RELATIONSHIPS

You can't develop a consistent international financial policy until you understand the reasons for the differences in exchange rates and interest rates. We will consider the following four problems:

- *Problem 1*. Why is the dollar rate of interest ($r_\$$) different from, say, the peso rate (r_{peso})?
- *Problem 2*. Why is the forward rate of exchange ($f_{peso/\$}$) different from the spot rate ($s_{peso/\$}$)?
- *Problem 3*. What determines next year's expected spot rate of exchange between dollars and pesos [$E(s_{peso/\$})$]?
- *Problem 4*. What is the relationship between the inflation rate in the United States ($i_\$$) and the inflation rate in Mexico (i_{peso})?

Suppose that individuals were not worried about risk and that there were no barriers or costs to international trade. In that case the spot exchange rates, forward exchange rates, interest rates, and inflation rates would stand in the following simple relationship to one another:

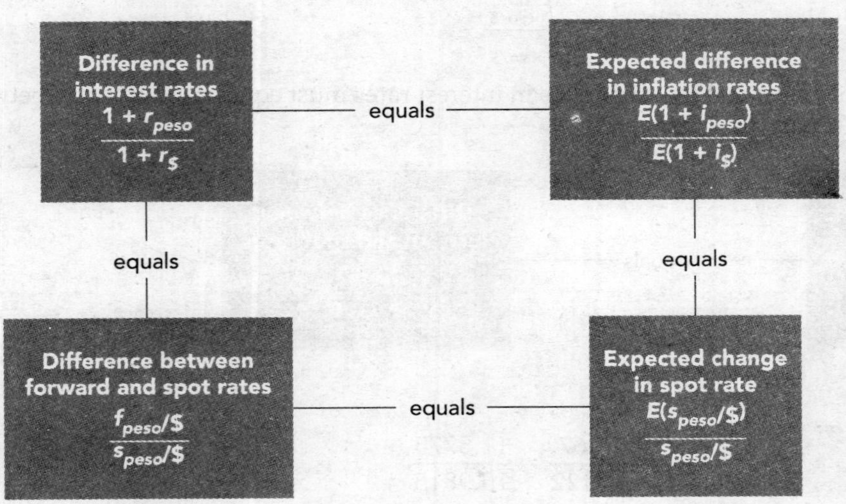

Why should this be so?

[4] Notice that spot and short-term forward trades are sometimes undertaken together. For example, a company might need the use of Mexican pesos for one month. In this case it would buy pesos spot and simultaneously sell them forward. Dealers refer to this as a *swap* trade. But do not confuse it with the longer term currency swaps that we described in Chapter 27.

[5] See Chapter 27 for a further discussion of the difference between forward and futures contracts.

Interest Rates and Exchange Rates

It is March 2004 and you have $1 million to invest for one year. U.S. dollar deposits are offering an interest rate of about 1.22 percent; Mexican peso deposits are offering an (attractive?) 6.70 percent. Where should you put your money? Does the answer sound obvious? Let's check:

- *Dollar loan.* The rate of interest on one-year dollar deposits is 1.22 percent. Therefore at the end of the year you get 1,000,000 × 1.0122 = $1,012,200.
- *Peso loan.* The current exchange rate is 10.9815/$. For $1 million, you can buy 1,000,000 × 10.9815 = peso 10,981,500. The rate of interest on a one-year peso deposit is 6.7 percent. Therefore at the end of the year you get 10,981,500 × 1.067 = peso 11,717,261. Of course, you don't know what the exchange rate is going to be in one year's time. But that doesn't matter. You can fix today the price at which you sell your pesos. The one-year forward rate is peso 11.5775/$. Therefore, by selling forward, you can make sure that you will receive 11,717,261/11.5775 = $1,012,072 at the end of the year.

Thus, the two investments offer almost exactly the same rate of return.[6] They have to—they are both risk-free. If the domestic interest rate were different from the *covered* foreign rate, you would have a money machine.

When you make the peso loan, you receive a higher interest rate. But you get an offsetting loss because you sell pesos forward at a lower price than you pay for them today. The interest rate differential is

$$\frac{1 + r_{\text{peso}}}{1 + r_{\$}}$$

And the differential between the forward and spot exchange rates is

$$\frac{f_{\text{peso}/\$}}{s_{\text{peso}/\$}}$$

Interest rate parity theory says that the difference in interest rates must equal the difference between the forward and spot exchange rates:

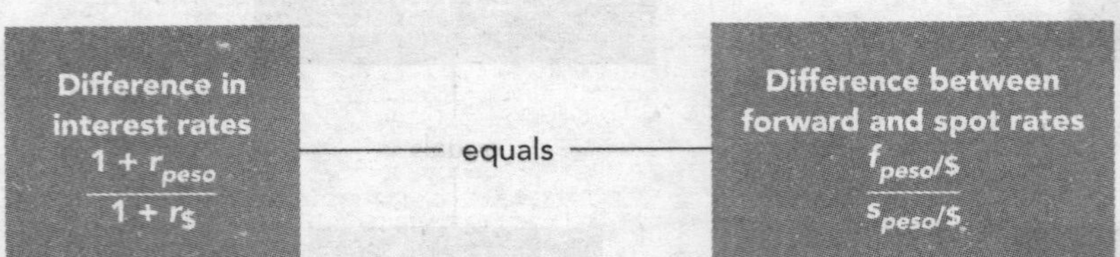

In our example,

$$\frac{1.067}{1.0122} = \frac{11.5775}{10.9815}$$

The Forward Premium and Changes in Spot Rates

Now let's consider how the forward premium is related to changes in spot rates of exchange. If people didn't care about risk, the forward rate of exchange would depend solely on what people expected the spot rate to be. For example, if the one-year forward rate on pesos is peso 11.5775/$, that

[6]The minor difference in our calculated end-of-year payoffs was mostly due to rounding in the interest rates.

could only be because traders expect the spot rate in one year's time to be peso 11.5775/\$. If they expected it to be, say, peso 12.0/\$, nobody would be willing to buy pesos forward. They could get more pesos for their dollar by waiting and buying spot.

Therefore the *expectations theory* of exchange rates tells us that the percentage difference between the forward rate and today's spot rate is equal to the expected change in the spot rate:

Difference between forward and spot rates — equals — **Expected change in spot rate**

$$\frac{f_{peso/\$}}{s_{peso/\$}} \quad \text{equals} \quad \frac{E(s_{peso/\$})}{s_{peso/\$}}$$

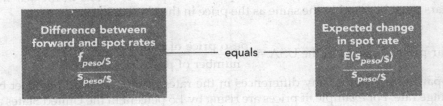

Of course, this assumes that traders don't care about risk. If they do care, the forward rate can be either higher or lower than the expected spot rate. For example, suppose that you have contracted to receive one million pesos in three months, You can wait until you receive the money before you change it into dollars, but this leaves you open to the risk that the price of the peso may fall over the next three months. Your alternative is to sell the peso forward. In this case, you are fixing today the price at which you will sell your pesos. Since you avoid risk by selling forward, you may be willing to do so even if the forward price of pesos is a little *lower* than the expected spot price.

Other companies may be in the opposite position. They may have contracted to pay out pesos in three months. They can wait until the end of the three months and then buy pesos, but this leaves them open to the risk that the price of the peso may rise. It is safer for these companies to fix the price today by *buying* pesos forward. These companies may, therefore, be willing to buy forward even if the forward price of the peso is a little *higher* than the expected spot price.

Thus some companies find it safer to *sell* the peso forward, while others find it safer to *buy* the peso forward. When the first group predominates, the forward price of pesos is likely to be less than the expected spot price. When the second group predominates, the forward price is likely to be greater than the expected spot price. On average you would expect the forward price to underestimate the expected spot price just about as often as it overestimates it.

Changes in the Exchange Rate and Inflation Rates

Now we come to the third side of our quadrilateral—the relationship between changes in the spot exchange rate and inflation rates. Suppose that you notice that silver can be bought in Mexico for peso 60 a troy ounce and sold in the United States for \$7.50. You think you may be on to a good thing. You take \$5,463.74 and exchange it for 5,463.74 × peso 10.9815 = peso 60,000. That's enough to buy 1,000 ounces of silver. You put this silver on the first plane to the United States, where you sell it for \$7,500. You have made a gross profit of just over \$2,000. Of course, you have to pay transportation and insurance costs out of this, but there should still be something left over for you.

Money machines don't exist—not for long, anyway. As others notice the disparity between the price of silver in Mexico and the price in the United States, the price will be forced up in Mexico and down in the United States until the profit opportunity disappears. Arbitrage ensures that the dollar price of silver is about the same in the two countries. Of course, silver is a standard and easily transportable commodity, but the same forces should act to equalize the domestic and foreign prices of other goods. Those goods that can be bought more cheaply abroad will be imported, and that will force down the price of domestic products. Similarly, those goods that can be bought more cheaply in the United States will be exported, and that will force down the price of the foreign products.

This is often called *purchasing power parity.*[7] Just as the price of goods in Safeway supermarkets must be roughly the same as the price of goods in A&P, so the price of goods in Mexico when converted into dollars must be roughly the same as the price in the United States:

$$\text{Dollar price of goods in the USA} = \frac{\text{peso price of goods in Mexico}}{\text{number of pesos per dollar}}$$

Purchasing power parity implies that any differences in the rates of inflation will be offset by a change in the exchange rate. For example, if prices are rising by 1.5 percent in the United States and by 6.5 percent in Mexico, the number of pesos that you can buy for \$1 must rise by 1.065/1.015 − 1, or about 5.0 percent. Therefore purchasing power parity says that to estimate changes in the spot rate of exchange, you need to estimate differences in inflation rates:[8]

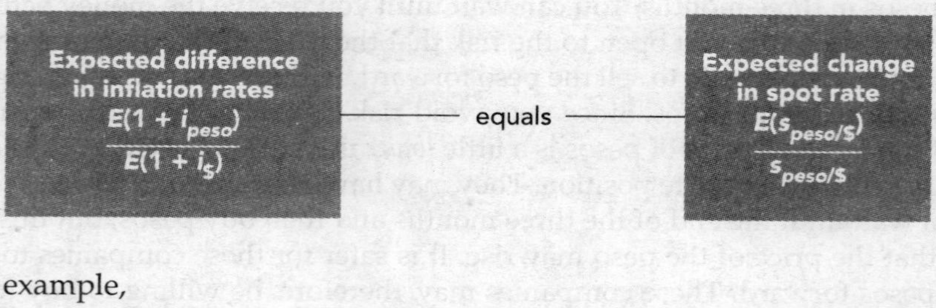

In our example,

$$\text{Current spot rate} \times \text{expected difference in inflation rates} = \text{expected spot rate}$$

$$10.9815 \times \frac{1.065}{1.015} = 11.5$$

Interest Rates and Inflation Rates

Now for the fourth leg! Just as water always flows downhill, so capital tends to flow where returns are greatest. But investors are not interested in *nominal* returns; they care about what their money will buy. So, if investors notice that real interest rates are higher in Mexico than in the United States, they will shift their savings into Mexico until the expected real returns are the same in the two countries. If the expected real interest rates are equal, then the difference in money rates must be equal to the difference in the expected inflation rates:[9]

[7]Economists use the term *purchasing power parity* to refer to the notion that the level of prices of goods in general must be the same in the two countries. They tend to use the phrase *law of one price* when they are talking about the price of a single good.

[8]In other words, the *expected* difference in inflation rates equals the *expected* change in the exchange rate. Strictly interpreted, purchasing power parity also implies that the *actual* difference in the inflation rates always equals the *actual* change in the exchange rate.

[9]In Section 23.1 we discussed Irving Fisher's theory that over time money interest rates change to reflect changes in anticipated inflation. Here we argue that international differences in money interest rates also reflect differences in anticipated inflation. This theory is sometimes known as the *international Fisher effect.*

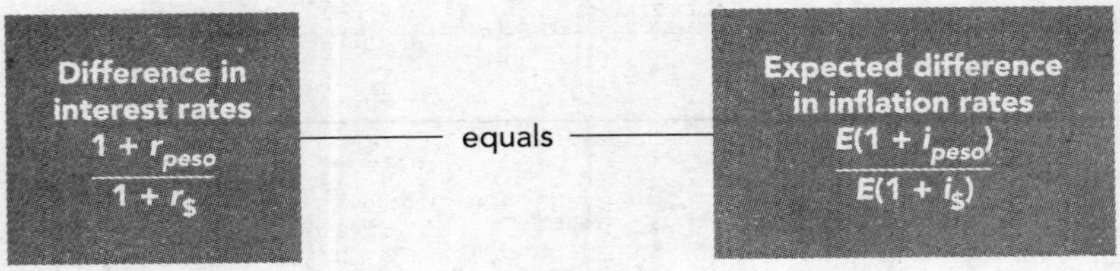

In Mexico the real one-year interest rate is close to zero:

$$r_{\text{peso}}(\text{real}) = \frac{1 + r_{\text{peso}}}{E(1 + i_{\text{peso}})} - 1 = \frac{1.067}{1.065} - 1 = .002$$

Ditto for the United States:

$$r_\$(real) = \frac{1 + r_\$}{E(1 + i_\$)} - 1 = \frac{1.0122}{1.015} - 1 = -.003$$

Is Life Really That Simple?

We have described above four theories that link interest rates, forward rates, spot exchange rates, and inflation rates. Of course, such simple economic theories are not going to provide an exact description of reality. We need to know how well they predict actual behavior. Let's check.

1. Interest Rate Parity Theory Interest rate parity theory says that the peso rate of interest covered for exchange risk should be the same as the dollar rate. As long as money can be moved easily between deposits in different currencies, interest rate parity almost always holds. In fact, dealers *set* the forward price of pesos by looking at the difference between the interest rates on deposits of dollars and pesos.

2. The Expectations Theory of Forward Rates How well does the expectations theory explain the level of forward rates? Scholars who have studied exchange rates have found that forward rates typically exaggerate the likely change in the spot rate. When the forward rate appears to predict a sharp rise in the spot rate (a forward premium), the forward rate tends to overestimate the rise in the spot rate. Conversely, when the forward rate appears to predict a fall in the currency (a forward discount), it tends to overestimate this fall.[10]

This finding is *not* consistent with the expectations theory. Instead it looks as if sometimes companies are prepared to give up return to *buy* forward currency and other times they are prepared to give up return to *sell* forward currency. In other words, forward rates seem to contain a risk premium, but the sign of this premium swings backward and forward.[11] You can see this from Figure 28.1. Almost half the time the forward rate for the Swiss franc *overstates* the likely future spot rate

[10]Many researchers have even found that, when the forward rate predicts a rise, the spot rate is more likely to fall, and vice versa. For a readable discussion of this puzzling finding, see K. A. Froot and R. H. Thaler, "Anomalies: Foreign Exchange," *Journal of Economic Perspectives* 4 (1990), pp. 179–192.

[11]For evidence that forward exchange rates contain risk premia that are sometimes positive and sometimes negative, see, for example, E. F. Fama, "Forward and Spot Exchange Rates," *Journal of Monetary Economics* 14 (1984), pp. 319–338.

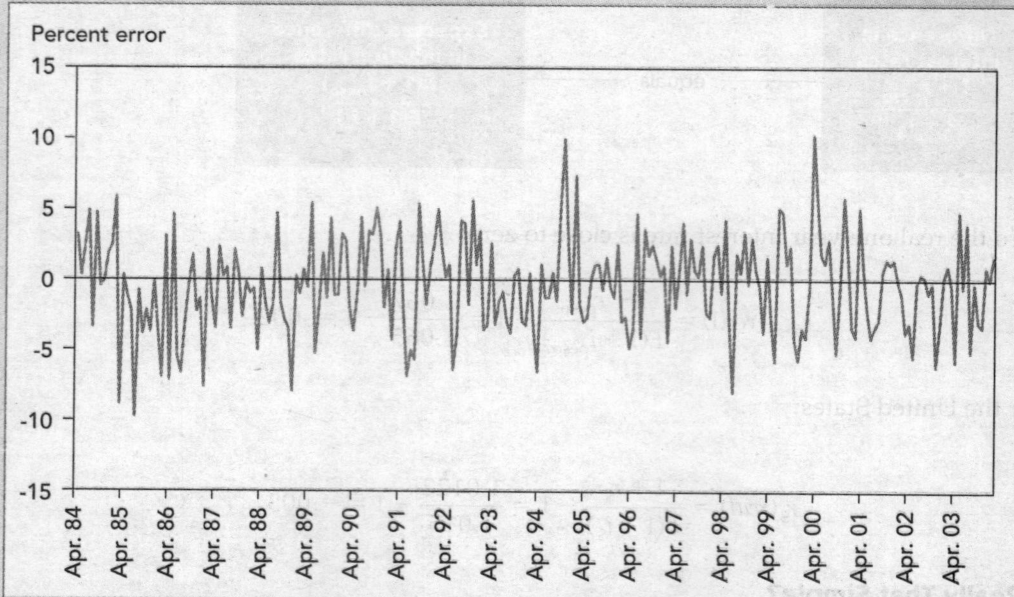

FIGURE 28.1

Percentage error from using the one-month forward rate for Swiss francs to forecast next month's spot rate. Note that the forward rate overestimates and underestimates the spot rate with about equal frequency.

and half the time it *understates* the likely spot rate. *On average* the forward rate and future spot rate are almost identical. This is important news for the financial manager; it means that a company that always uses the forward market to protect against exchange rate movements does not pay any extra for this insurance.

3. Purchasing Power Parity Theory What about the third side of our quadrilateral—purchasing power parity theory? No one who has compared prices in foreign stores with prices at home really believes that prices are the same throughout the world. Look, for example, at Table 28.2, which shows the price of a Big Mac in different countries. Notice that at current rates of exchange a Big Mac costs \$4.90 in Switzerland but only \$2.90 in the United States. To equalize prices in the two countries, the number of Swiss francs that you could buy for your dollar would need to increase by $4.90/2.90 - 1 = .69$, or 69 percent.

This suggests a possible way to make a quick buck. Why don't you buy a hamburger-to-go in (say) the Philippines for the equivalent of \$1.23 and take it for resale in Switzerland, where the price in dollars is \$4.90? The answer, of course, is that the gain would not cover the costs. The same good can be sold for different prices in different countries because transportation is costly and inconvenient.[12]

[12]Of course, even within a currency area there may be considerable price variations. The price of a Big Mac, for example, differs substantially from one part of the United States to another.

Country	Local Price Converted to U.S. Dollars	Country	Local Price Converted to U.S. Dollars
Canada	2.33	Philippines	1.23
China	1.26	Russia	1.45
Denmark	4.46	South Africa	1.86
Euro area	3.28	Switzerland	4.90
Japan	2.33	United Kingdom	3.37
Mexico	2.08	United States	2.90

TABLE 28.2

Price of Big Mac hamburgers in different countries.

Source: "The Big Mac Index: Food for Thought," *The Economist*, May 29, 2004, pp. 75–76. The Economist Newspaper Group, Inc. Reprinted with permission. Further reproduction prohibited (www.economist.com).

On the other hand, there is clearly some relationship between inflation and changes in exchange rates. For example, between 1999 and 2003 prices in Turkey rose 7.2 times. Or, to put it another way, you could say that the purchasing power of money in Turkey declined by about 86 percent. If exchange rates had not adjusted, Turkish exporters would have found it impossible to sell their goods. But, of course, exchange rates did adjust. In fact, the value of the Turkish currency declined by 79 percent relative to the U.S. dollar.

Turkey is a fairly extreme case, but in Figure 28.2 we have plotted the relative change in purchasing power for a sample of countries against the change in the exchange rate. Turkey is tucked in the bottom left-hand corner; the United States is closer to the top right.[13] You can see that although the relationship is far from exact, large differences in inflation rates are generally accompanied by an offsetting change in the exchange rate.[14]

Strictly speaking, purchasing power parity theory implies that the differential inflation rate is always identical to the change in the spot rate. But we don't need to go as far as that. We should be content if the *expected* difference in the inflation rates equals the *expected* change in the spot rate. That's all we wrote on the third side of our quadrilateral. Look, for example, at Figure 28.3. The blue line shows that in 2003 £1 sterling bought over 60 percent fewer dollars than it did one hundred years earlier. But this decline in the price of sterling was largely matched by the higher inflation rate in the United Kingdom. The green line shows that the inflation-adjusted, or *real*, exchange rate ended the century at roughly the same level as it began.[15] Of course, the real exchange rate *does* change, sometimes quite sharply. For example, the real value of sterling rose by a quarter between December 2001 and December 2003. However, if you were a financial manager called on to make a long-term forecast of the exchange rate, you could not have done much better than to assume that changes in the value of the currency would offset the difference in inflation rates.

[13]Turkey did not have the highest inflation rate or the most rapidly depreciating currency. That honor belonged to the Democratic Republic of the Congo, followed closely by Angola. These are shown by the two points in the extreme bottom left of Figure 28.2.

[14]Note that some of the countries represented in Figure 28.2 have highly controlled economies, so that their exchange rates are not those that would exist in an unrestricted market. The interest rates shown in Figure 28.4 are subject to a similar caveat.

[15]The real exchange rate is equal to the nominal exchange rate multiplied by the inflation differential. For example, suppose that the value of sterling falls from \$1.54 = £1 to \$1.40 = £1 at the same time that the price of goods rises 10 percent faster in the United Kingdom than in the United States. The inflation-adjusted, or real, exchange rate is unchanged at

$$\text{Nominal exchange rate} \times (1 + i_{£})/(1 + i_{\$}) = 1.40 \times 1.1 = \$1.54/£$$

FIGURE 28.2

A decline in the exchange rate and a decline in a currency's purchasing power usually go hand in hand. In this diagram, each of the 163 points represents the experience of a different country in the five years to 2002 or 2003. The vertical axis shows the change in the value of the foreign currency relative to the average. The horizontal axis shows the change in purchasing power relative to the average. The × at the lower left is Turkey; the United States is toward the top right.

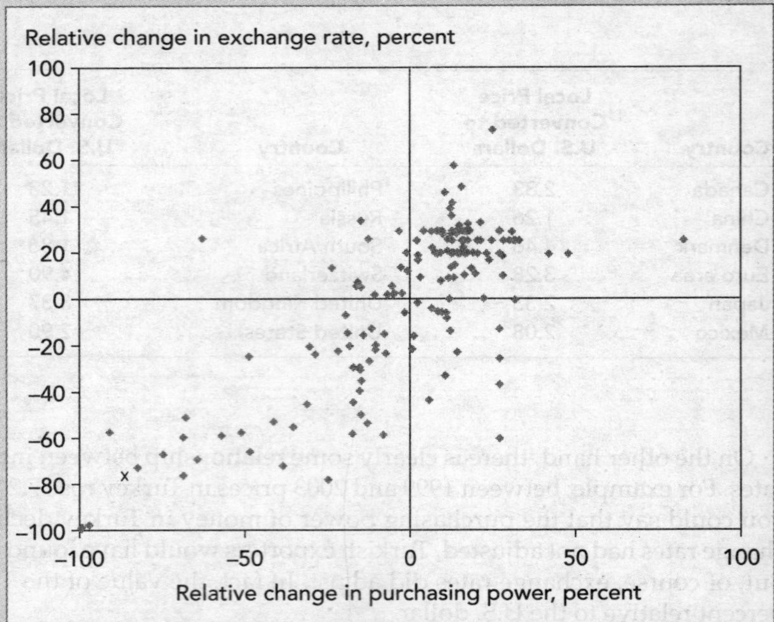

FIGURE 28.3

Since 1900 sterling has fallen sharply in value against the dollar. But this fall has largely offset the higher inflation rate in the U.K. The *real* value of sterling has been roughly constant.

Source: N. Abuaf and P. Jorion, "Purchasing Power Parity in the Long Run," *Journal of Finance* 45 (March 1990), pp. 157–174. We have revised and updated the data to 2003.

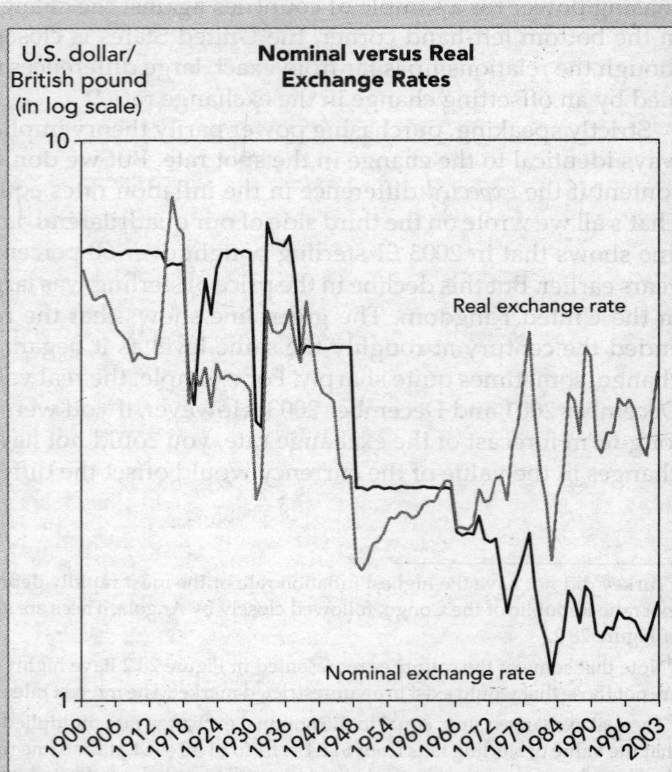

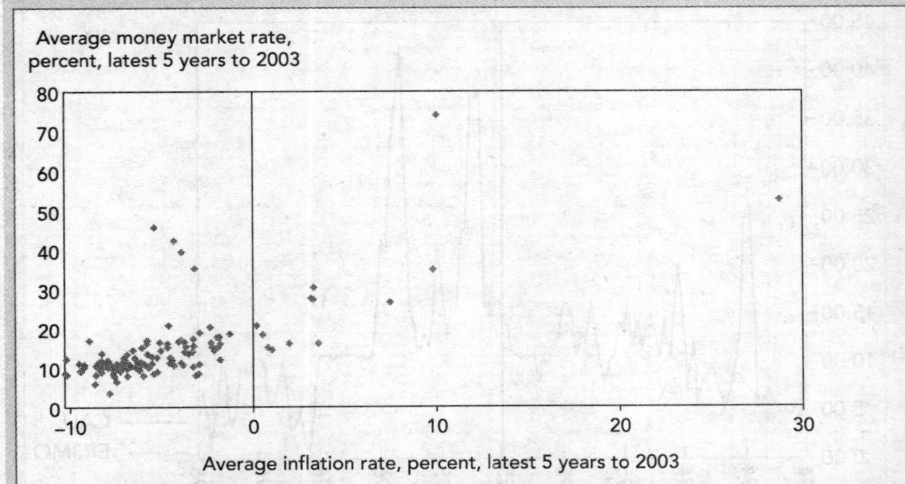

FIGURE 28.4

Countries with the highest interest rates generally have the highest inflation rates. In this diagram, each of the 129 points represents the experience of a different country.

4. Equal Real Interest Rates Finally we come to the relationship between interest rates in different countries. Do we have a single world capital market with the same *real* rate of interest in all countries? Does the difference in money interest rates equal the difference in the expected inflation rates?

This is not an easy question to answer since we cannot observe *expected* inflation. However, in Figure 28.4 we have plotted the average interest rate in each of 129 countries against the inflation that subsequently occurred. Japan is tucked into the bottom-left corner of the chart, while Malawi is represented by the dot in the top-right corner. You can see that, in general, the countries with the highest interest rates also had the highest inflation rates. There were much smaller differences between the real rates of interest than between the nominal (or money) rates.[16]

Interest Rate Parity in India

Prof. J R Varma observed that the theoretical linkage between interest rates and the foreign exchange markets were observed for the first time in India after September 1995. As Figure 28.5 shows, there was no relationship between the two markets prior to September 1995. Bhatt and Virmani similarly report linkage between the money market and the foreign currency market between 1993 and 2003. However, during periods of crisis (like Kargil war or Pokhran sanctions) when the RBI has intervened in the foreign currency market to stabilize the exchange rates, there was very weak relationship between the money market and the foreign currency rates. Figure 28.6 shows these findings.

28.3 HEDGING CURRENCY RISK

Sharp exchange rate movements can make a large dent in corporate profits. To illustrate how companies cope with this problem, we will look at a typical company in India, OLP Steel, and walk through its foreign exchange operations.

[16]In Chapter 24 we saw that in some countries the government has issued indexed bonds promising a fixed real return. The annual interest payment and the amount repaid at maturity increase with the rate of inflation. In these cases, therefore, we can observe and compare the real rate of interest. As we write this, real interest rates in Canada, France, Japan, Sweden, the U.K. and the United States cluster within the range of 1.2 to 2.4 percent. The exception is Australia, where the yield on indexed bonds is 3 percent.

FIGURE 28.5

Relationship between the implicit euro-rupee rate (estimated by Prof. J R Varma) and the call market interest rate in India. After September 1995, the two rates track each other fairly well.

Source: Varma, J.R., 1997, "Indian Money Market: Market Structure, Covered Parity, and Term Structure", *ICFAI Journal of Applied Finance*. pp.1–10

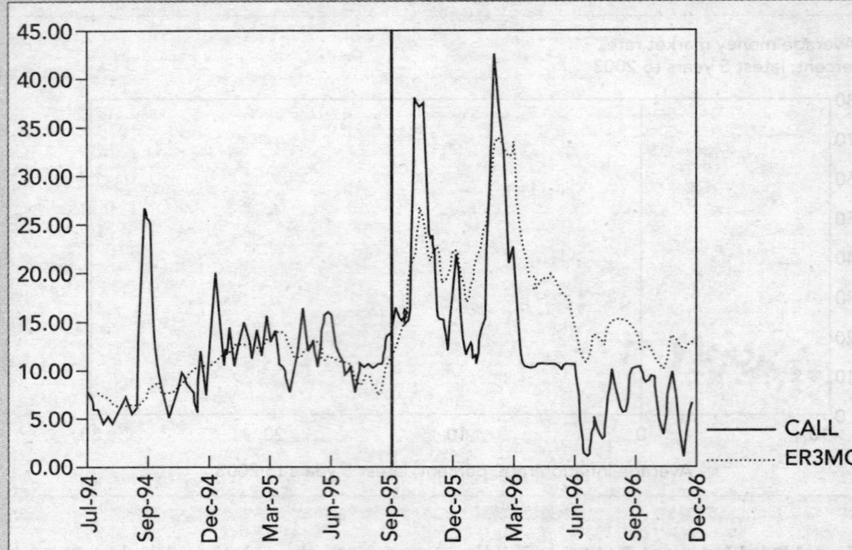

FIGURE 28.6

Three-month forward rate and India-U.S. interest differentials The sharp upward spikes represent RBI interventions.

Source: Bhatt, V., and A Virmani, 2005, "Global Integration of India's Money Market: Interest Rate Parity in India", ICRIER Working Paper, no 164, July 2005.

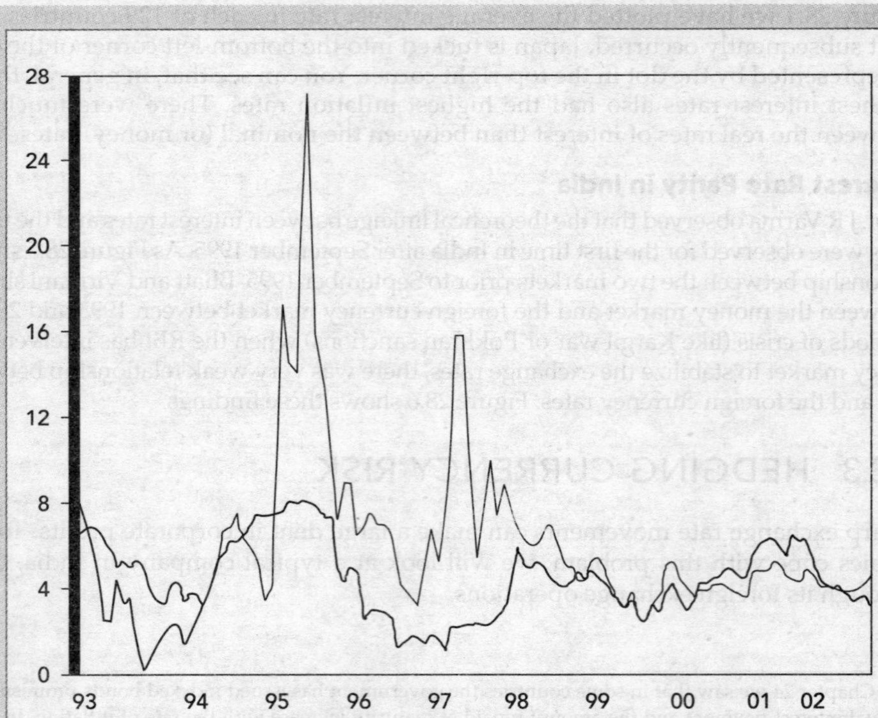

Example: OLP Steel OLP has a small but profitable export business. Contracts involve substantial delays in payment, but since the company has a policy of always invoicing in rupees, it is fully protected against changes in exchange rates. Recently the export department has become unhappy with this practice and believes that it is causing the company to lose valuable export orders to firms that are willing to quote in the customer's own currency.

You sympathize with these arguments, but you are worried about how the firm should price long-term export contracts when payment is to be made in foreign currency. If the value of that currency declines before payment is made, the company may suffer a large loss. You want to take the currency risk into account, but you also want to give the sales force as much freedom of action as possible.

Notice that OLP can insure against its currency risk by selling the foreign currency forward. This means that it can separate the problem of negotiating sales contracts from that of managing the company's foreign exchange exposure. The sales force can allow for currency risk by pricing on the basis of the forward exchange rate. And you, as financial manager, can decide whether the company *ought* to hedge.

What is the cost of hedging? You sometimes hear managers say that it is equal to the difference between the forward rate and *today's* spot rate. That is wrong. If OLP does not hedge, it will receive the spot rate at the time that the customer pays for the steel. Therefore, the cost of insurance is the difference between the forward rate and the expected spot rate when payment is received.

Insure or speculate? We generally vote for insurance. First, it makes life simpler for the firm and allows it to concentrate on its main business. Second, it does not cost much. (In fact, the cost is zero on average if the forward rate equals the expected spot rate, as the expectations theory of forward rates implies.) Third, the foreign currency market seems reasonably efficient, at least for the major currencies. Speculation should be a zero-NPV game, unless financial managers have information that is not available to the pros who make the market.

Is there any other way that OLP can protect itself against exchange loss? Of course. It can borrow foreign currency against its foreign receivables, sell the currency spot, and invest the proceeds in the India. Interest rate parity theory tells us that in free markets the difference between selling forward and selling spot should be equal to the difference between the interest that you have to pay overseas and the interest that you can earn at home.

Our discussion of OLP's export business illustrates four practical implications of our simple theories about forward exchange rates. First, you can use forward rates to adjust for exchange risk in contract pricing. Second, the expectations theory suggests that protection against exchange risk is usually worth having. Third, interest rate parity theory reminds us that you can hedge either by selling forward or by borrowing foreign currency and selling spot. Fourth, the cost of forward cover is not the difference between the forward rate and *today's* spot rate; it is the difference between the forward rate and the expected spot rate when the forward contract matures.

Perhaps we should add a fifth implication. You don't make money simply by buying currencies that go up in value and selling those that go down. For example, suppose that you buy Narnian leos and sell them after a year for 2 percent more than you paid for them. Should you give yourself a pat on the back? That depends on the interest that you have earned on your leos. If the interest rate on leos is 2 percentage points less than the interest rate on rupees, the profit on the currency is exactly canceled out by the reduction in interest income. Thus you make money from currency speculation only if you can predict whether the exchange rate will change by more or less than the interest rate differential. In other words, you must be able to predict whether the exchange rate will change by more or less than the forward premium or discount.

Transaction Exposure and Economic Exposure

The exchange risk from OLP's export business is due to delays in foreign currency payments and is therefore referred to as *transaction exposure*. Transaction exposure can be easily identified and hedged. Since a 1 percent fall in the value of the foreign currency results in a 1 percent fall in OLP's rupee receipts, for every euro or yen that OLP is owed by its customers, it needs to sell forward one euro or one yen.[17]

However, OLP may still be affected by currency fluctuations even if its customers do not owe it a cent. For example, OLP may be in competition with Swedish steel producers. If the value of the Swedish krona falls, OLP will need to cut its prices in order to compete.[18] OLP can protect itself against such an eventuality by selling the krona forward. In this case the loss on OLP's steel business will be offset by the profit on its forward sale.

Notice that OLP's exposure to the krona is not limited to specific transactions that have already been entered into. Financial managers often refer to this broader type of exposure as *economic exposure*.[19] Economic exposure is less easy to measure than transaction exposure. For example, it is clear that the value of OLP Steel is positively related to the value of the krona, so to hedge its position it needs to sell kronor forward. But in practice it may be hard to say exactly how many kronor OLP needs to sell.

Economic exposure is a major source of risk for many firms. For example, when the euro appreciated in value in 2003, European carmakers took a bath on their overseas sales. Volkswagen, Europe's biggest carmaker, calculated that the 20 percent rise in the euro had cut over $1 billion off its profits. American dealers that had a franchise to sell European cars also suffered, but competing producers, such as Ford and GM, benefited from their rivals' discomfiture. Thus European and American car producers and their dealers were all affected by exchange rate changes even though they may have had no fixed obligation to pay or receive dollars. They had economic exposure as well as possible transaction exposure.

DSM, a Dutch specialty-chemicals firm, is another company with economic exposure, since about two-thirds of its production is in the euro-zone, but four-fifths of its sales are in dollars. Consequently, a 1 percent fall in the value of the dollar reduces DSM's gross profits by an estimated €7–11 million. To protect itself against this economic exposure, DSM has sought to move more of its production out of the euro-zone and has bought an American pharmaceuticals firm partly to reduce its currency risk. The company has also increased the proportion of its debt that is in dollars and has swapped some of its euro debt into dollars. When the dollar falls, the impact on DSM's profits is partly offset by a reduction in the number of euros required to service its debt.[20]

Many of the software companies in India face similar problems as does DSM. A large part of the revenue comes from their international clients. However, their software testing centres are located mostly in India and hence their expenses are in Indian rupees. So they suffer revenue losses whenever rupee appreciates against the major international currencies. Thus for example, in the first quarter of 2006, Wipro suffered a revenue loss of Rs. 27 crores because of the appreciation of rupee.

Wipro and DSM's experience illustrates that companies with overseas sales can protect themselves against currency risk in two ways. They may hedge in the financial markets, either by borrowing in a foreign currency or by selling the currency forward.[21] Alternatively, they may construct overseas production facilities. If it becomes cheaper to produce overseas, some production may be shifted to the foreign plant.

[17]To put it another way, the hedge ratio is 1.0.

[18]Of course, if purchasing power parity always held, the fall in the value of the krona would be matched by higher inflation in Sweden. The risk for OLP is that the *real* value of the krona may decline, so that when measured in dollars Swedish costs are lower than previously. Unfortunately, it is much easier to hedge against a change in the *nominal* exchange rate than against a change in the *real* rate.

[19]Financial managers also refer to *translation exposure,* which measures the effect of an exchange rate change on the company's financial statements.

[20]The example of DSM is cited in "Tested by the Mighty Euro," *The Economist*, March 20–26, 2004, pp. 77–78.

[21]Notice that hedging in the financial markets reduces the risk, but it should not affect the firm's decision about where to produce and sell its products.

Currency Speculation

OLP Steel's currency exposure arose naturally from its business activity, but the risk was avoidable; it could have been hedged using either the forward markets or the loan markets. Sometimes, however, companies deliberately take on currency risk in the hope of gain. Now there is nothing wrong with that if you truly do have a forecasting edge, but we should warn you against the dangers of naive strategies.

Suppose, for example, that a company in India notices that the interest rate on the Swiss franc is lower than on the rupee. Does this mean that it is "cheaper" to borrow Swiss francs? Before jumping to that conclusion, you need to ask *why* the Swiss interest rate is so low. Unless the Swiss government is deliberately holding the rate down by restrictions on the export of capital, you should suspect that the real cost of capital is roughly the same in Switzerland as anywhere else. The nominal interest rate is low only because investors expect a low domestic rate of inflation and a strong currency. Therefore, the advantage of the low rate of interest is likely to be offset by the additional rupees required to buy the Swiss francs required to pay off the loan.

You cannot reliably make a profit simply by borrowing in countries with low nominal rates of interest and you may be taking on considerable currency exposure by doing so. If the currency subsequently appreciates *more* rapidly than investors expect, it could turn out to be very costly to buy the currency that you need to service the loan. In 1989 several Australian banks learned this lesson the hard way. They had induced their clients to borrow at the low Swiss interest rates. When the value of the Swiss franc rose sharply, the banks found themselves sued by irate clients for not having warned them of the risk of a rise in the price of Swiss francs.

28.4 EXCHANGE RISK AND INTERNATIONAL INVESTMENT DECISIONS

Suppose that the Swiss Pharmaceutical, Roche, is evaluating a proposal to build up a new plant in India. To calculate the project's net present value, Roche forecasts the following rupee cash flows from the project:

Cash Flows (Rs. millions)					
C_0	C_1	C_2	C_3	C_4	C_5
−1300	400	450	510	575	650

These cash flows are stated in rupees. So to calculate their net present value, Roche discounts them at the rupee cost of capital. (Remember rupees need to be discounted at a rupee rate, not the Swiss franc rate.) Suppose this cost of capital is 12 percent. Then

$$\text{NPV} = -1300 + \frac{400}{1.12} + \frac{450}{1.12^2} + \frac{510}{1.12^3} + \frac{575}{1.12^4} + \frac{650}{1.12^5} = \text{Rs. 513 million}$$

To convert this net present value to Swiss francs, the manager can simply divide the rupee NPV by the spot rate of exchange. For example, if the spot rate is Rs. 38/SFr, then the NPV in Swiss francs is

$$\text{NPV in francs} = \text{NPV in rupees/ Rs./SFr} = 513/38 = 13.5 \text{ million francs}$$

Notice one important point about this calculation. Roche does not need to forecast whether the rupee is likely to strengthen or weaken against the Swiss franc. No currency forecast is needed, because the company can hedge its foreign exchange exposure. In that case, the decision to accept or reject the pharmaceutical project in India is totally separate from the decision to bet on the outlook for the rupee. For example, it would be foolish for Roche to accept a poor project in India just because management is optimistic about the outlook for the rupee; if Roche wishes to speculate in this way it can simply buy rupees forward. Equally, it would be foolish for Roche to reject a good project just because management is pessimistic about the rupees. The company would do much better to go ahead with the project and sell rupees forward. In that way, it would get the best of both worlds.[22]

When Roche ignores currency risk and discounts the rupee cash flows at a rupee cost of capital, it is implicitly assuming that the currency risk is hedged. Let us check this by calculating the number of Swiss francs that Roche would receive if it hedged the currency risk by selling forward each future rupee cash flow.

We need first to calculate the forward rate of exchange between rupee and francs. This depends on the interest rates in India and Switzerland. For example, suppose that the rupee interest rate is 6 percent and the Swiss franc interest rate is 4 percent. Then interest rate parity theory tells us that the one-year forward exchange rate is

$$s_{Rs./SFr} \times (1 + r_{Rs.}) / (1 + r_{SFr}) = \frac{38 \times 1.06}{1.06} = 38.73$$

Similarly, the two-year forward rate is

$$s_{Rs./SFr} \times (1 + r_{Rs.})^2 / (1 + r_{SFr})^2 = \frac{38 \times 1.06^2}{1.04^2} = 39.47$$

So, if Roche hedges its cash flows against exchange rate risk, the number of Swiss francs it will receive in each year is equal to the rupee cash flow divided by the forward rate of exchange.

Cash Flows (millions of Swiss francs)					
C_0	C_1	C_2	C_3	C_4	C_5
−1300	400	450	510	575	650
−1300/38	400/38.731	450/39.476	510/40.235	575/41.008	650/41.797
=−34.21	=10.33	=11.40	=12.68	=14.02	=15.55

These cash flows are in Swiss francs and therefore they need to be discounted at the risk-adjusted Swiss franc discount rate. Since the Swiss rate of interest is lower than the rupee rate, the risk-adjusted rate must also be correspondingly lower. The formula for converting from the required rupee return to the required Swiss franc return is[23]

$$(1 + \text{Swiss franc return}) = (1 + \text{rupee return}) \times \frac{(1 + \text{Swiss franc interest rate})}{(1 + \text{rupee interest rate})}$$

[22]There is a general point here that is not confined to currency hedging. Whenever you face an investment that appears to have a positive NPV, decide what it is that you are betting on and then think whether there is a more direct way to place the bet. For example, if a copper mine looks profitable only because you are unusually optimistic about the price of copper, then maybe you would do better to buy copper futures or the shares of other copper producers rather than opening a copper mine.

[23]The following example should give you a feel for the idea behind this formula. Suppose the spot rate for Swiss francs is Rs.38/SFr. Interest rate parity tells us that the forward rate must be 38 × 1.06/1.04 = Rs.38.73/SFr. Now suppose that a share costs Rs.100 and will pay an expected Rs.112 at the end of the year. The cost to the Swiss investors of buying the share is 100/38 = SFr2.63. If the Swiss investors sell forward the expected payoff, they will receive an expected 112/38.73 = SFr2.89. The expected return in Swiss francs is 2.89 / 2.63 – 1= 0.099, or 9.99 percent. More simply, the Swiss franc return is 1.12 × 1.04/1.06 –1 = 0.099.

In our example

$$(1 + \text{Swiss franc return}) = 1.12 \times \frac{1.04}{1.06} = 1.099$$

Thus the risk-adjusted discount rate in rupees is 12 percent, but the discount rate in Swiss francs is only 9.9 percent.

All that remains is to discount the Swiss franc cash flows at the 9.9 percent risk-adjusted discount rate:

$$\text{NPV} = -34.21 + \frac{10.33}{1.099} + \frac{11.40}{1.099^2} + \frac{12.68}{1.099^3} + \frac{14.02}{1.099^4} + \frac{15.55}{1.099^5}$$
$$= 13.5 \text{ million francs}$$

Everything checks. We obtain exactly the same net present value by (a) ignoring currency risk and discounting Roche's rupee cash flows at the rupee cost of capital and (b) calculating the cash flows in francs on the assumption that Roche hedges the currency risk and then discounting these Swiss franc cash flows at the franc cost of capital.

To repeat: When deciding whether to invest overseas, separate out the investment decision from the decision to take on currency risk. This means that your views about future exchange rates should NOT enter into the investment decision. The simplest way to calculate the NPV of an overseas investment is to forecast the cash flows in the foreign currency and discount them at the foreign currency cost of capital. The alternative is to calculate the cash flows that you would receive if you hedged the foreign currency risk. In this case you need to translate the foreign currency cash flows into your own currency *using the forward exchange rate* and then discount these domestic currency cash flows at the domestic cost of capital. If the two methods don't give the same answer, you have made a mistake.

When Roche analyzes the proposal to build a plant in India, it is able to ignore the outlook for the rupee *only because it is free to hedge the currency risk.* Because investment in a pharmaceutical plant does not come packaged with an investment in the rupee, the opportunity for firms to hedge allows for better investment decisions.

More about the Cost of Capital

In our discussion of Roche's investment decision we did not explain how Roche estimated the cost of capital for its investment in India. There is no simple agreed-upon procedure for doing this but we suggest that you first estimate the cost of capital in Swiss francs and then convert it to a rupee cost.

We discussed the problem of estimating the required return on overseas investments in Chapter 9. You need to decide how risky an investment in the Indian pharmaceutical business would be to a Swiss investor. For example, a good starting point might be to look at the betas of a sample of Indian pharmaceutical companies *relative to the Swiss market index.*[24]

Suppose that you decide that the investment's beta relative to the Swiss market is .7 and that the market risk premium in Switzerland is 8.4 percent. Then the required return on the project can be estimated as

[24]We pointed out in Chapter 9 that when we use the beta relative to the Indian index to estimate the returns required by Indian investors, we are assuming that the Indian market index is an efficient portfolio for these investors. Similarly, when we use the beta relative to the Swiss index to estimate the returns that Swiss investors require, we are assuming that the Swiss market index is an efficient portfolio for these investors. Investors do invest largely, but not exclusively, in their home markets.

$$\text{Required return} = \text{Swiss interest rate} + (\text{beta} \times \text{Swiss market risk premium})$$
$$= 4 + (.7 \times 8.4) = 9.9\%$$

This is the project's cost of capital measured in Swiss francs. We used it above to discount the expected *Swiss franc* cash flows if Roche hedged the project against currency risk. We cannot use it to discount the *rupee* cash flows from the project.

To discount the expected *rupee* cash flows, we need to convert the Swiss franc cost of capital to a rupee cost of capital. This means running our earlier calculation in reverse:

$$(1 + \text{rupee return}) = (1 + \text{Swiss franc return}) \times \frac{(1 + \text{rupee interest rate})}{(1 + \text{Swiss franc interest rate})}$$

In our example,

$$(1 + \text{rupee return}) = 1.099 \times \frac{1.06}{1.04} = 1.12$$

We used this 12 percent rupee cost of capital to discount the forecasted rupee cash flows from the project.

28.5 POLITICAL RISK

So far we have focused on the management of exchange rate risk, but managers also worry about political risk. By this they mean the threat that a government will change the rules of the game—that is, break a promise or understanding—*after* the investment is made. Of course political risks are not confined to overseas investments. Businesses in every country are exposed to the risk of unanticipated actions by governments or the courts. But in some parts of the world foreign companies are particularly vulnerable.

A number of consultancy services offer analyses of political and economic risks and draw up country rankings.[25] For example, Table 28.3 is an extract from the 2003 political risk rankings provided by the PRS Group. You can see that each country is scored on 12 separate dimensions. Luxembourg comes top of the class overall, while Somalia languishes at the bottom.

Some managers dismiss political risk as an act of God, like a hurricane or earthquake. But the most successful multinational companies structure their business to reduce political risk. Foreign governments are not likely to expropriate a local business if it cannot operate without the support of its parent. For example, the foreign subsidiaries of American computer manufacturers or pharmaceutical companies would have relatively little value if they were cut off from the know-how of their parents. Such operations are much less likely to be expropriated than, say, a mining operation that can be operated as a stand-alone venture.

We are not recommending that you turn your silver mine into a pharmaceutical company, but you may be able to plan your overseas manufacturing operations to improve your bargaining position with foreign governments. For example, Ford has integrated its overseas operations so that the manufacture of components, subassemblies, and complete automobiles is spread across plants in a number of

[25]For a discussion of these services see C. Erb, C. R. Harvey, and T. Viskanta, "Political Risk, Financial Risk, and Economic Risk," *Financial Analysts Journal* 52 (1996), pp. 28–46. Campbell Harvey's Web page (**www.duke.edu/~charvey**) is also a useful source of information on political risk.

	A	B	C	D	E	F	G	H	I	J	K	L	Total
Maximum score	12	12	12	12	12	6	6	6	6	6	6	4	100
Luxembourg	11	11	12	12	12	5	6	6	6	5	5	4	95
Netherlands	9	11	12	11	12	5	6	5	6	5	6	4	91
Singapore	11	9	12	11	12	5	6	5	5	6	2	4	87
U.K.	9	10	12	10	9	5	6	6	6	4	6	4	86
Japan	11	8	12	12	10	4	6	6	5	6	5	4	86
Germany	9	8	12	11	10	5	6	6	5	4	5	4	83
United States	11	8	12	11	8	4	5	5	5	5	6	4	81
Italy	9	9	12	11	11	3	6	4	3	5	4	3	78
China	11	7	8	12	11	2	3	5	5	5	1	2	71
Brazil	9	6	8	11	11	4	4	6	2	3	5	2	69
Russia	12	7	9	9	10	2	5	6	4	2	4	1	68
India	9	4	9	8	9	2	4	1	4	2	6	3	59
Indonesia	9	4	6	8	11	1	3	1	2	2	4	2	52
Somalia	5	1	3	5	4	1	1	3	2	2	1	0	27

TABLE 28.3

Political risk scores for a sample of countries, 2003.

Key:
A Government stability
B Socioeconomic conditions
C Investment profile
D Internal conflict
E External conflict
F Corruption
G Military in politics
H Religious tensions
I Law and order
J Ethnic tensions
K Democratic accountability
L Bureaucracy quality

Source: International Country Risk Guide, a publication of the PRS Group (www.prsgroup.com), 2004.

countries. None of these plants would have much value on its own, and Ford can switch production between plants if the political climate in one country deteriorates.

Multinational corporations have also devised financing arrangements to help keep foreign governments honest. For example, suppose your firm is contemplating an investment of $500 million to reopen the San Tomé silver mine in Costaguana with modern machinery, smelting equipment, and shipping facilities.[26] The Costaguanan government agrees to invest in roads and other infrastructure and to take 20 percent of the silver produced by the mine in lieu of taxes. The agreement is to run for 25 years.

The project's NPV on these assumptions is quite attractive. But what happens if a new government comes into power five years from now and imposes a 50 percent tax on "any precious metals exported from the Republic of Costaguana"? Or changes the government's share of output from 20 to 50 percent? Or simply takes over the mine "with fair compensation to be determined in due course by the Minister of Natural Resources of the Republic of Costaguana"?

No contract can absolutely restrain sovereign power. But you can arrange project financing to make these acts as painful as possible for the foreign government. For example, you might set up the mine as a subsidiary corporation, which then borrows a large fraction of the required investment from a consortium of major international banks. If your firm guarantees the loan, make sure the guarantee stands only if the Costaguanan government honors its contract. The government will be reluctant to break the contract if that causes a default on the loans and undercuts the country's credit standing with the international banking system.

[26]The early history of the San Tomé mine is described in Joseph Conrad's *Nostromo*.

If possible, you should arrange for the World Bank (or one of its affiliates) to finance part of the project or to guarantee your loans against political risk.[27] Few governments have the guts to take on the World Bank. Here is another variation on the same theme. Arrange to borrow, say, $450 million through the Costaguanan Development Agency. In other words, the development agency borrows in international capital markets and relends to the San Tomé mine. Your firm agrees to stand behind the loan as long as the government keeps its promises. If it does keep them, the loan is your liability. If not, the loan is *its* liability.

Political risk is not confined to the risk of expropriation. Multinational companies are always exposed to the criticism that they siphon funds out of countries in which they do business, and, therefore, governments are tempted to limit their freedom to repatriate profits. This is most likely to happen when there is considerable uncertainty about the rate of exchange, which is usually when you would most like to get your money out. Here again a little forethought can help. For example, there are often more onerous restrictions on the payment of dividends to the parent than on the payment of interest or principal on debt. Royalty payments and management fees are less sensitive than dividends, particularly if they are levied equally on all foreign operations. A company can also, within limits, alter the price of goods that are bought or sold within the group, and it can require more or less prompt payment for such goods.

[27] In Section 25.7 we described how the World Bank provided the Hubco power project with a guarantee against political risk.

SUMMARY

The international financial manager has to cope with different currencies, interest rates, and inflation rates. To produce order out of chaos, the manager needs some model of how they are related. We described four very simple but useful theories.

Interest rate parity theory states that the interest differential between two countries must be equal to the difference between the forward and spot exchange rates. In the international markets, arbitrage ensures that parity almost always holds. There are two ways to hedge against exchange risk: One is to take out forward cover; the other is to borrow or lend abroad. Interest rate parity tells us that the costs of the two methods should be the same.

The expectations theory of exchange rates tells us that the forward rate equals the expected spot rate. In practice forward rates seem to incorporate a risk premium, but this premium is about equally likely to be negative as positive.

In its strict form, purchasing power parity states that $1 must have the same purchasing power in every country. That doesn't square well with the facts, for differences in inflation rates are not perfectly related to changes in exchange rates. This means that there may be some genuine exchange risks in doing business overseas. On the other hand, the difference in inflation rates is just as likely to be above as below the change in the exchange rate.

Finally, we saw that in an integrated world capital market real rates of interest would have to be the same. In practice government regulation and taxes can cause differences in real interest rates. But do not simply borrow where interest rates are lowest. Those countries are also likely to have the lowest inflation rates and the strongest currencies.

With these precepts in mind we showed how you can use forward markets or the loan markets to hedge transactions exposure, which arises from delays in foreign currency payments and receipts. But the company's financing choices also need to reflect the impact of a change in the exchange rate on the value of the entire business. This is known as economic exposure. Companies protect themselves against economic exposure either by hedging in the financial markets or by building plants overseas.

Because companies can hedge their currency risk, the decision to invest overseas does not involve currency forecasts. There are two ways for a company to calculate the NPV of an overseas project. The first is to forecast the foreign currency cash flows and to discount them at the foreign currency cost of capital. The second is to translate the foreign currency cash flows into domestic currency assuming that they are hedged against exchange rate risk. These domestic currency flows can then be discounted at the domestic cost of capital. The answers should be identical.

In addition to currency risk, overseas operations may be exposed to extra political risk. However, firms may be able to structure the financing to reduce the chances that government will change the rules of the game.

FURTHER READING

There are a number of useful textbooks in international finance. Here is a small selection:

D. K. Eiteman and A. I. Stonehill, *Multinational Business Finance*, 10th ed., (Reading, MA: Pearson Addison Wesley, 2003).

J. O. Grabbe, *International Financial Markets*, 3rd ed. (Englewood Cliffs, NJ: Prentice-Hall, Inc., 1995).

P. Sercu and R. Uppal, *International Financial Markets and the Firm*, (Cincinnati, OH: South-Western College Publishing, 1995).

A. C. Shapiro, *Multinational Financial Management*, 7th ed. (New York: John Wiley & Sons, 2002).

Here are some general discussions of international investment decisions and associated exchange risks:

D. R. Lessard, "Global Competition and Corporate Finance in the 1990s," *Journal of Applied Corporate Finance* 3 (Winter 1991), pp. 59–72.

M. D. Levi and P. Sercu, "Erroneous and Valid Reasons for Hedging Foreign Exchange Exposure," *Journal of Multinational Financial Management* 1 (1991), pp. 25–37.

A. C. Shapiro, "International Capital Budgeting," *Midland Corporate Finance Journal* 1 (Spring 1983), pp. 26–45.

Listed below are a few of the articles on the relationship between interest rates, exchange rates, and inflation:

Forward and spot exchange rates

M. D. Evans and K. K. Lewis, "Do Long-Term Swings in the Dollar Affect Estimates of the Risk Premia?" *Review of Financial Studies* 8 (1995), pp. 709–742.

E. F. Fama, "Forward and Spot Exchange Rates," *Journal of Monetary Economics* 14 (1984), pp. 319–338.

Interest-rate parity

K. Clinton, "Transaction Costs and Covered Interest Arbitrage: Theory and Evidence," *Journal of Political Economy* 96 (April 1988), pp. 358–370.

Purchasing power parity

K. Froot and K. Rogoff, "Perspectives on PPP and Long-run Real Exchange Rates," in G. Grossman and K. Rogoff (eds.), *Handbook of International Economics* (Amsterdam: North-Holland Publishing Company, 1995).

K. Rogoff, "The Purchasing Power Parity Puzzle," *Review of Economic Literature* 34 (June 1996), pp. 667–668.

WEB EXERCISE

1. The site **www.globalfindata.com** contains some excellent sample long-term data, including exchange rate and consumer price data for Australia, Canada, and Japan. Construct a chart similar to Figure 28.3 showing the nominal and real exchange rates for one of these countries against the U.S. dollar for the past century. (Warning: Check whether the exchange rates are direct or indirect quotes.) Has the country with the higher inflation had the weaker currency? Which is more stable—the nominal exchange rate or the real rate? (You will find that the answer is not always as clear-cut as in the case of sterling.)

CONCEPT REVIEW QUESTIONS

1. Explain the difference between a direct exchange rate quote and an indirect quote. (page 757)
2. Explain the difference between a spot exchange rate and a forward rate. If you buy pesos one-month forward, do you pay for them now or in one month? (page 758)
3. Explain purchasing power parity theory. If inflation is higher in India than in the UAE, would you expect each Indian rupee to buy more or fewer Dirham than in the past? (pages 762–763)

For additional Concept Review Questions, please visit us at www.mhhe.com/bmam8e or refer to your Student CD.

QUIZ

1. Look at Table 28.1.
   a. How many Singapore dollars do you get for your rupee?
   b. What is the one-month forward rate for Singapore dollar?
   c. Is the Singapore dollar at a forward discount or premium on the rupee?
   d. Use the six-month forward rate to calculate the six-month percentage discount or premium on Singapore dollar.
   e. If the six-month interest rate on rupees is 3.5 percent (about 7 percent per annum), what do you think is the six-month interest rate on Singapore dollar?
   f. According to the expectations theory, what is the expected spot rate for Singapore dollar in three months' time?
   g. According to the law of one price, then what is the expected difference in the three-month rate of price inflation in India and Singapore?
2. Define each of the following theories in a sentence or simple equation:
   a. Interest rate parity theory.
   b. Expectations theory of forward rates.
   c. Purchasing power parity.
   d. International capital market equilibrium (relationship of real and nominal interest rates in different countries).
3. In March 2004 the exchange rate between U.S. dollar and Indian rupee was Rs. 45.0179/$. Inflation in the year to March 2005 was about 4.78 percent in India and 2 percent in the United States.
   a. If purchasing power parity held, what should have been the nominal exchange rate in March 2005?
   b. The actual exchange rate in March 2005 was Rs. 43.6905/$. What was the change in the *real* exchange rate?
4. The following table shows interest rates and exchange rates for the U.S. dollar and the Philippine peso. The spot exchange rate is 56.46 pesos = $1. Complete the missing entries:

	1 Month	3 Months	1 Year
Dollar interest rate (annually compounded)	1.0	1.0	?
Peso interest rate (annually compounded)	9.42	?	9.32
Forward pesos per dollar	?	?	60.988
Forward premium on peso (% per year)	?	−7.98	?

5. An importer in India is due to take delivery of clothing from Mexico in six months. The price is fixed in Mexican pesos. Which of the following transactions could eliminate the importer's exchange risk?
   a. Sell six-month call options on pesos.
   b. Buy pesos forward.
   c. Sell pesos forward.
   d. Sell pesos in the currency futures market.
   e. Borrow pesos; buy rupees at the spot exchange rate.
   f. Sell pesos at the spot exchange rate; lend rupees.
6. An Indian company has committed to pay 10 million Australian dollars to an Australian company. What is the cost (in present value) of covering this liability by buying AUD forward? The Australian interest rate is 6.25 percent, and exchange rates are as shown in Table 28.1. Briefly explain.
7. A firm in the United States is due to receive payment of €1 million in eight years' time. It would like to protect itself against a decline in the value of the euro, but finds it difficult to get forward cover for such a long period. Is there any other way in which it can protect itself?
8. Suppose that two year interest rates are 7 percent in India and 0.06 percent in Japan. The spot exchange rate is Rs. 40/100 Yens. Suppose that one year later interest rates are 5 percent in both countries, while the value of yen has appreciated to Rs. 45/100 yens.
   a. Sanjay Dutta from Mumbai invested in an Indian two-year zero-coupon bond at the start of the period and sold it after one year. What was his return?
   b. Madame Butterfly from Tokyo bought some rupees. She also invested in the two-year Indian zero-coupon bond and sold it after one year. What was her return in yen?
   c. Suppose that Ms. Butterfly had correctly forecasted the price at which she sold her bond and that she hedged her investment against currency risk. How could she have done so? What would have been her return in yen?
9. It is the year 2006 and Indian Pork Barrel Company is considering construction of a new barrel plant in Spain. The forecasted cash flows in millions of euros are as follows:

C_0	C_1	C_2	C_3	C_4	C_5
−80	+10	+20	+23	+27	+25

   The spot exchange rate is Rs. 60 = €1. The interest rate in India is 7 percent and the euro interest rate is 6 percent. You can assume that pork barrel production is effectively risk-free.

   a. Calculate the NPV of the euro cash flows from the project. What is the NPV in rupees?
   b. What are the rupee cash flows from the project if the company hedges against exchange rate changes?
   c. Suppose that the company expects the euro to depreciate by 5 percent a year. How does this affect the value of the project?

PRACTICE QUESTIONS

1. Look at the foreign exchange table in a recent issue of *The Economic Times* or *The Business Line*. (You may like to visit the website of *The Business Line* at http://www.hinduonnet.com/businessline/banking/crcr-rate/exch.htm to get the quotes of foreign exchange for the previous day.)

   a. How many U.S. dollars are worth one Indian rupee today?
   b. Suppose that you arrange today to buy U.S. dollars in 90 days. How many U.S. dollars could you buy for each Indian rupee?
   c. If forward rates simply reflect market expectations, what is the likely spot exchange rate for the Hong Kong dollar in 90 days' time?

d. Look at the table of money rates in the same issue. What is the three-month interest rate on Indian rupees?
e. Can you deduce the likely three-month interest rate for the Swiss franc?

2. Table 28.1 shows the 6-month forward rate on Hong Kong dollar.
   a. Is rupee at a forward discount or premium on the Hong Kong dollar?
   b. What is the annual *percentage* discount or premium?
   c. If you have no other information about the two currencies, what is your best guess about the spot rate on the Hong Kong dollar six months hence?
   d. Suppose that you expect to receive 100,000 Hong Kong dollars in six months. How many rupees is this likely to be worth?
3. Look at Table 28.1. If the three-month interest rate on rupees is 2 percent, what do you think is the three-month interest rate on Singapore dollar? Explain what could happen if the rate were substantially above your figure.
4. Look in *The Economic Times* or *The Business Line*. How many Swiss francs can you buy for Rs. 100? How many euros can you buy? What rate do you think a Swiss bank would quote for buying or selling euros? Explain what would happen if it quoted a rate that was substantially above your figure.
5. Ms. Rosetta Stone, the treasurer of International Reprints, Inc., has noticed that the interest rate in Japan is below the rates in most other countries. She is, therefore, suggesting that the company should make an issue of Japanese yen bonds. Does this make sense?
6. Suppose you are the treasurer of Lufthansa, the German international airline. How is company value likely to be affected by exchange rate changes? What policies would you adopt to reduce exchange rate risk?
7. Companies may be affected by changes in the nominal exchange rate or in the real exchange rate. Explain how this can occur. Which risks are easiest to hedge against?
8. A Ford dealer in the United States may be exposed to a devaluation of the yen if this leads to a cut in the price of Japanese cars. Suppose that the dealer estimates that a 1 percent decline in the value of the yen would result in a permanent decline of 5 percent in the dealer's profits. How should she hedge against this risk, and how should she calculate the size of the hedge position? You may find it helpful to refer back to Section 27.5.
9. You have bid for a possible export order that would provide a cash inflow of €1 million in six months. The spot exchange rate is Rs. 60 = €1 and the six-month forward rate is Rs. 61 = €1. There are two sources of uncertainty: (1) the euro could appreciate or depreciate and (2) you may or may not receive the export order. Illustrate in each case the final payoffs if (a) you sell one million euros forward, and (b) you buy a six-month option to sell euros with an exercise price of Rs. 60/€1.
10. In August 2006, an American investor buys 1,000 shares in an Indian company at a price of Rs. 500 each. The share does not pay any dividend. A year later she sells the shares for Rs. 550 each. The exchange rates when she buys the stock are shown in Table 28.1. Suppose that the exchange rate at the time of sale is Rs. 48/$.
    a. How many dollars does she invest?
    b. What is her total return in Indian rupees? In dollars?
    c. Do you think that she has made an exchange rate profit or loss? Explain.
11. Table 28.4 shows the annual interest rate (annually compounded) and exchange rates against the dollar for different currencies. Are there any arbitrage opportunities? If so, how would you secure a positive cash flow today, while zeroing out all future cash flows?
12. "Last year we had a substantial income in sterling, which we hedged by selling sterling forward. In the event sterling rose, and our decision to sell forward cost us a lot of money. I think that in the future we should either stop hedging our currency exposure or just hedge when we think sterling is overvalued." As financial manager, how would you respond to your chief executive's comment?

TABLE 28.4

Interest rates and exchange rates.

*Number of units of foreign currency that can be exchanged for $1.

	Interest Rate (%)	Spot Exchange Rate	1-Year Forward Exchange Rate*
United States (dollar)	3	—	—
Costaguana (pulga)	23	10,000	11,942
Westonia (ruple)	5	2.6	2.65
Gloccamorra (pint)	8	17.1	18.2
Anglosaxophonia (wasp)	4.1	2.3	2.28

eXcel

Please visit us at www.mhhe.com/bmam8e or refer to your Student CD.

13. Carpet Baggers, Inc., of the US is proposing to construct a new bagging plant in a country in Europe. The two prime candidates are Germany and Switzerland. The forecasted cash flows from the proposed plants are as follows:

	C_0	C_1	C_2	C_3	C_4	C_5	C_6	IRR (%)
Germany (millions of euros)	−60	+10	+15	+15	+20	+20	+20	18.8
Switzerland (millions of Swiss francs)	−120	+20	+30	+30	+35	+35	+35	12.8

The spot exchange rate for euros is $1.3/€, while the rate for Swiss francs is SFr 1.5/$. The interest rate is 5 percent in the United States, 4 percent in Switzerland, and 6 percent in the euro countries. The financial manager has suggested that, if the cash flows were stated in dollars, a return in excess of 10 percent would be acceptable.

Should the company go ahead with either project? If it must choose between them, which should it take?

CHALLENGE QUESTIONS

1. If investors recognize the impact of inflation and exchange rate changes on a firm's cash flows, changes in exchange rates should be reflected in stock prices. How would the stock price of each of the following Swiss companies be affected by an unanticipated appreciation of the Swiss franc of 10 percent? Assume that only 2 percent of the appreciation can be attributed to increased inflation in the rest of the world (relative to the Swiss inflation rate).
   a. *A Swiss airline:* More than two-thirds of its employees are Swiss. Most revenues come from international fares set in U.S. dollars.
   b. *Nestlé:* Fewer than 5 percent of its employees are Swiss. Most revenues are derived from sales of consumer goods in a wide range of countries with competition from local producers.
   c. *UBS:* Forty percent of the employees work in Switzerland. The bank's Group Treasury periodically hedges any non-Swiss franc monetary positions.
2. Alpha and Omega are Indian corporations. Alpha has a plant in Dubai that imports components from India, assembles them, and then sells the finished products in Thailand. Omega is at the opposite extreme. It also has a plant in Dubai, but it buys raw material in Thailand and exports its output back to India. How is each firm likely to be affected by a fall in the value of Dirham? How could each firm hedge itself against exchange risk?

MINI-CASE

Exacta, s.a.

Exacta, s.a., is a major French producer, based in Lyons, of precision machine tools. About two-thirds of its output is exported. The majority of these sales is within the European Union. However, the company also has a thriving business in the United States, despite strong competition from several U.S. firms. Exacta usually receives payment for exported goods within two months of the invoice date, so that at any point in time only about one-sixth of annual exports to the United States is exposed to currency risk.

The company believes that its North American business is now large enough to justify a local manufacturing operation, and it has recently decided to establish a plant in South Carolina. Most of the output from this plant will be sold in the United States, but the company believes that there should also be opportunities for future sales in Canada and Mexico.

The South Carolina plant will involve a total investment of $380 million and is expected to be in operation by the year 2006. Annual revenues from the plant are expected to be about $420 million and the company forecasts net profits of $52 million a year. Once the plant is up and running, it should be able to operate for several years without substantial additional investment.

Although there is widespread enthusiasm for the project, several members of the management team have expressed anxiety about possible currency risk. M. Pangloss, the finance director, reassured them that the company was not a stranger to currency risk; after all, the company is already exporting about $320 million of machine tools each year to the United States and has managed to exchange its dollar revenue for euros without any major losses. But not everybody was convinced by this argument. For example, the CEO, M. B. Bardot, pointed out that the $380 million to be invested would substantially increase the amount of money at risk if the dollar fell relative to the euro. M. Bardot was notoriously risk-averse on financial matters and would push for complete hedging if practical.

M. Pangloss attempted to reassure the CEO. At the same time, he secretly shared some of the anxieties about exchange rate risk. Nearly all the revenues from the South Carolina plant would be in U.S. dollars and the bulk of the $380 million investment would likewise be incurred in the United States. About two-thirds of the operating costs would be in dollars, but the remaining one-third would represent payment for components brought in from Lyons plus the charge by head office for management services and use of patents. The company has yet to decide whether to invoice its U.S. operation in dollars or euros for these purchases from the parent company.

M. Pangloss is optimistic that the company can hedge itself against currency risk. His favored solution is for Exacta to finance the plant by a $380 million issue of dollar bonds. That way the dollar investment would be offset by a matching dollar liability. An alternative is for the company to sell forward at the beginning of each year the expected revenues from the U.S. plant. But he realizes from experience that these simple solutions might carry hidden dangers. He decides to slow down and think more systematically about the additional exchange risk from the U.S. operation.

QUESTIONS

1. What would Exacta's true exposure be from its new U.S. operations, and how would it change from the company's current exposure?
2. Given that exposure, what would be the most effective and inexpensive approach to hedging?

PART NINE RELATED WEB SITES

For an introductory guide to understanding financial statements see:

www.ibm.com/investor/financialguide

For financial ratios see:

www.jaxworks.com (simple illustrations of the calculation and interpretation of some common financial ratios)

edgarscan.pwcglobal.com (A very nice site that calculates company financial ratios. Use the Benchmarking Assistant to compare ratios across years and companies.)

For easy access to annual reports see:

www.reportgallery.com

www.prars.com (to order hard copies of annual reports)

Downloadable software for short- and long-term financial planning is available on:

www.crystalball.com

www.jaxworks.com (has a number of simple spreadsheets for financial planning)

www.toolkit.cch.com (another site with simple spreadsheets for financial planning)

The Web sites of the Bank of International Settlements and the central banks provide material on payment systems:

www.bis.org

www.federalreserve.gov

www.ecb.int (for material on the European Central Bank's "Target" payments system)

The Web sites of most major banks provide information on cash management services. See, for example:

www.bankone.com

www.bankofamerica.com

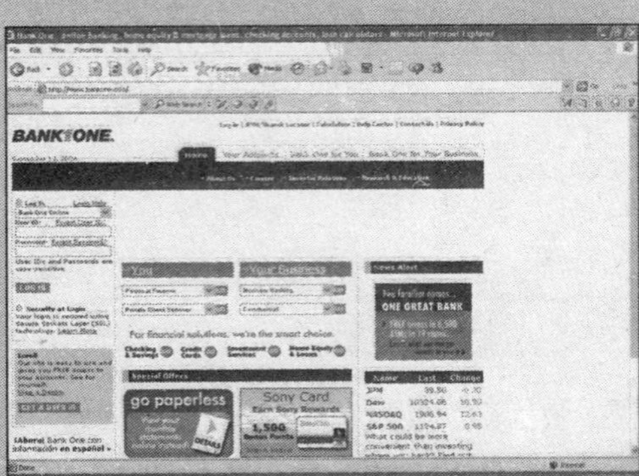

Other sites dealing with cash management include:

www.directpayment.org

www.nacha.org (material on electronic payments)

www.phoenixhecht.com (a comprehensive Web site on cash management with useful links)

GE's Web site contains information on sources and costs of short-term finance:

www.gecfosolutions.com

Central bank Web sites, such as those for the Federal Reserve and regional Feds, are generally good sources of reference for short-term interest rates:

www.federalreserve.gov (also contains results of the quarterly survey of the terms of business lending by banks)

www.ny.frb.org

www.stls.frb.org

www.oecd.org (the OECD Web site contains interest rate series for different countries)

Dun and Bradstreet and the three main credit-reporting agencies have useful Web sites:

www.dnb.com (examples of Dun and Bradstreet credit reports, articles on credit management, and an introductory guide to understanding financial statements)

www.equifax.com

www.experian.com

www.transunion.com

Fair Isaac Corporation is the leading provider of credit scoring for consumers. See:

www.fairisaac.com

www.myfico.com

finance.yahoo.com (Yahoo's credit analyzer allows you to estimate your personal credit rating)

Some other sources concerned with credit management:

www.creditworthy.com

www.nacm.org (includes links to sites on credit-related issues)

www.ftc.gov/bcp/conline/pubs/credit/scoring.htm (a guide to credit scoring)

PART [9]

FINANCIAL PLANNING AND THE MANAGEMENT OF WORKING CAPITAL

IN 1994 39-YEAR-OLD JEAN-MARIE MESSIER became CEO of the French company Generale des Eaux. He immediately set out to transform it from a sleepy water and sewage business into a multinational media and telecommunications group. The company, now renamed Vivendi, entered into a series of major acquisitions, including a $42 billion purchase of Seagram, owner of Universal Studios. To finance its expansion Vivendi increased its borrowing to $35 billion, and it increased its leverage further by repurchasing 104 million shares for $6.3 billion. Confident that its share price would rise, the company raised the stakes even more by selling a large number of put options on its own stock.

Vivendi's strategy made it very vulnerable to any decline in operating cash flow. As profits began to evaporate, the company faced a severe cash shortage. Its banks were reluctant to extend further credit and its bonds were downgraded to junk status. By July 2002 the share price had fallen to less than 10 percent of its level two years earlier. With the company facing imminent bankruptcy, M. Messier was ousted and the new management set about slashing costs and selling assets to reduce the debt burden.[1]

Vivendi's problems were exacerbated by considerable waste and ostentatious extravagance, but its brush with bankruptcy was a result of a lack of financial planning. The company's goals for growth were unsustainable and it had few options for surviving a decline in operating cash flow. Part 9 shows how firms can check that their growth strategy is consistent with their financing plans. Chapter 29 explains how managers monitor the company's financial health and develop long-term financial plans. Chapters 30 and 31 turn to short-term planning, first looking at the management of short-term assets and then at the construction of the cash budget.

[1]The rise and fall of Vivendi is chronicled in J. Johnson and M. Orange, *The Man Who Tried to Buy the World: Jean-Marie Messier and Vivendi Universal* (Portfolio, 2003).

CHAPTER [29]

FINANCIAL ANALYSIS AND PLANNING

A CAMEL LOOKS like an animal designed by a committee. If a firm made all its financial decisions piecemeal, it would end up with a financial camel. Therefore, smart financial managers consider the overall effect of financing and investment decisions and ensure that they have the financial strategies in place to support the firm's plans for future growth.

Knowing where you stand today is a necessary prelude to contemplating where you might be in the future. Therefore we start the chapter with a brief review of a company's financial statements and we show how you can use these statements to assess the firm's overall performance and its current financial standing.

To produce order out of chaos, financial analysts calculate a few key financial ratios that summarize the company's financial strengths and weaknesses. These ratios are no substitute for a crystal ball, but they do help you to ask the right questions. For example, when the firm needs a loan from the bank, the financial manager can expect some searching questions about the firm's debt ratio and the proportion of profits that is absorbed by interest. Likewise, financial ratios may alert senior management to potential problem areas. If a division is earning a low rate of return on its capital or its profit margins are under pressure, you can be sure that management will demand an explanation.

Growing firms need to invest in working capital, plant and equipment, product development, and so on. All this requires cash. We will, therefore, explain how firms use financial planning models to help them understand the financial implications of their business plans and to explore the consequences of alternative financial strategies.

Our focus in this chapter is on the long-term future. For example, firms may have a planning horizon of 5 or 10 years. In Chapter 31 we will look at how firms also develop more detailed strategies to ensure that they can get safely through the next few months.

29.1 FINANCIAL STATEMENTS

Public companies have a variety of stakeholders, such as shareholders, bondholders, bankers, suppliers, employees, and management. All these stakeholders need to monitor the firm and to ensure that their interests are being served. They rely on the company's financial statements to provide the necessary information.

When reviewing a company's financial statements, it is important to remember that accountants still have a fair degree of leeway in reporting earnings and book values. For example, accountants have discretion in the way they treat intangible assets, such as patents or franchises. Some believe that including these items on the balance sheet provides the best measure of the company's value as a going concern. Others take a more conservative approach and exclude intangible assets. They reason that, if the firm were liquidated, these assets would be largely valueless.

Although accountants around the world are working toward common practices, there are considerable variations in the accounting rules of different countries. In Anglo-Saxon countries such as the United States or the U.K. which have large and active equity markets, the rules have been designed with the shareholder very much in mind. By contrast, in Germany the focus of accounting standards is to verify that the creditors are properly protected.

Ray Ball has pointed out that differences between German and U.S. practice also arise because "German laws and institutional arrangements closely link German corporations' reported earnings to their dividend payments and to bonuses paid to managers and employees alike. The economic role of reported earnings is analogous to an annually-baked pie that is divided among the important stakeholders (government, employees, shareholders and managers alike), the size of the pie having first been determined with prudential regard for the financial stability of the corporation.... Reporting a loss would eliminate bonus, dividend and tax distributions, to the chagrin of all the stakeholders."[2]

Another difference is the way that taxes are shown in the income statement. For example, in Germany taxes are paid on the published profits and the depreciation method must therefore be approved by the revenue service. That is not so in countries like India, US and UK where the numbers shown in the published accounts are generally *not* the basis for calculating the company's tax payments. For instance, the depreciation method used to calculate the published profits may differ from the depreciation method used by the tax authorities.

Sometimes the effect of these differences in accounting rules can be substantial. When the German car manufacturer, Daimler-Benz, decided to list its shares on the New York Stock Exchange in 1993, it was required to revise its accounting practices to conform to U.S. standards. While it reported a modest profit in the first half of 1993 using German accounting rules, it reported a loss of $592 million under U.S. rules, primarily because of differences in the treatment of reserves.

For investors and multinational companies these variations in accounting rules can be irksome. Accounting bodies have therefore been getting together to see whether they can iron out some of the differences. It is not a simple task as the nearby box illustrates.

29.2 ACC'S FINANCIAL STATEMENTS

Your task is to assess the financial standing of ACC Limited, the cement company from India. Perhaps you are a financial analyst with ACC and are helping to develop a five-year financial plan. Perhaps you are employed by a rival company that is contemplating a takeover bid for ACC. Or perhaps you are a banker who needs to assess whether the bank should lend to the company. In each case your first step is to assess the company's current condition. You have before you the latest balance sheet, profit and loss account, and sources and uses of funds.

The Balance Sheet

ACC's balance sheet in Table 29.1 provides a snapshot of the company's assets and the sources of money used to buy those assets.

We show the items in the balance sheet in declining order of liquidity. For example, we first list those assets which are most likely to be turned into cash in the near future. They include cash itself, receivables (or sundry debtors), and inventories of raw materials, work in process, and finished goods. These assets are all known as *current* assets.

The remaining assets on the balance sheet consist of long-term assets such as land, building, plant, machinery, investments in shares, debentures, etc. The balance sheet does not show up-to-date market values of the fixed assets. Instead, the accountant records the amount that each asset

[2]See R. J. Ball, "Daimler-Benz (DaimlerChrysler) AG: Evolution of Corporate Governance from a Code-law 'Stakeholder' to a Common-law 'Shareholder Value' System," Graduate School of Business, University of Chicago.

FINANCE IN THE NEWS

A GLOBAL SET OF ACCOUNTING STANDARDS: THE SEARCH FOR THE HOLY GRAIL

While there remain substantial differences between accounting standards in different countries, accounting bodies have for some time been working together to narrow the gap between their regimes. The ultimate goal is to create one set of global accounting standards. Doing so, they say, will boost cross-border investment, deepen international capital markets and save multinational companies, who must currently report under multiple systems, a lot of time and money.

In December 2003 the Financial Accounting Standards Board (FASB) proposed changes intended to bring American rules nearer to international norms. Two days later, the International Accounting Standards Board (IASB) presented rules that would bring accounting for derivatives in line with American practice.

However, businesspeople and politicians are less happy than the standard-setters might have hoped. In America, business groups are already grumbling about at least one of the FASB's four proposals. This would require firms to restate prior years' earnings after any accounting changes, rather than permit just a one-off (i.e., cumulative) adjustment as they do now. Businesses say that, in the wake of the big accounting scams at Enron and WorldCom, investors are wary of any earnings restatements, even innocent ones.

But the big fight in America is likely to break out early next year, when the FASB is to reopen the debate over stock options, which are treated as an expense in Europe but not (yet) in America. The last time this battle was fought, in 1993, the FASB backed down after some lawmakers, pushed by deep-pocketed lobbyists for the technology industry, which was a heavy user of stock options for employees, threatened to strip the board of its rule-setting powers.

In Europe, the new accounting rules for derivatives are also controversial. Currently, European firms value derivatives at their original purchase price, which is often close to zero. The new standards would force firms to use the latest market values of these instruments instead, as American and Japanese firms already do. Banks and insurance companies, which are big users of financial instruments, are riled, claiming that the new rules will make their profits intolerably volatile. Political heavyweights such as Jean-Claude Trichet, president of the European Central Bank, and France's president, Jacques Chirac, agree.

Although the European Commission has said that all listed European companies should use the IASB's accounting rules from 2005, the European Parliament has the power to reject any standards not to its liking. So far it has not done so, but there is a chance that politics could stand in the way of new rules.

More worrying, the rules that have been proposed so far are the easier ones. The IASB and FASB have the longer-term intention of tackling trickier accounting issues such as the treatment of mergers and deciding when revenue should be recognised. When these more difficult changes are proposed, the resistance is likely to be even fiercer.

Source: Adapted from "A Move towards Global Accounting Standards Is Proving Controversial," *The Economist*, December 20, 2003, p. 115.

originally cost and deducts a fixed annual amount for depreciation. Indian companies however, report the aggregate market value of company's quoted investments.[3] The balance sheet does not include all the company's assets. Some of the most valuable ones are intangible, such as patents, reputation, a skilled management, and a well-trained labor force. Accountants are generally reluctant to record these assets in the balance sheet unless they can be readily identified and valued.

Now look at the bottom portion of ACC's balance sheet, which shows where the money to buy the assets came from.[4] We start by looking at the liabilities, that is, the money owed by the company. First come those liabilities that need to be paid off in the near future. These current liabilities include

[3]However, while finding the total value of all the assets, companies include only the book value of the investments.

[4] The Indians (following the British tradition) and Americans can never agree whether to keep to the left or to the right. American accountants list liabilities on the right and assets on the left. Of course, it does not matter. In any case, here, we show the balance sheet in a vertical format and first show the assets and then the liabilities.

	A	B	C	D	E	F
1	**Assets**	**Mar-2004**		**Mar-2005**		**Change**
2	Current Assets					
3	Cash and Bank	64.97		57.32		-7.65
4	Receivables	576.18		577.54		+ 1.36
5	Inventory	378.01		542.38		+ 164.37
6	Total current assets	1019.16		1177.24		+ 158.08
7						
8	Investments	375.74		326.69		-49.05
9						
10	Fixed Assets:					
11	Gross Fixed Assets	3899.58		4477.68		+ 578.1
12	*Less* accumulated depreciation	1406.93		1569.46		+ 162.53
13	Net Fixed Assets	2492.65		2908.22		+ 415.57
14						
15	Other assets	77.04		66.23		-10.81
16						
17	Total assets	3964.59		4478.38		+ 513.79
18						
19	**Liabilities and Shareholders' Equity**	**Mar-04**		**Mar-05**		**Change**
20	Current liabilities					
21	Debt due within 1 year	17.24		200		+ 182.76
22	Payables and provisions	851.71		1022.84		+ 171.13
23	Total current liabilities	868.95		1222.84		+ 353.89
24						
25	Long-term debt	1425.48		1309.07		-116.41
26	Other liabilities	316.97		349.28		+ 32.31
27	Shareholders' equity	1353.19		1597.19		+ 244
28						
29	Total liabilities & shareholders' equity	3964.59		4478.38		+ 513.79
30						
31	**Other financial information:**					
32	Market value of equity	4510.63		6434.03		1923.407
33	Average number of shares (crores)	17.72		17.85		0.13
34	Share price (Rs.)	254.55		360.45		105.9

TABLE 29.1

The balance sheet of ACC Limited (figures in Rs. crores).

eXcel

Please visit us at www.mhhe.com/bmam8e or refer to your Student CD

sundry creditors (or accounts payable), provisions. One should include the debts that are due to be repaid within the next year.[5]

The difference between the current assets and current liabilities is known as the *net current assets* or *net working capital* (or simply working capital). It roughly measures the company's potential reservoir of cash. For ACC in 2005

$$\text{Net working capital} = \text{current assets} - \text{current liabilities}$$
$$= 1177.24 - 1222.84 = -\text{ (minus) Rs. } 45.6 \text{ crores}$$

The bottom portion of the balance sheet shows the sources of the cash that was used to acquire the net working capital, investments, and fixed assets. Some of the cash has come from the issue of bonds that will not be paid for many years. After all these long-term liabilities have been paid off, the remaining assets belong to the common stockholders. The company's equity is simply the net working capital, investments, and fixed assets less the long-term liabilities. Part of this equity has

[5]Indian companies, however, include these debts under the head 'Secured and Unsecured Liabilities.'

	A	B
1		Rs. Crores
2	Sales	4548.92
3	Other Income	89.35
4	Total revenue	4638.27
5	Costs	3908.31
6	Depreciation	188.82
7	EBIT	541.14
8	Interest	96.32
9	Tax	66.43
10	Net Income (PAT)	378.39
11	Dividends	142.95
12	Retained Earnings	235.44
13	Earnings per share, rupees	21.20
14	Dividend per share, rupees	8.0

TABLE 29.2

The March 2005 profit and loss account of ACC Limited (figures in Rs. crores)

eXcel

Please visit us at www.mhhe.com/bmam8e or refer to your Student CD.

come from the sale of shares to investors and the remainder has come from earnings that the company has retained and invested on behalf of the shareholders.

Table 29.1 provides some other financial information about ACC. For example, it shows the market value of common stock. It is often helpful to compare the *book value* of the equity (shown in the company's accounts) with the *market value* established in the capital markets.

The Profit and Loss Account

If ACC's balance sheet resembles a snapshot of the firm at a particular point in time, its profit and loss account is like a video. It shows how profitable the firm has been over the past year.

Look at the summary profit and loss account in Table 29.2. You can see that during 2005, ACC sold goods worth Rs. 4548.92 crores and that the total costs of producing and selling these goods were Rs. 3908.31 crores. In addition to these out-of-pocket expenses, ACC also made a deduction of Rs. 188.82 crores for the value of the fixed assets used up in producing the goods. Thus ACC's earnings before interest and taxes (EBIT) were

$$\text{EBIT} = \text{Total revenues} - \text{costs} - \text{depreciation}$$
$$= 4638.27 - 3908.31 - 188.82 = \text{Rs. } 541.14 \text{ crores}$$

Of this sum Rs. 96.32 went to pay the interest on the short- and long-term debt (remember debt interest is paid out of pre-tax income) and a further Rs. 66.43 crores to the government in the form of taxes. The Rs. 378.39 crores that was left out belonged to the shareholders. ACC paid out Rs. 142.95 crores as dividends and dividend tax and reinvested the remaining Rs. 235.44 crores in the business.

Sources and Uses of Funds

Table 29.3 shows where ACC raised funds and how it spent them.[6] Beside each row in the table we have added a brief note on how the figure is calculated. We will explain each item in turn.

[6]Notice that in a *Sources and Uses of Funds* table the different components of net working capital are not separated out. When we discuss short-term planning in Chapter 31, we will show how to draw up a *Sources and Uses of Cash* table, which separates out different items of net working capital.

TABLE 29.3

Sources and uses of funds for ACC, 2005 (figures in Rs. crores)

Please visit us at www.mhhe.com/bmam8e or refer to your Student CD.

	A	B	C
1		Rs. Crores	Notes:
2	Sources:		
3	Profit after tax	378.39	See Table 29.2
4	Depreciation	188.82	See Table 29.2
5	Operating cash flow	567.21	
6	Issues of Other liabilities	32.31	See Table 29.1: 349.28 - 316.97
7	Issues of equity	8.56	See Tables 29.1 and 29.2: 1597.19 - 1353.19 - (378.39 - 142.95)
8	Decrease in Working Capital	195.81	See Table 29.1: -[(1177.24 - 1222.84) - (1019.16 - 868.95)]
9	Sale of Investments	49.05	See Table 29.1: -[326.69 - 375.74]
10	Decrease in other assets	10.81	See Table 29.1: -[66.23 - 77.04]
11			
12	Total Sources	863.75	
13			
14	Uses:		
15			
16	Investment in fixed assets	604.39	See Tables 29.1 and 29.2: 2908.22 - 2492.65 + 188.82
17	Redemption of long-term debt	116.41	See Table 29.1: 1309.07 - 1425.48
18	Dividends	142.95	See Table 29.2
19			
20	Total uses	863.75	

Look at the uses of funds. The money that ACC generates is invested in fixed assets or it is paid out to shareholders as dividends or is it is used to redeem part of the long-term debt. Thus

$$\begin{aligned}\text{Total uses of funds} &= \text{investment in fixed assets}\\ &\quad + \text{redemption of long-term debt}\\ &\quad + \text{dividends paid to shareholders}\end{aligned}$$

Table 29.1 shows that in 2004-05, fixed assets of ACC rose from Rs. 2492.65 crores to Rs. 2908.22 crores (after depreciation of Rs. 188.82 crores), implying a capital expenditure of Rs. 604.39 crores. During the same period, the long-term debt of ACC decreased from Rs. 1425.48 crores to Rs. 1309.07 crores. So ACC redeemed long-term debt of 1425.48 – 1309.07 = Rs. 116.41 crores during the year. Finally, the profit and loss account in Figure 29.2 shows that ACC distributed Rs. 142.95 crores as dividends and dividend distribution tax. Thus in total, ACC invested or paid out as dividends 604.39 + 116.41 + 142.95 = Rs. 863.75 crores.

Where did the funds come from? There are three sources – the cash generated from operations, cash generated from selling of assets and new money raised from investors:

$$\begin{aligned}\text{Total sources of funds} &= \text{operating cash flow} + \text{cash from sale of assets}\\ &\quad + \text{new issues of equity and other liabilities}\end{aligned}$$

The profit and loss account shows that in 2004-05 the company generated Rs. 567.21 crores from operations. This included Rs.188.82 crores of depreciation (remember depreciation is not a cash outflow) and Rs. 378.39 crores of profit after tax. Table 29.1 shows that in 2004-2005 ACC started the year with net working capital of 1019.16 – 868.95 = Rs. 150.21 crores. By the end of the year, it had decreased to 1177.24 – 1222.84 = minus Rs.45.6 crores. So the company liquidated Rs.195.81 crores of working capital in the year. In the year, the company also sold investments of Rs.49.05 crores and other assets of 10.81 crores. This left a deficiency of 863.75 – 567.21 – 195.81 – 49.05 – 10.81 = Rs. 40.87 crores that ACC needed to raise from the capital market. You can see from the balance sheet that

ACC raised Rs. 32.31 crores by the issue of other liabilities (other liabilities increased from Rs. 316.97 crores to Rs. 349.28 crores). ACC also raised the remaining Rs. 8.56 crores by the issue of equity capital. So why does the balance sheet show an increase in equity of 1597.19 – 1353.19 = Rs. 244 crores? The answer is that this increase in equity came from profit the company retained and plowed back on behalf of its shareholders (retained earnings = profit after tax – dividends and dividend tax = 378.39 – 142.95 = Rs. 235.44 crores).

29.3 MEASURING ACC'S FINANCIAL CONDITION

ACC's financial statements provide you with the basic information to assess its current financial standing. However, financial statements typically contain large amounts of data – far more than is contained in the simplified statements for ACC. To condense these data into a convenient form, financial managers generally focus on a few key financial ratios.

Table 29.4 summarizes the key financial ratios for ACC.[7] We will explain how to calculate these ratios and use them to shed light on five questions:

- How much has the company borrowed? Is the amount of debt likely to result in financial distress?
- How liquid is the company? Can it easily lay its hands on cash if needed?
- How productively is the company using its assets? Are there any signs that the assets are not being used efficiently?
- How profitable is the company?
- How highly is the firm valued by investors? Are investors' expectations reasonable?

When you calculate a company's financial ratios, you need some criteria to decide whether they are a cause for concern or a matter for congratulation. Unfortunately, there is no "right" set of financial ratios to which all companies should aspire. Take, for example, the company's capital structure. Debt has both advantages and disadvantages, and, even if there were an optimal level of debt for company A, it would not be appropriate for company B.

When managers review a company's financial position, they often start by comparing the current year's ratios with equivalent figures for earlier years. It is also helpful to look at how the company's financial position measures up to that of other firms in the same industry. Therefore, in Table 29.4 we have compared the financial ratios of ACC with those for the Indian cement industry.[8]

How Much Has ACC Borrowed?

When ACC borrows, it promises to make a series of fixed payments. Because its shareholders get only what is left over after the debt holders have been paid, the debt is said to create *financial leverage*. In extreme cases, if hard times come, a company may be unable to pay its debts.

The company's bankers and bondholders also want to make certain that ACC does not borrow excessively. So, if ACC wishes to take out a new loan, the lenders will scrutinize several measures of whether the company is borrowing too much and will demand that it keep its debt within reasonable bounds. Such borrowing limits are stated in terms of financial ratios.

[7]In addition to the ratios that we describe below, Table 29.4 includes a few other ratios that you may well encounter. Some are simply alternative ways to express the same result; others are variations on a theme.

[8]Financial ratios for different industries can be obtained from the Prowess database of CMIE.

		ACC	Cement Industry[b]
Leverage Ratios:			
Debt ratio	Long-term debt/(long-term debt + equity)	0.45	0.68
Debt ratio (including short-term debt)[a]	(Long-term debt + short-term debt)/(long-term debt + short-term debt + equity)	0.49	0.69
Debt-equity ratio	Long-term debt/equity	0.82	2.13
Times-interest-earned	(EBIT + depreciation)/interest	7.58	3.63
Liquidity Ratios:			
Net-working-capital-to-total assets[a]	(Current asset - current liabilities)/total assets	-0.01	0.04
Current ratio	Current assets/current liabilities	0.96	1.16
Quick ratio	(Cash + receivables + marketable securities)/current liabilities	0.52	0.81
Cash ratio	(Cash + marketable securities)/current liabilities	0.05	0.18
Interval measure[a]	(Cash+marketable securities+receivables)/(costs from operations/365)	56.56	150.55
Efficiency Ratios:			
Sales-to-assets ratio	Sales/average total assets	1.08	0.93
Sales-to-net-working-capital[a]	Sales/average net working capital	86.97	22.16
Days in inventory	Average inventory/(cost of goods sold/365)	55.70	71.74
Inventory turnover[a]	Cost of goods sold/average inventory	6.55	5.09
Average collection period (days)	Average receivables/(sales/365)	46.29	64.35
Receivables turnover[a]	Sales/average receivables	7.89	5.67
Profitability Ratios:			
Net profit margin	(EBIT-taxes)/sales	0.10	0.10
Return on assets (ROA)	(EBIT-taxes)/average total assets	0.11	0.09
Return on equity (ROE)	Earnings available for common stockholders/average equity	0.26	0.19
Payout ratio	Dividend per share/earnings per share	0.38	0.37
Market-Value Ratios:			
Price-earnings ratio (P/E)	Stock price/earnings per share	17.00	31.84
Dividend yield	Dividend per share/stock price	0.02	0.01
Market-to-book ratio	Stock price/book value per share	4.03	3.86

TABLE 29.4

Financial ratios for ACC, 2004-05.

[a]This ratio is an extra bonus not discussed in Section 29.2

[b]Average ratios for 82 Indian cement producing companies on the Prowess database.

Debt Ratio Financial leverage is usually measured by the ratio of long-term debt to total long-term capital. Since long-term lease agreements also commit the firm to a series of fixed payments, it makes sense to include the value of lease obligations with the long-term debt.

For ACC

$$\text{Debt ratio} = \frac{\text{long-term debt}}{\text{long-term debt} + \text{equity}}$$

$$= 1309.07 / (1309.07 + 1597.19) = 0.45$$

Another way to say the same thing is that ACC has a debt-to-equity ratio of 1309.07/1597.19 = 0.82:

$$\text{Debt-equity ratio} = \frac{\text{long-term debt}}{\text{equity}}$$

$$= 1309.07 / 1597.19 = 0.82$$

Notice that this measure makes use of book (i.e., accounting) values rather than market values. The market value of the company finally determines whether the debtholders get their money back, so you might expect analysts to look at the face amount of the debt as a proportion of the total market value of debt and equity. On the other hand, the market value includes the value of intangible assets generated by research and development, advertising, staff training, and so on. These assets are not readily salable, and if the company falls on hard times, their value may disappear altogether. For some purposes, it may be just as good to follow the accountant and ignore these intangible assets. This is what lenders do when they insist that the borrower should not allow the book debt ratio to exceed a specified limit.

Debt ratios are sometimes defined in other ways. For example, analysts may include short-term debt or other obligations such as payables. There is a general point here. There are a variety of ways to define most financial ratios and there is no law stating how they *should* be defined. So be warned: Don't accept a ratio at face value without understanding how it has been calculated.

Times-Interest-Earned (or Interest Cover) Another measure of financial leverage is the extent to which interest is covered by earnings before interest and taxes (EBIT) plus depreciation. For ACC,[9]

$$\text{Times-interest-earned} = \frac{(\text{EBIT} + \text{depreciation})}{\text{interest}}$$

$$= \frac{(541.14 + 188.82)}{96.32} = 7.58$$

The regular interest payment is a hurdle that companies must keep jumping if they are to avoid default. The times-interest-earned ratio measures how much clear air there is between hurdle and hurdler.

Is ACC borrowing in the ballpark of standard practice or is it a matter for concern? Table 29.4 provides some clues. You can see that the debt ratio is lower than the rest of the cement industry and the times-interest-earned is significantly higher.

[9]The numerator of times-interest-earned can be defined in several ways. Sometimes depreciation is excluded. Sometimes it is just earnings plus interest, that is, earnings before interest but *after* tax. This last definition seems nutty to us, because the point of interest earned is to assess the risk that the firm won't have enough money to pay interest. If EBIT falls below interest obligations, the firm won't have to worry about taxes. Interest is paid before the firm pays taxes.

How Liquid Is ACC?

If ACC is borrowing for a short period or has some large bills coming up for payment, you want to make sure that it can lay its hands on the cash when it is needed. The company's bankers and suppliers also need to keep an eye on ACC's liquidity. They know that illiquid firms are more likely to fail and default on their debts.

Another reason that analysts focus on liquid assets is that the figures are often more reliable. The book value of ACC's cement plants may be a poor guide to its true value, but at least you know what its cash in the bank's worth. Liquidity ratios also have some less desirable characteristics. Because short-term assets and liabilities are easily changed, measures of liquidity can rapidly become out-of-date. You may not know what the cement plant is worth, but you can be fairly sure that it won't disappear overnight.

Current Ratio ACC's current assets consist of cash and assets that can readily be turned into cash. Its current liabilities consist of payments that the company expects to make in the near future. Thus the ratio of current assets to the current liabilities measures the margin of liquidity. It is known as the *current ratio*:

$$\text{Current ratio} = \frac{\text{current assets}}{\text{current liabilities}} = \frac{1177.24}{1222.84} = 0.96$$

Rapid decreases in the current ratio sometimes signify trouble. However, they can also be misleading. For example, suppose that a company borrows a large sum from the bank and invests it in short-term securities. If nothing else happens, net working capital is unaffected, but the current ratio changes. For this reason it might be preferable to net off the short-term investments and the short-term debt when calculating the current ratio.

Quick (or Acid-Test) Ratio Some assets are closer to cash than others. If trouble comes, inventories may not sell at anything above fire-sale prices. (Trouble typically comes *because* customers are not buying and the firm's warehouse is stuffed with unwanted goods.) Thus, managers often focus only on cash, short-term securities, and bills that customers have not yet paid:

$$\text{Quick ratio} = \frac{(\text{cash} + \text{short-term securities} + \text{receivables})}{\text{current liabilities}}$$

$$= \frac{57.32 + 577.54}{1222.84} = 0.52$$

Cash Ratio A company's most liquid assets are its holdings of cash and marketable securities. That is why analysts also look at the cash ratio:

$$\text{Cash ratio} = \frac{(\text{cash} + \text{short-term securities})}{\text{current liabilities}} = \frac{57.32}{1222.84} = 0.05$$

Of course, these summary measures of liquidity are just that. They are no substitute for detailed plans to ensure that the company can pay its bills. In the next chapter we will describe how companies forecast their cash needs and draw up a short-term financial plan to deal with any cash shortage.

How Productively Is ACC Using Its Assets?

Financial analysts employ another set of ratios to judge how efficiently the firm is using its investment in current and fixed assets. Later in the chapter we will look at the financial implications of

ACC's ambitious plans to expand output, but understanding the investment in fixed assets and working capital that is needed to support ACC's current output may help to uncover inconsistencies in these plans for the future.

Sales-to-Assets (or Asset Turnover) Ratio The sales-to-assets ratio shows how hard the firm's assets are being put to use:

$$\frac{\text{Sales}}{\text{average total assets}} = \frac{4548.92}{(4478.38 + 3964.59)/2} = 1.08$$

Assets here are measured as the sum of current assets, fixed assets, investments and other assets. Notice that since assets are likely to change over the course of a year, we use the *average* of the assets at the beginning and end of the year. Averages are commonly used whenever a *flow* figure (in this case, sales) is compared with a *stock* or snapshot figure (total assets).

Notice that each rupee of investment in ACC generates Rs.1.08 of sales, a slightly higher figure than other cement companies. There are several possible explanations: (1) ACC uses its assets more efficiently; (2) ACC is working close to capacity, so that it may be difficult to increase sales without additional invested capital; (3) compared to its rivals, ACC produces high volume, low margin products. You need to dig deeper to know which explanation is correct. Remember our earlier comment – financial ratios help you ask the right questions, not to *answer* them.

Instead of looking at the ratio of sales to *total assets*, managers sometimes look at how hard particular types of capital are being put to use. For example, it turns out that ACC's ratio of sales to *net working capital* is much greater than that of other cement companies.

Days in Inventory The speed with which a company turns over its inventory is measured by the number of days that it takes for the goods to be produced and sold. First convert the cost of goods sold to a daily basis by dividing by 365. Then express inventories as a multiple of the daily cost of goods sold:

$$\text{Days in inventory} = \frac{\text{average inventory}}{\text{cost of goods sold} \div 365}$$

$$= \frac{(378.01 + 542.38)/2}{3015.76/365} = 55.7 \text{ days}$$

Average Collection Period The average collection period measures how quickly customers pay their bills:

$$\text{Average collection period} = \frac{\text{average reveivables}}{\text{sales} \div 365}$$

$$= \frac{(576.18 + 577.14)}{4548.92/365} = 46.29 \text{ days}$$

The collection period for ACC is much shorter than the industry average. The company may have a conscious policy of have stringent credit policy while selling to dealers. Alternatively, an average cement company may have a conscious policy of offering attractive credit terms to lure business, but it is also possible that the credit manager is lax in chasing up the slow payers.

How Profitable Is ACC?

Net Profit Margin If you want to know the proportion of sales that finds its way into profits, you look at the profit margin. Thus[10]

$$\text{Net profit margin} = \frac{(\text{EBIT - tax})}{\text{sales}} = \frac{541.14 - 66.43}{4589.92} = 0.1, \text{ or } 10\%$$

Return on Assets (ROA) Managers often measure the performance of the firm by the ratio of income to total assets (income is usually defined as earnings before interest but after taxes). This is known as the firm's *return on assets* (ROA) or *return on investment* (ROI):

$$\text{Return on assets} = \frac{(\text{EBIT} - \text{tax})}{(\text{average total assets})}$$

$$= \frac{541.14 - 66.43}{(3964.59 + 4478.38)/2} = 0.11, \text{ or } 11\%$$

Another measure focuses on the return on the firm's equity:

$$\text{Return on equity (ROE)} = \frac{(\text{earnings available for common stockholders})}{\text{average equity}}$$

$$= \frac{378.39}{(1353.19 + 1597.19)/2} = 0.26, \text{ or } 26\%$$

It is natural to compare the return earned by ACC with the opportunity cost of capital. Of course, the assets in the financial statements are shown at *net book value,* that is, original cost less depreciation.[11] So a low ROA does not necessarily imply that those assets could be better employed elsewhere. Nor would a high ROA necessarily mean that you could buy similar assets today and get a high return.

---

[10]Net profit margin is sometimes measured as profit after tax ÷ sales. This ignores the profits that are paid out to debtholders as interest and should therefore not be used to compare firms with different capital structures.

While making comparisons between firms, it makes sense to recognize that firms which pay more interest pay less tax. We suggest that you calculate the tax that the company would pay if it were all-equity-financed. To do this you need to adjust taxes by adding back interest tax shields (interest payments × marginal tax rate). Using an assumed tax rate of 30 percent,

$$\text{Net profit margin} = \frac{\text{EBIT} - (\text{tax} + \text{interest tax shields})}{\text{sales}}$$

$$= \frac{541.14 - [66.43 + 0.3 \times 96.32)]}{4548.92} = 0.098, \text{ or } 9.8\%$$

[11]When comparing the returns on total assets of firms with different capital structures, it makes sense to add back interest tax shields to tax payments (see footnote 9). This adjusted ratio then measures the returns that the company would have earned if it were all-equity-financed.

One other point about return on assets. Since profits are a flow figure and assets are a snapshot figure, analysts commonly divide profits by the average of assets at the start and end of the year. The reason that they do this is that the firm may raise large amounts of new capital during the year and then put it to work. Therefore part of the year's earnings is a return on this new capital.

However, this measure is potentially misleading and should not be compared closely with the cost of capital. After all, when we defined the return that shareholders require from investing in the capital market, we divided expected profit by the initial outlay, not by an average of starting and ending values.

In a competitive industry, firms can expect to earn only their cost of capital. Therefore, managers whose businesses are earning more than the cost of capital are likely to earn a pat on the back, while those that are earning a low return may face some tough questions or worse. Although shareholders like to see their companies earn a high return on assets, consumers' groups or regulators often regard a high return as evidence that the firm is charging excessive prices. Naturally, such conclusions are seldom cut and dried. There is plenty of room for argument as to whether the return on assets is properly measured or whether it exceeds the cost of capital.

Payout Ratio The payout ratio measures the proportion of earnings that is paid out as dividends. Thus

$$\text{Payout ratio} = \frac{\text{dividends}}{\text{earnings}} = \frac{142.95}{378.39} = 0.38$$

We saw in Section 16.3 that managers don't like to cut dividends if there is a shortfall in earnings. Therefore, if a company's earnings are particularly variable, management is likely to play it safe by setting a low average payout ratio. When earnings fall unexpectedly, the payout ratio will rise temporarily. Likewise, if earnings are expected to rise next year, management may feel that it can pay somewhat more generous dividends than it would otherwise have done.

How Highly Is ACC Valued by Investors?

There is no law that prohibits you from introducing data that are not in the company accounts. For example, when you are assessing ACC's efficiency, you might wish to look at the cost per ton of cement produced. Similarly, an airline might calculate revenue per passenger mile flown, and so on. If you want to gauge how highly ACC is valued by investors, then you will need to calculate ratios that combine accounting and stock market data. Here are three examples:

Price–Earnings Ratio The price-earnings, or P/E, ratio measures the price that investors are prepared to pay for each rupee of earnings. In the case of ACC

$$\text{P/E ratio} = \frac{\text{stock price}}{\text{earnings per share}} = \frac{360.45}{21.2} = 17$$

In Section 4.5 we explained that a high P/E ratio may indicate that investors think the firm has good growth opportunities or that its earnings are relatively safe and therefore more valuable. Of course, it may also mean that earnings are temporarily depressed. If a company just breaks even with zero earnings, its P/E ratio is infinite.

Dividend Yield ACC's dividend yield is simply its dividend as a proportion of the stock price. Thus

$$\text{Dividend yield} = \frac{\text{dividend per share}}{\text{stock price}} = \frac{8}{360.45} = .002, \text{ or } .2\%$$

Remember that the return to an investor comes in two forms – dividend yield and capital appreciation. ACC's relatively high dividend yield (vis-à-vis other cement companies) may indicate that investors are demanding a relatively high rate of return or that they are not expecting rapid dividend growth with consequent capital gain.

Market-to-Book Ratio The market-to-book ratio is the ratio of the stock price to book value per share. For ACC

$$\text{Market-to-book ratio} = \frac{\text{stock price}}{\text{book value per share}} = \frac{360.45}{1597.19 / 17.85} = 4.03$$

Book value per share is just stockholders' book equity divided by the number of shares outstanding. Book equity (or net worth) equals share capital plus retained earnings (or reserves and surpluses) – the net amount that the firm has received from stockholders or reinvested on their behalf.[12] Thus ACC's market-to-book ratio of 4.03 means that the firm is worth 303 percent more than past and present stockholders have put into it.

The Dupont System

Some of the profitability and efficiency ratios that we described above can be linked in useful ways. These relationships are often referred to as the **Dupont system,** in recognition of the chemical company that popularized them.

The first relationship links the return on assets (ROA) with the firm's sales-to-assets ratio and its profit margin:

$$\text{ROA} = \frac{\text{EBIT} - \text{tax}}{\text{assets}} = \underbrace{\frac{\text{sales}}{\text{assets}}}_{\text{sales-to-assets ratio}} \times \underbrace{\frac{\text{EBIT} - \text{tax}}{\text{sales}}}_{\text{profit margin}}$$

All firms would like to earn a higher return on assets but their ability to do so is limited by competition. If the expected return on assets is fixed by competition, firms face a trade-off between the sales-to-assets ratio and the profit margin. For example, fast-food chains, which turn over their capital frequently, also tend to operate on low profit margins. Classy hotels have relatively high margins, but this is offset by lower sales-to-assets ratios.

Firms often seek to increase their profit margins by becoming more vertically integrated; for example, they may acquire a supplier or one of their sales outlets. Unfortunately, unless they have some special skill in running these new businesses, they are likely to find that any gain in profit margin is offset by a decline in the sales-to-assets ratio.

The return on equity (ROE) can be broken down as follows:

$$\text{ROE} = \frac{\text{EBIT} - \text{tax} - \text{interest}}{\text{equity}}$$

$$= \underbrace{\frac{\text{assets}}{\text{equity}}}_{\text{leverage ratio}} \times \underbrace{\frac{\text{sales}}{\text{assets}}}_{\text{sales-to-assets ratio}} \times \underbrace{\frac{\text{EBIT} - \text{tax}}{\text{sales}}}_{\text{profit margin}} \times \underbrace{\frac{\text{EBIT} - \text{tax} - \text{interest}}{(\text{EBIT} - \text{tax})}}_{\text{"debt burden"}}$$

[12]Retained earnings are measured net of depreciation. They represent stockholders' new investment in the business over and above the amount needed to maintain the firm's existing stock of assets.

Notice that the product of the two middle terms is the return on assets. This depends on the firm's production and marketing skills and is unaffected by the financing mix. However, the first and fourth terms do depend on the debt–equity mix.[13] The first term measures the ratio of gross assets to equity, while the last term measures the extent to which profits are reduced by interest. If the firm is leveraged, the first term is greater than 1.0 (assets are greater than equity) and the fourth term is less than 1.0 (part of the profits are absorbed by interest). Thus, leverage can either increase or reduce the return on equity. In the case of ACC

$$\begin{aligned} \text{ROE} &= \text{leverage ratio} \times \text{sales-to-assets ratio} \times \text{profit margin} \times \text{debt burden} \\ &= 2.80 \times 1.08 \times 0.1 \times 0.8 = 0.26 \end{aligned}$$

So, for ACC the leverage ratio (2.80) more than offsets the debt burden (0.8). ACC's leverage increases its return on equity.

29.4 FINANCIAL PLANNING

Financial statements not only help you to understand the past but they also provide the starting point for developing a financial plan for the future. Here is where finance and strategy need to come together. A coherent financial plan demands an understanding of how the firm can generate superior long-term returns by its choice of industry and by the way that it positions itself within that industry.[14] Consider, for example, the case of Emerson Electric, a U.S.-based manufacturer of industrial products, such as electric motors and compressors.[15] A central feature of Emerson's business has been its sophisticated planning process, which integrates the tools of strategy and finance. Each division prepares a detailed five-year plan with projections of financial results and a discussion of why they are sensible. Emerson's divisional managers need to display an in-depth knowledge of how these plans will be implemented and why the projections are realistic in terms of the marketing and operating strategies involved.

When companies prepare a financial plan, they don't look just at the most likely outcomes. They also plan for the unexpected. One way to do this is to work through the consequences of the plan under the most likely set of circumstances and then use *sensitivity analysis* to vary the assumptions one at a time. Another approach is to look at the implications of different plausible scenarios.[16] For example, one scenario might envisage high interest rates leading to a slowdown in economic growth and lower commodity prices. Another scenario might involve a buoyant domestic economy, high inflation, and a weak currency. And so on.

---

[13]There is a complication here because the amount of tax paid does depend on the financing mix. We suggested in footnote 9 that it would be better to add back any interest tax shields to the tax payment when calculating the firm's profit margin.

[14]We discussed the sources of superior returns in Chapter 11.

[15]We are grateful to John Percival for pointing out this example. See C. F. Knight, "Emerson Electric: Consistent Profits, Consistently," *Harvard Business Review*, 70 (January–February 1992), pp. 57–71.

[16]For a description of the use of different planning scenarios in the Royal Dutch/Shell group, see P. Wack, "Scenarios: Uncharted Waters Ahead," *Harvard Business Review* 63 (September–October 1985) and "Scenarios: Shooting the Rapids," *Harvard Business Review* 64 (November–December 1985).

29.5 FINANCIAL PLANNING MODELS

Back to ACC. Suppose that the company management's analysis of the industry leads it to forecast a 30 percent annual growth in ACC's sales and profits over the next five years. Can the company realistically expect to finance this out of retained earnings and borrowings, or should it plan for an issue of equity? Spreadsheet programs are tailor-made for such questions. Let's investigate.

The basic sources and uses relationship tells us that

External capital required
= operating cash flow
− investment in net working capital
− investment in fixed assets
− dividends

Thus there are four steps to finding how much extra cash ACC will need and the implications for its debt ratio:

Step 1 Project next year's operating cash flow (depreciation provision plus net income) assuming the planned 20 percent increase in revenues. This gives the total sources of funds in the absence of any new issue of securities. Look, for example, at the second column of Table 29.5, which provides a forecast of operating cash flow in year 2006 for ACC.

Step 2 Project what additional investment in net working capital and fixed assets will be needed to support this increased activity and how much of the net income will be paid out as dividends. The sum of these expenditures gives you the total *uses* of funds. The second column of Table 29.6 provides a forecast of uses of funds for ACC.

Step 3 Calculate the difference between the projected operating cash flow (from Step 1) and the projected uses (Step 2). This is the cash that will need to be raised from new sales of securities. For example, you can see from Table 29.6 that ACC will need to issue Rs. 718.56 crores of debt in 2006 if it is to expand at the planned rate and not sell more shares.

Step 4 Finally, construct a pro forma balance sheet that incorporates the additional assets and the increase in debt and equity. This is done in the second column of Table 29.7. ACC's equity increases

TABLE 29.5

Latest and pro forma profit and loss account for ACC (figures in Rs. crores)

	A	B	C	G
1		**2005**	**2006**	**2010**
2	Sales	4548.92	5913.60	16889.82
3	Other Income (assumed constant)	89.35	89.35	89.35
4	Total revenue	4638.27	6002.95	16979.17
5	Costs (86% of sales)	3908.31	5085.69	14525.25
6	Depreciation (7.57% of fixed assets at start of year)	188.82	220.15	594.16
7	EBIT	541.14	697.10	1859.76
8	Interest (6.76% of long-term debt at start of year)	96.32	88.49	344.87
9	Tax (15% of pre-tax profit)	66.43	91.29	227.23
10	Net Income (PAT)	378.39	517.32	1287.66
11	Operating cash flow	567.21	737.47	1881.82

	A	B	C	G
1		2005	2006	2010
2	Increase in net working capital (NWC) assuming NWC is 5% of revenues	-195.81	345.75	194.88
3	Investment in fixed assets (FA) assuming FA = 60% of revenues	604.39	913.70	2932.75
4	Dividend (38% of profit after tax)	142.95	196.58	489.31
5	Total uses of funds	551.53	1456.03	3616.95
6	External capital required = total uses of funds - operating cash flow	-15.68	718.56	1735.13

TABLE 29.6

Latest and pro forma sources and uses of funds for ACC (figures in Rs. crores)

	A	B	C	G
1		2005	2006	2010
2	Net working capital (5% of revenues)	-45.6	300.15	848.96
3	Net fixed assets (60% of revenues)	2908.22	3601.77	10187.50
4	Other assets minus other liabilities (assumed constant)	43.64	43.64	43.64
5	Total net assets	2906.26	3945.55	11080.10
6	Long-term debt	1309.07	2027.63	6836.76
7	Equity	1597.19	1917.93	4243.35
8	Total long-term liabilities and equity	2906.26	3945.55	11080.10

TABLE 29.7

Latest and pro forma balance sheets for ACC (figures in Rs. crores)

by the additional retained earnings (profit after tax less dividends), while long-term debt is increased by the Rs. 718.56 crores new issue.

Once you have set up the spreadsheet, it is easy to run out your projections for several years. The final columns in Tables 29.5 – 29.7 show pro forma profit and loss account, sources and uses of funds, and balance sheet for the year 2010, assuming ACC continues to fund a 20 percent annual growth rate solely from retained earnings and new debt issues. Over the five-year period ACC would need to borrow an additional Rs. 5527.69 crores and by year 2010 its debt ratio would have increased to 62 percent. Many financial managers would consider this as sailing much too close to the wind, and the debt ratio would probably be above the limit set by the company's banks and bondholders. Of course, the projected debt ratio is still lower than the industry average. However, it is much higher than ACC's current debt ratio.

The obvious solution for ACC is to issue a mix of debt and equity, but there are other possibilities that the financial manager may want to explore. One option may be to hold back dividends during this period of rapid growth. An alternative might be to investigate whether the company could cut back on net working capital. This seems unlikely for ACC as its inventory turnover and average collection period are already far too below the industry average.

We stated earlier that financial planning is not just about exploring how to cope with the most likely outcomes. It also needs to ensure that the firm is prepared for unlikely ones. For example, the cement industry is notoriously exposed to economic downturn. So you would certainly wish to check that ACC could cope with a cyclical decline in sales and profit margins. Sensitivity analysis or scenario analysis can help you to do so.

Pitfalls in Model Design

The ACC model that we have developed is too simple for practical application. You probably have already thought of several ways to improve it—by keeping track of the outstanding shares, for example, and printing out earnings and dividends per share. Or you might want to distinguish between short-term lending and borrowing opportunities, now buried in working capital.

The model that we developed for ACC is known as a *percentage of sales model*. Almost all the forecasts for the company are proportional to the forecasted level of sales. However, in reality many variables will *not* be proportional to sales. For example, important components of working capital such as inventory and cash balances will generally rise less rapidly than sales. In addition, fixed assets such as plant and equipment are typically not added in small increments as sales increase. ACC's plant may well be operating at less than full capacity, so that the company can initially increase output without *any* additions to capacity. Eventually, however, if sales continue to increase, the firm may need to make a large new investment in plant and equipment.

But beware of adding too much complexity: There is always the temptation to make a model bigger and more detailed. You may end up with an exhaustive model that is too cumbersome for routine use. The fascination of detail, if you give in to it, distracts attention from crucial decisions like stock issues and payout policy.

There Is No Finance in Financial Planning Models

Why do we say there is no finance in these corporate financial models? The first reason is that they usually incorporate an accountant's view of the world. They are designed to forecast accounting statements. They do not emphasize the tools of financial analysis: incremental cash flow, present value, market risk, and so on.[17]

This may not matter as long as everyone recognizes the financial forecasts for what they are. However, you sometimes hear managers stating corporate goals in terms of accounting numbers. They may say, "Our objective is to achieve an annual sales growth of 20 percent," or "We want a 25 percent return on book equity and a profit margin of 10 percent." On the surface such objectives don't make sense. Shareholders want to be richer, not to have the satisfaction of a 10 percent profit margin. Also, a goal that is stated in terms of accounting ratios is not operational unless it is translated back into what the statement means for business decisions. For example, what does a 10 percent profit margin imply—higher prices, lower costs, increased vertical integration, or a move into new, high-margin products?

So why do managers define objectives in this way? In part such goals may be a mutual exhortation to try harder, like singing the company song before work. But we suspect that managers are often using a code to communicate real concerns. For example, the goal to increase sales rapidly may reflect managers' belief that increased market share is needed to achieve scale economies, or a target profit margin may be a way of saying that the firm has been pursuing sales growth at the expense of margins. The danger is that everyone may forget the code and the accounting targets may be seen as goals in themselves.

---

[17]Of course, there is no reason that the manager can't use the output to calculate the present value of the firm (given some assumption about growth beyond the planning period), and this is sometimes done.

The second reason for saying that there is no finance in these financing models is that they produce no signposts pointing toward optimal decisions. They do not even tell us which alternatives are worth examining. For example, we saw that ACC is planning for a rapid growth in sales and earnings per share. But is that good news for the shareholders? Well, not necessarily; it depends on the opportunity cost of capital that ACC needs to invest. If the new investment earns more than the cost of capital, it will have a positive NPV and add to shareholder wealth. The return that ACC is forecasting to earn on its new investment is much more than its cost of capital and hence its planned investments will make the shareholders better off.

The capital that ACC needs to raise depends on its decision to pay 38 percent of its earnings as dividends. But the financial planning model does not tell us whether this dividend payment makes sense or what mixture of equity or debt the company should issue. In the end the management has to decide. We would like to tell you exactly how to make the choice, but we can't. There is no model that encompasses all the complexities encountered in financial planning.

As a matter of fact, there never will be one. This bold statement is based on Brealey, Myers, and Allen's Third Law:[18]

- *Axiom:* The number of unsolved problems is infinite.
- *Axiom:* The number of unsolved problems that humans can hold in their minds is at any time limited to 10.
- *Law:* Therefore in any field there will always be 10 problems which can be addressed but which have no formal solution.

BMA's Third Law implies that no model can find the best of all financial strategies.[19]

29.6 GROWTH AND EXTERNAL FINANCING

We started this chapter by noting that financial plans force managers to be consistent in their goals for growth, investment, and financing. Before leaving the topic of financial planning, we should look at some general relationships between a firm's growth objectives and its financing needs.

Recall that ACC ended March 2005 with fixed assets, net working capital and other assets of Rs. 3255.54 crores. In 2006 it plans to plow back Rs. 320.74 crores, so net assets will increase by 320.74/3255.54, or 9.85 percent. Thus ACC can grow by 9.85 percent without needing to raise additional capital. The growth rate that a company can achieve without external funds is known as the internal growth rate. For ACC

$$\text{Internal growth rate} = \frac{\text{retained earnings}}{\text{net assets}} = 9.85\%$$

[18]The second law is presented in Section 12.2.

[19]It is possible to build linear programming models that help search for the best strategy subject to specified assumptions and constraints. These models can be more effective in screening alternative financial strategies.

We can gain more insight into what determines this growth rate by multiplying the top and bottom of the expression for internal growth rate by *net income* and *equity* as follows:

$$\text{Internal growth rate} = \frac{\text{retained earnings}}{\text{profit after tax}} \times \frac{\text{profit after tax}}{\text{equity}} \times \frac{\text{equity}}{\text{net assets}}$$

$$= \text{plowback ratio} \times \text{return on equity} \times \frac{\text{equity}}{\text{net assets}}$$

In 2006 ACC expects to plow back 62 percent of profit after tax and to earn a return of 32.39 percent on the equity with which it began the year. At the start of the year equity finances 49 percent of ACC's net assets. Therefore

$$\text{Internal growth rate} = 0.62 \times 0.3239 \times 0.49 = 0.0985, \text{ or } 9.85\%$$

Notice that if ACC wishes to grow faster than this without raising equity capital, it would need to (1) plowback a higher proportion of its earnings, (2) earn a higher return on equity, or (3) have a lower debt-to-equity ratio.[20]

Instead of focusing on how rapidly the company can grow without *any* external financing, ACC's financial manager may be interested in the growth rate that can be sustained without additional *equity* issues. Of course, if the firm is able to raise enough debt, virtually any growth rate can be financed. It makes more sense to assume that the firm has settled on an optimal capital structure which it will maintain as equity is increased by the retained earnings. Thus the firm issues only enough debt to keep the debt-equity ratio constant. The **sustainable growth rate** is the highest growth rate the firm can maintain without increasing its financial leverage. It turns out that the sustainable growth rate depends only on the plowback ratio and the return on equity.

$$\text{Sustainable growth rate} = \text{plowback ratio} \times \text{return on equity}$$

For ACC,

$$\text{Sustainable growth rate} = 0.62 \times 0.3239 = 0.2008, \text{ or } 20.08\%$$

We first encountered this formula in Chapter 4, where we used it to value common stocks.

These simple formulas remind us that financial plans need to be consistent. Firms may grow rapidly in the short term by relying on debt finance, but such growth cannot be maintained without incurring excessive debt levels.

[20]Notice that the internal growth rate does not stay constant. As the firm plows back earnings, the debt-to-equity ratio declines and the internal growth rate increases.

SUMMARY

Managers use financial statements to monitor their own company's performance, to help understand the policies of a competitor, or to check on the health of a customer. But there is a danger of being overwhelmed by the sheer volume of data. That is why managers use a few salient ratios to summarize the firm's leverage, liquidity, efficiency, profitability, and market valuation. We have described some of the more popular financial ratios.

We offer the following general advice to users of these ratios:

1. Financial ratios seldom provide answers, but they do help you to ask the right questions.
2. There is no international standard for financial ratios. A little thought and common sense are worth far more than blind application of formulas.
3. You need a benchmark for assessing a company's financial position. Compare financial ratios with the company's ratios in earlier years and with the ratios of other firms in the same business.

Understanding the past is the first step to being prepared for the future. Most firms prepare a financial plan that describes the firm's strategy and projects its future consequences by means of pro forma balance sheets, income statements, and statements of sources and uses of funds. The plan establishes financial goals and is a benchmark for evaluating subsequent performance.

The plan is the end result, but the process that produces the plan is valuable in its own right. First, planning forces the financial manager to consider the combined effects of all the firm's investment and financing decisions. This is important because these decisions interact and should not be made independently. Second, planning requires the manager to consider events that could upset the firm's progress and to devise strategies to be held in reserve for counterattack when unhappy surprises occur.

There is no theory or model that leads straight to *the* optimal financial strategy. Consequently, financial planning proceeds by trial and error. Many different strategies may be projected under a range of assumptions about the future. The dozens of separate projections that may be made during this trial-and-error process generate a heavy load of arithmetic. Firms have responded by developing corporate financial planning models to forecast the financial consequences of different strategies. We showed how you can use a simple spreadsheet model to analyze ACC's strategies. But remember there is no finance in these models. Their primary purpose is to produce accounting statements.

FURTHER READING

There are some good general texts on financial statement analysis. See, for example:

K. G. Palepu, V. L. Bernard, and P. M. Healy; *Business Analysis and Valuation*, 3rd ed. (Cincinnati, OH: South-Western College Publishing, 2003).

S. Penman, *Financial Statement Analysis and Security Valuation*, 2nd ed. (New York: McGraw-Hill/Irwin, 2003).

Corporate planning has an extensive literature of its own. Good books and articles include:

G. Donaldson: "Financial Goals and Strategic Consequences," *Harvard Business Review* 63 (May–June 1985), pp. 57–66.

G. Donaldson, *Strategy for Financial Mobility* (Boston: Harvard Business School Press, 1986).

A. C. Hax and N. S. Majluf, *The Strategy Concept and Process—A Pragmatic Approach*, 2nd ed., (Englewood Cliffs, NJ: Prentice-Hall, Inc., 1996).

The links between capital budgeting, strategy, and financial planning are discussed in:

S. C. Myers, "Finance Theory and Financial Strategy," *Interfaces* 14 (January–February, 1984), pp. 126–137.

Here are three references on corporate planning models:

W. T. Carleton, C. L. Dick, Jr., and D. H. Downes; "Financial Policy Models: Theory and Practice," *Journal of Financial and Quantitative Analysis* 8 (December 1973), pp. 691–709.

W. T. Carleton and J. M. McInnes, "Theory, Models and Implementation in Financial Management," *Management Science* 28 (September 1982), pp. 957–978.

S. C. Myers and G. A. Pogue, "A Programming Approach to Corporate Financial Management," *Journal of Finance* 29 (May 1974), pp. 579–599.

WEB EXERCISES

1. The Web site **edgarscan.pwcglobal.com** provides a very user-friendly way to compare financial ratios. Use the *Benchmarking Assistant* to enter the name of a large airline. Find and select some peer airlines and then graph their financial ratios. How does the company's financial strength stack up with that of other firms in the airline industry?
2. You can find financial ratios for different industries on the Market Insight database (**www.mhhe.com/edumarketinsight**) or on **www.census.gov/csd/qfr.** Can you account for some of the differences between industries?

CONCEPT REVIEW QUESTIONS

1. We said that financial ratios are designed to shed light on five questions. What are those questions? Give an example of each of the five categories of financial ratio. (page 793)
2. The Dupont system expresses the return on assets (ROA) in terms of the sales-to-assets ratio and the profit margin. What is this relationship? Would you expect firms with a high profit margin to have a high ratio of sales to assets? Why or why not? (page 800)
3. List the major elements of a completed financial plan. (page 801)

For additional Concept Review Questions, please visit us at www.mhhe.com/bmam8e or refer to your Student CD.

QUIZ

1. Table 29.8 gives abbreviated balance sheets and profit and loss accounts for Colgate Palmolive (India) Limited. Calculate the following ratios:
   - **a.** Debt ratio.
   - **b.** Times-interest-earned ratio.
   - **c.** Current ratio.
   - **d.** Quick ratio.
   - **e.** Net profit margin.
   - **f.** Days in inventory.
   - **g.** Return on equity.
   - **h.** Payout ratio.
2. There are no universally accepted definitions of financial ratios, but five of the following ratios make no sense at all. Substitute the correct definitions.
   - **a.** Debt–equity ratio = (long-term debt + value of leases)/(long-term debt + value of leases + equity)
   - **b.** Return on equity = (EBIT − tax)/average equity
   - **c.** Payout ratio = dividend/stock price
   - **d.** Profit margin = (EBIT − tax)/sales
   - **e.** Inventory turnover = sales/average inventory
   - **f.** Current ratio = current liabilities/current assets
   - **g.** Sales-to-net-working-capital = average sales/average net working capital
   - **h.** Average collection period = sales/(average receivables ÷ 365)
   - **i.** Quick ratio = (current assets − inventories)/current liabilities
3. True or false?
   - **a.** A company's debt–equity ratio is always less than 1.
   - **b.** The quick ratio is always less than the current ratio.
   - **c.** The return on equity is always less than the return on assets.
   - **d.** If a project is slow to reach full profitability, straight-line depreciation is likely to produce an overstatement of profits in the early years.

TABLE 29.8

Profit and loss account and balance sheet for Colgate Palmolive (India), 2005-06 (figures in Rs. crores)

Source: Prowess database

Profit and Loss Account	
Net Sales	Rs.3989.11
Other Income	632.75
Total Revenue	4621.86
Cost of Goods Sold	3341.08
Depreciation	348.65
Earnings before interest and tax (EBIT)	932.13
Net interest	191.88
Tax	89.91
Profit after tax	Rs.650.34
Dividends	120.85

Balance Sheet	Mar-06	Mar-05
Cash and Bank	5652.9	6045.37
Receivables	4466.1	2205.93
Inventories	396.33	389.14
Total current assets	10515.33	8640.44
Net Fixed Assets	2865.36	2910.94
Other assets	1315.84	795.62
Total assets	14696.53	12347
Short term debt	160	675
Payables	1659.06	2046.15
Provisions	713.43	479.9
Total current liabilities	2532.49	3201.05
Long-term debt	4130.47	3085.78
Other liabilities	248.53	288.69
Shareholders' equity	7785.04	5771.48
Total liabilities	Rs.14697	Rs.12347

e. A substantial new advertising campaign by a cosmetics company will tend to depress earnings and cause the stock to sell at a low price–earnings multiple.

4. A firm has Rs. 30,000 of inventory. If this represents 30 days' sales, what is the annual cost of goods sold? What is the inventory turnover ratio?

5. Bindu Cosmetics maintains a profit margin of 4 percent and a sales-to-assets ratio of 3.

a. What is its return on assets?

b. If its debt–equity ratio is 1.0, its interest payments and taxes are each Rs. 10,000, and EBIT is Rs. 40,000, what is the return on equity?

6. A firm has a long-term debt–equity ratio of .4. Shareholders' equity is Rs. 1 million. Current assets are Rs. 200,000, and the current ratio is 2.0. Long-term assets total Rs. 1.5 million. What is the ratio of debt to total long-term capital?

7. Magic Flutes has total receivables of Rs. 3,000, which represent 20 days' sales. Average total assets are Rs. 75,000. The firm's profit margin is 5 percent. Find the firm's sales-to-assets ratio and return on assets.

8. Consider this simplified balance sheet for Geomorph Trading:

Current assets	Rs. 100	Rs. 60	Current liabilities
		280	Long-term debt
Long-term assets	500	70	Other liabilities
		190	Equity
	Rs. 600	Rs. 600	

TABLE 29.9

Financial statement for Drake's Bowling Alleys, 2005 (figures in thousands).

*Assets at end-2004 were Rs.2,400,000.

†Debt at end-2004 was Rs.500,000.

Income Statement	
Sales	Rs.1,000 (40% of *average* assets)*
Costs	750 (75% of sales)
Interest	25 (5% of debt at start of year)†
Pretax profit	225
Tax	90 (40% of pretax profit)
Net income	Rs.135

Balance Sheet			
Assets	Rs.2,600	Debt	Rs.500
		Equity	2,100
Total	Rs.2,600	Total	Rs.2,600

TABLE 29.10

Financial statements for Archimedes Levers, 2004.

Income Statement	
Sales	Rs.4,000
Costs, including interest	3,500
Net income	Rs.500

Balance Sheet, Year-end	2004	2003		2004	2003
Assets	Rs.3,200	Rs.2,700	Debt	Rs.1,200	Rs.1,033
			Equity	2,000	1,667
Total	Rs.3,200	Rs.2,700	Total	Rs.3,200	Rs.2,700

a. Calculate the ratio of debt to equity.
b. What are Geomorph's net working capital and total long-term capital? Calculate the ratio of debt to total long-term capital.

9. Airlux Antarctica has current assets of $300 million, current liabilities of $200 million, and a crash—sorry—*cash* ratio of .05. How much cash and marketable securities does it hold?

10. On average, it takes Microlimp's customers 60 days to pay their bills. If Microlimp has annual sales of Rs. 500 million, what is the average value of unpaid bills?

11. True or false?
a. Financial planning should attempt to minimize risk.
b. The primary aim of financial planning is to obtain better forecasts of future cash flows and earnings.
c. Financial planning is necessary because financing and investment decisions interact and should not be made independently.
d. Firms' planning horizons rarely exceed three years.
e. Financial planning requires accurate forecasting.
f. Financial planning models should include as much detail as possible.

excel

Please visit us at www.mhhe.com/bmam8e or refer to your Student CD .

12. Table 29.9 summarizes the 2005 income statement and end-year balance sheet of Drake's Bowling Alleys. Drake's financial manager forecasts a 10 percent increase in sales and costs in 2006. The ratio of sales to *average* assets is expected to remain at 0.40. Interest is forecasted at 5 percent of debt at start of year.
a. What is the implied level of assets at the end of 2006?
b. If the company pays out 50 percent of net income as dividends, how much cash will Drake need to raise in the capital markets in 2006?
c. If Drake is unwilling to make an equity issue, what will be the debt ratio at the end of 2006?

13. Abbreviated financial statements for Archimedes Levers are shown in Table 29.10. If sales increase by 10 percent in 2005 and all other items, including debt, increase correspondingly, what must be the balancing item? What will be its value?

14. What is the maximum possible growth rate for Archimedes (see Quiz Question 13) if the payout ratio is set at 50 percent and (**a**) no external debt or equity is to be issued? (**b**) the firm maintains a fixed debt ratio but issues no equity?

PRACTICE QUESTIONS

1. Look up the latest financial statements for any company from its website and calculate the sources and uses of funds table for the latest year. You can also download financial statements from the website www.sebiedifar.nic.in. Don't be put off by the fact that annual financial statements are more complicated than the simplified ones we showed for ACC.

2. For the company identified for Q1 above, calculate the following ratios for the latest year:
   a. Debt ratio.
   b. Times-interest-earned.
   c. Current ratio.
   d. Quick ratio.
   e. Net profit margin.
   f. Days in inventory.
   g. Return on equity.
   h. Payout ratio.

3. Select a sample of companies from the website *www.sebiedifar.nic.in* and compare the days in inventory and the average collection period for receivables. Can you explain these differences?

4. This question reviews some of the difficulties encountered in interpreting accounting numbers.
   a. Give four examples of important assets, liabilities, or transactions which may not be shown on the company's books.
   b. How does investment in intangible assets, such as research and development, distort accounting ratios? Give at least two examples.

5. Discuss alternative measures of financial leverage. Should the market value of equity be used or the book value? Is it better to use the market value of debt, the book value, or the book value discounted at the risk-free interest rate? How should you treat off-balance-sheet obligations such as pension liabilities? How would you treat preferred stock, deferred tax reserves, and minority interest?

6. Suppose that as on 31 March 2006, ACC has unused lines of credit that would have allowed it to borrow a further Rs.500 crores. Suppose also that it used this line of credit to raise short-term loans of Rs. 500 crores and invested the proceeds in marketable securities (e.g., money market mutual funds). Would the company have appeared to be (a) more or less liquid? (b) more or less levered? Calculate the appropriate ratios.

7. How would the following actions affect a firm's current ratio?
   a. Inventory is sold.
   b. The firm takes out a bank loan to pay its suppliers.
   c. A customer pays its overdue bills.
   d. The firm uses cash to purchase additional inventories.

8. Sara Togas sells all its output to Federal Stores. The following table shows selected financial data, in millions, for the two firms:

	Sales	Profits	Assets
Federal Stores	$100	$10	$50
Sara Togas	20	4	20

Calculate the sales-to-assets ratio, the profit margin, and the return on the two firms. Now assume that the two companies merge. If Federal continues to sell goods worth $100 million, how will the three financial ratios change?

TABLE 29.11

Balance sheet and income statement of Transylvania Railroad (figures in $ millions).

	December 2004	December 2003
Balance Sheet		
Cash	[redacted]	20
Accounts receivable	[redacted]	34
Inventory	[redacted]	26
Total current assets	[redacted]	80
Fixed assets, net	[redacted]	25
Total	[redacted]	105
Notes payable	30	35
Accounts payable	25	20
Total current liabilities	[redacted]	55
Long-term debt	[redacted]	20
Equity	[redacted]	30
Total	115	105
Income Statement		
Sales	[redacted]	
Cost of goods sold	[redacted]	
Selling, general, and administrative expenses	10	
Depreciation	20	
EBIT	[redacted]	
Interest	[redacted]	
Earnings before tax	[redacted]	
Tax	[redacted]	
Earnings available for common stock	[redacted]	

Please visit us at www.mhhe.com/bmam8e or refer to your Student CD.

9. United Ratio's common stock has a dividend yield of 4 percent. Its dividend per share is Rs. 2, and it has 10 million shares outstanding. If the market-to-book ratio is 1.5, what is the total book value of the equity?

10. As you can see, someone has spilled ink over some of the entries in the balance sheet and income statement of Transylvania Railroad (Table 29.11). Can you use the following information to work out the missing entries?
    - Debt ratio: .4.
    - Times-interest-earned: 11.2.
    - Current ratio: 1.4.
    - Quick ratio: 1.0.
    - Cash ratio: .2.
    - Return on total assets: .18.
    - Return on equity: .41.
    - Inventory turnover: 5.0.
    - Receivables' collection period: 71.2 days.

11. Here are some data for five companies in the same industry:

	Company Code				
	A	B	C	D	E
Net income (millions)	Rs. 10	Rs. .5	Rs. 6.67	−Rs. 1	Rs. 6.67
Total book assets (millions)	Rs. 300	Rs. 30.0	Rs. 120.00	Rs. 50	Rs. 120.00
Shares outstanding (millions)	3	4	2	5	10
Share price	Rs. 100	Rs. 5	Rs. 50	Rs. 8	Rs. 10

You have been asked to calculate a measure of the industry price–earnings ratio. Discuss the possible ways that you might calculate such a measure. Does changing the method of calculation make a significant difference to the end result?

12. How would rapid inflation affect the accuracy and relevance of a manufacturing company's balance sheet and income statement? Does your answer depend on how much debt the company has issued?
13. Suppose you wish to use financial ratios to estimate the risk of a company's stock. Which of those that we have described in this chapter are likely to be helpful? Can you think of other accounting measures of risk?
14. Look up some firms that have been in trouble. Plot the changes over the preceding years in the principal financial ratios. Are there any patterns?
15. Our model of ACC is an example of top-down planning model. Some firms use a bottom-up financial planning model, which incorporates forecasts of revenues and costs of particular products, advertising plans, major investment projects, and so on. What sort of firms would you expect to use each type, and what would they use them for?
16. Corporate financial plans are often used as a basis for judging subsequent performance. What do you think can be learned from such comparisons? What problems are likely to arise, and how might you cope with these problems?
17. The balancing item in the ACC model is borrowing. What is meant by balancing item? How would the model change if dividends were made the balancing item instead? In that case how would you suggest that planned borrowing be determined?
18. Construct a new model for ACC based on your answer to Practice Question 17. Does your model generate a feasible financial plan for 2006? (Hint: If it doesn't, you may have to allow the firm to issue stock.)
19. a. Use the ACC model (Tables 29.5 – 29.7) to produce pro forma profit and loss account, balance sheets, and sources and uses of funds statement for 2006 and 2007. Assume business as usual except that now and sales and costs are planned to expand by 40 percent per year, as are fixed assets and net working capital. The interest rate is forecasted to remain at 9 percent and stock issues are ruled out. ACC also sticks to its 38 percent dividend payout ratio.
    b. What are the firm's debt ratio and interest coverage under this plan?
    c. Can the company continue to finance expansion by borrowing?
20. Table 29.12 shows the 2004 financial statements for the Executive Cheese Company. Annual depreciation is 10 percent of fixed assets at the beginning of the year, plus 10 percent of new investment. The company plans to invest a further Rs. 200 per year in fixed assets for the next five years and net working capital is expected to remain a constant proportion of fixed assets. The company forecasts that the ratio of revenues to total assets at the start of each year will remain at 1.75. Fixed costs are expected to remain at Rs. 53, and variable costs, at 80 percent of revenue. The company's policy is to pay out two-thirds of net income as dividends and to maintain a book debt ratio of 20 percent.
    a. Construct a model for Executive Cheese like the one in Tables 29.5–29.7.
    b. Use your model to produce a set of financial statements for 2005.
21. The financial statements of Eagle Sport Supply are shown in Table 29.13. For simplicity, "Costs" include interest. Assume that Eagle's assets are proportional to its sales.
    a. Find Eagle's required external funds if it maintains a dividend payout ratio of 60 percent and plans a growth rate of 15 percent in 2006.
    b. If Eagle chooses not to issue new shares of stock, what variable must be the balancing item? What will its value be?
    c. Now suppose that the firm plans instead to increase long-term debt only to $1,100 and does not wish to issue any new shares of stock. Why must the dividend payment now be the balancing item? What will its value be?

TABLE 29.12

Financial statements for Executive Cheese Company, 2004 (figures in thousands).

Income Statement	
Revenue	Rs. 1,785
Fixed costs	53
Variable costs (80% of revenue)	1,428
Depreciation	80
Interest (at 11.8%)	24
Taxes (at 40%)	80
Net income	Rs. 120

Sources and Uses of Funds	
Sources:	
Operating cash flow	Rs. 200
Borrowing	36
Stock issues	104
Total sources	Rs. 340
Uses:	
Increase in net working capital	Rs. 60
Investment	200
Dividends	80
Total uses	Rs. 340

Balance Sheet, Year-end	2004	2003
Assets:		
Net working capital	Rs. 400	Rs. 340
Fixed assets	800	680
Total assets	Rs. 1,200	Rs. 1,020
Liabilities:		
Debt	Rs. 240	Rs. 204
Book equity	960	816
Total liabilities	Rs. 1,200	Rs. 1,020

TABLE 29.13

Financial statements for Eagle Sport Supply, 2005.

Income Statement	
Sales	$950
Costs	250
EBIT	700
Taxes (tax rate = 28.6%)	200
Net income	$500

Balance Sheet, Year-end	2004	2005		2004	2005
Assets	$2,700	$3,000	Debt	$ 900	$1,000
			Equity	1,800	2,000
Total	$2,700	$3,000	Total	$2,700	$3,000

22. a. What is the internal growth rate of Eagle Sports (see Practice Problem 21) if the dividend payout ratio is fixed at 60 percent and the equity-to-asset ratio is fixed at 2/3?
    b. What is the sustainable growth rate?

23. Bio-Plasma Corp. is growing at 30 percent per year. It is all-equity-financed and has total assets of Rs. 1 million. Its return on equity is 20 percent. Its plowback ratio is 40 percent.
    a. What is the internal growth rate?
    b. What is the firm's need for external financing this year?
    c. By how much would the firm increase its internal growth rate if it reduced its payout rate to zero?
    d. By how much would such a move reduce the need for external financing? What do you conclude about the relationship between dividend policy and requirements for external financing?

CHALLENGE QUESTIONS

1. Take another look at Geomorph Trading's balance sheet in Quiz Question 8, and consider the following additional information:

Current Assets		**Current Liabilities**		**Other Liabilities**	
Cash	Rs. 15	Payables	Rs. 35	Deferred tax	Rs. 32
Inventories	35	Taxes due	10	Unfunded pensions	22
Receivables	50	Bank loan	15	R&R reserve	16
	Rs. 100		Rs. 60		Rs. 70

The "R&R reserve" covers the future costs of removal of an oil pipeline and environmental restoration of the pipeline route.

There are many ways to calculate a debt ratio for Geomorph. Suppose you are evaluating the safety of Geomorph's debt and want a debt ratio for comparison with the ratios of other companies in the same industry. Would you calculate the ratio in terms of total liabilities or total capitalization? What would you include in debt—the bank loan, the deferred tax account, the R&R reserve, the unfunded pension liability? Explain the pros and cons of these choices.

2. Take any firm whose financial statements for the year 2005-06 are available in the website *www.sebiedifar.nic.in* and make some plausible forecasts for future growth and the asset base needed to support the growth. Then use a spreadsheet program to develop a five-year financial plan. How vulnerable is the company to an error in your forecasts?

CHAPTER [30]

WORKING CAPITAL MANAGEMENT

MOST OF THIS BOOK is devoted to long-term financial decisions such as capital budgeting and the choice of capital structure. It is now time to look at the management of short-term assets and liabilities. Short-term, or *current*, assets and liabilities are collectively known as **working capital.** Table 30.1 gives a breakdown of working capital for all manufacturing corporations in India in 2005. Note that current assets are larger than current liabilities. **Net working capital** (current assets *less* current liabilities) is positive.

We begin our discussion of working capital management by focusing on the four principal types of current asset. We look first at **accounts receivable.** Companies frequently sell goods on credit, so that it may be weeks or even months before the company is paid. These unpaid bills are shown in the accounts as receivables. We will explain how the company's credit manager sets the terms for payment, decides which customers should be offered credit, and ensures that they pay promptly.

Our second task is to look at the management of inventory. To do business, firms need reserves of raw materials, work in process, and finished goods. But these inventories can be expensive to store and they tie up capital. Therefore, inventory management involves a trade-off between the advantages of holding large inventories and the costs. In manufacturing companies the production manager is best placed to make this judgment, and the financial manager is not usually directly involved in inventory management. So we will spend less time on this topic than on the management of other current assets.

Our next task is to discuss the firm's cash balances. The cash manager faces two principal problems. The first is to decide how much cash the firm needs to retain and therefore how much can be invested in interest-bearing securities. The second is to ensure that cash payments are handled efficiently. You don't want to stuff incoming checks into your desk drawer until you can walk them round to the bank; you want to get the money into your bank account as quickly as possible. We will describe some of the techniques that firms use to move money around efficiently.

Cash that is not required immediately is usually invested in a variety of short-term securities. Some of these literally pay off the next day; others may mature in a few months. In Section 30.4 we will describe the different features of these securities and show how to compare their yields.

The credit manager, the production manager, and the cash manager are all closely involved in the management of current assets. But, of course, their decisions cannot be made in isolation; the firm has to ensure that they add up to a sensible whole. Therefore in Chapter 31 we will look at how firms develop forecasts of their working capital over the coming months and how they raise short-term finance to cover any temporary cash deficiency.

TABLE 30.1

Current assets and liabilities for Indian manufacturing corporations, March 31, 2005 (figures in Rs. crores)

Current Assets			Current Liabilities
Cash	Rs.74651.53	Rs.26285.89	Current portion of long-term debt
Other short-term financial investments	30125.67	155962.85	Accounts payable
Accounts receivable	249097.79	29180.15	Income tax provisions
		16957.65	Dividend Provisions
Inventories	173214.88	63028.27	Other current liabilities
Total current assets	Rs.527089.87	Rs.291414.81	Total current liabilities

Net working capital (current assets - current liabilities) = 527089.87 - 291414.81 = Rs.235675.06 crores

Source: Compiled from Prowess database

30.1 CREDIT MANAGEMENT

We start our tour of current assets with the firm's *accounts receivable*. When one company sells goods to another, it does not usually expect to be paid immediately. These unpaid bills, or **trade credit,** compose the bulk of accounts receivable. The remainder is made up of **consumer credit,** that is, bills that are awaiting payment by the final customer.

Management of trade credit requires answers to five sets of questions:

1. How long are you going to give customers to pay their bills? Are you prepared to offer a cash discount for prompt payment?
2. Do you require some formal IOU from the buyer or do you just ask him to sign a receipt?
3. How do you determine which customers are likely to pay their bills?
4. How much credit are you prepared to extend to each customer? Do you play safe by turning down any doubtful prospects? Or do you accept the risk of a few bad debts as part of the cost of building a large regular clientele?
5. How do you collect the money when it becomes due? What do you do about reluctant payers or deadbeats?

We will discuss each of these topics in turn.

Terms of Sale

Not all sales involve credit. For example, if you are supplying goods to a wide variety of irregular customers, you may demand cash on delivery (COD). And, if your product is custom-designed, it may be sensible to ask for cash before delivery (CBD) or to ask for progress payments as the work is carried out.

When we look at transactions that do involve credit, we find that each industry seems to have its own particular practices.[1] These norms have a rough logic. For example, firms selling consumer durables may allow the buyer a month to pay, while those selling perishable goods, such as cheese or fresh fruit, typically demand payment in a week. Similarly, a seller may allow more extended payment if its customers are in a low-risk business, if their accounts are large, if they need time to check the quality of the goods, or if the goods are not quickly resold.

To encourage customers to pay before the final date, it is common to offer a cash discount for prompt settlement. For example, pharmaceutical companies commonly require payment within 30 days but may offer a 2 percent discount to customers who pay within 10 days. These terms are referred to as "2/10, net 30."

If goods are bought on a recurrent basis, it may be inconvenient to require separate payment for each delivery. A common solution is to pretend that all sales during the month in fact occur at the end of the month (EOM). Thus goods may be sold on terms of 8/10 EOM, net 60. This arrangement allows the customer a cash discount of 8 percent if the bill is paid within 10 days of the end of the month; otherwise, the full payment is due within 60 days of the invoice date.

---

[1]Standard credit terms in different industries in the US are reported in O. K. Ng, J. K. Smith, and R. L. Smith, "Evidence on the Determinants of Credit Terms Used in Interfirm Trade," *Journal of Finance* 54 (June 1999), pp. 1109–1129.

Cash discounts are often very large. For example, a customer who buys on terms of 2/10, net 30 may decide to forego the cash discount and pay on the thirtieth day. This means that the customer obtains an extra 20 days' credit but pays about 2 percent more for the goods. This is equivalent to borrowing money at a rate of 44.6 percent per annum.[2] Of course, any firm that delays payment beyond the due date gains a cheaper loan but damages its reputation.

The Promise to Pay

Repetitive sales to domestic customers are almost always made on *open account*. The only evidence of the customer's debt is the record in the seller's books and a receipt signed by the buyer.

If you want a clear commitment from the buyer before you deliver the goods, you can arrange a **commercial draft.**[3] This works as follows: You draw a draft ordering payment by the customer and send this to the customer's bank together with the shipping documents. If immediate payment is required, the draft is termed a *sight draft*; otherwise it is known as a *time draft*. Depending on whether it is a sight draft or a time draft, the customer either pays up or acknowledges the debt by signing it and adding the word *accepted*. The bank then hands the shipping documents to the customer and forwards the money or **trade acceptance** to you, the seller.

If your customer's credit may be shaky, you can ask the customer to arrange for a bank to *accept* the time draft and thereby guarantee the customer's debt. These **bankers' acceptances** are often used in overseas trade. The bank guarantee makes the debt easily marketable. If you don't want to wait for your money, you can sell the acceptance to a bank or to another firm that has surplus cash to invest.

An alternative when you are selling goods overseas is to ask the customer to arrange for an *irrevocable letter of credit*. In this case the customer's bank sends you a letter stating that it has established a credit in your favor at a bank in the United States. You then know that the money is available and already in the country. You therefore draw a draft on the customer's bank and present it to your bank together with the letter of credit and the shipping documents. Your bank arranges for this draft to be either accepted or paid, and forwards the documents to the customer's bank.

If you sell your goods to a customer who proves unable to pay, you cannot get your goods back. You simply become a general creditor of the company together with many other unfortunates. You may be able to avoid this situation by making a *conditional sale*, so that you remain the owner of the goods until payment has been made. The conditional sale is common practice in Europe. In India and the United States it is used only for goods that are bought on an installment basis. So, if you buy a new car and fail to make all the payments, the dealer can repossess the car.

---

[2]The cash discount allows you to pay Rs. 98 rather than Rs. 100. If you do not take the discount, you get a 20-day loan, but you pay $2/98 = 2.04$ percent more for your goods. The number of 20-day periods in a year is $365/20 = 18.25$. A rupee invested for 18.25 periods at 2.04 percent per period grows to $(1.0204)^{18.25}$ = Rs. 1.446, a 44.6 percent return on the original investment. If a customer is happy to borrow at this rate, it's a good bet that he or she is desperate for cash (or can't work out compound interest). For a discussion of this issue, see J. K. Smith, "Trade Credit and Information Asymmetry," *Journal of Finance* 42 (September 1987), pp. 863–872.

[3]Commercial drafts are sometimes known by the general term *bills of exchange*.

Credit Analysis

Firms may not be allowed to discriminate between customers by charging them different prices. Nor may they discriminate by offering the same prices but different credit terms. You *can* offer different terms of sale to different *classes* of buyer. For example, you can offer volume discounts or discounts to customers willing to enter into long-term purchase contracts. But as a rule, if you have a customer of doubtful standing, you should keep to your regular terms of sale and protect yourself by restricting the volume of goods that the customer may buy on credit.

There are a number of ways to find out whether customers are likely to pay their debts. For existing customers an obvious indication is whether they have paid promptly in the past. For new customers you can use the firm's financial statements to make your own assessment, or you may be able to look at how highly investors value the firm.[4] However, the simplest way to assess a customer's credit standing is to seek the views of a specialist in credit assessment. For example, in Chapter 24 we described how bond rating agencies, such as CRISIL and ICRA, provide a useful guide to the riskiness of the firm's bonds.

Bond ratings are usually available only for relatively large firms. However, you can obtain information on many smaller companies from a credit agency. Dun and Bradstreet is by far the largest of these agencies and its database contains credit information on 64 million businesses worldwide. In the US credit bureaus are another source of data on a customer's credit standing. In addition to providing data on small businesses, they also hold credit details on individual consumers, and provide an overall credit score for each individual based on his or her personal details and credit history.[5]

Finally, firms can also ask their bank to undertake a credit check. It will contact the customer's bank and ask for information on the customer's average balance, access to bank credit, and general reputation.

Of course you don't want to subject each order to the same credit analysis. It makes sense to concentrate your attention on the large and doubtful orders.

The Credit Decision

Let us suppose that you have taken the first three steps toward an effective credit operation. In other words, you have fixed your terms of sale; you have decided on the contract that customers must sign; and you have established a procedure for estimating the probability that they will pay up. Your next step is to work out which of your customers should be offered credit.

If there is no possibility of repeat orders, the decision is relatively simple. Figure 30.1 summarizes your choice. On one hand, you can refuse credit. In this case you make neither profit nor loss. The alternative is to offer credit. Suppose that the probability that the customer will pay up is p. If the customer does pay, you receive additional revenues (REV) and you incur additional costs; your net gain is the present value of REV − COST. Unfortunately, you can't be certain that the customer will pay; there is a probability $(1 - p)$ of default. Default means that you receive nothing and incur the additional costs. The *expected* profit from each course of action is therefore as follows:

---

[4]We discussed how you can use these sources of information in Section 24.3.

[5]We discussed credit scoring models in Section 24.3. Credit bureau scores are often called "FICO scores" because most credit bureaus use a credit scoring model developed by Fair Isaac and Company. FICO scores are provided by the three major credit bureaus—Equifax, Experian, and TransUnion.

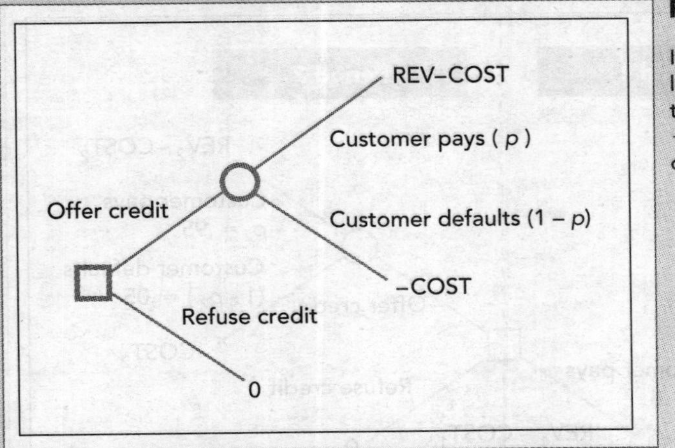

FIGURE 30.1

If you refuse credit, you make neither profit nor loss. If you offer credit, there is a probability p that the customer will pay and you will make REV – COST; there is a probability $(1 - p)$ that the customer will default and you will lose COST.

	Expected Profit
Refuse credit	0
Grant credit	pPV(REV – COST) – $(1 - p)$PV(COST)

You should grant credit if the expected gain from doing so is positive.

Consider, for example, the case of the Cast Iron Company. On each nondelinquent sale Cast Iron receives revenues with a present value of Rs. 1,200 and incurs costs with a value of Rs. 1,000. Therefore the company's expected profit if it offers credit is

$$p\text{PV(REV} - \text{COST)} - (1 - p)\text{PV(COST)} = p \times 200 - (1 - p) \times 1{,}000$$

If the probability of collection is 5/6, Cast Iron can expect to break even:

$$\text{Expected profit} = \frac{5}{6} \times 200 - \left(1 - \frac{5}{6}\right) \times 1{,}000 = 0$$

Therefore Cast Iron's policy should be to grant credit whenever the chances of collection are better than 5 out of 6.

So far we have ignored the possibility of repeat orders. But one of the reasons for offering credit today is that it may help to get yourself a good, regular customer. Figure 30.2 illustrates the problem.[6] Cast Iron has been asked to extend credit to a new customer. You can find little information on the firm, and you believe that the probability of payment is no better than .8. If you grant credit, the expected profit on this customer's order is

$$\begin{aligned}\text{Expected profit on initial order} &= p_1\text{PV(REV} - \text{COST)} - (1 - p_1)\text{PV(COST)}\\ &= (.8 \times 200) - (.2 \times 1{,}000) = -\text{Rs. } 40\end{aligned}$$

You decide to refuse credit.

[6] Our example is adapted from H. Bierman, Jr., and W. H. Hausman, "The Credit Granting Decision," *Management Science* 16 (April 1970), pp. B519–B532.

FIGURE 30.2

In this example there is only a .8 probability that your customer will pay in Period 1; but if payment is made, there will be another order in Period 2. The probability that the customer will pay for the second order is .95. The possibility of this good repeat order more than compensates for the expected loss in Period 1.

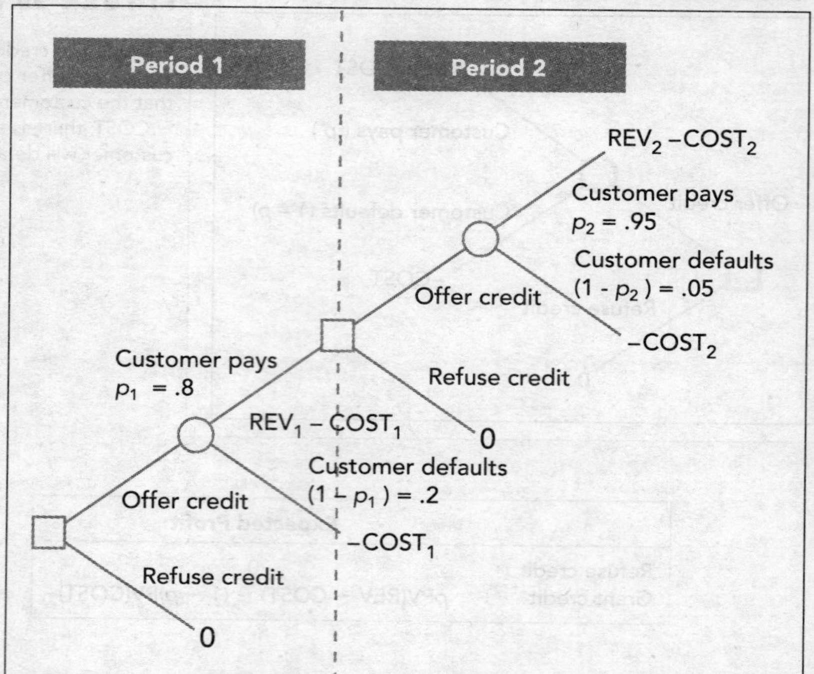

This is the correct decision if there is no chance of a repeat order. But look again at the decision tree in Figure 30.2. If the customer does pay up, there will be a repeat order next year. Because the customer has paid once, you can be 95 percent sure that he or she will pay again. For this reason any repeat order is very profitable:

$$\begin{aligned}\text{Next year's expected profit on repeat order} &= p_2\text{PV(REV} - \text{COST)} \\ &\quad - (1 - p_2)\text{PV(COST)} \\ &= (.95 \times 200) - (.05 \times 1{,}000) = \text{Rs. } 140\end{aligned}$$

Now you can reexamine today's credit decision. If you grant credit today, you receive the expected profit on the initial order *plus* the possible opportunity to extend credit next year:

$$\begin{aligned}\text{Total expected profit} &= \text{expected profit on initial order} \\ &\quad + \text{probability of payment and repeat order} \\ &\quad \times \text{PV(next year's expected profit on repeat order)} \\ &= -40 + .80 \times \text{PV}(140)\end{aligned}$$

At any reasonable discount rate, you ought to extend credit. Notice that you should do so even though you expect to take a loss on the initial order. The expected loss is more than outweighed by the possibility that you will secure a reliable and regular customer. Cast Iron is not committed to making further sales to the customer, but by extending credit today, it gains a valuable *option* to do so. It will exercise this option only if the customer demonstrates its creditworthiness by paying promptly.

Of course real-life situations are generally far more complex than our simple Cast Iron examples. Customers are not all good or all bad. Many of them pay consistently late; you get your money, but it costs more to collect and you lose a few months' interest. Then there is the uncertainty about repeat sales. There may be a good chance that the customer will give you further business, but you can't be sure of that and you don't know for how long she will continue to buy.

Like almost all financial decisions, credit allocation involves a strong dose of judgment. Our examples are intended as reminders of the issues involved rather than as cookbook formulas. Here are the basic things to remember.

1. *Maximize profit.* As credit manager, you should not focus on minimizing the number of bad accounts; your job is to maximize expected profit. You must face up to the following facts: The best that can happen is that the customer pays promptly; the worst is default. In the best case, the firm receives the full additional revenues from the sale less the additional costs; in the worst, it receives nothing and loses the costs. You must weigh the chances of these alternative outcomes. If the margin of profit is high, you are justified in a more liberal credit policy; if it is low, you cannot afford many bad debts.[7]
2. *Concentrate on the dangerous accounts.* You should not expend the same effort on analyzing all credit applications. If an application is small or clear-cut, your decision should be largely routine; if it is large or doubtful, you may do better to move straight to a detailed credit appraisal. Most credit managers don't make decisions on an order-by-order basis. Instead, they set a credit limit for each customer. The sales representative is required to refer the order for approval only if the customer exceeds this limit.
3. *Look beyond the immediate order.* The credit decision is a dynamic problem. You cannot look only at the present. Sometimes it may be worth accepting a relatively poor risk as long as there is a good chance that the customer will become a regular and reliable buyer. New businesses must, therefore, be prepared to incur more bad debts than established businesses. This is part of the cost of building a good customer list.

Collection Policy

The final step in credit management is to collect payment. When a customer is in arrears, the usual procedure is to send a statement of account and to follow this at intervals with increasingly insistent letters or telephone calls. If none of these has any effect, most companies turn the debt over to a collection agent or an attorney.

Large firms can reap economies of scale in record keeping, billing, and so on, but the small firm may not be able to support a fully fledged credit operation. However, the small firm may be able to obtain some scale economies by farming out part of the job to a **factor.** This arrangement is known as **factoring.**

Factoring typically works as follows: The factor and the client agree on credit limits for each customer and on the average collection period. The client then notifies each customer that the factor has purchased the debt. Thereafter, for any sale, the client sends a copy of the invoice to the factor,

[7]Look back at our Cast Iron example, where we concluded that the company is justified in granting credit if the probability of collection is greater than 5/6. If the customer pays, Cast Iron will earn a profit margin of 200/1200 = 1/6. In other words, the company is justified in granting credit if the probability of payment exceeds 1 − profit margin.

the customer makes payment directly to the factor, and the factor pays the client on the basis of the agreed average collection period regardless of whether the customer has paid. There are, of course, costs to such an operation, and the factor typically charges a fee of 1 to 2 percent of the value of the invoice.[8]

Factoring is slowly becoming very popular among the small and medium firms in India. The total size of funds deployed by the factoring companies in India is a little more than Rs. 1000 crores. Canbank Factors and SBI Factors are two of the leading players in the factoring market in India. They mostly cater to the requirements of the small and medium sized firms in India. Because a factor may be employed by a number of manufacturers, it sees a larger proportion of the transactions that any single firm and therefore is better placed to judge the creditworthiness of each customer.[9]

If you don't want help with collection but do want protection against bad debts, you can obtain credit insurance. For example, most governments have established agencies to insure export business. In India, the Export Credit Guarantee Corporation of India provides credit risk insurance covers to exporters against payment risks. It also offers guarantees to banks and financial institutions to enable exporters to obtain better facilities from them.

There is always a potential conflict of interest between the collection operation and the sales department. Sales representatives commonly complain that they no sooner win new customers than the collection department frightens them off with threatening letters. The collection manager, on the other hand, bemoans the fact that the sales force is concerned only with winning orders and does not care whether the goods are subsequently paid for.

There are also many instances of cooperation between the sales force and the collection department. For example, the specialty chemical division of a major pharmaceutical company actually made a business loan to an important customer that had been suddenly cut off by its bank. The pharmaceutical company bet that it knew its customer better than the customer's bank did. The bet paid off. The customer arranged alternative bank financing, paid back the pharmaceutical company, and became an even more loyal customer. It was a nice example of financial management supporting sales.

It is not common for suppliers to make business loans in this way, but they lend money indirectly whenever they allow a delay in payment. Trade credit can be an important source of funds for indigent customers that cannot obtain a bank loan. But that raises an important question: If the bank is unwilling to lend, does it make sense for you, the supplier, to continue to extend trade credit? Here are two possible reasons that it may make sense: First, as in the case of our pharmaceutical company, you may have more information than the bank about the customer's business. Second, you need to look beyond the immediate transaction and recognize that your firm may stand to lose some profitable future sales if the customer goes out of business.[10]

[8]Generally, the factor is also prepared to advance 70 to 80 percent of the value of the accounts receivable at an appropriate interest rate.

[9]This point is made in S. L. Mian and C. W. Smith, Jr., "Accounts Receivable Management Policy: Theory and Evidence," *Journal of Finance* 47 (March 1992), pp. 169–200.

[10]Of course, banks also need to recognize the possibility of continuing business from the firm. The question therefore is whether suppliers have a *greater* stake in the firm's continuing prosperity. For some evidence on the determinants of the supply and demand for trade credit, see M. A. Petersen and R. G. Rajan, "Trade Credit: Theories and Evidence," *Review of Financial Studies* 10 (Fall 1997), pp. 661–692.

30.2 INVENTORY MANAGEMENT

The second important current asset is *inventory*. Inventories may consist of raw materials, work in process, or finished goods awaiting sale and shipment. Firms are not obliged to carry these inventories. For example, they could buy materials day by day, as needed. But then they would pay higher prices for ordering in small lots, and they would risk production delays if the materials were not delivered on time. They can avoid that risk by ordering more than the firm's immediate needs. Similarly, firms could do away with inventories of finished goods by producing only what they expect to sell tomorrow. But this also could be a dangerous strategy. A producer with only a small inventory of finished goods is more likely to be caught short and unable to fill orders if demand is unexpectedly high. Moreover, a large inventory of finished goods may allow longer, more economical production runs.

But there are also costs to holding inventories that must be set against these benefits. Money tied up in inventories does not earn interest; storage and insurance must be paid for; and there may be a risk of spillage or obsolescence. Therefore, production managers need to strike a sensible balance between the benefits of holding inventory and the costs.

Corporations in the U.S. today get by with lower levels of inventory than they used to. Thirty years ago, inventories held by U.S. companies accounted for 12 percent of firm assets. Today the figure is little more than half of that. The ratio of inventory to total assets for a sample of 5259 manufacturing companies in India has however remained stagnant at 15 percent over the last ten years (1996-2005).

One way that companies in the US have reduced inventory levels is by moving to a **just-in-time approach.** Just-in-time was pioneered by Toyota in Japan. Toyota keeps inventories of auto parts to a minimum by ordering supplies only as they are needed. Thus deliveries of components to its plants are made throughout the day at intervals as short as one hour. Toyota is able to operate successfully with such low inventories only because it has a set of plans to ensure that strikes, traffic snarl-ups, or other hazards don't halt the flow of components and bring production to a standstill. Many companies in the United States have learned from Toyota's example. Thirty years ago Ford used to turn over its inventories about 5 times a year; today that figure is over 20 times.

The US firms are also finding that they can reduce their inventories of finished goods by producing their goods to order. For example, Dell Computer discovered that it did not need to keep a large stock of finished machines. Its customers are able to use the Internet to specify what features they want on their PC. The computer is then assembled to order and shipped to the customer.[11]

30.3 CASH

Short-term securities pay interest, cash doesn't. So why do corporations and individuals hold billions of dollars in cash and demand deposits? Why, for example, don't you take all *your* cash and invest it in interest-bearing securities? The answer of course is that cash gives you more *liquidity*

[11]These examples of just-in-time and build-to-order production are taken from T. Murphy, "JIT When ASAP Isn't Good Enough," *Ward's Auto World* (May 1999), pp. 67–73; R. Schreffler, "Alive and Well," *Ward's Auto World* (May 1999), pp. 73–77; "A Long March: Mass Customization," *The Economist*, July 14, 2001, pp. 63–65.

than do securities. You can use it to buy things. It is hard enough to get Mumbai taxi drivers to give you change for a Rs. 1000 bill, but try asking them to split a Treasury bill.

In equilibrium all assets in the same risk class are priced to give the same expected marginal benefit. The benefit from holding Treasury bills is the interest that you receive; the benefit from holding cash is that it gives you a convenient store of liquidity. In equilibrium the marginal value of this liquidity is equal to the marginal value of the interest on Treasury bills. This is just another way of saying that Treasury bills have zero net present value; they are fair value relative to cash.

Does this mean that it does not matter how much cash you hold? Of course not. The marginal value of liquidity declines as you hold increasing amounts of cash. When you have only a small proportion of your wealth in cash, a little extra can be extremely useful; when you have a substantial holding, any additional liquidity is not worth much. Therefore, as financial manager you want to hold cash balances up to the point where the marginal value of the liquidity is equal to the value of the interest foregone.

In choosing between cash and short-term securities, the financial manager faces a task like that of the production manager. After all, cash is just another raw material that you need to do business, and there are costs and benefits to holding large "inventories" of cash. If the cash were invested in securities, it would earn interest. On the other hand, you can't use those securities to pay the firm's bills. If you had to sell them every time you needed to pay a bill, you could incur heavy transactions costs. The financial manager must trade off the cost of keeping an inventory of cash (the lost interest) against the benefits (the saving on transactions costs).

For small firms this trade-off can be important. But for very large firms the transactions costs of buying and selling securities become trivial compared with the opportunity cost of holding idle cash balances. Suppose that the interest rate is 5 percent a year, or roughly 5/365 = .0137 percent per day. Then the daily interest earned by Rs.1 million is 0.000137 × 1,000,000 = Rs.137. Even at a cost of Rs. 50 per transaction, which is generously high, it pays to buy Treasury bills today and sell them tomorrow rather than to leave Rs.1 million idle overnight. Consider Wal-Mart, which has annual sales of about $250 billion and an average daily cash flow of $250,000,000,000/365, or nearly $700 million. Firms of this size generally end up buying or selling securities once a day every day.

Banks have developed ways to help firms to invest idle cash. For example, they may provide **sweep programs,** where the bank automatically "sweeps" surplus funds into a *money market deposit account* (MMDA), which pays interest. Banks are happy to do this because MMDA's avoid the reserve requirements on demand deposits.

Why then do large firms hold any significant amounts of cash? There are basically two reasons. First, cash may be left in non-interest-bearing accounts to compensate banks for the services they provide. Second, large corporations may have literally hundreds of accounts with dozens of different banks. It is often better to leave idle cash in these accounts than to monitor each account daily and make daily transfers among them.

One major reason for this proliferation of bank accounts is decentralized management. You cannot give a subsidiary operating autonomy without giving its managers the right to spend and receive cash. Good cash management nevertheless implies some degree of centralization. It is impossible to maintain your desired cash inventory if all the subsidiaries in the group are responsible for their own private pools of cash. And you certainly want to avoid situations in which one subsidiary is investing its spare cash at 5 percent while another is borrowing at 8 percent. It is not surprising, therefore, that even in highly decentralized companies there is generally central control over cash balances and bank relations.

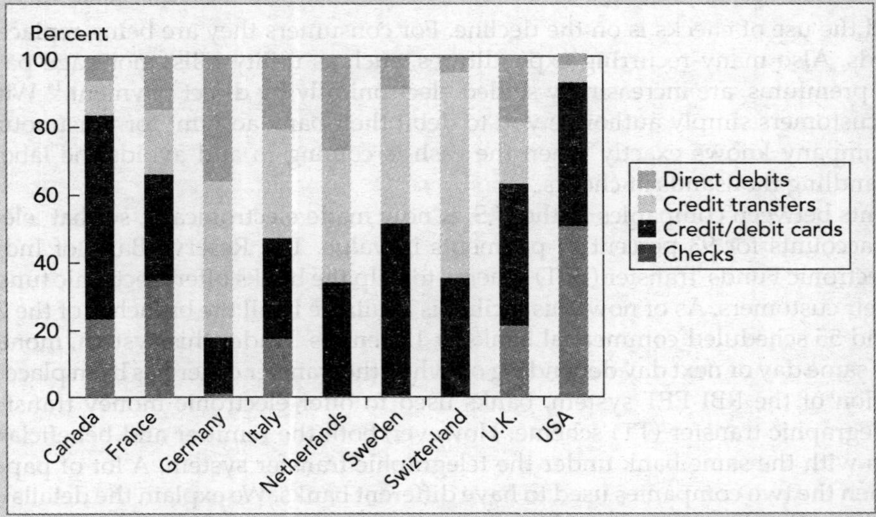

FIGURE 30.3

How purchases are paid for. Percentage of total *volume* of cashless transactions 2002. (Data exclude small usage of card-based e-money).

Source: Bank for International Settlements, "Statistics on Payment and Settlement Systems in Selected Countries," March 2004, **www.bis.org/publ.**

Using Cash Efficiently

In the United States the majority of small face-to-face purchases are made with dollar bills. The most popular alternative is to pay by check. Each year U.S. individuals and firms write about 70 billion checks.[12]

The United States is unusual in this heavy use of checks. Look, for example, at Figure 30.3, which shows how purchases are paid for in different countries. You can see that checks are almost unknown in countries like Germany, the Netherlands, and Sweden. Most payments in these countries are made by debit cards or credit transfer.[13]

Firms that receive a large volume of checks have devised a number of ways to make sure that the cash becomes available as quickly as possible. For example, many firms use **concentration banking** to speed up collections. In this case, all customers in a particular area make payment to a local branch office rather than to company headquarters. The branch then deposits the checks into a local bank account, and any surplus funds are transferred to a *concentration account* at one of the company's principal banks. There are two reasons that concentration banking allows the company to gain quicker use of its funds. First, because the branch office is nearer to the customer, the mailing time is reduced. Second, since the customer's check is likely to be drawn on a local bank, the time taken to clear the check is also reduced.

Concentration banking is often combined with a **lockbox system.** In this case the firm's customers are instructed to send their payments to a regional post-office box. The local bank then takes on the administrative chore of emptying the box and depositing the checks in the company's local account.

[12]"In India more than 90 percent of the total personal purchases are made by cash. The share of transactions made through debit and credit cards is just about 1 percent of the total personal expenditure. However, the total purchases made through debit and credit cards have increased at a rate of more than 68 percent in the last six years, and we believe that they will continue to account for bulk of the transactions in future."

[13]Debit cards allow the cardholder to transfer money to the receiver's bank account. With a credit transfer the payer initiates the transaction, for example, by giving her bank a standing order to make a regular payment. With a direct debit the transaction is initiated by the payee and is usually processed electronically.

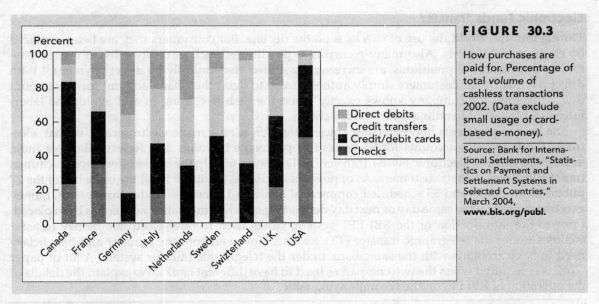

Electronic Funds Transfer

Throughout the world the use of checks is on the decline. For consumers they are being replaced by credit or debit cards. Also many recurring expenditures, such as utility bills, mortgage payments, and insurance premiums, are increasingly settled electronically by direct payment.[14] With direct payment your customers simply authorize you to debit their bank account for the amount due. Therefore, the company knows exactly when the cash is coming in and avoids the labor-intensive process of handling thousands of checks.

The bulk of payments between companies in the U.S. is now made electronically, so that electronic funds transfer accounts for 93 percent of payments in value. The Reserve Bank of India introduced the RBI Electronic Funds Transfer (EFT) scheme to help the banks offer electronic funds transfer facilities to their customers. As of now, this facility is available in all the branches of the 27 public sector banks and 55 scheduled commercial banks at 15 centres. Under this system, money gets transferred on the same day or next day depending on when the transfer order has been placed. Prior to the introduction of the RBI EFT system, banks used to offer electronic money transfer facilities under the telegraphic transfer (TT) scheme. However, both the remitter and beneficiary need to have accounts with the same bank under the telegraphic transfer system. A lot of paper work was required when the two companies used to have different banks. We explain the details of the operation of RBI EFT in the accompanying table.

Steps in RBI EFT System

Step-1: The remitter fills in the EFT Application form giving the particulars of the beneficiary (city, bank, branch, beneficiary's name, account type and account number) and authorizes the branch to remit a specified amount to the beneficiary by raising a debit to the remitter's account.
Step-2: The remitting branch prepares a schedule and sends the duplicate of the EFT application form to its Service branch for EFT data preparation. If the branch is equipped with a computer system, data preparation can be done at the branch level in the specified format.
Step-3: The Service branch prepares the EFT data file by using a software package supplied by RBI and transmits the same to the local RBI (National Clearing Cell) to be included for the settlement of 12 noon, 2 pm and 4 pm.
Step-4: The RBI at the remitting centre consolidates the files received from all banks, sorts the transactions city-wise and prepares vouchers for debiting the remitting banks on Day-1 itself. City-wise files are transmitted to the RBI offices at the respective destination centres.
Step-5: RBI at the destination centre receives the files from the originating centres, consolidates them and sorts them bank-wise. Thereafter, bank-wise remittance data files are transmitted to banks on Day 1 itself. Bank-wise vouchers are prepared for crediting the receiving banks' accounts the same day or next day.
Step-6: On Day 1/2 morning the receiving banks at the destination centres process the remittance files transmitted by RBI and forward credit reports to the destination branches for crediting the beneficiaries' accounts.

Source: www.rbi.org.in

[14]Consumers also may receive and pay bills electronically via their personal computer. Currently electronic bill presentment and payment (EBPP) accounts for only a small proportion of payments, but it is forecasted to grow rapidly.

Electronic funds transfer system has at least three advantages:

- Record keeping and routine transactions are easy to automate when money moves electronically.
- The marginal cost of transaction is very low. In fact, the RBI has waived the processing charges till March 31, 2007.
- Because companies do not need to wait for cheques to clear, they may get earlier access to their funds.

International Cash Management

Cash management in domestic firms is child's play compared with that in large multinational corporations operating in dozens of different countries, each with its own currency, banking system, and legal structure.

A single centralized cash management system is an unattainable ideal for these companies, although they are edging toward it. For example, suppose that you are treasurer of a large multinational company with operations throughout Europe. You could allow the separate businesses to manage their own cash, but that would be costly and would almost certainly result in each one accumulating little hoards of cash. The solution is to set up a regional system. In this case the company establishes a local concentration account with a bank in each country. Any surplus cash is swept daily into central multicurrency accounts in London or another European banking center. This cash is then invested in marketable securities or used to finance any subsidiaries that have a cash shortage.

Payments can also be made out of the regional center. For example, to pay wages in each European country, the company just needs to send its principal bank a computer file with details of the payments to be made. The bank then finds the least costly way to transfer the cash from the company's central accounts and arranges for the funds to be credited on the correct day to the employees in each country.

Companies that maintain separate balances in each country are liable to find that they have a cash surplus in one country and a shortage in another. In this case the company could lend the surplus and borrow the deficit. However, that is likely to be costly, since banks need to charge a higher rate to borrowers than they pay to lenders. One alternative is to convert the surplus cash pool into the currency which is in short supply, but a simpler solution is to arrange for the bank to *pool* all your cash surpluses and shortages. In this case no money is transferred among accounts. Instead, the bank just adds together the credit and debit balances, and pays you interest at its lending rate on the net surplus.

Most large multinationals have several banks in each country, but the more banks they use, the less control they have over their cash balances. So development of regional cash management systems favors banks that can offer a worldwide branch network. These banks can also afford the high costs of setting up computer systems for handling cash payments and receipts in different countries.

Paying for Bank Services

Much of the work of cash management—processing checks, transferring funds, running lockboxes, helping keep track of the company's accounts—is done by banks. And banks provide many other services not so directly linked to cash management, such as handling payments and receipts in foreign currency, or acting as custodian for securities.[15]

[15]Of course, banks also lend money or give firms the *option* to borrow under a line of credit. See Section 31.5.

All these services need to be paid for. Usually payment is in the form of a monthly fee, but banks may agree to waive the fee as long as the firm maintains a minimum average balance in an interest-free deposit. Banks are prepared to do this, because, after setting aside a portion of the money in a reserve account with the RBI, they can relend the money to earn interest. Demand deposits earmarked to pay for bank services are termed *compensating balances*. They used to be a very common way to pay for bank services, but there has been a steady trend away from using compensating balances and toward direct fees.

30.4 MARKETABLE SECURITIES

At the end of March 2006, Bajaj Auto was sitting on a Rs. 4830 crores mountain of cash, amounting to about half of the company's total assets.[16] The company kept Rs. 82 crores in the bank to support day-to-day operations and invested the surplus as follows:

Investment	Amount
Investment in mutual funds	Rs. 483.62 Crores
Investment in govt. securities	2957.5
Investment in debentures/PSU bonds	1307
Total	Rs. 4748.12 Crores

Most companies do not have the luxury of such huge cash surpluses, but they also park any cash that is not immediately needed in short-term investments. The market for these investments is known as the **money market.** The money market has no physical marketplace. It consists of a loose collection of banks and dealers linked together by telephones or through the Web. But a huge volume of securities is regularly traded on the money market, and competition is vigorous.

Most large corporations manage their own money-market investments, but small companies sometimes find it more convenient to hire a professional investment management firm or to put their cash into a money-market fund. This is a mutual fund that invests only in low-risk, short-term securities.[17]

Calculating the Yield on Money-Market Investments

Many money-market investments are pure discount securities. This means that they don't pay interest. The return consists of the difference between the amount you pay and the amount you receive at maturity. Unfortunately, it is no good trying to persuade the Income Tax Department that this difference represents capital gain. The Income Tax Department is wise to that one and will tax your return as ordinary income.

Interest rates on money-market investments are often quoted on a discount basis. For example, suppose that three-month bills are issued at a discount of 5 percent. This is a rather complicated way of saying that the price of a three-month bill is $100 - (3/12) \times 5 = 98.75$. Therefore, for every Rs. 98.75 that you invest today, you receive Rs. 100 at the end of three months. The return over three months is $1.25/98.75 = .0127$, or 1.27 percent. This is equivalent to an annual yield of 5.08 percent simple interest or 5.18 percent if interest is compounded annually. Note that the return is always higher than the discount. When you read that an investment is selling at a discount of 5 percent, it is very easy to slip into the mistake of thinking that this is its return.[18]

[16] In fact, in 2003, more than 60 percent of the total assets of Microsoft was in the form of cash. In July 2004, Microsoft decided to pay out a large part of its surplus cash to shareholders.

[17] We discussed money-market funds in Section 17.3.

[18] To confuse things even more, dealers in the money market often quote rates as if there were only 360 days in a year. So a discount of 5 percent on a bill maturing in 91 days translates into a price of $100 - 5 \times (91/360) = 98.74$ percent.

Yields on Money-Market Investments

When we value long-term debt, it is important to take account of default risk. Almost anything may happen in 30 years, and even today's most respectable company may get into trouble eventually. Therefore, corporate bonds offer higher yields than Treasury bonds.

Short-term debt is not risk-free either. When California was mired in the energy crisis of 2001, Southern California Edison and Pacific Gas and Electric were forced to suspend payments on nearly $1 billion of maturing commercial paper.[19] However, such examples are exceptions; in general, the danger of default is less for money-market securities issued by corporations than for corporate bonds. There are two reasons for this. First, the range of possible outcomes is smaller for short-term investments. Even though the distant future may be clouded, you can usually be confident that a particular company will survive for at least the next month. Second, for the most part only well-established companies can borrow in the money market. If you are going to lend money for just a few days, you can't afford to spend too much time in evaluating the loan. Thus, you will consider only blue-chip borrowers.

Despite the high quality of money-market investments, there are often significant differences in yield between corporate and government securities. Why is this? One answer is the risk of default. Another is that the investments have different degrees of liquidity or "moneyness." Investors like Treasury bills because they are easily turned into cash on short notice. Securities that cannot be converted so quickly and cheaply into cash need to offer relatively high yields.

During times of market turmoil investors may place a higher value on having ready access to cash. On these occasions the yield on illiquid securities can increase dramatically. This happened in the fall of 1998 when a large hedge fund, Long Term Capital Management (LTCM), came close to collapse.[20] Fearful that LTCM would be forced to liquidate its huge positions, investors shrank from illiquid securities, and there was a "flight to quality." The spread between the yield on commercial paper and Treasury bills rose to about 120 basis points (1.20 percent), almost four times its level at the beginning of the year.

The International Money Market

In Chapter 25 we pointed out that there are two main markets for dollar bonds. There is the domestic market in the United States and there is the eurobond market centered in London. Similarly, in addition to the domestic money market, there is also an international market for short-term dollar investments, which is known as the *eurodollar* market.

Eurodollars have nothing to do with the euro, the currency of the European Monetary Union (EMU). They are simply dollars deposited in a bank in Europe. For example, suppose that an American oil company buys crude oil from an Arab sheik and pays for it with a $1 million check drawn on JP Morgan Chase. The sheik then deposits the check with his account at Barclays Bank in London. As a result, Barclays has an asset in the form of a $1 million credit in its account with

[19]Commercial paper is short-term debt issued by corporations. We describe it in Section 31.5.

[20]Hedge funds specialize in making positive investments in securities that are believed to be underpriced, while selling short those that appear overvalued. The story of LTCM is told in R. Lowenstein, "*When Genius Failed: The Rise and Fall of Long Term Capital Management*, (New York: Random House, 2000); and N. Dunbar, *Inventing Money: The Story of Long Term Capital Management and the Legends behind It*, (New York: John Wiley, 2000).

JP Morgan Chase. It also has an offsetting liability in the form of a dollar deposit. Since that dollar deposit is placed in Europe, it is called a eurodollar deposit.[21]

Just as there is both a domestic U.S. money market and a eurodollar market, so there is both a domestic Japanese money market and a market in London for euroyen. So, if a U.S. corporation wishes to make a short-term investment in yen, it can deposit the yen with a bank in Tokyo or it can make a euroyen deposit in London. Similarly, there is both a domestic money market in the euro area as well as a money market for euros in London.[22] And so on.

Major international banks in London lend dollars to one another at the *London interbank offered rate* (LIBOR). Similarly, they lend yen to each other at the yen LIBOR interest rate, and they lend euros at the **euro interbank offered rate,** or **Euribor.** These interest rates are used as a benchmark for pricing many types of short-term loans in the United States and in other countries. For example, a corporation in the United States may issue a floating-rate note with interest payments tied to dollar LIBOR.

If we lived in a world without regulation and taxes, the interest rate on a eurodollar loan would have to be the same as the rate on an equivalent domestic dollar loan. However, the international debt markets thrive because governments attempt to regulate domestic bank lending. When the U.S. government limited the rate of interest that banks in the United States could pay on domestic deposits, companies could earn a higher rate of interest by keeping their dollars on deposit in Europe. As these restrictions have been removed, differences in interest rates have largely disappeared.

In the late 1970s the U.S. government was concerned that its regulations were driving business overseas to foreign banks and the overseas branches of American banks. To attract some of this business back to the States, the government in 1981 allowed U.S. and foreign banks to establish **international banking facilities (IBFs).** An IBF is the financial equivalent of a free-trade zone; it is physically located in the United States, but it is not required to maintain reserves with the Federal Reserve and depositors are not subject to any U.S. tax.[23] However, there are tight restrictions on what business an IBF can conduct. In particular, it cannot accept deposits from domestic U.S. corporations or make loans to them.

Money-Market Instruments

The principal money-market instruments are summarized in Table 30.2. We will describe each in turn.

Government of India Treasury Bills The first item in Table 30.2 is Government of India Treasury Bills. These are issued by the RBI on behalf of the Government of India. The RBI auctions 14-day and 91-day T-bills on a weekly basis (every Fridays) and 182-day and 364-day T-bills on a fortnightly basis (every alternative Wednesdays).[24] Before November 1998, all auctions were based on the multiple-price auction system (same as French auction). In case of multiple-price auctions,

[21]The sheik could equally well deposit the check with the London branch of a U.S. bank or a Japanese bank. He would still have made a eurodollar deposit.

[22]Occasionally (but only occasionally) referred to as "euroeuros."

[23]For these reasons dollars held on deposit in an IBF are classed as eurodollars.

[24]See http://www.rbi.org.in/scripts/FAQView.aspx?Id=48 for details.

successful bidders pay their own bid prices. However, after November 6, 1998, auction of 91-day T-bills are conducted based on uniform-price auction (same as Dutch auction) method. Under the uniform-price auction system, all bidders pay the same price, i.e., the cut-off price. Non-competitive bids (allowed only for specific entities like state governments and certain other statutory bodies) are filled-in at the same price as the successful competitive bids.

Bank Time Deposits and Certificates of Deposit If you make a time deposit with a bank, you are lending money to the bank for a fixed period. If you need the money before maturity, the bank will usually allow you to withdraw it but will exact a penalty in the form of a reduced rate of interest.

In June 1989, banks in India introduced the certificates of deposit (CD) with maturity value of Rs.1 lakh. The certificates of deposit are issued at a discount to the face value and have a maturity period ranging from 15 days to 1 year. In this case, when a bank borrows, it issues a certificate of deposit, which is simply evidence of a time deposit with that bank. The CDs are negotiable instruments. That means if a lender needs the money before maturity, it can sell the CD to another investor. When the CD matures, the new owner of the CD presents it to the bank and receives payment.

Commercial Paper and Medium-Term Notes These consist of unsecured, short- and medium-term debt issued by companies on a fairly regular basis. We will discuss both in more detail in the next chapter.

Bankers' Acceptances We saw earlier in the chapter how **bankers' acceptances (BAs)** may be used to finance exports or imports. An acceptance begins life as a written demand for the bank to pay a given sum at a future date. Once the bank accepts this demand, it becomes a negotiable security that can be bought or sold through money-market dealers. Acceptances by the large U.S. banks generally mature in one to six months and involve very low credit risk.

Repurchase Agreements **Repurchase agreements,** or *repos*, are effectively secured loans that are typically made to a government security dealer. They work as follows: The investor buys part of the dealer's holding of Treasury securities and simultaneously arranges to sell them back again at a later date at a specified higher price.[25] The borrower (the dealer) is said to have entered into a *repo*; the lender (who buys the securities) is said to have a *reverse repo*.

Under the Liquidity Adjustment Scheme (LAF), RBI is conducting repo and reverse-repo auctions daily (excepting on Saturdays and Sundays) since 5 June 2000. Excepting for the intervening holidays and Fridays, the repo tenure is one day. On Fridays repo auctions are held for three days maturity to cover the following Saturday and Sunday.

[25]To reduce the risk of repos, it is common to value the security at less than its market value. This difference is known as a *haircut*.

Investment	Borrower	Maturities When Issued	Marketability	Basis for Calculating Interest	Comments
Treasury Bills	Government of India	14-days, 91-days, 182-days, or 364 days	Good Secondary Market	Discount	14-day and 91-day T-Bills are auctioned weekly. The 182-days and 364-days T-Bills are auctioned fortnightly.
Certificates of Deposit	Banks	14 days to 1 year	Fair secondary market	Discount	The CDs are negotiable instruments
Commercial Papers	Industrial firms, financial institutions apart from primary dealers and satellite dealers	15 days to 1 year	Fair secondary market	Discount	Only companies with a CRISIL rating of P2 and above or equivalent rating can issue CPs
Repurchase agreements (repos)	Banks and primary dealers, and all entities having SGL and current account with RBI	1 day (2 to 3 days if issued on Fridays or holidays)	Excellent Secondary market	Repurchase price set higher than selling price; difference quoted as repo interest rate (adjusted for coupon)	Since June 2000, RBI is conducting Repo transactions every day under the Liquidity Adjustment Scheme

TABLE 30.2

Money-market investments in India.

SUMMARY

Companies invest in four principal short-term assets—accounts receivable, inventories, cash, and short-term securities. Each of these investments needs to be managed.

Credit management (the management of receivables) involves five steps:

1. Establish the length of the payment period and the size of any cash discounts for customers who pay promptly.
2. Decide the form of the contract with your customer. For example, if your customer's credit is somewhat shaky, you can ask the customer to arrange for a banker's acceptance. In this case payment is guaranteed by the customer's bank.
3. Assess your customer's creditworthiness. You can either do your own homework or rely on a credit agency or credit bureau that specializes in gathering information about the credit standing of firms or individuals.
4. Establish sensible credit limits. Remember your aim is not to minimize the number of bad debts, it is to maximize profits. Remember also not to be too shortsighted in reckoning the expected profit. It may be worth accepting marginal applicants if there is a chance that they may become regular and reliable customers.
5. Collect. You need to be resolute with the truly delinquent customers, but you do not want to offend the good ones by writing demanding letters just because their check has been delayed in the mail.

The second important current asset consists of inventories of raw materials, work in process, and finished goods. Inventories have benefits. For example, a stock of raw materials reduces the risk that the firm will be forced to shut down production because of an unexpected shortage. Inventories are also costly. They tie up capital and they are expensive to store. The task of the production manager is to strike a sensible balance between these benefits and costs. In recent years many companies have decided that they can get by on lower inventories than before. For example, some have adopted *just-in-time* systems that allow the firm to keep inventories to a minimum by receiving a regular flow of components and raw materials throughout the day.

You can think of cash as just another raw material that the firm needs to do business. There are always advantages to holding large "inventories" of cash. They reduce the risk of a sudden shortage and having to raise more at short notice. On the other hand, there is a cost to holding idle cash balances rather than putting the money to work in marketable securities. In balancing these benefits and costs the cash manager faces a task similar to that of the production manager. This trade-off is more important for small firms, for whom the costs of continually buying and selling securities are relatively large compared with the opportunity cost of holding idle cash balances.

Good cash management involves moving cash around efficiently. For example, if the firm receives a large number of small checks, it needs to ensure that they are not left lying about. We described how concentration banking and lockbox systems are used to speed up collections. Most large payments are made electronically by wire transfer. This allows companies to economize on the use of cash by transferring funds rapidly from local bank accounts to the firm's main *concentration* bank. Electronic funds transfer also speeds up payments and makes it possible to automate more of the cash management process.

If you have more cash than is currently needed, you can invest it in the money market. There is a wide choice of money-market investments, with different degrees of liquidity and risk. Remember that the interest rate on these investments is often quoted as a discount. The compound return is always higher than the rate of discount.

The principal money-market investments in the United States are:

- U.S. Treasury bills
- Federal agency notes
- Short-term tax exempts
- Time deposits and certificates of deposit
- Repurchase agreements
- Commercial paper
- Bankers' acceptances

The principal money-market investments in India are:

- Government of India Treasury Bills
- Certificates of Deposit
- Commercial paper
- Repurchase agreements

FURTHER READING

A standard text on the practice and institutional background of credit management is:

R. H. Cole and L. Mishler, *Consumer and Business Credit Management*, 11th ed. (New York: McGraw-Hill, 1998).

For a more analytical discussion of credit policy, see:

S. Mian and C. W. Smith, "Extending Trade Credit and Financing," *Journal of Applied Corporate Finance* 7 (Spring 1994), pp. 75–84.

M. A. Peterson and R. G. Rajan, "Trade Credit: Theories and Evidence," *Review of Financial Studies* 10 (Fall 1997), pp. 661–692.

Two classics on inventory models and their application to cash management are:

W. J. Baumol, "The Transactions Demand for Cash: An Inventory Theoretic Approach," *Quarterly Journal of Economics* 66 (November 1952), pp. 545–556.

M. H. Miller and D. Orr, "A Model of the Demand for Money by Firms," *Quarterly Journal of Economics* 80 (August 1966), pp. 413–435.

For descriptions of the money-market and short-term lending opportunities, see:

F. J. Fabozzi: *The Handbook of Fixed Income Securities*, 6th ed. (New York: McGraw-Hill, 2000).

F. J. Fabozzi, S. V. Mann and M. Choudhry, *The Global Money Market* (New York: John Wiley, 2002).

Chapter 4 of *U.S. Monetary Policy and Financial Markets*, available on the New York Federal Reserve Web site, **www.ny.frb.org.**

WEB EXERCISES

1. The Dun and Bradstreet Web site (**www.dnb.com**) contains a sample comprehensive report on a small business. Would you extend credit to the firm? Why or why not?
2. The three main credit bureaus maintain useful Web sites with examples of their business and consumer reports. Log in to **www.equifax.com** and look at the sample report on a small business. What information do you think would be most useful if you were considering granting credit to the firm?
3. Log on to the Reserve Bank of India site at *www.rbi.org.in* and look up current money market interest rates. Suppose your business has Rs. 70 crores set aside for an expenditure in three months. How would you choose to invest it in the meantime? Would your decision be different if there were some chance that you might need the money earlier?

CONCEPT REVIEW QUESTIONS

1. Vocabulary quiz. Define the following: (pages 823–833)
   a. Banker's acceptance
   b. Factor
   c. Just-in-time system
   d. Lockbox
   e. Eurodollar
   f. LIBOR
2. What do terms of 2/10/net 30 mean? (page 818)
3. What are the main sources of information about the credit standing of a small firm? (page 820)

For additional Concept Review Questions, please visit us at www.mhhe.com/bmam8e or refer to your Student CD.

QUIZ

1. Company X sells on a 1/30, net 60 basis. Customer Y buys goods invoiced at Rs. 1,000.
   a. How much can Y deduct from the bill if Y pays on day 30?
   b. What is the effective annual rate of interest if Y pays on the due date rather than on day 30?
   c. How would you expect payment terms to change if
      i. The goods are perishable.
      ii. The goods are not rapidly resold.
      iii. The goods are sold to high-risk firms.

2. The lag between the purchase date and the date on which payment is due is known as the *terms lag*. The lag between the due date and the date on which the buyer actually pays is the *due lag*, and the lag between the purchase and actual payment dates is the *pay lag*. Thus,

$$\text{Pay lag} = \text{terms lag} + \text{due lag}$$

State how you would expect the following events to affect each type of lag:
   a. The company imposes a service charge on late payers.
   b. A recession causes customers to be short of cash.
   c. The company changes its terms from net 10 to net 20.
3. The Branding Iron Company sells its iron for Rs. 2500 a piece wholesale. Production cost is Rs. 2000 per iron. There is a 25 percent chance that wholesaler Q will go bankrupt within the next year. Q orders 1,000 irons and asks for six months' credit. Should you accept the order? Assume that the discount rate is 10 percent per year, there is no chance of a repeat order, and Q will pay either in full or not at all.
4. Look back at Section 30.1. Cast Iron's costs have increased from Rs. 1,000 to Rs. 1,050. Assuming there is no possibility of repeat orders, answer the following:
   a. When should Cast Iron grant or refuse credit?
   b. If it costs Rs. 12 to determine whether a customer has been a prompt or slow payer in the past, when should Cast Iron undertake such a check?
5. Look back at the discussion in Section 30.1 of credit decisions with repeat orders. If $p_1 = .8$, what is the minimum level of p_2 at which Cast Iron is justified in extending credit?
6. True or False?
   a. Exporters who require greater certainty of payment arrange for the customers to sign a bill of lading in exchange for a sight draft.
   b. It makes sense to monitor the credit manager's performance by looking at the proportion of bad debts.
   c. If a customer refuses to pay despite repeated reminders, the company will usually turn the debt over to a factor or an attorney.
   d. The Foreign Credit Insurance Association insures export credits.
7. How should your willingness to grant credit be affected by differences in (a) the profit margin, (b) the interest rate, (c) the probability of repeat orders? In each case illustrate your answer with a simple example.
8. What are the trade-offs involved in the decision of how much inventory the firm should carry? In what way does the cash manager face a similar trade-off?
9. Anne Teak, the financial manager of a furniture manufacturer, is considering operating a lock-box system. She forecasts that 300 payments a day will be made to lock boxes, with an average payment size of $1,500. The bank's charge for operating the lock boxes is *either* $.40 a check *or* compensating balances of $800,000.
   a. If the interest rate is 9 percent, which method of payment is cheaper?
   b. What reduction in the time to collect and process each check is needed to justify use of the lock-box system?
10. Complete the passage that follows by choosing the appropriate terms from the following list: *lock-box banking, Fedwire, CHIPS, concentration banking.*

    Firms can increase their cash resources by speeding up collections. One way to do this is to arrange for payments to be made to regional offices which pay the checks into local banks. This is known as __________. Surplus funds are then transferred from the local bank to one of the company's main banks. Transfers can be made electronically by the __________ or __________ systems. Another technique is to arrange for a local bank to collect the checks directly from a post office box. This is known as __________.
11. Suppose that you can hold cash that pays no interest or invest in securities that pay interest at 8 percent. The securities are not easily sold on short notice; therefore, you must make up any cash deficiency by drawing on a bank line of credit which charges interest at 10 percent. Should you invest more or less in securities under each of the following circumstances?
    a. You are unusually uncertain about future cash flows.
    b. The interest rate on bank loans rises to 11 percent.

c. The interest rates on securities and on bank loans both rise by the same proportion.
d. You revise downward your forecast of future cash needs.

12. In July 2006, 91-day T-bills were issued at a discount of 6 percent. What is the annual yield?
13. For each item below, choose the investment that best fits the accompanying description:
a. Maturity often overnight (repurchase agreements / bankers' acceptances)
b. Maturity never more than 1 year (debentures / commercial papers)
c. Issued by RBI on behalf of Government of India (municipal bonds / Treasury bills)
d. Sold by auction (Treasury bills/ Certificates of deposit)
e. Quoted on a discount basis (Certificates of deposit / Treasury bills)
14. Consider three securities:
a. A floating-rate bond.
b. A preferred share paying a fixed dividend.
c. A floating-rate preferred.

A financial manager responsible for short-term investment of excess cash would probably choose the floating-rate preferred over *either* of the other two securities. Why? Explain briefly.

PRACTICE QUESTIONS

1. Listed below are some common terms of sale. Can you explain what each means?
a. 2/30, net 60.
b. 2/5, EOM, net 30.
c. COD.
2. Some of the items in Practice Question 1 involve a cash discount. For each of these, calculate the rate of interest paid by customers who pay on the due date instead of taking the cash discount.
3. Phoenix Lambert currently sells its goods cash on delivery. However, the financial manager believes that by offering credit terms of 2/10 net 30 the company can increase sales by 4 percent, without significant additional costs. If the interest rate is 6 percent and the profit margin is 5 percent, would you recommend offering credit? Assume first that all customers take the cash discount. Then assume that they all pay on day 30.
4. As treasurer of the Universal Bed Corporation, Aristotle Procrustes is worried about his bad debt ratio, which is currently running at 6 percent. He believes that imposing a more stringent credit policy might reduce sales by 5 percent and reduce the bad debt ratio to 4 percent. If the cost of goods sold is 80 percent of the selling price, should Mr. Procrustes adopt the more stringent policy?
5. Jim Khana, the credit manager of Velcro Saddles, is reappraising the company's credit policy. Velcro sells on terms of net 30. Cost of goods sold is 85 percent of sales, and fixed costs are a further 5 percent of sales. Velcro classifies customers on a scale of 1 to 4. During the past five years, the collection experience was as follows:

Classification	Defaults as Percent of Sales	Average Collection Period in Days for Nondefaulting Accounts
1	.0	45
2	2.0	42
3	10.0	40
4	20.0	80

The average interest rate was 15 percent.

What conclusions (if any) can you draw about Velcro's credit policy? What other factors should be taken into account before changing this policy?

6. Look again at Practice Question 5. Suppose (a) that it costs Rs. 95 to classify each new credit applicant and (b) that an almost equal proportion of new applicants falls into each of the four categories. In what circumstances should Mr. Khana not bother to undertake a credit check?

7. Until recently, Augean Cleaning Products sold its products on terms of net 60, with an average collection period of 75 days. In an attempt to induce customers to pay more promptly, it has changed its terms to 2/10, EOM, net 60. The initial effect of the changed terms is as follows:

	Average Collection Periods, Days	
Percent of Sales with Cash Discount	Cash Discount	Net
60	30*	80

*Some customers deduct the cash discount even though they pay after the specified date.

Calculate the effect of the changed terms. Assume

- Sales volume is unchanged.
- The interest rate is 12 percent.
- There are no defaults.
- Cost of goods sold is 80 percent of sales.

8. Look back at Practice Question 7. Assume that the change in credit terms results in a 2 percent increase in sales. Recalculate the effect of the changed credit terms.

9. From the website of www.sebiedifar.nic.in, download data on the average collection period of companies from the Indian tyre industry. Can you explain why some companies grant more credit than others?

10. Knob, Inc., is a nationwide distributor of furniture hardware. The company now uses a central billing system for credit sales of Rs. 180 million annually. First National, Knob's principal bank, offers to establish a new concentration banking system for a flat fee of Rs. 100,000 per year. The bank estimates that mailing and collection time can be reduced by three days. By how much will Knob's cash balances be increased under the new system? How much extra interest income will the new system generate if the extra funds are used to reduce borrowing under Knob's line of credit with First National? Assume that the borrowing rate is 12 percent. Finally, should Knob accept First National's offer if collection costs under the old system are Rs. 40,000 per year?

11. How would you expect a firm's cash balance to respond to the following changes?
    a. Interest rates increase.
    b. The volatility of daily cash flow decreases.
    c. The transaction cost of buying or selling marketable securities goes up.

12. A parent company settles the collection account balances of its subsidiaries once a week. (That is, each week it transfers any balances in the accounts to a central account.) The cost of a wire transfer is $10. A check costs $.80. Cash transferred by wire is available the same day, but the parent must wait three days for checks to clear. Cash can be invested at 12 percent per year. How much money must be in a collection account before it pays to use a wire transfer?

13. The financial manager of JAC Cosmetics is considering opening a lock box in Pittsburgh. Checks cleared through the lock box will amount to $300,000 per month. The lock box will make cash available to the company three days earlier than is currently the case.
    a. Suppose that the bank offers to run the lock box for a $20,000 compensating balance. Is the lock box worthwhile?
    b. Suppose that the bank offers to run the lock box for a fee of $.10 per check cleared instead of a compensating balance. What must the average check size be for the fee alternative to be less costly? Assume an interest rate of 6 percent per year.
    c. Why did you need to know the interest rate to answer (b) but not to answer (a)?

14. A three-month Treasury bill and a six-month bill both sell at a discount of 10 percent. Which offers the higher annual yield?
15. In Section 30.4 we described a three-month bill that was issued on an annually compounded yield of 5.18 percent. Suppose that one month has passed and the investment still offers the same annually compounded return. What is the percentage discount? What was your return over the month?
16. Look again at Practice Question 15. Suppose another month has passed, so the bill has only one month left to run. It is now selling at a discount of 5 percent. What is the yield calculated on a simple interest basis? What was your realized return over the two months?
17. Look up current interest rates offered by short-term investment alternatives. Suppose that your firm has Rs. 1 million excess cash to invest for the next two months. How would you invest this cash? How would your answer change if the excess cash were Rs. 5,000, Rs. 20,000, Rs. 100,000, or Rs. 100 million?
18. In February 2005, high-grade corporate bonds sold at a yield of 7.02 percent, while tax-exempt bonds issued by ICICI Bank of comparable maturity offered 6 percent annually. If an investor receives the same *after-tax* return from corporates and tax-exempts, what is the investor's marginal tax rate? What other factors might affect an investor's choice between the two types of securities?
19. The IRS in the US prohibits companies from borrowing money to buy tax-exempts and also deducting the interest payments on the borrowing from taxable income. Should the IRS prohibit such activity? If it didn't, would you advise the company to borrow to buy tax-exempts?
20. Suppose you are a wealthy individual paying 33.66 percent tax on income. What is the expected after-tax yield on each of the following investments?
    a. A municipal note yielding 7.0 percent pretax.
    b. A Treasury bill yielding 10 percent pretax.
    c. A floating-rate preferred stock yielding 7.5 percent pretax.

    How would your answer change if the investor is a corporation paying tax at 35 percent? What other factors would you need to take into account when deciding where to invest the corporation's spare cash?

CHALLENGE QUESTIONS

1. Reliant Pens has been approached by Plumpton Variety Stores of Hyderabad. Plumpton has expressed interest in an initial purchase of 5,000 pens at Rs. 10 each on Reliant's standard terms of 2/30, net 60. Plumpton estimates that if the pens prove popular with customers, its purchases could be in the region of 30,000 pens a year. After deductions for variable costs, this account would add Rs. 47,000 per year to Reliant's profits.

    Reliant has been anxious for some time to break into the lucrative Hyderabad market, but its credit manager has some doubts about Plumpton. In the past five years, Plumpton had embarked on an aggressive program of store openings. In 2004, however, it went into reverse. The recession, combined with aggressive price competition, caused a cash shortage. Plumpton laid off employees, closed one store, and deferred store openings. The company's Dun and Bradstreet rating is only fair, and a check with Plumpton's other suppliers reveals that, although Plumpton traditionally took cash discounts, it has recently been paying 30 days slow. A check through Reliant's bank indicates that Plumpton has unused credit lines of Rs. 350,000 but has entered into discussions with the banks for a renewal of a Rs. 1,500,000 term loan due at the end of the year. Table 30.3 summarizes Plumpton's latest financial statements.

    As credit manager of Reliant, how do you feel about extending credit to Plumpton?
2. Galenic, Inc., is a wholesaler for a range of pharmaceutical products. Before deducting any losses from bad debts, Galenic operates on a profit margin of 5 percent. For a long time the firm has employed a numerical credit scoring system based on a small number of key ratios. This has resulted in a bad debt ratio of 1 percent.

    Galenic has recently commissioned a detailed statistical study of the payment record of its customers over the past eight years and, after considerable experimentation, has identified five variables that could form the basis of a new credit scoring system. On the evidence of the past eight years, Galenic calculates that for every 10,000 accounts it would have experienced the following default rates:

Credit Score under Proposed System	Number of Accounts		
	Defaulting	Paying	Total
Greater than 80	60	9,100	9,160
Less than 80	40	800	840
Total	100	9,900	10,000

By refusing credit to firms with a low credit score (less than 80), Galenic calculates that it would reduce its bad debt ratio to 60/9,160, or just under .7 percent. While this may not seem like a big deal, Galenic's credit manager reasons that this is equivalent to a decrease of one-third in the bad debt ratio and would result in a significant improvement in the profit margin.

a. What is Galenic's current profit margin, allowing for bad debts?

b. Assuming that the firm's estimates of default rates are right, how would the new credit scoring system affect profits?

c. Why might you suspect that Galenic's estimates of default rates will not be realized in practice? What are the likely consequences of overestimating the accuracy of such a credit scoring scheme?

d. Suppose that one of the variables in the proposed scoring system is whether the customer has an existing account with Galenic (new customers are more likely to default). How would this affect your assessment of the proposal?

TABLE 30.3

Plumpton Variety Stores: summary financial statements (figures in millions).

	2004	2003		2004	2003
Cash	Rs. 1.0	Rs. 1.2	Payables	Rs. 2.3	Rs. 2.5
Receivables	1.5	1.6	Short-term loans	3.9	1.9
Inventory	10.9	11.6	Long-term debt	1.8	2.6
Fixed assets	5.1	4.3	Equity	10.5	11.7
Total assets	Rs. 18.5	Rs. 18.7	Total liabilities	Rs. 18.5	Rs. 18.7

	2004	2003
Sales	Rs. 55.0	Rs. 59.0
Cost of goods sold	32.6	35.9
Selling, general, and administrative expenses	20.8	20.2
Interest	.5	.3
Tax	.5	1.3
Net income	Rs .6	Rs. 1.3

CHAPTER [31]

SHORT-TERM FINANCIAL PLANNING

IN THE LAST CHAPTER we introduced you to the principal short-term assets—accounts receivable, inventory, cash, and marketable securities. But decisions on these assets cannot be made in isolation. For example, suppose that you decide to give your customers more time to pay for their purchases. That will reduce your future cash balances. Or perhaps you adopt a just-in-time system for ordering from suppliers. That will allow you to get by on smaller inventories and therefore free up cash. In this chapter we look at how the firm's financial decisions affect its working capital and cash balances, and we show how firms develop short-term financial plans.

Short-term financial decisions differ in two ways from long-term decisions such as capital investment and the choice of capital structure. First, they generally involve short-lived assets and liabilities, and, second, they are usually easily reversed. Compare, for example, a 60-day bank loan for Rs. 50 million with a Rs. 50 million issue of 20-year bonds. The bank loan is clearly a short-term decision. The firm can repay it two months later and be right back where it started. A firm might conceivably issue a 20-year bond in January and retire it in March, but it would be extremely inconvenient and expensive to do so. In practice, such a bond issue is a long-term decision, not only because of the bond's 20-year maturity but also because the decision to issue it cannot be reversed on short notice.

A financial manager responsible for short-term financial decisions does not have to look far into the future. The decision to take the 60-day bank loan could properly be based on cash-flow forecasts for the next few months only. The bond issue decision will normally reflect forecasted cash requirements 5, 10, or more years into the future.

Managers concerned with short-term financial decisions can avoid many of the difficult conceptual issues encountered elsewhere in this book. In a sense, short-term decisions are easier than long-term decisions, but they are not less important. A firm can identify extremely valuable capital investment opportunities, find the precise optimal debt ratio, follow the perfect dividend policy, and yet founder because no one bothers to raise the cash to pay this year's bills. Hence the need for short-term planning.

We start the chapter by showing how long-term financing decisions affect the firm's short-term financial planning problem. We describe how financial managers trace changes in cash and working capital, and we look at how they forecast month-by-month cash requirements or surpluses and develop short-term financing strategies. We conclude by examining more closely the principal sources of short-term finance.

31.1 LINKS BETWEEN LONG-TERM AND SHORT-TERM FINANCING DECISIONS

All businesses require capital, that is, money invested in plant, machinery, inventories, accounts receivable, and all the other assets it takes to run a business efficiently. Typically, these assets are not purchased all at once but obtained gradually over time. Let us call the total cost of these assets the firm's *cumulative capital requirement*.

For most firms the cumulative capital requirement grows irregularly, like the wavy line in Figure 31.1. This line shows a clear upward trend as the firm's business grows. But there is also seasonal variation around the trend: in the figure, the capital requirements peak late in each year. Finally, there would be unpredictable week-to-week and month-to-month fluctuations, but we have not attempted to show these in Figure 31.1.

The cumulative capital requirement can be met either from long-term or short-term financing. When long-term financing does not cover the cumulative capital requirement, the firm must raise

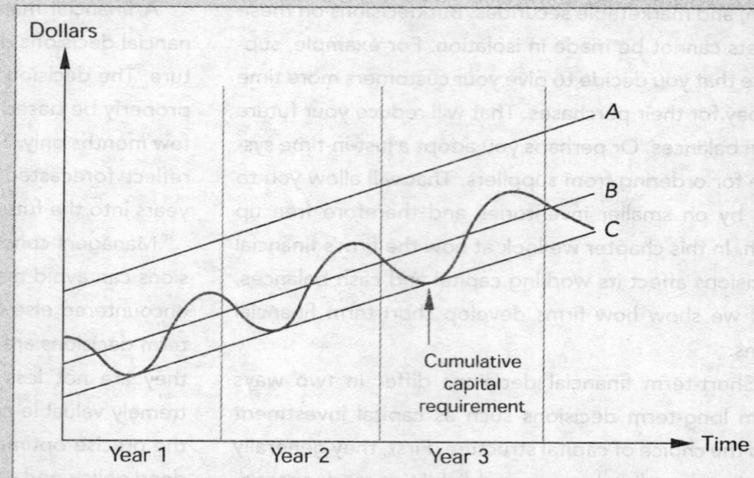

FIGURE 31.1

The firm's cumulative capital requirement (green line) is the cumulative investment in all the assets needed for the business. In this case the requirement grows year by year, but there is seasonal fluctuation within each year. The requirement for short-term financing is the difference between long-term financing (lines *A*, *B*, and *C*) and the cumulative capital requirement. If long-term financing follows line *C*, the firm always needs short-term financing. At line *B*, the need is seasonal. At line *A*, the firm never needs short-term financing. There is always extra cash to invest.

short-term capital to make up the difference. When long-term financing *more* than covers the cumulative capital requirement, the firm has surplus cash available. Thus the amount of long-term financing raised, given the capital requirement, determines whether the firm is a short-term borrower or lender.

Lines *A*, *B*, and *C* in Figure 31.1 illustrate this. Each depicts a different long-term financing strategy. Strategy *A* always implies a cash surplus, which can be invested in short-term securities. Strategy *C* implies a permanent need for short-term borrowing. Under *B*, which is probably the most common strategy, the firm is a short-term lender during part of the year and a borrower during the rest.

What is the *best* level of long-term financing relative to the cumulative capital requirement? It is hard to say. There is no convincing theoretical analysis of this question. We can make practical observations, however. First, most financial managers attempt to "match maturities" of assets and liabilities.[1] That is, they largely finance long-lived assets like plant and machinery with long-term borrowing and equity. Second, most firms make a permanent investment in net working capital (current assets less current liabilities). This investment is financed from long-term sources.

Current assets can be converted into cash more easily than can long-term assets. So firms with large holdings of current assets enjoy greater liquidity. Of course, some of these assets are more liquid than others. Inventories are converted into cash only when the goods are produced, sold, and paid for. Receivables are more liquid; they become cash as customers pay their outstanding bills. Short-term securities can generally be sold if the firm needs cash on short notice and are therefore more liquid still.

[1]A survey by Graham and Harvey found that managers considered that the desire to match the maturity of the debt with that of the assets was the single most important factor in their choice between short- and long-term debt. See J. R. Graham and C. R. Harvey, "The Theory and Practice of Finance: Evidence from the Field," *Journal of Financial Economics* 61 (May 2001), pp. 187–243. Stohs and Mauer confirm that firms with a preponderance of short-term assets do indeed tend to issue short-term debt. See M. H. Stohs and D. C. Mauer, "The Determinants of Corporate Debt Maturity Structure," *Journal of Business* 69 (July 1996), pp. 279–312.

Some firms choose to hold more liquidity than others. For example, many high-tech companies, such as Infosys and Wipro, hold huge amounts of short-term securities. On the other hand, firms in old-line manufacturing industries—such as chemicals, paper, or steel—manage with a far smaller reservoir of liquidity. Why is this? One reason is that companies with rapidly growing profits may generate cash faster than they can redeploy it in new positive-NPV investments. This produces a surplus of cash that can be invested in short-term securities. Of course, companies faced with a growing mountain of cash may eventually respond by adjusting their payout policies. For example, in Chapter 16 we saw how Microsoft reduced its cash mountain by paying a special dividend and repurchasing its stock.

There are some advantages to holding a large reservoir of cash, particularly for smaller firms that face relatively high costs to raise funds on short notice. For example, biotech firms require large amounts of cash if their drugs succeed in gaining regulatory approval. Therefore, these firms generally have substantial cash holdings to fund their possible investment needs. A reservoir of cash can also help to protect the firm against a rainy day and give it the breathing space to make changes to operations. That is not always in shareholders' interests; sometimes it simply helps to postpone the day of reckoning. The nearby box describes how the fashion company L. A. Gear was able to use its cash to survive six years of large losses and to employ a variety of radical, though ultimately unsuccessful, new strategies.

If this precautionary reason for holding liquid assets is important, we should find that small companies in relatively high-risk industries are more likely to hold large cash surpluses. A study by Tim Opler and others confirms that this is in fact the case.[2]

Financial managers of firms with a surplus of long-term financing and with cash in the bank don't have to worry about finding the money to pay next month's bills. But there are also costs to having surplus cash. Holdings of marketable securities are at best a zero-NPV investment for a taxpaying firm.[3] Also managers of firms with large cash surpluses may be tempted to run a less tight ship. If that is the case, firms with a permanent cash surplus should go on a diet and use the money to retire some of their long-term securities.

31.2 TRACING CHANGES IN CASH AND WORKING CAPITAL

Table 31.1 compares 2003 and 2004 year-end balance sheets for Dynamic Mattress Company. Table 31.2 shows the firm's income statement for 2004. Note that Dynamic's cash balance increased by Rs. 1 million during 2004. What caused this increase? Did the extra cash come from Dynamic Mattress Company's additional long-term borrowing, from reinvested earnings, from cash released by reducing inventory, or from extra credit extended by Dynamic's suppliers? (Note the increase in accounts payable.)

---

[2]T. Opler, L. Pinkowitz, R. Stulz, and R. Williamson, "The Determinants and Implications of Corporate Cash Holdings," *Journal of Financial Economics* 52 (April 1999), pp. 3–46.

[3]If there is a tax advantage to borrowing as most people believe, there must be a corresponding tax disadvantage to lending, since the firm must pay tax at the corporate rate on the interest that it receives from Treasury bills. In this case investment in Treasury bills has a negative NPV. See Section 18.1.

FINANCE IN THE NEWS

THE RISE AND FALL OF L. A. GEAR

Fashion company L. A. Gear was one of the stars of the 1980s. Teenie boppers loved its pink sequined sneakers and its silver and gold lamé workout shoes. Investors preferred the 1300 percent growth in the company's stock price in the space of four years. But as the company failed to react to changes in fashion during the 1990s, sales and profits fell away rapidly. In January 1998 L. A. Gear filed for Chapter 11 bankruptcy.

The decline of L. A. Gear illustrates how a company's liquid assets can provide the financial slack that allows it to evade market discipline and survive repeated losses. The following table summarizes the changes in L. A. Gear's profitability and its assets:

Sales, income, and assets of L. A. Gear 1989–1996 (figures in $ millions).

	1989	1990	1991	1992	1993	1994	1995	1996
Sales	617	820	619	430	398	416	297	196
Net income	55	31	−66	−72	−33	−22	−51	−62
Cash & securities	0	3	1	84	28	50	36	34
Receivables	101	156	112	56	73	77	47	24
Inventory	140	161	141	62	110	58	52	33
Current assets	257	338	297	230	220	194	138	93
Total assets	267	364	326	250	255	225	160	101

The first two rows of the table show that after 1990 L. A. Gear's sales declined sharply and the firm produced losses for the rest of its life. The remaining rows show the company's assets. Since L. A. Gear farmed out shoe and clothing production, it had few fixed assets and owned largely cash, receivables, and inventory. As sales declined, two things happened. First, the company was able to reduce its inventory of finished goods. Second, customers paid off their outstanding bills. Thus, despite making steady losses, the company's holdings of cash and short-term securities initially increased.

The following table shows L. A. Gear's capital structure. Notice that after 1991 the company had almost no short-term bank debt, so that it was largely free from the discipline that is exerted whenever a company has to approach its bank for a loan to be renewed.[4] As losses cumulated, common equity dwindled and the debt ratio climbed to 92 percent. Yet even in 1996 the company's cash holdings were over eight times that year's interest payments.

	1989	1990	1991	1992	1993	1994	1995	1996
Bank debt	37	94	20	0	4	1	1	0
Long-term debt	0	0	0	0	50	50	50	50
Preferred stock	0	0	100	100	100	100	108	116
Common equity	168	206	132	88	47	18	−41	−111

Because the company could liquidate its inventories and receivables and had no maturing debt, it was able to survive six years of large losses and to try a variety of radical new strategies, including a new emphasis on performance athletic shoes and then on children's shoes. All these strategies were ultimately unsuccessful. A company with large fixed assets that are not so easily liquidated would have found it less easy to survive so long.

[4]We saw in Chapter 25 that L. A. Gear had a line of credit with the Bank of America. This was used to provide the company's suppliers with letters of credit that guaranteed they would receive payment. Although the bank progressively reduced this line of credit, L. A. Gear's sales also fell and therefore reduced the extent to which the line of credit was needed.

Source: The decline of L. A. Gear is chronicled in H. DeAngelo, L. DeAngelo, and K. H. Wruck, "Asset Liquidity, Debt Covenants, and Managerial Discretion in Financial Distress: The Collapse of L. A. Gear," *Journal of Financial Economics* 64 (2002), pp. 3-34.

TABLE 31.1

Year-end balance sheets for 2003 and 2004 for Dynamic Mattress Company (figures in Rs. millions).

	2003	2004
Current assets:		
Cash	4	5
Marketable securities	0	5
Inventory	26	25
Accounts receivable	25	30
Total current assets	55	65
Fixed assets:		
Gross investment	56	70
Less depreciation	−16	−20
Net fixed assets	40	50
Total assets	95	115
Current liabilities:		
Bank loans	5	0
Accounts payable	20	27
Total current liabilities	25	27
Long-term debt	5	12
Net worth (equity and retained earnings)	65	76
Total liabilities and net worth	95	115

TABLE 31.2

Income statement for Dynamic Mattress Company, 2004 (figures in Rs. millions).

Sales	350
Operating costs	−321
	29
Depreciation	−4
	25
Interest	−1
Pretax income	24
Tax at 50%	−12
Net income	12

Note: Dividend = Rs. 1 million; retained earnings = Rs. 11 million.

The correct answer is "all the above." Financial analysts often summarize sources and uses of cash in a statement like the one shown in Table 31.3. The statement shows that Dynamic *generated* cash from the following sources:

1. It issued Rs. 7 million of long-term debt.
2. It reduced inventory, releasing Rs. 1 million.
3. It increased its accounts payable, in effect borrowing an additional Rs. 7 million from its suppliers.
4. By far the largest source of cash was Dynamic's operations, which generated Rs. 16 million. See Table 31.2, and note: Income (Rs. 12 million) understates cash flow because depreciation is deducted in calculating income. Depreciation is *not* a cash outlay. Thus, it must be added back in order to obtain operating cash flow.

TABLE 31.3

Sources and uses of cash for Dynamic Mattress Company, 2004 (figures in Rs. millions).

Sources:	
Issued long-term debt	7
Reduced inventories	1
Increased accounts payable	7
Cash from operations:	
Net income	12
Depreciation	4
Total sources	31
Uses:	
Repaid short-term bank loan	5
Invested in fixed assets	14
Purchased marketable securities	5
Increased accounts receivable	5
Dividend	1
Total uses	30
Increase in cash balance	1

Dynamic *used* cash for the following purposes:

1. It paid a Rs. 1 million dividend. (*Note:* The Rs. 11 million increase in Dynamic's equity is due to retained earnings: Rs. 12 million of equity income, less the Rs. 1 million dividend.)
2. It repaid a Rs. 5 million short-term bank loan.[5]
3. It invested Rs. 14 million. This shows up as the increase in gross fixed assets in Table 31.1.
4. It purchased Rs. 5 million of marketable securities.
5. It allowed accounts receivable to expand by Rs. 5 million. In effect, it lent this additional amount to its customers.

Tracing Changes in Net Working Capital

Financial analysts often find it useful to collapse all current assets and liabilities into a single figure for net working capital. Dynamic's net-working-capital balances were (in millions):

	Current Assets	Less	Current Liabilities	Equals	Net Working Capital
Year-end 2003	Rs. 55	–	Rs. 25	=	Rs. 30
Year-end 2004	Rs. 65	–	Rs. 27	=	Rs. 38

Table 31.4 gives balance sheets which report only net working capital, not individual current asset or liability items.

[5]This is principal repayment, not interest. Sometimes interest payments are explicitly recognized as a use of funds. If so, operating cash flow would be defined *before* interest, that is, as net income plus interest plus depreciation.

TABLE 31.4

Condensed year-end balance sheets for 2003 and 2004 for Dynamic Mattress Company (figures in Rs. millions).

	2003	2004
Net working capital	30	38
Fixed assets:		
Gross investment	56	70
Less depreciation	−16	−20
Net fixed assets	40	50
Total net assets	70	88
Long-term debt	5	12
Net worth (equity and retained earnings)	65	76
Long-term liabilities and net worth*	70	88

*When only *net* working capital appears on a firm's balance sheet, this figure (the sum of long-term liabilities and net worth) is often referred to as *total capitalization.*

TABLE 31.5

Sources and uses of funds (net working capital) for Dynamic Mattress Company, 2004 (figures in Rs. millions).

Sources:	
Issued long-term debt	7
Cash from operations:	
Net income	12
Depreciation	4
	23
Uses:	
Invested in fixed assets	14
Dividend	1
	15
Increase in net working capital	8

"Sources and uses" statements can likewise be simplified by defining *sources* as activities that contribute to net working capital and *uses* as activities that use up working capital. In this context working capital is usually referred to as *funds*, and a *sources and uses of funds statement* is presented.[6]

In 2003, Dynamic contributed to net working capital by

1. Issuing Rs. 7 million of long-term debt.
2. Generating Rs. 16 million from operations.

It used up net working capital by

1. Investing Rs. 14 million.
2. Paying a Rs. 1 million dividend.

The year's changes in net working capital are thus summarized by Dynamic Mattress Company's sources and uses of funds statement, given in Table 31.5.

Profits and Cash Flow

Now look back to Table 31.3, which shows sources and uses of *cash*. We want to register two warnings about the entry called *cash from operations*. It may not represent actual rupees—rupees you can buy beer with.

[6]We drew up a *sources and uses of funds* statement for Executive Paper in Section 29.2.

First, depreciation may not be the only noncash expense deducted in calculating income. For example, most firms use accounting procedures in their tax books different from those in their reports to shareholders. The point of special tax accounts is to minimize current taxable income. The effect is that the shareholder books overstate the firm's current cash tax liability,[7] and after-tax cash flow from operations is therefore understated.

Second, income statements record sales when made, not when the customer's payment is received. Think of what happens when Dynamic sells goods on credit. The company records a profit at the time of sale, but there is no cash inflow until the bills are paid. Since there is no cash inflow, there is no change in the company's cash balance, although there is an increase in working capital in the form of an increase in accounts receivable. No net addition to cash would be shown in a sources and uses statement like Table 31.3. The increase in cash from operations would be offset by an increase in accounts receivable.

Later, when the bills are paid, there is an increase in the cash balance. However, there is no further profit at this point and no increase in working capital. The increase in the cash balance is exactly matched by a decrease in accounts receivable.

That brings up an interesting characteristic of working capital. Imagine a company that conducts a very simple business. It buys raw materials for cash, processes them into finished goods, and then sells these goods on credit. The whole cycle of operations looks like this:

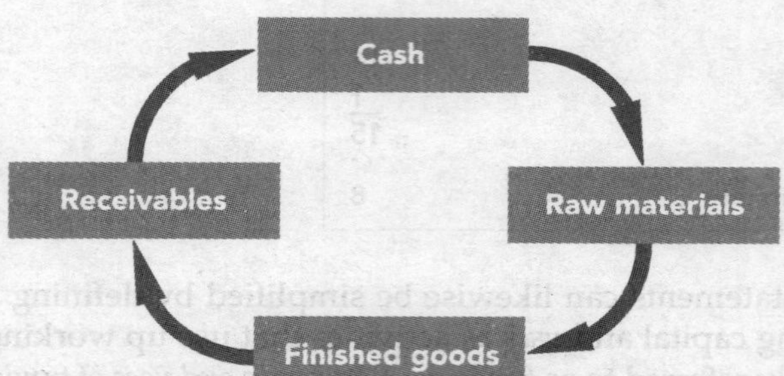

If you draw up a balance sheet at the beginning of the process, you see cash. If you delay a little, you find the cash replaced by inventories of raw materials and, still later, by inventories of finished goods. When the goods are sold, the inventories give way to accounts receivable, and finally, when the customers pay their bills, the firm draws out its profit and replenishes the cash balance.

There is only one constant in this process, namely, working capital. The components of working capital are constantly changing. That is one reason why (net) working capital is a useful summary measure of current assets and liabilities.

The strength of the working-capital measure is that it is unaffected by seasonal or other temporary movements between different current assets or liabilities. But the strength is also its weakness, for the working-capital figure hides a lot of interesting information. In our example cash was

[7]The difference between taxes reported and paid to the Internal Revenue Service shows up on the balance sheet as a deferred tax liability. The reason that a liability is recognized is that accelerated depreciation and other devices used to reduce current taxable income do not eliminate taxes; they only delay them. Of course, this reduces the present value of the firm's tax liability, but still the ultimate liability has to be recognized. In the sources and uses statements an increase in deferred taxes would be treated as a source of funds. In the Dynamic Mattress example we ignore deferred taxes.

transformed into inventory, then into receivables, and back into cash again. But these assets have different degrees of risk and liquidity. You can't pay bills with inventory or with receivables, you must pay with cash.

31.3 CASH BUDGETING

The past is interesting for what one can learn from it. The financial manager's problem is to forecast *future* sources and uses of cash. These forecasts serve two purposes. First, they provide a standard, or budget, against which subsequent performance can be judged. Second, they alert the manager to future cash-flow needs. Cash, as we all know, has a habit of disappearing fast.

Preparing the Cash Budget: Inflow

There are at least as many ways to produce a cash budget as there are to skin a cat. Many large firms have developed elaborate corporate models; others use a spreadsheet program to plan their cash needs. The procedures of smaller firms may be less formal. But there are common issues that all firms must face when they forecast. We will illustrate these issues by continuing the example of Dynamic Mattress.

Most of Dynamic's cash inflow comes from the sale of mattresses. We therefore start with a sales forecast by quarter[8] for 2005:

	First Quarter	Second Quarter	Third Quarter	Fourth Quarter
Sales (Rs. millions)	87.5	78.5	116	131

But sales become accounts receivable before they become cash. Cash flow comes from *collections* on accounts receivable.

Most firms keep track of the average time it takes customers to pay their bills. From this they can forecast what proportion of a quarter's sales is likely to be converted into cash in that quarter and what proportion is likely to be carried over to the next quarter as accounts receivable. Suppose that 80 percent of sales are "cashed in" in the immediate quarter and 20 percent are cashed in in the next. Table 31.6 shows forecasted collections under this assumption.

In the first quarter, for example, collections from current sales are 80 percent of Rs. 87.5, or Rs. 70 million. But the firm also collects 20 percent of the previous quarter's sales, or .2(75) = Rs. 15 million. Therefore total collections are Rs. 70 + Rs. 15 = Rs. 85 million.

Dynamic started the first quarter with Rs. 30 million of accounts receivable. The quarter's sales of Rs. 87.5 million were *added* to accounts receivable, but collections of Rs. 85 million were *subtracted*. Therefore, as Table 31.6 shows, Dynamic ended the quarter with accounts receivable of Rs. 30 + 87.5 − 85 = Rs. 32.5 million. The general formula is

Ending accounts receivable = beginning accounts receivable + sales − collections

[8]Most firms would forecast by month instead of by quarter. Sometimes weekly or even daily forecasts are made. But presenting a monthly forecast would triple the number of entries in Table 31.6 and subsequent tables. We wanted to keep the examples as simple as possible.

TABLE 31.6

To forecast Dynamic Mattress's collections on accounts receivable, you have to forecast sales and collection rates (figures in Rs. millions).

	First Quarter	Second Quarter	Third Quarter	Fourth Quarter
1. Receivables at start of period	30	32.5	30.7	38.2
2. Sales	87.5	78.5	116	131
3. Collections:				
Sales in current period (80%)	70	62.8	92.8	104.8
Sales in last period (20%)	15 [a]	17.5	15.7	23.2
Total collections	85	80.3	108.5	128
4. Receivables at end of period 1 + 2 - 3	32.5	30.7	38.2	41.2

[a]Sales in the fourth quarter of the previous year were Rs. 75 million.

eXcel

Please visit us at www.mhhe.com/bmam8e or refer to your Student CD.

The top section of Table 31.7 shows forecasted sources of cash for Dynamic Mattress. Collection of receivables is the main source, but it is not the only one. Perhaps the firm plans to dispose of some land or expects a tax refund or payment of an insurance claim. All such items are included as "other" sources. It is also possible that you may raise additional capital by borrowing or selling stock, but we don't want to prejudge that question. Therefore, for the moment we just assume that Dynamic will not raise further long-term finance.

Preparing the Cash Budget: Outflow

So much for the incoming cash. Now for the outgoing. There always seem to be many more uses for cash than there are sources. For simplicity, we have condensed the uses into four categories in Table 31.7.

1. *Payments on accounts payable.* You have to pay your bills for raw materials, parts, electricity, etc. The cash-flow forecast assumes all these bills are paid on time, although Dynamic could probably delay payment to some extent. Delayed payment is sometimes called *stretching your payables.* Stretching is one source of short-term financing, but for most firms it is an expensive source, because by stretching they lose discounts given to firms that pay promptly. This was discussed in more detail in Section 30.1.
2. *Labor, administrative, and other expenses.* This category includes all other regular business expenses.
3. *Capital expenditures.* Note that Dynamic Mattress plans a major capital outlay in the first quarter.
4. *Taxes, interest, and dividend payments.* This includes interest on presently outstanding long-term debt but does not include interest on any additional borrowing to meet cash requirements in 2005. At this stage in the analysis, Dynamic does not know how much it will have to borrow, or whether it will have to borrow at all.

The forecasted net inflow of cash (sources minus uses) is shown in the box in Table 31.7. Note the large negative figure for the first quarter: a Rs. 46.5 million forecasted *outflow.* There is a smaller forecasted outflow in the second quarter, and then substantial cash inflows in the second half of the year.

	First Quarter	Second Quarter	Third Quarter	Fourth Quarter
Sources of cash:				
Collections on accounts receivable	85	80.3	108.5	128
Other	0	0	12.5	0
Total sources	85	80.3	121	128
Uses of cash:				
Payments on accounts payable	65	60	55	50
Labor and other expenses	30	30	30	30
Capital expenditures	32.5	1.3	5.5	8
Taxes, interest, and dividends	4	4	4.5	5
Total uses	131.5	95.3	95	93
Sources minus uses	-46.5	-15.0	+26.0	+35.0
Calculation of short-term financing requirement:				
1. Cash at start of period	5	-41.5	-56.5	-30.5
2. Change in cash balance (sources less uses)	-46.5	-15	+26.0	+35.0
3. Cash at end of period[a] 1 + 2	-41.5	-56.5	-30.5	+4.5
4. Minimum operating balance	5	5	5	5
5. Cumulative financing required[b] 4 - 3	46.5	61.5	35.5	.5

TABLE 31.7

Dynamic Mattress's cash budget for 2005 (figures in Rs. millions).

[a]Of course, firms cannot literally hold a negative amount of cash. This is the amount the firm will have to raise to pay its bills.

[b]A negative sign would indicate a cash *surplus*. But in this example the firm must raise cash for all quarters.

eXcel

Please visit us at www.mhhe.com/bmam8e or refer to your Student CD

The bottom part of Table 31.7 (below the box) calculates how much financing Dynamic will have to raise if its cash-flow forecasts are right. It starts the year with Rs. 5 million in cash. There is a Rs. 46.5 million cash outflow in the first quarter, and so Dynamic will have to obtain at least Rs. 46.5 − 5 = Rs. 41.5 million of additional financing. This would leave the firm with a forecasted cash balance of exactly zero at the start of the second quarter.

Most financial managers regard a planned cash balance of zero as driving too close to the edge of the cliff. They establish a *minimum operating cash balance* to absorb unexpected cash inflows and outflows. We will assume that Dynamic's minimum operating cash balance is Rs. 5 million. That means it will have to raise the full Rs. 46.5 million cash outflow in the first quarter and Rs. 15 million more in the second quarter. Thus its cumulative financing requirement is Rs. 61.5 million in the second quarter. This is the peak, fortunately: The cumulative requirement declines in the third quarter by Rs. 26 million to Rs. 35.5 million. In the final quarter Dynamic is almost out of the woods: Its cash balance is Rs. 4.5 million, just Rs. 5 million shy of its minimum operating balance.

The next step is to develop a *short-term financing plan* that covers the forecasted requirements in the most economical way possible. We will move on to that topic after two general observations:

1. The large cash outflows in the first two quarters do not necessarily spell trouble for Dynamic Mattress. In part, they reflect the capital investment made in the first quarter: Dynamic is spending Rs. 32.5 million, but it should be acquiring an asset worth that much or more. In part, the cash outflows reflect low sales in the first half of the year; sales recover in the second half.[9] If this is a predictable seasonal pattern, the firm should have no trouble borrowing to tide it over the slow months.
2. Table 31.7 is only a best guess about future cash flows. It is a good idea to think about the *uncertainty* in your estimates. For example, you could undertake a sensitivity analysis, in which you inspect how Dynamic's cash requirements would be affected by a shortfall in sales or by a delay in collections. The trouble with such sensitivity analyses is that you are changing only one item at a time, whereas in practice a downturn in the economy might affect, say, sales levels *and* collection rates. An alternative but more complicated solution is to build a model of the cash budget and then to simulate to determine the probability of cash requirements significantly above or below the forecasts shown in Table 31.7.[10] If cash requirements are difficult to predict, you may wish to hold additional cash or marketable securities to cover a possible unexpected cash outflow.

31.4 THE SHORT-TERM FINANCING PLAN

Dynamic's cash budget defines its problem: Its financial manager must find short-term financing to cover the firm's forecasted cash requirements. There are dozens of sources of short-term financing, but for simplicity we assume that Dynamic has just two options.

Options for Short-Term Financing

1. *Bank loan:* Dynamic has an existing arrangement with its bank allowing it to borrow up to Rs. 38 million at an interest cost of 10 percent a year or 2.5 percent per quarter. The firm can borrow and repay whenever it wants to as long as it does not exceed its credit limit.
2. *Stretching payables:* Dynamic can also raise capital by putting off paying its bills. The financial manager believes that Dynamic can defer the following amounts in each quarter:

	First Quarter	Second Quarter	Third Quarter	Fourth Quarter
Amount deferrable (Rs. millions)	52	48	44	40

[9]Maybe people buy more mattresses late in the year when the nights are longer.

[10]In other words, you could use Monte Carlo simulation. See Section 10.2.

	First Quarter	Second Quarter	Third Quarter	Fourth Quarter
New borrowing:				
1. Bank loan	38.0	0.0	0.0	0.0
2. Stretching payables	3.5	19.7	0.0	0.0
3. Total	41.5	19.7	0.0	0.0
Repayments:				
4. Bank loan	0.0	0.0	4.2	33.8
5. Stretching payables	0.0	3.5	19.7	0.0
6. Total	0.0	3.5	24.0	33.8
7. Net new borrowing	41.5	16.2	-24.0	-33.8
8. Plus securities sold	5.0	0.0	0.0	0.0
9. Less securities bought	0.0	0.0	0.0	0.3
10. Total cash raised	46.5	16.2	-24.0	-34.1
Interest payments [a]				
11. Bank loan	0.0	1.0	1.0	0.8
12. Stretching payables	0.0	0.2	1.0	0.0
13. Interest on securities sold [b]	0.0	0.1	0.1	0.1
14. Net interest paid	0.0	1.2	2.0	0.9
15. Cash required for operations [c]	46.5	15.0	-26.0	-35.0
16. Total cash required	46.5	16.2	-24.0	-34.1

TABLE 31.8

Dynamic Mattress's financing plan (figures in Rs. millions).

[a]We assume that the first interest payment occurs one quarter after a loan is taken out.
[b]Dynamic sold Rs. 5 million of marketable securities in the first quarter. The yield is assumed to be 2 percent per quarter.
[c]From Table 31.7.

excel

Please visit us at www.mhhe.com/bmam8e or refer to your Student CD.

Thus, Rs. 52 million can be saved in the first quarter by *not* paying bills in that quarter. (Note that the cash-flow forecasts in Table 31.7 assumed that these bills *will* be paid in the first quarter.) If deferred, these payments *must* be made in the second quarter. Similarly, up to Rs. 48 million of the second quarter bills can be deferred to the third quarter, and so on.

Stretching payables is often costly, even if no ill will is incurred. The reason is that suppliers may offer discounts for prompt payment. Dynamic loses this discount if it pays late. In this example we assume the lost discount is 5 percent of the amount deferred. In other words, if a Rs. 100 payment is delayed, the firm must pay Rs. 105 in the next quarter.

Dynamic's Financing Plan

With these two options, the short-term financing strategy is obvious. Use the bank loan first, if necessary up to the Rs. 38 million limit. If there is still a shortage of cash, stretch payables.

Table 31.8 shows the resulting plan. In the first quarter the plan calls for borrowing the full amount available from the bank (Rs. 38 million) and stretching Rs. 3.5 million of payables (see lines 1 and 2 in the table). In addition the company sells the Rs. 5 million of marketable securities it held at the end of 2002 (line 8). Thus it raises 38 + 3.5 + 5 = Rs. 46.5 million of cash in the first quarter (line 10).

In the second quarter, the plan calls for Dynamic to continue to borrow Rs. 38 million from the bank and to stretch Rs. 19.7 million of payables. This raises a further Rs. 16.2 million after paying off the Rs. 3.5 million of bills deferred from the first quarter.

Why raise Rs. 16.2 million when Dynamic needs only an additional Rs. 15 million to finance its operations? The answer is that the company must pay interest on the borrowings that it undertook in the first quarter and it foregoes interest on the marketable securities that were sold.[11]

In the third and fourth quarters the plan calls for Dynamic to pay off its debt and to make a small purchase of marketable securities.

Evaluating the Plan

Does the plan shown in Table 31.8 solve Dynamic's short-term financing problem? No: The plan is feasible, but Dynamic can probably do better. The most glaring weakness is its reliance on stretching payables, an extremely expensive financing device. Remember that it costs Dynamic 5 percent *per quarter* to delay paying bills—20 percent per year at simple interest. The first plan would merely stimulate the financial manager to search for cheaper sources of short-term borrowing.

The financial manager would ask several other questions as well. For example:

1. Does the plan yield satisfactory current and quick ratios?[12] Its bankers may be worried if these ratios deteriorate.[13]
2. Are there intangible costs of stretching payables? Will suppliers begin to doubt Dynamic's creditworthiness?
3. Does the plan for 2005 leave Dynamic in good financial shape for 2006? (Here the answer is yes, since Dynamic will have paid off all short-term borrowing by the end of the year.)
4. Should Dynamic try to arrange long-term financing for the major capital expenditure in the first quarter? This seems sensible, following the rule of thumb that long-term assets deserve long-term financing. It would also reduce the need for short-term borrowing dramatically. A counterargument is that Dynamic is financing the capital investment *only temporarily* by short-term borrowing. By year-end, the investment is paid for by cash from operations. Thus Dynamic's initial decision not to seek immediate long-term financing may reflect a preference for ultimately financing the investment with retained earnings.
5. Perhaps the firm's operating and investment plans can be adjusted to make the short-term financing problem easier. Is there any easy way of deferring the first quarter's large cash outflow? For example, suppose that the large capital investment in the first quarter is for new mattress-stuffing machines to be delivered and installed in the first half of the year. The new machines are not scheduled to be ready for full-scale use until August. Perhaps the machine manufacturer could be persuaded to accept 60 percent of the purchase price on delivery and 40 percent when the machines are installed and operating satisfactorily.

---

[11]The bank loan calls for quarterly interest of .025 × 38 = Rs. 0.95 million; the lost discount on the stretched payables amounts to .05 × 3.5 = Rs. 0.175 million; and the interest lost on the marketable securities is .02 × 5 = Rs. 0.1 million.

[12]These ratios are discussed in Chapter 29.

[13]We have not worked out these ratios explicitly, but you can infer from Table 31.8 that they would be fine at the end of the year but relatively low midyear, when Dynamic's borrowing is high.

6. Dynamic may also be able to release cash by reducing the level of other current assets. For example, it could reduce receivables by getting tough with customers who are late paying their bills. (The cost is that in the future these customers may take their business elsewhere.) Or it may be able to get by with lower inventories of mattresses. (The cost is that it may lose business if there is a rush of orders that it cannot supply.)

Short-term financing plans are developed by trial and error. You lay out one plan, think about it, and then try again with different assumptions on financing and investment alternatives. You continue until you can think of no further improvements.

Trial and error is important because it helps you understand the real nature of the problem the firm faces. Here we can draw a useful analogy between the *process* of planning and Chapter 10, "A Project Is Not a Black Box." In Chapter 10 we described sensitivity analysis and other tools used by firms to find out what makes capital investment projects tick and what can go wrong with them. Dynamic's financial manager faces the same kind of task: not just to choose a plan but to understand what can go wrong with it and what will be done if conditions change unexpectedly.[14]

A Note on Short-Term Financial Planning Models

Working out a consistent short-term plan requires burdensome calculations.[15] Fortunately much of the arithmetic can be delegated to a computer. Many large firms have built *short-term financial planning models* to do this. Smaller companies like Dynamic Mattress do not face so much detail and complexity and find it easier to work with a spreadsheet program on a personal computer. In either case the financial manager specifies forecasted cash requirements or surpluses, interest rates, credit limits, etc., and the model grinds out a plan like the one shown in Table 31.8. The computer also produces balance sheets, income statements, and whatever special reports the financial manager may require.

Smaller firms that do not want custom-built models can rent general-purpose models offered by banks, accounting firms, management consultants, or specialized computer software firms.

Most of these models are *simulation* programs.[16] They simply work out the consequences of the assumptions and policies specified by the financial manager. *Optimization* models for short-term financial planning are also available. These models are usually linear programming models. They search for the *best* plan from a range of alternative policies identified by the financial manager. Optimization helps when the firm faces complex problems with many interdependent alternatives and restrictions for which trial and error might never identify the *best* combination of alternatives.

---

[14]This point is even more important in *long-term* financial planning. See Chapter 29.

[15]If you doubt that, look again at Table 31.8. Notice that the cash requirements in each quarter depend on borrowing in the previous quarter, because borrowing creates an obligation to pay interest. Moreover, the problem's complexity would have been tripled had we not simplified by forecasting per quarter rather than by month.

[16]Like the simulation models described in Section 10.2, except that the short-term planning models rarely include uncertainty explicitly. The models referred to here are built and used in the same way as the long-term financial planning models described in Section 29.5.

Of course the best plan for one set of assumptions may prove disastrous if the assumptions are wrong. Thus the financial manager has to explore the implications of alternative assumptions about future cash flows, interest rates, and so on. Linear programming can help identify good strategies, but even with an optimization model the financial plan is still sought by trial and error.

31.5 SOURCES OF SHORT-TERM BORROWING

Dynamic solved the greater part of its cash shortage by borrowing from a bank. But banks are not the only source of short-term loans. Financial Institutions are also a major source of cash, particularly for financing receivables and inventories.[17] In addition to borrowing from an intermediary like a bank or a financial institution, firms also sell short-term commercial paper directly to investors. It is time to look more closely at these sources of short-term funds.

Bank Loans

To finance its investment in current assets, a company may rely on a variety of short-term loans. Obviously, if you approach a bank for a loan, the bank's lending officer is likely to ask searching questions about your firm's financial position and its plans for the future. Also, the bank will want to monitor the firm's subsequent progress. There is, however, a good side to this. Other investors know that banks are hard to convince, and, therefore, when a company announces that it has arranged a large bank facility, the share price tends to rise.[18]

Bank loans come in a variety of flavors.[19] Here are a few of the ways that they differ.

Commitment Companies sometimes wait until they need the money before they apply for a bank loan, but nearly three-quarters of commercial loans are made under commitment. In this case the company establishes a line of credit that allows it to borrow from the bank up to an established unit. This line of credit is usually in the form of cash credit in India, where the firms withdraw funds from the banks up to the sanctioned credit limit. Banks charge interest only on the actual balance utilized by the company. The cash credit advances are given on the security of current assets. Usually, the stocks of inventory remain with the borrowing company and a floating charge over the inventory is created in favor of the bank. This type of cash credit facility is popularly known as the **cash credit hypothecation (CCH)**.

Such credit lines give guaranteed access to the bank's money at a given interest rate. This amounts to a put option, because the firm can sell its debt to the bank on fixed terms even if its creditworthiness deteriorates or the cost of credit rises. The growth in the use of credit lines is changing the role of banks. They are no longer simply lenders; they are also in the business of providing companies with liquidity insurance.

---

[17]Financial institutions in India started extending short-term loans to companies for financing working capital in the mid-90s.

[18]See C. James, "Some Evidence on the Uniqueness of Bank Loans," *Journal of Financial Economics* 19 (December 1987), pp. 217–235.

[19]The results of a survey of the terms of business lending by banks in the United States are published quarterly in the *Federal Reserve Bulletin* (see **www.federalreserve.gov/releases/E2**).

Many companies discovered the value of this insurance in 1998, when Russia defaulted on its borrowings and created turmoil in the world's debt markets. Companies in the United States suddenly found it much more expensive to issue their own debt to investors. Those who had arranged lines of credit with their banks rushed to take advantage of them. As a result, new debt issues languished, while bank lending boomed.[20]

Maturity Most bank loans are for only a few months. For example, a company may need a short-term **bridge loan** to finance the purchase of new equipment or the acquisition of another firm. In this case the loan serves as interim financing until the purchase is completed and long-term financing is arranged. Often a short-term loan may be needed to finance a temporary increase in inventory. Such a loan is described as **self-liquidating;** in other words, the sale of goods provides the cash to repay the loan.

Banks also provide longer-term loans, known as **term loans.** A term loan typically has a maturity of four to five years. Usually the loan is repaid in level amounts over this period, though there is sometimes a large final balloon payment or just a single bullet payment at maturity. Banks can accommodate the repayment pattern to the anticipated cash flows of the borrower. For example, the first repayment might be delayed a year until the new factory is completed. Term loans are often renegotiated before maturity. Banks are willing to do this if the borrower is an established customer, remains creditworthy, and has a sound business reason for making the change.[21]

Rate of Interest Short-term bank loans are often made at a fixed rate of interest, which is often quoted as a discount in the US. For example, if the interest rate on a one-year loan is stated as a discount of 5 percent, the borrower receives 100 − 5 = $95 and undertakes to pay $100 at the end of the year. The return on such a loan is not 5 percent, but 5/95 = .0526, or 5.26 percent.

For longer-term bank loans the interest rate is generally linked to the prime lending rate of the bank. Sometimes the interest rate is also linked to the general level of interest rates. Thus for example, the Bank of Baroda extends loans to companies (with credit rating of 'A' and above) at an interest rate equal to the MIBOR (Mumbai Inter Bank Offer Rate). It is standard practice in the U.S. to link the interest rate to LIBOR.[22] Thus, if the rate is set at "1 percent above LIBOR," the borrower may pay 5 percent for the first three months when LIBOR is 4 percent, 6 percent in the next three months when LIBOR is 5 percent, and so on.[23]

[20]The rush to draw on bank lines of credit is described in M. R. Saidenberg and P. E. Strahan, "Are Banks Still Important for Financing Large Businesses?" *Federal Reserve Bank of New York, Current Issues in Economics and Finance* 5 (August 1999), pp. 1–6.

[21]Term loans typically allow the borrower to repay early, but in many cases the loan agreement specifies that the firm must pay a penalty for early repayment.

[22]LIBOR is the rate of interest that major international banks offer each other on eurodollar deposits.

[23]In addition to paying interest, the borrower may be obliged to maintain a minimum interest-free deposit (*compensating balance*) with the bank. Compensating balances for bank loans are now relatively rare.

Syndicated Loans Some bank loans are far too large for a single bank. In these cases the loan may be arranged by one or more lead banks and then parceled out among a syndicate of banks. For example, when Vodafone Airtouch needed to borrow $24 billion (€25 billion) to help finance its bid for the German telephone company, Mannesmann, it engaged 11 banks from around the world to arrange a large syndicate of banks that would lend the cash.

Loan Sales Large banks in the US often have more demand for loans than they can satisfy; for smaller banks it is the other way around. Banks with an excess demand for loans may solve the problem by selling a portion of their existing loans to other institutions. Loan sales have mushroomed in recent years. In 1991 they totalled only $8 million; by 2003 they had reached $145 billion.[24]

These loan sales generally take one of two forms: *assignments* or *participations*. In the former case a portion of the loan is transferred with the agreement of the borrower. In the second case the lead bank maintains its relationship with its borrowers but agrees to pay over to the buyer a portion of the cash flows that it receives.

Participations often involve a single loan, but sometimes they can be huge deals involving hundreds of loans. Because these deals change a collection of nonmarketable bank loans into marketable securities, they are known as *securitizations*. For example, in 1996 the British bank Natwest securitized about one-sixth of its loan book. Natwest first put together a $5 billion package of about 200 loans to major firms in 17 different countries. It then sold notes, each of which promised to pay a proportion of the cash that it received from the package of loans. Because the notes provided the chance to share in a diversified portfolio of high-quality loans, they proved very popular with investors from around the world.

Security If a bank is concerned about a firm's credit risk, it will ask the firm to provide security for the loan. Since the bank is lending on a short-term basis, this security usually consist of liquid assets such as receivables, inventories, or securities. In India, banks usually accept a floating charge against these assets (inventories in case of cash credit hypothecation). This gives it a general claim if the firm defaults, but it does not specify the assets in detail, and it sets few restrictions on what the company can do with the assets.

More commonly, banks will require specific collateral. For example, suppose that there is a significant delay between the time that you ship your goods and when your customers pay you. If you need the money up front, you can borrow using these receivables as collateral. First, you must send the bank a copy of each invoice and provide it with a claim against the money that you receive from your customers.

Each day, as you make more sales, your collateral increases and you can borrow more money. Each day also some customers pay their bills. This money is placed in a special collateral account under the bank's control and is periodically used to reduce the size of the loan. Therefore, as the firm's business fluctuates, so does the amount of the collateral and the size of the loan.[25]

---

[24] Loan Pricing Corporation (**www.loanpricing.com**).

[25] In Chapter 30 we described how firms sometimes raise money by selling their receivables to a factor. The factor is responsible for collecting the debt and suffers any losses if the customers don't pay. When you pledge your receivables as collateral for a loan, *you* remain responsible for collecting the debt and *you* suffer if a customer is delinquent.

Banks also need to ensure that the collateral is kept safe and the borrower doesn't sell the assets and run off with the money. This is what happened in the great salad oil swindle. Fifty-one banks and companies made loans of nearly $200 million to the Allied Crude Vegetable Oil Refining Corporation. In return the company agreed to provide security in the form of storage tanks full of valuable salad oil. Unfortunately, the cursory inspections of the tanks failed to notice that they simply contained seawater and sludge. When the fraud was discovered, the president of Allied went to jail and the 51 lenders were left out in the cold, looking for their $200 million.[26] Lenders have been more careful since then, but Finance in the News shows that even old scams can still work.

Commercial Paper

Banks borrow money from one group of firms or individuals and relend the money to another group. They make their profit by charging the borrower a higher rate of interest than they offer the lender.

Sometimes it is convenient to have a bank in the middle. It saves the lenders the trouble of looking for borrowers and assessing their creditworthiness, and it saves borrowers the trouble of looking for lenders. Depositors do not care whom the bank lends to: They need only satisfy themselves that the bank as a whole is safe.

There are also occasions on which it is *not* worth paying an intermediary to perform these functions. Large well-known companies can bypass the banking system by issuing their own short-term unsecured notes. These notes are known as **commercial paper (CP).** The Reserve Bank of India introduced commercial papers in India following the recommendations of the Vagul working group in 1989. Highly rated companies (with a CRISIL rating of P2 and above or an equivalent rating from other rating agencies) can issue commercial papers in India. Initial issue of commercial papers is done primarily to the banks because of the differences in the stamp duties. The stamp duty on the primary issue of commercial papers is 0.25 percent for all investors, while it is only 0.05 percent for the banks. However, since the secondary market transactions do not attract stamp duties, other investors find it attractive to buy commercial papers in the secondary market. The secondary market transactions are usually done over the counter. The maturities of the commercial papers range between 15 days and 1 year.

Commercial paper is very popular with major companies in the U.S. By cutting out the intermediary they are able to borrow at rates that may be 1 to 1.5 percent below the prime rate charged by banks. Even after allowing for a dealer's commission and the cost of any backup line of credit, this is still a substantial savings. Banks have felt the competition from commercial paper and have been prepared to reduce their rates to blue-chip customers. As a result, "prime rate" doesn't mean what it used to. It once meant the rate banks charged their most creditworthy customers. Now the prime customers often pay less than the prime rate. In India though the bankers are the major buyers of the commercial papers (who otherwise would extend cash credit facilities to the banks), the interest rate on commercial papers is below the prime lending rate.

[26]See N. C. Miller, *The Great Salad Oil Swindle* (London: Gollancz, 1966).

FINANCE IN THE NEWS

THE HAZARDS OF SECURED BANK LENDING

The National Safety Council of Australia's Victoria Division had been a sleepy outfit until John Friedrich took over. Under its new management, NSC members trained like commandos and were prepared to go anywhere and do anything. They saved people from drowning, they fought fires, found lost bushwalkers and went down mines. Their lavish equipment included 22 helicopters, 8 aircraft and a mini-submarine. Soon the NSC began selling its services internationally.

Unfortunately the NSC's paramilitary outfit cost millions of dollars to run—far more than it earned in revenue. Friedrich bridged the gap by borrowing \$A236 million of debt. The banks were happy to lend because the NSC's debt appeared well secured. At one point the company showed \$A107 million of receivables (that is money owed by its customers), which it pledged as security for bank loans. Later checks revealed that many of these customers did not owe the NSC a cent. In other cases banks took comfort in the fact that their loans were secured by containers of valuable rescue gear. There were more than 100 containers stacked around the NSC's main base. Only a handful contained any equipment, but these were the ones that the bankers saw when they came to check that their loans were safe. Sometimes a suspicious banker would ask to inspect a particular container. Friedrich would then explain that it was away on exercise, fly the banker across the country in a light plane and point to a container well out in the bush. The container would of course be empty, but the banker had no way to know that.

Six years after Friedrich was appointed CEO, his massive fraud was uncovered. But a few days before a warrant could be issued, Friedrich disappeared. Although he was eventually caught and arrested, he shot himself before he could come to trial. Investigations revealed that Friedrich was operating under an assumed name, having fled from his native Germany, where he was wanted by the police. Many rumors continued to circulate about Friedrich. He was variously alleged to have been a plant of the CIA and the KGB and the NSC was said to have been behind an attempted counter-coup in Fiji. For the banks there was only one hard truth. Their loans to the NSC, which had appeared so well secured, would never be repaid.

Source: Adapted from Chapter 7 of T. Sykes, *The Bold Riders* (St. Leonards, NSW, Australia: Allen & Unwin, 1994).

Commercial paper is very popular with major companies in the US. By cutting out the intermediary, they are able to borrow at rates that may be 1 to 1.5 percent below the prime rate charged by banks. Even after allowing for a dealer's commission and the cost of any backup line of credit, this is still a substantial savings. Banks have felt the competition from commercial paper and have been prepared to reduce their rates to blue-chip customers. As a result, "prime rate" doesn't mean what it used to. It once meant the rate banks charged their most creditworthy customers. Now the prime customers often pay less than the prime rate. In India though the bankers are the major buyers of the commercial papers (who otherwise would extend cash credit facilities to the banks), the interest rate on commercial papers is below the prime lending rate.[27]

[27]The commercial paper rates are more directly related to money market rates and hence the companies are able to borrow at rates below the prime lending rates.

SUMMARY

Short-term financial planning is concerned with the management of the firm's short-term, or current, assets and liabilities. The most important current assets are cash, marketable securities, inventory, and accounts receivable. The most important current liabilities are short-term loans and accounts payable. The difference between current assets and current liabilities is called (net) working capital.

Current assets and liabilities are turned over much more rapidly than the other items on the balance sheet. Short-term financing and investment decisions are more quickly and easily reversed than long-term decisions. Consequently, the financial manager does not need to look so far into the future when making them.

The nature of the firm's short-term financial planning problem is determined by the amount of long-term capital it raises. A firm that issues large amounts of long-term debt or common stock, or which retains a large part of its earnings, may find that it has permanent excess cash. In such cases there is never any problem paying bills, and short-term financial planning consists of managing the firm's portfolio of marketable securities. A firm holding a reservoir of cash is able to buy itself time to react to a short-term crisis. This may be important for risky firms that find it difficult to raise cash on short notice. However, large cash holdings can lead to complacency. We suggest that firms with permanent cash surpluses ought to return the excess cash to their stockholders.

Other firms raise relatively little long-term capital and end up as permanent short-term debtors. Most firms attempt to find a golden mean by financing all fixed assets and part of current assets with equity and long-term debt. Such firms may invest cash surpluses during part of the year and borrow during the rest of the year.

The starting point for short-term financial planning is an understanding of sources and uses of cash.[28] Firms forecast their net cash requirements by forecasting collections on accounts receivable, adding other cash inflows, and subtracting all cash outlays. If the forecasted cash balance is insufficient to cover day-to-day operations and to provide a buffer against contingencies, the company will need to find additional finance. The search for the best short-term financial plan inevitably proceeds by trial and error. The financial manager must explore the consequences of different assumptions about cash requirements, interest rates, sources of finance, and so on. Firms are increasingly using computerized financial models to help in this process. The models range from simple spreadsheet programs that merely help with the arithmetic to linear programming models that help to find the best financial plan.

If you foresee a large and permanent cash deficiency, the financial plan may involve raising long-term finance. If the shortage is temporary, you may be able to finance it by not paying your bills for a while or you can choose from a variety of short- and medium-term loans.

Often firms arrange a *revolving line of credit* with a bank that allows them to borrow up to an agreed amount whenever they need financing. This is usually intended to tide the firm over a temporary shortage of cash and is therefore repaid in only a few months. However, banks also make *term loans* that sometimes extend for five years or more. In addition to borrowing from their domestic banks, companies may borrow rupees (or any other currency) from overseas banks or the foreign branches of Indian banks. These international bank loans often involve huge sums of money and in this case they may be *syndicated* among a group of major banks.

[28]We pointed out in Section 31.2 that sources and uses of *funds* are often analyzed rather than sources and uses of cash. Anything that contributes to working capital is called a *source of funds;* anything that diminishes working capital is called a *use of funds.* Sources and uses of funds statements are relatively simple because many sources and uses of cash are buried in changes in working capital. However, in forecasting, the emphasis is on cash flow. You pay bills with cash, not working capital.

Many bank loans are unsecured, but less-creditworthy borrowers may be asked to provide security. Sometimes this consists of a floating charge on receivables and inventories, but usually you will be asked to pledge specific assets. When you borrow against receivables, the bank is informed of all sales of goods and the resulting receivables are pledged to the bank. As the customers pay their bills, the money is paid into a special collateral account under the bank's control. Similarly, when you borrow against stocks of raw materials, the bank may insist that the goods are under the control of an independent warehouse company. As long as the bank holds the warehouse receipt for these goods, they cannot be released without the bank's permission.

The interest rate on very short-term bank loans is generally fixed for the life of the loan, but in other cases the rate floats with the general level of short-term interest rates. For example, it might be set at 1 percent over MIBOR (the Mumbai Interbank Offered Rate).

Of course, the interest rate that the bank charges must be sufficient to cover not only the opportunity cost of capital for the loan but also the costs of running the loan department. As a result, large regular borrowers have found it cheaper to bypass the banking system and issue their own short-term unsecured debt. This is called *commercial paper*. Longer-term loans that are marketed on a regular basis are known as *medium-term notes*.

FURTHER READING

Here are some general textbooks on working-capital management:

G. W. Gallinger and B. P. Healey, *Liquidity Analysis and Management*, 2nd. ed. (Reading, MA: Addison-Wesley 1991).

N. C. Hill and W. L. Sartoris, *Short-Term Financial Management: Text and Cases*, 3rd. ed. (Englewood Cliffs, NJ: Prentice-Hall, Inc. 1994).

K. V. Smith and G. W. Gallinger, *Readings on Short-Term Financial Management*, 3rd ed. (New York: West, 1988).

F. C. Scherr, *Modern Working Capital Management: Text and Cases* (Englewood Cliffs, NJ: Prentice-Hall, Inc. 1989).

CONCEPT REVIEW QUESTIONS

1. Growth firms commonly have relatively larger cash holdings than do old-line manufacturing firms. Why might this be so? (page 845)
2. What are the advantages and disadvantages of holding a large reservoir of cash? (page 845)
3. Why do we say that holdings of marketable securities are at best a zero-NPV investment for a taxpaying firm? (page 845)

For additional Concept Review Questions, please visit us at www.mhhe.com/bmam8e or refer to your Student CD.

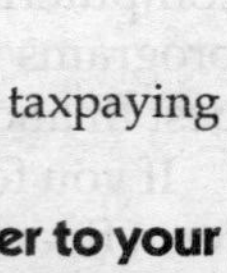

QUIZ

1. Listed below are six transactions that Dynamic Mattress might make. Indicate how each transaction would affect (a) cash and (b) working capital.

   The transactions are

   i. Pay out Rs. 2 million cash dividend.
   ii. Receive Rs. 2,500 from a customer who pays a bill resulting from a previous sale.
   iii. Pay Rs. 5,000 previously owed to one of its suppliers.
   iv. Borrow Rs. 1 million long term and invest the proceeds in inventory.
   v. Borrow Rs. 1 million short term and invest the proceeds in inventory.
   vi. Sell Rs. 5 million of marketable securities for cash.

2. State how each of the following events would affect the firm's balance sheet. State whether each change is a source or use of cash.
   a. An automobile manufacturer increases production in response to a forecasted increase in demand. Unfortunately, the demand does not increase.
   b. Competition forces the firm to give customers more time to pay for their purchases.
   c. Inflation increases the value of raw material inventories by 20 percent.
   d. The firm sells a parcel of land for Rs. 100,000. The land was purchased five years earlier for Rs. 200,000.
   e. The firm repurchases its own common stock.
   f. The firm doubles its quarterly dividend.
   g. The firm issues Rs. 1 million of long-term debt and uses the proceeds to repay a short-term bank loan.
3. Here is a forecast of sales by National Bromide for the first four months of 2006 (figures in Rs. thousands):

	Month 1	Month 2	Month 3	Month 4
Cash sales	15	24	18	14
Sales on credit	100	120	90	70

   On the average 50 percent of credit sales are paid for in the current month, 30 percent are paid in the next month, and the remainder are paid in the month after that. What is the expected cash inflow from operations in months 3 and 4?
4. Dynamic Futon forecasts the following purchases from suppliers:

	Jan.	Feb.	Mar.	Apr.	May	Jun.
Value of goods (Rs. millions)	32	28	25	22	20	20

   a. Forty percent of goods are supplied cash on delivery. The remainder are paid with an average delay of one month. If Dynamic Futon starts the year with payables of Rs. 22 million, what is the forecasted level of payables for each month?
   b. Suppose that from the start of the year the company stretches payables by paying 40 percent after one month and 20 percent after two months. (The remainder continue to be paid cash on delivery.) Recalculate payables for each month assuming that there are no cash penalties for late payment.
5. Each of the following events affects one or more tables in the chapter. Show the effects of each event by adjusting the tables listed in parentheses:
   a. Dynamic repays only Rs. 2 million of short-term debt in 2004. (Tables 31.1, 31.3–31.5)
   b. Dynamic issues an additional Rs. 10 million of long-term debt in 2004 and invests Rs. 12 million in a new warehouse. (Tables 31.1, 31.3–31.5)
   c. In 2004 Dynamic reduces the quantity of stuffing in each mattress. Customers don't notice, but operating costs fall by 10 percent. (Tables 31.1–31.5)
   d. Starting in the third quarter of 2005, Dynamic employs new staff members who will prove very effective in persuading customers to pay more promptly. As a result, 90 percent of sales are paid for immediately, and 10 percent are paid in the following quarter. (Tables 31.6 and 31.7)
   e. Starting in the first quarter of 2005, Dynamic cuts wages by Rs. 4 million a quarter. (Table 31.7)
   f. In the second quarter of 2005 a disused warehouse mysteriously catches fire. Dynamic receives a Rs. 10 million check from the insurance company. (Table 31.7)
   g. Dynamic's treasurer decides he can scrape by on a Rs. 2 million operating cash balance. (Table 31.7)
6. True or false?
   a. Most commercial bank loans are made under commitment.
   b. A line of credit provides the lender with a put option.
   c. Bank term loans typically have a maturity of several years.

d. If the interest rate on a one-year bank loan is stated as a discount of 10 percent, the actual yield on the loan is less than 10 percent.

e. The interest rate on term loans is usually linked to MIBOR, or the bank's prime lending rate.

7. Complete the passage below by selecting the most appropriate terms from the following list: *floating charge, commercial paper, warehouse receipt, collateral, commitment fee, line of credit, medium-term notes.*

Companies with fluctuating capital needs often arrange a ______ with their bank. This is relatively expensive because companies need to pay a ______ on any unused amount.

Secured short-term loans are sometimes covered by a ______ on all receivables and inventory. Generally, however, the borrower pledges specific assets as ______. For example, if goods are stored in a warehouse, an independent warehouse company may issue a ______ to the lender. The goods can then only be released with the lender's consent.

Banks are not the only source of short-term debt. Many large companies issue their own unsecured debt directly to investors, often on a regular basis. If the maturity is less than nine months, this debt is generally known as ______. Companies also make regular issues of longer term debt to investors. These are called ______.

PRACTICE QUESTIONS

eXcel
Please visit us at www.mhhe.com/bmam8e or refer to your Student CD.

1. Table 31.9 lists data from the budget of Ritewell Publishers. Half the company sales are for cash on the nail; the other half are paid for with a one-month delay. The company pays all its credit purchases with a one-month delay. Credit purchases in January were Rs. 30, and total sales in January were Rs. 180. Complete the cash budget in Table 31.10.
2. If a firm pays its bills with a 30-day delay, what fraction of its purchases will be paid in the current quarter? In the following quarter? What if the delay is 60 days?
3. Which items in Table 31.8 would be affected by the following events?
   a. There is a rise in interest rates.
   b. Suppliers demand interest for late payment.
   c. Dynamic receives an unexpected bill in the third quarter from the Income Tax Department for underpayment of taxes in previous years.

	February	March	April
Total sales	Rs. 200	Rs. 220	Rs.180
Purchases of materials			
For cash	70	80	60
For credit	40	30	40
Other expenses	30	30	30
Taxes, interest, and dividends	10	10	10
Capital investment	100	0	0

TABLE 31.9
Selected budget data for Ritewell Publishers.

TABLE 31.10

Cash budget for Ritewell Publishers.

	February	March	April
Sources of cash:			
Collections on cash sales			
Collections on accounts receivable	—	—	—
Total sources of cash			
Uses of cash:			
Payments of accounts payable			
Cash purchases of materials			
Other expenses			
Capital expenditures			
Taxes, interest, and dividends			
Total uses of cash	—	—	—
Net cash inflow			
Cash at start of period	100		
+ Net cash inflow			
= Cash at end of period			
+ Minimum operating cash balance	100	100	100
= Cumulative short-term financing required			

TABLE 31.11

Year-end balance sheet for Dynamic Mattress for 2002 (figures in Rs. millions).

Current assets:		**Current liabilities:**	
Cash	Rs. 4	Bank loans	Rs. 4
Marketable securities	2	Accounts payable	15
Inventory	20	Total current liabilities	19
Accounts receivable	22		
Total current assets	48	Long-term debt	5
		Net worth (equity and retained earnings)	60
Fixed assets:			
Gross investment	50		
Less depreciation	14		
Net fixed assets	36	Total liabilities	
Total assets	84	and net worth	84

TABLE 31.12

Income statement for Dynamic Mattress for 2003 (figures in Rs. millions).

Note: Dividend = Rs. 1 million; retained earnings = Rs. 5 million.

Sales	Rs. 300
Operating costs	−285
	15
Depreciation	−2
	13
Interest	−1
Pretax income	12
Tax at 50%	−6
Net income	6

4. Table 31.11 shows Dynamic Mattress's year-end 2002 balance sheet, and Table 31.12 shows its income statement for 2003. Work out statements of sources and uses of cash and sources and uses of funds for 2003.

5. Work out a short-term financing plan for Dynamic Mattress Company, assuming the limit on the line of credit is raised from Rs. 38 to Rs. 50 million. Otherwise keep to the assumptions used in developing Table 31.8.

6. Dynamic Mattress decides to lease its new mattress-stuffing machines rather than buy them. As a result, capital expenditure in the first quarter is reduced by Rs. 30 million, but the company must make lease payments of Rs. 1.5 million for each of the four quarters. Assume that the lease has no effect on tax payments until after the fourth quarter. Construct two tables like Tables 31.7 and 31.8 showing Dynamic's cumulative financing requirement and a new financing plan.

7. You need to borrow Rs.100 million for 90 days. You have the following alternatives:
   a. Issue high-grade commercial papers at a rate that is 0.5 percent below the prime lending rate of SBI
   b. Borrow from Corporation bank at an interest rate of 0.25 percent over LIBOR
   c. Borrow from Allahabad Bank at the prime lending rate.

   Given the rates currently prevailing in the market (visit the websites of the respective banks), which alternative would you choose?

8. Suppose that you are a banker responsible for approving corporate loans. Nine firms are seeking secured loans. They offer the following assets as collateral:
   a. Firm A, a heating oil distributor, offers a tanker load of fuel in transit from the Middle East.
   b. Firm B, a wine wholesaler, offers 1,000 cases of Beaujolais Nouveau, located in a warehouse.
   c. Firm C, a stationer, offers an account receivable for office supplies sold to the City of New York.
   d. Firm D, a bookstore, offers its entire inventory of 15,000 used books.
   e. Firm E, a wholesale grocer, offers a boxcar full of bananas.
   f. Firm F, an appliance dealer, offers its inventory of electric typewriters.
   g. Firm G, a jeweler, offers 100 ounces of gold.
   h. Firm H, a government securities dealer, offers its portfolio of Treasury bills.
   i. Firm I, a boat builder, offers a half-completed luxury yacht. The yacht will take four months more to complete.

   Which of these assets are most likely to be good collateral? Which are likely to be bad collateral? Explain.

9. From the website (www.sebiedifar.nic.in) download the balance sheets and profit and loss accounts for two companies. Draw up a sources and uses of cash statement and a sources and uses of funds statement as in Tables 31.3 and 31.5.

10. From the website (www.sebiedifar.nic.in) download the balance sheets of all the 30 companies that are part of Sensex. Compare the investment in current assets of these 30 companies. Which of these companies make a heavy investment in inventories and receivables? Can you explain why?

CHALLENGE QUESTIONS

1. Jaipur Chemical Corporation's treasurer has forecasted a Rs.1 million cash deficit for the next quarter. However, there is only a 50 percent chance this deficit will actually occur. The treasurer estimates that there is a 20 percent probability the company will have no deficit at all and a 30 percent probability that it will actually need Rs. 2 million in short-term financing. The company can either take out a 90-day unsecured loan for Rs. 2 million at 1 percent per month or establish a line of credit, costing 1.5 percent per month on the amount borrowed. If excess cash can be reinvested at 9 percent, which source of financing gives the lower expected cost?

2. Term loans usually require firms to pay a fluctuating interest rate. For example, the interest rate may be set at "1 percent above prime." The prime rate sometimes varies by several percentage points within a single year. Suppose that your firm has decided to borrow Rs. 40 million for five years. It has three alternatives. It can (a) borrow from a bank at the prime rate, currently 10 percent. The proposed loan agreement requires no principal repayments until the loan matures in five years. It can (b) issue 26-week commercial paper, currently yielding 9 percent. Since funds are required for five years, the commercial paper will have to be rolled over semiannually. That is, financing the Rs. 40 million requirement for five years will require 10 successive commercial paper sales. Or, finally, it can (c) borrow from an insurance company at a fixed rate of 11 percent. As in the bank loan, no principal has to be repaid until the end of the five-year period. What factors would you consider in analyzing these alternatives? Under what circumstances would you choose (a)? Under what circumstances would you choose (b) or (c)? (*Hint:* Don't forget Chapter 23.)

PART TEN RELATED WEB SITES

Most Web sites that provide market commentary (see list at start of Part One) also contain material on recent mergers. Other sites concerned with mergers include:

www.mergernetwork.com (information on businesses for sale)

www.mergerstat.com (some data on merger activity)

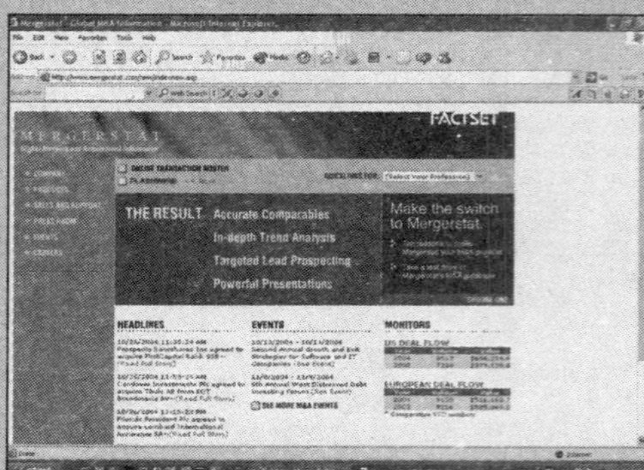

For material on bankruptcy see:

www.abiworld.org (web site of the American Bankruptcy Institute)

www.bankrupt.com

www.bankruptcydata.com
(largely a subscription site)

www.law.cornell.edu/uscode/11
(the bankruptcy code)

www.uscourts.gov/library/bankbasic.pdf
(a useful guide to the bankruptcy process)

PART [10]

MERGERS, CORPORATE CONTROL, AND GOVERNANCE

IN JANUARY 2000 AOL announced that it had reached agreement to acquire Time Warner for a record-breaking $156 billion of stock. Investors and commentators initially reacted with enthusiasm to the plan. The deal, reported the *Wall Street Journal,* "has potential synergies that make some observers drool. The merged company promises to offer consumers a soup-to-nuts menu of their media and information needs." But it proved difficult to realize these synergies and investor euphoria was short-lived. As profits of the merged company slumped, its stock price fell by more than 80 percent.

Mergers are the topic of Chapter 32. We look at the possible gains from merging and we show how managers can calculate the benefits and the costs. The AOL-Time Warner merger was an example of an amicable marriage, but sometimes one party is dragged unwillingly to the altar. We therefore describe some of the tactics employed by the bidder and target company in a hostile merger. We conclude by looking at why mergers occur and who gains and who loses.

Mergers are partly about economies from combining two businesses, but they are also about who gets to run the company. Chapter 33 circles back and considers other ways that companies can change their ownership and control. For example, we look at cases where a company spins off part of its business or where the firm is bought out by a group of investors who then take the business private.

In Chapter 34 we widen our discussion of company ownership and control by comparing company structures in the United States with those in other parts of the world. In the United States a large part of business is undertaken by public corporations with actively traded shares and relatively easy access to financial markets. But there are other ways to organize and finance business ventures. For example, in Germany and Japan stock markets are less important and banks play a much larger role in financing and monitoring businesses.

CHAPTER [32]

MERGERS

THE SCALE AND pace of merger activity in India have been remarkable. In 2005, a total of 467 deals were struck in India with total value exceeding $18.2 billion.[1] During such periods of intense merger activity, management spends significant amount of time either searching for firms to acquire or worrying about whether some other firm will acquire them.

A merger adds value only if the two companies are worth more together than apart. This chapter covers why two companies could be worth more together and how to get the merger deal done if they are. We proceed as follows.

- *Motives.* Sources of value added.
- *Dubious motives.* Don't be tempted.
- *Benefits and costs.* It's important to estimate them consistently.
- *Mechanics.* Legal, tax, and accounting issues.
- *Takeover battles and tactics.* We look back to several famous takeover battles. This history illustrates merger tactics and shows some of the economic forces driving merger activity.
- *Mergers and the economy.* How can we explain merger waves? Who gains and who loses as a result of mergers?

This chapter concentrates on ordinary mergers, that is, combinations of two established firms. We keep asking, What makes two firms worth more together than apart? But mergers also change *control* and *ownership.* Pick a merger, and you'll almost always find that one firm is the protagonist and the other is the target.

Financial economists now view mergers as part of a broader *market for corporate control.* The activity in this market goes far beyond ordinary mergers. It includes leveraged buyouts (LBOs), spin-offs and divestitures, and also privatizations, where a government-owned business is sold into the private sector. These are the subject of the next chapter.

[1]Source: Business Line, January 4, 2006

32.1 SENSIBLE MOTIVES FOR MERGERS

Table 32.1 lists a few recent mergers. Notice that most of these are **horizontal mergers,** that is combinations of two firms in the same line of business.[2] Two recent headline-grabbing examples are the acquisition of Aircel Limited by Maxis Communication and the promoters of Apollo Hospital (Reddy and family) for a consideration of Rs. 4860 crores and Oracle Global's takeover of I-Flex Solutions for a consideration of Rs. 3954.53 crores.

A **vertical merger** involves companies at different stages of production. The buyer expands back toward the source of raw materials or forward in the direction of the ultimate consumer. An example is Walt Disney's acquisition of the ABC television network. Disney planned to use the ABC network to show recent movies to huge audiences.

A **conglomerate merger** involves companies in unrelated lines of businesses. The principal mergers of the 1960s and 1970s were mostly conglomerate. Conglomerates are much less popular now, at least in the United States and other developed economies. Much of the action in the 1980s and 1990s has come from breaking up the conglomerates that had been formed 10 to 20 years earlier. Most of the mergers and acquisitions that have taken place in India between 2000-05 are actually horizontal mergers. In 1994 Bombay Dyeing made an unsuccessful bid for Union Carbide. Similarly, in 1995 it made another unsuccessful bid for Ahmedabad Electricity Corporation. Had these bids succeeded Bombay Dyeing would have been a larger conglomerate today.

With these distinctions in mind, we are about to consider motives for mergers, that is, reasons why two firms may be worth more together than apart. We proceed with some trepidation. The motives, though they often lead the way to real benefits, are sometimes just mirages that tempt unwary

[2]In India, sometimes a finance company makes a bid for a manufacturing company, thereby giving us the false impression that this is a conglomerate merger. However, quite often another company (from the same industry as that of the target) makes a bid indirectly through the finance company (in which it has substantial stake). So for all practical purposes, we can consider such mergers as horizontal mergers.

Industry	Acquiring Company	Selling Company	Payment (Rs.Crores)
Cement	Holdcem Cements Pvt Limited	Ambuja Cement	4885
Cement	Grasim	Ultratech Cement	1641
Petrochemicals	Indian Oil	IBP	1841
Petrochemicals	Reliance Industries	Controlling Stake in IPCL	2638
Technology	Oracle Global (Mauritius)	I-Flex Solutions	3955
Technology	Maxis Communications Berhad and Prathap Reddy (promoter of Apollo Hospital)	Aircel	4860

TABLE 32.1

Some important recent acquisitions

Source: Prowess Database

or overconfident managers into takeover disasters. This was the case for AT&T, which spent $7.5 billion to buy NCR. The aim was to shore up AT&T's computer business and to "link people, organizations and their information into a seamless, global computer network."[3] It didn't work. Even more embarrassing (on a smaller scale) was the acquisition of Apex One, a sporting apparel company, by Converse Inc. The purchase was made on May 18, 1995. Apex One was closed down on August 11, after Converse failed to produce new designs quickly enough to satisfy retailers. Converse lost an investment of over $40 million in 85 days.[4] Back in India, Jet Airways agreed to acquire Air Sahara for a consideration of Rs. 2300 crores in January 2006. However, the stock market did not perceive any synergy in the merger and within a span of five months, the stock price of Jet fell by more than 40 percent, when the broad based index, Nifty, increased by little more than 4 percent. The overall market capitalization of Jet fell by more than Rs. 4152 crores in the span of five months and as we write this chapter, Jet has decided to call off the agreement. This is a disaster-in-waiting that could be avoided because the management of Jet read the signal from the capital market.

Many mergers that seem to make economic sense fail because managers cannot handle the complex task of integrating two firms with different production processes, accounting methods, and corporate cultures. This was one of the problems in the AT&T–NCR merger. The nearby box shows how similar difficulties bedeviled the merger of three Japanese banks.

The value of most businesses depends on *human assets*—managers, skilled workers, scientists, and engineers. If these people are not happy in their new roles in the acquiring firm, the best of them will leave. One Portuguese bank (BCP) learned this lesson the hard way when it bought an investment management firm against the wishes of the firm's employees. The entire workforce immediately quit and set up a rival investment management firm with a similar name. Beware of paying too much for assets that go down in the elevator and out to the parking lot at the close of each business day. They may drive into the sunset and never return.

There are also occasions when the merger does achieve gains but the buyer nevertheless loses because it pays too much. For example, the buyer may overestimate the value of stale inventory or underestimate the costs of renovating old plant and equipment, or it may overlook the warranties on a defective product. Buyers need to be particularly careful about environmental liabilities. If

[3]Robert E. Allen, AT&T chairman, quoted in J. J. Keller, "Disconnected Line: Why AT&T Takeover of NCR Hasn't Been a Real Bell Ringer," *The Wall Street Journal*, September 9, 1995, p. A1.

[4]Mark Maremount, "How Converse Got Its Laces All Tangled," *BusinessWeek*, September 4, 1995, p. 37.

FINANCE IN THE NEWS

THOSE ELUSIVE SYNERGIES

When three of Japan's largest banks combined to form Mizuho Bank the result was a bank with assets of $1.5 trillion, more than twice those of the world leader Deutsche Bank. The name "Mizuho" means "rich rice harvest" and the bank's management forecasted that the merger would yield a rich harvest of synergies. In a message to shareholders, the bank president claimed that the merger would create "a comprehensive financial services group that will surge forward in the 21st century." He predicted that the bank would "lead the new era through cutting-edge comprehensive financial services . . . by exploiting to the fullest extent the Group's enormous strengths, which are backed by a powerful customer base and state-of-the-art financial and information technologies." The cost of putting the banks together was forecasted at ¥130 billion, but management predicted future benefits of ¥466 billion a year.

Within a few months of the announcement, reports began to emerge of squabbles among the three partners. One problem area was IT. Each of the three merging banks had a different supplier for its computer system. At first it was proposed to use just one of these three systems, but then the banks decided to connect the three different systems together using "relay" computers.

Three years after the initial announcement the new company opened for business on April 1, 2002. Five days later, computer glitches resulted in a spectacular foul-up. Some 7,000 of the bank's cash machines did not work, 60,000 accounts were debited twice for the same transaction, and millions of bills went unpaid. *The Economist* reported that two weeks later Tokyo Gas, the biggest gas company, was still missing ¥2.2 billion in payments, and the top telephone company, NTT, which was looking for ¥12.7 billion, was forced to send its customers receipts marked with asterisks in place of figures, since it did not know which of about 760,000 bills had been paid.

One of the objectives behind the formation of Mizuho was to exploit economies in its IT systems. The launch fiasco illustrated dramatically that it is easier to predict such merger synergies than to realize them.

Source: The creation of Mizuho Bank and its launch problems are described in "Undispensable: A Fine Merger Yields One Fine Mess," The Economist, April 27, 2002, p. 72; "Big, Bold, but ...", Euromoney, December 2000, pp. 30–35; and "Godzilla Bank," Forbes, March 20, 2000, pp. 132–133.

there is pollution from the seller's operations or toxic waste on its property, the costs of cleaning up will probably fall on the buyer.

Now we turn to the possible sources of merger *synergies*, that is, the possible sources of added value.

Economies of Scale

Just as most of us believe that we would be happier if only we were a little richer, so every manager seems to believe that his or her firm would be more competitive if only it were just a little bigger. Often this is true. One year after the merger of the oil and energy companies Chevron and Texaco, the firms' combined costs were cut by $1.8 billion per year, and $400 million per year of further savings were on the way. The savings came from consolidating operations and eliminating redundant costs.[5] (Some of these redundant "costs" were financial managers. For example, there were two chief financial officers (CFOs) before the merger and only one CFO afterward.)

[5] T. Herrick, "Chevron Texaco's Merger Savings Could Be as Much as $2.2 Billion," *The Wall Street Journal*, June 30, 2002, p. B4.

Achieving these *economies of scale* is the natural goal of horizontal mergers. But such economies have been claimed in conglomerate mergers, too. The architects of these mergers have pointed to the economies that come from sharing central services such as office management and accounting, financial control, executive development, and top-level management.[6]

Optimistic financial managers can see potential economies of scale in almost any industry. But it is easier to buy another business than to integrate it with yours afterward. Some companies that have gotten together in pursuit of scale economies still function as a collection of separate and sometimes competing operations with different production facilities, research efforts, and marketing forces. On the other hand, mergers can work out as planned if managed properly. When Hewlett-Packard bought Compaq Computer Corp., "A chorus of critics predicted that the deal would become . . . stalled in a mess of technical and personal tangles," and a rival executive foresaw "a slow-motion collision of two garbage trucks." But an integration plan was in place, and a team of managers set to work the day after the merger. Nine months later, annual savings were approaching $3 billion.[7]

Managing the merger becomes more important when the bidding and the target companies belong to different countries and different cultures. So when Tata Motors took over Daewoo in Korea, they used the locals in Korea to do most of the work. Similarly, when Tata Chemicals took over Brunner Mond with operations in the tribal areas of Masai, Kenya, its management made sure to be in good terms with the chiefs of the tribe.[8]

Economies of Vertical Integration

Vertical mergers seek economies in vertical integration. Some companies try to gain control over the production process by expanding back toward the output of the raw material and forward to the ultimate consumer. One way to achieve this is to merge with a supplier or a customer.

Vertical integration facilitates coordination and administration. We illustrate via an extreme example. Think of an airline that does not own any planes. If it schedules a flight from Boston to San Francisco, it sells tickets and then rents a plane for that flight from a separate company. This strategy might work on a small scale, but it would be an administrative nightmare for a major carrier, which would have to coordinate hundreds of rental agreements daily. In view of these difficulties, it is not surprising that all major airlines have integrated backward, away from the consumer, by buying and flying airplanes rather than patronizing rent-a-plane companies.

Do not assume that more vertical integration is better than less. Carried to extremes, it is absurdly inefficient, as in the case of LOT, the Polish state airline, which in the late 1980s found itself raising pigs to make sure that its employees had fresh meat on their tables. (Of course, in a centrally managed economy it may be necessary to raise your own cattle or pigs, since you can't be sure you'll be able to buy meat.)

Reliance Industries Limited was procuring naphtha and propane from Reliance Petroleum, a group company prior to their merger in 2002.[9] Prior to the merger, the Gujarat Government granted sales tax waiver to Reliance Petroleum. Since Indian Oil (IOL) was the distribution agent of RIL, the sales tax incidence was on falling on OIL. However, with the dismantling of the Administered Price Mechanism (APM) and after the renegotiation of the marketing deal, RIL was required to pay the sales tax. After the merger between RIL and RPL, the sales tax waiver granted to RPL would automatically come to the merged entity and hence RIL would not be required to pay any sales tax on the petroleum products sold out of Jamnagar in Gujarat.

---

[6]Economies of scale are enjoyed when the average unit cost of production goes down as production increases. One way to achieve economies of scale is to spread fixed costs over a larger volume of production.

[7]P-W Tam, "An Elaborate Plan Forces H-P Union to Stay on Target," *The Wall Street Journal*, April 28, 2003, pp. A1, A10. Hewlett-Packard had more time than usual to prepare the integration plan, because the takeover was delayed for several months by a proxy fight launched by the son of one of the company's founders.

[8]"For Corporate India, it's no longer a culture shock", Economic Times, June 29, 2006.

[9]"RIL – RPL Merger: Smartly Timed", Business Line, March 10, 2002.

Nowadays the tide of vertical integration seems to be flowing out. Companies are finding it more efficient to *outsource* the provision of many services and various types of production. For example, back in the 1950s and 1960s, General Motors was deemed to have a cost advantage over its main competitors, Ford and Chrysler, because a greater fraction of the parts used in GM's automobiles were produced in-house. By the 1990s, Ford and Chrysler had the advantage: They could buy the parts cheaper from outside suppliers. This was partly because the outside suppliers tended to use nonunion labor at lower wages. But it also appears that manufacturers have more bargaining power versus independent suppliers than versus a production facility that's part of the corporate family. In 1998 GM decided to spin off Delphi, its automotive parts division, as a separate company. After the spin-off, GM can continue to buy parts from Delphi in large volumes, but it negotiates the purchases at arm's length.[10]

Complementary Resources

Many small firms are acquired by large ones that can provide the missing ingredients necessary for the small firms' success. The small firm may have a unique product but lack the engineering and sales organization required to produce and market it on a large scale. The firm could develop engineering and sales talent from scratch, but it may be quicker and cheaper to merge with a firm that already has ample talent. The two firms have *complementary resources*—each has what the other needs—and so it may make sense for them to merge. Also, the merger may open up opportunities that neither firm would pursue otherwise.

Of course, two large firms may also merge because they have complementary resources. Consider the 1999 merger between two banks, HDFC Bank and Times Bank. HDFC Bank had branches mostly in the metros, whereas, Times Bank was predominantly present in the non-metro urban areas. Similarly, when ICICI Bank and Bank of Madura (present mostly in the rural areas of South India) merged in 2000, ICICI Bank got a strong hold on the lucrative South Indian market. These two mergers enabled the merged banks to enlarge the branch network in places in which they did not have a significant presence.

Surplus Funds

Here's another argument for mergers: Suppose that your firm is in a mature industry. It is generating a substantial amount of cash, but it has few profitable investment opportunities. Ideally such a firm should distribute the surplus cash to shareholders by increasing its dividend payment or repurchasing stock. Unfortunately, energetic managers are often reluctant to adopt a policy of shrinking their firm in this way. If the firm is not willing to purchase its own shares, it can instead purchase another company's shares. Firms with a surplus of cash and a shortage of good investment opportunities often turn to mergers *financed by cash* as a way of redeploying their capital. Hindustan Levers Limited (HLL) and Brooke Bond Lipton India Limited (BBLIL), for example, justified their merger in 1996 by arguing that the surplus cash of HLL can be "gainfully deployed to seek accelerated growth in processed foods".[11]

Some firms have excess cash and do not pay it out to stockholders or redeploy it by wise acquisitions. Such firms often find themselves targeted for takeover by other firms that propose to redeploy the cash for them. During the oil price slump of the early 1980s, many cash-rich oil companies found themselves threatened by takeover. This was not because their cash was a unique asset. The acquirers wanted to capture the companies' cash flow to make sure it was not frittered away on negative-NPV oil exploration projects. We return to this *free-cash-flow* motive for takeovers later in this chapter.

---

[10]Ford has also spun off its auto parts business as Visteon Corporation.

[11]See the Directors' Report, Annual Report of Brooke Bond Lipton India Limited, 1995.

Eliminating Inefficiencies

Cash is not the only asset that can be wasted by poor management. There are always firms with unexploited opportunities to cut costs and increase sales and earnings. Such firms are natural candidates for acquisition by other firms with better management. In some instances "better management" may simply mean the determination to force painful cuts or realign the company's operations. Notice that the motive for such acquisitions has nothing to do with benefits from combining two firms. Acquisition is simply the mechanism by which a new management team replaces the old one.

A merger is not the only way to improve management, but sometimes it is the only simple and practical way. Managers are naturally reluctant to fire or demote themselves, and stockholders of large public firms do not usually have much *direct* influence on how the firm is run or who runs it.[12]

If this motive for merger is important, one would expect to observe that acquisitions often precede a change in the management of the target firm. This seems to be the case. For example, Martin and McConnell found that the chief executive is four times more likely to be replaced in the year after a takeover than during earlier years.[13] The firms they studied had generally been poor performers; in the four years before acquisition their stock prices had lagged behind those of other firms in the same industry by 15 percent. Apparently many of these firms fell on bad times and were rescued, or reformed, by merger.

Industry Consolidation

The biggest opportunities to improve efficiency seem to come in industries with too many firms and too much capacity. These conditions seem to trigger a wave of mergers and acquisitions, which then force companies to cut capacity and employment and release capital for reinvestment elsewhere in the economy. For example, when U.S. defense budgets fell after the end of the Cold War, a round of consolidating takeovers followed in the defense industry. The consolidation was inevitable, but the takeovers accelerated it.

The banking industry is another example. You probably noticed the several banking mergers in Table 32.1. They are a symptom of a consolidating industry. The United States entered the 1980s with far too many banks, largely as a result of outdated restrictions on interstate banking. As these restrictions eroded and communications and technology improved, hundreds of small banks were swept up into regional or "super-regional" banks. For example, Bank of America's acquisition of FleetBoston Financial followed dozens of acquisitions by these two firms and their predecessors. Part of Bank of America's family tree is set out in Figure 32.1. The main motive in all of these acquisitions was to reduce costs.[14]

Banks are also consolidating in Japan,[15] the U.K., and other countries. For example, NatWest, one of the largest U.K. banks, was a takeover target in 1999. The BBC news described its defense:

[12]It is difficult to assemble a large-enough block of stockholders to effectively challenge management and the incumbent board of directors. Stockholders can have enormous indirect influence, however. Their displeasure shows up in the firm's stock price. A low stock price may encourage a takeover bid by another firm.

[13]K. J. Martin and J. J. McConnell, "Corporate Performance, Corporate Takeovers, and Management Turnover," *Journal of Finance* 46 (June 1991), pp. 671–687.

[14]A study of 41 large bank mergers estimated cost savings with present value averaging 12 percent of the combined market values of the merging banks. See J. F. Houston, C. M. James, and M. D. Ryngaert, "Where Do Merger Gains Come From? Bank Mergers from the Perspective of Insiders and Outsiders," *Journal of Financial Economics* 60 (May/June 2001), pp. 285–331.

[15]Most merging banks in the United States and U.K. have been financially healthy. This has not been the case in recent mergers of large Japanese banks, including the proposed acquisition of UFJ Holdings by Mitsubishi Tokyo Financial Group. UFJ was undercapitalized. It faced a cash shortage and government deadline to cut its portfolio of nonperforming loans in half by March 2005. The face value of the portfolio was ¥4.6 trillion, about $44 billion. These loans were a residue of aggressive lending in the late 1980s and early 1990s, combined with the stagnation of the Japanese economy throughout most of the 1990s.

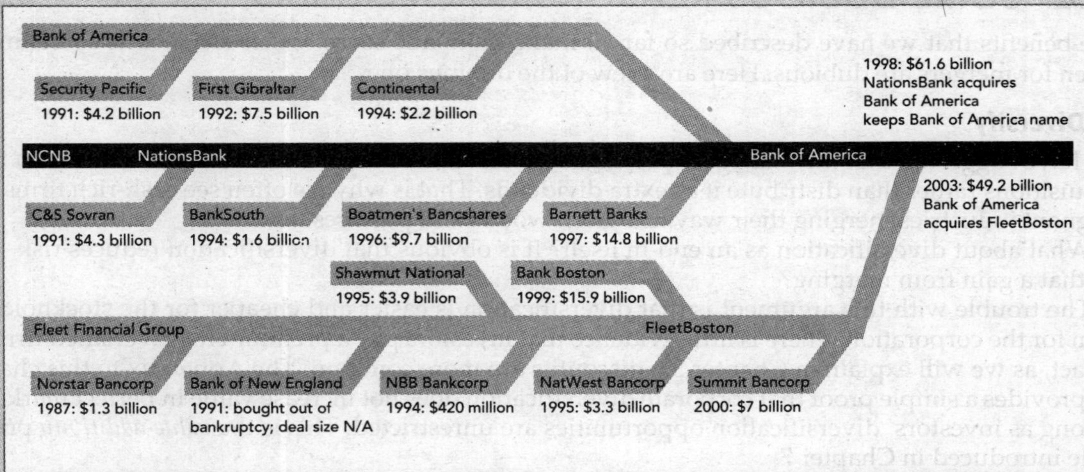

FIGURE 32.1

Part of Bank of America's family tree.

Source: Thomson Financial SDC M&A Database. © 2004 Reprinted by permission of Thompson Financial.

> NatWest has announced a further 1,650 job cuts as it launches details of its vigorous defense against the hostile £21 billion ($35 billion) Bank of Scotland takeover bid. The job cuts are on top of the already announced programme to cut 10,000 retail banking jobs by 2001. . . . Greenwich NatWest, Ulster Bank, Gartmore and NatWest Equity Partners are to be sold, with surplus capital returned to shareholders. . . . NatWest poured scorn on Bank of Scotland's claims regarding cost savings and merger benefits, saying that the Edinburgh firm was "attempting to hijack cost savings that belong to NatWest shareholders." (BBC, October 27, 1999)

All this was to no avail. NatWest was taken over by a much smaller rival and put on a stringent diet.[16]

In India, consolidation (via mergers and acquisitions) is taking in certain industries because of certain regulatory changes. The Industries (Development and Regulation) Act, 1951 has been changed now and the number of industries that require license now has been brought down to less than 10. The licensing regime determined the entry and exit of firms as well as the level of production capacity. The MRTP Act that effectively restricted the growth of large businesses was diluted in the early 1980s removing licensing restrictions, and allowing big businesses to expand in core areas like chemicals, drugs, ceramics and drugs.[17] The licensing policy was responsible for the industry becoming fragmented. In the cement industry, for example, more than 50 players were controlling 110 million ton capacity and out of these as many as 40 were marginal players controlling 1 million ton capacity each.[18] However, a number of the cement manufacturing firms have been merged with (taken over by) other cement firms in the last 13 years after the removal of the outdated licensing policy.

---

[16]The winning bidder was the Royal Bank of Scotland, which proved a more aggressive suitor than the Bank of Scotland, which launched the first attack.

[17]Kohli, A., 2006, "Politics of Economic Growth in India, 1980-2005", Economic and Political Weekly, April 1. pp 1361 – 1370.

[18]See Mergers and Acquisitions, International Financial Law Review, http://www.iflr.com/?Page=17&ISS=16166&SID=508005.

32.2 SOME DUBIOUS REASONS FOR MERGERS

The benefits that we have described so far all make economic sense. Other arguments sometimes given for mergers are dubious. Here are a few of the dubious ones.

To Diversify

We have suggested that the managers of a cash-rich company may prefer to see it use that cash for acquisitions rather than distribute it as extra dividends. That is why we often see cash-rich firms in stagnant industries merging their way into fresh woods and pastures new.

What about diversification as an end in itself? It is obvious that diversification reduces risk. Isn't that a gain from merging?

The trouble with this argument is that diversification is easier and cheaper for the stockholder than for the corporation. There is little evidence that investors pay a premium for diversified firms; in fact, as we will explain in Chapter 33, discounts are more common. The Appendix to this chapter provides a simple proof that corporate diversification does not increase value in perfect markets as long as investors' diversification opportunities are unrestricted. This is the *value-additivity* principle introduced in Chapter 7.

Increasing Earnings per Share: The Bootstrap Game

Some acquisitions that offer no evident economic gains nevertheless produce several years of rising earnings per share. To see how this can happen, let us look at the acquisition of Muck and Slurry by the well-known conglomerate World Enterprises.

The position before the merger is set out in the first two columns of Table 32.2. Because Muck and Slurry has relatively poor growth prospects, its stock's price–earnings ratio is lower than World Enterprises' (line 3). The merger, we assume, produces no economic benefits, and so the firms should be worth exactly the same together as they are apart. The market value of World Enterprises after the merger should be equal to the sum of the separate values of the two firms (line 6).

Since World Enterprises' stock is selling for double the price of Muck and Slurry stock (line 2), World Enterprises can acquire the 100,000 Muck and Slurry shares for 50,000 of its own shares. Thus World will have 150,000 shares outstanding after the merger.

Total earnings double as a result of the merger (line 5), but the number of shares increases by only 50 percent. Earnings *per share* rise from $2.00 to $2.67. We call this the *bootstrap effect* because there is no real gain created by the merger and no increase in the two firms' combined value. Since the stock price is unchanged, the price-earnings ratio falls (line 3).

Figure 32.2 illustrates what is going on here. Before the merger $1 invested in World Enterprises bought 5 cents of current earnings and rapid growth prospects. On the other hand, $1 invested in Muck and Slurry bought 10 cents of current earnings but slower growth prospects. If the *total* market value is not altered by the merger, then $1 invested in the merged firm gives 6.7 cents of immediate earnings but slower growth than World Enterprises offered alone. Muck and Slurry shareholders get lower immediate earnings but faster growth. Neither side gains or loses provided everybody understands the deal.

Financial manipulators sometimes try to ensure that the market does *not* understand the deal. Suppose that investors are fooled by the exuberance of the president of World Enterprises and by plans to introduce modern management techniques into its new Earth Sciences Division (formerly known as Muck and Slurry). They could easily mistake the 33 percent postmerger increase in earnings per share for real growth. If they do, the price of World Enterprises stock rises and the shareholders of both companies receive something for nothing.

This is a "bootstrap" or "chain letter" game. It generates earnings growth not from capital investment or improved profitability, but from purchase of slowly growing firms with low price-

TABLE 32.2

Impact of merger on market value and earnings per share of World Enterprises.

	World Enterprises before Merger	Muck and Slurry	World Enterprises after Merger
1. Earnings per share	$2.00	$2.00	$2.67
2. Price per share	$40	$20	$40
3. Price–earnings ratio	20	10	15
4. Number of shares	100,000	100,000	150,000
5. Total earnings	$200,000	$200,000	$400,000
6. Total market value	$4,000,000	$2,000,000	$6,000,000
7. Current earnings per dollar invested in stock (line 1 ÷ line 2)	$.05	$.10	$.067

Note: When World Enterprises purchases Muck and Slurry, there are no gains. Therefore, total earnings and total market value should be unaffected by the merger. But earnings per share increase. World Enterprises issues only 50,000 of its shares (priced at $40) to acquire the 100,000 Muck and Slurry shares (priced at $20).

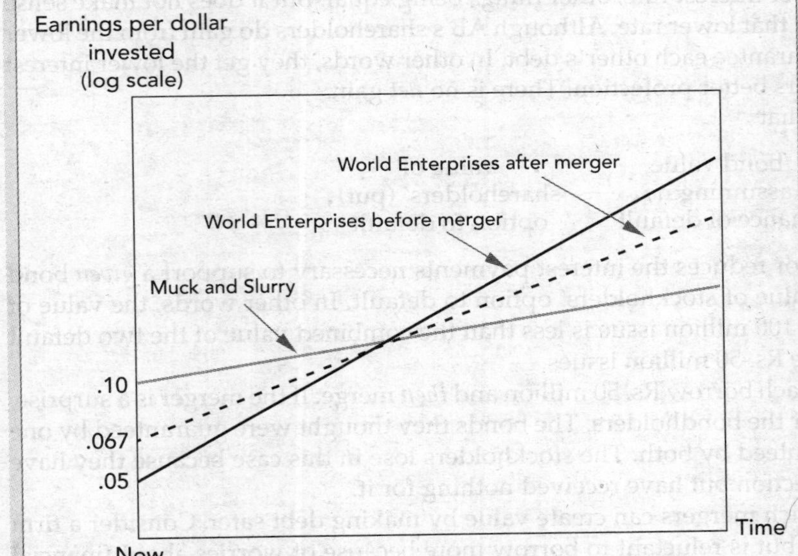

FIGURE 32.2

Effects of merger on earnings growth. By merging with Muck and Slurry, World Enterprises increases current earnings but accepts a slower rate of future growth. Its stockholders should be no better or worse off unless investors are fooled by the bootstrap effect.

Source: S. C. Myers, "A Framework for Evaluating Mergers," in S. C. Myers, ed., *Modern Developments in Financial Management*, (New York: Frederick A. Praeger, Inc., 1976), Figure 1, p. 639.

earnings ratios. If this fools investors, the financial manager may be able to puff up stock price artificially. But to keep fooling investors, the firm has to continue to expand by merger *at the same compound rate*. Clearly this cannot go on forever; one day expansion must slow down or stop. At this point earnings growth falls dramatically and the house of cards collapses.

This game is not often played these days, but you may still encounter managers who would rather acquire firms with low price–earnings ratios. Beware of false prophets who suggest that you can appraise mergers just by looking at their immediate impact on earnings per share.

Lower Financing Costs

You often hear it said that a merged firm is able to borrow more cheaply than its separate units could. In part this is true. We have already seen (in Section 15.4) that there are significant economies of scale in making new issues. Therefore, if firms can make fewer, larger security issues by merging, there are genuine savings.

But when people say that borrowing costs are lower for the merged firm, they usually mean something more than lower issue costs. They mean that when two firms merge, the combined company can borrow at lower interest rates than either firm could separately. This, of course, is exactly what we should expect in a well-functioning bond market. While the two firms are separate, they do not guarantee each other's debt; if one fails, the bondholder cannot ask the other for money. But after the merger each enterprise effectively does guarantee the other's debt; if one part of the business fails, the bondholders can still take their money out of the other part. Because these mutual guarantees make the debt less risky, lenders demand a lower interest rate.

Does the lower interest rate mean a net gain to the merger? Not necessarily. Compare the following two situations:

- *Separate issues.* Firm A and firm B each make a Rs. 50 million bond issue.
- *Single issue.* Firms A and B merge, and the new firm AB makes a single Rs. 100 million issue.

Of course AB would pay a lower interest rate, other things being equal. But it does not make sense for A and B to merge just to get that lower rate. Although AB's shareholders do gain from the lower rate, they lose by having to guarantee each other's debt. In other words, they get the lower interest rate only by giving bondholders better protection. There is no *net* gain.

In Section 24.1 we showed that

$$\text{Bond value} = \begin{array}{c}\text{bond value}\\ \text{assuming no}\\ \text{chance of default}\end{array} - \begin{array}{c}\text{value of}\\ \text{shareholders' (put)}\\ \text{option to default}\end{array}$$

Merger increases bond value (or reduces the interest payments necessary to support a *given* bond value) only by reducing the value of stockholders' option to default. In other words, the value of the default option for AB's Rs. 100 million issue is less than the combined value of the two default options on A's and B's separate Rs. 50 million issues.

Now suppose that A and B each borrow Rs. 50 million and *then* merge. If the merger is a surprise, it is likely to be a happy one for the bondholders. The bonds they thought were guaranteed by one of the two firms end up guaranteed by both. The stockholders lose in this case because they have given bondholders better protection but have received nothing for it.

There is one situation in which mergers can create value by making debt safer. Consider a firm that covets interest tax shields but is reluctant to borrow more because of worries about financial distress. (This is the trade-off theory described in Chapter 18.) Merging decreases the probability of financial distress, other things equal. If it allows increased borrowing, and increased value from the interest tax shields, there can be a net gain to the merger.[19]

In India, when Reliance Industries (RIL) and Reliance Petroleum (RPL) merged with each other, they could manage to reduce the financing costs by Rs. 0.45 billion because of the difference in the rating of the bonds issued by RIL and RPL. Prior to the merger, the non-convertible debentures of RPL of face value of about Rs. 60 billions had AA+ rating. After the merger, the rating of the bonds of RIL (the merged firm) was AAA (same as the pre-merger rating of the bonds of RIL), and this implied savings of about 75 basis points.

[19]This merger rationale was first suggested by W. G. Lewellen, "A Pure Financial Rationale for the Conglomerate Merger," *Journal of Finance* 26 (May 1971), pp. 521–537. If you want to see some of the controversy and discussion that this idea led to, look at R. C. Higgins and L. D. Schall, "Corporate Bankruptcy and Conglomerate Merger," *Journal of Finance* 30 (March 1975), pp. 93–114; and D. Galai and R. W. Masulis, "The Option Pricing Model and the Risk Factor of Stock," *Journal of Financial Economics* 3 (January–March 1976), especially pp. 66–69.

32.3 ESTIMATING MERGER GAINS AND COSTS

Suppose that you are the financial manager of firm A and you want to analyze the possible purchase of firm B.[20] The first thing to think about is whether there is an economic gain from the merger. There is an economic gain *only if the two firms are worth more together than apart*. For example, if you think that the combined firm would be worth PV_{AB} and that the separate firms are worth PV_A and PV_B, then

$$\text{Gain} = PV_{AB} - (PV_A + PV_B) = \Delta PV_{AB}$$

If this gain is positive, there is an economic justification for merger. But you also have to think about the *cost* of acquiring firm B. Take the easy case in which payment is made in cash. Then the cost of acquiring B is equal to the cash payment minus B's value as a separate entity. Thus

$$\text{Cost} = \text{cash paid} - PV_B$$

The net present value to A of a merger with B is measured by the difference between the gain and the cost. Therefore, you should go ahead with the merger if its net present value, defined as

$$\begin{aligned} \text{NPV} &= \text{gain} - \text{cost} \\ &= \Delta PV_{AB} - (\text{cash} - PV_B) \end{aligned}$$

is positive.

We like to write the merger criterion in this way because it focuses attention on two distinct questions. When you estimate the benefit, you concentrate on whether there are any gains to be made from the merger. When you estimate cost, you are concerned with the division of these gains between the two companies.

An example may help make this clear. Firm A has a value of Rs. 200 million, and B has a value of Rs. 50 million. Merging the two would allow cost savings with a present value of Rs. 25 million. This is the gain from the merger. Thus,

$$\begin{aligned} PV_A &= \text{Rs. } 200 \\ PV_B &= \text{Rs. } 50 \\ \text{Gain} = \Delta PV_{AB} &= +\text{Rs. } 25 \\ PV_{AB} &= \text{Rs. } 275 \text{ million} \end{aligned}$$

Suppose that B is bought for cash, say, for Rs. 65 million. The cost of the merger is

$$\begin{aligned} \text{Cost} &= \text{cash paid} - PV_B \\ &= 65 - 50 = \text{Rs. } 15 \text{ million} \end{aligned}$$

Note that the stockholders of firm B—the people on the other side of the transaction—are ahead by Rs. 15 million. *Their* gain is *your* cost. They have captured Rs. 15 million of the Rs. 25 million merger gain. Thus when we write down the NPV of the merger from A's viewpoint, we are really calculating the part of the gain that A's stockholders get to keep. The NPV to A's stockholders equals the overall gain from the merger less that part of the gain captured by B's stockholders:

$$\text{NPV} = 25 - 15 = +\text{Rs. } 10 \text{ million}$$

[20] This chapter's definitions and interpretations of the gains and costs of merger follow those set out in S. C. Myers, "A Framework for Evaluating Mergers," op. cit.

Just as a check, let's confirm that A's stockholders really come out Rs. 10 million ahead. They start with a firm worth PV_A = Rs. 200 million. They end up with a firm worth Rs. 275 million and then have to pay out Rs. 65 million to B's stockholders.[21] Thus their net gain is

$$\begin{aligned} \text{NPV} &= \text{wealth with merger} - \text{wealth without merger} \\ &= (PV_{AB} - \text{cash}) - PV_A \\ &= (\text{Rs. } 275 - \text{Rs. } 65) - \text{Rs. } 200 = +\text{Rs. } 10 \text{ million} \end{aligned}$$

Suppose investors do not anticipate the merger between A and B. The announcement will cause the value of B's stock to rise from Rs. 50 million to Rs. 65 million, a 30 percent increase. If investors share management's assessment of the merger gains, the market value of A's stock will increase by Rs. 10 million, only a 5 perçent increase.

It makes sense to keep an eye on what investors think the gains from merging are. If A's stock price falls when the deal is announced, then investors are sending the message that the merger benefits are doubtful or that A is paying too much for them.

Right and Wrong Ways to Estimate the Benefits of Mergers

Some companies begin their merger analyses with a forecast of the target firm's future cash flows. Any revenue increases or cost reductions attributable to the merger are included in the forecasts, which are then discounted back to the present and compared with the purchase price:

$$\begin{matrix}\text{Estimated} \\ \text{net gain}\end{matrix} = \begin{matrix}\text{DCF valuation} \\ \text{of target, including} \\ \text{merger benefits}\end{matrix} - \begin{matrix}\text{cash required} \\ \text{for acquisition}\end{matrix}$$

This is a dangerous procedure. Even the brightest and best-trained analyst can make large errors in valuing a business. The estimated net gain may come up positive not because the merger makes sense but simply because the analyst's cash-flow forecasts are too optimistic. On the other hand, a good merger may not be pursued if the analyst fails to recognize the target's potential as a stand-alone business.

Our procedure *starts* with the target's stand-alone market value (PV_B) and concentrates on the *changes* in cash flow that would result from the merger. *Ask yourself why the two firms should be worth more together than apart.*

The same advice holds when you are contemplating the sale of part of your business. There is no point in saying to yourself, This is an unprofitable business and should be sold. Unless the buyer can run the business better than you can, the price you receive will reflect the poor prospects.

Sometimes you may come across managers who believe that there are simple rules for identifying good acquisitions. They may say, for example, that they always try to buy into growth industries or that they have a policy of acquiring companies that are selling below book value. But our comments in Chapter 11 about the characteristics of a good investment decision also hold true when you are buying a whole company. *You add value only if you can generate additional economic rents—* some competitive edge that other firms can't match and the target firm's managers can't achieve on their own.

[21]We are assuming that PV_A includes enough cash to finance the deal, or that the cash can be borrowed at a market interest rate. Notice that the value to A's stockholders after the deal is done and paid for is Rs. 275 − 65 = Rs. 210 million—a gain of Rs. 10 million.

One final piece of horse sense: Often two companies bid against each other to acquire the same target firm. In effect, the target firm puts itself up for auction. In such cases, ask yourself whether the target is worth more to you than to the other bidder. If the answer is no, you should be cautious about getting into a bidding contest. Winning such a contest may be more expensive than losing it. If you lose, you have simply wasted your time, if you win, you have probably paid too much.

More on Estimating Costs—What If the Target's Stock Price Anticipates the Merger?

The cost of a merger is the premium that the buyer pays over the seller's stand-alone value. How can that value be determined? If the target is a public company, you can start with its market value; just observe price per share and multiply by the number of shares outstanding. But bear in mind that if investors *expect* A to acquire B, or if they expect *somebody* to acquire B, the market value of B may overstate its stand-alone value.

This is one of the few places in this book where we draw an important distinction between market value (MV) and the true, or "intrinsic," value (PV) of the firm as a separate entity. The problem here is not that the market value of B is wrong but that it may not be the value of firm B as a separate entity. Potential investors in B's stock will see two possible outcomes and two possible values:

Outcome	Market Value of B's Stock
1. No merger	PV_B: Value of B as a separate firm
2. Merger occurs	PV_B *plus* some part of the benefits of the merger

If the second outcome is possible, MV_B, the stock market value we observe for B, will overstate PV_B. This is exactly what *should* happen in a competitive capital market. Unfortunately, it complicates the task of a financial manager who is evaluating a merger.

Here is an example: Suppose that just before A and B's merger announcement we observe the following:

	Firm A	Firm B
Market price per share	Rs. 200	Rs. 100
Number of shares	1,000,000	500,000
Market value of firm	Rs. 200 million	Rs. 50 million

Firm A intends to pay Rs. 65 million cash for B. If B's market price reflects only its value as a separate entity, then

$$\text{Cost} = (\text{cash paid} - PV_B)$$
$$= (65 - 50) = \text{Rs. 15 million}$$

However, suppose that B's share price has *already* risen Rs. 12 because of rumors that B might get a favorable merger offer. That means that its intrinsic value is overstated by 12 × 500,000 = Rs. 6 million. Its true value, PV_B, is only Rs. 44 million. Then

$$\text{Cost} = (65 - 44) = \text{Rs. 21 million}$$

Since the merger gain is Rs. 25 million, this deal still makes A's stockholders better off, but B's stockholders are now capturing the lion's share of the gain.

Notice that if the market made a mistake, and the market value of B was *less* than B's true value as a separate entity, the cost could be negative. In other words, B would be a *bargain* and the merger would be worthwhile from A's point of view, even if the two firms were worth no more together than apart. Of course, A's stockholders' gain would be B's stockholders' loss, because B would be sold for less than its true value.

Firms have made acquisitions just because their managers believed they had spotted a company whose intrinsic value was not fully appreciated by the stock market. However, we know from the evidence on market efficiency that "cheap" stocks often turn out to be expensive. It is not easy for outsiders, whether investors or managers, to find firms that are truly undervalued by the market. Moreover, if the shares are bargain-priced, A doesn't need a merger to profit by its special knowledge. It can just buy up B's shares on the open market and hold them passively, waiting for other investors to wake up to B's true value.

If firm A is wise, it will not go ahead with a merger if the cost exceeds the gain. Firm B will not consent if A's gain is so big that B loses. This gives us a range of possible cash payments that would allow the merger to take place. Whether the payment is at the top or the bottom of this range depends on the relative bargaining power of the two participants.

Estimating Cost When the Merger Is Financed by Stock

In recent years about 70 percent of mergers have involved payment wholly or partly in the form of the acquirer's stock. When a merger is financed by stock, cost depends on the value of the shares in the new company received by the shareholders of the selling company. If the sellers receive *N* shares, each worth P_{AB}, the cost is

$$\text{Cost} = N \times P_{AB} - PV_B$$

Just be sure to use the price per share *after the merger is announced* and its benefits are appreciated by investors.

Suppose that A offers 325,000 (.325 million) shares instead of Rs. 65 million in cash. A's share price before the deal is announced is Rs. 200. If B is worth Rs. 50 million stand-alone,[22] the cost of the merger *appears* to be

$$\text{Apparent cost} = .325 \times 200 - 50 = \text{Rs. } 15 \text{ million}$$

However, the apparent cost may not be the true cost. A's stock price is Rs. 200 before the merger announcement. At the announcement it ought to go up.

Given the gain and the terms of the deal, we can calculate share prices and market values after the deal. The new firm will have 1.325 million shares outstanding and will be worth Rs. 275 million.[23] The new share price is 275/1.325 = Rs. 207.55. The true cost is

$$\text{Cost} = .325 \times 207.55 - 50 = \text{Rs. } 17.45 \text{ million}$$

[22]In this case we assume that B's stock price has *not* risen on merger rumors and accurately reflects B's stand-alone value.

[23]In this case no cash is leaving the firm to finance the merger. In our example of a cash offer, Rs. 65 million would be paid out to B's stockholders, leaving the final value of the firm at 275 − 65 = Rs. 210 million. There would only be one million shares outstanding, so share price would be Rs. 210. The cash deal is better for A's shareholders in this example.

This cost can also be calculated by figuring out the gain to B's shareholders. They end up with .325 million shares, or 24.5 percent of the new firm AB. Their gain is

$$.245(275) - 50 = \text{Rs. } 17.45 \text{ million}$$

In general, if B's shareholders are given the fraction x of the combined firms,

$$\text{Cost} = x\text{PV}_{AB} - \text{PV}_B$$

We can now understand the first key distinction between cash and stock as financing instruments. If cash is offered, the cost of the merger is unaffected by the merger gains. If stock is offered, the cost depends on the gains because the gains show up in the postmerger share price.

Stock financing also mitigates the effect of overvaluation or undervaluation of either firm. Suppose, for example, that A overestimates B's value as a separate entity, perhaps because it has overlooked some hidden liability. Thus A makes too generous an offer. Other things being equal, A's stockholders are better off if it is a stock offer rather than a cash offer. With a stock offer, the inevitable bad news about B's value will fall partly on the shoulders of B's stockholders.

Asymmetric Information

There is a second key difference between cash and stock financing for mergers. A's managers will usually have access to information about A's prospects that is not available to outsiders. Economists call this *asymmetric information*.

Suppose A's managers are more optimistic than outside investors. They may think that A's shares will really be worth Rs. 215 after the merger, Rs. 7.45 higher than the Rs. 207.55 market price we just calculated. If they are right, the true cost of a stock-financed merger with B is

$$\text{Cost} = .325 \times 215 - 50 = \text{Rs. } 19.88$$

B's shareholders would get a "free gift" of Rs. 7.45 for every A share they receive—an extra gain of Rs. 7.45 × .325 = 2.42, that is, Rs. 2.42 million.

Of course, if A's managers were really this optimistic, they would strongly prefer to finance the merger with cash. Financing with stock would be favored by *pessimistic* managers who think their company's shares are *over*valued.

Does this sound like "win-win" for A—just issue shares when overvalued, cash otherwise? No, it's not that easy, because B's shareholders, and outside investors generally, understand what's going on. Suppose you are negotiating on behalf of B. You find that A's managers keep suggesting stock rather than cash financing. You quickly infer A's managers' pessimism, mark down your own opinion of what the shares are worth, and drive a harder bargain.

This asymmetric-information story explains why buying-firms' share prices generally fall when stock-financed mergers are announced.[24] Andrade, Mitchell, and Stafford found an average market-adjusted fall of 1.5 percent on the announcement of stock-financed mergers between 1973 and 1998. There was a small *gain* (.4 percent) for a sample of cash-financed deals.[25]

---

[24]The same reasoning applies to stock issues. See Sections 15.4 and 18.4.

[25]See G. Andrade, M. Mitchell, and E. Stafford, "New Evidence and Perspectives on Mergers," *Journal of Economic Perspectives* 15 (Spring 2001), pp. 103–120. This result confirms earlier work, including N. Travlos, "Corporate Takeover Bids, Methods of Payment, and Bidding Firms' Stock Returns," *Journal of Finance* 42 (September 1987), pp. 943–963; and J. R. Franks, R. S. Harris, and S. Titman, "The Postmerger Share-Price Performance of Acquiring Firms," *Journal of Financial Economics* 29 (March 1991), pp. 81–96.

32.4 THE MECHANICS OF A MERGER

Buying a company is a much more complicated affair than buying a piece of machinery. Thus we should look at some of the problems encountered in arranging mergers. In practice, these arrangements are often *extremely* complex, and specialists must be consulted. We are not trying to replace those specialists; we simply want to alert you to the kinds of legal, tax, and accounting issues they deal with.

Mergers and Competition Act

Prior to 1991, pre-entry scrutiny of the mergers in India was required under the MRTP Act, 1969 in India. However, after the amendment of the MRTP Act, there is no provision under which mergers that give rise to monopoly situations are scrutinized and cleared by any legal authority.[26] This is in sharp contrast to the situation prevailing in many developed countries, including the U.S., where the Clayton Act of 1914[27] forbids an acquisition whenever "in any line of commerce or in any section of the country" the effect "*may be* substantially to lessen competition, or to *tend* to create a monopoly."

Antitrust law can be enforced by the federal government in either of two ways: by a civil suit brought by the Justice Department or by a proceeding initiated by the Federal Trade Commission (FTC).[28] The Hart–Scott–Rodino Antitrust Act of 1976 requires that these agencies be informed of all acquisitions of stock amounting to $15 million or 15 percent of the target's stock, whichever is less. Thus, almost all large mergers are reviewed at an early stage.[29] Both the Justice Department and the FTC then have the right to seek injunctions delaying a merger. An injunction is often enough to scupper the companies' plans.

Both the FTC and the Justice Department have been flexing their muscles in recent years. Here is an example. After the end of the Cold War, sharp declines in defense budgets triggered consolidation in the U.S. aerospace industry. By 1998 there remained just three giant companies—Boeing, Lockheed Martin, and Raytheon—plus several smaller ones, including Northrup Grumman. Thus, when Lockheed Martin and Northrup Grumman announced plans to get together, the Departments of Justice and Defense decided that this was a merger too far. In the face of this opposition, the two companies broke off their engagement.

The merger boom of the late 1990s has kept antitrust regulators busy. Other industries in which large mergers have been blocked on antitrust grounds include aluminum (Reynolds and Alcoa), telecoms (WorldCom and Sprint), supermarkets (Kroger and WinnDixie), video rentals (Hollywood Entertainment and Blockbuster), and office equipment (Office Depot and Staples).

Companies that do business outside the USA also have to worry about foreign antitrust laws. For example, GE's $46 billion takeover bid for Honeywell was blocked by the European Commission, which argued that the combined company would have too much power in the aircraft industry.

Sometimes trustbusters will object to a merger, but then relent if the companies agree to divest certain assets and operations. For example, the Justice Department has insisted that any joint venture between American Airlines and British Airways would be permitted to go ahead only if the airlines relinquished some of their take-off and landing slots at London's Heathrow airport.

---

[26]The Competition Bill, 2001, however, proposes to vest the Competition Commission of India (CCI) with power to examine the merger proposals and thereby bring back the regime of pre-merger scrutiny and clearance.

[27]This is the most important statute that can bog down any merger in the U.S.

[28]Competitors or third parties who think they will be injured by the merger can also bring antitrust suits.

[29]The target has to be notified also, and it in turn informs investors. Thus the Hart–Scott–Rodino Act effectively forces an acquiring company to "go public" with its bid.

The Form of Acquisition

Next, you will want to consider the form of acquisition. One possibility is literally to merge the two companies, in which case one company automatically assumes all the assets and all the liabilities of the other. Such a merger must have the approval of at least 75 percent of the stockholders (present and voting, in value terms) of each firm. Section 395 of the Companies Act in India further stipulates that the shareholding of the dissenting shareholders can be purchased provided at least 90 percent of the shareholders (present and voting, in value terms) agree to the scheme of the merger. In the U.S. a merger must have the approval of at least 50 percent of the shareholders of each firm.[30]

An alternative is simply to buy the seller's stock in exchange for cash, shares, or other securities.[31] In this case the buyer can deal individually with the shareholders of the selling company. The seller's managers may not be involved at all. Their approval and cooperation are generally sought, but if they resist, the buyer will attempt to acquire an effective majority of the outstanding shares. If successful, the buyer has control and can complete the merger and, if necessary, toss out the incumbent management. It is not necessary to buy 100 percent of the shares of the selling company to obtain effective management control over the selling company. In fact, in India, one rarely finds the buying company buying all the 100 percent of the shares of the target company. With 51 percent stake in the selling company, a buying company can effectively control the management decision making of the selling company. However, in the U.S. it is often a common practice to buy all the 100 percent of the shares of the selling company.

The third approach is to buy some or all of the seller's assets. In this case ownership of the assets needs to be transferred, and payment is made to the selling firm rather than directly to its shockholders.

Merger Accounting

When one company buys another, its management worries about how the purchase will show up in its financial statements. According to Accounting Standard 14 (AS 14) issued by the Institute of Chartered Accountants of India (ICAI), an amalgamation (same as merger) can be in the nature of pooling of interests (referred to as amalgamation in the nature of merger) or acquisition. AS 14 lays down five conditions that must be satisfied for an amalgamation to be in the nature of merger. The five conditions are:

1. All assets and liabilities of the "Transferor Company"[32] before amalgamation should become assets and liabilities of the "Transferee Company."
2. Shareholders holding not less than 90% of shares (in value terms) of the "Transferor Company" should become the shareholders of the "Transferee Company".
3. The consideration payable to the shareholders of the "Transferor Company" should be in the form of shares of the "Transferee Company" only; cash can however, be paid in respect of fractional shares.
4. Business of the "Transferor Company" is intended to be carried on by the "Transferee Company."
5. The "Transferee Company" incorporates, in its balance sheet, the book values of assets and liabilities of the "Transferor Company" without any adjustment except to the extent needed to ensure uniformity of accounting policies.

[30]Corporate charters and state laws sometimes specify a higher percentage.

[31]As per the SEBI (Substantial Acquisition of Shares and Takeovers) Regulations, 1997, the offer price shall be payable in (a) cash, (b) shares of the buying company, (c) secured instruments of the buying company with a minimum 'A' grade rating, (d) or any combination of (a), (b), (c). However, most acquisitions are financed with cash only.

[32]Here, the term 'transferor company' refers to the merging company or the selling company. The term 'transferee company' refers to the buying company or the merged company.

TABLE 32.3

Accounting for the merger of A Corporation and B Corporation assuming that (a) A Corporation issues shares to the shareholders of B Corporation (under the pooling of interest method) and (b) A Corporation pays Rs.18 million for B Corporation (Figures in Rs. millions) A corporation has raised Rs. 18 m by issuing debt.

Key: NWC = Net working capital (or net current assets)
FA: Net book value of fixed assets
D: debt
E: book value of equity

Initial Balance Sheets

A Corporation				B Corporation			
NWC	20	30	D	NWC	1	0	D
FA	80	70	E	FA	9	10	E
	100	100			10	10	

Balance Sheet of AB Corporation (Pooling of Interest Method)

NWC	21	30	D
FA	89	80	E
	110	110	

Balance Sheet of AB Corporation (Purchase Method)

NWC	21	48	D
FA	89	70	E
Goodwill	8		
	118	118	

An amalgamation which does not satisfy all the conditions stated above will be regarded as an "Acquisition". For a merger, the 'pooling of interests' method is used and for an acquisition, the 'purchase method' is used. The U.S. GAAP, however, allows only the purchase method.

We illustrate the difference between the two methods in Table 32.3, which shows what happens when A Corporation buys B Corporation, leading to a new AB Corporation. The two firms' initial balance sheets are shown at the top of the table. Below this we show what happens to the balance sheet when the two firms merge under the two different methods. We assume (under Purchase Method) that B Corporation has been purchased for Rs.18 million, 180 percent of the book value. Similarly, we assume that A Corporation issues shares to the shareholders of the B Corporation (under the Pooling of Interests Method).

Under the pooling of interest method, the balance sheet of AB Corporation is arrived at by a line-by-line addition of the corresponding line items of the balance sheets of both the companies. Under the purchase method, the A Corporation will treat B Corporation as an acquisition investment and hence reports the assets (wherever possible) at the market values.

We assume that A Corporation pays Rs.18 million to the shareholders of B Corporation under the 'Purchase Method'. Why did A Corporation pay an Rs.8 million premium over B's book value? There are two possible reasons. First, the true values of B's **tangible assets** – its working capital, fixed assets – may be greater than Rs.10 million. We will assume that this is *not* the reason; that is, we assume that the assets listed on its balance sheet are valued there correctly.[33]

Second, A Corporation may be paying for an **intangible asset** that is not listed on B Corporation's balance sheet. For example, the intangible asset may be a promising product or technology. Or it may be not more than B Corporation's share of the expected economic gains from the merger.

A Corporation is buying an asset worth Rs.18 million. The problem is to show that asset on the left-hand[34] side of AB Corporation's balance sheet. B Corporation's tangible assets are worth only Rs.10 million. This leaves Rs.8 million. Under the purchase method, the accountant takes care of this by creating a new asset category called **goodwill** and assigning Rs.8 million to it.[35] Goodwill amortization can have a substantial impact on the reported net income if the premium paid in an acquisition is very large.

[33] If B's tangible assets are worth more than their previous book values, they would be reappraised and their current values entered on AB Coporation's balance sheet.

[34] A die-hard fan of accounting in India may raise an objection to our showing assets on the left hand side. But how does it matter?

[35] If part of the Rs. 8 million consisted of payment for identifiable intangible assets such as patents, the accountant would place these under a separate category of assets. Identifiable intangible assets that have a finite life need to be written off over their life.

Income Tax Act	Mergers
Sec 2 (1B)	Explains which mergers will get some tax benefits under Section 35
Sec 35 (5),35A(6),35D(5),35E(7)	Benefits under these acts (which the merging company was getting prior to the merger) will continue to be available to the merged company,when merger satisfies the conditions laid down under Section 2(1B)
Sec 72A	If a profit making company acquires a loss making company,then it can continue to carry forward the business losses subject to certain considitions (including Section 32 of SICA)
Section 47	Explains when the exchange of shares in case of mergers will not be treated as capital gains

TABLE 32.4

A brief description of some of the sections under the Income Tax Act of India that affect mergers.

Some Tax Considerations[36]

In order to understand the tax implications of mergers under the Income Tax Act, 1961 we need to divide the mergers into two categories. Under Section 2(1B) of the IT Act, mergers satisfying the following conditions get different tax benefits mentioned under the various sections (Section 35, for example).

"All the property and liabilities of the amalgamating company (same as merging company) or companies immediately before the amalgamation (same as merger) must become part of the amalgamated company (same as merged company) by virtue of the amalgamation. Shareholders holding not less than nine-tenths in value of the shares in the amalgamating company or companies (other than shares already held therein immediately before the amalgamation by, or by a nominee for, the amalgamated company or its subsidiary) become shareholders of the amalgamated company by virtue of the amalgamation procedure."

Mergers that do not satisfy the above conditions do not get the tax benefits. It is therefore very important to design the merger transaction in such a way that the above conditions are satisfied. In most cases, when a merger is financed by the exchange of shares of the buying company, all the conditions will automatically get satisfied. However, special care needs to be taken when the buying company does not want to buy the entire business of the selling company. Let's assume that the selling company is into the manufacturing of cements and construction. The buying company is into cements only. Let's also assume that the buying company is not interested in acquiring the construction business of the selling company. However, in order to satisfy the requirements of Sec 2 (1B) of the Act, it needs to buy all the properties of the selling company, including the construction division. In India companies usually follow one of the two approaches to directly avoid the provisions of the above section. The buying company, can for example, first buy all the properties of the selling company and then sell the construction division to some other company. It can alternatively, ask the selling company to spin off the cements division into a separate company and then merge with the newly-created cement company.

The merging company loses its identity after a merger, and this has a great significance for the estimation of tax benefits arising out of mergers. Under the provisions of the Income Tax Act, only the loss-making company can carry-forward the loss. The right to carry-forward is attached to the company and not to the assets of the company. Thus for example, prior to the merger with Godrej Soaps Limited (GSL), Gujarat Godrej Innovative Chemicals Limited (GGICL) had accumulated losses of Rs. 95 crores in 1994. However, as per the IT Act in India, only GGICL could carry forward

[36]For a detailed discussion on the tax considerations in case of mergers, refer to "Mergers et al" by S Ramanujam (2000), Chapter 22. Tata McGraw-Hill. New Delhi.

these losses. So Godrej Soaps got merged with GGICL to ensure that the identity of the loss-making company remains intact after the merger. And the merged entity (that is GGICL) changed its name to Godrej Soaps Limited with effect from January 6, 1995. This way, Godrej Soaps managed to retain its brand name and at the same time managed to set off the accumulated losses of GGICL against its own profit. Of course, Godrej Soaps could have obtained an approval under Sec 72A of the IT Act to carry forward the business losses of GGICL. However, the reverse merger route (where GGICL and *not* GSL is the merged company) is a preferred route because the merged entity can carry forward both the business and capital losses and secondly, the merged entity does not have to face the bureaucratic hassles associated with managing BIFR.

Apart from income tax, one has also to consider stamp duties to be paid in case of mergers in India. In India, a few of the states like Maharashtra, Gujarat, Kerala, Karnataka and Rajasthan have their own stamp duty legislation. Other states have adopted the Indian Stamp Act, 1899 with appropriate amendments. Thus for example, the Rajasthan Government has fixed the stamp duty at 10 percent of the market value of the property to be conveyed and the market value is equal to the sum total of the value of shares issued by the merged company and the amount of consideration, if any, paid in the merger.

In Table 32.4, we mention the tax laws that one needs to keep in mind in the case of mergers in India.

32.5 TAKEOVER BATTLES AND TACTICS

Most mergers are negotiated by the two firms' top management and boards of directors. And in most cases, the top management will be under the same business groups in India. From a list of 190 mergers that were announced between 1993 and 2001, we find that as many as 177 were mergers where both the merged and the merging companies were controlled by the same business group or management. In only 13 cases, the merged and the merging companies were controlled by unrelated management. This is however, not the case internationally and hence in practice one of the management teams usually comes out on top.

If a negotiated merger appears impossible the acquirer can instead go over the heads of the target firm's management and appeal directly to its stockholders. There are two ways of doing this. First, the acquirer can seek the support of the target firm's stockholders at the next annual meeting. This is called a *proxy fight* because the right to vote someone else's share is called a *proxy.*[37]

Proxy fights are expensive and difficult to win. The alternative for the would-be acquirer is to make a *tender offer* directly to the shareholders. The management of the target firm may advise its shareholders to accept the tender, or it may attempt to fight the bid. Tender offers in India are regulated by the SEBI (Substantial Acquisition of Shares and Takeovers) Regulations, 1997. Tender offers in India can be made by a hostile bidder, by a friendly outside bidder, or by the promoters of the company. The promoters of a company, can for example, make a tender offer to the public shareholders of a company to increase their stake in the company.

In the US, tender battles resemble a complex game of poker. The rules are set mostly by the Williams Act of 1968, by state law, and by the courts. The problem in setting the rules is that it is unclear who requires protection. Should the management of the target firm be given more weapons to defend itself against unwelcome predators? Or should it simply be encouraged to sit the game out? Or should it be obliged to conduct an auction to obtain the highest price for its shareholders? And what about would-be acquirers? Should they be forced to reveal their intentions at an early

[37] Peter Dodd and Jerrold Warner have written a detailed description and analysis of proxy fights. See "On Corporate Governance: A Study of Proxy Contests," *Journal of Financial Economics* 2 (April 1985), pp. 401–438.

stage, or would that allow other firms to piggy-back on their good ideas and enter competing bids?[38]

Keep these questions in mind as we review one of the more interesting chapters in merger history.

Boone Pickens Tries to Take Over Cities Service, Gulf Oil, and Phillips Petroleum

The 1980s saw a series of pitched takeover battles in the oil industry. The most interesting and visible player in these battles was Boone Pickens, chairman of Mesa Petroleum and a self-styled advocate for shareholders everywhere. Pickens and Mesa didn't win many battles, but they made a lot of money losing them, and they helped force major changes in oil companies' investment and financing policies.

Mesa's attack on Cities Service[39] illustrates Pickens's *modus operandi*. The battle began in May 1982, when Mesa bought Cities shares in preparation for a takeover bid. Cities counterattacked. It issued more shares to dilute Mesa's holdings, and it made a retaliatory offer for Mesa. (This is called a *pacman defense*—try to take over the attacker before it takes over you!) Over the following month Mesa upped its bid for Cities, and Cities twice increased its bid for Mesa. But in the end Cities won: Mesa agreed to call off its bid and not to make another one for Cities for at least five years. In exchange, Cities agreed to repurchase Mesa's holdings at an $80 million profit to Mesa. This is called a **greenmail** payment.

Though Cities escaped Mesa, it was still in play. It looked for a **white knight,** that is, a friendly acquirer, and found one in Gulf Oil. But the Federal Trade Commission raised various objections to that deal, and Gulf backed out.

In the end, Cities was bought by Occidental Petroleum. Occidental made a tender offer of $55 per share in cash for 45 percent of Cities, followed by a package of fixed income securities for the remaining stock. This is called a *two-tier offer.* In effect, Occidental was saying, "Last one through the door does the washing up." Almost all Cities stockholders rushed to take advantage of the cash offer, and Occidental gained control.

One year after its brief engagement with Cities, Gulf itself became a takeover target. Pickens and Mesa were again on the warpath. At this point Chevron came to the rescue and acquired Gulf for $13.2 billion, more than double its value six months earlier. Chevron's bid gave Mesa a profit of $760 million on the Gulf shares it had bought. Asked for his views, Pickens commented, "Shucks, I guess we lost another one."

Pickens's next foray was against Phillips Petroleum. By 1984 Mesa had accumulated 6 percent of Phillips at an average price of $38 per share and made a bid for a further 15 percent at $60 per share. Phillips's first response was predictable: It bought out Mesa's shareholding. This greenmail payment gave Mesa a profit of $89 million.[40]

[38]The Williams Act obliges firms who own 5 percent or more of another company's shares to tip their hand by reporting their holding in a Schedule 13(d) filing with the SEC.

[39]See R. S. Ruback, "The Cities Service Takeover: A Case Study," *Journal of Finance* 38 (May 1983), pp. 319–330.

[40]Giving in to greenmail can be dangerous, as Phillips soon discovered. Just six weeks later another corporate raider, Carl Icahn, acquired nearly 5 percent of Phillips stock and made an offer for the remainder. Phillips responded with a second greenmail payment, buying out Icahn and his pals for a profit (to them) of about $35 million.

	1985	1984		1985	1984
Current assets	$ 3.1	$ 4.6	Current liabilities	$ 3.1	$ 5.3
Fixed assets	10.3	11.2	Long-term debt	6.5	2.8
Other	.6	1.2	Other long-term liabilities	2.8	2.3
			Equity	1.6	6.6
Total assets	$14.0	$17.0	Total liabilities	$14.0	$17.0

TABLE 32.5
Phillips's balance sheet was dramatically changed by its leveraged restructuring (figures in billions).

The other two responses reveal why Phillips was such an attractive target. It raised its dividend by 25 percent, reduced capital spending, and announced a program to sell $2 billion of assets. It also agreed to repurchase about 50 percent of its stock and to issue instead $4.5 billion of debt. Table 32.5 shows how this *leveraged* restructuring changed Phillips's balance sheet. The new debt ratio was about 80 percent, and book equity shrank by $5 billion to $1.6 billion.

This massive debt burden put Phillips on a strict cash diet. It was forced to sell assets and pinch pennies wherever possible. Capital expenditures were cut back from $1,065 million in 1985 to $646 million in 1986. In the same years, the number of employees fell from 25,300 to 21,800. Austerity continued through the late 1980s.

This restructuring removed the chief *motive* for takeover, which was to force Phillips to generate and pay out more cash to investors. Before the restructuring, investors sensed that Phillips was not running a tight ship and worried that it would plow back its ample operating cash flow into mediocre capital investments or ill-advised expansion. One can almost hear the potential raider thinking:

> So what if I have to pay a 30 or 40 percent premium to take over Phillips? I can borrow most of the purchase price and then pay off the loan by selling surplus assets, cutting out all but the best capital investments, and wringing out slack in the organization. It'll be a rough few years, but if surgery's necessary, I might as well be the doctor and get paid for doing it.

Phillips's managers did not agree that the company was slack or prone to overinvestment. Nevertheless, they bowed to pressure from the stock market and undertook the surgery themselves.

There are two lessons here. First, when the merger motive is to eliminate inefficiency or to distribute excess cash, the target's best defense is to do what the bidder would do, and thus avoid the cost, confusion, and random casualties of a takeover battle. Second, you can see why a company with ample free cash flow can be a tempting target for takeover.

The oil industry entered the 1980s with more-than-ample free cash flow. Rising oil prices had greatly increased revenues and operating profits. However, investment opportunities had not expanded proportionally and many companies overinvested. Investors foresaw massive, negative-NPV outlays and marked down the companies' stock prices accordingly. This created the opportunity for takeovers.

Pickens never succeeded in taking over a major oil company, but he and other "raiders" helped force the industry to cut back investment, reduce operating costs, and return cash to investors. Much of the cash was returned by stock repurchases.

Type of Defense	Description
	Preoffer Defenses
Shark-repellent charter amendments:	
Staggered board	The board is classified into three equal groups. Only one group is elected each year. Therefore the bidder cannot gain control of the target immediately.
Supermajority	A high percentage of shares is needed to approve a merger, typically 80%.
Fair price	Mergers are restricted unless a fair price (determined by formula or appraisal) is paid.
Restricted voting rights	Shareholders who acquire more than a specified proportion of the target have no voting rights unless approved by the target's board.
Waiting period	Unwelcome acquirers must wait for a specified number of years before they can complete the merger.
Other:	
Poison pill	Existing shareholders are issued rights which, if there is a significant purchase of shares by a bidder, can be used to purchase additional stock in the company at a bargain price.
Poison put	Existing bondholders can demand repayment if there is a change of control as a result of a hostile takeover.
	Postoffer Defenses
Litigation	File suit against bidder for violating antitrust or securities laws.
Asset restructuring	Buy assets that bidder does not want or that will create an antitrust problem.
Liability restructuring	Issue shares to a friendly third party or increase the number of shareholders. Repurchase shares from existing shareholders at a premium.

TABLE 32.6

A summary of takeover defenses.

Takeover Defenses

The Cities Service case illustrates several tactics managers use to fight takeover bids. Frequently they don't wait for a bid before taking defensive action. Instead, they deter potential bidders by devising **poison pills** that make their companies unappetizing or they persuade shareholders to agree to **shark-repellent** changes to the company charter. Table 32.6 summarizes the principal first and second levels of defense.

Why do managers contest takeover bids? One reason is to extract a higher price from the bidder. Another possible reason is that managers believe their jobs may be at risk in the merged company. These managers are not trying to obtain a better price; they want to stop the bid altogether.

Some companies reduce these conflicts of interest by offering their managers **golden parachutes,** that is, generous payoffs if the managers lose their jobs as the result of a takeover. It may seem odd to reward managers for being taken over. However, if a soft landing overcomes their opposition to takeover bids, a few million dollars may be a small price to pay.

Any management team that tries to develop improved weapons of defense must expect challenge in the courts. In the early 1980s the courts tended to give managers the benefit of the doubt and respect their business judgment about whether a takeover should be resisted. But the courts' attitudes to takeover battles have changed. For example, in 1993 a court blocked Viacom's agreed takeover of Paramount on the grounds that Paramount's directors did not do their homework before turning down a higher offer from QVC. Paramount was forced to give up its poison-pill defense and the stock options that it had offered to Viacom. Because of such decisions, managers have become much more careful in opposing bids, and they do not throw themselves blindly into the arms of any white knight.[41]

At the same time, state governments have provided some new defensive weapons. In 1987 the Supreme Court upheld state laws that allow companies to deprive an investor of voting rights as soon as the investor's share in the company exceeds a certain level. Since then state antitakeover laws have proliferated. Many allow boards of directors to block mergers with hostile bidders for several years and to consider the interests of employees, customers, suppliers, and their communities in deciding whether to try to block a hostile bid.

AlliedSignal vs. AMP

The hostile attacks of the 1980s were rarely repeated in the 1990s, when most mergers were friendly.[42] But now and then a battle flared up. The following example illustrates takeover tactics and defenses near the end of the millennium.

In the first week of August 1998, AlliedSignal, Inc., announced that it would bid $44.50 per share, or $9.8 billion, for AMP, Inc. AMP's stock price immediately jumped by nearly 50 percent to about $43 per share.

AMP was the world's largest producer of cables and connectors for computers and other electronic equipment. It had just announced a fall of nearly 50 percent in quarterly profits from the previous year. The immediate cause for this bad news was economic troubles in Southeast Asia, one of AMP's most important export markets. But longer-run performance had also disappointed investors, and the company was widely viewed as ripe for change in operations and management. AlliedSignal was betting that it could make these changes faster and better than the incumbent management.

AMP at first seemed impregnable. It was chartered in Pennsylvania, which had passed tough antitakeover laws. Pennsylvania corporations could "just say no" to takeovers that might adversely affect employees and local communities. The company also had a strong poison pill.[43]

AlliedSignal held out an olive branch, hinting that price was flexible if AMP was ready to talk turkey. But the offer was rebuffed. A tender offer went out to AMP shareholders, and 72 percent accepted. However, the terms of the offer did not require AlliedSignal to buy any shares until the poison pill was removed. In order to do that, AlliedSignal would have to appeal again to AMP's shareholders, asking them to approve a *solicitation of consent* blocking AMP's directors from enforcing the pill.

---

[41]In 1985 a shiver ran through many boardrooms when the directors of Trans Union Corporation were held personally liable for being too hasty in accepting a takeover bid.

[42]By contrast, a number of hostile takeovers took place in continental European countries where such activity had been almost unknown.

[43]It was a *dead-hand* poison pill: Even if AlliedSignal gained a majority of AMP's board of directors, only the *previous* directors were empowered to vote to remove the pill.

AMP fought back vigorously and imaginatively. It announced a plan to borrow $3 billion to repurchase its shares at $55 per share—its management's view of the true value of AMP stock. It convinced a federal court to delay AlliedSignal's solicitation of consent. At the same time it asked the Pennsylvania legislature to pass a law which would effectively bar the merger. The governor announced his support. Both companies sent teams of lobbyists to the state capitol. In October the bill was approved in the Pennsylvania House of Representatives and sent to the Senate for consideration.

Yet AlliedSignal discovered it had powerful allies. About 80 percent of AMP's shares were owned by mutual funds, pension funds, and other institutional investors. Many of these institutions bluntly and publicly disagreed with AMP's intransigence. The College Retirement Equities Fund (CREF), one of the largest U.S. pension funds, called AMP's defensive tactics "entirely inimical to the principles of shareholder democracy and good corporate governance." CREF then took an extraordinary step: It filed a legal brief supporting AlliedSignal's case in the federal court.[44] Then the Hixon family, descendants of AMP's cofounder, made public a letter to AMP's management and directors expressing "dismay," and asking, "Who do management and the board work for? The central issue is that AMP's management will not permit shareholders to voice their will."[45]

AMP had complained all along that AlliedSignal's bid was too low. AMP's chairman reiterated this point in his reply to the Hixons and also said, "As a board, we have an overarching responsibility to AMP, all of its shareholders, and its other constituencies—which we believe we are serving on a basis consistent with your interests."[46]

But as the weeks passed, AMP's defenses, while still intact, did not look quite so strong. By mid-October it became clear that AMP would not receive timely help from the Pennsylvania legislature. In November, the federal court finally gave AlliedSignal the go-ahead for its solicitation of consent to remove the poison pill. Remember, 72 percent of its stockholders had already accepted AlliedSignal's tender offer.

Then, suddenly, AMP gave up: It agreed to be acquired by a white knight, Tyco International, for $55 per AMP share, paid for in Tyco stock. AlliedSignal dropped out of the bidding; it didn't think AMP was worth that much.

What are the lessons? First is the strength of poison pills and other takeover defenses, especially in a state like Pennsylvania where the law leans in favor of local targets. AlliedSignal's offensive gained ground, but with great expense and effort and at a very slow pace.

The second lesson is the potential power of institutional investors. We believe AMP gave in not because its legal and procedural defenses failed but largely because of economic pressure from its major shareholders.

Did AMP's management and board act in shareholders' interests? In the end, yes. They said that AMP was worth more than AlliedSignal's offer, and they found another buyer to prove them right. However, they would not have searched for a white knight absent AlliedSignal's bid.

[44]G. Faircloth, "AMP's Tactics Against AlliedSignal Bid Are Criticized by Big Pension Fund," *The Wall Street Journal*, September 28, 1998, p. A17.

[45]S. Lipin and G. Faircloth, "AMP's Antitakeover Tactics Rile Holder," *The Wall Street Journal*, October 5, 1998, p. A18.

[46]Ibid.

Who Gains Most in Mergers?

As our brief history illustrates, in mergers sellers generally do better than buyers. Andrade, Mitchell, and Stafford found that following the announcement of the bid, selling shareholders received a healthy gain averaging 16 percent.[47] The overall value of the merging firms, buyer and seller combined, increases by about 2 percent on average. Thus the merging firms are worth more together than apart. But it seems that the stock prices of the acquiring firms *decline* on average.[48]

Why do so many firms make acquisitions that appear to destroy value? One explanation appeals to behavioral traits; the managers of acquiring firms may be driven by hubris or overconfidence in their ability to run the target firm better than its existing management.[49] This may well be so, but we should not dismiss more charitable explanations. For example, McCardle and Viswanathan have pointed out that firms can enter a market either by building a new plant or by buying an existing business. If the market is not growing, it makes more sense for the firm to expand by acquisition. Hence, when it announces the acquisition, firm value may drop simply because investors conclude that the market is no longer growing. The acquisition in this case does not destroy value; it just signals the stagnant state of the market.[50]

Why do sellers earn higher returns? There are two reasons. First, buying firms are typically larger than selling firms. In many mergers the buyer is so much larger that even substantial net benefits would not show up clearly in the buyer's share price. Suppose, for example, that company A buys company B, which is only one-tenth A's size. Suppose the dollar value of the net gain from the merger is split equally between A and B.[51] Each company's shareholders receive the same *dollar* profit, but B's receive 10 times A's *percentage* return.

The second, and more important, reason is the competition among potential bidders. Once the first bidder puts the target company "in play," one or more additional suitors often jump in, sometimes as white knights at the invitation of the target firm's management. Every time one suitor tops another's bid, more of the merger gain slides toward the target. At the same time, the target firm's management may mount various legal and financial counterattacks, ensuring that capitulation, if and when it comes, is at the highest attainable price.

Of course, bidders and targets are not the only possible winners. Unsuccessful bidders often win, too, by selling off their holdings in target companies at substantial profits.

Other winners include investment bankers, lawyers, accountants, and in some cases arbitrageurs, or "arbs," who speculate on the likely success of takeover bids.[52] "Speculate" has a negative ring, but it can be a useful social service. A tender offer may present shareholders with a difficult decision. Should they accept, should they wait to see if someone else produces a better offer, or should they sell their stock in the market? This dilemma presents an opportunity for the arbitrageurs, who

[47]G. Andrade, M. Mitchell, and E. Stafford, *op. cit.*, Table 3, p. 110.

[48]One recent study found that the losers were mainly the largest acquirers; the stockholders of the other acquirers appeared to gain. See S. B. Moeller, F. P. Schlingemann, and R. Stulz, "Firm Size and the Gains from Acquisitions," *Journal of Financial Economics* 73 (August 2004), pp. 201–228.

[49]See R. Roll, "The Hubris Hypothesis of Corporate Takeovers," *Journal of Business* 59 (April 1986), pp. 198–216.

[50]K. F. McCardle and S. Viswanathan, "The Direct Entry versus Takeover Decision and Stock Price Performance around Takeovers," *Journal of Business* 67 (January 1994), pp. 1–43.

[51]In other words, the *cost* of the merger to A is one-half the gain ΔPV_{AB}.

[52]Strictly speaking, an arbitrageur is an investor who takes a fully hedged, that is, riskless, position. But arbitrageurs in merger battles often take very large risks indeed. Their activities are oxymoronicly known as "risk arbitrage."

specialize in answering such questions. In other words, they buy from the target's shareholders and take on the risk that the deal will not go through.

As Ivan Boesky demonstrated before he went to jail, arbitrageurs can make even more money if they learn about the offer *before* it is publicly announced. Because arbitrageurs may accumulate large amounts of stock, they can have an important effect on whether a deal goes through, and the bidding company or its investment bankers may be tempted to take the arbitrageurs into their confidence. This is the point at which a legitimate and useful activity becomes an illegal and harmful one.

32.6 MERGERS AND THE ECONOMY

Merger Waves

Research shows that mergers come in waves in the US. The first episode of intense merger activity occurred at the start of the 20th century and the second occurred in the 1920s. There was a further boom from 1967 to 1969 and then again in the 1980s and 1990s (1999 and 2000 were record years). Each episode coincided with a period of buoyant stock prices, though there were substantial differences in the types of companies that merged and the ways they went about it.

We don't really understand why merger activity is so volatile. If mergers are prompted by economic motives, at least one of these motives must be "here today and gone tomorrow," and it must somehow be associated with high stock prices. But none of the economic motives that we review in this chapter has anything to do with the general level of the stock market. None burst on the scene in 1967, departed in 1970, and reappeared for most of the 1980s and again in the mid-1990s.

Some mergers may result from mistakes in valuation on the part of the stock market. In other words, the buyer may believe that investors have underestimated the value of the seller or may hope that they *will* overestimate the value of the combined firm. But we see (with hindsight) that mistakes are made in bear markets as well as bull markets. Why don't we see just as many firms hunting for bargain acquisitions when the stock market is low? It is possible that "suckers are born every minute," but it is difficult to believe that they can be harvested only in bull markets.

Merger activity tends to be concentrated in a relatively small number of industries and is often prompted by deregulation and by changes in technology or the pattern of demand. Deregulation of telecoms and banking earlier in the 1990s led to a spate of mergers in both industries. Andrade, Mitchell, and Stafford found that about half of the value of all U.S. mergers between 1988 and 1998 occurred in industries that had been deregulated.[53]

Do Mergers Generate Net Benefits?

There are undoubtedly good acquisitions and bad acquisitions, but economists find it hard to agree on whether acquisitions are beneficial *on balance*. Indeed, since there seem to be transient fashions in mergers, it would be surprising if economists could come up with simple generalizations.

[53] Andrade, Mitchell, and Stafford, *op. cit.*, pp. 108–109.

We do know that mergers generate substantial gains to acquired firms' stockholders and overall gains in the value of the two merging firms. But not everybody is convinced. Some believe that investors analyzing mergers react with short-run enthusiasm and don't give enough critical attention to long-term prospects.

Since we can't observe how companies would have fared in the absence of a merger, it is difficult to measure the long-run effects on profitability. Ravenscroft and Scherer, who looked at mergers during the 1960s and early 1970s, argued that productivity declined in the years following a merger.[54] But studies of subsequent merger activity suggest that mergers *do* seem to improve real productivity. For example, Paul Healy, Krishna Palepu, and Richard Ruback examined 50 large mergers between 1979 and 1983 and found an average increase of 2.4 percentage points in the companies' pretax returns.[55] They argue that this gain came from generating a higher level of sales from the same assets. There was no evidence that the companies were mortgaging their long-term future by cutting back on long-term investments; expenditures on capital equipment and research and development tracked industry averages.[56]

The most important effect of acquisitions may be felt by the managers of companies that are *not* taken over. Perhaps the threat of takeover spurs the whole of corporate America to try harder. Unfortunately, we don't know whether, on balance, the threat of merger makes for active days or sleepless nights.

The threat of takeover may be a spur to inefficient management, but it is also costly. It can soak up large amounts of management time and effort. In addition, the company needs to pay for the services provided by the investment bankers, lawyers, and accountants. In the year 2000 merging companies paid in total more than $2 billion for professional assistance.

[54]See D. J. Ravenscroft and F. M. Scherer, "Mergers and Managerial Performance," in J. C. Coffee, Jr., L. Lowenstein, and S. Rose-Ackerman (eds.), *Knights, Raiders, and Targets: The Impact of the Hostile Takeover,* (New York: Oxford University Press, 1988).

[55]See P. Healy, K. Palepu, and R. Ruback, "Does Corporate Performance Improve after Mergers?" *Journal of Financial Economics* 31 (April 1992), pp. 135–175. The study examined the pretax returns of the merged companies relative to industry averages. A study by Lichtenberg and Siegel came to similar conclusions. Before merger, acquired companies had lower levels of productivity than did other firms in their industries, but by seven years after the control change, two-thirds of the productivity gap had been eliminated. See F. Lichtenberg and D. Siegel, "The Effect of Control Changes on the Productivity of U.S. Manufacturing Plants," *Journal of Applied Corporate Finance* 2 (Summer 1989), pp. 60–67.

[56]Maintained levels of capital spending and R&D are also observed by Lichtenberg and Siegel, op. cit.; and B. H. Hall, "The Effect of Takeover Activity on Corporate Research and Development," in A. J. Auerbach (ed.), *Corporate Takeover: Causes and Consequences* (Chicago: University of Chicago Press, 1988).

SUMMARY

A merger generates synergies—that is, added value—if the two firms are worth more together than apart. Suppose that firms A and B merge to form a new entity, AB. Then the gain from the merger is

$$\text{Gain} = PV_{AB} - (PV_A + PV_B) = \Delta PV_{AB}$$

Gains from mergers may reflect economies of scale, economies of vertical integration, improved efficiency, the combination of complementary resources, or redeployment of surplus funds. In some cases the object is to install a more efficient management team or to force shrinkage and consolidation in an industry with excess capacity or too many small, inefficient companies. There are also dubious reasons for mergers. There is no value added by merging just to diversify risks, to reduce borrowing costs, or to pump up earnings per share.

You should go ahead with the acquisition if the gain exceeds the cost. Cost is the premium that the buyer pays for the selling firm over its value as a separate entity. It is easy to estimate when the merger is financed by cash. In that case,

$$\text{Cost} = \text{cash paid} - PV_B$$

When payment is in the form of shares, the cost naturally depends on what those shares are worth after the merger is complete. If the merger is a success, B's stockholders will share the merger gains.

The mechanics of buying a firm are much more complex than those of buying a machine. First, you have to make sure that the purchase does not fall afoul of the antitrust laws. Second, you have a choice of procedures: You can merge all the assets and liabilities of the seller into those of your own company; you can buy the stock of the seller rather than the company itself; or you can buy the individual assets of the seller. Third, you have to worry about the tax status of the merger.

Mergers are often amicably negotiated between the management and directors of the two companies; but if the seller is reluctant, the would-be buyer can decide to make a tender offer. We sketched some of the offensive and defensive tactics used in takeover battles. We also observed that when the target firm loses, its shareholders typically win: Selling shareholders earn large abnormal returns, while the bidding firm's shareholders roughly break even. The typical merger appears to generate positive net benefits for investors, but competition among bidders, plus active defense by target management, pushes most of the gains toward the selling shareholders.

Mergers come and go in waves. The most recent wave, which peaked in 2000, consisted mostly of horizontal mergers. Merger activity thrives in periods of economic expansion and buoyant stock prices. Mergers are most frequent in industries that are coping with change, for example, changes in technology or regulation. The wave of mergers in banking and telecoms, for instance, can be traced to deregulation of these industries in the 1990s.

APPENDIX

Conglomerate Mergers and Value Additivity

A pure conglomerate merger is one that has no effect on the operations or profitability of either firm. If corporate diversification is in stockholders' interests, a conglomerate merger would give a clear demonstration of its benefits. But if present values add up, the conglomerate merger would not make stockholders better or worse off.

In this appendix we examine more carefully our assertion that present values add. It turns out that values *do* add as long as capital markets are perfect and investors' diversification opportunities are unrestricted.

Call the merging firms A and B. Value additivity implies

$$PV_{AB} = PV_A + PV_B$$

where

PV_{AB} = market value of combined firms just after merger;

PV_A, PV_B = separate market values of A and B just before merger.

For example, we might have

$$PV_A = \$100 \text{ million } (\$200 \text{ per share} \times 500{,}000 \text{ shares outstanding})$$

and

$$PV_B = \$200 \text{ million } (\$200 \text{ per share} \times 1{,}000{,}000 \text{ shares outstanding})$$

Suppose A and B are merged into a new firm, AB, with one share in AB exchanged for each share of A or B. Thus there are 1,500,000 AB shares issued. *If* value additivity holds, then PV_{AB} must equal the sum of the separate values of A and B just before the merger, that is, \$300 million. That would imply a price of \$200 per share of AB stock.

But note that the AB shares represent a portfolio of the assets of A and B. Before the merger investors could have bought one share of A and two of B for \$600. Afterward they can obtain a claim on *exactly* the same real assets by buying three shares of AB.

Suppose that the opening price of AB shares just after the merger is \$200, so that $PV_{AB} = PV_A + PV_B$. Our problem is to determine if this is an equilibrium price, that is, whether we can rule out excess demand or supply at this price.

For there to be excess demand, there must be some investors who are willing to increase their holdings of A and B as a consequence of the merger. Who could they be? The only thing new created by the merger is diversification, but those investors who want to hold assets of A *and* B will have purchased A's and B's stock before the merger. The diversification is redundant and consequently won't attract new investment demand.

Is there a possibility of excess supply? The answer is yes. For example, there will be some shareholders in A who did not invest in B. After the merger they cannot invest solely in A, but only in a fixed combination of A and B. Their AB shares will be less attractive to them than the pure A shares, so they will sell part of or all their AB stock. In fact, the only AB shareholders who will *not* wish to sell are those who happened to hold A and B in exactly a 1:2 ratio in their premerger portfolios!

Since there is no possibility of excess demand but a definite possibility of excess supply, we seem to have

$$PV_{AB} \leq PV_A + PV_B$$

That is, corporate diversification can't help, but it may hurt investors by restricting the types of portfolios they can hold. This is not the whole story, however, since investment demand for AB shares might be attracted from other sources if PV_{AB} drops below $PV_A + PV_B$. To illustrate, suppose there are two other firms, A* and B*, which are judged by investors to have the same risk characteristics as A and B, respectively. Then before the merger,

$$r_A = r_{A^*} \text{ and } r_B = r_{B^*}$$

where r is the rate of return expected by investors. We'll assume $r_A = r_{A^*} = .08$ and $r_B = r_{B^*} = .20$.

Consider a portfolio invested one-third in A* and two-thirds in B*. This portfolio offers an expected return of 16 percent:

$$r = x_{A^*}r_{A^*} + x_{B^*}r_{B^*}$$
$$= \tfrac{1}{3}(.08) + \tfrac{2}{3}(.20) = .16$$

A similar portfolio of A and B before their merger also offered a 16 percent return.

As we have noted, a new firm AB is really a portfolio of firms A and B, with portfolio weights of ⅓ and ⅔. Thus it is equivalent in risk to the portfolio of A* and B*. Thus the price of AB shares must adjust so that it likewise offers a 16 percent return.

What if AB shares drop below $200, so that PV_{AB} is less than $PV_A + PV_B$? Since the assets and earnings of firms A and B are the same, the price drop means that the expected rate of return on AB shares has risen above the return offered by the A*B* portfolio. That is, if r_{AB} exceeds $\frac{1}{3}r_A + \frac{2}{3}r_B$, then r_{AB} must also exceed $\frac{1}{3}r_{A^*} + \frac{2}{3}r_{B^*}$. But this is untenable: Investors A* and B* could sell part of their holdings (in a 1:2 ratio), buy AB, and obtain a higher expected rate of return with no increase in risk.

On the other hand, if PV_{AB} rises above $PV_A + PV_B$, the AB shares will offer an expected return less than that offered by the A*B* portfolio. Investors will unload the AB shares, forcing their price down.

A stable result occurs only if AB shares stick at $200. Thus, value additivity will hold exactly in a perfect-market equilibrium if there are ample substitutes for the A and B assets. If A and B have unique risk characteristics, however, then PV_{AB} can fall below $PV_A + PV_B$. The reason is that the merger curtails investors' opportunity to custom-tailor their portfolios to their own needs and preferences. This makes investors worse off, reducing the attractiveness of holding the shares of firm AB.

In general, the condition for value additivity is that investors' opportunity set—that is, the range of risk characteristics attainable by investors through their portfolio choices—is independent of the particular portfolio of real assets held by the firm. Diversification per se can never expand the opportunity set given perfect security markets. Corporate diversification may reduce the investors' opportunity set, but only if the real assets the corporations hold lack substitutes among traded securities or portfolios.

In a few cases the firm may be able to expand the opportunity set. It can do so if it finds an investment opportunity that is unique—a real asset with risk characteristics shared by few or no other financial assets. In this lucky event the firm should not diversify, however. It should set up the unique asset as a separate firm so as to expand investors' opportunity set to the maximum extent. If Gallo by chance discovered that a small portion of its vineyards produced wine comparable to Chateau Margaux, it would not throw that wine into the Hearty Burgundy vat.

FURTHER READING

Here are three useful books on mergers:

R. Bruner, *Applied Mergers and Acquisitions* (Hoboken, NJ: John Wiley & Sons, 2004).

L. Herzel and R. Shepro, *Bidders and Targets: Mergers and Acquisitions in the U.S.* (Cambridge, MA: Basil Blackwell, Inc., 1990).

J. F. Weston, J. A. Siu, and B. A. Johnson: *Takeovers, Restructuring and Corporate Finance*, 3rd ed. (Upper Saddle River, NJ: Prentice-Hall 2000).

Recent merger waves are reviewed in:

G. Andrade, M. Mitchell, and E. Stafford, "New Evidence and Perspectives on Mergers," *Journal of Economic Perspectives* 15 (Spring 2001), pp. 103–120.

S. J. Everett, "The Cross-Border Mergers and Acquisitions Wave of the Late 1990s," in R. E. Baldwin and L. A. Winters (eds.), *Challenges to Globalization* (Chicago: University of Chicago Press, 2004).

B. Holmstrom and S. N. Kaplan, "Corporate Governance and Merger Activity in the U.S.: Making Sense of the 1980s and 1990s," *Journal of Economic Perspectives* 15 (Spring 2001), pp. 121–144.

Jensen and Ruback review the early empirical work on mergers. The April 1983 issue of the Journal of Financial Economics *also contains a collection of some of the more important empirical studies.*

M. C. Jensen and R. S. Ruback, "The Market for Corporate Control: The Scientific Evidence," *Journal of Financial Economics* 11 (April 1983), pp. 5–50.

Finally, here are some informative case studies:

S. N. Kaplan (ed), *Mergers and Productivity* (Chicago: University of Chicago Press, 2000). This is a collection of case studies.

R. Bruner, "An Analysis of Value Destruction and Recovery in the Alliance and Proposed Merger of Volvo and Renault," *Journal of Financial Economics* 51 (1999), pp. 125–166.

R. S. Ruback, "The Cities Service Takeover: A Case Study," *Journal of Finance* 38 (May 1983), pp. 319–330.

CONCEPT REVIEW QUESTIONS

1. Define *horizontal*, *vertical*, and *conglomerate mergers*. (page 873)
2. List some sensible reasons for merger. (pages 875–879)
3. List some dubious reasons for merger. (pages 879–882)

For additional Concept Review Questions, please visit us at www.mhhe.com/bmam8e or refer to your Student CD.

QUIZ

1. Are the following hypothetical mergers horizontal, vertical, or conglomerate?
   a. Infosys acquires TCS
   b. Wipro acquires Pritish Nandy Communications
   c. Tata Motors acquires Shriram Transport Finance Company
   d. Maruti Udyog Limited acquires MRF Tyres
2. Which of the following motives for mergers make economic sense?
   a. Merging to achieve economies of scale.
   b. Merging to reduce risk by diversification.
   c. Merging to redeploy cash generated by a firm with ample profits but limited growth opportunities.
   d. Merging to combine complementary resources.
   e. Merging just to increase earnings per share.
3. Velcro Saddles is contemplating the acquisition of Pogo Ski Sticks, Inc. The values of the two companies as separate entities are Rs. 20 million and Rs. 10 million, respectively. Velcro Saddles estimates that by combining the two companies, it will reduce marketing and administrative costs by Rs. 500,000 per year in perpetuity. Velcro Saddles can either pay Rs. 14 million cash for Pogo or offer Pogo a 50 percent holding in Velcro Saddles. The opportunity cost of capital is 10 percent.
   a. What is the gain from merger?
   b. What is the cost of the cash offer?
   c. What is the cost of the stock alternative?
   d. What is the NPV of the acquisition under the cash offer?
   e. What is its NPV under the stock offer?
4. In which of the following mergers, the merged company will not get Sec 2(1B) benefits of the Income Tax Act of India?
   a. The merged company acquires the merging company by exchanging preference shares for the equity shares of the merging company.
   b. The merged company acquires the merging company by exchanging zero-coupon bonds for the equity shares of the merging company.

5. True or false?
   a. Sellers almost always gain in mergers.
   b. Buyers usually gain more than sellers.
   c. Firms that do unusually well tend to be acquisition targets.
   d. Merger activity in the United States varies dramatically from year to year.
   e. On the average, mergers produce large economic gains.
   f. Tender offers require the approval of the selling firm's management.
   g. The cost of a merger to the buyer equals the gain realized by the seller.
6. Briefly define the following terms:
   a. Purchase accounting
   b. Tender offer
   c. Poison pill
   d. Greenmail
   e. Synergy

PRACTICE QUESTIONS

1. Examine several recent mergers and suggest the principal motives for merging in each case.
2. Examine a recent merger in which the payment made to the seller was in the form of stock. Use stock market prices to obtain an estimate of the gain from the merger and the cost of the merger.
3. Respond to the following comments.
   a. "Our cost of debt is too darn high, but our banks won't reduce interest rates as long as we're stuck in this volatile widget-trading business. We've got to acquire other companies with safer income streams."
   b. "Merge with Fledgling Electronics? No way! Their P/E's too high. That deal would knock 20 percent off our earnings per share."
   c. "Our stock's at an all-time high. It's time to make our offer for Digital Organics. Sure, we'll have to offer a hefty premium to Digital stockholders, but we don't have to pay in cash. We'll give them new shares of our stock."
4. Sometimes the stock price of a possible target company rises in anticipation of a merger bid. Explain how this complicates the bidder's evaluation of the target company.
5. Suppose you obtain special information—information unavailable to investors—indicating that L&T's stock price is 40 percent undervalued. Is that a reason to launch a takeover bid for L&T? Explain carefully.
6. As treasurer of Leisure Products, Inc., you are investigating the possible acquisition of Plastitoys. You have the following basic data:

	Leisure Products	Plastitoys
Earnings per share	Rs. 5.00	Rs. 1.50
Dividend per share	Rs. 3.00	Rs. .80
Number of shares	1,000,000	600,000
Stock price	Rs. 90	Rs. 20

   You estimate that investors currently expect a steady growth of about 6 percent in Plastitoys' earnings and dividends. Under new management this growth rate would be increased to 8 percent per year, without any additional capital investment required.
   a. What is the gain from the acquisition?
   b. What is the cost of the acquisition if Leisure Products pays Rs. 25 in cash for each share of Plastitoys?

c. What is the cost of the acquisition if Leisure Products offers one share of Leisure Products for every three shares of Plastitoys?
d. How would the cost of the cash offer and the share offer alter if the expected growth rate of Plastitoys were not changed by the merger?

7. The Muck and Slurry merger has fallen through (see Section 32.2). But World Enterprises is determined to report earnings per share of $2.67. It therefore acquires the Wheelrim and Axle Company. You are given the following facts:

	World Enterprises	Wheelrim and Axle	Merged Firm
Earnings per share	$2.00	$2.50	$2.67
Price per share	$40	$25	?
Price–earnings ratio	20	10	?
Number of shares	100,000	200,000	?
Total earnings	$200,000	$500,000	?
Total market value	$4,000,000	$5,000,000	?

Once again there are no gains from merging. In exchange for Wheelrim and Axle shares, World Enterprises issues just enough of its own shares to ensure its $2.67 earnings per share objective.
a. Complete the above table for the merged firm.
b. How many shares of World Enterprises are exchanged for each share of Wheelrim and Axle?
c. What is the cost of the merger to World Enterprises?
d. What is the change in the total market value of the World Enterprises shares that were outstanding before the merger?

8. Explain the difference between merger and reverse merger. If you are the CFO of a company that plans to acquire a sick company, what factors (pertaining to the Income Tax Act of India) should you take into consideration?

9. Look again at Table 32.3. Suppose that B Corporation's fixed assets are reexamined and found to be worth Rs. 12 million instead of Rs. 9 million. How would that affect the AB Corporation's balance sheet under the purchase accounting? How about pooling of interest accounting? How would the value of AB Corporation change under the purchase method?

10. What was the common theme in Boone Pickens's attempts to take over Cities Service, Gulf Oil, and Phillips Petroleum? Did his efforts create value for these companies' shareholders? How? Was economic efficiency enhanced?

CHALLENGE QUESTIONS

1. Examine a hostile acquisition in the US and discuss the tactics employed by both the predator and the target companies. Do you think that the management of the target firm was trying to defeat the bid or to secure the highest price for its stockholders? How did each announcement by the protagonists affect their stock prices?

2. How do you think mergers should be regulated? For example, what defenses should target companies be allowed to employ? Should managers of target firms be compelled to seek out the highest bids? Should they simply be passive and watch from the sidelines?

CHAPTER 33

CORPORATE RESTRUCTURING

IN THE LAST CHAPTER we described how mergers and acquisitions enable companies to change their ownership and management teams, and often force major shifts in corporate strategy. But this is not the only way that company structure can be altered. In this chapter we will look at a variety of other mechanisms for changing ownership and control, including leveraged buyouts (LBOs), spin-offs and carve-outs, privatizations, workouts, and bankruptcy.

The first section starts with a famous takeover battle, the leveraged buyout of RJR Nabisco. The remainder of Sections 33.1 and 33.2 offer a general review of LBOs, spin-offs, and privatizations. The main point of these transactions is not just to change control, although existing management is often booted out, but also to change incentives for managers and improve financial performance.

Section 33.3 looks at conglomerates. Conglomerates bring together a number of unrelated businesses under one set of owners and managers. Although conglomerates have been a declining species in the United States, there are a number of successful temporary conglomerates.[1]

Some companies choose to restructure but others have it thrust upon them. None more so than those that fall on hard times and can no longer service their debts. The chapter therefore concludes by looking at how distressed companies either work out a solution with their debtors or go through a formal bankruptcy process.

[1]What is a temporary conglomerate? Sorry, you'll have to wait for the punch line.

33.1 LEVERAGED BUYOUTS

Leveraged buyouts (LBOs) differ from ordinary acquisitions in two immediately obvious ways. First, a large fraction of the purchase price is financed by debt. Some, if not all, of its debt is usually junk, that is, below investment-grade. Thus for example, when Tata Tea acquired Tetley, €200 million of the total acquisition cost of €271 million was financed by debt. Second, the company goes private and its shares no longer trade on the open market. The LBO's stock is held by partnership of (usually institutional) investors and is often referred to as **private equity**. In the case of Tata Tea's acquisition of Tetley, the shares of Tetley were held by Tata Tea Great Britain after the LBO. When the group is led by the company's management, the transaction is called a **management buyout (MBO).**

In the 1970s and 1980s many MBOs in the US were arranged for unwanted divisions of large diversified companies. Smaller divisions outside the companies' main line of business sometimes failed to attract top management's interest and commitment, and divisional management chafed under corporate bureaucracy. Many such divisions flowered when spun off as MBOs. Their managers, pushed by the need to generate cash for debt service and encouraged by a substantial personal stake in the business, found ways to cut costs and compete more effectively.

In the 1980s, LBO activity shifted to buyouts of entire businesses, including large, mature, public corporations. Table 33.1 lists the largest LBOs of the 1980s, plus a sample of more-recent transactions. Today's LBOs are generally smaller and not leveraged as aggressively as the deals of the 1980s.[2] But LBO activity is still impressive in aggregate. Buyouts involved $89 billion of new capital in 2003.

Table 33.1 starts with the largest, most dramatic, and best documented LBO of all time, the $25 billion takeover of RJR Nabisco by Kohlberg, Kravis, Roberts (KKR). The players, tactics, and controversies of LBOs are writ large in this case.

[2]In 1988 LBOs were on average financed with 90 percent debt. In more-recent LBOs the figure is about 60 percent.

Acquirer	Target	Industry	Year	Value
KKR	RJR Nabisco	Food, tobacco	1989	$24,720
KKR	Beatrice	Food	1986	6,250
KKR	Safeway	Supermarkets	1986	4,240
Thompson Co.	Southland (7–11)	Convenience stores	1987	4,000
KKR	Owens-Illinois	Glass	1987	4,680
Wings Holdings	NWA, Inc.	Airlines	1989	3,690
TF Investments	Hospital Corp. of America	Hospitals	1989	3,600
Macy Acquisitions Corp.	R. H. Macy & Co.	Department stores	1986	3,500
Carlyle Group & Welsh, Carson, Anderson and Stowe	Qwest Dex	Yellow pages	2002	7,050
Blackstone Group	TRW Automotive Holdings	Auto parts	2002	4,700
KKR	PanAmSat	Satellites	2004	4,380
Texas Pacific Group, Bain Capital, & Goldman Sachs	Burger King	Fast food	2002	2,260

TABLE 33.1

The 10 largest LBOs of the 1980s, plus examples of more-recent deals (values in $ millions).

Source: A. Kaufman and E. J. Englander, "Kohlberg Kravis Roberts & Co. and the Restructuring of American Capitalism," *Business History Review* 67 (Spring 1993), p. 78; and *Mergers and Acquisitions*, various issues.

RJR Nabisco

In October 1988 the board of directors of RJR Nabisco revealed that Ross Johnson, the company's chief executive officer, had formed a group of investors that proposed to buy all RJR's stock for $75 per share in cash and take the company private. RJR's share price immediately moved to about $75, handing shareholders a 36 percent gain over the previous day's price of $56. At the same time RJR's bonds fell, since it was clear that existing bondholders would soon have a lot more company.[3]

Johnson's offer lifted RJR onto the auction block. Once the company was in play, its board of directors was obliged to consider other offers, which were not long in coming. Four days later, KKR bid $90 per share, $79 in cash plus PIK preferred stock valued at $11. (PIK means "pay in kind." The company could choose to pay preferred dividends in more preferred shares rather than cash.)

The resulting bidding contest had as many turns and surprises as a Dickens novel. In the end it was Johnson's group against KKR. KKR bid $109 per share, after adding $1 per share (roughly $230 million) in the last hour.[4] The KKR bid was $81 in cash, convertible subordinated bonds valued at about $10, and PIK preferred shares valued at about $18. Johnson's group bid $112 in cash and securities.

But the RJR board chose KKR. Although Johnson's group had offered $3 a share more, its security valuations were viewed as "softer" and perhaps overstated. The Johnson group's proposal also contained a management compensation package that seemed extremely generous and had generated an avalanche of bad press.

[3] N. Mohan and C. R. Chen track the abnormal returns of RJR securities in "A Review of the RJR Nabisco Buyout," *Journal of Applied Corporate Finance* 3 (Summer 1990), pp. 102–108.

[4] The whole story is reconstructed by B. Burrough and J. Helyar in *Barbarians at the Gate: The Fall of RJR Nabisco* (New York: Harper & Row 1990)—see especially chapter 18—and in a movie with the same title.

But where did the merger benefits come from? What could justify offering $109 per share, about $25 billion in all, for a company that only 33 days previously was selling for $56 per share? KKR and other bidders were betting on two things. First, they expected to generate billions in additional cash from interest tax shields, reduced capital expenditures, and sales of assets that were not strictly necessary to RJR's core businesses. Asset sales alone were projected to generate $5 billion. Second, they expected to make the core businesses significantly more profitable, mainly by cutting back on expenses and bureaucracy. Apparently, there was plenty to cut, including the RJR "Air Force," which at one point included 10 corporate jets.

In the year after KKR took over, a new management team set out to sell assets and cut back operating expenses and capital spending. There were also layoffs. As expected, high interest charges meant a net loss of nearly a billion dollars in the first year, but pretax operating income actually increased, despite extensive asset sales.

Inside the firm, things were going well. But outside there was confusion and prices in the junk bond market were declining rapidly, implying much higher future interest charges for RJR and stricter terms on any refinancing. In 1990 KKR made an additional equity investment in the firm and the company retired some of its junk bonds. RJR's chief financial officer described the move as "one further step in the deleveraging of the company."[5] For RJR, the world's largest LBO, it seemed that high debt was a temporary, not a permanent, virtue.

RJR, like many other firms that were taken private through LBOs, enjoyed only a short period as a private company. In 1991 it went public again with the sale of $1.1 billion of stock.[6] KKR progressively sold off its investment, and its last remaining stake in the company was sold in 1995 at roughly the original purchase price.

Barbarians at the Gate?

The RJR Nabisco LBO crystallized views on LBOs, the junk bond market, and the takeover business. For many it exemplified all that was wrong with finance in the late 1980s, especially the willingness of "raiders" to carve up established companies, leaving them with enormous debt burdens, basically in order to get rich quick.

There was plenty of confusion, stupidity, and greed in the LBO business. Not all the people involved were nice. On the other hand, LBOs generated large increases in market value, and most of the gains went to the selling shareholders, not to the raiders. For example, the biggest winners in the RJR Nabisco LBO were the company's stockholders.

The most important sources of added value came from making RJR Nabisco leaner and meaner. The company's new management was obliged to pay out massive amounts of cash to service the LBO debt. It also had an equity stake in the business and therefore strong incentives to sell off nonessential assets, cut costs, and improve operating profits.

LBOs are almost by definition *diet deals*. But there were other motives. Here are some of them.

---

[5]C. Andress, "RJR Swallows Hard, Offers $5-a-Share Stock," *The Wall Street Journal*, December 18, 1990, pp. C1–C2.

[6]Northwest Airlines, Safeway Stores, Kaiser Aluminum, and Burlington Industries are other examples of LBOs that reverted to being public companies.

The Junk Bond Markets LBOs and debt-financed takeovers may have been driven by artificially cheap funding from the junk bond markets. With hindsight, it seems that investors underestimated the risks of default in junk bonds. Default rates climbed painfully, reaching 10.3 percent in 1991.[7] The market also became temporarily much less liquid after the demise in 1990 of Drexel Burnham, the investment banking firm that was the chief market maker in junk bonds.

Leverage and Taxes Borrowing money saves taxes, as we explained in Chapter 18. But taxes were not the main driving force behind LBOs. The value of interest tax shields was simply not big enough to explain the observed gains in market value.[8] For example, Richard Ruback estimated the present value of additional interest tax shields generated by the RJR LBO at $1.8 billion.[9] But the gain in market value to RJR stockholders was about $8 billion.

Of course, if interest tax shields were the main motive for LBO's high debt, then LBO managers would not be so concerned to pay off debt. We saw that this was one of the first tasks facing RJR Nabisco's new management.

Other Stakeholders We should look at the total gain to all investors in an LBO, not just to the selling stockholders. It's possible that the latter's gain is just someone else's loss and that no value is generated overall.

Bondholders are the obvious losers. The debt that they thought was secure may turn into junk when the borrower goes through an LBO. We noted how market prices of RJR debt fell sharply when Ross Johnson's first LBO offer was announced. But again, the losses suffered by bondholders in LBOs are not nearly large enough to explain stockholder gains. For example, Mohan and Chen's estimate of losses to RJR bondholders was at most $575 million[10]—painful to the bondholders, but far below the stockholders' gain.

Leverage and Incentives Managers and employees of LBOs work harder and often smarter. They have to generate cash for debt service. Moreover, managers' personal fortunes are riding on the LBO's success. They become owners rather than organization men and women.

It's hard to measure the payoff from better incentives, but there is some evidence of improved operating efficiency in LBOs. Kaplan, who studied 48 MBOs during the 1980s, found average increases in operating income of 24 percent three years after the buyouts. Ratios of operating income and net cash flow to assets and sales increased dramatically. He observed cutbacks in capital expenditures but not in employment. Kaplan concludes that these "operating changes are due to improved incentives rather than layoffs."[11]

---

[7]See E. I. Altman and G. Fanjul, "Defaults and Returns in the High Yield Bond Market: The Year 2003 in Review and Market Outlook," Monograph, Salomon Center, Leonard N. Stern School of Business, New York University, 2004.

[8]Moreover, there are some tax costs to LBOs. For example, selling shareholders realize capital gains and pay taxes that otherwise would be deferred. See L. Stiglin, S. N. Kaplan, and M. C. Jensen, "Effects of LBOs on Tax Revenues of the U.S. Treasury," *Tax Notes* 42 (February 6 1989), pp. 727–733.

[9]R. J. Ruback, "RJR Nabisco," case study, Harvard Business School, Cambridge, MA, 1989.

[10]Mohan and Chen, op. cit.

[11]S. Kaplan, "The Effects of Management Buyouts on Operating Performance and Value," *Journal of Financial Economics* 24 (October 1989), pp. 217–254.

We have reviewed several motives for LBOs. We do not say that all LBOs are good. On the contrary, there have been many mistakes, and even soundly motivated LBOs are risky, as the bankruptcies of a number of highly leveraged transactions have demonstrated. Yet, we do quarrel with those who portray LBOs solely as undertaken by Wall Street barbarians breaking up the traditional strengths of corporate America.

Leveraged Restructurings

The essence of a leveraged buyout is of course leverage. So why not take on the leverage and dispense with the buyout? Here is how Sealed Air did just that and put itself on a diet by changing its capital structure.[12]

In 1989 Sealed Air was a very profitable company. The problem was that its profits were coming too easily because its main products were protected by patents. When the patents expired, strong competition was inevitable, and the company was not ready for it. The years of relatively easy profits had resulted in too much slack:

> We didn't need to manufacture efficiently; we didn't need to worry about cash. At Sealed Air, capital tended to have limited value attached to it—cash was perceived as being free and abundant.

The company's solution was to borrow the money to pay a \$328 million special cash dividend. In one stroke the company's debt increased 10 times. Its book equity went from \$162 million to *minus* \$161 million. Debt went from 13 percent of total book assets to 136 percent. The company hoped that this leveraged restructuring would "disrupt the status quo, promote internal change," and simulate "the pressures of Sealed Air's more competitive future." The shakeup was reinforced by new performance measures and incentives, including increases in stock ownership by employees.

It worked. Sales and operating profits increased steadily without major new capital investments, and net working capital *fell* by half, releasing cash to help service the company's debt. The stock price quadrupled in the five years following the restructuring.

Sealed Air's restructuring was not typical. It is an exemplar chosen with hindsight. It was also undertaken by a successful firm under no outside pressure. But it clearly shows the motive for most leveraged restructurings. They are designed to force mature, successful, but overweight companies to disgorge cash, reduce operating costs, and use assets more efficiently.[13]

LBOs and Leveraged Restructurings

The financial characteristics of LBOs and leveraged restructurings are similar. The three main characteristics of LBOs are

1. *High debt*. The debt is not intended to be permanent. It is designed to be paid down. The requirement to generate cash for debt service is intended to curb wasteful investment and force improvements in operating efficiency. Of course, this solution only makes sense in the case of companies that are generating lots of cash and have few investment opportunities.
2. *Incentives*. Managers are given a greater stake in the business via stock options or direct ownership of shares.

[12]K. H. Wruck, "Financial Policy as a Catalyst for Organizational Change: Sealed Air's Leveraged Special Dividend," *Journal of Applied Corporate Finance* 7 (Winter 1995), pp. 20–37.

[13]Look back to the last chapter for a description of another leveraged restructuring by Phillips Petroleum.

3. *Private ownership*. The LBO goes private. It is owned by a partnership of private investors who monitor performance and can act right away if something goes awry. But private ownership is not intended to be permanent. The most successful LBOs go public again as soon as debt has been paid down sufficiently and improvements in operating performance have been demonstrated.

Leveraged restructurings share the first two characteristics but continue as public companies.

33.2 FUSION AND FISSION IN CORPORATE FINANCE

Figure 33.1 shows some of AT&T's acquisitions and divestitures. Before 1984, AT&T controlled most of the local and virtually all of the long-distance telephone service in the United States. (Customers used to speak of the ubiquitous "Ma Bell.") Then in 1984 the company accepted an antitrust settlement requiring local telephone services to be spun off to seven new, independent companies.[14] AT&T was left with its long-distance business plus Bell Laboratories, Western Electric (telecommunications manufacturing), and various other assets. As the communications industry became increasingly competitive, AT&T acquired several other businesses, notably in computers, cellular telephone service, and cable television. Some of these acquisitions are shown as the green incoming arrows in Figure 33.1.

AT&T was an unusually active acquirer. It was a giant company trying to respond to rapidly changing technologies and markets. But AT&T was simultaneously *divesting* dozens of other businesses. For example, its credit card operations (the AT&T Universal Card) were sold to Citicorp. AT&T also created several new companies by spinning off parts of its business. For example, in 1996 it spun off Lucent (incorporating Bell Laboratories and Western Electric) and its computer business (NCR). Only six years earlier AT&T had paid $7.5 billion to acquire NCR. These and several other important divestitures are shown as the green outgoing arrows in Figure 33.1.

In the market for corporate control, fusion—mergers and acquisitions—gets most publicity. But fission—the disposal of assets or entire businesses—can be just as important. We will now see how these separations are carried out by spin-offs, carve-outs, asset sales, and privatizations.

Spin-offs

A **spin-off** (or *split-up*) is a new, independent company created by detaching part of a parent company's assets and operations. Shares in the new company are distributed to the parent company's stockholders.[15] For example, in May 2004 Abbott Laboratories spun off Hospira, a manufacturer of hospital products. Abbott shareholders were sent 1 share in the new company for each 10 Abbott shares that they held. They were then free to trade their shares in Hospira as well as those of the slimmed-down Abbott Labs.[16]

[14]Subsequent mergers reduced these seven companies to four: Bell South, SBC Communications, Qwest, and Verizon.

[15]The value of the shares that shareholders receive is taxed as a dividend unless they are given at least 80 percent of the shares in the new company.

[16]Instead of undertaking a spin-off, some companies have given their shareholders *tracking stock* tied to the performance of particular divisions. For example, in 2000 AT&T distributed a special class of shares tied to the performance of its wireless business. But tracking stocks did not prove popular with investors, and a year later AT&T went whole hog and spun off AT&T Wireless into a separate company.

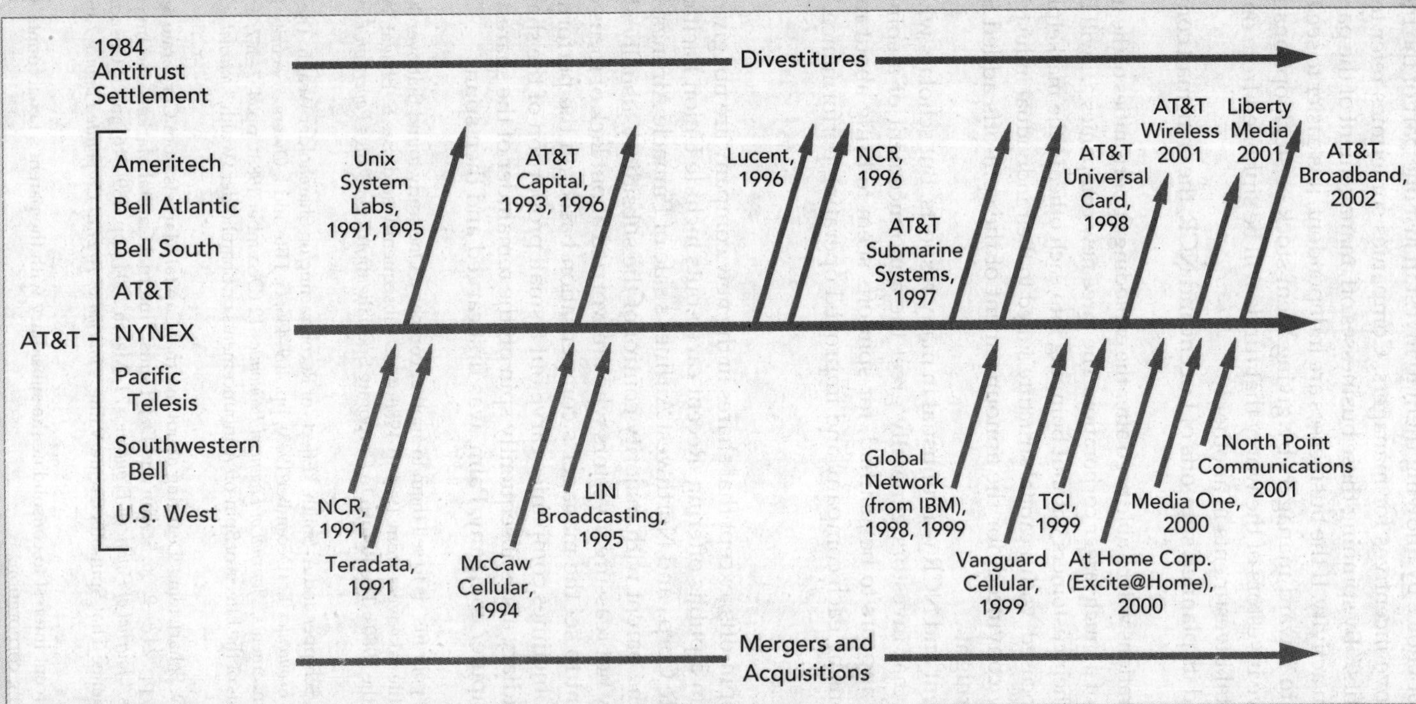

FIGURE 33.1

The effects of AT&T's antitrust settlement in 1984, and a few of AT&T's acquisitions and divestitures from 1991 to 2003. Divestitures are shown by the outgoing green arrows. When two years are given, the transaction was completed in two steps.

Spin-offs widen investor choice by allowing them to invest in just one part of the business. More important, they can improve incentives for managers. Companies sometimes refer to divisions or lines of business as "poor fits." By spinning these businesses off, management of the parent company can concentrate on its main activity. If the businesses are independent, it is easier to see the value and performance of each and to reward managers by giving them stock or stock options in their company. Also, spin-offs relieve investors of the worry that funds will be siphoned from one business to support unprofitable capital investments in another.[17]

When AT&T announced its planned spin-offs of Lucent and NCR, the chairman commented that the

> three independent corporations will be able to go after the exploding opportunities of the industry faster than they could as parts of a much larger corporation. The three new companies . . . will be free to pursue the best interests of their customers without bumping into each other in the marketplace. They are designed to be fast and focused, with a capital structure suited to their individual industries.

Investors were apparently convinced, for the announcement of the spin-offs added $10 billion to the value of the stock overnight.

AT&T's spin-off of Lucent and NCR was unusual in many respects. But scholars who have studied the topic have found that investors generally greet the announcement of a spin-off as good news.[18] Their enthusiasm appears to be justified, for spin-offs seem to bring about more efficient capital investment decisions by each company and improved operating performance.[19]

Carve-outs

Carve-outs are similar to spin-offs, except that shares in the new company are not given to existing shareholders but are sold in a public offering. Recent carve-outs include Union Pacific's sale of its trucking business, Overnite Corp., and Northwest Airlines's sale of Pinnacle Airlines.

Most carve-outs leave the parent with majority control of the subsidiary, usually about 80 percent ownership.[20] This may not reassure investors who are worried about lack of focus or a poor fit, but it does allow the parent to set the manager's compensation based on the performance of the subsidiary's stock price. Sometimes companies carve out a small proportion of the shares to establish the market in the subsidiary and subsequently spin off the remainder of the shares. The nearby box describes how the computer company, Palm, was first carved and then spun.

---

[17]The other way of getting rid of "poor fits" is to sell them to another company. One study found that over 30 percent of assets acquired in a sample of hostile takeovers from 1984 to 1986 were subsequently sold. See S. Bhagat, A. Shleifer, and R. Vishny, "Hostile Takeovers in the 1980s: The Return to Corporate Specialization," *Brookings Papers on Economic Activity: Microeconomics*, 1990, pp. 1–12.

[18]Research on spin-offs includes K. Schipper and A. Smith, "Effects of Recontracting on Shareholder Wealth: The Case of Voluntary Spin-offs," *Journal of Financial Economics* 12 (December 1983), pp. 409–436; G. Hite and J. Owers, "Security Price Reactions around Corporate Spin-off Announcements," *Journal of Financial Economics* 12 (December 1983), pp. 437–467; and J. Miles and J. Rosenfeld, "An Empirical Analysis of the Effects of Spin-off Announcements on Shareholder Wealth," *Journal of Finance* 38 (December 1983), pp. 1597–1615.

[19]See R. Gertner, E. Powers, and D. Scharfstein, "Learning about Internal Capital Markets from Corporate Spin-offs," *Journal of Finance* 57 (December 2002), pp. 2479–2506; S. Ahn and D. J. Denis, "Internal Capital Markets and Investment Policy: Evidence from Corporate Spinoffs," *Journal of Financial Economics* 71 (March 2004), pp. 489–516; and P. Cusatis, J. Miles, and J. R. Woolridge, "Some New Evidence That Spin-offs Create Value," *Journal of Applied Corporate Finance* 7 (Summer 1994), pp. 100–107.

[20]The parent must retain an 80 percent interest to consolidate the subsidiary with the parent's tax accounts. Otherwise the subsidiary is taxed as a freestanding corporation.

FINANCE IN THE NEWS

HOW PALM WAS CARVED AND SPUN

When 3Com acquired U.S. Robotics in 1997, it also became the owner of Palm, a small start-up business developing handheld computers. It was a lucky purchase, for over the next three years the Palm Pilot came to dominate the market for handheld computers. But as Palm began to take up an increasing amount of management time, 3Com concluded that it needed to return to its knitting and focus on its basic business of selling computer network systems. In 2000 it announced that it would carve out 5 percent of its holding of Palm through an initial public offering, and then spin off the remaining 95 percent of Palm shares by giving 3Com shareholders about 1.5 Palm shares for each 3Com share that they owned.

The Palm carve-out occurred at close to the peak of the high-tech boom and got off to a dazzling start. The shares were issued in the IPO at \$38 each. On the first day of trading the stock price touched \$165 before closing at \$95. Therefore, anyone owning a share of 3Com stock could look forward later in the year to receiving about 1.5 shares of Palm worth $1.5 \times 95 =$ \$142.50. But apparently 3Com's shareholders were not fully convinced that their newfound wealth was for real, for on the same day 3Com's stock price closed at \$82, or more than \$60 a share less than the market value of the shares in Palm that they were due to receive.[21]

Three years after 3Com spun off its holding in Palm, Palm itself entered the spin-off business by giving shareholders stock in PalmSource, a subsidiary that was responsible for developing and licensing the Palm™ operating system. The remaining business, renamed palmOne, would focus on making mobile gadgets. The company gave three reasons for its decision to split into two. First, like 3Com's management, Palm's management believed that the company would benefit from clarity of focus and mission. Second, it argued that shareholder value could "be enhanced if investors could evaluate and choose between both businesses separately, thereby attracting new and different investors." Finally, it seemed that Palm's rivals were reluctant to buy software from a company that competed with them in making handheld hardware.

[21] This difference would seem to present an arbitrage opportunity. An investor who bought 1 share of 3Com and sold short 1.5 shares of Palm would earn a profit of \$60 *and* own 3Com's other assets for free. The difficulty in executing this arbitrage is explored in O. A. Lamont and R. H. Thaler, "Can the Market Add and Subtract? Mispricing in Tech Stock Carve-Outs," *Journal of Political Economy* 111 (April 2003), pp. 227–268.

Perhaps the most enthusiastic carver-outer of the 1980s and 1990s was Thermo Electron, with operations in health care, power generation equipment, instrumentation, environmental protection, and various other areas. By 1997 it had carved out stakes in seven publicly traded subsidiaries, which in turn had carved out 15 further public companies. The 15 were grandchildren of the ultimate parent, Thermo Electron. The company's management reasoned that the carve-outs would give each company's managers responsibility for their own decisions and expose their actions to the scrutiny of the capital markets. For a while the strategy seemed to work, and Thermo Electron's stock was a star performer. But the complex structure began to lead to inefficiencies, and in 2000 Thermo Electron went into reverse. It reacquired many of the subsidiaries that the company had carved out only a few years earlier, and it spun off several of its progeny, including Viasis Health Care and Kadant Corp., a manufacturer of papermaking and paper-recycling equipment.

Asset Sales

The simplest way to divest an asset is to sell it. **Asset sale** refers to the sale of *part* of one firm to another. This may consist of the odd store or plant, but sometimes the assets of a whole divisions may be sold. The record asset sale is AT&T's disposal of its cable television division to Comcast in 2001 for \$42 billion.

Asset sales are common in manufacturing. Maksimovic and Phillips examined a sample of about 50,000 U.S. manufacturing plants each year from 1974 to 1992. About 35,000 plants in the sample changed hands during that period. One-half of the ownership changes were the result of mergers or acquisitions of entire firms. The other half of the ownership changes resulted from asset sales, that is, sale of part or all of a division.[22]

Announcements of asset sales are good news for investors in the selling firm and on average the assets are employed more productively after the sale.[23] It appears that asset sales transfer business units to the companies that can manage them most effectively.

Demerger

A demerger is very similar to an asset sale. The parent company sells off a division to another company and the buying company issues shares (instead of paying cash to the parent company) to the shareholders of the parent company. Thus for example, in September 1998, the Aditya Birla group, as part of its restructuring exercise, transferred the cement division of Indian Rayon to Grasim in a share-swap transaction. The shareholders of Indian Rayon received 3 shares of Grasim for every 10 shares in Indian Rayon held by them. This transaction is very similar to a spin off or equity carve out. The parent company that transfers the division becomes more focused after the transaction and hence can focus on its core competency.

In India, often companies resort to spin-offs, demergers or asset sales just before (or sometimes after) a merger for some tax-related reasons. Let's assume that Company B wants to acquire Company A in a share-swap transaction. 'A' manufactures steel and cement and 'B' manufacturers cement only. Here, B may not be interested in the steel division of A. As per Sec 2 (1B) of the Income Tax Act in India, a merged company gets some of the tax benefits (like carrying forward expenditure on acquisition of patent rights, preliminary expenses, etc) only if, among other things, all the assets of the merging company become assets of the merged company by virtue of the amalgamation. So here, B has the choice of either asking A to spin off the cement division into a cement company before the merger. Alternatively, B can first takeover A and then demerge the steel division. Thus for example, in 1993, Voltas first got Hyderabad Allwyn Limited (HAL) merged with itself and then transferred the watch division of HAL to Allwyn Watches Limited.

Privatization

A **privatization** is a sale of a government-owned company to private investors. In recent years almost every government in the world seems to have a privatization program. Here are some examples of recent privatization news:

- Thailand privatizes Thai Airways (November 2003).
- Pakistan sells a majority stake in Habib Bank (February 2004).
- Japan sells the West Japan Railway Company (March 2004).
- India sells a stake in ONGC, an oil exploration and production company (March 2004).
- Turkey starts the process of selling a stake in Turk Telecom (May 2004).
- Ukraine sells steel company Kryvorizhstal (June 2004).
- Germany privatizes Postbank, the country's largest retail bank (June 2004).
- The French government announces its plans to privatize EDF (Electricité de France; June 2004).

[22]V. Maksimovic and G. Phillips, "The Market for Corporate Assets: Who Engages in Mergers and Asset Sales and Are There Efficiency Gains?" *Journal of Finance* 56 (December 2001), Table 1, p. 2000.

[23]Ibid.

Most privatizations are more like carve-outs than spin-offs, because shares are sold for cash rather than distributed to the ultimate "shareholders," that is, the citizens of the selling country. But several former Communist countries, including Russia, Poland, and the Czech Republic, privatized by means of vouchers distributed to citizens. The vouchers could be used to bid for shares in the companies that were being privatized. Thus the companies were not sold for cash, but for vouchers.[24]

Privatizations have raised enormous sums for selling governments. France raised $17.6 billion in two share issues for France Telecom in 1997 and 1998. Japan raised over $80 billion in the privatization of NTT (Nippon Telephone and Telegraph) in 1987 and 1988.

The motives for privatization seem to boil down to the following three points:

1. *Increased efficiency*. Through privatization, the enterprise is exposed to the discipline of competition and insulated from political influence on investment and operating decisions.[25] Managers and employees can be given stronger incentives to cut costs and add value.
2. *Share ownership*. Privatizations encourage share ownership. Many privatizations give special terms or allotments to employees or small investors.
3. *Revenue for the government*. Last but not least.

There were fears that privatizations would lead to massive layoffs and unemployment, but that does not appear to be the case. While it is true that privatized companies operate more efficiently and thus reduce employment, they also grow faster as privatized companies, which increases employment. In many cases the net effect on employment is positive.

On other dimensions, the impact of privatization is almost always positive. A review of research on privatization concludes that the firms "almost always become more efficient, more profitable, . . . financially healthier and increase their capital investment spending."[26]

33.3 CONGLOMERATES

As firms merge and divest, ownership and control changes. But restructuring may also change the spread of markets in which the firm operates. For example, the effect of the 1960s merger boom was to create a number of sprawling conglomerates operating in a variety of unrelated industries. Table 33.2 shows that by the 1970s some of these conglomerates had achieved amazing spans of activity. The largest conglomerate, ITT, was operating in 38 different industries and ranked eighth in total sales among U.S. corporations.

Most of the conglomerates created in the 1960s were broken up in the 1980s and 1990s. In 1995 ITT, which had already sold or spun off several lines of business, split its remaining operations into three separate firms. One acquired ITT's interests in hotels and gambling; a second took over ITT's automotive parts, defense, and electronics businesses; and a third specialized in insurance and financial services.

What advantages were claimed for conglomerates? First, diversification across industries was supposed to stabilize earnings and reduce risk. That's hardly compelling, because shareholders can diversify much more efficiently on their own.[27] Second, and more important, was the idea that good

[24] There is extensive research on voucher privatizations. See, for example, M. Boyco, A. Shleifer, and R. Vishny, "Voucher Privatizations," *Journal of Financial Economics* 35 (April 1994), pp. 249–266; and R. Aggarwal and J. T. Harper, "Equity Valuation in the Czech Voucher Privatization Auctions," *Financial Management* 29 (Winter 2000), pp. 77–100.

[25] The relative merits of state and private ownership and control are surveyed in R. A. Brealey, I. A. Cooper, and M. A. Habib, "Investment Appraisal in the Public Sector," *Oxford Review of Economic Policy* 13 (1997), pp. 12–28.

[26] W. L. Megginson and J. M. Netter, "From State to Market: A Survey of Empirical Studies on Privatization," *Journal of Economic Literature* 39 (June 2001), p. 381.

[27] See the Appendix to Chapter 32.

TABLE 33.2

The largest conglomerates of 1979, ranked by sales compared with U.S. industrial corporations. Most of these companies have been broken up.

Source: A. Chandler and R. S. Tetlow (eds.), *The Coming of Managerial Capitalism* (Homewood, IL: Richard D. Irwin, Inc., 1985), p. 772. See also J. Baskin and P. J. Miranti, Jr., *A History of Corporate Finance* (Cambridge, U.K.: Cambridge University Press, 1997), ch. 7.

Sales Rank	Company	Number of Industries
8	International Telephone & Telegraph (ITT)	38
15	Tenneco	28
42	Gulf & Western Industries	4
51	Litton Industries	19
66	LTV	18

managers were fungible; in other words, it was suggested that modern management would work as well in the manufacture of auto parts as in running a hotel chain. Thus the conglomerates of the 1960s were supposed to add value by removing old-fashioned managers and replacing them with ones schooled in the new management science.

There was some truth in this. The most successful early conglomerates did force improvements in some mature and slackly managed businesses. The problem, of course, is that a company doesn't need to be diversified to take over and improve a lagging business.

Third, a widely diversified firm could operate an *internal capital market*. Free cash flow generated by divisions in mature industries (*cash cows*) could be funneled within the company to those divisions (*stars*) with plenty of profitable growth opportunities. Consequently, there was no need for fast-growing divisions to raise finance from outside investors.

There are some good arguments for internal capital markets. The company's managers probably know more about its investment opportunities than outside investors do, and transaction costs of issuing securities are avoided. Nevertheless, it appears that attempts by conglomerates to allocate capital investment across many unrelated industries are more likely to subtract value than add it. Trouble is, internal capital markets are not really markets but combinations of central planning (by the conglomerate's top management and financial staff) and intracompany bargaining. Divisional capital budgets depend on politics as well as pure economics. Large, profitable divisions with plenty of free cash flow may have the most bargaining power; they may get generous capital budgets while smaller divisions with good growth opportunities are reined in.

Conglomerates face further problems. Their divisions' market values can't be observed independently, and it is difficult to set incentives for divisional managers. This is particularly serious when managers are asked to commit to risky ventures. For example, how would a biotech startup fare as a division of a traditional conglomerate? Would the conglomerate be as patient and risk-tolerant as investors in the stock market? How are the scientists and clinicians doing the biotech R&D rewarded if they succeed? We don't mean to say that high-tech innovation and risk-taking are impossible in public conglomerates, but the difficulties are evident.

Economists have tried to measure whether corporate diversification destroys value. For example, Berger and Ofek estimate the average conglomerate discount at 12 to 15 percent.[28] *Conglomerate discount* means that the market value of the whole conglomerate is less than the sum of the values of the parts. The chief cause of this discount, at least in Berger and Ofek's sample, seemed to be overinvestment and misallocation of investment. In other words, investors were marking down the value of the conglomerates' shares from worry that their managements would make negative-NPV investments in mature divisions and forego positive-NPV opportunities elsewhere. But not

[28] P. Berger and E. Ofek, "Diversification's Effect on Firm Value," *Journal of Financial Economics* 37 (January 1995), pp. 39–65.

everybody is convinced by Berger and Ofek's estimates. Many researchers have found a somewhat smaller discount, while others have concluded that conglomerates may even sell at a premium.[29]

Internal Capital Markets in the Oil Business Misallocation in internal capital markets is not restricted to pure conglomerates. For example, Lamont found that, when oil prices fell by half in 1986, diversified oil companies cut back capital investment in their *non-oil* divisions.[30] The non-oil divisions were forced to "share the pain," even though the drop in oil prices did not diminish their investment opportunities. The *Wall Street Journal* reported one example:[31]

> Chevron Corp. cut its planned 1986 capital and exploratory budget by about 30 percent because of the plunge in oil prices. . . . A Chevron spokesman said that the spending cuts would be across the board and that no particular operations will bear the brunt.
>
> About 65 percent of the $3.5 billion budget will be spent on oil and gas exploration and production—about the same proportion as before the budget revision.
>
> Chevron also will cut spending for refining and marketing, oil and natural gas pipelines, minerals, chemicals, and shipping operations.

Why cut back on capital outlays for minerals, say, or chemicals? Low oil prices are generally good news, not bad, for chemical manufacturing, because oil distillates are an important raw material.

By the way, most of the oil companies in Lamont's sample were large, blue-chip companies. They could have raised additional capital from investors to maintain spending in their non-oil divisions. They chose not to. We do not understand why.

All large companies must allocate capital among divisions or lines of business. Therefore, they all have internal capital markets and must worry about mistakes and misallocations. But the danger probably increases as the company moves from a focus on one, or a few related industries, to unrelated conglomerate diversification. Look again at Table 33.2: How could top management of ITT keep accurate track of investment opportunities in 38 different industries?

Group Diversification in India

Unlike in the U.S., we see a different type of diversification in India. The Indian business groups (e.g., Tatas and Birlas) are diversified across a wide range of businesses and hence are not focused business groups.[32] Thus for example, the Tata Group has interests in engineering, automobiles, steel, software, etc. Khanna and Palepu argue that diversification makes sense in emerging countries like India where the different institutions like product market, capital market, etc. are ill-developed.[33] The business groups add value by effectively mediating between the group companies and the rest of the economy. In this sense the business groups serve the functions of the different institutions that are not well developed.

Khanna and Palepu argue that the different institutions like the capital market, the labor market, the product market, government regulation and contract enforcement are not well-developed in the emerging countries. Successful business groups can fill the void created by the lack of good institutions and hence can create value for the investors. Thus for example, the capital markets are illiquid and underdeveloped. This creates problems for companies from raising equity capital from the primary market. However, the business groups can serve the role of a venture capital company and

[29]See, for example, J. M. Campa and S. Kedia, "Explaining the Diversification Discount," *Journal of Finance* 57 (August 2002), pp. 1731–1762; and B. Villalonga, "Diversification Discount or Premium? New Evidence from the Business Information Tracking Service," *Journal of Finance* 59 (April 2004), pp. 479–506.

[30]O. Lamont, "Cash Flow and Investment: Evidence from Internal Capital Markets," *Journal of Finance* 52 (March 1997), pp. 83–109.

[31]Ibid. pp. 89–90, as cited therein.

[32]It is possible that the different companies operating under the banner of a particular business group are all focused companies.

[33]See Khanna, T., and K Palepu (1997), "Why Focused Strategies May be Wrong for Emerging Markets," Harvard Business Review, July – August.

provide necessary funds to the group companies. Similarly, despite underdeveloped labor market, the business groups can serve management competency to the different groups companies. Many of the Tata group companies, for example, benefit by borrowing skilled managers from Tata Administrative Service.

Fifteen Years after Reading This Chapter

You have just seized control of Establishment Industries, the blue-chip conglomerate, after a high-stakes, high-profile takeover battle. You are a financial celebrity, hounded by business reporters every time you step out of your stretch limo. You're contemplating a Ferrari and a trophy spouse. Fundraisers from your college or university are suddenly very attentive. But first you've got to deliver on promises to add shareholder value to your renamed New Establishment Corporation.

Fortunately you remember *Principles of Corporate Finance*. First, you identify New Establishment's neglected divisions—the poor fits that have not received their share of capital or top-management attention. These you spin off; no more internal capital market. As independent companies, these divisions can set their own capital budgets, but to obtain financing, they have to convince outside investors that their growth opportunities are truly positive-NPV. The managers of these spun-off companies can buy stock or be given stock options as part of their compensation packages. Therefore, incentives to maximize value are stronger. Investors understand this, so New Establishment's stock price jumps as soon as the spin-offs are announced.

New Establishment also has some large, mature, cash-cow businesses. You add still more value by selling some of these to LBO partnerships. You bargain hard and get a good price, so the stock price jumps again.

The remaining divisions will be the core of New Establishment. You consider pushing through a leveraged restructuring of these core activities to make sure that free cash flow is paid out to investors rather than invested in negative-NPV ventures. But you decide instead to implement a performance measurement and compensation system based on residual income.[34] You also make sure managers and key employees have sensible equity stakes. You take over as CEO, and New Establishment prospers. Your celebrity status fades away, except that once a year you are listed in *Forbes* magazine's compilation of the 400 wealthiest executives and investors. It could happen.

Financial Architecture of Traditional U.S. Conglomerates

This fanciful tale sums up the argument for *focus* and against conglomerate diversification. But we must be careful not to push the argument too far. For example, GE, a very successful company, operates in a wide range of unrelated industries, including jet engines, equipment leasing, television, home appliances, and medical equipment.

To succeed, conglomerates need to tackle two tasks: (1) Make sure divisional management and operating performance are better than could be achieved if the divisions were independent companies, and (2) operate an internal capital market that beats the external capital market. In other words, management of a conglomerate has to make better capital investment decisions than could be achieved by independent companies responsible for their own financing.

Task 1 is difficult because divisions' market values can't be observed separately, and it is harder to set incentives for divisional managers. Task 2 is difficult because the conglomerate's central planners have to fully understand investment opportunities in many different industries and because internal capital markets are prone to allocations by bargaining and politics.

Now we turn to a class of conglomerates that does seem to add value. We will find, however, that they have a very different structure.

---

[34]That is, on EVA. See Section 12.4.

Industry	Number of Companies	Industry	Number of Companies
Chemicals	2	Home building	1
Communications	6	Hotel and leisure	1
Consumer products	3	Industrial and manufacturing	8
Energy	2	Media	1
Financial services	4	Education	1
Health care	3		

TABLE 33.3

In 2004 KKR and its partners held private equity investments in 32 companies in the following industries. The fund was a (temporary) conglomerate.

Source: Kohlberg Kravis Roberts & Company, www.kkr.com.

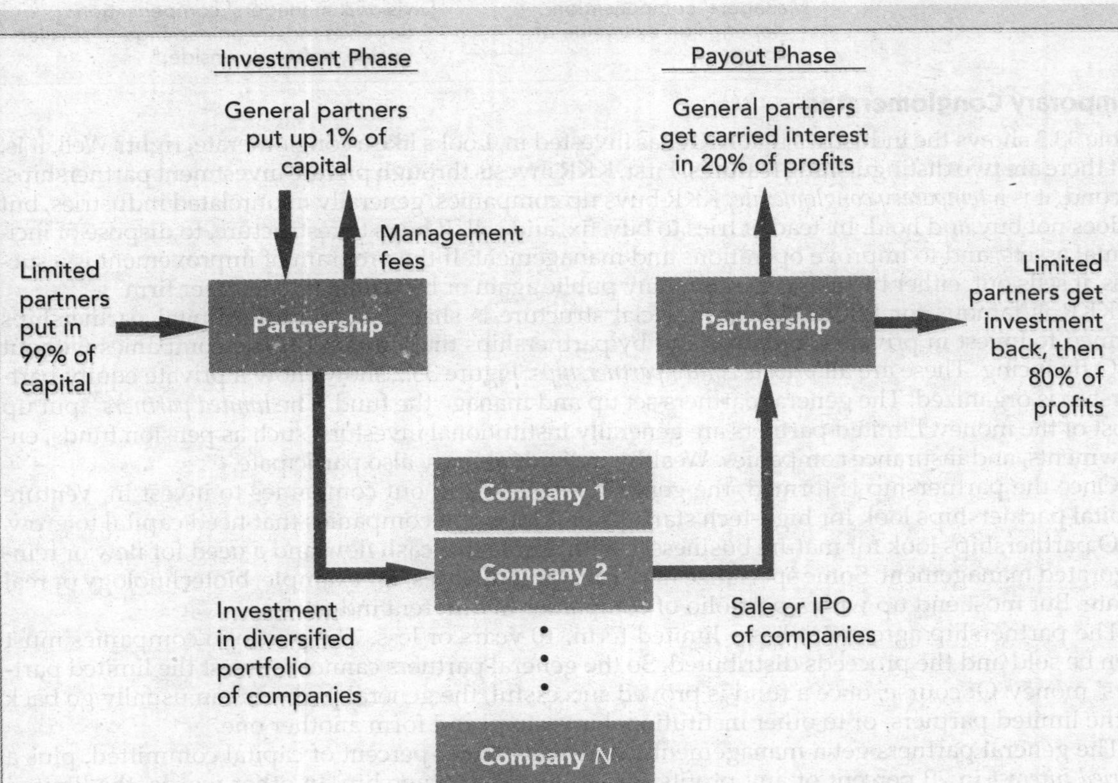

FIGURE 33.2

Organization of a typical private equity partnership. The limited partners, having put up almost all of the money, get first crack at the proceeds from sale or IPO of the portfolio companies. Once their investment is returned, they get 80 percent of any profits. The general partners, who organize and manage the partnership, get a 20 percent carried interest in profits.

923

TABLE 33.4

LBO fund vs. public conglomerate. Both diversify, investing in a portfolio of unrelated businesses, but their financial structures are otherwise fundamentally different.

Source: Adapted from G. Baker and C. Montgomery, "Conglomerates and LBO Associations: A Comparison of Organizational Forms," working paper, Harvard Business School, Cambridge, MA, July 1996.

LBO Partnership	Public Conglomerate
Widely diversified, investment in unrelated industries	Widely diversified, investment in unrelated industries
Limited-life partnership forces sale of portfolio companies.	Public corporations designed to operate divisions for the long run
No financial links or transfers between portfolio companies	Internal capital market
General partners "do the deal," then monitor; lenders also monitor.	Hierarchy of corporate staff evaluates divisions' plans and performance.
Managers' compensation depends on exit value of company.	Divisional managers' compensation depends mostly on earnings—"smaller upside, softer downside."

Temporary Conglomerates

Table 33.3 shows the industries that KKR has invested in. Looks like a conglomerate, right? Well, it is, but there are two distinguishing features. First, KKR invests through private investment partnerships. Second, it is a *temporary conglomerate.* KKR buys up companies, generally in unrelated industries, but it does not buy and hold. Instead, it tries to buy, fix, and sell. It buys to restructure, to dispose of incidental assets, and to improve operations and management. If the program of improvement is a success, it sells out, either by taking the company public again or by selling it to another firm.

KKR is famous for LBOs. But its financial structure is shared by venture capital partnerships formed to invest in private companies and by partnerships that buy up private companies without LBO financing. These are all *private equity partnerships.* Figure 33.2 shows how a private equity partnership is organized. The general partners set up and manage the fund. The *limited partners*[35] put up most of the money. Limited partners are generally institutional investors, such as pension funds, endowments, and insurance companies. Wealthy individuals may also participate.

Once the partnership is formed, the general partners seek out companies to invest in. Venture capital partnerships look for high-tech startups or adolescent companies that need capital to grow. LBO partnerships look for mature businesses with ample free cash flow and a need for new or reinvigorated management. Some specialize in particular industries, for example, biotechnology or real estate. But most end up with a portfolio of companies in different industries.

The partnership agreement has a limited term, 10 years or less. The portfolio companies must then be sold and the proceeds distributed. So the general partners cannot reinvest the limited partners' money. Of course, once a fund is proved successful, the general partners can usually go back to the limited partners, or to other institutional investors, and form another one.

The general partners get a management fee, usually 1 or 2 percent of capital committed, plus a *carried interest* in 20 percent of any profits earned by the partnership. In other words, the limited partners get paid off first, but then get only 80 percent of any further returns.[36]

Table 33.4 summarizes a comparison by Baker and Montgomery of the financial structure of an LBO fund and of a typical public conglomerate. Both are diversified, but the fund's limited partners do not have to worry that free cash flow will be plowed back into unprofitable investments. The fund has no internal capital market. Monitoring and compensation of management also differ. In the LBO fund, each company is run as a separate business. The managers report directly to the owners, the fund's

[35]Limited partners enjoy limited liability. See Section 14.2.

[36]This means that the general partners have a call option on 20 percent of the partnership's value, with an exercise price equal to the limited partners' investment.

partners. Each company's managers own shares or stock options in that company, not in the fund. Their compensation depends on their firm's market value in a sale or IPO.

In a public conglomerate, these businesses would be divisions, not freestanding companies. Ownership of the conglomerate would be dispersed, not concentrated. The divisions would not be valued separately by investors in the stock market, but by the conglomerate's corporate staff, the very people who run the internal capital market. Managers' compensation wouldn't depend on divisions' market values because no shares in the divisions would be traded and the conglomerate would not be committed to selling the divisions or spinning them off.

The advantages of LBO partnerships are obvious: strong incentives for management, concentrated ownership (no separation of ownership and control), and limited life, which reassures the investors that cash flow will not be reinvested wastefully.

These advantages carry over to other types of private equity partnerships, such as venture capital. We don't say that the structure is appropriate for most businesses. It is designed for change, not for the long run. But traditional conglomerates don't seem to work well for the long run either, at least in the United States (But in the next chapter we will find that conglomerates are common, and apparently successful, in many other parts of the world.)

33.4 BANKRUPTCY

Some firms are forced to reorganize by the onset of financial distress. At this point they need to agree to a reorganization plan with their creditors or file for bankruptcy. We list the largest U.S. bankruptcies in Table 33.5.

Bankruptcy proceedings in the United States may be initiated by the creditors, but usually it is the firm itself that decides to file. It can choose one of two procedures, which are set out in Chapters 7 and 11 of the 1978 Bankruptcy Reform Act. The purpose of Chapter 7 is to oversee the firm's death and dismemberment, while Chapter 11 seeks to nurse the firm back to health.

Most small firms make use of Chapter 7. In this case the bankruptcy judge appoints a trustee, who then closes the firm down and auctions off the assets. The proceeds from the auction are used to pay off the creditors. Secured creditors can recover the value of their collateral. Whatever is left over goes to the unsecured creditors, who take assigned places in a queue. The court and the trustee are first in line. Wages come next, followed by federal and state taxes and debts to some government agencies such as the Pension Benefit Guarantee Corporation. The remaining unsecured creditors mop up any remaining crumbs from the table.[37] Frequently the trustee will need to prevent some creditors from trying to jump the gun and collect on their debts, and sometimes the trustee will retrieve property that a creditor has recently seized.

Managers of small firms that are in trouble know that Chapter 7 bankruptcy means the end of the road and, therefore, will try to put off filing as long as possible. For this reason, Chapter 7 proceedings are often launched not by the firm but by its creditors.

When large public companies can't pay their debts, they generally attempt to rehabilitate the business. This is in the shareholders' interests; they have nothing to lose if things deteriorate further and everything to gain if the firm recovers. The procedures for rehabilitation are set out in Chapter 11 of the 1978 Act. Their purpose is to keep the firm alive and operating and to protect the value of the assets while a plan of reorganization is worked out.[38] During this period, other proceedings against the

[37]On average there isn't much left. See M. J. White, "Survey Evidence on Business Bankruptcy," in J. S. Bhandari and L. A. Weiss (eds.), *Corporate Bankruptcy* (Cambridge, U.K.: Cambridge University Press, 1996).

[38]To keep the firm alive, it may be necessary to continue to use assets that were offered as collateral, but this denies secured creditors access to their collateral. To resolve this problem, the Bankruptcy Reform Act makes it possible for a firm operating under Chapter 11 to keep such assets as long as the creditors who have a claim on them are compensated for any decline in their value. Thus, the firm might make cash payments to the secured creditors to cover economic depreciation of the assets.

TABLE 33.5

The largest U.S. bankruptcies.

Source: New Generation Research, Inc., **www.bankruptcydata.com.**

Company	Bankruptcy Date	Total Assets Prebankruptcy ($ billions)
WorldCom	July 2002	$103.9
Enron Corp.	December 2001	63.4
Conseco	December 2002	61.4
Texaco	April 1987	35.9
Financial Corp. of America	September 1988	33.9
Global Crossing	January 2002	30.2
Pacific Gas and Electric	April 2001	29.8
UAL	December 2002	25.2

firm are halted, and the company usually continues to be run by its existing management.[39] The responsibility for developing the plan falls on the debtor firm but, if it cannot devise an acceptable plan, the court may invite anyone to do so—for example, a committee of creditors.

The plan goes into effect if it is accepted by the creditors and confirmed by the court. Each *class* of creditors votes separately on the plan. Acceptance requires approval by at least one-half of votes cast in each class, and those voting "aye" must represent two-thirds of the value of the creditors' aggregate claim against the firm. The plan also needs to be approved by two-thirds of the shareholders. Once the creditors and the shareholders have accepted the plan, the court normally approves it, provided that each class of creditors is in favor and that the creditors will be no worse off under the plan than they would be if the firm's assets were liquidated and the proceeds distributed. Under certain conditions the court may confirm a plan even if one or more classes of creditors votes against it,[40] but the rules for a "cram-down" are complicated and we will not attempt to cover them here.

The reorganization plan is basically a statement of who gets what; each class of creditors gives up its claim in exchange for new securities or a mixture of new securities and cash. The problem is to design a new capital structure for the firm that will (1) satisfy the creditors and (2) allow the firm to solve the *business* problems that got the firm into trouble in the first place.[41] Sometimes satisfying these two conditions requires a plan of baroque complexity, involving the creation of a dozen or more new securities.

The Securities and Exchange Commission (SEC) plays a role in many reorganizations, particularly for large, public companies. Its interest is to ensure that all relevant and material information is disclosed to the creditors before they vote on the proposed plan of reorganization.

Chapter 11 proceedings are often successful, and the patient emerges fit and healthy. But in other cases rehabilitation proves impossible, and the assets are liquidated under Chapter 7. Sometimes the firm may emerge from Chapter 11 for a brief period before it is once again submerged by

[39]Occasionally the court will appoint a trustee to manage the firm.

[40]But at least one class of creditors must vote for the plan; otherwise the court cannot approve it.

[41]Although Chapter 11 is designed to keep the firm in business, the reorganization plan often involves the sale or closure of large parts of the business.

disaster and back in the bankruptcy court. For example, TWA came out of Chapter 11 bankruptcy at the end of 1993, was back again less than two years later, and then for a third time in 1998, prompting jokes about "Chapter 22" and "Chapter 33."[42]

Is Chapter 11 Efficient?

Here is a simple view of the bankruptcy decision: Whenever a payment is due to creditors, management checks the value of the equity. If the value is positive, the firm makes the payment (if necessary, raising the cash by an issue of shares). If the equity is valueless, the firm defaults on its debt and files for bankruptcy. If the assets of the bankrupt firm can be put to better use elsewhere, the firm is liquidated and the proceeds are used to pay off the creditors; otherwise the creditors become the new owners and the firm continues to operate.[43]

In practice, matters are rarely so simple. For example, we observe that firms often petition for bankruptcy even when the equity has a positive value. And firms often continue to operate even when the assets could be used more efficiently elsewhere. The problems in Chapter 11 usually arise because the goal of paying off the creditors conflicts with the goal of maintaining the business as a going concern. We described in Chapter 18 how the assets of Eastern Airlines seeped away as the court attempted to keep the airline flying. When the company filed for bankruptcy, its assets were more than sufficient to repay in full its liabilities of $3.7 billion. But the bankruptcy judge was determined to keep Eastern flying. When it finally became clear that Eastern was a terminal case, the assets were sold off and the creditors received less than $.9 billion. The creditors would clearly have been better off if Eastern had been liquidated immediately; the unsuccessful attempt at resuscitation cost the creditors $2.8 billion.[44]

Here are some reasons that Chapter 11 proceedings do not always achieve an efficient solution:

1. Although the reorganized firm is legally a new entity, it is entitled to the tax-loss carryforwards belonging to the old firm. If the firm is liquidated rather than reorganized, the tax-loss carryforwards disappear. Thus there is a tax incentive to continue operating the firm even when its assets could be sold and put to better use elsewhere.
2. If the firm's assets are sold, it is easy to determine what is available to pay the creditors. However, when the company is reorganized, it needs to conserve cash. Therefore, claimants are generally paid in a mixture of cash and securities. This makes it less easy to judge

[42]One study found that after emerging from Chapter 11, about one in three firms reentered bankruptcy or privately restructured their debt. See E. S. Hotchkiss, "Postbankruptcy Reform and Management Turnover," *Journal of Finance* 50 (March 1995), pp. 3–21.

[43]If there are several classes of creditors in this simplistic model, the junior creditors initially become the owners of the company and are responsible for paying off the senior debt. They now face exactly the same decision as the original owners. If their newly acquired equity is valueless, they will also default and turn over ownership to the next class of creditors.

[44]These estimates of creditor losses are taken from L. A. Weiss and K. H. Wruck, "Information Problems, Conflicts of Interest, and Asset Stripping: Chapter 11's Failure in the Case of *Eastern Airlines*," *Journal of Financial Economics* 48 (April 1998), pp. 55–97.

whether they receive a fair shake. For example, each bondholder may be offered $300 in cash and $700 in a new bond that pays no interest for the first two years and a low rate of interest thereafter. A bond of this kind in a company that is struggling to survive may not be worth much, but the bankruptcy court usually looks at the face value of the new bonds and may therefore regard the bondholders as paid off in full.

3. Senior creditors who know they are likely to get a raw deal in a reorganization are likely to press for a liquidation. Shareholders and junior creditors prefer a reorganization. They hope that the court will not interpret the creditors' pecking order too strictly and that they will receive consolation prizes when the firm's remaining value is sliced up. Such prizes are common.[45]
4. Although shareholders and junior creditors are at the bottom of the pecking order, they have a secret weapon—they can play for time. On average it takes about two years before a plan is presented to the court and agreed to by each class of creditor. When they use delaying tactics, the junior claimants are betting on a stroke of luck that will rescue their investment. On the other hand, the senior claimants know that time is working against them, so they may be prepared to settle for a lower payoff as part of the price for getting the plan accepted. Also, prolonged bankruptcy cases are costly, as we pointed out in Chapter 18. Senior claimants may see their money seeping into lawyers' pockets and decide to settle quickly.
5. While a reorganization is being drawn up, the company is likely to need additional working capital. It is therefore allowed to buy goods on credit and borrow money (known as *debtor-in-possession*, or *DIP*, debt). The new creditors have priority over the old creditors, and their debt may even be secured by assets that are already mortgaged to existing debtholders. This also gives existing debtholders an incentive to settle quickly, before their claims are diluted by the new debt.
6. When the firm is in Chapter 11, secured debt receives interest but unsecured debt does not. For unsecured debtholders that is another reason for a fast settlement.
7. Sometimes profitable companies have filed for Chapter 11 bankruptcy to protect themselves against burdensome contracts or suits. For example, Continental Airlines, which was bedeviled by a costly labor contract, filed for Chapter 11 in 1982 and immediately cut pay by up to 50 percent.[46] In 1995 Dow Corning was threatened with costly litigation for damage allegedly caused by its silicone-gel breast implants. Dow filed for bankruptcy under Chapter 11, and the bankruptcy judge agreed to stay the damage suits. Needless to say, lawyers and legislators worry that these actions were contrary to the original intent of the bankruptcy acts.

[45]Franks and Torous found that stockholders received some payoff—usually securities—in two-thirds of Chapter 11 reorganizations. See J. R. Franks and W. N. Torous, "An Empirical Investigation of U.S. Firms in Reorganization," *Journal of Finance* 44 (July 1989), pp. 747–770. A similar study concluded that in a third of the cases shareholders received more than 25 percent of the equity in the new firm. See L. A. Weiss, "Bankruptcy Resolution, Direct Costs and Violation of Priority of Claims," *Journal of Financial Economics* 27 (October 1990), pp. 285–314.

[46]The pay cut enabled Continental to reduce fares aggressively and improve its load factors, but it did not solve Continental's problems. Shortly after emerging from Chapter 11, it was back in the bankruptcy court.

Workouts

If Chapter 11 reorganizations are not efficient, why don't firms bypass the bankruptcy courts and get together with their creditors to work out a solution? Many firms that are in distress *do* first seek a negotiated settlement, or **workout.** For example, they can seek to delay payment of the debt or negotiate an interest rate holiday. However, shareholders and junior creditors know that senior creditors are anxious to avoid formal bankruptcy proceedings. So they are likely to be tough negotiators, and senior creditors generally need to make concessions to reach agreement.[47] The larger the firm, and the more complicated its capital structure, the less likely it is that everyone will agree to any proposal. For example, Wickes Corporation, a Californian-based retailer, tried to reach a negotiated settlement with its creditors when it fell on hard times. Unfortunately, it had 250,000 creditors, and the negotiations failed. In 1982 Wickes ended up in an unusually complex bankruptcy proceeding that soaked up about $250 million in legal and administrative costs.

Sometimes the firm does agree to an informal workout with its creditors and then files under Chapter 11 to obtain the approval of the bankruptcy court. Such *prepackaged bankruptcies* reduce the likelihood of subsequent litigation and allow the firm to gain the special tax advantages of Chapter 11. For example, in 2004 Trump Hotels & Casino Resorts arranged a *prepack* after reaching agreement with its creditors.

Alternative Bankruptcy Procedures

The United States bankruptcy system is often described as a debtor-friendly system. Its principal focus is on rescuing firms in distress. But this comes at a cost, for there are many instances in which the firm's assets would be better deployed in other uses. Michael Jensen, a critic of Chapter 11, has argued that "the U.S. bankruptcy code is fundamentally flawed. It is expensive, it exacerbates conflicts of interest among different classes of creditors, and it often takes years to resolve individual cases."[48] Jensen's proposed solution is to require that any bankrupt company be put immediately on the auction block and the proceeds distributed to claimants in accordance with the priority of their claims.[49]

In some countries the bankruptcy system is even more friendly to debtors. For example, in France the primary duties of the bankruptcy court are to keep the firm in business and preserve employment. Only once these duties have been performed does the court have a responsibility to creditors. Creditors have minimal control over the process, and it is the court that decides whether the firm should be liquidated or preserved. If the court chooses liquidation, it may select a bidder who offers a lower price but better prospects for employment.

The U.K. is just about at the other end of the scale. When a British firm is unable to pay its debts, the control rights pass to the creditors. Most commonly, a designated secured creditor appoints a *receiver,* who assumes direction of the firm, sells sufficient assets to repay the secured creditors, and

[47] Franks and Torous show that creditors make even greater concessions to junior creditors in informal workouts than in Chapter 11. See J. R. Franks and W. N. Torous, "How Shareholders and Creditors Fare in Workouts and Chapter 11 Reorganizations," *Journal of Financial Economics* 35 (May 1994), pp. 13–33.

[48] M. C. Jensen, "Corporate Control and the Politics of Finance," *Journal of Applied Corporate Finance* 4 (Summer 1991), pp. 13–33.

[49] An ingenious alternative set of bankruptcy procedures is proposed in L. Bebchuk, "A New Approach to Corporate Reorganizations, *Harvard Law Review* 101 (1988), pp. 775–804; and P. Aghion, O. Hart, and J. Moore, "The Economics of Bankruptcy Reform," *Journal of Law, Economics and Organization* 8 (1992), pp. 523–546.

ensures that any excess funds are used to pay off the other creditors according to the priority of their claims.

Franks and Davydenko, who have examined alternative bankruptcy systems, found that banks responded to these differences in the bankruptcy code by adjusting their lending practices.[50] Nevertheless, as you would expect, lenders recover a smaller proportion of their money in those countries that have a debtor-friendly bankruptcy system. For example, in France the banks recover on average only 47 percent of the money owed by bankrupt firms, while in the U.K. the corresponding figure is 69 percent.

Of course, the grass is always greener elsewhere. In the United States and France, critics complain about the costs of trying to save businesses that are no longer viable. By contrast, in countries such as the U.K., bankruptcy laws are blamed for the demise of healthy businesses and Chapter 11 is held up as a model of an efficient bankruptcy system.

Bankruptcy Regulations in India

Unlike in the U.S., India did not have one law dealing with bankruptcy of companies. The Sick Industries Companies Act, 1985 (SICA) was dealing with revival and rehabilitation of sick companies. The Companies Act, 1956 was dealing with the winding up (or liquidation) of the companies. Following the recommendation of the Eradi Committee (Justice V.B. Eradi Committee, set up in 1999), the Bill to Repeal SICA was passed in the Parliament in 2003. It also got the President's assent in 2004. However, due to a delay in setting up an alternative mechanism, i.e., the National Company Law Tribunal (NCLT), the Ministry of Finance has asked BIFR (under SICA) to continue in its existing form.

Under SICA, a sick industrial company was defined as one with negative net worth. Therefore under SICA, it was possible that a company had defaulted in its debt payments and still was not defined as a sick company simply because its net worth was positive. Once a firm was referred to BIFR, the creditors could not take any action against the company to recover their dues because all claims against the firm were automatically stayed. This provision enabled many unscrupulous managers to manipulate their accounts and show negative net worth and refer the company to BIFR. This ensured that the creditors of the firm could no longer seize the assets of the company. This virtually made any debt covenant meaningless.

Under the SICA, a company had to register with BIFR within 60 days after its net worth became negative. Then BIFR used to decide in another 60 days whether the firm registered with it was indeed sick. Then BIFR would appoint an Operating Agency (OA) to investigate into the matter and recommend a suitable rehabilitation scheme. The OA would design an appropriate rehabilitation scheme in another 90 days' time. Once a plan was proposed, it required a lot of time in implementing it.

In 2002 the Government of India enacted the Securitisation and Reconstruction of Financial Assets and Enforcement of Security Interest Act.[51] This Act gave some leeway to the creditors. Chapter III of the Act, for example, says that "*...any security interest created in favor of any secured creditor may be enforced without the intervention of the court or tribunal, by such creditor in accordance with the provisions of this Act.*"

The new Act allows for the creation of **Asset Reconstruction Companies (ARCs)** with the objective to acquire the non-performing assets from banks and financial institutions and try maximizing the recovery through improved management. The banks and financial institutions can

[50]J. R. Franks and S. Davydenko, "Do Bankruptcy Codes Matter? A Study of Defaults in France, Germany, and the UK," unpublished working paper, London Business School, June 2004.

[51]Downloadable from www.arcil.co.in

transfer all financial assets (loans issued to the defaulting company) to an ARC and the ARC in turn will issue debentures and bonds to the banks and financial institutions. This way the ARC takes the responsibility of recovering the dues from the defaulting companies. The ARC can take over the management of the borrowing company, can sale or lease its assets, can reschedule the payments to be made to the borrowers, can take possession of secured assets, etc. ICICI bank, State Bank of India, IDBI Bank, etc. set up the first asset reconstruction company, namely the Asset Reconstruction Company of India Limited (ARCIL). Thus for example, in January 2005, the Asset Reconstruction Company of India took over the assets of the ailing company Kumar Metallurgical Corporation Limited of Hyderabad.

SUMMARY

A corporation's structure is not immutable. Companies frequently reorganize by adding new businesses or disposing of existing ones. They may alter their capital structure and they may change their ownership and control. In this chapter we looked at some of the mechanisms by which companies transform themselves.

We started with leveraged buyouts (LBOs). An LBO is a takeover or buyout of a company or division that is financed mostly with debt. The LBO is owned privately, usually by an investment partnership. Debt financing is not the objective of most LBOs; it is a means to an end. Most LBOs are diet deals. The cash requirements for debt service force managers to shed unneeded assets, improve operating efficiency, and forego wasteful expenditure. The managers and employees are given a significant stake in the business, so they have strong incentives to make these improvements.

A leveraged restructuring is in many ways similar to an LBO. In this case the company puts *itself* on a diet. Large amounts of debt are added and the proceeds are paid out to shareholders. The company is forced to generate cash to service the debt, but there is no change in control and the company stays public.

Most investments in LBOs are made by private equity partnerships. We called these "temporary conglomerates." They are conglomerates because they create a portfolio of companies in unrelated industries. They are temporary because the partnership has a limited life, usually about 10 years. At the end of this period, the partnership's investments must be sold or taken public again in IPOs. Private equity funds do not buy and hold; they buy, fix, and sell. Investors in the partnership therefore do not have to worry about wasteful reinvestment of free cash flow. LBO managers know that they will be able to cash out their equity stakes if their company succeeds in improving efficiency and paying down debt.

The private equity partnership is also common in venture capital. The limited partners, who put up almost all of the money, are mostly institutional investors such as pension funds, endowments, and insurance companies. The limited partners are first in line when the partnership's investments are sold. The general partners, who organize and manage the fund, receive a regular fee and get a carried interest in the fund's profits.

The private equity market has been growing steadily. In contrast to these temporary conglomerates, public conglomerates have been declining in the United States. In public companies, unrelated diversification seems to destroy value—the whole is worth less than the sum of its parts. There are two possible reasons for this. First, since the value of the parts can't be observed separately, it is harder to set incentives for divisional managers. Second, conglomerates' internal capital markets are inefficient. It is difficult for management to appreciate investment opportunities in many different industries, and internal capital markets are prone to overinvestment and cross-subsidies. The difficulties of running internal capital markets are not restricted to pure conglomerates, but they are most acute there.

Of course, companies shed assets as well as acquire them. Assets may be divested by spin-offs, carve-outs, or asset sales. In a spin-off the parent firm splits off part of its business into a separate public company and gives its shareholders stock in the company. In a carve-out the parent raises cash by separating off part of its business and selling shares in this business through an IPO. These divestitures are generally good news to investors; it appears that the divisions are moving to better homes, where they can be well managed and more profitable. The same improvements in efficiency and profitability are observed in privatizations, which are spin-offs or carve-outs of businesses owned by governments.

Companies in distress may reorganize by getting together with their creditors to arrange a workout. For example, they may agree to a delay in repayment. If a workout proves impossible, the company will need to file for bankruptcy. Chapter 11 of the Bankruptcy Act, which is used by most large public companies, seeks to reorganize the company and put it back on its feet again. Proceedings are often successful. However, the goal of paying off the company's creditors often conflicts with the aim of keeping the business going. As a result, Chapter 11 sometimes allows a firm to continue to operate when its assets could be better used elsewhere and the proceeds used to pay off creditors.

Chapter 11 tends to favor the debtor. But in some other countries the bankruptcy system is designed almost exclusively to recover as much cash as possible for the lenders. While U.S. critics of Chapter 11 complain about the costs of saving businesses that are not worth saving, commentators elsewhere bemoan the fact that their bankruptcy laws are causing the break up of potentially healthy businesses.

FURTHER READING

The paper by Kaplan povides evidence on the evolution and performance of LBOs. Jensen, the chief proponent of the free-cash-flow theory of takeovers, gives a spirited and controversial defense of LBOs:

S. N. Kaplan and J. C. Stein, "The Evolution of Buyout Pricing and Financial Structure (Or, What Went Wrong) in the 1980s," *Journal of Applied Corporate Finance* 6 (Spring 1993), pp. 72–88.

M. C. Jensen, "The Eclipse of the Public Corporation," *Harvard Business Review* 67 (September/October 1989), pp. 61–74.

Papers on divestitures include:

P. Cusatis, J. Miles, and R. Woolridge, "Some New Evidence That Spinoffs Create Value," *Journal of Applied Corporate Finance* 7 (Summer 1994), pp. 100–107.

Privatization is reviewed in:

W. I. Megginson and J. M. Netter, "From State to Market: A Survey of Empirical Studies on Privatization," *Journal of Economic Literature* 39 (June 2001), pp. 321–389.

Altman's book and the Senbet and Seward article provide good general surveys of the bankruptcy decision, while Bhandari and Weiss offer a useful collection of readings. Also listed are several studies of the conflicting interests of security holders and the costs and consequences of reorganization:

E. I. Altman, *Corporate Financial Distress and Bankruptcy: A Complete Guide to Predicting and Avoiding Distress and Profiting from Bankruptcy* 2nd ed. (New York: John Wiley & Sons, 1993).

L. Senbet and J. Seward, "Financial Distress, Bankruptcy and Reorganization," in R. A. Jarrow, V. Maksimovic, and W. T. Ziemba (eds), *North-Holland Handbooks of Operations Research and Management Science: Finance*, vol. 9 (New York: Elsevier, 1995), pp. 921–961.

J. S. Bhandari, L. A. Weiss, and B. E. Adler (eds.), *Corporate Bankruptcy: Economic and Legal Perspectives* (Cambridge, U.K.: Cambridge University Press, 1996).

M. J. White, "The Corporate Bankruptcy Decision," *Journal of Economic Perspectives* 3 (Spring 1989), pp. 129–152.

S. C. Gilson, "Managing Default: Some Evidence on How Firms Choose between Workouts and Bankruptcy," *Journal of Applied Corporate Finance* 4 (Summer 1991), pp. 62–70.

L. A. Weiss, "The Bankruptcy Code and Violations of Absolute Priority," *Journal of Applied Corporate Finance* 4 (Summer 1991), pp. 71–78.

There are a number of excellent case studies of reorganization. Here are a few:

B. Burrough and J. Helyar, *Barbarians at the Gate: The Fall of RJR Nabisco* (New York: Harper & Row, 1990).

G. P. Baker, "Beatrice: A Study in the Creation and Destruction of Value," *Journal of Finance* 47 (July 1992), pp. 1081–1120.

K. H. Wruck, "Financial Policy as a Catalyst for Organizational Change: Sealed Air's Leveraged Special Dividend," *Journal of Applied Corporate Finance* 7 (Winter 1995), pp. 20–37.

J. Allen, "Reinventing the Corporation: The Satellite Structure of Thermo Electron," *Journal of Applied Corporate Finance* 11 (Summer 1998), pp. 38–47.

R. Parrino, "Spinoffs and Wealth Transfers: The Marriott Case," *Journal of Financial Economics* 43 (February 1997), pp. 241–274.

C. Eckel, D. Eckel, and V. Singal, "Privatization and Efficiency: Industry Effects of the Sale of British Airways," *Journal of Financial Economics* 43 (February 1997), pp. 275–298.

L. A. Weiss and K. H. Wruck, "Information Problems, Conflicts of Interest, and Asset Stripping: Chapter 11's Failure in the Case of Eastern Airlines," *Journal of Financial Economics* 48 (April 1998), pp. 55–97.

CONCEPT REVIEW QUESTIONS

1. What are the distinguishing features of an LBO? Why did we describe LBOs as diet deals? (pages 909–914)
2. How is a private equity partnership organized? Who is the general partner and who are the limited partners? (pages 923–925)
3. Why did we describe the private equity partnership as a temporary conglomerate? What advantages does this structure have compared with normal public conglomerates? (pages 924–925)

For additional Concept Review Questions, please visit us at www.mhhe.com/bmam8e or refer to your Student CD.

QUIZ

1. Define the following terms:
   a. LBO
   b. MBO
   c. spin-off
   d. carve-out
   e. asset sale
   f. privatization
   g. leveraged restructuring
2. True or false?
   a. One of the first tasks of an LBO's financial manager is to pay down debt.
   b. Once an LBO or MBO goes private, it almost always stays private.
   c. Targets for LBOs in the 1980s tended to be profitable companies in mature industries.
   d. "Carried interest" refers to the deferral of interest payments on LBO debt.

e. By the early 2000s, new LBO transactions were extremely rare.
f. The announcement of a spin-off is generally followed by a sharp fall in the stock price.
g. Privatizations are generally followed by massive layoffs.
h. On average, privatization seems to improve efficiency and add value.

3. What are the government's motives in a privatization?
4. List the *disadvantages* of a conglomerate in the United States.
5. What is the difference between Chapter 7 and Chapter 11 bankruptcy?
6. True or false?
   a. When a company becomes bankrupt, it is usually in the interests of the equityholders to seek a liquidation rather than a reorganization.
   b. In Chapter 11 a reorganization plan must be presented for approval by each class of creditor.
   c. In a reorganization, creditors may be paid off with a mixture of cash and securities.
   d. When a company is liquidated, one of the most valuable assets to be sold off is the tax-loss carryforward.
7. Explain why equity can sometimes have a positive value even when companies file for bankruptcy.

PRACTICE QUESTIONS

1. True, false, or "It depends on . . ."?
   a. Carve-out or spin-off of a division improves incentives for the division's managers.
   b. Private equity partnerships have limited lives. The main purpose is to force the general partners to seek out quick payback investments.
   c. Managers of private equity partnerships have an incentive to make risky investments.
2. For what kinds of firm would an LBO or MBO transaction *not* be productive?
3. Outline the similarities and differences between the RJR Nabisco LBO and the Sealed Air leveraged restructuring. Were the economic motives the same? Were the results the same? Do you think it was an advantage for Sealed Air to remain a public company?
4. Examine some recent examples of divestitures. What do you think were the underlying reasons for them? How did investors react to the news?
5. Read *Barbarians at the Gate* (Further Reading). What agency costs can you identify? *Hint:* See Chapter 12. Do you think the LBO was well-designed to reduce these costs?
6. Explain the structure of a private equity partnership. Pay particular attention to incentives and compensation. What types of investment were such partnerships designed to make?
7. "Privatization appears to bring efficiency gains because public companies are better able to reduce agency costs." Why do you think this may (or may not) be true?
8. We described several problems with Chapter 11 bankruptcy. Which of these problems could be mitigated by negotiating a prepackaged bankruptcy?

CHAPTER [34]

GOVERNANCE AND CORPORATE CONTROL AROUND THE WORLD

MUCH OF CORPORATE finance (and much of this book) assumes a particular financial structure—public corporations with actively traded shares and relatively easy access to financial markets. But there are other ways to organize and finance business ventures. The arrangements for ownership, control, and financing vary greatly around the world. In this chapter we consider some of these differences.

Corporations raise cash from financial markets and also from financial institutions. Markets are relatively more important in the U.S., U.K., and other "Anglo Saxon" economies. Financial institutions, particularly banks, are relatively more important in many other countries, including Germany and Japan. In bank-based systems, individual investors are less likely to hold corporate debt and equity directly. Instead ownership passes through banks, insurance companies, and other financial intermediaries.

This chapter starts with an overview of financial markets, financial institutions, and sources of financing. We contrast Europe, Japan, and the rest of Asia to the United States and U.K. Then Section 34.2 looks more closely at ownership, control, and governance. Here we start with the United States and United Kingdom and then turn to Japan, Germany, and the rest of the world. Section 34.3 asks whether these differences matter. For example, do well-functioning financial markets and institutions contribute to economic development and growth? What are the advantages and disadvantages of market-based versus bank-based systems?

Before starting on this worldwide tour, remember that the principles of financial management apply throughout the journey. The concepts and basic tools of the trade do not vary. For example, all companies in all countries should recognize the opportunity cost of capital (although the cost of capital is even harder to measure where stock markets are small or sleepy). Discounted cash flow still makes sense. Real options are encountered everywhere. And even in bank-based financial systems, corporations participate in world financial markets—by trading foreign exchange or hedging risks in futures markets, for instance.

34.1 FINANCIAL MARKETS AND INSTITUTIONS

In most of this book we have assumed that debt financing comes from public bond markets. Nothing in principle changes when a firm borrows from a bank instead. But in some countries bond markets are stunted and bank financing is more important. Figure 34.1 shows the total values of bank loans, private (nongovernment) bonds, and stock markets in different parts of the world in 2003. To measure these financial claims on a comparable basis, the amounts are scaled by gross domestic product (GDP).[1]

Company financing in the United States is different from that in most other countries. The United States not only has a large amount of bank loans outstanding, but there is also a large stock market *and* a large corporate bond market. Thus the United States is said to have a market-based financial system. Stock market value is also high in the United Kingdom and Asia,[2] but bank loans are much

[1]For more detailed data and discussion of the material in this section, see F. Allen, M. Chui, and A. Maddaloni, "Financial Systems in Europe, the US and Asia," *Oxford Review of Economic Policy,* forthcoming November 2004.
[2]Asia here includes Hong Kong, Indonesia, Korea, Malaysia, the Philippines, Singapore, Taiwan, and Thailand.

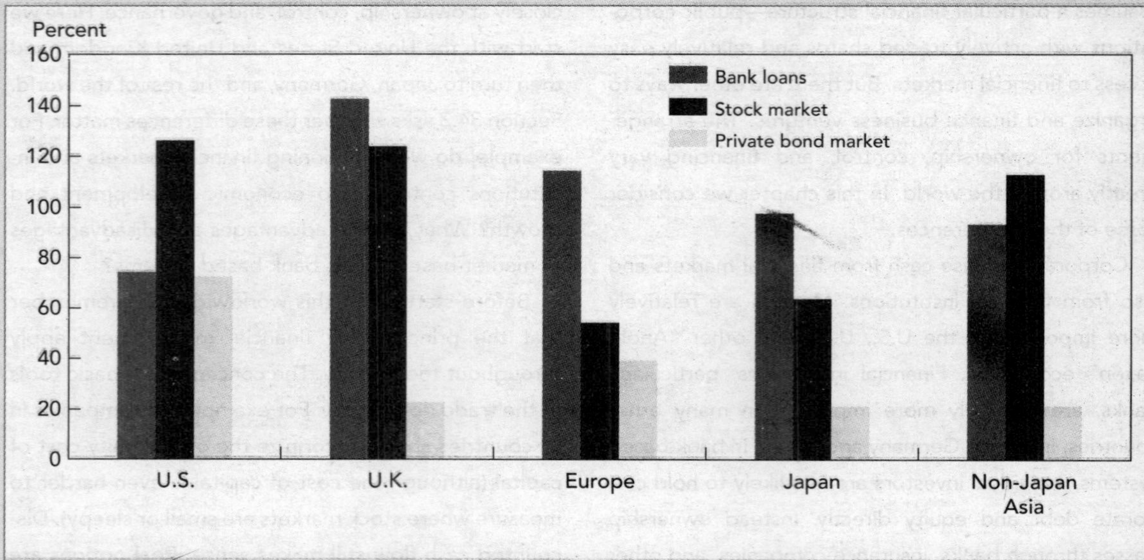

FIGURE 34.1

Value of financial claims in 2003, percentage of GDP.

Sources: CEIC Data Ltd, International Financial Statistics, and national sources.

more important than the bond market in these countries. In Europe[3] and Japan, bank financing again outpaces bond markets, but the stock market is relatively small. Most countries in Europe, including Germany, France, Italy, and Spain, have bank-based financial systems. So does Japan.

Let's look at these regions from a different perspective. Figure 34.2 shows the financial investments made by households, again scaled by GDP.[4] ("Households" means individual investors.) Household portfolios are divided into four categories: bank deposits; insurance policies and mutual and pension funds; equity securities; and "other." Notice in Figure 34.2 the differences in the total amounts of financial assets. Summing the columns for each country and region, the amount of financial assets is 327 percent of GDP in the United States, 306 percent in the United Kingdom, 267 percent in Japan, and 192 percent in Europe. This does not mean that European investors are poor, just that they hold less wealth in the form of financial assets. Figure 34.2 excludes other important investment categories, such as real estate or privately owned businesses. It also excludes the value of pensions provided by governments. In many countries companies are not obliged to establish pension funds. Instead they pay pensions out of regular income. When this happens, institutional investment in securities is reduced.

[3]Europe here includes the countries that have adopted the euro currency: Austria, Belgium, Finland, France, Germany, Greece, Ireland, Italy, Luxembourg, the Netherlands, Portugal, and Spain.

[4]Data for Asia are not available for this and the following figures that summarize portfolio allocations.

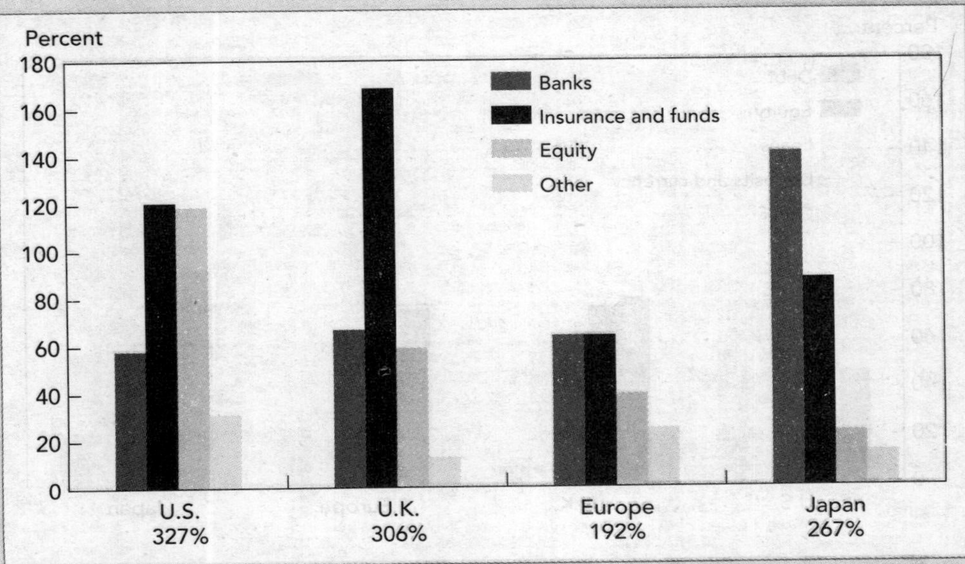

FIGURE 34.2

Household portfolio allocations, 1995–2002, percentage of GDP.

Source: European Central Bank Federal Reserve Board, and Bank of Japan.

In the United States, a large fraction of households' portfolios is held directly in equity securities, mostly common stocks. Therefore individual investors can potentially play an important role in corporate governance. Direct equity holdings are smaller in the United Kingdom, smaller still in Europe, and smallest in Japan. Japanese households could not play a significant direct role in corporate governance even if they wanted to. They can't vote shares that they don't own.

Where direct equity investment is small, household investments in bank deposits, insurance policies, and mutual and pension funds are correspondingly large. In the United Kingdom, the insurance and funds category dominates, with bank deposits in second place. In Europe, bank deposits and insurance and funds run a close race for first. In Japan, bank deposits win by a mile, with insurance and funds in second place and equities a distant third.

Figure 34.2 tells us that in many parts of the world there are relatively few individual stockholders. Most individuals don't invest directly in equity markets, but indirectly, through insurance companies, mutual funds, banks, and other financial intermediaries. Of course the thread of ownership traces back through these intermediaries to individual investors. All assets are ultimately owned by individuals. There are no Martian or extra-terrestrial investors that we know of.[5]

Now let's look at financial institutions. Figure 34.3 shows the financial assets held by financial institutions, including banks, mutual funds, insurance companies, pension funds, and other

[5]There may be owners not yet present on this planet, however. For example, endowments of educational, charitable, and religious organizations are partly held in trust for future generations.

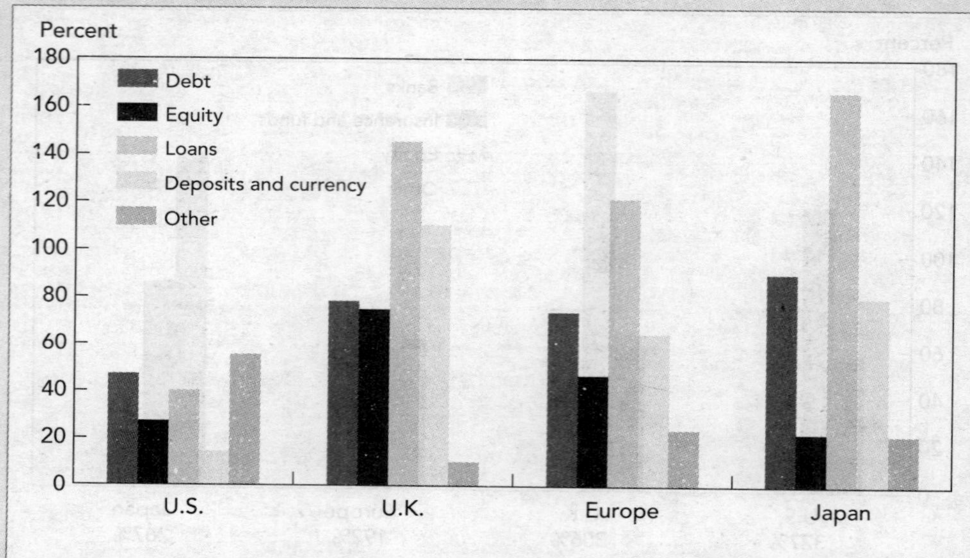

FIGURE 34.3

Financial institutions' portfolio allocations, 1995–2002, percentage of GDP.

Source: European Central Bank, Federal Reserve Board, and Bank of Japan.

intermediaries. These investments are smaller in the United States, relative to GDP, than in other countries (as expected in the U.S. market-based system). Financial institutions in the United Kingdom, Europe, and Japan have invested large sums in loans and in deposits and currency. Holdings of equity are highest in the United Kingdom. These holdings are mainly owned by insurance companies and pension funds.

We've covered households and financial institutions. Is there any other source for corporate financing? Yes, financing can come from other corporations. Take a look at Figure 34.4, which shows the financial assets held by nonfinancial corporations. Perhaps the most striking feature is the large amount of equity held by firms in Europe. The amount of equity held in Japan and the United Kingdom is also large. In the United States it is relatively small. As we will see, these holdings of shares by other nonfinancial corporations have important implications for corporate ownership and governance.

Another interesting aspect of Figure 34.4 is the large amount of intercompany loans and trade credit (mostly trade credit) in Japan. Many Japanese firms rely heavily on trade-credit financing, that is, on accounts payable to other firms. Of course the other firms see the reverse side of trade credit: They are providing financing in the form of accounts receivable.

Figures 34.1 to 34.4 show that just drawing a line between market-based, "Anglo-Saxon" financial systems and bank-based financial systems is simplistic. We need to dig a little deeper when comparing financial systems. For example, more equity is held directly by households in the United States than in the United Kingdom and the portfolio allocations of households, nonfinancial corporations, and financial institutions are also significantly different. In addition, we noted the large

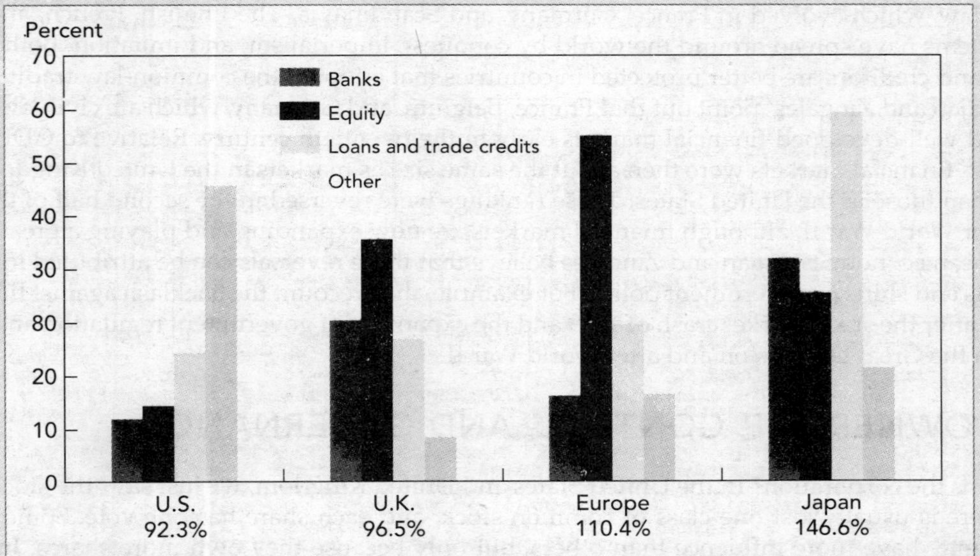

FIGURE 34.4

Nonfinancial corporations' portfolio allocations, 1995–2002, percentage of GDP.

Source: European Central Bank, Federal Reserve Board, and Bank of Japan.

cross-holdings of shares among European corporations. Finally, Japanese households put significantly more of their savings in banks and Japanese corporations use trade credit much more than do other advanced economies.

Investor Protection and the Development of Financial Markets

What explains the importance of financial markets in some countries, while other countries rely less on markets and more on banks and other financial institutions? One answer is investor protection. Stock and bond markets thrive where investors in these markets are protected reasonably well.

Investors' property rights are much better protected in some parts of the world than others. La Porta, Lopez-de-Silanes, Shleifer, and Vishny have developed quantitative measures of investor protection based on shareholders' and creditors' rights and the quality of law enforcement. Countries with poor scores generally have smaller stock markets, measured by aggregate market value relative to GDP and the number of listed firms and initial public offerings relative to population. Poor scores also mean less debt financing to private firms.[6]

It's easy to understand why poor protection of outside investors stunts the growth of financial markets. The next question is why protection is good in some countries and poor in others. La Porta, Lopez-de-Silanes, Shleifer, and Vishny point to the origin of legal systems.They distinguish legal

[6]R. La Porta, F. Lopez-de-Silanes, A. Shleifer, and R. Vishny, "Legal Determinants of External Finance," *Journal of Finance* 52 (July 1997) pp. 1131–1150; and "Law and Finance," *Journal of Political Economy* 106 (December 1998), pp. 1113–1155.

systems derived from the common-law tradition, which originated in England, from systems based on civil law, which evolved in France, Germany, and Scandinavia. The English, French, and German systems have spread around the world by conquest, imperialism, and imitation. Both shareholders and creditors are better protected in countries that adopted the common-law tradition.

But Rajan and Zingales[7] point out that France, Belgium, and Germany, which are civil-law countries, had well-developed financial markets early in the twentieth century. Relative to GDP, these countries' financial markets were then about the same size as markets in the United Kingdom and bigger than those in the United States. These rankings were reversed in the second half of the century, after World War II, although financial markets are now expanding and playing a greater role in European economies. Rajan and Zingales believe that these reversals can be attributed to political trends and shifts in government policy. For example, they recount the backlash against financial markets after the stock market crash of 1929 and the expansion of government regulation and ownership in the Great Depression and after World War II.

34.2 OWNERSHIP, CONTROL, AND GOVERNANCE

Who owns the corporation? In the United States and United Kingdom, we just say "the stockholders." There is usually just one class of common stock, and each share has one vote. Some stockholders may have more influence than others, but only because they own more shares. In other countries, ownership is not so simple, as we will see later in this section.

What is the corporation's financial objective? Normally we just say "to maximize stockholder value." According to U.S. and U.K. corporation law, managers have a *fiduciary duty* to the shareholders. In other words, they are legally required to act in the interests of shareholders. Consider the classic illustration provided by an early case involving the Ford Motor Company. Henry Ford announced a special dividend, but then reneged, saying that the cash earmarked for the dividend would be spent for the benefit of employees. A shareholder sued on the grounds that corporations existed for the benefit of shareholders and the management did not have the right to improve the lot of workers at shareholders' expense. Ford lost the case.[8]

The idea that the corporation should be run in the interests of the shareholders is thus embedded in the law in the United States and United Kingdom. The board of directors is supposed to represent shareholders' interests. But laws and customs differ in other countries. Now we will look at some of these differences. We start with Japan.

Ownership and Control in India

One notable feature about corporate ownership in India is the concentration of control in the hands of the promoters. One can divide the companies in India into the following four broad categories:

- Companies controlled by the Indian Business Groups
- Companies controlled by Government of India and the different state governments
- Companies controlled by MNCs and NRIs
- Other Companies

[7] R. Rajan and L. Zingales, *Saving Capitalism from the Capitalists* (New York: Crown Business, 2003).

[8] Subsequently it appeared that Henry Ford reneged on the dividend so that he could purchase blocks of shares at depressed prices!

Ninety-three percent of the total corporate assets are controlled by the first three categories of companies leaving aside only 7 percent of the assets for the non-promoter controlled companies. A quick survey of 9703 companies from the Prowess database shows that in July 2006, the Indian Business Groups controlled 38 percent of the total corporate assets, the government controlled companies (both Central and State government) controlled another 48 percent of the total corporate assets. We show the results in Table 34.1 below.

Types of Companies	No. of Companies	Total Assets Controlled (Rs. Crores)	% of Aggregated Assets Controlled
Indian Business Groups	2959	893454.61	38
Top 50 Indian Business Groups	1151	452590.35	19
Government Controlled Companies	462	1121816.48	48
Foreign Companies	593	153373.82	7
Other Companies	5689	171307.64	7
Total	9703	2339952.55	100

TABLE 34.1

Types of Indian Companies and assets controlled by them.

Source: Compiled from Prowess database

Shareholders	Indian Business Groups Controlled Companies(%)	Government Controlled Companies (%)	Foreign Companies (%)
Promoters	51.86	64.71	63.01
Mutual Funds	2.40	1.95	2.37
Banks and Insurance Companies	5.18	8.24	2.92
FIIs	3.64	6.06	2.95
Public	23.85	13.18	19.68
Others	13.07	5.86	9.06
Total	100	100	100

TABLE 34.2

Shareholding Pattern in Indian Companies.

Source: Compiled from Prowess database

From Table 34.2 we can see that promoters control most of the shares in the respective companies. Thus for example, Indian promoters control 52 percent of the shares in the companies managed by them. Promoters in the foreign companies and government-controlled companies control about 64 percent of the shares leaving aside only 36 percent of the shares to be controlled by others.

This gives tremendous power to the promoters as they can pass any ordinary resolution in the company irrespective of whether the other shareholders agree to it or not. This also makes the market for corporate control virtually ineffective in disciplining the management. That is why, we normally observe mergers taking place between companies belonging to the same business groups in India. In only about 6 percent of the mergers that have taken place between 1991 and 2000, the promoters of the merged and merging companies are different.

Though the average stake of the Indian promoters is about 52 percent, in about 15 percent of the companies, the promoters control less than 30 percent of the total shares. In about 30 percent of the companies, the promoters control less than 40 percent of the shares. The promoters in such companies, however manage to maintain their control over such company because of the tacit support they receive from the financial institutions. The Indian business groups also manage to control the different group companies by effectively using the concept of **cross-holdings**. This way the promoter can increase its stake in the different companies indirectly without having to spend anything while acquiring the shares. Thus for example, in 2006, Tata Sons had 20.04 percent stake in Tata Steel and 21.98 percent stake in Tata Motors. Tata Steel had 8.46 percent stake in Tata Motors and Tata Motors in turn had 4.66 percent stake in Tata Steel. We show this cross-holding pattern here.

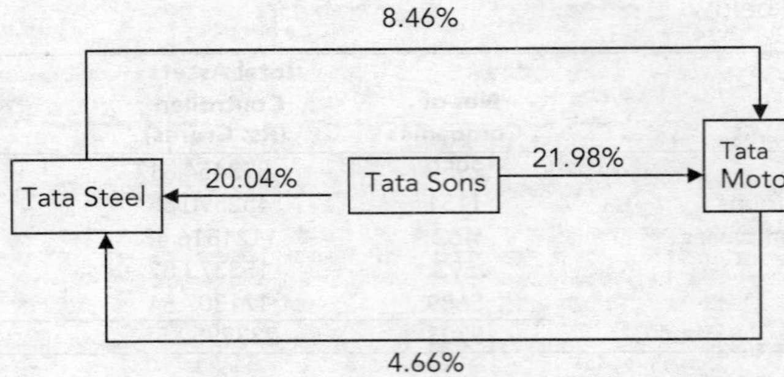

In emerging markets like India, some of the institutions like capital market or labor market are not well-developed. As we discussed in Chapter 33, the successful business groups have managed to create shareholders' wealth by performing the role of these institutions. It has a negative side also. As we discussed in Chapter 1, there is always a conflict of interest between the minority shareholders and the promoters and hence the promoters may take investment decisions that are not in the overall interest of the company.

Ownership and Control in Japan

The most notable feature of Japanese corporate finance is the **keiretsu.** A keiretsu is a network of companies, usually organized around a major bank. Japan is said to have a *main bank* system, with long-standing relationships between banks and firms. There are also long-standing business relationships between a keiretsu's companies. For example, a manufacturing company might buy most of its raw materials from group suppliers and in turn sell much of its output to other group companies.

The bank and other financial institutions at the keiretsu's center own shares in most of the group companies (though a commercial bank in Japan is limited to 5 percent ownership of each company). Those companies may in turn hold the bank's shares or each others' shares. See, for example, the cross-holdings in 2000 among Sumitomo Bank, the Sumitomo Corporation (a trading company), and Sumitomo Trust, which concentrates on investment management:

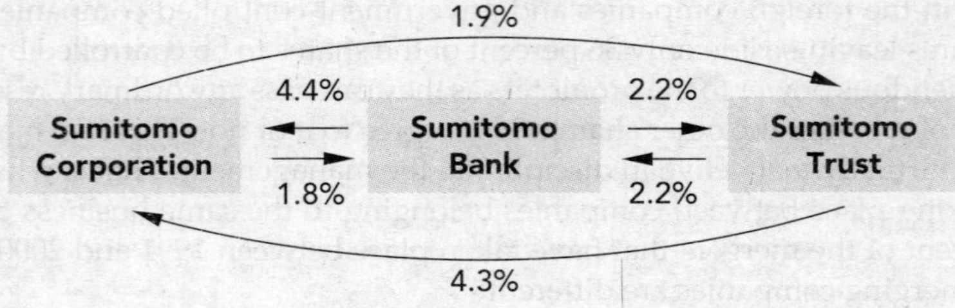

Thus, the bank owns 4.8 percent of Sumitomo Corporation, which owns 1.8 percent of the bank. Both own shares in Sumitomo Trust . . . and so on. Table 34.3 illustrates the myriad of cross-holdings in the Sumitomo keiretsu. Because of the cross-holdings, the number of shares available for purchase by outside investors is much lower than the total number outstanding.

The keiretsu is tied together in other ways. Most debt financing comes from the keiretsu's main bank or from affiliated financial institutions. Managers may sit on the boards of directors of other group companies, and a "presidents' council" of the CEOs of the most important group companies meets regularly.

Think of the keiretsu as a system of corporate governance, where power is divided among the main bank, the group's largest companies, and the group as a whole. This confers certain financial advantages. First, firms have access to additional "internal" financing—internal to the group, that is. Thus a company with a capital budget exceeding operating cash flows can turn to the main bank or other keiretsu companies for financing. This avoids the cost or possible bad-news signal of a public sale of securities. Second, when a keiretsu firm falls into financial distress, with insufficient cash to pay its bills or fund necessary capital investments, a workout can usually be arranged. New management can be brought in from elsewhere in the group, and financing can be obtained, again "internally."

Hoshi, Kashyap, and Scharfstein tracked capital expenditure programs of a large sample of Japanese firms—many, but not all, members of keiretsus. The keiretsu companies' investments were more stable and less exposed to the ups and downs of operating cash flows or to episodes of financial distress.[9] It seems that the financial support of the keiretsus enabled members to invest for the long run, regardless of temporary setbacks.

Shareholder	Sumitomo Bank	Sumitomo Trust	Sumitomo Corporation	Sumitomo Metal Industries	Sumitomo Chemical	NEC
S. Bank	—	2.2	4.4	3.4	4.7	3.0
S. Trust	2.2	—	4.3	6.8	5.0	3.2
S. Corporation	1.8	1.9	—	2.1		
S. Metal Industries				—		
S. Chemical					—	—
NEC		1.9	2.7			
Other S. Group	7.5	3.8	9.5	4.3	7.8	6.8
Total	11.5	9.8	20.9	16.6	17.5	13.0

TABLE 34.3

Cross-holdings of common stock among six companies in the Sumitomo Group in 2000 (percentage of shares outstanding). Read down the columns to see holdings of each of the companies by the five others. Thus 4.6 percent of Sumitomo Metal Industries was held by Sumitomo Bank, 6.8 percent by Sumitomo Trust, 2.1 percent by Sumitomo Corporation, and 4.3 percent by other Sumitomo Group companies not included in the table. The data for this table reflect only the 10 largest share holdings in each company.

Source: Compiled from *Industrial Groupings in Japan: The Changing Face of Keiretsu* (Tokyo: Brown & Co. Ltd., 2001).

[9] T. Hoshi, A. Kashyap, and D. Scharfstein, "Corporate Structure, Liquidity and Investment: Evidence from Japanese Industrial Groups," *Quarterly Journal of Economics* 106 (February 1991), pp. 33–60; and "The Role of Banks in Reducing the Costs of Financial Distress in Japan," *Journal of Financial Economics* 27 (September 1990), pp. 67–88.

Corporation law in Japan resembles that in the United States, but there are some important differences. For example, in Japan it is easier for shareholders to nominate and elect directors. Also, management remuneration must be approved at general meetings of shareholders.[10] Nevertheless, ordinary shareholders do not in fact have much influence. Japanese boards may have 40 or 50 members, with only a handful who are potentially independent of management.[11] The CEO effectively controls nominations to the board. As long as the financial position of a Japanese corporation is sound, the CEO and senior management control the corporation. Outside stockholders have very little influence.

Given this control, plus the cross-holdings within industrial groups, it's no surprise that takeovers are exceedingly rare in Japan. Also, Japanese corporations have been stingy with dividends, which probably reflects the relative lack of influence of outside shareholders. On the other hand, Japanese CEOs do not use their power to generate large sums of personal wealth. They are not well paid, compared to CEOs in most other developed countries. (Look back to Figure 12.1 for average top-management compensation levels for Japan and other countries.)

Ownership and Control in Germany

Figure 34.5 summarizes the ownership in 1990 of Daimler-Benz, one of the largest German companies.[12] The immediate owners were Deutsche Bank, the largest German Bank, with 28 percent; Mercedes Automobil Holding, with 25 percent; and the Kuwait government, with 14 percent. The remaining 32 percent of the shares were widely held by about 300,000 individual and institutional investors.

But this was only the top layer. Mercedes Automobil Holding was half owned by two holding companies, "Stella" and "Stern" for short. The rest of its shares were widely held. Stella's shares were in turn split four ways: between two banks; Robert Bosch, an industrial company; and another holding company, "Komet." Stern's ownership was split four ways too, but we ran out of space.[13]

The differences between German and U.S. ownership patterns leap out from Figure 34.5. Note the concentration of ownership of Daimler-Benz shares in large blocks and the several layers of owners. A similar figure for General Motors would just say "General Motors, 100 percent widely held."

In Germany these blocks are held by other companies or by holding companies on behalf of families. Franks and Mayer, who examined the ownership of 171 large companies in 1990, found 47 with blocks of shares held by other companies and 35 with blocks owned by families. Only 26 of the companies did not have a substantial block of stock held by some company or institution.[14]

Note also the bank ownership of Daimler-Benz. This would be impossible in the United States, where federal law prohibits equity investment by banks in nonfinancial corporations. Germany's *universal banking* system allows such investments. In addition, German banks customarily hold shares for safekeeping on behalf of individual and institutional investors and usually acquire proxies to vote these shares on the investors' behalf. For example, Deutsche Bank held 28 percent of

---

[10]These requirements have led to a unique feature of Japanese corporate life, the *sokaiya,* who are racketeers who demand payment in exchange for not disrupting shareholders' meetings.

[11]In recent years some Japanese companies such as Sony have changed to U.S.-style boards with fewer members and more independent directors.

[12]Corporate ownership in Germany is typical of continental Europe. For example, an ownership diagram for a large French company would resemble Figure 34.5. See J. Franks and C. Mayer, "Corporate Ownership and Control in the U.K., Germany and France," *Journal of Applied Corporate Finance* 9 (Winter 1997), pp. 30–45.

[13]A five-layer ownership tree for Daimler-Benz is given in S. Prowse, "Corporate Governance in an International Perspective: A Survey of Corporate Control Mechanisms among Large Firms in the U.S., U.K., Japan and Germany," *Financial Markets, Institutions, and Instruments* 4 (February 1995), Table 16.

[14]See J. Franks and C. Mayer, "The Ownership and Control of German Corporations," *Review of Financial Studies* 14 (Winter 2001), Table 1, p. 947.

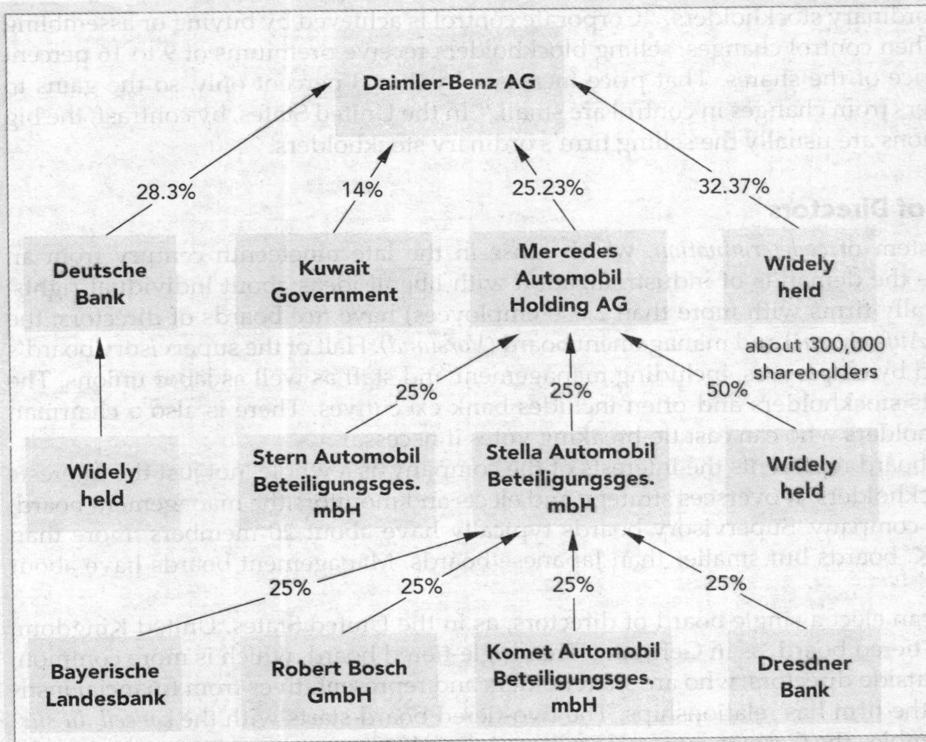

FIGURE 34.5

Ownership of Daimler-Benz, 1990.

Source: J. Franks and C. Mayer, "The Ownership and Control of German Corporations," *Review of Financial Studies* 14 (Winter 2001), Figure 1, p. 949. Reprinted by permission of the Oxford University Press.

Daimler-Benz for its own account and had proxies for 14 percent more. Therefore, it *voted* 42 percent, which approaches a majority.

German banks have close ties with industry. They form long-run relationships with firms, not only because of the loans they make and the shares they own directly but also because of the proxies they are able to exercise. This *hausbank* system can provide effective outside monitoring and reduce agency problems between the firm's managers and its ultimate owners.[15] But the banks may have their own agency problems. In effect, they control themselves; at one point in the 1990s, Deutsche Bank held voting rights for 47 percent of its own shares. Dresdner Bank voted 59 percent of its shares and Commerzbank voted 30 percent of its shares.[16]

Daimler-Benz, now DaimlerChrysler, is an interesting case study of the effects of globalization on firms and financial markets. In the mid-1990s it reversed an unsuccessful diversification strategy that had led it into several other industries, including aerospace and defense. In 1998 it took over Chrysler. It listed its shares on the New York Stock Exchange and issued financial statements conforming to U.S. accounting standards. It turned to international capital markets for financing, including a share issue in the United States. At the same time Deutsche Bank was reducing its stake in the company. DaimlerChrysler has formally announced a commitment to increasing shareholder value.

Nevertheless, the multilayered ownership structures as in Figure 34.5 are still common for large German corporations. Control rests mainly with banks, insurance companies, and holders of blocks

[15]See R. Elsas and J. P. Krahnen, "Universal Banks and Relationships with Firms," in J. P. Krahnen and R. H. Schmidt (eds.), *The German Financial System* (Oxford: Oxford University Press, 2004), pp. 197–232.

[16]J. Charkham, *Keeping Good Company: A Study of Corporate Governance in Five Countries* (Oxford: Clarendon Press, 1994).

of shares, not with ordinary stockholders.[17] Corporate control is achieved by buying or assembling blocks of shares. When control changes, selling blockholders receive premiums of 9 to 16 percent over the trading price of the shares. That price increases by 2 or 3 percent only, so the gains to ordinary stockholders from changes in control are small.[18] In the United States, by contrast, the big winners in acquisitions are usually the selling firm's ordinary stockholders.

European Boards of Directors

Germany has a system of *codetermination,* which arose in the late nineteenth century from an attempt to reconcile the demands of industrialization with liberal ideas about individual rights. Larger firms (generally firms with more than 2,000 employees) have *two* boards of directors: the supervisory board *(Aufsichtsrat)* and management board *(Vorstand).* Half of the supervisory board's members are elected by employees, including management and staff as well as labor unions. The other half represents stockholders and often includes bank executives. There is also a chairman appointed by stockholders who can cast tie-breaking votes if necessary.

The supervisory board represents the interests of the company as a whole, not just the interests of employees or stockholders. It oversees strategy and elects and monitors the management board, which operates the company. Supervisory boards typically have about 20 members, more than typical U.S. and U.K. boards but smaller than Japanese boards. Management boards have about 10 members.

In France, firms can elect a single board of directors, as in the United States, United Kingdom, and Japan, or a two-tiered board, as in Germany. The single-tiered board, which is more common, consists mostly of outside directors, who are shareholders and representatives from financial institutions with which the firm has relationships. The two-tiered board starts with the *conseil du surveillance,* which resembles the German supervisory board. Employees are not represented directly, although workers' representatives have the right to attend board meetings as observers in all companies with at least 50 employees. This conseil du surveillance appoints the *directoire,* which is responsible for the management of the company.

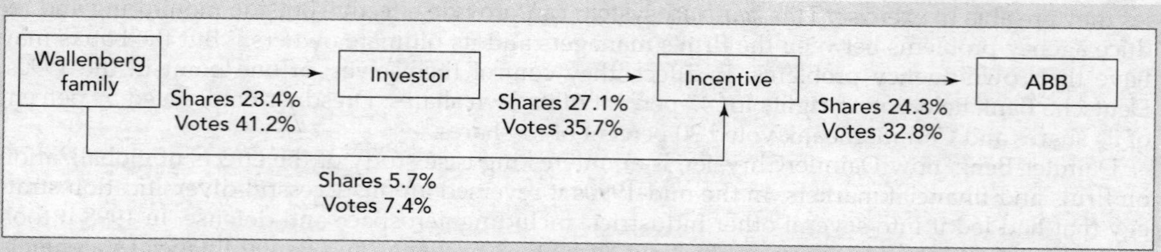

FIGURE 34.6

The pyramid that controls ABB, one of Sweden's largest companies.

Source: R. La Porta, F. Lopez-Silanes, and A. Shleifer, "Corporate Ownership Around the World," *Journal of Finance* 54 (April 1999), Figure 8, p. 488. Reprinted by permission from Blackwell Publishers Journal Rights.

[17]For example, the largest five stockholders in a sample of German companies controlled about 42 percent of outstanding shares on average, compared to 25 percent in the U.S., 21 percent in the U.K., and 33 percent in Japan. Also, about 25 percent of the German companies were majority owned by a *single* stockholder. See Prowse, *op. cit.,* Tables 9 and 10, pp. 25, 29.

[18]Franks and Mayer, op. cit., Table 9, p. 969.

Ownership and Control in Other Countries

La Porta, Lopez-de-Silanes, and Shleifer surveyed corporate ownership in 27 developed economies.[19] They found relatively few firms with actively traded shares and dispersed ownership. The German pattern of significant ownership by banks and other financial institutions is also uncommon. Instead, firms are typically controlled by wealthy families or the state. The ultimate controlling shareholders typically have secure voting control even when they do not have the majority stake in earnings, dividends, or asset values.

	Number of Firms in Sample	Control[a]			Percentage of Assets[b] Controlled by Top 10 Families
		Family	State	Widely Held	
Hong Kong	330	66.7%	1.4%	7.0%	32.1%
Indonesia	178	71.5	8.2	5.1	57.7
Japan	1,240	9.7	0.8	79.8	2.4
Korea	345	48.4	1.6	43.2	36.8
Malaysia	238	67.2	13.4	10.3	24.8
Philippines	120	44.6	2.1	19.2	52.5
Singapore	221	55.4	23.5	5.4	26.6
Taiwan	141	48.2	2.8	26.2	18.4
Thailand	167	61.6	8.0	6.6	46.2

TABLE 34.4

Family control in Asia.

[a]"Control" means ownership of shares with at least 20 percent of voting rights. Percentages controlled by widely held financial institutions or corporations are not reported.
[b]Percentage of total assets of all sample firms in each country.
Source: S. Claessens, S. Djankov, and L. H. P. Lang, "The Separation of Ownership and Control in East Asian Corporations," *Journal of Financial Economics* 58 (October/November 2000), Table 6, p. 103, and Table 9, p. 108.

Family control is common in Europe and also in Asia. Table 34.4 summarizes a study by Claessens, Djankov, and Lang, who traced ownership in 1996 for a sample of nearly 3,000 Asian companies. Except in Japan, a high proportion of public firms were family controlled. Thus wealthy families control large fractions of many Asian economies. For example, in Hong Kong, the 10 largest family groups control 32 percent of the assets of all listed firms. In Thailand, the top 10 families control 46 percent of assets. In Indonesia, they control nearly 58 percent of assets.

Family control does not usually mean a direct majority stake in the public firm. Control is usually exercised by cross-shareholdings, pyramids, and dual-class shares. We have already seen an example of cross-holdings in Table 34.3. Pyramids and dual-class shares need further explanation.

Pyramids Pyramids are common in Asian countries as well as several European countries.[20] In a pyramid, control is exercised through a sequence of controlling positions in several layers of companies. The actual operating companies are at the bottom of the pyramid. Above each operating

[19]R. La Porta, F. Lopez-de-Silanes, and A. Shleifer, "Corporate Ownership around the World," *Journal of Finance* 54 (1999), pp. 471–517.

[20]L. A. Bebchuk, R. Kraakman, and G. R. Triantis, "Stock Pyramids, Cross-Ownership, and Dual Class Equity," in R. Morck (ed.), *Concentrated Corporate Ownership* (Chicago: University of Chicago Press, 2000), pp. 295–318.

company is a first holding company, then a second one, then perhaps others still higher in the pyramid.[21] Consider a three-tier pyramid and a single operating company. Assume that 51 percent of the votes confer control at each tier. Suppose that the second holding company—the highest one in the pyramid—holds a 51 percent controlling stake in a lower holding company, which in turn holds a 51 percent controlling stake in the operating company. A 51 percent stake in the highest holding company is really only a 26 percent stake in the operating company ($.51 \times .51 = .26$, or 26 percent). Thus an investor in the top holding company could control an operating company worth $100 million with an investment of only $26 million. By adding another layer, the required investment falls to $.51 \times 26 =$ $13 million.

Usually less than 51 percent of shares are needed for effective control, so the shareholders of the topmost holding company may be able to maintain control with an even smaller investment. Figure 34.6 shows how the Wallenberg family controls ABB, one of Sweden's largest companies. ABB, the operating company, is shown at the right of the diagram. ABB is controlled by Incentive, which holds 24 percent of ABB's shares but controls about 33 percent of the shareholder votes. Incentive is in turn controlled by Investor, an investment holding company, and by the Wallenberg family directly. The family also holds about 41 percent of Investor. At each stage the family's voting control is at least 33 percent, which is amply sufficient to control the next layer of the pyramid.[22]

Australia	.23	Italy	.29
Brazil	.23	Korea	.48
Canada	.03	Mexico	.36
Chile	.23	Norway	.06
Denmark	.01	South Africa	.07
Finland	.00	Sweden	.01
France	.28	Switzerland	.06
Germany	.09	U.K.	.10
Hong Kong	−.03	U.S.	.02

TABLE 34.5

The value of control-block votes as a proportion of firm value.

Source: T. Nenova, "The Value of Corporate Voting Rights and Control: A Cross-Country Analysis," *Journal of Financial Economics* 68 (June 2003), Table 4, p. 336.

Dual-Class Equity Another way to maintain control is to hold stock with extra voting rights. (Note the voting rights at each level of the pyramid in Figure 34.6.) Extra votes can be attached to a special class of shares. For example, a firm's Class A shares could have 10 votes and the Class B shares only 1. *Dual-class equity* occurs frequently in many countries, including Brazil, Canada, Denmark, Finland, Germany, Italy, Mexico, Norway, South Korea, Sweden, and Switzerland. Stocks with different voting rights also occur (but less frequently) in Australia, Chile, France, Hong Kong, South Africa, the United Kingdom, and the United States. For example, the Ford Motor Company is still controlled by the Ford family, who hold a special class of shares with 40 percent of the voting power. Dual-class equity is forbidden in Belgium, China, Japan, Singapore, and Spain.

[21]A holding company is a firm whose only assets are controlling blocks of shares in other companies.

[22]Figure 34.6 shows only part of the Wallenberg group's holdings. The group controls companies whose shares account for about 50 percent of the value of the Stockholm Stock Exchange. See J. Agnblad, E. Berglof, P. Hogfeld, and H. Svancar, "Ownership and Control in Sweden: Strong Owners, Weak Minorities and Social Control," in F. Barca and M. Becht (eds.), *The Control of Corporate Europe* (Oxford: Oxford University Press, 2001).

As we briefly discussed in Chapter 14, there is a wide variation in the value of votes across countries. Table 34.5 shows Tatiana Nenova's estimates of the value of controlling blocks in different countries, calculated as a fraction of firms' market values.[23] These values are calculated from the differences in prices between ordinary shares and shares with extra votes. The range of values is large. For example, the Scandinavian countries have uniformly low premiums for control. South Korea and Mexico have very high control premiums.

Why is shareholder control valuable? For two reasons, one positive and one negative. The controlling-shareholder may maximize value by monitoring management and making sure that the firm pursues the best operating and investment strategies. On the other hand, a controlling shareholder may be tempted to *capture* value by extracting private benefits at other shareholders' expense.

Conglomerates Revisited

Of course there are also examples of U.S. companies that are controlled by families or by investors holding large blocks of stock. But in these cases control is exercised for a single firm, not a group of firms. Elsewhere in the world, and particularly in countries without fully developed financial markets, control extends to groups of firms in several different industries. These industrial groups are really conglomerates.

In Korea, for example, the 10 largest conglomerates control roughly two-thirds of the corporate economy. These *chaebols* are also strong exporters: names like Samsung and Hyundai are recognized worldwide. Conglomerates are also common in Latin America. One of the more successful, the Chilean holding company Quinenco, is a dizzying variety of businesses, including hotels and brewing, mobile telephone services, banking, and the manufacture of copper cable. Widely diversified groups are also common in India. The largest, the Tata Group, spans 80 companies in various industries, including steel, electric power, real estate, telecommunications, and financial services. All of these companies are public, but control rests with the group and ultimately with the Tata family.

The United States had a conglomerate merger wave in the 1960s and 1970s, but diversification didn't deliver value in the longer run, and most of the conglomerates of that era have dissolved. But conglomerates survive and grow in developing economies. Why?

Family ownership is part of the answer. A wealthy family can reduce risk, while maintaining control, expanding the family business into new industries. Of course the family could also diversify by buying shares of other companies. But where financial markets are limited and investor protection is poor, internal diversification may come before financial diversification. Of course internal diversification means running an internal capital market, but if a country's financial markets and institutions are substandard, an internal capital market may not be so bad after all.

"Substandard" does not just mean lack of scale or trading activity. It may mean government regulations limiting access to bank financing or requiring government approval before bonds or shares are issued.[24] It may mean poor information. If accounting standards are loose and companies are secretive, monitoring by outside investors becomes especially costly and difficult, and agency costs proliferate.

Internal diversification may also be the only practical way to grow. You can't be big *and* focused in a small, closed economy, because the scale of one-industry companies is limited by the local

[23] T. Nenova, "The Value of Corporate Voting Rights and Control: A Cross-Country Analysis," *Journal of Financial Economics* 68 (June 2003), pp. 325–351.

[24] In the United States, the SEC does *not* have the power to deny share issues. Its mandate is only to assure that investors are given adequate information.

market. Size can be an advantage if larger companies have easier access to international financial markets. This is important if local financial markets are inefficient.

Size also means political power, which is especially important in managed economies or in countries where the government economic policy is unpredictable. In Korea, for example, the government has controlled access to bank loans. Bank lending has been directed to government-approved uses. The Korean conglomerate chaebols have usually been first in line.

Many widely diversified business groups have been efficient and successful, particularly in countries like Korea that have grown rapidly. But there is also a dark side. Sometimes conglomerate business groups *tunnel* resources between the group companies at the expense of outside minority shareholders. Group company X can transfer value to Y by lending it money at a low interest rate, buying some of Y's output at high prices or selling X's assets to Y at low prices. Bertrand, Mehta, and Mullainathan found evidence of widespread tunneling in India.[25] Johnson, Boone, Breach, and Friedman note that the temptation to tunnel is stronger during a recession or financial crisis and argue that tunneling—and poor corporate governance in general—contributed to the Asian crisis of 1997–1998.[26]

34.3 DO THESE DIFFERENCES MATTER?

A good financial system appears to accelerate economic growth.[27] In fact, at least rudimentary finance may be necessary for any growth at all. Raghu Rajan and Luigi Zingales give the example of a bamboo-stool maker in Bangladesh, who needed 22 cents to buy the raw materials for each stool. Unfortunately, she did not have the 22 cents and had to borrow it from middlemen. She was forced to sell back the stools to the lenders in repayment for the loans and was left with only 2 cents' profit. Because of a lack of finance, she was never able to break out of this cycle of poverty. In contrast, they give the example of Kevin Taweel and Jim Ellis, two Stanford MBAs, who were able to purchase their own business soon after graduating. They had insufficient capital of their own but were able to raise seed funding to search for the right acquisition, and then additional funding to complete it.[28] Taweel and Ellis were the beneficiaries of a modern financial system, including a sophisticated private equity market.

It is easy to understand the connection between financial and economic development by considering a very simple financial decision. Suppose you need to decide whether to extend credit to a small business. If you are in the United States, you can almost instantaneously pull down a Dun and Bradstreet report via the Internet on any one of 10 million businesses. This report will show the company's financial statements, the average size of its bank balances, and whether it pays its bills on time. You will also receive an overall credit score for the company. Such widely available credit information reduces the cost of lending and increases the availability of credit. It also means that no one lender has a monopoly of information, which increases competition among suppliers of credit and reduces the costs to borrowers.

---

[25]M. Bertrand, P. Mehta, and S. Mullainathan, "Ferreting out Tunneling: An Application to Indian Business Groups," *Quarterly Journal of Economics* 117 (February 2002), pp. 121–148.

[26]S. Johnson, P. Boone, A. Breach, and E. Friedman, "Corporate Governance in the Asian Financial Crisis," *Journal of Financial Economics* 58 (October/November 2000), pp. 141–186.

[27]R. Levine, "Financial Development and Economic Growth: Views and Agenda," *Journal of Economic Literature* 35 (1997), pp. 688–726; and R. Rajan and L. Zingales, "Financial Dependence and Growth," *American Economic Review* 88 (1998), pp. 559–586.

[28]R. Rajan and L. Zingales, *Saving Capitalism from the Capitalists* (New York: Crown Business, 2003), pp. 4–8.

Of course finance matters. But does the nature of a country's financial system matter as long as it is advanced? Does it matter whether a developed country has a market-based or bank-based system? Both types are effective, but each has potential advantages.

Risk and Short-termism

If you look back to Figure 34.2, you will see that in different countries the amount of risk borne by households from their financial portfolios varies significantly. At one extreme is Japan. Here households hold over half of their financial assets in bank accounts. Much of the remainder is in insurance and pension funds, which in Japan mainly make fixed payments and are not linked to the stock market. Only a small proportion of household portfolios are linked to the stock market and to the business risk of Japanese corporations. European households also have relatively little direct exposure to the risks of the corporate sector. At the other extreme, households in the United States have large investments in shares and mutual funds.

Of course someone has to bear business risks. The risks that are not borne directly by households are passed on to banks and other financial institutions, and finally to the government. In most countries, the government guarantees bank deposits either explicitly or implicitly. If the banks get into trouble, the government steps in and society as a whole bears the burden.[29]

Some people argue that firms are free to "invest for the long run" in bank-based systems where financial institutions absorb business risks and few individuals invest directly in the stock market. The close ties of Japanese and German companies to banks are supposed to prevent the dreaded disease of *short-termism*. Firms in the United States and United Kingdom are supposedly held captive by shareholders' demands for quick payoffs and therefore have to deliver quick earnings growth at the expense of long-term competitive advantage. Many found this argument persuasive in the late 1980s when the Japanese and German economies were especially robust.[30] But market-based economies surged ahead in the 1990s, and views have changed accordingly.

Growth Industries and Declining Industries

Market-based systems seem to be particularly successful in developing brand-new industries. For example, railways were first developed in the United Kingdom in the nineteenth century, financed largely through the London Stock Exchange. In the twentieth century, the United States led development of mass production in the automobile industry, even though the automobile was invented in Germany. The commercial aircraft industry was also mainly developed in the United States, as was the computer industry after World War II, and more recently the biotechnology and Internet industries.[31] On the other hand, Germany and Japan, two countries with bank-based financial systems, have sustained their competitive advantages in established industries. Recent examples include automobiles in both countries and electronics in Japan.

---

[29]Another possibility is that banks that take a long-run view and are not subject to intense competition can smooth risk across different generations by building up reserves when returns are high and running them down when returns are low. Competition from financial markets prevents this type of intergenerational risk sharing. Generations with high returns want to receive their full returns and will not be willing to have reserves built up. See F. Allen and D. Gale, "Financial Markets, Intermediaries, and Intertemporal Smoothing," *Journal of Political Economy* 105 (June 1997), pp. 523–546.

[30]See M. Porter, "Capital Disadvantage: America's Failing Capital Investment System," *Harvard Business Review*, (September/October 1992), pp. 65–82.

[31]There are counter examples, such as the development of the chemical industry on a large scale in nineteenth-century Germany.

Why are financial markets better at fostering innovative industries?[32] When new products or processes are discovered, there is a wide diversity of opinion about the prospects for a new industry and the best way to develop it. Financial markets accommodate this diversity, allowing young, ambitious companies to search out like-minded investors to fund their growth. This is less likely when financing has to come through a few major banks.

Market-based systems also seem to be more effective at forcing companies in declining industries to shrink and release capital.[33] When a company cannot earn its cost of capital and further growth would destroy value, stock price drops, and the drop sends a clear negative signal. But in bank-based financial systems, uneconomic firms are often bailed out. When Mazda faltered in the 1970s, Sumitomo Bank guaranteed Mazda's debts and orchestrated a rescue, in part by exhorting employees within its keiretsu to purchase Mazda cars. Sumitomo Bank had an incentive to undertake the rescue, because it knew that it would keep Mazda's business when it recovered. In the 1990s, Japanese banks continued to lend to "zombie" firms long after it became clear that prospects for their recovery were hopeless. For example, a coalition of banks kept the Japanese retailer Sogo afloat for years, despite clear evidence of insolvency. When Sogo finally failed in 2000, its debts had accumulated to ¥1.9 trillion.[34]

Transparency and Governance

Despite all the advantages of market-based systems, serious accidents happen. Think of the many sudden, costly corporate meltdowns after the telecom and dot.com boom of the late 1990s. In the last chapter we noted the $100 billion bankruptcy of WorldCom (now reorganized as MCI). But the most notorious meltdown was Enron, which failed in late 2001.

Enron started as a gas pipeline company, but expanded rapidly into trading energy and commodities, and made large investments in electricity generation, broadband communications, and water companies. By the end of 2000, its total stock market value was about $60 billion. A year later, it was bankrupt. But that $60 billion wasn't really lost when Enron failed, because most of that value wasn't there in the first place. By late 2001, Enron was in many ways an empty shell. Its stock price was supported more by investors' enthusiasm than by profitable operating businesses. The company had also accumulated large hidden debts. For example, Enron borrowed aggressively through *special purpose entities* (SPEs). The SPE debts were not reported on its balance sheet, even though the SPEs did not meet the requirements for off-balance-sheet accounting. (The fall of Enron also brought down its accounting firm, Arthur Andersen.)

The bad news started to leak out in the last months of 2001. In October, Enron announced a $1 billion write-down of its water and broadband businesses. In November, it consolidated its SPEs retroactively, which increased the debt on its balance sheet by $658 million and reduced past earnings by $591 million.[35] Its public debt was downgraded to junk ratings on November 28 and on December 2 it filed for bankruptcy.

---

[32]See F. Allen and D. Gale, "Diversity of Opinion and the Financing of New Technologies," *Journal of Financial Intermediation* 8 (April 1999), pp. 68–89.

[33]See R. Rajan and L. Zingales, "Banks and Markets: The Changing Character of European Finance," in *European Central Bank 2nd Annual Conference*, 2003.

[34]T. Hoshi and A. Kashyap, "Japan's Financial Crisis and Economic Stagnation," *Journal of Economic Perspectives* 18 (Winter 2004), pp. 3–26.

[35]Enron faced many further financial problems. For example, it told investors that it had hedged business risks in SPE transactions, but failed to say that many of the SPEs were backed up by pledges of Enron shares. When Enron's stock price fell, the hedges unraveled. See P. Healy and K. Palepu, "The Fall of Enron," *Journal of Economic Perspectives* 17 (Spring 2003), pp. 3–26.

Enron demonstrated the importance of *transparency* in market-based financial systems. If a firm is transparent to outside investors—if the investors can see its true profitability and prospects—then problems will show up right away in a falling stock price. That in turn generates extra scrutiny from security analysts, bond rating agencies, and investors. It may also lead to a takeover.

With transparency, corporate troubles generally lead to corrective action. But the top management of a troubled opaque company may be able to maintain its stock price and postpone the discipline of the market. Market discipline caught up with Enron only a month or two before bankruptcy.

Opaqueness is not so dangerous in a bank-based system. Firms will have long-standing relationships with banks, which can monitor the firm closely and urge it to staunch losses or to cancel excessively risky strategies. But no financial system can avoid occasional corporate meltdowns.

Parmalat, the Italian food company, appeared to be a solidly profitable firm with good growth prospects. It had expanded around the world, and by 2003 was operating in 30 countries with 36,000 employees. It reported about €2 billion in debt but also claimed to hold large portfolios of cash and short-term liquid securities. But doubts about the company's financial strength began to accumulate. On December 19, 2003, it was revealed that a €3.9 billion bank deposit reported by Parmalat had never existed. Parmalat's stock price fell by 80 percent in two weeks, and it was placed in administration (the Italian bankruptcy process) on December 24. Investors learned later that Parmalat's true debts exceeded €14 billion, that additional billions of euros of asset value had disappeared into a black hole, and that its sales and earnings had been overstated.

It's nice to dream of a financial system that would completely protect investors against nasty surprises like Enron and Parmalat. Complete protection of investors is impossible, however. In fact, complete protection would be unwise and inefficient even if it were feasible. Why? Because outside investors cannot know everything that managers are doing or why they are doing it. Laws and regulations can specify what managers can't do but can't tell them what they should do. Therefore managers have to be given discretion to act in response to unanticipated problems and opportunities.

Once managers have discretion, they will consider their self-interest as well as investors' interests. Agency problems are inevitable. The best a financial system can do is to protect investors reasonably well and to try to keep managers' and investors' interests congruent. We have discussed agency problems at several points in this book, but it won't hurt to reiterate the mechanisms that keep these problems under control:

- Laws and regulations that protect outside investors from self-dealing by insiders.
- Disclosure requirements and accounting standards that keep public firms reasonably transparent.
- Monitoring by banks and other financial intermediaries.
- Monitoring by boards of directors.
- The threat of takeover (although takeovers are very rare in some countries).
- Compensation tied to earnings and stock price.

In this chapter we have stressed the importance of investor protection for the development of financial markets. But don't assume that more protection for investors is always a good thing. A corporation is a kind of partnership between outside investors and the managers and employees who operate the firm. The managers and employees are investors too: they commit human capital instead of financial capital. A successful firm requires coinvestment of human and financial capital.

If you give the financial capital too much power, the human capital doesn't show up—or if it does show up, it won't be properly motivated.[36]

[36]It is difficult to observe effort and the value of human capital, and therefore difficult to set up compensation schemes that reward effort and human capital appropriately. Thus it can be better to allow managers some leeway to act in their own interests to preserve their incentives. Stockholders can provide this leeway by relaxing some of their rights and committing not to interfere if managers and employees capture private benefits when the firm is successful. How to commit? One way is to take the firm public. Direct intervention by public stockholders in the operation of the firm is difficult and therefore rare. See M. Burkart, D. Gromb, and F. Panunzi, "Large Shareholders, Monitoring and the Value of the Firm," *Quarterly Journal of Economics* 112 (1997), pp. 693–728; S. Myers, "Outside Equity," *Journal of Finance* 55 (June 2000), pp. 1005–1037; and S. Myers, "Financial Architecture," *European Financial Management* 5 (July 1999), pp. 133–142.

SUMMARY

It's customary to distinguish market-based and bank-based financial systems. The United States has a market-based system, because it has large stock and bond markets. The United Kingdom also has a market-based system: its bond market is less important, but the U.K. stock market still plays a crucial role in corporate finance and governance. Germany and Japan have bank-based systems, because most debt financing comes from banks and these countries' stock markets are less important.

Of course the simple distinction between banks and markets is far from the end of the story. For example:

- U.K. households tend to hold shares indirectly, through equity-linked insurance and pensions. Direct investment in shares is much less common than in the United States.
- Japanese households bear relatively little equity risk. Most of their savings goes into bank accounts and insurance policies.
- In Europe, large blocks of a company's stock are often held by other corporations.
- In Japan, companies rely heavily on trade-credit financing, that is, on accounts payable to other companies.

In Japan and Germany, the role of banks goes far beyond just lending money. The largest Japanese banks are the hubs of *keiretsus*, large, cooperative groups of firms. Each keiretsu is tied together by long-standing ties to the main bank and by extensive cross-shareholdings within group companies. German banks also have long-standing ties to the their corporate customers (the *hausbank* system). The banks hold large blocks of shares in these companies and end up voting shares held for other investors.

Ownership of large, public corporations in the United States and United Kingdom is pretty simple: there is one class of shares, which trade actively, and ownership is dispersed. In Japan, there is usually one class of shares, but a significant fraction of the shares is locked up in cross-shareholdings within keiretsus. Japanese stockholders have little say in corporate governance. European stockholders likewise have little say, given the concentration of ownership by banks and other corporations.

In the United States and United Kingdom, the law puts shareholders' interests first. Managers and boards of directors have a fiduciary duty to shareholders. But in Germany, the management board, which runs the business, answers to a supervisory board, which represents all employees as well as investors. The company as a whole is supposed to come first.

Outside these major countries, a rather different pattern of ownership emerges. Groups of companies are controlled by families, and sometimes by the state. Control is maintained by cross-shareholdings, by pyramids, and by issue of shares with extra voting rights. Wealthy families control large fractions of the corporate sector in many developing economies. These family groups operate as conglomerates. Conglomerates are a declining species in the United States, but a conglomerate's internal capital market can make sense where financial markets and institutions are not well-developed. The conglomerates' scale and scope may also provide political power, which can add value in countries where the government tries to manage the economy or where laws and regulations are enforced erratically.

Concentrated family control can be a good thing, if it is used to force managers to run a tight ship and focus on value-maximizing investments. But concentration of control can also open the door to tunneling of resources out of the firm at the expense of minority investors.

Protection for outside investors varies greatly around the world. Where protection is good, market-based systems flourish. These systems have certain advantages: they appear to foster innovation and to encourage the release of capital from declining industries. On the other hand, market-based systems may end up investing too much in trendy innovations, as the collapse of the dot.com and telecom boom has recently illustrated. Bank-based systems may be better-suited to established industries. These systems also help shield individuals from direct exposure to stock market risk.

Market-based systems work only when public firms are reasonably transparent to investors. When they are opaque, like Enron, occasional meltdowns can be expected. Bank-based financial systems may have an advantage in monitoring and controlling opaque firms. The banks have long-standing relationships with their corporate customers, and therefore have better information than outside investors.

FURTHER READING

The following studies survey or compare financial systems:

F. Allen and D. Gale, *Comparing Financial Systems* (Cambridge, MA: MIT Press, 2000).

T. Hoshi and A. Kasyap, *Corporate Financing and Governance in Japan: The Road to the Future* (Cambridge, MA: MIT Press, 2001).

J. P. Krahnen and R. H. Schmidt (eds.), *The German Financial System* (Oxford: Oxford University Press, 2004).

R. La Porta, F. Lopez-de-Silanes, and A. Shleifer, "Corporate Ownership around the World," *Journal of Finance* 54 (April 1999), pp. 471–517.

For excellent discussions of corporate governance, see:

M. Becht, P. Bolton, and A. Röell, "Corporate Governance and Control" in G. Constantinides, M. Harris, and R. Stulz (eds.), *Handbook of the Economics of Finance* (Amsterdam: North-Holland, 2003), pp. 1–109.

S. Prowse, "Corporate Governance in an International Perspective: A Survey of Corporate Control Mechanisms among Large Firms in the U.S., U.K., Japan and Germany," *Financial Markets, Institutions, and Instruments* 4 (February 1995), pp. 1–63.

A. Shleifer and R. W. Vishny, "A Survey of Corporate Governance," *Journal of Finance* 52 (June 1997), pp. 737–783.

For discussions of the role of law, politics, and finance see:

R. La Porta, F. Lopez de Silanes, A. Shleifer, and R. Vishny, "Legal Determinants of External Finance," *Journal of Finance* 52 (July 1997), pp. 1131–1150.

R. Rajan and L. Zingales, *Saving Capitalism from the Capitalists* (New York: Crown Business, 2003).

For the evidence on why finance matters for growth, see:

R. Levine, "Financial Development and Economic Growth: Views and Agenda," *Journal of Economic Literature* 35 (1997), pp. 688–726.

R. Rajan and L. Zingales, "Financial Dependence and Growth," *American Economic Review* 88 (June 1998), pp. 559–586.

Finally, if you'd like to read about corporate governance gone wrong . . .
P. Healy and K. Palepu, "The Fall of Enron," *Journal of Economic Perspectives* 17 (Spring 2003), pp. 3–26.
S. Johnson, R. La Porta, F. Lopez de Silanes, and A. Shleifer, "Tunneling," *American Economic Review* 90 (May 2000), pp. 22–27.

CONCEPT REVIEW QUESTIONS

1. How does the relative importance of common stocks, bank loans and corporate bonds vary between different countries? (page 938)
2. What factors may explain the fact that some countries have more developed financial markets than others? (pages 941–942)
3. What are the main advantages of a keiretsu? List its advantages and disadvantages. (pages 944–946)

For additional Concept Review Questions, please visit us at www.mhhe.com/bmam8e or refer to your Student CD.

QUIZ

1. Which countries have:
   a. The largest stock markets?
   b. The largest bond markets?
   c. The smallest direct holdings of shares by individual investors?
   d. The largest holdings of bank deposits by individual investors?
   e. The largest holdings of shares by other corporations?
   f. The largest use of trade credit for financing?

   In each case, define "largest" or "smallest" as total value relative to GDP.
2. What is a keiretsu? Give a brief description.
3. Do Japanese investors play an important role in corporate financial policy and governance? If not, could they?
4. German banks often control a large fraction of the shareholder votes for German businesses. How do they get that voting power?
5. What is meant by the German system of *codetermination*?
6. What is the most common form of ownership of corporations worldwide?
7. Suppose that a shareholder can gain effective control of a company with 30 percent of the shares. Explain how a shareholder might gain control of company Z by setting up a holding company X^2 which holds shares in a second holding company X, which in turn holds shares in Z.
8. Why may market-based financial systems be better in supporting innovation and in releasing capital from declining industries?
9. What is tunneling? Why does the threat of tunneling impede the development of financial markets?

PRACTICE QUESTIONS

1. Agency problems are inevitable. That is, we can never expect managers to give 100 percent weight to shareholders' interests and none to their own.
   a. Why not?
   b. List the mechanisms that are used around the world to keep agency problems under control.

2. Banks are not the only financial intermediary from which corporations can obtain financing. What are the other intermediaries? How much financing do they supply, relative to banks, in the United Kingdom, Germany, and Japan?
3. Why is transparency important in a market-based financial system? Why is it less important in a bank-based system?
4. What is meant by dual-class equity? Do you think it should be allowed or outlawed?
5. What kind of industries do you think should thrive in a market-based financial system? In a bank-based system?
6. Why are pyramids common in many countries but not in the United States or United Kingdom?
7. What are some of the advantages and disadvantages of Japanese keiretsus?
8. What are some of the advantages and disadvantages of Indian Business Groups?

PART [11]

CONCLUSION

The end is nigh!

CHAPTER [35]

CONCLUSION: WHAT WE DO AND DO NOT KNOW ABOUT FINANCE

It is time to sign off. Let us finish by thinking about some of the things that we do and do not know about finance.

35.1 WHAT WE DO KNOW: THE SEVEN MOST IMPORTANT IDEAS IN FINANCE

What would you say if you were asked to name the seven most important ideas in finance? Here is our list.

1. Net Present Value

When you wish to know the value of a used car, you look at prices in the secondhand car market. Similarly, when you wish to know the value of a future cash flow, you look at prices quoted in the capital markets, where claims to future cash flows are traded (remember, those highly paid investment bankers are just secondhand cash-flow dealers). If you can buy cash flows for your shareholders at a cheaper price than they would have to pay in the capital market, you have increased the value of their investment.

This is the simple idea behind *net present value* (NPV). When we calculate a project's NPV, we are asking whether the project is worth more than it costs. We are estimating its value by calculating what its cash flows would be worth if a claim on them were offered separately to investors and traded in the capital markets.

That is why we calculate NPV by discounting future cash flows at the opportunity cost of capital—that is, at the expected rate of return offered by securities having the same degree of risk as the project. In well-functioning capital markets, all equivalent-risk assets are priced to offer the same expected return. By discounting at the opportunity cost of capital, we calculate the price at which investors in the project could expect to earn that rate of return.

Like most good ideas, the net present value rule is "obvious when you think about it." But notice what an important idea it is. The NPV rule allows thousands of shareholders, who may have vastly different levels of wealth and attitudes toward risk, to participate in the same enterprise and to delegate its operation to a professional manager. They give the manager one simple instruction: "Maximize present value."

2. The Capital Asset Pricing Model

Some people say that modern finance is all about the capital asset pricing model. That's nonsense. If the capital asset pricing model had never been invented, our advice to financial managers would be essentially the same. The attraction of the model is that it gives us a manageable way of thinking about the required return on a risky investment.

Again, it is an attractively simple idea. There are two kinds of risk: risks that you can diversify away and those that you can't. You can measure the *nondiversifiable*, or *market*, risk of an investment by the extent to which the value of the investment is affected by a change in the *aggregate* value of all the assets in the economy. This is called the *beta* of the investment. The only risks that people care about are the ones that they can't get rid of—the nondiversifiable ones. This is why the required return on an asset increases in line with its beta.

Many people are worried by some of the rather strong assumptions behind the capital asset pricing model, or they are concerned about the difficulties of estimating a project's beta. They are right to be worried about these things. In 10 or 20 years' time we may have much better theories than we do now. But we will be extremely surprised if those future theories do not still insist on the crucial distinction between diversifiable and nondiversifiable risks—and that, after all, is the main idea underlying the capital asset pricing model.

3. Efficient Capital Markets

The third fundamental idea is that security prices accurately reflect available information and respond rapidly to new information as soon as it becomes available. This *efficient-market theory* comes in three flavors, corresponding to different definitions of "available information." The weak form (or random-walk theory) says that prices reflect all the information in past prices. The semistrong form says that prices reflect all publicly available information, and the strong form holds that prices reflect all acquirable information.

Don't misunderstand the efficient-market idea. It doesn't say that there are no taxes or costs; it doesn't say that there aren't some clever people and some stupid ones. It merely implies that competition in capital markets is very tough—there are no money machines or arbitrage opportunities, and security prices reflect the true underlying values of assets.

Extensive empirical testing of the efficient-market hypothesis began around 1970. By 2004, after 30 years of work, the tests have uncovered dozens of statistically significant anomalies. Sorry, but this work does *not* translate into dozens of ways to make easy money. Superior returns are elusive. For example, only a few mutual fund managers can generate superior returns for a few years in a row, and then only in small amounts.[1] Statisticians can beat the market, but real investors have a much harder time of it.

4. Value Additivity and the Law of Conservation of Value

The principle of **value additivity** states that the value of the whole is equal to the sum of the values of the parts. It is sometimes called the *law of the conservation of value.*

When we appraise a project that produces a succession of cash flows, we always assume that values add up. In other words, we assume

$$\text{PV(project)} = \text{PV}(C_1) + \text{PV}(C_2) + \cdots + \text{PV}(C_t) + \cdots$$

$$= \frac{C_1}{1+r} + \frac{C_2}{(1+r)^2} + \cdots + \frac{C_t}{(1+r)^t} + \cdots$$

[1]See, for example, M. J. Gruber, "Another Puzzle: The Growth in Actively Managed Mutual Funds," *Journal of Finance* 51 (July 1996), pp. 783–810.

We similarly assume that the sum of the present values of projects A and B equals the present value of a composite project AB.[2] But value additivity also means that you can't increase value by putting two whole companies together unless you thereby increase the total cash flow. In other words, there are no benefits to mergers solely for diversification.

5. Capital Structure Theory

If the law of the conservation of value works when you add up cash flows, it must also work when you subtract them.[3] Therefore, financing decisions that simply divide up operating cash flows don't increase overall firm value. This is the basic idea behind Modigliani and Miller's famous proposition 1: In perfect markets changes in capital structure do not affect value. As long as the *total* cash flow generated by the firm's assets is unchanged by capital structure, value is independent of capital structure. The value of the whole pie does not depend on how it is sliced.

Of course, MM's proposition is not The Answer, but it does tell us where to look for reasons why capital structure decisions may matter. Taxes are one possibility. Debt provides a corporate interest tax shield, and this tax shield may more than compensate for any extra personal tax that the investor has to pay on debt interest. Also, high debt levels may spur managers to work harder and to run a tighter ship. But debt has its drawbacks if it leads to costly financial distress.

6. Option Theory

In everyday conversation we often use the word *option* as synonymous with *choice* or *alternative;* thus we speak of someone as "having a number of options." In finance *option* refers specifically to the opportunity to trade in the future on terms that are fixed today. Smart managers know that it is often worth paying today for the option to buy or sell an asset tomorrow.

Since options are so important, the financial manager needs to know how to value them. Finance experts always knew the relevant variables—the exercise price and the exercise date of the option, the risk of the underlying asset, and the rate of interest. But it was Black and Scholes who first showed how these can be put together in a usable formula.

The Black–Scholes formula was developed for simple call options and does not directly apply to the more complicated options often encountered in corporate finance. But Black and Scholes's most basic ideas—for example, the risk-neutral valuation method implied by their formula—work even where the formula doesn't. Valuing the real options described in Chapter 22 may require extra number crunching but no extra concepts.

---

[2]That is, if

$$PV(A) = PV[C_1(A)] + PV[C_2(A)] + \ldots + PV[C_t(A)] + \ldots$$

$$PV(B) = PV[C_1(B)] + PV[C_2(B)] + \ldots + PV[C_t(B)] + \ldots$$

and if for each period t, $C_t(AB) = C_t(A) + C_t(B)$, then

$$PV(AB) = PV(A) + PV(B)$$

[3]If you *start* with the cash flow $C_t(AB)$ and split it into two pieces, $C_t(A)$ and $C_t(B)$, then total value is unchanged. That is, $PV[C_t(A)] + PV[C_t(B)] = PV[C_t(AB)]$. See footnote 2.

7. Agency Theory

A modern corporation is a team effort involving a number of players, such as managers, employees, shareholders, and bondholders. For a long time economists used to assume without question that all these players acted for the common good, but in the last 30 years they have had a lot more to say about the possible conflicts of interest and how companies attempt to overcome such conflicts. These ideas are known collectively as *agency theory.*

Consider, for example, the relationship between the shareholders and the managers. The shareholders (the *principals*) want managers (their *agents*) to maximize firm value. In the United States the ownership of major corporations is widely dispersed and no single shareholder can check on the managers or reprimand those who are slacking. So, to encourage managers to pull their weight, firms seek to tie the managers' compensation to the value that they have added. For those managers who persistently neglect shareholders' interests, there is the threat that their firm will be taken over and they will be turfed out.

In some other countries corporations are more likely to be owned by a few major shareholders and therefore there is less distance between ownership and control. For example, the families, companies, and banks that hold large stakes in many German companies can review top management's plans and decisions as insiders. In most cases they have the power to force changes as necessary. However, hostile takeovers in Germany are rare.

We discussed the problems of management incentives and corporate control in Chapters 12, 14, 33 and 34, but they were not the only places in the book where agency issues arose. For example, in Chapters 18 and 25 we looked at some of the conflicts that arise between shareholders and bondholders, and we described how loan agreements try to anticipate and minimize these conflicts.

Are these seven ideas exciting theories or plain common sense? Call them what you will, they are basic to the financial manager's job. If by reading this book you really understand these ideas and know how to apply them, you have learned a great deal.

35.2 WHAT WE DO NOT KNOW: 10 UNSOLVED PROBLEMS IN FINANCE

Since the unknown is never exhausted, the list of what we do not know about finance could go on forever. But, following Brealey, Myers and Allen's Third Law (see Section 29.5), we will list and briefly discuss 10 unsolved problems that seem ripe for productive research.

1. What Determines Project Risk and Present Value?

A good capital investment is one that has a positive NPV. We have talked at some length about how to calculate NPV, but we have given you very little guidance about how to find positive-NPV projects, except to say in Section 11.2 that projects have positive NPVs when the firm can earn economic rents. But why do some companies earn economic rents while others in the same industry do not? Are the rents merely windfall gains, or can they be anticipated and planned for? What is their source, and how long do they persist before competition destroys them? Very little is known about any of these important questions.

Here is a related question: Why are some real assets risky and others relatively safe? In Section 9.3 we suggested a few reasons for differences in project betas—differences in operating leverage, for example, or in the extent to which a project's cash flows respond to the performance of the national economy. These are useful clues, but we have as yet no general procedure for estimating project betas. Assessing project risk is therefore still largely a seat-of-the-pants matter.

2. Risk and Return—What Have We Missed?

In 1848 John Stuart Mill wrote, "Happily there is nothing in the laws of value which remains for the present or any future writer to clear up; the theory is complete." Economists today are not so sure about that. For example, the capital asset pricing model is an enormous step toward understanding the effect of risk on the value of an asset, but there are many puzzles left, some statistical and some theoretical.

The statistical problems arise because the capital asset pricing model is hard to prove or disprove conclusively. It appears that average returns from low-beta stocks are too high (that is, higher than the capital asset pricing model predicts) and that those from high-beta stocks are too low; but this could be a problem with the way that the tests are conducted and not with the model itself.[4] We also described the puzzling discovery by Fama and French that expected returns appear to be related to the firm's size and to the ratio of the book value of the stock to its market value. Nobody understands why this should be so; perhaps these variables are related to variable x, that mysterious second risk variable that investors may rationally take into account in pricing shares.[5]

Meanwhile scholars toil on the theoretical front. We discussed some of their work in Section 8.4. But just for fun, here is another example: Suppose that you love fine wine. It may make sense for you to buy shares in a grand cru chateau, even if doing so soaks up a large fraction of your personal wealth and leaves you with a relatively undiversified portfolio. However, you are *hedged* against a rise in the price of fine wine: Your hobby will cost you more in a bull market for wine, but your stake in the chateau will make you correspondingly richer. Thus you are holding a relatively undiversified portfolio for a good reason. We would not expect you to demand a premium for bearing that portfolio's undiversifiable risk.

In general, if two people have different tastes, it may make sense for them to hold different portfolios. You may hedge your consumption needs with an investment in wine making, whereas somebody else may do better to invest in Baskin-Robbins. The capital asset pricing model isn't rich enough to deal with such a world. It assumes that all investors have similar tastes: The "hedging motive" does not enter, and therefore they hold the same portfolio of risky assets.

---

[4]See R. Roll, "A Critique of the Asset Pricing Theory's Tests: Part 1: On Past and Potential Testability of the Theory," *Journal of Financial Economics* 4 (March 1977), pp. 129–176; and, for a critique of the critique, see D. Mayers and E. M. Rice, "Measuring Portfolio Performance and the Empirical Content of Asset Pricing Models," *Journal of Financial Economics* 7 (March 1979), pp. 3–28.

[5]Fama and French point out that small firms, and firms with high book-to-market ratios, are also low-profitability firms. Such firms may suffer more in downturns in the economy. Thus size and book-to-market measures may be proxies for exposure to business-cycle risk. See E. F. Fama and K. R. French, "Size and Book-to-Market Factors in Earnings and Returns," *Journal of Finance* 50 (March 1995), pp. 131–155.

Merton has extended the capital asset pricing model to accommodate the hedging motive.[6] If enough investors are attempting to hedge against the same thing, the model implies a more complicated risk–return relationship. However, it is not yet clear who is hedging against what, and so the model remains difficult to test.

So the capital asset pricing model survives not from a lack of competition but from a surfeit. There are too many plausible alternative risk measures, and so far no consensus exists on the right course to plot if we abandon beta.

In the meantime we must recognize the capital asset pricing model for what it is: an incomplete but extremely useful way of linking risk and return. Recognize too that the model's most basic message, that diversifiable risk doesn't matter, is accepted by nearly everyone.

3. How Important Are the Exceptions to the Efficient-Market Theory?

The efficient-market theory is strong, but no theory is perfect; there must be exceptions.

Now some of the apparent exceptions could simply be coincidences, for the more that researchers study stock performance, the more strange coincidences they are likely to find. For example, there is evidence that daily returns around new moons have been roughly double those around full moons.[7] It seems difficult to believe that this is anything other than a chance relationship—fun to read about but not a concern for serious investors or financial managers. But not all exceptions can be dismissed so easily. We saw that the stocks of firms which announce unexpectedly good earnings continue to perform well for a couple of months after the announcement date. Some scholars believe that this may mean that the stock market is inefficient and investors have consistently been slow to react to earnings announcements. Of course, we can't expect investors never to make mistakes. If they have been slow to react in the past, perhaps they will learn from this mistake and price the stocks more efficiently in the future.

Some researchers believe that the efficient-market hypothesis ignores important aspects of human behavior. For example, psychologists find that people tend to place too much emphasis on recent events when they are predicting the future. If so, we may find that investors are liable to overreact to new information. It will be interesting to see how far such behavioral observations can help us to understand apparent anomalies.

During the dot.com boom of the late 1990s stock prices rose to astronomic levels. The Nasdaq Composite Index rose 580 percent from the beginning of 1995 to its peak in March 2000 and then fell by nearly 80 percent. Such gyrations were not confined to the United States. For example, stock prices on Germany's Neuer Markt rose 1,600 percent in the three years from its foundation in 1997, before falling by 95 percent by October 2002.

This is not the only occasion that asset prices have reached unsustainable levels. In the late 1980s there was a surge in the prices of Japanese stock and real estate. At one point the land that the Imperial Palace stands on in central Tokyo was worth the same as all the land in California or in the whole of Canada![8]

Maybe such extreme price movements can be explained by standard valuation techniques.[9] However, others argue that stock prices are liable to speculative bubbles, where investors are caught up

[6]See R. Merton, "An Intertemporal Capital Asset Pricing Model," *Econometrica* 41 (1973), pp. 867–887.

[7]K. Yuan, L. Zheng and Q. Zhu, "Are Investors Moonstruck? Lunar Phases and Stock Returns," working paper, University of Michigan, September 2001.

[8]See W. Ziemba and S. Schwartz, *Invest Japan* (Chicago, Illinois: Probus, 1992), p. 109.

[9]For example, Peter Garber argues that tulipmania was not obvious madness. See P. Garber, "Tulipmania" *Journal of Political Economy* 97 (1989), pp. 535–560.

in a scatty whirl of irrational exuberance.[10] Now that may be true of your uncle Harry or aunt Hetty, but why don't hard-headed professional investors bail out of the overpriced stocks? Perhaps they would do so if it was their money at stake, but maybe there is something in the way their performance is measured and rewarded that encourages them to run with the herd.[11]

These are important questions. Much more research is needed before we have a full understanding of why asset prices sometimes get so out of line with what appears to be their discounted future payoffs.

4. Is Management an Off-Balance-Sheet Liability?

Closed-end funds are firms whose only asset is a portfolio of common stocks. One might think that if you knew the value of these common stocks, you would also know the value of the firm. However, this is not the case. The stock of the closed-end fund often sells for substantially less than the value of the fund's portfolio.[12]

All this might not matter much except that it could be just the tip of the iceberg. For example, real estate stocks appear to sell for less than the market values of the firms' net assets. In the late 1970s and early 1980s the market values of many large oil companies were less than the market values of their oil reserves. Analysts joked that you could buy oil cheaper on Wall Street than in west Texas.

All these are special cases in which it was possible to compare the market value of the whole firm with the values of its separate assets. But perhaps if we could observe the values of other firms' separate parts, we might find that the value of the whole was often less than the sum of the values of the parts.

Whenever firms calculate the net present value of a project, they implicitly assume that the value of the whole project is simply the sum of the values of all the years' cash flows. We referred to this earlier as the law of the conservation of value. If we cannot rely on that law, the tip of the iceberg could turn out to be a hot potato.

We don't understand why closed-end investment companies or any of the other firms sell at a discount on the market values of their assets. One explanation is that the value added by the firm's management is less than the cost of the management. That is why we suggest that management may be an off-balance-sheet liability. For example, the discount of oil company shares from oil-in-the-ground value can be explained if investors expected the profits from oil production to be frittered away in negative-NPV investments and bureaucratic excess. The present value of growth opportunities (PVGO) was negative!

We do not mean to portray managers as leeches soaking up cash flows meant for investors. Managers commit their human capital to the firm and rightfully expect a reasonable cash return on these personal investments. If investors extract too great a share of the firm's cash flow, the personal investments are discouraged, and the long-run health and growth of the firm can be damaged.

[10]See C. Kindleberger, *Manias, Panics, and Crashes: A History of Financial Crises* (New York: Basic Books, 1978); and R. Shiller, *Irrational Exuberance* (Princeton, NJ: Princeton University Press, 2000).

[11]Investment managers may reason that if the stocks continue to do well, they will benefit from increased business in the future; on the other hand, if the stocks do badly, it is the customers who incur the losses and the worst that can happen to the managers is that they have to find new jobs. See F. Allen, "Do Financial Institutions Matter?" *Journal of Finance* 56 (August 2001), pp. 1165–1174.

[12]There are relatively few closed-end funds. Most mutual funds are *open-end*. This means that they stand ready to buy or sell additional shares at a price equal to the fund's net asset value per share. Therefore the share price of an open-end fund always equals net asset value.

In most firms, managers and employees coinvest with stockholders and creditors—human capital from the insiders and financial capital from outside investors. So far we know very little about how this coinvestment works.

5. How Can We Explain the Success of New Securities and New Markets?

In the last 20 years companies and the securities exchanges have created an enormous number of new securities: options, futures, options on futures; zero-coupon bonds, floating-rate bonds; bonds with collars and caps, asset-backed bonds; catastrophe bonds, . . . the list is endless. In some cases, it is easy to explain the success of new markets or securities; perhaps they allow investors to insure themselves against new risks or they result from a change in tax or in regulation. Sometimes a market develops because of a change in the costs of issuing or trading different securities. But there are many successful innovations that cannot be explained so easily. Why do investment bankers continue to invent, and successfully sell, complex new securities that outstrip our ability to value them? The truth is we don't understand why some innovations in markets succeed and others never get off the ground.

6. How Can We Resolve the Payout Controversy?

We spent all of Chapter 16 on payout policy without being able to resolve the payout controversy. Many people believe dividends are good; others believe dividends are bad and repurchases are good; and still others believe that, as long as the firm's investment decisions are unaffected, the payout decision is irrelevant. If pressed, we largely take the middle view, but we can't be dogmatic about it.

We don't mean to disparage existing research; rather we say that more is in order. Whether future research will change anybody's mind is another matter. The problem is to disentangle several possible reasons that payout policy *may* matter. The recent change in the U.S. tax law that lowered the tax on dividends and equated the rate with that on capital gains may provide useful evidence that allows this to be done.

In recent years the way that companies distribute cash has been changing. An increasing number of companies do not pay any dividends, while the volume of stock repurchases has mushroomed. The tax law change may reverse this trend. But to be sure of this, we need to understand better both how companies determine their payout policy and how that policy affects firm value.

7. What Risks Should a Firm Take?

Financial managers end up managing risk. For example,

- When a firm expands production, managers often reduce the cost of failure by building in the option to alter the product mix or to bail out of the project altogether.
- By reducing the firm's borrowing, managers can spread operating risks over a larger equity base.
- Most businesses take out insurance against a variety of specific hazards.
- Managers often use futures or other derivatives to protect against adverse movements in commodity prices, interest rates, and exchange rates.

All these actions reduce risk. But less risk can't always be better. The point of risk management is not to reduce risk but to add value. We wish we could give general guidance on what bets the firm should place and what the *appropriate* level of risk is.

In practice, risk management decisions interact in complicated ways. For example, firms that are hedged against commodity price fluctuations may be able to afford more debt than those that are not hedged. Hedging can make sense if it allows the firm to take greater advantage of interest tax shields, provided the costs of hedging are sufficiently low.

How can a company set a risk management strategy that adds up to a sensible whole?

8. What Is the Value of Liquidity?

Unlike Treasury bills, cash pays no interest. On the other hand, cash provides more liquidity than Treasury bills. People who hold cash must believe that this additional liquidity offsets the loss of interest. In equilibrium, the marginal value of the additional liquidity must equal the interest rate on bills.

Now what can we say about corporate holdings of cash? It is wrong to ignore the liquidity gain and to say that the cost of holding cash is the lost interest. This would imply that cash always has a *negative* NPV. It is equally foolish to say that, because the marginal value of liquidity is equal to the loss of interest, it doesn't matter how much cash the firm holds. This would imply that cash always has a *zero* NPV. We know that the marginal value of cash to a holder declines with the size of the cash holding, but we don't really understand how to value the liquidity service of cash and therefore we can't say how much cash is enough or how readily the firm should be able to raise it. To complicate matters further, we note that cash can be raised on short notice by borrowing, or by issuing other new securities, as well as by selling assets. The financial manager with a $1 million unused line of credit may sleep just as soundly as one whose firm holds $1 million in marketable securities. In our chapters on working-capital management we largely finessed these questions by presenting models that are really too simple or by speaking vaguely of the need to ensure an "adequate" liquidity reserve.

A better knowledge of liquidity would also help us to understand better how corporate bonds are priced. We already know part of the reason that corporate bonds sell for lower prices than Treasury bonds—companies have the option to walk away from their debts. However, the differences between the prices of corporate bonds and Treasury bonds are too large to be explained just by the company's default option. It seems likely that the price difference is partly due to the fact that corporate bonds are less liquid than Treasury bonds. But, until we know how to price differences in liquidity, we can't really say much more than this.

Investors seem to value liquidity much more highly at some times than at others. When liquidity suddenly dries up, asset prices can become very volatile. This happened in 1998 when Long Term Capital Management, a large hedge fund, collapsed.[13] Since its formation four years earlier LTCM had generated high returns by holding large positions in "cheap" illiquid assets, which it hedged by

[13]Hedge funds attempt to buy underpriced securities and to sell short overpriced ones. They are typically organized as partnerships and owned by a small number of institutions or wealthy individuals.

selling liquid assets. LTCM, therefore, served as a supplier of liquidity to other investors. When Russia defaulted on its debt in 1998, there was a rush by investors to get out of illiquid assets. As the value of LTCM's holdings declined, its banks demanded additional collateral for their loans and LTCM was forced to liquidate its positions in a market that was already short of liquidity. Eventually, the New York Fed encouraged a group of institutions to take over LTCM, but not before there had been very sharp swings in asset prices.

9. How Can We Explain Merger Waves?

In 1968 at the first peak of the postwar merger movement, Joel Segall noted: "There is no single hypothesis which is both plausible and general and which shows promise of explaining the current merger movement. If so, it is correct to say that there is nothing known about mergers; there are no useful generalizations."[14] Of course there are many plausible motives for merging. If you single out a *particular* merger, it is usually possible to think up a reason why that merger could make sense. But that leaves us with a special hypothesis for each merger. What we need is a general hypothesis to explain merger waves. For example, in the late 1990s everybody seemed to be merging, while at the beginning of the twenty-first century mergers were out of fashion.

There are other instances of apparent financial fashions. For example, from time to time there are hot new-issue periods when there seems to be an insatiable supply of speculative new issues and an equally insatiable demand for them. We don't understand why hard-headed businessmen sometimes seem to behave like a flock of sheep, but the following story may contain the seeds of an explanation.

It is early evening and George is trying to decide between two restaurants, the Hungry Horse and the Golden Trough. Both are empty and, since there seems to be little reason to prefer one to the other, George tosses a coin and opts for the Hungry Horse. Shortly afterward Georgina pauses outside the two restaurants. She somewhat prefers the Golden Trough, but observing George inside the Hungry Horse while the other restaurant is empty, she decides that George may know something that she doesn't and therefore the rational decision is to copy George. Fred is the third person to arrive. He sees that George and Georgina have both chosen the Hungry Horse, and, putting aside his own judgment, decides to go with the flow. And so it is with subsequent diners, who simply look at the packed tables in the one restaurant and the empty tables elsewhere and draw the obvious conclusions. Each diner behaves fully rationally in balancing his or her own views with the revealed preferences of the other diners. Yet the popularity of the Hungry Horse owed much to the toss of George's coin. If Georgina had been the first to arrive or if all diners could have pooled their information before coming to a decision, the Hungry Horse might not have scooped the jackpot.

Economists refer to this imitative behavior as a **cascade.**[15] It remains to be seen how far cascades or some alternative theory can help to explain financial fashions.

[14] J. Segall, "Merging for Fun and Profit," *Industrial Management Review* 9 (Winter 1968), pp. 17–30.

[15] For an introduction to cascades, see S. Bikhchandani, D. Hirschleifer and I. Welch, "Learning from the Behavior of Others: Conformity, Fads, and Informational Cascades," *Journal of Economic Perspectives* 12 (Summer 1998), pp. 151–170.

10. How Can We Explain International Differences in Financial Architecture?

In Chapter 34 we showed how financial architecture varies internationally. By this we mean that there are important international differences in the legal form of the business, its ownership, governance, and sources of financing. In the United States and most other English-speaking countries large firms are commonly organized as public corporations with actively traded shares, dispersed ownership, and relatively easy access to financial markets. In other countries businesses are often more closely held, and the owners have more say in how the business is run. Banks often play a much larger role in financing businesses and keeping an eye on their progress. Also, in many countries businesses are combined together into diversified conglomerates which can allocate capital from the parts that have a capital surplus to those that are short of capital.

We don't fully understand why these differences in organizational structure exist, though we suggested that part of the answer may lie in differences in legal and political systems. We also made some qualitative statements about the advantages and disadvantages of different structures, but commentators continue to debate which arrangements are most efficient. Some worry that the preoccupation of managers in the United States with enhancing shareholder value leads to a focus on short-term profits; others assert that too cozy a relationship between a company and its sources of capital can lead to a lack of discipline in managers.

35.3 A FINAL WORD

That concludes our list of unsolved problems. We have given you the 10 uppermost in our minds. If there are others that you find more interesting and challenging, by all means construct your own list and start thinking about it.

It will take years for our 10 problems to be finally solved and replaced with a fresh list. In the meantime, we invite you to go on to further study what we *already* know about finance. We also invite you to apply what you have learned from reading this book.

Now that the book is done, we sympathize with Huckleberry Finn. At the end of his book he says:

> So there ain't nothing more to write, and I am rotten glad of it, because if I'd a' knowed what a trouble it was to make a book I wouldn't a' tackled it, and I ain't a'going to no more.

APPENDIX A

PRESENT VALUE TABLES

APPENDIX TABLE 1

Discount factors: Present value of $1 to be received after t years = $1/(1 + r)^t$.

Number of Years	Interest Rate per Year 1%	2%	3%	4%	5%	6%	7%	8%	9%	10%	11%	12%	13%	14%	15%
1	.990	.980	.971	.962	.952	.943	.935	.926	.917	.909	.901	.893	.885	.877	.870
2	.980	.961	.943	.925	.907	.890	.873	.857	.842	.826	.812	.797	.783	.769	.756
3	.971	.942	.915	.889	.864	.840	.816	.794	.772	.751	.731	.712	.693	.675	.658
4	.961	.924	.888	.855	.823	.792	.763	.735	.708	.683	.659	.636	.613	.592	.572
5	.951	.906	.863	.822	.784	.747	.713	.681	.650	.621	.593	.567	.543	.519	.497
6	.942	.888	.837	.790	.746	.705	.666	.630	.596	.564	.535	.507	.480	.456	.432
7	.933	.871	.813	.760	.711	.665	.623	.583	.547	.513	.482	.452	.425	.400	.376
8	.923	.853	.789	.731	.677	.627	.582	.540	.502	.467	.434	.404	.376	.351	.327
9	.914	.837	.766	.703	.645	.592	.544	.500	.460	.424	.391	.361	.333	.308	.284
10	.905	.820	.744	.676	.614	.558	.508	.463	.422	.386	.352	.322	.295	.270	.247
11	.896	.804	.722	.650	.585	.527	.475	.429	.388	.350	.317	.287	.261	.237	.215
12	.887	.788	.701	.625	.557	.497	.444	.397	.356	.319	.286	.257	.231	.208	.187
13	.879	.773	.681	.601	.530	.469	.415	.368	.326	.290	.258	.229	.204	.182	.163
14	.870	.758	.661	.577	.505	.442	.388	.340	.299	.263	.232	.205	.181	.160	.141
15	.861	.743	.642	.555	.481	.417	.362	.315	.275	.239	.209	.183	.160	.140	.123
16	.853	.728	.623	.534	.458	.394	.339	.292	.252	.218	.188	.163	.141	.123	.107
17	.844	.714	.605	.513	.436	.371	.317	.270	.231	.198	.170	.146	.125	.108	.093
18	.836	.700	.587	.494	.416	.350	.296	.250	.212	.180	.153	.130	.111	.095	.081
19	.828	.686	.570	.475	.396	.331	.277	.232	.194	.164	.138	.116	.098	.083	.070
20	.820	.673	.554	.456	.377	.312	.258	.215	.178	.149	.124	.104	.087	.073	.061

Number of Years	Interest Rate per Year 16%	17%	18%	19%	20%	21%	22%	23%	24%	25%	26%	27%	28%	29%	30%
1	.862	.855	.847	.840	.833	.826	.820	.813	.806	.800	.794	.787	.781	.775	.769
2	.743	.731	.718	.706	.694	.683	.672	.661	.650	.640	.630	.620	.610	.601	.592
3	.641	.624	.609	.593	.579	.564	.551	.537	.524	.512	.500	.488	.477	.466	.455
4	.552	.534	.516	.499	.482	.467	.451	.437	.423	.410	.397	.384	.373	.361	.350
5	.476	.456	.437	.419	.402	.386	.370	.355	.341	.328	.315	.303	.291	.280	.269
6	.410	.390	.370	.352	.335	.319	.303	.289	.275	.262	.250	.238	.227	.217	.207
7	.354	.333	.314	.296	.279	.263	.249	.235	.222	.210	.198	.188	.178	.168	.159
8	.305	.285	.266	.249	.233	.218	.204	.191	.179	.168	.157	.148	.139	.130	.123
9	.263	.243	.225	.209	.194	.180	.167	.155	.144	.134	.125	.116	.108	.101	.094
10	.227	.208	.191	.176	.162	.149	.137	.126	.116	.107	.099	.092	.085	.078	.073
11	.195	.178	.162	.148	.135	.123	.112	.103	.094	.086	.079	.072	.066	.061	.056
12	.168	.152	.137	.124	.112	.102	.092	.083	.076	.069	.062	.057	.052	.047	.043
13	.145	.130	.116	.104	.093	.084	.075	.068	.061	.055	.050	.045	.040	.037	.033
14	.125	.111	.099	.088	.078	.069	.062	.055	.049	.044	.039	.035	.032	.028	.025
15	.108	.095	.084	.074	.065	.057	.051	.045	.040	.035	.031	.028	.025	.022	.020
16	.093	.081	.071	.062	.054	.047	.042	.036	.032	.028	.025	.022	.019	.017	.015
17	.080	.069	.060	.052	.045	.039	.034	.030	.026	.023	.020	.017	.015	.013	.012
18	.069	.059	.051	.044	.038	.032	.028	.024	.021	.018	.016	.014	.012	.010	.009
19	.060	.051	.043	.037	.031	.027	.023	.020	.017	.014	.012	.011	.009	.008	.007
20	.051	.043	.037	.031	.026	.022	.019	.016	.014	.012	.010	.008	.007	.006	.005

Note: For example, if the interest rate is 10 percent per year, the present value of $1 received at year 5 is $.621.

APPENDIX TABLE 2

Future value of $1 after t years = $(1 + r)^t$.

Number of Years	1%	2%	3%	4%	5%	6%	7%	8%	9%	10%	11%	12%	13%	14%	15%
	Interest Rate per Year														
1	1.010	1.020	1.030	1.040	1.050	1.060	1.070	1.080	1.090	1.100	1.110	1.120	1.130	1.140	1.150
2	1.020	1.040	1.061	1.082	1.102	1.124	1.145	1.166	1.188	1.210	1.232	1.254	1.277	1.300	1.323
3	1.030	1.061	1.093	1.125	1.158	1.191	1.225	1.260	1.295	1.331	1.368	1.405	1.443	1.482	1.521
4	1.041	1.082	1.126	1.170	1.216	1.262	1.311	1.360	1.412	1.464	1.518	1.574	1.630	1.689	1.749
5	1.051	1.104	1.159	1.217	1.276	1.338	1.403	1.469	1.539	1.611	1.685	1.762	1.842	1.925	2.011
6	1.062	1.126	1.194	1.265	1.340	1.419	1.501	1.587	1.677	1.772	1.870	1.974	2.082	2.195	2.313
7	1.072	1.149	1.230	1.316	1.407	1.504	1.606	1.714	1.828	1.949	2.076	2.211	2.353	2.502	2.660
8	1.083	1.172	1.267	1.369	1.477	1.594	1.718	1.851	1.993	2.144	2.305	2.476	2.658	2.853	3.059
9	1.094	1.195	1.305	1.423	1.551	1.689	1.838	1.999	2.172	2.358	2.558	2.773	3.004	3.252	3.518
10	1.105	1.219	1.344	1.480	1.629	1.791	1.967	2.159	2.367	2.594	2.839	3.106	3.395	3.707	4.046
11	1.116	1.243	1.384	1.539	1.710	1.898	2.105	2.332	2.580	2.853	3.152	3.479	3.836	4.226	4.652
12	1.127	1.268	1.426	1.601	1.796	2.012	2.252	2.518	2.813	3.138	3.498	3.896	4.335	4.818	5.350
13	1.138	1.294	1.469	1.665	1.886	2.133	2.410	2.720	3.066	3.452	3.883	4.363	4.898	5.492	6.153
14	1.149	1.319	1.513	1.732	1.980	2.261	2.579	2.937	3.342	3.797	4.310	4.887	5.535	6.261	7.076
15	1.161	1.346	1.558	1.801	2.079	2.397	2.759	3.172	3.642	4.177	4.785	5.474	6.254	7.138	8.137
16	1.173	1.373	1.605	1.873	2.183	2.540	2.952	3.426	3.970	4.595	5.311	6.130	7.067	8.137	9.358
17	1.184	1.400	1.653	1.948	2.292	2.693	3.159	3.700	4.328	5.054	5.895	6.866	7.986	9.276	10.76
18	1.196	1.428	1.702	2.026	2.407	2.854	3.380	3.996	4.717	5.560	6.544	7.690	9.024	10.58	12.38
19	1.208	1.457	1.754	2.107	2.527	3.026	3.617	4.316	5.142	6.116	7.263	8.613	10.20	12.06	14.23
20	1.220	1.486	1.806	2.191	2.653	3.207	3.870	4.661	5.604	6.727	8.062	9.646	11.52	13.74	16.37

Number of Years	16%	17%	18%	19%	20%	21%	22%	23%	24%	25%	26%	27%	28%	29%	30%
	Interest Rate per Year														
1	1.160	1.170	1.180	1.190	1.200	1.210	1.220	1.230	1.240	1.250	1.260	1.270	1.280	1.290	1.300
2	1.346	1.369	1.392	1.416	1.440	1.464	1.488	1.513	1.538	1.563	1.588	1.613	1.638	1.664	1.690
3	1.561	1.602	1.643	1.685	1.728	1.772	1.816	1.861	1.907	1.953	2.000	2.048	2.097	2.147	2.197
4	1.811	1.874	1.939	2.005	2.074	2.144	2.215	2.289	2.364	2.441	2.520	2.601	2.684	2.769	2.856
5	2.100	2.192	2.288	2.386	2.488	2.594	2.703	2.815	2.932	3.052	3.176	3.304	3.436	3.572	3.713
6	2.436	2.565	2.700	2.840	2.986	3.138	3.297	3.463	3.635	3.815	4.002	4.196	4.398	4.608	4.827
7	2.826	3.001	3.185	3.379	3.583	3.797	4.023	4.259	4.508	4.768	5.042	5.329	5.629	5.945	6.275
8	3.278	3.511	3.759	4.021	4.300	4.595	4.908	5.239	5.590	5.960	6.353	6.768	7.206	7.669	8.157
9	3.803	4.108	4.435	4.785	5.160	5.560	5.987	6.444	6.931	7.451	8.005	8.595	9.223	9.893	10.60
10	4.411	4.807	5.234	5.695	6.192	6.728	7.305	7.926	8.594	9.313	10.09	10.92	11.81	12.76	13.79
11	5.117	5.624	6.176	6.777	7.430	8.140	8.912	9.749	10.66	11.64	12.71	13.86	15.11	16.46	17.92
12	5.936	6.580	7.288	8.064	8.916	9.850	10.87	11.99	13.21	14.55	16.01	17.61	19.34	21.24	23.30
13	6.886	7.699	8.599	9.596	10.70	11.92	13.26	14.75	16.39	18.19	20.18	22.36	24.76	27.39	30.29
14	7.988	9.007	10.15	11.42	12.84	14.42	16.18	18.14	20.32	22.74	25.42	28.40	31.69	35.34	39.37
15	9.266	10.54	11.97	13.59	15.41	17.45	19.74	22.31	25.20	28.42	32.03	36.06	40.56	45.59	51.19
16	10.75	12.33	14.13	16.17	18.49	21.11	24.09	27.45	31.24	35.53	40.36	45.80	51.92	58.81	66.54
17	12.47	14.43	16.67	19.24	22.19	25.55	29.38	33.76	38.74	44.41	50.85	58.17	66.46	75.86	86.50
18	14.46	16.88	19.67	22.90	26.62	30.91	35.85	41.52	48.04	55.51	64.07	73.87	85.07	97.86	112.5
19	16.78	19.75	23.21	27.25	31.95	37.40	43.74	51.07	59.57	69.39	80.73	93.81	108.9	126.2	146.2
20	19.46	23.11	27.39	32.43	38.34	45.26	53.36	62.82	73.86	86.74	101.7	119.1	139.4	162.9	190.0

Note: For example, if the interest rate is 10 percent per year, the investment of $1 today will be worth $1.611 at year 5.

APPENDIX TABLE 3

Annuity table: Present value of $1 per year for each of t years = $1/r - 1/[r(1 + r)^t]$.

Number of Years	1%	2%	3%	4%	5%	6%	7%	8%	9%	10%	11%	12%	13%	14%	15%
1	.990	.980	.971	.962	.952	.943	.935	.926	.917	.909	.901	.893	.885	.877	.870
2	1.970	1.942	1.913	1.886	1.859	1.833	1.808	1.783	1.759	1.736	1.713	1.690	1.668	1.647	1.626
3	2.941	2.884	2.829	2.775	2.723	2.673	2.624	2.577	2.531	2.487	2.444	2.402	2.361	2.322	2.283
4	3.902	3.808	3.717	3.630	3.546	3.465	3.387	3.312	3.240	3.170	3.102	3.037	2.974	2.914	2.855
5	4.853	4.713	4.580	4.452	4.329	4.212	4.100	3.993	3.890	3.791	3.696	3.605	3.517	3.433	3.352
6	5.795	5.601	5.417	5.242	5.076	4.917	4.767	4.623	4.486	4.355	4.231	4.111	3.998	3.889	3.784
7	6.728	6.472	6.230	6.002	5.786	5.582	5.389	5.206	5.033	4.868	4.712	4.564	4.423	4.288	4.160
8	7.652	7.325	7.020	6.733	6.463	6.210	5.971	5.747	5.535	5.335	5.146	4.968	4.799	4.639	4.487
9	8.566	8.162	7.786	7.435	7.108	6.802	6.515	6.247	5.995	5.759	5.537	5.328	5.132	4.946	4.772
10	9.471	8.983	8.530	8.111	7.722	7.360	7.024	6.710	6.418	6.145	5.889	5.650	5.426	5.216	5.019
11	10.37	9.787	9.253	8.760	8.306	7.887	7.499	7.139	6.805	6.495	6.207	5.938	5.687	5.453	5.234
12	11.26	10.58	9.954	9.385	8.863	8.384	7.943	7.536	7.161	6.814	6.492	6.194	5.918	5.660	5.421
13	12.13	11.35	10.63	9.986	9.394	8.853	8.358	7.904	7.487	7.103	6.750	6.424	6.122	5.842	5.583
14	13.00	12.11	11.30	10.56	9.899	9.295	8.745	8.244	7.786	7.367	6.982	6.628	6.302	6.002	5.724
15	13.87	12.85	11.94	11.12	10.38	9.712	9.108	8.559	8.061	7.606	7.191	6.811	6.462	6.142	5.847
16	14.72	13.58	12.56	11.65	10.84	10.11	9.447	8.851	8.313	7.824	7.379	6.974	6.604	6.265	5.954
17	15.56	14.29	13.17	12.17	11.27	10.48	9.763	9.122	8.544	8.022	7.549	7.120	6.729	6.373	6.047
18	16.40	14.99	13.75	12.66	11.69	10.83	10.06	9.372	8.756	8.201	7.702	7.250	6.840	6.467	6.128
19	17.23	15.68	14.32	13.13	12.09	11.16	10.34	9.604	8.950	8.365	7.839	7.366	6.938	6.550	6.198
20	18.05	16.35	14.88	13.59	12.46	11.47	10.59	9.818	9.129	8.514	7.963	7.469	7.025	6.623	6.259

Number of Years	16%	17%	18%	19%	20%	21%	22%	23%	24%	25%	26%	27%	28%	29%	30%
1	.862	.855	.847	.840	.833	.826	.820	.813	.806	.800	.794	.787	.781	.775	.769
2	1.605	1.585	1.566	1.547	1.528	1.509	1.492	1.474	1.457	1.440	1.424	1.407	1.392	1.376	1.361
3	2.246	2.210	2.174	2.140	2.106	2.074	2.042	2.011	1.981	1.952	1.923	1.896	1.868	1.842	1.816
4	2.798	2.743	2.690	2.639	2.589	2.540	2.494	2.448	2.404	2.362	2.320	2.280	2.241	2.203	2.166
5	3.274	3.199	3.127	3.058	2.991	2.926	2.864	2.803	2.745	2.689	2.635	2.583	2.532	2.483	2.436
6	3.685	3.589	3.498	3.410	3.326	3.245	3.167	3.092	3.020	2.951	2.885	2.821	2.759	2.700	2.643
7	4.039	3.922	3.812	3.706	3.605	3.508	3.416	3.327	3.242	3.161	3.083	3.009	2.937	2.868	2.802
8	4.344	4.207	4.078	3.954	3.837	3.726	3.619	3.518	3.421	3.329	3.241	3.156	3.076	2.999	2.925
9	4.607	4.451	4.303	4.163	4.031	3.905	3.786	3.673	3.566	3.463	3.366	3.273	3.184	3.100	3.019
10	4.833	4.659	4.494	4.339	4.192	4.054	3.923	3.799	3.682	3.571	3.465	3.364	3.269	3.178	3.092
11	5.029	4.836	4.656	4.486	4.327	4.177	4.035	3.902	3.776	3.656	3.543	3.437	3.335	3.239	3.147
12	5.197	4.988	4.793	4.611	4.439	4.278	4.127	3.985	3.851	3.725	3.606	3.493	3.387	3.286	3.190
13	5.342	5.118	4.910	4.715	4.533	4.362	4.203	4.053	3.912	3.780	3.656	3.538	3.427	3.322	3.223
14	5.468	5.229	5.008	4.802	4.611	4.432	4.265	4.108	3.962	3.824	3.695	3.573	3.459	3.351	3.249
15	5.575	5.324	5.092	4.876	4.675	4.489	4.315	4.153	4.001	3.859	3.726	3.601	3.483	3.373	3.268
16	5.668	5.405	5.162	4.938	4.730	4.536	4.357	4.189	4.033	3.887	3.751	3.623	3.503	3.390	3.283
17	5.749	5.475	5.222	4.990	4.775	4.576	4.391	4.219	4.059	3.910	3.771	3.640	3.518	3.403	3.295
18	5.818	5.534	5.273	5.033	4.812	4.608	4.419	4.243	4.080	3.928	3.786	3.654	3.529	3.413	3.304
19	5.877	5.584	5.316	5.070	4.843	4.635	4.442	4.263	4.097	3.942	3.799	3.664	3.539	3.421	3.311
20	5.929	5.628	5.353	5.101	4.870	4.657	4.460	4.279	4.110	3.954	3.808	3.673	3.546	3.427	3.316

Note: For example, if the interest rate is 10 percent per year, the investment of $1 received in each of the next 5 years is $3.791.

APPENDIX TABLE 4

Values of e^{rt}. Future value of $1 invested at a *continuously compounded* rate *r* for *t* years.

rt	.00	.01	.02	.03	.04	.05	.06	.07	.08	.09
.00	1.000	1.010	1.020	1.030	1.041	1.051	1.062	1.073	1.083	1.094
.10	1.105	1.116	1.127	1.139	1.150	1.162	1.174	1.185	1.197	1.209
.20	1.221	1.234	1.246	1.259	1.271	1.284	1.297	1.310	1.323	1.336
.30	1.350	1.363	1.377	1.391	1.405	1.419	1.433	1.448	1.462	1.477
.40	1.492	1.507	1.522	1.537	1.553	1.568	1.584	1.600	1.616	1.632
.50	1.649	1.665	1.682	1.699	1.716	1.733	1.751	1.768	1.786	1.804
.60	1.822	1.840	1.859	1.878	1.896	1.916	1.935	1.954	1.974	1.994
.70	2.014	2.034	2.054	2.075	2.096	2.117	2.138	2.160	2.181	2.203
.80	2.226	2.248	2.271	2.293	2.316	2.340	2.363	2.387	2.411	2.435
.90	2.460	2.484	2.509	2.535	2.560	2.586	2.612	2.638	2.664	2.691
1.00	2.718	2.746	2.773	2.801	2.829	2.858	2.886	2.915	2.945	2.974
1.10	3.004	3.034	3.065	3.096	3.127	3.158	3.190	3.222	3.254	3.287
1.20	3.320	3.353	3.387	3.421	3.456	3.490	3.525	3.561	3.597	3.633
1.30	3.669	3.706	3.743	3.781	3.819	3.857	3.896	3.935	3.975	4.015
1.40	4.055	4.096	4.137	4.179	4.221	4.263	4.306	4.349	4.393	4.437
1.50	4.482	4.527	4.572	4.618	4.665	4.711	4.759	4.807	4.855	4.904
1.60	4.953	5.003	5.053	5.104	5.155	5.207	5.259	5.312	5.366	5.419
1.70	5.474	5.529	5.585	5.641	5.697	5.755	5.812	5.871	5.930	5.989
1.80	6.050	6.110	6.172	6.234	6.297	6.360	6.424	6.488	6.553	6.619
1.90	6.686	6.753	6.821	6.890	6.959	7.029	7.099	7.171	7.243	7.316
2.00	7.389	7.463	7.538	7.614	7.691	7.768	7.846	7.925	8.004	8.085
2.10	8.166	8.248	8.331	8.415	8.499	8.585	8.671	8.758	8.846	8.935
2.20	9.025	9.116	9.207	9.300	9.393	9.488	9.583	9.679	9.777	9.875
2.30	9.974	10.07	10.18	10.28	10.38	10.49	10.59	10.70	10.80	10.91
2.40	11.02	11.13	11.25	11.36	11.47	11.59	11.70	11.82	11.94	12.06
2.50	12.18	12.30	12.43	12.55	12.68	12.81	12.94	13.07	13.20	13.33
2.60	13.46	13.60	13.74	13.87	14.01	14.15	14.30	14.44	14.59	14.73
2.70	14.88	15.03	15.18	15.33	15.49	15.64	15.80	15.96	16.12	16.28
2.80	16.44	16.61	16.78	16.95	17.12	17.29	17.46	17.64	17.81	17.99
2.90	18.17	18.36	18.54	18.73	18.92	19.11	19.30	19.49	19.69	19.89
3.00	20.09	20.29	20.49	20.70	20.91	21.12	21.33	21.54	21.76	21.98
3.10	22.20	22.42	22.65	22.87	23.10	23.34	23.57	23.81	24.05	24.29
3.20	24.53	24.78	25.03	25.28	25.53	25.79	26.05	26.31	26.58	26.84
3.30	27.11	27.39	27.66	27.94	28.22	28.50	28.79	29.08	29.37	29.67
3.40	29.96	30.27	30.57	30.88	31.19	31.50	31.82	32.14	32.46	32.79
3.50	33.12	33.45	33.78	34.12	34.47	34.81	35.16	35.52	35.87	36.23
3.60	36.60	36.97	37.34	37.71	38.09	38.47	38.86	39.25	39.65	40.04
3.70	40.45	40.85	41.26	41.68	42.10	42.52	42.95	43.38	43.82	44.26
3.80	44.70	45.15	45.60	46.06	46.53	46.99	47.47	47.94	48.42	48.91
3.90	49.40	49.90	50.40	50.91	51.42	51.94	52.46	52.98	53.52	54.05

Note: For example, if the continuously compounded interest rate is 10 percent per year, the investment of $1 today will be worth $1.105 at year 1 and $1.221 at year 2.

APPENDIX TABLE 5

Present value of $1 per year received in a continuous stream for each of *t* years (discounted at an *annually compounded* rate *r*) = $\{1 - 1/(1 + r)^t\}/\{\ln(1 + r)\}$.

Number of Years	Interest Rate per Year														
	1%	2%	3%	4%	5%	6%	7%	8%	9%	10%	11%	12%	13%	14%	15%
1	.995	.990	.985	.981	.976	.971	.967	.962	.958	.954	.950	.945	.941	.937	.933
2	1.980	1.961	1.942	1.924	1.906	1.888	1.871	1.854	1.837	1.821	1.805	1.790	1.774	1.759	1.745
3	2.956	2.913	2.871	2.830	2.791	2.752	2.715	2.679	2.644	2.609	2.576	2.543	2.512	2.481	2.450
4	3.922	3.846	3.773	3.702	3.634	3.568	3.504	3.443	3.383	3.326	3.270	3.216	3.164	3.113	3.064
5	4.878	4.760	4.648	4.540	4.437	4.337	4.242	4.150	4.062	3.977	3.896	3.817	3.741	3.668	3.598
6	5.825	5.657	5.498	5.346	5.202	5.063	4.931	4.805	4.685	4.570	4.459	4.353	4.252	4.155	4.062
7	6.762	6.536	6.323	6.121	5.930	5.748	5.576	5.412	5.256	5.108	4.967	4.832	4.704	4.582	4.465
8	7.690	7.398	7.124	6.867	6.623	6.394	6.178	5.974	5.780	5.597	5.424	5.260	5.104	4.956	4.816
9	8.609	8.243	7.902	7.583	7.284	7.004	6.741	6.494	6.261	6.042	5.836	5.642	5.458	5.285	5.121
10	9.519	9.072	8.657	8.272	7.913	7.579	7.267	6.975	6.702	6.447	6.208	5.983	5.772	5.573	5.386
11	10.42	9.884	9.391	8.935	8.512	8.121	7.758	7.421	7.107	6.815	6.542	6.287	6.049	5.826	5.617
12	11.31	10.68	10.10	9.572	9.083	8.633	8.218	7.834	7.478	7.149	6.843	6.559	6.294	6.048	5.818
13	12.19	11.46	10.79	10.18	9.627	9.116	8.647	8.216	7.819	7.453	7.115	6.802	6.512	6.242	5.992
14	13.07	12.23	11.46	10.77	10.14	9.571	9.048	8.570	8.131	7.729	7.359	7.018	6.704	6.413	6.144
15	13.93	12.98	12.12	11.34	10.64	10.00	9.423	8.897	8.418	7.980	7.579	7.212	6.874	6.563	6.276
16	14.79	13.71	12.75	11.88	11.11	10.41	9.774	9.201	8.681	8.209	7.778	7.385	7.024	6.694	6.390
17	15.64	14.43	13.36	12.41	11.55	10.79	10.10	9.482	8.923	8.416	7.957	7.539	7.158	6.809	6.490
18	16.48	15.14	13.96	12.91	11.98	11.15	10.41	9.742	9.144	8.605	8.118	7.676	7.275	6.910	6.577
19	17.31	15.83	14.54	13.39	12.39	11.49	10.69	9.983	9.347	8.777	8.263	7.799	7.380	6.999	6.652
20	18.14	16.51	15.10	13.86	12.77	11.81	10.96	10.21	9.533	8.932	8.394	7.909	7.472	7.077	6.718

Number of Years	Interest Rate per Year														
	16%	17%	18%	19%	20%	21%	22%	23%	24%	25%	26%	27%	28%	29%	30%
1	.929	.925	.922	.918	.914	.910	.907	.903	.900	.896	.893	.889	.886	.883	.880
2	1.730	1.716	1.703	1.689	1.676	1.663	1.650	1.638	1.625	1.613	1.601	1.590	1.578	1.567	1.556
3	2.421	2.392	2.365	2.337	2.311	2.285	2.259	2.235	2.211	2.187	2.164	2.141	2.119	2.098	2.077
4	3.016	2.970	2.925	2.882	2.840	2.799	2.759	2.720	2.682	2.646	2.610	2.576	2.542	2.509	2.477
5	3.530	3.464	3.401	3.340	3.281	3.223	3.168	3.115	3.063	3.013	2.964	2.917	2.872	2.828	2.785
6	3.972	3.886	3.804	3.724	3.648	3.574	3.504	3.436	3.370	3.307	3.246	3.187	3.130	3.075	3.022
7	4.354	4.247	4.145	4.048	3.954	3.865	3.779	3.696	3.617	3.542	3.469	3.399	3.331	3.266	3.204
8	4.682	4.555	4.434	4.319	4.209	4.104	4.004	3.909	3.817	3.730	3.646	3.566	3.489	3.415	3.344
9	4.966	4.819	4.680	4.547	4.422	4.302	4.189	4.081	3.978	3.880	3.786	3.697	3.612	3.530	3.452
10	5.210	5.044	4.887	4.739	4.599	4.466	4.340	4.221	4.108	4.000	3.898	3.801	3.708	3.619	3.535
11	5.421	5.237	5.063	4.900	4.747	4.602	4.465	4.335	4.213	4.096	3.986	3.882	3.783	3.689	3.599
12	5.603	5.401	5.213	5.036	4.870	4.713	4.566	4.428	4.297	4.173	4.057	3.946	3.841	3.742	3.648
13	5.759	5.542	5.339	5.150	4.972	4.806	4.650	4.503	4.365	4.235	4.112	3.997	3.887	3.784	3.686
14	5.894	5.662	5.446	5.245	5.058	4.882	4.718	4.564	4.420	4.284	4.157	4.036	3.923	3.816	3.715
15	6.010	5.765	5.537	5.326	5.129	4.945	4.774	4.614	4.464	4.324	4.192	4.068	3.951	3.841	3.737
16	6.111	5.853	5.614	5.393	5.188	4.998	4.820	4.655	4.500	4.355	4.220	4.092	3.973	3.860	3.754
17	6.197	5.928	5.679	5.450	5.238	5.041	4.858	4.687	4.529	4.381	4.242	4.112	3.990	3.875	3.767
18	6.272	5.992	5.735	5.498	5.279	5.076	4.889	4.714	4.552	4.401	4.259	4.127	4.003	3.887	3.778
19	6.336	6.047	5.781	5.538	5.313	5.106	4.914	4.736	4.571	4.417	4.273	4.139	4.014	3.896	3.785
20	6.391	6.094	5.821	5.571	5.342	5.130	4.935	4.754	4.586	4.430	4.284	4.149	4.022	3.903	3.791

Note: For example, if the interest rate is 10 percent per year, a continuous cash flow of $1 a year for each of 5 years is worth $3.977. A continuous flow of $1 in year 5 only is worth $3.977 − $3.326 = $.651.

APPENDIX TABLE 6

Cumulative probability [*N*(*d*)] that a normally distributed variable will be less than *d* standard deviations above the mean.

d	0	0.01	0.02	0.03	0.04	0.05	0.06	0.07	0.08	0.09
0	.5000	.5040	.5080	.5120	.5160	.5199	.5239	.5279	.5319	.5359
0.1	.5398	.5438	.5478	.5517	.5557	.5596	.5636	.5675	.5714	.5753
0.2	.5793	.5832	.5871	.5910	.5948	.5987	.6026	.6064	.6103	.6141
0.3	.6179	.6217	.6255	.6293	.6331	.6368	.6406	.6443	.6480	.6517
0.4	.6554	.6591	.6628	.6664	.6700	.6736	.6772	.6808	.6844	.6879
0.5	.6915	.6950	.6985	.7019	.7054	.7088	.7123	.7157	.7190	.7224
0.6	.7257	.7291	.7324	.7357	.7389	.7422	.7454	.7486	.7517	.7549
0.7	.7580	.7611	.7642	.7673	.7704	.7734	.7764	.7794	.7823	.7852
0.8	.7881	.7910	.7939	.7967	.7995	.8023	.8051	.8078	.8106	.8133
0.9	.8159	.8186	.8212	.8238	.8264	.8289	.8315	.8340	.8365	.8389
1	.8413	.8438	.8461	.8485	.8508	.8531	.8554	.8577	.8599	.8621
1.1	.8643	.8665	.8686	.8708	.8729	.8749	.8770	.8790	.8810	.8830
1.2	.8849	.8869	.8888	.8907	.8925	.8944	.8962	.8980	.8997	.9015
1.3	.9032	.9049	.9066	.9082	.9099	.9115	.9131	.9147	.9162	.9177
1.4	.9192	.9207	.9222	.9236	.9251	.9265	.9279	.9292	.9306	.9319
1.5	.9332	.9345	.9357	.9370	.9382	.9394	.9406	.9418	.9429	.9441
1.6	.9452	.9463	.9474	.9484	.9495	.9505	.9515	.9525	.9535	.9545
1.7	.9554	.9564	.9573	.9582	.9591	.9599	.9608	.9616	.9625	.9633
1.8	.9641	.9649	.9656	.9664	.9671	.9678	.9686	.9693	.9699	.9706
1.9	.9713	.9719	.9726	.9732	.9738	.9744	.9750	.9756	.9761	.9767
2	.9772	.9778	.9783	.9788	.9793	.9798	.9803	.9808	.9812	.9817
2.1	.9821	.9826	.9830	.9834	.9838	.9842	.9846	.9850	.9854	.9857
2.2	.9861	.9864	.9868	.9871	.9875	.9878	.9881	.9884	.9887	.9890
2.3	.9893	.9896	.9898	.9901	.9904	.9906	.9909	.9911	.9913	.9916
2.4	.9918	.9920	.9922	.9925	.9927	.9929	.9931	.9932	.9934	.9936
2.5	.9938	.9940	.9941	.9943	.9945	.9946	.9948	.9949	.9951	.9952

Note: For example, if *d* = .22, *N*(*d*) = .5871 (i.e., there is a .5871 probability that a normally distributed variable will be less than .22 standard deviations above the mean).

APPENDIX B

ANSWERS TO QUIZZES

Chapter 1

1. (a) Real; (b) executive airplanes; (c) brand names; (d) financial; (e) bonds; (f) investment; (g) capital budgeting; (h) financing.
2. **a.** Financial assets, such as stocks or bank loans, are claims held by investors. Corporations sell financial assets to raise the cash to invest in real assets such as plant and equipment. Some real assets are intangible.
   b. Capital budgeting means investment in real assets. Financing means raising the cash for this investment.
   c. The shares of public corporations are traded on stock exchanges and can be purchased by a wide range of investors. The shares of closely held corporations are not traded and are not generally available to investors.
   d. Unlimited liability: investors are responsible for all the firm's debts. A sole proprietor has unlimited liability. Investors in corporations have limited liability. They can lose their investment, but no more.
   e. A corporation is a separate legal "person" with unlimited life. Its owners hold shares in the business. A partnership is a limited-life agreement to establish and run a business.
3. *c, d, e,* and *g* are real assets. Others are financial.
4. Double taxation and agency costs due to separation of ownership and control. Public organizations also face the higher costs of complying with legal requirements and communicating with dispersed shareholders.
5. *a, c, d.*
6. *c, d.*
7. Principal–agent issues, often amplified by asymmetric information.

Chapter 2

1. (a) Negative; (b) $PV = C_1/(1 + r)$; (c) $NPV = C_0 + (C_1/(1 + r))$; (d) r is the return foregone by investing in the project rather than the capital market; (e) the return offered by default-free U.S. Treasury securities.
2. $DF_1 = .867$; discount rate = .154, or 15.4%.
3. (a) .909; (b) .833; (c) .769.
4. (a) Return = profit/investment = (132 − 100)/100 = .32, or 32%; (b) Negative (if the rate of interest r equals 32%, NPV = 0); (c) PV = 132/1.10 = 120, or Rs.120,000; (d) NPV = −100 + 120 = 20, or Rs.20,000.
5. The return foregone by investing in a project rather than in securities. The opportunity cost of capital for a risk-free investment is the interest rate on government bonds. For risky investments firms need to estimate the return expected by investors from securities of similar risk.
6. Neither should invest in the office building. The ant should lend and receive 1.2 × 185,000 = Rs. 222,000 at the end of the year (compared with a payoff of Rs. 210,000 from the building). The grasshopper should consume his Rs. 185,000 today rather than borrow 210,000/1.2 = Rs. 175,000 against the future value of the office building.
7. They will vote for *a* only. The other tasks can be carried out just as efficiently by stockholders.
8. To protect and enhance their reputations; because compensation is tied to earnings and stock price; supervision by the board of directors; the threat of takeover.
9. More. The additional loss would reflect the damage to its reputation which would affect its ability to hire staff and attract customers.

Chapter 3

1. Rs. 1.00.
2. 125/139 = .899.
3. $374/(1.09)^9$ = Rs. 172.
4. PV = $432/1.15 + 137/(1.15)^2 + 797/(1.15)^3$ = 376 + 104 + 524 = 1,003.
5. $100 \times (1.15)^8$ = Rs. 305.90.
6. NPV = −1,548 + 138/.09 = −Rs. 14.67.
7. PV = 4/(.14 − .04) = Rs. 40.
8. Each installment is 194/25 = Rs. 7.76 million. If installments are paid at the *end* of each year, PV = 7.76 × 25-year annuity factor = 7.76 × 9.823 = Rs. 76.23 million. Since payments are at the *beginning* of each year, PV = 76.23 × 1.09 = Rs. 83.08 million.
9. **(a)** PV = 1/.10 = Rs. 10; **(b)** PV = $(1/.10)/(1.10)^7$ = 10/2 = Rs. 5 (approximately); **(c)** PV = 10 − 5 = Rs. 5 (approximately); **(d)** PV = $C/(r-g)$ = 10,000/(.10 − .05) = Rs. 200,000.
10. **(a)** $10{,}000/1.05^5$ = Rs. 7,840.
    (b) You need to set aside (12,000 × 6-year annuity factor) = 12,000 × 4.623 = Rs. 55,476.
    (c) At the end of 6 years you would have $1.08^6 \times$ (60,476 − 55,476) = Rs. 7,934.
11. (1.25)/(1.21) − 1 = .033, or 3.3%.
12. **(a)** $1{,}000e^{.12 \times 5} = 1{,}000e^{.6}$ = Rs. 1,822; **(b)** PV = $5e^{-.12 \times 8} = 5e^{-.96}$ = Rs. 1.914 million;
    (c) $$\text{PV} = C\left(\frac{1}{r} - \frac{1}{re^{rt}}\right) = 2{,}000\left(\frac{1}{.12} - \frac{1}{.12e^{.12\times15}}\right)$$ = Rs. 13,912
13. **(a)** Rs. 12.625 million; **(b)** Rs. 12.705 million; **(c)** Rs. 12.712 million.

Chapter 4

1. **(a)** Does not change; **(b)** Price falls; **(c)** Yield rises.
2. More than 8 percent.
3. **(a)** True; **(b)** true.
4. Investors who buy stocks may get their return from capital gains as well as dividends. But the future stock price always depends on subsequent dividends. There is no inconsistency.
5. P_0 = (10 + 110)/1.10 = Rs. 109.09.
6. r = 5/40 = .125.
7. P_0 = 10/(.08 − .05) = Rs. 333.33.
8. By year 5, earnings will grow to Rs.18.23 per share. Forecasted price per share at year 4 is 18.23/.08 = Rs. 227.91.
   $$P_0 = \frac{10}{1.08} + \frac{10.50}{(1.08)^2} + \frac{11.03}{(1.08)^3} + \frac{11.58}{(1.08)^4} + \frac{227.91}{(1.08)^4} = 203.05.$$
9. 15/.08 + PVGO = 333.33; therefore PVGO = Rs. 145.83.
10. Z's forecasted dividends and prices grow as follows:

	Year 1	Year 2	Year 3
Dividend	10	10.50	11.03
Price	350	367.50	385.88

Calculate the expected rates of return:

$$\text{From year 0 to 1: } \frac{10+(350-333.33)}{333.33} = .08.$$

$$\text{From year 1 to 2: } \frac{10.50+(367.50-350)}{350} = .08.$$

$$\text{From year 2 to 3: } \frac{11.03+(385.88-367.50)}{367.50} = .08$$

Double expects 8% in *each* of the first 2 years. Triple expects 8% in *each* of the first 3 years.

11. **(a)** False; **(b)** true.
12. PVGO = 0, and EPS_1 equals the average future earnings the firm could generate under no-growth policy.

Chapter 5

1. **(a)** A = 3 years, B = 2 years, C = 3 years; **(b)** B; **(c)** A, B, and C; **(d)** B and C (NPV_B = Rs. 3,378; NPV_C = Rs. 2,405); **(e)** true; **(f)** It will accept no negative-NPV projects but will turn down some with positive NPVs. A project can have positive NPV if all future cash flows are considered but still not meet the stated cutoff period.
2. Given the cash flows $C_0, C_1, \ldots, C_T$, IRR is defined by
   $$\text{NPV} = C_0 + \frac{C_1}{1+\text{IRR}} + \frac{C_2}{(1+\text{IRR})^2} + \cdots + \frac{C_T}{(1+\text{IRR})^T} = 0.$$

It is calculated by trial and error, by financial calculators, or by spreadsheet programs.

3. (a) Rs. 15,750; Rs. 4,250; Rs. 0; (b) 100%.
4. No (you are effectively "borrowing" at a rate of interest higher than the opportunity cost of capital).
5. (a) Two; (b) −50% and +50%; (c) yes, NPV = +14.6.
6. The incremental flows from investing in Alpha rather than Beta are −200,000; +110,000; and 121,000. The IRR on the incremental cash flow is 10 percent (i.e., $-200 + 110/1.10 + 121/1.10^2 = 0$). The IRR on Beta exceeds the cost of capital and so does the IRR on the incremental investment in Alpha. Choose Alpha.
7. 1, 2, 4, and 6.

Chapter 6

1. *a, b, d, g, h.*
2. Real cash flow = 100,000/1.04 = Rs. 96,154; real discount rate = 1.08/1.04 − 1 = .03846

$$PV = \frac{96,154}{1.03846} = \text{Rs. } 92,593$$

3. (a) False; (b) false; (c) false; (d) false.
4. If additional depreciation is allowed throughout the life of the asset, then the company will be able to charge a higher amount as depreciation in the initial years of the life of the asset. This will increase the present value of the depreciation tax shields. If the company is allowed normal depreciation only, then it will be able to charge lesser depreciation in the first year of the life of the asset and more in the subsequent years of the life of the asset. Unless the tax rate is very high, this method will always produce a higher present value of the depreciation tax shields.
5.

	2004	2005	2006	2007	2008
Working capital	50,000	230,000	305,000	250,000	0
Cash flows	+50,000	+180,000	+75,000	−55,000	−250,000

6. Comparing present values can be misleading when projects have different economic lives and the projects are part of an ongoing business. For example, a machine that costs Rs. 100,000 per year to buy and lasts 5 years is not necessarily more expensive than a machine that costs Rs. 75,000 per year to buy but lasts only 3 years. Calculating the machines' equivalent annual costs allows an unbiased comparison.
7. PV cost = 1.5 + .2 × 14.09 = Rs. 4.319 million. Equivalent annual cost = 4.319/14.09 = .306, or Rs. 306,000.
8. (a) NPV_A = Rs. 100,000; NPV_B = Rs. 180,000.
(b) Equivalent cash flow of A = 100,000/1.736 = Rs. 57,604; equivalent cash flow of B = 180,000/2.487 = Rs. 72,376.
(c) Machine B.
9. Replace at end of 5 years (Rs. 80,000 > Rs. 72,376).

Chapter 7

1. Expected payoff is Rs. 100 and expected return is zero. Variance is 20,000 (percent squared) and standard deviation is 141%.
2. a. Standard deviation = 21.37 percent
b. Average real return = −0.74 percent
3. The fund had an average return of 6.47 percent and a standard deviation of 23.4 percent. The market had a lower return (0.69 percent) and a higher standard deviation (24.36 percent). Mr. Sabharwal's fund performed better than the market.
4. (a) False; (b) true; (c) true; (d) true; (e) false.
5. *d*
6.

$x_1^2\sigma_1^2$	$x_1x_2\sigma_{12}$	$x_1x_3\sigma_{13}$
$x_1x_2\sigma_{12}$	$x_2^2\sigma_2^2$	$x_2x_3\sigma_{23}$
$x_1x_3\sigma_{13}$	$x_2x_3\sigma_{23}$	$x_3^2\sigma_3^2$

7. (a) 26%; (b) zero; (c) .75; (d) less than 1.0 (the portfolio's risk is the same as the market, but some of this risk is unique risk).
8. 1.3 (Diversification does not affect market risk.)
9. A, 1.0; B, 2.0; C, 1.5; D, 0; E, −1.0.

Chapter 8

1. (a) 7%; (b) 27% with perfect positive correlation; 1% with perfect negative correlation; 19.1% with no correlation; (c) See Figure 1; (d) No, measure risk by beta, not by standard deviation.

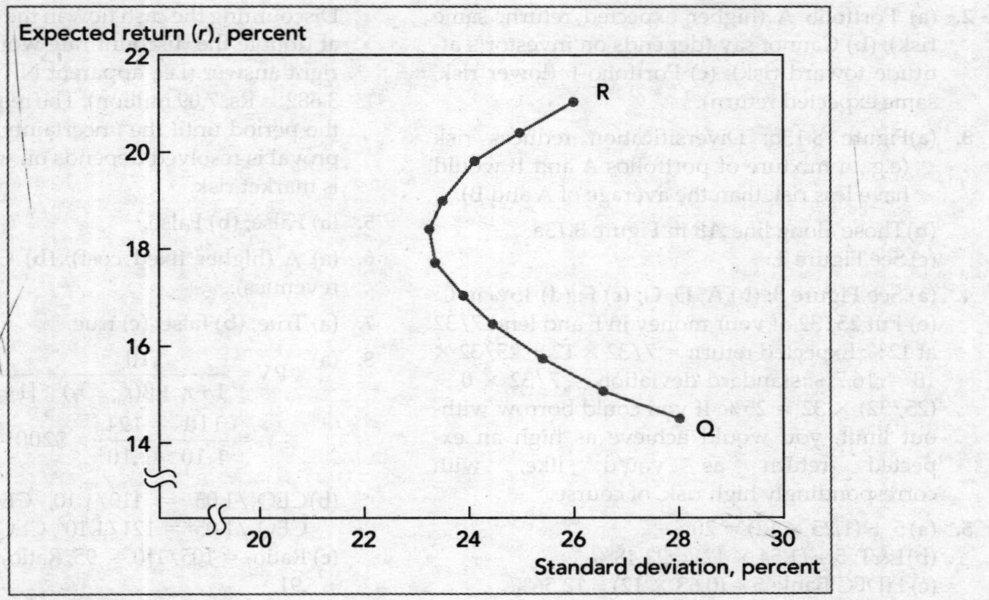

FIGURE 1

Chapter 8, Quiz question 1(c).

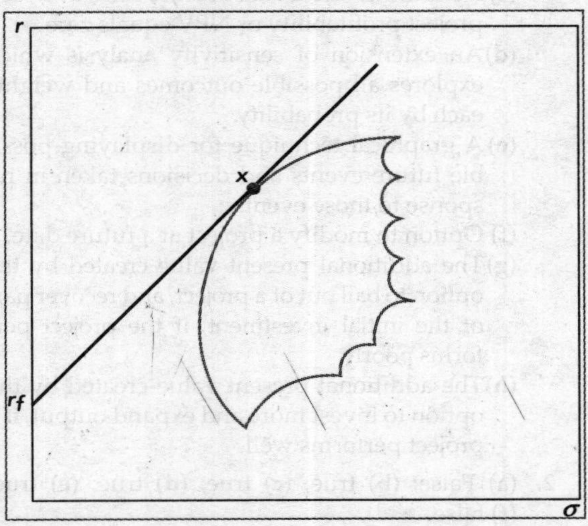

FIGURE 2

Chapter 8, Quiz question 3(c).

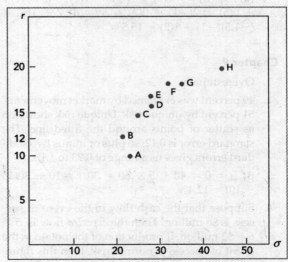

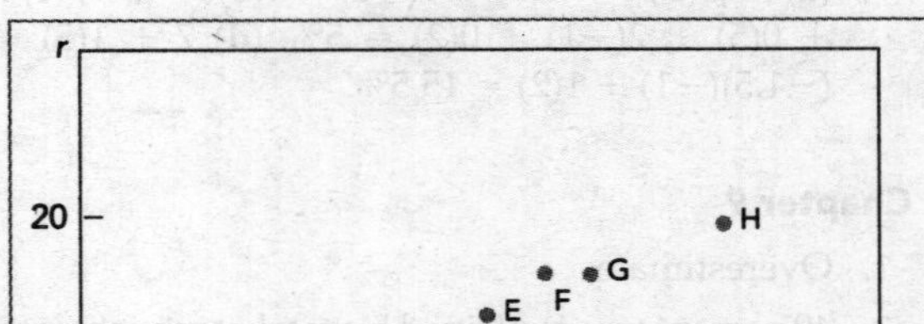

FIGURE 3

Chapter 8, Quiz question 4(a).

2. (**a**) Portfolio A (higher expected return, same risk); (**b**) Cannot say (depends on investor's attitude toward risk); (**c**) Portfolio F (lower risk, same expected return).

3. (**a**) Figure 8.13b: Diversification reduces risk (e.g., a mixture of portfolios A and B would have less risk than the average of A and B).

   (**b**) Those along line *AB* in Figure 8.13a.

   (**c**) See Figure 2.

4. (**a**) See Figure 3; (**b**) A, D, G; (**c**) F; (**d**) 15% in C. (**e**) Put 25/32 of your money in F and lend 7/32 at 12%: Expected return = 7/32 × 12 + 25/32 × 18 = 16.7%; standard deviation = 7/32 × 0 + (25/32) × 32 = 25%. If you could borrow without limit, you would achieve as high an expected return as you'd like, with correspondingly high risk, of course.

5. (**a**) 5 + (1.25 × 12) = 20%

   (**b**) L&T: 5 + (1.54 × 12) = 23.48%

   (**c**) HDFC Bank: 5 + (0.63 × 12) = 12.56%

   (**d**) Higher: If interest rate is 6%, $r = 6 + (0.73 * 11) = 14.03\%$; if rate = 5%, $r = 5 + (0.73 \times 12) = 13.76\%$

   (**e**) Lower: If interest rate is 6%, $r = 6 + (1.47 * 11) = 22.17\%$; if rate = 5%, $r = 5 + (1.47 \times 12) = 22.64\%$

6. (**a**) True; (**b**) false (it offers twice the market *risk premium*); (**c**) false.

7. (**a**) 7%; (**b**) 7 + 1(5) + 1(−1) + 1(2) = 13%; (**c**) 7 + 0(5) + 2(−1) + 0(2) = 5%; (**d**) 7 + 1(5) + (−1.5)(−1) + 1(2) = 15.5%.

Chapter 9

1. Overestimate.

2. 49 percent was explained by market movements, 51 percent by unique risk. Unique risk shows up as scatter of points around the fitted line. The standard error is 0.12, so plus or minus two standard errors gives us a range of 0.73 to 1.15.

3. $\beta_{assets} = 0 \times .40 + .5 \times .60 = .30$, $r = 10 + .30(18 - 10) = 12.4\%$.

4. Suppose that the cash flow in the event of success is $6 million. Then the *expected* flow is .5 × 6 = $3 million. If production of the potato in the event of success is normal risk, then this figure can be discounted back to the start of production at the company's ordinary cost of capital. For example, suppose the project lasts for 10 years. Then NPV = −15 + 3 × 5.65 = $1.95 million. Discounting the cash flow in the event of success at double the discount rate would not give the right answer (i.e., apparent NPV = −15 + 6 × 3.682 = Rs. 7.09 million). The required return for the period until the uncertainty about FDA approval is resolved depends on whether this risk is market risk.

5. (**a**) False; (**b**) False.

6. (**a**) A (higher fixed cost); (**b**) C (more cyclical revenues).

7. (**a**) True; (**b**) false; (**c**) true.

8. (**a**)

$$PV = \frac{110}{1 + r_f + \beta(r_m - r_f)} + \frac{121}{[1 + r_f + \beta(r_m - r_f)]^2} = \frac{110}{1.10} + \frac{121}{1.10^2} = \$200.$$

   (**b**) $CEQ_1/1.05 = 110/1.10$, CEQ_1 = Rs. 105; $CEQ_2/1.05^2 = 121/1.10^2$, CEQ_2 = Rs. 110.25.

   (**c**) $Ratio_1 = 105/110 = .95$; $Ratio_2 = 110.25/121 = .91$.

Chapter 10

1. (**a**) Analysis of how project profitability and NPV change if different assumptions are made about sales, cost, and other key variables.

   (**b**) Project NPV is recalculated by changing several inputs to new, but consistent, values.

   (**c**) Determines the level of future sales at which project profitability or NPV equals zero.

   (**d**) An extension of sensitivity analysis which explores all possible outcomes and weights each by its probability.

   (**e**) A graphical technique for displaying possible future events and decisions taken in response to those events.

   (**f**) Option to modify a project at a future date.

   (**g**) The additional present value created by the option to bail out of a project, and recover part of the initial investment, if the project performs poorly.

   (**h**) The additional present value created by the option to invest more and expand output, if a project performs well.

2. (**a**) False; (**b**) true; (**c**) true; (**d**) true; (**e**) true; (**f**) false.

3. (**a**) Describe how project cash flow depends on the underlying variables.

   (**b**) Specify probability distributions for forecast errors for these cash flows.

(c) Draw from the probability distributions to simulate the cash flows.

4. (a) True; (b) true; (c) false; (d) false.

Chapter 11

1. (a) False; (b) true; (c) true; (d) false.
2. Rs. 15
3. First consider whether *renting* the building and opening the Taco Palace is positive NPV. Then consider whether to buy (instead of renting) based on your optimistic view of local real estate.
4. (a) 160/1.05 = Rs. 152.4 million; (b) The expected rate of return is $r_f + \beta(r_m - r_f) = .05 + 1.2(.12 - .05) = .134$, or 13.4%. The expected price is 1,524 × 1.134 = 1,728. The certainty equivalent price is 1,600.
5. The second-hand market value of older planes falls by enough to make up for their higher fuel consumption. Also, the older planes are used on routes where fuel efficiency is relatively less important.

Chapter 12

1. (a) False; (b) true; (c) true; (d) false; (e) true (e.g., marketing programs and training); (f) false.
2. (a) Can lead to investment in negative-NPV projects.
   (b) Confuses the relative NPVs of projects proposed by different business units.
   (c) Project interactions may be ignored. Some opportunities, such as the closing or sale of a division, will not be considered. Strategic investments may be missed.
   (d) Creates a bias in favor of quick payback projects and against long-lived projects that may have large NPVs.
3. (a) *Agency costs:* value lost when managers do not act to maximize value. This includes costs of monitoring and control.
   (b) *Private benefits:* perks or other advantages enjoyed by managers.
   (c) *Empire building:* investing for size, not NPV.
   (d) *Free-rider problem:* when one shareholder, or group of shareholders, acts to monitor and control management, all shareholders benefit.
   (e) *Entrenching investment:* managers choose or design investment projects which increase the managers' value to the firm.
   (f) *Delegated monitoring:* monitoring on behalf of principals. For example, the board of directors monitors management performance on behalf of stockholders.
4. Monitoring is costly and encounters diminishing returns. Also, completely effective monitoring would require perfect information.
5. (a) Rupee amount; (b) EVA = Income earned − (cost of capital × investment); (c) They are essentially the same; (d) EVA makes the cost of capital visible to managers. Compensation based on EVA encourages them to dispose of unnecessary assets and to forego investment unless it earns more than the cost of capital; (e) Yes.
6. Return on investment = 1.6/20 = .08 or 8%. Net return = 8 − 11.5 = −3.5%. EVA = 1.6 − (.115 × 20) = −Rs. 7 million. EVA is negative.
7. Cash flow, economic, less, greater.
8.

	Year 1	Year 2	Year 3
Cash flow	0	78.55	78.55
PV at start of year	100.00	120.00	65.45
PV at end of year	120.00	65.45	0
Change in value during year	+20.00	−54.55	−65.45
Expected economic income	+20.00	+24.00	+13.10

Chapter 13

1. *c*
2. Weak, semistrong, strong, strong, weak.
3. (a) False; (b) false; (c) true; (d) false; (e) false; (f) true.
4. (a) False; (b) false; (c) true; (d) false.
5. 6 − (1.49 + 0.83 × 5) = 0.36%
6. (a) True; (b) false; (c) true; (d) true.
7. Decrease. The stock price already reflects an expected 25% increase. The 20% increase conveys bad news relative to expectations.

8. (a) An investor should not buy or sell shares based on apparent trends or cycles in returns.
(b) A CFO should not speculate on changes in interest rates or foreign exchange rates. There is no reason to think that the CFO has superior information.
(c) A financial manager evaluating the creditworthiness of a large customer could check the customer's stock price and the yield on its debt. A falling stock price or a high yield could indicate trouble ahead.
(d) Don't assume that accounting choices which increase or decrease earnings will have any effect on stock price.
(e) The company should not seek diversification just to reduce risk. Investors can diversify on their own.
(f) Stock issues do not depress price if investors believe the issuer has no private information.

Chapter 14

1. (a) True; (b) true; (c) False.
2. (a) 1393.09 / 10 = 139.309 crore shares; (b) 139.309 crores; (c) When some of the investors have not paid the purchased shares issued to them or when they have partially paid; (d) 250 crores (authorized) – 139.309 (issued) = 110.691 crore shares; (e) Rs.40403.32 crores / 139.309 crores shares = Rs.290 per share; (f) It will remain unchanged; (g) Book value per share will be (Rs.40403.32 crores – 10 crores)/(139.309 – 0.1) = Rs.290.16 per share.
3. (a) 80 votes; (b) 10 × 80 = 800 votes.
4. (a) subordinated; (b) floating rate; (c) convertible; (d) warrant; (e) common stock; preferred stock.
5. (a) False; (b) true;

Chapter 15

1. (a) Further sale of an already publicly traded stock; (b) U.S. bond issue by foreign corporation; (c) Bond issue by industrial company; (d) Bond issue by large financial institution.
2. (a) B; (b) A; (c) D; (d) C.
3. (a) Financing of startup companies.
(b) Sale of a security by the firm to investors.
(c) Sale of a security by existing shareholder.
(d) Description of a security offering filed with the SEC.
(e) Winning bidders for a new issue tend to overpay.
4. (a) A large issue; (b) a bond issue; (c) subsequent issue of stock; (d) a small private placement of bonds.
5. (a) False; (b) true; (c) true.
6. (a) 135,000 shares; (b) primary: 500,000 shares; secondary: 400,000 shares; (c) \$25 or 31%, which is higher than the average underpricing.
(d)

	Millions
Underwriting cost	Rs. 5.04
Administrative cost	.82
Underpricing	22.5
Total	Rs. 28.36

Note: Calculation ignores cost of shares sold under greenshoe option.

7. (a) Net proceeds of public issue = 10,000,000 – 150,000 – 80,000 = Rs. 9,770,000; net proceeds of private placement = Rs. 9,970,000.
(b) PV of extra interest on private placement =

$$\sum_{t=1}^{10} \frac{.005 \times 10{,}000{,}000}{1.085^t} = \text{Rs.}\,328{,}000,$$

i.e., extra cost of higher interest on private placement more than outweighs saving in issue costs. N.b. We ignore taxes.
(c) Private placement debt can be custom-tailored and the terms more easily renegotiated.
8. (a) Number of new shares, 50,000; (b) Amount of new investment, Rs. 500,000; (c) Total value of company after issue, Rs. 4,500,000; (d) Total number of shares after issue, 150,000; (e) Stock price after issue, Rs. 4,500,000/150,000 = Rs. 30; (f) The opportunity to buy one share is worth Rs. 20.

Chapter 16

1. (a) A1, B5; A2, B4; A3, B3; A4,B1; A5,B2; (b) May 6 = ex-dividend date; (c) (.18 × 4)/88.17 = .0082 or .82 percent; (d) (.18 × 4)/4.95 = .145 or 14.5 percent; (e) The price would fall to 88.17/1.1 = 80.15.
2. (a) False. The dividend depends on past dividends and current and forecasted earnings.
   (b) True. This target does reflect growth opportunities and capital expenditure requirements.
   (c) False. Dividends are adjusted gradually to a target. The target is based on current or forecasted earnings multiplied by the target payout ratio.
   (d) True. Dividend changes convey information to investors.
   (e) False. Dividends are "smoothed." Managers rarely increase regular dividends temporarily. They may pay a special dividend, however.
   (f) False. Dividends are rarely cut when repurchases are being made.
3. (a) Reinvest 1,000 × Rs. 50 = Rs. 500 in the stock. If the ex-dividend price is Rs. 150 – Rs. 2.50, this should involve the purchase of 500/147.50, or about 3.4 shares.
   (b) Sell shares worth 1,000 × Rs. 3 = Rs. 3,000. If the ex-dividend price is Rs. 200 – Rs. 5, this should involve the sale of 3,000/195, or about 15 shares.
4. Reduce repurchases by Rs. 10 million or issue new shares for Rs. 10 million.
5. (a) Company value is unchanged at 5,000 × 140 = $700,000. Share price stays at $140.
   (b) The discount rate $r = (DIV_1/P_0) + g = (20/140) + .05 = .193$. The price at which shares are repurchased in year 1 is 140 × (1 + r) = 140 × 1.193 = $167. Therefore the firm repurchases 50,000/167 = 299 shares. Total dividend payments in year 1 fall to 5,000 × 10 = $50,000, which is equivalent to 50,000/(5000 – 299) = $10.64 a share. Similarly, in year 2 the firm repurchases 281 shares at $186.52 and the dividend per share increases by 11.7% to $11.88. In each subsequent year, total dividends increase by 5%, the number of shares declines by 6% and, therefore, dividends per share increase by 11.7%. The constant growth model gives PV share = 10.64/(.193 – .117) = $140.
6. (a) $127.25.
   (b) Nothing; the stock price will stay at $130. 846,154 shares will be repurchased.
   (c) The with-dividend price stays at $130. Ex dividend it drops to $124.50; 883,534 shares will be issued.
7. *Current tax law (assuming dividend distribution tax rate of 14.025% and securities transaction tax of 0.15%):* All will prefer 'Lo'.
   Alternative tax law (assuming dividends are taxed in the hands of investors at a rate of 30 percent and capital gains tax of 20%): All will prefer 'Lo' again.

Chapter 17

1. Note the market value of Copper Corporation is far in excess of its book value:

	Market Value
Equity (8 million shares at Rs. 20)	Rs. 160
Short-term loans	Rs. 20 million

Ms. Pooja owns 0.625% of the firm, which proposes to increase equity to Rs.170 million and cut short-term debt. Ms. Pooja can offset this by (a) borrowing 0.00625 × 10,000,000 = Rs. 62,500, and (b) buying that much more Copper stock.

2. (a) $.5r_E + .5 \times 5\% = 12.5\%$; $r_E = 20\%$; (b) 12.5%; (c) E/P = 20%; P/E = 5; (d) Rs. 50; (e) $.5 \times \beta_E + .5 \times 0 = 1.0$; $\beta_E = 2.0$.
3. Expected return on assets is $r_A = .08 \times 30/80 + .16 \times 50/80 = .13$. The new return on equity will be $r_E = .13 + (20/60)(.13 - .08) = .147$.
4. a.

Operating income (Rs.)	500	1,000	1,500	2,000
Interest (Rs.)	250	250	250	250
Equity earnings (Rs.)	250	750	1,250	1,750
Earnings per share	.33	1.00	1.67	2.33
Return on shares (%)	3.3	10	16.7	23.3

b. $\beta_A = \left(\frac{D}{D+E} \times \beta_D\right) + \left(\frac{E}{D+E} \times \beta_E\right)$

$.8 = (.25 \times 0) + (.75 \times \beta_E)$

$\beta_E = 1.07$

5. **(a)** True; **(b)** True (as long as the return earned by the company is greater than the interest payment, earnings per share increase, but the P/E falls to reflect the higher risk); **(c)** False (the cost of equity increases with the ratio D/E); **(d)** False (the formula $r_E = r_A + (D/E)(r_A - r_D)$ does not require r_D to be constant); **(e)** False (debt amplifies variations in equity income); **(f)** False (value increases only if clientele is not satisfied).

6. **(a)** $r_A = .15$, $r_E = .175$; **(b)** $\beta_A = .6$ (unchanged), $\beta_D = .3$, $\beta_E = .9$.

7. See Figure 17.3.

8. Currently $r_A = r_E = .14$, or 14%. From proposition 2 the leverage causes r_E to increase to $r_E = r_A + (r_A - r_D)(D/E) = .14 + (.14 - .095) \times (45/55) = .1768$, or 17.68%.

After-tax WACC $= .095 \times (1 - .40) \times .45 + .1768 \times .55 = .1229$, or 12.29%.

Chapter 18

1. **a.** $\text{PV tax shield} = \frac{T_C(r_D D)}{1+r_D} = \frac{.35(.08 \times 1000)}{1.08} = 25.93.$

b. $\text{PV tax shield} = \sum_{t=1}^{5} \frac{.35(.08 \times 1000)}{(1.08)^t} = \text{Rs. } 11.80$

c. PV tax shield $= T_C D =$ Rs. 350.

2. **a.** PV tax shield $= T_C D =$ Rs. 16.

b. $T_C \times 20 =$ Rs. 8.

3. $\text{Relative advantage of debt} = \frac{1 - T_p}{(1 - T_{pE})(1 - T_C)} = \frac{.65}{(1)(.65)} = 1.00$

$\text{Relative advantage} = \frac{.65}{(.85)(.65)} = 1.18$

4. A firm with no taxable income saves no taxes by borrowing and paying interest. The interest payments would simply add to its tax-loss carryforwards. Such a firm would have little tax incentive to borrow.

5. **a.** Direct costs of financial distress are the legal and administrative costs of bankruptcy. Indirect costs include possible delays in liquidation (Eastern Airlines) or poor investment or operating decisions while bankruptcy is being resolved. Also the *threat* of bankruptcy can lead to costs.

b. If financial distress increases odds of default, managers' and shareholders' incentives change. This can lead to poor investment or financing decisions.

c. See the answer to 5(*b*). Examples are the "games" described in Section 18.3.

6. Not necessarily. Announcement of bankruptcy can send a message of poor profits and prospects. Part of the share price drop can be attributed to anticipated bankruptcy costs, however.

7. **a.** Stockholders win. Bond value falls, since the value of assets securing the bond has fallen.

b. Bondholder wins if we assume the cash is left invested in Treasury bills. The bondholder is sure to get Rs. 26 plus interest. Stock value is zero, because there is no chance that firm value can rise above Rs. 50.

c. The bondholders lose. The firm adds assets worth Rs. 10 and debt worth Rs. 10. This would increase Circular's debt ratio, leaving the old bondholders more exposed. The old bondholders' loss is the stockholders' gain.

d. Both bondholders and stockholders win. They share the (net) increase in firm value. The bondholders' position is not eroded by the issue of a junior security. (We assume that the preferred does not lead to still more game playing and that the new investment does not make the firm's *assets* safer or riskier.)

e. Bondholders lose because they are at risk for longer. Stockholders win.

8. More profitable firms have more taxable income to shield and are less likely to incur the costs of distress. Therefore the trade-off theory predicts high (book) debt ratios. In practice the more profitable companies borrow least.

9. When a company issues securities, outside investors worry that management may have unfavorable information. If so the securities can be overpriced. This worry is much less with debt than equity. Debt securities are safer than equity, and their price is less affected if unfavorable news comes out later.

A company that can borrow (without incurring substantial costs of financial distress) usually does so. An issue of equity would be read as "bad news" by investors, and the new stock could be sold only at a discount to the previous market price.

10. Financial slack is most valuable to growth companies with good but uncertain investment opportunities. Slack means that financing can be raised quickly for positive-NPV investments. But too much financial slack can tempt mature companies to overinvest. Increased borrowing can force such firms to pay out cash to investors.

Chapter 19

1. Market values of debt and equity are: D = 0.9 × 75 = Rs. 67.5 million and E = 42 × 2.5 = Rs. 105 million. D/V = 0.39

   WACC = 0.09 × (1 – 0.3366) × 0.39 + 0.18 × 0.61 = 0.133, or 13.3 percent

2. Step 1: r = 0.09 × 0.39 + 0.18 × 0.61 = 0.145

   Step 2: r_D = 0.086, r_E = 0.145 + (0.145 – 0.086) (15/85) = 0.155

   Step 3: WACC = 0.086 × (1 – 0.3366) × 0.15 + 0.155 × 0.85 = 0.1403, or 14.03%

3. (a) False; (b) true; (c) true.

4. The method values the equity of a company by discounting cash flows to stockholders at the cost of equity. See Section 19.2 for more details. The method assumes that the debt-to-equity ratio will remain constant.

5. (a) True; (b) false, if interest tax shields are valued separately; (c) true.

6. APV = base-case NPV ± PV financing side effects

   a. APV = 0 – .15(500,000) = –75,000;

   b. APV = 0 + 76,000 = +76,000.

7. **a.** 12%, of course.

   b. r_E = .12 + (.12 – .075)(30/70) = .139, WACC = .075(1 – .35)(.30) + .139(.70) = .112, or 11.2%.

8. **a.** Base-case NPV = –1,000 + 1200/1.20 = 0.

   b. PV tax shield = (.35 × .1 × .3(1000))/1.1 = 9.55. APV = 0 + 9.55 = $9.55.

9. No. The more debt you use, the higher rate of return equity investors will require. (Lenders may demand more also.) Thus there is a hidden cost of the "cheap" debt: It makes equity more expensive.

10. Howrah Trucking does not have 90 percent debt capacity. Kolkata Motors is borrowing Rs. 45 million partly on the strength of its existing assets. Also the decision to raise bank finance for the purchase does not mean that Howrah Trucking has changed its target debt ratio. An APV valuation of Kolkata Motors would probably assume 50 percent debt ratio.

Chapter 20

1. Call; exercise; put; European.

2. Figure 20.13*a* represents a call seller; Figure 20.13*b* represents a call buyer.

3. **a.** The exercise price of the put option (i.e., you'd sell stock for the exercise price);

   b. The value of the stock (i.e., you would throw away the put and keep the stock).

4. Value of call + PV(exercise price) = value of put + value of asset (e.g., share). See table below. Relationship holds only for European options with same exercise price.

At Maturity:	Share Price Exceeds Exercise Price		Share Price Below Exercise Price	
	Action	Value	Action	Value
Call + PV(EX)	Exercise call	Stock price	Don't exercise call	Exercise price
Put + share	Don't exercise put	Stock price	Exercise put	Exercise price

5. Buy a call and lend the present value of the exercise price.

6. **a.** Keep gold stocks and buy 6-month puts with an exercise price equal to 83.3% of the current price.

   b. Sell gold stocks, invest £485,000 for 6 months at 6%. The remaining £115,000 can be used to buy calls on the gold stocks with the same exercise price.

7. (a) See Figure 4; (b) stock price − PV(EX) = 100 − 100/1.1 = Rs. 9.09.

8. Figure 20.13(b) doesn't show the cost of purchasing the call. The profit from call purchase would be negative for all stock prices less than exercise price plus cost of call. Figure 20.13(a) doesn't record the proceeds from selling the call.

9. (a) Zero; (b) Stock price less the present value of the exercise price.

10. The call price (a) increases; (b) decreases; (c) increases; (d) increases; (e) decreases; (f) decreases.

11. a. All investors, however risk-averse, should value more highly an option on a volatile stock. For both ExxonMobil and Amgen the option is valueless if final stock price is below the exercise price, but the option on Amgen has more upside potential.
    b. Other things equal, stockholders lose and debtholders gain if the company shifts to safer assets. When the assets are risky, the option to default is more valuable. Debtholders bear much of the losses if asset value declines, but shareholders get the gains if asset value increases.

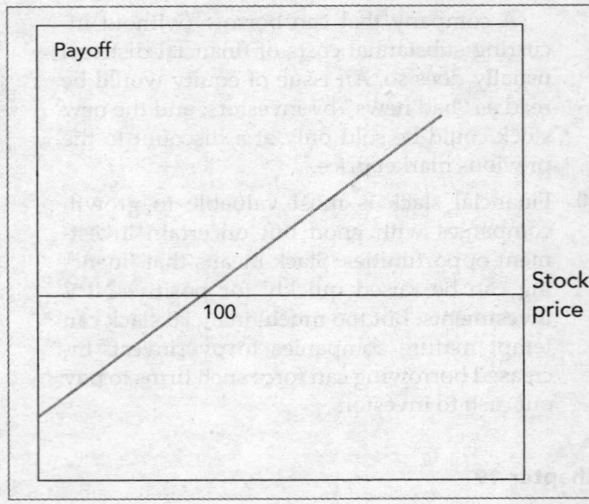

FIGURE 4
Chapter 20, Quiz Question 7.

Chapter 21

1. (a) Using risk-neutral method, $(p \times 20) + (1 - p)(-16.7) = 1$, $p = .48$.

$$\text{Value of call} = \frac{(.48 \times 8) + (.52 \times 0)}{1.01} = 3.8.$$

(b) $$\text{Delta} = \frac{\text{spread of option prices}}{\text{spread of stock prices}} = \frac{8}{14.7} = .544.$$

(c)

	Current Cash Flow	Possible Future Cash Flows	
Buy call	−3.8	0	+8.0
equals			
Buy .544 shares	−21.8	−18.2	+26.2
Borrow 18.0	+18.0	−18.2	−18.2
	−3.8	0	+8.0

(d) Possible stock prices with call option prices in parentheses.

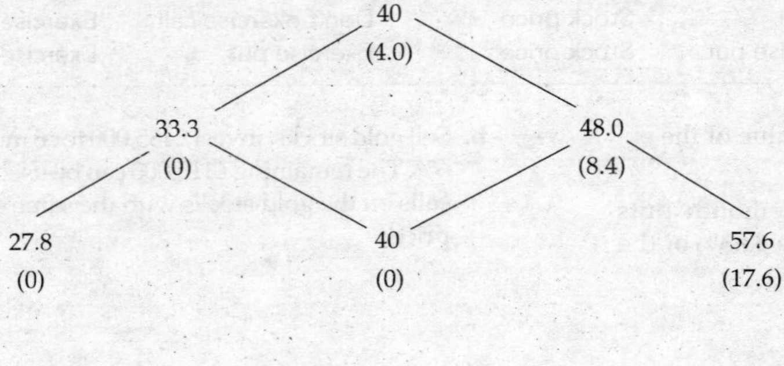

Option prices were calculated as follows:

$$Month\ 1: \text{(i)} \frac{(.48\times 0)+(.52\times 0)}{1.01}=0,$$

$$\text{(ii)} \frac{(.48\times 17.6)+(.52\times 0)}{1.01}=8.4.$$

$$Month\ 0: =\frac{(.48\times 8.4)+(.52\times 0)}{1.01}=4.0.$$

e. $\text{Delta}=\dfrac{\text{spread of option prices}}{\text{spread of stock prices}}=\dfrac{8.4}{14.7}=.57.$

2. (a) No. The maximum delta is 1.0 when the ratio of stock price to exercise price is very high. (b) No. (c) Delta increases. (d) Delta increases.

3. Using the replicating portfolio method, delta = (25 – 0) / (80 – 45) = 0.7143.

	Current Cash Flow	Possible Future Cash Flows	
Buy call	−11.27	0	+25
equals			
Buy 0.7143 shares	−42.86	+32.14	+57.14
Borrow 31.59	+31.59	−32.14	−32.14
	−11.27	0	+25

Using risk-neutral method, (1.0175 – 0.75) / (1.33 – 0.75) = 0.4612

$$\text{Value of call}=\frac{(0.4612\times 25)+(0.5388\times 0)}{1.07}=11.27$$

The put value is 11.27 + 55/1.0175 − 60 = 5.32.

4. Using the replicating portfolio method, delta = (15 – 0) / (75 – 48) = 0.556

	Current Cash Flow	Possible Future Cash Flows	
Buy call	−7.12	0	+15
equals			
Buy .556 shares	−33.33	+26.67	+41.67
Borrow 26.21	+26.21	−26.67	−26.67
	−7.12	0	+15

Using the risk-neutral method, p = (1.0175 – 0.8) / (1.25 – 0.8) = 0.4833

$$\text{Value of call}=\frac{0.4833\times 15+0.5167\times 0}{1.0175}=7.12$$

Lower risk means less upside for the call option. Thus option value falls.

5. a. Delta = 100/(200 − 50) = .667.
   b.

	Current Cash Flow	Possible Future Cash Flows	
Buy call	−36.36	0	+100
equals			
Buy .667 shares	−66.67	+33.33	+133.33
Borrow 30.30	+30.30	−33.33	−33.33
	−36.36	0	+100

   c. $(p \times 100) + (1 - p)(-50) = 10$, $p = .4$.
   d. $\text{Value of call} = \dfrac{(.4 \times 100) + (.6 \times 0)}{1.10} = 36.36.$
   e. No. The true probability of a price rise is almost certainly higher than the risk-neutral probability, but it does not help to value the option.
6. a. Call value = Rs. 3.44.
   b. Put value = call value + PV(exercise price) − stock price = Rs. 1.67.
7. True; as the stock price rises, the risk of the option falls.
8. a. You would exercise early if the stock price was sufficiently low. There may be little opportunity for further gains in the option value and it would be better to invest the exercise price to earn interest.
   b. Don't exercise early. The interest savings from delaying payment of the exercise price is larger than the dividend foregone.
   c. If the stock price and dividend are sufficiently high, it may pay to exercise early to capture the dividend.

Chapter 22

1. a. Increase value (unless the cash flows from the Mark II needed to be discounted at a higher rate).
   b. Increase value.
   c. Reduce value.
2. a. You can't use *any* single discount rate for option payoffs. The risk of an option changes as asset price changes and time passes.
   b. The risky *asset* may be worth less as a result, but the option owner can capitalize from up moves while not losing from down moves.
   c. Option value depends on value of underlying asset. DCF is needed to get this value.
3. a. You learn more about land prices and best use of the land.
   b. By developing immediately, you capture rents immediately.

Chapter 23

1. There are 12 semi-annual coupons of 5.515 plus a principal repayment of 100. With a discount rate of 5.434 / 2 = 2.717%, PV is

$$\frac{5.515}{1.02717} + \frac{5.515}{1.02717^2} + \ldots + \frac{105.515}{1.02717^{12}} = 128.33$$

2. a. The yields on the four bonds are: 6.72% bond, 4.61%; 7.37% bond, 4.46%; 10% bond, 4.58%; 10.5% bond, 4.22% (i.e., the 6.72% bond had the highest yield and the 10.5% bond had the lowest yield)
   b. The 6.72% bond had the longest duration (6.26 years) and the 10.5% bond the shortest (5.91 years).

	PV			Proportion of PV			Proportion × Time		
Year	2s	4s	8s	2s	4s	8s	2s	4s	8s
1	1.92	3.84	7.70	0.023	0.039	0.058	0.023	0.039	0.058
2	1.84	3.68	7.41	0.023	0.037	0.056	0.045	0.075	0.111
3	1.76	3.54	7.13	0.022	0.036	0.053	0.065	0.108	0.160
4	1.69	3.39	6.86	0.021	0.034	0.051	0.083	0.138	0.206
5	1.62	3.26	6.61	0.020	0.033	0.050	0.099	0.165	0.248
6	1.55	3.12	6.36	0.019	0.032	0.048	0.114	0.191	0.286
7	1.49	3.00	6.12	0.018	0.030	0.046	0.128	0.213	0.321
8	1.43	2.88	5.89	0.017	0.029	0.044	0.140	0.234	0.353
9	1.37	2.76	5.67	0.017	0.028	0.042	0.151	0.253	0.382
10	66.95	68.92	73.67	0.820	0.700	0.552	8.203	7.005	5.521
	81.62	98.39	133.42	1.000	1.000	1.000	9.051	8.420	7.647
								▲ Durations	

3. a. $PV = \frac{50}{1+r_1} + \frac{1,050}{(1+r_2)^2}$
   b. $PV = \frac{50}{1+y} + \frac{1,050}{(1+y)^2}$
   c. Less (it is between the 1-year and 2-year spot rates).
   d. Yield to maturity; spot rate.
4. a. Fall (e.g., 1-year 10% bond is worth 110/1.1 = 100 if r = 10% and is worth 110/1.15 = 95.65 if r = 15%).
   b. Less (e.g., see 4(*a*)).
   c. Less (e.g., with r = 5%, 1-year 10% bond is worth 110/1.05 = 104.76).
   d. Higher (e.g., if r = 10%, 1-year 10% bond is worth 110/1.1 = 100, while 1-year 8% bond is worth 108/1.1 = 98.18).
   e. No, low-coupon bonds have longer durations (unless there is only one period to maturity) and are therefore more volatile (e.g., if r falls from 10% to 5%, the value of a 2-year 10% bond rises from 100 to 109.3 (a rise of 9.3%). The value of a 2-year 5% bond rises from 91.3 to 100 (a rise of 9.5%).
5. a. $(100/95.56)^{(1/2)}$ = .0230, or 2.30%
   $(100/92.30)^{(1/3)}$ = .0271, or 2.71%
   $(100/88.62)^{(1/4)}$ = .0307, or 3.07%
   $(100/64.42)^{(1/10)}$ = .0450, or 4.50%
   b. Upward.
   c. Lower (the yield is a complicated average of the different spot rates).
   d. 95.56/92.30 − 1 = .0353, or 3.53%; 92.30/88.62 − 1 = .0415, or 4.15%.
6. a. Price today is 108.425; price after 1 year is 106.930.
   b. Return = (106.930 + 8)/108.425 − 1 = .06, or 6%.
   c. If a bond's yield to maturity is unchanged, the return to the bondholder is equal to the yield.
7. a. False. Duration depends on the coupon as well as the maturity.
   b. False. Given the yield to maturity, volatility is proportional to duration.
   c. True. A lower coupon rate means longer duration and therefore higher volatility.
   d. False. A higher interest rate reduces the relative present value of (distant) principal repayments.
8.

	Year	C_t	$PV(C_t)$	Proportion of Total Value	Proportion × Time
Security A	1	40	37.04	.359	.359
	2	40	34.29	.333	.666
	3	40	31.75	.308	.924
		V =	103.08	1.0	Duration = 1.949 years
Security B	1	20	18.52	.141	.141
	2	20	17.15	.131	.262
	3	120	95.26	.728	2.184
		V =	130.93	1.0	Duration = 2.587 years
Security C	1	10	9.26	.088	.088
	2	10	8.57	.082	.164
	3	110	87.32	.830	2.490
		V =	105.15	1.0	Duration = 2.742 years

Volatilities: A, 1.80; B, 2.40; C, 2.49.

9. a. $(1 + r_2)^2 = (1 + r_1)(1 + f_2)$
$1.03^2 = 1.01 \times (1 + f_2)$
$f_2 = .05$, or 5%.
b. The expected 1-year spot rate at time 1 equals the forward rate f_2.
c. Against (unless one believes that investors have generally expected interest rates to rise).
d. The forward rate equals the expected spot rate *plus* a liquidity premium.
e. Long-term bonds.
f. Short-term bonds.

Chapter 24

1. Promised yield = 12.72 percent; expected yield = 9.37 percent.
2. (a) Increase; (b) increase.
3. Put option on company's assets with an exercise price equal to the face value of the bond.
4. Company A: Z-score = .400 + .058 + .365 + .381 + .168 = 1.371 (grey area) Company B: Z-score = −.027 + .004 + .082 + .008 + .497 = .564 (bankrupt)
5. The expected growth in the market value of the assets, the face value and maturity of the debt, and the variability of future asset values. (In practice, compromises need to be made if, for example, the company has issued bonds with different maturities.)
6. 97.24% (from Table 24.4); 2.76%.
7. Both bonds are more likely to be downrated.
8. The value at risk of a loan portfolio depends on the correlation between their returns.

Chapter 25

1. (**a**) Bonds; (**b**) Bond; (**c**) an asset-backed security; (**d**) project finance
2. a. You would like an issue of junior debt.
b. You prefer it not to do so (unless it is also junior debt). The existing property may not be sufficient to pay off your debt.
3. (**a**) First Boston Corporation; (**b**) Bank of America National Trust and Savings Association; (**c**) $986.14; (**d**) registered; (**e**) 103.0%.
4. (**a**) Approximately 99.489 + 8.25/12 = 100.18%; (**b**) .04125 × 250 = $10.3 million on Feb 15, 1993; (**c**) After making earlier sinking fund payments, $12.5 million remains to be repaid on Aug 15, 2022; (**d**) 2008 (but see footnote 23 for some possible complications).
5. Private placements: typically have simpler loan agreements—which may nevertheless contain "custom" features; have more stringent covenants; are more easily renegotiated.
6. a. False. Lenders usually retain some recourse; e.g., they may demand a completion guarantee.
b. True, but some new securities (e.g., euro bonds) survive even when the original motive for issuing them disappears.
c. False. The borrower has the option.
d. True. But debt issues with weak covenants suffered in such takeovers.
e. True. The costs of renegotiation are less for private placements.
7. (**a**) 1,000/47 = 21.28; (**b**) 1,000/50 = Rs. 20.00; (**c**) 21.28 × 41.50 = Rs. 883.12, or 88.31%; (**d**) 650/21.28 = Rs. 30.55; (**e**) no (not if the investor is free to convert immediately); (**f**) Rs. 12.22 (i.e., (910 − 650)/21.28; (**g**) (47/41.50) − 1 = .13, or 13%; (**h**) when the price reaches 102.75% of face value.
8. (**a**) False; (**b**) true; (**c**) false; (**d**) true.

Chapter 26

1. *A, c; B, d* or *i; C, b* or *e; D, f; E, a; F, h; G, g.*
2. *a, b, d, f,* and *h* (though there may be other ways to reduce AMT).
3. a. The lessor must charge enough to cover the present value of the costs of owning and operating the asset over its expected economic life. In a competitive leasing market the present value of rentals cannot exceed the present value of costs. The competitive rental payment ends up equal to the lessor's equivalent annual cost.
b. The user's equivalent annual cost is the annual cost to the user of owning and operating the asset. If the operating lease rate is less than this cost, it pays to lease.
4. (**a**) True; (**b**) true; (**c**) true, but compare after-tax rates; (**d**) true; (**e**) true; (**f**) true; (**g**) true.

5. The present value of depreciation tax shields on the Rs. 75,000 desk, using 20% WDV rate for 6 years (the entire net block at the end of the fifth year written off in the sixth year), is

PV (at 9 percent) = 0.35 × PV (6 years' depreciation)

= Rs. 19,377.

After-tax administrative costs are 1000 *(1-0.35) = Rs. 650 per year for six years. If the first costs are incurred immediately, their present value is Rs. 3178. Thus the present value of all costs is Rs. 75,000 – Rs. 19,377 + Rs. 3,178 = Rs. 58,801. The break-even rate is about Rs. 12,026. In other words, the present value of six payments of Rs. 12,026, with the first payment due immediately, is about Rs. 58,801. The break-even rate pre-tax is Rs. 12,026/0.65 = Rs. 18,501.

6. Administrative costs drop to Rs. 500 per year. Moreover, the lease payments are a fixed commitment of the blue-chip company. The six lease payments are discounted at the after-tax rate at which Shriram would lend money; that is 6(1 – 0.35) = 3.9%. The break-even lease rent falls to about Rs. 10,210 after tax. The pre-tax break-even rate is Rs. 15,706.

7. **a.** Rs. 59,307; the present value of the lease cash flows from $t = 1$ to $t = 3$, discounted at $r(1 - T_c) = .10(1 - .35) = .065$.
   b. Rs. 62,000 – 59,307 = Rs. 2,693.
   c. It should not invest. The lease's value of +2,693 does not offset the machine's negative NPV. It would be happy to sign the same lease on a more attractive asset.

Chapter 27

1. **a.** Price paid for immediate delivery.
   b. Forward contracts are contracts to buy or sell at a specified future date at a specified price. Futures differ from forwards in two main ways. They are traded on an exchange and they are marked to market.
   c. Investors who are long have agreed to buy the asset. Investors who are short have contracted to sell;
   d. The risk that arises because the price of the asset used to hedge is not perfectly correlated with that of the asset that is being hedged.
   e. Profits and losses on a position are settled on a regular basis (e.g., daily).
   f. The advantage from owning the commodity rather than the promise of future delivery *less* the cost of storing the commodity.

2. (**a**) True; (**b**) false (you pay at delivery); (**c**) true; (**d**) true.

3. She is asking you to pay money (your sale is showing a loss).

4. $F = S(1 + r_f - y) = 95(1 + .049 - 4/95) = 95.655$.

5. A farmer, who sells wheat futures to hedge his crop, has fixed the price that he will receive for his wheat (we ignore possible basis risk). Because he now has a certain income, he gives up the possibility of pleasant surprises as well as unpleasant ones.

6. $F = S(1 + r_f + s_c - c_y)$. Therefore, $110 = 116(1.03 + 1/116 - c_y)$ and $c_y = 10.48 / 116 = 0.09$, or 9 percent.

7. **a.** A shortage of heating oil increases net convenience yield and reduces the futures price relative to spot price.
   b. Spot and futures prices decrease. The futures price rises relative to spot because convenience yield falls and storage costs rise.

8. Storage costs are likely to be high. Other things equal, firms will prefer to hold the future rather than the spot commodity, and net convenience yield will be low.

9. (**a**) Profit; (**b**) If the bank took out a new 4-year swap, it would need to pay an extra Rs. 25 million a year. At the new interest rate of 6.5%, the extra payment has a present value of Rs. 856,000. This is the amount that the bank should charge to terminate.

10. Basis risk means that the hedging instrument is imperfectly correlated with the risk to be

hedged. It is highest in a, because Tata Motors stock has considerable nonmarket risk. In *b* basis risk is likely to be small, and in *c* it should disappear.

11. Sell short Rs. 1.2 million of the market portfolio. In practice rather than "sell the market" you would sell futures on Rs. 1.2 million of the market index.

12. (a) Sell; (b) sell 3-month bond futures.

Chapter 28

1. **(a)** 0.0338; **(b)** Rs.29.58 / Singapore dollar; **(c)** Singapore dollar is at a forward premium (rupee is at a discount); **(d)** premium = 29.9 / 29.55 – 1= 0.0118, or 1.18 percent; **(e)** By interest rate parity $1 + r_{SG\$} = 1.035 \times (29.55 / 29.9) = 1.0229$; $r_{SG\$} = 0.229$, or 2.29%; **(f)** Rs.29.695 / Singapore dollar; **(g)** If the real exchange rate is expected to be constant, expected difference in inflation 29.695 / 29.55 – 1 = 0.0049, i.e., inflation in India over the 3 months is expected to be 0.49% higher than in Singapore.

2. **a.** The interest rate differential equals the forward premium or discount, i.e.,

$$\frac{1+r_x}{1+r_\$} = \frac{f_{x/\$}}{s_{x/\$}}$$

b. The expected change in the spot rate equals the forward premium or discount, i.e.,

$$\frac{f_{x/\$}}{s_{x/\$}} = \frac{E(s_{x/\$})}{s_{x/\$}}$$

c. Prices of goods in different countries are equal when measured in terms of the same currency. It follows that the expected change in the spot rate equals the expected inflation differential; i.e.,

$$\frac{E(1+i_x)}{E(1+i_\$)} = \frac{E(s_{x/\$})}{s_{x/\$}}$$

d. Expected real interest rates in different countries are equal; i.e.,

$$\frac{1+r_x}{1+r_\$} = \frac{E(1+i_x)}{E(1+i_\$)}$$

3. **a.** 45.0179 × 1.0478 / 1.02 = Rs. 46.2448/$
b. Real value of rupee increased by 46.2448 / 43.6905 – 1 = 0.058, or 5.8 percent

4.

	1 Month	3 Months	1 Year
Dollar interest rate, %	1.0	1.0	1.2
Peso interest rate, %	9.42	9.48	9.32
Forward pesos per dollar	56.84	57.61	60.99
Forward premium on peso (% per year)	–7.98	–7.98	–7.42

5. *b*.

6. Zero, of course. You don't need to do any calculations.

7. It can borrow the present value of €1 million, sell the euros in the spot market, and invest the proceeds in an 8-year dollar loan.

8. **a.** Sanjay Dutta's return is: (100 / 1.05) / (100 / 1.072) –1 = 0.0904, or 9.4%
b. Butterfly's return is 1.0904 × (40 / 45) –1 = –0.0275, or 2.74%
c. She can borrow against her rupee receipts, convert the proceeds to yen and lend the yen. Her return is 1.0904 × (1.006 / 1.07) – 1 = 0.025, or 2.5%

9. **a.** NPV = 6.61 × 60 = Rs. 396.6 million.

b.

Year	0	1	2	3	4	5
Forward rate	60	60.57	61.14	61.71	62.30	62.88
Rs. Million	–4800	605.66	1222.75	1419.43	1682.00	1572.10

c. It doesn't. The company can always hedge against a fall in the euro.

Chapter 29

1. **(a)** 4130.47 / (4130.47 + 7785.04) = 0.35; **(b)** (348.65 + 932.13) / 191.88 = 6.67; **(c)** 10515.33 / 2532.49 = 4.15; **(d)** (5652.9 + 4466.1)/2532.49 = 3.99; **(e)** (932.13 – 89.91) / 3989.11 = 0.211, or 21.1%; **(f)** [(396.33 + 389.14)/2] / (3341.08 / 365) = 42.9 days; **(g)** 650.34 / [(7785.04 + 5771.48)/2] = 0.096, or 9.6 percent; **(h)** 120.85 / 650.34 = 0.1858

2. The illogical ratios are *a*, *b*, *c*, *f*, and *i*. The correct definitions are

$$\text{Debt-equity ratio} = \frac{\text{long-term debt + value of leases}}{\text{equity}}$$

$$\text{Return on equity} = \frac{\text{earnings available for common stock holders}}{\text{average eqiuty}}$$

$$\text{payout ratio} = \frac{\text{dividend per share}}{\text{earnings per share}}$$

$$\text{current ratio} = \frac{\text{current assets}}{\text{current liabilities}}$$

$$\text{Average collection period} = \frac{\text{average receivables}}{\text{sales} \div 365}$$

3. (**a**) False; (**b**) true; (**c**) false; (**d**) false; (**e**) false—it will tend to increase the price–earnings multiple.

4. Rs. 365,000; 12.2.

5. (**a**) 12%; (**b**) 16%.

6. .25.

7. .73.; 3.65%

8. (**a**) 1.47; (**b**) Net working capital = 40. Total capitalization = 540. Debt to total capitalization = .52.

9. $10 million.

10. Rs. 82 million.

11. **a.** False (it is a process of deciding which risks to take).
b. False (financial planning is concerned with possible surprises as well as expected outcomes).
c. True (financial planning considers both the investment and financing decisions).
d. False (a typical horizon for long-term planning is 5 years).
e. True (perfect accuracy is unlikely to be obtainable, but the firm needs to produce the best possible consistent forecasts).
f. False (excessive detail distracts attention from the crucial decisions).

12. (**a**) $2,900,000; (**b**) $225,000; (**c**) .25.

13. Archimedes will earn $550 and invest $320 to expand assets. Additional borrowing is $120, so retained earnings is $320 − 120 = $200. The residual dividend is $550 − 200 = $350.

14. (**a**) 8.6%; (**b**) 13.75%.

Chapter 30

1. **a.** 1% of Rs.1,000 = Rs.10.
b. 1% for 30 days = 12.2% per annum simple interest or 12.9% compound interest.
c. (i) Shorter; (ii) longer; (iii) shorter.

2. **a.** Due lag decreases, therefore pay lag decreases;
b. Due lag increases, therefore pay lag increases;
c. Terms lag increases, therefore pay lag increases.

3. Reject the order because PV of Q's order = (0.75 × 2500) / 1.101/2 – 2000 = –Rs. 212.26 per iron, or –Rs. 212, 258 in total.

4. **a.** Expected profit = $p(1{,}200 - 1{,}050) - 1{,}050(1 - p) = 0$

$$p = .875$$

Therefore, grant credit if probability of payment exceeds 87.5%.

b. Expected profit from selling to slow payer: $.8(150) - .2(1{,}050) = -90$. Break-even point for credit check: $(.05 \times 90 \times \text{units}) - 12 = 0$. Units = 2.67.

5. Total expected profit on initial order $= -40 + .8[(p_2 \times 200) - 1{,}000(1 - p_2)]/1.2 = 0$

$$p_2 = .88, \text{ or } 88\%.$$

6. (**a**) False; (**b**) false; (**c**) false—should be collection agency or attorney; (**d**) true.

7. If variable increases (**a**) more willing; (**b**) less willing; (**c**) more willing.

8. By holding large inventories, the firm avoids the risk of running out of materials and finished goods. It can order materials in larger quantities and arrange longer production runs. On the other hand, inventories tie up capital, must be stored and insured, and may be subject to damage.

Similarly, large cash inventories reduce the risk of running out of cash or having to sell securities at short notice. The firm needs to make less frequent sales of securities and therefore minimize the fixed costs of such sales. On the other hand, inventories of cash tie up capital.

9. **a.** The $.40 per check fee is cheaper at 300 × .40 = $120 per day. The cost of putting up $800,000 of compensating balances is .09 × 800,000 = $72,000 per year, or 72,000/365 = $197 per day.
b. The lock-box system costs $120 per day, or $43,800 per year. You would need $486,700 additional cash to generate this much interest. Thus the lock-box system must generate at least this much cash. The cash flow is 300 × 1,500 = $450,000 per day. Thus the lock box must speed up average collection time by 486,700/450,000 = 1.08 days.

10. Concentration banking; Fedwire; CHIPS; lock-box banking.
11. (a) Less; (b) less; (c) invest the same amount; (d) more.
12. Price = 100 − (6 × 0.25) = 98.5. Compound annual return = (100 / 98.5)4 − 1 = 0.0623, or 6.23%
13. (a) Repurchase agreements; (b) commercial papers; (c) Treasury bills; (d) Treasury bills; (e) Treasury bills
14. Only 30% of the floating-rate preferred dividend is taxed versus 100% of bond interest. The fixed-dividend preferred also has this advantage but its price fluctuates more than that of the floating-rate preferred.

Chapter 31

1.

Cash	Working Capital
1. Rs. 2 million decline	Rs. 2 million decline
2. Rs. 2,500 increase	Unchanged
3. Rs. 5,000 decline	Unchanged
4. Unchanged	Rs. 1 million increase
5. Unchanged	Unchanged
6. Rs. 5 million increase	Unchanged

2. (a) Inventories go up (use). (b) Accounts receivable go up (use). (c) No change shown on the firm's books. (d) Increase in cash (source) and reduction in assets. A loss of Rs.100,000 is deducted from retained earnings. (e) Cash declines (use) and equity declines. (f) Cash declines (use) (g) Cash unchanged, although net working capital increases (the debt issue is a source of *funds*).
3. Month 3: 18 + (.5 × 90) + (.3 × 120) + (.2 × 100) = Rs. 119,000.
Month 4: 14 + (.5 × 70) + (.3 × 90) + (.2 × 120) = Rs. 100,000.
4. (a) 19.2, 16.8, 15, 13.2, 12, 12; (b) 19.2, 23.2, 20.6, 18.2, 16.4, 16.
5. a. Table 31.1: Bank loans = 3, Cash = 8, Current assets = 68, Current liabilities = 30, Total assets = Total liabilities and net worth = 118. Table 31.3 Repaid short-term bank loan = 2, Increase in cash balance = 4. Tables 31.4 and 31.5 unchanged.
   b. Table 31.1: Long-term debt = 22, Gross investment = 82, Net fixed assets = 62, Cash = 3, Total assets = Total liabilities and net worth = 125. Table 31.3: Issued long-term debt = 17, Total sources = 41, Invested in fixed assets = 26, Total uses = 42, Increases in cash balance = −1. Table 31.4: Fixed and Total assets change as in Table 31.1, as do Long-term debt and Total liabilities and net worth. Table 31.5: same changes as in Table 31.3, except Increase in net working capital = 6.
   c. Table 31.2: Operating costs = 289, Pretax income = 56, Net income = 28, Retained earnings = 27. Table 31.1: Net worth = 92, Total liabilities and net worth = Total assets = 131; Inventory = 22.5, Cash = 23.5. Table 31.4: Net worth = 92, Long-term liabilities and net worth = Total assets = 104, Net working capital = 54. Table 31.5: Net income = 28, increase in Net working capital = 24.
   d. Table 31.6: Third quarter, Total collections = 120.1, Ending receivables = 26.6. Fourth quarter, Total collections = 129.5, Ending receivables = 28.1. Table 31.7: Third quarter: Sources minus uses and Cash at end of period increase by 11.6, Cumulative financing required decreases by 11.6. Fourth quarter: Sources minus uses increase by 1.5, Cumulative financing required decreases by 13.1 to −12.6.
   e. Table 31.7: Labor, etc. = 26, Sources minus uses decrease by 4 in each quarter. Cumulative financing required decreases by 4 in first quarter, 8 in second, etc.
   f. Table 31.7: Other sources of cash increase by 10 in the second quarter, increasing Sources minus uses and decreasing Cumulative financing required.
   g. Table 31.7: Minimum operating cash balance = 2, Cumulative financing required decreases by 2 in all quarters.
6. (a) True; (b) false (borrower has a call); (c) true; (d) false (100/90 − 1 = .111, or 11.1%); (e) true.
7. (a) Line of credit; (b) commitment fee; (c) floating charge; (d) collateral; (e) warehouse receipt; (f) commercial paper; (g) medium-term notes.

Chapter 32

1. (a) Horizontal; (b) conglomerate; (c) vertical; (d) vertical.

2. *a* and *d; c* can also make sense, although merging is not the only way to redeploy excess cash.

3. (a) Rs. 5 million (We assume that the Rs. 500,000 saving is an after-tax figure.); (b) Rs. 4 million; (c) Rs. 7.5 million; (d) +Rs. 1 million; (e) −Rs. 2.5 million.

4. *b*.

5. (a) True; (b) false; (c) false; (d) true; (e) false (They may produce gains, but "large" is stretching it.); (f) false; (g) true.

6. **a.** Any premium paid by the bidder over the book value of the target's equity is reflected in the bidder's balance sheet, e.g., it is shown as "goodwill."
   b. The bidder offers to buy the target's stock directly from its shareholders.
   c. The target's stockholders can purchase additional shares at a bargain price.
   d. The target purchases shares held by the bidder; the bidder agrees to go away.
   e. The gain from combining two firms.

Chapter 33

1. **a.** Purchase of a business using mostly debt financing. The company goes private. Management is given a substantial equity stake.
   b. An LBO undertaken by management.
   c. A parent company creates a new company with part of its assets and operations. Shares in the new business are distributed to the parent's stockholders.
   d. Like a spin-off, but shares in the new business are sold to investors.
   e. Sale of specific assets rather than entire firm.
   f. A government-owned business is sold to private investors.
   g. A company moves to a much higher debt ratio. Proceeds of additional borrowing are paid out to stockholders.

2. (a) True; (b) false; (c) true; (d) false; (e) false; (f) false; (g) false (h) true.

3. Increased efficiency, broader share ownership, and revenue for the government.

4. Internal capital markets often misallocate capital. The market values of the conglomerate's divisions can't be observed separately, so it's hard to set incentives and to reward risk-taking.

5. Chapter 7 usually leads to liquidation. Chapter 11 protects the firm from its creditors while a reorganization plan is developed.

6. (a) False; (b) true; (c) true; (d) false (tax-loss carry-forwards do not survive liquidation).

7. There is always a chance that the company can recover, allowing creditors to be paid off and leaving something for shareholders. Also, the court may not observe *absolute priority*, so shareholders may be given some crumbs in a Chapter 11 reorganization.

Chapter 34

1. (a) USA and UK; (b) USA; (c) Japan and Europe; (d) Japan; (e) Europe; (f) Japan. (Note: answers exclude countries not separately shown in Figures 34.1–34.4)

2. A network of companies, organized around a major bank, which supplies finance to the rest of the keiretsu. Members of the keiretsu may have holdings in each other's stock and have long-standing business relationships with one another.

3. No. Individual investors hold relatively little common stock directly. Also the cross-holdings of stock by Japanese companies limits the opportunities for individuals to play an important role in governance.

4. German banks often have large shareholdings in industrial companies and also hold proxies to vote those shares that they hold in safekeeping for individual and institutional investors.

5. German firms have two boards of directors: a management board and a supervisory board, half of whose members are elected by employees. The supervisory board represents the interests of the company as a whole, not just the interests of employees or stockholders.

6. Family ownership.

7. The shareholder has a .3 holding in x_2. x_2 has a .3 holding in x, which has a .3 holding in z. The shareholder really has only a $.3^3$ or .027 holding in z.

8. Financial markets offer entrepreneurs greater diversity of financing sources. They also send clearer signals when an industry is in decline and are less likely to bail the firms out.

9. If firm *y* as a large stake in *x*, it may be able to transfer value from *x* by borrowing from *x* at a low interest rate, selling materials to *x* at excessive prices, or buying *x*'s output at low prices.

SOME USEFUL INDIAN WEBSITES

Data on Bond Markets are available in:

www.rbi.org.in (Website of the Reserve Bank of India)

www.fimmda.org (Website of Fixed Income Money Market and Derivatives Association)

www.ccilindia.com (Website of the Clearing Corporation of India)

Websites of the Premier Indian Stock Exchanges

www.bseindia.com (Website of Mumbai Stock Exchange)

www.nseindia.com (Website of National Stock Exchange of India)

Websites of the Premier Commodity Exchanges

www.ncdex.com (Website of National Commodity and Derivatives Exchange)

www.mcxindia.com (Website of Multi-commodity Exchange of India)

www.nmce.com (Website of National Multi-commodity Exchange of India)

Useful Websites for Company and Industry Data

www.icicidirect.com/research (Select company snapshot to get company data)

www.valuenotes.com (Extremely useful site for quick reference)

www.sebiedifar.nic.in (Can download companies' annual report filings)

www.in.finance.yahoo.com (useful for getting quick reference)

www.equitymaster.com (You can get company information and some research reports)

www.myiris.com (Useful for getting company and industry data)

www.indiainfoline.com (You can get data on companies, industries, and commodities here)

www.sify.com/finance (Useful website for getting company and mutual fund information)

Websites of Online Brokerage Houses (You can get a lot of useful company data from these sites.)

www.icicidirect.com
www.5paisa.com
www.indiabulls.com
www.sharekhan.com
www.kotakstreet.com
www.motilaloswal.com
www.stockmarkit.com (Look at the exact spelling here)

Websites of Regulators

www.sebi.gov.in (Website of Security Exchange Board of India)
www.rbi.org.in (Website of RBI)
www.clb.nic.in (Website of Company Law Board)
www.irdaindia.org (Website of Insurance Regulatory and Development Authority of India)
www.fmc.gov.in (Website of Forward Market Commission of India)

Websites Containing Useful Data about Indian Economy

www.rbi.org.in (Extremely useful)
www.ibef.org (India Resource Centre)
www.indiastat.com (Source for Indian statistics)
www.dot.gov.in/usefullinks.htm (Links to some of the useful Government sites)
www.finmin.nic.in/stats_data/monthly_economic_report/ (Monthly economic report the Ministry of Finance)

Some other Useful Websites

www.utimf.com (Website of UTI Mutual Fund)
www.kotakmahindra.com (Website of Kotak Mahindra)
http://www.emecklai.com/ (useful website for foreign-currency)
http://www.tradingpicks.com/beginners_guide.htm (Beginner's guide to commodities)
www.finance.indiamart.com (You get useful finance links and data)
http://www.indiainbusiness.nic.in/invest-india/invrellinks.htm (Links to banks, Indian laws, etc.)

GLOSSARY*

A

Abnormal return Part of return that is not due to systematic influences, e.g., marketwide price movements.

Absolute priority Rule in bankruptcy proceedings whereby senior creditors are required to be paid in full before junior creditors receive any payment.

Accelerated depreciation Any *depreciation* method that produces larger deductions for depreciation in the early years of a project's life.

Accounts payable (payables, trade debt) Money owed to suppliers.

Accounts receivable (receivables, trade credit) Money owed by customers.

Accrued interest Interest that has been earned but not yet paid.

ACH *Automated Clearinghouse.*

Acid-test ratio *Quick ratio.*

Adjusted present value (APV) *Net present value* of an asset if financed solely by equity plus the *present value* of any financing side effects.

ADR *American depository receipt.*

Adverse selection A situation in which a pricing policy causes only the less desirable customers to do business, e.g., a rise in insurance prices that leads only the worst risks to buy insurance.

Affirmative covenant Loan *covenant* specifying certain actions that the borrower must take.

Agency theory Theory of the relationship between a principal, e.g., a shareholder, and an agent of the principal, e.g., the company's manager.

AIBD Association of International Bond Dealers.

All-or-none underwriting An arrangement whereby a security issue is canceled if the *underwriter* is unable to resell the entire issue.

Alternative Minimum Tax (AMT) A separately calculated minimum amount of tax that must be paid by corporations or individuals.

American depository receipt (ADR) A security issued in the United States to represent shares of a foreign company.

American option *Option* that can be exercised any time before the final exercise date (cf. *European option*).

Amex American Stock Exchange.

Amortization (1) Repayment of a loan by installments; (2) allowance for *depreciation.*

AMT *Alternative Minimum Tax.*

Angel investor Wealthy individual who provides capital for small start-up businesses.

Annual percentage rate (APR) Annual interest rate calculated using *simple interest.*

Annuity Investment that produces a level stream of cash flows for a limited number of periods.

Annuity due *Annuity* whose payments occur at the start of each period.

Annuity factor *Present value* of $1 paid for each of t periods.

Anticipation Arrangement whereby customers who pay before the final date may be entitled to deduct a normal rate of interest.

Appraisal rights A right of shareholders in a *merger* to demand the payment of a fair price for their shares, as determined independently.

Appropriation request Formal request for funds for a capital investment project.

APR *Annual percentage rate.*

APT *Arbitrage pricing theory.*

APV *Adjusted present value.*

Arbitrage Purchase of one security and simultaneous sale of another to give a risk-free profit.

"Arbitrage" or "risk arbitrage" Often used loosely to describe the taking of offsetting positions in related securities, e.g., at the time of a takeover bid.

Arbitrage pricing theory (APT) Model in which expected returns increase linearly with an asset's sensitivity to a small number of pervasive factors.

Articles of incorporation Legal document establishing a corporation and its structure and purpose.

Asian currency units Dollar deposits held in Singapore or other Asian centers.

Asian option *Option* based on the average price of the asset during the life of the option.

**Italicized* words are listed elsewhere in the glossary.
A number of websites contain comprehensive financial glossaries. See, for example, www.finance-glossary.com and www.duke.edu/~charvey/Classes/wpg/glossary.htm.

Ask price (offer price) Price at which a dealer is willing to sell (cf. *bid price*).

Asset-backed securities Securities issued by a special purpose company that holds a package of low-risk assets whose cash flows are sufficient to service the *bonds*.

Asset stripper Acquirer who takes over firms in order to sell off a large part of their assets.

At-the-money option Option whose exercise price equals the current asset price (cf. *in-the-money option, out-of-the-money option*).

Auction-rate preferred A variant of *floating-rate preferred* stock where the dividend is reset every 49 days by auction.

Authorized share capital Maximum number of shares that a company can issue, as specified in the firm's *articles of incorporation*.

Automated Clearinghouse (ACH) Private electronic system run by banks for high-volume, low-value payments.

Availability float Checks deposited by a company that have not yet been cleared.

Aval Bank guarantee for debt purchased by *forfaiter*.

B

BA *Banker's acceptance.*

Backwardation Condition in which *spot price* of commodity exceeds price of *future* (cf. *contango*).

Balloon payment Large final payment (e.g., when a loan is repaid in installments).

Bank discount Interest deducted from the initial amount of a loan.

Banker's acceptance (BA) Written demand that has been accepted by a bank to pay a given sum at a future date (cf. *trade acceptance*).

Barrier option *Option* whose existence depends on asset price hitting some specified barrier (cf. *down-and-out option, down-and-in option*).

Basel Accord International agreement on the amount of capital to be maintained by large banks to support their risky loans.

Basis point (bp) 0.01 percent.

Basis risk Residual risk that results when the two sides of a hedge do not move exactly together.

Bearer security Security for which primary evidence of ownership is possession of the certificate (cf. *registered security*).

Bear market Widespread decline in security prices (cf. *bull market*).

Behavioral finance Branch of finance that stresses aspects of investor irrationality.

Benchmark maturity Maturity of a newly issued Treasury bond.

Benefit–cost ratio One plus *profitability index*.

Best-efforts underwriting An arrangement whereby *underwriters* do not commit themselves to selling a security issue but promise only to use best efforts.

Beta Measure of *market risk*.

Bid price Price at which a dealer is willing to buy (cf. *ask price*).

Big Board Colloquial term for the New York Stock Exchange.

Bill of exchange General term for a document demanding payment.

Bill of lading Document establishing ownership of goods in transit.

Blue-chip company Large and creditworthy company.

Blue-sky laws State laws covering the issue and trading of securities.

Boilerplate Standard terms and conditions, e.g., in a debt contract.

Bond Long-term debt.

Bond rating Rating of the likelihood of bond's default.

Bookbuilding The procedure whereby *underwriters* gather nonbinding indications of demand for a new issue.

Book entry Registered ownership of stock without issue of stock certificate.

Book runner The managing *underwriter* for a new issue. The book runner maintains the book of securities sold.

Bought deal Security issue where one or two *underwriters* buy the entire issue.

bp *Basis point.*

Bracket A term signifying the extent of an *underwriter's* commitment in a new issue, e.g., major bracket, minor bracket.

Break-even analysis Analysis of the level of sales at which a project would just break even.

Bridging loan Short-term loan to provide temporary financing until more permanent financing is arranged.

Bull–bear bond *Bond* whose *principal* repayment is linked to the price of another security. The bonds are issued in two *tranches:* In the first the repayment increases with the price of the other security; in the second the repayment decreases with the price of the other security.

Bulldog bond *Foreign bond* issue made in London.

Bullet payment Single final payment, e.g., of a loan (in contrast to payment in installments).

Bull market Widespread rise in security prices (cf. *bear market*).

Bund Long-term German government *bond*.

Buyback *Repurchase agreement*.

C

Cable The exchange rate between U.S. dollars and sterling.

Call option Option to buy an asset at a specified exercise price on or before a specified exercise date (cf. *put option*).

Call premium (1) Difference between the price at which a company can call its *bonds* and their *face value;* (2) price of a call *option*.

Call provision Provision that allows an issuer to buy back the *bond* issue at a stated price.

Cap An upper limit on the interest rate on a *floating-rate note*.

Capital asset pricing model Model in which expected returns increase linearly with an asset's *beta*.

Capital budget List of planned investment projects, usually prepared annually.

Capitalization Long-term debt plus *preferred stock* plus *net worth*.

Capital lease *Financial lease*.

Capital market Financial market (particularly the market for long-term securities).

Capital rationing Shortage of funds that forces a company to choose between worthwhile projects.

Capital structure Mix of different securities issued by a firm.

CAPM *Capital asset pricing model*.

Captive finance company Subsidiary whose function is to provide finance for purchases from the parent company.

CAR Cumulative *abnormal return*.

CARDs (Certificates for Amortizing Revolving Debt) *Pass-through securities* backed by credit card *receivables*.

Carried interest A proportion of the profits to which *private equity* partnerships etc. are entitled.

CARs (Certificates of Automobile Receivables) *Pass-through securities* backed by automobile *receivables*.

Carve-out Public offering of shares in a subsidiary.

Cascade Rational herding in which each individual deduces that previous decisions by others may have been based on extra information.

Cash and carry Purchase of a security and simultaneous sale of a *future,* with the balance being financed with a loan or *repo*.

Cash budget Forecast of sources and uses of cash.

Cash cow Mature company producing a large *free cash flow*.

Cash-deficiency arrangement Arrangement whereby a project's shareholders agree to provide the operating company with sufficient *net working capital*.

CAT bond *Catastrophe bond*.

Catastrophe bond (CAT bond) *Bond* whose payoffs are linked to a measure of catastrophe losses such as insurance claims.

CD *Certificate of deposit*.

CEO Chief executive officer.

Certainty equivalent A certain cash flow that has the same present value as a specified risky cash flow.

Certificate of deposit (CD) A certificate providing evidence of a bank time deposit.

CFTC Commodity Futures Trading Commission.

CFO Chief financial officer.

Chaebol A Korean conglomerate.

Chapter 7 Bankruptcy procedure whereby a debtor's assets are sold and the proceeds are used to repay creditors.

CHIPS *Clearinghouse Interbank Payments System*.

Chapter 11 Bankruptcy procedure designed to reorganize and rehabilitate defaulting firm.

Clean price (flat price) *Bond* price excluding *accrued interest* (cf. *dirty price*).

Clearinghouse Interbank Payments System (CHIPS) An international wire transfer system operated by a group of major banks for high-value dollar payments.

Closed-end fund Company whose assets consist of investments in a number of industrial and commercial companies.

Closed-end mortgage Mortgage against which no additional debt may be issued (cf. *open-end mortgage*).

CMOs *Collateralized mortgage obligations*.

COD Cash on delivery.

Collar An upper and lower limit on the interest rate on a *floating-rate note*.

Collateral Assets that are given as security for a loan.

Collateralized mortgage obligations (CMOs) A variation on the mortgage *pass-through security* in which the cash flows from a pool of mortgages are repackaged into several *tranches* of *bonds* with different maturities.

Collateral trust bonds *Bonds* secured by *common stocks* or other securities that are owned by the borrower.

Collection float Customer-written checks that have not been received, deposited, and added to the company's available balance (cf. *payment float*).

Commercial draft (bill of exchange) Demand for payment.

Commercial paper Unsecured *notes* issued by companies and maturing within nine months.

Commitment fee Fee charged by bank on an unused *line of credit*.

Common-size financial statements Balance sheet where entries are expressed as proportion of total assets and income statement where entries are expressed as a proportion of revenues.

Common stock Security representing ownership of a *corporation*.

Company cost of capital The expected return on a portfolio of all the firm's securities.

Compensating balance Non-interest-bearing demand deposits to compensate banks for bank loans or services.

Competitive bidding Means by which public utility *holding companies* are required to choose their *underwriter* (cf. *negotiated underwriting*).

Completion bonding Insurance that a construction contract will be successfully completed.

Composition Voluntary agreement to reduce payments on a firm's debt.

Compound interest Reinvestment of each interest payment on money invested to earn more interest (cf. *simple interest*).

Compound option Option on an *option*.

Concentration banking System whereby customers make payments to a regional collection center. The collection center pays the funds into a regional bank account and surplus money is transferred to the company's principal bank.

Conditional sale Sale in which ownership does not pass to the buyer until payment is completed.

Conglomerate merger *Merger* between two companies in unrelated businesses (cf. *horizontal merger, vertical merger*).

Consol Name of a perpetual *bond* issued by the British government. Sometimes used as a general term for *perpetuity*.

Contango Condition in which spot price of a commodity is below that of the *future* (cf. *backwardation*).

Contingent claim Claim whose value depends on the value of another asset.

Contingent project Project that cannot be undertaken unless another project is also undertaken.

Continuous compounding Interest compounded continuously rather than at fixed intervals.

Controller Officer responsible for budgeting, accounting, and auditing in a firm (cf. *treasurer*).

Convenience yield The extra advantage that firms derive from holding the commodity rather than the *future*.

Conversion price *Par value* of a *convertible bond* divided by the number of shares into which it may be exchanged.

Conversion ratio Number of shares for which a *convertible bond* may be exchanged.

Convertible bond *Bond* that may be converted into another security at the holder's option. Similarly convertible *preferred stock*.

Convexity Term often used to describe the fact that the effect of an interest rate change on *bond* prices declines as the interest rate rises.

Corporate venturing Practice by which a large manufacturer provides financial support to new companies.

Correlation coefficient Measure of the closeness of the relationship between two variables.

Corporation A business that is legally separate from its owners.

Cost company arrangement Arrangement whereby the shareholders of a project receive output free of charge but agree to pay all operating and financing charges of the project.

Cost of capital *Opportunity cost of capital*.

Counterparty Party on the other side of a *derivative* contract.

Coupon (1) Specifically, an attachment to the certificate of a *bearer security* that must be surrendered to collect interest payment; (2) more generally, interest payment on debt.

Covariance Measure of the co-movement between two variables.

Covenant Clause in a loan agreement.

Covered option *Option* position with an offsetting position in the underlying asset.

Cramdown Action by a bankruptcy court to enforce a plan of reorganization.

Credit derivative Contract for *hedging* against loan default or changes in credit risk (see *default swap, credit option*).

Credit option Similar to a long-term insurance policy against loan default.

Credit scoring A procedure for assigning scores to borrowers on the basis of the risk of default.

Cross-default clause Clause in a loan agreement stating that the company is in default if it fails to meet its obligation on any other debt issue.

Cum dividend *With dividend.*

Cum rights *With rights.*

Cumulative preferred stock Stock that takes priority over *common stock* in regard to dividend payments. Dividends may not be paid on the common stock until all past *dividends* on the *preferred stock* have been paid.

Cumulative voting Voting system under which a stockholder may cast all of his or her votes for one candidate for the board of directors (cf. *majority voting*).

Current asset Asset that will normally be turned into cash within a year.

Current liability Liability that will normally be repaid within a year.

Current ratio *Current assets* divided by *current liabilities*—a measure of liquidity.

D

Data mining (data snooping) Excessive search to find interesting (but probably coincidental) behavior in a body of data.

DCF *Discounted cash flow.*

DDM *Dividend discount model.*

Debenture Unsecured *bond*.

Death spiral convertible *Convertible bond* exchangeable for shares with a specified market value.

Debtor-in–possession financing (DIP financing) Debt issued by a company in *Chapter 11* bankruptcy.

Decision tree Method of representing alternative sequential decisions and the possible outcomes from these decisions.

Default swap *Credit derivative* in which one party makes fixed payments while the payments by the other party depend on the occurrence of a loan default.

Defeasance Practice whereby the borrower sets aside cash or *bonds* sufficient to service the borrower's debt. Both the borrower's debt and the offsetting cash or bonds are removed from the balance sheet.

Delta *Hedge ratio.*

Depository transfer check (DTC) Check made out directly by a local bank to a particular company.

Depreciation (1) Reduction in the book or market value of an asset; (2) portion of an investment that can be deducted from taxable income.

Derivative Asset whose value derives from that of some other asset (e.g., a *future* or an *option*).

Diff *Differential swap.*

Differential swap (diff, quanto swap) Swap between two *LIBOR* rates of interest, e.g., yen LIBOR for dollar LIBOR. Payments are in one currency.

Dilution Diminution in the proportion of income to which each share is entitled.

DIP financing *Debtor-in–possession financing.*

Direct lease *Lease* in which the *lessor* purchases new equipment from the manufacturer and leases it to the *lessee* (cf. *sale and lease-back*).

Direct quote For foreign exchange, the number of U.S. dollars needed to buy one unit of a foreign currency (cf. *indirect quote*).

Dirty price *Bond* price including *accrued interest*, i.e., the price paid by the bond buyer (cf. *clean price*).

Discount bond Debt sold for less than its *principal* value. If a discount bond pays no interest, it is called a "pure" discount, or *zero-coupon*, bond.

Discounted cash flow (DCF) Future cash flows multiplied by *discount factors* to obtain *present value.*

Discount factor *Present value* of $1 received at a stated future date.

Discount rate Rate used to calculate the *present value* of future cash flows.

Discounted payback rule Requirement that discounted values of cash flows should be sufficient to pay back initial investment within a specified time.

Discriminatory price auction Auction in which successful bidders pay the price that they bid (cf. *uniform price auction*).

Disintermediation Withdrawal of funds from a financial institution in order to invest them directly (cf. *intermediation*).

Dividend Payment by a company to its stockholders.

Dividend discount model Model showing that the value of a share is equal to the discounted value of future *dividends.*

Dividend reinvestment plan (DRIP) Plan that allows shareholders to reinvest dividends automatically.

Dividend yield Annual *dividend* divided by share price.

Double-declining-balance depreciation Method of *accelerated depreciation.*

Double-tax agreement Agreement between two countries that taxes paid abroad can be offset against domestic taxes levied on foreign *dividends.*

Down-and-in option *Barrier option* that comes into existence if asset price hits a barrier.

Down-and-out option *Barrier option* that expires if asset price hits a barrier.

DRIP *Dividend reinvestment plan.*

Drop lock An arrangement whereby the interest rate on a *floating-rate note* or *preferred stock* becomes fixed if it falls to a specified level.

DTC *Depository transfer check.*

Dual-class equity Shares with different voting rights.

Dual-currency bond *Bond* with interest paid in one currency and *principal* paid in another.

Duration The average number of years to an asset's *discounted cash flows.*

E

EBIT Earnings before interest and taxes.

EBITDA Earnings before interest, taxes, depreciation, and *amortization.*

Economic exposure Risk that arises from changes in real exchange rates (cf. *transaction exposure, translation exposure*).

Economic income Cash flow plus change in *present value.*

Economic rents Profits in excess of the competitive level.

Economic value added (EVA) A measure of *residual income* implemented by the consulting firm Stern Stewart.

Efficient market Market in which security prices reflect information instantaneously.

Efficient portfolio Portfolio that offers the lowest risk (*standard deviation*) for its *expected return* and the highest expected return for its level of risk.

EFT *Electronic funds transfer.*

Electronic funds transfer (EFT) Transfer of money electronically (e.g., by *Fedwire*).

Employee stock ownership plan (ESOP) A company contributes to a trust fund that buys stock on behalf of employees.

Entrenching investment An investment that makes particular use of the skills of existing management.

EPS Earnings per share.

Equipment trust certificate Form of *secured debt* generally used to finance railroad equipment. The trustee retains ownership of the equipment until the debt is repaid.

Equity (1) *Common stock* and *preferred stock.* Often used to refer to common stock only. (2) *Net worth.*

Equivalent annual cash flow (or cost) *Annuity* with the same *net present value* as the company's proposed investment.

ESOP *Employee stock ownership plan.*

Euribor *Euro Interbank Offered Rate.*

Euro interbank offered rate (Euribor) The interest rate at which major international banks in Europe lend euros to each other.

Eurobond *Bond* that is marketed internationally.

Eurodollar deposit Dollar deposit with a bank outside the United States.

European option *Option* that can be exercised only on final exercise date (cf. *American option*).

EVA *Economic value added.*

Event risk The risk that an unanticipated event (e.g. a takeover) will lead to a debt default.

Evergreen credit *Revolving credit* without maturity.

Exchange of assets Acquisition of another company by purchase of its assets in exchange for cash or shares.

Exchange of stock Acquisition of another company by purchase of its stock in exchange for cash or shares.

Ex dividend Purchase of shares in which the buyer is not entitled to the forthcoming *dividend* (cf. *with dividend, cum dividend*).

Exercise price (striking price) Price at which a *call option* or *put option* may be exercised.

Expectations theory Theory that *forward interest rate* (*forward exchange rate*) equals expected *spot rate.*

Expected return Average of possible returns weighted by their probabilities.

Ex rights Purchase of shares in which the buyer is not entitled to the rights to buy shares in the company's *rights issue* (cf. *with rights, cum rights, rights on*).

Extendable bond *Bond* whose maturity can be extended at the option of the lender (or issuer).

External finance Finance that is not generated by the firm: new borrowing or an issue of stock (cf. *internal finance*).

Extra dividend *Dividend* that may or may not be repeated (cf. *regular dividend*).

F

Face value *Par value.*

Factoring Arrangement whereby a financial institution buys a company's *accounts receivable* and collects the debt.

Fair price provision *Appraisal rights.*

Fallen angel *Junk bond* that was formerly *investment grade.*

FASB Financial Accounting Standards Board.

FCIA Foreign Credit Insurance Association.

FDIC Federal Deposit Insurance Corporation.

Federal funds Non-interest-bearing deposits by banks at the Federal Reserve. Excess reserves are lent by banks to each other.

Fedwire A wire transfer system for high-value payments operated by the Federal Reserve System (cf. *CHIPS*).

Field warehouse Warehouse rented by a warehouse company on another firm's premises (cf. *public warehouse*).

Financial assets Claims on *real assets*.

Financial engineering Combining or dividing existing instruments to create new financial products.

Financial lease (capital lease, full-payout lease) Long-term, noncancelable lease (cf. *operating lease*).

Financial leverage (gearing) Use of debt to increase the *expected return* on *equity*. Financial leverage is measured by the ratio of debt to debt plus equity (cf. *operating leverage*).

Fiscal agency agreement An alternative to a bond *trust deed*. Unlike the trustee, the fiscal agent acts as an agent of the borrower.

Flat price *Clean price*.

Flipping Buying shares in an *IPO* and selling immediately.

Float *See availability float, collection float, payment float.*

Floating lien General *lien* against a company's assets or against a particular class of assets.

Floating-rate note (FRN) *Note* whose interest payment varies with the short-term interest rate.

Floating-rate preferred *Preferred stock* paying dividends that vary with short-term interest rates.

Floor planning Arrangement used to finance inventory. A finance company buys the inventory, which is then held in trust by the user.

Foreign bond A *bond* issued on the domestic *capital market* of another country.

Forex Foreign exchange.

Forfaiter Purchaser of promises to pay (e.g., *bills of exchange* or *promissory notes*) issued by importers.

Forward cover Purchase or sale of forward foreign currency in order to offset a known future cash flow.

Forward exchange rate Exchange rate fixed today for exchanging currency at some future date (cf. *spot exchange rate*).

Forward interest rate Interest rate fixed today on a loan to be made at some future date (cf. *spot interest rate*).

Forward rate agreement (FRA) Agreement to borrow or lend at a specified future date at an interest rate that is fixed today.

FRA *Forward rate agreement*.

Free cash flow Cash not required for operations or for reinvestment.

Free-rider problem The temptation not to incur the costs of participating in a decision when one's influence on that decision is small.

FRN *Floating-rate note.*

Full-payout lease *Financial lease.*

Full-service lease (rental lease) *Lease* in which the *lessor* promises to maintain and insure the equipment (cf. *net lease*).

Fundamental analysis Security analysis that seeks to detect misvalued securities by an analysis of the firm's business prospects (cf. *technical analysis*).

Funded debt Debt maturing after more than one year (cf. *unfunded debt*).

Futures contract A contract to buy a commodity or security on a future date at a price that is fixed today. Unlike forward contracts, futures are generally traded on organized exchanges and are *marked to market* daily.

G

GAAP Generally accepted accounting principles.

Gearing *Financial leverage.*

General cash offer Issue of securities offered to all investors (cf. *rights issue*).

Golden parachute A large termination payment due to a company's officers if they lose their jobs as a result of a *merger.*

Goodwill The difference between the amount paid for a firm in a *merger* and its book value.

Governance The oversight of a firm's management.

Gray market Purchases and sales of *eurobonds* that occur before the issue price is set.

Greenmail Situation in which a large block of stock is held by an unfriendly company, forcing the target company to repurchase the stock at a substantial premium to prevent a takeover.

Greenshoe option *Option* that allows the *underwriter* for a new issue to buy and resell additional shares.

Growth stock *Common stock* of a company that has an opportunity to invest money to earn more than the *opportunity cost of capital* (cf. *income stock*).

H

Haircut An additional margin of *collateral* for a loan.

Hedge ratio (delta, option delta) The number of shares to buy for each *option* sold in order to create a safe position; more generally, the number of units of an asset that should be bought to hedge one unit of a liability.

Hedging Buying one security and selling another in order to reduce risk. A perfect hedge produces a riskless portfolio.

Hell-or-high-water clause Clause in a *lease* agreement that obligates the *lessee* to make payments regardless of what happens to the *lessor* or the equipment.

Highly leveraged transaction (HLT) Bank loan to a highly leveraged firm (formerly needed to be separately reported to the Federal Reserve Board).

HLT *Highly leveraged transaction.*

Holding company Company whose sole function is to hold stock in other companies or subsidiaries.

Horizontal merger *Merger* between two companies that manufacture similar products (cf. *vertical merger, conglomerate merger*).

Horizontal spread The simultaneous purchase and sale of two *options* that differ only in their exercise date (cf. *vertical spread*).

Hurdle rate Minimum acceptable rate of return on a project.

I

IBF *International banking facility.*

IMM *International monetary market.*

Immunization The construction of an asset and a liability that are subject to offsetting changes in value.

Imputation tax system Arrangement by which investors who receive a *dividend* also receive a tax credit for corporate taxes that the firm has paid.

Income bond *Bond* on which interest is payable only if earned.

Income stock *Common stock* with high *dividend yield* and few profitable investment opportunities (cf. *growth stock*).

Indenture Formal agreement, e.g., establishing the terms of a *bond* issue.

Indexed bond *Bond* whose payments are linked to an index, e.g., a consumer price index (see *TIPs*).

Index fund Investment fund designed to match the returns on a stockmarket index.

Indirect quote For foreign exchange, the number of units of a foreign currency needed to buy one U.S. dollar (cf. *direct quote*).

Industrial revenue bond (IRB) Bond issued by local government agencies on behalf of *corporations.*

Initial public offering (IPO) A company's first public issue of *common stock.*

In-substance defeasance *Defeasance* whereby debt is removed from the balance sheet but not canceled (cf. *novation*).

Intangible asset Nonmaterial asset, such as technical expertise, a trademark, or a patent (cf. *tangible asset*).

Integer programming Variant of *linear programming* whereby the solution values must be integers.

Interest cover *Times interest earned.*

Interest rate parity Theory that the differential between the *forward exchange rate* and the *spot exchange rate* is equal to the differential between the foreign and domestic interest rates.

Intermediation Investment through a financial institution (cf. *disintermediation*).

Internal finance Finance generated within a firm by *retained earnings* and *depreciation* (cf. *external finance*).

Internal growth rate The maximum rate of firm growth without *external finance* (cf. *sustainable growth rate*).

Internal rate of return (IRR) *Discount rate* at which investment has zero *net present value.*

International banking facility (IBF) A branch that an American bank establishes in the United States to do eurocurrency business.

International monetary market (IMM) The financial futures market within the Chicago Mercantile Exchange.

Interval measure The number of days that a firm can finance operations without additional cash income.

In-the-money option An *option* that would be worth exercising if it expired immediately (cf. *out-of-the-money option*).

Inverse FRN *Floating-rate note* whose payments rise as the general level of interest rates falls and vice versa.

Investment-grade bond *Bond* rated at least Baa by Moody's or BBB by Standard and Poor's or Fitch.

IPO *Initial public offering.*

IRB *Industrial revenue bond.*

IRR *Internal rate of return.*

IRS Internal Revenue Service.

ISDA International Swap and Derivatives Association.

ISMA International Securities Market Association.

Issued share capital Total amount of shares that are in issue (cf. *outstanding share capital*).

J

Junior debt *Subordinated debt.*

Junk bond Debt that is rated below an *investment-grade bond.*

Just-in-time System of inventory management that requires minimum inventories of materials and very frequent deliveries by suppliers.

K

Keiretsu A network of Japanese companies organized around a major bank.

L

LBO *Leveraged buyout.*

Lease Long-term rental agreement.

Legal capital Value at which a company's shares are recorded in its books.

Legal defeasance *Novation.*

Lessee User of a leased asset (cf. *lessor*).

Lessor Owner of a leased asset (cf. *lessee*).

Letter of credit Letter from a bank stating that it has established a credit in the company's favor.

Letter stock Privately placed *common stock,* so-called because the *SEC* requires a letter from the purchaser that the stock is not intended for resale.

Leverage See *financial leverage, operating leverage.*

Leveraged buyout (LBO) Acquisition in which (1) a large part of the purchase price is debt-financed and (2) the remaining *equity* is privately held by a small group of investors.

Leveraged lease *Lease* in which the *lessor* finances part of the cost of the asset by an issue of debt secured by the asset and the lease payments.

Liabilities, total liabilities Total value of financial claims on a firm's assets. Equals (1) total assets or (2) total assets minus *net worth.*

LIBOR *London interbank offered rate.*

Lien Lender's claims on specified assets.

Limited liability Limitation of a shareholder's losses to the amount invested.

Limited partnership *Partnership* in which some partners have *limited liability* and general partners have unlimited liability.

Linear programming (LP) Technique for finding the maximum value of some objective function subject to stated linear constraints.

Line of credit Agreement by a bank that a company may borrow at any time up to an established limit.

Liquid asset Asset that is easily and cheaply turned into cash—notably cash itself and short-term securities.

Liquidating dividend *Dividend* that represents a return of capital.

Liquidator Person appointed by unsecured creditors in the United Kingdom to oversee the sale of an insolvent firm's assets and the repayment of debts.

Liquidity-preference theory Theory that investors demand a higher yield to compensate for the extra risk of long-term *bonds.*

Liquidity premium (1) Additional return for investing in a security that cannot easily be turned into cash; (2) difference between the *forward interest rate* and the expected *spot interest rate.*

Liquid yield option note (LYON) *Zero-coupon,* callable, puttable, *convertible bond.*

Lockbox system Form of *concentration banking.* Customers send payments to a post office box. A local bank collects and processes the checks and transfers surplus funds to the company's principal bank.

London interbank offered rate (LIBOR) The interest rate at which major international banks in London lend to each other. (LIBID is London interbank bid rate; LIMEAN is mean of bid and offered rate.)

Long hedge Purchase of a *hedging* instrument (e.g., a *future*) to hedge a short position in the underlying asset (cf. *short hedge*).

Lookback option *Option* whose payoff depends on the highest asset price recorded over the life of the option.

LP *Linear programming.*

LYON *Liquid yield option note.*

M

MACRS *Modified accelerated cost recovery system.*

Maintenance margin Minimum margin that must be maintained on a *futures* contract.

Majority voting Voting system under which each director is voted upon separately (cf. *cumulative voting*).

Management buyout (MBO) *Leveraged buyout* whereby the acquiring group is led by the firm's management.

Margin Cash or securities set aside by an investor as evidence that he or she can honor a commitment.

Marked to market An arrangement whereby the profits or losses on a *futures* contract are settled up each day.

Market capitalization rate *Expected return* on a security.

Market model Model suggesting a linear relationship between actual returns on a stock and on the market portfolio.

Market risk (systematic risk) Risk that cannot be diversified away.

Maturity factoring *Factoring* arrangement that provides collection and insurance of *accounts receivable.*

MBO *Management buyout.*

MDA *Multiple-discriminant analysis.*

Medium-term note (MTN) Debt with a typical maturity of 1 to 10 years offered regularly by a company using the same procedure as *commercial paper.*

Merger (1) Acquisition in which all assets and liabilities are absorbed by the buyer (cf. *exchange of assets, exchange of stock*); (2) more generally, any combination of two companies.

MIP (Monthly income preferred security) *Preferred stock* issued by a subsidiary located in a tax haven. The subsidiary relends the money to the parent.

Mismatch bond *Floating-rate note* whose interest rate is reset at more frequent intervals than the rollover period (e.g., a note whose payments are set quarterly on the basis of the one-year interest rate).

Modified accelerated cost recovery system (MACRS) Schedule of *depreciation* deductions allowed for tax purposes.

Modified IRR *Internal rate of return* calculated by first discounting later cash flows back to earlier periods so that there remains only one change in the sign of the cash flows.

Money center bank A major U.S. bank that undertakes a wide range of banking activities.

Money market Market for short-term safe investments.

Money market deposit account (MMDA) A bank account paying *money-market* interest rate.

Money-market fund *Mutual fund* that invests solely in short-term safe securities.

Monte Carlo simulation Method for calculating the probability distribution of possible outcomes, e.g., from a project.

Moral hazard The risk that the existence of a contract will change the behavior of one or both parties to the contract; e.g., an insured firm may take fewer fire precautions.

Mortgage bond *Bond* secured against plant and equipment.

MTN *Medium-term note.*

Multiple-discriminant analysis (MDA) Statistical technique for distinguishing between two groups on the basis of their observed characteristics.

Mutual fund Managed investment fund whose shares are sold to investors.

Mutually exclusive projects Two projects that cannot both be undertaken.

N

Naked option *Option* held on its own, i.e., not used for *hedging* a holding in the asset or other options.

Nasdaq National Association of Security Dealers Automated Quote System. A U.S. stock exchange, whose dealers tend to specialize in high-tech stocks.

Negative pledge clause Clause under which the borrower agrees not to permit an exclusive *lien* on any of its assets.

Negotiated underwriting Method of choosing an *underwriter.* Most firms may choose their *underwriter* by negotiation (cf. *competitive bidding*).

Net lease *Lease* in which the *lessee* promises to maintain and insure the equipment (cf. *full-service lease*).

Net present value (NPV) A project's net contribution to wealth—*present value* minus initial investment.

Net working capital *Current assets* minus *current liabilities.*

Net worth Book value of a company's *common stock,* surplus, and *retained earnings.*

Nominal interest rate Interest rate expressed in money terms (cf. *real interest rate*).

Nonrefundable debt Debt that may not be called in order to replace it with another issue at a lower interest cost.

Normal distribution Symmetric bell-shaped distribution that can be completely defined by its mean and *standard deviation.*

Note Unsecured debt with a maturity of up to 10 years.

Novation (legal defeasance) *Defeasance* whereby the firm's debt is canceled (cf. *in-substance defeasance*).

NPV *Net present value.*

NYSE New York Stock Exchange.

O

Odd lot A trade of less than 100 shares (cf. *round lot*).

Off-balance-sheet financing Financing that is not shown as a liability in a company's balance sheet.

Offer price *Ask price.*

OID debt *Original issue discount debt.*

Old-line factoring *Factoring* arrangement that provides collection, insurance, and finance for *accounts receivable.*

On the run The most recently issued (and, therefore, typically the most liquid) government *bond* in a particular maturity range.

Open account Arrangement whereby sales are made with no formal debt contract. The buyer signs a receipt, and the seller records the sale in the sales ledger.

Open-end mortgage Mortgage against which additional debt may be issued (cf. *closed-end mortgage*).

Open interest The number of currently outstanding *futures* contracts.

Operating lease Short-term, cancelable *lease* (cf. *financial lease*).

Operating leverage Fixed operating costs, so-called because they accentuate variations in profits (cf. *financial leverage*).

Opportunity cost of capital (hurdle rate, cost of capital) *Expected return* that is foregone by investing in a project rather than in comparable financial securities.

Option See *call option, put option.*

Option delta *Hedge ratio.*

Original issue discount debt (OID debt) Debt that is initially offered at a price below *face value.*

OTC *Over-the-counter.*

Out-of-the-money option An *option* that would not be worth exercising if it matured immediately (cf. *in-the-money option*).

Outstanding share capital *Issued share capital* less the *par value* of shares that are held in the company's treasury.

Oversubscription privilege In a *rights issue,* arrangement by which shareholders are given the right to apply for any shares that are not taken up.

Over-the-counter (OTC) Informal market that does not involve a securities exchange. Specifically used to refer to the Nasdaq dealer market for *common stocks.*

P

Partnership Joint ownership of business whereby general partners have unlimited liability.

Par value (face value) Value of a security shown on the certificate.

Pass-through securities *Notes* or *bonds* backed by a package of assets (e.g., mortgage pass-throughs, *CARs, CARDs*).

Path-dependent option *Option* whose value depends on the sequence of prices of the underlying asset rather than just the final price of the asset.

Payables *Accounts payable.*

Payback rule Requirement that project should recover its initial investment within a specified time.

Pay-in-kind bond (PIK) *Bond* that allows the issuer to choose to make interest payments in the form of additional bonds.

Payment float Company-written checks that have not yet cleared (cf. *availability float*).

Payout ratio *Dividend* as a proportion of earnings per share.

PBGC Pension Benefit Guarantee Corporation.

P/E ratio Share price divided by earnings per share.

PERC (Preferred equity redemption cumulative stock) *Preferred stock* that converts automatically into equity at a stated date. A limit is placed on the value of the shares that the investor receives.

Perpetuity Investment offering a level stream of cash flows in perpetuity (cf. *consol*).

PIK *Pay-in-kind bond.*

PN *Project note.*

Poison pill An issue of securities that is convertible, in the event of a *merger,* into the shares of the acquiring firm or must be repurchased by the acquiring firm.

Poison put A *covenant* allowing the *bond*holder to demand repayment in the event of a hostile *merger.*

Pooling of interest Method of accounting for *mergers* (no longer available in the USA). The consolidated balance sheet of the merged firm is obtained by combining the balance sheets of the separate firms (cf. *purchase accounting*).

Position diagram Diagram showing the possible payoffs from a *derivative* investment.

Postaudit Evaluation of an investment project after it has been undertaken.

Preemptive right Common stockholder's right to anything of value distributed by the company.

Preferred stock Stock that takes priority over common stock in regard to *dividends.* Dividends may not be paid on *common stock* unless the dividend is paid on all preferred stock (cf. *cumulative preferred stock*). The dividend rate on preferred is usually fixed at time of issue.

Prepack *Prepackaged bankruptcy.*

Prepackaged bankruptcy (prepack) Bankruptcy proceedings intended to confirm a reorganization plan that has already been agreed to informally.

Present value Discounted value of future cash flows.

Present value of growth opportunities (PVGO) *Net present value* of investments the firm is expected to make in the future.

PRIDE Similar to a *PERC* except that as the equity price rises beyond a specified point, the investor shares in the stock appreciation.

Primary issue Issue of new securities by a firm (cf. *secondary issue*).

Prime rate Benchmark lending rate set by U.S. banks.

Principal Amount of debt that must be repaid.

Principal–agent problem Problem faced by a principal (e.g., shareholder) in ensuring that an agent (e.g., manager) acts on his or her behalf.

Private equity *Equity* that is not publicly traded and that is used to finance business start-ups, *leveraged buy-outs*, etc.

Privileged subscription issue *Rights issue.*

Production payment Loan in the form of advance payment for future delivery of a product.

Profitability index Ratio of a project's *NPV* to the initial investment.

Pro forma Projected.

Project finance Debt that is largely a claim against the cash flows from a particular project rather than against the firm as a whole.

Project note (PN) *Note* issued by public housing or urban renewal agencies.

Promissory note Promise to pay.

Prospect theory A theory of asset pricing suggested by the observation of behavioral psychologists that investors have a particular aversion to losses even if very small.

Prospectus Summary of the *registration* statement providing information on an issue of securities.

Proxy vote Vote cast by one person on behalf of another.

Public warehouse (terminal warehouse) Warehouse operated by an independent warehouse company on its own premises (cf. *field warehouse*).

Purchase accounting Method of accounting for *mergers*. The assets of the acquired firm are shown at market value on the balance sheet of the acquirer (cf. *pooling of interest*).

Purchase fund Resembles a *sinking fund* except that money is used only to purchase bonds if they are selling below their *par value*.

Put option *Option* to sell an asset at a specified *exercise price* on or before a specified exercise date (cf. *call option*).

PVGO *Present value of growth opportunities.*

Pyramid Created by forming a *holding company* whose only asset is a controlling interest in a second holding company, which in turn has a controlling interest in an operating company.

Q

q Ratio of the market value of an asset to its replacement cost.

QIBs *Qualified institutional buyers.*

Quadratic programming Variant of *linear programming* whereby the equations are quadratic rather than linear.

Qualified institutional buyers (QIBs) Institutions that are allowed to trade unregistered stock among themselves.

Quanto swap *Differential swap.*

Quick ratio (acid-test ratio) Measure of liquidity: (*current assets* − inventory) divided by *current liabilities*.

R

Range forward A *forward exchange rate* contract that places upper and lower bounds on the cost of foreign exchange.

Ratchet bonds Floating-rate *bonds* whose coupon can only be reset downwards.

Rate-sensitive bonds *Bonds* whose coupon rate changes as issuer's credit-rating changes.

Real assets *Tangible assets* and *intangible assets* used to carry on business (cf. *financial assets*).

Real estate investment trust (REIT) Trust company formed to invest in real estate.

Real interest rate Interest rate expressed in terms of real goods, i.e., *nominal interest rate* adjusted for inflation.

Real option The flexibility to modify, postpone, expand or abandon a project.

Receivables *Accounts receivable.*

Receiver A bankruptcy practitioner appointed by secured creditors in the United Kingdom to oversee the repayment of debts.

Record date Date set by directors when making dividend payment. *Dividends* are sent to stockholders who are registered on the record date.

Recourse Term describing a type of loan. If a loan is with recourse, the lender has a general claim against the parent company if the *collateral* is insufficient to repay the debt.

Red herring Preliminary *prospectus*.

Refunding Replacement of existing debt with a new issue of debt.

Registered security Security whose ownership is recorded by the company's *registrar* (cf. *bearer security*).

Registrar Financial institution appointed to record issue and ownership of company securities.

Registration Process of obtaining *SEC* approval for a public issue of securities.

Regression analysis In statistics, a technique for finding the line of best fit.

Regular dividend *Dividend* that the company expects to maintain in the future.

Regulation A issue Small security issues that are partially exempt from *SEC registration* requirements.

REIT *Real estate investment trust.*

Rental lease *Full-service lease.*

Repo *Repurchase agreement.*

Repurchase agreement (RP, repo, buy-back) Purchase of Treasury securities from a securities dealer with an agreement that the dealer will repurchase them at a specified price.

Residual income After-tax profit less the *opportunity cost of capital* employed by the business (see also *Economic Value Added*).

Residual risk *Unique risk.*

Retained earnings Earnings not paid out as *dividends.*

Return on equity Usually, equity earnings as a proportion of the book value of equity.

Return on investment (ROI) Generally, book income as a proportion of net book value.

Reverse convertible Bond that gives the issuer the right to convert it into common stock.

Revolving credit Legally assured *line of credit* with a bank.

Rights issue (privileged subscription issue) Issue of securities offered to current stockholders (cf. *general cash offer*).

Rights on *With rights.*

Risk premium Expected additional return for making a risky investment rather than a safe one.

ROI *Return on investment.*

Roll-over CD A package of successive *certificates of deposit.*

Round lot A trade of 100 shares (cf. *odd lot*).

RP *Repurchase agreement.*

R squared (R^2) Square of the *correlation coefficient*—the proportion of the variability in one series that can be explained by the variability of one or more other series.

Rule 144a *SEC* rule allowing *qualified institutional buyers* to buy and trade unregistered securities.

S

Sale and lease-back Sale of an existing asset to a financial institution that then *leases* it back to the user (cf. *direct lease*).

Salvage value Scrap value of plant and equipment.

Samurai bond A yen *bond* issued in Tokyo by a non-Japanese borrower (cf. *bulldog bond, Yankee bond*).

SBIC Small Business Investment Company.

Scenario analysis Analysis of the profitability of a project under alternative economic scenarios.

Seasoned issue Issue of a security for which there is an existing market (cf. *unseasoned issue*).

Season datings Extended credit for customers who order goods out of the peak season.

SEC Securities and Exchange Commission.

Secondary issue (1) Procedure for selling blocks of *seasoned issues* of stock; (2) more generally, sale of already issued stock.

Secondary market Market in which one can buy or sell *seasoned issues* of securities.

Secured debt Debt that, in the event of default, has first claim on specified assets.

Securitization Substitution of tradable securities for privately negotiated instruments.

Security market line Line representing the relationship between *expected return* and *market risk.*

Self-liquidating loan Loan to finance *current assets.* The sale of the current assets provides the cash to repay the loan.

Self-selection Consequence of a contract that induces only one group (e.g., low-risk individuals) to participate.

Semistrong-form efficient market Market in which security prices reflect all publicly available information (cf. *weak-form efficient market* and *strong-form efficient market*).

Senior debt Debt that, in the event of bankruptcy, must be repaid before *subordinated debt* receives any payment.

Sensitivity analysis Analysis of the effect on project profitability of possible changes in sales, costs, and so on.

Serial bonds Package of *bonds* that mature in successive years.

Series bond *Bond* that may be issued in several series under the same *indenture.*

Shark repellant Amendment to company charter intended to protect against takeover.

Shelf registration A procedure that allows firms to file one *registration* statement covering several issues of the same security.

Shogun bond Dollar *bond* issued in Japan by a nonresident.

Short hedge Sale of a *hedging* instrument (e.g., a *future*) to *hedge* a long position in the underlying asset (cf. *long hedge*).

Short sale Sale of a security the investor does not own.

Sight draft Demand for immediate payment (cf. *time draft*).

Signal Action that demonstrates an individual's unobservable characteristics (because it would be unduly costly for someone without those characteristics to take the action).

Simple interest Interest calculated only on the initial investment (cf. *compound interest*).

Simulation *Monte Carlo simulation.*

Sinker *Sinking fund.*

Sinking fund (sinker) Fund established by a company to retire debt before maturity.

Skewed distribution Probability distribution in which an unequal number of observations lie below and above the mean.

SPE *Special purpose entity.*

Special dividend (extra dividend) *Dividend* that is unlikely to be repeated.

Special purpose entity *Partnerships* established by companies to hold certain assets and obtain funding. May be used to obtain off-balance-sheet debt for the parent.

Specific risk *Unique risk.*

Specialist The individual who conducts the auction of a set of securities on the New York Stock Exchange.

Spin-off Distribution of shares in a subsidiary to the company's shareholders so that they hold shares separately in the two firms.

Spot exchange rate Exchange rate on currency for immediate delivery (cf. *forward exchange rate*).

Spot interest rate Interest rate fixed today on a loan that is made today (cf. *forward interest rate*).

Spot price Price of asset for immediate delivery (in contrast to forward or futures price).

Spread Difference between the price at which an *underwriter* buys an issue from a firm and the price at which the underwriter sells it to the public.

Standard deviation Square root of the*variance*—a measure of variability.

Standard error In statistics, a measure of the possible error in an estimate.

Standby agreement In a *rights issue*, agreement that the *underwriter* will purchase any stock not purchased by investors.

Step-up bond *Bond* whose *coupon* is stepped up over time (also step-down bond).

Stock dividend *Dividend* in the form of stock rather than cash.

Stock split "Free" issue of shares to existing shareholders.

Straddle The combination of a *put option* and a *call option* with the same *exercise price.*

Straight-line depreciation An equal dollar amount of *depreciation* in each period.

Striking price *Exercise price* of an *option.*

Stripped bond *Bond* that is subdivided into a series of *zero-coupon bonds.*

Strong-form efficient market Market in which security prices reflect instantaneously all information available to investors (cf. *weak-form efficient market* and *semistrong-form efficient market*).

Structured debt Debt that has been customized for the buyer, often by incorporating unusual *options.*

Subordinated debt (junior debt) Debt over which *senior debt* takes priority. In the event of bankruptcy, subordinated debtholders receive payment only after senior debt is paid off in full.

Sum-of-the-years'-digits depreciation Method of *accelerated depreciation.*

Sunk costs Costs that have been incurred and cannot be reversed.

Supermajority Provision in a company's charter requiring a majority of, say, 80 percent of shareholders to approve certain changes, such as a *merger.*

Sushi bond A *eurobond* issued by a Japanese corporation.

Sustainable growth rate Maximum rate of firm growth without increasing financial leverage (cf. *internal growth rate*).

Swap An arrangement whereby two companies lend to each other on different terms, e.g., in different currencies, or one at a fixed rate and the other at a floating rate.

Swaption *Option* on a *swap.*

Sweep program Arrangement whereby bank invests a company's available cash at the end of each day.

Swingline facility Bank borrowing facility to provide finance while the firm replaces U.S. *commercial paper* with eurocommercial paper.

Systematic risk *Market risk.*

T

Take-or-pay In *project finance*, arrangement where parent company agrees to pay for output of project even if it chooses not to take delivery.

Take-up fee Fee paid to *underwriters* of a *rights issue* on any stock they are obliged to purchase.

Tangible asset Physical asset, such as plant, machinery, and offices (cf. *intangible assets*).

Tax-anticipation bill Short-term bill issued by the U.S. Treasury that can be surrendered at *face value* in payment of taxes.

T-bill *Treasury bill.*

Technical analysis Security analysis that seeks to detect and interpret patterns in past security prices (cf. *fundamental analysis*).

TED spread Difference between *LIBOR* and U.S. *Treasury bill* rate.

Tender offer General offer made directly to a firm's shareholders to buy their stock.

Tenor Maturity of a loan.

Terminal warehouse *Public warehouse.*

Term loan Medium-term, privately placed loan, usually made by a bank.

Term structure of interest rates Relationship between interest rates on loans of different maturities (cf. *yield curve*).

Throughput arrangement Arrangement by which shareholders of a pipeline company agree to make sufficient use of pipeline to enable the pipeline company to service its debt.

Tick Minimum amount the price of a security may change.

Time draft Demand for payment at a stated future date (cf. *sight draft*).

Times interest earned (interest cover) Earnings before interest and tax, divided by interest payments.

TIPS (Treasury Inflation Protected Securities) U.S. Treasury *bonds* whose *coupon* and *principal* payments are linked to the Consumer Price Index.

Tolling contract In *project finance*, arrangement whereby parent company promises to deliver materials to project for processing and then to repurchase them.

Tombstone Advertisement listing the *underwriters* to a security issue.

Trade acceptance Written demand that has been accepted by an industrial company to pay a given sum at a future date (cf. *banker's acceptance*).

Trade credit *Accounts receivable.*

Trade debt *Accounts payable.*

Tranche Portion of a new issue sold at a point in time different from the remainder or that has different terms.

Transaction exposure Risk to a firm with known future cash flows in a foreign currency that arises from possible changes in the exchange rate (cf. *economic exposure, translation exposure*).

Transfer agent Individual or institution appointed by a company to look after the transfer of securities.

Translation exposure Risk of adverse effects on a firm's financial statements that may arise from changes in exchange rates (cf. *economic exposure, transaction exposure*).

Treasurer Principal financial manager (cf. *controller*).

Treasury bill (T-bill) Short-term discount debt maturing in less than one year, issued regularly by the government.

Treasury stock *Common stock* that has been repurchased by the company and held in the company's treasury.

Trust deed Agreement between trustee and borrower setting out terms of *bond*.

Trust receipt Receipt for goods that are to be held in trust for the lender.

Tunneling Actions by a controlling shareholder to transfer wealth out of the firm (e.g., by supplying goods at an inflated price).

U

Underpricing Issue of securities below their market value.

Underwriter Firm that buys an issue of securities from a company and resells it to investors.

Unfunded debt Debt maturing within one year (cf. *funded debt*).

Uniform price auction Auction in which all successful bidders pay the same price (cf. *discriminatory price auction*).

Unique risk (residual risk, specific risk, unsystematic risk) Risk that can be eliminated by diversification.

Unseasoned issue Issue of a security for which there is no existing market (cf. *seasoned issue*).

Unsystematic risk *Unique risk.*

V

Value additivity Rule that the value of the whole must equal the sum of the values of the parts.

Value-at-risk (VAR) The probability of portfolio losses exceeding some specified proportion.

Vanilla issue Issue without unusual features.

Variable-rate demand bond (VRDB) Floating-rate *bond* that can be sold back periodically to the issuer.

Variance Mean squared deviation from the expected value—a measure of variability.

Variation margin The daily gains or losses on a *futures* contract credited to the investor's margin account.

VAR *Value-at-risk.*

Venture capital Capital to finance a new firm.

Vertical merger *Merger* between a supplier and its customer (cf. *horizontal merger, conglomerate merger*).

Vertical spread Simultaneous purchase and sale of two options that differ only in their *exercise price* (cf. *horizontal spread*).

VRDB *Variable rate demand bond.*

W

WACC *Weighted-average cost of capital.*

Warehouse receipt Evidence that a firm owns goods stored in a warehouse.

Warrant Long-term *call option* issued by a company.

Weak-form efficient market Market in which security prices instantaneously reflect the information in the history of security prices. In such a market security prices follow a random walk (cf. *semistrong-form efficient market* and *strong-form efficient market*).

Weighted-average cost of capital (WACC) *Expected return* on a portfolio of all the firm's securities. Used as *hurdle rate* for capital investment.

White knight A friendly potential acquirer sought out by a target company threatened by a less welcome suitor.

Wi. When issued.

Winner's curse Problem faced by uninformed bidders. For example, in an *initial public offering* uninformed participants are likely to receive larger allotments of issues that informed participants know are overpriced.

With dividend (cum dividend) Purchase of shares in which the buyer is entitled to the forthcoming *dividend* (cf. *ex dividend*).

Withholding tax Tax levied on *dividends* paid abroad.

With rights (cum rights, rights on) Purchase of shares in which the buyer is entitled to the rights to buy shares in the company's *rights issue* (cf. *ex rights*).

Working capital *Current assets* and *current liabilities.* The term is commonly used as synonymous with *net working capital.*

Workout Informal arrangement between a borrower and creditors.

Writer *Option* seller.

X

xd *Ex dividend.*

xr *Ex rights.*

Y

Yankee bond A dollar *bond* issued in the United States by a non-U.S. borrower (cf. *bulldog bond, Samurai bond*).

Yield curve *Term structure of interest rates.*

Yield to maturity *Internal rate of return* on a bond.

Z

Zero-coupon bond *Discount bond* making no *coupon* payments.

Z-score Measure of the likelihood of bankruptcy.

INDEX

D

E

F

G

Q

R